DATE DUE

	PRINTED IN U.S.A.

International Encyclopedia of the
Social Sciences, 2nd edition

International Encyclopedia of the Social Sciences, 2nd edition

VOLUME 5
MASCULINITY–NYERERE, JULIUS

William A. Darity Jr.
EDITOR IN CHIEF

MACMILLAN REFERENCE USA
A part of Gale, Cengage Learning

GALE
CENGAGE Learning

Detroit • New York • San Francisco • New Haven, Conn • Waterville, Maine • London

International Encyclopedia of the Social Sciences, 2nd edition
William A. Darity Jr., Editor in Chief

For permission to use material from this product, submit your request via Web at http://www.gale-edit.com/permissions, or you may download our Permissions Request form and submit your request by fax or mail to:

Permissions Department
Gale 27500 Drake Rd.
Farmington Hills, MI 48331-3535
Permissions Hotline:
248-699-8006 or 800-877-4253 ext. 8006
Fax: 248-699-8074 or 800-762-4058

Since this page cannot legibly accommodate all copyright notices, the credits constitute an extension of the copyright notice.

While every effort has been made to ensure the reliability of the information presented in this publication, Gale does not guarantee the accuracy of the data contained herein. Gale accepts no payment for listing; and inclusion in the publication of any organization, agency, institution, publication, service, or individual does not imply endorsement of the editors or publisher. Errors brought to the attention of the publisher and verified to the satisfaction of the publisher will be corrected in future editions.

LIBRARY OF CONGRESS CATALOGING-IN-PUBLICATION DATA

International encyclopedia of the social sciences / William A. Darity, Jr., editor in chief.—2nd ed. v. cm. Rev. ed. of: International encyclopedia of the social sciences / David L. Sills, editor. c1968–c1991.
   Includes bibliographical references and index.
   ISBN 978-0-02-865965-7 (set hardcover : alk. paper)—ISBN 978-0-02-865966-4 (v. 1 hardcover : alk. paper)—ISBN 978-0-02-865967-1 (v. 2 hardcover : alk. paper)—ISBN 978-0-02-865968-8 (v. 3 hardcover : alk. paper)—ISBN 978-0-02-865969-5 (v. 4 hardcover : alk. paper)—ISBN 978-0-02-865970-1 (v. 5 hardcover : alk. paper)—ISBN 978-0-02-865971-8 (v. 6 hardcover : alk. paper)—ISBN 978-0-02-865972-5 (v. 7 hardcover : alk. paper)—ISBN 978-0-02-865973-2 (v. 8 hardcover : alk. paper)—ISBN 978-0-02-866141-4 (v. 9 hardcover : alk. paper)—ISBN 978-0-02-866117-9 (ebook : alk. paper)
   1. Social sciences—Dictionaries. 2. Social sciences—Encyclopedias. I. Darity, William A., 1953– II. Title: Encyclopedia of the social sciences.
   H40.A2I5 2008
   300.3–dc22

                                                                    2007031829

0-02-865965-1 (set)   0-02-865970-8 (v. 5)
0-02-865966-X (v. 1)   0-02-865971-6 (v. 6)
0-02-865967-8 (v. 2)   0-02-865972-4 (v. 7)
0-02-865968-6 (v. 3)   0-02-865973-2 (v. 8)
0-02-865969-4 (v. 4)   0-02-866141-9 (v. 9)

This title is also available as an e-book.
ISBN 978-0-02-866117-9; 0-02-866117-6
Contact your Gale representative for ordering information.

Printed in the United States of America
3 4 5 6 7 8 14 13 12 11 10 09 08

Editorial Board

Contents

Contents

M

MASCULINITY

Masculinity refers to the social roles, behaviors, and meanings prescribed for men in any given society at any one time. As such, it emphasizes gender, not biological sex, and the diversity of identities among different groups of men. Although we experience gender to be an internal facet of identity, the concept of masculinity is produced within the institutions of society and through our daily interactions (Kimmel 2000).

SEX VS. GENDER

Much popular discourse assumes that biological sex determines one's gender identity, the experience and expression of masculinity and femininity. Instead of focusing on biological universals, social and behavioral scientists are concerned with the different ways in which biological sex comes to mean different things in different contexts. *Sex* refers to the biological apparatus, the male and the female—our chromosomal, chemical, anatomical, organization. *Gender* refers to the meanings that are attached to those differences within a culture. *Sex* is male and female; *gender* is masculinity and femininity—what it means to be a man or a woman. Whereas biological sex varies very little, gender varies enormously. Sex is biological; gender is socially constructed. Gender takes shape only within specific social and cultural contexts.

PLURAL MASCULINITIES

The use of the plural—*masculinities*—recognizes the dramatic variation in how different groups define masculinity, even in the same society at the same time, as well as individual differences. Although social forces operate to create systematic differences between men and women, on average, these differences *between* women and men are not as great as the differences *among* men or *among* women.

The meanings of masculinity vary over four different dimensions; thus four different disciplines are involved in understanding gender—anthropology, history, psychology, and sociology.

First, masculinities vary across cultures. Anthropologists have documented the ways that gender varies cross-culturally. Some cultures encourage men to be stoic and to prove masculinity, especially by sexual conquest. Other cultures prescribe a more relaxed definition of masculinity based on civic participation, emotional responsiveness, and collective provision for the community's needs. What it means to be a man in France or among Aboriginal peoples in the Australian outback are so far apart that it belies any notion that gender identity is determined mostly by biological sex differences. The differences between two cultures' version of masculinity is often greater than the differences between the two genders.

Second, definitions of masculinity vary considerably in any one country over time. Historians have explored how these definitions have shifted in response to changes in levels of industrialization and urbanization, in a nation's position in the larger world's geopolitical and economic context, and with the development of new technologies. What it meant to be a man in seventeenth-century France or in Hellenic Greece is certainly different from what it might mean to be a French or Greek man today.

Third, definitions of masculinity change over the course of a person's life. Developmental psychologists have examined how a set of developmental milestones leads to differences in our experiences and our expressions of gender identity. Both chronological age and life stage require different enactments of gender. In the West, the issues confronting a man about proving himself and feeling successful change as he ages, as do the social institutions in which he attempts to enact those experiences. A young single man defines masculinity differently than do a middle-aged father and an elderly grandfather.

Finally, the meanings of masculinity vary considerably within any given society at any one time. At any given moment, several meanings of masculinity coexist. Simply put, not all American or Brazilian or Senegalese men are the same. Sociologists have explored the ways in which class, race, ethnicity, age, sexuality, and region all shape gender identity. Each of these axes modifies the others. For example, an older, black, gay man in Chicago and a young, white, heterosexual farm boy in Iowa would likely have different definitions of masculinity and different ideas about what it means to be a woman. Yet each of these people is deeply affected by the gender norms and power arrangements of their society.

Because gender varies so significantly—across cultures, over historical time, among men and women within any one culture, and over the life course—we cannot speak of masculinity as though it is a constant, universal essence, common to all men. Gender must be seen as an ever-changing, fluid assemblage of meanings and behaviors; we must speak of *masculinities*. By pluralizing the term we acknowledge that masculinity means different things to different groups of people at different times.

GENDER IDENTITY

Recognizing diversity ought not to obscure the ways in which gender definitions are constructed in a field of power. Simply put, all masculinities are not created equal. In every culture, men contend with a definition that is held up as the model against which all are expected to measure themselves. This "hegemonic" definition of masculinity is "constructed in relation to various subordinated masculinities as well as in relation to women," writes sociologist R. W. Connell (1987, p. 183). As Erving Goffman once described it,

> In an important sense there is only one complete unblushing male in America: a young, married, white, urban, northern, heterosexual, Protestant, father, of college education, fully employed, of good complexion, weight, and height, and a recent record in sports.... Any male who fails to

qualify in any one of these ways is likely to view himself—during moments at least—as unworthy, incomplete, and inferior. (1967, p. 128)

Definitions of masculinity are not simply constructed in relation to the hegemonic ideals of that gender, but also in constant reference to each other. Gender is not only plural, it is also relational. Surveys in Western countries indicate that men construct their ideas of what it means to be men in constant reference to definitions of femininity. What it means to be a man is to be unlike a woman; indeed, social psychologists have emphasized that although different groups of men may disagree about other traits and their significance in gender definitions, the "antifemininity" component of masculinity is perhaps the single dominant and universal characteristic.

Gender difference and gender inequality are both produced through our relationships. Nancy Chodorow argued that the structural arrangements by which women are primarily responsible for raising children creates unconscious, internalized desires in both boys and girls that reproduce male dominance and female mothering (1978). For boys, gender identity requires emotional detachment from mother, a process of individuation through separation. The boy comes to define himself as a boy by rejecting whatever he sees as female, by devaluing the feminine in himself (separation) and in others (male superiority). This cycle of men defining themselves through their distance from and devaluation of femininity can end, Chodorow argues, only when parents participate equally in child rearing.

GENDER AS AN INSTITUTION

Although we recognize gender diversity, we still may conceive masculinities as attributes of identity only. We think of gendered individuals who bring with them all the attributes and behavioral characteristics of their gendered identity into gender-neutral institutional arenas. But because gender is plural and relational, it is also situational: What it means to be a man varies in different institutional contexts, and those different institutional contexts demand and produce different forms of masculinity. "Boys may be boys," writes feminist legal theorist Deborah Rhode, "but they express that identity differently in fraternity parties than in job interviews with a female manager" (Rhode 1997, p. 142). Gender is thus not only a property of individuals, some "thing" one has, but a specific set of behaviors that are produced in specific social situations. Thus gender changes as the situation changes.

Institutions are themselves gendered. Institutions create gendered normative standards and express a gendered institutional logic, and are major factors in the reproduction of gender inequality. The gendered identity of individuals shapes those gendered institutions, and the gendered institutions express and reproduce the inequalities that compose gender identity. Institutions themselves express a logic—a dynamic—that reproduces gender relations between women and men and the gender order of hierarchy and power.

Not only do gendered individuals negotiate their identities within gendered institutions, but also those institutions produce the very differences we assume are the properties of individuals. Thus, "the extent to which women and men do different tasks, play widely disparate concrete social roles, strongly influences the extent to which the two sexes develop and/or are expected to manifest widely disparate personal behaviors and characteristics" (Chafetz 1980, p. 112). Different structured experiences produce the gender differences that we often attribute to people (Chafetz 1980).

For example, take the workplace. In her now classic work *Men and Women of the Corporation* (1977), Rosebeth Moss Kanter argued that the differences in men's and women's behaviors in organizations had far less to do with their characteristics as individuals than with the structure of the organization itself and the different jobs men and women held. Organizational positions "carry characteristic images of the kinds of people that should occupy them," she argued, and those who do occupy them, whether women or men, exhibited those necessary behaviors (Kanter 1977, p. 21). Though the criteria for evaluation of job performance, promotion, and effectiveness seem to be gender neutral, they are, in fact, deeply gendered. "While organizations were being defined as sex-neutral machines," she writes, "masculine principles were dominating their authority structures" (p. 241). Once again, masculinity—the norm—was invisible (Kanter 1975, 1977). For example, secretaries seemed to stress personal loyalty to their bosses more than did other workers, which led some observers to attribute this to women's greater level of personalism. But Kanter pointed out that the best way for a secretary—of either gender—to get promoted was for the boss to decide to take the secretary with him to the higher job. Thus the structure of the women's jobs, not the gender of the job holder, dictated their responses.

Sociologist Joan Acker has expanded on Kanter's early insights and has specified the interplay of structure and gender. It is through our experiences in the workplace, Acker maintains, that the differences between women and men are reproduced, and in this way the inequality between women and men is legitimated. Institutions are like factories, and one of the things that they produce is gender difference. The overall effect of this is the reproduction of the gender order as a whole (see Acker 1987, 1988, 1989, 1990).

Institutions accomplish the creation of gender difference and the reproduction of the gender order through several gendered processes. Thus, "advantage and disadvantage, exploitation and control, action and emotion, meaning and identity, are patterned through and in terms of a distinction between male and female, masculine and feminine" (Acker 1990, p. 146). We would err to assume that gendered individuals enter gender-neutral sites, thus maintaining the invisibility of gender-as-hierarchy, and specifically the invisible masculine organizational logic. At the same time, we would be just as incorrect to assume that genderless "people" occupy those gender-neutral sites. The problem is that such genderless people are assumed to be able to devote themselves single-mindedly to their jobs, to have no children or family responsibilities, and perhaps even to have familial supports for such single-minded workplace devotion. Thus, the "genderless" job holder turns out to be gendered as a man.

Take, for example, the field of medicine. Many doctors complete college by age twenty-one or twenty-two, and medical school by age twenty-five to twenty-seven, and then face three more years of internship and residency, during which time they are occasionally on call for long stretches of time, sometimes for even two or three days straight. They thus complete their residencies by their late twenties or early thirties. Such a program is designed for a male doctor—one who is not pressured by the ticking of a biological clock, for whom the birth of children will not disrupt these time demands, and who may even have someone at home taking care of his children while he sleeps at the hospital. No wonder women in medical school—who number nearly one half of all medical students today—began to complain that they were not able to balance pregnancy and motherhood with their medical training.

In another example, in a typical academic career a scholar completes a PhD about six to seven years after the BA, roughly by age thirty, and then begins a career as an assistant professor with six more years to earn tenure and promotion. This is usually the most intense academic work period of a scholar's life and also the most likely childbearing years for professional women. The tenure clock is thus set to a man's rhythms—not just any man, but one with a wife to relieve him of family obligations as he establishes his credentials. To academics struggling to make tenure, it often feels that publishing requires that family life perish.

Embedded in organizational structures that are gendered, subject to gendered organizational processes, and evaluated by gendered criteria, then, the differences between women and men appear to be the differences solely between gendered individuals. When gender boundaries seem permeable, other dynamics and processes can reproduce the gender order. When women do not meet these criteria (or, perhaps more accurately, when the criteria do not meet women's specific needs), we see a gender-segregated workforce and wage, hiring, and promotional disparities as the "natural" outcomes of already present differences between women and men. It is in this way that those differences are generated and the inequalities between women and men are legitimated and reproduced.

"DOING" GENDER

There remains one more element in the sociological explanation of masculinities. Some psychologists and sociologists believe that early childhood gender socialization leads to gender identities that become fixed, permanent, and inherent in our personalities. However, many sociologists disagree with this notion today. As they see it, gender is less a component of identity—fixed, static—that we take with us into our interactions and more the product *of* those interactions. In an important article, "Doing Gender," Candace West and Don Zimmerman argued that "a person's gender is not simply an aspect of what one is, but, more fundamentally, it is something that one *does*, and does recurrently, in interaction with others" (1987, p. 140). We are constantly "doing" gender, performing the activities and exhibiting the traits that are prescribed for us.

Doing gender is a lifelong process of performances. As we interact with others we are held accountable to display behavior that is consistent with gender norms, at least for that situation. Thus consistent gender behavior is less a response to deeply internalized norms or personality characteristics and more a negotiated response to the consistency with which others demand that we act in a recognizable masculine or feminine way. Gender is not an emanation of identity that bubbles up from below in concrete expression; rather, it is an emergent property of interactions, coerced from us by others.

Understanding how we do masculinities, then, requires that we make visible the performative elements of identity, and also the audience for those performances. It also opens up unimaginable possibilities for social change, as Suzanne Kessler points out in her study of "intersexed" people (hermaphrodites, those born with anatomical characteristics of both sexes or with ambiguous genitalia):

> If authenticity for gender rests not in a discoverable nature but in someone else's proclamation, then the power to proclaim something else is available. If physicians recognized that implicit in their management of gender is the notion that finally, and always, people construct gender as

well as the social systems that are grounded in gender-based concepts, the possibilities for real societal transformations would be unlimited. (Kessler 1990, p. 25)

Kessler's gender utopianism raises an important issue. In saying that we "do" gender we are saying that gender is not only something that is done *to* us. We create and re-create our own gendered identities within the contexts of our interactions with others and within the institutions we inhabit.

BIBLIOGRAPHY

Acker, Joan. 1987. Sex Bias in Job Evaluation: A Comparable Worth Issue. In *Ingredients for Women's Employment Policy,* eds. Christine Bose and Glenna Spitze, 183–196. Albany: State University of New York Press.

Acker, Joan. 1988. Class, Gender, and the Relations of Distribution. *Signs: Journal of Women in Culture and Society* 13: 473–497.

Acker, Joan. 1989. *Doing Comparable Worth: Gender, Class, and Pay Equity.* Philadelphia: Temple University Press.

Acker, Joan. 1990. Hierarchies, Jobs, Bodies: A Theory of Gendered Organizations. *Gender and Society* 4 (2): 149–158.

Acker, Joan, and Donald R. Van Houten. 1974. Differential Recruitment and Control: The Sex Structuring of Organizations. *Administrative Science Quarterly* 19 (2): 152–163.

Chafetz, Janet. 1980. Toward a Macro-Level Theory of Sexual Stratification. *Current Perspectives in Social Theory* 1: 103–126.

Chodorow, Nancy. 1978. *The Reproduction of Mothering: Psychoanalysis and the Sociology of Gender.* Berkeley: University of California Press.

Connell, R. W. 1987. *Gender and Power.* Stanford, CA: Stanford University Press.

Goffman, Erving. 1963. *Stigma.* Englewood Cliffs, NJ: Prentice-Hall.

Kanter, Rosabeth Moss. 1975. Women and the Structure of Organizations: Explorations in Theory and Behavior. In *Another Voice: Feminist Perspectives on Social Life and Social Science,* eds. Marcia Millman and Rosabeth Moss Kanter, 34–74. New York: Anchor Books.

Kanter, Rosabeth Moss. 1977. *Men and Women of the Corporation.* New York: Basic Books.

Kessler, Suzanne J. 1990. The Medical Construction of Gender: Case Management of Intersexed Infants. *Signs* 16 (1): 3–26.

Kimmel, Michael. 2000. *The Gendered Society.* New York: Oxford University Press.

Rhode, Deborah. 1997. *Speaking of Sex.* Cambridge, MA: Harvard University Press.

Risman, Barbara. 1999. *Gender Vertigo.* New Haven, CT: Yale University Press.

West, Candace, and Don H. Zimmerman. 1987. Doing Gender. *Gender and Society* 1 (2): 125–151.

Michael Kimmel

MASCULINITY STUDIES

Masculinity refers most commonly to socially constructed expectations of appropriate behaviors, beliefs, expressions, and styles of social interaction for men in a culture or sub-culture at a given time. The substantive meanings associated with masculinity are culturally specific, and refer to social arrangements and institutionalized practices as well as individual actions and embodiments. Historically, these meanings have been premised on ideologies and symbolism that cast women as "opposite" and inferior to men, and that position some men as superior to other men. This is due, in large part, to the framing of gender expectations by dominant groups in ways that endorse dominant group practices—and the personal characteristics that presumably represent the embodiment of those practices—while at the same time devaluing the practices and characteristics of other out-groups. Evelyn Nakano Glenn (2002) and Eduardo Bonilla-Silva (2001) explain, for example, that Anglo or white men in industrialized Europe, North America, and other parts of the world support practices and social constructs that endorse their own position as superior to nonwhite men and men with little or no material resources.

Despite its complexity and relational character, popular conceptualizations continue to view masculinity narrowly as a unified set of personal characteristics, behaviors, and beliefs—including physical strength, assertiveness, emotional detachment, competition, and the belief that men are better suited than women for positions of leadership and decision making. Though unsupported by scientific evidence, many also believe that masculinity is derived from biology. The notion of essential differences between men and women, and corresponding notions of women's and men's different abilities and proclivities, has its origins in late nineteenth-century political movements in Western Europe and the United States. As more women joined the struggle for basic human rights, such as the right to vote and the right to own land, white male scholars focused increasing attention on notions of biological sex difference as a means for supporting ideologies of female inferiority (Carrigan, Connell, and Lee 1985; Fausto-Sterling 2000; MacInnes 2001). Men already in positions of power and privilege relative to women, men of color, men with fewer material advantages, noncitizens, and the disenfranchised, used ideologies of innate differ-ences to justify discriminatory laws and practices (Glenn 2002).

The highly visible women's movement, as well as the loss of control and opportunity that many men—particularly white men—were experiencing as industrial work processes became more routine and competition for work from immigrants and migrant workers became more intense (Glenn 2002; Kimmel 1996; Roper 1994), also fed into a perceived "crisis of [white] masculinity" in both Europe and the United States at the beginning of the twentieth century (Chauncey 1985; D'Emilio and Freedman 1988). The perception of crisis added fuel to the search for biological evidence of male superiority and white racial superiority (Fausto-Sterling 2000, p. 156; hooks 2004).

Biologically based explanations for sex differences, notes François Nielsen (1994), were pervasive by the mid-twentieth century, and persist still. The logic behind these arguments is that evolutionary processes produce two distinct categories of humans, one that is more physically aggressive, competitive, emotionally independent, and instrumentally decisive, and another that is more passive, cooperative, interdependent, and nurturing. Persons categorized as male are assumed to fit the former, and those categorized as female to fit the latter. Scientific studies reveal many problems with the assumption that biology produces opposite sexes, that gender differences are derived from biology, and that males are innately superior to females. For example, the characteristics and traits that are supposed to differentiate women and men have much more in common than not (Fausto-Sterling 2000; Kemper 1990; Kessler and McKenna 1978).

EARLY VIEWS ON MASCULINITY AS IDENTITY

Not all scholars of the early twentieth century viewed masculinity as a direct function of biology. The foundations of masculinity as identity were established in the early 1900s with the work of Sigmund Freud (1905, 1923). Freud posited that the personality people most commonly associate with masculinity results from complex processes of unconscious conflict resolution and emotional development that start early in life. "The outcome of the differently structured Oedipal crises," explains Raewyn Connell, "are the bases of Freudian accounts of femininity and masculinity" (1987, p. 204). Freud's work has been variously elaborated by gender scholars. Nancy Chodorow (1978) focuses on how the division of labor within the family shapes how females and males process unconscious motivations and repressed desire. Given a gendered division of labor in industrial capitalist Western society, explains Chodorow, and a nuclear heterosexual family with a male primary wage earner, young boys construct a sense of self in relation to a mother figure whose presence is consistent and intense, and a father figure that is more distant because of his role in paid labor. This arrangement leads infants to associate the mother with the fulfillment of desires. Boys' emotional attachment to the mother, however, transforms from one of oneness with her to a form of individuality-with-attachment that is intensely possessive. These possessive feelings for the mother lead the boy to view the father as a competitor for the mother's affections (Di Stefano 1991, pp. 45–48). The feelings of threat that the boy experiences in relation to the father (castration anxiety), along with the need to establish self and not-female, evoke ambivalence, which in turn requires that the boy identify with the father. And to develop a sense of self apart from mother, the boy seeks to establish himself as that which women/females are not (Chodorow 1978, pp. 96–97; Parsons 1964). Emotional detachment, competitiveness, and desire to control self and others become central to his identity (Gilligan 1982; Messner 1992).

Other theorists point out that psychoanalytic object relations views, such as Chodorow's, posit an overly unified concept of self and identity. Connell (1987, 1995) argues that Freud did not assert that processes of personality development produce two clear-cut, stable categories of personality characteristics. Connell agrees that fear of castration at the hands of the father leads boys to repress erotic feelings for the mother, to identify with the powerful father figure, to internalize prohibitions against desire for the mother, and to develop a strong superego, but argues that these are not fail-safe or immanent steps (Connell 1987, p. 204). Many contingencies and conflicts characterize these processes.

Building on existential psychoanalytic theory, Connell proposes the concept of gender projects, which views gender not as a fixed identity but rather as "a system of symbolic relationships" (1995, p. 20). From this view, past attachments, though often repressed, have consequences for future actions. The emotional contradictions and conflicts that arise as a boy goes through the pre-Oedipal and Oedipal stages produce a range of possible outcomes for the individual. The many conflicting emotions that a boy experiences in the development of his sense of self will influence how he projects himself into the future, and thus, the position he takes up in the symbolic order (Connell 1987, p. 211). Boys' and men's gender projects take many forms, some of which are consistent with dominant ideals of masculinity, and others of which are not. "The point," argues Connell, "is that no one pattern of development can be taken as universal even within the specific social context Freud studied" (Connell 1987, p. 206). Not all boys and men take up the same gender project (Chen 1999; Collinson 2003; Majors and Billson 1992; Messerschmidt 2000).

SOCIALIZATION THEORIES AND MASCULINITY AS GENDER ROLE

The most common social science frameworks for understanding masculinity since the mid-twentieth century have been sex role (later referred to as gender role) and socialization theories. The concept of sex roles was popularized in the work of Talcott Parsons (Parsons 1964; Parsons and Bales 1955). Underlying the logic of masculinity as a role is the assumption that significant differences separate men from women as social actors. According to Parsons, structural differentiation is a requirement of society, and the division of labor within the family between "instrumental" men and "expressive" women was necessary to ensure proper socialization of children. Boys are also taught within the family, peer groups, schools, and other social organizations and institutions the behaviors and traits that are considered appropriate for boys and men. Boys internalize gender-specific, "appropriate" personalities and behaviors as a result. Masculinity is the identity that corresponds with the position (or role) of man in societal structures.

Modeling behaviors and the rewards and punishments boys receive for their actions facilitate socialization processes. Cognitive approaches to gender socialization posit, further, that once boys embrace the male sex category for themselves, they actively seek activities, behaviors, and modes of presentation that facilitate feedback from others that affirm maleness (Kohlberg 1966). Social cognition models assume that in order to manage the wealth of information to which individuals are exposed in daily life, they look for ways to effectively prioritize the inputs to which they must pay the most attention, which in turn leads to the use of social categories for organizing the social world. Sex categories and corresponding gender schemas, or cognitive structures that allow individuals to organize social information about self and about groupings of people in society, shape what individuals pay attention to, remember, and expect of themselves and other people (Bem 1983, 1993). From this view, prevailing stereotypes about and expectations for men and women in society persist in large part because they provide cognitive road maps and a sense of ontological security for people (Howard and Hollander 1997, p. 88).

One critique of socialization theories is that they equate masculinity with that which men in the most powerful positions in society do (Howard and Hollander 1997; Smiler 2004). By assuming that "normal" males internalize "normative" masculinity, this perspective removes the issue of structural power from the analysis of gender (Connell 1987; Gerson and Peiss 1985; Lopata and Thorne 1978). Boys and men who fail to follow these prescribed paths are thus viewed as deviant (Schur 1984). Socialization is cast as an explanation without explicit discussion of the power struggles between differently empowered social groups (Howard 1988; Howard and Hollander 1997).

Socialization and role theories, in addition, reify the notion of gender dualisms, thereby minimizing and obscuring differences between men and other men, and between women and other women, and fail to address the intersections of social categories of difference and inequality—such as class, race, and sexual orientation—and how these shape negotiations of dominant masculinity imperatives (Chen 1999; Collinson and Hearn 1994; Martin 1996; Nonn 2004). The notion that masculinity exists as a "role" into which boys and men are socialized obscures how power structures mediate individual negotiations of identity and self.

Throughout U.S. history, for example, boys and men of color have resisted many of the practices and beliefs constructed by white and middle- to upper-class men as appropriate and ideal for "true" men, especially those practices and beliefs that cast men of color as inferior. Men oppressed by other men on the basis of race, ethnicity, and national origin have approached power hierarchies and the men whose positions of structural power enable them to mobilize resources in their own favor with what the American educator and writer W. E. B. Du Bois (1903) identified as "double consciousness." Double consciousness is born out of the experience of being constrained not by actual personal inabilities but by structures and practices constructed and reinforced by those who control material and symbolic resources. This two-sided consciousness allows members of systematically subordinated groups to understand the dominant group's constructions of status differences and related expectations for social behavior while at the same time resisting the dominant culture's construction of the subordinated group as inferior. The notion that masculinity exists as a role that boys and men fit to varying degrees, however, backgrounds the continual negotiations among men and between women and men over the actual meanings that constitute what is commonly referred to as masculinity.

MASCULINITIES, HEGEMONIC MASCULINITY, AND GENDER AS RELATIONAL

The limitations of identity and role theories of gender have led many late twentieth- and early twenty-first-century scholars to argue that masculinity does not consist of a single unified set of practices, beliefs, or characteristics. Rather, masculin*ities* are multiple and exist not only as embodied practices, characteristics, and beliefs, but also as routinized and institutionalized practices and symbols. As such, masculinities are constructed and negotiated via discourse and material relations, and are the object of contes-

tation by groups and individuals (Carrigan, Connell, and Lee 1985; Collinson and Hearn 1994; Hearn 1998; Whitehead 2002). This scholarship emphasizes the relational and hierarchical character of socially constructed genders (Connell and Messerschmidt 2005; Collinson and Hearn 1994; Martin 2001; Whitehead 2002).

Gender as a relational concept acknowledges that while bodies are sex-differentiated (i.e., they produce some different physiological needs), these differences do not determine the actual practices in which people engage. Instead, social embodiment transforms bodies (Connell 2002, p. 50). Masculinities and femininities are sets of practices constrained but not fully dictated by "the structure of social relations that centers on the reproductive arena" (Connell 2002, p.10). The reproductive arena refers not to a biological base for gender but rather an arena in which social processes occur. Practices exist as patterns of relationships that connect and separate individuals, and constrain the practices in which individuals engage.

Gender as a relational concept also acknowledges the "different material interests that groups have in an unequal society" (Connell 2002, p. 71). Men have less interest in changing the social structures that give them a collective advantage over women and are more invested than women in maintaining the category "woman" as the "other" against which men are defined because this distinction supports the illusion of gender difference and male/masculine superiority (Bordo 1993). Similarly, Anglo and middle- and upper-class men are more invested in maintaining the structures that sustain their collective advantage over oppressed race and ethnic groups, and over lower socioeconomic classes of men (Lewis 2003; MacLeod 1995; Majors and Billson 1992; Willis 1977).

Hegemonic masculinity, the conceptual framework used commonly to express gendered relations of domination and subordination, refers to "the configuration of gender practice which embodies the currently accepted answer to the problem of the legitimacy of patriarchy, which guarantees (or is taken to guarantee) the dominant position of men and the subordination of women" (Connell 1995, p. 77). Hegemonic masculinity is composed of practices that enable and sustain the status and power of men over women collectively (external dimension) and of some men over other men (internal dimension) (Demetriou 2001). All males (and those who pass as male; Halberstam 1998) are subject to prevailing expectations of hegemonic masculinity, though few actually live up to these expectations (Bird 2003; Dellinger 2004; Messerschmidt 2000; Messner 1992). Few men fit hegemonic ideals of masculinity for any extended period because these ideals and standards change over time and vary by social context, and because men's bodies and minds also change over the life course.

Supporting a family financially, exercising autonomy and authority in paid labor, and superior athleticism are all examples of practices that commonly align with hegemonic masculinity in many contemporary Western nations. Most men support the idea that these are practices that distinguish men as different from and superior to women (and lesser men), and confer legitimacy and status upon men who are exemplars of these practices (Chen 1999; Gerschick and Miller 1994; Henson and Rogers 2001). This is the case even though hierarchies of class, race, ethnicity, sexual orientation, gender expression, religion, and able-bodiedness ensure that not all men exercise the same level of power or status over women. Most men remain complicit with hegemonic masculinity because as long as the category "man" is constructed as distinct from and superior to the category "female," dominant as well as subordinated men will continue to benefit from the status of being male (Whitehead 2002).

Resistance to and even rejection of hegemonic masculinity imperatives does, however, exist (Gerschick 1998; Majors and Billson 1992). Thomas Gerschick explains, for example, that while some men with physical disabilities embrace fully ideals of masculinity that only fully able-bodied men can attain, others reject these ideals and construct meanings of their own. Whether and the extent to which one embodies hegemonic practices is partly a matter of having the resources to do so, partly a matter of being allowed to embody such practices, and partly a matter of wanting to embody them.

Research also shows, however, that while there are many forms of resistance to hegemonic ideals and imperatives of masculinity (Boyd 1997; Garcia 2004; Majors and Billson 1992; Mirandé 1997; Neal 2005), complete rejection of all elements of hegemonic patriarchal masculinity is rare (Carby 1998); hooks 2004; Neal 2005). Scholars including Hazel Carby, Anthony Chen (1999), Jerry Garcia (2004), bell hooks (2004), and Mark Anthony Neal demonstrate, for example, how African American, Latino, and Asian American men often adopt patriarchal sexism even as they are struggling against white men for racial and ethnic equality.

Since the 1990s, scholarship has examined the themes outlined above in a variety of contexts, including work organizations (Bird 2003; Britton 2003; Dellinger 2004; Kerfoot and Knights 1993, 1998; Martin 1996, 2001; Pierce 1995; Williams 1995), families (Adams and Coltrane 2005; Marsiglio and Pleck 2005), sports (Messner 1992, 2004), crime and violence (Messerschmidt 2000), the media (McKay, Mokosza, and Hutchins 2005), education (Ferguson 2000; Lewis 2003; McGuffey and Rich 1999; Swain 2005), and leisure settings (Bird 1996; Bird and Sokolofski 2005; Campbell 2000). Gender theorists have called for a greater focus beyond the level of organizations, institutions, and cross-cultural comparative ethnographies. Scholars, including Sikata Banerjee (2005), Wendy Bracewell (2000), Charlotte Hooper (1998, 1999), Joane Nagel (1998, 2005), Raewyn Connell (2005), and Sergei Zherebkin (2006), illuminate macro constructions of masculinity and the relationships between nationalism, imperialism, and globalization. Nations seeking to construct and/or sustain national unity, loyalty, and strength, especially military strength, draw upon the imagery, power relations, division of labor, and emotional relations associated with emerging global patterns of hegemonic masculinity. While Connell (2005) argues that an emerging global hegemonic masculinity focuses on transnational business practices, Hooper (1999) asserts that practices in the arena of international power politics are the basis for a global hegemonic masculinity. These and other scholars note the need for further collaborations across continents and nations in the study of masculinities (Committee for Research on Men and Masculinities in Europe 2005; Gutmann and Viveros Vigoya 2005; Morrell and Swart 2005; Taga 2005).

EVOLVING SCHOLARSHIP

In this brief overview, some of the key theoretical issues regarding the study of masculinities have been presented. During the twentieth century, scholarship moved away from theories that posit biological determinism and toward a greater understanding of masculinities as social constructs that exist not simply as personality characteristics but as practices that are variously taken up by individuals and, at the same time, are embedded in organizations, institutions, and global systems. Twenty-first-century scholars study multifaceted "masculinities" that, in conjunction with multifaceted "femininities," organize every aspect of social life.

SEE ALSO *Du Bois, W. E. B.; Femininity; Feminism; Freud, Sigmund; Gender; Gender, Alternatives to Binary; Gender Gap; Gender Studies; Men; Women's Studies*

BIBLIOGRAPHY

Adams, Michele, and Scott Coltrane. 2005. Boys and Men in Families: The Domestic Production of Gender, Power and Privilege. In *Handbook of Studies on Men and Masculinities*, ed. Michael S. Kimmel, Jeff Hearn, and Raewyn Connell, 230–248. Thousand Oaks, CA: Sage.

Banerjee, Sikata. 2005. *Make Me a Man!: Masculinity, Hinduism, and Nationalism in India*. Albany: State University of New York Press.

Bem, Sandra L. 1983. Gender Schema Theory and Its Implications for Child Development: Raising Gender-Aschematic Children in a Gender-Schematic Society. *Signs* 8: 598–616.

Bem, Sandra L. 1993. *The Lenses of Gender*. New Haven, CT: Yale University Press.

Bird, Sharon R. 1996. Welcome to the Men's Club: Homosociality and the Maintenance of Hegemonic Masculinity. *Gender & Society* 10 (2): 120–132.

Bird, Sharon R. 2003. Sex Composition, Masculinities and the Quality of Men's Workplace Social Relations. *Gender, Work and Organization* 10 (5): 579–604.

Bird, Sharon R., and Leah K. Sokolofski. 2005. Gendered Socio-Spatial Practices in Public Eating and Drinking Establishments in the United States. *Gender, Place and Culture* 12 (2): 213–230.

Bonilla-Silva, Eduardo. 2001. *White Supremacy and Racism in the Post–Civil Rights Era*. Boulder, CO: Lynne Rienner.

Bordo, Susan. 1993. *Unbearable Weight: Feminism, Western Culture, and the Body*. Berkeley: University of California Press.

Boyd, Todd. 1997. *Am I Black Enough for You? Popular Culture from the 'Hood and Beyond*. Bloomington: Indiana University Press.

Bracewell, Wendy. 2000. Rape in Kosovo: Masculinity and Serbian Nationalism. *Nations and Nationalism* 6(4): 563–590.

Britton, Dana M. 2003. *At Work in the Iron Cage: The Prison as Gendered Organization*. New York: New York University Press.

Campbell, Hugh. 2000. The Glass Phallus: Pub(lic) Masculinity and Drinking in Rural New Zealand. *Rural Sociology* 65 (4): 562–581.

Carby, Hazel. 1998. *Race Men*. Cambridge, MA: Harvard University Press.

Carrigan, Tim, Robert W. Connell, and John Lee. 1985. Toward a New Sociology of Masculinity. *Theory and Society* 14 (5): 551–604.

Chauncey, George, Jr. 1985. Christian Brotherhood or Sexual Perversion? Homosexual Identities and the Construction of Sexual Boundaries in the World War I Era. *Journal of Social History* 19: 189–212.

Chen, Anthony S. 1999. Lives at the Center of the Periphery, Lives at the Periphery of the Center: Chinese American Masculinities and Bargaining with Hegemony. *Gender & Society* 13 (5): 584–607.

Chodorow, Nancy. 1978. *The Reproduction of Mothering: Psychoanalysis and the Sociology of Gender*. Berkeley: University of California Press.

Collinson, David L. 2003. Identities and Insecurities: Selves at Work. *Organization* 10 (3): 527–547.

Collinson, David L., and Jeff Hearn. 1994. Naming Men as Men: Implications for Work, Organization and Management. *Gender, Work and Organization* 1 (1): 2–22.

Committee for Research on Men and Masculinities in Europe. 2005. Men, Masculinities, and "Europe." In *Handbook of Studies on Men and Masculinities*, ed. Michael S. Kimmel, Jeff Hearn, and Raewyn Connell, 141–162. Thousand Oaks, CA: Sage.

Connell, Raewyn. 1987. *Gender and Power*. Stanford, CA: Stanford University Press.

Connell, Raewyn. 1995. *Masculinities*. Berkeley: University of California Press.

Connell, Raewyn. 1998. Masculinities and Globalization. *Men and Masculinities* 1 (1): 3–23.

Connell, Raewyn. 2002. *Gender*. Cambridge, U.K.: Polity Press.

Connell, Raewyn. 2005. Globalization, Imperialism, and Masculinities. In *Handbook of Studies on Men and Masculinities*, ed. Michael S. Kimmel, Jeff Hearn, and Raewyn Connell, 71–89. Thousand Oaks, CA: Sage.

Connell, Raewyn, and James W. Messerschmidt. 2005. Hegemonic Masculinity: Rethinking the Concept. *Gender & Society* 19 (6): 829–859.

Dellinger, Kirsten. 2004. Masculinities in "Safe" and "Embattled" Organizations: Accounting for Pornographic and Feminist Magazines. *Gender & Society* 18 (5): 545–566.

Demetriou, Demetrakis Z. 2001. Connell's Concept of Hegemonic Masculinity: A Critique. *Theory and Society* 30: 377–361.

D'Emilio, John, and Estelle B. Freedman. 1988. *Intimate Matters: A History of Sexuality in America*. New York: Harper and Row.

Di Stefano, Christine. 1991. *Configurations of Masculinity: A Feminist Perspective on Modern Political Theory*. Ithaca, NY: Cornell University Press.

Du Bois, W. E. B. 1903. *The Souls of Black Folk*. Chicago: McClurg.

Fausto-Sterling, Anne. 2000. *Sexing the Body: Gender Politics and the Construction of Sexuality*. New York: Basic Books.

Ferguson, Ann Arnett. 2000. *Bad Boys: Public Schools in the Making of Black Masculinity*. Ann Arbor: University of Michigan Press.

Ferree, Myra Marx, and Elaine J. Hall. 1996. Rethinking Stratification from a Feminist Perspective: Gender, Race, and Class in Mainstream Textbooks. *American Sociological Review* 61 (6): 929–950.

Freud, Sigmund. 1905. Three Essays on the Theory of Sexuality. In Vol. 7 of *The Standard Edition of the Complete Psychological Works of Sigmund Freud*, trans. and ed. James Strachey, 125–245. London: Hogarth Press. (Orig. pub. 1919.)

Freud, Sigmund. 1923. The Ego and the Id. In Vol. 19 of *The Standard Edition of the Complete Psychological Works of Sigmund Freud*, trans. and ed. James Strachey, 3–59. London: Hogarth Press. (Orig. pub. 1919.)

Garcia, Jerry. 2004. The Measure of a Cock: Mexican Cockfighting, Culture, and Masculinity. In *I Am Aztlán: The Personal Essay in Chicano Studies*, ed. Chon A. Noriega and Wendy Belcher, 109–138. Los Angeles: UCLA Chicano Studies Research Center Press.

Gerschick, Thomas J. 1998. Sisyphus in a Wheelchair: Men with Physical Disabilities Confront Gender Domination. In *Everyday Inequalities: Critical Inquiries*, ed. Jodi O'Brien and Judith A. Howard, 189–211. Malden, MA: Blackwell.

Gerschick, Thomas J., and Adam Stephen Miller. 1994. Gender Identities at the Crossroads of Masculinity and Physical Disability. *Masculinities* 2 (1): 34–55.

Gerson, Judith M., and Kathy Peiss. 1985. Boundaries, Negotiation, Consciousness: Reconceptualizing Gender Relations. *Social Problems* 32 (4): 317–331.

Gilligan, Carol. 1982. *In a Different Voice: Psychological Theory and Women's Development.* Cambridge, MA: Harvard University Press.

Glenn, Evelyn Nakano. 2002. *Unequal Freedom: How Race and Gender Shaped American Citizenship and Labor.* Cambridge, MA: Harvard University Press.

Gutmann, Matthew C., and Mara Viveros Vigoya. 2005. Masculinities in Latin America. In *Handbook of Studies on Men and Masculinities*, ed. Michael S. Kimmel, Jeff Hearn, and Raewyn Connell, 114–128. Thousand Oaks, CA: Sage.

Halberstam, Judith. 1998. *Female Masculinity.* Durham, NC: Duke University Press.

Hearn, Jeff. 1998. Theorizing Men and Men's Theorizing: Men's Discursive Practices in Theorizing Men. *Theory and Society* 27 (6): 781–816.

Henson, Kevin D., and Jackie Krasas Rogers. 2001. "Why Marcia You've Changed!": Male Clerical Temporary Workers Doing Masculinity in a Feminized Occupation. *Gender & Society* 15 (2): 218–238.

hooks, bell. 2004. *We Real Cool: Black Men and Masculinity.* New York: Routledge.

Hooper, Charlotte. 1998. Masculinist Practices and Gender Politics: The Operation of Multiple Masculinities in International Relations. In *The "Man Question" in International Relations*, ed. Marysia Zalewski and Jane Parpart, 28–53. Boulder, CO: Westview.

Hooper, Charlotte. 1999. Masculinities, IR and the "Gender Variable." *Review of International Studies* 25 (3): 475–491.

Howard, Judith. 1988. Gender Differences in Sexual Attitudes: Conservatism or Powerlessness? *Gender & Society* 2 (1): 103–114.

Howard, Judith A., and Jocelyn A. Hollander. 1997. *Gendered Situations, Gendered Selves.* Thousand Oaks, CA: Sage.

Kemper, Theodore D. 1990. *Social Structure and Testosterone: Explorations of the Socio-Bio-Social Chain.* New Brunswick, NJ: Rutgers University Press.

Kerfoot, Deborah, and David Knights. 1993. Management, Masculinity and Manipulation: From Paternalism to Corporate Strategy in Financial Services in Britain. *Journal of Management Studies* 30 (4): 659–667.

Kerfoot, Deborah, and David Knights. 1998. Managing Masculinity in Contemporary Organizational Life. *Organization* 5 (1): 7–26.

Kessler, Suzanne J., and Wendy McKenna. 1978. *Gender: An Ethnomethodological Approach.* Chicago: University of Chicago Press.

Kimmel, Michael S. 1996. *Manhood in America.* New York: Free Press.

Kohlberg, Lawrence A. 1966. A Cognitive-Developmental Analysis of Children's Sex Role Concepts and Attitudes. In *The Development of Sex Differences*, ed. Eleanor E. Maccoby, 82–172. Stanford, CA: Stanford University Press.

Lewis, Amanda E. 2003. *Race in the Schoolyard: Negotiating the Color Line in Classrooms and Communities.* New Brunswick, NJ: Rutgers University Press.

Lopata, Helena Z., and Barrie Thorne. 1978. On the Term "Sex Roles." *Signs* 3 (3): 718–721.

MacInnes, John. 2001. The Crisis of Masculinity and the Politics of Identity. In *The Masculinities Reader*, ed. Stephen M. Whitehead and Frank J. Barrett, 311–329. Cambridge, U.K.: Polity Press.

MacLeod, Jay. 1995. *Ain't No Makin' It: Aspirations and Attainment in a Low-Income Neighborhood.* Boulder, CO: Westview.

Majors, Richard, and Janet Mancini Billson. 1992. *Cool Pose: The Dilemmas of Black Manhood in America.* New York: Lexington.

Marsiglio, William, and Joseph H. Pleck. 2005. Fatherhood and Masculinities. In *Handbook of Studies on Men and Masculinities*, ed. Michael S. Kimmel, Jeff Hearn, and Raewyn Connell, 249–269. Thousand Oaks, CA: Sage.

Martin, Patricia Yancey. 1996. Gendering and Evaluating Dynamics: Men, Masculinities and Managements. In *Men as Managers, Managers as Men: Critical Perspectives on Men, Masculinities, and Managements*, ed. David L. Collinson and Jeff Hearn, 186–209. London: Sage.

Martin, Patricia Yancey. 2001. "Mobilizing Masculinities": Women's Experiences of Men at Work. *Organization* 8 (4): 587–618.

McGuffey, C. Shawn, and B. Lindsay Rich. 1999. Playing in the Gender Transgression Zone: Race, Class, and Hegemonic Masculinity in Middle Childhood. *Gender & Society* 13 (5): 608–627.

McKay, Jim, Janine Mokosza, and Brett Hutchins. 2005. "Gentlemen, the Lunchbox Has Landed": Representations of Masculinities in Popular Media. In *Handbook of Studies on Men and Masculinities*, ed. Michael S. Kimmel, Jeff Hearn, and Raewyn Connell, 270–288. Thousand Oaks, CA: Sage.

Messerschmidt, James W. 2000. *Nine Lives: Adolescent Masculinities, the Body, and Violence.* Boulder, CO: Westview.

Messner, Michael A. 1992. *Power at Play: Sports and the Problem of Masculinity.* Boston: Beacon.

Messner, Michael A. 2004. Still a Man's World? Studying Masculinities and Sport. In *Handbook of Studies on Men and Masculinities*, ed. Michael S. Kimmel, Jeff Hearn, and Raewyn Connell, 313–325. Thousand Oaks, CA: Sage.

Mirandé, Alfredo. 1997. *Hombres y Machos: Masculinity and Latino Culture.* Boulder, CO: Westview.

Morrell, Robert, and Sandra Swart. 2005. Men in the Third World: Postcolonial Perspectives on Masculinity. In *Handbook of Studies on Men and Masculinities*, ed. Michael S. Kimmel, Jeff Hearn, and Raewyn Connell, 90–113. Thousand Oaks, CA: Sage.

Nagel, Joane. 1998. Masculinity and Nationalism: Gender and Sexuality in the Making of Nations. *Ethnic and Racial Studies* 21 (2): 242–269.

Nagel, Joane. 2005. Nation. In *Handbook of Studies on Men and Masculinities*, ed. Michael S. Kimmel, Jeff Hearn, and Raewyn Connell, 397–413. Thousand Oaks, CA: Sage.

Neal, Mark Anthony. 2005. *New Black Man*. New York: Routledge.

Nielsen, François. 1994. Sociobiology and Sociology. *Annual Review of Sociology* 20: 267–303.

Nonn, Timothy. 2004. Hitting Bottom: Homelessness, Poverty, and Masculinity. In *Men's Lives*, ed. Michael S. Kimmel and Michael A. Messner, 258–267. 6th ed. Boston: Allyn and Bacon.

Parsons, Talcott. 1964. *Essays in Sociological Theory*. New York: Free Press.

Parsons, Talcott. 1964. *Social Structure and Personality*. New York: Free Press.

Parsons, Talcott, and Robert F. Bales. 1955. *Family, Socialization and Interaction Process*. Glencoe, IL: Free Press.

Pierce, Jennifer L. 1995. *Gender Trials*. Berkeley: University of California Press.

Ridgeway, Cecilia L., and Lynn Smith-Lovin. 1999. The Gender System and Interaction. *Annual Review of Sociology* 25: 191–216.

Roper, Michael. 1994. *Masculinity and the British Organization Man since 1945*. New York: Oxford University Press.

Rotundo, E. Anthony. 1993. *American Manhood*. New York: Basic Books.

Schur, Edwin M. 1984. *Labeling Women Deviant: Gender, Stigma and Social Control*. New York: Random House.

Smiler, Andrew P. 2004. Thirty Years after the Discovery of Gender: Psychological Concepts and Measures of Masculinity. *Sex Roles* 50 (1/2): 15–26.

Swain, Jon. 2005. Masculinities in Education. In *Handbook of Studies on Men and Masculinities*, ed. Michael S. Kimmel, Jeff Hearn, and Raewyn Connell, 213–229. Thousand Oaks, CA: Sage.

Taga, Futoshi. 2005. East Asian Masculinities. In *Handbook of Studies on Men and Masculinities*, ed. Michael S. Kimmel, Jeff Hearn, and Raewyn Connell, 129–140. Thousand Oaks, CA: Sage.

Whitehead, Stephen M. 2002. *Men and Masculinities: Key Themes and New Directions*. Cambridge, U.K.: Polity Press.

Williams, Christine L. 1995. *Still a Man's World: Men Who Do "Women's Work."* Berkeley: University of California Press.

Willis, Paul. 1977. *Learning to Labour*. London: Saxon House.

Zherebkin, Sergei. 2006. "Male Fantasies" in Ukraine: "Fucking Women and Building Nation." *Gender Studies Journal* (Eastern Europe) 14:38–59.

Sharon R. Bird

MASLOW, ABRAHAM
1908–1970

Abraham Harold Maslow, often referred to as the "father of humanist psychology," was born in Brooklyn, New York, on April 1, 1908. He was the first of seven children born to Jewish immigrants from Russia. Maslow completed his BA, MA, and PhD, all in psychology, at the University of Wisconsin. After graduating, he held various academic positions, spending the bulk of his career at Brandeis University in Waltham, Massachusetts. Maslow served as the chair of the Brandeis Psychology Department from 1951 until 1969. An avid researcher, lecturer, and writer, he published extensively, authoring more than thirty-one articles and eight books. Maslow died of a heart attack at the age of sixty-two on June 8, 1970. His work remains among the most influential in humanist psychology and enjoys continued recognition and application in myriad disciplines, including education, marketing, management, psychology, sociology, and communications.

Maslow is best known for his *hierarchy of human needs*, first proposed in 1943 in "A Theory of Human Motivation." In the original paper, Maslow concluded that humans have five sets of basic needs:

Physiological needs: These are the most basic of all human needs and include air, food, shelter, water, sex, and sleep.

Safety needs: This need category includes physical and psychological safety. Issues of personal safety and security of family, property, and employment are all included.

Love needs: Although Maslow originally labeled this as *love*, later interpretations expanded the notion and renamed it *belongingness*. Maslow stated that all individuals desire affection and a sense of belonging.

Esteem needs: Maslow argued that all individuals have a need for self-respect and the respect of others. This need category was divided into two subsidiary sets: (1) the need for strength, achievement, and adequacy; and (2) the desire for reputation and prestige, recognition, attention, and appreciation.

The need for self-actualization: Maslow described this as the need for individuals to do what they were meant to do, and argued that individuals could not be truly satisfied unless they became all that they were capable of becoming. He noted that a singer must sing and a poet must write if they are to be truly healthy and happy.

Maslow argued that these needs are arranged in a hierarchy of prepotency, and that individuals are motivated to fulfill lower-level needs before they are motivated to fulfill higher-level needs. For example, an individual experiencing thirst will be motivated to satisfy that need before other (higher) needs are considered. Once all physiological needs are met, the individual will be motivated by safety needs. According to Maslow, the four lowest levels are deficiency needs, and the top level is a growth need.

Most modern-day depictions of Maslow's hierarchy place the five levels of needs in a triangle or pyramid formation, with the lowest level of needs (physiological) at the bottom and self-actualization at the top. In many texts, this is all we see of Maslow's work, and his name has become almost synonymous with the *motivation triangle*.

Despite the widespread use and adaptation of Maslow's hierarchy of needs, it is not without its critics. Much of the criticism lies in the lack of empirical support for the hierarchy. Other criticisms stem from the methods used in Maslow's research, citing small sample sizes and "pseudoscientific" methods. Maslow himself argued that his theories were overused and understudied. In his personal journals, he wrote about limitations of reliability, validity, and small sample sizes and urged people to replicate his research to address these issues. Despite these criticisms, the hierarchy still holds a prominent place in motivation theory and can be found in many university textbooks. Many new theories of motivation have been introduced since Maslow's work was completed. Although these theories claim better reliability and validity, and have more empirical support, Maslow's conceptualization of a needs-based theory of motivation lies at the core of many of the new theories.

The hierarchy of needs is but a small sample of Maslow's contribution. Although best known for his work on the hierarchy of needs, Maslow was much more concerned with moving members of society beyond the basic needs, through self-actualization, to a more enlightened existence that he called *eupsychia*. Maslow's work also offered insights into leadership theory, psychotherapy, organizational change, dominance and sexuality, and the meaning of work. Influenced by such great thinkers as Sigmund Freud (1856–1939), Karl Marx (1818–1883), Kurt Goldstein (1878–1965), Alfred Adler (1870–1937), Erich Fromm (1900–1980), and Karen Horney (1885–1952), Abraham Maslow's contribution to humanist psychology is undeniable. Indeed, many credit him with founding the "third force" of psychology, following on the heels of the behaviorism and psychoanalytic schools of thought.

SEE ALSO *Motivation; Needs; Psychology; Reliability, Statistical; Self-Actualization; Validity, Statistical*

BIBLIOGRAPHY

Dye, Kelly, Albert J. Mills, and Terrance Weatherbee. 2005. Maslow: Man Interrupted: Reading Management Theory in Context. *Management Decision* 43 (10): 1375–1395.

Lowry, Richard, ed. 1979. *The Journals of A. H. Maslow*. 2 vols. Monterey, CA: Brooks/Cole.

Maslow, Abraham H. 1943. A Theory of Human Motivation. *Psychological Review* 50: 370–396.

Maslow, Abraham H. 1970. *Motivation and Personality*. 2nd ed. New York: Harper and Row.

Wilson, Colin. 1972. *New Pathways in Psychology: Maslow and the Post-Freudian Revolution*. New York: Taplinger.

Kelly Dye

MASSIVE RESISTANCE
SEE *Brown v. Board of Education, 1955.*

MASTER-SERVANT RELATIONSHIP
SEE *Servitude.*

MATERIAL CULTURE

Material culture consists of any physical manifestation or product of culture. Culture as a conceptual category exists in opposition to material culture, with culture sometimes distinguished as *mental culture* or *nonmaterial culture*, although some scholars take issue with such a Cartesian distinction. Alternatively material culture can be taken as a subset of a primary category, culture. Following the gist of E. B. Tylor's ([1871] 1974) classic 1871 definition, culture, in social science usage, comprises a complex whole of patterned knowledge and behavior: that which is traditional but also emergent, cumulated, learned, and acquired by members of society. By the mid-twentieth century culture could be defined and understood in literally hundreds of ways (Kroeber and Kluckhohn 1952); by the late twentieth century the term had been deconstructed by some postmodernist thinkers as totalizing, hegemonic, essentialist, and an imagined figment. Tylor employed the term *material culture* as early as 1871, although he apparently neglected to define it (Reynolds 1987, p. 155; for a commentary on the concept, see Buchli 2002, pp. 2–8).

Culture resides in the mind and is shared across minds. Material culture renders culture manifest in physical, palpable, measurable form. For archaeologists, folklorists, historians, museum curators, and others, material culture evidences the cultural. Material culture includes what archaeologists typically refer to as *artifacts*, collectors as *relics*, and art historians as *objets d'art*. Artifacts include such objects as stone tools, potsherds, bottles, beads, buttons, fibulae, coins, clay pipes, paintings, and textiles. To this list of conventionally recognized artifacts one should add such large-scale examples of material culture as buildings, monuments, gardens, gravestones, watercraft, roads, bridges, tunnels, dams, irrigation ditches, fences, wharves, landfills, and landscapes—all part of the intentionally built environment. For some scholars, any modification of the environment resulting from cultural activity, deliberate or not, counts as material culture: trash middens, oil spills, crop marks, cultigens, particulate emissions, food bones, human skeletal remains, manuports (materials moved out of their original location by human agency, like moon rocks brought to earth), and ecofacts of all sorts and conditions (such as flower pollen in Neanderthal burials or oyster shells filling in a road pothole). All writing and symbolic expression, from pictographs, graffiti, iconography (Munn 1973), and tattoos to cuneiform tablets and comic books can be considered material culture. The anthropologist and archaeologist James Deetz has suggested that spoken language be thought of as material culture in its "gaseous state" (Deetz 1996, p. 36), because sounds physically set air in motion during speech, if only briefly. Whether or not one wants to go so far as to accept spoken language as material culture, one can certainly admit records, tapes, and DVDs.

Material culture—past and present, partial and entire, in situ at an archaeological dig, on or of the landscape, or cached in a museum—illuminates cultural phenomena in many ways. Material culture communicates, expresses meaning, conveys experience, disciplines, and exhibits agency. Just as material culture is various, so too the study of material culture reflects a broad array of perspectives, analytical stances, and underlying philosophical traditions.

DESCRIPTION

Description remains foundational to material culture studies. The anthropologist Franz Boas ([1888] 1964), in one of the first formal ethnographies, recorded material as well as nonmaterial culture by describing such items as igloos, harpoons, and dolls, which were illustrated with sketches. For archaeologists, time, space, and form constitute three important descriptive dimensions of material culture. It is essential to know how old an object is and when it was used, recycled, or discarded. Chronology supplies part of the crucial cultural context of material culture. Dozens of dating methods yield relative and absolute chronologies. Relative dating, which establishes that something is older than, newer than, or contemporaneous with something else, is exemplified by cross dating derived from stratigraphy and an examination of stylistic change. Absolute dating methods, which assign age in calendar years, include obsidian hydration, dendrochronology

(using tree rings), and radiometric techniques such as radiocarbon dating.

It is also invaluable to know an object's spatial location—its point of origin or place of discovery. Provenance, like chronology, constitutes prime contextual data. Location might be variously logged as a cultural area, city, or country name, an archaeological excavation's grid/stratum designation, or a set of latitude and longitude points in a geographical positioning system. Lack of provenance is problematical because it means spatial context has been lost.

Form involves the attributes or characteristics of an object. Description of form entails acquiring and recording data concerning factors such as dimension, color, texture, chemical composition, and stylistic elements. Taxonomy, typology, or classification may draw on numerous methods, such as the type-variety concept, modal analysis, numerical taxonomy, and linguistic models. The widely applied type-variety approach identifies configurations of associated attributes to generate categories of types and varieties. In modal analysis, single attributes such as stylistic motifs can be traced through time and space. Numerical taxonomy codes for multiple attributes and tests for clustering or correlations by means of statistical routines. Typology based on linguistic models posits parallels to language, using either constituent units analogous to phonemes or morphemes or a set of grammatical rules for object construction. The results of typological analysis end up in such formats as exhibit catalogs, databases, museum labels, and archaeological site reports.

TECHNOLOGY AND FUNCTION

Considerations of technology and function are vital to material culture studies. Some typologies, such as the first ones developed in the second half of the nineteenth century to describe European Paleolithic assemblages, posit functions for stone tools, such as scraper, graver, and burin. The approach known as experimental archaeology (see Coles 1973; Reynolds 1979; Gould 1980; Ingersoll, Yellen, and Macdonald 1977) features rigorous testing of technology and function, applied to areas as diverse as flint-tool knapping and the experience of building and living in an Iron Age village. To discover aspects of technology or function, sophisticated laboratory analysis may be performed, as was the case with Arlene Fraikor et al. (1971), who showed that the copper in Hopewell earspools (Ohio, c. 100 BCE–550 CE) was shaped both by annealing and cold hammering. Thomas Loy and James Dixon (1998) contributed to the understanding of the function of 11,000-year-old Alaskan fluted projectile points when they identified species like mammoth, Dall sheep, and bison from blood cell residues preserved in the tools' crevices.

DIFFUSION AND DISTRIBUTION

Some of the earliest material culture studies, conducted during the late nineteenth and early twentieth centuries, focused on the distribution of elements of material and nonmaterial culture. The British heliocentric diffusionist school of Grafton Elliot Smith and William J. Perry and the German/Austrian diffusionist school of Friedrich Ratzel, Fritz Graebner, Leo Frobenius, and Wilhelm Schmidt identified complexes or *culture circles* of material and nonmaterial culture traits and used migration and borrowing to account for cultural differences. Similarly the twentieth-century American anthropologists A. L. Kroeber ([1939] 1952), Clark Wissler (1914), and Harold Driver (1961) linked cultural traits—with material items figuring prominently—to geographical areas, yielding *culture areas*. Nonmaterial elements like kinship terminology and language were combined with material culture categories, such as housing types, crafts, and art, and were mapped across culture areas. Material items from the Arctic culture area, for example, might include igloos, kayaks, and ivory tools. The culture area approach still finds expression (Kehoe 2006) as an organizational principle for ethnological surveys. One notable continuation of diffusionist analysis is the early work of the folklorist Henry Glassie (1968), which, in the tradition of the geographer Fred Kniffen, traces the diffusion of vernacular buildings, musical instruments, and tools across the eastern United States. The focus on culture element distributions still finds representation in twenty-first-century cultural and material culture studies in the extensive ethnological and archaeological databases at Yale. Known as the Human Relation Area Files (HRAF), these were initially published in book form but are available on the Web by subscription (http://www.yale.edu/hraf/).

PROCESS

Part of a much larger system, material culture can be viewed as performing certain systemic functions, such as fulfilling human needs or adapting to environmental change. Early twentieth-century functionalism, largely descriptive and static, was somewhat displaced during the 1960s by positivist and processual approaches, often fortified by conflict theory and cultural ecology. Processual archaeology seeks, by means of the hypothetico-deductive approach, to explain relationships within specific cultures as well as the evolutionary record across cultures. In a pioneering study Sally Binford and Lewis Binford (1969) employed factor analysis to relate clusters of tools to climate and environmental change. Susan Kent (1984) compared spatial patterning of domestic activity areas in Navajo, Euro-American, and Spanish American sites in the Southwest. William Rathje and Cullen Murphy (1992) contrasted what people presume to be in urban landfills with what really is there by means of laboratory-based quantification.

HISTORY, ART HISTORY, ARCHITECTURE, AND AMERICAN STUDIES

Many material culture studies simultaneously examine art, folk art, history, and technology. For example, the Winterthur Museum and Country Estate has published numerous books and conference papers on material culture and the decorative arts, examining categories such as clocks, ceramics, glass, furniture, architecture, gardens, and silver. A collection of material culture studies edited by Ian Quimby (1978) illustrates this approach. J. Ritchie Garrison (1991) followed the approach of Fernand Braudel to the local, individual level when he tracked the development of wealth and social status in Franklin County, Massachusetts, through an analysis of crops, architecture, and farmsteads. Robert Thompson and Joseph Cornet (1981) combined field and informant-based data, study of museum collections, and documentary research to decipher the meanings and social context of *maboondo*, bottomless cylindrical vessels placed on some Ki-Kongo graves (in Zaire) to symbolize the wisdom of deceased leaders. The art historian Thompson finds echoes of this Ki-Kongo tradition in the seashells and mugs with broken-out bottoms found on some African American graves in the southeastern United States.

MATERIAL CULTURE AS COMMUNICATION SYSTEM

Material culture, even when it appears to us as mere technology, communicates. Whatever culture needs or aspires to communicate or signal can be represented or reflected in material culture. Consider material culture as an alternative to spoken language and gesture—a medium less flexible but more enduring (McCracken 1987). Expressions and symbols of social and cultural identity, affiliation, role, rank, wealth, status, age, gender, values, and beliefs constitute a major area of interest for scholars of material culture. Material culture, from this perspective, can be thought of as providing a parallel record of a culture's worldview, values, and beliefs. A study by the geographer Peter Hugill (1984) showed how material culture can communicate about and correlate with social indicators. Looking at the evolution of the landscape in the Cazenovia area of New York, Hugill revealed ways the old elite maintain status over the newly wealthy by means of a "full range of gestures in the 'aesthetic-historical-genealogical' complex" (Hugill 1984, p. 29). Among that range of "gestures" are old homesteads infused with family history, something not readily attained by the newly wealthy. The creaky homes of the old elite proclaim a status beyond the purchasable.

Material culture systems may also be at variance with the nonmaterial, however. For example, language and material culture distributions do not necessarily predict each other (Welsch, Terrell, and Nadolski 1992); likewise, in traditional societies ownership of modern material culture may fail to correlate with values of modernity (Robbins and Pollnac 1974). Furthermore, although material culture exists in a sense as *doubly* cultural—first as a pattern in minds, second as material representation—not all material culture communications are intentional or even consciously understood. The plain, unadorned cross of the Southern Baptist church and the Christ on the cross of Latin American Catholicism symbolize, respectively, the ethereal (risen) Pentecostal Christ and the earthbound, suffering Christ (Richardson 2003, p. 122)—but few churchgoers consciously register these theological messages.

MATERIAL CULTURE AS MEANING AND COGNITION SYSTEM

One prominent approach to meaning in social science, structuralism, emphasizes patterned cultural meanings and central symbols and focuses on cultural abstraction or culture as knowledge system. By contrast, symbolic interactionism investigates the active behavioral processes of socialization and the realm of social actors. Each yields different pictures when applied to material culture. Inspired by the work of the structuralist anthropologist Claude Lévi-Strauss and the linguist Noam Chomsky, Henry Glassie (1975) analyzed vernacular Virginia houses and deduced a grammar of spatial proportion and function through which symbolic oppositions inherent in Western culture—such as natural/artificial and public/private—were expressed. The anthropologist Claire Farrer (1991) encountered expressions of the Mescalero Apache "base metaphor" throughout Apache culture, including in material forms, such as baskets, the tribal museum's layout, and the Holy Lodge. Sunwise directionality, circularity, sound and silence, harmony and disharmony, colors, gender, and the number 4 are among the integrated symbolic qualities of the Apache base metaphor. (See Hodder 1982 for a host of structuralist-oriented material culture studies by archaeologists.)

As for the social interactionist perspective, one can point to Rhys Isaac, who, influenced by the sociologist Erving Goffman, conducted a dramaturgical analysis of an eighteenth-century Virginia house "Sabine Hall" and of a diary from the 1760s written by Colonel Landon Carter. From these two sources, Isaac reconstructed webs of social relationships and daily rituals. Sabine Hall and its spaces appear as a stage with props, part of the material "definition of the situation" conditioning social action in eighteenth-century daily dramas. In a similar vein Miles Richardson (1987; see also Low 2000), influenced by the work of Goffman and the philosopher George Herbert Mead, contrasted the preliminary definitions of the situation and socially generated meanings of contemporary markets and plazas in Spanish America and then, guided by the concept of artifact as "collapsed act," outlined how archaeologists might rediscover the lost social world of a burial mound.

Akin to structuralism and symbolic interactionism is what is sometimes called cognitivism. For cognitivist archaeologists the question is: How did people of the past think? Through inferences drawn largely from the analysis of material culture, archaeologists reconstruct cultural thought processes. At Pincevent and other French sites of the Magdalenian age, C. Karlin and M. Julien (1994) found evidence of stages of "apprenticeship" in regard to lithic stone tool–making ability, which may reveal age and skill-level communication within a system of groups.

MATERIAL CULTURE AS COMMODITY SYSTEM

A universal category of human experience, *exchange*, incorporates material culture in both economic and symbolic ways. The work of two scholars, Igor Kopytoff and Daniel Miller, exemplifies the focus on exchange in material culture studies. If one follows their trajectories, things accumulate their own biographies just as people do, Kopytoff (1986) has suggested. One process Kopytoff has identified, *commoditization*, brings a wide range of objects into the orbit of one common exchange medium, such as money. But commoditization, as convenient and expansive as it tends to be, may threaten other social interests; hence some objects may undergo the nearly opposite process of *singularization* in order to be protected from commoditization. An artist's commoditized painting is bought and sold half a dozen times; after the artist becomes famous, the painting is purchased by a museum and becomes, at least temporarily, singularized.

For his part, Miller challenged the common assumption that globalization is an entirely homogenizing process. In his 1998 study of Coca-Cola in Trinidad, he observed that Coca-Cola furnished only one of several ways of preparing locally defined and preferred "black sweet drinks" (such as rum and Coke). The powerful locally owned distributor of Coca-Cola followed its own strategy—not Coca Cola's—when it came to marketing.

AGENCY AND POWER

Some analysts treat material culture as taken for granted or received (as with nonmaterial culture). Others, however, see material culture as imbued with the power to direct human thought and behavior or to reinforce class, gender, or other inequalities (McGuire and Paynter 1991). Inverting the Hegelian dialectic, Karl Marx set the stage for the materialist analysis of technology and material culture by proclaiming, "It is not the articles made, but how they are made, and by what instruments, that enables us to distinguish different economic epochs" (Marx [1887] 1967, p. 180). Marx incorporated the evolutionary scheme of Lewis Henry Morgan ([1887] 1985) to extend into prehistory the relations of modes of production, and in the process he provided an enduring model for Soviet archaeology, material culture studies, American cultural materialism (see Harris 1979), and of course numerous versions of conflict theory and critical theory. Continuing in this materialist vein and informed also by the work of Immanuel Wallerstein, Fernand Braudel ([1967] 1973, 1977) has traced the history of evolving relationships, on a worldwide scale, between economics and material culture categories, such as towns, housing, motive power sources (steam engines, water wheels, etc.), food, and money.

In his study of the material culture of seventeenth-through nineteenth-century Annapolis, the archaeologist Paul Shackel (1993) argued that clocks, scientific instruments, and items such as individual dinner plates, knives, forks, and spoons all enforce "discipline" and etiquette systems. At first only owned by the elite, clocks and scientific instruments such as telescopes served to "measure" time. Because it is measured, time can be made to appear as if it exists externally in nature rather than being a human construct; clocks then are used to set discipline parameters for everyday life, such as the beginning of a factory shift or a unit of pay (the hourly wage). Eventually all people come to possess clocks and to conceptualize time as located in nature.

Not all such analysis derives from conflict theory. In his evaluation of New York City public parks and plazas, the sociologist William Whyte (1980) documented the power of spatial layout and architecture to either invite or repel users. Places to sit, sun, shade, and water (in fountains and pools) invite human presence; fences, walls too high to sit on, immovable and uncomfortable benches, or threatening signs repel.

CONTESTED MATERIAL CULTURE

As mentioned in the above discussion of agency, analysts of material culture frequently draw on conflict theory and deconstruction theory (in anthropology the latter is sometimes referred to as post-structuralism). A collection of essays edited by Christopher Tilley (1990) explores ways the work of deconstructionists like Jacques Derrida and Michel Foucault might be applied to archaeology. Deconstruction places social power and systems of control front and center, and not surprisingly, material culture is very much taken into consideration. John Dorst (1989) detailed the properties of postmodern life represented by material culture found in the booths and exhibits of the annual Chadds Ford Days living history fair. As the visitors moved through the exhibits at the fair, observing and purchasing souvenirs, they marked or enacted difference and engaged the fair's "controlling image" of the late-eighteenth-century domestic sphere. At Chadds Ford the struggle to legitimize and represent the social order manifested itself at several levels: as a competition between the Brandywine River Museum, the Historical Society, and the Chris Sanderson Museum and on the landscape itself, where the projected nostalgic images of the Wyeth school wrestled with the suburban dream.

Courtney Workman (2001) documented the tortured politics surrounding a statue, *The Woman Movement*, designed by Adelaide Johnson in 1921 and portraying Elizabeth Cady Stanton, Susan Brownwall Anthony, and Lucretia Mott. On display briefly in the rotunda of the Capitol building, it was then removed to a basement closet, where it resided until 1997 in spite of numerous lobbying efforts over the years. The National Political Congress of Black Women sought to block relocation, demanding that Sojourner Truth first be added to an unfinished part of the monument. Even the way material culture is represented by archaeologists to archaeologists may be contested; for example, Janet Spector (1993) attempted to correct the underrepresentation of women's presence and activities in the archaeological record of a Wahpeton Dakota village.

"EXPERIENCE-NEAR" MATERIAL CULTURE

Material culture can also be presented in a way that is "experience-near," to use Clifford Geertz's term—that is, from the perspective of those who create it or experience it firsthand. Folklorist Simon Bronner helps one to encounter the "evidence of tangible things" (1986, p. 1) whether it's entering a house, making turtle soup, or carving gravemarkers. Henry Glassie's (1999) sensitive reporting allows one to enter into the mind of Hagop Barin, a Turkish Oriental carpet restorer working in Istanbul and Philadelphia. For Hagop, the good rugs evoke memories, create a mood and a feel. They are not just rugs but works of art with the hearts and thoughts of their creators woven into them.

CONCLUSION

Material culture can be analyzed from many perspectives. Its study is pursued by many disciplines both within and outside of the social sciences: anthropology, archaeology, architecture, art history, folklore/folklife, history, American studies, geography, cultural history, historic preservation, museology, and sociology. What is common to these perspectives and disciplines? For all, material culture serves as the principal source of data (Deetz 1977, p. 10). Material culture is habitually contrasted and related to nonmaterial culture. Space/time/culture boundaries are relaxed and transcended, such that material culture from any time, place, or culture becomes an object of interest. The focus is on comprehending material culture for its cultural and social significance, not on objects as things to be assessed, possessed, or appreciated. Material culture constitutes a "supercategory of objects," to apply differently a term employed by Victor Buchli (Buchli 2002, p. 6). Surprisingly, even as disciplines, schools, and perspectives proliferate, those studying that supercategory of objects, material culture, appear to readily cross disciplinary lines and read and cite each other's work (see Lubar and Kingery 1993; Miller 1998; Reynolds and Stott 1987; Richardson 1974; Schlereth 1982).

SEE ALSO *Anthropology; Anthropology, Linguistic; Archaeology; Architecture; Boas, Franz; Chomsky, Noam; Cognition; Culture; Ethnography; Goffman, Erving; Levi-Strauss, Claude; Marx, Karl; Materialism; Materialism, Dialectical; Mead, George Herbert; Meaning; Navajos; Symbols; Truth, Sojourner; Wallerstein, Immanuel*

BIBLIOGRAPHY

Binford, Sally R., and Lewis R. Binford. 1969. Stone Tools and Human Behavior. *Scientific American* 220 (4): 70–84.

Boas, Franz. [1888] 1964. *The Central Eskimo.* Lincoln: University of Nebraska Press.

Braudel, Fernand. [1967] 1973. *Capitalism and Material Life, 1400–1800.* Trans. Miriam Kochan. New York: Harper and Row.

Braudel, Fernand. 1977. *Afterthoughts on Material Civilization and Capitalism.* Trans. Patricia M. Ranum. Baltimore, MD: Johns Hopkins University Press.

Bronner, Simon J. 1986. *Grasping Things: Folk Material Culture and Mass Society in America.* Lexington: University of Kentucky Press.

Buchli, Victor, ed. 2002. *The Material Culture Reader.* Oxford: Berg.

Coles, John M. 1973. *Archaeology by Experiment.* London: Hutchinson.

Deetz, James. 1977. Material Culture and Archaeology: What's the Difference? In *Historical Archaeology and the Importance of Material Things,* ed. Leland Ferguson, 9-13. Society for

Historical Archaeology Special Publication Series, no. 2. Lansing, MI: Society for Historical Archaeology.

Deetz, James. 1996. *In Small Things Forgotten: An Archaeology of Early American Life.* New York: Anchor Books/Doubleday.

Dorst, John D. 1989. *The Written Suburb: An American Site, an Ethnographic Dilemma.* Philadelphia: University of Pennsylvania Press.

Driver, Harold E. 1961. *Indians of North America.* Chicago: University of Chicago Press.

Farrer, Claire R. 1991. *Living Life's Circle: Mescalero Apache Cosmovision.* Albuquerque: University of New Mexico Press.

Fraikor, Arlene L., James J. Hester, and Frederick J. Fraikor. 1971. Metallurgical Analysis of a Hopewell Copper Earspool. *American Antiquity* 36 (3): 358–361.

Garrison, J. Ritchie. 1991. *Landscape and Material Life in Franklin County, Massachusetts, 1770–1860.* Knoxville: University of Tennessee Press.

Glassie, Henry. 1968. *Pattern in the Material Folk Culture of the Eastern United States.* Philadelphia: University of Pennsylvania Press.

Glassie, Henry. 1975. *Folk Housing in Middle Virginia: A Structural Analysis of Historic Artifacts.* Knoxville: University of Tennessee Press.

Glassie, Henry. 1999. *Material Culture.* Bloomington: Indiana University Press.

Gould, R. A. 1980. *Living Archaeology.* Cambridge, U.K.: Cambridge University Press.

Harris, Marvin. 1979. *Cultural Materialism: The Struggle for a Science of Culture.* New York: Random House.

Hodder, Ian, ed. 1982. *Symbolic and Structural Archaeology.* Cambridge, U.K.: Cambridge University Press.

Hugill, Peter. 1984. The Landscape as a Code for Conduct: Reflections on Its Role in Walter Firey's "Aesthetic-Historical-Genealogical Complex." In *Place: Experience and Symbol,* ed. Miles Richardson, 21–30. Baton Rouge: Geoscience Publications, Department of Geography and Anthropology, Louisiana State University.

Ingersoll, Daniel W., John E. Yellen, and William Macdonald, eds. 1977. *Experimental Archeology.* New York: Columbia University Press.

Isaac, Rhys. 1988. Ethnographic Method in History: An Action Approach. In *Material Life in America, 1600–1860,* ed. Robert Blair St. George, 39–61. Boston: Northeastern University Press.

Karlin, C., and M. Julien. 1994. Prehistoric Technology: A Cognitive Science? In *The Ancient Mind: Elements of Cognitive Archaeology,* eds. Colin Renfrew and Ezra B. W. Zubrow, 152–164. Cambridge, U.K.: Cambridge University Press.

Kehoe, Alice Beck. 2006. *North American Indians: A Comprehensive Account.* 3rd ed. Englewood Cliffs, NJ: Prentice-Hall.

Kent, Susan. 1984. *Analyzing Activity Areas: An Ethnoarchaeological Study of the Use of Space.* Albuquerque: University of New Mexico Press.

Kopytoff, Igor. 1986. The Cultural Biography of Things: Commoditization as Process. In *The Social Life of Things:*

Commodities in Cultural Perspective, ed. Arjun Appadurai, 64–91. Cambridge, U.K., and New York: Cambridge University Press.

Kroeber, A. L. [1939] 1952. Cultural Intensity and Climax. In *The Nature of Culture*, 337–343. Chicago: University of Chicago Press.

Kroeber, A. L., and Clyde Kluckhohn. 1952. *Culture: A Critical Review of Concepts and Definitions*. New York: Vintage Books.

Low, Setha M. 2000. *On the Plaza: The Politics of Public Space and Culture*. Austin: University of Texas Press.

Loy, Thomas H., and E. James Dixon. 1998. Blood Residues on Fluted Points from Eastern Beringia. *American Antiquity* 63 (1): 21–46.

Lubar, Steven, and W. David Kingery, eds. 1993. *History from Things: Essays on Material Culture*. Washington, DC: Smithsonian Institution Press.

Marx, Karl. [1887] 1967. *The Process of Capitalist Production*. Vol. 1 of *Capital: A Critique of Political Economy*, ed. Frederick Engels, trans. Samuel Moore and Edward Aveling. New York: International Publishers.

McCracken, Grant. 1987. Clothing as Language: An Object Lesson in the Study of the Expressive Properties of Material Culture. In *Material Anthropology: Contemporary Approaches to Material Culture*, eds. Barrie Reynolds and Margaret A. Stott, 103–128. Lanham, MD: University Press of America.

McGuire, Randall H., and Robert Paynter, eds. 1991. *The Archaeology of Inequality*. Oxford: Basil Blackwell.

Miller, Daniel. 1998. Coca-Cola: A Black Sweet Drink from Trinidad. In *Material Cultures: Why Some Things Matter*, ed. Daniel Miller, 169–187. London: UCL Press.

Morgan, Lewis Henry. [1877] 1985. *Ancient Society*. Tucson: University of Arizona Press.

Munn, Nancy D. 1973. *Walbiri Iconography: Graphic Representation and Cultural Symbolism in a Central Australian Society*. Ithaca, NY: Cornell University Press. Reprint, Chicago: University of Chicago Press, 1986.

Quimby, Ian M. G., ed. 1978. *Material Culture and the Study of American Life*. New York: Norton.

Rathje, William L., and Cullen Murphy. 1992. *Rubbish: The Archaeology of Garbage*. New York: HarperCollins.

Reynolds, Barrie. 1987. Material Systems: An Approach to the Study of Kwandu Material Culture. In *Material Anthropology: Contemporary Approaches to Material Culture*, eds. Barrie Reynolds and Margaret A. Stott, 155–187. Lanham, MD: University Press of America.

Reynolds, Peter J. 1979. *Iron-Age Farm: The Butser Experiment*. London: Colonnade Book/British Museum Publications.

Richardson, Miles. 1987. A Social (Ideational-Behavioral) Interpretation of Material Culture and Its Application to Archaeology. In *Mirror and Metaphor: Material and Social Constructions of Reality*, eds. Daniel W. Ingersoll Jr. and Gordon Bronitsky, 381–403. Lanham, MD: University Press of America.

Richardson, Miles. 2003. *Being-in-Christ and Putting Death in Its Place: An Anthropologist's Account of Christian Performance in Spanish America and the American South*. Baton Rouge: Louisiana State University Press.

Robbins, Michael C., and Richard B. Pollnac. 1974. A Multivariate Analysis of the Relationship of Artifactual to Cultural Modernity in Rural Buganda. In *The Human Mirror: Material and Spatial Images of Man*, ed. Miles Richardson, 174–195. Baton Rouge: Louisiana State University Press.

Schlereth, Thomas J., ed. 1982. *Material Culture Studies in America*. Nashville, TN: AASLH.

Shackel, Paul A. 1993. *Personal Discipline and Material Culture: An Archaeology of Annapolis, Maryland, 1695–1870*. Knoxville: University of Tennessee Press.

Spector, Janet D. 1993. *What This Awl Means: Feminist Archaeology at a Wahpeton Dakota Village*. St. Paul: Minnesota Historical Society Press.

Thompson, Robert Farris, and Joseph Cornet. 1981. *The Four Moments of the Sun: Kongo Art in Two Worlds*. Washington, DC: National Gallery of Art.

Tilley, Christopher, ed. 1990. *Reading Material Culture: Structuralism, Hermeneutics, and Post-Structuralism*. Oxford: Basil Blackwell.

Tylor, Edward B. [1871] 1974. *Primitive Culture: Researches into the Development of Mythology, Philosophy, Religion, Language, Art, and Custom*. New York: Gordon.

Welsch, Robert L., John Terrell, and John A. Nadolski. 1992. Language and Culture on the North Coast of New Guinea. *American Anthropologist* 94 (3): 568–600.

Whyte, William H. 1980. *The Social Life of Small Urban Spaces*. Washington, DC: Conservation Foundation.

Wissler, Clark. 1914. The Influence of the Horse in the Development of Plains Culture. *American Anthropologist*, n.s., 16 (1): 1–25.

Workman, Courtney. 2001. *The Woman Movement*: Memorial to Women's Rights Leaders and the Perceived Images of the Women's Movement. In *Myth, Memory, and the Making of the American Landscape*, ed. Paul A. Shackel, 47–66. Gainesville: University of Florida Press.

Daniel W. Ingersoll Jr.

MATERIALISM

Materialism is a philosophical doctrine of existence that argues that human consciousness is determined either principally or exclusively by matter and its change or manipulation. This "primacy" of matter has its foundation in an early philosophical argument that while material being (or the body) can exist without the mind, the mind is unable to exist without corporeality. Because materialism in its most basic and unifying sense as a doctrine relies on the denial of the nonmaterial (and thus a mechanistic relationship between the nature and its manipulation), many view it as quite different from other conceptualizations of existence (or ontologies) that analyze the relationship between entities such as mind, body, and spirit. It is seen rather as a philosophical assertion in juxtaposition to a doctrine of idealism, and in particular its invocation of the supernatural or disembodied existence. Later forms of materialism proved far less reductionist with respect to the mind and subjective experience; still, at its most basic, materialism implicitly denies the possibly of any Cartesian mind/body dualism, as processes of the mind are subordinated to the physical environment in which they must take place, and not to some disembodied realm of existence.

Questions of materiality are among the oldest of philosophical inquiries. Epicurus and Democritus, the Greek philosophers on whom the noted historical materialist Karl Marx based his doctoral thesis, were among the earliest thinkers to expound a metaphysical doctrine of materialism. Early forms of materialism sought to explain human experience in terms of how atoms interacted with one another in nature to manifest different objects. This type of thinking was opposed to that of some of their Hellenic contemporaries (notably Plato and Aristotle) who proposed the existence of immateriality. It is the implicit denial of a spirit or otherworldly embodiment of the mind in these early forms of materialism that has led many to argue that materialism is an intrinsically atheistic philosophy. This point about the tension between religion and intellectual inquiry is significant, because materialism's emergence as a significant doctrine occurred as a product of Enlightenment questions about the role of science and religion in social life.

MATERIALISM: SCIENTIFIC VERSUS DIALECTIC

Materialism has had a propensity for misrepresentation as teleological and deterministic philosophical doctrine, wherein critics warn of insinuations that matter is being afforded a kind of unmediated rationality in guiding action and history. This is in part attributable to a misunderstanding of the major philosophical and social scientific debates that have taken place since the introduction of the concept of dialectics in the nineteenth century. A common error, for instance, rests on characterizing Marx's *historical materialism* (a term in fact coined by Friedrich Engels) as such by referencing his introduction to his *Contribution to a Critique of Political Economy* (1859), in which he concludes that legal and political superstructures arise out of the economic base (infrastructure) of society. Of course, Marx had a lifelong engagement with Hegelian dialectics, and was more centrally concerned philosophically with trying to make sense of the social relations through a theory of praxis, not through a mechanistic determinism. And it is important to understand how such dialectical interventions emerging at that time engaged, and continue to engage, with materialist approaches unabashed in their determinism. The materialist anthro-

pologist Marvin Harris once remarked that Marx's materialism would be palatable if he could just get the Hegelian monkey off his back (Harris 1979). An extreme position (and anticipatory of Harris's reductionist cultural materialism), it does however underscore a fundamental difference about what role ideas, beliefs, or immaterial states have to different kinds of materialists.

Scientific materialism emerged most notably in nineteenth-century Germany as a response to idealism and clerical domination over intellectual life. Ludwig Feuerbach (1804–1872), a student of Hegel best known as the inspiration for Marx's *Theses on Feuerbach* (1845), catalyzed a materialist movement that had important consequences for the future relationship between the sciences and religion. Materialists of this ilk believed that the rapid advances in science and medicine occurring at this time constituted evidence of the power of science to answer questions about the material and immaterial alike as reflections of biological, chemical, and physical processes. Such atheism worried many advocates of science and led to the caricaturing of evolution as an antireligious doctrine. The devoutly religious Charles Darwin (1809–1882) declined Marx's invitation to dedicate *Capital* (1867) to him because he feared further associations with materialism and social evolutionism.

Scientific materialism did anticipate further problems in philosophy. Indeed, claims about determinism and physicalism remain important to the *identity thesis* in materialist philosophy, the view that "there are no philosophical considerations that rule out the possibility that future scientific inquiry will show that *every mental state and event is identical with some material state or event*" (Rosenthal 2000, pp. 8–9; emphasis added). Eliminative materialism, for example, has been a subject of interest to some of the most important philosophers of the twentieth century (e.g., Richard Rorty, Paul Feyerabend, W. V. O. Quine, Paul Churchland, and Wilfrid Sellars) who have been concerned with the legitimacy of separating mental states apart from the physical state in which they take place.

Georgi Plekhanov and Vladimir Lenin are famous for developing the concept of *dialectical materialism*. In his *Materialism and Empirio-Criticism* ([1909] 1947) Lenin sought to develop a philosophy of materialism that relied less on the reductionist claims of nineteenth-century "vulgar materialism." He eschewed the trivializing analogies of the scientific materialists—such as that thoughts were to the brain as bile was to the liver—evoked to assert that nothing other than matter existed, in favor of a materialism that saw mental processes as emanating from material ones. Although also clearly influenced by Feuerbach, Lenin claimed that the material world (nature) was primary and the mind and spirit were secondary in a dependent relationship for the development of knowledge.

Some contemporary materialist philosophers remain wary of mind/body dualism generally, in particular of theories that "either deny causal interaction between the mental and the physical, deny causal efficacy to mental states, picture the mental and the physical as being two wholly distinct realms of being, or fail to give integrity to one term of the mind-body relationship" (Peters 1995, p. 8). Notwithstanding philosophical debates as to the efficacy of mental and material realms as categories of analysis, the legacy of materialist philosophy for the social sciences can be said to be twofold. First, materialism abjectly underscores empirical method and observation as essential for an adequate understanding of human societies. And second, it has legitimated the innovation and honing of viable methods for comprehending human action through an emphasis on materiality (and the manipulation thereof) as an entry point of social analysis.

MATERIALITY AND THE METHODOLOGICAL IMPORTANCE OF THINGS

To understand the significance of materialism to contemporary social science, it is necessary to identify the fundamental changes that the academy has undergone in the last two centuries toward the formation of sciences of social processes. In the nineteenth century Auguste Comte (1798–1857) authored a theory of "social physics," a primitive social science method based on an analogy to the physical sciences that had a profound influence on the development of positivism. The vitality of empirical and positivist theory during this period was aided by the derivation and development of empirical methods that proved successful in their capacity for establishing laws for social processes. The philosopher Ian Hacking (1990) has argued that the honing of techniques for prediction and the establishment of probability in both the physical and social sciences created conditions of possibility for contemporary ways of thinking about the knowability of the world. Among materialist scholars there remains much difference with respect to the degree to which the world is exhaustively knowable. Cultural materialism, for instance, rejects dialectics outright, prioritizing instead positivism, probability, and the primacy of human use of the environment for the understanding of social process. Still, materialist doctrine in the social sciences has become more of an operationalization of a particular positivist method than an outright philosophical account of human activity.

There are a number of methodical approaches to the study of materiality that have become increasingly popular in the social sciences, particularly as all of its disciplines have sought to make sense of social processes that are increasingly informed by global flows of information,

communication, and technology. Economics for the most part has always remained unabashedly materialist, methodologically individualist, and positivist as a discipline. Cultural ecological approaches historically have been significant traditions in anthropology and geography. And long-standing subdisciplines such as economic sociology and economic anthropology have gained increased visibility as scholars throughout the social sciences have increasingly queried the meanings and impacts of globalization. Two relevant approaches to the contemporary study of materiality in the social sciences merit particular notice.

Since the mid-1980s there have been numerous studies devoted to the study of a single material object with the aim of understanding the complexities of human global relationships. These commodity biographies have traced the social and economic importance of various globally significant commodities, including tobacco, coal, potatoes, cod, bananas, and salt (see Mantz and Smith 2006, pp. 78–80 for summary). Some of these scholars were influenced by Arjun Appadurai's groundbreaking anthology *The Social Life of Things* (1986), and accordingly tend to orient themselves to discussions of how consumption of material objects frames political economic relationships. Others, emphasizing the importance of global production systems to the origination of political economic inequalities, originate their work in Sidney Mintz's *The Sweetness of Power* (1985), or more broadly in the cultural ecology and political economic traditions from which it came. Mintz's account shows how sugar played an instrumental role in building the economies of industrial Europe around extractive plantation production regimes in the Caribbean. A more recent study has attempted to understand how political economic structural inequalities developed under capitalism are taking on a parallel form in the digital age with the extraction of Congolese coltan, an ore essential to digital technologies such as mobile phones (Mantz and Smith 2006).

At the same time, a growing field of material culture studies has emerged with a specific interest in the consumptive dimensions of human social economic practice (e.g., Miller 2004). Though many of these scholars certainly would not recognize themselves or their approaches as materialist per se, the fact that their entry point remains largely concerned with the human use of material objects indicates their importance to the legacy of materialism in the social sciences. With influences from linguistics and semiotics, and a foundation that engages (at times both sympathetically and critically) with the Frankfurt school, this school of thought has been concerned principally with attempting to unravel the social meaning of objects. This tradition represents a radical break from the traditional domination of studies of the material by materialists. The departure is reflected in a philosophical heritage indebted to the early-twentieth-century German sociologist Georg Simmel (1858–1918), as a purported alternative to the materialism of Marxian political economy. A number of the commodity biographies approaches likewise endeavor to move the focus of the study of objects away from their productive sites and instead into the consumptive realms in which they have discernible semiotic and sociological meaning.

There are a number of reasons why the study of material objects has moved away from the materialist philosophy in which it was once firmly ensconced. First, approaches having determinist legacies or "metanarrative" claims have become unpopular among a large number of social scientists, particularly given the influence of postmodernism in the late twentieth and early twenty-first centuries. Second, the end of the cold war has precipitated an increased discomfort with dialectical materialist approaches that were influential to the creation and development of Soviet socialism. At the same time, the scientific materialist approaches of the nineteenth century, as well as the more orthodox approaches of the twentieth century such as cultural materialism, have not been appealing to social scientists uncomfortable with their unwavering dedication to physicalism. And finally, a historic divide between the humanities and sciences—a rift separating what C. P. Snow referred as "two cultures" (1959)—remains unresolved and taxing for the development of a unified and truly interdisciplinary social scientific theory and method. Nonetheless, there remain dedicated approaches to political economy principally influenced by materialist philosophy and method that hold great possibility for unifying various approaches to the study of material objects in the social sciences.

SEE ALSO *Marx, Karl; Marxism; Materialism, Dialectical*

BIBLIOGRAPHY

Appadurai, Arjun, ed. 1986. *The Social Life of Things.* Cambridge, U.K.: Cambridge University Press.

Armstrong, David M. 1968. *A Materialist Theory of the Mind.* New York: Routledge and Kegan Paul.

Campbell, Keith. 1984. *Body and Mind.* 2nd ed. Notre Dame, IN: University of Notre Dame Press.

Hacking, Ian. 1990. *The Taming of Chance.* Cambridge, U.K.: Cambridge University Press.

Harris, Marvin. 1979. *Cultural Materialism: The Struggle for a Science of Culture.* New York: Random House.

Lenin, Vladimir I. [1909] 1947. *Materialism and Empirio-Criticism: Critical Comments on a Reactionary Philosophy.* Moscow: Foreign Languages Publishing.

Mantz, Jeff W., and Jim H. Smith. 2006. Do Cellular Phones Dream of Civil War? The Mystification of Production and the Consequences of Technology Fetishism in the Eastern Congo. In *Inclusion and Exclusion in the Global Arena*, ed. Max Kirsch, 71–93. New York: Routledge.

Marx, Karl. [1845] 1969. Theses on Feuerbach. In *Marx/Engels Selected Works*, vol. 1, trans. W. Lough, 13–15. Moscow: Progress Publishers.

Marx, Karl. [1859] 1971. *A Contribution to a Critique of Political Economy.* London: Lawrence and Wishart.

Marx, Karl. [1867] 1990. *Capital: A Critique of Political Economy.* Vol. 1. Trans. Ben Fowkes. New York: Penguin Books in association with New Left Review.

Miller, Daniel, ed. 2004. *Materiality.* Durham, NC: Duke University Press.

Miller, Richard W. 1984. *Analyzing Marx.* Princeton, NJ: Princeton University Press.

Mintz, Sidney W. 1985. *Sweetness and Power: The Place of Sugar in Modern History.* New York: Viking.

Peters, Selton L. 1995. *Emergent Materialism: A Proposed Solution to the Mind/Body Problem.* Lanham, MD: University Press of America.

Rosenthal, David M., ed. 2000. *Materialism and the Mind-Body Problem.* 2nd ed. Indianapolis, IN: Hackett.

Snow, C. P. 1959. *The Two Cultures and the Scientific Revolution.* Cambridge, U.K.: Cambridge University Press.

Jeffrey Mantz

MATERIALISM, DIALECTICAL

Dialectical materialism was the name given by the doctrinaires and political stalwarts of the Communist Party of the Soviet Union (CPSU) to official Soviet philosophy. Others regarded it more as an ideology, but either way dialectical materialism was a constituent part of the major political innovation of the twentieth-century, official Soviet Marxism. Whether or not dialectical materialism was well formed enough to give adequate or appropriate support to the Soviet experiment is, of course, another question, and a much-debated one. Because CPSU officials and stalwarts were powerful enough to impose their definitions on a captive audience, dialectical materialism—which was commonly given the acronymic form DiaMat—enjoyed a remarkable shelf life during the mid-twentieth century. But, as a concept, its sell-by date is by now long past.

Dialectical was often confused with historical materialism. (In *Dialectical and Historical Materialism*, a book supposedly written by Joseph Stalin during the 1930s, it is unclear whether the author wishes to separate the two or run them together.) Their conflation was and is mistaken: Historical materialism's register is historiographical—it is a mode of historical and sociopolitical analysis—whereas dialectical materialism, whose register is philosophical and scientific, throws nature and its laws, along with the supposed "laws" of thought, into the mix. One might say that whereas dialectical encompasses historical materialism, the latter can and did flourish among thinkers to whom dialectical materialism was an embarrassment—Western Marxists and critical theorists prominent among them. The addition of nature and thought, which was first and foremost the contribution of Friedrich Engels (1820–1895), did nothing to make DiaMat philosophically coherent. DiaMat was, rather, a hodgepodge of philosophy and science that confused the pursuit or advance of (mainly scientific) knowledge *in* the world with the attainment of truth *about* the world.

At a basic level, DiaMat regarded historical or social evolution as an aspect or facet of natural evolution, and as being subject to the same "laws" as those that govern natural evolution—laws that are said but not shown to be "dialectical" in character. (Engels was as uncomfortable as many other Victorian gentlemen with the aleatory, non-teleological character of Darwin's principle of natural selection.) When we ask who was the first to run together natural laws, historical laws, and the "laws" of thought, it is Engels, not Marx, who instantly snaps into focus. (Marx, for the record, never even used the term *historical materialism*, though he did not protest when Engels in a review designated Marx's method as an instance of "the materialist interpretation of history.")

While it was Georgi Plekhanov, "the father of Russian Marxism," who coined the term *dialectical materialism*, the concept was first authoritatively enacted by V. I. Lenin (1870–1924), who regarded Engels's and Plekhanov's legacy as giving intellectual ballast to the copy-theory of perception he advanced in *Materialism and Empirio-Criticism* (1908). In fact, Lenin's theory of perception

> involved a divergence from Engels's account, since materialism to Engels was not the same as epistemological realism. … [Engels's] medley of metaphysical materialism and Hegelian dialectics … was conserved by Lenin, but [Lenin's] own theory of cognition—which was all that really mattered to him—was not strictly speaking dependent on it. Matter as an absolute substance, or constitutive element of the universe, is not required for a doctrine which merely postulates that the mind is able to arrive at universally true conclusions about the external world given to the senses (Lichtheim 1974, pp. 70–71).

(As an aside, the contemporary philosopher Donald Davidson argues that the question whether an accurate representation of reality in thought is possible, let alone desirable—Lenin thought it was both—is undecidable and should be discarded from philosophy altogether.) The compatibility of Lenin with Engels (or Marx, for that

matter) was in the event eclipsed by Russian Marxist notables' need to establish "orthodoxy," to produce a canon, a continuous, unbroken line of succession stretching from Hegel through Marx through Engels through Plekhanov through Lenin through Stalin (and whoever else was *à la page* at the time).

Engels of course could have had no foreknowledge of what Soviet stalwarts would do with his doctrine. His sights had been set, not on a nonexistent CPSU, but on German social democracy and, by extension, the Second International (1885–1914). Engels cannot be held directly responsible for the transformation of his speculations into a state dogma imposed on a captive audience. Even so, at a less direct level Engels has much to answer for. He did much to make the sorry Soviet sequence of DiaMat luminaries possible. These swiftly awarded Engels canonical status, and presented him as enjoying a status he had never claimed, as someone coeval and on an equal footing with Marx.

There can be no doubt that Engels's presentation of his intellectual partnership with Marx, "second fiddle" or no second fiddle, aided and abetted the spurious continuity between Marx and Stalin that DiaMat required. (This continuity was celebrated by cold warriors in the West as well as the East, for it provided the former with an easy—arguably, too easy—target). Such continuity depended throughout on an idea Engels encouraged after Marx's death in 1883: that in writing about (and conflating) the laws of nature, history, and thought, Engels was faithfully fulfilling his part in an agreed-upon division of labor, according to which Engels produced texts that were interchangeable with Marx's texts on some subjects and supplementary to, but always compatible with, and true to Marx's works on others. Without this supposition DiaMat would not and could not have taken the seamless form it took; but there is no evidence that the supposition itself could withstand serious, critical examination.

The disservice done to Marx by the later Engels was a disservice to philosophy at large: It turned Marxism at the official level into the kind of universal *weltanschauung* or worldview that Marx never intended to provide. Marxism-Leninism constructed around Marx's writings, to the extent that these were made available (and they were not rushed into print as Engels's were), a key to unlock every door, a grand theory concerned with the ultimate laws and constituents of the universe. Marx himself had maintained discretion on such cosmic questions. Naturalism and cosmology were domains distant from the critique of political economy that was Marx's lifework. Worse still, it was in a sense precisely because Marx had remained reticent on these issues that his self-styled Soviet epigones—to whom such silence seemed unnerving—felt the need to fill in nonexistent gaps and construct a coherent, comprehensive system of materialist metaphysics. Marx's considered reticence, it could be (and was) argued, constituted not a failure of scholarly nerve but a well-judged reluctance to extend his arguments into areas where they could have no meaningful application.

Even though Engels's interpretation of Marxism is in significant respects at variance with what Marx had bequeathed him (and us), Engels took care to advance it in Marx's name. This immeasurably helped DiaMat set the tone for more than a generation of "official" Soviet Marxists. While DiaMat did not pass unquestioned in the West, particularly among Western Marxists and critical theorists, it ruled the roost and attained canonical status in the USSR, its satellites, and China. There was throughout its elaboration an inbuilt, fatal flaw: If nature is conceived materialistically, it does not lend itself to dialectical method, and if, conversely, the dialectic (a category that Hegel had confined within logic, and that was to be of no real use to Marx) is read back into nature, there is no real place or need for materialism. The misapplication of the dialectic into natural processes then either endows the structure of reality with a purposive, teleological striving (which would fly in the face of Darwin, if not of Darwinism), or it stretches the concept of dialectical change to the point of tautology: Anything that happens is said to be a "development" involving qualitative as well as quantitative change (see Lichtheim 1965, p. 254; cf. 247–248).

Paid positions for philosophers who accepted the precepts of DiaMat (or who said they did) came into existence as the fledgling Soviet régime consolidated itself. But, unsurprisingly, "between 1930–1955, philosophical discussions among (Soviet) Marxists were stifled, the publication of books and articles became virtually nonexistent, and the teaching of philosophy in the USSR was greatly reduced" (Loone 1993, p. 158). Engels's third law of dialectics (the negation of the negation) was unceremoniously jettisoned by Stalin, and Engels's first law (the transformation of quantity into quality) was relegated by Chairman Mao to the status of a special instance of Engels's second law (the interpenetration of opposites). These doctrinal modifications could be regarded as refinements, or as signs that DiaMat was beginning to collapse beneath its own weight—even before the political system it was said to uphold imploded at the institutional level. Lichtheim has called DiaMat an "intellectual disaster," and it is not hard to see why. It was also, after all, a kind of politically charged quodlibet for the philosophically tone-deaf.

SEE ALSO *Marxism*

BIBLIOGRAPHY

Bhaskar, Roy. 1993. Dialectic. In *The Blackwell Dictionary of Twentieth-Century Social Thought*, ed. William Outhwaite and Tom Bottomore, 154–157. Oxford: Blackwell.

Graham, Loren R. 1972. *Science and Philosophy in the Soviet Union*. New York: Knopf.

Jordan, Z. A. 1967. *The Evolution of Dialectical Materialism: A Philosophical and Sociological Analysis*. London and New York: Macmillan.

Kuusinen, O. W., et al. 1960. *Fundamentals of Marxism-Leninism*. Trans. and ed. Clemens Dutt. Moscow: Foreign Language Publishing House.

Lichtheim, George. 1965. Dialectical Materialism. In his *Marxism: An Historical and Critical Study*, 244–248. 2nd rev. ed. New York: Praeger.

Lichtheim, George. 1974 (1971). On the Interpretation of Marx's Thought. In his *From Marx to Hegel*, 63–79. New York: Seabury.

Loone, Eero. 1993. "Dialectical Materialism." In *The Blackwell Dictionary of Twentieth Century Social Thought*, ed. William Outhwaite and Tom Bottomore, 157–158. Oxford: Blackwell.

Marcuse, Herbert. 1958. *Soviet Marxism*. London and New York: Columbia University Press.

Thomas, Paul. 1999. Engels and 'Scientific Socialism'. In *Engels after Marx*, ed. Manfred B. Steger and Terrell Carver, 215–231. University Park: Pennsylvania State University Press.

Wetter, Gustav A. 1958. *Dialectical Materialism: A Historical and Systematic Survey of Philosophy in the Soviet Union*. Trans. Peter Heath. Rev. ed. London and New York: Routledge and Kegan Paul.

Paul Thomas

MATHEMATICAL ECONOMICS

In a narrow sense, mathematical economics, as represented by the *Journal of Mathematical Economics* or the North-Holland *Handbook of Mathematical Economics*, is the specialization within advanced economic theory using sophisticated mathematical techniques such as functional analysis and topology. In a wider, more general sense, mathematical economics refers to the application of mathematical methods within economics (other than the application of probability theory and mathematical statistics in economics, which has acquired separate disciplinary status as econometrics). The use of mathematics, together with emphasis on formal economic theory, has become increasingly pervasive in economics since World War II (1939–1945), as general equilibrium analysis, game theory, and operations research became prominent. Training in at least calculus, matrix algebra, and constrained optimization (as well as econometrics) is now indispensable for comprehension of articles in general economics journals, not just journals specializing in economic theory.

There were numerous early attempts to use mathematics to analyze questions in political economy before a receptive audience existed for such works (see Baumol and Goldfeld 1968 for selections from this literature). A few of these early efforts, notably Antoine Augustin Cournot's 1838 analysis of oligopoly, Francis Ysidro Edgeworth's 1881 study of bilateral exchange, and Louis Bachelier's 1900 dissertation on financial speculation and stochastic processes, have been rediscovered and reinterpreted in light of solution concepts developed much later (Cournot oligopoly being viewed by some as a special case of Nash equilibrium, Edgeworth's analysis being related to the game-theoretic concept of the core), but their contemporary readership and influence was slight. Alfred Marshall was educated as a mathematician (Second Wrangler at Cambridge, ranked behind only the physicist Lord Rayleigh) but, unlike his contemporary Edgeworth, he relegated mathematics to a mathematical appendix in his *Principles of Economics* that, in eight editions from 1890 to 1920, dominated the teaching of economics in English. Although he advocated mathematics as an aid to thought, Marshall distrusted mathematical economics that could not be translated into plain English, and worried about restricting attention only to those considerations that can be quantified. Similarly, as late as 1939, J. R. Hicks restricted formal mathematics to an appendix in his *Value and Capital*, which brought the continental European tradition of general equilibrium analysis associated with Léon Walras and Vilfredo Pareto in Lausanne to the attention of English-language economists. Along with Roy Harrod, James Meade, and others, Hicks (1937) took a leading role in translating John Maynard Keynes's theory of employment into a small system of simultaneous equations, which Hicks's accompanying diagrams (later modified by Alvin Hansen) turned into the trained intuition of two generations of economists. Keynes himself had made such a translation into a four-equation system in his Cambridge lectures in December 1933 (and the first two published versions of such a model were by David Champernowne and Brian Reddaway, who had both attended that series of lectures), but following Marshall's precedent, Keynes did not include such a formalized model in his *General Theory of Employment, Interest, and Money* in 1936.

The American economist Irving Fisher had proposed in 1912 the formation of an international society to promote the formal use of mathematics and statistics in economics, but it was only at the end of 1930 that the Econometric Society was founded with Fisher as president (succeeded by the French index-number theorist François Divisia). The Econometric Society's U.S. and European conferences, and its journal *Econometrica* (founded 1933), provided a forum for mathematical economics and econometrics, as did the closely associated Cowles Commission

for Research in Economics (in Colorado from 1933 to 1939, and then in Chicago from 1939 to 1955). The publication of Paul Samuelson's *Foundations of Economic Analysis* in 1947 (based on his 1941 Harvard dissertation) was a turning point in general acceptance of formal, mathematical economic theory. Samuelson's restatement and extension of neoclassical comparative static and dynamic analysis, introducing a generation of economists to difference and differential equations, emphasized Walrasian general equilibrium analysis, in which all markets are linked through the budget constraints of individual agents. Following from work by John von Neumann and Abraham Wald in Karl Menger's mathematical colloquium in Vienna in the 1930s (see Baumol and Goldfeld 1968, Weintraub 2002), Kenneth Arrow, Gerard Debreu, and Lionel McKenzie provided formal proofs of the existence of general competitive equilibrium in the 1950s, but such works as the 1959 Cowles monograph *The Theory of Value* by Debreu could be read and understood by very few economists. Gradually, general equilibrium theory, requiring formal mathematics for its statement and application, came to dominate graduate courses in microeconomics (until challenged by game theory since the 1980s), with Marshallian partial equilibrium, susceptible to diagrammatic treatment, prominent only in undergraduate courses.

Military applications encouraged operations research in the United States (and operational research in Britain) during World War II, and postwar research in related fields was supported by the Office of Naval Research, the U.S. Air Force (initially the sole client of the RAND Corporation), and the U.S. Army through the Stanford Research Institute, later SRI (see Mirowski 2002). Discrete optimization (linear and nonlinear programming) was widely used in economics to implement the neoclassical paradigm of agents maximizing an objective function (expected utility) subject to budget and other constraints, as by Robert Dorfman, Paul Samuelson, and Robert Solow in their 1958 RAND study *Linear Programming and Economic Analysis*. Linear programming and related techniques were entrenched in business schools as operations research, management science, or decision science, and in the Soviet Union and other centrally planned economies as planometrics. Within economics, however, attention shifted from activity analysis (including linear programming) to game theory from the 1970s onward.

Game theory, the formal modeling of conflict and cooperation, emerged as a distinct field of study in applied mathematics and in economics and other social sciences with John von Neumann and Oskar Morgenstern's *Theory of Games and Economic Behavior* in 1944. This work built on the minimax solution for two-player, zero-sum games, whose existence von Neumann had proved in 1928 (with a much simpler, non-topological proof provided by Jean Ville in 1938), and with John F. Nash Jr.'s equilibrium concept for n-player, general-sum games. Game theory stressed strategic interaction: the payoffs for each player depend not only on the strategy (a rule for selecting an action in response to a particular information set) chosen by that player, but also on the strategies chosen by all the other players (see "Strategic Games"). Nash equilibrium for a noncooperative game (one in which binding contracts, externally enforced, are not possible) requires that no player can gain from changing his or her strategy under the assumption that no other player changes strategy. Game theory, with its emphasis on strategic interaction among players, contrasts with general competitive equilibrium analysis, which assumes a single agent to be too small to affect market outcomes. In the 1950s and 1960s, game theoretic research, often published in the *Journal of Conflict Resolution* and some funded by the U.S. Arms Control and Disarmament Agency, focused on the understanding and control of arms races. Game theory is now pervasive in economics from industrial organization to trade policy and the credibility of macroeconomic policy, and is influential in other fields from political science and law to evolutionary biology.

BIBLIOGRAPHY

Baumol, William J., and Stephen M. Goldfeld, eds. 1968. *Precursors in Mathematical Economics: An Anthology*. London: London School of Economics and Political Science.

Blaug, Mark. 2003. The Formalist Revolution of the 1950s. In *A Companion to the History of Economic Thought*, ed. Warren J. Samuels, Jeff E. Biddle, and John B. Davis, 395–410. Malden, MA, and Oxford: Blackwell.

Mirowski, Philip. 2002. *Machine Dreams: Economics becomes a Cyborg Science*. Cambridge, U.K.: Cambridge University Press.

Samuelson, Paul A. 1947. *Foundations of Economic Analysis*. Cambridge, MA: Harvard University Press (enlarged edition, 1983).

Weintraub, E. Roy. 2002. *How Economics Became a Mathematical Science*. Durham, NC: Duke University Press.

Hichem Ben-El-Mechaiekh
Robert W. Dimand

MATHEMATICS IN THE SOCIAL SCIENCES

Methodologically, scientists think that the social sciences differ from the physical sciences in degree but not in kind. The commonality among the sciences is best expressed by Paul A. Samuelson: "All sciences have the common task of describing and summarizing empirical reality.... There are no separate methodological problems that face the social scientist different in kind from those that face any other scientist" (Samuelson 1966, Vol. 3, p. 1756). Another common feature among the sciences is that they use mathematics as a language.

Joseph Schumpeter (1954, p. 955) asserted that in studying quantitative relationships, the knowledge of a handful of simple concepts in calculus—variables, functions, limits, continuity, derivatives, differentials, maxima, minima, system of equations, determinateness, and stability—change one's attitude to the problem. The applied interest of social scientists is piqued by advances in the frontiers of mathematics and includes, besides calculus, linear programming; information, game, and network theories; and Markov processes, which have industrial, political, social, economic, and military applications (Tucker 1963).

Some have identified stages in the development of mathematics in economics. According to John Hicks, "All through the first period of mathematical economics—the age of Marshall, of Pareto, of Wicksell, even that of Pigou and Keynes—the economist's main mathematical tool was the differential calculus.... Most economics problems were problems of maxima and minima" (Hicks 1983, pp. 247–248). As in the physical sciences, the approaches to mathematical modeling in the social sciences follow broad methodologies. One simple approach is reductionism, where the laws of one discipline are transplanted to that of another. The physicist Stephen Hawking abides by that rule (Hawking [1997] 2000, p. 169), and so does Samuelson (1966, Vol. 3, p. 1755).

In the social sciences, an abstraction from reality is made in the form of a model that can be expressed in mathematical form. Social scientists tend to divide into two camps in their fundamental belief in the use of mathematical models: Some build models that follow the principle that nature does not make any leaps, and others believe in a dialectical or chaotic process. In either case, a good grasp of the history, statistics, and theory required to function in the social sciences in turn depends on a good understanding of mathematics (Schumpeter 1954, p. 14). In editing mathematical models of the social sciences, James R. Newman (1956) selected classical contributions from the fields of psychology, economics, and sociology. A later book by Kenneth Arrow, Samuel Karlin, and Patrick Suppes (1960) tackles topics in economics, management science, and psychology.

MODELING IN PSYCHOLOGY

An early form of an inner observation model in psychology is Fechner's Law, after Gustav Theodor Fechner (1801–1887). This law is traced to the work of Ernst

Heinrich Weber (1795–1878), who had conducted several experiments giving subjects weights to hold and asking them to report when they sensed an increase in weight (sensation, *S*). Because sensations cannot be measured, Fechner proposed to observe noticeable differences in sensation. (The expressions that follow use the symbols of Edwin Boring [1956, pp. 1159–1160]). One can measure the stimulus, *R*, as so many pounds of weight, and then record the constant point, *c*, where the stimulus has created a noticeable difference as $dR/R = c$. This relationship takes the form $dS = c(dR/R)$. The implication here is that all changes in stimulus are homogeneous and can be aggregated. One can, therefore, integrate the equation to measure sensation. The integration constant can be approximated by choosing a threshold value of the stimulus, *r*, such that when $R = r$, then $S = 0$. This will yield the expression $S = c \log_e(R/r)$. By moving to a different base of logarithms and by measuring stimuli in units *r*, Fechner's Law is expressed in a more compact form as $S = k \log R$. The equation states that as stimulus multiplies in strength, such as in tripling (3×1), the corresponding perception will increase additively, say twice stronger ($1 + 1$).

By the use of combinatorial mathematics, Kenneth Arrow developed a possibility theorem to show that consistent voting behavior is impossible, even in a democracy. He was preceded by a long line of political theorists who were trying to aggregate individual preferences for a group or society. Attempts by Jean-Charles de Borda (1733–1799) and Marie Jean Antoine Nicolas Caritat (1743–1794) established that the law of transitive reasoning does not hold up when voting preferences are aggregated. A set of voters may choose the candidate A over B, and B over C, but not A over C. Arrow postulated a set of consistent axioms that cannot all be met in the aggregation of social preferences. Besides the transitivity axiom, he required that there be no dictator, that when two choices are ranked their outcome should not depend on the third choice, and finally, that if everyone prefers one outcome over another, the preferred outcome should dominate.

To illustrate Arrow's model, consider two persons, X and Y, who are voting on three candidates, A, B, and C. We can create thirty-six profiles of their ranking, because two persons can rank three outcomes in $6 \times 6 = 36$ ways. Of these thirty-six profiles, X and Y can make only six unanimous rankings, where their first, second, and third rankings can be {A,B,C}, {A,C,B}, {B,A,C}, {B,C,A}, {C,A,B}, and {C,B,A}. In many instances, however, X and Y will not be able to rank the candidates the same. Although they both may rank A first, X might rank B second, and Y may rank B third. The aggregation of these preferences will not, therefore, be unanimous, and this may require a benevolent dictator to pick the final candidate.

MODELING IN SOCIOLOGY

As an example of mathematical models from sociology, we take one developed by Arnold Faden (1977, p. 266) as in Alfred Lotka's predator-prey model, which explains how crime spreads. Loosely speaking, the density of crime at a location has a three-population functional relationship $f[v(s), c(s), p(s)]$, where *v, c, p, s* represent victims, criminals, policemen, and location, respectively. A particular explicit relation of this model can take the form of $f(v, c, p) = vce^{-p}$. One implication of the model is that a crime is possible when a potential victim meets a criminal, assuming no policing, $p = 0$.

From the game perspective, several implications can be modeled. Faden examined cases where victims and criminals follow their individual rationality, where they collude in the absence of police, and where the police and criminals collude, given the distribution of victims. Such modeling represents only the beginning of a complex social problem. The assumption about the size and distribution of the three populations, the functions that relate them, and their motivations can vary. For instance, if we focus on the struggle for existence between two populations, say victims and criminals, the increment of the former will add to the possibility of the latter, yielding a simple system of differential equations such as $(dv/dt)1/v = f(c)$ and $(dc/dt)1/c = f(v)$. As Samuelson pointed out (1972, p. 474), solutions for these types of equations can lead to perpetual movement in a circle around an equilibrium value. However, the potential for such modeling is on the increase. In the global economy, a country enforcing international trade law can represent the police variable. Consumers, countries, or agents may be the victims, and criminals may be engaged in international piracy of intellectual property rights.

MODELING IN ECONOMICS

The classical economists were concerned with how the economy is interconnected. Prices of commodities depend on cost of production (the price of inputs), and output is what is demanded at existing prices. Antoine Augustin Cournot ([1838] 1956, p. 1215) was the first to use calculus in determining both prices and quantities in his model. He formulated quantity demanded as a function of price $D = F(p)$, and foreshadowed the development of the Marshallian elasticity concept by advancing that $\frac{\Delta D}{\Delta p} < or > \frac{D}{p}$. Taking the differential of demand to yield $F(p) + pF'(p) = 0$, Cournot proceeded to analyze maximum problems.

Cournot has bequeathed a behavioral assumption that makes possible the solution of rivalry problems in modern economics. Each firm assumes that the other firms' output is fixed. The expected output of the other firms now enters into the one firm's own demand curve. If costs are given, the calculus method can be used to find optimal price and output. Variations in demand and cost curves are prominent exemplars in intermediate microeconomics and managerial textbooks.

The founders of the marginal revolution in economics, Léon Walras, Stanley Jevons, and Karl Menger, were influenced by Cournot. They extended Cournot's model into the theory of the firm, consumer behavior, and general equilibrium analysis. Walras (1954, pp. 103, 110–111) indicated equilibrium where supply and demand curves cross. The markets are related because a change in price in one market affects changes in other markets. A general equilibrium is sought for all markets through the process of *tatonnement*—raising the price in cases of excess demand and lowering it in cases of excess supply until equilibrium is attained.

Paul Samuelson (1966, Vol. 1, p. 544) explained how stability in a Walrasian system can be achieved using differential equations. Solving the equation $dp/dt = H(q_D - q_s)$, the term on the left is the rate of change of prices, dp, with respect to changes of time, dt. Given that H is a proportional constant, q is quantity, S is supply, and D is demand, one can find the time path. Stability occurs when, as time goes to infinity, the solution of the differential equation breaks down, which in economic terms means that the supply curve must cut the demand curve from below. Solving for quantity in terms of price, one can also find the Marshallian stability conditions under which quantity adjusts to clear the market. Malthus's demographic model used differential equations to show stability. If a population, x, grows at an exponential rate, c, over time, t, then $dx/dt = cx$. If food supply, y, grows at a constant rate, k, over time, t, then $dy/dt = k$. Thus, the ratio of $y/x = (y_0 + kt)/(x_0 e^{ct})$ will break down as t approaches infinity, implying misery (Hirsch 1984, p. 14).

Mathematical modeling in economics climaxed with the Arrow-Debreu theorem (1954). In this system, a fixed-point mapping method was used instead of counting equations and unknowns in the Walrasian system. The idea of a fixed point is that, in the process of transforming a rubber sheet, say by stretching it, one point will not move. It will be mapped onto itself. William Baumol (1965, p. 494) explained this process for the case of the demand and supply curves. Starting with demand and supply curves on two separate graphs, let Q_s be the quantity supplied, and Q_d the quantity demanded. Then, tracing up from the two-quantity axes to the demand and the supply curves, one finds two prices, say a supply price, P_s, and a demand price, P_d. If we can find a function, a map of $f(P_s) = P_d$ or $f(Q_s) = Q_d$, then we have a fixed point mapping for the equilibrium problem.

The application of the fixed point theorem to the Arrow-Debreu general equilibrium required that convex assumptions be applied on consumers' and producers' sets, as well as special ideas of continuity, and the idea of separating planes in Euclidean space. For instance, a commodity has spatiotemporal and physically differentiated characteristics, which can be represented by a point in space. If there are L amounts of commodities, one can imbed them in the Euclidian space, R^L. As Debreu put it, "By focusing attention on changes of dates one obtains ... a theory of savings, investment, capital, and interest. Similarly by focusing attention on changes of locations one obtains ... a theory of location, transportation, international trade and exchange" (Debreu 1959, p. 32). In his *Theory of Value* (1959) Debreu relied on a lemma of Hukukane Nikaido (1956) to prove equilibrium. The lemma assumes a referee that sets the price, P. Consumers will maximize their utility, $U_i(x)$, subject to $PX = PA$, where A is endowment and goods X is in space $E = (X|0 \leq X \leq C)$, C being an arbitrary bundle such that $C > A$. All acceptable bundles with respect to P are labeled $\varphi_i(P)$, the ith individual demand function. Its sum is just $\varphi(P)$. If total demand, X, does not match total available bundles, A, the referee must make an adjustment. The difference is $X - A$. Its value is $P(X - A)$. The referee's objective is to pay a person a value PX that is greater than the endowment value PA. In other words, choose a price, Q, that will maximize the price-manipulating function $\theta X = (P|P(X - A)) = \max(Q(X - A))$ for all Q in S^k, where X is total demand lying in Γ. We now have the following demand function and a price-adjustment function:

$S^k \ni P \rightarrow \varphi(P) \subset \Gamma$ (Demand function)

$\Gamma \ni X \rightarrow \theta(X) \subset S^k$ (Price-manipulating function).

We want to choose (X, P) in this demand and price adjustment space, $\Gamma \times S^k$, such that $\varphi(P) \times \theta(X)$ is contained in $\Gamma \times S^k$. This is possible because the mapping is upper semicontinuous. Therefore, the equilibrium price exists.

Upper semicontinuity is easy to show for $\theta(X)$. Given $P_n \rightarrow P$ in S^k, $X_n \rightarrow X$ in Γ and $P_n \in \theta(X_n)$, then $P \in \theta(X)$. The proof is that, for any Q price-constellation, $P_n(X_n - A) \geq Q(X_n - A)$, and, for the whole sequence, as $n \rightarrow \infty$, we get $P(X - A) \geq Q(X - A)$. Therefore, the existence of $P \in \theta(X)$ is demonstrated.

A model developed by Karl Marx has been used as a material balance approach to modeling the economy. Total value is the sum of c = constant capital (depreciation), v = variable capital (wage bill), and s = surplus, and the cost price of total capital to produce the commodity is $c + v$. Assuming turnover rates of 1 for both c and v, let the total invested capital in one department be 100 units of capital distributed as $80c + 20v$, and $70c + 30v$ in the other. The average rate of profits is $s/(c + v)$, and the average rate of surplus value is s/v. For the first department, $80c + 20v$, $s/v = 20$, or 100 percent of variable capital, and $s/(c + v)$ is 20 percent. For the second department, $70c + 30v$, the rate of profit becomes 30 percent.

Because of competition, the sum of the profits, $20 + 30 = 50$, will have to be distributed evenly across the two departments discussed above, in this case 25 each. Adding this average profit of 25 to the cost price of total capital ($c + v$) yields prices of $125 for each department. Adding s to the cost price of total capital yields values of 120 for the first department, and 130 for the second department. The price-value differences are $5 and $–5, respectively, whereas the total values and total prices are the same, each equal to 250. This difference between price and value has been called the "transformation problem" in Marxian economics. Tremendous efforts have been made to solve this problem, and to extend this model to show growth. All in all, the mathematization of the social sciences deepens their ability to probe the human condition.

SEE ALSO *Arrow Possibility Theorem; Arrow-Debreu Model; Economics; Economics, Marxian; Economics, Neoclassical; General Equilibrium; Hicks, John R.; Marginalism; Marxism; Models and Modeling; Psychology; Samuelson, Paul A.; Schumpeter, Joseph Alois; Social Science; Statistics in the Social Sciences; Walras, Léon*

BIBLIOGRAPHY

Arrow, Kenneth J. 1963. *Social Choice and Individual Value.* New York: John Wiley and Sons.

Arrow, Kenneth J., and Gerard Debreu. 1954. Existence of an Equilibrium for a Competitive Economy. *Econometrica* 22: 265–290.

Arrow, Kenneth J., Samuel Karlin, and Patrick Suppes, eds. 1960. *Mathematical Methods in the Social Sciences.* Stanford, CA: Stanford University Press.

Baumol, William J. 1965. *Economic Theory and Operations Analysis.* 2nd ed. Englewood Cliffs, NJ: Prentice Hall.

Boring, Edwin G. 1956. Gustav Theodor Fechner. In *The World of Mathematics*, Vol. 2, ed. James R. Newman, 1148–1166. New York: Simon and Schuster.

Cournot, Antoine Augustin. [1838] 1956. Researches into the Mathematical Principles of the Theory of Wealth. Trans. N. T. Bacon. In *The World of Mathematics*, Vol. 2, ed. James R. Newman, 1203–1216. New York: Simon and Schuster.

Debreu, Gerard. 1959. *Theory of Value.* New York: John Wiley and Sons.

Faden, Arnold M. 1977. *Economics of Space and Time: The Measure-Theoretic Foundations of Social Sciences.* Ames: Iowa State University Press.

Hawking, Stephen. [1997] 2000. The Objections of an Unashamed Reductionist. In *The Large, the Small and the Human Mind*, ed. Malcolm Longair, 169–172. Cambridge, U.K.: Cambridge University Press.

Hicks, John R. 1983. *Classics and Moderns: Collected Essays in Economic Theory.* Oxford: Basil Blackwell.

Hirsch, Morris. 1984. The Dynamical Systems Approach to Differential Equations. *Bulletin of the American Mathematical Society* (July 11): 1–64.

Koopmans, Tjalling C. 1947. Measurement without Theory. *Review of Economic Statistics* 29: 161–172.

Marshall, Alfred. [1890] 1920. *Principles of Economics.* 8th edition. London: Macmillan.

Newman, James R. 1956. *The World of Mathematics.* Vol. 2. New York: Simon and Schuster.

Nikaido, Hukukane. 1956. On the Classical Multilateral Exchange Problem. *Metroeconomica* 8: 135–145.

Samuelson, Paul A. 1966. *The Collected Scientific Papers of Paul A. Samuelson.* 3 vols., eds. Joseph E. Stiglitz and Robert C. Merton. Cambridge, MA: MIT Press.

Schumpeter, Joseph A. 1954. *History of Economic Analysis*, ed. Elizabeth Boody. New York: Oxford University Press.

Tucker, A. W. 1963. New Directions in Applied Mathematics. In *New Directions in Mathematics*, eds. John G. Kemeny, Robin Robinson, and Robert W. Ritchie. Englewood Cliffs, NJ: Prentice Hall.

Walras, Léon. [1874] 1954. *Elements of Pure Economics, or the Theory of Social Wealth.* Trans. William Jaffe. Homewood, IL: Richard D. Irwin.

Lall Ramrattan
Michael Szenberg

MATRIARCHY

Matriarchy is a complex and controversial term. It is emotionally and politically loaded, and has been seen as suppressed history (Walker 1996b), utopian theory (Perkins Gilman [1915] 1992), deluded fantasy (Marshall 1998), and dangerous degeneration or dysfunction (Frazier 1949; Moynihan 1965). Barbara Walker, citing Wolfgang Lederer's *Fear of Women*, argues that *Amazon* was a "Greek name for Goddess-worshipping tribes in North Africa, Anatolia, and the Black Sea area" whose women were "warlike" (1996a, p. 24). In Eurasian Scythia women were not only warriors, but also important in politics (Walker 1996a). Similarly, Lewis Henry Morgan's, whose work was a basis for that of Engel's, description of the Iroquois certainly points to women holding an important base of power in choosing the leadership and controlling resources, which are contexts of political control of a society (Engels [1884] 1972).

These are relative descriptions, made by those writing the history and/or anthropology of the Other. The fact that there are a variety of versions of mythological and popular renderings of, for example, the Amazons—that they removed a breast for better archery, that they disallowed adult men from living with them, that they practiced infanticide on males—as well as actual evidence of women engaged in both war and politics outside of classical Greek society and ideals, suggests distortional bias. That both the Greeks and the Americans excluded women from soldier and politician roles would make any comparative society in which women were found in these roles on a regular and ordinary basis seem to us like the world turned upside down, and indeed monstrous.

The concept of matriarchy encompasses several component parts that delineate arenas of power and control granted to women. Matriarchy is of course based on motherhood, and how social relations are arranged—especially in terms of the distribution of resources—in relation to how motherhood (and thus fatherhood and other kin relationships) is understood. The two most important components of matriarchy are matrilineal descent or inheritance, and matrilocal living patterns.

If a group determines descent or distribution with a focus on the mother or the mother's kin network, we refer to this focus as *matrilineal.* If a group determines where a new couple or family will live with a focus on the mother or the mother's kin network, we refer to this focus as *matrilocal.* If these practices are determined with a focus upon the father, they are termed their opposite, *patrilineal* and *patrilocal.* Neither matrilineal nor matrilocal practices necessarily add up to matriarchy in the sense of woman-domination of politics, which brings us to the first dilemma in discussing matriarchy, wherein arguments over the meaning of social practices come to the fore. Why is evidence of patrilineal and patrilocal arrangements taken at face value to equal patriarchy (male-domination)? Why does evidence of their opposites (which are abundant) not equal matriarchy? Matriarchy is often discussed as nonexistent, with scholars insisting that there is "no evidence" of it, that it has never existed in any human society (Marshall 1998, p. 402).

In his synopsis of matriarchy, Gordon Marshall points to Friedrich Engels's reliance upon a notion of evolutionary progress from mother-right to father-right that is now out of favor (1998). Thomas Laquer argues this point from a very different perspective, arguing that patriarchy was embedded in valuing the idea over matter (the body)—historically, fatherhood was considered far more "factual" than motherhood. Thus materiality (bearing the child) does not always make for the logical understanding of connection, where "mother" is assumed as a natural fact and ontologically, whereas fatherhood is often an idea, and not understood as a physical connection (Laquer 1992, pp. 158–164). However, there is more to the Engels argument than Marshall discusses.

As noted above, Engels relied heavily on the anthropology of the Iroquois developed by the American anthro-

pologist Lewis Henry Morgan ([1884] 1972). Morgan noted that Iroquois kinship and economy was organized matrilineally, and thus that the women held considerable political power, although they were by no means all-powerful. He interpreted this situation as a matriarchy comparable to the more familiar patriarchal male-domination in his own culture, and interpreted matriarchy as a universal stage that preceded patriarchy in the development in human civilization. Engels took this idea of stages of family development and connected it to the Marxist idea of progressive stages of economic development. Certainly, interpreting a contemporaneous social situation—the existence of women's political power in the Iroquois confederation—as evidence of a worldwide historical stage of evolutionary development in social structure is problematic. However, it is at least equally problematic to ignore what is certainly evidence of a very differently gendered system of distributing power and resources.

Although it is repeatedly stated by scholarly authorities that there are no matriarchal societies in the world today (and many argue there never were), Heide Göttner-Abendroth and the International Academy for Modern Matriarchy Studies and Matriarchal Studies contest this position. Göttner-Abendroth traces the discussion of matriarchal societies to J. J. Bachofen in 1861 (2004; see also Walker 1996). She argues that one of the root words of matriarchy—*arche*—has a double meaning in Greek: both "beginning" and "domination." She argues that *matriarchy* can thus mean "the mothers from the beginning." But Göttner-Abendroth also asserts that *patriarchy* is correctly translated as "domination of the fathers." Her interpretation seems to be a feminist understanding of woman's power that is always more benevolent than that of man's. She defines matriarchy as women "hav[ing] the power of disposition over the goods of the clan, especially the power to control the sources of nourishment," and distinguishes this actual distributive power from "mere" matrilineality or matrilocality (2004). Although in this situation women have this power—and men do not—Göttner-Abendroth and others define matriarchy as egalitarian or consensus-based (see also Walker 1996, and Perkins Gilman's fictional utopia *Herland*).

Göttner-Abendroth's outline of the criteria for a matriarchy is highly formal and detailed. She incorporates a fundamentally different diffusion of the power of women in these societies, one that is based upon consensus in which women are key, because "even the process of *taking a political decision* is organized along the lines of matriarchal kinship" (2004). She argues further,

> In contrast to the frequent ethnological mistakes made about these men, they are not the "chiefs" and do not, in fact, decide.... Therefore, from the political point of view, I call matriarchies *egalitar-*

ian societies or *societies of consensus.* These political patterns do not allow the accumulation of political power. In *exactly* this sense, they are free of domination: They have no class of rulers and no class of suppressed people, i.e., they do not know *enforcement bodies*, which are necessary to establish domination. (2004; emphasis in the original)

Thus, according to a definition that takes into account matri-based kinship strategies, there have indeed been any number of matriarchal societies. According to this definition, there are contemporary matriarchal societies, but they are exceedingly rare, indeed endangered (Jacobs 2003).

Matriarchy and patriarchy are systems of distributing resources and arranging status. In writing about the African American family structure, Robert Staples asks an important question: "does the family determine the economic status of individuals, or does the economy determine the structure of a family?" (1999, p. 19). This emphasis on the relationship between the economy, the family, and the economic success or survival of particular families—and particular individuals in families—is useful. Staples's argument is problematic in that he labels the entire continent of Africa "patriarchal"—without ever defining the term—and never notes from where exactly on that continent the vast majority of African Americans came (West Africa, where there were and are several cultures that can be characterized as "matriarchal" at least in terms of matrilineal descent, and some in the more robust usage of Göttner-Abendroth; see especially Bergstrom 2002). Although critical of both racism and sexism, Staples's structural view of the situation tends to assume that the conventional patriarchal marriage pattern is the one deviants must adhere to, and assumes that pattern to be an inherently stable (read "normal") one, as did Talcott Parsons, Daniel Patrick Moynihan, and E. Franklin Frazier, among others.

When discussing matriarchy (or more accurately, female-headed families) as a deviation from the norm of patriarchy, Staples does not descend into labeling matriarchy as a dangerous degeneration or a pathology, but he compares the dictatorship of patriarchy to the democracy of gender equality—equality is here valued, but recognized as more of a struggle to maintain (1999, pp. 20–21; see also Frazier 1949 and Dill 1990). Although Moynihan's report "The Negro Family" also was in part an indictment of a racist system that deprived blacks of the normative family relations of their society, its language of pathology tended to normalize what many had already argued—and would continue to argue—was also a pathological social system—patriarchy itself (see Perkins Gilman [1915] 1992, Beauvoir [1949] 1972, and Friedan [1963] 1983).

It is possible to examine the arrangements of sexuality, procreation, management of land and resources, and other essentially political processes as they have existed in every group of people that is an ongoing concern (see Allen 2000). Although we can trace the historical (or even at times the prehistorical) development of particular practices among humans, it is a mistake to view history as inevitable evolution or progression. It is also a mistake to uncritically use one social standard as a measurement device for all others (see Dill [1979] 1990, Dilworth Anderson et al. 1993, and Allen 2000). In the end, both matriarchy and patriarchy may be overly polarizing ideal types that make it difficult for scholarly and everyday analysis of social, cultural, and political arrangements of power. Getting at the nuances of both systemic and individual-level arrangements of power is arguably what is needed here (see Genovese 1972 and Mann 1990 for a brief study that does this admirably).

SEE ALSO *Frazier, E. Franklin; Gender; Hierarchy; Patriarchy*

BIBLIOGRAPHY

Allen, Walter. 2000. African-American Family Life in Societal Context: Crisis and Hope. In *Upon These Shores: Themes in the African-American Experience, 1600 to the Present*, ed. William Scott, 303–318. New York and London: Routledge.

Beauvoir, Simone de. [1949] 1972. *The Second Sex.* Trans. H. M. Parshley. New York: Penguin.

Bergstrom, Kari. 2002. Legacies of Colonialism and Islam for Hausa Women: An Historical Analysis, 1804–1960. http://www.wid.msu.edu/resources/papers/pdf/WP276.pdf.

Dill, Bonnie Thornton. [1979] 1990. The Dialectics of Black Womanhood. In *Black Women in America: Social Science Perspectives*, ed. Micheline R. Malson, Elisabeth Mudimbe-Boyi, Jean F. O'Barr, and Mary Wyer, 65–78. Chicago: University of Chicago Press.

Dilworth-Anderson, Peggye, Linda M. Burton, and Leanor Boulin Johnson. 1993. Reframing Theories for Understanding Race, Ethnicity, and Families. In *Sourcebook of Family Theories and Methods: A Contextual Approach*, ed. Pauline G. Boss, William J. Doherty, Ralph LaRossa, Walter R. Schumm, and Suzanne S. K. Steinmetz, 627–649. New York: Plenum.

Engels, Friedrich. [1884] 1972. *The Origin of the Family, Private Property, and the State.* New York: Pathfinder.

Frazier, E. Franklin. 1949. *The Negro Family in the United States.* New York: Macmillan.

Friedan, Betty. [1963] 1983. *The Feminine Mystique.* New York: Laurel/Dell.

Genovese, Eugene. 1972. *Roll, Jordan, Roll: The World the Slaves Made.* New York: Pantheon/Random House.

Göttner-Abendroth, Heide. 2004. Matriarchal Society: Definition and Theory. In *The Gift*, ed. Genevieve Vaughan. Rome: Athanor. http://www.hagia.de/en/index.php?page=matriarchy.

International Academy for Modern Matriarchy Studies and Matriarchal Spirituality. Winzer, Germany. http://www.hagia.de/en/.

Jacobs, Marie-Josée. 2003. Opening Words of the First World Congress on Matriarchal Studies: Matriarchy and Gender. http://www.congress-matriarchal-studies.com/en/index.html.

Laquer, Thomas. 1992. The Facts of Fatherhood. In *Rethinking the Family: Some Feminist Questions*, ed. Barrie Thorne and Marilyn Yalom, 155–175. Boston: Northeastern University Press.

Lederer, Wolfgang. 1968. *The Fear of Women*. New York: Harcourt Brace Jovanovich.

Mann, Susan A. 1990. Slavery, Sharecropping, and Sexual Inequality. In *Black Women in America: Social Science Perspectives*, ed. Micheline R. Malson, Elisabeth Mudimbe-Boyi, Jean F. O'Barr, and Mary Wyer, 133–158. Chicago: University of Chicago Press.

Marshall, Gordon. 1998. Matriarchy. In *Oxford Dictionary of Sociology*, 402. Oxford: Oxford University Press.

Moynihan, Daniel Patrick. 1965. The Negro Family: The Case for National Action. Washington, DC: Office of Policy Planning and Research, U.S. Department of Labor. http://dol.gov/oasam/programs/history/webid-meynihan.htm.

Parsons, Talcott. [1949] 1954. The Kinship System of the Contemporary United States. In *Essays in Sociological Theory*, 2nd ed., 189–194. Glencoe, IL: Free Press.

Perkins Gilman, Charlotte. [1915] 1992. Herland. In *Herland and Selected Stories by Charlotte Perkins Gilman*, ed. Barbara H. Solomon, 1–148. New York: Penguin.

Staples, Robert. 1999. Sociocultural Factors in Black Family Transformation: Toward a Redefinition of Family Functions. In *The Black Family*, ed. Robert Staples, 18–24. Belmont, CA: Wadsworth.

Walker, Barbara G. [1983] 1996a. Amazons. In *The Women's Encyclopedia of Myths and Secrets*, 24–27. Edison, NJ: Castle Books.

Walker, Barbara G. [1983] 1996b. Matrilineal Inheritance. In *The Women's Encyclopedia of Myths and Secrets*, 620–624. Edison, NJ: Castle Books.

Sarah N. Gatson

MATRIX, THE

The Matrix (1999), a science fiction action movie written and directed by Larry and Andy Wachowski, has been called the masterpiece of "cyperpunk" cinema for the twenty-first century. Cyberpunk, a science fiction sub-genre, deals with the adventures of rebellious hackers in the computerized realm of "virtual reality." The subgenre was founded in the early 1980s by a group of American science fiction writers, foremost among them the novelist William Gibson in his novel *Neuromancer* (1984). Gibson coined the terms "cyberspace" and "the matrix" to refer to virtual reality. *The Matrix* is a central film dealing with the

philosophical issues concerning virtual reality: What is happening to the nature of the human within the new electronic universe humans have created? How can people tell the difference between the real world and a computerized reality? Which is preferable?

The Matrix is the first film of a trilogy about a hacker superhero called Neo who is prophesied to be the savior who will defeat the computers that have enslaved humanity. The film blends the old mythology of the coming of a messiah with the new mythology of virtual reality to create a new kind of religious hero. The first film is the origin story of Neo, who discovers he is living in a computer-constructed world, escapes to the real world, and begins to exercise his extraordinary powers against the agents of the machine. The first third of the film takes the form of a mystery: Both Neo and the audience are at first bewildered by fantastic events. As Neo slowly learns the truth about his world and the nature of his powers, so too does the audience. Gradually the audience realizes that it is 2199 and the surface of the earth has been destroyed in a war with artificially intelligent machines. Deep underground, human beings are bred as a source of energy for the machines and kept lifelong in an embryonic state, dreaming that they are living in an American city in 1999. The dream world of the Matrix is a computer simulation to keep the populace docile.

A few humans remain in Zion, the last human city. Morpheus, the rebel leader, and his crew rescue from the Matrix Thomas Anderson, by day an obscure computer programmer working for a large corporation, by night an outlaw hacker called "Neo." Morpheus believes Anderson is "the One" who it is foretold can defeat the agents of the machine. But first Neo must be extracted from the Matrix, reborn in the real world, reeducated, and trained.

Today, because of formidable technological obstacles, a program sufficiently complex to simulate real life, including all five senses, well enough to fool people does not exist. *The Matrix* assumes that in the future these obstacles have been overcome. Many commentators imagine virtual reality as a transcendent space better than ordinary reality, promising a utopian existence. And, in fact, in *The Matrix* the character Cypher knowingly chooses the Matrix over meager existence in the real world; however, Cypher is a villain who betrays and murders his comrades. Other contemporary critics argue that virtual reality, if it ever exists, would not be transcendent but merely a secondhand existence in a world of shadows, like life in Plato's cave.

Science fiction and other contemporary cultural concerns about virtual reality project fears and hopes about life inside the machine or life augmented by the machine in the cybernetic age. Humans live now in a new electronic age, not simply the postmodern but "the posthuman." As the boundary lines break down, people fear that the human may be taken over by the machine, or, at the opposite extreme, hope that the human may be made transcendent by the machine. As critic David Porush (1996) says, virtual reality is "a new mythology" in which the new frontier is not outer space but the "inner space" of the computer and of the human mind and the interface between the two (p. 109).

In Gibson's novel *Neuromancer*, cyberspace is a transcendent realm that, for hardcore hackers, is better than drugs or sex. *The Matrix* taps into this new mythology but inverts Gibson's notion of cyberspace, creating not a New Jerusalem but a virtual prison, a cyber-hell. Instead, the film openly borrows the ideas of French philosopher Jean Baudrillard, one of the theoreticians of the new order of simulation or virtual reality.

Baudrillard's central idea is that, in the postmodern world, the real has been almost totally displaced by the simulated, or what he calls the "hyperreal" (1994, p. 1). The real, he believes, has been irretrievably lost, replaced by the electronic and other forms of simulation. Even if people wanted to, they could not distinguish anymore between the simulation and the real. America is in the vanguard of the hyperreal, and the future promises only more and more simulation, he claims.

According to philosopher Slavoj Žižek, *The Matrix* is not about the future but about the unreality of present-day America in the oppressive, all-enveloping world of virtual capitalism: "The material reality we all experience and see around us is a virtual one, generated and coordinated by a gigantic computer to which we are all attached" (2001, p. 25).

SEE ALSO *Cyberspace; Film Industry; Reality; Totalitarianism; Utopianism*

BIBLIOGRAPHY

Baudrillard, Jean. 1994. *Simulacra and Simulation,* trans. Sheila Faria Glaser. Ann Arbor: University of Michigan Press.

Gibson, William. 1984. *Neuromancer.* New York: Ace.

Hayles, N. Katherine. 1999. *How We Became Posthuman: Virtual Bodies in Cybernetics, Literature, and Informatics.* Chicago: University of Chicago Press.

Matrix, The. 1999. Written and directed by the Wachowski Brothers. Burbank, CA: Warner Home Video.

Porush, David. 1996. Hacking the Brainstem: Postmodern Metaphysics and Stephenson's *Snow Crash.* In *Virtual Realities and Their Discontents,* ed. Robert Markley, 107–141. Baltimore, MD: Johns Hopkins University Press.

Yeffeth, Glenn, ed. 2003. *Taking the Red Pill: Science, Philosophy and Religion in* The Matrix. Dallas, TX: BenBella Books.

Žižek, Slavoj. 2001. The Desert of the Real. *In These Times,* October 29: 25–27.

Andrew Gordon

MATRIX ALGEBRA

Real numbers can be used to convey one-dimensional information, such as a family's total expenditure in a month. However, if one wants to record the monthly expenditures of two families (indexed by 1, 2) on three items—food, entertainment, and health (indexed by 1, 2, 3)—then one needs to use a rectangular array of real numbers, or a matrix. A *matrix* (A) is defined as a rectangular array of numbers, parameters, or variables. The members of the array are referred to as the *elements* of the matrix and are usually enclosed in brackets, parentheses, or double vertical lines.

$$A = \begin{bmatrix} a_{11} & a_{12} & a_{13} \\ a_{21} & a_{22} & a_{23} \end{bmatrix}$$

The first row of matrix A provides information on the first family's expenditures on food, entertainment, and health, and the second row gives similar information related to the second family. For instance, a_{23} is the expenditure of the second family on health, and a_{12} is the first family's expenditure on entertainment. Matrix is a concept of linear algebra, and it has wide applications in many fields, including economics, statistics, computer programming, operations research, industrial organization, and engineering.

Like numbers, elementary operations such as addition and multiplication can also be performed on matrices. A typical element in matrix A is written as a_{ij}, which is the element located in row i and column j of the matrix. For instance, a_{13} is the element in the first row and third column, or the first family's expenditure on health in the first month. Matrix A is also written as $\{a_{ij}\}_{2 \times 3}$, which simply means that A is a matrix with two rows and three columns whose typical element is a_{ij}. The expenditures of the two families in the second month on food, entertainment, and health can be written as another matrix, $B = \{b_{ij}\}_{2 \times 3}$. Then, the *sum* of two months' expenditures for both families on all three items can be written in the form of a third matrix C, which is the sum of the corresponding elements of A and B; it is defined as:

$$C = \{a_{ij} + b_{ij}\}_{2 \times 3} = A + B$$

Let us now assume that in the third month the two families spend exactly the same amount of money on every item as they spent in the first month. In other words, the matrix of expenditure in the third month is the same as the matrix of expenditure in the first month. Then we can write a matrix D, which will tell us the total expenditure of the two families in three months on each of the three items as:

$$D = \{2a_{ij} + b_{ij}\}_{2 \times 3} = 2A + B.$$

2A is called *scalar multiplication* of a matrix, in which every element of A is multiplied by the scalar 2.

Multiplication of two matrices can be illustrated from *input-output* models used to illustrate producer theory in economics. Let us suppose that there are two firms, each producing three goods (indexed by 1, 2, 3) with two factors of production (indexed by 1, 2). Let $A = \{a_{ij}\}_{2 \times 3}$ be the matrix of input-output coefficients. Thus, a_{ij} is the amount of factor i needed to produce one unit of good j. The first firm wants to produce X_1, X_2, X_3 and the second firm wants to produce Y_1, Y_2, Y_3 quantities of the three goods. Let us define a matrix of these outputs as:

$$Z = \begin{bmatrix} X_1 & Y_1 \\ X_2 & Y_2 \\ X_3 & Y_3 \end{bmatrix}$$

Then the *matrix multiplication* of A and Z can be written as:

$$AZ = \begin{bmatrix} a_{11} & a_{12} & a_{13} \\ a_{21} & a_{22} & a_{23} \end{bmatrix} \begin{bmatrix} X_1 & Y_1 \\ X_2 & Y_2 \\ X_3 & Y_3 \end{bmatrix}$$

$$= \begin{bmatrix} a_{11}X_1 + a_{12}X_2 + a_{13}X_3 & a_{11}Y_1 + a_{12}Y_2 + a_{13}Y_3 \\ a_{21}X_1 + a_{22}X_2 + a_{23}X_3 & a_{21}Y_1 + a_{22}Y_2 + a_{23}Y_3 \end{bmatrix}$$

It may be noticed that A is a 2×3 and Z is a 3×2 matrix. Their product will be a 2×2 matrix. The general rule is that if A is $m \times n$ and Z is $n \times q$ then their product will be a matrix of the order of $m \times q$. The number of columns of A must be equal to the number of rows of Z. If this condition is not satisfied, matrix multiplication is not possible. The meaning of the product matrix (AZ) is very simple. Suppose labor and capital are the two factors of production. The first column of AZ gives the total quantities of labor and capital used by the first firm to produce all three goods, and the second column of AZ gives the amounts of all factors used by the second firm to produce these three goods.

The *transpose* of a matrix A^T is obtained by interchanging the rows and columns of A. The ith row of A is the ith column of A^T. For instance, the transpose of A, written as A^T, is:

$$A^T = \begin{bmatrix} a_{11} & a_{21} \\ a_{12} & a_{22} \\ a_{13} & a_{23} \end{bmatrix}$$

A *square matrix* is a matrix with an equal number of rows and columns. The equivalent of the number one is an identity matrix I, which is a square matrix with 1 in its principle diagonal and 0 elsewhere. The following identity matrix is of dimension 3×3:

$$I = \begin{bmatrix} 1 & 0 & 0 \\ 0 & 1 & 0 \\ 0 & 0 & 1 \end{bmatrix}$$

Obviously, $I^T = I$, $AI = IA = A$, for any matrix A for which these products are defined. A *null matrix* (written as O) is a matrix whose elements are all zero.

Matrix operations satisfy certain mathematical laws:

1. A + (B+C) = (A+B) + C (associative law for addition)
2. A(BC) = (AB)C (associative law for multiplication)
3. A + B = B + A (commutative law)
4. c(A+B) = cA + cB, where c is a scalar (distributive law for scalar products)
5. C(A+B) = CA + CB, provided the products are defined (distributive law for matrix multiplication)

A crucial application of matrices is that matrix algebra can be used to solve a system of linear simultaneous equations of the form: AX = B. A is a matrix of order $m \times n$ whose elements are real numbers, X is an $n \times 1$ matrix of variables whose values have to be solved, and B is an $m \times 1$ matrix of right-hand-side constant terms of m linear equations. An example of these equations for the case m = n = 3 follows:

$$x + y + z = 4$$
$$3x + y - z = 6$$
$$x + y - 2z = 4$$

In the above system of equations,

$$A = \begin{bmatrix} 1 & 1 & 1 \\ 3 & 1 & -1 \\ 1 & 1 & -2 \end{bmatrix}; X^T = \begin{bmatrix} x & y & z \end{bmatrix}; B^T = \begin{bmatrix} 4 & 6 & 4 \end{bmatrix}$$

Something that is equivalent to division for real numbers is called *matrix inversion* in matrix algebra. Only a square matrix can be inverted. If A is a square matrix of order $n \times n$, then its inverse, A^{-1}, is a matrix such that A $A^{-1} = A^{-1} A = I$. If there is a system of linear simultaneous equations AX = B, where A is $n \times n$, X is $n \times 1$, and B is $n \times 1$, then the solution is $X = A^{-1} B$, provided A^{-1} exists.

SEE ALSO *Cholesky Decomposition; Hessian Matrix; Input-Output Matrix; Inverse Matrix; Jacobian Matrix; Linear Systems; Mathematical Economics; Programming, Linear and Nonlinear; Vectors*

BIBLIOGRAPHY

Chiang, Alpha C., and Kevin Wainwright. 2005. *Fundamental Methods of Mathematical Economics*. 4th ed. Boston: McGraw Hill/Irwin.

Monica Das

MATRIX INVERSION

SEE *Inverse Matrix.*

MATURATION

The term *maturation* comes from *maturatio*, a Latin word for ripening; thus, many dictionaries describe maturation as the process of "becoming ripe" or "mature," and being mature as "being ripe." In the social sciences, when we describe developmental changes as maturational, we are describing the change as having three characteristics: First, maturational change is an intrinsically teleological or end-goal oriented process. Second, maturational change is a systematic process. Finally, the end-goal of maturational change is an adaptive state. *Maturity* represents this goal-like apex of adaptive functioning, and *maturation* describes the systematic and time-consuming processes that achieve maturity. Consequently, maturity does not just "happen"; it is a time-consuming and organized growth process.

This definition of maturation is broader than it has been defined historically. For example, the Child Study Movement of the first half of the twentieth century sought to describe child development as a maturational process that is independent of experience and learning. The goal of much of early developmental psychology (e.g., the work of Arnold Gessell and Nancy Bayley) was to chart the course of average and atypical child maturation. This approach, while providing information on the "what and when" of child development, does not explain "why" children develop as they do. Subsequent research has shown that human development is never a purely biological process. For example, there is a documented decrease of about four years in the age of menarche (the onset of menstruation in girls) in Europe and North America over the last century. This is called a secular trend (a trend over a long period of time) and appears to have leveled off in developed nations. However, in the United States there is some evidence that breast development is occurring earlier, although average age at menarche (twelve and one-half years) is not declining. Age at menarche is typically half a year later in most parts of Europe (thirteen years). Age at menarche in nations currently struggling with high rates of disease and malnutrition can be as high as seventeen—where Europe was in the early 1800s. Environmental improvements in nutrition and disease control have the capacity to act on the genetically based timing of female reproductive maturation. Similarly, experiences such as paternal sexual abuse, chemical exposure, obesity, and ongoing stress can speed up pubertal development. On the other hand, severe caloric deprivation (e.g., an eating disorder or famine) can delay the onset of menarche, or even return an adolescent to prepubescent levels of hormonal functioning.

Development is multiply determined; genomes, physical environment, social environment, culture, adaptive history, and even our efforts to retain volitional control by the creation of meanings all contribute to the timing and expression of human development. Genetic code does not have sole control of even physical maturation; instead, the flexible capacity to act on the environment and be acted on by the environment is a core attribute of the human genome. It is increasingly apparent that no aspect of human psychological growth can be understood simply in terms of genetic input. In short, debates that push for allegiance to either nature or nurture no longer fit the data of human development.

Conceiving maturation as a purely biological process shares the same untenable assumption as nature versus nurture debates do; both assume that we can neatly untangle these forces. It is rather like trying to separate conjoined twins who share a brain or heart; each requires something owned by the other. Human development emerges out of dynamic interaction between forces inside and outside our bodies. Additionally, we must remember that there are also less deterministic players in the ring—for example, volition and the cognitive processes of meaning-making. "Purely biological" maturation is an impossibility. As Irving Gottesman and Daniel Hanson put it: "Everything that is genetic is biological, but not all things biological are genetic" (2005). We have probably underestimated the degree to which ever-popular nature-versus-nurture debates have blinded us to the profound and lively interaction of internal and external causes development. At best, these debates are artificial; at worst, they create a peculiar lens through which observations become myopic.

So where does this leave the word *maturation*? Social scientists still use it to draw attention to biological aspects of development, but few would say they are speaking of purely genetically driven development. Is this word a historical artifact—no longer precise enough for science? If we drop the "purely biological" restriction, does it become a simple synonym of development?

MATURATION VERSUS DEVELOPMENT

Although the term *maturation* is similar to the term *development*, from a lifespan perspective it is not synonymous with *development*. Unsystematic changes and declines can still be developmental changes, but they do not have the goal-based character of maturational change. For example, entropic changes toward lesser functionality and greater chaos are developmental changes, but not maturational because they are not systematic and teleological. Lifespan development is quite inclusive; it can include trajectories of gain or decline, systematic or chaotic processes, goal-directed or random ends. If we drop the dysfunctional aspects of maturation's historic definition (i.e., excluding purely biological assumptions), maturation still includes only growthlike, purposeful, and maximally adaptive changes. For example, throughout a lifespan we find maturational growth in many domains of adaptation, but in the final years of life, nonmaturational developmental change increasingly overshadows maturational development. In contrast, maturational change dominates the pubertal, cognitive, emotional, and social developments of the first two decades of life. Declines of aging also have predictable developmental trajectories, but they less frequently include the systematic, goal-directed, adaptive changes characteristic of maturation. Ultimately death occurs because the organism, at all levels, can no longer maintain the goal-directed and systematic functions that preserve equilibrium.

CAVEATS ABOUT IDENTIFYING MATURATIONAL PROCESSES

When we designate a segment of development as a maturational change, we must remember that we have done just that—designated. Any dissection of human development into segments imposes onto it our own interests and timelines. In nature, maturation is an integrated whole, but when we describe maturation we would be overwhelmed if we did not focus on particular points of maturity within specific domains. For example, indicators of maturity and their maturational processes will differ depending upon whether one is looking at cognitive maturation, sexual maturation, or emotional maturation; each has its own "maturity" endpoint, yet in reality they are not as distinct as their separate titles would suggest. We may discuss them as separate maturational processes, but from the perspective of the developing organism (e.g., an adolescent), they are a single, dramatically integrated process.

A less obvious relativity is our choice of end goals or mature attributes. For example, the word *ripe* conjures images of fruit that has reached a stage of maturity we subjectively find delicious. Some say a mango is not ripe until it drops off the tree, because "sweet and juicy" is their conception of maturity. Others like mangos picked a little earlier because they prefer tangy mangos. A mango exporter defines maturity by factoring in shipping time and shelf life. The mango tree, if it could reflect on such things, might wonder at our fuss about its intact fruit; its goal is reproduction—rotting, sprouting, and such things. Reflecting back on human development, if we value maximally efficacious child development, then a mother is reproductively mature when she herself has reached an acceptable level of psychological maturity. If, however, we are only concerned with basic sexual reproduction, then human females generally reach reproductive maturity during the year following menarche. Similarly, if the maturity or "ripeness" being defined is wisdom, our descriptions of what constitutes maturity and the processes needed to achieve maturation may vary considerably across cultures, religions, and historical period.

MATURATION—AN EPIGENETIC PROCESS

Maturation is an epigenetic process because it involves the emergence of new structures and functions through bidirectional relations between all levels of biological and experiential variables. According to Gottlieb: "Individual development is characterized by an increase of complexity of organization (that is, the emergence of new structural and functional properties and competencies) at all levels of analysis (molecular, subcellular, cellular, organismic) as a consequence of horizontal and vertical coactions among the organism's parts, including organism-environment coactions" (Gottlieb 1991, p. 7).

Genetic determinants of behavior are not fixed or immutable; rather, they have the capacity to respond adaptively, to turn off and on as required by circumstances. More than one gene determines the expression of most attributes, and each gene is embedded in a maturational system that is determined by a multitude of other genetic and environmental inputs. For example, Eric Turkheimer and his colleagues (2003) have found that the genetic heritability of intelligence is influenced by socioeconomic status. In impoverished families, shared environment explained most of the IQ variability among seven-year-old twins and almost none was explained genetically. They found the opposite among affluent families; shared genes accounted for most of the variation in intelligence, while environment accounted for very little. Only bidirectional influence between genetic, experiential, and volitional inputs, or epigenesis, can explain this apparent effect of socioeconomic status on genetic expression.

MATURATION—TIMING AND SEQUENCE

The fact that maturational timing is highly variable, while process or stage sequence is generally invariant, is a fascinating characteristic of the first two decades of life. For example, the sequence of motor skills developed before an infant is able to walk is quite consistent across individuals, but the rate at which infants learn to walk is quite variable. Similarly, pubertal maturation follows a predictable sequence of physical changes, but the rate of maturation is highly variable. One adolescent may start and finish pubertal development in a year, while another can take five years to go through the same sequence of change. The timing of female reproductive maturation is more sensitive to environmental and experiential inputs than is male reproductive maturation. This sequential regularity supports the inclusion of systematicity as a characteristic of maturation.

The timing of pubertal maturation has a significant impact on both male and female psychosocial adjustment. In Western cultures, girls who begin pubertal maturation ahead of their peers are more likely to experience depression, premature and exploitive sexual experiences, delinquency, low academic achievement, and school dropout. Because a heavier body type is associated with early pubertal maturation, these girls also experience more body image disturbances and eating disorders. However, early-maturing girls attending same-sex schools do not seem to experience these problems. Boys who mature early experience life differently; they tend to be given more leadership experience, have more success in sports, attract more positive female attention, and have more confidence. The downside of early male pubertal development is greater involvement in delinquent behavior and substance abuse. There is little negative impact of late development on girls. They tend to have the slimmer body type preferred in Western cultures, thus avoiding the body image problems of early developers. Their academic achievement is also significantly higher than that of their early-developing peers. Late-developing boys have more difficulty, with less confidence and more depressive affect, but they do tend to be more creative and achieve more in the end.

CO-OCCURRENCE OF MATURATIONAL PROCESSES

Maturational processes can be correlated or uncorrelated despite occurring during the same period of life. For example, pubertal maturation and the final stages of musculoskeletal and cardiovascular maturation generally co-occur. Other co-occurring maturational processes can be quite independent of each other. For example, the timing of pubertal maturation and adolescent cognitive maturation seem to be unrelated. Adolescent pubertal maturation and its influence on emotion processing (e.g., limbic system) can occur before, during, or after the prefrontal cortex maturation that underlies gains in abstract thinking and self-regulation. Consequently, adolescents whose pubertal maturation precedes their cognitive development are more vulnerable to risk-taking and poor social choices because they have the drives and emotions of puberty without the cognitive maturity to help control their expression.

LIFESPAN PERSPECTIVES ON MATURATION

Developmentalists also use maturation to describe the attainment of skills and capacities achieved later in life. For the adult, both the domains of maturation and the level of maturation reached become individualized. One adult may focus on attaining mature financial skills, while another may focus on attaining mature interpersonal skills or "wisdom." Experiential opportunities and demands do play a stronger role in adult maturation than they do in childhood, but genetic input is still substantial. Both genes and prior developmental outcomes contribute to cognitive and physical capacity, and choice of environments, experiences, and acquaintances. Another input that may grow in strength across adulthood is volition. The adult capacity for meaning making and thus control over choices creates maturational opportunities that are not available to the young. These opportunities increase individual differences in both areas of competence and the levels of skill (maturity) reached. These individual differences are part of the study of personality and the study of clinical and counseling applications. For all of these areas, maturity refers to maximally adaptive social, emotional, or cognitive functioning, and maturation is the process of achieving it.

SEE ALSO *Child Development; Children; Developmental Psychology; Malnutrition; Nutrition; Undereating*

BIBLIOGRAPHY

Gottesman, Irving I., and Daniel R. Hanson. 2005. Human Development: Biological and Genetic Processes. *Annual Review of Psychology* 56: 263–286.

Gottlieb, Gilbert. 1991. Experiential Canalization of Behavioral Development: Theory. *Developmental Psychology* 27: 4–13.

Turkheimer, Eric, Andreana Haley, Mary Waldron, et al. 2003. Socioeconomic Status Modifies Heritability of IQ in Young Children. *Psychological Science* 14 (6): 623–628.

Joan M. Martin

MAU MAU

The Mau Mau movement of Kenya was a nationalist armed peasant revolt against the British colonial state, its policies, and its local supporters. The overwhelming majority of the Mau Mau fighters and of their supporters, who formed the "passive wing," came from the Kikuyu ethnic group in Central Province. There was also representation in the movement from the Embu, Kamba, and Meru ethnic groups. In addition, available evidence shows that some individual members of the Luo, Luyia, and even Maasai ethnic groups participated in the revolt as well.

Most of the Mau Mau guerrillas were young men and landless peasants. Some of these peasants had lost land to corrupt chiefs and other "landed gentry" in Central Province, while others were victims of land appropriation carried out to enable European settlement. Repatriated African squatters from the white farms in the Rift Valley fueled the ranks of the guerrillas, as did the economically desperate and unemployed Kikuyu in Nairobi and the surrounding urban centers. During the post–World War II period, there was massive African unemployment in the urban areas of Kenya, along with very poor housing (or no housing at all) and high inflation.

Among the Kikuyu, the embrace of a radical political posture was symbolized by taking the oath of unity with and allegiance to the Mau Mau movement. This oath, initially administered at Kiambu in 1950, was supposed to "inject courage into those who were initiated" (Edgerton 1989). It was also supposed to be administered to as many Kikuyu as possible. By July 1952 a new oath, the *Batuni* oath ("platoon oath"), was introduced. This was a warrior oath and it marked a further radicalization of the Mau Mau, which still remained an underground movement. When the colonial government, in a panic, declared a state of emergency in October 1952, the Mau Mau were not yet prepared to launch an all-out armed revolt. This started in earnest only after the declaration of a state of emergency, and the arrest and detention of most of the major African political leaders, including Jomo Kenyatta, Fred Kubai, Bildad Kaggia, and Ramogi Achieng' Oneko.

Throughout the revolt, the Mau Mau guerrillas referred to themselves as the *land and freedom army*. This description indeed summarized the revolt's principal causes, which were both economic and political. Scarcity of land, especially in Central Province, remained a major African grievance against the colonial government and white settlers. Hence, the attainment of fertile land, which signified general economic welfare and prosperity for African families, was a major objective of the revolt. To this must be added the demand for vastly expanded opportunities in education, training, housing, and employment. Politically, the Mau Mau guerrillas remained steadfast in their demand for Kenya's political independence from Britain. The Mau Mau movement's political objectives and even its ideology did not differ from the aims and objectives of the mainstream political independence party, the Kenya African Union (KAU); both sought political freedom (*Uhuru*) and the restoration of African dignity. From 1944, when it was formed, until 1953, when it was banned, KAU was the preeminent

African political organization in Kenya. Its formation represented the "first attempt at territorial nationalism," and also the most prominent "legitimate political outlet" for Africans (Maloba 1993, p. 51). Still, KAU's political agitation did not lead to any remarkable victories. By 1947 none of its leaders, including Kenyatta, expected Kenya to achieve its political freedom during their lifetime.

One of the distinguishing features of the Mau Mau is that it remains perhaps the only major nationalist revolutionary movement to have been led almost entirely by peasants, many of them illiterate. The movement had no external sources of political or material support. Even the British government arrived at this conclusion, having determined that the Soviet Embassy in Addis Ababa, Ethiopia, had not provided any help whatsoever to the revolt or even established any verifiable contacts. The movement also lacked any propaganda machinery to spread its message beyond Central Province. Together with the British government in London, the colonial government in Nairobi took advantage of this weakness, and launched a harsh and effective propaganda campaign against the Mau Mau and Kenyan nationalism. The revolt was portrayed as irrational, and as a reversion to primitive savagery by Africans traumatized by the stress of modern (Western) civilization. The British government firmly maintained the position that the revolt was not caused by economic conditions, but rather an organized criminal enterprise. In this propaganda offensive, a lot of emphasis was placed on the oaths taken by the supporters of the revolt; almost routinely, many of these oaths were described as "bestial." It is this image as a senseless, savage, murderous enterprise that would haunt the Mau Mau for many years to come. In the West, major newspapers and magazines carried stories on the Mau Mau that reinforced British propaganda. Robert Ruark's *Something of Value* (1955), a novel read widely in Britain and the United States, also echoed official propaganda by contrasting "white heroism" with "black savagery."

For four years from October 1952 to 1956, the Mau Mau guerrillas operated from the forests of Mount Kenya and the Aberdares. Although they were outgunned throughout the duration of the revolt, these guerrillas fought with singular courage and determination against the combined forces of the colonial government's army, British troops, and the Home Guards (paramilitary units of local Kikuyu/Embu/Meru people supporting the colonial government's military and political objectives against the Mau Mau fighters and their objectives). One of the most celebrated leaders of the Mau Mau was Dedan Kimathi, who was based in the Aberdares, and who sought, in 1953 and 1954, to establish some unity among the various guerrilla units operating in the forests. These efforts did not succeed, and as a result the Mau Mau never had an overall leader or commander.

In response to the revolt, the British government undertook a major rehabilitation campaign in Central Province in order to "remake Kenya" by defeating radicalism and reinforcing the power of the conservative Kikuyu "landed gentry" and the Home Guards. Members of these groups would emerge triumphant in the post-emergency period. The rehabilitation campaign was carried out in the detention camps and even in the Kikuyu reserve. Its objective was to get the detained and arrested Kikuyu to renounce the Mau Mau and its radicalism. Christian religious indoctrination, sanctioned by the colonial government, played a major role in the rehabilitation process.

Although defeated militarily, the Mau Mau revolt was clearly instrumental in forcing the British government to undertake immediate political reforms. These reforms included the reinstatement of African political parties in 1955, and then the promulgation of several constitutional reforms that eventually led to the attainment of political independence on December 12, 1963.

The legacy of the Mau Mau revolt in Kenya remains a very complex and controversial subject. The controversy revolves around the following issues: What role did the revolt play in the decolonization of Kenya? Did Mau Mau bring *Uhuru*? Who benefited from *Uhuru*, the Home Guards and their descendants or the actual Mau Mau supporters and fighters? Was the Mau Mau a Kikuyu affair or a national movement? And lastly, how should this very complex movement be remembered in Kenya?

SEE ALSO *Anticolonial Movements; Colonialism; Decolonization; Guerrilla Warfare; Kenyatta, Jomo; Kimathi, Dedan; Liberation Movements; Nationalism and Nationality; Peasantry; Propaganda; Protest; Resistance; Revolution; Terrorists; Violence; Violence, Frantz Fanon on*

BIBLIOGRAPHY

Anderson, David. 2005. *Histories of the Hanged: Britain's Dirty War and the End of Empire.* London: Weidenfeld and Nicolson.

Barnett, Donald L., and Karari Njama. 1966. *Mau Mau from Within: Autobiography and Analysis of Kenya's Peasant Revolt.* New York: Monthly Review Press.

Berman, Bruce, and John Lonsdale. 1992. *Unhappy Valley: Conflict in Kenya and Africa.* London: James Currey; Nairobi: Heinemann Kenya; Athens: Ohio University Press.

Buijtenhuijs, Rob. 1982. *Essays on Mau Mau: Contributions to Mau Mau Historiography.* Leiden, Netherlands: African Studies Center.

Clayton, Anthony. 1976. *Counter-Insurgency in Kenya, 1952–60: A Study of Military Operations against Mau Mau.* Nairobi: Transafrica Publishers.

Edgerton, Robert B. 1989. *Mau Mau: An African Crucible.* New York: Free Press; London: Collier Macmillan.

Elkins, Caroline. 2005. *Imperial Reckoning: The Untold Story of Britain's Gulag in Kenya.* New York: Henry Holt.

Furedi, Frank. 1974. The Social Composition of the Mau Mau Movement in the White Highlands. *Journal of Peasant Studies* 1 (4): 492–502.

Gikoyo, Gucu G. 1979. *We Fought for Freedom.* Nairobi: East African Publishing House.

Kanogo, Tabitha. 1987. *Squatters and the Roots of Mau Mau, 1905–63.* London: James Currey; Nairobi: Heinemann Kenya; Athens: Ohio University Press.

Maloba, Wunyabari O. 1993. *Mau Mau and Kenya: An Analysis of a Peasant Revolt.* Bloomington: Indiana University Press.

W. O. Maloba

MAUSS, MARCEL

SEE *Dance.*

MAXIMIN PRINCIPLE

The maximin principle is a principle for making choices when one is not sure of the outcome that will result from one's choice. The principle says to evaluate each option in terms of the worst possible outcome that could result from choosing that option, and to pick the option that offers the best worst outcome (the maximum minimum or maximin). Rational choice theory generally divides situations in which agents do not know for sure the outcome of their choices into three types: risk, uncertainty, and games. In situations of risk, the probabilities of various outcomes resulting from particular choices are known. In situations of uncertainty, those probabilities are not known, and in some cases the possible outcomes are also unknown. Games are strategic interactions, where the outcome that results from each player's choice is determined not merely by external—possibly random—factors, but by the play of other rational agents.

Maximin is both risk and uncertainty averse, because it minimizes the degree of risk or uncertainty faced by the agent. Many rational choice theorists argue that risk aversion is irrational, as it involves a kind of double counting, valuing the mere avoidance of risk over and above its effect on the expected value of the possible outcomes. Subjects in psychological tests display a fair range of attitudes toward risk, from positively valuing it to extreme risk adversity. Some rational choice theorists argue that aversion to uncertainty is more rational, and experimental results confirm that aversion to uncertainty is more widespread. Finally, in the case of games where the gains of one's opponents are one's own losses (so-called zero-sum games), maximin strategies are more clearly rational. If player one's opponent, player two, is rational, and player two's maximizing behavior will have the effect of giving player one the minimal result that can arrive from the options that player one faces, then it is rational for player one to try to maximize over those minimums. Furthermore, if such games have what is called a pure-strategy equilibrium, it will result from all players adopting a maximin strategy.

The importance and notoriety of the maximin principle outside of rational choice theory is due in large part to its connection with John Rawls's *A Theory of Justice* (1971). Something resembling a maximin principle appears at two crucial moments in Rawls's argument for the conception of justice he calls justice as fairness. First, at the heart of justice as fairness are two principles of justice, part of the second of which is the so-called difference principle. The difference principle states that social and economic inequalities are to be arranged to give the greatest benefit to the least advantaged members of society. Because the difference principle requires maximizing the share of goods that go to those with the smallest share, it is often described as a maximin principle of justice. Rawls rejected that name, however, because of its tendency to be confused with the maximin principle of choice.

Second, Rawls's argument for the two principles, from what he calls the original position, is often thought to involve an invocation of the maximin principle. In the original position, artificial rational agents must make a unanimous choice about principles of justice for a society, and do so without any particular knowledge about the people they represent or their society. Rawls argues that in such a situation, purely rational agents would choose his principles of justice over utilitarian principles. Many have read that argument as resting on the claim that it would be rational to use the maximin principle for choice in the original position. Such critics as John Harsanyi then argue that because the maximin principle is not a rational principle for choice under risk, Rawls's argument fails. Defenders of Rawls's theory (including Rawls himself) have offered three sorts of replies: (1) Risk aversion in the original position is rational because of the stakes and finality of the choice; (2) the choice in the original position is really one under uncertainty, not risk, and aversion to uncertainty is a much weaker and thus more defensible assumption to make than aversion to risk; (3) the original position is best thought of as a game, whose players are looking for an equilibrium, and this justifies their adoption of the maximin principle. In his *Justice as Fairness: A Restatement* (2001), Rawls further clarifies the role of the maximin principle in his argument, arguing in addition that its role is limited to supporting the adoption of his first principle, which guarantees adequate liberties to all, rather than the second principle, which includes the difference principle.

SEE ALSO *Gambling; Game Theory; Justice; Justice, Distributive; Justice, Social; Maximization; Minimization; Rawls, John; Risk; Social Contract; Uncertainty*

BIBLIOGRAPHY

Harsanyi, John. 1975. Can the Maximin Principle Serve as a Basis for Morality? A Critique of John Rawls's Theory. *American Political Science Review* 69(2): 594–606.

Luce, R. Duncan, and Howard Raiffa. 1957. *Games and Decisions.* New York: Wiley.

Rawls, John. 2001. *Justice as Fairness: A Restatement.* Ed. Erin Kelly. Cambridge, MA: Harvard University Press.

Anthony Laden

MAXIMIZATION

In modern economics agents are assumed to maximize, so naturally the structure of the maximization assumption has had a significant impact on the structure of modern economics. On one hand, the widespread use of maximization has given economics an intellectual unity not seen in most of the social sciences; on the other hand, the reliance on maximization threatens to halt empirical and theoretical progress in economics.

Nobel Prize winner Paul Samuelson should be credited with making maximization the foundation of modern economics. In his influential *Foundations of Economic Analysis* (1947), Samuelson demonstrates that consumer and firm behavior could be usefully modeled as solutions to what are now known, in mathematics, as classical programming problems.

In general, the classical programming problem takes the following mathematical form:

$$\text{Max}_{x_1, x_2, \ldots, x_n} F(x_1, x_2, \ldots, x_n) \text{ subject to:}$$
$$g_1(x_1, x_2, \ldots, x_n) = b_1$$
$$g_2(x_1, x_2, \ldots, x_n) = b_2$$
$$\ldots$$
$$g_m(x_1, x_2, \ldots, x_n) = b_m.$$

The n variables $x_1, x_2, \ldots, x_n$ are the instruments. The function $F(\cdot)$ is the objective function, and the m functions $g_1(\cdot), g_2(\cdot), \ldots, g_m(\cdot)$ are the constraint functions. The constants $b_1, b_2, \ldots, b_m$ are the constraint constants. Interpret the instruments as a representation of the choices available to the agent. Interpret the objective function as a representation of the agent's desires with respect to the choices. Finally, interpret the constraint functions and constants as a representation of the limits the environment imposes upon the agent's choices. Under these interpretations, the classical programming problem becomes a model of constrained maximization by an agent. If certain mathematical assumptions are met, a solution to the classical programming problem exists (Intriligator 1971). The method of LaGrange multipliers can be used to find a solution. Once a solution is deduced, compare its characteristics against the agent's observable behavior. If there is a match, the agent's behavior has been explained. If not, change the mathematical structure and repeat the process.

It is important to recognize that although the classical programming version of constrained maximization was new to most economists at the time of Samuelson's *Foundations*, the idea of constrained maximization was familiar. Constrained maximization is merely a sophisticated version of what the philosopher Daniel Dennett (1987) calls the "intentional stance." The intentional stance is a strategy for prediction and explanation. The first step in taking an intentional stance toward something—call it Z—is to attribute beliefs, desires, and rationality to Z. Since Z is assumed to be rational, the attributed beliefs and desires ought to make sense in the context of Z's circumstances. One can then predict (or explain) Z's behavior by determining what is rational given Z's attributed beliefs and desires. Since there is always leeway in the attribution of beliefs and desires, if a prediction turns out wrong, or an explanation does not impress, the intentional stance need not be questioned for we can always revise the beliefs and desire we attribute to Z. The intentional stance is practically irrefutable.

As Dennett notes, there is nothing particularly profound about the intentional stance. It is "folk psychology," "familiar to us since childhood and used effortlessly by us all every day" (Dennett 1987, p. 7). Yet when Samuelson merged the intentional stance with classical programming, he elevated this folk psychology to science. Think of Thomas Kuhn's (1962) definition of normal science as the relatively routine puzzle-solving activity of trained professionals. All can use the intentional stance effortlessly; few can do classical programming effortlessly, even with training.

Economic theorists at the research frontier quickly mastered the classical programming version of constrained maximization and began rapidly to transform the discipline. Mechanisms were created to select and reward mathematical skill. In one generation—the late 1940s to the late 1970s—the leading periodicals in economics, the leading economics departments in America, the minimal mathematical proficiency levels of American graduate students in economics, and the standards defining scholarly success in economics all changed. The mathematical goals of rigor, generality, and simplicity became widely shared imperatives in economics. The Nobel Prize winner Gerard

Debreu uses the term: "the mathematization of economic theory" (Debreu 1991) to refer to this evolution.

To illustrate the nature of this evolution, consider the discovery of nonlinear programming by Harold Kuhn and Albert Tucker (1951). The nonlinear programming problem is similar to the classical programming problem described above; the only differences are that the constraint functions are inequalities ($\leq$) and the instruments x_i ($i = 1, 2, \ldots, n$) are nonnegative (≥ 0). However, surface similarities mask deep differences; mathematically, nonlinear programming is better than classical programming. Nonlinear programming imposes fewer restrictions than classical programming, and it is based on a less complex mathematical foundation (convexity) than classical programming (differentiability). Given the new emphasis on rigor, generality, and simplicity in economics, on the battlefield of economic theory, nonlinear programming wiped out classical programming. Yet empirically speaking there is no difference between the two types of mathematical programming. Not surprisingly, modeling with nonlinear programming did not lead to new empirical generalizations.

Once maximization opened the gate to mathematization, constrained maximization became even more entrenched as the preferred method of doing economics. If you like rigor, generality, and simplicity then you like mathematical programming. So after years of selecting and rewarding mathematical skill, by the late 1970s the field of economics had as much consensus in the National Science Foundation's peer review system as the fields of chemical dynamics and solid-state physics (Cole, Cole, and Simon 1981).

Of course the consensus is incomplete. One of the earliest and most profound critics of constrained maximization is the Nobel Prize winner Herbert Simon. In 1955 Simon proposed satisficing as an alternative explanation of economic behavior, and throughout his career he urged economists to take a more empirical approach to their science. For more than four decades Simon carefully observed agents making choices, created theories, and devised experiments and computer simulations to test his theories. His work helped create two brand-new disciplines: artificial intelligence and cognitive science. Further, the primarily empirical research produced by two cognitive scientists inspired by Simon—Daniel Kahneman and Amos Tversky—received one of the 2002 Nobel Prizes in economics.

The work of Simon, Kahneman, and Tversky is very different from the economics produced after mathematization. To explain the difference, let us return to Dennett. In developing his notion of the intentional stance, Dennett has often referred to a contrasting strategy for prediction and explanation; he calls this strategy the

	Price theory	Applications of price theory	Behavioral economics
Empirical	40	27	6
Theoretical	10	20	10

design stance (Dennett 1987, pp. 16–17). Simon, Kahneman, and Tversky can be interpreted as applying the design stance toward human beings, and the first step in taking this sort of design stance is to figure out "how the machinery which Nature has provided us works" (Dennett 1987, p. 33). Figuring out the human machinery and implementing the intentional stance on a system of mathematical objects are two tasks divergent in empirical content. In which direction will economics go? Will it remain on the deeply mathematical track of constrained maximization, or will it move toward Simon and become more empirical?

Pierre-Andre Chiappori and Steven Levitt (2003) categorized every microeconomics paper in three prestigious economics journals between the years of 1999 and 2001. Consider three of their categories: (1) *price theory*, which "refers to basic economic principles and techniques used by economists in the 1950s and before" (p. 152); (2) *applications of price theory*, which "refer to the testing of simple economic ideas … in domains outside the traditional purview of the field" (p. 152); and (3) *behavioral economics*, which gives us a rough indicator of research in the spirit of Simon, Kahneman, and Tversky. The table includes the percentages of the paper types that Chiappori and Levitt placed in these three categories.

The pattern displayed in the table invites the question: If a high proportion of the most talented current economists are exploring economic ideas that were well known a half century ago, and few seem inspired by the current revolutions in cognitive science and artificial intelligence, will economics continue to achieve empirical and theoretical progress?

SEE ALSO *Debreu, Gerard; Economics, Neoclassical; Kuhn, Thomas; Maximin Principle; Minimization; Optimizing Behavior; Programming, Linear and Nonlinear; Samuelson, Paul A.; Satisficing Behavior; Science*

BIBLIOGRAPHY

Chiappori, Pierre-Andre, and Steven D. Levitt. 2003. An Examination of the Influence of Theory and Individual Theorists on Empirical Research in Microeconomics. *American Economic Review* 93 (2): 151–155.

Cole, Stephen, Jonathan R. Cole, and Gary A. Simon. 1981. Chance and Consensus in Peer Review. *Science* 214 (November): 881–886.

Debreu, Gerard. 1991. Economic Theory in the Mathematical Mode. *American Economic Review* 74 (3): 267–278.

Dennett, Daniel. 1987. *The Intentional Stance.* Cambridge, MA: MIT Press.

Intriligator, Michael. 1971. *Mathematical Optimization and Economic Theory.* Englewood Cliffs, NJ: Prentice Hall.

Kuhn, H. W., and A. W. Tucker. 1951. Nonlinear Programming. In *Proceedings of the Second Berkeley Symposium on Mathematical Statistics and Probability*, ed. J. Neyman. Berkeley: University of California Press.

Kuhn, Thomas. 1962. *The Structure of Scientific Revolutions.* Chicago: University of Chicago Press.

Samuelson, Paul. 1947. *Foundations of Economic Analysis.* Cambridge, MA: Harvard University Press.

Simon, Herbert. 1955. A Behavioral Model of Rational Choice. *Quarterly Journal of Economics* 69 (1): 99–118.

Gregory A. Lilly

MAXIMUM LIKELIHOOD REGRESSION

Maximum likelihood is a methodology used to estimate the parameters of an econometric or statistical model. It was first proposed by Ronald Aylmer Fisher (1890–1962) and is now considered the workhorse of modern econometrics, not only because of its flexibility but also due to the availability of computer power, which has permitted the resolution of complicated numerical problems associated with this technique. *Maximum likelihood estimation* seeks to determine the parameters of a statistical process that have the highest probability of generating the observed sample of data.

Consider the following regression model: $Y_i = \beta_0 + \beta_1 X_{1i} + \ldots \beta_k X_{ki} + \varepsilon_i$ for $i = 1, 2, \ldots . n$. In the simplest case, one can assume that the error term ε_i is an independent and identically distributed (iid) normal random variable with variance σ^2; that is, $\varepsilon_i \to N(0, \sigma^2)$. It will be shown below that the assumption of a particular density function for ε_i is paramount to write the likelihood function. Under the assumption of normality, the probability density function of the error term is written as

$$f(\varepsilon_i) = \frac{1}{\sqrt{2\pi\sigma^2}} \exp\left(-\frac{\varepsilon_i^2}{2\sigma^2}\right).$$

Since $\varepsilon_i = Y_i - \beta_0 - \beta_1 X_{1i} - \ldots - \beta_k X_{ki}$, the assumption of normality of the error term is equivalent to the assumption of normality for the conditional probability density function of Y given X: $f(Y_i \mid X_{1i}, X_{2i}, \ldots X_{ki}; \beta_0, \beta_1, \ldots \beta_k, \sigma^2) \to N(\beta_0 + \beta_1 X_{1i} + \ldots \beta_k X_{ki}, \sigma^2)$—that is,

$$f(Y_i \mid X_{1i}, X_{2i}, \ldots\ldots X_{ki}) =$$

$$\frac{1}{\sqrt{2\pi\sigma^2}} \exp\left(-\frac{(Y_i - \beta_0 - \beta_1 X_{1i} - \ldots \beta_k X_{ki})^2}{2\sigma^2}\right).$$

The objective is to estimate the parameter vector $\theta \equiv (\beta_0, \beta_1, \beta_2, \ldots .\beta_k, \sigma^2)'$. For a sample of size n, and because of the iid assumption, the joint probability density function of $\varepsilon_1, \varepsilon_2, \ldots .\varepsilon_n$, is then the product of the marginal densities: $f(\varepsilon_1, \varepsilon_2, \ldots .\varepsilon_n; \theta) = f(\varepsilon_1; \theta) f(\varepsilon_2; \theta) \ldots .. f(\varepsilon_n; \theta)$. The *likelihood function* $L(\theta; \varepsilon_1, \varepsilon_2, \ldots .\varepsilon_n)$ is based on the joint probability density function of $\varepsilon_1, \varepsilon_2, \ldots .\varepsilon_n$, where $\varepsilon_1, \varepsilon_2, \ldots .\varepsilon_n$ is taken as fixed data and the parameter vector θ is the argument of the function: $L(\theta; \varepsilon_1, \varepsilon_2, \ldots .\varepsilon_n) = f(\varepsilon_1; \theta) f(\varepsilon_2; \theta) \ldots .. f(\varepsilon_n; \theta)$. Note that $\varepsilon_1, \varepsilon_2, \ldots .\varepsilon_n$ is a function of the data $(Y_i, X_{1i}, X_{2i}, \ldots .X_{ki})$ through the regression model; that is to say, $\varepsilon_i = Y_i - \beta_0 - \beta_1 X_{1i} - \beta_2 X_{2i} - \ldots .. - \beta_k X_{ki}$

Though the aforementioned regression model deals with a cross-sectional data set, the maximum likelihood principle also applies to time-series data and panel data. For instance, a time-series regression such as $Y_t = \Phi Y_{t-1} + \varepsilon_t$ for $t = 1, 2 \ldots T$, with iid $\varepsilon_t \rightarrow N(0, \sigma^2)$, implies that the conditional density function of Y_t given Y_{t-1} is also normal, $f(Y_t \mid Y_{t-1}) \rightarrow N(\Phi Y_{t-1}, \sigma^2)$, that is,

$$f(Y_t \mid Y_{t-1}) = \frac{1}{\sqrt{2\pi\sigma^2}} \exp\left(-\frac{(Y_t - \phi Y_{t-1})^2}{2\sigma^2}\right)$$

As before, the object of interest is to estimate $\theta \equiv (\Phi, \sigma^2)'$ and the likelihood function for a sample of size T is $L(\theta; Y_1, Y_2, \ldots Y_T) = f(Y_1; \theta) f(Y_2 \mid Y_1; \theta) \ldots \ldots f(Y_T \mid Y_{T-1}; \theta)$. This function requires the knowledge of the marginal density of the first observation $f(Y_1; \theta)$. When the sample size is very large, the contribution of the first observation is almost negligible for any practical purposes. Conditioning on the first observation (Y_1 is known) we define the *conditional likelihood function* as $L(\theta; Y_T, Y_{T-1} \ldots . Y_2 \mid Y_1) = f(Y_2 \mid Y_1; \theta) \ldots \ldots f(Y_T \mid Y_{T-1}; \theta)$.

Mathematically, it is more convenient to work with the logarithm of the likelihood function. The *log-likelihood function* is defined as:

$$\lambda(\theta) \equiv \log L(\theta; \varepsilon_1, \varepsilon_2, \ldots \varepsilon_n) = \sum_{i=1}^{n} \log f(\varepsilon_i; \theta)$$

The *maximum likelihood estimator* (MLE) of θ is the value of θ that maximizes the likelihood of observing the sample $(Y_i, X_{1i}, X_{2i}, \ldots .X_{ki})$ $i = 1 \ldots n$. In estimating a regression model using maximum likelihood, the question is which value of $\theta \equiv (\beta_0, \beta_1, \beta_2, \ldots .\beta_k, \sigma^2)'$, out of all the possible values, makes the possibility of occurrence of the observed data the largest. Since the log transformation is

monotonic, the value of θ that maximizes the likelihood function is the same as the one that maximizes the log-likelihood function. The statistical inference problem is reduced to a mathematical problem, which under the assumption of normality, looks like:

$$\max_{\theta} \lambda(\theta) = \max_{\theta} \sum_{i=1}^{n} \log f(\varepsilon_i; \theta)$$

$$= \max_{\theta} \left[-\frac{n}{2} \log (2\pi\sigma^2) \right.$$

$$\left. -\frac{1}{2} \sum_{i=1}^{n} \frac{(Y_i - \beta_0 - \beta_1 X_{1i} - \ldots - \beta_k X_{ki})^2}{\sigma^2} \right].$$

Equating the first-order conditions (the score vector of first-order partial derivatives) to zero results in a system of $k + 2$ equations with $k + 2$ unknowns. The solution to this system is the maximum likelihood estimator. The solution is the maximum of the function if the Hessian (the matrix of second-order partial derivatives) is negative semi-definite.

For a linear regression model, the MLE is very easy to compute. First, we compute the solution for the system of equations corresponding to the parameter vector $(\beta_0, \beta_1, \ldots .\beta_k)'$. This system is linear, and its solution is identical to the ordinary least squares (OLS) estimator that is, $\hat{\beta}_{mle} = \hat{\beta}_{ols} = (X'X)^{-1} X'Y$. Second, the maximum likelihood estimator of the variance is straightforward to compute once the MLE $\hat{\beta}_i$'s are obtained. The MLE $\hat{\sigma}^2$ corresponds to the sample variance of the residuals $\hat{\sigma}^2_{mle} = \sum_i \hat{\varepsilon}_i^2 / n$, which is a biased estimator of the population variance. The $\hat{\beta}_{mle}$ is identical to the $\hat{\beta}_{ols}$ when the likelihood function is constructed under the assumption of normality.

For a nonlinear regression model, the system of equations is usually nonlinear, and to obtain the MLE solution numerical optimization methods are needed. In addition, there is the possibility of heteroscedasticity. This is the case when the variance of the error term is not constant but it depends on a set of variables, for instance, $\sigma^2(X, \gamma)$. In this instance, there is an additional set of parameters γ to estimate. The system of equations will be nonlinear and the solution will again be obtained by numerical optimization. In nonlinear models, the system of equations may have several solutions, for the likelihood function may exhibit a complicated profile with several local maxima. In this case, the researcher needs to make sure that the global maximum has been achieved by either plotting the profile of the likelihood function (when possible), or by using different initial values to start the iterative procedures within the optimization routine.

The significance of the maximum likelihood estimator derives from its optimal asymptotic properties. In large samples and under correct model specification, the MLE $\hat{\theta}_{mle}$ is in most cases consistent, asymptotically efficient, and asymptotically normal. Among these properties, *maximum efficiency* (estimators with the smallest variance) is the most significant property of the ML estimator. Maximum efficiency is a very desirable property because it allows the construction of more powerful tests and smaller confidence intervals than those based in less efficient estimators.

Within the maximum likelihood framework and after obtaining the ML estimators, we can also perform hypothesis testing by comparing the value of the estimates with other fixed values. The *likelihood ratio test* assesses the likelihood that the data may have been generated by a different set of parameter values (those under the null hypothesis). The test compares the value of the likelihood function under the null hypothesis with that under the alternative. The test is computed as two times the difference of the log-likelihood functions and it is asymptotically distributed as a chi-square with as many degrees of freedom as the number of parameters under the null.

The maximum likelihood estimator is also known as a *full information estimator* because the estimation is based on the most comprehensive characterization of a random variable, which is the specification of its probability density function. In practice, it is not known what density function should be assumed, and a potential shortcoming of the maximum likelihood estimator is that one could write a likelihood function under a false probability density function. The consequences of this are severe, for the asymptotic properties will not hold anymore. However, one can still apply *quasi-maximum likelihood estimation* (QMLE). The QML estimator requires that the conditional mean and conditional variance are correctly specified. It assumes that the error is normally distributed, though this may be a false assumption. The quasi-maximum likelihood estimator is still consistent, though the maximum efficiency property is lost. The efficiency loss depends on how far the normal density is from the true density. In practice, estimation is done within the quasi-maximum likelihood framework, because a full knowledge of the density is rare. Other estimators can recover some of the efficiency loss but, these belong to the family of nonparametric and semiparametric estimators.

SEE ALSO *Linear Regression; Models and Modeling; Probability Distributions; Properties of Estimators (Asymptotic and Exact); Regression; Regression Analysis*

BIBLIOGRAPHY

González-Rivera, Gloria, and Feike C. Drost. 1999. Efficiency Comparisons of Maximum-Likelihood-Based Estimators in GARCH Models. *Journal of Econometrics* 93 (1): 93–111.

White, Halbert L. 1994. *Estimation, Inference, and Specification Analysis.* Cambridge, UK: Cambridge University Press.

Gloria González-Rivera

MAYANS

SEE *Pre-Columbian Peoples.*

McCARTHYISM

The term *McCarthyism* refers to an accusatory campaign based on unfair allegations, fear tactics, innuendo, and sensationalized threats of guilt by association. *McCarthyism* was coined by political cartoonist Herbert Block (1909–2001) in a March 29, 1950, *Washington Post* cartoon lampooning the anticommunist campaigns of Senator Joseph Raymond McCarthy (1908–1957), a Republican from Wisconsin, in the 1950s. McCarthy was elected to the U.S. Senate in 1946 and rose to national prominence after newspapers reported on a speech he made in Wheeling, West Virginia, on February 9, 1950, in which he claimed to have a list of 205 State Department employees who were members of the Communist Party. McCarthy's list later shrunk to eighty-one, then fifty-seven, but McCarthy's facts mattered little to the press or his public.

When McCarthy became the chair of the Permanent Investigations Subcommittee of the Senate Committee on Governmental Operations in 1952, he used this position to investigate alleged Communists. In 1953 the committee identified "subversive" books held at American embassy libraries around the world. Books by authors such as Owen Lattimore (1900–1989), Lillian Hellman (1905–1984), Langston Hughes (1902–1967), and Dorothy Parker (1893–1967) were removed from libraries because of allegations that the authors were either fellow travelers or Communists. In late 1953 McCarthy investigated the U.S. Army after an army dentist was promoted despite his refusal to answer questions on a federal loyalty oath. McCarthy's inquiries soon led to investigations of a number of army officers.

Journalist Edward R. Murrow (1908–1965) broadcast a critical analysis of Senator McCarthy's tactics in March 1954 on the CBS program *See It Now*. This broadcast brought increased public scrutiny of McCarthy. In April 1954 the Senate began the Army-McCarthy hearings, investigating McCarthy's claims that the army was promoting Communists in its ranks. The hearings were nationally televised, allowing the nation to witness McCarthy's bullying and fabricating of evidence. On June 9, 1954, McCarthy's rapid descent began after a televised hearing showed army special council Joseph Welch (1890–1960) rebuffing McCarthy for his scurrilous tactics. Welch berated McCarthy before the cameras for his reckless bullying, rhetorically asking, "Have you no sense of decency, sir, at long last? Have you left no sense of decency?"

The Senate censured McCarthy on December 2, 1954, by a vote of seventy-six to twenty-two. McCarthy remained in the Senate, but his power was greatly diminished. He died of sclerosis of the liver in 1957. For all his bluster and claims to hold secret evidence of American Communism, McCarthy never identified a single Communist spy.

The social impacts of McCarthyism were significant. Some victims of McCarthyism lost jobs, were blacklisted, were alienated from friends and associates, or committed suicide. McCarthyism generated a climate of self-censorship. President Dwight D. Eisenhower (1890–1969), members of Congress, intellectuals, celebrities, and everyday citizens muted criticisms of McCarthy out of fear of being called procommunist (Schrecker 1998).

The Federal Bureau of Investigation (FBI) had a symbiotic relationship with Senator McCarthy. FBI director J. Edgar Hoover (1895–1972) had conducted free-ranging investigations of the American political Left since the 1930s, and the FBI secretly and illegally provided Senator McCarthy with records and names of individuals.

Functionally, McCarthyism deadened what might have been a critical activist edge in American social science as those who fought for racial or economic justice or who studied social stratification were routinely interrogated by the House Un-American Activities Committee (HUAC) or subjected to FBI surveillance and harassment (Harris 1980; Keen 2004; Price 2004). Proponents of McCarthyism were not simply interested in exposing and destroying Communists. McCarthyism's outcomes were much broader and included attacking labor union leaders, as well as discrediting a wide range of social activists working for gender, racial, and economic equality.

Loyalty hearings made examples out of public figures associated with progressive causes. In 1952 playwright Arthur Miller (1915–2005) began work on his play *The Crucible*, set during the 1692 Salem witch trials. *The Crucible*, which opened in New York in 1953, used the past to examine the 1950s climate of fear, accusations by informers, guilt by association, and the right of communities to bring moral judgments.

McCarthyism's mechanisms of social control extend beyond the mid-twentieth century's "Red Scare." The use of fear, guilt by association, vague accusations, and claims that dissent is dangerously unpatriotic to generate silence and compliance is a recurrent instrument of social control employed in various societies before and since the 1950s (Garfinkel 1956).

BIBLIOGRAPHY

Garfinkel, Harold. 1956. Conditions of Successful Degradation Ceremonies. *American Journal of Sociology* 61 (1): 420–424.

Harris, Benjamin. 1980. The FBI's Files on APA and SPSSI. *American Psychologist* 35: 1141–1144.

Keen, Mike. 2004. *Stalking Sociologists: J. Edgar Hoover's FBI Surveillance of American Sociology.* New Brunswick, NJ: Transaction.

Miller, Arthur. 1953. *The Crucible: A Play in Four Acts.* New York: Viking.

Price, David H. 2004. *Threatening Anthropology: McCarthyism and the FBI's Surveillance of Activist Anthropologists.* Durham, NC: Duke University Press.

Schrecker, Ellen. 1998. *Many Are the Crimes: McCarthyism in America.* New York: Little, Brown.

David H. Price

McFADDEN, DANIEL L.
1937–

Daniel L. McFadden, a physics undergraduate who switched to behavioral science (economics) in graduate school, won the Nobel Prize in economics (Bank of Sweden Prize in Honor of Alfred Nobel) in 2000. McFadden's best-known economic contribution and the one that led to his winning the Nobel Prize was the theoretical development and econometric evaluation of discrete choices involving multiple outcomes.

Discrete choice outcomes had been a vexing problem in economic analysis. Typically, economic decisions have been framed as trade-offs between goods in which quantities of goods could be traded over relatively continuous ranges. Discrete choices, by contrast, are "lumpy": One choice precludes the possibility of choosing another option. For example, the same consumer cannot choose simultaneously to drive and to take the train to work on the same morning.

Modeling discrete outcomes requires a theoretical framework for discrete choice and empirical innovations that allow researchers to investigate the factors that influence the outcomes of choices. McFadden provided the theoretical linkage by adopting the basic precepts of a random utility model in which the agent is assumed to maximize utility but the researcher cannot observe the full set of factors that lead to the choice; the agent also cannot do this because of cognitive and information limitations.

The limited decision-making capacity of the agent, along with the limited information researchers have about the factors that lead to a decision, results in a set of determinants that are unobservable in the modeling process.

This insight implies that the errors associated with decision-making are especially important in estimating discrete choice models. The idea of unobserved preference heterogeneity serves as the theoretical foundation of McFadden's well-known multinomial logit model.

In a multinomial logit model McFadden assumes that there is a latent (unobserved) variable that represents the indirect utility (satisfaction) associated with each discrete choice. One set of independent variables measures the attributes of the choice. A second set of variables measures the individual attributes affecting tastes. A fundamental assumption of McFadden's discrete choice models is that current economic conditions affect the feasibility of a choice through the budget constraint but not the preferences of the individual. Thus, prestige goods, or "snob" goods, are not modeled adequately using McFadden's theoretical foundation.

Although the theoretical foundations for the multinomial logit model are complex, the empirical estimation of that model has become increasingly simple. Most of the empirical methods developed by McFadden, such as multinomial logit, conditional logit, and other nested models, have been standardized enough that they are easy to estimate. However, the interpretation of the results is less straightforward. Estimates are interpreted relative to the "base" category (often the most common choice), and every other outcome has its own set of parameter estimates. One consequence of this is that when there are many choice outcomes, interpretation of the results is difficult. In particular, neither the sign nor the magnitude of the parameter estimates indicates the direction of the influence of the independent variable on the outcome. Typically, marginal effects must be calculated for each variable of interest.

A second difficulty with the multinomial logit model is that the observed attributes of the choices must provide a systematic mapping onto the agent's preferences. If arbitrary attributes are used to categorize choices, the multinomial logit model will provide incorrect estimates of the effects of independent variables. This difficulty is known as the independence of irrelevant alternatives (IIA) problem. The issue of IIA points to the importance of understanding, classifying, and defining the choice set.

SEE ALSO *Choice in Economics; Economics, Nobel Prize in; Information, Economics of; Logistic Regression; Variables, Latent*

BIBLIOGRAPHY

McFadden, Daniel. 2000. Economic Choices. *American Economic Review* 91 (3): 351–378.

Jeffrey B. Wenger

McLUHAN, MARSHALL
1911–1980

In 1964, when Canadian educator and social theorist Marshall McLuhan's *Understanding Media* appeared, the terms *medium* and *media* were generally understood in the sense of intermediary or intermediate. The *media* were not recognized as a subject of study; reviewers and teachers cautioned that the word was obscure and needed definition. McLuhan's radical observation was that it is the medium (not the program content) that shapes and controls the scale and form of human association and action:

> The message of any medium or technology is the change of scale or pace or pattern that it introduces into human affairs. The railway did not introduce movement or transportation or wheel or road into human society, but it accelerated and enlarged the scale of previous human functions, creating totally new kinds of cities and new kinds of work and leisure. This happened whether the railway functioned in a tropical or northern environment, and is quite independent of the freight or content of the railway medium. (McLuhan 1964, p. 8)

This is essentially a sociological outlook, though it has not been adopted by that field. Yet *Understanding Media* did serve to found the field of media study in North America and ultimately throughout the world.

Among its groundbreaking insights were that some media involve the user deeply ("cool media"), while others ("hot media") do not: The involvement takes place on the sensory level, below consciousness. For example, the movie viewer must supply all of the movement that occurs on the screen between frames while the screen is black. The television viewer or computer user supplies most of the mosaic image from moment to moment and nearly all of the color. These effects, which occur independently of the content or uses, shape the sensory preferences of the users and supply new perceptual biases that affect how they construe their cultures and societies.

McLuhan was the first to study advertising seriously: In his first book, *The Mechanical Bride* (1951), he called advertising the "Folklore of Industrial Man." This work applies then-new critical techniques (practical criticism, developed in England) for the first time to ads and other facets of North American popular culture. McLuhan followed it with *Culture Is Our Business* (1970), a companion study of advertising *after* television.

The Gutenberg Galaxy (1962) delved into the manner in which print and the press reshaped culture and sensibility in the centuries that followed their introduction and showed how to study the social-environmental actions of new media. *Take Today: The Executive as Dropout* (1972) examined the effects of electric media on management practice and business culture.

Laws of Media: The New Science (1988), written with his son Eric, sought to place McLuhan's style of environmental media study on a scientific basis for the first time. In it, the authors proposed that four invariable laws govern the action of all media—and also of all human artifacts. Briefly, every human artifact extends or amplifies some process or faculty; obsolesces some established pattern; reinvigorates or retrieves some older, previously obsolesced form that now returns in a new shape or guise; and reverses its characteristics when pushed to its limit. The four laws exhibit an inner relation to each other as A is to B as C is to D.

During his life, McLuhan was a controversial figure, not least because his techniques of media study departed so radically from the established methods, which focused on content analysis and research into the desires and motivations of audiences. McLuhan, in contrast, approached media study from the angle of perception and changes in sensibility occasioned by media as forms and as extensions of the users' senses. Although McLuhan's work remains controversial, his techniques work as well now as they did in his time, to the chagrin of those who have tried to apply them superficially, without first understanding how perception is modified by media.

SEE ALSO *Critical Theory; Cultural Studies; Film Industry; Journalism; Media; Popular Culture; Television; Theater; Visual Arts*

BIBLIOGRAPHY

McLuhan, Marshall. 1951. *The Mechanical Bride: Folklore of Industrial Man.* New York: Vanguard.

McLuhan, Marshall. 1962. *The Gutenberg Galaxy: The Making of Typographic Man.* Toronto, ON: University of Toronto Press.

McLuhan, Marshall. 1964. *Understanding Media: The Extensions of Man.* New York: McGraw-Hill.

McLuhan, Marshall. 1970. *Culture Is Our Business.* New York: McGraw-Hill.

McLuhan, Marshall. 1999. *The Medium and the Light: Reflections on Religion*, eds. Eric McLuhan and Jacek Szklarek. Toronto, ON: Stoddart.

McLuhan, Marshall, and Quentin Fiore. 1967. *The Medium is the Massage.* New York: Random House.

McLuhan, Marshall, and Quentin Fiore. 1968. *War and Peace in the Global Village: An Inventory of Some of the Current Spastic Situations That Could Be Eliminated by More Feedforward.* New York: Random House.

McLuhan, Marshall, and Eric McLuhan. 1988. *Laws of Media: The New Science.* Toronto, ON: University of Toronto Press.

McLuhan, Marshall, and Barrington Nevitt. 1972. *Take Today: The Executive as Dropout.* New York: Harcourt.

McLuhan, Marshall, and Harley Parker. 1968. *Through the Vanishing Point: Space in Poetry and Painting.* New York: Harper.

McLuhan, Marshall, and Wilfred Watson. 1970. *From Cliché to Archetype.* New York: Viking.

Eric McLuhan

MEAD, GEORGE HERBERT
1863–1931

George Herbert Mead was one of the core founders of pragmatism, a distinctively American philosophy. Mead was a professor of philosophy at the University of Chicago (1894–1931), but he had a powerful influence on both philosophy and sociology. He is also recognized as one of the originators of symbolic interactionism, an important discipline within sociology. In this regard, he is famous for showing the relationships between mind, self, and society: Our minds and selves are gifts we receive from society, though we can augment and alter mind, self, and society in countless ways (Mead 1934).

Mead and the other pragmatists argued that the scientific method is the most powerful tool humans have ever discovered for analyzing knowledge, and they applied empirical methods to all knowledge—including science, philosophy, government, religion, ideologies, and everyday life. Mead argued that we should treat all ideas as hypotheses that are open to analysis in terms of the consequences associated with using them. It is true that many religious people and ideologues are not used to thinking that their favorite ideas are hypotheses that can be tested by examining how well they work, but pragmatists treat all knowledge as tentative and open to investigation.

Any ideas that work well when we act on them are tentatively supported as useful and valid. On the other hand, ideas that lead to failures are identified as problematic. This is most obvious in the realm of science. A medical procedure that prolongs life without problematic reactions is seen as valuable, but a procedure with adverse side effects alerts researchers to either abandon the technique or rework it until the problems are overcome. Pragmatists treat all ideas in a similar manner. For example, many American professors defended Marxism and communism during the mid-1900s, and pragmatists are not surprised that some abandoned these theories after the collapse of the Soviet Union and the Communist nations of Eastern Europe. Even if an idea was once popular, pragmatists emphasize that a series of failures often leads people to abandon or revise prior views: Countless positive claims about an idea are not as powerful as a succession of failings.

No theory can ever be proven so conclusively as to be completely above question and possible future revision. Pragmatists argue that tentative and flexible truths are in fact more useful than the dogmas or static "truths" that ideologues defend. Our physical, biological, and social worlds are in constant change; hence, it is wise to approach all knowledge as likely to need modification as we attempt to track our ever changing and evolving world.

Pragmatism has had major influences on philosophy, sociology, science, and many other domains of thought. Mead's version of pragmatism is highly nuanced because, as the youngest of the pragmatists, he benefited from the best ideas of his predecessors.

SEE ALSO *Philosophy; Philosophy, Political; Pragmatism; Science; Society; Sociology*

BIBLIOGRAPHY

Mead, George Herbert. 1932. *Philosophy of the Present*, ed. Arthur E. Murphy. Chicago and London: Open Court.

Mead, George Herbert. 1934. *Mind, Self and Society*, ed. Charles W. Morris. Chicago: University of Chicago Press.

John D. Baldwin

MEAD, MARGARET
1901–1978

Margaret Mead was an American anthropologist whose career as a social scientist and public intellectual spanned the greater part of the twentieth century. She was an indefatigable fieldworker whose ethnographic research focused primarily on the study of small-scale societies in the South Pacific and Bali, but she was also well known for her insights about and prescriptions for American society. Mead received her PhD in anthropology in 1925 from Columbia University, where she worked with Dr. Franz Boas and Dr. Ruth Benedict, two anthropologists well known for their work on race and cultural relativism, or the idea that no culture or racial group is inherently superior to another and that any cultural practice can be understood within the context of the larger social structure and cultural whole of which it is a part. Along with Benedict, Mead was a major contributor to the development of the school of culture and personality, a subfield of cultural anthropology that sought to understand the role that culture played in shaping the personality of individual members of a particular society. Influenced by neo-Freudian theory of the 1930s and 1940s, Mead sought to apply psychoanalytic concepts about the individual—especially the development of a child into an adult—to the study of socialization in non-Western societies. Although aspects of culture and personality theory have been disparaged, many of the topics that Mead first investigated formed the basis for today's subfield of psychological anthropology.

After Mead returned from her first field trip to Samoa in 1926, she became curator of anthropology at the American Museum of Natural History. She remained at the museum for the rest of her lengthy career. Mead's fame arose from her ability to write books that captured the general public's interest with their engaging prose and provocative and timely choice of topics. Beginning with her first book—*Coming of Age in Samoa*—published in 1928, Mead became a best-selling author and an increasingly well-known expert on the topics of primitive cultures, adolescence, gender and sexuality, education, child development, and culture change. While *Coming of Age in Samoa* established Mead's reputation as an anthropologist who studied sexuality, especially the sexual behavior of adolescent girls, subsequent books focused on education in so-called primitive cultures (*Growing Up in New Guinea*), gender roles and male-female relations (*Sex and Temperament in Three Primitive Societies* and *Male and Female*), acculturation (*The Changing Culture of an Indian Tribe*), the relationship between culture and the development of adult personality (*Balinese Character*), national character (*And Keep Your Powder Dry*, Mead's first anthropological book about American culture), *New Lives for Old* (about cultural transformation and the impact of Western development on traditional societies), and *Culture and Commitment* (Mead's analysis of the generation gap).

During World War II (1939–1945) Mead worked for the U.S. government, contributing studies on American food habits, morale building, and the interpretation of British and American culture for British civilians and American soldiers in the United Kingdom. After the war Mead shifted her focus to the application of anthropological methods to the study of American society, the Soviet Union, and the problems of development faced by newly independent nations. As a result of her increasing media presence on television, in popular magazines, and the radio, by the time she died Mead was famous worldwide and eulogized as "grandmother to the world."

In 1983, five years after Mead's death, Australian anthropologist Derek Freeman published a detailed critique of Mead's Samoan research, ultimately claiming that Mead's informants had duped her and that her conclusions about the relative freedom toward premarital sex she had claimed characterized Samoan society were false. Moreover, Freeman concluded that if Mead's Samoan findings were false, so too was the larger claim she had made about the relative importance of nurturance versus biologically innate characteristics of human behavior. Although Mead was not able to respond to Freeman's critique herself, many anthropologists who had worked in Samoa, or who were proponents of the importance of cultural factors in shaping human behavior, came to her defense. They did so despite their acknowledgment of some factual errors in her Samoan research, which they claimed were of minor significance and the result of her youth and the infancy of anthropology as a social science. (For a detailed discussion of the critique of Freeman's argument and defense of Mead's work, see Caton [1990], Orans [1996], and Lapsley [1999]). In November 1983 the American Anthropological Association censured Freeman, citing inconsistencies and errors in his critique of Mead's Samoan research. However, although the media coverage of the Mead-Freeman controversy damaged Mead's public image, in 2001 the American Anthropological Association and the media honored Mead during her centennial year. This asserted her prominence as a public figure whose major contribution had been to apply anthropological methods and insights gleaned from the study of remote small-scale societies into the analysis of contemporary American society and the solution of problems that vexed complex modern societies in general.

SEE ALSO *Anthropology, U.S.; Benedict, Ruth; Boas, Franz; Psychoanalytic Theory*

BIBLIOGRAPHY

Bateson, Gregory, and Margaret Mead. 1942. *Balinese Character.* New York: New York Academy of Sciences.

Caton, Hiram, ed. 1990. *The Samoa Reader: Anthropologists Take Stock.* Latham, MD: University Press of America.

Freeman, Derek. 1983. *Margaret Mead and Samoa: The Making and Unmaking of an Anthropological Myth* (reprinted as *Margaret Mead and the Heretic*). Cambridge, MA: Harvard University Press.

Freeman, Derek. 1999. *The Fateful Hoaxing of Margaret Mead: A Historical Analysis of Her Samoan Research.* Boulder, CO: Westview Press.

Lapsley, Hilary. 1999. *Margaret Mead and Ruth Benedict: The Kinship of Women.* Amherst: University of Massachusetts Press.

Lutkehaus, Nancy. 1995. Introduction. In *Blackberry Winter: My Earlier Years*, by Margaret Mead. New York: Kodansha International.

Lutkehaus, Nancy. 1995. Margaret Mead and the "Rustling-of-the-Wind-in-the-Palm-Trees" School of Ethnographic Writing. In *Women Writing Culture*, eds. Ruth Behar and Deborah A. Gordon, 186–206. Berkeley: University of California Press.

Mead, Margaret. 1928. *Coming of Age in Samoa: A Psychological Study of Primitive Youth for Western Civilization.* New York: William Morrow. Reprinted 2001. New York: Perennial Classics, HarperCollins.

Mead, Margaret. 1930. *Growing Up in New Guinea: A Comparative Study of Primitive Education.* New York: William Morrow. Reprinted 2001. New York: Perennial Classics, HarperCollins.

Mead, Margaret. 1932. *The Changing Culture of an Indian Tribe.* New York: Columbia University Press.

Mead, Margaret. 1935. *Sex and Temperament in Three Primitive Societies.* New York: William Morrow. Reprinted 2001. New York: Perennial Classics, HarperCollins.

Mead, Margaret. 1942. *And Keep Your Powder Dry: An Anthropologist Looks at America.* New York: William Morrow.

Mead, Margaret. 1949. *Male and Female: A Study of the Sexes in a Changing World.* New York: William Morrow. Reprinted 2001. New York: Perennial Classics, HarperCollins.

Mead, Margaret. 1956. *New Lives for Old: Cultural Transformation—Manus, 1928–1953.* New York: William Morrow. Reprinted 2001. New York: Perennial Classics HarperCollins.

Mead, Margaret. 1970. *Culture and Commitment: A Study of the Generation Gap.* Garden City, NY: Natural History Press.

Mead, Margaret. 1972. *Blackberry Winter: My Earlier Years.* New York: William Morrow. Reprinted 1995. New York and Tokyo: Kodansha Press.

Orans, Martin. 1996. *Not Even Wrong: Margaret Mead, Derek Freeman, and the Samoans.* Novato, CA: Chandler and Sharp.

Nancy Lutkehaus

MEADE, JAMES
1907–1995

During his long career as an economist, James Edward Meade made major contributions to many fields, including national income accounting, economic growth, public finance, and welfare economics, as well as the two most important, for the discipline and for the world economy, macroeconomics and international economics (trade and finance). For his contribution to international trade and finance he was awarded the 1977 Nobel Memorial Prize in Economics jointly with Swedish economist Bertil Ohlin (1899–1979).

As an undergraduate at Oriel College, Oxford, Meade switched from the study of classics to economics, motivated by the serious unemployment problem in Britain in the 1920s. Upon graduation with first-class honors in 1930, he was appointed to a fellowship in economics at Hertford College, which first allowed him a postgraduate year at Trinity College, Cambridge. He swiftly became a member of the Cambridge "circus" of young economists—including Richard Kahn (1905–1989), Austin Robinson (1897–1993), Joan Robinson

(1903–1983), and Piero Sraffa (1898–1983)—whose criticism of John Maynard Keynes's (1883–1946) *A Treatise on Money* (1930) set Keynes on the path to *The General Theory of Employment, Interest, and Money* (1936). Meade returned to Oxford already a "Keynesian" in the modern (i.e., post-1936) sense, and published the first Keynesian economics textbook, *An Introduction to Economic Analysis and Policy*, in 1936. Throughout his career his main concern was with the contribution economic analysis can make to practical economic policy. One of several young Oxford economists advising the Labour Party in the 1930s, he was a "liberal socialist" who believed in using the market mechanism for egalitarian ends. He was also a convinced believer in international political and economic cooperation.

In 1937 Meade joined the Financial Section of the League of Nations and wrote two of its *World Economic Surveys* before World War II (1939–1945), when he returned to England to work for the British government. In government, he and Richard Stone (1913–1991) prepared the first modern double-entry social accounts for any country, published as *An Analysis of the Sources of War Finance and an Estimate of the National Income and Expenditure in 1938 and 1940*, accompanying the first "Keynesian" budget of April 1941. He then concerned himself with planning postwar macroeconomic policy. It was Meade who wrote, in March 1943, the first draft of what became the wartime coalition government's *Employment Policy* (1944). He was also a founding father of the GATT (General Agreement on Tariffs and Trade). To complement Keynes's "clearing union" plan for the postwar international currency system, Meade proposed an "international commercial union" to restore multilateral trade and remove trade restrictions after the war. The two plans formed the basis of the British contributions to wartime Anglo-American discussions on the postwar international economic order. Meade's ideas bore fruit in the Anglo-American *Proposals for Consideration by an International Conference on Trade and Employment* of December 1945, and he served on the preparatory commission for the conference that drew up the charter for an International Trade Organization. Although the charter was not ratified, its main principles were incorporated in the GATT, negotiated in Geneva in 1947.

Meade returned to academic life in 1947 as Cassel Professor of Commerce with special reference to international trade at the London School of Economics. There, as a direct result of his wartime work on economic policy, he was to make his most lasting contributions to economic theory when he began to write on international economic policy. He began by constructing a general-equilibrium comparative static model for an economy open to trade and capital flows, synthesizing Keynesian and classical theory and extending it in order to analyze the effects of different policy instruments and other variables on internal and external balance. The result, *The Theory of International Economic Policy*, Volume 1: *The Balance of Payments* (1951a), and its supplement containing the mathematical model (1951b), was the first systematic exploration of the relationship between domestic and international equilibrium. The model has become "part of the baggage of every economist" (Corden and Atkinson 1979, p. 529), the most important single influence behind the development of open-economy macroeconomics in the next four decades.

The equally pathbreaking second volume, *Trade and Welfare* (1955a, 1955b), made three major and lasting contributions to economics: a fundamental reformulation of the theory of economic welfare to make it both operational and more widely applicable; the use of this new theory to analyze controls on factor movements as well as controls of trade; and the extension of the analysis from two-country models to a many-country world, including its application to the theory of customs unions (1955c). He originally drafted much of the book on the basis of the "new welfare economics" of the late 1930s, but he rewrote it to utilize the work (1951) of his former wartime colleague, Marcus Fleming (1911–1976). "It was a brilliant feat of imagination ... to realize ... [Fleming's method] was capable of large-scale generalization into a powerful tool for welfare analysis of practical policy problems, and an act of great intellectual honesty and courage for him to scrap his existing draft and rework the whole problem on the new approach" (Johnson 1978, p. 73).

From 1968 Meade was based in Cambridge, first as professor of political economy in succession to Dennis Robertson (1890–1963), A. C. Pigou (1877–1959), and Alfred Marshall (1842–1924). He worked on the theory of economic growth (1961a) and income distribution for ten years before returning to macroeconomics to lead a major research project on *Stagflation* (Meade 1982; Vines et al. 1983). He concentrated on the reform of wage-fixing arrangements, in order to solve the problem of the dual function of the price mechanism: The prices of goods and factors of production that promote the most efficient use of resources may well produce an unacceptably unequal distribution of income. His consistent concern for both efficiency and equality is spelled out most clearly in *Efficiency, Equality, and the Ownership of Property* (1964), which he himself regarded as his best book. It was also a feature of two "Meade Reports," *The Economic and Social Structure of Mauritius* (1961b) and *The Structure and Reform of Direct Taxation* (1978), and his final book *Full Employment Regained? An Agathotopian Dream* (1995). An inveterate explorer of improvements in economic arrangements, he should be remembered for his practical contributions as well as for his theoretical achievements.

SEE ALSO *Economics, International; Economics, Keynesian; Economics, Nobel Prize in; Exchange Rates; General Agreement on Tariffs and Trade; Kahn, Richard F.; Keynes, John Maynard; League of Nations; Marshall, Alfred; Robinson, Joan; Sraffa, Piero; Trade*

BIBLIOGRAPHY

PRIMARY WORKS

Meade, James E. 1936. *An Introduction to Economic Analysis and Policy.* London: Oxford University Press.

Meade, James E. 1951a. *The Theory of International Economic Policy.* Vol. 1: *The Balance of Payments.* London: Oxford University Press.

Meade, James E. 1951b. *The Theory of International Economic Policy.* Vol. 1: *The Balance of Payments, Mathematical Supplement.* London: Oxford University Press.

Meade, James E. 1955a. *The Theory of International Economic Policy.* Vol. 2: *Trade and Welfare.* London: Oxford University Press.

Meade, James E. 1955b. *The Theory of International Economic Policy.* Vol. 2: *Trade and Welfare, Mathematical Supplement.* London: Oxford University Press.

Meade, James E. 1955c. *The Theory of Customs Unions.* Amsterdam: North-Holland.

Meade, James E. 1961a. *A Neo-Classical Theory of Economic Growth.* London: Allen & Unwin.

Meade, James E., et al. 1961b. *The Economic and Social Structure of Mauritius: Report to the Governor of Mauritius.* London: Methuen.

Meade, James E. 1964. *Efficiency, Equality, and the Ownership of Property.* London: Allen & Unwin.

Meade, James E., et al. 1978. *The Structure and Reform of Direct Taxation.* London: Allen & Unwin for the Institute of Fiscal Studies.

Meade, James E. 1982. *Stagflation.* Vol. 1: *Wage-Fixing.* London: Allen & Unwin.

Meade, James E. 1988. *The Collected Papers of James Meade.* Vol. 1: *Employment and Inflation.* Vol. 2: *Value, Distribution, and Growth.* Vol. 3: *International Economics,* ed. Susan Howson. London: Unwin Hyman.

Meade, James E. 1990a. The Law Mission, September–October 1943. In *The Wartime Diaries of Lionel Robbins and James Meade, 1943–45,* eds. Susan Howson and Donald Moggridge, 92–155. London: Macmillan.

Meade, James E. 1990b. *The Collected Papers of James Meade.* Vol. 4: *The Cabinet Office Diary, 1944–46,* eds. Susan Howson and Donald Moggridge. London: Unwin Hyman.

Meade, James E. 1995. *Full Employment Regained? An Agathotopian Dream.* Cambridge, U.K.: Cambridge University Press.

Vines, David, Jan Maciejowski, and James E. Meade. 1983. *Stagflation.* Vol. 2: *Demand Management.* London: Allen & Unwin.

SECONDARY WORKS

Corden, W. M., and A. B. Atkinson. 1979. James E. Meade. In *International Encyclopedia of the Social Sciences, Biographical Supplement,* vol. 18, ed. David L. Sills, 528–532. New York: Free Press.

Fleming, J. Marcus. 1951. On Making the Best of Balance of Payments Restrictions on Imports. *Economic Journal* 61: 48–69.

Johnson, Harry G. 1978. James Meade's Contribution to Economics. *Scandinavian Journal of Economics* 80: 64–85.

Keynes, John Maynard. 1930. *A Treatise on Money.* 2 vols. London: Macmillan.

Keynes, John Maynard. 1936. *The General Theory of Employment, Interest, and Money.* London: Macmillan.

Vines, David. 1987. Meade, James Edward. In *The New Palgrave Dictionary of Economics,* eds. John Eatwell, Murray Milgate, and Peter Newman, vol. 3, 410–417. London: Macmillan.

Susan Howson

MEAN

SEE *Descriptive Statistics.*

MEAN, THE

The mean is widely used throughout the social sciences and is the arithmetic average of a set of scores. It is simply the sum of all the scores of interest divided by the number of scores. In casual conversation this calculation is referred to as "getting the average." The capital letter M is commonly used in journal articles to represent the mean. The formula for the mean is quite simple: $M = \Sigma X/N$, where M is the mean, ΣX is the sum of all the scores of interest, and N is the number of the scores.

In general, what is sought is a single value that represents the location of the set of scores on some scale. The mean describes the central tendency of a distribution of scores. In other words, it describes where the scores tend to cluster together or the arithmetic middle point of the scores. This measure of central tendency is sometimes referred to as the index of location.

The mode and the median are also used to describe central tendency; they lack, however, the mathematical properties of the mean. These other measures are most useful when the distribution of scores is multimodal or skewed.

A simple example will illustrate the mean. Assume one has five scores: 6, 5, 4, 3, and 2. The sum of these scores is 20. The mean is 20/5, which equals 4. In this case the median is also 4 (it is the score that divides all the scores in half). This is usually the case when the distribution of scores is symmetrical. This example can also illustrate an advantage of the mean over the median. The mean is sensitive to all the scores in the distribution, while the median is not. Look at what happens if the score of 6 is changed to a score of 16. The new sum of the scores is now 30, and the mean is 30/5, which is 6. But the median is still 4. The mean reflects the value of every score in the distribution. Of course, in the social sciences one often encounters distributions that are essentially normal, in which case all three measures of central tendency (mode, median, and mean) will be the same.

For many variables in the social sciences the mean is the standard descriptor of central tendency. For example, the mean may be used to describe a person's average grade in a course of study or a person's average weight over a given period. The mean is useful in describing groups as well. Demographic data are often presented as means (e.g., mean age, height, weight, number of children, or siblings). The average performance of a class of students, a school, a school district, a state, or the whole country may be reported on some measure of academic achievement. Even countries may be compared on average academic skills.

In research or evaluation the characteristics of a population of interest often need to be described. Populations, however, are typically very large (sometimes infinitely so) and impossible to measure completely. The truth about a population may only be inferred. For this reason a sample is collected from the population, with the intent of generalizing the results to the whole population. Once the sample scores have been obtained, the data need to be described in such a way as to communicate the essential characteristics and also allow inferences about the population—briefly but informatively.

The sample mean is an unbiased estimator of the population mean. It determines a center point of the set of scores that includes the value of every score in the set. Because the mean includes all the scores, it is the point of balance or center of gravity of the distribution.

Much research is concerned with trying to determine how different or how similar people or groups may be. The mean is used to do this. The measurement of how far individuals are from their group mean is taken, and also the measurement of how far group means are from the mean of all the samples. The resulting scores are called deviation scores, and are obtained by subtracting the mean from the individual score. These deviation scores can be used to calculate another average called the variance (because the sum of the deviation scores is always zero, they must be squared before being added together and dividing by the number). The square root of the variance is called the standard deviation. This average tells one

about the amount of variability in a set of scores or among a set of means.

This property of the mean is critical because much research is concerned with examining how much sample means deviate from some point or from each other. If the means deviate from each other by a large enough amount, they are said to be "significantly different." This is the basis for significance testing between groups. These significance tests are commonly found in published research, although there is debate about which approach to use and how results should be reported.

The mean is arguably the most widely used measure of central tendency. It requires interval or ratio level of measurement, works best with distributions that are unimodal and roughly symmetrical, and is the basis for much statistical decision-making.

SEE ALSO *Decision-making; Population Studies; Standard Deviation*

BIBLIOGRAPHY

Aron, Arthur, and Elaine N. Aron. 2003. *Statistics for Psychology.* 3rd ed. Upper Saddle River, NJ: Prentice Hall.

Hays, William L. 1973. *Statistics for the Social Sciences.* 2nd ed. New York: Holt, Rinehart and Winston.

Oaks, Michael W. 1986. *Statistical Inference: A Commentary for the Social and Behavioural Sciences.* Chichester, U.K.: Wiley.

Samuel K. Rock Jr.

MEAN SQUARE EFFICIENCY

SEE *Properties of Estimators (Asymptotic and Exact).*

MEANING

In the social sciences, the concept of meaning has been understood theoretically in three different ways, which can be called the *mirroring, constructivist,* and *production* perspectives.

The mirroring perspective derives from the work of Max Weber (1864–1920), who called attention to the subjective interpretations that people create to describe or explain their social experience. Whether or not these meanings are conveyed to others, they are social to the extent that they are broadly characteristic of those who share a similar position within the structure of social relationships. For example, according to a study of television audiences in Israel, the meanings viewers ascribed to the

American television series *Dallas* had much more to do with ethnicity than with whatever meanings might have been intended by the show's scriptwriters and directors. Arabs saw the show as a moral drama exemplifying how American immorality inexorably led to chaos in interpersonal relationships, while Jews who recently immigrated from Russia saw it as a social drama portraying the evils of the capitalist system (Liebes and Katz 1990). Similarly, in the United States and United Kingdom, men and women have been repeatedly found to view corporate leadership roles differently. For most men, effective leadership means setting up a forceful and consistently applied system of rewards and punishments. For most women, it means showing others how to transform one's individual goals into group goals so that teams can work more effectively and harmoniously (Alimo-Metcalfe 1995). In the mirroring perspective, the social meanings that people are found to have about the social world are seen to stem from their differing experience of a social structure in which prestige, wealth, and power are unequally distributed. Although shared social meanings can foster a sense of shared identity, when viewed through the lens of the mirroring perspective, they are essentially epiphenomenal and close to irrelevant for explanatory purposes. For example, studies of corporate leadership styles have largely failed to demonstrate that these differing meanings are related to the style female leaders actually choose.

The constructivist perspective, in contrast, emphasizes how people employ agency in order to create and deploy social meanings within fields of social relations that are contentious, fluid, and imperfectly defined: a world of becoming rather than being. This perspective derives from a variety of 1960s theoretical innovations, including symbolic interactionism, phenomenology, sociolinguistics, anthropological linguistics, ethnomethodology, structuralism, social movement theory, pragmatics, and social constructivism. The constructivist perspective turns the mirroring perspective on its head: Social structure is seen as the *consequence* of the constant and contentious efforts people make to create meanings and, by means of communicative behaviors, to frame social situations in terms of those meanings. In its most radical forms, constructivists deny that what Émile Durkheim (1858–1917) would call "social facts"—objectively measurable patterns of social behavior that are external to individual motivations—have any a priori existence whatsoever. For example, medicine has struggled unsuccessfully for decades to define a "self-neglect syndrome" in objective, medical terms. If a self-neglect syndrome can be said to exist in an objective sense, it is only because, within the field of medical relations, some patients have emphasized "self-neglect" behaviors in order to frame the situation in light of their understanding of it; alternatively, a medical organization has identified certain patient behav-iors as "self-neglect" in order to alter the patient's position and rights within a medical organization.

The production perspective, the most recent of the three, derives from the work of British sociologist Anthony Giddens (1993) and, more recently, the flourishing subfield of cultural sociology. It seeks to strike a balance between the mirroring and constructivist perspectives by emphasizing the dialectic between, on the one hand, social forces that really are larger than the individual (such as institutionalized discrimination), and, on the other hand, the attempts by individuals and groups to try to frame situations to their advantage. In order to do so, they draw on the stock of meanings at hand, but they also create new ones or repackage the old ones in new ways. From the production perspective, the interpretation of *Dallas* offered by Arab citizens of Israel is part of a broader meaning-formation strategy that is being pursued by Sunni Arab communities throughout the Middle East: It involves a rejection of the secularism and perceived immorality of Western societies in favor of a radically reformulated, fundamentalist version of Islam known as Wahhabism. In contrast to constructivist approaches, which almost invariably emphasize interpersonal interaction as the medium in which meanings are defined, the production perspective is equally attuned to the institutions, technologies, and media that meaning-producers appropriate as they attempt to frame the meaning of situations. For example, the rise of Islamic moral and religious fundamentalism in Sunni Arab communities is clearly related to Saudi Arabia's lavishly funded and influential system of religious schools and to the rise of Arabic media, including satellite television stations, that are independent of Western control and censorship.

SEE ALSO *Anthropology; Constructivism; Durkheim, Émile; Giddens, Anthony; Identity; Islam, Shia and Sunni; Linguistic Turn; Media; Phenomenology; Representation; Television; Weber, Max*

BIBLIOGRAPHY

Alimo-Metcalfe, Beverly. 1995. An Investigation of Female and Male Constructs of Leadership and Empowerment. *Women in Management Review* 10 (2): 3–8.

Giddens, Anthony. 1993. *New Rules of Sociological Method: A Positive Critique of Interpretative Sociologies.* 2nd ed. Stanford, CA: Stanford University Press.

Liebes, Tamar, and Elihu Katz. 1990. *The Export of Meaning: Cross-Cultural Readings of* Dallas. New York: Oxford University Press.

Weber, Max. [1921] 1968. *Economy and Society.* Trans. Guenther Roth and Claus Wittich. New York: Bedminster.

Bryan Pfaffenberger

MEANS, RUSSELL
1939–

Russell Means, an Oglala Sioux, is one of the most lionized and controversial American Indians of the twentieth century. Means rose to national prominence as an American Indian Movement (AIM) spokesperson and negotiator during the 1973 Wounded Knee occupation on the Pine Ridge reservation in South Dakota. The occupation lasted seventy-one days, ending with two occupiers dead and two federal officials seriously injured. Means faced several charges stemming from the Wounded Knee occupation, but they were eventually dismissed.

Means was not a founding member of AIM, an American Indian civil rights organization started in Minneapolis in 1968, but he did establish a local chapter in Cleveland and became the group's first national director in 1970. His other political activities include a 1970 lawsuit against the Cleveland Indians baseball team over the Chief Wahoo mascot; the 1972 takeover of the Bureau of Indian Affairs (BIA) office in Washington D.C.; and protests against Columbus Day observances and parades in 1992.

His relationship with AIM became strained over the years, and he resigned in 1986. By 1993, AIM factions had officially split, with Means developing the International Confederation of Autonomous Chapters of the American Indian Movement; and fellow American Indian activists Vernon Bellecourt (b. 1931) and Clyde Bellecourt (b. 1939) heading up the American Indian Movement–Grand Governing Council.

Means admitted to criminal activity in his 1995 autobiography, *Where White Men Fear to Tread*; his legal troubles include several arrests and trials, a felony conviction for the 1974 Sioux Falls courthouse riot, and a 1975 murder charge. Although Means served one year in prison for the riot conviction, he was pardoned in 2002 by South Dakota governor Bill Janklow; he was acquitted on the murder charge.

In 1997 he was arrested on the Navajo reservation for assaulting his father-in-law. Scheduled to be tried in the Navajo Nation court system, Means argued that he was not subject to its jurisdiction. In 2005 the U.S. Court of Appeals for the Ninth Circuit ruled the Navajo Nation does have misdemeanor criminal jurisdiction over non-member American Indians, including Means. Critics contend that Means's effort to thwart Navajo jurisdiction was an attack on tribal sovereignty to further his own interests, whereas Means argues that he was attempting to uphold Navajo treaty rights with respect to jurisdiction over lawbreakers. The U.S. Supreme Court declined to hear the case.

Means has also made several attempts to work within the political system. He made three unsuccessful bids for the presidency of the Oglala Sioux Nation in 1974, 1984, and 2002. In 1984, Means was *Hustler* magazine publisher Larry Flynt's running mate in the latter's unsuccessful attempt to secure the Republican nomination for president of the United States. In 1988 Means lost his bid to be the Libertarian Party's presidential nominee. He entered the New Mexico gubernatorial race as an independent in 2002 but ultimately withdrew.

Means is also an actor, securing roles in *The Last of the Mohicans* (1992), *Pocahontas* (1995), and *Thomas and the Magic Railroad* (2000). Means prefers the term American Indian over Native American because he believes "anyone born in the Western hemisphere is a Native American" (Means 1998).

SEE ALSO *American Indian Movement; Indigenous Rights; Native Americans; Tribe*

BIBLIOGRAPHY

Means, Russell. 1995. *Where White Men Fear to Tread: The Autobiography of Russell Means.* Written with Marvin J. Wolf. New York: St. Martin's.

Means, Russell. 1998. I Am an American Indian, Not a Native American! Russell Means Web site, January 16, 1998. http://www.russellmeans.com/russell.html.

Wilson, Raymond. 2001. Russell Means/Lakota. In *The New Warriors: Native American Leaders since 1900*, ed. R. David Edmunds, 147–169. Lincoln: University of Nebraska Press.

Elizabeth Arbuckle Wabindato

MEANS OF PRODUCTION
SEE *Forces of Production.*

MEASUREMENT

Measurement is the evaluation or estimation of degree, extent, dimension, or capacity in relation to certain standards (i.e., units of measurement). As one of the most important inventions in human history, the process of measuring involves every aspect of our lives, such as time, mass, length, and space. The Greeks first developed the "foot" as their fundamental unit of length during the fourth millennium BCE. The ancient peoples of Mesopotamia, Egypt, and the Indus Valley seem to have all created systems of weight around the same period. Zero, the crucial number in the history of measurement, was first regarded as a true number by Aristotle.

The ancient Egyptians first developed a systematic method of measuring objects, which they used in the construction of pyramids. During the long period during which their civilization thrived in northeastern Africa, they also cultivated the earliest thoughts on earth measurement: geometry. Euclid of Alexandria (c. 330–c. 275 BCE), a Greek mathematician who lived in Egypt and who is regarded as the "father of geometry," provided the proofs of geometric rules that Egyptians had devised in building their monuments. His most famous work, *Elements*, covers the basic definitions, postulates, propositions, and proofs of mathematical and geometric theorems. Euclid's *Elements* has proven instrumental in the development of modern science and measurement.

Another great mathematician who contributed to modern measurement was Karl Friedrich Gauss. He was born on April 30, 1777, in Brunswick, Germany. At age twenty-four, Gauss published a brilliant work, *Disquisitiones Arithmeticae*, in which he established basic concepts and methods of number theory. In 1801, Gauss developed the method of least squares in calculating the orbital component of the motion of celestial bodies with high accuracy. Since that time the method of least squares has been the most widely used method in all of science to estimate the impact of measurement error. He was able to prove that a bell-shaped, normally distributed error curve is a basic assumption of statistical probability analysis (Gauss-Markov theorem).

Among all science and social science disciplines, there are three broad measurement theories (Michell 1986, 1990). The first and most commonly used is the classical theory of measurement. Measurement is defined by the magnitudes of the quantity and expressed as real numbers. An object's quantitative properties are estimated in relation to one another, and ratios of quantities can be determined by the unit of measurement. The classical concept of measurement can be traced back to early theorists and mathematicians, including Isaac Newton and Euclid. The classical approach assumes that the underlying reality exists, but only quantitative attributes are measurable, and the meaningfulness of scientific theories can, and only can, be supported by the empirical relationships of various measurements.

The second theory, the representational approach, defines measurement as "the correlation of numbers and entities that are not numbers" (Nagel [1932] 1960, p. 121). For example, IQ scores can be used to measure intelligence, and the Likert scale measures personal attitudes based on a set of statements. The representational approach assumes that a reality exists and can be measured, and the goal of science is to understand this reality. However, the representational approach does not insist that only quantitative properties are measurable. Instead, measurements can be used to reflect differences at multiple levels.

Unlike the classical and representational approaches, the third approach, called the operational approach, avoids the assumption of objective reality. Instead, it emphasizes only the precisely specified operational process, such as the measurement of reliability and validity. The main concern of scientific theories is only the relationships indicated by the measurements rather than the distance between the reality and measures.

According to the different properties and relationships of the numbers, there are four different levels of measurement: nominal, ordinal, interval, and ratio. In nominal (also called categorical) measurement, names or symbols are assigned to objects, and this assignment is determined by the similarity of the to-be-measured values or attributes. The categories of assignment in most situations are defined arbitrarily, for instance, numbers assigned to individual marital status: single = 1, married = 2, separated = 3, divorced = 4, and so on, or to religious preference: Christian = 1, Jewish = 2, Muslim = 3, Buddhist = 4, and so on.

In ordinal measurement, the number assigned to the objects based on their attributes reflects an order relation among them. Examples include grades for academic performance (A, B, C …), the results of sporting events and the awarding of gold, silver, and bronze medals, and many measurements in psychology and other social science disciplines.

Interval measurements have all the features of ordinal measurements, but in addition the difference between the numbers reflects the equivalent interval of the attributes being measured. This property makes comparison among different measures of an attribute or characteristic meaningful and operations such as addition and subtraction possible. Temperature in Fahrenheit or Celsius degrees, calendar dates, and standardized intelligence tests (IQ) are a few examples of interval measurements.

In ratio measurement, objects are assigned numbers that have all the features of interval measurements, but in addition there are meaningful ratios between the numbers. In other words, the zero value is a meaningful point on the measurement scale, and operations of multiplication and division are therefore also meaningful. Examples include income in dollars, length or distance in meters or feet, age, and duration in seconds or hours.

Because measurement can be arbitrarily defined by the government, researchers, or cultural norms, it is socially constructed. The social construction of measurement is frequently encountered in social science disciplines. For instance, the U.S. Census Bureau has redefined the measure of race several times. Before the 1980 census, census forms contained questions about racial categories, but the categories included only white, black, American Indian, and specified Asian categories. The census was based on the Office of Management and Budget's (OMB) 1977 Statistical Policy Directive Number 15, Race and Ethnic Standards for Federal Statistics and Administrative Reporting, defining four mutually exclusive single-race categories: white, black, American Indian or Alaska Native, and Asian or Pacific Islander. In addition, the standards also provided two ethnicity categories: Hispanic origin and Not of Hispanic origin. The 1980 and 1990 censuses were collected according to these standards.

By 1997, OMB modified the race/ethnicity measurement again by splitting the Asian or Pacific Islander category into two groups, creating five race categories: white, African American, American Indian or Alaska Native, Asian, and Native Hawaiian or Other Pacific Islander. In addition, the 2000 census allowed people to identify themselves as belonging to two or more races. It also created six single races and fifty-seven multiple race categories. The ethnicity measure for Hispanic doubled the total number of the race/ethnicity categories to 126. However, such an extensive number of measures causes even more problems. Many Hispanics consider their ethnic origin as a racial category and therefore choose "some other race" on the census form, leading to over 40 percent of the Texas population reported as "some other race." The misconstruction of the categories of race and ethnicity in the U.S. census illustrates the fluid and subjective nature of measurement.

SEE ALSO *Econometrics; Ethnicity; Gender; Likert Scale; Mathematics in the Social Sciences; Measurement Error; Methods, Quantitative; Racial Classification; Regression Analysis; Sampling; Scales; Survey*

BIBLIOGRAPHY

Michell, J. 1986. Measurement Scales and Statistics: A Clash of Paradigms. *Psychological Bulletin* 100: 398–407.

Michell, J. 1990. *An Introduction to the Logic of Psychological Measurement*. Hillsdale, NJ: Erlbaum.

Nagel, E. [1932] 1960. Measurement. In *Philosophy of Sciences*, ed. A. Danto and S. Morgenbesser, 121–140. New York: Meridian.

Xi Chen

MEASUREMENT ERROR

Measurement error refers to a circumstance in which the true empirical value of a variable cannot be observed or measured precisely. The error is thus the difference between the actual value of that variable and what can be observed or measured. For instance, household consump-

tion/expenditures over some interval are often of great empirical interest (in many applications because of the theoretical role they play under the forward-looking theories of consumption). These are usually observed or measured via household surveys in which respondents are asked to catalog their consumption/expenditures over some recall window. However, these respondents often cannot recall precisely how much they spent on the various items over that window. Their reported consumption/expenditures are thus unlikely to reflect precisely what they or their households actually spent over the recall interval.

Unfortunately measurement error is not without consequence in many empirical applications. Perhaps the most widely recognized difficulty associated with measurement error is bias to estimates of regression parameters. Consider the following regression model:

$$y = \beta_0 + \beta_1 \cdot x + \varepsilon$$

If y and x are observed precisely (and assuming no other complications), β_0 and β_1 can be estimated via straightforward linear regression techniques. Suppose, however, that we actually observe x^*, which is x plus some randomly distributed error v:

$$x^* = x + v$$

In terms of observed variables, our regression model now becomes

$$y = \beta_0 + \beta_1 \cdot (x^* - v) + \varepsilon$$
$$= \beta_0 + \beta_1 \cdot x^* + \varepsilon - \beta_1 \cdot v$$
$$= \beta_0 + \beta_1 \cdot x^* + \zeta$$

where $\zeta = \varepsilon - \beta_1 \cdot v$. From this setup, a problem should be immediately apparent. Because $x^* = x + v$ and $\zeta = \varepsilon - \beta_1 \cdot v$, x^* is correlated with the error term ζ, violating a central assumption of linear regression (that is, independence between regressors and the regression error) required to recover consistent, unbiased estimates of regression parameters. If one were to regress y on what we can observe (that is, x^*), the probability limit of the estimate of β_1, $\hat{\beta}_1$, would be

$$p \lim (\hat{\beta}_1) = \left(\frac{\sigma_x^2}{\sigma_x^2 + \sigma_v^2} \right) \cdot \beta_1$$

Using x^* thus does not yield a consistent estimate of β_1:

$$| p \lim (\hat{\beta}_1) | < | \beta_1 |$$

If both v and ε are normally distributed or if the conditional expectation from the regression model is linear, then this holds even in small samples as an expectation (Hausman 2001):

$$E(\hat{\beta}_1) = \left(\frac{\sigma_x^2}{\sigma_x^2 + \sigma_v^2} \right) \cdot \beta_1$$

This is generally referred to as attenuation bias. While measurement error to right-hand side explanatory variables will also result in biased and inconsistent estimates in a multiple regression framework, the direction of bias is less clear and will depend on the correlations between the measurement errors of the various regressors. Similarly, biased and inconsistent estimates will obtain when the measurement error v is correlated with ε or x, although once again the sign of the bias will no longer be clear a priori.

Measurement error in left-hand side, dependent variables has a different consequence. To cleanly separate issues, imagine that x can now be observed perfectly but that we cannot observe the dependent variable y precisely, but only with a degree of error, as follows:

$$y^* = y + v$$

Here y^* is the observed variable. Thus we cannot observe y directly because of some measurement error v. Returning to our regression framework, we have

$$y = \beta_0 + \beta_1 \cdot x + \varepsilon$$

which, in terms of observed variables, yields

$$y^* - v = \beta_0 + \beta_1 \cdot x + \varepsilon$$

or

$$y^* = \beta_0 + \beta_1 \cdot x + \zeta$$

where $\zeta = \varepsilon + v$. Since x is still uncorrelated with the new regression error ζ, straightforward linear regression of y^* on x will still yield unbiased and consistent estimates of the regression parameters β_0 and β_1. However, the variance of ζ will in general exceed that of ε, implying more uncertain estimates (and hence higher standard errors and lower t-statistics for those parameters).

Because it is likely a ubiquitous condition (particularly with many variables typically found in microlevel data, often based on interviews at the household, firm, or individual level), many econometric remedies for measurement error have been proposed. Here we focus on the case of measurement errors in right-hand side explanatory variables x because it is errors in these that will actually lead to biased and inconsistent (as opposed to merely inefficient) estimates. While a variety of practical solutions has been proposed, in practice one has become particularly popular: instrumental variables.

In some sense the instrumental variables approach is rooted in part in the contributions of Vincent Geraci (1976, 1977), who explored identification and estimation of systems of simultaneous equations with generalized measurement error. Geraci established the necessary conditions for identification and efficient estimation under such circumstances. Of particular importance, his work stressed the need for prior restrictions sufficiently numerous to compensate for the additional parameters introduced by the measurement error.

Despite the rather elaborate work in the context of systems of equations by Geraci and others, in practice most instrumental variables estimation to surmount measurement error is carried out in a simple, two-stage setting. Once again, to isolate issues, let us assume that y is observed without error but that x is; specifically, assume that we actually observe x^*, where

$$x^* = x + v.$$

To implement the instrumental variables remedy for this sort of measurement error, one must have some variable z (an instrument) that is correlated with the true value x and not the measurement error v. Furthermore z must be correlated with y only through its correlation with x. (Following standard results for instrumental variables estimation, z can be correlated with other observed determinants of y; what it cannot be correlated with is the regression error $\zeta = \varepsilon - \beta_1 \cdot v$.) Once such an instrument has been identified, the standard two-stage least squares procedure can be adopted: Regress x^* on z, use the fitted model to predict x^*, and finally, regress y on the predicted x^*. For example, the case of mismeasured household consumption is often addressed through instruments such as household income (often measured in a separate survey module), local prices (which influence consumption, given income), and the like. What is required is a variable correlated with the true measure and not the error. All the concerns regarding the predictive power of instruments (see, for example, Staiger and Stock 1997) apply.

The result that mismeasured explanatory variables leads to biased and inconsistent estimates generalizes to nonlinear regression and limited-dependent variable models (such as logit and probit), although the instrumental variables solution discussed above is no longer effective. See Jerry Hausman (2001) for further discussion of the case of nonlinear regression and Douglas Rivers and Quang Vuong (1988) for solutions in the case of limited dependent variable models. Interestingly measurement error in dependent variables can lead to biased and inconsistent estimates of model parameters in limited dependent variable models. See Hausman (2001) for further discussion.

SEE ALSO *Descriptive Statistics; Distribution, Normal; Hypothesis and Hypothesis Testing; Instrumental Variables Regression; Probability, Limits in; Properties of Estimators (Asymptotic and Exact); Specification Error; Test Statistics*

BIBLIOGRAPHY

Deaton, Angus. 1997. *The Analysis of Household Surveys: A Microeconometric Approach to Development Policy.* Baltimore, MD: World Bank and Johns Hopkins University Press.

Geraci, Vincent. 1976. Identification of Simultaneous Equation Models with Measurement Error. *Journal of Econometrics* 4: 262–283.

Geraci, Vincent. 1977. Estimation of Simultaneous Equation Models with Measurement Error. *Econometrica* 45 (5): 1243–1255.

Hausman, Jerry. 2001. Mismeasured Variables in Econometric Analysis: Problems from the Right and Problems from the Left. *Journal of Econometric Perspectives* 15 (4): 57–67.

Rivers, Douglas, and Quang Vuong. 1988. Limited Information Estimators and Exogeneity Tests for Simultaneous Probit Models. *Journal of Econometrics* 39 (3): 347–366.

Staiger, Douglas, and James Stock. 1997. Instrumental Variables Regression with Weak Instruments. *Econometrica* 65 (3): 557–586.

Peter M. Lance

MECCA

Makkah al-Mukarramah, or "Mecca the blessed," as it is called by the government of Saudi Arabia, is the holiest city in Islam. Its unique status derives from its links to the rise of monotheism and the triumph of Islam in Arabia, and its role as a pilgrimage destination for all Muslims.

The pilgrimage to Mecca (*hajj*)—once in one's lifetime—is a religious duty for Muslims who can afford it. Pilgrimages to the vicinity predate the founding of Islam (there were evidently pre-Islamic pilgrimages to nearby Arafat and Mina, and the Kaaba was a religious site before it became a focus of worship for Muslims), but the Islamic Mecca hajj is more than 1,300 years old. Muhammad himself completed the pilgrimage in year 10 of the Muslim calendar (632 CE). In modern times, several million Muslims converge on Mecca each year during the last month of the Muslim calendar (Dhu al-Hijjah, literally "Lord of the Pilgrimage") to perform the necessary rituals, demonstrate and renew their faith, and seek forgiveness for sins. This huge annual gathering of believers from every continent is unique among contemporary religions. Located about 80 kilometers inland from the Red Sea in a desert valley, Mecca could be reached by pilgrims only after extraordinary travels and hardships before the rise of modern transportation in the twentieth century, but now it is serviced by an international airport at nearby Jeddah.

The experience of the pilgrimage combines obedience to prescribed rites, some unavoidable discomfort or even suffering, and, frequently, the exhilaration of religious renewal. As with all major historical pilgrimages, commerce and services have always flourished within and around the hajj. In the contemporary world the hajj also strengthens the sense among Muslims of a worldwide community of believers. The hajj is a leveler: men and women wear the same simple forms of clothing for the rituals (for men, two white cloths wrapped around the body; for women, a simple dress with a head covering). Differences of wealth and status are temporarily put aside as the worshippers submerge themselves in a sea of believers who are—as pilgrims—equal before God. In addition to wearing these simple white clothes, pilgrims must also refrain from anger, disputes, and sexual relations so that they may focus on obedience and devotion to God.

The specific rituals of the hajj cannot be understood without reference to ancient traditions about Ibrahim (Abraham), his wife Hagar, and his son Isma'il (Ishmael), the supposed progenitors of the peoples of Arabia. Some of the rituals reenact the struggles of Hagar and Isma'il to survive in the desert: for example, pilgrims walk and run seven times between the sites of two ancient hills near Mecca, as Hagar did to seek water for her son. The rituals also include stoning a pillar representing the devil, to commemorate Ibrahim's attempts to fulfill what he believed to be his mission to sacrifice his son. This sacrifice proved to be unnecessary, and Ibrahim was allowed to substitute the sacrifice of an animal. Subsequently, Ibrahim and Isma'il established a holy shrine in the desert that became the cubical structure known as the Kaaba, in Mecca. Although that shrine incorporated icons used for polytheistic worship in pre-Islamic times, these elements were removed after the conquest of Mecca by the Muslim army, led by Muhammad, in 630 CE.

Some elements of the hajj have been modernized. For example, the sacrifice of animals by small groups of worshippers in the traditional hajj (for piety and the sustenance of believers, as the Qur'an asserts, not as offerings sent to God) has been replaced by a sanitized industrial slaughter, after which the meat is packed and shipped to developing Muslim countries overseas. However, the hajj remains an extraordinary demonstration of adherence to ritual traditions as worshippers reenact and remember the struggles and piety of the founders of an ancient and still vibrant monotheism.

SEE ALSO *Muhammad*

BIBLIOGRAPHY

Hassaballa, Hesham A., and Kabir Helminski. 2006. *The Beliefnet Guide to Islam.* New York: Three Leaves Press, Doubleday.

Peters, F. E. 1994. *The Hajj.* Princeton, NJ: Princeton University Press.

Graeme Lang

MECHANISM DESIGN

Mechanism design deals with the problem of how to design a "mechanism" or a game that has an equilibrium whose outcome maximizes some objective function, such as the maximization of social welfare, subject to certain constraints that depend on the specific problem.

Mechanism design begins with the assumption that each one of the agents for whom the mechanism is designed has access to a different piece of private information, and that elicitation of this information is important for achieving the desired objective. Mechanism design is thus all about incentives: about how to provide the agents with incentives to reveal their private information, and to act in accordance with the designer's objectives. Accordingly, the most important constraint in mechanism design is called "incentive compatibility," or IC. The IC constraint obliges the designer to take into account the fact that the agents will try to manipulate the mechanism to their advantage. For example, in one famous mechanism design problem the challenge is how to design an auction that maximizes the expected revenue to the seller under the assumption that the willingness of the potential buyers' to pay for the auctioned object is their private information.

The roots of the question of how to collect decentralized information for the purpose of allocating resources can be found in economists' early debates regarding the feasibility of a centralized socialist economy. These early discussions emphasized the complexity of the systems involved, but it soon became evident that any system for making decisions over the allocation of resources might be open to manipulation. One of the first to recognize the importance of incentives in this context was Leonid Hurwicz (b. 1917), who coined the term *incentive compatibility* in 1959.

Mechanism design was established as a field of study in the early 1970s as a result of Hurwicz's work on the possibility of attaining efficient outcomes in dominant strategy equilibria in "economic environments"; the investigation by James Mirrlees into optimal income taxation schemes; and the studies by Edward H. Clarke and Theodore Groves of efficient dominant strategy mechanisms for the provision of public goods, which are known as "Vickrey-Clarke-Groves," or VCG, mechanisms (William Vickrey studied such mechanisms in the 1960s in the context of his work on auctions). In the late 1970s Kenneth Arrow and Claude d'Aspremont and Louis-André Gerard-Varet showed that it was possible to obtain incentive compatible, efficient, and budget-balanced mechanisms. However, in 1983, in their research into optimal mechanisms for bilateral trade, Roger Myerson and Mark Satterthwaite showed that these earlier possibility results might break down if the agents were permitted to refrain from participation in the mechanism if it does not give them an expected utility that is larger than their reservation utility. In 1982 Myerson published a paper on optimal auctions that to this day serves as the model for implementing mechanism design. The literature on mechanism design continued to expand, and presently encompasses price discrimination, regulation, public-good provision, taxation, auction design, procurement, the organization of markets and trade, and more.

Mechanism design has not had the effect on policy anticipated by its early practitioners. This is probably because many of its main results are not robust against changes in the details of the underlying environment (as argued by Robert Wilson in the so-called Wilson Critique). It still remains to be seen whether the current work on "robust mechanism design" would make the theory more practicable.

SEE ALSO *Game Theory; Mixed Strategy; Multiple Equilibria; Nash Equilibrium*

BIBLIOGRAPHY

Arrow, Kenneth J. 1979. The Property Rights Doctrine and Demand Revelation Under Incomplete Information. In *Economics and Human Welfare*, ed. Michael J. Boskin, 23, 29–31. New York: Academic Press.

Clarke, Edward H. 1971. Multipart Pricing of Public Goods. *Public Choice* 8: 19–33.

D'Aspremont, Claude, and Louis-André Gerard-Varet. 1979. Incentives and Incomplete Information. *Journal of Public Economics* 11: 25–45.

Groves, Theodore. 1973. Incentives in Teams. *Econometrica* 41: 617–631.

Hurwicz, Leonid. 1959. Optimality and Informational Efficiency in Resource Allocation Processes. In *Mathematical Methods in the Social Sciences*, ed. Kenneth Arrow et al., 27–46. Stanford, CA: Stanford University Press.

Hurwicz, Leonid. 1972. On Informationally Decentralized Systems. In *Decision and Organization*, ed. Charles B. McGuire and Roy Radner, 297–333. Amsterdam: North-Holland.

Mirrlees, James. 1971. An Exploration in the Theory of Optimum Income Taxation. *Review of Economic Studies* 38: 175–208.

Myerson, Roger B. 1981. Optimal Auction Design. *Mathematics of Operations Research* 6: 58–73.

Myerson, Roger B., and Mark A. Satterthwaite. 1983. Efficient Mechanisms for Bilateral Trading. *Journal of Economic Theory* 28: 265–281.

Vickrey, William. 1961. Counterspeculation, Auctions, and Competitive Sealed Tenders. *Journal of Finance* 16: 8–37.

Wilson, Robert. 1987. Game-Theoretic Analyses of Trading Processes. In *Advances in Economic Theory: Fifth World Congress*, ed. Truman Bewley, 33–77. Cambridge, U.K.: Cambridge University Press.

Zvika Neeman

MEDIA

In conversation, the term *the media* generally refers to communication media or mass media, which are available to a plurality of recipients and are conceived collectively, as a single, all-encompassing and pervasive entity. Originally meaning an intermediary or a middle quantity, the word *medium* has been in use since the sixteenth century. By the 1700s, the term was used to refer to currency and a medium of exchange. In the nineteenth century, *medium* tended to indicate a material used in creative expression and a "channel of mass communication." Since the early twentieth century, *medium* has referred to "any physical material … used for recording or reproducing data, images, or sound" (Oxford English Dictionary Online). The term *media* carries different meanings in various fields. In the field of natural science, a *medium* is a substrate, whereas in the arts it is a material with distinctive physical properties. In media studies and other social sciences, *media* typically refer to "the means of communication" (print or broadcast media) or "certain technical forms by which these means are actualized" (books, newspapers, television, radio, film, and now the Internet and video games) (O'Sullivan et al. 1994, p. 176).

Each medium—from the newspaper to the telephone to the personal digital assistant—has its own formal properties and preferred content, arises from distinctive political, economic, and cultural matrices, and holds the potential to influence individuals and society in varying ways. There are obvious limitations to regarding media only as technical devices for delivering content to receivers or audiences. The functions and impact of the media can be sufficiently understood only if broader social dimensions of communication are taken into account.

MEDIA AND SOCIETY

Today there is widespread recognition that the media have had significant impacts—both beneficial and deleterious—on individuals and societies through all stages of their development, playing key roles in socialization and education. They have been variously charged with watering down political debate while also opening up new political forums, and with debasing popular discourse while also facilitating more democratic access to educational resources.

Throughout the history of communication, each era's predominant media have reflected the shape and character of the civilizations that created and made of use them. Harold Innis (1894–1952), a Canadian economic historian, regards media as "staples" allowing for the creation of monopolies of knowledge, and he explores the impact of the media on the spatial and temporal organization of power. Durable, or what he calls "time-biased," media, like stone and clay tablets, make a society or empire tend toward longevity (e.g., the Egyptian civilization), whereas light, portable, "space-biased" media, like papyrus, allow for territorial expansion, as with the Roman Empire. In the latter part of the fourteenth century, block printing techniques, first developed in East Asia, reached Europe, where, by the 1450s, metal printing was developed by Johannes Gutenberg. Printing technology revolutionized religion and education in Europe by bringing the word, printed in vernacular languages, to the public. Print culture has been essential to the development of such aspects of Western modernity as rational individualism, scientific knowledge, the nation-state, and capitalism. The emergence of radio broadcasting in the 1920s ushered in a new era in the development of electronic communication media. The ability of radio to reach, simultaneously, unprecedented numbers of people was soon exploited by totalitarian regimes. The rise of film necessitated the creation of a massive industry and new communal exhibition spaces, forged new relationships between media makers and politicians (e.g., the Committee on Public Information), and provided a new form for addressing timely social issues. In the mid-twentieth century, television, through both its form and content, reinforced postwar consumerism and a turn inward, to the private suburban home and the nuclear family.

THEORIES OF MEDIA

Not until recently have the media received sufficient critical attention in academic fields. Classical thinkers such as Karl Marx (1818–1883), Max Weber (1864–1920), and Emile Durkheim (1858–1917) neglected the role of the media in the development of modern societies. With industrialization, urbanization, and modernization, the growth of the media accelerated, as did scholars' interest in it. Communication studies programs began appearing in Western universities in the early twentieth century. These early programs tended to focus on the use of media in public address—during the war years, for propaganda—and on media's effects on its audiences. A critical analysis of the medium itself—and not on the process of communication or rhetoric—is a relatively new development, one that distinguishes media studies from communication studies. The various approaches to the media can be divided into three general categories, in accordance with their particular focus—though it should be noted that these are not mutually exclusive and are commonly applied in combination.

Media and Political Economics The political economics approach advanced studies of media in the mid-twentieth century. Walter Lippmann (1889–1974) studied the formation of public opinion through propaganda, while Harold Lasswell (1902–1978) conducted empirical analyses of communication, commonly through content analyses of propaganda in the two World Wars. Yet this early work tended to focus on the effects of a medium's message on the audiences and paid little attention to the nature of the medium itself. Through his investigation of the transformation of the public sphere, Jürgen Habermas (b. 1929) critically examined the political role of the print media—such as the periodical press—during the transition from absolutism to liberal democracy in the late eighteenth and early nineteenth centuries. The conventional Marxist theory of the media is also one of the main schools of the political economic approach. More recent political economic media scholarship, including the work of Noam Chomsky (b. 1928) and Robert McChesney (b. 1952), focuses on ownership of media organization and argues that the consolidation of ownership in the hands of a few large media corporations limits the variety of ideas presented to the public. Theorists of this type also emphasize the institutional nature of media, focusing on the labor of media production (e.g., work in the newsroom or on the film set).

Media and Technology The technological approach focuses attention on the material substance of the media. This approach tends to examine the technological attributes, the form, of the medium, and the impact that those material qualities have on individual and social development. The famous dictum of Marshall McLuhan (1911–1980), "The Medium is the Message," illustrates the importance of the technical form of media irrespective of their content. Understanding media as extensions of the human body, McLuhan argued that media technologies encourage distinctive modes of thought and perception, which has profound social consequences. Print, for instance, encourages rational, linear thinking, and portable books, which can be read in private, tend to promote atomization. He also devised the concepts of "hot" and "cool" media to describe how particular media forms encourage more or less participation in the communication process.

Media and Culture The cultural approach to media tends to examine the interplay between cultural production, identity politics, media representation, and reception, often in quotidian settings and situation. The theorists of the Frankfurt school made significant contributions to the early development of cultural analysis of the media in the 1930s and 1940s. Max Horkheimer (1895–1973) and Theodor W. Adorno (1903–1969) critically investigated the ideological function of communication media as a tool of social domination. According to them, the culture industry, a central characteristic of a new configuration of capitalist modernity, ultimately induced compliance with dominant social relations by utilizing mass communica-

tion. Compared to their overly negative view of mass media, Walter Benjamin (1892–1940) put more emphasis on the positive role of the media. Benjamin argued that while communication technologies such as photography and cinema have tended to destroy the authentic and unique character of artwork, they have also created new forms of media culture that provide the modern masses with the opportunity for aesthetic experience and thereby stimulate their critical political consciousness. More recently, scholars like Raymond Williams (1921–1988), James Carey (1934–2006), and those of the Birmingham school have conceived of communication as *culture*, and have endeavored to combine media studies with cultural studies. They examine how dominant ideologies are embedded in, and produce meaning in, popular culture by virtue of mass media. Rejecting elitist perspectives that regard audiences as inert masses engaging in passive reception, these scholars emphasize that media consumers actively produce meaning by accepting, negotiating, or rejecting a medium's dominant meaning.

NEW MEDIA AND POSTMODERNISM

Electronic and digital media have indeed made their mark on contemporary societies around the globe, introducing new challenges and opportunities. Yet long-lived concerns, including the independence of media from government and corporate control, are extant not only in the postindustrial world, but particularly in developing nations. The role of the media, from the local to the international level, in contemporary political conflicts, from terrorism to political coups, has garnered much attention inside and outside the academy. Meanwhile, video games, often charged with promoting violence and encouraging sedentary lifestyles, are championed by some designers and educators as a revolutionary new tool for hands-on learning. Video cameras, when used as surveillance media, and Internet spyware have also raised political and ethical questions about the uses to which technologies are put: to protect children from potential sexual predators in online chat rooms, to monitor employees' business-related correspondence, or to track people traffic in urban public places. Personal media technologies such as cellular phones, digital cameras, and MP3 players—many of which come equipped with global positioning technology—shape users' conceptions of time and space, changing the way people schedule their daily activities, interact with friends and family, and navigate through space. These new media are influencing the way people learn, create personal identities and social networks, and engage in politics, and the way governments and economies evolve in response to global flows of capital and culture. Jean Baudrillard (1929–2007), a French philosopher, sees the emergence of cyberspace and new media technologies as creating what he calls *simulation* and *hypperreality*. In the age of postmodern society, he argues, the new media-saturated culture becomes predominant over the "real" world, replacing conventional social relations grounded in political economics.

Media—regarded either as a collective, encompassing, mass entity or as individual technologies with distinctive forms and unique political, economic, and cultural characteristics—interact with individuals and societies in ways that have attracted attention both within popular culture and across academic disciplines. And in what is regarded as an increasingly mediated world, their influence will undoubtedly continue to be subjected to scholarly examination and critique.

SEE ALSO *Chomsky, Noam; Communication; Cultural Studies; Cyberspace; Frankfurt School; Habermas, Jürgen; Hall, Stuart; Information, Economics of; Internet; Journalism; Lasswell, Harold; Marxism; Medium Is the Message; Postmodernism; Public Sphere; Repressive Tolerance; Television*

BIBLIOGRAPHY

Baudrillard, Jean. [1981] 1994. *Simulacra and Simulation.* Trans. Sheila Faria Glaser. Ann Arbor: University of Michigan Press.

Benjamin, Walter. [1936] 2002. The Work of Art in the Age of Its Technological Reproducibility. In *Walter Benjamin: Selected Writings,* Vol. 3: *1935–1938,* trans. Edmund Jephcott, Howard Eiland, et al., 101–133. Cambridge, MA: Harvard University Press.

Carey, James W. 1989. *Communication as Culture: Essays on Media and Society.* New York: Routledge.

Habermas, Jürgen. [1962] 1989. *The Structural Transformation of the Public Sphere: An Inquiry into a Category of Bourgeois Society.* Trans. Thomas Burger. Cambridge, MA: MIT Press.

Hall, Stuart, et al., eds. 1980. *Culture, Media, Language.* New York: Routledge.

Herman, Edward S., and Noam Chomsky. 1988. *Manufacturing Consent: The Political Economy of the Mass Media.* New York: Pantheon.

Horkheimer, Max, and Theodor W. Adorno. [1947] 1997. *Dialectic of Enlightenment.* Trans. Edmund Jephcott. London and New York: Verso.

Innis, Harold. 1951. *The Bias of Communication.* Toronto: University of Toronto Press.

Lasswell, Harold D. 1938. *Propaganda Technique in the World War.* New York: Peter Smith.

Lippmann, Walter. 1922. *Public Opinion.* New York: Free Press.

McChesney, Robert W. 1999. *Rich Media, Poor Democracy: Communication Politics in Dubious Times.* Urbana: University of Illinois Press.

McLuhan, Marshall. 1964. *Understanding Media: The Extensions of Man.* New York: McGraw-Hill.

O'Sullivan, Tim, et al., eds. 1994. *Key Concepts in Communication and Cultural Studies.* 2nd ed. London and New York: Routledge.

Thompson, John B. 1995. *The Media and Modernity: A Social Theory of the Media.* Cambridge, U.K.: Polity Press.

Williams, Raymond. 1962. *Communications.* Harmondsworth, U.K.: Penguin.

Shannon Mattern
Jae Ho Kang

MEDIAN
SEE *Descriptive Statistics.*

MEDIAN, THE
SEE *Descriptive Statistics.*

MEDIATED STABILITY
SEE *Stability, Psychological.*

MEDICAID

The U.S. Medicaid program was enacted in 1965 as Title XIX of the Social Security Act. It is a federal-state program of health-care coverage for some low-income Americans, administered at the federal level by the Centers for Medicare and Medicaid Services. There are distinct Medicaid programs in every state, the District of Columbia, and the U.S. territories, but every program operates within guidelines set at the federal level. Medicaid is financed through federal and state general revenue funds using a formula (based on a state's per capita income) whereby federal dollars are matched to state dollars at a rate of between 50 and 77 percent. In fiscal year 2004, Medicaid served approximately fifty-two million recipients at a cost of $288 billion.

Medicaid is a highly complex program, in part because there is considerable variation among states. Federal law requires states to cover some populations, referred to as *categorically needy*, and some services, referred to as *mandatory*. States may also cover medically needy and special populations and optional services and still receive federal matching funds. The major categorically needy groups are pregnant women and children under age six with family income at or below 133 percent of the federal poverty level (FPL); children ages six to nineteen with family income up to 100 percent of the FPL; and aged or disabled people who meet the income eligibility standards for the Supplemental Security Income program. Although there are many more recipients in the first two categories, the largest share of Medicaid dollars is spent on behalf of the third. Aged and disabled Medicaid recipients may also be eligible for Medicare, in which case Medicaid covers what Medicare does not.

Mandatory services for the categorically needy population comprise a comprehensive medical benefit, including inpatient and outpatient hospital, physician, prenatal, and postpartum care, as well as laboratory and x-ray, home-health, and nursing-facility services. Because Medicaid is a means-tested program vying with other state programs for general revenue funds, however, Medicaid reimbursement rates are typically substantially lower than those paid by Medicare and private insurers. Consequently, many Medicaid recipients have difficulty finding providers who will treat them for what the program will pay. Some states have addressed the access problem by requiring that Medicaid enroll recipients in managed-care organizations that contract to serve the program population in return for a yearly per capita payment. Managed care is also viewed as a cost-containment strategy.

Medicaid pays for almost half of all nursing-home care, compared with approximately 12 percent by Medicare and 8 percent by private insurers. Although Medicaid coverage is limited to low-income elders, program rules allow residents to qualify for nursing-home benefits by "spending down" their resources first and then turning to the program for assistance. Because Medicare covers only short-term and medically involved nursing-home stays and because private long-term care insurance is costly and time-limited, even middle-class elderly seek Medicaid benefits in a nursing home. In recent years, states have received federal waivers of some program requirements in order to provide comprehensive long-term care in recipients' homes.

SEE ALSO *Medicare; Medicine, Socialized; National Health Insurance; Poverty; Poverty, Indices of; Public Health; Welfare; Welfare State*

BIBLIOGRAPHY

Centers for Medicare and Medicaid Services. *Medicaid-At-a-Glance 2005: A Medicaid Information Source.* http://www.cms.hhs.gov/MedicaidGenInfo/.

Grogan, Colleen, and Eric Patashnik. 2003. Between Welfare Medicine and Mainstream Entitlement: Medicaid at the Political Crossroads. *Journal of Health Politics, Policy, and Law* 28 (5): 821–858.

Kaiser Commission on Medicaid and the Uninsured. May 2006. *Medicaid Enrollment and Spending Trends.* http://www.kff.org/medicaid/7523.cfm.

Sandra J. Tanenbaum

MEDICARE

Medicare is the name given to public health insurance programs in Canada, Australia, and the United States. In Canada and Australia, the program covers the vast majority of health services for all citizens. The Canadian provinces administer medicare (with a lowercase *m*) for their inhabitants, and provincial health plans vary in some respects, but in both Canada and Australia, health-care coverage is universal and financed primarily through general tax revenues.

In the United States, Medicare is a public program that provides health insurance for people who are age sixty-five or older, considered disabled by the Social Security Administration (after a two-year wait), or diagnosed with end-stage renal disease. Medicare was enacted in 1965 as Title XVIII of the Social Security Act. In 2005, 42.5 million Medicare beneficiaries were covered at a cost of $330 billion. Despite its primarily elderly clientele, Medicare does not pay for long-term care, except for brief, medically involved stays in a skilled nursing facility.

Medicare is organized into parts A through D, each of which corresponds to a different service type with a different financing scheme. Part A is a program of inpatient hospital insurance available to all Medicare beneficiaries; there is no premium, although beneficiaries are required to pay deductibles and co-payments when they use covered services. Part A is financed through a payroll tax of 2.9 percent, paid half by employers and half by employees. Part B provides coverage for outpatient services, including physician visits, therapies, and laboratory tests. Enrollment is voluntary, and beneficiaries pay a monthly premium for coverage and deductibles and co-payments at the point of service. Part B is financed through premiums and general tax revenues. Part C concerns itself with managed care plans. Part D, passed in 2003, represents the largest expansion of Medicare benefits since 1965; as of January 1, 2006, it covers some of the cost of prescription drugs for beneficiaries who enroll. In a departure from earlier Medicare policy, enrollees receive Part D benefits through private insurance plans that offer coverage for different drugs (within limits set by the government) at different premium amounts. Like Part B, Part D is financed through premiums and general revenue funds. Medicare beneficiaries may also purchase private supplementary, or Medigap, insurance policies to cover deductibles, co-payments, and uncovered services.

Medicare is administered at the federal level by the Centers for Medicare and Medicaid Services. The Medicare program's passage followed a decades-long attempt to enact national health insurance for all Americans. Medicare proponents hoped and expected that the program would be a first step toward that end; as of 2007, Medicare for all remained just one of many proposals for health-care reform.

Among other strengths, Medicare has substantially lower administrative costs than private insurers and has instituted innovative payment systems in the form of diagnosis related groups (DRGs) for hospitals and the resource-based relative value scale (RBRVS) for physicians. Under DRGs, hospitals are paid on a prospective basis to encourage efficiency. The RBRVS makes it possible to redress payment imbalances between generalist and specialist physicians.

SEE ALSO *Medicaid; Welfare; Welfare State*

BIBLIOGRAPHY

Centers for Medicare & Medicaid Services. http://www.cms.gov.

Henry J. Kaiser Family Foundation. 2005. *Medicare Chartbook.* 3rd ed. http://www.kff.org/medicare/upload/Medicare-Chart-Book-3rd-Edition-Summer-2005-Report.pdf.

Marmor, Theodore R. 2000. *The Politics of Medicare.* 2nd ed. New York: de Gruyter.

Oberlander, Jonathan. 2003. *The Political Life of Medicare.* Chicago: University of Chicago Press.

Sandra J. Tanenbaum

MEDICINE

In its broadest sense, medicine denotes ideas relating to diagnoses, causes, and cures of illness, as well as the practice of restoring and maintaining health, and the substances used in the treatment of disease. Medicine is both a domain of knowledge and the application of that knowledge. Medical ideas and practices as well as the social institutions relating to health compose a medical system. Medical systems include ways of classifying disease (cancer, a cold, soul loss, and spirit possession), health specialists (doctors, herbalists, and shamans), and therapies to end illness (pharmaceuticals, meditation, acupuncture, and divination).

Western medicine, or biomedicine, is currently the most widespread medical system, but thousands of others exist throughout the world. Although each tradition is different, diagnosis and treatment often consist of both mag-

ical and herbal components. For instance, many societies believe that ill health can be attributed to supernatural forces, which can be meted out by spirits, gods, ancestors, sorcerers, or witches. These forces are capable of causing both the body and the soul to become ill. To combat disease, patients and healers can also invoke magical substances, rituals, or supernatural beings. Another common method of healing is herbalism, using plants to treat illness. An immense variety of plant species are employed as remedies and include decongestants, pain relievers, and antiseptics. Plants in the Americas have been used to derive important drugs including aspirin, quinine, and novocaine. Although nonbiomedical traditions were once regarded as ineffective and superstitious, they are now acknowledged as providing new sources of medicinal plants as well as information regarding the social lives, environments, and experiences of humans.

Medical ideas and practices both constitute and are constituted by social and cultural beliefs and concerns. Arthur Kleinman notes that medicine is a cultural system "of symbolic meanings anchored in particular arrangements of social institutions and patterns of interpersonal interactions" (1990, p. 24). Illness dialogues, diagnoses, and treatments can express ideas regarding religion, morality, power, politics, identity, economics, and gender. Consequently, social scientists are able to examine medical systems and their components as one method of understanding societal norms, attitudes, and practices. For instance, in *The Birth of the Clinic* (1973) Michel Foucault examines what he calls the "clinical gaze," to show how medicine is linked to power. In *AIDS and Accusation* (1992) Paul Farmer explores how AIDS dialogues in the United States and Haiti reflect attitudes of colonialism, capitalism, and poverty. Social science research regarding the conceptions and use of medicine can focus on both local environments and global ones.

HISTORY OF MEDICINE

The purposeful treatment of illness has probably occurred throughout the entire span of human existence. However, without written records, it is impossible to know for certain what the earliest types of medical treatment were. The first written evidence of medical knowledge, including lists of symptoms, diagnoses, and treatments, comes from Mesopotamia and Egypt, dating to more than four thousand years ago. In ancient Mesopotamia 250 vegetable and 120 mineral drugs were documented (Magner 1992, p. 19). But it is ancient Egypt that can claim both the first real physician known by name, Imhotep (c. 2980 BCE), and, later, the first formalized medical system, which included medical schools, medical insurance, sick leave, and registered physicians of both sexes. The ancient Mesopotamian and the Egyptian medical systems also incorporated magical remedies. These were the first of a number of codified medical traditions that developed around the world.

The ancient medical systems of India and China were developed later than those of Mesopotamia and Egypt but they are still practiced today. In India, Ayurveda (the science of life) was intended to maintain health, not simply treat disease. Ayurvedic practitioners believe that health is the result of the balance of three *doshas* (elemental manifestations in the physical body) that govern body processes. Magner notes that ancient texts list more than one thousand diseases and almost one thousand drugs, and describe advanced surgical procedures including cesarean section, amputation, lithotomy, cauterization, tonsillectomy, and plastic surgery (p. 43). Like Ayurveda, traditional Chinese medicine also views disease as the result of an imbalance in the body, which is composed of *yin* and *yang* elements. Doctors often made diagnoses by studying the pulses of patients and were aware that the heart was responsible for circulating blood long before Europeans were. Chinese medicine employs a variety of treatments including more than five thousand medicinal herbs (such as ginseng), acupuncture (inserting needles into the body at specific points), and moxibustion (applying a burning tinder to the skin).

In classical Greece, Hippocrates (460–361 BCE), sometimes called the "Father of Medicine," wrote that health was the result of a balance between the four humors (basic bodily fluids) of phlegm, yellow bile, black bile, and blood. During the Roman Empire the humoral approach was used by many physicians, including Galen (130–200 CE). His writings were used as important medical texts throughout Rome, the Islamic world, and Europe for centuries. Islamic doctors further embraced and modified the Greek tradition and spread it from Spain to India. The medical writings of the doctor and philosopher Ibn Sina (Avicenna, 980–1037) became standard texts throughout the Arab conquests and Medieval Europe. In Europe it was not until the scientific revolution of the sixteenth and seventeenth centuries that the Greco-Islamic tradition was fully abandoned.

In 1628 William Harvey (1578–1657) challenged the Galenic tradition when he published what was then an unorthodox idea: that the pumping heart moved a continuous flow of blood through the body. Almost one hundred years later the Turkish and African practice of purposefully exposing individuals to mild strains of smallpox to achieve inoculation caught the attention of Europeans and Americans, leading to the development of the first vaccine. Nonetheless, it was not until the nineteenth century that advances in chemistry and medical technology led to the discovery of microbial sources of disease and their cures. This allowed researchers to isolate, treat, and create vaccines for diseases such as tuberculosis, tetanus, cholera, and rabies. The introduction of general anesthesia (1840s) and antisepsis (1870s) precipitated the growth of surgery and hospitals, but it was not until the twentieth century that significant advances were made.

MEDICINE TODAY

The product of a specific historic and cultural past, biomedicine is currently used around the globe. The biomedical system includes professional, scientific, educational, legal, financial, and ethical frameworks. Biomedicine can be characterized by a number of features. One is its almost exclusive use of science and technology to fight disease. Unlike many other traditions, biomedicine views disease as caused by only natural factors. Supernatural or magical sources of illness or treatments are absent. Most biomedical treatments involve the use of synthesized pharmaceuticals and some require hospitalization. Furthermore, the physical body, not the soul, is considered to be the only locus of illness. Given its early history, biomedical practitioners often have a tendency to look for and find a single cause of an illness (such as a microbe) and then to treat it with a single cure (such as antibiotics). Deborah Gordon (1988) notes that the scientific approach of biomedicine is not only a way to treat illness; it is also a way of conceptualizing the world.

The focus of biomedicine is illness and not health, which is often defined as the absence of disease. Critics charge that because biomedicine almost exclusively treats the body and disease, it lacks a holistic approach to well-being that engages with the social individual. Patients who feel that biomedicine is not meeting their needs have a number of other therapeutic options from which to choose. In developed counties such as the United States, complementary and alternative medicines are widely used. In 1998 Eisenberg et al. estimated that number of visits to alternative medicine practitioners exceeded the total number of consultations with primary care physicians in the United States. These therapies, which include herbalism, meditation, yoga, massage, acupuncture, aromatherapy, and chiropractic medicine, are used either in conjunction with, or as a substitute for, biomedical treatment. They are often provided by nonlicensed healers and can incorporate religious or non-Western traditions.

Throughout much of the world, the majority of medical consultations are still with traditional healers and not biomedical personnel. Nevertheless, indigenous and local healing traditions are often used in conjunction with biomedicine. For instance, in India and China, Ayurveda and traditional Chinese medicine, respectively, continue to play important roles in the public health care systems alongside biomedicine. Magner notes that in the 1960s acupuncture anesthesia was used in 60 percent of all surgeries in China (1992, p. 59). Australian Aboriginal people have the choice of going to a biomedical clinic, using local plants as remedies, or consulting local healers to cure spiritual sickness. In Africa herbalists and diviners, as well as doctors and nurses, are regularly consulted. Throughout our history, humans have employed a variety of techniques to treat illness, and this process continues today.

SEE ALSO *AIDS; AIDS/HIV in Developing Countries, Impact of; Anthropology, Medical; Disease; Magic; Medicaid; Medicare; Medicine, Socialized; Public Health*

BIBLIOGRAPHY

Eisenberg, David, Rodger Davis, Susan Ettner, et al. 1998. Trends in Alternative Medicine Use in the United States, 1990–1997: Results of a Follow-Up National Survey. *Journal of the American Medical Association* 280 (18): 1569–1575.

Farmer, Paul. 1992. *AIDS and Accusation.* Berkeley: University of California Press.

Foucault, Michel. 1973. *The Birth of the Clinic: An Archaeology of Medical Perception.* London: Routledge.

Gordon, Deborah. 1988. Tenacious Assumptions in Western Medicine. In *Biomedicine Examined,* ed. Margaret Lock and Deborah Gordon, 19–56. Dordrecht, Netherlands: Kluwer Academic Publishers.

Kleinman, Arthur. 1980. *Patients and Healers in the Context of Culture: An Exploration of the Borderland Between Anthropology, Medicine, and Psychiatry.* Berkeley: University of California Press.

Magner, Lois. 1992. *A History of Medicine.* New York: Marcel Dekker.

Eirik J. Saethre

MEDICINE, SOCIALIZED

The *American Heritage Dictionary* (4th ed., 2001) defines socialized medicine as "a system for providing medical and hospital care for all at a nominal cost by means of government regulation." This leaves room for considerable craftsmanship in the construction of socialist systems. Indeed existing socialized medical systems in, for example, Great Britain, Cuba, Finland, and Switzerland conform to this definition, but are far from monolithic.

Because every aspect of a socialized health care industry is controlled and provided by the government—most doctors, nurses, medics, and administrators are government employees—the system, such as the National Health Service (NHS) in Britain, determines where, when, and how services are provided. Of course citizens may seek care outside the system, in the private sector.

Socialized medical systems are designed to eliminate the insurance industry and marginalize profit while providing health care for all. According to many recent studies, socialized systems outperform free-market profit-driven systems in terms of availability, quality, and cost of care. In addition a report from the Johns Hopkins University Bloomberg School of Public Health stated that the United Kingdom's socialized medical system outperforms the U.S. system in patient-reported perceptions (Blendon, Schoen, DesRoches, et al. 2003). In other words, the people with direct experiences report greater satisfaction with their health services under a socialized system than they do in a free-market system. These results must be considered along with the fact that the U.S. per capita health care expenditures ($4,887) are nearly triple those in the United Kingdom ($1,992). In the year 2000 the United States spent 44 percent more on health care than Switzerland, the nation with the next highest per capita health care costs. Nevertheless, Americans had fewer physician visits, and hospital stays were shorter compared with those in most other industrialized nations. The study suggests that the difference in spending is caused mostly by higher prices for health care goods and services in the United States.

The British system is probably the most instructive example for Americans to evaluate because of the similarities in economy and government structure between the two nations. According to the NHS Web site, the system "was set up on the 5th July 1948 to provide healthcare for all citizens, based on need, not the ability to pay" (National Health Service 2007). Originally conceived as a response to the massive casualties of World War II (1939–1945), the system survives and continues to evolve in the early twenty-first century. The NHS is funded by taxpayers and managed by the Department of Health, which sets overall policy on health issues. Individual patients are assigned a primary care center (with doctors, dentists, optician, pharmacist, and a walk-in center) managed by a primary care trust (PCT). The NHS explains its system of referrals this way: "If a health problem cannot be sorted out through primary care, or there is an emergency, the next stop is hospital. If you need hospital treatment, a general practitioner will normally arrange it for you" (National Health Service 2007).

The PCTs are responsible for planning secondary care. They look at the health needs of the local community and develop plans to set priorities locally. They then decide which secondary care services to commission to meet people's needs and work closely with the providers of the secondary care services to agree about delivering those services.

The NHS may be the world's most sophisticated socialized medical system, but the modern world's first such system was established by the former Soviet Union in the 1920s. Whereas the NHS demonstrates that socialized medicine can exist within a capitalist economy, the failures of Soviet medicine demonstrated how corruption within a society can distort any system. China, Cuba, Sweden, and most of Scandinavia have successful and completely socialized health care systems.

Life expectancy and infant mortality rates are two of the best indicators of overall health. Average life expectancy in Great Britain was 77.4 years in 1998; in comparison, life expectancy for the U.S. population reached 76.9 years in 2000. Infant mortality in Finland is below 4 percent; in the United States it is 7 percent. Health services are available to all in Finland, regardless of their financial situations.

Single-payer systems such as Medicare are not socialized medicine. In socialized systems the government owns, operates, and provides every aspect of the health care services. Although it is true that in a single-payer system the government collects and disperses the capital for services rendered, its decision-making responsibilities end there. Even without socialized medicine's additional powers to limit corporate profits, studies by the U.S. General Accounting Office and the Congressional Budget Office show that single-payer universal health care would save $100 to $200 billion dollars per year while covering every currently uninsured American and increasing health care benefits to those already insured (U.S. Government Accounting Office 1991; Congressional Budget Office 1993).

Outside of the United States, health care in the twenty-first century is increasingly seen as a basic human right that deserves to be protected and provided at an affordable fee to all citizens of civilized societies. This idea—that medical procedures and health care in general should not be subject to or motivated by market forces—is one that, in the late twentieth century, evolved back into favor only after repeated experiments with the capitalization of health care led to systematic and catastrophic failures, resulting in grotesque profits on the supply side contrasted with the suffering of millions of disenfranchised patients on the demand side of the equation. Socialized medicine is an egalitarian system that addresses these iniquities.

SEE ALSO *Egalitarianism; Human Rights; Medicine; Morbidity and Mortality; National Health Insurance; Public Health; Socialism; Union of Soviet Socialist Republics*

BIBLIOGRAPHY

Anderson, Gerard, and Peter Hussey. 2001. Comparing Health System Performance in OECD Countries. *Health Affairs* 20 (3): 219–232.

Blendon, Robert J., Cathy Schoen, Catherine DesRoches, et al. 2003. Common Concerns amid Diverse Systems: Health Care Experiences in Five Countries. *Health Affairs* 22 (3): 106–121.

Congressional Budget Office. 1993. *Single-Payer and All-Payer Insurance Systems Using Medicare's Payment Rates*. Washington, DC: Author.

National Health Service. 2007. NHS in England. http://www.nhs.uk.

U.S. Government Accounting Office. *Canadian Health Insurance: Lessons for the United States*. Document GAO/HRD-91-90. Washington, DC: Author.

Woolhandeler, Steffie, and David Himmelstein. 1991. The Deteriorating Administrative Efficiency of the U.S. Health Care System. *New England Journal of Medicine* 324: 1253–1258.

World Health Organization. 2000. *The World Health Report 2000: Health Systems Improving Performance*. Geneva: Author.

Eugene Straus

MEDICIS, THE

The story of the Medici family is closely associated with four historical developments of great interest to scholars in the social sciences: the history of Florence, Italy, and the Florentine "republic" in particular; the development of humanism and the attendant rise of a new association of humanist scholars and artists; the life story and scholarly career of Niccolò Machiavelli; and the history of the Roman Catholic Church.

The Medicis first arrived in Florence around 1200 CE from the Mugello region north of Florence. During the thirteenth century the city of Florence became increasingly famous and prosperous due to its success in the cloth and woolen trade, but also became increasingly divided between those who supported the pope, the Guelphs, and those who supported the German emperor, the Ghibellines. These developments provided the framework for two changes central to an understanding of Florentine history and to the rise of the Medici to power. Success in commerce and trade led to the creation of trade guilds, among which was the guild of bankers (*Arte del Cambio*), and the division between papal and imperial partisans continued to plague Florence well into the sixteenth century. The Medicis made their fortune and achieved their status in the banking business and within the greater guilds of Florence. And, for the most part, the Medicis aligned themselves with the interests of the papacy.

The first reference to the Medicis in the records of the city is to Ugo de Medici in the year 1280. He was banished from the city for disturbing the peace. Shortly after, in 1293, the city adopted the Ordinances of Justice, which all but guaranteed that the most important guilds, the *Arti Maggiori*, would govern Florence. Most workers, the *ciompi* (wool combers), were ineligible for membership in these guilds and had no share in city governance. Following a revolt of the *ciompi* and a brief period of shared rule (1378–1381) the trade guilds reasserted control and came to be dominated by the Albizzi family, all in the name of a "republican" form of government. The Medici family, under the leadership of Giovanni di Bicci de Medici (1360–1429), emerged in the late fourteenth century as a challenger to the Albizzi, eventually replacing them as the dominant family in the republic. With the death of Giovanni, his son Cosimo assumed leadership of the family and the city of Florence.

For reasons having to do with excessive wealth and ambition, Cosimo de Medici (1389–1464) was exiled from the city in 1433 along with his younger brother Lorenzo. Largely due to his wealth and influence outside of Florence, however, Cosimo was able to have his exile decree lifted a year later, and upon his return to the city worked with the *signoria*, city executives, to encourage legal and political reforms to strengthen Florence's independence and free the city from outside threats. Within this more stable political climate, and for the next thirty years, Cosimo began to act as generous patron to the artists and scholars who began to gather in the city.

For his many contributions to Florence, Cosimo de Medici earned the honorific title *Pater patriae*, father of the country. Among his most notable deeds was his patronage of artists and scholars such as Leonardo Bruni (1370–1444), Sandro Botticelli (1445–1510), Poggio Bracciolini (1380–1459), and the famous Platonist Marsilio Ficino (1433–1499). Botticelli's *Adoration of the Magi* (c. 1476) depicts four generations of the Medici as models for characters at the birth of Jesus. Cosimo also funded the construction and filled the shelves of Europe's first public library, a library dedicated primarily to housing classical and early Christian manuscripts. Cosimo had two sons, Piero (1416–1469) and Giovanni (1421–1453). Piero suffered throughout his life with a severe case of gout and served as head of the family only briefly (1464–1469). It was Piero's son Lorenzo, however, who assumed leadership of the family from 1469 and who came to be called *il Magnifico*, the magnificent.

Lorenzo the Magnificent (1449–1492) was only twenty years old when he assumed his duties as both head of the Medici family and shaper of Florentine policy. Following his grandfather Cosimo's lead, Lorenzo dedicated himself to assisting the rising generation of young artists and scholars. Among the numerous recipients of his patronage were some of the leading creative spirits of the Italian Renaissance, including Michelangelo Buonarroti (1475–1564), Pico della Mirandola (1463–1494), and

Leonardo da Vinci (1452–1519). As a young man in his teens, Michelangelo actually lived in the Medici house. He later sculpted the Medici tombs and designed the New Sacristy Chapel of San Lorenzo, which houses them. Lorenzo is also credited with establishing internal stability and external diplomacy to secure Florence's independence. Soon after Lorenzo's death, however, Charles VIII entered Florence with his French army, the Medici were banished from Florence, and the Dominican monk Savonarola (1452–1498) became the charismatic leader of the republic for the next three years. It would be another fifteen years before the Medicis returned in 1512. The years 1498 to 1512 are widely regarded as the period of the republic, though Florence had been nominally a republic from the late thirteenth century. The dominant figures during this period of Medici absence were Piero Soderini (1450–1513) and Niccolò Machiavelli (1469–1527).

Machiavelli is most famously associated with the Medici family for his dedication of *Il Principe* (*The Prince*; originally *De Principatibus, About Principalities*) to Lorenzo (1492–1519), the Duke of Urbino, grandson of Lorenzo the Magnificent, and father of Catherine de Medici (1519–1589). Catherine, as wife of King Henry II, would serve as queen of France. According to a famous letter of December 10, 1513, Machiavelli originally intended to dedicate the work to Giuliano de Medici (1479–1516), but Giuliano died unexpectedly in 1516. So the dedication went to Giuliano's nephew instead. In either case, the dedication was intended to curry favor with the Medicis, who were back in control of Florence. Though Machiavelli never returned to a position of authority in Florence under the Medicis, he did go on minor diplomatic missions on their behalf, to Lucca in 1520, and to Carpi in 1521. He was also commissioned by the Medici to write one of his most famous works, the *Istorie fiorentine* (*History of Florence*). It is somewhat ironic that in the last years of Machiavelli's life, from 1523 to his death in 1527, Florence was for all practical purposes under the rule of Ippolito and Alessandro, the illegitimate sons of Giuliano and Lorenzo de Medici, the two dedicatees of *The Prince*.

The Medici family also played an important role in the history of the Roman Catholic Church. Indeed, Lorenzo the Magnificent's son, Giovanni, and nephew, Giulio, were elected pope. Giovanni de Medici (1475–1521), brother of Giuliano, for whom Machiavelli originally intended *The Prince*, became Pope Leo X in 1513. He is perhaps best remembered as the pope who excommunicated Martin Luther (1483–1546) in 1521. Giulio, who was a cardinal and close associate during his cousin's reign as pope (1513–1521), became Pope Clement VII in 1523. Pope Clement VII is the pope who famously refused to grant King Henry VIII (1491–1547) of England a divorce from Catherine of Aragon

(1485–1536), which prepared the ground for the establishment of the Church of England.

SEE ALSO *Banking; Enlightenment; Humanism; Machiavelli, Niccolò; Roman Catholic Church*

BIBLIOGRAPHY

Hale, John R. 1960. *Machiavelli and Renaissance Italy.* New York: Macmillan.

Kent, Dale. 1978. *The Rise of the Medici: Faction in Florence, 1426–1434.* Oxford: Oxford University Press.

Rubinstein, Nicolai. 1968. *The Government of Florence Under the Medicis (1434–1494).* Oxford: Clarendon Press.

Young, Colonel G. F. 2005. *The Medicis.* 2 vols. Whitefish, MT: Kessinger.

Timothy Hoye

MEDITATION
SEE *Buddhism.*

MEDIUM IS THE MESSAGE

"The medium is the message" is one of the most famous—yet controversial—statements in the field of media and communication studies. The Canadian literary scholar and pioneering media analyst Herbert Marshall McLuhan (1911–1981) coined the phrase after hearing the anthropologist Ashley Montagu (1905–1999) deliver a talk on science titled "The Method is the Message." McLuhan's expression refers to the significance of the form of communication media irrespective of its content; that is, the communication medium itself has the potential to influence the way a particular medium's content is perceived and to shape cultures dominated by particular media. This dictum, which is also the title of the first chapter of McLuhan's provocative book *Understanding Media: The Extensions of Man* (1964), encapsulates the central foundations of his broader analyses of the profound impact of communication technology on society, culture, and human senses.

Until the mid-1950s McLuhan's work primarily consisted of literary and cultural criticism that examined new forms of popular culture, with an emphasis on the increasing role of mass media in the emergence of consumerism, as well illustrated in *The Mechanical Bride* (1951). From the later 1950s on, McLuhan turned more attention to the technological properties of communication and the vast effects of the media on human cognition and sensation. Conventional communication studies, he thought, were preoccupied with analyzing media content, while taking for granted the medium as a mere technical device to deliver the message to the receiver. McLuhan, instead, privileged the medium over the message, or form over content; even content is form. He argued that the content of any medium is not only a message, but also, more importantly, always another medium. For instance, the written word is the content of print and, at the same time, the medium of speech. McLuhan defined *medium* broadly, regarding many cultural artifacts as media and arguing that their work as "media" extended beyond the mere conveyance of content. The electric light, McLuhan explained, functions as a medium, as it renders possible certain forms of human activities such as night football or brain surgery. These activities themselves are the "content" of the electric light because they cannot exist without it. In his terminology, the medium designates something that "shapes and controls the scale and form of human association and action" (McLuhan 1964, p. 9). As such, McLuhan extended the term *media* to mean any forms of technology that function to extend and widen the human senses and limbs by abolishing temporal-spatial limitations. For instance, the telephone is the extension of the ear, just as the wheel is the extension of foot and leg, and clothing is that of skin. McLuhan's approach sees media as including all technologically constructed artifacts such as buildings, roads, planes, automation, and so on.

Drawing on the work of his mentor, the economic historian Harold Innis (1894–1952), who in his work on the "bias of communication" examined the material substance of communication and its impact on the spatial-temporal organization of societies, McLuhan presented the history of communication as a history of the medium, rather than as a history of the message. McLuhan maintained that the major phases of civilization tended to accord with the introduction and rise to popularity of particular modes of communication technology and consequent changes of the human sensorium at a social level. With the rise of the printing press, social life shifted from a traditional society based upon oral communication to a modern, visual typographic culture that, because of its emphasis on literacy and uniformity, made possible the rise of rational individualism and western nationalism. Since then, electronic media pushed culture into an unprecedented, turbulent media revolution—a techno-cultural society in which communication technology itself has become the central nervous system. It is an age of global communication mediated through radio and TV (and the Internet), which has generated diverse and heterogeneous social relations and brought about the retribalization of the world—the "global village," as McLuhan famously characterized.

The startling new insight implicated in McLuhan's statement predated the postmodern turn in media studies, which is typified in the work of Jean Baudrillard (1929–2007). Some critics point out that McLuhan's technological determinist perspective ignores vital questions related to the functions of various media institutions and the ideological effects of the media on the audience. His erratic and poetic style of writing also makes it difficult to formulate a comprehensive theory of the media and society. Yet, the core aspects of his insight contributed to the development of "medium theory" and "media ecology," elaborated more systematically by later theorists.

BIBLIOGRAPHY

Innis, Harold. 1951. *The Bias of Communication.* Toronto: University of Toronto Press.

McLuhan, Marshall. 1951. *The Mechanical Bride: Folklore of Industrial Man.* New York: Vanguard.

McLuhan, Marshall. 1962. *The Gutenberg Galaxy: The Making of Typographic Man.* Toronto: University of Toronto Press.

McLuhan, Marshall. 1964. *Understanding Media: The Extensions of Man.* New York: McGraw-Hill.

McLuhan, Marshall, and Bruce B. Powers. 1989. *The Global Village: Transformations in World Life and Media in the Twenty-First Century.* New York: Oxford University Press.

Meyrowitz, Joshua. 1985. *No Sense of Place: The Impact of Electronic Media on Social Behavior.* New York: Oxford University Press.

Ong, Walter. 1982. *Orality and Literacy.* London: Methuen.

Theall, Donald F. 2001. *The Virtual McLuhan.* Montreal: McGill-Queen's University Press.

Jae Ho Kang

MEIJI RESTORATION

The Meiji Restoration of 1868 marked the beginning of Japan's revolutionary turn away from medieval and early-modern patterns of development, which had been characterized by samurai domination of virtually every aspect of society. Narrowly conceived, the Restoration amounted to little more than the coup d'état of 1868, which forced the resignation of the last Tokugawa (1600–1868) shogun and elevated Emperor Meiji (Mutsuhito, 1852–1912), then a teenager, to sovereign administrative rule. Viewed expansively, however, the Meiji Restoration was more than a mere regime change: It initiated a revolutionary transformation, achieved during the Meiji period (1868–1912), that was comparable in scope to the mid-sixth-century introduction of Buddhism and Chinese civilization. In the mid-nineteenth century, however, the new model for civilization came from the West. The Meiji Restoration brought about a revolution that led to the westernization of virtually all aspects of national life.

Meiji Japan's embrace of the West reflected its determination to remake itself so as to acquire the power of, and achieve recognition as an equal to, the Western nation-states that dominated it in the 1850s and 1860s. Indeed, the downfall of the last samurai regime, the Tokugawa, resulted largely from its inability to mediate, without internal upheaval, the imperialistic demands of nations such as the United States, made powerful by the Industrial Revolution and seeking trade and diplomatic exchanges with Japan. Until the 1850s the Tokugawa shoguns, fearing the kind of domination that occurred in the Philippines, had effectively minimized contacts with the West. The only Western power permitted to trade with Japanese merchants were the Dutch, and even they were restricted to the artificial island of Dejima, created in Nagasaki Bay to circumscribe the presence of Dutch traders on Japanese soil. As long as maritime technology depended upon the winds, this approach was relatively successful. With the development of steam-powered vessels carrying heavy cannon, Western nations—Great Britain and the United States in particular—were able to dominate East Asia at will, with little significant opposition.

Through the Dutch, the Tokugawa regime was informed of Britain's defeat of China in the Opium War (1840–1842) and the resulting Treaty of Nanjing (1842). When Commodore Matthew Perry's flotilla arrived near Edo (Tokyo) in 1852 demanding treaty relations providing for exchanges between Japan and the United States, the Tokugawa regime realized that it had little choice but to comply, despite the fact that doing so violated its raison d'être: defending the realm against barbarian incursions. The resulting Treaty of Kanagawa (1853), though a sensible accommodation, marked the beginning of the end for the Tokugawa insofar as it became the target of unrelenting critiques from anti-Tokugawa forces. Significant opposition emerged from the "outer" (*tozama*) domains of Chōshū and Satsuma, centers of long-standing animosities toward the Tokugawa.

Opposing the regime's strategy of negotiating with the foreigners rather than fighting them, anti-Tokugawa forces called on the shogunate to do its duty: "Revere the emperor and repel the barbarian" (*sonnō jōi*). When the Americans returned with demands for fuller diplomatic and trade relations, anti-Tokugawa forces intensified their opposition through terrorist attacks. Radical opposition was strong in Chōshū, which launched two military challenges to the Tokugawa in the 1860s. Although the first round of fighting resulted in defeat for Chōshū, in the second it was joined by forces from Satsuma and Tosa domains. The result was the military defeat of the

Tokugawa in 1866. Within two years, the last of the Tokugawa shoguns, Yoshinobu (1837–1913), had turned over administrative authority over the realm to Emperor Meiji and his backers.

The new regime, ostensibly led by Emperor Meiji, was dominated by opposition leaders from Chōshū, Satsuma, and Tosa who had played instrumental roles in the military strikes that had forced the Tokugawa into a state of collapse. Though often described as statesmen, they remained in significant respects revolutionary leaders, defining a radically new political course that resulted in the creation of a modern nation-state. Ironically enough, once the pro-imperial forces had forced the collapse of the Tokugawa shogunate, the rebels-turned-statesmen proceeded to throw the gates open to the West in a search for knowledge and power. By the end of Emperor Meiji's reign in 1912, this assimilation of Western knowledge had resulted in across-the-board achievements that impressed the world.

Socially, the imperial regime abolished the old hereditary social hierarchy that had been decreed by the Tokugawa. Economically, it created the yen, Japan's first national currency, and the Bank of Japan to regulate economic growth. The development of a modern, centralized economy amounted to a revolutionary transformation of earlier economic relations in which the only equivalent to a national currency had been the rice bushel. At the same time, the imperial state induced an industrial revolution by promoting the development of heavy industries such as mining, shipping, and rail transport. Politically, the new regime, under the leadership of Itō Hirobumi (1841–1909), created a representative, constitutionally defined political system. The Meiji government instituted compulsory elementary education at schools created nationwide and established a Western-style conscript force, developed by Yamagata Aritomo (1838–1922) to replace the now-abolished samurai estate. Modeled after the Prussian military, Meiji forces proved effective in defeating internal rebellions and the armies of much larger nations, as seen in the Sino-Japanese War (1894–1895) and the Russo-Japanese War (1904–1905). With the latter victory, imperial Japan finally received the kind of respect internationally that it had long sought. By the end of the Meiji period, Japan was recognized as the leading military and imperial power among East Asian nations.

Geopolitically, Japan was reconfigured during the Meiji period, first with the move of the imperial capital away from its home for over a millennium, Kyoto, to a new center, Edo, the capital of the Tokugawa shoguns, now renamed Tokyo. In the countryside, imperial prefectures replaced the old *daimyō* domains. Before the Meiji period had ended, the beginnings of an empire were evident in the acquisition of Taiwan in 1895, following the

Sino-Japanese War, and the annexation of Korea in 1910, a consequence of the Russo-Japanese War. Japan became a strategic player in the world of military alliances with the Anglo-Japanese Alliance of 1902, in which both nations pledged to support the other in the event of multinational military aggression.

Though not billed in traditional historiography as a revolutionary movement, the Meiji Restoration entailed nothing less than a wholesale transformation of Japan. If there were flaws in the revolution that flowed from the restoration of imperial rule, they had to do with the extent to which military power was increasingly viewed as an expedient means to national power, prestige, and wealth.

SEE ALSO *Imperialism; Industrialization; Revolution*

BIBLIOGRAPHY

Beasley, W. G. 1972. *The Meiji Restoration.* Stanford, CA: Stanford University Press.

Craig, Albert M.. 1961. *Chōshū in the Meiji Restoration.* Cambridge, MA: Harvard University Press.

Fujitani, Takashi. 1996. *Splendid Monarchy: Power and Pageantry in Modern Japan.* Berkeley: University of California Press.

Keene, Donald. 2002. *Emperor of Japan: Meiji and His World, 1852–1912.* New York: Columbia University Press.

Norman, E. H. 1975. *Origins of the Modern Japanese State: Selected Writings of E. H. Norman.* Ed. by John W. Dower. New York: Pantheon.

Totman, Conrad. 1980. *The Collapse of the Tokugawa Bakufu, 1862–1868.* Honolulu: University of Hawaii Press.

John Tucker

MEIR, GOLDA
1898–1978

Golda Meir was born Golda Mabovitz on May 3, 1898, in Kiev, Russia (now Ukraine). Due to terrible hardship, Golda's family immigrated in 1906 to Milwaukee, Wisconsin, where Golda graduated from a teachers' college and worked as a public-school teacher. She joined the Labor Zionist Party in 1915 and married Morris Meyerson in 1917. In 1921 they immigrated to Palestine, where they joined Kibbutz Merhavia. In 1956 she adopted the Hebrew name Meir ("to burn brightly").

Believing that Jews should make their "Just Society" through their own physical labor, Meir was a prominent socialist Zionist figure in the Histadrut (the Israeli Trade Union Congress) and the Jewish Agency, a Zionist organization founded in 1929 to provide services for Jewish immigration and assimilation into Palestine. Being proficient in English, Meir was sent to the United States in the

1930s on a mission to raise funds for building the state of Israel.

After the establishment of Israel on May 14, 1948, Meir played a central role in domestic politics as well as on the diplomatic front. In the same year, she paid a secret, yet unsuccessful, visit to Jordan to persuade its king, Abdullah (1882–1951), not to attack Israel. David Ben-Gurion (1886–1973), a leader in the struggle to establish the state of Israel and later the first prime minister of Israel, appointed Meir a member of the Provisional Government and then, in June 1948, ambassador to the Soviet Union. In 1949 she was elected to the first Knesset as a member of Mapai, the Israeli Workers Party. Meir served as minister of labor from 1949 to 1956, a period of high unemployment and social unrest that resulted from mass immigration. She served as foreign minister from 1956 to 1966. While in office, Meir sought to strengthen Israel's relationship with the United States, create bilateral relationships with Latin American countries, and provide African countries with Israeli know-how in nation building.

Meir became secretary-general of Mapai in 1966, before taking the helm of the newly formed Labor Party. After the death of Prime Minister Levi Eshkol (1895–1969), Meir was appointed prime minister; thus becoming the third female prime minister in the world (after Sirimavo Bandaranaike [1916–2000] of Sri Lanka and Indira Gandhi [1917–1984] of India). Reelected prime minister in October 1969, Meir proved highly successful in consolidating American political and financial support for Israel.

Meir took a rigid stance toward the Arabs. She also adopted the so-called open-door immigration policy, which encouraged thousands of people to leave the Soviet Union and other places to settle in Israel and the occupied territories. She believed that Israelis could not return the occupied territories because there was nobody to return them to. In a June 15, 1969, interview with the *Sunday Times* of London, she said, "There was no such thing as Palestinians … they did not exist," a statement that Arabs often quote to refer to what they think to be bias. Moreover, she wrote in *My Life*, her 1975 autobiography, that she did not believe that "the Jews 'stole' land from Arabs in Palestine," since "a lot of good money changed hands, and a lot of Arabs became very rich indeed" (p. 63).

The most critical event during her term was the 1973 Arab-Israeli War, when Egypt and Syria attacked Israeli forces in Sinai and the Golan Heights. Although she won the elections once more in December 1973, and despite the fact that the Agranant Inquiry Commission did not hold her responsible for the war, Meir's performance was widely criticized for overestimating Israel's preparedness and underestimating Arab power. Meir resigned in mid-1974 and withdrew from public life. She died in Jerusalem in December 1978.

SEE ALSO *Rabin, Yitzhak; Zionism*

BIBLIOGRAPHY

Agress, Eliyahu. 1969. *Golda Meir: Portrait of a Prime Minister*. Trans. Israel Taslitt. New York: Sabra.

Avallone, Michael. 1982. *A Woman Called Golda*. New York: Leisure Books.

Gelvin, James L. 2005. *The Israel-Palestine Conflict: One Hundred Years of War*. New York: Cambridge University Press.

Mann, Peggy. 1971. *Golda: The Life of Israel's Prime Minister*. New York: Coward, McCann, and Geoghegan.

Meir, Golda. 1962. *This Is Our Strength: Selected Papers of Golda Meir*. Ed. Henry Cristman. New York: Macmillan.

Meir, Golda. 1969. Interviewed by the *Sunday Times*, London, June 15.

Meir, Golda. 1973. *A Land of Our Own: An Oral Autobiography of Golda Meir*. Ed. Marie Syrkin. New York: Putnam.

Meir, Golda. 1975. *My Life*. London: Weidenfeld and Nicolson.

Meir, Menahem. 1983. *My Mother Golda Meir: A Son's Evocation of Life with Golda Meir*. New York: Arbor House.

Opfell, Olga. 1993. Golda Meir. In *Women Prime Ministers and Presidents*, ed. Olga S. Opfell, 33–49. Jefferson, NC: McFarland.

Pogrebin, Letty Cottin. 1991. *Deborah, Golda, and Me: Being Female and Jewish in America*. New York: Crown.

Pogrebin, Letty Cottin. 1997. Golda Meir. In *Jewish Women in America: An Historical Encyclopedia*, ed. Paula Hyman and Deborah Dash Moore. New York: Routledge.

Segev, Tom. 1986. *1949, The First Israelis*. New York: Free Press; London: Collier Macmillan.

Slater, Robert. 1981. *Golda: The Uncrowned Queen of Israel*. Middle Village, NY: Jonathan David.

Syrkin, Marie. 1969. *Golda Meir: Israel's Leader*. New York: Putnam.

Syrkin, Marie, ed. 1973. *Golda Meir Speaks Out*. London: Weidenfeld and Nicolson.

Thompson, Seth. 1993. Golda Meir: A Very Public Life. In *Women as National Leaders*, ed. Michael Genovese, 135–160. Newbury Park, CA: Sage.

Abdel-Fattah Mady

MELTING POT

Amalgamation of settlers of diverse national origin has long been linked with the idealistic self-image of America as a new type of nation-state. The French-born immigrant J. Hector St. John de Crèvecoeur (1735–1813), in *Letters from an American Farmer* (1782), described America as a country where "individuals of all nations are melted into a new race of men." Though the nationalities included in the early expression of the melting pot ideal were largely limited to northwestern Europe, the vision of American national identity as based on cross-ethnic amalgamation eventually came to include nearly all European nationalities. British writer Israel Zangwill's (1864–1926) early twentieth-century play *The Melting Pot* was the first to use the term as a metaphor of assimilation in the American context of mass immigration from Europe. The melting pot ideal was depicted in an illustration featured on the play's theater program, which shows many strands of people walking past the Statue of Liberty into a huge boiling pot. As an ideology of immigrant assimilation, the melting pot has persisted as an idealistic vision of the inclusive nature of assimilation in America.

The melting pot ideal is often referred to as an alternative conception of immigrant incorporation in a continuum of idealized conception of assimilation as a cultural belief. At one end of the continuum is *Anglo-conformity*, a belief associated with the normative requirement that individual members of immigrant groups adapt to the culture and institutions established by the early Anglo-Saxon settlers of colonial America. Milton Gordon in *Assimilation in American Life* (1964) interpreted *Anglo-conformity* to mean that immigrants and their descendants adopt the beliefs and norms of middle-class Anglo-American culture, which he maintained remained largely unchanged despite successive waves of immigration from Europe, except for minor changes in cuisine and place names. Anglo-conformity tacitly rules out the viability of intact Old World identities and cultural practices outside of the Anglo-American mold. It emphasizes the need for immigrants to "unlearn" their cultural traits in order to learn the new social practices necessary for acceptance. In the Anglo-conformity formulation, critics underline that this approach to assimilation tacitly assumes the superiority of Anglo-American culture. Anglo-conformity is often associated with the public policy of "pressure-cooker" Americanization during and immediately after World War I (1914–1918).

At the other end of the continuum is *cultural pluralism*, an ideology that conceives of American society as a quiltlike mosaic of diverse cultural traditions and ethnic identities that coexist as subcultures alongside a dominant Anglo-American mainstream. According to cultural pluralism, an ideology of immigrant incorporation first espoused by the philosopher Horace Kallen (1882–1974) in the early twentieth century, the strength and durability of American democracy stems from extending equality of rights, religious belief, and cultural expression to all citizens. The basic idea was that a society benefited when the ethnic groups retained cultural distinctiveness, contributing to the cultural richness and diversity of American soci-

ety. Multiculturalism is the contemporary expression of this vision of civil society.

Sociological studies by Stanley Lieberson, Herbert Gans, Richard Alba, and Mary Waters of the "twilight of ethnicity" of descendants of mass immigration from eastern and southern Europe document that the melting pot ideal of amalgamation has conformed broadly to the historical experiences of white ethnics. Old World identities and cultural practices have become mostly a symbolic attachment for white ethnics as cross-ethnic social life increasingly blurred ethnic boundaries and identities. Cross-ethnic marriages among white ethnics have become so commonplace that many identify as "American" in ethnicity and no longer list the Old World ethnic identities in response to the decennial census questionnaire item on ethnic origin.

Whether conceived as the effects of the beliefs and norms of Anglo-conformity or the melting pot, assimilation has been the primary pattern of incorporation for the European groups that migrated to America. For the descendants of mass immigration from Europe in the late nineteenth century, however, it is likely that the social process of assimilation was a protracted process taking place through incremental changes across generations. The pattern of increasing cross-ethnic marriage within religious boundaries was first identified in analysis of quantitative evidence for the 1940s. Since the historic passage of the Immigration Act of 1965, more than twenty-five million immigrants have settled in expansive immigrant metropolises, greatly increasing the ethnic diversity of American cities. Nearly one out of five Americans are now either foreign-born or children of immigrant parents. The new immigration, largely from Latin America and Asia, has driven a rapid demographic transformation of major urban centers.

Skeptics of the applicability of the melting pot ideal to post-1965 immigrants have justifiably pointed to serious problems in the assumption of assimilation of new immigrants and their children. Although the post-1965 immigrants have often settled in mixed neighborhoods and established ongoing social relationships not only with members of their own ethnic group but also with individuals outside of their ethnic group, the sheer numbers of immigrants concentrated in inner cities suggests that much of the cross-ethnic social interactions are with members of other ethnic groups that are also part of the new immigration.

Post-1965 immigration is more diverse than that of the past, in terms of human and financial capital, race, and legal status. Members of some ethnic groups enter American society at a high level almost from the start because they bring wealth or educational and professional credentials that provide an initial advantage. These immigrants and their children are in a position to benefit from the opportunities open to minorities in the wake of the civil rights movement of the 1960s. It is not uncommon for the families of immigrant professionals and entrepreneurs to establish domicile in middle-class suburban communities and for their children to attend selective American schools and pursue professional occupations themselves. The melting pot ideal remains a compelling metaphor of assimilation for the children of immigrants from professional and entrepreneurial backgrounds. But intermarriage often takes place among native-born children of immigrant parents, similar to the pattern of intermarriage within religious groups observed for European Americans in the twentieth century.

The pattern of incorporation is different for the native-born children of labor migrants from the Caribbean and Central America. With low levels of formal schooling, labor migrants compete for positional advantage at the bottom rungs of the labor market. The reliance of labor migrants on ethnic-based social capital, moreover, leads to incorporation within immigrant ethnic enclaves where initial disadvantages in human capital are likely to be passed on to the second generation, increasing the risk of a melting pot experience that results in amalgamation with downtrodden domestic minorities in the inner cities. This bifurcation of the melting pot experience of children of advantaged human-capital immigrants and disadvantaged labor migrants is the focus of studies of *segmented assimilation*. However, the extent of downward mobility may be overstated in the segmented assimilation literature, as horizontal mobility even within the same occupational groups often leads to substantial socioeconomic gains for the second generation.

In conclusion, the melting pot ideal has a long history as a cultural belief in the viability of the amalgamation of diverse ethnic groups in the making of the American nation-state. With successive waves of immigration, the ideology of the melting pot has emphasized a hybrid vision of American society and culture stemming from intermarriage across ethnic groups and cultural mixing resulting from structural assimilation.

SEE ALSO *Assimilation; Conformity; Ellis Island; Ethnicity; Glazer, Nathan; Immigrants to North America; Immigration; Migration; Mobility; Moynihan, Daniel Patrick; Multiculturalism; Nationalism and Nationality; Whiteness*

BIBLIOGRAPHY

Alba, Richard, and Victor Nee. 2003. *Remaking the American Mainstream: Assimilation and Contemporary Immigration.* Cambridge, MA: Harvard University Press.

Glazer, Nathan, and Daniel Patrick Moynihan. 1963. *Beyond the Melting Pot: The Negroes, Puerto Ricans, Jews, Italians, and Irish of New York City.* Cambridge, MA: MIT Press.

Gordon, Milton M. 1964. *Assimilation in American Life: The Role of Race, Religion, and National Origins.* New York: Oxford University Press.

Lieberson, Stanley, and Mary C. Waters. 1988. *From Many Strands: Ethnic and Racial Groups in Contemporary America.* New York: Russell Sage Foundation.

St. John de Crèvecoeur, J. Hector. 1782. Letter III: What Is an American. In *Letters from an American Farmer.* London: T. Davies. http://www.yale.edu/lawweb/avalon/treatise/american_farmer /letters.htm.

Victor Nee
Richard Alba

MEMÍN PINGUÍN

Memín Pinguín is one of the most popular fictional characters in Latin American comics. He is intellectually significant because he has inspired transnational polemics over racial identity, racism, and racial stereotypes in the region. The Mexican writer Yolanda Vargas Dulché (1926–1999) created the character in the mid-1940s in response to a request from the magazine *Pepín* for a children's comic strip. *Memín* is a contracted nickname for Guillermo, the name of Guillermo de la Parra Loya, who would become the writer's husband. One interpretation of Vargas Dulché's adoption of *Pinguín* is that it refers to a slang term for mischievous, but in some parts of Latin America the name's proximity to another slang word for penis meant that some editions of the comic book spelt the last name as "Pingüín," giving it a closer association with the Spanish word for penguin (*pingüino*).

It was largely due to the success of the Memín Pinguín series and other comic books that Grupo Editorial Vid (the company founded by the couple) was able to become established as one of the most successful publishers in Latin America. The company produced about 25 million comic books a month at the height of the popularity of the genre in the 1970s and 1980s. Grupo Editorial Vid produced 372 Memín Pinguín comic book stories over a period of over 30 years. Memín, the chief protagonist of the stories, is an elementary-school-aged child intended by his creator to be likeable and clever. His *cuatachos* (buddies)—Ernestillo, Carlangas, and Ricardo—partner him in mischief and adventures that are always resolved successfully by Memín by the end of each story.

Memín has phenotypically black features that are exaggerated by the artists to make him appear similar to a monkey. The only other character in the stories with the Negroid phenotype is his mother. The Memín Pinguín series deployed archetypes derived from American minstrel shows, specifically the *pickaninny* (to depict Memín) and the *nanny* (to depict his mother, Eufrosina). It is specifically this dimension of the comic books that provoked American President George W. Bush and civil rights activists to denounce the Memín character as racist when the Mexican government issued a stamp to honor Memín in 2005. A substantial amount of empirical and theoretical research had been amassed at that time by such scholars as Marilyn Kern-Foxworth, Donald Bogle, and Jan Nederveen Pieterse to show not only the popularity of such archetypal depictions of blacks in the history of American popular culture, but also how such depictions are deployed to justify the dehumanization and exploitation of blacks.

Ironically, the creators of Memín Pinguín adopted a creative device that was developed in the United States and then disseminated to other parts of the world, including Mexico. The defense of these depictions in Mexico and several other Latin American countries, where such archetypal depictions of blacks are still quite common and popular, has been a range of arguments within a paradigm known as *mestizaje*. These arguments are most directly associated with the writings of the early twentieth-century Mexican intellectual José Vasconcelos, and they include the claims that malicious racial intent is not to blame because black communities are small or nonexistent in their countries, and that Latin American ruling classes cannot be racist because they themselves have a mixed racial ancestry. The fact that some Latin American countries have had heads of state of color is given as evidence that these societies have been more progressive on the issue of race than the United States. One problem with the *mestizaje* paradigm is its deployment of essentialized notions of race and racial hierarchy (with Europeans at the top and blacks at the bottom) as its basic intellectual premise. This point leaves Memín Pinguín and other Latin American pop culture icons that deploy racial archetypes as targets for activists within and outside Latin America who would like to see them eliminated.

BIBLIOGRAPHY

Pieterse, Jan Nederveen. 1992. *White on Black: Images of Africa and Blacks in Western Popular Culture.* New Haven, CT: Yale University Press.

Vasconcelos, José. 1997. *The Cosmic Race.* Baltimore, MD: Johns Hopkins University Press.

Mark D. Alleyne

MEMORY

Since the 1980s, collective memory has become an intensely studied topic across the social sciences. This sudden remarkable interest may be attributed to a rising preoccupation with dissolving collective identities in the face of new historical realities—globalizing economic and cultural trends, the reconfiguration of gender relations, and a media revolution with far-reaching implications for the organization of knowledge. The scholarly discourse about collective memory parallels another about the distinguishing traits of a "postmodernism" temper.

Serious efforts in the social sciences to understand the dynamics of collective memory, however, date from the early twentieth century in the research of the French sociologist Maurice Halbwachs (1877–1945). He contended that memory must be investigated within its social settings. The present attitudes, beliefs, and traditions of social groups determine the way memories are evoked, and these are continually remodeled as the interests and fortunes of such groups change. The strength of a collective memory is a function of the relative power of such social forces.

By placing his accent on collective memory, Halbwachs took issue with the Viennese neurologist Sigmund Freud (1856–1939), who a generation before had addressed the issue of memory as a task of exploring the workings of the individual mind. Freud believed in the autonomy of personal memory, and developed an analytical technique for recovering repressed memories from the unconscious psyches of his patients. His critics claim that he never worked out a plausible theory of collective memory. For Halbwachs, by contrast, all memory is socially conditioned in that personal memories are always evoked within specific social settings. Without these social props, personal memories tend to fade away.

In explaining the malleability of memory in the face of social forces, Halbwachs proposed that social groups—families, religious cults, political organizations, and other communities—develop strategies to hold fast to their images of the past through places, monuments, and rituals of commemoration. His *La topographie légendaire des évangiles en terre sainte* (The Legendary Topography of the Gospels in the Holy Land, 1941) was a pioneering case study of the way an imagined past is localized, conflated, and idealized over time in a commemorative landscape. In his theory, the ancient art of memory as a technique of mnemonic displacement was reinvented as a political strategy for anchoring cultural traditions.

For several decades, Halbwachs's theory of collective memory was largely ignored. But it was rediscovered during the 1970s, to become a working model for burgeoning scholarship in this field. The newfound interest in collective memory has had three principal venues of research: the politics of memory; the changing uses of memory that followed from the invention of new technologies of communication; and a deepening meditation on the memory of the Holocaust.

THE POLITICS OF COMMEMORATION

This interest reflected an emerging critical perspective on modern traditions once naively honored as the remembered heritage of a commonly imagined past. In France, for example, a lively debate emerged during the 1980s about how, and even whether, to celebrate the bicentenary of the French Revolution (1789–1799), hitherto conceived as the enduring moral touchstone of modern French national identity. Many of these studies investigated the making of the identity of the modern state. The most influential was *The Invention of Tradition* (1983), an anthology edited by English scholars Eric Hobsbawm and Terence Ranger that explored the political uses of tradition in the construction of collective identity. They challenged the long-standing interpretation of tradition as a heritage that impinges on the present through its inertial power and argued that traditions are conceptions of the past invented in the present and periodically refashioned to serve reformulated political goals. Collective memory, they argued, is inspired by present circumstances, and calls into being a serviceable past. In like manner, the anthropologist Benedict Anderson wrote an influential study of the way "imagined communities" are constructed as public memories to give concrete affirmation to otherwise abstract ideals. From a somewhat different perspective, the sociologist Mary Douglas examined the workings of institutional memory, in which bureaucratic solutions to organizational problems are rapidly forgotten only to be invented anew.

By the turn of the twenty-first century, a vast scholarly literature had been produced on the politics of memory, extending investigations beyond commemoration into a wide range of institutional and cultural practices. Noteworthy among these are studies of the making of national identity by Pierre Nora, *Les lieux de mémoire* (Places of Memory, 1984–1992) for France; Michael Kammen, *Mystic Chords of Memory* (1991) for the United States; Yael Zerubavel, *Recovered Roots* (1995) for Israel; and Wulf Kansteiner, *In Pursuit of German Memory* (2006). All display intellectual sophistication in moving beyond commemorative rites to the many cultural forms in which collective memory is embedded. Over time, the study of collective memory has become an impressive strategy for interpreting cultural history.

THE USES OF MEMORY IN CHANGING TECHNOLOGIES OF COMMUNICATION

A parallel but independent line of scholarly inquiry has explored the cultural consequences of advances in the technologies of communication. This research was inspired by the media revolution of the late twentieth century, which stimulated curiosity about earlier thresholds in the process—notably from orality to manuscript literacy in antiquity, and the democratization of print culture during the eighteenth century. Contributors to this scholarship have been varied—classicists interested in Homer as a collective name for epic storytellers, anthropologists in the living oral traditions of Africa, intellectual historians in the emergence of the republic of letters during the Enlightenment, literary critics in the reflective autobiographical soul searching that print culture for the first time made possible. Less has been written to date on the effects of media on cultural memory, but J. David Bolter has pointed out the way electronic memory localized in the icons and Web sites of the computer screen mimics the organizational technique of the ancient art of memory in its images and places. Though contributions to this field were made by specialists, the cumulative effect has been to produce a sweeping new perspective on cultural history from antiquity to the present.

TRAUMA AND MEMORY

Somewhat apart are scholarly reflections on the painful process through which Holocaust survivors sought to deal with the trauma they had suffered. This topic reintroduced Freud's psychoanalytic approach in that it exposed the need for survivors to work through repressed memories of their ordeal before the historical meaning of the Holocaust could be adequately addressed. Beyond inventorying such living testimony, scholars raised the question of how these recovered memories might be historicized within the narratives of modern history. This scholarship provoked the "historians' controversy" of the mid-1980s in Germany about whether such an atrocity could be conveyed within the limits of historical representation. The Holocaust, initially viewed as one among the many horrors of World War II (1939–1945), came toward century's end to be reconceived as a singular experience whose memory needed to be processed collectively before an account of its nature could be integrated into any acceptable historical narrative.

MEMORY AND HISTORY

The debate about the limits of historical representation shows how the study of collective memory has unsettled the established conventions of historical narration. During the 1970s, the American scholar Hayden White launched an inquiry into the strategies through which historians compose their interpretations, and so shifted historiographical interest from the evidentiary content of historical research to the rhetorical forms of historical writing. One consequence was to reveal the mnemonic character of historical narrative as a technique for selecting and ordering judgments about what is worth remembering out of the past. Challenging the "noble dream" of historical objectivity, historiographers such as Peter Novick turned to the task of exposing the bias, distortions, and omissions of the master narratives of modern history. Novick points out how American historians once naively presented a past they wanted to remember. From the founding of the American Historical Association in 1884 until well into the twentieth century, eminent historians tended to favor a patriotic view of American identity that denied the divisive realities of class conflict, racial and ethnic discrimination, and the diverse viewpoints of an expanding immigrant population.

As this historiography of patriotic consensus fragmented from the mid-twentieth century, a new generation of practicing historians sought to reclaim the forgotten past of women, African Americans, and other marginalized groups, while those with a theoretical bent proposed new categories of conceptualization to frame a more complex historical memory, notably through models for gender studies, the history of collective mentalities, and global history. In the process, they subverted the political identities previously highlighted by modern historiography. The conventional model of a directional modern history, originally conceived as a story of ongoing progress, became an uncertain guide to historical writing. This loss of direction coupled with a sense of accelerating time promoted by larger contemporary trends—advertising that incites the fads of consumerism, the ongoing technological innovations through which global communication approaches the instantaneous—led to the collapse of the future-oriented conception of historical time in favor of one that stresses the urgency of present-day problems. The French historiographer François Hartog has characterized this rethinking of the mnemonics of historical time as a "new regime of historicity," one that privileges present concerns over past intentions as a point of departure for historical inquiry.

Memory's subversion of the grand narrative of modern history has legitimized some novel approaches to historical interpretation—an encounter model in global history, a shift from history's story to history's topics in historical exposition, the genealogical reading of the past to point out its discontinuities vis-à-vis the present, and efforts to recapture "sublime" moments of historical experience through historical reenactment.

The scholarly discourse about memory across the curriculum in the late twentieth century reveals its essential paradox—the fragility of its representations of the past in relation to the durability of its resources to imagine that past anew.

SEE ALSO *Collective Memory; Freud, Sigmund; History, Social; Holocaust, The; Psychoanalytic Theory*

BIBLIOGRAPHY

Anderson, Benedict. 2006. *Imagined Communities: Reflections on the Origin and Spread of Nationalism.* Rev. ed. London: Verso.

Confino, Alon, and Peter Fritzsche, eds. 2002. *The Work of Memory: New Directions in the Study of German Society and Culture.* Urbana: University of Illinois Press.

Douglas, Mary. 1986. *How Institutions Think.* Syracuse, NY: Syracuse University Press.

Friedlander, Saul, ed. 1992. *Probing the Limits of Representation: Nazism and the "Final Solution."* Cambridge, MA: Harvard University Press.

Hartog, François. 2003. *Régimes d'historicité: Présentisme et expériences du temps.* Paris: Seuil.

Hobsbawm, Eric, and Terence Ranger, eds. 1983. *The Invention of Tradition.* Cambridge, U.K.: Cambridge University Press.

Hutton, Patrick. 1993. *History as an Art of Memory.* Hanover, NH: University Press of New England.

Matsuda, Matt. 1996. *The Memory of the Modern.* New York: Oxford University Press.

Nora, Pierre, ed. 1984–1992. *Les lieux de mémoire.* 3 vols. Paris: Gallimard.

Novick, Peter. 1988. *That Noble Dream: The "Objectivity Question" and the American Historical Profession.* Cambridge, U.K: Cambridge University Press.

Ong, Walter. 1982. *Orality and Literacy: The Technologizing of the Word.* London: Methuen.

Schacter, Daniel. 2001. *The Seven Sins of Memory: How the Mind Forgets and Remembers.* Boston: Houghton Mifflin.

Patrick H. Hutton

MEMORY IN PSYCHOLOGY

The creation of new memories is an ability that occurs minute to minute in human beings (and some researchers would argue millisecond to millisecond) as people go about their daily lives encountering new information. In fact, although people sometimes need to intentionally remember an appointment date or a phone number, many of life's everyday experiences are not intentionally rehearsed at the time for later remembering, but are created without intentional awareness. Human recall of certain events is not perfect, nor always detailed. This transformation of past events is influenced by many factors relating to events occurring in one's environment and in the brain itself.

BRAIN/MEMORY RELATIONSHIPS

In 1968 Richard Atkinson and Richard Shiffrin were among the first researchers to propose that the formation of memories proceeds by passing through a series of stages. Information from the environment first flows through one's sensory organs (responsible for vision, hearing, smell, touch, and taste) into what Atkinson and Shiffrin termed the *sensory store*. Memories are considered to be stored very briefly in this processing step because the flow of information through the sensory organs leaves only a temporary trace of the information—this is why waving a sparkler at night gives the illusion of a light trail. If an individual pays further attention to the incoming information, it enters a short-term or working memory system that allows additional processing (e.g., analyzing the meaning of a letter one is reading). When one "thinks" or works through a problem mentally, one is using working memory. This working memory system is limited in capacity so that there is only so much information that can be processed at one time. Another important function of working memory is to transfer information to long-term memory, where an infinite number of memories are capable of being stored indefinitely.

The process of storing memories is ultimately dependent on biological brain structures. Although it is still unknown "where" personal memories are stored in the brain, it is clear that certain brain structures are critical for storing and retrieving memories. A structure in the medial temporal region of the brain called the hippocampus has long been known to be important for the development of new memories. Numerous case studies have demonstrated that damage to the hippocampus leads to profound memory impairment. The most famous case study is that of an epileptic patient, H.M., whose hippocampus was surgically removed, leaving him with the inability to form any new memories despite the fact that he could remember events that occurred before the surgery and otherwise had a normal intelligence quotient (IQ).

STORAGE AND RETRIEVAL OF MEMORIES

The ability to remember information is based on two fundamental processes, encoding and retrieval. During encoding, incoming information is transmitted to the brain and is consolidated and prepared in the hippocampus and surrounding medial temporal regions for long-term memory storage. Although these regions play a primary role in preparing memories for long-term storage, the memories themselves are not stored there, but are dis-

tributed throughout the brain in a network. Once information has been properly encoded and stored in long-term memory, recalling these past events relies, in part, on the frontal lobes of the brain, responsible for organizational and strategic processing of information. Neuroimaging research suggests that the fontal lobes play a key role in memory processes because both encoding and retrieval processes are inherently strategic. That is, when one remembers an event, one often must remember when the event occurred relative to other events, how individual details contributed to the overall meaning of the events, and where the event occurred. In 1994 Endel Tulving and colleagues reported that the left frontal lobe may play a more active role during information encoding, whereas the right frontal lobe may be more responsible for retrieval.

The distinction between encoding and retrieval processes is key because if either process fails, a memory cannot be experienced. In the case of H.M. encoding processes were impaired so that new experiences were not stored in long-term memory. Other forms of disease-related damage to medial temporal brain regions (e.g., Korsakoff's syndrome) also lead to an impaired ability to recall previously stored memories, often attributable to a retrieval, rather than an encoding, problem. Evidence from healthy individuals indicates that problems during encoding may be more responsible for memory failures relative to problems during retrieval. For example, it is common for a person to fail to remember the name of a recently met person, even though the introduction may have occurred only minutes before. When meeting someone new, one's attention is drawn to many aspects of the person other than the name—what the person looks like, whom he or she knows, whom he or she is with, and other details of the encounter. Because one's working memory is also engaged in these other processes, the specific name information may not be encoded sufficiently, so that no matter how hard one tries to later remember the name, that information is not accessible. In 1996 Fergus Craik and his colleagues substantiated these findings, showing that memory performance is much poorer when people are distracted when encoding information compared to distraction during retrieval.

In addition to conscious recollection of past experiences, memory can also be demonstrated subconsciously or automatically. The ability to ride a bike, type, read, and accomplish other familiar tasks relies on a memory of how to do these things. Psychologists in the past have used a number of terms to define the distinction between these learned skills and memories that are consciously recalled. In 1985 Tulving used the term *procedural memory* to describe these memories that were skill-based and learned through repetition over time. In contrast, Tulving used the term *episodic memory* to describe the conscious recollection of past events, and the term *semantic memory* to refer to memory of word meanings, facts, and concepts. Semantic and procedural memories have been shown to be more resistant to brain injury, disease, and aging than episodic memories. For example, although H.M. was unable to recall any new events that he experienced after his surgery, his vocabulary system was unaffected, and he was able to learn new complex skills as efficiently as others his age.

AGING AND MEMORY

As people age, they typically notice that their memory is not quite as strong as it used to be. One theory proposed by Lynn Hasher and Rose Zacks in 1979 states that remembering often requires the use of substantial working memory resources and effort, which may decline as people age. Thus, recalling one's new doctor's name may be relatively more difficult as one ages because doing so requires one to engage these limited mental resources. When memory tasks, however, place less of a burden on these mental resources, an older adult's memory performance is similar to that of a younger adult. For example, although one may have difficulty recalling a doctor's name without prompts, one may easily identify the name on a directory list at the doctor's health center. Research conducted in 1987 by Fergus Craik and Joan McDowd has confirmed that when presented with a list of words, young adults perform significantly better than older adults if required to later recall the words without assistance. The two age groups, however, often show similar memory performance when participants are later presented with the words and have to simply recognize those that were previously seen.

Hasher and Zacks proposed that this decline in working memory could be due to either a shrinkage in capacity with normal aging or to a difficulty inhibiting irrelevant information while remembering. Everyone has thoughts that drift in and out of consciousness during the day, but Hasher and Zacks believe that younger adults may be more efficient in inhibiting such thoughts when needed, leading to a less cluttered working memory space. In fact, in studies conducted by Zacks and colleagues in 1996, when told to purposefully forget information they had previously been instructed to remember, younger adults were more successful at this forgetting than older adults. Another theory of declining memory with age, put forth by Timothy Salthouse in 1996, suggests that brain cells (neurons) undergo the same degradation with age as the nerves in one's arms and legs that move the muscles associated with these areas. Consequently, Salthouse argued, declining memory processes are the result of a "general slowing," so that information in the brain is transmitted more slowly. In a sense, information can get backed-up and fade from

memory before it can be used. Although there may be a gradual progression of general slowing as a person ages, other factors appear to either slow down or speed up memory declines. Educational status, social activity, exercise, cardiovascular disease, diabetes, and medications may all influence memory ability in old age.

AUTOBIOGRAPHICAL MEMORIES

Although older adults may have difficulty recalling more recently experienced events and information, they are nonetheless able to recall distant memories with clarity and detail. Psychological researchers typically refer to memories related to one's self as *autobiographical memories*. Autobiographical memories may be distinct from other types of explicit memories because autobiographical memories are rich with contextual or situational detail. For example, recalling one's wedding requires not just remembering information about the event (e.g., what food was served), but also recall of the time in one's life that it occurred. This time-tag on the memory may also serve to help one recall other events surrounding the event (e.g., remembering the date of the event can help one remember where the event happened). These memories are not just organized by time period, but may also be organized around themes (e.g., "that happened during my long-haired hippie days"). Perhaps the most critical component of autobiographical memories is that they contain information related to the individual person and his or her own sense of self. Research conducted in 1997 by Cynthia Symons and Blair Johnson showed that people exhibit better memory performance when they are required to learn a list of adjectives (e.g., assertive) by how well each adjective applies to their own personality compared to conditions where they remember other similar words without self-reference.

This latter finding may explain why a reminiscence "bump" is observed when older adults are asked to recall as many events as they can from their life. Although people tend to recall many events from the most recent year, the number of memories recalled declines the older the memories are except for a bump (or period) that occurs during the teenage years through the mid-twenties of which people recall a good deal of memories. Martin Conway and David Rubin believe that this pattern may exist because the adolescent and early adult years are a time when the self is formed and thus this time becomes a dominant theme in one's life resulting in more vivid memories of this period.

THE RECONSTRUCTIVE NATURE OF MEMORY

When studying autobiographical memories it is very difficult to establish whether a reported memory actually occurred—usually there is no one available to confirm or deny the accuracy of the memory. Further compounding this problem is the fact that human memory is not exact, but reconstructive in nature. That is, one's recall of details surrounding an event is a combination of what actually happened and what one believes happened. These beliefs may or may not be true. Memory researcher Elizabeth Loftus has studied how people can come to "remember" events that never happened to them.

In 1978 Loftus and her colleagues first observed that participants' memory of an actual event can be contaminated and changed when they hear a different account of the same memory from someone else. Loftus termed this phenomenon the misinformation effect. Perhaps more troubling is the finding that not only can memory be distorted by post-event information, but through the power of suggestion people can come to remember things that never even happened to them. A 2004 review by Loftus notes that even in laboratory settings people can come to believe that as children they were attacked by an animal or almost drowned in a pool, and come to remember things that never could have happened, such as seeing Warner Bros.' Bugs Bunny at Disney World. Telling the participants that the following story they are about to hear came from a family member implants such memories. Participants then come to believe, with great confidence, that the story is true. Some therapists have been critical of Loftus's theory, concerned that it may minimize or discount truly recovered memories of abuse that may occur in therapy sessions. Loftus, however, did not suggest that all recovered memories are necessarily false, but rather that some people may remember some things that did not happen if questioned in a particular way.

Not all participants in such studies adopt false memories—the range being around 20 to 50 percent for false memory adoption, depending on other variables, according to Loftus. Further, some individuals appear to be more susceptible than others. Those who have more creative imaginations and those who are more prone to memory or attentional lapses appear most susceptible. Studies involving false memories have received considerable attention from the media due to their relevance to judicial cases involving childhood sexual abuse and rape. Based solely on the testimony of children, day care workers at the Little Rascals day care center in Edenton, North Carolina, in 1988 were accused, charged, and convicted of orchestrating a child sexual abuse ring. Higher courts eventually overturned the cases involving the staff because the children's accusations were the result of leading questions by investigators and therapists and were fueled by the children's imaginations.

The Little Rascals day care case reveals the fluid and malleable nature of memory, especially during childhood, and how it is often difficult to distinguish between what actually happened and what sounds familiar due to repeated and leading questioning. In 1993 Marcia Johnson and her colleagues suggested that such problems can be attributed to internal source monitoring, or difficulties identifying the source of internalized experiences (e.g., whether the experience was real or imagined). The ability to make these internal source distinctions appears to be more difficult for children and older adults, compared to younger adults. Human memories are thus a product of what an individual actually experiences (or sometimes does not actually experience), and intervening information received after the event. How a person reflects on these memories later in life can also come to influence and change the perception of memory.

BIBLIOGRAPHY

Atkinson, Richard C., and Richard M. Shiffrin. 1968. Human Memory: A Proposed System and Its Control Processes. In *The Psychology of Learning and Motivation: Advances in Research and Theory*, Vol. 2, ed. Kenneth W. Spence and Janet T. Spence. New York: Academic Press.

Bäckman, Lars, Brent J. Small, Åke Wahlin, and Maria Larsson. 2000. Cognitive Functioning in Very Old Age. In *The Handbook of Aging and Cognition*, ed. Fergus I. M. Craik and Timothy A. Salthouse. 2nd ed. Mahwah, NJ: Erlbaum.

Bloom, Floyd, Charles A. Nelson, and Arlyne Lazerson. 2001. *Brain, Mind, and Behavior*. 3rd ed. New York: Worth.

Conway, Martin A., and David C. Rubin. 1993. The Structure of Autobiographical Memory. In *Theories of Memory*, ed. A. F. Collins and S. E. Gathercole. Hillsdale, NJ: Erlbaum.

Craik, Fergus I. M., Richard Govoni, Moshe Naveh-Benjamin, and Nicole D. Anderson. 1996. The Effects of Divided Attention on Encoding and Retrieval Processes in Human Memory. *Journal of Experimental Psychology: General* 125 (2): 159–180.

Craik, Fergus I. M., and Joan M. McDowd. 1987. Age Differences in Recall and Recognition. *Journal of Experimental Psychology: Learning, Memory, and Cognition* 13 (3): 474–479.

Hasher, Lynn, and Rose T. Zacks. 1979. Automatic and Effortful Processes in Memory. *Journal of Experimental Psychology: General* 108 (3): 356–388.

Johnson, Marcia K., Shahin Hashtroudi, and D. Stephen Lindsay. 1993. Source Monitoring. *Psychological Bulletin* 114 (1): 3–28.

Loftus, Elizabeth F. 1997. Memories for a Past That Never Was. *Current Directions in Psychological Science* 6 (3): 60–65.

Loftus, Elizabeth F. 2004. Memories of Things Unseen. *Current Directions in Psychological Science* 13 (4): 145–147.

Loftus, Elizabeth F., David G. Miller, and Helen J. Burns. 1978. Semantic Integrations of Verbal Information into a Visual Memory. *Journal of Experimental Psychology: Human Learning and Memory* 4 (1): 19–31.

Parkin, Alan J., and Nicholas R. C. Leng. 1993. Neuropsychology of the Amnesic Syndrome. In *Brain*

Damage, Behavior and Cognition: Developments in Clinical Neuropsychology. Hillsdale, NJ: Erlbaum.

Salthouse, Timothy A. 1996. The Processing-Speed Theory of Adult Age Differences in Cognition. *Psychological Review* 103 (3): 403–428.

Symons, Cynthia S., and Blair T. Johnson. 1997. The Self-Reference Effect in Memory: A Meta-Analysis. *Psychological Bulletin* 121 (3): 371–394.

Tulving, Endel. 1985. How Many Memory Systems Are There? *American Psychologist* 40 (4): 385–398.

Tulving, Endel, Shitij Kapur, Fergus I. M. Craik, et al. 1994. Hemispheric Encoding/Retrieval Asymmetry in Episodic Memory: Positron Emission Tomography Findings. *Proceedings of the National Academy of Sciences USA* 91 (6): 2016–2020.

Zacks, Rose T., Gabriel Radvansky, and Lynn Hasher. 1996. Studies of Directed Forgetting in Older Adults. *Journal of Experimental Psychology: Learning, Memory, & Cognition* 22 (1): 143–156.

Wythe L. Whiting
David J. Madden

MEN

Open any newspaper, and you can see a pattern so widespread that it is rarely noticed: Almost all the "serious" stories are about men. In societies scholars label *patriarchies*, men dominate the most important public institutions, including law, politics, business, science, and the military; men also control economic and political decisions in more private realms, such as the family. Yet patriarchy is not universal, and the forms of masculinity that it perpetuates are neither natural nor inevitable.

CONSTRUCTING MANHOOD

According to sociocultural theories of gender, while sex (physical characteristics) is biologically inherited, gender (behaviors and attitudes associated with a given sex) is socially learned. What it means to be a man, or masculinity, varies both within and across eras and cultures by race, ethnicity, class, sexual orientation, occupation, education, age, geography, and other social characteristics (Kimmel and Messner 2004). For this reason, although biology interacts with the social and physical environment to produce these variations, scholars acknowledge that masculinity is predominantly learned rather than genetically inherited (Coltrane 1998; Connell 1995; Lorber 1994). Despite the many versions of masculinity in existence, scholars have identified common characteristics that distinguish masculinities in egalitarian societies from masculinities in patriarchal societies. In egalitarian societies, women tend to share in the control of property and polit-

ical decision-making, and men are taught to be soft-spoken and nonviolent, taking part in child care while generally avoiding exclusively male initiation rituals and displays of masculine bravado and male superiority. As exemplified by select tribes in the South Pacific islands, the African rain forest, and the Amazon river valley, egalitarian societies have existed in every major region of the world (Coltrane 1992). Modern societies have adopted some egalitarian practices, as exemplified in the social policies of several Nordic countries.

Yet, partially due to colonial exploitation, the vast majority of societies assume a patriarchal form, ranging from ancient agrarian civilizations to modern industrialized nations. Patriarchal societies have existed around the world and on every major continent. Patriarchies, literally translated as "rule by the father," are defined by male control of resources and symbolic privileging of the masculine over the feminine (Coltrane 1992; Connell 2005; Gutmann 1997). In patriarchal societies, men rule by virtue of their power in family and kinship systems, and masculinity revolves around hierarchal male power. Beyond the family, men in patriarchal societies rule the public institutions by writing and enforcing the laws, controlling the political system, occupying the highest posts in government, running the businesses, monopolizing the highest paying jobs, shaping access to and the focus of science, and dictating funding and execution of war-related activities. Meanwhile, women are expected to perform household chores and provide child care, tasks that are rarely rewarded with financial or political power. In addition, men in patriarchal societies often treat wives as sexual property and tend to exploit the labor and sexuality of women who do not have male protectors (Barnett, Miller-Perrin, and Perrin 2005; Coltrane 1992; Coltrane 1996; Coltrane and Collins 2001).

Men not only dominate women in the public and private realms of these societies, but they also shun femininity. As such, feminine characteristics of nurturance and collaboration are treated by men as symbols of weakness to be avoided. Masculinity instead encourages men to focus on achieving power through independence, aggression, and violence (David and Brannon 1976; Maccoby 1998). Each of these gendered behaviors serves to help men maintain control of society at the expense of women. First, the disdain for anything feminine leads men in power to value the opinions of men over women. Second, the desire for power instilled in men and the desire for serving others instilled in women help men to obtain and hold positions of authority. Third, the masculine value of independence helps men take leadership roles as well as avoid sharing influence with women and less powerful men. Fourth, men use aggression and violence to control and intimidate women and less powerful men. For example, women are much more likely than men to be victims of child sexual abuse, rape, and partner violence, and their abusers are almost always men (Barnett, Miller-Perrin, and Perrin 2005).

In patriarchal societies, men begin learning masculine styles of behavior at birth and continue to be reinforced for masculine traits and behaviors well into adulthood. For instance, in modern industrialized nations, experiments show that only after being notified of a baby's sex will children and adults tend to label baby boys as stronger, bigger, and noisier than girls (Coltrane 1998). By expecting that "boys will be boys," male offspring are treated as already embodying masculinity. They are given greater encouragement in sports and other whole-body stimulation while girls are given more verbalization, interpersonal stimulation, and nurturance. As boys grow into men, the people in their lives (parents, siblings, relatives, friends, teachers) continue modeling and teaching acceptable masculine behavior, rewarding compliance and punishing deviance by granting or denying social acceptance. Cultural influences (stories, media, schools, politics, religion, customs, and rituals) also illustrate and model acceptable masculinity and, in addition, provide arenas in which men can practice the gendered behavior they have been taught (Adams and Coltrane 2004). While gender is malleable in the sense that men can stray from it in small ways without retribution, deviations are not tolerated (especially when compared to "tomboy" behavior in girls). Eventually, men realize that their happiness and success depend upon their ability to demonstrate masculinity on their own, so they no longer require external incentives and reminders to enforce gendered behavior (Bem 1993; Coltrane 1998; Connell 1990). In reproducing masculinity, men are given the tools to maintain positions of power in patriarchal societies.

COSTS OF MASCULINITY

Both women and men experience the costs of masculinity. Despite increases in equality between men and women in the past century, most patriarchal societies, the United States included, still endorse the idea that men are naturally superior to women in public affairs and that they deserve authority over women in the home. As a result, being born a woman carries penalties in most societies. Furthermore, men in patriarchal societies are also harmed by the pressure to maintain high levels of masculinity. First, men take more risks than women, helping explain why men are far more likely than women to die in car crashes (Powell-Griner, Anderson, and Murphy 1997; National Center for Health Statistics 2006). Second, masculinity demands that men be physically strong, inhibiting them from acknowledging and addressing serious medical problems or following prescribed medical regimens (Courtenay 2003). In part because of this, men are

more likely than women to die of heart disease, cancer, respiratory disease, and pneumonia (National Center for Health Statistics 2006). Third, masculinity confines and isolates men emotionally; they have higher suicide rates than women, and cross-national research shows that men report greater loneliness than women when without a romantic partner or children (Stack 1998; National Center for Health Statistics 2006). Fourth, masculinity encourages men to be violent, a leading reason men are more likely than women to suffer injury, commit violence, be the victims of violence, die from homicide, and have a shorter life span (Federal Bureau of Investigation 2004; Centers for Disease Control 2004; National Center for Health Statistics 2006).

PROSPECTS FOR CHANGE

Despite widely held beliefs that "boys will be boys" and that men are naturally violent and unemotional, comparative scholarship shows that manhood ideals are culturally conceived and that boys are turned into manly men through a combination of family, social, and personal processes. Perhaps taking a cue from past egalitarian societies, new models of masculinity in industrialized societies are emerging, with gradual recognition that women can be the equals of men and should enjoy similar public and private rights and obligations. Because masculinity itself is socially constructed, with time and effort, men can discard the negative aspects of masculinity that promote subjugation of women and deterioration of their own emotional and physical health.

SEE ALSO *Aggression; Alpha-male; Family; Fatherhood; Femininity; Gender; Gender Gap; Masculinity; Masculinity Studies; Militarism; Patriarchy; Sexual Orientation, Determinants of; Sexual Orientation, Social and Economic Consequences; Social Dominance Orientation; Violence*

BIBLIOGRAPHY

Adams, Michele, and Scott Coltrane. 2004. Boys and Men in Families: The Domestic Production of Gender, Power, and Privilege. *The Handbook of Studies on Men and Masculinities*, ed. R. W. Connell, Jeff Hearn, and Michael Kimmel, 230–248. Thousand Oaks, CA: Sage.

Barnett, Ola, Cindy L. Miller-Perrin, and Robin D. Perrin. 2005. *Family Violence Across the Lifespan: An Introduction.* 2nd ed. Thousand Oaks, CA: Sage.

Bem, Sandra L. 1993. *The Lenses of Gender: Transforming the Debate on Sexual Inequality.* New Haven, CT: Yale University Press.

Centers for Disease Control. 2004. Surveillance for Fatal and Nonfatal Injuries: United States, 2001. *Morbidity and Mortality Weekly Report* 53 (S S07): 1–57.

Coltrane, Scott. 1992. The Micropolitics of Gender in Nonindustrial Societies. *Gender and Society* 6 (1): 86–107.

Coltrane, Scott. 1996. *Family Man: Fatherhood, Housework, and Gender Equity.* New York: Oxford University Press.

Coltrane, Scott. 1998. *Gender and Families.* Thousand Oaks, CA: Pine Forge Press.

Coltrane, Scott, and Randall Collins. 2001. *Sociology of Marriage and the Family: Gender, Love, and Property.* 5th ed. Belmont, CA: Wadsworth/Thomson Learning.

Connell, Robert W. 1990. The State, Gender, and Sexual Politics. *Theory and Society* 19 (5): 507–544.

Connell, Robert W. 1995. *Masculinities.* Berkeley: University of California Press.

Connell, Robert W. 2005. Change Among the Gatekeepers: Men, Masculinities, and Gender Equality in the Global Arena. *Signs: Journal of Women in Culture and Society* 30 (3): 1801–1825.

Courtenay, William H. 2003. Key Determinants of the Health and Well-Being of Men and Boys. *International Journal of Men's Health* 2 (1): 1–30.

David, Deborah S., and Robert Brannon, eds. 1976. *The Forty-Nine Percent Majority: The Male Sex Role.* Reading, MA: Addison-Wesley.

Federal Bureau of Investigation. 2004. Crime in the United States, 2003: Uniform Crime Reports. Washington, DC: Author.

Gutmann, Matthew C. 1997. Trafficking in Men: The Anthropology of Masculinity. *Annual Review of Anthropology* 26: 385–409.

Kimmel, Michael S., and Michael A. Messner, eds. 2004. *Men's Lives.* 6th ed. Boston: Pearson A and B.

Lorber, Judith. 1994. *Paradoxes of Gender.* New Haven, CT: Yale University Press.

Maccoby, Eleanor E. 1998. *The Two Sexes: Growing Up Apart, Coming Together.* Cambridge, MA: Harvard University Press.

National Center for Health Statistics. 2006. *Health, United States, 2005: With Chartbook on Trends in the Health of Americans.* Hyattsville, MD: Author.

Powell-Griner, E., J. E. Anderson, and W. Murphy. 1997. State- and Sex-Specific Prevalence of Selected Characteristic— Behavioral Risk Factor Surveillance System, 1994 and 1995. *Morbidity and Mortality Weekly Report* (Surveillance Summaries SS-3) 46: 1–31.

Stack, Steven. 1998. Marriage, Family, and Loneliness: A Cross-National Study. *Sociological Perspectives* 41 (2): 415–432.

Scott Coltrane
Adam Messinger

MENDACITY

SEE *Lying.*

MENDEL'S LAW

Gregor Mendel (1822–1884), an Austrian monk, conducted experiments on 28,000 pea plants in his monastery garden between 1856 and 1863. His results, outlined in his essay "Experiments on Plant Hybridization," were read to the Natural History Society of Brno (Brunn) in February and March of 1865 and were published in 1866 in the proceedings of the society. These experiments involved studying variations in peas across successive generations of true breeding plants in terms of their shape, size, and color. In simple terms, through close observation and good record keeping, he discovered that, for example, the size of a plant was passed on as a separate trait in a competition for the dominance between traits. These variations were caused by what Mendel called "factors" but what we now call "genes."

The results of these experiments were initially neglected, but then "rediscovered" in 1900 by three European scientists, Hugo de Vries, Carl Correns, and Erich von Tschermak. However, it was William Bateson (1861–1926) who promoted these research findings and who coined the key terms of modern genetic science, namely "genetics," "gene," and "allele." Genetics is that branch of biology that studies both hereditary and variation in organisms. It was Thomas Hunt Morgan (1866–1945) who would later integrate Mendel's theoretical model with the chromosome theory of inheritance. Morgan's experiments with the fruit fly showed that genes are carried by chromosomes, which are the mechanisms of hereditary. His account of hereditary particles created what is now referred to as "classical genetics."

Mendel's First Law, or Law of Segregation, states that members of a pair of homologous chromosomes separate during the formation of gametes such that every gamete receives only one member of the pair. The law can be broken down into four components: (1) alternative versions of genes account for variations in inherited characters; (2) for each characteristic, an organism inherits two alleles, one from each parent; (3) if the two alleles differ, then the dominant allele is fully expressed in the organism's appearance, while the recessive allele has no noticeable effect; and (4) the two alleles for each characteristic segregate during gamete production.

Mendel's Second Law, or Law of Independent Assortment, states that the emergence of one trait will not affect the emergence of another. For example, the eye color and height of a human are not necessarily connected but random.

These laws can only be fully understood in terms of the behavior of chromosomes in reproduction. A cell nucleus is composed of several chromosomes that carry genetic traits, and in a normal cell these chromosomes have two parts, or chromatids. A reproductive cell contains only one of these chromatids, but when two cells (normally male and female) are merged, the genes are mixed and the new cell becomes an embryo. Mendelian laws explain how this new cellular life has half the genes of each parent, and also explain the varying dominance of different genes, resulting in the uneven distribution of traits across generations.

The reproductive advantages of Mendelian-type hereditary are that it creates greater evolutionary opportunities that are beneficial. For example, cell mutations can produce positive side effects such as disease resistance. It is also the case that mutation in a single gene can cause an inherited disease such as sickle-cell anemia or cystic fibrosis. However, this outcome can also be treated as consistent with Mendelian hereditary advantages. Whereas sickle cell disease is a crippling ailment, the sickle cell trait, more prevalent in populations that have a greater geographic likelihood of exposure to mosquitoes, is associated with some resistance to malaria.

Mendelian theories of hereditary have proved to be hugely controversial in modern society. For one thing, Mendelian genetic theories offered additional support to the theory of natural selection in the evolutionary science of Charles Darwin (1809–1882) in which human development was to be explained by secular causes such as the blind adaptation of species to the natural environment rather than by conscious or intentional design. In addition, following Francis Galton (1822–1911), Mendelian theories have become associated with eugenics, or the science that aims to improve the quality of the human stock by increasing "good genes." Eugenics, though, also became an arm of European fascism in which sterilization and selective breeding would improve the Aryan race. Mendelian laws also underpin the pressure from parents in affluent societies for so-called "designer babies," leading critics to fear the creation of a master race. Application of the findings of the Human Genome Project will give scientists increasing control over reproductive outcomes. However, these fears can be exaggerated, since genetic counseling is directed at the prevention of crippling disease (specifically Huntington's disease) rather than designing aesthetically pleasing or highly intelligent offspring. These fears of course are influenced by the accuracy of the content of the genetic counseling and on the impact and effectiveness of such counseling.

SEE ALSO *Eugenics; Galton, Francis; Genetic Testing; Genomics; Heredity; Phenotype*

BIBLIOGRAPHY

Bowler, Peter J. 1989. *The Mendelian Revolution: The Emergence of Hereditarian Concepts in Modern Science and Society.* Baltimore, MD: Johns Hopkins University Press.

Fisher, Ronald A. 1936. Has Mendel's Work Been Rediscovered? *Annals of Science* 1: 115–137.

Fukuyama, Francis. 2002. *Our Posthuman Future: Consequences of the Biotechnological Revolution.* New York: Farrar, Straus and Giroux.

Warnock, Mary. 2002. *Making Babies: Is There a Right to Have Children?* Oxford: Oxford University Press.

Bryan S. Turner

MENTAL HEALTH

Mental health has attracted considerable attention from social scientists. Poor mental health frequently creates personal distress for the individual and those around that individual; often has social causes; has significant social costs in the form of dependency, incapacity, and unemployment; and may also lead, on occasion, to social disturbance and disruption. Consequently social scientists have contributed to a series of related debates about the validity and boundaries of the concepts of mental health and illness, the social distribution and causes of mental illness, and the appropriate care and treatment of mental illness. To a more limited extent, social scientists have also added to discussions about the ways to facilitate and enhance mental health.

When defined positively, mental health tends to be described rather loosely as a state of psychological well-being or satisfactory psychological functioning. More frequently, however, much as with health generally, it is simply defined negatively as the absence of mental illness. Based on an analogy with physical illness, mental illness refers to mental functioning that is considered disordered and described in lay terms as mad, disturbed, or disruptive or as anxiety and unhappiness that is more extensive than usual. While the indicators of mental illness often take the form of behavior that seems inexplicable or unintelligible, the judgment made is of some pathology of mental functioning. In *Madness and Civilization* the social theorist Michel Foucault (1926–1984) argued that unreason is the defining characteristic of madness, although whether this applies to the full range of mental disorders that are now identified, which extends well beyond the narrower category of madness, is contested. In severe cases, mental illness impairs the individual's capacity to carry out some ordinary tasks of living, although symptoms are often episodic. Mental illness can also generate behavior dangerous to self or others, which may be used to justify legal powers of detention on the grounds of the person's lack of reason and the perceived threat to his or her own safety or that of the public. In less severe cases, it can lead to distress and suffering and difficulties with certain aspects of daily living. Consequently satisfactory performance of normal tasks of living often becomes a key indicator of mental health.

CHANGING UNDERSTANDINGS

The use of the language of health and illness reflects the role doctors have played in offering care and treatment for psychological problems. In European and North American societies medical understandings, which draw on a range of scientific ideas, tend to be dominant and inform much lay discourse, especially about mental illness. However, in many contexts the term *mental disorder*, which has fewer medical connotations, is used. The impact of scientific ideas, as well as the ideas themselves, has varied historically and cross-culturally, and there have been times and places when the understandings have been magical or religious rather than scientific. Magical or religious ideas relating to mental illness have not entirely disappeared from lay understandings, such as when people think a mental or physical illness is a judgment of God or that health is a matter of luck and good fortune.

Modern-day medical ideas about mental illness have largely been developed in psychiatry, a medical specialty that emerged as a profession in the mid-nineteenth century from the associations of doctors working in charitable and public asylums that catered for "lunatics" and had powers of detention. In Europe a few institutions for lunatics were set up in the medieval period; these were followed first by small private madhouses in the sixteenth and seventeenth centuries and then, from the beginning of the nineteenth century, by charitable and public asylums. As the century progressed asylums became increasingly large-scale. They were mainly staffed by untrained attendants, with doctors usually the key figure of authority.

In the twentieth century asylum attendants were transformed into mental health nurses, and a range of other professionals (e.g., mental health social workers, psychotherapists, and clinical and health psychologists) started to contribute to the care and treatment of those with mental health problems and to understandings about mental health and illness. Mental health practice outside the asylum also expanded in the twentieth century. In the mid-twentieth century there was a move toward "community care," which is the provision of services within community settings, even for those with more severe disorders, with far fewer mentally ill admitted to a psychiatric bed (where compulsory powers of detention are frequently used). The extent and quality of community services have often been questioned.

The types of mental illness identified by psychiatrists are diverse, ranging from the relatively severe and less common, such as schizophrenia, to the less severe and far more common, such as mild forms of depression and anxiety. Classifications have varied enormously over time, and during the second half of the twentieth century there were major attempts to systematize and standardize mental illnesses in order to improve the reliability of psychiatric diagnosis. In the twenty-first century two major classifications were developed: the American *Diagnostic and Statistical Manual of Mental Disorders* (DSM) and the listing of mental disorders in *The International Classification of Diseases*. The two classifications do not group mental disorders in the same way.

An earlier distinction widely used in the early postwar decades was between psychoses and neuroses, a contrast between more and less severe disorders that linked to symptom differences and ideas about causation. Psychoses were held to be primarily disorders of thought (i.e., Foucault's unreason) and caused by biological factors. Psychoses were typified by the delusions and hallucinations of schizophrenia, the archetypical madness, associated with disturbed and sometimes difficult behavior. Bipolar disorder (formerly referred to as manic depression) is also placed in this category, as are usually disorders where there is clear brain pathology, such as the senile dementias. Neuroses, such as anxiety states and phobias, were considered primarily disorders of emotion (usually called "affect" or "mood" by psychiatrists) rather than thought and were held to have psychological causes. However, in its third edition in 1980, the DSM decided (not entirely successfully) to eschew etiology as a basis for classification shifting to a symptomatological categorization and excluding the term *neurosis*. Official classifications also include a range of conduct or personality disorders in which the main symptoms relate to behavior, such as "antisocial personality disorder," anorexia nervosa, and substance use disorders, including alcoholism and drug addiction. Comparison of the different editions of the DSM is salutary. According to Allan V. Horwitz, the number of mental disorders listed in the 1918 edition of the DSM was 22, whereas by the fourth edition in 1995 it was nearly 400. Such increases necessarily broaden the boundaries of mental disorder and narrow those of mental health.

PHYSICAL AND PSYCHOLOGICAL VIEWS

Consistent with medicine's interest in the body, psychiatry has developed a "biomedical" model of mental illness. The biomedical model focuses on physical causes and the provision of physical treatments, although psychiatrists often deploy a wider range of understandings in their practice. The search for physical causes has concentrated on inheritance, brain pathology, and biochemistry. While there is strong evidence of a genetic tendency for more severe mental disorders, there can be no doubt that environmental factors play a part in causation, even with severe disorders, and are important to mental health. For instance, the evidence from a range of studies has shown that genetic factors play a role in the etiology of schizophrenia, but there is also evidence of environmental factors having a role. Biochemical processes in the brain have been shown to underpin some mental illnesses, most obviously conditions such as Alzheimer's disease. However, significantly data also indicate that social and behavioral factors, such as exercise (physical and mental) as well as diet and obesity, play a part in the complex etiology of Alzheimer's disease.

Biochemical changes in the brain are associated with other mental disorders. There is evidence, for instance, that serotonin levels play a role in depression. But in contrast to Alzheimer's, it is not clear that brain pathology is the cause of depression. The build up of serotonin may be a consequence of social and psychological experiences that are themselves better viewed as the cause of the depression. Such examples indicate that the causes of any mental illness are multifactorial and are not the same for one disorder as for another. They also indicate that debates about causation that have so vexed discussions of mental illness depend in part on the choice of which causes to examine. Psychiatrists have tended to focus on physical causes and to give them primacy, downplaying social and psychological factors.

Evidence of the importance of social and psychological factors to mental health comes from a range of studies. Many studies show that early childhood experiences affect mental health and that external stresses (stressful life events or ongoing difficulties, whether in childhood or later) can lead to mental disorder, although some would argue that in some disorders stress is more a precipitating factor than a cause. Data on the distribution of mental disorders across populations also display a marked social patterning. International studies show that a condition similar to schizophrenia is common across a wide range of societies. However, within any given society data indicate that schizophrenia is more common among groups with lower socioeconomic status and that this difference cannot be adequately accounted for by individuals with schizophrenia drifting down the socioeconomic scale. The link between socioeconomic status and mental illness applies to other disorders, such as depression. It has been argued that depression is due not only to the frequency of adverse life events but also to difficult circumstances and low levels of social support, which affect coping and its adverse vulnerability. There is also a marked patterning by gender. Whereas levels of schizophrenia are roughly the same for men and women, depression and anxiety are far more common in women than men, and personality and conduct disorders are more common in men. Part of this difference appears to be due to gender socialization and

differing expectations as to appropriate emotions and behavior. There are also ethnic differences in the patterning of mental disorder. In the United Kingdom, for instance, a 1997 study by James Nazroo showed that schizophrenia is more commonly diagnosed in Afro-Caribbean men than in other social groups, though the reasons for this are not entirely clear.

Equally controversial have been related issues around the validity and boundaries of mental illness. A number of authors from different theoretical perspectives have argued that it is only reasonable to talk of illness when there is a clear physical pathology. For the psychiatrist Thomas Szasz, who famously argued in 1961 that mental illness was a myth, this meant recognizing that disorders such as senile dementia are diseases of the brain. Where there is no biological pathology, Szasz stated, psychological problems should be termed "problems in living" and not regarded as illnesses at all. From a rather different perspective, a range of sociologists has argued that mental illness, with its overtly behavioral symptoms, is best understood as a form of deviance (i.e., a behavior that breaks social norms) and not as illness. This position was developed by the psychotherapist T. J. Scheff in his well-known 1966 study *Being Mentally Ill*. These two positions reflect a long-standing contest between those who espouse the biomedical model of mental disorder and wish to appropriate psychological problems to the domain of physical illness—a process sociologists term medicalization and which is reflected in the expansion of psychiatric categories—and those who wish to appropriate mental disorder to the social (or psychological) domain of behavior considered unacceptable or difficult. Horwitz, in *Creating Mental Illness*, accepts that the boundaries of mental health and illness are set by society and tries to resolve the conflict between the two positions by stating that a condition is a valid mental illness or disorder if (a) it involves a psychological dysfunction that is defined as socially inappropriate, and (b) it is socially useful to define the dysfunction as a disease.

CARE AND TREATMENT

Given such disputes, not surprisingly a further major area of controversy concerns care and treatment. When charitable and public asylums were first established, the most influential therapeutic model was that of "moral treatment." This was a set of ideas about the importance for "lunatics" to live in a supportive, well-ordered, and well-staffed environment that built on the individual's capacity for self-control to facilitate his or her return to health. However, this social model, which was an important component of the pro-institutional discourse that underpinned the establishment of asylums, was resource intensive and difficult to implement in practice, especially when asylums became large-scale. The challenges of asylums were among the reasons they were increasingly replaced by biomedical approaches. Treatments in the early twentieth century included drugs, such as morphine and chloral hydrate, and various forms of hydro and electrical therapy. In the late 1930s electro-convulsive therapy (ECT) and psychosurgery (which involves the cutting of certain brain tissues) were introduced, and from the mid-1950s a range of synthesized drugs began to be used starting with chlorpromazine, an antipsychotic. In the beginning of the twenty-first century psychotropic medications provide the dominant form of treatment for mental health problems, from the most to the least severe, although many professionals accept that the drugs control symptoms rather than provide cures. Some medications, notably the antipsychotics, have unpleasant side effects, and patients may be reluctant to take them except by compulsion; they are also often prescribed on a long-term basis, which increases the risks to patients. Yet a number of factors encourage the medical reliance on drugs: efficacy in controlling symptoms; the scope of doctors' expertise with its concentration on the physical at the expense of the psychological and social; pressures of time that make more intensive therapies seem harder to provide; and heavy marketing by the pharmaceutical industry.

Psychological theories and therapies have, however, played an important role in ideas about mental health and the treatment of the less severe forms of mental illness. In the first half of the twentieth century psychoanalysis had a major impact, and "talking cures" began to be used by trained psychoanalysts, especially for private patients (in the United States psychoanalysis had widespread acceptance within psychiatry). Psychological theories also informed child and educational psychology and the "mental hygiene" movement that flourished in the United States in the early decades of the twentieth century, in which the focus was on improving and sustaining mental health through education, early treatment, and public health.

However, some psychologists, highly critical of psychoanalysis, developed their own therapies based on the behaviorist ideas that swept academic psychology from the early decades of the twentieth century. Early behavior therapy excluded attention to thought and meaning but was gradually replaced by cognitive behavior therapy (CBT), which concentrates on the individual's ways of thinking and is seen by some as offering a relatively speedy and effective route to mental health, especially for less severe disorders. CBT has been influenced by "positive psychology," which is a set of ideas that seeks to encourage individuals to focus on what can give meaning in life, especially their strengths. Some also argue that CBT can be of value in treating psychosis. Yet psychological therapies such as physical remedies mainly concentrate on dealing with mental health problems that have already developed and not on mental health maintenance and prevention, the area to which social scientists have arguably more to contribute.

SEE ALSO *Cognition; Disease; Emotion; Foucault, Michel; Intelligence; Madness; Medicine; Mental Illness; Personality; Personality, Type A/Type B; Psychoanalytic Theory; Psychotherapy; Stress; Trauma*

BIBLIOGRAPHY

American Psychiatric Association. 1994. *Diagnostic and Statistical Manual of Mental Disorders: DSM-IV*. Washington, DC: Author.

Brown, George, and Tirril Harris. 1978. *Social Origins of Depression*. London: Tavistock.

Foucault, Michel. 1967. *Madness and Civilization*. London: Tavistock.

Hollingshead, August, and Fredrick C. Redlich. 1958. *Social Class and Mental Illness*. New York: John Wiley.

Horwitz, Allan V. 2002. *Creating Mental Illness*. Chicago: University of Chicago Press.

Nazroo, James. 1997. *Ethnicity and Mental Health*. London: Policy Studies Institute.

Scheff, Thomas J. [1996] 1999. *Being Mentally Ill: A Sociological Theory*. 3rd ed. New York: Aldine de Gruyter.

Szasz, Thomas. 1961. The Myth of Mental Illness. *American Psychologist* 15: 113–118.

World Health Organization. 1992. *The ICD-10 Classification of Mental and Behavioural Disorders: Cultural Descriptions and Diagnostic Guidelines*. Geneva: Author.

Joan Busfield

MENTAL ILLNESS

Mental illness is a global term for disorders of thought, mood, affect, and behavior that impair normal functioning, social relationships, and productivity. Worldwide, mental illnesses account for four of the ten leading causes of premature death or of disability in terms of lost years of healthy life. Major depression is the leading cause of disability worldwide, as measured by years of living with this disorder. Mental illnesses, including suicide, account for over 15 percent of disease burden, more than the burden from cancers, in established market economies such as the United States and Europe (National Institute of Mental Health 2006).

Mental illnesses such as schizophrenia and other psychotic disorders, mood disorders, anxiety disorders, and adjustment, identity, and personality disorders, are defined by discrete, clinically meaningful clusters of behavioral symptoms. The German psychiatrist Emil Kraepelin (1856–1926) was the first to develop a unified classification of the psychoses. His emphasis on precision and objective behavioral criteria greatly influenced the current diagnostic system, the American Psychiatric Association's periodically updated and revised *Diagnostic and Statistical Manual of Mental Disorders* (*DSM*-IV-TR, 2000). The *DSM* codes are fully compatible with those in the mental disorders section of the World Health Organization's *International Classification of Diseases* (*ICD*-10, 2005), with worldwide applicability. Patients are assessed on five axes:

Axis I—clinical disorders and other conditions that may be a focus of clinical attention;

Axis II—personality disorders and mental retardation;

Axis III—general medical conditions;

Axis IV—psychosocial and environmental problems; and

Axis V—global assessment of functioning.

Multiaxial assessment yields multiple domains of information that indicate possible comorbidities and permit comprehensive treatment planning.

Mental illnesses vary in severity, duration, and degree of incapacitation. Some specialists distinguish between acute reactive (brief nonrecurring) and chronic (long-term episodic) mental illness. The term *chronic*, disavowed by consumers (present and former psychiatric patients) as promoting hopelessness, has largely been replaced by "severe and persistent mental illness." This description typically applies to persons with major Axis I disorders who manifest long-term disability.

Despite increasing evidence that most major mental illnesses appear to be biologically based, vulnerability and prognosis seem highly sensitive to the social environment. Epidemiologic studies indicate that major mental illnesses such as schizophrenia, depression, and bipolar or manic-depressive illness are found in all cultures throughout the world. However, there is considerable variability based on immigrant and socioeconomic status, and on urban versus rural living. Studies in Great Britain have found significantly higher prevalence rates for psychotic disorders in immigrants, city dwellers, and black and ethnic minority groups than in white British natives (Kirkbride et al. 2006). Incidence rates for schizophrenia drawn from 158 studies of 32 countries were significantly higher for males, migrants, city dwellers, and individuals born in the winter months (McGrath 2006), the latter presumably because of greater exposure of fetuses and neonates to viral insults to developing brain structures. Internationally, female gender and income inequality are major risk factors for depression (Patel 2001). World Health Organization studies indicate that although the diagnostic criteria for schizophrenia are applicable cross-culturally, prognosis and recovery rates are significantly better in the developing world than in Western industrialized nations (Jablensky et al. 1992)

Prolonged hospitalization for mental illness has long been on the decline in the industrialized world. Most mental disorders currently are treated on an outpatient basis, with various forms of individual, group, and family psychotherapy and in most cases, psychotropic medications. These include antipsychotic, antidepressant, antianxiety, and antiobsessional agents, as well as mood stabilizers and psychostimulants. More disabling disorders may require brief hospitalizations and rehabilitative interventions such as supported housing, supported employment, social-skills training, and combined mental health and substance abuse treatment. There is increasing demand for research-supported evidence-based treatments. Among these, psychotropic medications, cognitive and behavioral psychotherapies, family psychoeducation, and rehabilitative interventions have yielded the most empirical validation. However, studies also suggest that the patient-therapist relationship may be more salient than particular therapeutic models. Some mental health systems are promoting the involvement of consumers as service providers in rehabilitation and in peer counseling. Persons in recovery are able to share experiences and coping strategies, provide role models, and help reduce self-stigmatization.

The concept of mental illness as a biomedical condition distinct from social context has been subject to extensive criticism by social scientists and by some psychiatrists. Prominent writers such as Michel Foucault (1926–1984), R. D. Laing (1927–1989), and Thomas Szasz (b. 1920) have disputed the validity of a concept based on cultural definitions of normalcy and often mediated by social and economic concerns. Every culture has some concept of "madness," defined as negatively perceived deviant behaviors that are distinguished from merely antisocial behaviors because they are incomprehensible within that cultural idiom. Despite transnational acceptance of *ICD* codes, the identification of a behavior or behavioral syndrome as denoting mental illness by ordinary citizens, as opposed to mental health professionals, is still to a considerable extent culture-bound. In certain individuals, religious delusions or hallucinations may be viewed as extraordinary gifts rather than symptoms. It is only when the symptoms impair role functioning and productivity that the person is labeled as mentally ill. Depression is sometimes manifested as somatization (diffuse bodily complaints) in some traditional cultures and is conceptualized by the sufferer as a physical rather than psychological condition. Stigmatization of mental illness is ubiquitous, yet research shows that social factors may affect perceptions of deviance and subsequent labeling and discrimination. In many cultures stigma seems to be related to chronic dysfunction and dependency, or to assumed threat, rather than to bizarre behaviors.

There is also a substantial literature on culture-bound syndromes—seemingly unique patterns of disordered or psychotic behaviors that are manifested only in particular cultural settings. Whether or not these are unique syndromes or variant forms of universal diagnostic categories, the behaviors are locally perceived as mental disturbances with specific names. The *DSM*-IV-TR lists twenty-five culture-bound syndromes found in various parts of the world, most of which appear as temporary delusional or dissociative states in which the person acts out in culturally aberrant and sometimes self-harmful ways. Some culture-bound syndromes appear as anxiety states with paranoid ideation about external malevolence or sorcery, or possession by spirits, accompanied by debilitating somatic symptoms. Still others are manifested as panic reactions, sexual fears, or paralyzing phobias. Most culture-bound syndromes are time-limited and do not seem to engender stigma. If they prove to be ongoing or potentially life-threatening, remedies are sought primarily in traditional healing rituals rather than in Western medicine.

Despite local variants, there is compelling evidence of universality and genetic predisposition in major Axis I and some Axis II disorders. The literature on schizophrenia also offers proliferating research findings from neuroradiology, neuropathology, neurochemistry, hematology, and psychopharmacology, indicating biological parameters of what was once considered a psychogenic or sociogenic disorder. Depression is associated with catecholamine deficits or excess, and hormonal imbalance. Obsessive-compulsive disorders have unique neurological substrates. Lesions in the orbitofrontal cortex have been linked to the impulsivity and affective instability of borderline personality disorder and other disorders of impulse control. Many mental illnesses show abnormalities in the serotonin neurotransmitter system. The permanent effects of these biological anomalies is still in question. There is increasing evidence of recovery from disorders that were once considered lifetime disabilities with a deteriorating course. Three major long-term outcome studies of formerly hospitalized persons with schizophrenia in Europe and the United States indicated a recovery or mild impairment rate ranging from 50 percent to 66 percent (Harding 1988). Representing a heterogeneous body of behavioral symptoms varying widely in severity and potential for remission, the term *mental illness* remains a concept in flux and the subject of ongoing research.

BIBLIOGRAPHY

American Psychiatric Association. 2000. *Diagnostic and Statistical Manual of Mental Disorders.* 4th ed., text revision. Washington, DC: Author.

Harding, Courtenay M. 1988. Course Types in Schizophrenia: An Analysis of European and American Studies. *Schizophrenia Bulletin* 14: 633–643.

International Statistical Classification of Diseases. 2005. *ICD-10-Classification of Mental and Behavioral Disorders and Related Health Problems.* Geneva, Switzerland: World Health Organization.

Jablensky, Assen, Norman Sartorius, Georg Ernberg, et al. 1992. Schizophrenia; Manifestations, Incidence, and Course in Different Cultures: A World Health Organization 10-Country Study. *Psychological Medicine* Monograph Supplement 20: 1–97.

Kirkbride, James B., Paul Fearon, Craig Morgan, et al. 2006. Heterogeneity in Incidence Rates of Schizophrenia and Other Psychotic Syndromes: Findings from the 3-Center AESOP Study. *Archives of General Psychiatry* 63 (3): 250–258.

McGrath, John J. 2006. Variations in the Incidence of Schizophrenia: Data Versus Dogma. *Schizophrenia Bulletin* 32 (1): 195–197.

National Institute of Mental Health. 2006. The Impact of Mental Illness on Society. NIH publication no. 01-4586. http://www.nimh.nih.gov/publicat/burden.cfm.

Patel, Vikram. 2001. Cultural Factors and International Epidemiology. *British Medical Bulletin* 57 (1): 33–45.

Harriet P. Lefley

MENTAL LEXICON

SEE *Psycholinguistics.*

MENTAL RETARDATION

The U.S. Department of Education defines *mental retardation* as "significantly subaverage general intellectual functioning existing concurrently with deficits in adaptive behavior and manifested during the developmental period that adversely affects a child's educational performance" (34 C.F.R., Sec. 300.7[b][5]). The American Association on Mental Retardation (AAMR) defines it in a similar way: "Mental retardation is a disability characterized by significant limitations both in intellectual functioning and in adaptive behavior as expressed in conceptual, social, and practical adaptive skills. This disability originates before age 18" (AAMR 2002, p. 1). Finally, the *Diagnostic and Statistical Manual of Mental Disorders* (*DSM*-IV) of the American Psychiatric Association (APA) describes the disorder as "characterized by significantly subaverage intellectual functioning (an IQ of approximately 70 or below) with onset before age 18 years and concurrent with deficits or impairments in adaptive functioning" (APA 2000, p. 37). Each of the three definitions has the inclusion of an impairment of adaptive functioning in common, while only the *DSM*-IV lists a specific intellectual quotient (IQ) score. Thus, the two major characteristics of mental retardation are limitations in intellectual functioning and limitation in adaptive behavior.

LIMITATIONS IN INTELLECTUAL FUNCTIONING

Intelligence refers to an individual's cognitive ability to think, reason, problem solve, remember information, learn skills, and generalize knowledge from one setting or situation to another. This ability level is often described using an intelligence quotient obtained from assessment with one or more individually administered standardized intelligence tests, such as the Wechsler Intelligence Scale for Children III or the Stanford-Binet Intelligence Scales (SB5). Significantly subaverage intellectual functioning is defined as an IQ of 70 or below (approximately two standard deviations below the mean). Regardless of IQ, individuals with mental retardation have impaired functioning in memory (especially short-term memory), generalization (transferring learned knowledge or behavior from one task to another or from one setting to another), and decreased motivation (which may result from repeated failures).

LIMITATIONS IN ADAPTIVE BEHAVIOR

Adaptive behavior refers to an individual's ability to perform successfully in various environments. Skill limitations occur in three primary domains as defined by AAMR (2002)—conceptual, social, and practical adaptive skills. Conceptual skills include self-determination, reading, and writing, while social skills involve taking responsibility and following rules. The individual with mental retardation will also have difficulty with daily living and employment skills. Age, cultural expectations, and environmental demands will all influence the individual's adaptive behavior.

CLASSIFICATIONS

Several classification systems have been developed to more clearly define the range of mental retardation. Each method reflects the attempts of a particular discipline (e.g., education or medicine) to explain the needs of the individual with mental retardation. Most classification systems are based on the necessary supports required by these individuals to function optimally in the home and community. Severity of condition is characterized in the *DSM*-IV (2000) as *mild*, *moderate*, *severe*, and *profound*, with *mild* describing the highest level of performance and *profound* describing the lowest level. Separate codes are provided for each level, as well as for *mental retardation, severity unspecified*.

Individuals with mild mental retardation have been termed educationally as *educable* in the past, with an IQ range of 50–55 to approximately 70. This constitutes the largest segment (about 85 percent) of the group of individuals with mental retardation.

Individuals with *moderate* mental retardation have an IQ range of 35–40 to 50–55, and were once referred to by the outdated educational term *trainable*. This term wrongly implies that these individuals can only be "trained" and will not benefit from educational programming. Approximately 10 percent of the population of individuals with mental retardation is classified in this range.

The group categorized as *severe* makes up 3 to 4 percent of the population with mental retardation, while those with *profound* mental retardation constitute extremely low numbers of individuals (1–2 percent). The IQ level for *severe* mental retardation ranges from 20–25 to 35–40, and the IQ range for *profound* mental retardation is below 20–25.

Mental retardation, severity unspecified is used most often when there is a strong indication of mental retardation, but the individual's intelligence is untestable using standardized assessments. This occurs when individuals are too impaired or uncooperative for testing.

EDUCATIONAL OPTIONS

Public education for students with mental retardation is a relatively new concept, particularly for those with the most significant disabilities. In the past, the emphasis on academic achievement (i.e., reading, writing, and arithmetic) in public school programs made access difficult for these students. With the passage in 1975 of the Education for All Handicapped Children Act, Public Law 94-142 (now called the Individuals with Disabilities Education Act, or IDEA), public schools were required to provide both access and an appropriate education for all students, including those with mental retardation. The U.S. Department of Education (2002) indicated that approximately 94 percent of students with mental retardation between age six and twenty-one attend general education school, with 14 percent being served in a regular class at least 80 percent of the time.

The 1986 amendments to the Education for All Handicapped Children Act provided services to preschool-age children with disabilities, while the 1997 amendments provided for programming for infants and toddlers (birth to age two). Children with mild mental retardation may exhibit developmental delays when compared to their same-age peers. Intervention based on a developmental milestone approach is provided in either the natural environment (home-based intervention for infants and toddlers) or in preschool programs. Education focuses on assisting young children to develop, remedy, or adapt the skills appropriate for their chronological age.

Educational programs at the elementary level for children with mental retardation focus on decreasing the child's dependence on others and teaching adaptation to the environment. This generally includes facilitating the development of motor, self-help, social, communication, and academic skills. Students with mental retardation benefit from either basic or functional academic programs. A significant relationship exists between the level of retardation present and success in both reading and mathematics. The critical element is the teaching of functional academics that will aid the child's independence. For example, Diane Browder and Martha Snell describe functional academics as "simply the most useful parts of the three R's—reading, writing, and arithmetic" (2000, p. 497). *Useful* is defined on an individual basis, and is determined by that which will support the child's current daily routines, predicted future needs, and the priorities of the family.

The goal of programs for adolescents with mental retardation is to increase independence, enhance opportunities for participation in the community, prepare for future employment, and aid in the student's transition from school to adult life. Programming includes the development of skills in personal care and self-help, leisure activities, and access to community programs and supports. Employment preparation is undertaken with consideration of both functioning level and preference—the environment and tasks the individual enjoys.

DETERMINING THE CAUSES OF MENTAL RETARDATION

There are two categories of causes of mental retardation according to the American Association on Mental Retardation (2002, p. 126). One category involves *timing*, when the mental retardation occurred, and the other involves *type*, what factors were responsible for the mental retardation.

Timing is determined by onset of the disability—prenatal (before birth), perinatal (at birth), or postnatal (after birth). While research by Marshalyn Yeargin-Allsopp and colleagues (1997) showed that 12 percent of school-age children with mental retardation had a prenatal cause, 6 percent had a perinatal cause, and 4 percent had a postnatal cause, probable cause could not be determined for 78 percent of the children.

Type of cause is divided into four separate categories. *Biomedical* factors relate to biologic processes such as genetic disorders or nutrition. Down syndrome is a well-known genetic disorder for which mental retardation is characteristic. Mark Batshaw and Bruce Shapiro (2002) describe *social* factors that involve adverse influences related to social, behavioral, and educational areas, such as stimulation and adult responsiveness. *Behavioral* factors relate to behaviors with the potential to cause mental retardation, such as dangerous activities or maternal substance abuse. Finally, *educational* factors are related to the availability of supports that promote mental development. For example, mothers who lack information about prenatal health are more likely to have children with mental retardation. There is also a strong relationship between poverty and mental retardation. Of course, many of these factors evoke the age-old argument of "nature versus nurture" and whether ability is related more to sociocultural influences or genetics.

SOCIETAL STIGMA AND LABELING

There is considerable controversy about labeling and its consequences on both the individual and his or her family. Labels can be helpful in acquiring services, but the stigma attached to mental retardation can cause others to regard the individual as less than what they truly are. Stereotypical images of mental retardation are extremely difficult to change. People with mental retardation are at a higher risk of wrongful convictions for crimes. The label can also lead to segregation in educational placement, work, and the community. Because of the stigma attached to mental retardation, people with this disability often become adept at hiding it. Focus must be placed on the supports necessary for independence and success rather than on the individual's limitations.

SEE ALSO *Disability; Intelligence; Psychometrics; Scales; Stigma*

BIBLIOGRAPHY

American Association on Mental Retardation (AAMR). 2002. *Mental Retardation: Definition, Classification, and Systems of Supports.* 10th ed. Washington, DC: Author.

American Psychiatric Association (APA). 2000. *Diagnostic and Statistical Manual of Mental Disorders* (DSM-IV-TR). 4th ed., text rev. Washington, DC: Author.

Batshaw, Mark L., and Bruce K. Shapiro. 2002. Mental Retardation. In *Children with Disabilities*, ed. Mark L. Batshaw. 5th ed., 287–305. Baltimore, MD: Brookes.

Browder, Diane M., and Martha E. Snell. 2000. Teaching Functional Academics. In *Instruction of Students with Severe Disabilities*, eds. Martha E. Snell and Fredda Brown, 493–542. Upper Saddle River, NJ: Merrill.

Education for All Handicapped Children Act, 20 U.S.C. 1400. 1975.

Individuals with Disabilities Education Act (IDEA) (Public Law 105–17), C.F.R. 300. 1997.

Roid, Gale H. 2003. *Stanford-Binet Intelligence Scales* (SB5). 5th ed. Itasca, IL: Riverside.

U.S. Office of Special Education and Rehabilitative Service. 1987. To Assure the Free Appropriate Education of All Handicapped Children. In *Ninth Annual Report to Congress on the Implementation of the Education of the Handicapped Act*. Washington, DC: Office of Special Education Programs.

U.S. Department of Education. 2001. *To Assure the Free Appropriate Public Education of All Children with Disabilities: Twenty-third Annual Report to Congress on the Implementation of the Individuals with Disabilities Education Act*. Washington, DC: Author.

U.S. Department of Education. 2002. *To Assure the Free Appropriate Public Education of All Children with Disabilities: Twenty-fourth Annual Report to Congress on the Implementation of the Individuals with Disabilities Education Act*. Washington, DC: U.S. Government Printing Office.

Wechsler, David. 1991. *Wechsler Intelligence Scale for Children III (WISC-III)*. San Antonio, TX: Psychological Corporation.

Yeargin-Allsopp, Marshalyn, Catherine Murphy, José Cordero, et al. 1997. Reported Biomedical Causes and Associated Medical Conditions for Mental Retardation among 10-year-old Children, Metropolitan Atlanta, 1985 to 1987. *Developmental Medicine and Child Neurology* 39 (3): 142–149.

Sally Roberts

MENTORING

Mentors produce mentees, or protégés, who ultimately become mentors and perpetuate a cycle that has long-term and lasting effects on generations to come. Flaws and imperfections as well as strengths in the mentor are often passed along to future generations by the products of mentoring, protégés. As such, and as with many other skills-based human behaviors, it is important to understand the history and process of mentoring to make it more efficient and produce better and more consistent human outcomes.

The term *mentor* describes a person who consciously and with purpose fosters a relationship between the target of such efforts, the protégé, and the mentor. Mentors typically are older or more seasoned and having a level of experience that allows them to provide guidance, support, and a frame of comparison for protégés to guide their behaviors, choices, thoughts, attitudes, and emotions.

It was not until the mid-1980s that social and cultural researchers began formally to study mentoring using scientific methodology. Research on mentoring has histor-

ically focused on the products of mentoring, or the protégé. The term *protégé* refers to the individual receiving advice and guidance from the more senior participant.

Characteristics such as openness in the protégé are associated with better outcomes. Much of the research on mentoring suggests that it has a positive impact on career development, including salary level, promotion rate, and job satisfaction. Although the consequences of mentoring in formal and informal settings are beginning to be understood, much remains to be learned about the process of mentoring.

It is known, for example, that in the mentor-protégé relationship the mentor has two primary functions: (1) goal attainment (academic, career, relationships, and so forth) and (2) psychosocial support. In the goal-attainment function, the mentor provides advice and models of success and management to help the protégé facilitate achievement of professional and personal goals. This function is designed to produce achievements and help the protégé focus his or her professional aspirations and attain targeted outcomes. Notably in this area we know the most about the outcomes and process of mentoring.

Less well understood is the psychosocial and support-related function. This function is more personally oriented and is based on such complex factors as friendship, power, mutual respect, authority, and admiration. Mentors often provide informal counseling and manage a wide range of emotional and cognitive sequelae (frustration, doubt, and the like) in the protégé associated with both success and failure.

Mentoring is best understood in two forms: informal and formal. Informal mentoring usually develops spontaneously and depends on individuals having some common interests. The protégé may need short-term guidance and support for academic, career, and other decisions, to include personal situations.

Formal mentoring is based on the organizational structure that dictates the relationship. Formal mentoring programs were established to compensate and provide resources to groups that historically have been excluded from informal mentoring relationships because of their gender, ethnicity, social status, or sexual orientation. For example, in corporate situations individuals with powerful positions are often less than willing or excited to mentor those who are perceived to be "different."

There are six primary characteristics of formal mentoring: (1) formal program objectives, (2) formal selection of participants, (3) matching of mentors and protégés, (4) training, (5) guidelines for meeting frequency, and (6) formal goal setting and goal monitoring. Regardless of the mentoring type, the key component of a successful mentoring relationship is that it must meet the developmental needs, skills, and aspirations of both the mentor and protégé.

It is often the case that mentors may not be able to meet all the developmental needs of the protégé, thus requiring more than one mentor or the establishment of a mentoring network. This network of mentors can provide a variety of skills and knowledge and competently provide for the developmental needs of one or more protégés. In 2006 Tammy D. Allen, Lillian T. Eby, and Elizabeth Lentz developed a theoretical framework that incorporates a multimodal conceptualization of successful mentoring based on two key dimensions.

The first relates to the diversity of the social system. Individual mentors and networks are most effective when their characteristics can be matched to that of the protégé. The more diverse the social system in which mentoring occurs, the better the chance of getting the correct match. The second factor relates to the strength of mentoring relationships. Particularly in a mentoring network, when a protégé is having multiple contacts with a range of mentors, the strength of the relationships can vary greatly. This conceptualization of mentoring has received significant recent attention and may become critical as multidisciplinary mentoring becomes more common in business and academic settings.

Integrating and extending previous knowledge, the American Psychological Association Centering on Mentoring Presidential Task Force (2006) identified five critical stages associated with the mentoring process. The *initiation stage* is characterized by the initiation and emergence of the mentor–protégé relationship. During this stage protégés identify experienced and successful people to whom they can prove their worth. Ultimately both parties explore and evaluate the appropriateness of the mentor-protégé match. Next is the *cultivation stage*, where learning and development take place. During this stage the mentor provides advice and guidance to the protégé. Both the personal and professional relationship is developed and intensified during this time, and attainment and psychosocial goals are achieved. This is usually a positive stage for both participants and often results in the maturation of a strong friendship. The *separation stage* generally refers to the end of the mentoring relationship. This often signals that protégés want to establish their independence. At this stage problems may sometimes arise when only one party wants to terminate the mentoring relationship. A protégé may sometimes feel unprepared to venture out independently, or the mentor may feel betrayed when the protégé no longer seeks guidance and counsel. When both parties successfully matriculate separation, a *redefinition stage* can occur toward the development of a new and more parsimonious relationship. It is during this stage that protégés have established themselves as worthy colleagues and the focus of the relationship is no longer the protégé's development.

A few studies have examined factors that influence the nature and magnitude of the mentoring relationship (Ragins and Cotton 1999; Ragins 1997). For example, it is now known that gender may influence the interactions—and consequently mentoring outcomes—of mentors and protégés. Some have suggested that there may be more perceived similarity, greater identification, and intensified effects of role modeling in same-gender mentoring relationships. In partial contrast and certainly less well understood, both male and female protégés with a history of male mentors reported greater compensation in the workplace than those with female mentors (Ragins and Cotton 1999). Even with this finding, many advocate for female-female mentor-protégé relationships and suggest that the modeling of success and coping that they provide exceeds the benefit of increased salary.

Ethnicity is also an important consideration in mentoring outcomes. The benefits of formal mentoring, particularly for women and ethnic minorities, are significant and are often based on the premise of providing an equal opportunity to advance through perceived and real "glass ceilings." However, some sociocultural variables within the formal mentoring paradigm may ultimately put women and ethnic minorities at a significant disadvantage.

Lastly, a position of power appears to be an important variable for mentoring outcomes. The protégé may be more likely to respect and respond to a person who has perceived power and who gained that power through a process that led from where the protégé is currently positioned to where the mentor is currently positioned.

In conclusion, sufficient evidence supports the notion that mentoring is a powerful tool for the development of the protégé. Successful mentoring can often influence indicators such as compensation, promotion, exposure, and visibility. However, these outcomes are influenced by the strength and effectiveness of the mentoring relationship and psychosocial and sociocultural variables. The relationship is dynamic and changes to provide benefit to the mentor and protégé over time.

BIBLIOGRAPHY

Allen, Tammy D., Lillian T. Eby, and Elizabeth Lentz. 2006. Mentorship Behaviors and Mentorship Quality Associated with Formal Mentoring Programs: Closing the Gap between Research and Practice. *Journal of Applied Psychology* 91: 367–578.

Allen, Tammy D., Lillian T. Eby, Mark L. Poteet, Elizabeth Lentz, et al. 2004. Career Benefits Associated with Mentoring Protégés: A Meta-Analysis. *Journal of Applied Psychology* 89: 127–136.

American Psychological Association. 2006. Introduction to Mentoring: A Guide for Mentors and Mentees. Centering on

Mentoring Presidential Taskforce, Washington, DC. http://mentoring.apa.org/intromentoring.pdf.

Ragins, Belle Rose. 1997. Diversified Mentoring Relationships in Organizations: A Power Perspective. *Academy of Management Review* 22 (2): 482–521.

Ragins, Belle Rose, and J. L. Cotton. 1999. Mentor Functions and Outcomes: A Comparison of Men and Women in Formal and Informal Mentoring Relationships. *Journal of Applied Psychology* 84 (4): 529–550.

Stephanie R. Johnson
Christopher L. Edwards

MERCANTILISM

The term *mercantilism* designates a system of economic policy as well as an epoch in the development of economic doctrines, lasting from the sixteenth to the eighteenth century. It first appeared in print in Marquis de Mirabeau's *Philosophie rurale* in 1763 as *système mercantile*. The main popularizer of the "commercial system"—as he preferred to call it—was Adam Smith. According to him the core of the mercantile system consisted of the folly of confusing wealth with money. Despite the practical orientation of the mercantilist writers, they did propose a principle: the so-called *positive balance of trade* theory, which implied that a country must export more than it imported. According to Smith, the mercantile system was put into place by a mercantile special interest that would be able to profit from duties on imports, tariffs, and bounties.

From Smith onward, the view of the mercantile system, or simply mercantilism, as state *dirigism* and protectionism serving a special interest through the maintenance of positive balances of trade was developed further by classical political economy. During the nineteenth century this viewpoint was contested by the German historical school, which preferred to define mercantilism as statemaking in a general sense. According to its view mercantilism as a system of theory was the rational expression of nation-building during the early modern period. An attempt to combine these two interpretations was made by the Swedish economic historian Eli Heckscher in his *Mercantilism* ([1935] 1994). A response to Heckscher's wide definition of mercantilism was to altogether reject the notion of a particular mercantilist system.

This latter position goes too far, however. It is certainly correct that mercantilism was not a finished system or coherent doctrine in the nineteenth- and twentieth-century sense. It is better described as a literature of pamphlets and books that mainly dealt with practical political economy, published roughly between the late sixteenth century and 1750. The underlying issue dealt with in this literature was the question of how to achieve national wealth and power. This general agenda can be traced in English, Italian, and French economic texts from the sixteenth century onward. From this point of view, Italian writers such as Giovanni Botero (1544–1617) and Antonio Serra (1580–?), as well as sixteenth-century Spanish writers such as de Vitorias, de Soto, de Azpilcueta, and Luis de Ortiz were perhaps the first "mercantilists." In England, the most well-known mercantilists in the middle of the seventeenth century were Thomas Mun (1571–1641) and Edward Misselden (1608–1654). Later well-known mercantilist writers include Josiah Child (1630–1699), Nicholas Barbon (1640–1698), Charles Davenant (1656–1714), Malachy Postlethwayt (1707–1767), and James Steuart (1713–1780) in England and Antoine Montchrètien (1575–1621) and Jean Baptiste Colbert (1619–1683) in France. Most of these writers shared the view that the increase of trade and manufacture could only be accomplished through state intervention, and that it was not possible to rely only on the self-equilibrating forces of the marketplace.

From Adam Smith onward the view has been repeated that the mercantilist writers confused money with wealth. However, recent research has shown that this conception of the mercantilists is highly questionable. For the bulk of seventeenth-century writers on economic and trade issues, the quantity theory of money was a standard presupposition. Moreover, there were very few price inflationists among the mercantilists. Instead, a majority agreed that high prices would cause lower exports—that is, they argued that the effect of elasticity of demand was considerable on most export markets. However, Mun as well as many others during this period seems to have feared that without a steady inflow of money originating from a favorable balance of trade, trade and industry would stagnate and the price of land would fall. To counter this shortage of bullion in circulation, a steady inflow of money through a net trade surplus was necessary.

However, most writers had abandoned the favorable balance of trade theory in its simple form by the end of the seventeenth century. Some argued that the principle was impractical as a policy goal, as it was impossible to account for a trade surplus in quantitative terms. Others found problems on more theoretical grounds—that is, they directly or indirectly admitted to the argument later known as the *specie-flow* argument. Instead, from the 1690s writers such as Josiah Child (1630–1699), Charles Davenant (1656–1714), and Nicholas Barbon (1640–1698) developed a new idea that alternatively has been called the theory of *foreign-paid incomes*, the *labor balance of trade* theory, or the *export of work* theory. Instead of holding on to the dogma that a country should receive an inflow of bullion through the balance of trade, these authors stressed that a country should export products with as much value-added content as possible and import as little of such products as they could. The profit would come from the fact that the buyer—Spain, Portugal, or other countries—would not only pay England for its raw materials, but also for its laborers.

Hence, what makes it legitimate to speak of a specific "mercantile system" was its proponents' preoccupation with the question of how a nation could become rich, and thus also achieve greater national power and glory. In the broader sense of an ideology promoting economic protection in order to achieve domestic growth, the term *mercantilism* is not applicable only to the period before Adam Smith. Mercantilist ideas can also be found in modern forms of protectionism that have appeared since the nineteenth century. For example, the period between World Wars I and II was characterized by protectionism and economic nationalism; it was this that led to Heckscher's synthesis, which he intended as advocacy in favor of liberal and free-trade ideas. Despite Heckscher's insistence that mercantilism was a false ideology—free trade, he argued, was better for economic growth, at least in the long run—mercantilism was hailed as a form of popular economics of common sense. As such, it still exists to some degree, though it has reappeared most clearly during periods of economic crisis, such as the 1920s and 1930s. Mercantilist theory has found only a very few proponents among more modern schools of economics. Some economists inspired by institutional economics have referred sympathetically to mercantilist doctrines concerning population growth (for example Joseph J. Spengler), as have others inspired by radical development economics (for example, Cosimo Perrotta).

After World War II, mercantilist ideas have instead largely recurred in the form of neomercantilism and strategic-trade theory. From the end of the 1970s, strategic-trade theorists such as Lester Thurow, James Brander, Barbara Spencer, and Paul Krugman sought to replace the theory of comparative advantages with a theory of "competitive advantage." Their argument is that the pattern of international trade cannot be explained on the basis of comparative advantage or with the help of the simple Heckscher-Ohlin theorem. Instead, the flow of international trade is a consequence of scale and scope, economic muscle, and increasing returns to scale. The political implications of this were straightforward: Governmental support is appropriate when used to bring about a competitive advantage for an industry that would benefit its nation in the long term. Certainly, this was another way to defend the infant-industry argument, with clear implications for trade policy.

SEE ALSO *Beggar-Thy-Neighbor; Postlethwayt, Malachy; Smith, Adam; Zero-sum Game*

BIBLIOGRAPHY

Heckscher, Eli F. [1935] 1994. *Mercantilism*. London and New York: Routledge.

Hutchison, Terence W. 1988. *Before Adam Smith*. Oxford: Blackwell.

Magnusson, Lars. 1994. *Mercantilism. The Shaping of an Economic Language*. London and New York: Routledge.

Lars Magnusson

MERGERS AND ACQUISITIONS

SEE *Corporate Strategies.*

MERIT

At its most general level, merit is a value system that delineates qualities that are recognized and rewarded by societies. The most specific and significant reward under consideration in this system is the selection for public office on the basis of ability and character, rather than on the basis of class, caste, patronage, patrimony, ideology, or wealth. Such reward has profound implications for the structure of society and for the functioning of polities.

DEFINITIONS

The essential meaning of *merit* is generally underdefined, raising continuing questions about its content. In most political and administrative literature, merit is frequently discussed primarily in terms of its implementing mechanisms. Principles of merit are reasonably well documented and understood to include competitive examinations, protection from political influence, equal opportunity to compete for appointment, and fairness and equity in the treatment of civil servants.

In some recent literature, the term *meritocracy* is used as a synonym for the broader merit concept in its instrumental social and political connotations. Meritocracy was originally a pejorative term coined by Michael Young (1915–2002) in 1958 as a satirical indictment of a utopian system of rule governed by test results and devoid of human political impulse. More recently, the term has entered common discourse to denote any public or private employment system that makes job-related decisions on some calculation of character, ability, and potential.

A universal definition of merit is complicated by its apparent dependence on the mores, values, and accepted ethical standards in differing temporal, social, political, and cultural settings (Riccucci 1991, p. 88). Despite the relativistic argument, an approach to a universal definition may be found in the literature of philosophy, where merit is dually associated with concepts of ethics, morality, and justice, as well as with judgments regarding competent performance.

In the moral and ethical aspects of merit, Immanuel Kant (1724–1804) emphasized the importance of moral goodness, as stated in his lectures on ethics in 1793 and 1794: "[To] make myself worthy of honor … the dutifulness of action must be supplemented by moral goodness.… Toward men we realize more morality than is incumbent on us, and in this, therefore, lies at the same time the merit of our actions" (quoted in Guyer 2000, p. 328). This formulation gives no hint as to how moral goodness is to be measured as a basis for societal reward. The answer, deriving from Plato's *Republic* (c. 400 BCE) and practiced in many civil service systems throughout the world, has been through careful and comprehensive education and indoctrination in the regime values of the polity. This answer, however, raises questions regarding the eligibility of individuals from all strata of society. John Rawls (1921–2002) relates merit to justice only if every member of society has the opportunity and means to attain the requisite knowledge and abilities (1999, pp. 91-93).

Gregory Vlastos (1907–1991) identifies merit as a grading concept with judgment based on the measurement of valued qualities and performances (1969). The introduction of measurement and grading sharpens the definition. Vlastos, however, offers no help in defining the qualities and performances. Nor does he speculate on how measurement could be achieved. The conventional answer to this last question is found in the development and implementation of testing and performance appraisal processes; however, these processes raise serious questions as to their validity and effects (Cronbach 1980; Lemann 1999; Riccucci 1991).

A significant differentiation between two forms of merit has been provided by Amartya Sen. He identifies an internal conflict within the concept of merit, described as the tension between: "(1) the inclination to see merit in fixed and absolute terms, and (2) the ultimately instrumental character of merit—its dependence on the concept of 'the good' in the relevant society" (2000, p. 5). This differentiation is echoed by Hugh Heclo in his analysis of "substantive" and "instrumental" merit (2000).

The instrumental "good" is defined within every society primarily by historical and intellectual influences as interpreted and reinforced by the elite opinion makers of the society. The fixed and absolute idea of merit can be a subversive influence on established patterns of social and political hierarchy and status. The substantive concept of merit logically leads to the advocacy of an open society and some degree of democratic governance; however, it must be recognized that merit is not in itself a democratic concept. Its base is aristocratic in the Jeffersonian sense of being grounded in virtue and talent. The connection to democracy applies by linkage to the substantive, moral aspect of merit. Conversely, instrumental merit is a useful tool for achieving competence in government regardless of type of regime.

Societal definitions of merit through much of recorded history have been restrictive in terms of class and status and thus inimical to social movement. Since the latter part of the twentieth century, this has led to an antagonistic relationship of equal opportunity to merit-based employment systems because such systems are frequently viewed as discriminating against less-advantaged segments of society. If such discrimination does occur, then the opportunity that is implicit in merit theory is in fact not equal (Roemer 2000).

Nonetheless, the basic philosophical premise of merit is recognition of ability wherever found in the society. This is potentially regime changing and socially revolutionary as demonstrated by the development of merit-based systems in the United States, Great Britain, and France in the nineteenth century, and in Japan in the early twentieth century. The socially restrictive aspects of merit-based systems are due not to the basic premise of merit but, rather, to the hierarchical structure of societies and the rigidity and exclusionary nature of the implementing mechanisms.

ORIGINS AND EVOLUTION OF THE MERIT CONCEPT

The origin of the concept of merit in both Eastern and Western culture has ancient roots, preceding its dynamic emergence in the nineteenth century as a significant political and social force. In Asia, the origin of the merit concept is found in the *Analects* of Confucius (c. 551–479 BCE), and the subsequent interpretation of Confucian doctrine through centuries of dynastic change in China. Merit became institutionalized in traditional Chinese and Korean political cultures by the creation and implementation of rigorous examination processes for the selection of entrants into official positions; however, in practice, success in the examinations was almost entirely limited to upper-class candidates. Since 1950, the Peoples Republic of China has alternatively weakened and then strengthened the use of examinations for appointment to office. The turmoil has fostered a greater degree of political influence and greater inclusion of individuals with worker and peasant backgrounds in the appointment process (Klitgaard 1986, pp. 10–32).

In Tokugawa, Japan (1603–1868), the Confucian merit concept was recognized, but access to official positions was confined to the samurai class. Within a few years after the Meiji restoration in 1868, the merit principle was instituted as the basis for office, and access to a competitive process was substantially broadened (Koh 1989). The erosion of social and economic barriers was a necessary component of Japan's successful impulse to modernization and industrialization.

In Western culture, the origin of the merit concept is found in pre-Socratic Greece with the early identification of valued virtues and excellences (*arete*) (Adkins 1960). The ideal of merit found expression in, among other texts, the funeral oration of the statesman Pericles (c. 495–429 BCE) as related by Thucydides (d. c. 401 BCE), in Plato's *Republic* and *Gorgias*, and in Aristotle's (384–322 BCE) *Politics*. The normative power of the concept was assumed by the Roman Republic and ultimately defined by Cicero (106–43 BCE) in his *De Officiis*, ironically as the republic was dissolving in chaos.

After the fall of the Roman Republic, merit as a primary political value declined and virtually disappeared for seventeen centuries. The values that predominated for government service became those of servitude and obedience to the ruler, as outlined by Niccolò Machiavelli (1469–1527) in *The Prince* (1513, chap. 22) and Thomas Hobbes (1588–1679) in *Leviathan* (1651, chap. 23). To be sure, ability remained a factor, but subservient to obedience. For example, Oliver Cromwell's (1599–1658) brief English Republic (1649–1660) did not change the royal practice of awarding office on the basis of the "unholy three P's—Patrimony, Patronage, and Purchase" (Aylmer 1973, p. 61). This practice continued in Britain until the mid-nineteenth century.

Beginning in the late eighteenth century, the merit concept reemerged and developed both as a moral imperative and as a practical necessity. The philosophy of the Enlightenment and the new production systems of the Industrial Revolution demanded rationalism in the staffing of governmental enterprise by demonstrably competent people. No longer would nepotism and patronage suffice. The endorsement and application of merit as a primary value in staffing governmental positions became a necessary condition for national modernization and commercial and social progress. By the mid-twentieth century, the merit concept, with its implementing processes, was dominant in developed societies around the world.

In recent years, the definition of merit has changed to meet current societal and political trends. In a new time of postmodernism and postindustrialism, the established value and practices of merit have been altered as political leadership in democracies around the world has attempted to secure greater control over public bureaucracies through politicization of the appointment process (Peters and Pierre 2004). In many ways, this is a regression to earlier formulations of the primacy of political obedience over the rationality and morality that is inherent in the concept of merit-based civil service. Once again, responsiveness and obedience have become primary values. Merit practices have remained viable in their instrumental meaning as continuing emphasis is placed on performance measurement; however, substantive merit is in decline (Heclo 2000; Lane and Woodard 2001). In the long view, these developments are not unprecedented, nor do they alter the fact that the merit concept is an enduring value grounded in the very origins of both Eastern and Western civilization.

SEE ALSO *Affirmative Action; Discrimination; Meritocracy; Stratification*

BIBLIOGRAPHY

Adkins, Arthur W. H. 1960. *Merit and Responsibility: A Study in Greek Values.* London: Clarendon.

Aylmer, G. E. 1973. *The State's Servants: The Civil Service of the English Republic 1649–1660* London: Routledge and Kegan Paul.

Cronbach, Lee J. 1980. Selection Theory for a Political World. *Public Personnel Management* 9: 37–50.

Guyer, Paul. 2000. *Kant on Freedom, Law, and Happiness.* Cambridge, U.K.: Cambridge University Press.

Heclo, Hugh. 2000. The Future of Merit. In *The Future of Merit: Twenty Years After the Civil Service Reform Act*, eds. James P. Pfiffner and Douglas A Brook, 226–237. Washington, DC: Woodrow Wilson Center Press.

Klitgaard, Robert. 1986. *Elitism and Meritocracy in Developing Countries: Selection Policies for Higher Education.* Baltimore, MD: Johns Hopkins University Press.

Koh, B. C. 1989. *Japan's Administrative Elite.* Berkeley: University of California Press.

Lane, Larry M., and Colleen Woodard. 2001. Merit without the System: An Emergent Model for Public Sector HRM. In *Radical Reform of the Civil Service*, eds. Stephen E. Condrey and Robert Maranto, 127–149. Lanham, MD: Lexington.

Lemann, Nicholas. 1999. *The Big Test: The Secret History of the American Meritocracy.* New York: Farrar, Straus, and Giroux.

Peters, B. Guy, and Jon Pierre, eds. 2004. *Politicization of the Civil Service in Comparative Perspective: The Quest for Control.* London: Routledge.

Rawls, John. [1971] 1999. *A Theory of Justice.* Rev. ed. Cambridge, MA: Belknap.

Riccucci, Norma M. 1991. Merit, Equity, and Test Validity: A New Look at an Old Problem. *Administration and Society* 23 (1): 74–93.

Roemer, John E. 2000. Equality of Opportunity. In *Meritocracy and Economic Inequality*, eds. Kenneth Arrow, Samuel Bowles, and Steven Durlauf, 17–32. Princeton, NJ: Princeton University Press.

Sen, Amartya. 2000. Merit and Justice. In *Meritocracy and Economic Inequality*, eds. Kenneth Arrow, Samuel Bowles, and Steven Durlauf, 5–16. Princeton, NJ: Princeton University Press.

Vlastos, Gregory. 1969. Human Worth, Merit, and Equality. In *Moral Concepts*, ed. Joel Feinberg, 141–152. Oxford: Oxford University Press.

Young, Michael. 1958. *The Rise of the Meritocracy, 1870–2033: An Essay on Education and Equality*. London: Thames and Hudson.

Larry M. Lane

MERIT GOODS

The concept of merit wants or merit goods was first proposed by Richard A. Musgrave (1910–2007) in 1957 in an article on budget determination in *FinanzArchiv*; he revisited the concept in his *Theory of Public Finance* in 1959. For Musgrave, merit goods are goods that are "considered so meritorious that their satisfaction is provided for through the public budget, over and above what is provided for through the market and paid for by private buyers" (1959, p. 13; Musgrave 1998). Musgrave identified education, free school lunches, low-cost housing, and health care as important and common examples of merit goods.

While Musgrave coined the term *merit goods*, he was by no means the first to propose a role for the government in the provision of education. Adam Smith (1723–1790) was concerned in the *Wealth of Nations* (1776) with the dulling effect of the deepening division of labor on the intellectual faculties of the common people, and he promoted public provision of education as a remedy to the situation (Smith [1776] 1937, p. 737). Later, in the middle of the nineteenth century, John Stuart Mill (1806–1873) argued that:

> Any well-intentioned and tolerably civilized government may think, without presumption, that it does or ought to possess a degree of cultivation above the average of the community which it rules, and that it should therefore be capable of offering better education and better instruction to the people, than the greater number of them would spontaneously demand.... The case is one to which the reasons of the non-interference principle do not necessarily or universally extend. (Mill [1848] 1970, p. 318)

While seeking to justify government provision of education, Mill at the same time denied the legitimacy of government monopoly in education (Mill [1848] 1970, p. 320).

Merit goods have had a somewhat contested position in economics, but perhaps less so in policy practice. The traditional economic view of governmental tasks involving public good provision (later resource allocation), redistribution, and stabilization did not leave an easy niche for the provision of merit goods. Merit goods are "private goods" in the sense that their consumption is rival and exclusion from them is easy. Therefore, merit goods can be and often are privately provided on the market, which for many raises the question of why they should be provided publicly. The provision of merit goods also overrules consumer preferences and thus bypasses consumer sovereignty as a normative cornerstone of economic policy (McClure 1968). But this view sanctifies markets as the way to generate a social welfare function: Other ways to do so include collective decisions in representative democratic decision-making arenas.

One argument for the involvement of the government in the provision of merit goods is based on the view that, due to imperfect information, irrationality, or other reasons, people's preferences regarding merit goods can be ill-informed to serve their own best interests (Head 1966). In this light, overriding the preferences of, for example, deprived groups in the society may benefit them. A second argument treats the provision of merit goods as in-kind redistribution that expands the transfer recipients' consumption of goods that are identified as important by those who are funding the transfers. A third argument reconciles the notion of merit goods with standard welfare economics. It suggests that the consumption of certain goods involves positive (or negative) externalities, which justifies their subsidized (or taxed) provision in the name of maximization of social welfare (Culyer 1971). Yet another explanation, albeit not necessarily a justification, of merit goods is that their provision may enhance the utility of those who impose their "nosy" preferences on others.

A common criticism of public provision of merit goods is that they are inefficient public substitutes for goods that could be provided more efficiently privately. However, on this issue the jury seems to be out. Some studies have concluded that public provision of merit goods is substitutive (diminishing) of private provision of the same goods, while other studies have found that public and private provision are complementary (Fiorito and Kollintzas 2004). This means that public provision of merit goods increases the consumption of privately provided goods. Merit good provision accounts for a significant proportion of the gross domestic product (GDP) and government expenditure in developed countries that have substantial welfare states. Many European countries spent about 9 to 15 percent of their GDP on the provision of merit goods in the 1990s. Merit good provision made up about two-thirds of government consumption, an element of government expenditure that excludes transfers, public investments, and interest payments (Fiorito and Kollintzas 2004). The rest was used to provide public goods. Education and health care are the most significant merit goods from an expenditure point of view. However, their public provision does not necessarily mean public production: Public provision can be based on private production. For example, nonprofit organizations such as the Church of England offer free primary education with state support in the United Kingdom. Similarly, in a number of countries, national health-insurance schemes rely in part on private health-care service producers.

SEE ALSO *Education, USA; Externality; Markets; Mill, John Stuart; Public Goods; Social Welfare Functions; Welfare Economics*

BIBLIOGRAPHY

Culyer, A. J. 1971. Merit Goods and the Welfare Economics of Coercion. *Public Finance* 26: 546–571.

Fiorito, Riccardo, and Tryphon Kollintzas. 2004. Public Goods, Merit Goods, and the Relation between Private and Government Consumption. *European Economic Review* 48: 1367–1398.

Head, John G. 1966. On Merit Goods. *FinanzArchiv* 25: 1–29.

McClure, Charles E. 1968. Merit Wants: A Normatively Empty Box. *FinanzArchiv* 27: 474–483.

Mill, John Stuart. [1848] 1970. *Principles of Political Economy.* Harmondsworth, U.K.: Penguin.

Musgrave, Richard A. 1957. A Multiple Theory of Budget Determination. *FinanzArchiv* 17: 333–343.

Musgrave, Richard A. 1959. *The Theory of Public Finance: A Study in Public Economy.* New York: McGraw-Hill.

Musgrave, Richard A. 1998. Merit Goods. In *The New Palgrave: A Dictionary of Economics,* eds. John Eatwell, Murray Milgate, and Peter Newman, vol. 2, 452–453. London: Macmillan.

Smith, Adam. [1776] 1937. *An Inquiry into the Nature and Causes of the Wealth of Nations.* New York: Random House.

Jouni Paavola

MERITOCRACY

Meritocracy refers to a social system in which individuals advance and earn rewards in direct proportion to their individual abilities and efforts. The term *meritocracy* was coined by British sociologist Michael Young (1915–2002) in his book, *The Rise of the Meritocracy, 1870–2033: An Essay on Education and Equality* (1958). The book is a satirical novel about a futuristic society in which elites and leaders ascend to positions of dominance and authority based on their scores on intelligence and effort tests (I + E = M, where I = intelligence, E = effort, and M = merit). In this imagined society, tests have been devised that accurately and precisely identify the most capable and competent individuals within the total population. Young's portrayal of a meritocracy is necessarily futuristic, because no such society has been realized anywhere in practice. In every known human society, nonmeritocratic factors such as seniority, inheritance, nepotism, favoritism, discrimination, and sheer randomness either wholly or partially determine who is in charge.

The neologism, meritocracy, created for Young an implicit juxtaposition with the term *aristocracy*. While aristocracy characterizes a system in which statuses are ascribed, meritocracy characterizes a system in which statuses are achieved. As societies industrialize, there is a gradual shift away from ascription toward achievement, however incomplete. Merit is widely seen as inherently fair, because under such a system individuals get what they deserve based on their contributions to society. Such a system is also seen as inherently efficient because it results in an optimum match between the collective tasks in society that need to get done and the available pool of talent needed to perform them.

While seemingly fair on the surface, Young portrays a system of meritocracy that ultimately degenerates into an oppressive regime. In Young's future meritocracy, elites become arrogant and ruthless in the pursuit of their own ends while remaining callous or indifferent toward the needs and suffering of those they dominate. Self-assured in their own sense of inherent superiority, the elite feel smugly justified in their subjugation of the masses.

In a later reflection in 1998, Young noted that he wrote *The Rise of the Meritocracy* based on the model of Aldous Huxley's *Brave New World. Brave New World* (1932) depicts a future eugenic "World State" in which individuals are bred into one of five castes that, in turn, are assigned tasks consistent with their programmed capacities. The World State functions in essence as a meritocracy, albeit a biologically engineered one. In this futuristic world order, war, poverty, and other social ills have been eliminated. With nothing to fight over or worry about, individuals are free to derive pleasure from promiscuous sex and recreational drug use. Doped and duped into submission and complacency, however, individuals are systematically deprived of both individual freedom and intellectual curiosity. As with Young's imagined meritocracy, there is a devastating price to pay for life in

Huxley's *Brave New World*—giving both novels an ironically dystopian quality.

EMPIRICAL DEBATE

These novels have drawn attention to the empirical debate about whether or not or to what extent meritocracy has been realized in advanced industrial societies. Several prominent books have since made the case for a rising meritocracy. In *The Coming of Post-Industrial Society: A Venture in Social Forecasting* (1976), Daniel Bell contends that advanced industrial countries are moving beyond an industrial to a postindustrial stage of development. Postindustrial societies are characterized by a shift from goods production to service production, with an increasing premium on scientific and technical knowledge. Bell posits that a new knowledge class centered in universities is gradually replacing business and propertied elites that dominated in the industrial era. Similarly, in *The Bell Curve: Intelligence and Class Structure in American Life* (1994), Richard Herrnstein and Charles Murray suggest that barriers to mobility based on innate talent in advanced societies such as the United States have mostly been eliminated and that a new cognitive elite is emerging. Herrnstein and Murray argue further that intelligence is largely genetically inherited and differences in intelligence are principally responsible for differences in socioeconomic status. Others, such as Paul Kamolnick (2005) and Peter Saunders (1996), have made similar arguments.

Some critics (Arrow, Bowles, and Durlauf 2000; Breen and Goldthorpe 1999, 2002; McNamee and Miller 2004; Oliver and Shapiro 1995), however, have countered that nonmerit factors still largely determine social outcomes. These nonmerit factors include the influence of family background and economic inheritance, social networks, discrimination, the number and types of jobs available in society as a whole, and random luck. Economic inheritance, broadly defined as initial social class placement, is chief among these nonmerit factors. Nonmerit advantages are passed on in varying degrees to children from families with more relatively privileged backgrounds. Parents with the most resources can invest the most in securing their children's futures. To the extent that parents are successful in advancing the futures of their children through educational and other investments, meritocracy does not exist.

Discrimination in its varying forms is also antithetical to meritocracy. In an attempt to redress the effects of past and present forms of discrimination, various affirmative action initiatives have been adopted in advanced industrial societies. These measures, however, have themselves been labeled as reverse discrimination, to the extent that they are perceived as giving preferential treatment to so-called protected classes, especially women and racial minorities.

Central to this empirical debate is what is meant by merit and the extent to which merit factors are genetically innate or culturally acquired. It is generally acknowledged, for instance, that intelligence as measured by intelligence quotient (IQ) tests, reflects an interplay of both innate intellectual capacities and learned experiences. Beyond intelligence, other talents such as artistic creativity or athletic prowess are also probably the result of combinations of innate capacity and learned experience. Whatever innate talents or capacities that individuals have are of no use unless put into effect. And as Young initially noted, effort, apart from capacity, is also relevant to merit. In addition, social skills might in some circumstances be considered individually meritorious. Other acquired skills, knowledge, or experience could also be considered meritorious, even though the opportunity to acquire such traits is typically not equally available to all. Finally, merit has also been associated with particular attitudes or values such as diligence, perseverance, and willingness to take risks and defer gratification. It is not always clear, however, how these attitudes are acquired, how they might be causally linked to achievement, or how they interact with other factors in predicting outcomes.

The weight of the evidence suggests that both merit and nonmerit factors influence social and economic outcomes in advanced industrial societies. On the one hand, broad historical trends in industrialized societies toward a decline in overt discrimination and wider access to education have no doubt contributed to greater individual opportunity and prospects for mobility. On the other hand, the persistent and substantial influence of family background and economic inheritance, the effects of past and continued discrimination, social networks, randomness, and other structural barriers to individual mobility means that meritocracy is still far from being fully realized.

SEE ALSO *Affirmative Action; Discrimination; Equality; Meritocracy, Multiracial; Social Status*

BIBLIOGRAPHY

Arrow, Kenneth, Samuel Bowles, and Steven Durlauf, eds. 2000. *Meritocracy and Economic Inequality*. Princeton, NJ: Princeton University Press.

Bell, Daniel. 1976. *The Coming of Post-Industrial Society: A Venture in Social Forecasting*. New York: Basic Books.

Breen, Richard, and John H. Goldthorpe. 1999. Class Inequality and Meritocracy: A Critique of Saunders and an Alternative Analysis. *British Journal of Sociology*. 50 (1): 1–27.

Breen, Richard, and John H. Goldthorpe. 2002. Merit, Mobility and Method: Another Reply to Saunders. *British Journal of Sociology* 53 (4): 575–582.

Herrnstein, Richard J., and Charles Murray. 1994. *The Bell Curve: Intelligence and Class Structure in American Life*. New York: Free Press.

Huxley, Aldous. [1932] 1946. *Brave New World*. New York: Modern Library.

Kamolnick, Paul. 2005. *The Just Meritocracy: IQ, Class Mobility, and American Social Policy*. Westport, CT: Praeger.

McNamee, Stephen J., and Robert K. Miller Jr. 2004. *The Meritocracy Myth*. Lanham, MD: Rowman and Littlefield.

Oliver, Melvin L., and Thomas M. Shapiro. 1995. *Black Wealth/White Wealth: A New Perspective on Racial Inequality*. New York: Routledge.

Saunders, Peter. 1995. Might Britain Be a Meritocracy? *Sociology* 29 (1): 23–41.

Saunders, Peter. 1996. *Unequal but Fair? A Study of Class Barriers in Britain*. London: Institute of Economic Affairs.

Saunders, Peter. 1997. Social Mobility in Britain: An Empirical Evaluation of Two Competing Explanations. *Sociology* 31 (2): 261–288.

Young, Michael [1958] 1961. *The Rise of the Meritocracy, 1870–2033: An Essay on Education and Equality*. Baltimore, MD: Penguin.

Young, Michael. 1998. Meritocracy Revisited. *Society* 35 (2): 377–379.

Stephen McNamee

MERITOCRACY, MULTIRACIAL

Singapore is unusual among developed capitalist countries because its social system and its system of governance rest on the twin principles of multiracialism and meritocracy.

Multiracialism in this context is not the same as multiculturalism as it is usually understood. In Singapore, multiracialism refers to the conceptual division of society into discrete communal groups and the conviction that the only way to ensure peace, stability, and fairness between and among these groups is through close government management of communal relations and affairs. It is presumed that without heavy-handed interference the Chinese (76.8% of the population) would oppress the minority Malays (13.6%), Indians (8.7%), and others (2.1%), and that the minorities—especially the Muslim community (14.9%, mostly Malays)—would be a disturbing, if not a seditious, influence. Concerns about racial harmony are reinforced by the undisputed existence of a racial hierarchy in educational, professional, and financial achievement, in which Chinese lead, followed by Indians and then Malays.

R. Quinn Moore argued in 2000 that the operation of multiracialism has itself perpetuated and reinforced the communal divides by insisting that people see themselves and operate as members of their ethnic communities. This is achieved through the operation of race-and-religion-based self-help groups, race-based quotas in public housing estates, and language-cum-race-based allocation of resources and places in education (with Chinese receiving most resources). Michael D. Barr and Jevon Low went further in 2005, arguing that since the beginning of the 1980s the operation of multiracialism has acted as a cover for a deliberate policy of privileging the Chinese majority. They also argued that since about 1978 the nation-building mythology has been increasingly based on a Chinese-centered ethno-nationalism that the minorities can only mimic from the sidelines, and that this has replaced racially blind civic nationalism as the social foundation of the country.

Multiracialism operates in close harmony with meritocracy, between them assuring the minority communities that the system is fair to all regardless of race, religion, language, or socioeconomic background. The Singapore system of "meritocracy" rewards people on the basis of their academic performance in school. The government claims that selection into the economic, administrative, and political elites in adulthood is based on a level, "meritocratic" playing field, but these claims do not withstand close scrutiny. The socioeconomic status of one's parents is of tremendous importance in determining success in school, and scholars such as Lily Rahim (1998) have demonstrated unequivocally that there is no level playing field across ethnic boundaries, with Chinese children enjoying immense advantages.

It would be misleading, however, to suggest that this program sets out to create an economic or social underclass of minority races. Alongside discrimination in favor of the majority Chinese, the minorities are cajoled and coaxed to become more "like the Chinese" and so to share more fully in the fruits of this prosperous society. They are not under pressure to adopt the outward manifestations of being Chinese (diet, religion, language), but they are pressured to adopt a set of supposedly superior values that are routinely identified with Singapore's Chinese population: being materialistic, concerned with education as measured by grades and certificates, obsessively concerned with social mobility and, above all, being *kiasu*—a Chinese word meaning "afraid to lose." Children are pressured to immerse themselves in these values from nursery and kindergarten onward. Indian and Malay children who succeed under the system of meritocracy and who are successfully assimilated are appointed in adulthood as leaders of their communities, ensuring that the minorities are led by people who have a stake in maintaining the status quo.

Yet the irony is that even members of minority communities who immerse themselves in these values still suffer discrimination and marginalization because of their race, sometimes because of their ethnic dress (especially Muslim women wearing headscarves), and—most commonly—their language. Language is highly significant because this element arises as a direct result of the operation of multiracialism itself, whereby members of minority communities are generally not given an opportunity to learn Mandarin (the language of the dominant majority) in school and are forced to learn their racially ascribed mother tongue in an effort to reinforce their communal identities. These minority languages (Tamil and Malay) are of little economic value and make Indians and Malays vulnerable to social and economic exclusion from mainstream society (though the effects of this policy are diluted by the promotion of English as a lingua franca across the communal divide). Prime Minister Lee Hsien Loong, who took office in 2004, hoped to discourage discrimination in the workplace on the basis of race, dress, or language, but he was unwilling to consider an end to the language policies and the celebration of "Chinese values" that generated the problem in the first instance.

The Singapore example indicates how policies of assimilation and discrimination against ethnic minorities can be pursued in a modern capitalist society without either lapsing into overt persecution or provoking destabilizing reactions.

BIBLIOGRAPHY

Barr, Michael D., and Jevon Low. 2005. Assimilation as Multiracialism: The Case of Singapore's Malays. *Asian Ethnicity* 6 (3): 161–182.

Lai Ah Eng, ed. 2004. *Beyond Rituals and Riots: Ethnic Pluralism and Social Cohesion in Singapore*. Singapore: Eastern Universities Press.

Moore, R. Quinn. 2000. Multiracialism and Meritocracy: Singapore's Approach to Race and Inequality. *Review of Social Economy* 63 (3): 339–360.

Rahim, Lily Zubaidah. 1998. *The Singapore Dilemma: The Political and Educational Marginality of the Malay Community*. Kuala Lumpur and New York: Oxford University Press.

Michael D. Barr

MERRIAM, CHARLES EDWARD, JR.
1874–1953

Charles E. Merriam Jr. was a key figure in the development of the political science profession. He combined groundbreaking analytic, systematic, and objective social science approaches to research concerning pragmatic national and community problems. Merriam was professor of political science at the University of Chicago from 1900 to 1940, and emeritus after, and his chairmanship of that department from the early 1920s to 1940 laid the foundation for the behavioral movement in political science. This movement developed theoretical approaches based on principles of observation, hypothesis testing, and measurement to study individual and group political activities. Further, these systematic approaches to government activities led to an enhanced study of public administration. Both of these political science research areas—behavioral movement and public administration—remain prominent in political science studies.

He held many leadership roles in the political science profession, including president of the American Political Science Association (1925), cofounder and president of the Social Science Research Council (1924–1927), and cofounder of the Public Administration Clearinghouse in the first quarter of the twentieth century. The latter two organizations brought together a wide range of public and private experts to address critical societal issues.

Merriam argued that political science research should connect academic and practical matters to solve problems stemming from democratic political systems. His initial foray was in the realm of political thought through a study of the theory of sovereignty since Jean-Jacques Rousseau and studies in the development of U.S. political thought. Merriam focused on dimensions of political power ranging from political party leaders to public and private governing systems. These ideas led him to promote and conduct research on progressive ideas during the post–World War I era, such as reforming urban political machines, urban and regional planning, and democracy based upon citizen participation. His focus on and participation in urban politics, especially the rough-and-tumble politics of Chicago, enhanced his research in several areas of political science, such as political parties in the United States, the role of politics in social change, and public administration. His systematic understanding of politics and political change, based on new developing social science methodologies, was the basis of his research and often led to progressive prescriptions for civic reform and social change.

Merriam was a regular participant in public affairs, both in Chicago and in key national commissions during the Hoover, Franklin Roosevelt, and Truman presidencies. In Chicago he was an alderman and served on several investigating commissions that attempted to develop responsible governmental approaches to social programs that would replace corrupt government practices. Merriam relied on his progressive politics in an attempt to become mayor of Chicago, but he was defeated in the

1919 Republican mayoral primary. He applied these participatory experiences to understand complex interactions in the political process, especially how public administration practices affect governmental outcomes. Merriam's national prominence was enhanced by his service on President Hoover's Research Committee on Social Trends, President Franklin Roosevelt's National Resources Planning Board, and President Truman's Committee on Administrative Management (the Brownlow Commission). The latter commission held key debates concerning executive office reorganization. This national commission service allowed Merriam to apply political science research to central national issues and social change. He also sought to connect university research to public administration practices.

Merriam conducted a career that combined the development of an academic political science discipline, active citizen involvement, and proposals to reform of municipal and national government. In 1975 the American Political Science Association awarded its first Merriam Award, for "a person whose work and career represent a significant contribution to the art of government and social science research."

SEE ALSO *Chicago School*

BIBLIOGRAPHY

Karl, Barry D. 1974. *Charles E. Merriam and the Study of Politics.* Chicago: University of Chicago Press.

Merriam, Charles E. 1900. *History of Sovereignty since Rousseau.* New York: Columbia University Press.

Merriam, Charles E. 1920. *American Political Ideas: Studies in the Development of American Political Thought, 1865–1917.* New York: Macmillan.

Merriam, Charles E. 1925. *New Aspects of Politics.* Chicago: University of Chicago Press.

Merriam, Charles E. 1922. *The American Party System: An Introduction to the Study of Political Parties in the United States.* New York: Macmillan.

Merriam, Charles E., and Robert Merriam. 1945. *Systematic Politics.* Chicago: University of Chicago Press.

Steven Puro

MERTON, ROBERT K.
1910–2003

Robert K. Merton was the founder of the sociology of science and one of the twentieth century's most influential sociological theorists. Born Meyer R. Schkolnick to poor Jewish immigrants in South Philadelphia, Merton was part of an extraordinary generation of sociologists whose work shaped the basic contours of the discipline in the mid-twentieth century.

Merton eschewed the building of grand theoretical systems in favor of what he called "middle-range theories," explanations that transcend mere hypotheses, are designed to guide and be improved by empirical inquiry, and are potentially compatible with multiple larger theoretical systems. Thus, extending the idea of reference groups, he showed restricted interpersonal comparisons to be basic to judgments on a variety of matters from job satisfaction to educational choices, and to be no more specific to functional analysis than to Marxism. Likewise, the theory of bureaucracy originally introduced by Weber could be advanced by either structural or functional analysis. Merton emphasized the distinction between "manifest" and "latent" functions to clarify the contrast between analyzing intentions and consequences and to make functional analysis more precise. He also integrated analysis of social conflict into structural-functionalist analysis.

As a student at Harvard, Merton joined Talcott Parsons's first sociology seminar and participated alongside Parsons (and George C. Homans, Joseph Schumpeter, Crane Brinton, and Elton Mayo) in Lawrence J. Henderson's famed Pareto reading group. Pareto's idea of "motivating sentiments" was an enduring influence. Merton's main mentors, however, were Pitirim Sorokin and George Sarton. Under their tutelage, he helped found the sociology of science.

Merton argued that science is misunderstood as the product of individual geniuses able to break free from conventions and norms. Instead, he stressed the "ethos of science," the normative structure specific to the field that encouraged productivity, critical thinking, and pursuit of continually improved understanding. His dissertation, published as *Science, Technology and Society in Seventeenth Century England* (1938a), also introduced the famous "Merton thesis." Narrowly, this was that "Puritanism, and ascetic Protestantism generally, emerges as an emotionally consistent system of beliefs, sentiments and action which played no small part in arousing a sustained interest in science" (Merton 1938a, p. 495). More broadly, Merton argued that social and cultural factors (including religion, economics, and military pursuits) shaped interest in science, scientific problem choice, and the public reception and influence of science. He resisted, however, the relativist conclusion that such external influences so shaped the internal content of science as to undermine its truth value.

Working with his Columbia colleague Paul F. Lazarsfeld, Merton studied a range of policy questions from housing integration to medical education. He also carried out studies of propaganda and mass communications during World War II and wrote the classic *Mass*

Persuasion (1946). Merton and Lazarsfeld also played crucial institutional roles, training generations of students at Columbia and helping found the Center for Advanced Study in the Social and Behavioral Sciences.

Merton's contributions shaped not only the sociology of science and the general perspective of structural-functionalism but also a range of specific empirical fields, including the analysis of bureaucracy, deviance, and social psychology. He showed how social structure produced anomic responses in individuals whom the social structure deprived of resources for more normatively approved action and analyzed deviance as the pursuit of normative objectives by normatively disapproved means. In the course of his simultaneously theoretical and empirical analyses, Merton coined such now common phrases as "self-fulfilling prophecy," "role model," and "the unanticipated consequences of purposive social action" (1968, 1936).

Merton not only coined but studied memorable phrases and the patterns of association and evocation in which they were passed on—not least as they informed scholarly reference and the development of reputations. One of his most famous books traced the sentence "If I have seen farther it is by standing on the shoulders of giants" through centuries of use. The phrase was most commonly associated with Sir Isaac Newton, but what Merton showed with dazzling erudition and more than a few entertaining digressions was that the aphorism originated with Bernard of Chartres in the twelfth century. This corrected not only those who cited merely Newton but those who credited the phrase to ancient authors, including apparently nonexistent ancient authors, perhaps thinking thereby to accord it greater dignity and impress readers with their Latin references.

Merton continued to address the relationship between the first appearances of ideas and the occasions when they begin to have more serious influence, noting how many basic scientific advances were anticipated by "prediscoveries" that failed to change the way scientists thought. The role of chance connections—serendipity—in scientific breakthroughs became another enduring focus for Merton's boundless curiosity and careful scholarship (Merton and Barber 2004). But Merton was ambivalent about the many offspring of one of his own most famous innovations. With Marjorie Fiske and Patricia Kendall (1956), he invented the "focused group interview" that gave rise to the now ubiquitous and not always systematic focus groups of political and market research.

From the 1970s, the sociology of science turned in large part away from the study of institutions and toward microsociology of scientific practice. Many in the field were critical of Merton's emphasis on the norms of science because they saw these often violated. More generally,

structural-functionalism was challenged by a variety of perspectives placing greater stress on self-interest and conflict. Merton's work was often cited as emblematic of the now diverted "mainstream," though this was somewhat ironic because among leading functionalists he was particularly attentive to dysfunction, historical change, and conflict. Late in his life he worried that the approach of many in science studies was one-sidedly focused on debunking and sufficiently relativist that it made it hard to see the importance of the relative autonomy of science as a social institution.

SEE ALSO *Deviance; Functionalism; Lazarsfeld, Paul Felix; Pareto, Vilfredo; Parsons, Talcott; Persuasion; Propaganda; Role Models; Science; Social Science; Sociology*

BIBLIOGRAPHY

Merton, Robert K. 1936. The Unanticipated Consequences of Purposive Social Action. *American Sociological Review* 1 (6): 894–904.

Merton, Robert K. 1938a. Science, Technology and Society in Seventeenth Century England. *Osiris* 4: 360–632.

Merton, Robert K. 1938b. Science and the Social Order. *Philosophy of Science* 5 (3): 321–337.

Merton, Robert K. 1942. A Note on Science and Democracy. *Journal of Legal and Political Sociology* 1: 115–126.

Merton, Robert K. 1949. *Social Theory and Social Structure*. New York: Free Press, 1968.

Merton, Robert K. 1965. *On the Shoulders of Giants: A Shandean Postscript*. New York: Harcourt, Brace and World.

Merton, Robert K., and Elinor Barber. 2004. *The Travels and Adventures of Serendipity*. Princeton, NJ: Princeton University Press.

Merton, Robert K., with Marjorie Fiske and Alberta Curtis. 1946. *Mass Persuasion: The Social Psychology of a War Bond Drive*. New York: Harper.

Merton, Robert K., with Marjorie Fiske and Patricia Kendall. 1956. *The Focused Interview*. New York: Free Press.

Craig Calhoun

MESMER, FRANZ ANTON
SEE *Psychotherapy.*

MESO-AMERICA
SEE *Pre-Columbian Peoples.*

MESTIZO/MESTIZAJE

SEE *Blackness; Identification, Racial; Racial Classification.*

META-ANALYSIS

The American educational psychologist Gene V. Glass (1976) coined the term *meta-analysis* to stand for a method of statistically combining the results of multiple studies in order to arrive at a quantitative conclusion about a body of literature. The English statistician Karl Pearson (1857–1936) conducted what is believed to be one of the first statistical syntheses of results from a collection of studies when he gathered data from eleven studies on the effect of a vaccine against typhoid fever (1904). For each study, Pearson calculated a new statistic called the *correlation coefficient.* He then averaged the correlations across the studies and concluded that other vaccines were more effective than the new one.

Early work on quantitative procedures for integrating results of independent studies was ignored for decades. Instead, scholars typically carried out narrative reviews. These reviews often involved short summaries of studies considered "relevant," with the operational definition of that term usually based on arbitrary and unspecified criteria. Scholars would then arrive at an impressionistic conclusion regarding the overall findings of those studies, usually based largely on the statistical significance of the findings in the individual studies. This latter aspect of narrative reviews is especially problematic. Given that the findings from individual studies are based on samples, it is expected that they will vary from one another even if the studies are estimating the same underlying population parameter. Often, however, scholars misinterpreted expected sampling variability as evidence that the results of studies were "mixed" and therefore inconclusive. In addition, scholars generally did not think to account for the power of the statistical tests in their studies. In the social sciences, statistical power is often not high, resulting in an unacceptably high rate of Type II errors (i.e., the failure to reject a false null hypothesis). In a collection of studies with typical statistical power characteristics, ignoring power can lead to the appearance that the intervention has no effect even if it really does.

Further, narrative reviews were usually not conducted with the same level of explicitness as is required in primary studies. For example, scholars were rarely explicit about either the decision rules invoked in a review or the pattern of results across studies that would be used to accept or reject a hypothesis. In addition, narrative literature reviews typically could not impart a defensible sense of the magnitude of the overall relations they investigated, nor did they adequately account for potential factors that might influence the direction or magnitude of the relations.

The explosion of research in the social and medical sciences that occurred in the 1960s and 1970s created conditions that highlighted another of the difficulties associated with narrative reviews, specifically that it is virtually impossible for humans to make sense out of a body of literature when it is large. Robert Rosenthal and Donald Rubin (1978), for example, were interested in research on the effects of interpersonal expectancies on behavior and found over three hundred studies. Glass and Mary L. Smith (1979) found over seven hundred estimates of the relation between class size and academic achievement. Jack Hunter and his colleagues (1979) uncovered more than eight hundred comparisons of the differential validity of employment tests. It is not reasonable to expect that these scholars could have examined all of the evidence they uncovered and made decisions about what that evidence said in an unbiased and efficient manner.

Meta-analysis addresses the problem of how to combine and weight evidence from independent studies by relying on *effect sizes* and on statistical procedures for weighting research evidence. Effect sizes are statistics that express how much impact an intervention had (e.g., the average increase on an achievement test), and as such, they give reviewers a way to quantify both the findings from individual studies and the findings aggregated across a body of studies. Effect sizes can also be standardized to allow for comparisons between measures of the same outcome with different scaling properties (e.g., two different math achievement tests).

Effect sizes with known distribution properties can be weighted to arrive at a better estimate of the population parameter when they are combined. The most common method involves weighting each effect size by the inverse of its squared standard error. Using this method, larger studies contribute more to the analysis than do smaller studies. As such, a study with one hundred participants contributes more to the overall analysis than a study with ten participants. The rationale for this procedure is that the study with one hundred participants estimates the population effect more precisely (i.e., has less random variability) and is therefore a better estimate of that population effect.

To carry out a meta-analysis, an average of the weighted effect sizes is computed. A confidence interval can be placed around the weighted average effect size; if the confidence interval does not include zero, then the null hypothesis that the population effect size is zero can be rejected at the given level of confidence. In addition, scholars usually conduct a statistical test to assess the plausibility that the observed effect sizes appear to be drawn from the same population. If the null hypothesis of effect size homogeneity is rejected, then the reviewer has reasonable cause to conduct follow-up tests that attempt to localize the sources of variation. Generally, these correlational analyses attempt to relate variability in study outcomes to characteristics of interventions (e.g., intensity), as well as to study design, sampling, and measurement characteristics.

Finally, representing study results as weighted effect sizes allows scholars to conduct tests of the plausibility of *publication bias* on study results. Publication bias is the tendency for studies lacking a statistically significant effect not to appear in published literature. Therefore, these studies are more difficult to uncover during a literature search. All else being equal, studies that do not result in a rejection of the null hypothesis have smaller effects than those that do reject the null hypothesis. As such, failing to locate these studies at a rate similar to that of published studies means that the overall estimate arising from a body of studies might be positively biased. Several statistical methods (e.g., the trim-and-fill analysis) are available to help scholars assess the potential impact of publication bias on their conclusions.

SEE ALSO *Methods, Quantitative*

BIBLIOGRAPHY

Cooper, Harris, and Larry V. Hedges, eds. 1994. *Handbook of Research Synthesis*. New York: Russell Sage Foundation.

Glass, Gene V. 1976. Primary, Secondary, and Meta-analysis of Research. *Educational Researcher* 5: 3–8.

Glass, Gene V., and Mary L. Smith. 1979. Meta-analysis of Research on Class Size and Achievement. *Educational Evaluation and Policy Analysis* 1: 2–16.

Hunter, Jack E., Frank L. Schmidt, and R. Hunter. 1979. Differential Validity of Employment Tests by Race: A Comprehensive Review and Analysis. *Psychological Bulletin* 86: 721–735.

Lipsey, Mark W., and David B. Wilson. 2001. *Practical Meta-analysis*. Thousand Oaks, CA: Sage.

Pearson, Karl. 1904. Report on Certain Enteric Fever Inoculation Statistics. *British Medical Journal* 3: 1243–1246.

Rosenthal, Robert, and Donald Rubin. 1978. Interpersonal Expectancy Effects: The First 345 Studies. *Behavioral and Brain Sciences* 3: 377–415.

Jeffrey C. Valentine

METAPHOR

SEE *Symbols*.

METAPHYSICS

SEE *Philosophy; Reality*.

METHOD VARIANCE

SEE *Self-Report Method*.

METHOD OF MOMENTS

Both the method of moments and its generalization, namely the generalized method of moments (GMM), have taken a prominent place in statistical inference in the social sciences and have been applied in almost every field of economics, including asset pricing, business cycle, commodity market, education, and labor market. The (standard) method of moments consists of estimating a parameter β by equating sample moments with population moments and solving these equations for β. This method was introduced at the end of the nineteenth century by the British mathematician Karl Pearson and was partly abandoned when the British biologist Ronald Fisher (1890–1962) showed that the maximum likelihood estimator (MLE) is more efficient than the method of moments estimator because its variance is smaller. Since its introduction by Lars Peter Hansen in 1982, however, GMM has been extremely popular in economics for three reasons. The first reason is that economic models are often too complex to be completely specified and an attempt to describe the full model is likely to yield misspecification errors. GMM provides a way to estimate partially specified models. The second reason is that, even if the model is completely specified, MLE may be too cumbersome to implement, whereas GMM provides a practical method to perform inference. Finally, GMM embeds many familiar estimation techniques as special cases, including the method of moments, ordinary least squares, instrumental variables estimation, and even maximum likelihood estimation.

THE ESTIMATION METHOD

GMM may be illustrated in a time series context where observations $x_1, x_2, \ldots, x_T$ are available. Assume that for a given function g, the moment condition $E[g(x_t, \beta)] = 0$ holds for a unique solution β. To solve this equation, the population mean needs to be replaced by the sample mean $g_T(\beta) = \frac{1}{T} \sum_{t=1}^{T} g(x_t, \beta)$. Two cases are distinguished, depending on whether the dimension of g is the same as or larger than the dimension of β. In the first case (just identified), the equation $g_T(\beta) = 0$ can be solved to obtain the method of moments estimator of β. In the second case (overidentified), the previous equation does not have a solution and the standard method of moments needs to be modified. The GMM estimator is defined as the solution

$$b_T = \underset{\beta}{\arg\min}\, g_T(\beta)' W_T g_T(\beta)$$ where W_T is a positive definite matrix that attaches weights to moments. For any W_T, b_T is consistent, that is, it approaches the true value β as the sample size T grows. Additionally, the GMM estimator has minimal variance if W_T is an estimator of the inverse of the variance of $g_T(\beta)$.

In the overidentified case, $g_T(b_T)$ is not exactly equal to zero but should go to zero as T goes to infinity. This provides the basis for the overidentifying restrictions test. This test consists of rejecting the hypothesis that the moment conditions hold in the population if $T g_T(b_T)' W_T g_T(b_T)$ is greater than the critical value given by a chi-square distribution with degrees of freedom equal to the difference in the dimensions of g and β.

GMM provides a framework that encompasses most estimation techniques used in economics. Instrumental variables estimation, although a predecessor to GMM, can be recast as a special case of GMM. Consider the regression

$$y_t = x_t'\beta + \varepsilon_t$$

where x_t is endogenous, that is, correlated with the residual ε_t. As a consequence of endogeneity, the ordinary least squares estimator is not consistent. A consistent estimator, however, may be obtained by using a vector of so-called instruments z_t. To be a valid instrument, z_t must be correlated with x_t but not with the error ε_t. Then, β can be estimated by GMM using $g(y_t, x_t, z_t, \beta) = (y_t - x_t'\beta)z_t$. The resulting estimator is called the instrumental variables estimator.

MLE itself can be interpreted as a GMM estimator because the expectation of the derivative of the log-likelihood is equal to zero, giving rise to a moment condition.

To overcome computational difficulties, Daniel McFadden (1989) and Ariel Pakes and David Pollard (1989) have proposed the method of simulated moments (MSM), which consists of replacing population moments with moments computed from simulated data.

MIXED POPULATION EXAMPLE

Consider a population where each subject is equally likely to be a male or a female. We observe a measure x (for instance, the weight) but not the sex and we wish to estimate the difference between males and females. This is particularly relevant in anthropology where most fossil specimens lack indicators of sex. Assume that observations are normally independently distributed with mean μ_F and

variance σ^2 if the subject is a female and with mean μ_M and the same variance σ^2 if the subject is a male. The method of moments that matches the expectations of x, x^2, and x^4 with their sample counterparts permits to estimate μ_F, μ_M, and σ^2.

CONSUMPTION-BASED ASSET PRICING MODEL

Lars Peter Hansen and Kenneth Singleton (1982) explain how to apply GMM to estimate behavioral parameters of economic agents in a general equilibrium model, without having to describe the full economic environment. This approach may be used to study how agents allocate their spending. Consider an economy where a representative agent chooses consumption and investment plans so as to maximize $E\left[\sum_{i=0}^{\infty} \delta^i U(c_{t+i}) \mid \Omega_t\right]$, where c_t is consumption in period t, U is a utility function, δ is a discount factor, and Ω_t is the information at t. Maximization is performed under a budget constraint $c_t + p_t q_t = r_t q_{t-1} + w_t$ where w_t is the income, q_t the quantity of asset held at the end of period t, p_t the price of this asset, and r_t its return. The first order condition is

$$E\left[\delta \frac{r_{t+1}}{p_t} \frac{U'(c_{t+1})}{U'(c_t)} - 1 \mid \Omega_t\right] = 0.$$

Assume that $U(c_t) = (c_t^{\gamma} - 1)/\gamma$. The parameter of interest $\beta = (\delta, \gamma)$ may be estimated by GMM using

$$g(r_{t+1}, p_t, c_{t+1}, c_t, z_t, \beta) = \left(\delta \frac{r_{t+1}}{p_t}\left(\frac{c_{t+1}}{c_t}\right)^{\gamma-1} - 1\right)z_t$$

where z_t is a vector of instruments. Any element of Ω_t may be used as instrument, for example the constant and

$$\frac{r_{t+1-j}}{p_{t-j}}, \frac{c_{t+1-j}}{c_{t-j}}, j = 1, 2, \ldots, L.$$

DISCRETE CHOICE MODEL

Consider a model where each individual has the choice among J alternatives (for example, occupations or means of transportation). The individual chooses the alternative with the greatest value. The value u_{ij} of occupation j for individual i depends on a set of observed variables x_{ij} (such as sex, race, age, and education) so that $u_{ij} = x_{ij}\beta^j + \varepsilon_{ij}$ where $\varepsilon_j = (\varepsilon_{1j}, \varepsilon_{2j}, \ldots, \varepsilon_{nj})$ is normally distributed with mean zero and covariance matrix Σ. We observe that individual i chooses alternative j, if $u_{ij} \geq u_{il}$ for $l = 1, \ldots, J$. The probability of choosing alternative j, denoted by P_{ij}, involves a $J-1$ dimensional integral. If J is large, this integral is cumbersome to compute and hence maximum likelihood estimation is intractable. By contrast, P_{ij} can be estimated using simulations. Let ε_j^r, $r = 1, \ldots, R$ be independently drawn from a normal distribution with mean zero and covariance Σ, and let $u_{ij}^\gamma = x_{ij}\beta^j + \varepsilon_{ij}^\gamma$. Then, an estimate $\hat{P}_{ij}$ of P_{ij} is given by the proportion of cases where u_{ij}^γ exceeds u_{il}^γ for all l different from j. An MSM estimator of $(\beta^1, \beta^2, ..., \beta^J)$, is given by the solution to

$$\frac{1}{n}\sum_{i=1}^{n}\sum_{j=1}^{J} z_{ij}\left(y_{ij} - \hat{P}_{ij}\right) = 0$$ where z_{ij} is exogenous (equal to x_{ij}, for instance).

SEE ALSO *Inference, Statistical; Instrumental Variables Regression; Large Sample Properties; Pearson, Karl*

BIBLIOGRAPHY

Hansen, Lars Peter. 1982. Large Sample Properties of Generalized Method of Moments Estimators. *Econometrica* 50 (4): 1029–1054.

Hansen, Lars Peter, and Kenneth J. Singleton. 1982. Generalized Instrumental Variables Estimation of Nonlinear Rational Expectations Models. *Econometrica* 50 (5): 1269–1286.

McFadden, Daniel L. 1989. A Method of Simulated Moments for Estimation of Discrete Response Models without Numerical Integration. *Econometrica* 57(5): 995–1026.

Pakes, Ariel, and David Pollard. 1989. Simulation and the Asymptotics of Optimization Estimators. *Econometrica* 57 (5): 1027–1057.

Marine Carrasco

METHODOLOGY

The term *methodology* may be defined in at least three ways: (1) a body of rules and postulates that are employed by researchers in a discipline of study; (2) a particular procedure or set of procedures; and (3) the analysis of the principles of procedures of inquiry that are followed by researchers in a discipline of study. This entry will first discuss each of these definitions. It will then cover the debate among philosophers of science about general methodological assumptions. Finally, the entry will review some of the issues pertaining to the quantitative versus qualitative debate about methods.

A BODY OF RULES AND POSTULATES

Methodology refers to the behavior of scientists and scholars when examining phenomena relevant to their specific disciplines. The *American Heritage Dictionary* offers the following formal definition for *methodology:* "the theoretical analysis of the methods appropriate to a field of study or to the body of methods and principles particular to a branch of knowledge" (Pickett 2000, p. 2074). Methodology in the social sciences is usually characterized

by the following: (1) it defines the information to be analyzed; (2) it provides the conceptual tools and procedures necessary to perform an analysis; and (3) it sets forth the limits of the analysis. Methodology necessarily encompasses the three facets of exploration, description, and explanation (Babbie 2001, p. 91).

When scholars undertake research projects, they usually follow a well-defined procedure known as the *research process*. The research process begins when a researcher determines his or her research topic and formulates the research question or questions. For example, the research question of a social scientist could be: Are minority children in the United States more profoundly effected by poverty than their white counterparts? Once the research question has been determined, it is necessary to construct a study design. This is where the researcher decides the type of research to be undertaken. In the social sciences, there are two broad types of research: quantitative and qualitative. The former relies on numerical and statistical techniques and data garnered through the analysis of large groups of subjects. The latter often involves in-depth interviews that are designed to probe and produce extensive information about small numbers of subjects. Inductive and deductive reasoning also come into play when the researcher decides to follow a predetermined framework for the duration of the project (deduction), or instead formulates the research question and allows the remainder of the research to unfold as it may (induction). Once the researcher has decided which method to use, the next step is to collect the data. Finally, the data are analyzed, interpreted, and put into a format accessible to others.

Many of the social science subfields (e.g., economics, psychology, sociology, etc.) have developed specific models for the collection and organization of knowledge. Economics and psychology were the first to develop mathematical models of inquiry. Many subfields have borrowed heavily from one another. Beginning around 1970, a general system of models for all the social sciences was developed following guidelines proposed by the Social Science Research Council (Hekman 1980). The social sciences have also borrowed heavily from statistics, as is evident in the quantification of information obtained in the research process.

A PARTICULAR PROCEDURE OR SET OF PROCEDURES

The social sciences use an assortment of research methods. These include, but are not limited to, experiments, surveys, field research, content analysis, analysis of existing data, comparative research, and evaluative research (Mouton and Marais 1988). Each of these types of analysis needs to be systematized.

The first and most important step in any methodology is the formulation of the research question. It is with this step that the researcher determines the direction and approach of analysis. This step involves exploration, is crucial to understanding the topic, gives an idea of the feasibility of the research, and identifies the methods to be used (Babbie 2001, p. 92).

Once the researcher determines what the research will entail, it is then necessary to address the study design. During this step, the *unit of analysis* is determined. The unit of analysis is often an individual or group of individuals that is sampled from the larger population to which the researcher wishes to generalize his or her findings. For example, if one's research were to focus on the above question concerning whether American minority children are more profoundly effected by poverty than white children, the appropriate unit of analysis would be the child, and a sample of children would be drawn from the larger population of minority and white children. In this example, the use of quantitative methods would be most appropriate and would enable the researcher to develop generalizations about the general population.

However, even if the researcher chooses to use inductive methods, it would still be necessary to address many of the above issues. The study design portion of the process would involve determining sample size, who or what should be studied, and how the study would be conducted. Researchers must create a framework for their study for a number of reasons, including the need to coordinate the activities of more than one researcher and to obtain funding, among other things.

The next step in the research process is the collection of the data. This is accomplished according to the framework that has already been prescribed. In a quantitative study, researchers will most likely use a survey or some other type of questionnaire. In qualitative research, a list of questions would probably be employed, along with less-structured interviews. An important function of scientific inquiry is description. Qualitative studies in particular enable the researcher to describe situations and events in detail.

After the research data have been collected and organized, it is necessary to undertake the analysis. This may include statistical analyses of data gathered via quantitative methods, or more straightforward descriptive analyses of data obtained via qualitative methods. The data are then interpreted and summarized so the results of the research will be more accessible and available to others. Explanation is the natural by-product of research, and researchers hope that their projects provide information that answers the original research question.

ANALYSIS OF PRINCIPLES

All methodologies include a system of analysis that is used as a backdrop for organizing, collecting, and interpreting data. Data are usually systematized through either inductive and deductive reasoning. In most research projects, the system of analysis is determined in the first step of the research process because the researcher must at that point choose how he or she intends to collect data. Deductive reasoning begins with the idea that the researcher has a predetermined framework and uses it as a model to guide the research (Mouton and Marais 1988; Babbie 2001). Inductive reasoning, on the other hand, allows the researcher to begin a project with a general question but without a clear outline or framework.

METHODOLOGICAL ISSUES IN THE PHILOSOPHY OF SCIENCE

One of the major issues when conducting social science research is validity. Some argue that the social sciences do not deal in empirical fact and as such are not as valid as the so-called hard sciences. It is believed that researchers are human and can therefore never be fully objective. Max Weber (1864–1920) argued for value-free sociology and urged researchers to contribute information free from subjective opinions (Mouton and Marais 1988; Weber 1962). This is a central debate in social science research. Many researchers strive to separate research from value judgments, and the idea behind quantification within the social sciences is a nod toward value-free judgments. In fact, the idea of creating a methodology with clear procedures and principles is the embodiment of the necessity to make the social sciences more objective in the eyes of the public.

Approaches to methodology in the social sciences generally fall into three categories: positivist, interpretive, and critical social science. William Neumann writes that the positivist approach is the most widespread and is based on the methods of the natural sciences. In the social sciences, this approach was first used by Auguste Comte (1798–1857) and was later expanded by Émile Durkheim (1858–1917) (Neumann 2003; Smith 1983). The positivist approach is most strongly linked to the quantitative realm of social science research and strives for objectivity. It is argued that only when the social sciences follow the models prescribed by the natural sciences can the findings be valid and reliable. According to Neumann, *positivism* as it relates to social science can be defined as "an organized method for combining deductive logic with precise empirical observations of individual behavior in order to discover and confirm a set of probabilistic causal laws that can be used to predict general patterns of human activity" (2003, p. 71).

Interpretive social science originated with Max Weber and is focused on discovering the meaning behind social action. There are many facets of interpretivism, including hermeneutics, constructionism, ethnomethodology, and qualitative sociology. This school of thought argues that the social sciences cannot be analyzed using the methods of the natural sciences because they are inadequate for studying the meaning behind human behavior (Lee 1991). As stated previously, this approach focuses on meaning. As such, qualitative work is often considered an interpretive method. Neumann defines the interpretive approach as "the systematic analysis of socially meaningful action through the direct detailed observation of people in natural settings in order to arrive at understandings and interpretations of how people create and maintain their social worlds" (2003, p. 77).

Critical social science is associated with Karl Marx (1818–1883) and Sigmund Freud (1856–1939). Practitioners of this approach criticize the positivist approach for its inability to focus on meaning in the human context, and the interpretive approach for "being too subjective and relativist"(Neumann 2003, p. 81). Neumann defines this approach as "a critical process of inquiry that goes beyond surface illusions to uncover the real structures in the material world in order to help people change conditions and build a better world for themselves" (2003, p. 81).

QUANTITATIVE VERSUS QUALITATIVE ANALYSIS

Quantitative researchers are mostly concerned with measurement and sampling and often use deductive reasoning. In addition, it is important to identify facts and laws that can be used as predictive tools. In contrast, qualitative researchers tend to be more interested in content and use induction with more frequency (Neumann 2003). In this case, the meanings associated with human behavior are taken into consideration. Though quantitative and qualitative research differ in many ways, both types of research make important contributions that benefit the other. Quantitative research provides data in numerical form and allows for the manipulation of the data using statistical procedures. That information can then be combined with the descriptive data provided through qualitative research to provide more meaningful results.

Many social science researchers use both methods to provide fuller and more complete explanations. Indeed, since the 1980s, there has been a convergence of the two approaches, and many analyses use both methods (for examples in demography, see Massey 1987, 1990; and Knodel et al. 1987). The argument here is that qualitative research enriches purely quantitative research by filling in gaps created by the sole use of straightforward statistical

methods. On the other hand, quantitative research can enhance qualitative work by providing validity in the form of numbers. And qualitative work can enhance quantitative work by providing detail in the explanation of certain trends that is not possible through a strict analysis of the numerical data.

Qualitative methods examine social data without quantifying the data. Qualitative researchers often examine the links between theory and analysis and seek to discover general patterns among and between their variables. Some of the methods involved in qualitative research include grounded theory, semiotics, and conversation analysis (Mouton and Marais 1988). Qualitative researchers more frequently use an interpretive or critical approach and are interested in allowing the meaning of their work to develop as they conduct more research. They are further interested in using their research to explain and predict. Their data usually take the form of words, rather than numbers, and such researchers most often reason via induction (Neumann 2003).

In contrast, researchers using quantitative methods seek to transform the collected data numerically so the data can then be analyzed using statistical methods. Quantitative researchers most often use a positivist approach because accuracy is an important requirement. The data are first described using measures of central tendency, such as the mean, median, and mode. In most cases, the quantitative researcher next moves to multivariate analyses that examine several variables simultaneously. Quantitative research begins with the formulation of a research question and then a hypothesis or hypotheses. The researcher then identifies and operationalizes the desired variables, creates a standardized data set, defines procedures with which to analyze the data, and finally undertakes analysis using the statistical methods described above.

SEE ALSO *Quantification; Scientific Method*

BIBLIOGRAPHY

Babbie, Earl. 2001. *The Practice of Social Research.* 9th ed. Belmont, CA: Wadsworth/Thomson Learning. 10th ed., 2004.

Hekman, Susan. 1980. Phenomenology, Ordinary Language, and the Methodology of the Social Sciences. *Western Political Quarterly* 33 (3): 341–356.

Knodel, John, Aphichat Chamratrithirong, and Nibhon Debavalya. 1987. *Thailand's Reproductive Revolution: Rapid Fertility Decline in a Third-world Setting.* Madison: University of Wisconsin Press.

Lee, Allen S. 1991. Integrating Positivist and Interpretive Approaches to Organizational Research. *Organization Science* 2 (4): 342–365.

Massey, Douglas S. 1987. The Ethnosurvey in Theory and Practice. *International Migration Review* 21: 1498–1522.

Massey, Douglas S. 1990. Social Structure, Household Strategies, and the Cumulative Causation of Migration. *Population Index* 56: 3–26.

Mouton, Johann, and H. C. Marais. 1988. *Basic Concepts in the Methodology of the Social Sciences.* Trans. K. F. Mauer. Pretoria, South Africa: Human Sciences Research Council.

Neumann, William Lawrence. 2003. *Social Research Methods: Qualitative and Quantitative Approaches.* 5th ed. Boston: Allyn and Bacon.

Pickett, Joseph P., ed. 2000. *The American Heritage Dictionary of the English Language.* 4th ed. Boston: Houghton Mifflin.

Smith, John K. 1983. Quantitative versus Qualitative Research: An Attempt to Clarify the Issue. *Educational Researcher* 12 (30): 6–13.

Weber, Max. 1962. *Basic Concepts in Sociology.* Trans. H. P. Secher. New York: Citadel.

Ginny E. Garcia
Dudley L. Poston Jr.

METHODS, QUALITATIVE

Qualitative methodology is used by social scientists in the study of human behavior. This methodology may be used in addition to or in place of quantitative methods. The use of qualitative methods by social scientists allows the researcher to obtain a rich set of data that is not easily obtainable with the use of quantitative methods. Qualitative methods encompass a variety of methodologies, including observation, interviewing, document analysis, and archival document analysis.

OBSERVATION AND INTERVIEWING

Two key methods used in the social sciences are observation and interviewing. Observation involves the examination of research subjects in the natural social environment, with particular attention paid to the subject's behavior and actions. These observations are made firsthand by the researcher. An important element of observation is to study the subject's unmodified, natural behavior. Observational methods include several types of examination. Unobtrusive observation is one in which the researcher does not directly participate in the activities that are being observed. Unobtrusive measures are often used to prevent researcher influence on the subject's behavior. Participant observation allows the researcher to take part in the activities that are being observed and to gain familiarity with the subject's experiences. Researchers can become fully involved in the activities being observed

or they may observe activities they are involved in themselves.

Adrian Holliday, in "What Counts as Data" (2002), creates a schema of the different types of data that may be collected and the methods in which they are collected. Data may include description of (1) behaviors, in which the researcher describes the subject's behaviors and verbalizations; (2) events, in which the researcher or the subject involved in the event describes the behaviors observed; (3) institutions, in which the researcher describes the rules, regulations, or rituals of the institution; (4) appearance, in which the researcher describes how the environment or the subjects in the environment appear; (5) research events, in which the researcher describes what subjects say or how they behave in the research setting, such as those occurring in interviews; and (6) settings, in which the researcher describes what is actually occurring in a particular setting. These types of data can be obtained through observation notes, research diaries, photographs, or video recordings.

The use of observation as a method of research is valuable for several reasons. Observation allows the investigator to study human behavior as it naturally occurs, with or without the researcher's influence on the behavior. In other words, human activity is observed without the filtering effects of the subject's interpretation of their interactions.

Interviewing involves direct interaction between the investigator and the research subject. The investigator speaks directly with the subject asking questions related to a specific topical area. Interviews are generally recorded utilizing audiotapes, videotapes, or written notations. Interviewing may take the form of structured or semi-structured interviews.

Andrea Fonatna and James H. Frey, in "The Interview: From Structured Questions to Negotiated Text" (2000), note that structured interviewing allows the researcher to ask targeted questions of the research subjects. This form of interviewing consists of a prepared series of questions asked of all subjects. The subjects' responses are limited, leaving little room for variation among the answers. The questions are directed at obtaining answers to specific topics of interest for the researcher. Semi-structured interviewing, by contrast, allows for more freedom of discussion with the subject and aims for a greater understanding of the subject. Questions are prepared to prompt topical areas of dialogue. The goal of these questions is to allow the subject to expand upon the question and reveal information that cannot be achieved with a structured interview.

Interviews have several benefits to research. They allow the researcher to discover the meanings of experience that subjects create in relation to the research topics.

Interviews provide richer understandings of human behavior by providing real-life examples.

METHODS OF ANALYSIS

Document analysis and archival document analysis are two additional methods utilized in qualitative analysis. Document analysis entails the study of photographs, diaries, newspapers, government documents, books, memorandums, and other written documents. Archival document analysis involves the study of historical documents, including historical examples of those listed above. Importance is placed on analysis of original documents, as opposed to photocopies or other reproductions. While this method allows access to difficult study subjects such as historical figures or societal elites, the study of documents does not allow the investigator to speak to the individual who has created the document. This may lead the investigator to theorize the meanings of the documents and the motivations underlying their creation. These types of studies require the researcher to hypothesize the relationship of the document to the social environment of the time.

The analysis of qualitative data includes a variety of methods, including grounded theory, narrative analysis, and computer-based approaches. As Kathy Charmaz notes in "Grounded Theory: Objectivist and Constructivist Methods" (2000), grounded theory involves an ongoing analysis of the data as it is collected. The data are coded as they are collected and categories begin to emerge. With these categories, theories begin to develop related to the data. These then guide further data collection.

Narrative analysis focuses on the narratives, or stories and experiences, of subjects. Through narrative analysis the researcher endeavors to understand the meaning attached to the experiences of the subject. The researcher may also analyze the specific words employed to describe these experiences.

Computer-based analytic approaches look to the burgeoning World Wide Web for new research subjects. Innovative research is being conducted on subjects found in a variety of Internet communities and through a variety of methods, including online chat rooms, online or e-mail based interviews, and document-type analysis of Web sites. These approaches allow the investigator to contact communities of individuals with similar interests and individuals located outside the investigator's region or around the world.

RESEARCH VALIDITY, RELIABILITY, AND ETHICS

The use of qualitative methods, however, can be challenging in several respects. As Valerie Janesick notes in "The Choreography of Qualitative Research Design" (2000), qualitative researchers have struggled to address issues of validity and reliability. These terms are used primarily in the interpretation of quantitative data, yet qualitative researchers too are called upon to adhere to these standards of research.

For research to be considered valid it must actually measure what it proposes to measure, and the results should reflect the activity being studied. In other words, the data should accurately reflect the topic being studied. The notion of validity as it relates to qualitative methodology differs from its understanding in quantitative methodology. As Janesick contends, validity in qualitative research asks whether the description and the explanation fit. In an effort to achieve qualitative validity, researchers may permit participants to review the data for accuracy or ask a fellow researcher to do so.

For research to be considered reliable it must yield similar results in subsequent tests. Quantitative reliability is achieved when results are found to be consistent in subsequent tests. Unlike qualitative studies, quantitative reliability is determined through the use of mathematical equations to determine reliability, such as the determination of alpha. Qualitative tests are considered reliable when similar findings are achieved in subsequent tests. However, some debate exists as to whether reliability is pertinent in conducting qualitative studies, particularly since qualitative studies target the meanings and interpretations of experience by the subject and may involve investigator bias. One argument made by some researchers, including Caroline Stenbacka, is that, owing to the nature of qualitative studies and their aim at understanding rather than explaining human experience, the reliability of qualitative research is difficult to assess. Other researchers, such as James F. Davis, Robert Hagedorn, Morton B. King, Jerome Kirk and Marc L. Miller argue that a form of reliability is achievable in qualitative research.

Ethical issues are a concern when using qualitative methods. The protection of the research subject is of the highest priority. Ethical concerns include whether or not the subjects should know they are being observed, how investigator involvement may influence the behaviors under study, how the investigator-interviewee relationship may influence research results, and the bias involved in interpreting qualitative data, as well as protection of subjects' identities.

In particular, the influence of the investigator on responses given by a subject in interview has been an ongoing concern. Subjects may provide answers they believe the interviewer prefers rather than providing their own unique answers. Subjects may construct answers due to a lack of knowledge of the topical area. Interviewers may unintentionally influence the subject's answers through their body language, facial gestures, or other responses. As well as the information garnered from interviews is information that has been filtered and interpreted by both the subject and the researcher, calling into question the validity or reliability of the data obtained.

SEE ALSO *Ethnography; Methodology; Methods, Research (in Sociology)*

BIBLIOGRAPHY

Charmaz, Kathy. 2000. Grounded Theory: Objectivist and Constructivist Methods. In *Handbook of Qualitative Research.* 2nd ed. Eds. Norman K. Denzin and Yvonna S. Lincoln, 509–535. Thousand Oaks, CA: Sage Publications.

Crittenden, Kathleen S., and Richard J. Hill. 1971. Coding Reliability and Validity of Interview Data. *American Sociological Review* 36 (6): 1073–1080.

Davis, F. James, and Robert Hagedorn. 1954. Testing the Reliability of Systematic Field Observations. *American Sociological Review* 19 (3): 345–348.

Ellis, Carolyn, and Arthur P. Bochner. 2000. Autoethnography, Personal Narrative, Reflexivity: Researcher as Subject. In *Handbook of Qualitative Research.* 2nd ed. Eds. Norman K. Denzin and Yvonna S. Lincoln, 751. Thousand Oaks, CA: Sage Publications.

Fonatna, Andrea, and James H. Frey. 2000. The Interview: From Structured Questions to Negotiated Text. In *Handbook of Qualitative Research.* 2nd ed. Eds. Norman K. Denzin and Yvonna S. Lincoln, 649–651. Thousand Oaks, CA: Sage Publications.

Holliday, Adrian. 2002. What Counts as Data? In *Doing and Writing Qualitative Research.* Thousand Oaks, CA: Sage Publications.

Janesick, Valerie. 2000. The Choreography of Qualitative Research Design. In *Handbook of Qualitative Research.* 2nd ed. Eds. Norman K. Denzin and Yvonna S. Lincoln, 379–399. Thousand Oaks, CA: Sage Publications.

King, Morton B., Jr. 1944. Reliability of the Idea-Centered Question in Interview Schedules. *American Sociological Review* 9 (1): 57–64.

Kirk, Jerome, and Marc L. Miller. 1986. *Reliability and Validity in Qualitative Research.* Beverly Hills, CA: Sage Publications.

Stenbacka, Caroline. 2001. Qualitative Research Requires Quality Concepts of Its Own. *Management Decision* 39 (7): 551–556.

Gabriela Guazzo

METHODS, QUANTITATIVE

In the social sciences, quantitative research can be defined as any research that uses numbers as the basis for making inferences about the phenomenon under study. The hallmarks of quantitative research are control over extraneous influences (often involving experimental manipulation) and, more generally, statistical approaches to sampling, measurement, and data analysis. However, the simplicity of this general definition does not do justice to the full range of methodologies and data-analysis strategies that fall under the umbrella of quantitative research.

The goals of research represent a convenient way to discuss different types of quantitative research. Researchers employ a *descriptive research* strategy when they are interested in a numerical description of an object, event, or situation. For example, if a scholar were interested in the average class size of elementary schools in Spain, he or she might design a survey asking about the number of students and the number of classrooms (possibly among other variables) and send that survey to every elementary school in Spain. That researcher might also be interested in describing patterns of class sizes across different countries and parts of the world. Researchers employ a *relational research* strategy when they are interested in the extent to which two or more variables tend to co-occur. For instance, the scholar interested in class sizes may also be interested in the relationship between class size and the socioeconomic status of the neighborhood from which the students are drawn. One way to answer this question would be to survey schools and determine their average class size and the socioeconomic status of the surrounding neighborhood. The researcher could then compute a correlation coefficient that describes the magnitude of this relationship. Researchers employ an *experimental research* strategy when they are interested in causal relations. For example, a scholar might be interested in whether or not reducing class sizes will increase student achievement. One way to answer this question would be to randomly assign classrooms to be rather small or rather large, then measure student achievement after an appropriate interval of time. The performance of students in the smaller classes can then be compared to the performance of students in the larger classes.

A second useful distinction implied by the discussion above is between experimental and nonexperimental quantitative research. Experimental research is typified by the manipulation of a variable. For most questions that interest social scientists, the best way to explore the effects of manipulating a variable involves randomly assigning study participants to different levels of the variable, such as by randomly assigning a teacher to have a relatively large or a relatively small number of students. Nonexperimental research lacks this essential feature (and may not even involve a group comparison at all). In the social sciences, a common type of study known as a quasi-experiment bridges these two categories. The quasi-experiment shares many features with an experiment yet does not involve random assignment of study participants. In the class size example, teachers may choose to teach smaller or larger classes, school principals may choose which teachers teach which classes, and so on.

A final distinction evident in quantitative research is between cross-sectional and longitudinal research. Cross-sectional research involves participants at one point in time (e.g., immediately before a political election). Longitudinal research involves participants at multiple points in time. An example of cross-sectional research is the political poll in which voters are surveyed for their preferences one time. In a longitudinal approach, researchers assess participants at multiple points in time. For example, researchers might identify likely voters one year before an election and track their expressed preferences one time a week until the election occurs. Cross-sectional research, therefore, provides a snapshot of participants at a single point in time, while longitudinal research allows for an analysis of change over time.

The branch of mathematics known as statistics is widely employed in quantitative research. Statistics is relevant to quantitative approaches to social science in three major ways. First, researchers rarely work with entire populations (e.g., all elementary students in a country), as these are generally too large to study. Instead, researchers work with samples, and statistics provides a way of quantifying the expected range of differences between a randomly drawn sample and the population. This is best illustrated in political polling, for example, when researchers telephone a random sample of households to assess voting intentions. Results are then reported in terms of the percentage of respondents who endorsed each candidate. They are accompanied by a "margin of error" that expresses the expected range of the differences between the actual sample of respondents and the population from which the sample was drawn.

A second major use of statistics in quantitative research is in group comparisons. In the effects of class size on academic achievement example above, the academic performance of students in small classrooms would be compared to the academic performance of students in larger classrooms. A statistical test (such as a t-test or an analysis of variance) could be conducted to assess whether the group averages differ more than would be expected if the groups differ only because of chance (that is, if class size does not affect student achievement).

A third major use of statistics in quantitative research involves statistical modeling of the interrelationships between variables. For instance, a clinical psychologist might be interested in how client personality, therapist personality and skill, and the quality of the relationship between the client and the therapist all work to affect the client's mental health. The psychologist might postulate a theoretical model involving these variables. Then, the psychologist would collect data on these variables and use techniques (such as structural equation modeling) to determine if the observed pattern of interrelations fits the theoretical model.

Quantitative research is often contrasted with qualitative research. The latter overlaps somewhat with descriptive approaches to quantitative research, but instead of resulting in numerical and statistical descriptions, qualitative research often is presented in narrative form. Historically, the distinction between qualitative and quantitative research created a rift among social scientists. At the extremes, quantitative social scientists have argued that a question is not truly scientific unless it can be formulated in mathematical or statistical terms, while qualitative social scientists have argued that quantitative approaches are too crude and can therefore never result in valid knowledge. Neither of these extreme views reflects the practice of scientists in other scientific disciplines (such as biology), and most modern social scientists believe that qualitative and quantitative methods can complement one another (Kuhn 1961). This recognition is reflected in the growing use of so-called "mixed method research," in which both qualitative and quantitative methods are employed in the same research study (see Tashakkori and Teddlie 2003).

SEE ALSO *Data; Data, Longitudinal; Experiments; Methodology; Methods, Qualitative; Methods, Research (in Sociology); Polling; Polls, Opinion; Regression; Regression Analysis; Social Science; Statistics; Structural Equation Models; Survey; Test Statistics*

BIBLIOGRAPHY

Kuhn, Thomas S. 1961. The Function of Measurement in Modern Physical Science. *Isis* 52 (2): 161–193.

Shadish, William R., Thomas D. Cook, and Donald T. Campbell. 2002. *Experimental and Quasi-experimental Designs for Generalized Causal Inference*. Boston: Houghton Mifflin.

Tashakkori, Abbas, and Charles Teddlie, eds. 2003. *Handbook of Mixed Methods in Social and Behavioral Research*. Thousand Oaks, CA: Sage Publications.

Jeffrey C. Valentine

METHODS, RESEARCH (IN SOCIOLOGY)

Various sociological methodologies are used when designing and executing research. Each of these methods, including comparative-historical sociology, ethnomethodology, ethnography, evaluation research, qualitative methods, and survey research, has strengths and weaknesses. While debate surrounds qualitative versus quantitative methods, the best sociological research often integrates both kinds of methods to test hypotheses.

COMPARATIVE-HISTORICAL SOCIOLOGY

Most nineteenth-century social scientists, including Emile Durkheim, Herbert Spencer, and Karl Marx, engaged in analyses of historical data and made cross-cultural comparisons in their studies of human society. The work of these early historical sociologists was guided by the belief that societies were evolving and that the western European societies were the most advanced. The premise was that societies progressed via evolution and that progress was good. Comparisons were used as a tool for the development of social facts based on cross-cultural and/or historical data. In modern times cross-cultural comparisons serve to provide a better understanding of the structures and institutions of different societies.

The primary strength of comparative-historical research is its use of an interdisciplinary approach. If the scope conditions are clear and the criteria are specified and defined, then this approach is an important method for obtaining "social facts."

Data available for cross-cultural and historical analyses face multiple hurdles. To illustrate, one must remember that information from a culture is embedded in the language, status sets, and expectations for the use of the data, as well as the time and place where the data were collected. There is always the issue of making sure that data sets are comparable and that the variables are equivalent. One primary limitation noted by Etienne Van de Walle (2005) is that although historical demographers have access to volumes of information, they are frequently limited by only including information on elite male populations with little or no information about females or the common man.

QUALITATIVE METHODS AND ETHNOGRAPHY

The primary qualitative methods sociologists use are ethnography interviews and direct observations. Interviews with research participants may range from open-ended interviews with flexible content directed by the interviewer to more structured questions asked by multiple researchers; in the latter case there is an obvious requirement for internal consistency so that all interviewers ask the same questions in the same way, and hopefully obtain comparable data. Researchers engaged in direct observations may have varying levels of participation, ranging from covert observation to participant observa-

tion where the researcher becomes an active member of the group.

Many ethnographers agree that to fully understand a complex social situation, one must enter into an unbiased observation or interaction with the society being studied. William Foote Whyte (1955) argued in his classic *Street Corner Society: The Social Structure of an Italian Slum*, that the only way to describe a society is to live in it, learn to speak the language, and participate in its social events and everyday life. Some of the most well known ethnographies have been guided by similar principles, for example, Elliott Liebow's *Tally's Corner* (1967), Margery Wolf's *The House of Lim* (1968), and Laud Humphrey's *Tearoom Trade* (1975), to mention only a few. A quantitative counting using preconceived survey questions only provides answers to the questions and could well be biased by the selection process as well as by the perceived social desirability of the responses by the researcher. In contrast, a qualitative analysis provides detailed description and information and new perspectives necessary for hypothesis development. An issue that should be addressed is the role of the researcher in the ethnographic research and whether or not an external observer can really study the internal workings of a society without bias. Also, a weakness of ethnographic field studies is generalization. But this weakness is often resolved by integrating the qualitative results of the fieldwork with quantitative results obtained in research in which a large population is systematically and randomly sampled and surveyed (see the work of Knodel, Chamratrithirong, and Debavalya [1987] as an example of such integration).

ETHNOMETHODOLOGY

The term *ethnomethodology* was first used in the 1960s by Harold Garfinkel (1967) in research determining how people make sense of their worlds. Garfinkel noted that for interactions to be smooth, everyday communication and interpersonal interactions have to be based on prior assumptions. Ethnomethodologists commonly study the normal through the use of techniques such as conversation analysis and breaching experiments, which force an examination of the usual, accepted, and unquestioned. The documented reactions of others to these experiments confirm which behaviors are normative (Cohen 2006).

The strength of ethnomethodology is that it permits the researcher to analyze the normal. For example, Allen Smith and Sherry Kleinman (1989) use narratives to demonstrate the patterns of discourse in conversations, which can be used to train medical personnel in the delivery of bad news and desexualizing gynecological exams. The weakness is that assumptions about what is normal and what is expected are in continual flux so that generalizability is sometimes limited.

EVALUATION RESEARCH

Organizational sociologists, following a long-standing positivistic agenda, often use evaluation research to determine whether the programs and routines of such groups as corporate organizations, social agencies, and educational institutions actually perform as planned. Evaluation research techniques involve formative research; setting the agenda, goals, and strategies for the organization; determining how these can be quantified and hence evaluated; and summative evaluation, determining if these quantifiable outcomes of both the steps and the goals meet the predetermined standards. Evaluation researchers usually use multiple techniques, including ethnography and survey instruments (see Rossi, Lipsey, and Freeman 2003). The strength of evaluation research is that it is used to minimize expenses while improving the quality of the accepted standards set by formative research. One weakness is that organizations have multiple systems and the research may not target the critical part of the systems. Organizations are in continual flux so that their evaluations must be ongoing and easily modifiable to respond to changing conditions.

SURVEY RESEARCH

Survey research involves the "systematic gathering of information on a defined social group" (Rapley and Hansen 2006, p. 616). The group is typically sampled from a larger population; information is obtained by asking standard questions about previously operationalized variables. One reason for the use of survey research is its simplicity; if one wants to know information, ask. Questions may be either closed-ended or open-ended. The strengths of the analysis and the generalizations from the findings are determined in part by the sample size and selection. Samples may range from small convenience samples to large randomized representative samples. Surveys may be administered via interviews, mailed questionnaires, telephone calls or online. Don Dillman (2000) argues that mail surveys using the "tailored design method," a detailed methodology of multiple contacts ensuring compliance, often have the greatest likelihood of being understood, completed, and returned; these are all characteristics necessary for the survey results to be truly representative of the population.

Surveys are usually used after one has developed hypotheses to be tested quantitatively. The best-known surveys have an efficient methodology and obtain accurate and current information about the population. Examples include the U.S. Current Population Survey, the World Fertility Surveys, and the U.S. National Surveys of Family Growth.

A strength of survey research, if done correctly, is its potential for strong and generalizable statistical analysis. However, the best surveys require randomization, ade-quate sample size, and a high completion rate. It must be remembered, however, that survey methods provide only a "partial description of complex social issues.... They are but one tool, of many, in the [social scientist's] armamentarium" (Rapley and Hansen 2006, p. 617).

SEE ALSO *Chicago School; Communication; Conversational Analysis; Discourse; Ethnography; Ethnomethodology; Hypothesis and Hypothesis Testing; Methods, Qualitative; Methods, Quantitative; Observation, Participant; Positivism; Sampling; Sociology; Survey; Tally's Corner*

BIBLIOGRAPHY

Agar, Michael. 1996. *The Professional Stranger: An Informal Introduction to Ethnography*. New York: Academic Press.

Cohen, Ira. 2006. Ethnomethodology. In *The Cambridge Dictionary of Sociology*, ed. Bryan S. Turner, 177–180. New York: Cambridge University Press.

Garfinkel, Harold. 1967. *Studies in Ethnomethodology*. Englewood Cliffs, NJ: Prentice-Hall.

Denzin, Norman K., and Yvonna S. Lincoln. 1994. *Handbook of Qualitative Research*. Thousand Oaks, CA: Sage Publications.

Dillman, Don A. 2000. *Mail and Internet Surveys: The Tailored Design Method*, 2nd ed. New York: Wiley.

Fowler, Floyd J. Jr. 1995. *Improving Survey Questions: Design and Evaluation*. Thousand Oaks, CA: Sage Publications.

Humphreys, Laud. 1975. *Tearoom Trade: Impersonal Sex in Public Places*. Chicago: Aldine.

Knodel, John, Aphichat Chamratrithirong, and Nibhon Debavalya. 1987. *Thailand's Reproductive Revolution*. Madison: University of Wisconsin Press.

Liebow, Elliot. 1967. *Tally's Corner: A Study of Negro Streetcorner Men*. Boston: Little and Brown.

Rapley, Mark, and Susan Hansen. 2006. Surveys. In *The Cambridge Dictionary of Sociology*, ed. Bryan S. Turner, 616–617. New York: Cambridge University Press.

Rossi, Peter, Mark W. Lipsey, and Howard E. Freeman. 2003. *Evaluation: A Systematic Approach*, 7th ed. Thousand Oaks, CA: Sage Publications.

Smith, Allen C., and Sherry Kleinman. 1989. Managing Emotions in Medical School: Students' Contacts with the Living and the Dead. *Social Psychology Quarterly* 52: 56–69.

Van de Walle, Etienne. 2005. Historical Demography. In *The Handbook of Population*, eds. Dudley L. Poston, Jr., and Michael Micklin, 577–600. New York: Kluwer Academic/Plenum Publishers.

Whyte, William Foote. 1955. *Street Corner Society: The Social Structure of an Italian Slum*. Chicago: University of Chicago Press.

Wolf, Margery. 1968. *The House of Lim: A Study of a Chinese Farm Family*. Englewood Cliffs, NJ: Prentice-Hall.

Mary Ann Davis
Dudley L. Poston Jr.

METHODS, SURVEY

A survey is a data collection instrument that generates data through the responses provided by respondents to survey questions. Some researchers connect the term *sample* with the term *survey*, arguing that the primary use of surveys is to draw inferences about a population from whom a sample of respondents have been surveyed. Surveys administered to relatively small, random samples permit the drawing of inferences about large populations.

HISTORY

According to Jean Converse's *Survey Research in the United States* (1987), historians generally believe the first surveys were used by governments in order to know who to tax and who to draft into military service. Later surveys were used to document conditions of poverty, using open-ended questions and convenience samples. In the early twentieth century, opinion polls were conducted by newspaper organizations; again convenience samples were employed.

As interest developed in measuring opinions and other subjective states, surveyors became interested in question wording. Since the 1930s, systematic efforts have been made to develop questions and answer choices on questionnaires that are relevant, understandable, and unambiguous.

Types of data collected by sample surveys include, for example: beliefs, attitudes, values, resource possession, socioeconomic status, time use, characteristics of members of social networks, and self-reports of behavior. Surveys frequently contain scales of items designed to measure concepts that are multidimensional. Many of these scales have been validated in prior research and have a solid track record in terms of reliability. Survey data also lend themselves to sophisticated types of statistical analyses.

All surveys, however, contain a certain amount of error. The term *measurement error* refers to those errors directly associated with the questions in the questionnaire. Two types of measurement error exist: systematic error (the respondent falsely reports drinking alcohol infrequently) and random error (a fatigued respondent mistakenly checks the wrong answer to a question).

TYPES OF SURVEYS

The variety of survey modes include: (1) self-administered questionnaires; (2) telephone and other communication-assisted interviewing surveys; and (3) personal or face-to-face interviews. These types differ in terms of the amount of motivation a respondent must have in order complete a given survey, cost, research staff requirements, and length and complexity. Personal interviews, for example, can be longer and more complex than self-administered questionnaires. Additional complexity is added to this picture by means of technological intermediary delivery devices, such Internet/Web site surveys and computer-assisted interviewing. In addition, mixed mode surveys, which use two or more survey types, are used to increase response rates across differing subpopulations and across differing data collection needs. Thus some respondents fill out questionnaires while others are interviewed by telephone or in person. Mixed modes can be used with the same respondents in which, for example, subjects are interviewed about their health and other topics and then those subjects are asked to maintain a time diary over a several-day period. Optical scanning technology permits wider-scale distribution of surveys because of the labor savings this type of survey represents.

The type of survey employed depends on factors such as: (1) cost; (2) goals of the survey; (3) length and complexity of the instrument; and (4) accessibility of the population (related to cost). Personal interviews require trained, well-paid interviewers. Such skilled labor is relatively expensive when compared with minimum wages offered student workers on college campuses, a frequent source of interviews for university surveys.

Surveys are conducted by individuals and research teams; often these surveys are conducted with a small sample, limiting generalization to larger populations. At the same time, federally funded national surveys have increased in number since the mid-twentieth century; these surveys are conducted across multiple points in time making possible longitudinal studies and panel studies. The General Social Survey (GSS) has provided data on key social issues since 1972. The Current Population Survey (CPS), an excellent data source regarding employment issues, has collected data each quarter of every year since 1937. A time expenditure recall has been added to the CPS in order to study trends in time use. Other surveys provide data on crime victimization (National Crime Victimization Survey), families (National Survey of Families and Households), and health (National Health Interview; National Health and Nutrition Examination Survey).

OPEN-ENDED QUESTIONS VERSUS CLOSE-ENDED QUESTIONS

Researchers are often unsure as to what answer choices to a given question provide the full range of possible valid answers. In addition, the provision of such answers by the researchers is thought by some to bias the answer chosen by respondents. Under such circumstances, open-ended questions are utilized. Such questions inquire but provide no guidance as to what the researcher considers an acceptable answer. The weaknesses associated with open-ended questions include: respondents must be highly motivated in order to fully access their thoughts; and respondents may ask for assistance in order for them to provide an answer. At this point the interviewer is trained in probing, a technique designed to guide the respondent toward an answer. However, if the probing comes across in a directive manner, the respondent may be biased toward providing an answer that does not represent his or her answer. There is also debate over the issue of standardized interviewing, during which the interviewer is required to stick to the "survey text" as written, versus flexible interviewing, which permits the interviewer to diverge from the survey text and reword the question when respondents are unable to understand a given question.

LIMITATIONS

Early-twenty-first-century criticism observes that respondent attitudes often conflict with societal norms. One of the issues is the discrepancy between the liberal attitudes that respondents frequently express toward ethnic groups and the behavior shown by, for example, whites toward blacks. Social desirability bias may lead to this discrepancy. Equally plausible is the observation from social psychology that norms may conflict with attitudes unless those norms result from membership in a salient in-group, according to Katherine White and her colleagues in their 2002 study. Eduardo Bonilla-Silva, in his work *Racism without Racists* (2003), suggests the most important reason is that while it is less socially acceptable to express "prejudicial attitudes," whites discriminate against minority groups when their material interests are threatened. Other problems relate to cognitive issues such as memory; respondents typically have difficulty remembering details regarding mundane activities such as eating and remembering activities that have taken place over longer time periods. Much experimental work is taking place in universities and other research settings in order to reduce survey error, including enhancing memory and reducing social desirability bias. Other problems have to do with response rates: people are less willing than in the past to participate in survey research.

THE ISSUE OF CAUSALITY

Social scientists, including those who test hypotheses using survey data, are frequently accused of making causal claims inappropriately. Surveys are most often used in a cross-sectional setting; that is data is collected from the respondent at one point in time. In his research published in 2004, Andrew Abbott describes this in terms of "vision of causality quite dominant in U.S. quantitative research … arrays causes by their impact on that outcome, explicitly separating the immediate from the distant both in social time and social space" (Abbott 2004, p. 398). At the

same time, survey data can be collected over time, which allows the study of change over time. A number of large-scale surveys, including the General Social Survey and the Current Population Survey, permit such studies.

Time (temporal process) and context are frequently not captured by survey instruments. However, certain aspects of time can be captured by having respondents maintain time diaries. The Current Population Survey includes a twenty-four-hour time recall. In addition, survey data may be supplemented with information from other data sources (observations made of groups and neighborhoods; secondary data sources such as the Census of Population) that describe the group, neighborhood, and societal context, as multilevel statistical models have demonstrated.

Surveys generally fail to tap issues that may be salient to the researcher's goals, but are not captured in the survey's questions. Qualitative methods including participant observation and open-ended interviewing offer a means for capturing those issues. In some studies, researchers begin with open-ended interviews and then use information (respondents' word choices; issues that are important to respondents) to construct a survey instrument. Surveys also fail to capture historical context. To some degree this problem can be alleviated by use of historical materials (including census and other surveys done in the past) to place survey findings in a broader context.

THE FUTURE OF SURVEYS

With the development of new national surveys designed to study socioeconomic circumstances and other aspects of society, the prospects for the availability of national level data, collected given time periods, are good. Survey methodology continues to reduce survey error, as Robert M. Groves and Don Dillman describe in their works. Other trends suggest problems for survey researchers: refusal rates to traditional types of surveys have increased over time. The technology-assisted techniques, while offering new avenues for obtaining data from hard-to-reach respondents, appear to have a poor track record in terms of response rate.

SEE ALSO *Data; Methods, Qualitative; Methods, Research (in Sociology); Survey*

BIBLIOGRAPHY

Abbott, Andrew. 2004. Process and Temporality in Sociology: The Idea Outcome in Sociology. In *The Politics of Method in the Human Sciences: Positivism and Its Epistemological Others*, ed. George Steinmetz. Durham, NC: Duke University Press.

Bonilla-Silva, Eduardo. 2003. *Racism without Racists: Color-Blind Racism and the Persistence of Racial Inequality in the United States.* New York: Rowan and Littlefield.

Converse, Jean. 1987. *Survey Research in the United States: Roots and Emergence.* Berkeley: University of California Press.

Dillman, Don A. 2000. *Mail and Internet Surveys: The Tailored Design Method.* 2nd ed. New York: John Wiley and Sons.

Groves, Robert M., Floyd J. Fowler Jr., Mick P. Couper, et al. 2004. *Survey Methodology.* Hoboken, NJ: Wiley.

House, James S., F. Thomas Juster, Robert L. Kahn, et al. 2004. *A Telescope on Society: Survey Research and Social Science at the University of Michigan and Beyond.* Ann Arbor: University of Michigan Press.

White, Katherine M., Michael A. Hogg, and Deborah J. Terry. 2002. Improving Attitude-Behavior Correspondence through Exposure to Normative Support from a Salient Ingroup. *Basic and Applied Social Psychology* 24 (2): 91–103.

Wm. Alex McIntosh

METHUEN TREATY
SEE *Corn Laws.*

METONYM
SEE *Symbols.*

METROPOLIS

The term *metropolis* refers to a giant city, an urban center that supersedes its more provincial counterparts in population, economic strength, and political influence. One remarkable ancient model was Megalopolis, built in Arcadia between 371 and 368 BCE. The giant city, both as an urban form and an idea, runs through much of recorded history. The Babylon metaphor—known from the Old Testament and frequently applied to the "New Babylons" of the nineteenth and twentieth centuries—describes a place of total chaos and disorder. The persistence of the image indicates the relevance of the negative connotation attached to the notion of a metropolis; it is a "parasitic city," a dangerous entity that rules society without contributing to its wealth and stability. At the same time, throughout its historical existence the giant city has had an enormous—and beneficial—impact on the national or imperial area surrounding it. Often three, four, or even ten times larger than the second largest city in the state or empire, the geographers' "primate city" invariably becomes the driving force behind economic and cultural innovation. The European metropolises of the early modern and modern era in particular may end up exercising the same positive influence as did London in the sixteenth and seventeenth, Paris in the nineteenth, and Los Angeles in the twentieth centuries—by effectively shaping aesthetic taste and mass consumption patterns worldwide. This is precisely what happened when an urban center such as New York City after the Civil War became, in the words of Lewis Mumford, "an imperial metropolis, sucking into its own whirlpool the wealth and the wreckage of the rest of the country, and of the lands beyond the sea" (Mumford 1945, p. 28). The global influence, however, often goes hand in hand with negative consequences. A case in point is again New York, a financial force capable, in 1929, for example, of threatening the economic stability of the entire world.

The metropolis as a "primate city" gains its disproportionate size and enhanced importance by sharply separating itself from, and standing above, all other cities in the area. However, it maintains close ties with giant cities whose territories are even more extensive. The metropolises, seeing themselves as "world cities"—the term originated in nineteenth-century Germany—tend to form interregional and supranational communication networks. The idea of the metropolis as the physical representation of an entire universe (Jerusalem, Rome) has always been an important part of the way these centers are perceived and thought about. In the age of the Industrial Revolution, for example, the term *Industrial City* was generally applied to them. In spite of the unambiguous industrialization of many of these cities, they did their best to define their physical appearance more in opposition to the industrialization than in terms of its inevitable consequences. That is why the modern metropolis may also be perceived as a work of art, consciously conveying images of national or imperial glory. An additional frequent image is that of the chaotic place represented by American novelist John Dos Passos in *Manhattan Transfer* (1925) and Friedrich Anton Christian Lang's silent film, *Metropolis* (1927). Lang's science fiction vision, also inspired by New York City under the influence of German expressionism, depicts alike the magnificent and the dreadful sides of modernity. The world of the rulers is characterized by a cityscape with suspended streets, zigzagged buildings, and a bustling city; in contrast is the life of the repressed, poor people, who live underground and monotonously run the machines that keep the Metropolis in working order.

SEE ALSO *Architecture; Cities; Modernism; Modernity; Popular Culture; Urban Renewal; Urban Sprawl; Urban Studies; Urbanization*

BIBLIOGRAPHY

Mumford, Lewis. 1945. *City Development: Studies in Disintegration and Renewal.* New York: Harcourt, Brace.

Olsen, Donald J. 1986. *The City as a Work of Art: London, Paris, Vienna.* New Haven and London: Yale University Press.

Gábor Gyáni

MEXICAN AMERICANS

Mexican Americans (also known as Chicanos and Chicanas) are one of the oldest population groups in the United States, and simultaneously one of the newest as a result of ongoing immigration from Mexico. Indeed, the immigration of Mexicans into the United States is considered the longest sustained migration of labor anywhere in the world. The 2005 mid-decade census counted 42 million Hispanics in the United States, representing 14.5 percent of the national population. Mexican Americans represent 64 percent of the total Hispanic American population, or 27 million people.

The historical background of Mexican Americans is complex due to the mixed heritage that was forged through *mestizaje*, or the process that fused Indians, Europeans, Africans, and Asians biologically and culturally during three hundred years of colonialism in the Americas. The indigenous background of Mexican Americans includes numerous groups from the Mexica (Aztecs), Maya, and Tarahumara, as well as many of the indigenous populations of the American Southwest. Long before the arrival of Europeans in the Americas in the late fifteenth and early sixteenth centuries, indigenous groups created magnificent societies that ranged from the Pueblos of the Four Corners region of the American Southwest to the Mayan culture of southern Mexico. This diversity created for Mexican Americans a multilayered identity based primarily on Spanish and indigenous culture.

EUROPEAN INVASION

The region known as Mesoamerica, or that area stretching from central Mexico to the borders of Central America, has been inhabited by numerous indigenous groups for thousands of years. Indeed, this region is considered one of the "cradles" of civilization, and saw the emergence of highly sophisticated and complex societies, such as the Olmecas, the Teotihuacán, the Maya, the Toltecs, and the Aztecs. European contact with the Americas began with the arrival of Cristóbal Colón (Christopher Columbus, 1451–1506) in 1492. The Spanish invasion and conquest of what is now Mexico began with the arrival of Hernán Cortés (c. 1484–1547) in the spring of 1519 in what is today Veracruz. During this period, the Aztec Empire controlled large areas of the Valley of Mexico. The Aztecs were under the control of an indigenous group known as the Mexica, who had migrated from a homeland known as Aztlán north of the Valley of Mexico. The arrival of Cortés and his conquistadores led to the downfall of indigenous control of the region. Initially, the Aztecs were able to repel the Spanish invasion, but when the Spaniards regrouped and returned to Tenochtitlán in 1521, they found the Aztec capital in the midst of an epidemic of smallpox contracted from earlier European visitors. The Aztecs' lack of immunity to European diseases decimated the population of the capital, and with the help of Indian allies, the Spaniards were able topple the Aztec Empire in August 1521.

EUROPEAN COLONIZATION

The Mexican American experience can be linked directly to the colonial period by the process of *mestizaje*. This process also included the mixing of Africans with Europeans and Indians. *Mestizaje* created not only multiple heritages, it layered the Mexican American experience with multiple identities. In conjunction with the mixing of various population groups, the colonial Spaniards developed racial hierarchies that were based on the concept of whiteness. Thus, those who could claim a so-called pure European ancestry were accorded special privileges and access to power. In its most basic form, this hierarchy had *peninsulares* (Spaniards born in Spain) at the top, followed by criollos (Spaniards born in the Americas), mestizos (those of mixed Indian and European descent), and indigenous people, with blacks at the bottom. This system was based on class, race, and stereotypes developed by the Spaniards about mestizos, Indians, and blacks. These positions were not static, and the Spanish colonial system allowed for movement up and down this racial hierarchy. This movement through the hierarchy occurred over time by the process of miscegenation where offspring could be "whitened" or the reverse. There are also recorded instances where colonial subjects paid officials for documents authenticating their "whiteness."

Mexican independence from Spain is connected with the political turmoil in Europe that emerged in the early nineteenth century. Although Mexico gained independence in 1821, the Republic of Mexico was not born until 1824. At the time, Mexico's territory stretched from the Pacific Northwest to northern Central America. As a newborn republic, Mexico faced many challenges from European and European American powers that coveted Mexican territory. Not long after gaining independence, Mexico found itself fighting for its sovereignty in a civil war in its northern territories in 1836, followed by a war against the United States from 1846 to 1848.

THE TEXAS-MEXICAN WAR AND THE NORTH AMERICAN INTERVENTION

With independence, Mexico became concerned with possible invasion not only by the United States but also by European powers seeking to colonize regions of what is now the American West. Another concern for Mexico was the various indigenous groups who were raiding Mexican settlements in Texas. During this period most Mexicans refused to settle in Mexico's northern territories because of the hostile environment and only a small population existed in Texas. Mexico addressed some of these worries by inviting European Americans to settle in the Texas territory in the early 1820s under the premise that an increase in population would create a buffer against the United States and other groups vying for Mexican territory. Under conditions of colonization European Americans that settled in Mexico agreed to become Mexican citizens and swore an oath of loyalty. U.S. citizens jumped at this opportunity, and by the 1830s more than twenty thousand Anglo settlers, primarily from the American South, were living in Mexico's Texas territory, along with about five thousand of their slaves. Mexican citizens in the same region numbered fewer than five thousand. Before long, Mexico became concerned with the growing Anglo population, and attempted to stem the flow by outlawing slavery in the Texas territory in 1829 and repealing the colonization law in 1830. When the central government of Mexico denied the Texas territory statehood, Anglos and their Tejano allies opted to fight for independence from Mexico.

The 1836 Texas-Mexican War lasted a few short months, but in the end Texas gained its independence from Mexico and for nine years was an independent nation. The Texas-Mexican War—in particular the battles at the Alamo, Goliad, and San Jacinto—led to a lasting animosity between Mexicans and Anglos. On April 21 at San Jacinto, Anglo forces crying "Remember the Alamo" massacred over seven hundred Mexican soldiers in retaliation for the earlier Anglo defeat at the Alamo. The defeat of the Mexican Army at San Jacinto and Texas's declaration of independence did not prevent Mexico from continuing to claim the Texas territory. When the United States annexed Texas in 1845, Mexico considered it an act of aggression and intervention.

The American government's annexation of Texas was part of a grand design of invasion, conquest, and movement toward the Pacific Ocean. This movement was imbued with the notion of manifest destiny, in which the United States and its citizens believed that God had given the nation a mission to spread democracy throughout North America. This concept also encompassed ethnocentric views of non-Europeans, and was thus inherently racist. When Mexico refused to sell California to the United States during this period, the American government, determined to gain this land, used a skirmish between U.S and Mexican troops along disputed territory in Texas as a pretext to declare war on Mexico.

The Mexican-American War (1846–1848) left thousands dead on both sides. The United States occupied the remaining northern territories of Mexico, and U.S. troops laid siege to Mexico City. The war ended on February 2, 1848, with the Treaty of Guadalupe Hidalgo, which gave California, Arizona, New Mexico, Colorado, Nevada, Utah, and parts of Colorado and Wyoming to the United States. More than 100,000 Mexicans remained in these conquered territories and became U.S. citizens. The treaty included a number of articles to protect the liberties of these new Mexican Americans, but like other treaties signed by the U.S. government, these provisions were mostly ignored or circumvented. Article X of the treaty, which would have protected all titles to land grants issued by the Spanish and Mexican authorities, was eliminated by the U.S. Senate. As a result of the war, Mexico lost approximately half of its territory to the United States, leaving a legacy of animosity between the two nations. The Mexican American experience within the confines of the United States begins during this period.

THE TRANSFORMATION

Between 1848 and 1910, the lives of Mexicans and their descendants in the conquered territories underwent a profound change. Mexicans lost millions of acres of land to the U.S. government, land speculators, railroads, industrialists, thieves, and squatters, whose efforts were abetted by the U.S. judicial system. This enormous loss of land created a Mexican American population that was displaced from the small farms where they made a subsistence living. By the beginning of the twentieth century, most had become day laborers.

Structural changes also occurred at the social level. As more Anglos arrived in the conquered territories, the culture and customs of Mexicans diminished, while those of the new Anglo settlers became dominant. Over time, the majority of Mexican Americans began to lose position in the social, economic, and political structure of the United States. However, a small elite class of Mexican Americans that resided in enclaves in Texas, New Mexico, and southern California was able to maintain its viability at all levels through strong economic interests.

Furthermore, as racial animosity and oppression increased, many Mexicans in the conquered territories resorted to resistance, which has often been labeled by Anglos as banditry. Such individuals as Josefa, who in 1851 became the first woman lynched in California, resisted oppression by defending herself against Anglo aggressors, killing an attacker. Others, including Turbucio Vasquez and Juan Cortina and a group known as Las Gorras Blancas ("The White Caps"), resorted to armed resistance and rebellion to challenge Anglo hegemony in the conquered areas. State and territorial governments reacted by unleashing such units as the Texas Rangers to indiscriminately round up and kill Mexicans. Similar organizations were raised in Arizona and California. Anglo hegemony of the region included not only political control, but also an ideological philosophy that viewed all non-Europeans as inferior. The Mexican American experience in the second half of the nineteenth century was marked by racial strife.

CITIZENSHIP

Although the Treaty of Guadalupe Hidalgo conferred U.S. citizenship on Mexicans living in the conquered territories, Mexican Americans were often denied the rights of citizens. Like American blacks and indigenous groups, they were relegated to a second-class status. The government of California, for example, made attempts in the early twentieth century to reclassify Mexican Americans as Indians so they could be denied their legal rights.

It was counter to the prevailing ideology of the period to grant U.S. citizenship to individuals who were considered nonwhite. However, there was a question in the minds of the American public: Were Mexicans "white" or not? This question plagued Mexicans in the United States well into the twentieth century. The Mexicans that were incorporated into the United States in 1848 were not natural-born citizens of the country, and therefore did not fall under jus soli, a British common law used by the United States that stipulated that citizenship is granted to those born within the nation's jurisdiction. But this concept did not include racial minorities for the first one hundred or more years of U.S history, and jus soli did not become part of the organic law of the United States until after the Civil War (1861–1865) and the adoption in 1868 of the Fourteenth Amendment to the U.S. Constitution. The "whiteness" of Mexicans became an important legal question when Mexican immigrants began to enter the United States in larger numbers in the late nineteenth century. The Treaty of Guadalupe Hidalgo, as well as state and territorial constitutions, clearly included resident Mexicans as citizens. What remained unclear was whether or not Mexicans fit the legal definition of *white* in accordance with the 1870 Naturalization Act, which stipulated that a "white person" and "persons of African nativity, or African descent" could become naturalized citizens of the United States, but not others. This question was finally addressed in 1897 in a Texas federal court.

In the 1897 case, known as *In re Rodriguez*, Ricardo Rodriguez, who had resided in San Antonio, Texas, for ten years, petitioned the court to grant him naturalization. The court described Rodriguez using language typical of the day, pointing to various phenotypes to label him Indian or Asian, but not white. Rodriguez described himself as "pure-blooded Mexican," meaning neither purely Spanish nor purely Indian. One court brief characterized him as Asian by referring to the so-called Bering Strait hypothesis, according to which Indians originated in Asia and walked across an ice-bridge between present-day Russia and Alaska tens of thousands of years ago. Since Indians and Asians were barred from naturalization, attempts were made to categorize Rodriguez into one of those groups. In the end, the court relied on legal precedent, treaties that affirmed the citizenship of Mexican Americans, and various constitutions, such as that of the Republic of Texas, which conferred citizenship upon Mexicans in 1836. The court stated, "Citizens of Mexico are eligible for American naturalization, and may be individually naturalized by complying with the provisions of our laws." The court did not confer "whiteness" on Mexicans, but stated "if the strict scientific classification of the anthropologist should be adopted, he [Rodriguez] would probably not be classified as white." Thus, with reference to Mexicans and naturalization, the courts decided to use national origin, rather than race. However, despite the admission of Rodriguez to citizenship, Mexicans in the United States suffered considerable legal repression in the decades after the U.S. conquest and well into the twentieth century.

THE MEXICAN REVOLUTION AND MEXICAN IMMIGRATION

By the beginning of the twentieth century, the Mexican-descent population in the United States was estimated at between 380,000 to 560,000, with the majority living in the Southwest. The first four decades of the twentieth century had a profound effect on Mexican Americans and Mexican immigrants. The discontent of the Mexican population exploded into the first revolution of the twentieth century in 1910. By 1911 Mexican president Porfirio Díaz (1830–1915) was forced into exile and Mexico was plunged into a violent political struggle among numerous factions that continued for over a decade.

While Mexico was engaged in civil war, the United States was developing the Southwest. The impact of the Mexican Revolution and U.S. economic development of the Southwest resulted in: (1) more than 500,000 Mexicans immigrating to the United States as war refugees; (2) U.S. agricultural growers and other industries drawing Mexican laborers into such states as California and Arizona; and (3) an increase in the Mexican population along the border region, leading to the first large-scale exodus of Mexicans to other parts of the United States, including the Midwest, the Rocky Mountain region, the Pacific Northwest, and as far east as Pennsylvania and New York.

By the early 1920s the Mexican population in the United States was estimated by the Census Bureau at 766,000. However, many sources consider this figure to be an undercount because the census only counted Mexican immigrants and the first generation of U.S.-born Mexicans. Overall, Mexicans accounted for roughly 2 percent of all immigrants entering the United States during the decade leading up to 1920. However, this period also saw a rise in nativism and the passage of legislation aimed at curtailing the arrival of "undesirable" immigrants. The categorization of "undesirability" can be traced to the eugenics movement of the early twentieth century, when groups of scientists and such individuals as Charles Davenport (1866–1944) and Harry Laughlin (1880–1943) promoted a theory of racial betterment that became known as *scientific racism*.

The height of the influence of the eugenics movement came with the passage of the 1924 U.S. Immigration Act, which essentially halted immigration from eastern and southern Europe. According to the views of eugenicists, these groups represented a pollutant to the gene pool of the United States, and their immigration needed to be restricted. Immigrants from the countries of the Western Hemisphere were not included in this legislation because of the U.S. need for a reliable and temporary workforce, primarily from Mexico. However, beginning in 1925, Mexican immigration became the next target of opportunity for exclusion. From this period until the end of the 1920s, numerous congressional hearings were held to determine the "desirability" of Mexican immigrants and whether an immigration quota should be attached to Mexico. By 1930 the Mexican-origin population in the United States had grown to approximately 1.5 million. The Great Depression of the 1930s brought to a temporary conclusion the discussion on Mexican immigration.

THE DEPORTATIONS OF THE 1930s

Regardless of the rationalization that has been used to explain the repatriation and deportation of Mexicans in the 1930s, the fact remains that 360,000 to 500,000 individuals of Mexican origin were deported or strongly encouraged to leave the United States. At least half of those deported or repatriated were U.S. citizens whose constitutional rights were thus violated. The 1930s were not an aberration: deportations of Mexicans had begun as early as the 1920s when the U.S. experienced a recession. Close to one million Mexicans may have been deported during the 1920s and 1930s.

Yet, not all Mexicans were victims of these deportations. In fact, as Mexicans in such cities as Detroit and Chicago were being deported, Mexican labor was badly needed to harvest crops in California, Idaho, and elsewhere. During the 1930s, Mexican Americans became heavily involved in U.S. labor issues, as exemplified by the efforts of activists such as Emma Tenayuca (1916–1999), who organized a strike in 1938 at the Southern Pecan Shell Company in Texas. Throughout the country, the Mexican American community resorted to insulation and mobilization as protection from the economic fallout of the Great Depression. The 1940s brought further change for the Mexican American community.

WORLD WAR II AND THE MEXICAN AMERICAN GENERATION

The entry of the United States into World War II (1939–1945) changed the lives of Mexican Americans dramatically. As the United States mobilized for the war, more than 500,000 Mexican Americans either were drafted or volunteered for service. Mexican American men and women served with distinction, earning the highest percentage of medals of honor of any minority group. Mexican nationals known as *braceros* ("those who work with their arms") also served with distinction on the home front. The Bracero Program was initiated in 1942 to fill a labor shortage in the United States. Although braceros came from such places as Puerto Rico, Haiti, and Newfoundland, the overwhelming numbers were Mexican nationals. The Mexican *braceros* worked primarily in the agriculture and railroad industries throughout the war period. Due to easy access to a supply of labor, growers petitioned the U.S. government to extend the bracero program beyond the war years. The U.S. government agreed, but after 1947 growers were responsible for the transportation to and from Mexico. Between 1942 and 1964 approximately five million Mexican braceros entered the country under contract for six to twelve months. When their contract expired they were returned to Mexico. Congress, under pressure from various groups and unions, allowed the program to expire on December 31, 1964. There is a direct correlation between the conclusion of the bracero program and the increase in undocumented immigration from Mexico. However, because the program brought in a temporary and cheap labor force, it continued to operate after the war, and lasted until 1964. In addition, Mexican Americans throughout the country were mobilized to work for war industries. Mexican American women were prominent in these industries, earning the moniker Rosita the Riveter.

However, as Mexican American servicemen and women were fighting for liberty and democracy, many Mexican Americans in the United States were not afforded basic civil liberties. Segregation was rampant and Jim Crow laws prevented Mexican Americans from entering many establishments in the Southwest. During the war, intense racism against Mexicans became manifest in riots instigated in Los Angeles, California, between June 3 and 9, 1943 by U.S. military personnel. The primary targets of these riots were Mexican American youth wearing zoot suits, whose apparel was seen as not conforming to cultural norms. Large groups of U.S. sailors rampaged through barrios seeking Mexican American men and women to assault. When the riots ended on June 9, 1943, hundreds of Mexican Americans had been violated, but they were blamed by the police and media for starting the riots.

The end of the 1940s brought significant victories against the segregation of Mexican American schoolchildren. A 1948 district court decision, *Delgado v. Bastrop*, made it illegal to segregate children of Mexican descent in Texas schools. This and other accomplishments of the 1940s, plus the return of Mexican American war veterans, set the stage for additional civil rights struggles in the next decade.

THE MEXICAN AMERICAN CIVIL RIGHTS MOVEMENT

By the 1950s the Mexican population in the United States had reached approximately 2.2 million. Texas and California had the largest population of Mexican Americans, and although Mexican Americans were dispersed throughout the United States, the largest concentrations continued to reside in the five southwestern states. The small gains achieved by the Mexican American community during the 1950s were overshadowed by continuing residential segregation and a lack of housing, racism, job discrimination, segregation and disparities in education, attacks on Mexican American unions, and poverty.

Despite being oppressed, one of the singular characteristics of the Mexican American community has been its resiliency. Since the nineteenth century, Mexican Americans have resisted oppression at every opportunity. During the twentieth century, such organizations as the League of United Latin American Citizens (LULAC), La Confederación de Uniones de Campesinos y Obreros Mexicanos (the Confederation of Mexican Farmworkers and Laborers Unions, CUCOM), the American G.I. Forum, and the United Cannery, Agricultural, Packing, and Allied Workers of America (UCAPAWA) fought for the civil rights of Mexican Americans on a variety of fronts. Dennis Chávez Jr. (1888–1962) was elected a U.S. senator from New Mexico in 1936 and held the seat until his death in 1962. In California, Edward R. Roybal (1916–2005) became an influential politician at the grassroots level, and rose to national prominence when he was elected to Congress in 1962.

For a small segment of U.S. society, the 1950s represented a period of conformity, upward mobility, and security. But for others, including most Mexican Americans, the 1950s was characterized by government attacks on unions. Luisa Moreno (1907–1992), a Latina labor activist, was deported by the U.S. government in the 1950s for alleged ties to the Communist Party and so-called un-American activities. Furthermore, as civil liberties were diminished and "witch hunts" for suspected communists curtailed activism, Mexican immigrants were again rounded up and deported under a military action dubbed Operation Wetback. Despite the landmark court case of *Brown v. Board of Education* (1954), which called for the desegregation of educational institutions nationally, Mexican Americans continued to find themselves marginalized. In 1950 the average median education for Mexican Americans was 6.1 years, compared to 11.8 for European Americans.

In reaction to widespread racial discrimination, some Mexican Americans demanded to be classified as white. A number of civil rights organizations, however, sought legal relief from racial discrimination by petitioning the courts to classify Mexicans and Mexican Americans as ethnically and linguistically distinct and nonwhite (Martinez 2001, p. 76). The landmark case of *Hernández v. Texas* (1954) officially classified Mexican Americans as a distinct ethnic group, opening the way for lawsuits fighting racial discrimination under the Fourteenth Amendment.

Labor issues were another major concern for Mexican Americans during the 1950s, but gains were few. However, the 1950–1951 "Salt of the Earth" strike by the International Union of Mine, Mill, and Smelter Workers against Empire Zinc Company of Silver City, New Mexico, was a significant victory during a decade of union busting by the government. Mexican American political activists also became more visible during this decade. Groups such as La Alianza Hispano-Americana (the Hispanic-American Alliance), the Community Service Organization (CSO), LULAC, the American G.I. Forum, and an umbrella organization called the National Spanish-Speaking Council all continued to develop grassroots movements to bring about change within and outside of the Mexican American community.

According to the 1960 U.S. Census, there were approximately 3.5 million Spanish-surnamed persons in the United States, residing primarily in the Southwest. The per capita annual income for Mexican Americans at this time was $968, compared to $2,047 for European Americans. The median educational attainment for Mexicans was 8.1 years of education, compared to 12.0 for European Americans. Mexican Americans also had higher unemployment rates, higher poverty, and less access to adequate housing. The 1960s also saw discontent among Mexican Americans with the increasing involvement of the United States in Vietnam and continued neglect at all levels of education. In addition, social and economic inequality continued unabated, and Mexican Americans struggled to make their voices heard in national politics.

It was during this period that a significant portion of the Mexican American community emerged to challenge the status quo. Along with a new approach to the issues faced by Mexican Americans, the labels of *Chicano* and *Chicana* were adopted when Mexican Americans sought to embrace their indigenous background. The Chicano civil rights movement that developed in the 1960s had its roots primarily in the early twentieth century. The 1960s represented a continuation of the struggle that had been fought for generations. Yet this decade also represented a different approach to the economic, social, and political issues facing Chicanos. This approach has been characterized as militant and confrontational as Mexican Americans began to assert their rights and demand equal treatment. Additionally, the Chicano movement contained strong elements of cultural nationalism as Mexican Americans began to embrace their indigenous past.

The movement included a variety of organizations and issues. The ending of the Bracero Program in 1964 had two effects: (1) an increase in the number of Mexicans entering the United States outside of proper channels; and (2) a lack of a steady form of cheap Mexican labor that enabled César Chávez (1927–1993) and Dolores Huerta to establish the National Farm Workers Association (NFWA) in 1962. With the help of Filipino workers and the Agricultural Organizing Committee (AWOC) Chávez and Huerta organized the first major strike in 1965 known as the Delano Grape Strike, which lasted five years. This organization championed the rights of agricultural workers throughout many regions of the United States. In 1966, the NFWA and AWOC merged to become the United Farm Workers and the symbol for the Chicano movement.

Reies López Tijerina founded La Alianza Federal de Mercedes (the Federal Alliance of Autonomous Land Grants) in 1962. Tijerina's objective was to reclaim land grants that were stolen by a variety of groups, organizations, and institutions in New Mexico after 1848. La Alianza used a variety of tactics that included occupying Carson National Forest in northern New Mexico, arresting game wardens, and confronting authorities who attempted to impede these actions. Tijerina was eventually arrested for inciting a riot and sentenced to three years in prison. However, his efforts in New Mexico brought national exposure to the Chicano movement, and other organizations emerged as a result.

Two other interrelated groups that emerged in the late 1960s had a profound influence on the Mexican American experience. In 1969 the Crusade for Justice, an organization established by Rodolfo "Corky" Gonzales (1928–2005), held the First National Chicano Youth Liberation Conference in Denver, Colorado. From this meeting came an important manifesto for self-determination, *El Plan Espiritual de Aztlán* (the spiritual plan of Aztlan), which described the American Southwest as the symbolic homeland of Mexican Americans. The manifesto took its name from the Mexica place of origin, Aztlán, and adopted the term *Chicano* as a symbol of resistance. During this period, La Raza Unida Party (LRUP) was established by Luz Gutiérrez and José Angel Gutiérrez in Crystal City, Texas. LRUP became an important political party in many regions of the American Southwest, winning a number of local and regional elections.

The Chicano movement reached its height with the August 1970 moratorium against the Vietnam War (1957–1975). The disproportionate number of Chicano casualties resonated throughout the community. Mexican Americans in the 1960s represented only 8 percent of the population of the Southwest, yet accounted for 20 percent of all casualties in Vietnam. Thousands of Chicanos and Chicanas from throughout the country marched in Los Angeles demanding policy changes ranging from a reduction in the number of Chicanos serving in Vietnam to the opening of higher education to more Mexican Americans. The moratorium, like the military riots of the 1940s, turned into chaos when police officers attacked the peaceful marchers. In the end, many Chicanos and Chicanas were injured, and *Los Angeles Times* reporter Rubén Salazar (1928–1970) was killed when Los Angeles Sheriff deputies fired a tear gas canister into a crowded bar hitting Salazar in the head. The brutality of the police left many of the marchers further disillusioned.

Overall, the Chicano movement had a lasting impact. Mexican Americans realized that the community could be mobilized, and important organizations, such as the student group El Movimiento Estudantil Chicano de Aztlán (the Chicano Student Movement of Aztlán), were created. Mexican American culture and history became more open and prevalent throughout the country. The UFW remains vital to agriculture workers in the contemporary period. LRUP remained relevant until the mid-1970s. The Crusade for Justice receded to Colorado, but continues its activism. And Tijerina's movement spawned lawsuits from Mexican American families to reclaim their land from the U.S. government.

THE CONTEMPORARY PERIOD

In 1980 the U.S. Census Bureau began to use the term *Hispanic* for Mexican Americans. The 1980 Census counted 8.7 million Mexican Americans in the United States, and by 1990 that population had risen to 13.5 million. Between 1980 and 1990, the overall Hispanic population grew by 42 percent, approaching almost 10 percent of the nation's population. The unemployment rate for Hispanics was 11.9 percent in 1990, which was lower than the 16.5 percentage of 1980 but higher than the national average of 7.1 percent. According to census reports, 50 percent of Hispanics over twenty-five years of age had high school diplomas, compared to 82 percent of non-Hispanics of the same age. Furthermore, the median income for Mexican Americans remained lower and increased less than non-Hispanics during the 1980s.

Geographically, the number of Mexican Americans increased in regions outside of the American Southwest. In 1990 Washington state had the tenth-largest Mexican American population in the United States at 155,864. In the Midwest, states such as Illinois (623,688) and Michigan (132,312) had significant clusters of Mexican Americans. New York (93,244) and Florida (161,499) also saw sizeable increases in their Mexican American populations. These increases were largely the result of a dramatic rise in Mexican immigration to the United States between 1970 and 1990.

The Mexican-origin population in the United States saw a further surge between 1990 and 2000. By 2005, the Mexican American population in the United States had reached twenty-seven million, not including a sizeable number of undocumented Mexican immigrants, estimated at between ten and twelve million. This increase has resulted primarily from high immigration rates, but also from high fertility rates among the young Latino American population, whose median age is twenty-five years compared to thirty-six for white Americans. According to the 2000 U.S. Census this population increase has made Hispanics the largest minority group in the country and the second-largest labor force at 13 percent, after whites. However, 36 percent of the Hispanic labor force lacks a high school diploma, compared to fewer than 9 percent of non-Hispanic workers. This translates into Mexican Americans working in low-skilled jobs in areas such as private household services, construction, agriculture, forestry and fishing, and manufacturing.

The distribution of the Mexican population has reached virtually every region of the country. Some of the largest increases have occurred in the American South, where economic opportunities have drawn many Mexicans. States that saw rapid and sizeable increases were Oregon, Washington, Nevada, Georgia, North Carolina, Virginia, and Massachusetts. The fast growth of the Hispanic population has also increased the number of Hispanic schoolchildren in U.S. schools. By 2005 there was a noticeable increase in the number of Hispanics completing high school and enrolling in college; however, Latinos continue to lag behind white students at all key milestones of their educational journey (Pew Hispanic Center 2005, p. 3).

Since a large portion of America's Mexican-origin population is made up of either recent arrivals or first-generation citizens, assimilation is a factor in various economic indicators. The process of assimilation, whereby immigrants and their offspring adopt some of the values, beliefs, and behaviors more characteristic of mainstream U.S. culture, is not monolithic, and some individuals change more than others. Studies completed by the Pew Hispanic Center (2005) have shown that the attitudes of Hispanics who speak primarily English are much more like those held by non-Latinos than are the attitudes of Spanish-dominant Latinos.

The immigration debate in the United States has been a major issue since the 1980s, and Mexicans and Mexican Americans have felt the impact of increasingly restrictive immigration laws, including the 1986 Immigration Reform and Control Act, California's 1993 Proposition 187, and the 1996 Illegal Immigration Reform and Immigrant Responsibility Act. These were followed by post–September 11 hysteria over immigration and the 2006 Secure Fence Act. Latinos nationwide responded to this immigration backlash by holding large rallies that attracted millions in the spring of 2006, a demonstration that was dubbed "A Day Without a Mexican."

However, the long-established Mexican American community has made great gains in the political arena, and Mexican American politicians have become influential at the local, regional, and national levels. The ability of the community to mobilize and organize constituents was vital in electing Mexican Americans to office. There are 24 members of the 109th Congress of the United States out of 435 total members. In the House of Representatives there are nineteen Democrats and five Republicans of Hispanic origin, and two U.S. Senators of Hispanic descent (one Democrat, one Republican). In Texas, Mexican Americans hold 20 percent of state house seats and 19 percent of all state senate positions in 2007. In California, Mexican Americans hold over one-fourth of all Senate seats as of 2007. In the California Assembly, Mexican Americans hold 25 percent of the seats as of 2007. However, according to the current census figures, Hispanics comprise 35 percent of California's total population. California also has elected a number of Mexican American women into the U.S. Congress, including Loretta Sanchez, first elected in 1997. In 1999 California voters elected Cruz Bustamante as the first Mexican American lieutenant governor of the state since 1875, and in 2005 the city of Los Angeles elected Antonio

Villaraigosa as the first Mexican American mayor since 1872. Most of these politicians ran on Democratic Party tickets.

Since the 1980s the Republican Party has also made gains within the Mexican American community. However, George W. Bush's presidency, the wars in Afghanistan and Iraq, and the Republican Party's position on immigration has slowed any momentum the party may have enjoyed shortly after 2000. Overall, it is clear that people of Mexican origin are becoming a strong demographic and political force in the United States. The projected demographics indicate that Latinos will constitute 25 percent of the U.S. population by 2050, a population growth that should translate into stronger political power. Simultaneously, Mexican Americans will continue to face many of the challenges of the previous decades, but they will confront those challenges with the same resiliency that carried them through adverse conditions in the past.

SEE ALSO *Annexation;* Brown v. Board of Education, *1954;* Brown v. Board of Education, *1955; Chávez, César; Colonialism;* Hernandez v. Texas; *Immigration; Latinos; Malinchistas; Mexican Revolution (1910–1920); Politics, Latino; Protest; Social Movements*

BIBLIOGRAPHY

Acuña, Rodolfo F. 2006. *Occupied America: A History of Chicanos.* 6th ed. New York: Pearson Longman.

Garcia, Jerry, and Gilberto Garcia, eds. 2005. *Memory, Community, and Activism: Mexican Migration and Labor in the Pacific Northwest.* Lansing: Julian Samora Research Institute and Michigan State University Press.

Gutiérrez, David G. 1995. *Walls and Mirrors: Mexican Americans, Mexican Immigrants, and the Politics of Ethnicity.* Berkeley: University of California Press.

Haney-López, Ian. 2006. *White by Law: The Legal Construction of Race.* Rev. ed. New York: New York University Press.

Martínez, Oscar J. 2001. *Mexican-Origin People in the United States: A Topical History.* Tucson: University of Arizona Press.

McWilliams, Carey. [1948] 1968. *North from Mexico: The Spanish-Speaking People of the United States.* New York: Greenwood.

Menchaca, Martha. 2001. *Recovering History, Constructing Race: The Indian, Black, and White Roots of Mexican Americans.* Austin: University of Texas Press.

Padilla, Fernando V. 1980. Early Chicano Legal Recognition: 1846–1897. *Journal of Popular Culture* 13 (3): 564–574.

Pew Hispanic Center. 2005. Hispanics: A People in Motion. http://pewhispanic.org/files/reports/40.pdf.

Pew Hispanic Center. 2006. A Statistical Portrait of Hispanics at Mid-Decade. http://pewhispanic.org/reports/middecade/.

Ruíz, Vicki L. 1987. *Cannery Women, Cannery Lives: Mexican Women, Unionization, and the California Food Processing Industry, 1930–1950.* Albuquerque: University of New Mexico Press.

Valdés, Dennis Nodín. 1991. *Al Norte: Agricultural Workers in the Great Lakes Region, 1917–1970.* Austin: University of Texas Press.

Valencia, Reynaldo Anaya, Sonia R. García, Henry Flores, and José Roberto Juárez Jr. 2004. *Mexican Americans and the Law: El pueblo unido jama será vencido! (A People United Cannot Be Divided!).* Tucson: University of Arizona Press.

Jerry Garcia

MEXICAN-AMERICAN WAR

The Mexican-American War commenced on May 13, 1846, after President James Knox Polk (1795–1849) pressured Congress for an immediate declaration of war on Mexico. The road to war with Mexico represents a complicated period in U.S. history. By late 1845 political upheaval between the Whigs and the Democrats had reached a crescendo in Congress. The most pressing political issue surrounding war with Mexico had been the potential expansion of slavery to the U.S. Southwest. Many prowar congressional leaders favored battle as a means by which they could increase the influence and lucrative potential of slavery; meanwhile other hawkish war supporters understood the conflict to be a moral struggle for the purpose of spreading freedom and liberty in the absence of servitude. Former president John Quincy Adams (1825–1829), an ardent antislavery advocate, became one of the few voices of dissent in the House of Representatives then dominated by congressmen arguing for war.

By 1803 Texas had become a disputed territory between the United States and Mexico. Many Americans loudly proclaimed Texas a part of the Louisiana Purchase brokered by President Thomas Jefferson on April 30, 1803. In 1821 Mexico achieved independence from Spanish control. Most of the Spanish leaders, pejoratively labeled *gachupines*, were deposed, and in their place native mestizo rulers assumed control of the government. (*Gachupines* were native Spaniards who oppressed, enslaved, and exploited indigenous Mexicans. This is a pejorative term referring to Spanish imperialists, similar to the word *gringo*.) The mestizos became known as *criollos,* most of whom demonstrated ineptitude due to their initial inexperience at governing, for under Spanish rule few indigenous citizens had achieved positions of power (Faulk and Stout 1973, p. xiii). Political turmoil and chronic factionalism followed the Mexican independence movement. Approximately thirty-six changes in leadership occurred between 1833 and 1855. The military remained dominant in political affairs, a circumstance that facilitated the rise of Mexican general turned president Antonio López de Santa Anna (1794–1876), who was elected president of Mexico by a majority vote in 1833. Santa Anna began his military career in 1810 as a cadet under the command of Joaquín de Arredondo. Mexican historians differ on whether he was vulgar and corrupt or a brave and skillful leader.

Provoked by the aggressive movements of volunteer soldiers from Texas in 1836, the fiery Santa Anna set his sights on attacking Texan forces garrisoned at the Alamo mission in San Antonio. A bloody battle ensued at the Alamo. The most popular American interpretation of this incident depicts a small but death-defying American force of roughly three hundred soldiers led by Sam Houston and Davy Crockett pitted against Santa Anna's roughly eight thousand bloodthirsty attackers (Mexican historians present a significantly different version of the battle). The battle officially lasted for thirteen days, from February 23 to March 6, 1836. There is some debate as to whether the Mexican general ordered the execution of American forces surrendering peacefully or if the Americans chose to fight until the bitter conclusion. The undeniable historical result of this tragic event is that no Americans were left alive. Consequently Santa Anna became a virtual public enemy in the United States.

While the battle raged at the Alamo, a group of sixty councilmen representing the U.S. citizens of Texas gathered at the "General Convention" in the town of Washington and unanimously declared independence. All sixty signatories to the Texas Declaration of Independence (March 2, 1836), including Sam Houston, declared their independence from the "evil rulers" who brought "oppression" and removed even "the semblance of freedom."

Compassion among U.S. observers of the Texans' struggle further developed because of Mexico's Goliad campaign of 1836 (also referred to as the "Goliad massacre"). This event has taken second place to the Alamo in American memory. One of Santa Anna's commanders, General José de Urrea (1795–1848), succeeded in taking prisoner 230 American soldiers who surrendered voluntarily on March 20, 1846. Santa Anna betrayed Urrea's promise of their safety by ordering the execution of many of the unarmed Texas fighters. Their deaths were justified by Santa Anna, who labeled them "foreign pirates" who had attacked a sovereign government without legal cause (Faulk and Stout 1973, p. xv).

At the battle of San Jacinto on April 21, 1836, Santa Anna's forces suffered defeat at the hands of an outraged Texan army. Santa Anna sought to avoid capture and punishment by dressing in plain clothing and hiding in the fields. Eventually U.S. forces recognized and seized him.

This battle for all intents and purposes secured Texan independence and halted Santa Anna's onslaught. In 1836 Anglo-Americans residing in Texas declared independence. Mexican leaders immediately recognized the danger in the United States receiving an unfettered pass to annex the former Mexican territory. Many feared the U.S. spirit of expansion would whet the appetite of expansionists in Congress and expedite the annexation movement.

Meanwhile, in order for Mexican leaders to maintain power, they had to continually promise embittered constituents a reconquest of Texas. Mexico refused to acknowledge Texas as an independent state and asserted both its claims to the disputed territory and its willingness to defend against U.S. violation of its sovereignty. Nevertheless, the U.S. government did not express an absolute commitment to sending military forces to defend Texas against an onslaught. This prompted volunteer soldiers, also known as "soldiers of fortune," to flood into the disputed region (Haynes 2002, p. 115). Despite promises to recover San Antonio and other lost territories, Mexico's promised assaults failed to materialize. In early 1845 the voters of Texas approved the Annexation Ordinance, which prompted a congressional authorization known as the Joint Resolution to Admit Texas as a State; this was subsequently signed into effect by President Polk on December 29, 1845. Northern abolitionists feared that the admittance of Texas into the Union would encourage the expansion of slavery and destabilize the nation. John R. Collins writes that "a small group of Whig abolitionists … viewed the war as a 'slavocracy conspiracy'" (Faulk and Stout 1973, p. 70).

Born in Mecklenburg County, North Carolina, in 1795, Polk became president of the United States in 1844. His political platform consisted primarily of a belligerent attitude toward Mexico's reluctance to relinquish the southwestern territories and an aggressive stance toward Great Britain, who refused to budge on the issue of sharing or relinquishing the Oregon Territory. As a candidate for president, Polk had promised both to reannex Texas and to occupy Oregon from the California boundary to the 54'40" latitudinal line. At this time the theory of manifest destiny was on the rise. The term, coined by the influential Democratic writer and strategist John L. O'Sullivan, addressed the right of the United States to spread freedom and liberty across the North American continent. Supporters of this ideology believed that God, or divine Providence, had empowered the American people with the ability to conquer the continent and thereby civilize and Christianize the world. Although not completely materialized by 1844, the spirit of manifest destiny, teamed with Polk's campaign promises, seemingly offered a mandate to the incipient president to engage those who stood in America's pathway to continental dominance.

The United States persisted in its assertion that the Rio Grande represented the legal southern border of Texas, despite the obvious lack of evidence to validate the claim. Polk dispatched minister plenipotentiary John Slidell (1793–1871) to Mexico with the express purpose of settling the border dispute in favor of the Rio Grande rather than the Nueces River, as demanded by the Mexican government. Slidell was also instructed to purchase New Mexico and California. At least two previous presidential administrations, those of John Quincy Adams and Andrew Jackson, had sent negotiators to purchase Texas and possibly the surrounding territories from Mexico; their offers were soundly rejected and seemed only to antagonize Mexican leaders. Polk offered $5 million to redraw the boundary of Texas to the Rio Grande and $25 million for the California Territory. The Mexican government repudiated Slidell and the offer. Consequently President Polk decided to station General Zachary Taylor (1784–1850) with U.S. forces along the Rio Grande. In turn Mexican general Mariano Arista (1802–1855) guarded the Mexican side of the river. Border provocations on April 24 and the refusal of the Mexican government to negotiate with the president's ambassador instigated war. After President Polk delivered a war message to Congress, the United States officially declared war on Mexico on May 13, 1846.

Combat had already commenced, with Colonel Stephen Kearny's Army of the West traveling to New Mexico and then to California to secure those territories for U.S. migration and General Zachary Taylor's army crushing the Mexican forces in battles at Palo Alto and Resaca de Palma. Kearny fully controlled Santa Fe by August 18, 1846. In California a group of American settlers, along with an exploring party led by John C. Frémont (1813–1890), joined Kearny in what became known as the "Bear Flag Revolution" (Brinkley 2003, p. 352). U.S. soldiers experimented with flying artillery at Palo Alto, and hand-to-hand fighting erupted at Resaca de Palma. The U.S. Navy seized control of Monterey and Los Angeles thanks to Commodore John Drake Sloat (1781–1867). During these tempestuous days of battle, the former Mexican general Santa Anna returned from exile to prepare an army of roughly twenty thousand men with the express purpose of fighting the invaders until any defense would become untenable. Enthusiasm for war in the United States led to 200,000 volunteers responding to the secretary of war's call to arms (Haynes 2002, p. 155).

U.S. forces entered battle outnumbered in almost every engagement with Mexico (Eisenhower 1986, p. 35). The most recognizable casualties of war were "Henry Clay, Jr., and Archibald Yell, former governor of Arkansas (both at Buena Vista), and Captain Samuel Walker of the Texas Rangers, at Huamantia" (Eisenhower 1986, p. 36). Volunteer forces received only a rudimentary training,

and due to the sporadic popularity of the war, many of the soldiers, themselves from different states, never trained together. Many of the volunteers were not supplied with the bare essentials, and this led to sickness and disease. Statistically the greatest challenge to the army, and the most damage inflicted on it, was caused by outbreaks of disease. Of the approximately 100,182 soldiers who fought in the war, nearly 10,790 died from disease and exposure to inclement weather. A much smaller number, 1,548 volunteers, died on the battlefield. Generals George B. McClellan (1826–1885) and Winfield Scott (1786–1866) marveled at the destruction wrought on their forces by rampant diseases. The historian Thomas Irey asserts that nearly 10 percent of all "noncombat" deaths were caused by disease and infection (Faulk and Stout 1973, p. 110). President Polk's troubled relationships with generals Scott and Taylor further challenged the U.S. military's already troubled tactics (Haynes 2002, p. 152). On November 19, 1846, the president reappointed General Scott commander of the army, displacing Taylor.

On March 9, 1847, General Scott landed at Veracruz with ten thousand soldiers, finally entering Mexican territory to compel surrender. Scott eventually advanced 260 miles across the Mexican National Highway to Mexico City. This major amphibious assault was the first of its kind in U.S. history (Brinkley 2003, p. 352). On April 18 Scott's forces pushed forward at Cerro Gordo, flanking Santa Anna's forces and forcing his retreat, embarrassingly without his artificial leg. Some of the most famous future Civil War generals planned this mission, including Robert E. Lee (1807–1870), McClellan, Joseph E. Johnston (1807–1891), and P. G. T. Beauregard (1818–1893). At Churubusco on August 20, Scott's army defeated a Mexican defensive force of twenty thousand soldiers. The last major confrontation before Scott's forces marched on Mexico City was the battle of Molino del Rey, in which twelve thousand Mexican soldiers lost the battle and the overall struggle and Scott took Chapultepec, overlooking Mexico City. Nevertheless, by September 1847 many Americans had become frustrated by Mexico's refusal to accept terms of surrender (Davis 1999, p. 316).

In the summer of 1847 Mexico received Polk's special peace envoy Nicholas P. Trist (1800–1874). In July, Mexico stalled, then rebuffed the ambassador's offer. Although Polk recalled Trist and sought to demand more from Mexico, on February 2, 1848, the Treaty of Guadalupe Hidalgo was negotiated by the envoy. The treaty ceded to the United States 500,000 miles of Mexican territory that would become the U.S. states of New Mexico, California, Arizona, Nevada, Wyoming, and Colorado (Davis 2003, p. 192). Mexico also conceded that the Rio Grande would become the permanent border of Texas. The United States compensated Mexico with

$15 million in exchange for the lost territory and $3.25 million in remuneration. The Senate ratified the treaty by a vote of 38 to 14 on March 10, 1848 (National Archives 2003, p. 72).

More so than the Mexican-American War itself, the events that roused the bellicose passions of the American people have been captured in cinematic history. Walt Disney produced a three-episode television series about Davy Crockett that included *Davy Crockett at the Alamo* (1955), a romantic story depicting a group of outnumbered Americans surrounded by a marauding army waiting to pummel them. There also have been more than twenty major motion pictures produced about Crockett's famous execution after or death in battle at the Alamo. In 1960 John Wayne directed and starred as Crockett in *The Alamo*. In 2004 Billy Bob Thornton starred as Crockett in another film titled *The Alamo* alongside Dennis Quaid, who was cast as General Sam Houston. Most of the films on this subject depict a mythologized version of historical events.

Many political theorists point to U.S. imperialism and the insatiable southern drive to further the institution of slavery as the motivations for war with Mexico. Utilizing the writings of the then-congressman Abraham Lincoln, some political scientists assert that Mexican provocations led to the shedding of American blood to be sure but on the Mexican side of the border, thus negating the American claim that Mexico had trespassed on U.S. soil illegally, prompting the U.S. declaration of war. More traditional historians assert that the Mexican leadership believed their nation to be omnipotent because of their enormous success in expelling the Spanish leadership and that, given Britain's inclination to stir up trouble in the region in order to attain California and to retain the Oregon territories, Mexican leaders felt assured of their assistance should their own forces suffer serious setbacks. The British never offered such assistance.

According to the historian Kyle Ward, who examines changes in the content of textbooks on U.S. history, late-twentieth-century American political scientists portrayed the U.S. South in a detestable light, alleging that a plot existed to encompass all of Mexico's territory into their slavocracy (Ward 2006, p. 158). Following this line of logic, many historians believe that President Polk and his cohorts would have seized more territory and imposed a harsher indemnity on Mexico if there had not been such widespread domestic and congressional opposition to his policy of expansion. This is why, according to some, Polk never requested a straightforward yes or no vote on the war (Silverstone 2004, p. 198). In lieu of an up-or-down vote, the president asked for reinforcements and war materials for a war that had already been provoked and

threatened to engulf the U.S. territory if Congress failed to act quickly and decisively.

BIBLIOGRAPHY

Brinkley, Alan. 2003. *American History: A Survey.* Boston: McGraw-Hill.

Davis, Kenneth C. 2003. *Don't Know Much about History.* New York: HarperCollins.

Davis, Paul K. 1999. *100 Decisive Battles from Ancient Times to the Present.* New York: Oxford University Press.

Eisenhower, John S. D. 1986. Polk and His Generals. In *Essays on the Mexican War,* ed. Douglas W. Richmond, John S. D. Eisenhower, Miguel E. Soto, and Wayne Cutler, 34–65. College Station: Texas A&M Press.

Faulk, Odie B., and Joseph A. Stout Jr. 1973. *The Mexican War: Changing Interpretations.* Chicago: Sage.

Haynes, Sam W. 2002. *James K. Polk and the Expansionist Impulse.* New York: Longman.

National Archives. 2003. *Our Documents: 100 Milestone Documents from the National Archives.* Foreword by Michael Beschloss. New York: Oxford University Press.

Silverstone, Scott A. 2004. *Divided Union: The Politics of War in the Early American Republic.* Ithaca, NY: Cornell University Press.

Ward, Kyle. 2006 *History in the Making: An Absorbing Look at How American History Has Changed in the Telling over the Last 200 Years.* New York: New Press.

Jonathan A. Jacobs

MEXICAN REVOLUTION (1910–1920)

Scholars have long debated whether the Mexican Revolution was a social revolution, a civil war, a nationalist movement, a struggle for unrealized liberal ideals, or a meaningless rebellion. The revolution is quite universally seen as beginning with the 1910 issuance of Francisco Madero's Plan of San Luis Potosí, calling for free elections, but there is no universal agreement on its terminal point. Many of the revolution's demands were codified in a progressive 1917 constitution that for some marks the revolution's culmination. Those who view revolution as military warfare rather than ideology often view the cessation of fighting in 1920 as the endpoint. In either case, many of the promised social reforms were not realized until the 1930s, under the Lázaro Cárdenas government. The entrenchment of a conservative regime in 1940 largely ended revolutionary social policy, though not necessarily its rhetoric. In 1968 the massacre of protesting students at Tlatelolco in Mexico City demonstrated definitively that Mexico had left its revolutionary heritage behind. The defeat of the ruling Institutional Revolutionary Party (PRI) in 2000 brought an end to the hegemonic institutional legacy of the early revolutionary leaders. Nonetheless, some contend that Mexico continues to be shaped by various legacies of the 1910 popular uprising against Porfirio Díaz's dictatorship.

PORFIRIO DÍAZ

General Porfirio Díaz's entrenched dictatorship, the *Porfiriato*, lasted from 1876 to 1911. Díaz rose through the political ranks as a liberal leader, but in contrast to the anticlericalism of most nineteenth-century liberals he developed close relations with the Catholic Church and relied on conservative and wealthy elites to assure his political survival. His feared police forces (the *rurales*) viciously suppressed dissent, but equally significantly Díaz used the mechanisms of a large (and expensive) government bureaucracy to gain popular support. This dual strategy of *pan o palo* (literally, "bread or the club," or "carrot or a stick") successfully eliminated any significant opposition. As Díaz acquired more power, elections increasingly became a farce. The result was one of the longest dictatorships in Latin American history.

FRANCISCO MADERO

In a 1908 interview with a U.S. journalist, James Creelman, Díaz indicated that Mexico was ready for a multiparty democratic system and that he would welcome opposition in the 1910 elections. Apparently the statement was only meant to improve his image abroad, but local dissidents jumped at the chance to remove Díaz from power. Francisco Madero, a wealthy landowner from the northern state of Coahuila who had studied in the United States and France, emerged as the leading opposition candidate. Hardly a revolutionary, Madero championed a liberal democratic ideology and pushed for open, fair, and transparent elections. Before the June 1910 elections, Díaz arrested and imprisoned Madero. As in previous elections, Díaz rigged the vote and won almost unanimously. The blatant fraud convinced Madero that the dictator could only be removed through armed struggle.

When released from prison after the elections, Madero fled north to Texas where he drafted his Plan of San Luis Potosí. The plan made vague references to agrarian and other social reforms, but mostly focused on political reforms. Most significantly, Madero declared the 1910 elections null and void, proclaimed himself provisional president, and called for free elections. With this plan in place, Madero returned to Mexico to launch a guerrilla war. After Madero's forces won decisive victories in May 1911, Díaz resigned the presidency and sailed for Europe. His reported parting words were, "Madero has unleashed

the tiger; let's see if he can tame it." In 1915 the former dictator died peacefully in Paris at the age of eighty-five, the only significant figure in the Mexican Revolution not to meet a violent death.

Once in power, Madero faced pressure from both the Left and Right. He had stirred the passions of agrarian rebels who wanted the return of their communal *ejido* lands. In Morelos, south of Mexico City, Emiliano Zapata confiscated estates and distributed land to peasants. In the north, Francisco (Pancho) Villa also demanded deep social and political changes. Madero, responding to his elite class interests, opposed radical reforms and encouraged his rural supporters to regain their lands through legal and institutional means. Madero insisted that the guerrillas disarm, but they refused. In response, in 1911 Zapata issued his Plan of Ayala, which denounced Madero, called for agrarian reform, and introduced one of the revolution's most noted slogans, *Land and Liberty*.

VICTORIANO HUERTA

Madero's legalization of labor unions and inability to confine peasant revolts alienated conservatives. U.S. Ambassador Henry Lane Wilson, favoring political stability and economic development over democracy, threatened to invade to protect U.S. property. With Wilson's tactical approval and the support of Mexican conservatives, in February 1913 General Victoriano Huerta launched a coup against Madero. A ten-day battle (called the *Decena Trágica*) heavily damaged Mexico City and resulted in high civilian casualties, culminating in the overthrow and assassination of the former leader. Huerta's time in office ushered in a period of chaotic and extreme political violence, with the conflict assuming aspects of a civil war rather than an ideologically driven revolutionary struggle. In April 1914 the United States occupied Mexico's principal port of Veracruz, an act that drew widespread condemnation. New weapons, including machine guns, brought an unprecedented level of carnage to the battlefield. Various armies moved across the country drafting people and stealing food along the way. These great migrations broke through Mexico's provincial isolation, creating for the first time a national identity.

Wealthy landowner and former Madero supporter Venustiano Carranza merged the forces of Zapata, Villa, and Alvaro Obregón into a Constitutionalist Army against the new dictator. Together they defeated Huerta and forced him to flee the country. With a common enemy gone, the revolutionaries fought among themselves. Carranza felt threatened by his rival Villa, who proposed much more radical social policies. In October 1914 delegates representing Villa and Zapata met at Aguascalientes to unify their forces and drive Carranza from power. Under the impression that the United States was supporting his enemy Carranza, Villa raided Columbus, New Mexico. In response, U.S. president Woodrow Wilson sent General John J. "Black Jack" Pershing into Mexico to capture Villa. Pershing's pursuit was a fiasco and Villa's popularity increased. Under Obregón's military leadership, however, Carranza gained the upper hand over Villa and Zapata.

1917 MEXICAN CONSTITUTION

Once in power, Carranza convoked a new constitutional convention that debated many key issues of the revolution, including the roles of the church and state, property rights, agrarian reforms, labor reforms, education, foreign investments, subsoil rights, and the political participation of Indians and women. Carranza wanted a conservative document, but delegates drafted a constitution embodying the aspirations of more radical revolutionaries that attacked large landholders, the church, and foreign capitalists. Even though many of its provisions were only slowly, if ever, implemented, it was a surprisingly progressive document that influenced subsequent social reforms in other Latin American countries.

The constitution codified much of the revolution's nationalist ideology. Article 27 claimed mineral rights for the state. In a reversal of policies under the Díaz regime, it tightly restricted foreign and church ownership of property and returned *ejido* lands to rural communities. In what some view as the high point of the revolution, in 1938 Lázaro Cárdenas used these provisions to nationalize Standard Oil and establish the state oil company Petróleos Mexicanos (PEMEX). Article 123 incorporated a labor code that instituted an eight-hour workday, set a minimum salary, abolished company stores and debt peonage, defended the right to organize and strike, outlawed child labor, and provided for generous pregnancy leaves. Article 130 provided for freedom of religion and separation of church and state. Other articles extended the constitution's liberal anticlericalism, including provisions outlawing religious control over education.

AFTERMATHS

Carranza assumed power under the new constitution as the first constitutionally elected president since Madero. In 1919 he rid himself of one of his primary enemies by killing Zapata. Carranza had moved significantly to the right by then, and attempted to manipulate the electoral apparatus to maintain himself in power. In response, Obregón, who had by then become more liberal, overthrew Carranza, who was then killed in an ambush. With Carranza gone, Obregón won the 1920 elections and made concessions that largely brought the ten years of fighting to an end. In 1923 Villa, who had retired to a comfortable estate in the northern state of Chihuahua,

was assassinated in an attack that seemed to trace back to old feuds between revolutionary leaders. In the first peaceful transfer of power since the revolution began, Plutarco Elías Calles became president in 1924. His time in office witnessed increased conflict between the government and the Catholic Church hierarchy, leading to the 1926–1929 Cristero rebellion. In 1928 Obregón was once again elected president, but was then assassinated a few months later. Facing endless violence that seemed to be claiming the lives of all the revolutionary leaders, politicians devised a system that would assure their continued hold on power. In 1929 Calles formed the National Revolutionary Party, the forerunner of the PRI that ruled Mexico for the next seventy years. This opened the way for Lázaro Cárdenas (1934–1940), who not only implemented progressive agrarian and social reforms, but also consolidated control over the country.

By the time Cárdenas handed power to his conservative successor Manuel Ávila Camacho, the governing party had developed a corporate state that held more absolute control than had Díaz. Although the government introduced successful reforms in education and health care and created political stability, for many marginalized peoples the revolution had brought few changes. Although women participated massively in a variety of roles in the revolution—most notably as *soldaderas* who accompanied their husbands, providing domestic and other services—they ultimately gained little. Indigenous peasants were still confronted with authoritarian political structures and racial discrimination.

SEE ALSO *Civil Wars; Communalism; Coup d'Etat; Guerrilla Warfare; Land Claims; Land Reform; Partido Revolucionario Institucional; Politics, Gender; Socialism; Villa, Francisco (Pancho); Zapata, Emiliano*

BIBLIOGRAPHY

Brunk, Samuel. 1995. *Emiliano Zapata: Revolution and Betrayal in Mexico*. Albuquerque: University of New Mexico Press.

Gilly, Adolfo. 2005. *The Mexican Revolution*. Trans. Patrick Camiller. New York: New Press.

Gonzales, Michael J. 2002. *The Mexican Revolution, 1910–1940*. Albuquerque: University of New Mexico Press.

Knight, Alan. 1986. *The Mexican Revolution*. 2 vols. Cambridge, U.K.: Cambridge University Press.

McLynn, Frank. 2001. *Villa and Zapata: A History of the Mexican Revolution*. New York: Carroll and Graf.

Salas, Elizabeth. 1990. *Soldaderas in the Mexican Military: Myth and History*. Austin: University of Texas Press.

Womack, John, Jr. 1968. *Zapata and the Mexican Revolution*. New York: Vintage.

Marc Becker

MICHELS, ROBERT
1876–1936

Robert Michels was a German sociologist born in Cologne. His major work was *Zur Soziologie des Parteiwesens in der modernen Demokratie* (1911), published in 1915 in the United States under the name *Political Parties*. While Michels wrote hundreds more works (most of which are obscure articles published by various socialist groups during the early 1900s), only *Political Parties* is still highly regarded today. In this book, Michels formulated his famous "iron law of oligarchy."

During his early life, Michels came under the influence of French culture, which later seems to have had an impact on his writings. He was educated in Paris, Munich, Leipzig, and Halle, where he received his PhD. Around this time, he became involved with the German Social Democratic Party, which he joined in 1903. Because of his socialist activities, he was not allowed to teach history in German universities when he first began his career. Michels wrote close to two hundred articles between 1901 and 1907, many of which criticize the socialist parties to which he belonged. Michels argued that these parties were failing to accomplish the goals of socialism, and, while he was an active member at various points in his life, he felt that these shortcomings kept socialists from achieving any real change in society. Michels is characterized (as were most of his writings) as a syndicalist. In other words, he subscribed to the revolutionary idea that workers could seize both the economy and the government in order to further their interests. His beliefs were heavily influenced by Marxism, but also by Max Weber (1864–1920), with whom he corresponded regularly.

Near the end of his life, Michels became disillusioned with socialist politics and many of the foundational ideas upon which his works were written. Having resigned from both the German and Italian socialist parties by 1907, he continued to teach at the university level until 1928. Then, at the invitation of Benito Mussolini (1883–1945), he moved to Italy where he became an apologist for fascism. He died in 1936, after receiving chairs at the universities of Perugia and Rome.

Political Parties was first published in German in 1911. Within four years, it had been translated into French, Italian, and English. Michels's major theory in the book, the iron law of oligarchy, caused considerable scholarly debate because Michels failed to provide an exact definition of either the theory or the terms *oligarchy* or *organization*. On the most basic level, the theory holds that as groups begin to formally organize, they move toward oligarchy as a result of a number of technical and psychological factors. Oligarchy develops because organization prevents the masses from participating in decision making, and creates a need for specialized positions that not everyone is able to fill, as well as a leadership whose will and desires are easily fulfilled by the organization without input from others. Michels contends that this situation leads to a paradox because, although organization is necessary to achieve democracy, the organization that is essential to democracy also creates its antitype, oligarchy.

Political Parties had a significant impact on the research of social scientists, especially in the United States during the mid-1900s when Michels's book experienced a revival among political scientists. At the same time, however, this renewed interest outside the context of the original writing led to much debate over the book's original intent. Michels's writings cannot be divorced from his experiences with the socialist parties of Italy and Germany and his desire for them to achieve democracy in those two countries, as well as his eventual disillusionment with them.

SEE ALSO *Fascism; Mussolini, Benito; Oligarchy; Oligarchy, Iron Law of; Sociology, Political; Syndicalism*

BIBLIOGRAPHY

Cassinelli, C. W. 1953. The Law of Oligarchy. *The American Political Science Review* 47 (3): 773–784.

Cook, Philip J. 1971. Robert Michels's Political Parties in Perspective. *The Journal of Politics* 33 (3): 773–796.

May, John D. 1965. Democracy, Organization, Michels. *The American Political Science Review* 59 (2): 417–429.

Michels, Robert. [1915] 1968. *Political Parties: A Sociological Study of the Oligarchical Tendencies of Modern Democracies.* 2nd ed. Trans. Eden and Cedar Paul. New York: Free Press.

Mitzman, Arthur. 1973. *Sociology and Estrangement: Three Sociologists of Imperial Germany.* New York: Knopf.

Thomas K. Bias

MICROANALYSIS

Microanalysis represents not only a distinctive methodology, but also a distinctive way of thinking about communication (Bull 2002). Of particular importance has been the belief in the value of studying social interaction through detailed analysis of film, audiotape, and videotape recordings. Indeed, the effect of the videorecorder has been likened to that of the microscope in the biological sciences. Through the use of recorded data that can repeatedly be examined and dissected in the finest detail, interpersonal communication has become an object of study in its own right.

But microanalysis did not develop simply as a consequence of innovations in technology. It also reflects fundamental changes in the way in which we think about human communication (Kendon 1982). Microanalytic research has been conducted in a wide variety of academic disciplines, most notably social psychology, psychiatry, anthropology, linguistics, sociology, ethology, and communications. Within these disciplines, a number of distinctive approaches may be distinguished: in particular, conversation analysis (e.g., Sacks 1992), discourse analysis (e.g., Potter and Wetherell 1987), speech act theory (Austin 1962), ethology (e.g., Fridlund 1997), and the social skills approach (e.g., Hargie 1997). Despite substantial disagreements and differences, these approaches do also share a number of common assumptions. The key features of the microanalytic approach are:

1. Communication is studied as it actually occurs.

2. Communication can be studied as an activity in its own right.

3. All features of interaction are potentially significant.

4. Communication has a structure.

5. Conversation can be regarded as a form of action.

6. Communication can be understood in an evolutionary context.

7. Communication is best studied in naturally occurring contexts.

8. Communication can be regarded as a form of skill.

9. Communication can be taught like any other skill.

10. Macro issues (such as racism or politics) can be studied through microanalysis. (Bull 2002)

Not all of these features characterize all microanalytic research. For example, there are many studies that do not concern themselves with the evolutionary context of behavior. But an evolutionary perspective has played an important part in our understanding of the facial expressions of emotion (e.g., Ekman 2002).

Similarly, not all microanalysts concern themselves with macro issues. Indeed, microanalysts are open to criticism for ignoring larger structural factors that may influence behavior. But significant insights into macro issues can be gained through microanalysis. For example, according to interaction ritual theory (Collins 2004), it is social rituals that hold society together as a pattern of stratified and conflicting groups. Through the microanalysis of such rituals in situational context, Randall Collins argues that we can acquire a deeper understanding of macro issues such as social stratification and conflict at the societal or even global level. Again, according to expectation states theory, beliefs about how men and women differ in competence affect the emergence and exercise of social hierarchy and leadership (Ridgeway 2001). But through microanalysis, it may be possible to identify how those beliefs and expectations are manifest in behavior and affect social interaction. Thus, microanalysis is not incompatible with a macro perspective; indeed, our understanding of macro issues may be enhanced through the application of a microanalytic approach.

SEE ALSO *Individualism; Methodology; Microeconomics; Reductionism; Sociology*

BIBLIOGRAPHY

Austin, John L. 1962. *How to Do Things With Words.* Cambridge, MA: Harvard University Press.

Bull, Peter. 2002. *Communication under the Microscope: The Theory and Practice of Microanalysis.* London: Psychology Press.

Collins, Randall. 2004. *Interaction Ritual Chains.* Princeton, NJ: Princeton University Press.

Darwin, Charles. [1872] 2002. *The Expression of the Emotions in Man and Animals,* 3rd ed., ed. Paul Ekman. Oxford: Oxford University Press

Fridlund, Alan J. 1997. The New Ethology of Human Facial Expressions. In *The Psychology of Facial Expression,* eds. James A. Russell and José-Miguel Fernández-Dols, 103–129. New York: Cambridge University Press.

Hargie, Owen D.W. 1997. Interpersonal Communication: A Theoretical Framework. In *The Handbook of Communication Skills,* 2nd ed., ed. Owen D. W. Hargie, 29–63. London: Routledge.

Kendon, Adam. 1982. Organization of Behaviour in Face-to-Face Interaction. In *Handbook of Methods in Nonverbal Behaviour Research,* eds. Klaus R. Scherer and Paul Ekman, 440–505. Cambridge, U.K.: Cambridge University Press.

Marey, Étienne-Jules. 1895. *Movement.* New York: D. Appleton.

Muybridge, Eadweard. [1899] 1957. *Animals in Motion.* New York: Dover Publications.

Muybridge, Eadweard. [1901] 1957. *The Human Figure in Motion.* New York: Dover Publications.

Potter, Jonathan, and Margaret Wetherell. 1987. *Discourse and Social Psychology: Beyond Attitudes and Behaviour.* London: Sage.

Sacks, Harvey. 1992. *Lectures on Conversation,* ed. Gail Jefferson. Oxford: Blackwell.

Peter Bull

MICROECONOMICS

Microeconomics refers to the behavior of individual actors, using economic reasoning. Economic reasoning refers to the specification of individuals as purposeful decision makers. In economics, observed behaviors are typically interpreted as the outcomes of decision problems. At this level of abstraction, such a conceptualization of individuals is purely tautological. Microeconomic theories have content because of the way in which these decisions are specified; in other words, from the ways in which individuals are assumed to behave and from the description of the environment in which they function.

BASIC IDEAS

While the behavioral assumptions embodied in theoretical economic models vary widely, there are common elements that provide a heuristic description of individual decisions. First, agents are assumed to have preferences over the outcomes of their actions. By itself, this is again tautological until structure is placed on the preferences. In neoclassical economic theory, where preferences are defined over different commodity vectors, such as consumer durables to leisure, standard assumptions include: (1) completeness, the idea that an individual can compare all possible pairs of commodities and determine that which he or she prefers; and (2) transitivity, the idea that if an individual prefers commodity vector *a* to *b* and prefers *b* to *c*, then he or she will prefer *a* to *c*. These assumptions on preferences can, with certain technical assumptions, mean that individuals may be modeled as possessing utility functions; that is, that an individual acts "as if" there is a function that assigns numbers to different commodity bundles such that higher numbers are always preferred. While microeconomic environments typically start with utility functions, the reason for this is not a belief in their literal existence, but the fact that preference orderings may be represented by them.

Second, agents are assumed to face constraints. Simply put, an agent cannot choose the best of all possible outcomes. In the context of consumption, constraints are usually represented as a budget constraint, which requires that the expenditures required for a group of commodities are affordable. Constraints can be less transparent. In labor economics, when there is imperfect information about jobs, an unemployed worker can either choose among those jobs of which he or she is aware or alter the constraint by engaging in search.

Third, decisions are affected by an agent's beliefs. The preferences that an agent has over outcomes will be mediated by his or her beliefs as to how these outcomes affect him or her. For example, if an individual is deciding on whether to attend college or begin work after graduating high school, this decision will be affected by his or her beliefs as to the trajectories of earned wages under the two scenarios. An obvious reason why beliefs and realizations may differ is time, where decisions are made today before their future consequences are known. While the baseline assumptions on beliefs in economics are some form of consistent beliefs such as rational expectations, recent research has stressed various forms of learning and adaptation, such as the 2001 work of George Evans and Seppo Honkapohja.

EQUILIBRIA AND THE PRICE SYSTEM

Individual decisions are made in larger contexts. Traditionally the context for microeconomics was that of markets, in which buyers and sellers transact commodities. General equilibrium theory represents the apex of the market-based approach to microeconomics, in which the individual behaviors of buyers and sellers is simultaneously considered. In the classical environment studied by Kenneth Arrow, Gerard Debreu, and Lionel McKenzie, the key feature linking these decisions is the presence of a common price for all buyers and sellers in a given market. In general equilibrium theory, classic questions include whether an equilibrium exists (that is, whether there is a set of prices such that aggregate demand and aggregate supply are equated in every market) and whether the equilibrium is Pareto Optimal (that is, whether the allocation of goods at an equilibrium is efficient in the sense that there is no other allocation where everyone is equally well off and at least one person better off).

In classical general equilibrium theory prices do not convey information; no one learns from prices. The classical theory has been extended to include an informational role for prices. This is of great importance as it addresses the question of how information is aggregated in a decentralized economy. As Friedrich Hayek wrote in a classic statement, "How can the combination of fragments of knowledge bring about results which, if they were to be brought about deliberately, would require a knowledge on the part of the directing mind which no single person can possess?" (Hayek 1948, p. 54). Hayek's profound suggestion was that the price system aggregates information across agents in a way to produce collectively efficient allocations; modern microeconomic theory, pioneered by Sanford Grossman, has provided both a formalization and a description of the cases where this aggregation property does and does not hold. This is especially true for asset markets, where, as Grossman observed in 1989, a trader will wish to change his or her demand function for an asset evaluated at a particular price after observing that price cleared the market, in contrast to the standard formulation of a demand function in classical Walrasian general equilibrium theory.

Grossman's own work shows that the extension of classical general equilibrium theory to include the informational role of prices leads to: (1) results that show how equilibrium prices aggregate private information held by individual traders and renders key portions of it publicly available to all traders; (2) results that help resolve key information paradoxes in efficient markets theory; and (3) results that show key distinctions between synthetic securities (e.g., those synthetic securities produced by program trading strategies) and real securities and the policy importance of this distinction. The importance of prices as conveyors of information originally arose in the context of debates, primarily between Hayek and Oskar Lange, on whether socialist economies could replicate the efficiency of capitalist ones; economists conjecture they are important in thinking about transition by postcommunist economies today.

In contrast to general equilibrium theory, game theory does not focus on the role of markets in adjudicating individual decisions or in the transmission of information in a world where agents take prices as given beyond their individual control, but rather examines how individuals choose strategies when others are also choosing strategies. In such environments, important institutional features include the specification of whether or not agents can communicate with one another and form contracts with one another. Game theory has proven particularly useful in understanding the consequences of imperfect competition; that is, cases where individual firms do not act as passive price takers.

APPLICATIONS

Virtually all forms of economic decisions have been studied using microeconomics, with particular attention to their implications for behaviors that are observed in equilibrium. One example of this is the analysis of decision making under uncertainty. In order to understand how, for example, financial markets price risk, it is necessary to specify how individual agents react to risk as well as the riskiness of assets that are available. When placed in an integrated general equilibrium framework that takes into account the informational role of prices, one has the basis for the theory of finance, which has provided a complete theory of how asset returns are interrelated. Celebrated results such as the capital asset pricing model, which describes how financial markets price risk and the Black-Scholes option pricing model, which relates the prices of a stock option to the price of the stock and the interest rate on risk free bonds, have proven to have great practical as well as scholarly value.

Much of the research in microeconomics since the 1970s has focused on the relaxation of the behavioral assumptions that are traditionally associated with neoclassical economic theory. A particularly important body of work is often referred to as information economics and explores the implications for imperfect and differential information for the functioning of market and nonmarket interactions. A classic example is George Akerlof's 1970 analysis of the market for used cars when some cars are known by their owners to be lemons. Two ideas that

emerge from this literature that are standard in the study of insurance and related markets are adverse selection (the idea that certain market arrangements influence the composition of market participants such as individuals who privately know they are ill being more likely to seek medical insurance but vendors of such insurance are unable to observe the health of the individual) and moral hazard (the idea that market arrangements can lead to undesirable behaviors, such as an insured person taking more risks because he or she has the insurance).

The newly influential school of behavioral economics has challenged many of the rationality assumptions that agents face. Behavioral economists have attempted both to document how actual behaviors deviate from traditional notions of rationality as well as to understand how these deviations can explain phenomena such as investment behavior. Recent work on social interactions has attempted to expand microeconomics to incorporate substantive sociological perspectives. A recent survey of this type of work and the related empirical measurement problems is produced in William Brock and Steven Durlauf's article for the *Handbook of Econometrics* (2001).

In addition to efforts to expand the behavioral richness of microeconomics, research has attempted to apply microeconomic reasoning to new contexts; much of this was pioneered by Gary Becker. It is standard for economists to study decisions ranging from childbearing to religious behavior to crime using microeconomic reasoning. This work is sometimes regarded as "economic imperialism" but is perhaps better regarded as a recognition that purposeful decision making is not simply an economic concept but rather an important element of human nature. The notion of purposeful decision making that lies at the heart of microeconomics is compatible with the use of substantive ideas from psychology and sociology to enrich the specification of how these decisions are made.

An equally important development concerns the integration of microeconomics into macroeconomics. Modern macroeconomic theory, as exemplified in the work of Robert Lucas, Edward Prescott, and Thomas Sargent, has to a large extent been defined by the requirement that microeconomics provides the basis for macroeconomic modeling relationships. This integration has been of fundamental importance providing a coherent view of macroeconomic dynamics, including the role of expectations and intertemporal decision making in understanding the effects of macroeconomic policies. The integration of microeconomics and macroeconomics is not complete in the sense that issues of aggregation are typically ignored, but the importance of microeconomic reasoning in conditioning the modeling of macroeconomic relations is clear.

Finally, it is important to note that microeconomics has an extraordinarily active empirical side. Specific microeconomic theories are constantly being subjected to testing and evaluation. More generally, microeconomic reasoning has been used to strengthen the inferences drawn for what might appear initially as purely statistical questions, such as the effect of a job-training program on its participants. As exemplified in the work of James Heckman, microeconomic reasoning is required whenever one is interested in discussing causal aspects of individual behavior.

FURTHER READING

Neoclassical economic theory is comprehensively surveyed in Andreu Mas-Collel, Michael Whinston, and Jerry Green's *Microeconomic Theory* (1995). J. Darrell Duffie's *Dynamic Asset Pricing Theory* (2001) is a deep treatment of the modern theory of finance. Becker surveyed his fundamental contributions to the extension of neoclassical microeconomics to the study of the family and reproduced them in *A Treatise on the Family* (1993). Nancy Stokey, Robert Lucas, and Edward Prescott in *Recursive Methods in Economic Dynamics* (1989) and Thomas Sargent in *Dynamic Macroeconomic Theory* (1987) provide full coverage of the contemporary microfoundations of macroeconomics. Colin Camerer described the contemporary behavioral economics and contrasted it with more traditional approaches in his 2003 work. Heckman's 2001 article is an overview of his scholarship and is in many ways a summary of the achievements of modern microeconometrics. In their book *Microeconometrics* (2005), A. Colin Cameron and Pravin Trivedi describe many statistical methods that have been employed to evaluate microeconomic data.

SEE ALSO *Arrow-Debreu Model; Economics, Neoclassical; Game Theory; General Equilibrium; Macroeconomics; Microfoundations; Rationality*

BIBLIOGRAPHY

Akerlof, George. 1970. The Market for Lemons: Quality Uncertainty and the Market Mechanism. *Quarterly Journal of Economics* 89: 488–500.

Becker, Gary. 1993. *A Treatise on the Family*. Enlarged ed. Cambridge, MA: Harvard University Press.

Brock, William, and Steven Durlauf. 2001. Interactions-Based Models. In *Handbook of Econometrics*. Vol. 5, ed. James Heckman and Edward Leamer, 3297–3380. Amsterdam: North Holland.

Camerer, Colin. 2003. *Behavioral Game Theory: Experiments in Strategic Interaction*. Princeton, NJ: Princeton University Press.

Cameron, A. Colin, and Pravin Trivedi. 2005. *Microeconometrics: Methods and Applications*. New York: Cambridge University Press.

Duffie, J. Darrell. 2001. *Dynamic Asset Pricing Theory*. 3rd ed. Princeton, NJ: Princeton University Press.

Evans, George, and Seppo Honkapohja. 2001. *Learning and Expectations in Macroeconomics*. Princeton, NJ: Princeton University Press.

Grossman, Sanford. 1989. *The Informational Role of Prices*. Cambridge: MIT Press.

Hayek, Friedrich. 1948. *Individualism and Economic Order*. Chicago: University of Chicago Press.

Heckman, James. 2001. Micro Data, Heterogeneity, and the Evaluation of Public Policy: Nobel Lecture. *Journal of Political Economy* 109: 673–748.

Mas-Collel, Andreu, Michael Whinston, and Jerry Green. 1995. *Microeconomic Theory*. New York: Oxford University Press.

Sargent, Thomas. 1987. *Dynamic Macroeconomic Theory*. Cambridge, MA: Harvard University Press.

Stokey, Nancy, Robert Lucas, and Edward Prescott. 1989. *Recursive Methods in Economic Dynamics*. Cambridge, MA: Harvard University Press.

William A. Brock
Steven N. Durlauf

MICROELECTRONICS INDUSTRY

The global Internet economy had its origins in the microelectronics industry and the innovation of the microchip in its various versions. In the stages of optoelectronics, the use of electrical energy to generate optical energy or vice versa such as light-emitting diodes (LEDs), the microelectronic chip, as developed by Intel Corporation, assumed enormous importance for the world of information and telecommunications.

Since 1970, Moore's Law concerning the pace of technological innovation relative to cost gave significance to the power of the microchip and its contribution to all technological innovations, from the calculator to the computer, to voice and data over the Internet, and to the "magical" downloading of pictures from satellites onto the computer screen. Now known as *digital convergence*, most technological innovations in this sector originated from the microchip. The transformative innovation of the microchip led to the many innovations that emerged from Silicon Valley and other centers of technology in the United States, Europe, and Asia. Specifically, the microchip enabled computing and telecommunications to interlock in transforming data and information into digits that can be stored, processed, and transmitted over long distances instantaneously. The microchip has transformed manufacturing, health-care appliances, gadgets for domestic use, and tools and machines of every description. It has led to surges of wealth creation and employment, and it has transformed the ways in which people communicate, learn, and integrate across political borders.

Inevitably, the global Internet economy was the outcome of the transformative technology of the semiconductor. It enables the creation of new technologies in new sectors of the economy and in the daily activities of the population. In essence, the microchip is an extremely flexible technology capable of being customized to many different kinds of users and applications. As the United States witnessed the innovative dynamism generated by the microchip in the locality of Palo Alto, California, Sweden did as well near Stockholm, India in Bangalore, and Taiwan in Taipei.

PRODUCTS AND COMPETITION

The progress of the microchip industry led to the growth of multimedia services and operations. Due to this progress, the cost characteristics of the new technologies changed, and these technologies enhanced new economies of scope and reduced the economies of scale as miniaturization grew. Borrowing a term from William Gibson's novel *Neuromancer* (1984), *cyberspace* has changed the entire world and rendered many of the previously basic tools of strategy, planning, and information systems obsolete.

The newest innovations originated not in corporate headquarters but in consumer markets in which proprietary communication networks were built; these in turn were overtaken by the power of the Internet and its global connectivity. New electronic markets were exploding overnight and technology had become "not the solution, but the problem" (Downes and Mui 2000). In a process described by J. A. Schumpeter (1942) as "creative destruction," new technologies appearing in a capitalist society replaced old technologies, leading to the creation of new economies that added to the accumulation of wealth and prosperity. This change occurred under competition when the microchip became a "killer app" (application), and gave rise to the revolution in information technology and the transformation of the entire telecommunications industry.

As computing devices became smaller, less expensive, and more powerful, digital technology became the most disruptive force in modern society. Gordon Moore, who founded Intel, witnessed the decrease in the size of the product—the microchip—with each succeeding decade. He realized that as size decreases, power increases geometrically because more circuits can be placed on a single chip. Moore articulated the theory, which came to be known as Moore's Law, that processing power doubles every eighteen months, while cost holds constant. Moore's

Law applies to many other aspects of digital technology, including memory and storage devices.

THE ROLE OF THE MICROPROCESSOR

Many aspects of the telecommunications industry, such as bandwidth, the speed at which data can be transmitted, the use of high-speed fiber optic cable, and satellite and wireless communications, rely on the microchip in one way or another. As of 2006, one gigabyte of storage could fit on a credit card–sized device that cost no more than $200.

Moore's Law is supported by Metcalf's Law, according to which the more users a particular technology draws, the more valuable the technology becomes. Robert Metcalf was the founder in 1979 of 3Com Corporation, a Massachusetts-based manufacturer of computer networking products, and the designer of the Ethernet protocol for computers. Metcalf calculated that the usefulness of a network is equal to the square of the number of users, an insight that led to the explosion of the Internet in the digital age and the development of multimedia firms and services.

As a result of the cost characteristics of new technologies based on greater economies of scope and reduced economies of scale, it became possible to place greater reliance on competition, which benefits economic activities, rather than regulation. In the new information economy, the rules of market pricing have changed as transaction costs are reduced and the concept of what constitutes public goods has changed. The power of information as a public good has radically altered its impact on consumers; information is no longer a proprietary good due to its availability in cyberspace. In the multimedia age, "content" is now a public good, but its distribution costs have an impact on competition and business models.

Although the term *multimedia* has no single definition, it covers three trends in communication products. One is the delivery by a single medium of different types of content, including text, video, sound, graphics, and data. The second trend depends on the way in which content is delivered, because digitization allows more information to be stored on the same chip and pushed through the same channels, either wire line or wireless. The third trend is determined by telecommunications and media companies, which are motivated to offer consumers integrated packages from a single vendor. In such a case, transaction costs dominate both the supply-side and the demand-side identities. Multimedia firms have an advantage in market competition in which the basic feature of their products—the microchip—gains greater power for both transmission and storage.

SMART CARDS

As the microelectronics industry advances, companies have introduced multifunctional *smart cards*. Such cards are used for the payment for services, public transportation, access to health and government services, public telephones, and so on. Using smart cards, electronic payments are made at point of sale, and through the Internet and home-banking sessions (Berkvens 1997). The data on the chip would include general information to be used by application providers and card acceptors. Data is stored on the chip, as well as in the back office of the card-scheme participants. Biometrics makes identification of the user on the chip even easier and more reliable.

THE ROLE OF THE CHIP IN TRADE

Microprocessor-related trade talks between the United States and Japan became critical in 1986 when Japan agreed to open up to 20 percent of its market to foreign supplies of microprocessors. It was initially difficult to make inroads into the Japanese market for computer chips, but by 1996, 80 percent of foreign chips sold in Japan were made in the United States (Cooper and Takahashi 1996). Renewal of the 1986 agreement was sought by the administration of President Bill Clinton ten years after the initial agreement was signed. By this time, however, Japanese companies had access to lower-cost capital and subsidies from the Japanese government, and they could produce better-quality chips. The American company Cray Research, then the largest producer of supercomputers, lost a bid against Japan's Nippon Electronic Corporation to build a weather-forecasting computer for the U.S. National Science Foundation in 1996.

The spread of the production of microprocessors in Japan, China, and Taiwan, and to some extent India, has "transformed Asia into a global factory for diverse goods including microelectronics, which has led to Asia's emergence as a location for innovation offshoring" (Ernst 2004, p. 3). According to William J. Baumol (2002), new actors from Asia are entering the global innovations race, and Taiwan has accumulated a competitive advantage in digital circuit designs. Intel remained the leading chipmaker in the world as of 2006; its chips direct the inner workings of most personal computers, and it is responsible for changing the function of the personal computer to an entertainment device. Intel began positioning its platform to provide online entertainment to the digital living room, and was prepared to expand its operations in India. Domestic firms in India can benefit from the rapid growth of the domestic information technology market.

THE ERA OF MOBILE COMMUNICATIONS

Wireless technologies, including Wi-Fi (wireless Internet connectivity), Blue Tooth, and 3G, provide faster and longer-range transmissions. Competing with them is a communication technology called *near-field system*, which fuses tickets, key cards, and cash with mobile phones. This device requires different types of microprocessors and may displace existing wireless technologies. By 2006, it had become possible to install a "contactless" chip and its reader into a mobile phone, thereby making possible such operations as using a screen and connecting to the Internet with a phone. Devices are in use in Hong Kong (Octopus cards) and Japan (DoCoMo) that offer wallet phones with a FeliCa chip. A FeliCa chip is a contactless card for an electronic wallet developed by Sony. From the word *felicity* the card cannot be forged and helps send and receive data at high speed and security.

These innovations are a consequence of a global production system based on vertical specialization in which many of the functions can be relocated to low-cost and low-wage regions. Beyond manufacturing, most of the production innovation in the electronics industry has given rise to the development of mass-production facilities in developing Asian countries. The models for chip design and manufacturing, for example, are developed in Korea, Taiwan, and Singapore, and then transmitted to other countries, such as Malaysia and China, as well as such eastern European countries as Hungary, Poland, and Romania.

The restructuring of global design chains has created wide-ranging links across countries, and these can vary between manufacturing-based innovation, product innovation, and infrastructure (Ernst 2004). Chip design has become strategically important for telecommunications and computer networking, mobile handsets and entertainment devices, and automobile electronics. In the past, chip design and manufacturing was considered the monopoly of the Japanese microelectronics industry, but Japan's innovation prowess failed in the software and biotechnology arena during the 1990s. Japanese researchers had better luck with robotics, aerospace technology, and other burgeoning technologies (Competing Through Innovation 2005, p. 65).

In order to regain its competitive strength, Japan aimed to innovate in its microelectronics industry. Japanese companies also began conducting research in the robotics sector with robots designed to enter the health-care industry and search-and-rescue operations. Japan's position as a leading innovator in chip design is being challenged by other Asian countries, especially Taiwan, as well as countries in eastern Europe. In the early years of the twenty-first century, Japan continued to lead the world in its investment in research and development, with approximately 3.2 percent of its gross national product devoted to research and development, compared with 2.6 percent in the United States and 2 percent in the European Union. Japan also leads other countries in obtaining patents in the electronics industry, but it lags in management skills and university research.

At the same time, India and China were racing to obtain foreign investment for chips manufacturing. In 2005 the California-based company Advanced Micro Devices (AMD) joined a consortium to build India's first semiconductor plant, as well as an assembly and testing plant in the Chinese city of Chengdu. In 2004 Lenovo, China's leading personal computer manufacturer, agreed to use AMD chips in its desktops. In addition, AMD agreed to open a chip-testing facility in India, gaining contracts from India's railways, schools, and government.

Intel also has a commanding market presence in both India and China. Intel aimed at developing a low-cost personal computer to be used in rural multimedia kiosks found across India. The product could also prove successful in China. Competition between AMD and Intel would keep down costs for rural applications. In addition, both India and China were making a push for the faster spread of broadband with affordable Internet applications and e-initiatives.

CHIP MANUFACTURE AND HEALTH CARE

There has been continuing opposition to the use of computing in health care, a prospect that involves far greater use of computers by the medical profession. Some critics argue that a systematic use of software to diagnose and care for patients could be disruptive. However, in *telehealth* projects, computing plays a vital role because diagnoses can be transmitted via the Internet to distant places through the use of satellites or even microwaves. The goal of this process is to use software that matches a patient's symptoms and health history against a catalogue of computerized medical knowledge. This idea has been supported and propagated by Dr. Larry Weed, who believes that doctors need technology to facilitate their absorption and retention of new medical information. As governments push for health-care automation, resistance to the use of information technology could finally crumble.

DISPERSION OF CHIP DESIGN AND MANUFACTURE

As chip design centers become geographically disbursed, the links between engineers and markets have to be established. Market demand for microelectronic chips is growing phenomenally because of the wide use of chips in consumer products and in the entertainment industry. New models of

software development are leading to a new breed of knowledge workers, adding to the complications already inherent in chip design and innovation. As the number of knowledge workers grows in developing countries, there is a shift in production in the microelectronics industry, with product chains also growing in number and intensity. These developments have had a major impact on the telecommunications industry, as well as in mobile communications, automobile production, and the health sector.

The convergence of digital technologies has created a new environment—cyberspace—for transacting business, providing entertainment, forming links with customers, and creating and distributing wealth. The development of digital technology has been fueled by the conditions expressed in Moore's Law and Metcalf's Law, as well as the economic effects of the Schumpeterian process of creative destruction. As a consequence, the microelectronics industry has touched all lives, both real and virtual. A new generation of knowledge workers is entering cyberspace armed with the Internet and the ability to change the economic dynamics of the business world and markets worldwide. The ability to reach new frontiers in microelectronics research is no longer determined by geography, but by free computing power, free bandwidth, free software, and a society that values such an environment for its business interests and its livelihood.

SEE ALSO *Bubbles; Industry; Internet; Technology, Adoption of*

BIBLIOGRAPHY

Baumol, William J. 2002. *The Free Market Innovation Machine: Analyzing the Growth Miracle of Capitalism.* Princeton, NJ: Princeton University Press.

Berkvens, Jan. 1997. Consumer Trust and Multifunctional Chip Cards. *I-Ways: Digest of Electronic Commerce Policy and Regulation* 20 (4): 22.

Competing Through Innovation: The Future of Japanese Business. 2005. *The Economist* 377 (8457), December 17: 65–68.

Cooper, Helene, and Dean Takahashi. 1996. Politics to Color U.S.-Japan Chip Talks. *The Wall Street Journal* Eastern edition 228 (20), July 29: A2.

Ernst, Dieter. 2004. Internationalisation of Innovation: Why Is Chip Design Moving to Asia? East-West Center Working Papers, Economics Series, No. 64. Honolulu, HI: East-West Center.

Downes, Larry, and Chunka Mui. 2000. *Unleashing the Killer App: Digital Strategies for Market Dominance.* Boston: Harvard Business School Press.

Gibson, William. 1984. *Neuromancer.* New York: Ace.

Schumpeter J. A. 1942. *Capitalism, Socialism, and Democracy.* New York and London: Harper.

Meheroo Jussawalla

MICROFINANCE

Microfinance, also termed microcredit, refers primarily to small, development-oriented loans made to low-income borrowers with the aim of helping them to develop commercial activities or start businesses.

The concept of microcredit originated with the economist Muhammad Yunus. He made a small loan to a woman in Chittagong, Bangladesh, who used it to increase her family's income by making and selling bamboo furniture. Established formal-sector banks were not interested in making loans of such small amounts, especially to borrowers who were highly risky because they lacked both collateral and business experience. Yunus founded the Grameen Bank in 1976 as a lending institution that specialized in loans of this type.

The Grameen Bank organized potential borrowers into small groups, and put them through a training program emphasizing both personal habits and enterprise-related skills. All members of the group made regular deposits; one member of the group would be selected to receive a loan. The next loan would be made to a group member only when the outstanding loan was repaid. In effect, the social pressure of the borrower group provided a form of collateral.

Pooling savings to facilitate rotating borrowing for in-group members is not unique to Grameen Bank; migrants and co-ethnics, in particular, often make such arrangements. What is distinctive about the Grameen approach is that these pooled savings are used to facilitate entrepreneurial activity, and that women are targeted. Indeed, this bank's design highlighted the problem of the exclusion of women from participation in markets, and the potential economic-development impact of fully engaging the resources, energy, and initiative of women once these women were freed to create their own enterprises.

Grameen's loan program quickly became well known and found global imitators and adaptors. Economic theorists have been fascinated by the Grameen Bank, as the design of its lending-saving mechanism has interesting aspects from the perspectives of game theory and information theory. And as the Grameen model spread to other nations, a critical academic discussion has ensued about the potential and limitations of this model. One debate, summarized by Dale Adams and J. D. Von Pischke in 1992, involves whether microcredit represents a new element in developing economies, and can serve as a stand-alone poverty-alleviation program. A related debate, expressed by Anne Marie Goetz and Rina Sen Gupta in 1996, discusses the net impact of Grameen-type programs on women, primarily because women-centered microcredit programs may have complex and unintended effects on gender relations, and specifically on intra-household power relations and resource and debt allocations.

These controversies notwithstanding, microcredit has been broadly embraced by many development agencies and governments. The United Nations (UN) declared 2005 the Year of Microcredit, recognizing and initiating microcredit programs in more than ninety countries. The World Bank set a goal of reaching "100 million of the world's poorest families by 2005." Microcredit programs have received strong support from national governments: for example, the Community Development Financial Institution program in the United States, initiated in 1996, channels money to microcredit; in 2003, Brazil's federal government began requiring all banks to set aside 2 percent of their assets for use in funding microcredit activities.

Microcredit has become a central element in the efforts of global, national, and local organizations to increase self-employment prospects for low-income people, and for providing access to credit. In October 2005, UN secretary general Kofi Annan stated that microfinance has "an untapped opportunity to create markets, bring people in from the margin, and give them the tools with which to help themselves." He called for "scaling up" microcredit practices "without losing sight of the poorest and most vulnerable members of our society" (States News Service 2005).

With this growing government and agency attention, and these shifting expectations about what microcredit can do, most contemporary microcredit programs have only a partial resemblance to Grameen's original program: the focus on female borrowers, on the very poor, and on extensive training of participants often disappears.

The combination of financial deregulation, proliferating publicly sponsored programs, and public officials' shifting expectations has blurred the line between microcredit and other financial markets for lower-income people. Microcredit sometimes denotes small-denomination loans made to very small businesses, or to businesses operating in informally settled areas such as Brazil's *favelas* (slums or shantytowns). In this usage, microcredit supports working-capital needs, not business creation as in the Grameen model. And in some nations, such as South Africa, the term microcredit refers generally to loan markets in which non-bank lenders provide credit to borrowers in unregulated or high-risk, low-sum credit markets. This multiplication of usages has led to the creation of a distinction between productive and nonproductive microcredit.

BIBLIOGRAPHY

Adams, Dale W., and J. D. Von Pischke. 1992. Microenterprise Credit Programs: Déja Vu. *World Development* 20 (10): 1463–1470.

Besley, Timothy, Stephen Coate, and Glenn Loury. 1993. The Economics of Rotating Savings and Credit Associations. *American Economic Review* 83 (4): 792–810.

Goetz, A. M., and R. Sen Gupta. 1996. Who Takes the Credit? Gender, Power, and Control Over Loan Use in Rural Credit Programs in Bangladesh. *World Development* 24 (1): 45–64.

States News Service. 2005. Annan Calls for Small Loans to Millions of People with Unmet Borrowing Needs. New York, October 10.

World Bank. 1998. Council of International Financial Institutions—The World Bank. In *Countdown 2005: The Newsletter of the Microcredit Summit Campaign*, September 1998. http://www.microcreditsummit.org/newsletter/serageldin.htm.

Yunus, Muhammad, with Alan Jolis. 2001. *Banker to the Poor: The Autobiography of Muhammad Yunus, Founder of Grameen Bank*. New York: Oxford University Press.

Gary Dymski

MICROFOUNDATIONS

Microfoundations refers to a concept in economics associated with a research program that developed in the 1940s and which apparently became uninteresting to economists by the 1980s. If macroeconomics is associated with aggregate economic models, and microeconomics is associated with the individual behavior of households and firms, microfoundations was taken to be the demand that macroeconomic models have microeconomic foundations. That is, no macroeconomic model was to be deemed acceptable if it could not be derived from underlying individual choice behavior.

Though this seems unobjectionable, it in fact carried some intellectual baggage. In the 1940s, there were two strands of economics that vied for the attention of theorists: the first was the economics of John Maynard Keynes, associated with managing the economy as a whole. The second was general equilibrium theory, a view of the economy as built on the optimizing behavior of individuals and firms, which investigated whether all their independent decisions could possibly lead, as Adam Smith had suggested, to coherent social outcomes. General equilibrium analysis was part of the tradition of the Cowles Commission, then located at the University of Chicago. For Cowles's economists, Keynesian macroeconomic theory needed to be derived from the foundational work in general equilibrium theory else it would be an ad hoc theory. The neoclassical synthesis, the marriage of neoclassical general equilibrium with Keynesian macroeconomics, begun with Oscar Lange's *Price Flexibility and Unemployment* (1944) was further developed in Lawrence Klein's *The Keynesian Revolution* (1947), and was com-

pleted by Don Patinkin's *Money, Interest, and Prices* (1956). Keynesian models "fell out" as special cases of aggregated general equilibrium models with money.

In the 1950s and 1960s many Keynesians were opposed to general equilibrium analysis out of a belief that Keynesian economics was not a special case of rigidities and market failures in those models, and for them *microfoundations* became the code word for a desire to reconstruct microeconomics to support Keynesian macroeconomics. At the same time, anti-Keynesians like monetarist Milton Friedman began constructing equilibrium expectations models that ruled out the idea of the Phillips Curve trade-off between unemployment and inflation that then played a role in standard Keynesian models.

Microfoundations thus became part of the monetarists versus Keynesians debate of the 1960s, with the Keynesians asking for disequilibrium or Marshallian partial equilibrium microfoundations to be developed, and the monetarists asking that Keynesian analysis be reconstructed to accommodate rational expectations equilibrium models.

As is the case for most controversies in economics whose bases are oversimplifications of complex analytic positions, neither perspective on the microfoundations of macroeconomics made contact with much of what was actually going on in economic analysis. In the first decade of the twenty-first century, economists do not produce arguments about microfoundations as such. The reconstruction of macroeconomic analysis in the post–Robert Lucas period has resulted in the general acceptability, indeed general requirement, that macroeconomic models be based on optimizing behavior by (perhaps representative) economic agents. Microfoundations now gives only a residual hint of earlier foundationalist thinking, and merely suggests that the choice structure of any particular economic model be clear and well specified. To the degree that the term *microfoundations* has a meaning today, it is that agents' decisions and choices should not be based on ad hoc specifications.

SEE ALSO *Macroeconomics; Macrofoundations; Microeconomics*

BIBLIOGRAPHY

Klein, Lawrence R. 1947. *The Keynesian Revolution*. New York: Macmillan.

Lange, Oscar. 1944. *Price Flexibility and Employment*. Bloomington, IN: Principia Press.

Patinkin, Don. 1956. *Money, Interest, and Prices*. New York: Harper and Row.

Weintraub, E. Roy. 1979. *Microfoundations: The Compatibility of Microeconomics and Macroeconomics*. New York: Cambridge University Press.

E. Roy Weintraub

MICROSOFT

The spread of computerization in the late twentieth century ushered in a new, third, industrial revolution, which redefined the environment and relationships of industrial capitalism. The computer hardware and software industries have been among the most dynamic and rapidly developing of any industries. The origins of the microcomputer industry are typically acknowledged as dating to 1975 with the release of the MITS/Altair in specialist hobby magazine *Popular Electronics*. It was for this computer that William (Bill) Gates, while still a student at Harvard, succeeded in writing an operating system (Langlois and Robertson 1985). Formed in 1975 by Gates and Paul Allen, with Steve Ballmer joining later, Microsoft Corporation became the world's largest computer operating system and software company. Annual turnover increased from $140 million in 1985 to over $2.7 billion by 1992 and more than $44 billion by 2006. Pretax revenue as a percentage of turnover was 37 percent in 2006 (Microsoft 2006). By the early 1990s, the firm had gained a dominant position in the market for computer software with 44 percent of sales (Wallace and Erickson 1992). The U.S. Department of Justice, however, brought an antitrust case in October 1998, arguing that Microsoft had succeeded in achieving a monopolistic position in the supply of computer operating systems with a market share of over 90 percent of Intel-based PC (personal computer) operating systems (U.S. Department of Justice 1999).

ORGANIZATIONAL CULTURE AND BILL GATES

The culture and organization of the company was synonymous with informality and openness to top management, despite its being an organization of over 76,000 employees. From the beginning, casual dress, group working, and a lack of hierarchy were its trademarks. The corporation's offices in Redmond, Washington, are arranged in a campus style, imitating a university where staff would feel a sense of familiarity and "belonging." The company actively sought to recruit bright and ambitious programmers and graduates from leading universities. This flat managerial structure and openness is, however, only one side of the coin. Microsoft employees were expected to work extremely long hours. Strong pressure existed to ensure employees were focused solely on the work they did for the company. More draconically, the company used a biannual peer review process whose result was the sacking of the worst performing 5 percent of staff in each review.

Gates's entrepreneurship, often discussed in Schumpeterian terms, highlights the importance of social networks and social capital. Born in Seattle in 1955 into a wealthy family with a father who was a successful lawyer, Gates attended Lakeside School, a prestigious private school, and later Harvard University with the aim of becoming a lawyer like his father. Gates was thus not simply an exceedingly bright student, he was also well connected. He was able, through his father, to gain contacts with leading lawyers and raise capital through venture capitalists.

COMPETITIVE ADVANTAGE: LICENSING IN OPERATING SYSTEMS AND SOFTWARE

Microsoft released its first disk operating system, called Microsoft Disk Operating System (MS-DOS), in 1981. The decision of IBM to adopt MS-DOS as its operating system for preinstallation on IBM computers proved crucial in allowing Microsoft to establish MS-DOS as the industry standard. MS-DOS was not the most technologically advanced product available in the early 1980s. Icon-based interfaces (using a graphical user interface), developed at the Xerox research labs and adopted by Apple Computer, Inc., were not matched by Microsoft until the release of Microsoft Windows in 1985. However, the superiority of the icon-based system encouraged Apple to maintain close proprietorial control over its operating system, resulting in the Apple operating system being only available on Apple Mac machines. Unlike Apple, Microsoft saw in licensing a commercial mechanism for the establishment of an industry standard, as well as a strategy and competitive advantage based upon the creation of positive externalities and the networking effects deriving from the establishment of an industry standard (Langlois and Robertson 1985, pp. 68–101). Thus the licensing and success of Microsoft Windows was such that by 1990 Microsoft had achieved a dominant position in the supply of operating systems running on Intel-based PCs.

Microsoft also found competitive advantage in closely monitoring and responding to new developments in the software industry. As a result, however, Microsoft has been continually accused—as with the antitrust case described above and in a lawsuit brought by Apple in 1988—of anti-competitive practices, copying and even stealing new developments. Microsoft developed close contacts with small innovative firms, only to release alternative versions of the small firms' software. Intuit, a producer of a money-management software package, claimed that after its software began outselling rivals by six to one, Microsoft approached the company in early 1990 to discuss a possible takeover or joint venture whereby Microsoft would produce the software, licensing the

Intuit brand name. However, by the end of 1990, Microsoft had abandoned all negotiations and announced the release of its own finance product, Microsoft Money.

Microsoft's practice of licensing software, and increasing the price to manufacturers for older versions of Microsoft software and operating systems, has been effective at encouraging the spread of the newest versions of its software, thereby reinforcing its market position. Microsoft's success brought it into conflict with the antitrust authorities in both the United States and Europe, where its monopoly power was subject to extensive government investigation. In the European case, Microsoft was fined €280.5 million in 1996, with another €497 million levied in 2004. European authorities also restricted Microsoft's ability to bundle software (Tran 2006).

As of 2007, the company is organized into three divisions—Microsoft Platforms and Services, Microsoft Business, and Microsoft Entertainment and Devices—reflecting the evolution of the company from its initial development of operating systems and software toward the provision of Internet, media, and entertainment services. By 2007 Microsoft had expanded its operations into ninety countries. However, this expansion has brought new regulatory problems, notably the Chinese government's demands that the company restrict access to Internet services and news. Thus Microsoft's expansion worldwide and into new markets is, almost uniquely, inherently interlinked with regulatory and competitive interaction between the company and host governments.

SEE ALSO *Computers: Science and Society; Digital Divide; Entrepreneurship; Globalization, Social and Economic Aspects of; Information, Economics of; Internet; Management; Networks; Organizations; Social Capital; Venture Capital*

BIBLIOGRAPHY

Langlois, Richard N., and Paul L. Robertson. 1995. *Firms, Markets, and Economic Change: A Dynamic Theory of Business Institutions.* London: Routledge.

Microsoft Corporation. 2006. Microsoft Corporate Annual Report 2006: Financial Highlights. http://www.microsoft.com/msft/reports/ar06/flashversion/10 k_fh_fin.html.

Tran, Mark. 2006. EU Hits Microsoft with €280.5m Antitrust Fine. *Guardian Unlimited*, July 12.

U.S. Department of Justice, Antitrust Division. 1999. *United States v. Microsoft*: Findings of Fact. http://www.usdoj.gov/atr/cases/ms_findings.htm.

Wallace, James, and Jim Erickson. 1992. *Hard Drive: Bill Gates and the Making of the Microsoft Empire.* New York: Wiley.

Carlo Morelli

MIDDLE CLASS

Class is perhaps the most crucial concept in the social sciences; class location affects everyone's life, and class struggles are at the core of social dynamics in all societies. Class can be viewed as a dichotomous system in which each class presupposes the other (e.g., there can be no masters without slaves and vice versa) or as a gradational system with a continuous ordering or ranking of people, from low to high, on the basis of income, skill levels, occupation, education, and so on (Ossowski 1963). The middle class can be identified on a purely descriptive, ad hoc basis, using a gradational approach to divide the population into aggregates sharing similar characteristics. The "middle class" is, then, the population aggregate that falls in the middle of the income, educational, and occupational profiles of a research sample, a given community, a region, or a nation-state. This descriptive approach yields only a superficial picture of the middle class, however. Theoretical analysis is required to identify the basis for the location of the middle class in the social and economic structures that, in turn, affect its economic, social, and political behavior and ideological commitments. Karl Marx (1818–1883) and Max Weber (1864–1920) set the foundations for the analysis of class. A discussion of their main ideas must precede consideration of more recent theories about the middle class.

MARX AND WEBER ON CLASS

Marx identifies two main classes in capitalist societies: the bourgeoisie or capitalist class (owners of the means of production), and the proletariat or working class (owners only of labor power or the capacity to work). Prior to capitalism, there was a "manifold gradation of social rank" (e.g., feudal lords, apprentices, serfs, etc.), and within each of these ranks there were "subordinate gradations" (Marx and Engels [1848] 1998, p. 2). In reply to the question, "What makes wage-laborers, capitalists, and landlords constitute the great social classes?" Marx offers a preliminary answer: "the identity of revenues and sources of revenues." He rejects this conclusion because it would lead to defining as a class any group whose income has the same origin. Marx gives the example of physicians and officials and ends by stating, "the same would also be true of the infinite fragmentation of interest and rank into which the division of labor splits laborers as well as capitalists and landlords" (Marx [1894] 1967, pp. 885–886). For Marx, a social class is not an income group, but a necessary and unequal relationship between people, mediated or shaped by their relationship to the means of production. The relationship between capitalists and workers is necessary (they presuppose each other), it is exploitative (capitalists appropriate the surplus value produced by the workers), and it places the capitalist class in a position of power over the working class.

When examining capitalism theoretically, Marx uses a dichotomous concept of class. Empirically, he observed, classes do not appear in "pure form"; in England, for example, they were fragmented by the division of labor into "middle and intermediate strata" (Marx [1894] 1967, p. 885). The middle class, Marx's writings suggest, is a descriptive concept that refers to an empirically variable, heterogeneous set of strata located in an intermediate position between workers and capitalists.

Weber's concept of class is neither relational nor centered on exploitation. Weber's focus is the effect of class situation on life chances, that is, on an individual's economic and social opportunities. Classes are aggregates of individuals who, because they bring similar resources to the market (e.g., ownership of different kinds of property, different skills, etc.), they share similar life chances. "The term 'class' refers to any group of people that is found in the same class situation" (Gerth and Mills [1946] 1973, p. 181). In market exchanges, ownership of property gives power to owners over nonowners, that is, those who must sell their labor or goods made with their labor in order to survive. This is why " 'property' and 'lack of property' are … the basic categories of all class situations" (Gerth and Mills [1946] 1973, pp. 181–182). These categories, however, are extremely differentiated according to the kinds and quantity of property and the type of skills individuals bring to the market. Weber provides an elaborate taxonomy of propertied, commercial, and social classes. The middle classes are located between the "positively" and "negatively" privileged propertied and commercial classes—for example, small property owners, craftsmen, self-employed farmers, public officials, professionals, and credentialed and highly skilled workers (Weber 1978, pp. 302–307).

Weber theorized about classes at the level of what Marx called "the Eden of the innate rights of man" (Marx [1867] 1967, p. 176), meaning the market, where capitalists and workers meet freely as buyers and sellers of commodities. Marx focused on the level of production, where capitalists exploit workers. Both levels of analysis are important for the study of class.

TWENTIETH-CENTURY THINKING ABOUT THE MIDDLE CLASS

As capitalism developed in western Europe and the United States, it brought not only an increase in the size of the working class, but, especially during the first half of the twentieth century, a relatively greater increase in the number of nonmanual waged and salaried employees. Some of these "white-collar" workers were highly educated, well paid, and in positions of authority; others were

poorly paid and differed from manual "blue-collar" workers mainly in the kind of work they did. Sociologist C. Wright Mills (1916–1962) referred to these workers as a "new" middle class, different in its dependent status and source of income (salaried work) from the economically self-reliant "old" middle class prevalent in the nineteenth century, composed of independent professionals, small farmers, small entrepreneurs, and property owners (Mills 1951). This new and growing intermediate strata or middle class, because of its heterogeneity in terms of occupation, education, income, and authority in the workplace, is difficult to categorize and identify.

Among Marxist analysts, the most important work has been done by Erik Olin Wright, who introduced complexity into the two-class schema by examining, in the context of concrete capitalist societies, variations in the extent to which the three dimensions of capitalist power—ownership and control over money capital, physical capital, and labor—coincide or not to form different kinds of class locations. There are, in light of this analysis, three "pure" classes: capitalists, the working class, and the petty bourgeoisie or owners of means of production who do not employ labor (Wright 2001, pp. 112–113). The middle classes are propertyless employees whose levels of skill and knowledge, and position in the authority structure, place them in "contradictory" class locations. As well-paid managers or experts, they are in a "privileged location within relations of exploitation" (Wright 1997, p. 22); they are exploited (as workers), while simultaneously sharing capitalist privileges that vary with their degree of authority and expertise.

A different criterion for separating the working class from the middle class is whether or not workers engage in productive labor, that is, whether they produce exchange values and, therefore, surplus value. Arguing that only productive workers are members of the working class, Nicos Poulantzas (1936–1979) considers all other wage and salary earners, those who only contribute to the circulation and realization of surplus value (i.e., those employed in banking, commerce, research, advertising, services, etc.), as unproductive workers: the middle classes are composed of such workers (Poulantzas 1973, pp. 30–31).

Today's neo-Weberian analysis of class has to focus on the relationship between class or market situation and life chances. Given the exceedingly large number of possible market situations, social scientists have to identify clusters of those positions that could be considered classes (Breen 2005, p. 35). Aage Sørensen, for example, defines classes as "sets of structural positions. Social relationships within markets, especially within labor markets, and within firms define these positions" (Sørensen 1991, p. 72; cited in

Breen 2005, p. 35). The nature of those positions and the number of classes that can be constructed vary.

POLITICS AND THE MIDDLE CLASS

Class location objectively determines people's economic and political interests and influences, not their subjectivity, political consciousness, beliefs, behavior, and so forth. But classes, as Weber observed, are not communities; they are not groups whose members share a sense of belonging and a set of objectives. Classes are aggregates of people in the same "class situation," and they become mobilized and politicized only under certain circumstances, such as, for example, interclass confrontations or rapid economic and technological change that undermines their life chances. The middle classes, like all classes in "contradictory" class locations, can vary in their political allegiances. Simultaneously placed in relations of subordination, domination, and relative autonomy, they are more likely to be motivated by ideological political commitments, values, beliefs, religion, and so on than by "objective" interests.

The paradoxical behavior of American voters who, despite their economic vulnerability, vote for a party that protects the interests of the capitalist class, illustrates the weight of politics, culture, and religion in shaping the political behavior of the middle classes (see, for example, Frank 2004). As long as the ruling classes continue to control the media and the production and dissemination of ideologies in harmony with the value commitments of the middle strata, these sectors of the population will most likely be swayed towards conservatism unless a sudden economic crisis, like the Great Depression of the 1930s, undermines their understanding of their real conditions of existence.

SEE ALSO *Autonomy; Black Middle Class; Blue Collar and White Collar; Bourgeoisie, Petty; Class; Gramsci, Antonio; Hegemony; Jacobinism; Managerial Class; Marx, Karl; Middleman Minorities; Middlemen Minorities; Poulantzas, Nicos; Professionalization; Professionals; Stratification; Voting; Voting Patterns; Weber, Max; Working Class*

BIBLIOGRAPHY

Breen, Richard. 2005. Foundations of a Neo-Weberian Class Analysis. In *Approaches to Class Analysis*, ed. Erik Olin Wright, 31–50. Cambridge, U.K.: Cambridge University Press.

Corey, Lewis. [1935] 1992. *The Crisis of the Middle Class.* New York: Columbia University Press.

Frank, Thomas. 2004. *What's the Matter With Kansas? How Conservatives Won the Heart of America.* New York: Metropolitan.

Gerth, Hans, and C. Wright Mills, eds. and trans. [1946] 1973. *From Max Weber: Essays in Sociology.* New York: Oxford University Press.

Marx, Karl. [1867] 1967. *Capital.* Vol. 1. New York: International Publishers.

Marx, Karl. [1894] 1967. *Capital.* Vol. 3. New York: International Publishers.

Marx, Karl, and Frederick Engels. [1845–1846] 1947. *The German Ideology.* New York: International Publishers.

Marx, Karl, and Friedrich Engels. [1848] 1998. *The Communist Manifesto.* New York: Monthly Review Press.

Mills, C. Wright. 1951. *White Collar: The American Middle Classes.* New York: Oxford University Press.

Ossowski, Stanislaw. 1963. *Class Structure in the Social Consciousness.* Trans. Sheila Patterson. New York: Free Press of Glencoe.

Poulantzas, Nicos. 1973. On Social Classes. *New Left Review* 78: 27–54.

Sørensen, Aage B. 1991. On the Usefulness of Class Analysis in Research on Social Mobility and Socioeconomic Inequality. *Acta Sociologica* 34:2; cited in Breen, Richard. 2005. Foundations of a Neo-Weberian Class Analysis. In *Approaches to Class Analysis*, ed. Erik Olin Wright. London: Cambridge University Press.

Weber, Max. 1978. *Economy and Society: An Outline of Interpretive Sociology,* eds. Guenter Roth and Claus Wittich. Berkeley: University of California Press.

Wright, Erik Olin. 1997. *Class Counts: Comparative Studies in Class Analysis.* Cambridge, U.K.: Cambridge University Press.

Wright, Erik Olin. 2001. Varieties of Marxist Conceptions of Class Structure. In *Social Stratification: Class, Race, and Gender in Sociological Perspective*, ed. David B. Grusky, 112–115. 2nd ed. Boulder, CO: Westview.

Wright, Erik Olin, ed. 2005. *Approaches to Class Analysis.* Cambridge, U.K.: Cambridge University Press.

Martha Gimenez

MIDDLE CLASS, BLACK
SEE *Black Middle Class.*

MIDDLE WAY

Within the religio-philosophical traditions of Asia, the term *middle way* is associated with both Confucian and Buddhist teachings. In Confucianism, the *Doctrine of the Mean* (*Zhongyong*) advanced a vision of the goodness of human nature in terms of its "centeredness" (*zhong*) prior to the arousal of the feelings, and its harmoniousness (*yong*) when balanced after the feelings are aroused. Through "sincerity" (*cheng*) in thought and deed, the centrality of this original state is preserved in a harmonious relationship to all things, making possible a mystic unity with everything between heaven and earth. However, the *Doctrine of the Mean* only came to be emphasized as a canonical text with the appearance of neo-Confucianism, a post-Buddhist development, during the Song dynasty (960–1279). Though the "mean" as the course of moderation and balance had been a part of the teachings of Confucius (551–479 BCE), the importance assigned to the *Doctrine of the Mean* can be viewed as an indication of the extent to which neo-Confucians felt compelled to respond to themes that had been more emphasized by the Buddhists. Mention of the "middle way" first and foremost brings to mind the teachings of Siddhārtha Gautama (563–483 BCE), the historical Buddha, and later Mahāyāna Buddhist philosophers such as Nāgārjuna (c. 150–250).

After having been raised in luxury, as the son of the king of the Shakya tribe, Siddhārtha Gautama left his family and embarked on a search for the meaning of life, one that involved him in a prolonged period of ascetic practice. Icons representing the extent to which Siddhārtha pursued this course depict him as an emaciated figure, sitting in meditation, with a taut layer of flesh binding his pronounced skeleton. Ultimately, however, Siddhārtha accepted a small portion of rice-milk from a goatherd, Sumedha. Though he continued his search for meaning, Siddhārtha abandoned extreme asceticism, as he had earlier abandoned his life of luxury, in favor of a "middle way," or a search for understanding and liberation based on balance and moderation.

Not long after taking up this middle course, Siddhārtha achieved enlightenment. In his first sermon, Siddhārtha praised the middle way as superior to both the life of luxury and that of asceticism. He then related his realization of the Four Noble Truths: that life is suffering; that there is a cause of suffering, desire and attachment; that there is a cure, elimination of attachment; and that the path to such elimination is the Eightfold Noble Path. The latter can be summarized as a way of life that flows from the practitioner's realization that there is no self (the absence of self is referred to as *anātman*), that all things lack self-nature, and that everything is transitory. With these insights into the meaning of life, Siddhārtha was able to achieve *nirvāna*, or liberation from the cycle of reincarnation through the "putting out of the flame" of existence. He thus became known as "the awakened one," or "the Buddha." The implication of the Buddha beginning his first sermon with praise for the middle way is that the entirety of his teachings should be understood as an expression of the course that steers clear of extreme practices that lead to rebirth and continued suffering. More particularly, however, the middle way, lauded as the source

of wisdom, peace, and *nirvāna*, was identified with the practical way of the Eightfold Path.

The philosopher Nāgārjuna made the teaching of the middle way virtually identical with Mahāyāna Buddhism as it came to be understood metaphysically. Nāgārjuna's most famous work, the *Mūlamadhyamaka kārikā*, or *Treatise on the Middle Way*, explained "the middle way" (*mādhyamaka*) in terms of an eightfold process of negation systematically denying all theses and their antitheses. Nāgārjuna viewed both thesis and antithesis as extreme positions that could be mediated only by denial of both. Furthermore, he insisted that the denial of both thesis and antithesis be denied, as well as the affirmation of both thesis and antithesis. Ultimately, Nāgārjuna affirms the middle way as *śūnyatā*, or emptiness, the state of all aspects of existence that is midway between independent, self-sustaining existence and utter nonexistence. *Śūnyatā* properly understood is neither absolute existence nor absolute nonexistence, but instead the middle way that recognizes the dependent nature of any aspect of existence in relation to all other aspects of existence. Rather than being a negation of reality, *śūnyatā* makes possible the phenomenal world as we know it. Nāgārjuna's metaphysical interpretation of the middle way as applied to all categories and things—including time, space, causality, suffering, the self, *samsāra*, the Buddha, the Four Noble Truths, the Eightfold Noble Path, *nirvāna*, and so on—complemented the earlier practical interpretation of the middle path as an existential course of moderation, one avoiding the extremes of indulgence in luxury or excessive asceticism. Followers of Nāgārjuna's "middle way" teachings, known as *Mādhyamikas*, found comfort especially in knowing that suffering and *samsāra* are empty in the sense that they have no independent existence. Alternatively, they have found in the emptiness of the self, the Buddha, and *nirvāna* an absence of obstacles that might otherwise hinder their unity with them.

SEE ALSO *Buddha; Buddhism; Religion*

BIBLIOGRAPHY

Cheng, Hsueh-li. 1982. *Nāgārjuna's* Twelve Gate Treatise; *Translated, with Introductory Essays, Comments, and Notes.* Boston: D. Reidel.

Garfield, Jay L. 1995. *The Fundamental Wisdom of the Middle Way: Nāgārjuna's* Mūlamadhyamakakārikā. New York: Oxford University Press.

Inada, Kenneth. 1970. *Nāgārjuna: A Translation of His* Mūlamadhyamakakārikā *with an Introductory Essay.* Tokyo: Hokuseido.

Kalupahana, David J. 1975. *Buddhist Philosophy: A Historical Analysis.* Honolulu: University of Hawaii Press.

Kalupahana, David J. 1999. Mūlamadhyamakakārikā *of Nāgārjuna: The Philosophy of the Middle Way.* Motilal Banarsidass.

John Tucker

MIDDLEMAN MINORITIES

The term *middleman minorities*, coined by Hubert Blalock (1967), refers to minority entrepreneurs who mediate between the dominant and subordinate groups. Their customers are typically members of marginalized racial or ethnic groups that are segregated from the majority group.

EARLY DEVELOPMENT OF MIDDLEMAN MINORITIES

Edna Bonacich's article "A Theory of Middleman Minorities" (1973) remains the seminal work on the topic. Bonacich offers an explanation for the development and persistence of middleman minorities as minority groups serving an intermediary position between the majority group and other segregated minority groups. She notes several commonalities among various middleman groups (e.g., Armenians, Indians, Chinese, Japanese, and Jews) in selected occupations (e.g., bankers, barbers, brokers, launderers, and restaurateurs). A key characteristic for Bonacich is the tendency of middleman minorities to be sojourners—people who intend to return to their country of origin.

Because they are sojourners and their migration is economically driven, middleman minorities are thrifty while amassing capital. Moreover, they maintain strong ties with their compatriots in the host and origin countries while remaining detached from the host society. In short, middleman minorities have little incentive to develop ties to the host society. Furthermore, they tend toward businesses in which assets are quickly accumulated and liquidated.

Due to their sojourner status and their strong in-group ties, middleman minorities develop a competitive business edge. In particular, these entrepreneurs minimize their labor costs through their reliance on family members and fellow ethnic workers willing to work long hours for little pay. These circumstances allow middleman minorities to establish positions of economic dominance.

Their success places middleman minorities in conflict with different sectors of the host society. Entrepreneurs from other groups cannot readily compete with the middleman minorities' cheap labor. Also, workers in the mainstream labor force view the workforce of middleman minorities as a threat to their own ability to negotiate higher wages and better working conditions. Finally, the minority clientele of middleman minorities resent them for not hiring members of their group and for not being vested in their communities.

Consequently, their success as entrepreneurs creates a paradox. Middleman minorities sometimes abandon their intentions to return to their country of origin, transitioning from sojourners to settlers. As settlers, they tend to become more integrated into the host society, a fate of many Jews, Chinese, Indians, and Japanese in the United States (Bonacich 1973). However, due to continued antagonism from the host society some middleman minority groups remain perpetual middlemen, maintaining their sojourner intentions and residential separation (Blalock 1967).

CULTURE, BLOCKED OPPORTUNITIES, AND MIDDLEMAN MINORITIES

Bonacich (1973) posits that the culture of the country of origin is important in the development of middleman minority. She asserts that the cultures of some groups tend to predispose them to the role of middleman minorities, regardless of location. Similarly, Thomas Sowell (1996) highlights the role that culture plays in the entrepreneurial activities of middleman minorities such as Chinese and Jews.

While culture may be an important ingredient in the formation of middleman minorities, blocked access to opportunity structures represents an equally—if not more—important component in the making of middleman minorities. Traditional middleman minorities have experienced discrimination and hostility in different parts of the world. For example, during the "coolie" period in the United States, segregation laws during the nineteenth century hindered Chinese immigrants from learning English and the dominant group's culture and norms (Wang 1991; Ha 1998). Sowell (1996) also describes the discrimination and violence directed against Chinese in gold rush communities. Chinese were also barred from immigrating to the United States and from becoming citizens. Due to virulent anti-Asian sentiment, Chinese clustered in enclaves where they fended for their survival. Even today, Asians fail to receive appropriate returns to their educational levels in the labor market, with many opting to become entrepreneurs, increasingly in black neighborhoods (Min 2002).

RECENT DEVELOPMENTS REGARDING MIDDLEMAN MINORITIES

The conceptualization of middleman minorities has some shortcomings today. For example, the term generally describes the experiences of certain immigrant groups historically. The extent to which the perspective can be fully applied to immigrant groups now is open to debate. Furthermore, the emphasis on sojourning requires some adaptation, as many middleman minorities in the United States have settled or intend to settle in this country while others are transnational migrants, maintaining ties in the countries of origin and destination.

Since the appearance of Bonacich's 1973 article, there have been shifts in immigration patterns to the United States, with some groups especially likely to become entrepreneurs (e.g., Cubans and Koreans). Due to the diverse experiences of such groups, other terms have emerged to capture their varying realities. For instance, *ethnic enclave* describes a geographic setting where ethnic groups are concentrated (see Portes and Rumbaut 1990). The term captures the economic, social, cultural, and language activities associated with ethnic concentrations. With respect to ethnic entrepreneurial activities, the main distinction between "ethnic enclave" and "middleman minorities" concerns the ethnic background of the clientele and the residence of ethnic entrepreneurs. Middleman minorities share neither an ethnicity nor a residential area with their clientele: they typically live outside of the neighborhoods where their segregated minority clientele live. In contrast, ethnic entrepreneurs in ethnic enclaves share an ethnicity and residential area with their clientele. Thus, ethnic entrepreneurs are members of the neighborhoods where their businesses reside. Two groups illustrate these concepts. Korean business owners serving predominantly African American areas in Los Angeles exemplify middleman minorities. Cuban business owners in predominantly Cuban areas in Miami illustrate ethnic entrepreneurs in ethnic enclaves. For further discussion regarding these terms see Feagin and Feagin (2003).

In sum, despite the changing nature of immigration and the context in which immigrants exist in the host society, the term *middleman minority* endures. An analysis of the entries in *Sociological Abstracts* suggests a general increasing usage of the term since its inception (1960–1969, 0.3 average annual entries; 1970–1979, 1.4; 1980–1989, 2.9; 1990–1999, 3.9; and 2000–2005, 2.8). The continued changing nature of immigration and racial/ethnic relations is likely to result in future modifications to the conceptualization of middleman minorities.

SEE ALSO *Ethnic Enclave*

BIBLIOGRAPHY

Blalock, Hubert M. 1967. *Toward a Theory of Minority-Group Relations.* New York: Wiley.

Bonacich, Edna. 1973. A Theory of Middleman Minorities. *American Sociological Review* 38: 583–594.

Feagin, Joe R., and Clairece Booher Feagin. 2003. *Racial and Ethnic Relations.* 7th ed. Upper Saddle River, NJ: Prentice Hall.

Ha, Marie-Paule. 1998. Cultural Identities in the Chinese Diaspora. *Mots pluriels* 7. http://www.arts.uwa.edu.au/MotsPluriels/MP798mph.html.

Min, Pyong Gap. 2002. A Comparison of Pre- and Post-1965 Asian Immigrant Businesses. In *Mass Migration to the United States: Classical and Contemporary Periods*, ed. Pyong Gap Min, 285–308. Walnut Creek, CA: AltaMira.

Portes, Alejandro, and Ruben Rumbaut. 1990. *Immigrant America: A Portrait.* Berkeley: University of California Press.

Sowell, Thomas. 1996. *Migrations and Cultures: A World View.* New York: Basic Books.

Wang Gungwu. 1991 *China and the Chinese Overseas.* Singapore: Times Academic Press.

Karen Manges Douglas
Rogelio Saenz

MIDDLETOWN

SEE *Community Power Studies; Lynd, Robert and Helen.*

MIDLIFE CRISIS

Psychologist Elliot Jaques has been given credit for coining the term *midlife crisis*, now heavily embedded in psychodynamic theory, in a 1965 article entitled "Death and the Midlife Crisis," written for the *International Journal of Psychoanalysis*. Jaques suggested that *midlife*, analogous to the top of the "hill" in the common saying "over the hill," is a time when adults retrospectively analyze their lives, project future autonomy, functionality, and life expectancy, and realize their mortality as an intimate reality.

This initial conceptualization highlighted two important implied points. The first was that a midlife crisis is part of a continuing developmental process of maturation and adaptation that characterizes aging. This suggests that the factors that precede, precipitate, and follow a midlife crisis may reoccur. The second point is that perceived proximity to decreasing functionality or mortality may be a more salient initiator of retrospective analysis than age alone. For example, there is evidence among populations where lifespan is truncated by disease that factors associated with a midlife crisis may occur much earlier in life.

Carl Jung (1875–1961), in his extensive writings, identified five stages associated with an innate, normal, and expected midlife transition: accommodation, separation, liminality, reintegration, and individuation. In *accommodation*, a pretransition stage, individuals present adaptive characteristics (personae) that are based on environmental demands and expectations, and acquire definitions of self based on what is most adaptive. Using enormous mental energy, individuals engage in a continual attempt to balance their persona with fundamental preferences and desires. This stage is typically characteristic of younger years, when the expectations of others are a more significant influence on preferences and behavior.

For many, what is needed to be functional in a specific environmental context is in significant conflict with fundamental preferences. During a period of reevaluation, often occurring around midlife, individuals begin to challenge and slowly disassemble the persona and order their lives based on fundamental preferences. This process, known as *separation*, is filled with questions about underlying preferences and how closely they align with what has been presented to the world for the sake of adaptation. The greater the distance is between these innate motives and the external persona, the greater the tendency for this period to be defined as a "crisis" and for dramatic changes in overt behavior and preferences to occur.

In *liminality*, the next stage in cases where there is substantial distance between the adaptive persona and personal preferences, the previously adaptive persona is fully rejected, if only for a short period, and certain societal and cultural demands are largely ignored. Individuals often question their essence, lack a sense of self, and are much more reliant on new external sources—both property and people—for the definition of who they are, as they work toward the establishment of a new persona.

It is notable that the stages of separation and liminality are most associated with the modern era and with the developed countries. Symptoms of midlife crises in Western cultures may include increased boredom and self-doubt, compulsivity, major changes in the libido and sexual preferences, a change in the people, places, and things that define personal success, increased insecurity, increased rumination about past relationships and personal/professional decisions, restlessness, and an intense desire to make change without a clear sense of direction. For those with closely aligned persona and personal preferences, moderate changes in perception, priorities, and behavior may not necessarily be negative and can be associated with a productive realignment of resources and behavior congruent with age.

During the stage of *reintegration*, individuals adopt a new persona. For some, the new persona is congruent with previous roles and responsibilities; for others, it is in conflict. Uncertainty about self is reduced, but not always eliminated, and confidence about the direction of life is established. Individuals frequently achieve a new level of stability and functioning that is reflective of a better balance between the persona and personal preferences.

In the final stage of a midlife transition, known as *individuation*, individuals become increasingly re-aware of societal and cultural demands, and come to a clearer understanding of their recent choices. It is often during this stage that the financial, interpersonal, personal, and professional consequences of the previous stages are realized. This stage is also characterized by new attempts to maintain minimal distance between the persona and fundamental preferences.

There appears to be tremendous individual variability in the incidence and sequence of stages associated with midlife crisis. Jung's five-stage schema provides a conceptual context for understanding midlife transitions but does not imply a definitive sequence or timing of events. Individuals, as a function of a range of internal and external, environmental factors, may move back and forth from separation to liminality over a long period of time. Furthermore, successful movement through a stage does not preclude revisiting previous stages based on subsequent events. For example, introspection brought on by a job promotion or change in career may precipitate a sequence of separation, liminality, and finally individuation over a period of no more than a few days. In contrast, the death of a spouse or close friend may bring about a return to separation and liminality lasting months or even years. In other cases, sequential life changes can result in a healthy and painless reevaluation of priorities and resources, and a quick and successful movement to a new functional and a well-integrated persona.

Since the early psychodynamic attempts to grapple with midlife transitions, and certainly after Elliot Jacques's introduction of the concept of midlife crisis, several other conceptualizations have been put forth. For example, the midlife crisis has been conceptualized by more cognitively oriented professionals as an emotional state characterized by intense self-doubt and anxiety, occurring usually between the ages of thirty and forty years old. The crisis is either thought to occur naturally or to be precipitated by sudden and major change in status or life circumstance (job promotion, grandchildren, etc.) or a period of extensive introspection (brought on by loss of a job, shrinking interpersonal network as the result of morbidities or mortality, etc.). Other factors thought to precipitate crises include financial problems, the death of a spouse, parent, sibling, or friend, and diagnoses of potentially life-threatening or lifestyle-altering age-related morbidities (sexual impotence, hypertension, obesity, diabetes, etc.).

Not all cultures respond to the midlife transition as a crisis, in part because of their more positive perceptions of aging. For example, in many Eastern cultures where advanced age is equated with experience and wisdom and aging increases status in the family and society, midlife transitions are thought of as a time of celebration, not crisis. In contrast, in Western cultures senior status is often equated with disability and lack of autonomy—hence it is no surprise that the midlife crisis appears to be much more prevalent in the West. In addition to differences in perceptions of aging, it has been suggested that cultural variations in the epidemiology of the midlife crisis may also reflect the greater distance between the persona and fundamental preferences in Western cultures.

Although the midlife crisis is frequently associated primarily with men, both men and women experience potentially difficult midlife transitions. For those men and women for whom transition rises to the level of crisis, the process lasts from approximately three to ten years among men and two to five years among women. The women who appear to be most likely to experience a midlife crisis are Westerners of childbearing age who are heavily engaged in their careers, and who have presented a persona for many years that is inconsistent with their fundamental preferences. In these cases, and sometimes in others initiated by menopause or a change in reproductive status, women often experience boredom and engage in a process of self-reflection through which professional and personal achievements are reevaluated and new priorities are established. Women may suddenly prefer younger sexual and interpersonal partners, may devalue established and ongoing personal and professional relationships, pursue changes in their career, experience increased affective disturbance, pursue substantial modifications to their appearance including plastic and cosmetic surgeries (breast implants, face-lifts, changes in makeup, etc.), or experience a sudden onset of maternal instincts including the desire to have a child.

The midlife crisis in men is most frequently characterized by a difficult and intense transition *process* involving the reassessment of expected longevity, the realization of death as intimate and an inevitable future event, the reevaluation of life priorities, values, and goals, and attempts to project future functionality and the quality of the second half of life. Onset is most often caused by decreased libido or work-related issues. Men may become concerned about their physical appearance and initiate a program of exercise and dieting; they may consider hair implantation if balding and hair coloring if graying; they may abuse alcohol and illicit substances, or engage in domestic violence, or seek the attention of younger friends, coworkers, and sexual partners to confirm their vitality and youth. Because men often define themselves through their career, and until recently mostly pursued only one career throughout their lifetime, feelings of being stuck in a single career with limited prospects for advancement frequently precipitates midlife crisis. One can only speculate what impact recent increases in the number of lifetime careers an employee is expected to have prior to retirement will have on the incidence of midlife crisis in the United States.

There is evidence that only between 8 and 25 percent of Americans over the age of thirty-five experience a midlife crisis, which suggests at the very least that the midlife crisis is not an inevitable and natural process. Indeed, some researchers suggest that the midlife crisis is a chimera, and occurs for self-serving reasons and not because it is a genuine crisis. It gives white middle class people in North America and Europe, who value leisure time, prosperity, and self-indulgence, permission to act out, ignore traditions, and pursue new self-indulgent directions later in life. Experiencing a midlife crisis allows them to sidestep societal expectations about age-appropriate behavior and life stages.

For the minority of individuals who experience a midlife crisis—"real" or not, and whatever the causes—managing behavioral symptoms and distress becomes important. This can be achieved through a process of introspection—alone or with the aid of friends or relatives—but in more extreme cases, the aid of mental health specialists and other professional care providers may be necessary.

In summary, the midlife crisis is perhaps best viewed as a special manifestation of a developmentally normal midlife transition that provides individuals a time to reevaluate expectations and make age-appropriate adjustments to roles and resources. For many, this transition is very productive and leads to needed decisions and changes, and to a focus on the value of interpersonal and intimate relationships. It can also be an opportunity to move beyond previously accepted boundaries and societal constraints.

SEE ALSO *Developmental Psychology; Jung, Carl; Maturation; Psychotherapy; Social Psychology*

BIBLIOGRAPHY

Becker, Daniel. 2006. Therapy for the Middle-Aged: The Relevance of Existential Issues. *American Journal of Psychotherapy* 60 (1): 87–99.

Epperly, Ted D., and Kevin E. Moore. 2000. Health Issues in Men: Part II: Common Psychosocial Disorders. *American Family Physician* 62 (1): 117–124.

Kruger, Arnold. 1994. The Mid-Life Transition: Crisis or Chimera? *Psychological Reports* 75: 1299–1305.

Oles, Piotr K. 1999. Towards a Psychological Model of Midlife Crisis. *Psychological Reports* 84 (3, pt. 2): 1059–1069.

Samuels, S. C. 1997. Midlife Crisis: Helping Patients Cope with Stress, Anxiety, and Depression. *Geriatrics* 52 (7): 55–56; 59–63.

Shek, Daniel T. L. 1996. Middle Age. In *Academic American Encyclopedia* 13: 390–391. Danbury, CT: Grolier.

Woods, Nancy Fugate, Anne Mariella, and Ellen Sullivan Mitchell. 2002. Patterns of Depressed Mood across the Menopausal Transition: Approaches to Studying Patterns in Longitudinal Data. 2002. *Acta Obstetricia et Gynecologia Scandinavica* 81 (7): 623–632.

Woods, Nancy Fugate, and Ellen Sullivan Mitchell. 1997. Pathways to Depressed Mood for Midlife Women: Observations from the Seattle Midlife Women's Health Study. *Research in Nursing and Health* 20 (2): 119–129.

Woods, Nancy Fugate, and Ellen Sullivan Mitchell. 1997. Women's Images of Midlife: Observations from the Seattle Midlife Women's Health Study. *Health Care for Women International* 18 (5): 439–453.

Christopher L. Edwards
Goldie Byrd

MIDWIFERY

Midwife, an Anglo-Saxon term meaning "with woman," aptly describes the role that women have long assumed as birth attendants. Throughout history and across cultures, women have traditionally provided direct assistance and support during childbirth; men were generally excluded. Attendance at birth has been suggested to be essential in facilitating mother-child survival as the physiology of birth changed during human evolutionary history. The upright stance necessary for bipedal locomotion made human birth more complicated than the births of other higher primates, whose quadrupedal locomotion allows a pelvis aligned for the direct descent of the fetal head, whereas the human infant must rotate as it descends through the pelvis, causing pain to the laboring woman. Immediately after birth primate babies can climb onto their mothers' backs and cling; human infants, born earlier in their developmental cycle because of their larger brains, are relatively helpless at birth and require immediate nurturance. These factors encouraged the evolution of birth as a highly social process; in few societies do women give birth alone and unaided. Indeed it is reasonable to assume that midwifery must have evolved right along with *Homo sapien* birth. The presence of other females would have enhanced the success of the birth process as they acquired such skills as turning the baby in utero, providing emotional support to the mother through the pain of labor, assisting rotation of the head and shoulders at birth, massaging the mother's uterus, and administering herbs to stop postpartum bleeding. Such skills typify the traditional midwifery of thousands of cultures throughout human history.

The birth attendant is not always a specialist, and some cultures do not have specifically delineated roles for midwives; in Nepal and Bangladesh, for example, family members are often the ones to care for the birthing mother. But thousands of traditional societies, and the vast majority of industrialized societies, do have a specific category of career that translates into English as *midwife*. Broadly speaking, a midwife is defined as a skilled practitioner who cares for the mother during pregnancy, birth, and the postpartum period and is recognized by her government or her community as such. In traditional societies midwives often serve additional roles as community healers, and in industrialized societies as specialists in primary health care, gynecological well-woman care, and sometimes also in complementary therapies such as homeopathy, herbalism, and nutrition.

According to the International Definition of a Midwife endorsed by the International Confederation of Midwives (ICM) and various development agencies, the midwife's sphere of practice generally includes supervision, care, and advice to the pregnant woman; attending births on her own responsibility; caring for the newborn and mother after birth; identifying risks or abnormalities; taking preventive measures; procuring medical assistance when necessary; and dealing with emergencies in the absence of medical help. She also takes an active role in counseling and education not only for women but also for families and communities. She may practice in hospitals, clinics, health units, freestanding birth centers, homes, or any place her services are needed. Her government, her community, insurance companies, or individuals may pay for her services; traditional midwives often barter for their care, accepting whatever the family might offer.

OBSTETRICS AND MIDWIFERY

Throughout the world, during the nineteenth and twentieth centuries, biomedical obstetrics took over much of the care and "management" of pregnancy and birth. Biomedical personnel tend to attribute the dramatic decline in maternal and infant mortality of the twentieth century, especially in developed countries, to medical and technological advances. Yet public health experts insist that much of this decline is due to public health measures such as improvements in sanitation and hygiene, better nutrition, higher education, and better working conditions for women. They note that in the developing world, clean water would do far more to promote maternal health than the expensive high-tech hospital. Nevertheless, biomedicalization equates to modernization, so such hospitals continue to be built in modernizing countries, and governments continue to encourage or insist that women give birth in them.

One direct result is that the rates of obstetrical intervention in birth are rising worldwide. For example, national cesarean rates in Taiwan, China, Brazil, Argentina, Chile, Mexico, and Puerto Rico are between 40 and 50 percent. In the United States, the cesarean rate has risen since the early 2000s from 23 percent to 29.1 percent; most European countries, Canada, and Australia have cesarean rates in the mid-20 percent range. Although professional midwives attend the majority of births in some of these countries, they are biomedically socialized and often overworked, and have been unable to stem the rising cesarean tide, which is largely obstetrician-driven. The exceptions include the Scandinavian/Nordic countries and Japan, where cesarean rates range from 12 to 17 percent; in those countries, both midwives and obstetricians have worked hard to preserve normal vaginal delivery.

Obstetrical dominance over birthing represents not a neutral substitution of one care provider by another, but rather a fundamentally different and opposing philosophical approach to birthing care—one that takes a mechanistic approach to birth, treating the laboring body as a dysfunctional machine unable to work properly without technological intervention. The high rates of unnecessary intervention in birth and the resultant iatrogenic damage to mother and child have spurred professional midwives around the world to develop, articulate, and practice a "midwifery model of care"—a woman-centered, humanistic, and physiological approach to birth based on respect and compassion for the woman, and on the large body of scientific evidence that demonstrates the much better outcomes that result when the woman is encouraged to birth in the place of her choice, to move about freely, eat and drink at will during labor, and give birth in upright positions. Application of this model has been shown in multiple studies to result in far less technological intervention in birth, greater maternal satisfaction, higher rates of breast-feeding after birth, and low rates of cesarean section and perinatal mortality.

In Europe and Australia, midwives have always been and continue to be the primary attendants at the majority of births, yet during the 1900s their education became heavily medicalized and their practices moved almost entirely into the hospital. In Canada and the United States, the obstetrical takeover of birth in the early 1900s resulted in the near-elimination of midwifery. In all these countries, home birth has become rare (around 1% of all births) in spite of much evidence demonstrating planned, midwife-attended home birth to be as safe as, or safer than, hospital birth for women without serious complications. Many professional midwives are engaged in a

process of self-examination, attempting to reclaim the autonomy they lost with the obstetrical takeover of birth in the nineteenth and twentieth centuries, to return to attending out-of-hospital births at homes and in birth centers, and to work in nonhierarchical collaborative relationships with obstetricians.

NURSE- AND DIRECT-ENTRY MIDWIFERY

The early British combination of nursing and midwifery has long been the model for the profession of nurse-midwifery in many developed and developing nations, but many have come to critique this model because education in nursing first tends to heavily socialize midwives into the hierarchical, interventionist biomedical model of birth. Such critics have worked to generate or regenerate direct-entry midwifery, in which midwives are not first educated in nursing, but instead are educationally grounded in the midwifery model of care. The best-known example of this kind of midwifery comes from the Netherlands, where for centuries midwives have been trained in their own midwifery schools and have enjoyed full integration into the health care system as autonomous practitioners, maintaining in the 2000s a 30 percent home birth rate in their country. Since the 1970s midwives in Canada, the United States, Australia, New Zealand, Mexico, and other countries, inspired in part by the Dutch model, have developed new models of direct-entry education and autonomous practice for midwives based on the midwifery model of care. This reclaiming and revitalization of midwifery has resulted from alliances between activist consumers, midwives, public health officials, and many others working to humanize birth.

TRADITIONAL AND PROFESSIONAL MIDWIVES

There is a sharp distinction made in international literature and discourse between professional midwives and traditional birth attendants (TBAs). The definition created by the professional midwives of the ICM stresses the completion of prescribed course(s) of studies in midwifery and registration and/or legal licensing to practice midwifery.

Professional midwives who meet these criteria, including both nurse- and direct-entry midwives, are usually fully incorporated into health care systems. Traditional midwives, who still attend the majority of births in many developing countries, have no such formal education; they suffer multiple forms of discrimination within biomedical systems. The World Health Organization (WHO) does not recognize the traditional midwife as a midwife, but rather as a TBA—"the term TBA refers only to traditional, independent (of the health system), non-formally trained and community-based providers of care during pregnancy, childbirth, and the postnatal period" (WHO 2004, p. 8). WHO suggests that TBAs are stopgap measures until more "qualified" personnel are available (and indeed, traditional midwives have been largely eliminated or greatly reduced in number and scope of practice in, for example, Thailand, Costa Rica, Venezuela, Argentina, Chile, and Brazil, with the exception of the Amazon region). Health authorities tend to accept this distinction, while social scientists reject or contest it, examining the social roles of definitions as tools of power to determine insiders and outsiders, and studying and documenting the vital roles traditional midwives still play in many societies.

Since the mid-twentieth century nongovernmental organizations, multilaterals, and bilaterals have invested heavily in professional midwife and TBA training in their efforts to reduce maternal and perinatal mortality in the third world. The social science of midwifery grew out of this trend, and reflects social scientists' roles in analyzing training programs for development organizations and the impact of new models on both quality of care and health outcomes. Social scientists find that women trained as professional midwives are usually young and have borne no children themselves. In developing countries, they are educated in an urban environment, usually in two-year programs, then sent out to serve in a rural village, where they wear the white coat and expect respect from the townspeople for their professional, educated status. They usually work in underfunded and understaffed government-built clinics, but for an extra sum of money will sometimes attend a home birth if they are called. Workloads and stress levels in such clinics are high, often resulting in maltreatment of women and early burnout on the part of the professional midwife.

Thus even though the governments of almost all developing countries have embarked on massive programs to bring birth into the clinics and hospitals under the care of professional midwives and obstetricians, many rural women resist because of inadequate and impersonal care. For example, women are forced to birth flat on their backs in very exposed positions, usually receiving an episiotomy to widen the vaginal outlet and speed the birth. To the apparent bewilderment of governments and biomedical personnel, many women in developing countries prefer the more nurturing and culturally appropriate care provided by the local traditional midwife/TBA, usually an older woman who has given birth several times and has earned the respect and trust of her community through years of midwifery practice.

Training courses intended to educate TBAs in how to identify risks and to improve their prenatal and maternity care have been strongly criticized. Designed by biomedical personnel, course content is often inappropriate to local circumstances and realities. Courses often assume access to material resources that are lacking locally, are taught in a style inappropriate to the literacy skills and learning styles of midwives, and fail to provide TBAs a respected and effective place within an integrated system of medicine. Additionally, TBA trainings emphasize transporting the woman to a hospital for a large number of risk factors, in places where transport is often unavailable and hospital care is inadequate. Traditional midwives take such courses to seek additional skills to cope with emergencies; in many countries, traditional midwives are very aware that their community-based care is the only viable alternative to an unnecessary cesarean and an unpleasant hospital experience.

In some places, professional midwives and physicians scorn and denigrate TBAs, treating them and their clients disrespectfully when they transport to a hospital or clinic. But sometimes professional midwives make a sincere effort to learn about and honor local customs and traditions, approach local people with an attitude of respect, and cooperate with traditional midwives; in such situations of mutual accommodation between the biomedical and traditional systems, TBAs and their clients are more willing to transport to the hospital in case of need, and birth outcomes improve.

It is important not to romanticize or demonize professional or traditional midwives. Both work under discriminatory biomedical systems and both usually try to give skilled and considerate care and remain, in many parts of the world, the only viable option for millions of women. Social scientists question the wisdom of dividing professional midwives and TBAs in a hierarchical manner that allows government agencies and development planners to support one group while trying to exterminate the other, suggesting that a "real midwife" may be recognized either by her government or her community as such, and that all midwives should have access to adequate, scientifically based, and culturally appropriate training.

Changes in midwifery in the developing world are intimately linked to debates over midwifery in the developed world, where professional midwives provide care for the majority of pregnant women. Their education is generally university-based and often postgraduate, giving them skills in research and publication unavailable to midwives in the developing world. They practice in hospitals that are usually well staffed, well funded, and replete with medical technologies. Their major dilemmas are ideological: they struggle both in thought and in practice with the tension between what they themselves call the "medical" and the "midwifery" models of care. Many professional midwives are working to support and sustain traditional midwifery and its future development. Many weave elements of traditional midwifery knowledge, such as the use of herbs for aiding labor or stopping a postpartum hemorrhage, manual techniques for turning breech babies and facilitating the delivery of "stuck" babies, and upright positions for birth, into their practices.

In general, midwives spend more time than physicians with women during pregnancy, answering their questions and providing emotional reassurance, and know more about how to facilitate normal labor and birth without drugs or surgery than obstetricians. The vast body of epidemiological evidence demonstrating the benefits of midwifery care in many countries will prove key to midwives' maintenance of their roles and their identities as being "with women" in the new millennium.

SEE ALSO *Medicine; Natural Childbirth*

BIBLIOGRAPHY

Davis-Floyd, Robbie E., and Carolyn Sargent. 1997. *Childbirth and Authoritative Knowledge: Cross-Cultural Perspectives.* Berkeley: University of California Press.

Davis-Floyd, Robbie, Stacy Leigh Pigg, and Sheila Cosminsky, eds. 2001. Daughters of Time: The Shifting Identities of Contemporary Midwives. Spec. issue, *Medical Anthropology* 20 (2–4).

DeVries, Raymond, Edwin van Teijlingen, Sirpa Wrede, and Cecilia Benoit, eds. 2001. *Birth by Design: Pregnancy, Maternity Care and Midwifery in North America and Europe.* New York: Routledge.

Jordan, Brigitte. [1978] 1993. *Birth in Four Cultures: A Cross-Cultural Investigation of Childbirth in Yucatan, Holland, Sweden, and the United States.* 4th ed. Prospect Heights, IL: Waveland.

Kitzinger, Sheila, ed. 1991. *The Midwife Challenge.* London: Pandora.

Lefeber, Yvonne. 1994. *Midwives without Training: Practices and Beliefs of Traditional Birth Attendants in Africa, Asia and Latin-America.* Assen, The Netherlands: Van Gorcum.

Luckere, Vicki, and Margaret Jolly, eds. 2002. *Birthing in the Pacific: Beyond Tradition and Modernity?* Honolulu: University of Hawaii Press.

World Health Organization. 2004. *Making Pregnancy Safer: The Critical Role of the Skilled Birth Attendant—A Joint Statement by WHO, ICM, and FIGO.* Geneva: WHO. www.who.int/reproductive-health/publications/2004/skilled_attendant.pdf.

Robbie E. Davis-Floyd
Gwynne L. Jenkins

MIGRANT LABOR

During the Dust Bowl migration, more than half a million people left the American Plains and migrated to the western United States. John Steinbeck's (1902–1968) novel *The Grapes of Wrath* (1939) describes vividly the large migration of poor whites from Oklahoma to California during the 1930s. His book captures how individuals were affected by dramatic changes in agriculture. "Now farming was an industry.... They imported slaves although they did not call them slaves: Chinese, Japanese, Mexicans, and Filipinos" (Steinbeck 1939, p. 298). This quotation from Steinbeck's novel points out that farming had changed. Industrialization in the United States in the late nineteenth century set the stage for changes in agriculture during the early twentieth century. Farm sizes grew across the United States, and farming became mechanized. Crops that previously required hand labor for harvesting, like cotton and beans, were being harvested by machines, which resulted in fewer jobs. These new mechanized farms were described as "factories in the fields." At the same time, the need for hand labor became increasingly seasonal, creating a high demand for migrant labor that could follow specialty crops, like berries and grapes.

Steinbeck's quotation also captures the racial and ethnic changes that farming in the United States experienced. Unlike the racial and ethnic composition of farm labor at the beginning of the twenty-first century, during the early twentieth century, farm labor was racially and ethnically diverse, and included whites and African Americans, as well as Mexican, Filipino, Japanese, Italian, and West Indian immigrants. Changes in U.S. laws regarding immigration and the impact of two world wars greatly affected the racial and ethnic composition of American farm labor. For instance, as World War I began in 1914 and as the United States attempted to halt immigration in the 1920s, the demand for farm laborers increased, and African American workers filled the need. Similarly, when the United States entered World War II in 1941, workers entered defense jobs and shipyards, which created a labor shortage in the fields. To fill this shortage, the United States created the Bracero Program, a temporary guest-worker program to recruit Mexican workers to the fields. The Bracero Program, instituted in the 1940s and ending in the 1960s, ensured that a large number of Mexican-origin people entered the agriculture industry in California as laborers. It is estimated that four million Mexican farm laborers began working in the United States during the program's twenty-two-year tenure. Even though the Bracero Program was meant to supply temporary employment, many *braceros* settled permanently in the United States.

In 2007 the majority of migrant laborers in the United States are of Mexican descent. Their poor treatment is compounded by racial/ethnic discrimination and xenophobic attitudes. Migrant workers are viewed by some as a drain on social services, even though they often do not use these services. At the same time, the demand for low-skilled labor has legislators ready to implement another guest-worker program. In March 2007,

Representatives Luis V. Gutierrez (D-Ill.) and Jeff Flake (R-Ariz.) introduced an immigrant worker visa bill in the U.S. House of Representatives, which allows foreigners to enter the United States legally to temporarily fill low-skill jobs, including agriculture and seasonal jobs. Guest-worker programs provide temporary labor without offering citizenship rights to workers. In essence, workers are expected to work and not create families or settle in the United States, but return home when their work visa ends. However, service workers, who work in hotels and restaurants, are not included in this provision, leaving them no way to work legally in the United States. The fear of another wave of settlement leaves undocumented immigration as the main alternative for workers, which ensures the denial of citizenship rights and makes them more vulnerable to exploitation.

Migrant farmworkers and their families are among the most vulnerable groups in society. Migrant workers face dangerous and poor working conditions. Basic necessities, like adequate drinking water, are not provided by employers, even though laborers may work in extreme heat. Many are forced to work without access to toilet or hand-washing facilities, even though washing hands regularly is important to avoid pesticide poisoning. Living conditions are also difficult for migrant farmworkers. Wages for farmwork have not kept up with inflation; consequently, it is difficult for families to afford basic necessities like housing, food, health care, and education for their children. In 2006 the United States Department of Labor findings from the National Farmworker Survey (collected in 1994 and 1995) reported that farmworkers have low individual earnings; the median annual income is between $2,500 and $5,000, and about three-fourths of all workers earn less than $10,000 annually.

The children of farmworkers are often found working with family members, despite laws outlawing child labor. Human Rights Watch (a nonprofit civil rights organization) estimates that there are between 300,000 and 800,000 child farmworkers in the United States. Children work an average of twelve hours a day, and during peak seasons as much as fourteen hours a day. Children report having difficulty getting paid minimum wages; some earn as little as $2 an hour. Children are routinely exposed to harmful pesticides, and report experiencing rashes, headaches, dizziness, nausea, and vomiting. In addition to the demanding physical conditions, the children of migrant laborers lack access to education. When children work in the fields, it is nearly impossible for them to attend school. Children who do not work but migrate with their families have their education disrupted because of the constant need to relocate.

For many years, farmworkers sought to form a union. The creation of United Farm Workers by César Chávez (1927–1993) and Dolores Huerta was the result of a long struggle to unionize farmworkers. The Agricultural Workers Organizing Committee (AWOC), founded by Huerta, and the National Farm Workers Association (NFWA), founded by Chávez, were the first groups that attempted to organize farmworkers. By 1965 both were successful in obtaining wage increases after staging strikes and walkouts, but the organizations had not received union recognition from growers. In the summer of 1965, AWOC led Filipino farmworkers on a strike in Delano, California. They approached the NFWA and asked the mainly Chicano workers to join the strike. The NFWA agreed, and with the new strength in membership they launched a strike, with several thousand workers leaving the field. The growers offered to raise wages, but the organizations also wanted a union. To aid the effort, Chávez called on the American public to boycott grapes without union labels. Millions of Americans responded and stopped buying grapes. The workers won the long strike and established a union-run hiring hall, a health clinic and health plan, a credit union, a community center, and a cooperative gas station, as well as higher wages. The two unions merged into the United Farm Workers Organizing Committee in 1966.

In 2004, the International Labor Office (ILO) estimated that eighty-six million migrant and refugee adults work across the globe. Migration affects countries around the world because nearly every country serves as either a place of origin, destination, transit, or sometimes all of these at once. Each country struggles with the government's role in regulating migrant workers and with the social and economic incorporation of such workers. Guest-worker programs are often used to attract and regulate low-skilled and high-skilled workers. But there are concerns about the social and economic consequences of migrant labor. Migrant laborers leave families behind in their home countries, creating fragmented families and communities. In addition, men and women face differing labor opportunities, with women sometimes limited to factory or domestic labor. The economic consequences of migration are severe in developing countries. Nearly 400,000 scientists and engineers from developing countries are employed in research and development jobs in industrial countries. This migration of highly skilled workers creates a "brain drain," leaving developing countries without highly skilled workers. Migrant workers face a risk to their human rights and fundamental freedoms, but this does not deter their migration; the hope of a better life ensures a steady flow of migrant laborers.

SEE ALSO *Agricultural Industry; Bracero Program; Brain Drain; Chávez, César; Citizenship; Labor; Migration*

BIBLIOGRAPHY

Akers Chacón, Justin, and Mike Davis. 2006. *No One Is Illegal: Fighting Racism and State Violence on the U.S.-Mexico Border.* Chicago: Haymarket.

Castles, Stephen. 2006. Guestworkers in Europe: A Resurrection? *International Migration Review* 40: 741–766.

Hahamovitch, Cindy. 1997. *The Fruits of Their Labor: Atlantic Coast Farmworkers and the Making of Migrant Poverty, 1870–1945.* Chapel Hill: University of North Carolina Press.

Lan, Pei-Chia. 2003. Maid or Madam? Filipina Migrant Workers and the Continuity of Domestic Labor. *Gender & Society* 17: 187–208.

Liow, Joseph. 2003. Malaysia's Illegal Indonesian Migrant Labour Problem: In Search of Solutions. *Contemporary Southeast Asia* 25: 44–64.

Martin, Philip. 1997. Guest Worker Policies for the Twenty-first Century: Lessons from U.S. and German Foreign Worker Programs. *New Community* 23: 483–495.

McWilliams, Carey. 1939. *Factories in the Field.* Boston: Little, Brown.

Pun, Ngai. 2005. *Made in China: Women Factory Workers in a Global Workplace.* Durham, NC: Duke University Press; Hong Kong: Hong Kong University Press.

Roberts, Kenneth D. 1997. China's "Tidal Wave" of Migrant Labor: What Can We Learn from Mexican Undocumented Migration to the United States? *International Migration Review* 31: 249–293.

Steinbeck, John. 1939. *The Grapes of Wrath.* London: Heinemann.

Weinstein, Eric. 2002. Migration for the Benefit of All: Towards a New Paradigm for Economic Immigration. *International Labour Review* 141: 225–252.

Katy M. Pinto

MIGRATION

Migration is a demographic process that has played an increasingly important role in the changing populations of many countries around the world. Much of the geographic shift in populations occurs from rural areas to urban areas, as well as from less developed countries to more developed countries. Since the mid-twentieth century, an expanding literature has been developed to understand migration. In particular, many scholars have focused not only on the forces encouraging people to migrate, but also on the impact that this migration has had on the migrants themselves and on their places of origin and destination. This interest in the topic of migration emerges not only from the increasing prevalence of people migrating, but also the relevance of migration in shaping demographic, social, economic, and political spheres worldwide.

DEFINING MIGRATION

Migration has been defined generally as a "permanent or semi permanent change of residence" (Lee 1966, p. 49). This definition places no restriction "upon the distance of the move or upon the voluntary or involuntary nature of the act, and no distinction is made between external and internal migration" (Lee 1966, p. 49). However, such a broad definition obscures the heterogeneous types of movements that exist based on geographical distance, as well as the factors involved in the different types of movements. For example, some people move within a community, others move across counties within the same state, others move across states, and others move across international boundaries. The U.S. Census Bureau collects information on the migration activities of people using the five-year migration question (location of present residence and location of residence five years earlier). Furthermore, the U.S. Census Bureau defines *movers* as those who lived in a different house but within the same county in the five-year period, *migrants* as those that moved at least across counties within the country during the period, and *international migrants* as those that were living outside of the United States five years earlier. The five-year migration question has numerous shortcomings, most notably that it is based on only two points in time. For instance, persons living in the same county in 1995 and 2000 but who lived in another county in the interim are classified as *nonmigrants.*

The process of accounting for the continuous movement of people has become complicated by technological advances in the areas of transportation and communications. For example, immigrants increasingly engage in *transnational migration*, which involves the continuous movement between the community of origin in the home country and the community of destination in the host country (Levitt 1998). This type of movement has important implications beyond the migrant's experience because it produces a variety of changes for both the sending and the receiving community.

THEORETICAL DEVELOPMENTS

The theorizing of explanations for the movement of people extends back to the late nineteenth century with geographer E. G. Ravenstein's (1834–1913) article "The Laws of Migration" (1885). Interest in the development of theoretical perspectives to explain migration resurfaced between the 1950s and 1970s with important works by William Petersen (1958), Everett Lee (1966), and P. N. Ritchey (1976). However, the changing nature of migration—especially the increasing prevalence of international migration—has seen the development of theoretical perspectives that place greater attention on immigration since the 1960s (see Massey et al. 1993). This entry describes some of the most prominent perspectives.

World-Systems Perspective The world-system perspective is a structural-macrolevel perspective developed by sociologist Immanuel Wallerstein. This perspective views international migration as the result of the expansion of the market economy throughout the world, as capitalists from core countries make inroads into peripheral and semiperipheral countries (Brettell 2000; Massey and Espinosa 1997; Portes 1998; Sassen 2001; Wallerstein 1974). Accordingly, the flow of capital into peripheral and semiperipheral countries, such as Mexico, results in a countermovement of labor from such countries to core countries, such as the United States (Massey and Espinosa 1997). This perspective highlights the links between the movement of capital and the countermovement of labor. To a large extent, emigrants from periphery countries migrate to "global cities" (Sassen 2001), which are urban centers in which "banking, finance, administration, professional services, and high-tech production tend to be concentrated" (Massey et al. 1993, p. 447). However, by focusing exclusively on the macrolevel, the world-systems perspective ignores the microlevel factors that encourage people to migrate, while also neglecting the role of politics and the state in social and economic change (Brettell 2000).

Dual Labor-Market Perspective The dual labor-market perspective emphasizes the demands of advanced industrial countries for low-skilled and low-wage labor (Massey et al. 1993). This perspective suggests that immigrants fill jobs that natives shun due to low wages, lack of mobility ladders, lack of benefits, and the arduous and dangerous nature of such jobs. The dual labor-market perspective asserts that the movement of immigrants from less developed to more developed countries is driven by the constant demand for cheap labor in developed countries.

Neoclassical Economics Perspective The neoclassical economics perspective is characterized by attention to both the macrolevel and the microlevel. At the macrolevel, this perspective suggests that migration occurs as a response to a disequilibrium between labor supply and labor demand. Thus, some labor markets have a surplus of labor, which results in high levels of unemployment and low wages. Other labor markets have greater labor demands than the existing labor pool can supply, which results in low levels of unemployment and high wages. This perspective suggests that workers gravitate from labor markets with a greater surplus of labor toward those with a greater demand for labor.

In contrast, the microlevel form of the neoclassical economics perspective focuses on the cost-benefit calculations that individuals undertake when making decisions regarding migration. This perspective treats individuals as utility maximizers who attempt to obtain the highest wages in relation to investments. In considering migration, people weigh the costs of relocation against the benefits that they are likely to receive from moving. People are expected to migrate when the benefits outweigh the costs, whereas they are presumed to remain stable when costs outweigh benefits.

The New Economics-of-Migration Perspective The new economics-of-migration perspective shifts the context to the household and focuses on how such units organize themselves to maximize economic returns while minimizing risks (see Massey et al. 1993). In settings without readily accessible unemployment benefits, bank loans, and insurance to protect against potential failure (e.g., loss of crops due to weather), households are especially vulnerable to a variety of economic and physical calamities. The new economics-of-migration perspective suggests that household members are deployed to undertake a wide variety of employment activities to ensure that the household generates economic resources while minimizing risks. Thus, some household members may remain at home to conduct subsistence agricultural activities, while other household members work locally in the private sector, others migrate to urban areas within the country, and still others move abroad and send remittances to the household. Essentially, the new economics-of-migration perspective proposes that households diversify their investment portfolios to protect themselves against risks and uncertainties.

Social-Network Perspective The social-network perspective emphasizes the interpersonal ties linking potential migrants and former migrants, as well as the migrants' communities of origin and destination. In particular, the social-network perspective focuses on social relations that exist among family or community members, with special attention to social capital. Alejandro Portes notes that social capital is made up of "those expectations for action within a collectivity that affect economic goals and goal-seeking behavior of its members, even if these expectations are not oriented to the economic sphere" (1993, p. 1322). This perspective places primary importance on the social networks that potential migrants have with people who have previously migrated as the most important factor influencing people's decision to migrate (Massey and Espinosa 1997). Hence, social networks affect the decision of individuals to migrate based on interpersonal ties. Migration is facilitated by sharing information about destination communities, reducing the expected costs and risks of migration, and increasing the expected benefits of migration (Rivero Fuentes 2003). In contrast to the neoclassical economics perspective, the social-network perspective recognizes the nonrational elements involved in people's migration decision. However, sociologists have also been careful to recognize the shortcomings of this perspective. For example, social capital may prevent the creation of new networks by excluding outsiders, restricting individual freedom, and promoting downward leveling norms (Portes 1998).

Cumulative Migration (or the Migration Syndrome) Perspective Closely connected to the social-network perspective is the cumulative migration (or migration syndrome) perspective. According to this perspective, originating from the social-movements framework, every act of immigration has the potential to facilitate the migration of other people by decreasing the cost of immigration (Massey et al. 1993). Carried to its fullest, migration becomes cumulative and natural when it becomes embedded in the culture of sending communities. In such instances, it is completely expected that certain segments of the population (e.g., the young in many parts of Mexico, especially males) will emigrate. In the case of Mexico, for example, many communities have relatively few working-age men because they have followed the trek of friends and relatives to the United States.

IMPLICATIONS OF MIGRATION FOR SENDING AND RECEIVING AREAS

While migration represents an important life-changing event for migrants, it also poses important demographic, social, economic, and political implications for sending and receiving communities. In demographic terms, international migration is responsible for changing the racial and ethnic composition of the communities of destination. For example, the American Latino and Asian populations have expanded tremendously through immigration into the United States since the 1960s (Alba 1999). In addition, with respect to the social implications of immigration, much discussion has focused on issues such as language and racial and ethnic boundaries as examined through the assimilation and multiculturalism models (Alba 1999).

Furthermore, migration has tremendous economic implications for communities, states, and countries around the globe. For example, Peggy Levitt and Rafael de la Dehesa (2003) have pointed out that much public policy on immigration is due to the recognition of migrants and their remittances as crucial elements in the state's economy. Because of this, many states are reinventing themselves by expanding the boundaries of citizenship

and nationality, granting migrants the right to vote, establishing bureaucratic reforms, and making investments that allow states to become more efficient in aiding migrants within and across their own borders.

FUTURE TRENDS

As noted earlier, and as predicted by contemporary theoretical perspectives on migration, people generally move from less developed to more developed countries. The future points increasingly to this scenario. Of the 2.8 billion people that are projected to be added to the world's population between 2005 and 2050, nearly all (98.6%) are expected to be added to the populations of developing countries (Population Reference Bureau 2005). Developed countries, with increasingly aging populations and low fertility rates, are projected to account for only 1.4 percent of the world's population growth between 2005 and 2050. Given continued economic disparities across the developed and developing worlds, increasing global population shifts are likely.

SEE ALSO *Immigrants to North America; Migrant Labor*

BIBLIOGRAPHY

Alba, Richard. 1999. Immigration and the American Realities of Assimilation and Multiculturalism. *Sociological Forum* 14 (1): 3–25.

Brettell, Caroline B., and James F. Hollifield. 2000. Migration Theory: Talking across Disciplines. In *Migration Theory: Talking across Disciplines*, eds. Caroline B. Brettell and James F. Hollifield, 1–26. New York: Routledge.

Brown, David L. 2002. Migration and Community: Social Networks in a Multilevel World. *Rural Sociology* 67 (1): 1–23.

Conway, Karen Smith, and Andrew J. Houtenville. 1998. Do the Elderly "Vote with Their Feet?" *Public Choice* 97: 663–685.

De Jong, Gordon F., Rex H. Warland, and Brenda Davis Root. 1998. Family Interaction and Migration Decision Making. *Research in Rural Sociology and Development* 7: 155–167.

Lee, Everett S. 1966. A Theory of Migration. *Demography* 3: 47–57.

Levitt, Peggy. 1998. Social Remittances: Migration Driven Local-Level Forms of Cultural Diffusion. *International Migration Review* 32 (4): 926–948.

Levitt, Peggy, and Rafael de la Dehesa. 2003. Transnational Migration and the Redefinition of the State: Variations and Explanations. *Ethnic and Racial Studies* 26 (4): 587–611.

Massey, Douglas S., and Kristin Espinosa. 1997. What's Driving Mexico-U.S. Migration? A Theoretical, Empirical, and Policy Analysis. *American Journal of Sociology* 4 (102): 939–999.

Massey, Douglas S., et al. 1993. Theories of International Migration: A Review and Appraisal. *Population and Development Review* 19 (3): 431–466.

Petersen, William. 1958. A General Typology of Migration. *American Sociological Review* 23 (3): 256–266.

Plane, David A., and Peter A. Rogerson. 1994. *The Geographical Analysis of Population with Applications to Planning and Business.* New York: Wiley.

Population Reference Bureau. 2005. *2005 World Population Data Sheet.* Washington, DC: Author. http://www.prb.org/pdf05/05WorldDataSheet_Eng.pdf.

Portes, Alejandro. 1998. Social Capital: Its Origins and Applications in Modern Sociology. *Annual Review of Sociology* 24: 1–24.

Portes, Alejandro, and Julia Sensenbrenner. 1993. Embeddedness and Immigration: Notes on the Social Determinants of Economic Action. *American Journal of Sociology* 98(6): 1320–1350.

Portes, Alejandro, and Min Zhou. 1993. The New Second Generation: Segmented Assimilation and Its Variants. *Annals of the American Academy of Political and Social Sciences* 530: 74–96.

Ravenstein, E. G. 1885. The Laws of Migration. *Journal of the Statistical Society* 48 (2): 167–235.

Ritchey, P. N. 1976. Explanations of Migration. *Annual Review of Sociology* 2: 363–404.

Rivero Fuentes, Estela. 2003. Engendering Migrant Networks: The Case of Mexican Migration. *Demography* 40 (2): 289–307.

Sassen, Saskia. 2001. *The Global City: New York, London, Tokyo.* 2nd ed. Princeton, NJ: Princeton University Press.

Wallerstein, Immanuel. 1974. *The Modern World-System. Capitalist Agriculture and the Origins of the European World Economy in the Sixteenth Century.* New York: Academic Press.

Rogelio Saenz
Maria Isabel Ayala

MIGRATION, RURAL TO URBAN

Rural to urban migration has historically been the most classic pattern of human migration. This form of migration began in preindustrial times and persists into the mid-2000s. Nevertheless, despite the movement of people to urban areas, there have been periodic exceptions over the last several decades.

Gideon Sjoberg (1960) provides an exceptional account of the formation of cities extending back to preindustrial times. He argues that such cities emerged because of an ecological base favorable to the development of agriculture, improved technology, and a complex social organization. Cities at this time represented the hub of social, economic, political, religious, educational, communication, and family activity. Sjoberg notes that preindustrial cities depended heavily on rural–urban migration for their growth.

Similarly, E. G. Ravenstein's (1885) laws of migration, drawn from analyses of the 1871 U.K. census, identify the prevalence of rural-to-urban migration and the influence of technology and economic factors on this movement. His laws of migration include the following: (1) migration takes place in steps, in short distance from remote areas toward the city; (2) long-distance migrants move to the centers of commerce and industry; and (3) urban inhabitants are less migratory than their rural counterparts.

CONTEMPORARY URBANIZATION

The movement of people from rural to urban areas has been re-created throughout the world beginning at varying periods alongside industrialization and economic development. Over the period from 1950 to 2005, the percentage of the world's inhabitants living in urban areas increased from 29 percent to 49 percent (United Nations 2006). Yet there is great variation in the degree of urbanization, with 74 percent of people in more developed regions (MDRs) living in urban locations in 2005 compared to only 43 percent of those in less developed regions (LDRs) and still fewer (27 percent) people in the least developed countries (LDCs) (United Nations 2004). As a whole, the most urbanized countries are located in the following regions: Australia/New Zealand (88 percent), northern Europe (84 percent), South America (82 percent), North America (81 percent), and western Europe (77 percent) (United Nations 2004).

The massive growth of urban areas has been associated with a variety of problems ranging from overcrowding, pressures on the environment (e.g., demand from natural resources, noise pollution, air pollution, and sanitation problems), lack of housing, and increasing inequality between different segments of the population. In addition, rural areas often lack social and economic infrastructures to support their dwindling populations.

THE RURAL TURNAROUND

Throughout most of the twentieth century the United States consistently witnessed the net movement of people from rural to urban areas. However, demographers and rural sociologists were surprised in the 1970s when this trend reversed. Indeed, during this period, rural areas were net importers of migrants while urban areas were net exporters (Brown and Wardwell 1980). Terms such as *rural renaissance* and *rural turnaround* were used to describe this unprecedented phenomenon. While the 1980s returned to historic migration patterns, the 1990s witnessed a new non-metropolitan migration "rebound" with renewed migration gains in these areas (Johnson 2003).

Many explanations have been proposed to account for this anomaly (Fuguitt et al. 1998). Frey and Speare (1992) group these explanations into three main categories: period effects, regional restructuring, and deconcentration explanations. Common to these explanations are two types of underlying causes: restructuring of employment opportunities and changes in residential preferences. The most important cause of the rural turnaround appears to be the restructuring of industries, especially manufacturing, which brought jobs to rural areas during the 1970s (Hawley and Mazie 1981). The development of infrastructure and narrowing wage differences between rural and urban areas facilitated migration to rural areas during this period.

Furthermore, the rural turnaround also seems to be associated with people's continued romantic attachments to bucolic settings. It has been suggested that the overcrowding of large cities and concomitant social problems during the 1960s and 1970s drove people out of central cities, especially when transportation and communication technologies made it possible for them to realize their residential preferences (Campbell and Garkovich 1984). Moreover, migrants have consistently been attracted to rural communities in scenic areas, such as those located near mountains and bodies of water.

More recently, rural communities in the South and the Midwest have experienced significant growth associated with the movement of Latino immigrants. Jobs in such industries as meat processing and construction have attracted these newcomers to new destinations for Latinos (Millard and Chapa 2004; Saenz et al. 2003; Zúñiga and Hernández-León 2005).

TRENDS IN LITERATURE

There is a major and expanding literature on rural-urban migration. We conducted a literature search using the following combination of terms in *Sociological Abstracts*: "rural" or "nonmetropolitan" or "nonmetro"; "urban" or "metropolitan" or "metro"; and "migration." We identified 1,542 entries (based on journal articles, book chapters, dissertations, papers presented at professional meetings, and a few books) between 1950 and 2005. Yet, the first entry that we identified was published in 1934—an article titled "Rural-Urban Migration in the Tennessee Valley Beyond 1920 and 1930," which appeared in *Social Forces* (Hamilton 1934).

Interest in rural–urban migration increased significantly in the 1975–1979 period, reflecting the rural-turnaround era, when the number of entries (145) nearly tripled compared to those (54) in the 1970–1974 period. The overall upward trend in interest on the topic can be seen by examining the average number of entries across five-year periods (6 in the case of the 2000–2005 interval)

beginning in 1950: 1950–1954, 4.2; 1955–1959, 11.8; 1960–1964, 6.0; 1965–1969, 10.2; 1970–1974, 10.8; 1975–1979, 29.0; 1980–1984, 19.0; 1985–1989, 32.0; 1990–1994, 40.8; 1995–1999, 58.2; and 2000–2005, 72.0. Two trends emerge from this literature review. First, nearly half (47%) of all entries appeared since 1995. Second, there has been a shift from works based almost exclusively on the United States toward a greater representation of international settings.

Economists have also made important contributions to the understanding of rural–urban migration. For example, Harris and Todaro (1970) developed a model—the Harris-Todaro model—to understand the flow of workers in tropical Africa from rural to urban locales. This movement challenged traditional thinking in economics because it involved the movement of rural workers to urban areas in light of the existence of employment in agriculture in rural settings and relatively high levels of unemployment in urban areas. The Harris-Todaro model points out that such migrants are behaving rationally because the expected wages in urban area—even in the presence of high unemployment—are higher than in rural areas. While the Harris-Todaro model focuses on individuals maximizing their utility without taking into account other members of their households, other economists have pointed out that migration is a household, rather than individual, decision. For example, in their study of rural-to-urban migration in Kenya, Agesa and Kim (2001) focus on the household unit maximizing its utility through various forms of migration. They observe that because of large households, including numerous dependents, the majority of rural-to-urban migrants engage in split migration. In this form of movement, the husband typically moves to an urban area initially without his family. The rest of the household joins him only after he has accumulated enough money to afford the move

SEE ALSO *Cities; Harris-Todaro Model; Migration; Urbanization*

BIBLIOGRAPHY

Agesa, Richard U., and Sunwoong Kim. 2001. Rural to Urban Migration as a Household Decision: Evidence from Kenya. *Review of Development Economics* 5 (1): 60–75.

Brown, David L., and John M. Wardwell, eds. 1981. *New Directions in Urban-Rural Migration: The Population Turnaround in Rural America.* New York: Academic Press.

Campbell, Rex R., and Lorraine Garkovich. 1984. Turnaround Migration as an Episode of Collective Behavior. *Rural Sociology* 49 (1): 89–105.

Frey, William H., and Alden Speare, 1992. The Revival of Metropolitan Growth in the United Sates: An Assessment of Findings from the 1990 Census. *Population and Development Review* 18 (1): 129–146.

Fuguitt, Glenn V., Calvin L. Beale, John A. Fulton, and Richard M. Gibson. 1998. Recent Population Trends in Nonmetropolitan Cities and Villages: From the Turnaround, Through Reversal to the Rebound. In *Research in Rural Sociology and Development*, ed. H. K. Schwarzweller and B. Mullan, 1–21. Greenwich, CT: JAI Press.

Hamilton, C. Horace. 1934. Rural-Urban Migration in the Tennessee Valley beyond 1920 and 1930. *Social Forces* 13: 57–64.

Harris, John R., and Michael P. Todaro. 1970. Migration, Unemployment and Development: A Two-Sector Analysis. *American Economic Review* 60 (1): 126–142.

Hawley, Amos H., and Sara Mills Mazie, eds. 1981. *Nonmetropolitan America in Transition.* Chapel Hill: University of North Carolina Press.

Johnson, Kenneth M. 2003. Unpredictable Directions of Population Growth and Migration. In *Challenges for Rural America in the 21st Century*, ed. D. L. Brown and L. Swanson, 19–31. University Park: Pennsylvania State University Press.

Millard, Ann V., and Jorge Chapa. 2004. *Apple Pie and Enchiladas: Latino Newcomers in the Rural Midwest.* Austin: University of Texas Press.

Ravenstein, E. G. 1885. The Laws of Migration. *Journal of the Statistical Society of London* 48 (2): 167–235.

Saenz, Rogelio, Katharine M. Donato, Lourdes Gouveia, and Cruz Torres. 2003. Latinos in the South: A Glimpse of Ongoing Trends and Research. *Southern Rural Sociology* 19 (1): 1–19.

Sjoberg, Gideon. 1960. *The Preindustrial City: Past and Present.* New York: Free Press.

United Nations. 2004. *Urban and Rural Areas 2003.* New York: United Nations, Population Division.

United Nations. 2006. *World Urbanization Prospects: The 2005 Revision Population Database.* New York: United Nations, Population Division.

Zuñiga, Victor, and Rubén Hernández-León, eds. 2005. *New Destinations: Mexican Immigration in the United States.* New York: Russell Sage Foundation.

Rogelio Saenz
Isao Takei
Xiaodong Wang

MILGRAM, STANLEY
1933–1984

Stanley Milgram was born on August 15, 1933, in the Bronx, New York, the second of three children of Samuel and Adele Milgram, who had both emigrated from Eastern Europe around the time of World War I. Samuel was a baker and cake decorator, and Adele assisted him in the bakery, in addition to being a homemaker.

Stanley's superior intelligence was already discernible in elementary school, and he graduated from James Monroe High School in only three years. While there, one of his extracurricular activities was working on stagecraft—an experience that helped him infuse his experiments with the dramatic elements that made them powerfully realistic experiences for his subjects. He obtained his BA in political science from Queens College. He continued his graduate education in the Department of Social Relations at Harvard University, where Gordon Allport (1897–1967), a leading figure in personality and social psychology, became his mentor and, later, the chairman of his doctoral dissertation, beginning a lifetime relationship of mutual admiration.

During the 1955 to 1956 academic year, Solomon Asch (1907–1996), a social psychologist who was already well known for his groundbreaking research on conformity, came to Harvard as a visiting lecturer, and Allport assigned Milgram to be Asch's teaching and research assistant. Several years later, in 1959 to 1960, Milgram worked for Asch again, helping him edit a book on conformity at the Institute for Advanced Study in Princeton. As a result of these repeated contacts with Asch, Milgram came to regard him as his main scientific influence.

Milgram was awarded his PhD in social psychology in the spring of 1960, and in the fall began his academic career as an assistant professor in the Department of Psychology at Yale University. It was there that he conducted his very first and most important experimental work—a series of experiments on obedience to authority.

Although a secular Jew, throughout his lifetime Milgram maintained a strong sense of connectedness to Judaism, which included an identification with the millions of his fellow Jews murdered by the Nazis during World War II. In the speech he wrote and gave at his bar mitzvah celebration in 1946, a year after the end of the war, he said: "As I come of age and find happiness in joining the ranks of Israel, the knowledge of the tragic suffering of my fellow Jews throughout war-torn Europe makes this also a solemn event and an occasion to reflect upon the heritage of my people" (quoted in Blass 2004, p. 8). Milgram's obedience experiments were clearly motivated by an attempt to shed new light on the horrors of the Holocaust.

In these experiments, conducted from August 1961 to April 1962, subjects were to teach another subject a list of adjective-noun pairs by punishing him with electric shocks of increasing voltage every time he made a mistake, by pressing one of thirty switches on a "shock machine." Each subsequent switch represented a 15-volt increase in shock intensity—ranging from 15 to 450 volts. What the volunteer subject did not know was that the realistic-looking shock apparatus was merely a prop that did not deliver shocks, that the learner was an accomplice who gave right and wrong answers according to a predetermined schedule, and that the increasingly pitiful screams of the learner were actually scripted, prerecorded complaints. The result: more than 60 percent of the subjects went to the end of the shock scale—that is, ended up fully obedient to the experimenter's commands to keep increasing the punishment—even after the learner fell silent and, perhaps, lost consciousness. This was the central revelatory finding of the obedience studies—the extreme willingness of individuals to obey an authority who had no coercive means to enforce his commands, to commit acts that were in conflict with their moral principles. A secondary but also important finding was that the amount of obedience varied as a function of changes in the social situation. For example, in one set of experimental variations, Milgram gradually reduced the distance between teacher and learner, which resulted in a corresponding decrease in subjects' obedience. Altogether, Milgram carried out more than twenty different variations of the obedience experiment.

The results of the Yale experiments led Milgram to conclude that it was unnecessary to invoke sadism or psychopathology to explain the barbaric behavior of Nazi perpetrators and their allies during the Holocaust. They showed, he argued, that "ordinary people, simply doing their jobs, and without any particular hostility on their part, can become agents in a terrible destructive process.... A substantial proportion of people do what they are told to do, irrespective of the content of the act and without limitations of conscience as long as they perceive that the command comes from a legitimate authority" (Milgram 1974, pp. 6, 189).

Milgram's obedience experiments, whose consequences are still with us today, provoked a controversy that revolved around the ethical aspects of his research methods. Some critics questioned Milgram's right to expose his subjects to an intensive, stressful experience that they had not anticipated, and to deceive them into believing that they had inflicted painful shocks to, and perhaps had harmed, an innocent victim. In his defense, one can note that Milgram operated in an ethical vacuum; at the time, there were no formal rules about what was permissible in research with human subjects. Also, some months after their participation, Milgram sent his subjects a postexperimental questionnaire that included a question inquiring about their well-being, something which is rarely done in social-psychological research. About 84 percent of his respondents indicated that they were glad to have been in the experiment, and only 1.3 percent said that they were sorry to have participated (see Milgram 1974, p. 195). Nonetheless, during the experiment itself, as Milgram himself noted, "in a large number of cases the degree of tension reached extremes that are rarely seen in

sociopsychological laboratory studies" (Milgram 1963, p. 375). The safeguards we have in place today to ensure the welfare of human research subjects, as embodied in the American Psychological Association's guidelines and federal regulations, can be traced to the concerns evoked by Milgram's obedience experiments, together with a handful of other ethically questionable studies from the same era.

In the fall of 1963 Milgram returned as an assistant professor to Harvard, where he became involved in two new areas of research. One, already begun at Yale, was the lost-letter technique, which became the most widely used unobtrusive measure of attitudes. The second was the creation of the small-world method (now commonly termed "six degrees of separation"), in which a group of "starters" in one part of the United States were asked to send mailings to a designated stranger in another part of the country, via a chain of acquaintances. Among the completed chains it took a surprisingly small number of intermediaries—about six—to reach the target.

In 1966 Milgram came up for tenure, and—after some lengthy and contentious deliberations by the committee evaluating him—he was turned down. Some committee members still held the ethical indiscretions of the obedience experiments against him. In the fall of 1967 Milgram accepted an offer to head a newly developing doctoral program in social psychology at the Graduate Center of the City University of New York (CUNY). There he turned his attention to the systematic study of city life, in particular the norms—the intangible, unspoken rules—that guide everyday social interactions. Among the studies he conducted was one that investigated subway riders' willingness to give up their seats when asked to (more than 50% did). Another set of studies compared city and small-town residents' willingness to help strangers.

With the urban environment now Milgram's "laboratory," the field experiment became his primary research tool at CUNY, and he contributed to the growth of field experimentation in social psychology by demonstrating how a wide diversity of everyday phenomena could be studied—even within the structural confines of the experimental method. Milgram died of heart failure at the age of 51 on December 20, 1984.

SEE ALSO *Authority; Conformity; Ethics in Experimentation; Experiments, Human; Experiments, Shock*

BIBLIOGRAPHY

Blass, Thomas. 2004. *The Man Who Shocked the World: The Life and Legacy of Stanley Milgram.* New York: Basic Books.

Blass, Thomas, ed. 2000. *Obedience to Authority: Current Perspectives on the Milgram Paradigm.* Mahwah, NJ: Erlbaum.

Milgram, Stanley, 1963. Behavioral Study of Obedience. *Journal of Abnormal and Social Psychology* 67: 371–378.

Milgram, Stanley, 1974. *Obedience to Authority: An Experimental View*. New York: Harper and Row.

Milgram, Stanley, 1992. *The Individual in a Social World: Essays and Experiments*. 2nd ed. Ed. John Sabini and Maury Silver. New York: McGraw-Hill.

Thomas Blass

MILITANTS

Militant, in contemporary academic, activist, and journalistic interpretations, refers to an individual (as a noun) or to a party, a struggle or a state (as an adjective), engaged in aggressive forms of social and political resistance. This aggression is demonstrated in a range of behavior: from oral abuse, to the threat of violence, to physical attacks on people and property. The word has its origin in the fifteenth-century Latin word *militare*, the latter signifying civilians acting as soldiers during war, conflict, famine, and other periods of crises. Militant was used in the English language to represent public activism, as an assertion of speech, ideas, and self-determination (for example, human rights activism, militant environmentalism); but the moderate meaning of the term has undergone substantial change. In popular usage, militants are described as people with an ideology who are forceful, energetic, and dynamic supporters of their collective principles. This ideology may be personal or political. The individual militant, however, is increasingly lost in the clamor of rising global violence.

More recent understanding of militants implies that they are forced or voluntary recruits in an organization/militia. Their methods of action rarely have similar patterns. Some militants may be rigorously trained for serving a particular cause, and may easily employ force as a form of offense. For example, the Liberation Tigers of the Tamil Eelam (LTTE), a militant secessionist movement in the north of Sri Lanka, help their recruits to acquire skills in guerrilla warfare against the state (Daniel 1996). Other militant groups may use the display of arms or antagonistic body language to sustain their movement. A depleted police force and rise in crime has given birth to militant citizens' organizations in urban Nicaragua. This form of vigilantism, endorsed by Nicaraguan youth, involves armed patrolling of neighborhoods at night (Rodgers 2006). This is an example of how militants manipulate notions of counterviolence and retaliation in pursuit of their cause, organizing their activities around the mere promise of violent action. Thus, militancy can also be a performance to contest the vast indeterminacies of everyday social life.

The definition of *militant* raises some vital questions. Do militants always rationalize overt or covert violence? Gandhi's resistance to colonial rule in India was described as militant nonviolence by scholars and administrators alike. So militancy may involve promoting intolerance, but the task of militants may be to collect in preordained spaces and take part peacefully in civil disobedience. Buddhist nationalism in Southeast Asia is also an example of passive resistance to oppressive state rule. Do militants remain within movements for ideological reasons? Many men within militant movements remain committed, not to the ideology, but to "violence as sport" (Tambiah 1996). Several scholars exploring the worlds of militant outfits show how the members get pleasure from indulging in violence for voyeurism, entertainment, and excitement. Further, loyalty to militant philosophies is usually a reflection of masculinity, especially in conflict-riddled societies where membership of warring factions is a rite of passage into manhood. In this context of gendered identity politics, who is the woman militant? During the moderate use of the term, feminist activists, right-wing and left-wing demonstrators, and campaigners for women's rights were known to be militant women. However, research into the changing nature of female militancy has shown that women are the new recruits into self-styled militia. Often entering the movement due to a shortage in manpower, women can even offer militant leadership. Statistics from United Nations (UN) surveys show that 40 percent of suicide bombers are women, affiliated with various national and international militant organizations (UN Report on Suicide Bombers, 2006). Most women militants can enter public places without raising suspicion, and their engagement in violence stems from a determination to display their equality with male counterparts. The final goal of all militants, however, is to assert or establish their own social and political worldview, whether by influencing state policies or taking over a government through force or passive resistance.

Changing alliances between world leaders and chaotic political events are transforming the flexible definition of the term *militant*. Before the attack on the twin towers of the World Trade Center in New York (September 11, 2001), terrorists were characterized as having covert collective missions, and they carried out indiscriminate, violent attacks on civilian targets. They could be placed across a broad spectrum of faiths and convictions, from white xenophobia to radical fundamentalism. However, the media nowadays readily use the label *militant* as synonymous with *terrorist*, suggesting that militancy in the modern world necessarily involves extreme forms of political action. The term *militant* is intricately tied to notions of international law, the Geneva

Convention, the human rights discourse and, of course, Islam. "The militant Muslim" is the new label being attached to nationalistic activities especially in Palestine, Iraq, and Afghanistan. While militancy could earlier be used to describe subversive activities by marginalized groups and "a weapon of the weak," to use Scott's celebrated phrase (1985), it has now developed a negative connotation in being reinterpreted in the context of the War on Terror. Sadly, this adherence to a static meaning relegates the broader concept to the fringes of scholarly debate.

SEE ALSO *Black Panthers; Black Power; Civil Disobedience; Liberation; Liberation Movements; Palestine Liberation Organization (PLO); Passive Resistance; Performance; Protest; Resistance; Revolution; Social Movements; Suicide Bombers; Terror; Violence; Women's Liberation; Women's Movement*

BIBLIOGRAPHY

Daniel, E. Valentine 1996. *Charred Lullabies: Chapters in an Anthropography of Violence.* Princeton, NJ: Princeton University Press.

Rodgers, Dennis. 2006. Living in the Shadow of Death: Gangs, Violence and Social Order in Urban Nicaragua, 1996–2002. *Journal of Latin American Studies* 38 (2): 267–292.

Scott, James C. 1985. *Weapons of the Weak: Everyday Forms of Peasant Resistance.* New Haven, CT and London: Yale University Press.

Tambiah, Stanley J. 1996. *Leveling Crowds: Ethnonationalist Conflicts and Collective Violence in South Asia.* Berkeley: University of California Press.

Atreyee Sen

MILITARISM

Traditionally, militarism is a behavior or condition in which states resort quickly to the use of their armed forces in response to international or domestic threats or go to great lengths to mobilize people and resources for war. Militarism is also the belief that military responses are usually the best ones, and that the military is the most important institution in the state. However, *militarism* has different connotations depending on the era and field of scholarship. The traditional meaning of *militarism* is common in much of the standard international-relations literature and histories of Great Power wars. In feminist analyses, intellectual and cultural histories, or "bottom-up" historical accounts, militarism is a factor of inequality or an aspect of cultural hegemony. In the comparative politics field, militarism usually refers to interventionism in politics.

War has been the object of criticism since the time of the ancient Chinese, Hebrews, and Greeks, yet the term *militarism* did not come into common usage in the West until the latter half of the nineteenth century. As war-making became industrialized, and as states took on more and more nonmilitary functions, such as building economic infrastructure or providing social services, a growing chorus of political leaders and intellectuals began attributing war and social ills to militarism. These critics, often from a liberal or Marxist perspective, considered a state militaristic if its leaders dedicated a great deal of the government budget to the armed forces, employed a large proportion of the populace in the military or in military-related industries, and encouraged a martial spirit among its subjects. These antimilitarists worried that training so many in the methods of organized violence, along with arms races and naval competition, only increased the likelihood of war. All of those resources and people used up in the armed forces only meant less for dealing with the challenges and victims of drastic economic and social change. Moreover, given its authoritarian structure, a powerful military may be inimical to democracy. Militarism, then, from the start has been a pejorative term.

Twentieth-century Germany and Japan are oft-cited cases of militarism. Germany twice attempted to gain regional hegemony over Europe by force of arms—from 1914 to 1919 under the kaiser and the military, and from 1939 to 1945 under Adolf Hitler's (1889–1945) fascist regime. Japan's military government made a bloody bid for empire in Asia from 1931 to 1945. To attempt ambitious expansion, these two countries harnessed their economies and citizens to war-making, as well as the resources and peoples of captured lands. In doing so they wreaked staggering, irreparable harm on millions of people. Hence, for those who attribute—rightly or wrongly—these wars to militarism, the term is not just a pejorative, it is a pathology. For those averse to war on principle, such as strict pacifists, states are inherently militaristic.

When states mobilize for war, they depend on taxation, recruitment, and coercion to get enough resources and people to pay for and staff their armed forces. States must also convince their subjects of the necessity of preparing for or actually going to war. This is an aspect of state militarism particularly important in democracies. Watching the German Weimar republic crumble in the 1930s, or the U.S. government expand its security powers as it geared up for the cold war, or the impact of constant war or preparation for war on Israel's democracy, social scientists have long worried that war-making and accompanying militarism might weaken democratic government. Some scholars have envisioned a grim "garrison state" in which experts on violence have more power than elected officials, and in which national security becomes more important than the safety, liberties, and rights of citizens. U.S. president Dwight Eisenhower (1890–1969) worried about this possibility. Just before leaving office in 1961, this former general warned the nation to "guard against the acquisition of unwarranted influence, whether sought or unsought, by the military-industrial complex," oddly anticipating the critique of American and European antiwar and student movements of the late 1960s and early 1970s, or the later "nuclear freeze" movement in the 1980s. Other scholars have debated this thesis, arguing that democracy by its nature has hindered militarism and prevented the rise of garrison states, even in places with large militaries, such as the United States.

President Woodrow Wilson (1856–1924) was not worried about garrison states, but he did blame war on militarism. In his famous Fourteen Points speech before the U.S. Congress in 1918, he argued that only through transparent diplomacy, mutual security agreements, and disarmament could the world hope to diminish the causes of war. Others have since then kept this liberal banner flying. Since 1957, for example, the interdisciplinary *Journal of Conflict Resolution* has been publishing research on military affairs and international relations, theorizing the conditions of war and peace. Other groups have compiled data on military employment and spending, armament levels, and the number and scope of armed conflicts to measure levels of militarism. Scholars in Sweden established the Stockholm International Peace Research Institute in 1966 and began publishing its annual yearbook on armaments, disarmament, and international security in 1969. A similar series, *World Military and Social Expenditures*, has been published since 1974.

Reactions to militaristic behavior or ideology are also easily found in literature and other arts. Erich Maria Remarque's (1898–1970) novel *All Quiet on the Western Front* (1929) remains a trenchant account of World War I (1914–1918) and of the militaristic creed underlying the violence. Pablo Picasso's (1881–1974) painting *Guernica* (1937) was an angry reaction to the Nazi German bombing of the city of Guernica during the Spanish Civil War (1936–1939), and it attributed the tragedy in part to militaristic elements in Spanish culture. The painting later became a symbolic reference for movements against U.S. involvement in the Vietnam War (1957–1975) and the U.S. war in Iraq that began in 2003. In the Stanley Kubrick (1928–1999) films *Dr. Strangelove* (1964) and *Full Metal Jacket* (1987), the military is but a step away from fascism. Kubrick's soldiers and officers, in facing dehumanizing treatment or the dehumanization of the enemy, run the risk of psychosis, if they are not already psychotic.

Not all studies link militarism to the state and war-making. Some see a predominant military and martial spirit as products of civil society or culture, or of particular social groups. The indicators of militarism, or "militarization" some insist, are the same, but its cause lies more in socialization or cultural institutions than in state officials. In short, civilians are to blame for militarism, not the state or its soldiers.

With postmodernism and the cultural turn in the social sciences, another variant of militarism has appeared. In some scholarship, militarism is not about war-making per se, but the replication of military organization and values in the society at large—not just to increase the capacity to wage war, but for some ulterior purpose, such as to maintain social order, promote economic development, or further national integration. This "social" militarism may be said to exist in nations in which the military is the primary institution responsible for integrating diverse ethnic populations, for training workers, or for spearheading colonization and other development projects. Some scholars also employ this definition to argue that the spread of military organization and values into society contributes to patriarchy, elitism, or other forms of social inequality.

A fourth kind of militarism appears in the field of comparative politics in the developing world. Militarism in this field often means military interventionism in politics, and social scientists are typically concerned with the amount of independence the armed forces has from civilian rule, the level of socioeconomic segregation (that is, how many more material benefits and privileges the military receives in comparison to civilians), and the number of responsibilities the armed forces have beyond national defense. As the military's independence, benefits, and responsibilities increase, so too does the likelihood of militaristic behavior or attitudes. The greater the military's stake in politics, the greater its willingness and ability to intervene in politics, whether through backroom pressure or a dramatic coup.

SEE ALSO *Authoritarianism; Civil-Military Relation; Culture; Fascism; Imperialism; Industrialization; League of Nations; Liberalism; Masculinity; Military; Military Regimes; Nationalism and Nationality; Patriarchy; Patriotism; Politics, Comparative; Postmodernism; United Nations; War; War and Peace; Wilson, Woodrow*

BIBLIOGRAPHY

Bacevich, Andrew J. 2005. *The New American Militarism: How Americans are Seduced by War.* New York: Oxford University Press.

Berghahn, Volker R. 1981. *Militarism: The History of an International Debate, 1861–1979.* New York: Cambridge University Press.

Eisenhower, Dwight D. 1961. Farewell Radio and Television Address to the American People by President Dwight D. Eisenhower, January 17, 1961. http://www.eisenhower.archives.gov/farewell.htm.

Enloe, Cynthia. 1983. *Does Khaki Become You? The Militarisation of Women's Lives*. Boston: South End.

Friedburg, Aaron L. 2000. *In the Shadow of the Garrison State: America's Anti-Statism and Its Cold War Grand Strategy*. Princeton, NJ: Princeton University Press.

Gillis, John R., ed. 1989. *Militarization of the Western World*. New Brunswick, NJ: Rutgers University Press.

Lasswell, Harold D. 1941. The Garrison State. *American Journal of Sociology* 46: 455–468.

NcNeill, William. 1982. *The Pursuit of Power: Technology, Armed Force, and Society since A.D. 1000*. Chicago: University of Chicago Press.

Nunn, Frederick M. 1992. *The Time of the Generals: Latin American Professional Militarism in World Perspective*. Lincoln: University of Nebraska Press.

Rouquié, Alain. 1987. *The Military and the State in Latin America*. Trans. Paul E. Sigmund. Berkeley: University of California Press.

Tilly, Charles. 1992. *Coercion, Capital, and European States, AD 990–1990*. Cambridge, MA: Blackwell.

Vagts, Alfred. 1959. *A History of Militarism: Civilian and Military*. Rev. ed. New York: Meridian.

Andrew J. Schlewitz

MILITARY

Scholars and practitioners in the social and behavioral sciences have studied military systems for over a century. Archaeologists and anthropologists have offered insights into the war making of prehistoric humankind as well as modern primary group dynamics (the ways soldiers develop their own methods of making sense of and appraising what they do) and the ways modern societies celebrate and memorialize warriors (Keeley 1996; Divale 1973; Mosse 1990; Ben-Ari 1998). Historians have explored the relationships between the social, economic, and geographic contexts of ancient and modern states and the military institutions they generated as well as the relationship between technological changes in weaponry and changes or the absence of change in the ways states and their military leaders prepare for and wage war (Mumford 1961; Mann 1986; Vagts 1959; Lynn 1984). Political scientists have delved into the relationships between political and military elites and the presence or absence of military coup making. (Finer 1988; Huntington 1957; Stepan 1971; Peri 1983; Karsten 1997; Feaver and Kohn 2001). Sociologists and social psychologists have asked how soldiers are recruited, trained, and motivated; how racial and

gender integration is achieved; how morale is sustained or lost; what combat does to those who experience it; and how military institutions and personnel interact with the rest of society (Andrzejewski 1954; Janowitz 1960; Moskos et al. 2000; Stouffer 1949; Kindsvatter 2003; Gal and Mangelsdorff 1991; Cronin 1998). Geographers and economists have attempted to measure the costs and benefits of military institutions and warfare on regions, with their attendant impacts on domestic economies (Nef 1950; Melman 1985; Knorr 1956; Russett 1970; Rockoff 2005; Kirby 1992). Cultural studies/literary history scholars have mined the memoirs, poems, and novels of veterans (Wilson 1962; Fussell 1975; Fussell 1989; Lewis 1985).

THE MILITARY-SOCIETY SYMBIOSIS

For millennia organization for warfare has been one of the central activities of humankind. Military institutions, however simple they were in prehistoric times, were among the first social institutions. Bands of hunter-gatherers employed simple weapons and tactics in fights with other hunter-gatherers. The kinship-centered, cooperative propensities of earlier humankind coupled with the effective use of verbal communication offer better explanations of the combat effectiveness of early human communities than do studies relying solely on theories of aggressiveness (Bigelow 1969; Dawson 1986).

Simple, subsistence-level societies did not all wage war in the same manner. Resource availability and cultural differences among those societies were important factors in war making. The decision of some communities to house new couples in the wife's mother's community (matrilocality) as opposed to the husband's father's community (patrilocality) has been found to be associated strongly with a low level of local conflict as a result of the constant breaking up of extremely localistic war bands and a higher degree of effectiveness in longer-range warfare as a result of the creation of more cosmopolitan intercommunity trust and affiliation (Divale 1973).

Simple settled agricultural communities defended their fields with every-man-a-warrior militias. The first city-states tended to emerge in fertile alluvial valleys, where warlords dominated and fortified central market towns that had a surplus large enough to enable them to retain a professional military retinue. Those warlords centralized the acquisition and distribution of weapons, attacked and held nearby towns and cities, and extended their power into the pastoral hinterland. Virtually the entire budget of the first known warlord, Sargon of Akkad, the conqueror of Sumer, went to his army, but his military "pacification" also produced secure trade routes, law courts, uniform weights and measures, and a common coinage. (In later periods up to 70 percent of the budget would go to the military, as in the cases of the Roman Empire, Charlemagne, Edward III, and Louis XIV.) In the process those warlords developed symbiotic relations with agrarian and mercantile elites. "Civilization" had arrived (O'Connell 1995; Mumford 1961).

In the Middle Ages the armies of city-states and monarchies served elites who in several areas ruled relatively decentralized feudal communities dominated by aristocratic lords with their own armed retinues. Eventually most of the nominal kingly leaders of those feudal states, utilizing new military technologies and "standing armies" paid for in innovative ways, defeated their aristocratic rivals and claimed a monopoly on military violence. Many of those monarchic rulers later yielded to revolutionary forces employing conscript armies. Most of those military forces reverted in time to the modern model of "all-volunteer" forces, and the more affluent of those states developed increasingly sophisticated weapons, strategic planners, and logistic systems (Redlich 1964–1965; Black 1998; Tilly 1992; McNeill 1982).

The early modern state emerged in areas where monarchs were able to overcome the medieval constitutional traditions of sharing their power with a parliament composed of the gentry and the aristocracy. As commerce, riches from the New World, and more efficient European farming techniques generated economic surpluses, those resources were taxed for military purposes. *Intendants* loyal to the French monarchy slowly bled power from the nobility to fuel royal ambitions throughout the seventeenth century. King Gustavus Adolphus successfully conscripted Swedes for the seven armies he threw against the Hapsburgs in the second quarter of that century, paying for the effort with the sale of war bonds and monopolies, the appropriation of farms, the rationing of food, and the debasement of the currency, all accomplished by a ruthless bureaucracy. As Charles Tilly put it, "War made the State, and the State made war" (Tilly 1992, p. 213).

In the Netherlands sixteenth-century Calvinist wool manufacturers and merchants organized the first modern professional army. The forces of their Spanish foe had been raised in the venture-capitalism fashion of most early modern forces: The crown paid a fixed sum to professional military entrepreneurs to raise regiments. However, the primary remuneration for those men in the course of the campaign was understood to be booty under the maxim *bellum se ipsum alet* ("war should feed itself"). The Dutch force was conceived differently. Its mission was defensive and of indefinite tenure. Its commanders tried to avoid the chaotic behavior characteristic of looting soldiers in order to maintain discipline. Hence its men were paid regular salaries and enjoyed the benefits of a fledgling commissariat. Its employers included some of the world's first assembly-line (woolen clothing) manufacturers. Thus it is not surprising that Dutch infantrymen were trained to present the enemy with a continuous and lethal series of musket volleys through the use of training manuals that offered a recruit dozens of by-the-number engravings of the steps that all the ranks of musketeers were to take simultaneously in a load-and-fire countermarch (Feld 1975).

THE ROLE OF TECHNOLOGY

Some technological innovations transformed both military methods and social and political structures. Bronze weapons were expensive. Thus Bronze Age armies were aristocratic, and their states were oligarchies. The advent of cheaper iron weapons meant that men of more modest means could bear arms. In ancient Greece this eventually resulted in more democratic polities. The stirrup enabled armored men to fight more effectively from horseback, but armor and large horses were expensive. Only an oligarchy could afford to field that type of force in Europe, Asia, or Africa.

By 1350, however, pikemen and crossbowmen had dealt the armored cavalry of feudalism devastating blows, and although the landed nobles resisted, their role as cavalry in military systems began to decline. The introduction of firearms into western Africa and Maori New Zealand significantly transformed the social and political structures of those peoples. In Europe and the Middle East firearms grew in significance as the rate and rainproof reliability of fire increased tenfold between the early sixteenth century and the late seventeenth century. By 1600 the ratio of infantry to cavalry in Europe had risen to almost 8 to 1. Military demands continued to influence and be aided by developments in the clothing industry, the metals trades, nautical technology, land transportation, and high finance (Vasillopulos 1995; Nef 1950; Van Creveld 1983).

The evolution and growth of military institutions appears to some to have followed a steady linear path from the simple to the sophisticated, but there were many exceptions. Indeed the European feudal and nineteenth-century Chinese warlord military systems were retrogressions from the more complex and effective armies of the Roman and Chinese imperial states that preceded them. Technological advances in warfare were not adopted readily by many military elites (Goldman 2006). Eighteenth-century and early nineteenth-century Mameluke warriors in Egypt clung to swordsmanship, sixteenth-century Japanese shoguns embraced firearms with great success but then abandoned and suppressed their use out of respect for the ethos of the elite class of samurai swordsmen, and medieval European aristocrats disdained improvements in infantry weapons and tactics for similar reasons (Stone 2004).

Armies grew in size as well as complexity over the course of several centuries, but those increases were not driven by technological breakthroughs. They came about only when political leaderships decided that such increases were appropriate. Empire builders such as Louis XIV and Phillip II increased the size of their armies, whereas leaders in Poland, Britain, and the United States held back. The leadership of the fledgling state of Israel produced a military with a high participation ratio because of its sense that Israel was beleaguered. Revolutionaries such as those in the French Committee of Public Safety and the Chinese Kuomintang and the Chinese Communists opted for mass armies for political purposes. Political leaders decide to add weapons and manpower at times of opportunity or threat; they also decide to reduce their expenditures and forces when that seems to be the right course. Examples include the Swedish decision in the eighteenth century to reduce the national military and the decision by the Chinese Empire in the sixteenth century to withdraw its massive navy from the Indian Ocean (Lynn 1990; Stone 2004; Vagts 1959; Perrin 1979).

Conscription of Frenchmen in the 1790s for the revolutionary infantry advanced the role of the common soldier. The conscription act called on those with new rights to satisfy new obligations. However, that massive and recurring mobilization did not lead to greater democracy. The musket had not "made the democrat," in J. F. C. Fuller's formulation (Fuller 1961, p. 33), in revolutionary France any more than it had in early modern Japan, Russia, or Prussia. Although it ended the battlefield supremacy of the samurai and the knight, they reemerged as the officer corps of the new standing armies.

Although the intensity of warfare and the military participation rates of male citizens both increased throughout the nineteenth and twentieth centuries, the share of both the gross national product and the resources of the state devoted to military expenditures began to decline in the late twentieth century. Social welfare and other nonmilitary lobbies grew more effective at the expense of the military-industrial complex. Civilian experts and technicians provided an increasing number of services to military institutions as the "tooth to tail" ratio of support personnel to combatants grew. Those in technical military specialties became increasingly vital to the maintenance and functioning of increasingly sophisticated military equipment (Wool 1968). Private contractors began to replace some military personnel. The ratio of American contract personnel to military personnel in the Gulf War was 1 to 60; by late 2006 in the war in Iraq it was virtually 1 to 1 (Hemingway 2006).

THE RECRUITMENT PROCESS

Military personnel have been recruited as volunteers or conscripted by the state. At different times and in different places volunteers have had a variety of reasons for offering themselves for service, and nations have employed a number of philosophical and technical approaches to the recruitment process, ranging from a total reliance on volunteerism to the most brutal sort of compulsion, with a host of intermediate formulas (Levi 1996).

In the absence of conscription, individuals have chosen to serve for monetary rewards or economic security, adventure or glory, and religious or political idealism. The soldiers of ancient Greece and Rome, those of medieval and early modern magnates, and those of more modern armies of empire were motivated largely by economic considerations; in fact some were foreign mercenaries. However, those economic motives could be intermingled with more culture-driven ones. Many Irish, Sikhs, and Gurkhas in the service of the nineteenth-century and early twentieth-century British armed forces, for example, conceived of themselves as people with a warrior tradition, a self-image that was not lost on British recruiters (Karsten 1983; Enloe 1980). Similarly the Crow, Pawnee, and Shoshoni braves who volunteered to serve as scouts for the U.S. Army in the 1870s felt both the push of tribal need and the pull of a warrior tradition (Dunlay 1982). Some members of the untouchable caste (*harijan*) were recruited for British military service in India after the mutiny of elite Indian troops in the Bombay army in 1857. Untouchables saw military service as a vehicle for social mobility, and the thought of being used against Brahmins might have been appealing to some (Cohen 1990). Black Americans first volunteered largely for ideological reasons during the Civil War. Later many found military service to be a clear avenue for economic and social mobility, though they faced disappointment at the hands of racist recruiters and commanders until the second half of the twentieth century.

Within socioethnic communities that do not see themselves as warlike and in subcultures and families that are not impoverished, the individual act of volunteering in peacetime cannot be explained as easily. The first surge of wartime patriotic fervor in modern nation-states has led millions to enlist, but patriotic behavior also has been inspired by other motives. Many colonial New England recruits during the French and Indian War were younger sons who had not inherited land. Their response to offers of enlistment bounties consequently was informed by their desire to acquire a nest egg and personal independence from parental control. Most of those who served in the Continental army were more interested in the size of the bounty offered than in "the Cause" (Anderson 1984;

Lender 1986). Conversely, many Confederate volunteers who rode with the guerrilla commander William Quantrill in western Missouri and Kansas during the Civil War were the eldest sons of substantial slave owners, defending their world against what they perceived to be a serious threat to its survival (Bowen 1977).

In any event patriotism alone does not explain why many have selected the military calling in peacetime in a host of historical periods. The spirit of adventure and the martial spirit notwithstanding, economic security clearly has been the primary motive for peacetime enlistments in voluntary military institutions (with the exception of officer candidate academies) (Karsten 1982).

When the question of recruitment is approached from the perspective of the recruiter, there are clear correlations between policy and sociopolitical structure. Mercantilist reasoning led several early modern European states to seek foreign paid volunteers (mercenaries) to keep their subjects employed productively on their farms and at their trades. Machiavelli argued for a militia drawn from both the propertied classes and the masses to defend the liberty of a city-state, but that reasoning did not impress most seventeenth- and eighteenth-century rulers and their bureaucracies. Thus in 1776 Adam Smith maintained in his *Wealth of Nations* that militias were inefficient. Such a system drew people from their fields and trades to train and failed to bring them up to the standards of professional soldiers (Smith 1937, pp. 653–668). The solution was the creation of a professional military.

The modern nation-state rediscovered the power of local and regional loyalties in recruiting volunteers. Great Britain reorganized its regiments in 1873 by basing one of its two battalions permanently in locales with which they thereafter would be identified. The usefulness of that step for both recruitment and morale was proved quickly, and in the first two years of World War I the massive British volunteer army was raised largely through the private actions of committees and individuals drawing on "local pride," the "taproot of English nationality" (Simkins 1988, pp. 82, 97, 186). The National Guard Association of the United States, created in the 1870s, lobbied for volunteer units of the various states seeking resources from Congress. The regular U.S. Army, recognizing the recruiting and political power of the guard's local roots, drew on the same source in the local basing of its army reserve units in the twentieth century. Early twentieth-century Japanese military planners used the strong social bonds of village life to reinforce motivation in organizing army reserve units (Smethurst 1974).

Volunteerism was not always sufficient for raising military forces. Consequently Britain was subjected to a conscription of sorts during the Seven Years' War and the wars of the French Revolution and Empire. However, the English Militia Act of 1757 and its later English and Irish counterparts of the 1790s, like the American Union army drafts of 1863 and 1864, were designed essentially to spur enlistment by coaxing either service or the purchase of insurance to provide the required "commutation fee" or pay for a substitute. The conscription policies of other eighteenth- and nineteenth-century nations offered fewer options. The peasants of Russia, Hesse-Damstadt, Prussia, and some Latin American dictatorships were subjected to long terms of service.

Black Americans conscripted for segregated service in World Wars I and II faced both the fear and anger of southern whites and the distrust of white officers who regarded blacks as irresponsible and panicky. However, on the basis of their reading of massive surveys of the opinions of World War II soldiers, social psychologists advising the American military in the 1940s recommended the integration of black and white units to boost morale and improve performance levels. They were supported by white officer combat veterans who had developed respect for their men and had become confident in their ability, a phenomenon reminiscent of the experience of many white officers and their black troops in the Civil War. The integration of the services during the Korean War proved successful (Dalfiume 1969; Mandelbaum 1952). In the early 1960s the John F. Kennedy administration took the next step, requiring the desegregation of housing for military families near bases throughout the South.

WOMEN COMBATANTS

On rare occasions women have been used as combatants, as in nineteenth-century Benin and early modern Japan, and as guerrillas by the Soviet Union in World War II. More often they have served as auxiliaries in support, clerical, and nursing roles. In the late twentieth century and the early twenty-first century the armed services in the United States have recruited women more aggressively for a wider range of tasks, including combat support. Simultaneously women have been admitted to the nation's federal and state service academies. There was considerable resistance to this change, but academy leadership later began to crack down on sexual harassment and selective hazing (Alpern 1998; Sherrow 1996; Gelfand 2006).

TRAINING AND SOCIALIZATION

The process of socializing military inductees into the service's norms and mores while preparing them to perform their new duties always has had two dimensions: the goals and practices of the military and the impact of the process on the inductees. Certain features of the first dimension have been persistent and unmistakable. Discipline, collective action, the transmission of unit traditions, physical conditioning, and the acquisition of specific military skills always have been objectives of those responsible for the integration of recruits into military forces.

Modern boot camps are assumed by some social psychologists to be sophisticated versions of this process of reorienting individuals into the regimen and mores of the warrior culture with its male bonding. However, a study of U.S. Marine Corps basic training at Parris Island, South Carolina, in the 1940s and 1950s established the fact that marine officers for generations had felt it best to leave the process entirely in the hands of drill instructor sergeants (DIs), who trained the next generation of DIs without formal manuals or officer-led instruction. As one officer put it: "Probably it's a good thing we don't know how it's done. If we knew, we might fiddlebitch and tinker with the process until we ruined it" (Fleming 1990, pp. 24–25; see also pp. 140–155).

The military always has reinforced training with disciplinary codes and leadership methods to ensure that missions are accomplished. Those codes and methods sometimes change, reflecting changes in the value system of the larger society or new demands within the military. The patterns of organizational authority in the modern military have changed since World War II. As the military became more technologically sophisticated, employing more specialists, the need to reenlist those specialists grew, but the specialists were often averse to arbitrary authority. Many former specialists indicated in the 1950s and 1960s that they had left the military because of its coercive ways (Wool 1968). Simultaneously soldier resistance movements, some developing into military unions, grew in the technologically advanced Western states in the 1960s and 1970s (Cortright and Watts 1991). Hence out of need, military elites slowly devised and provided less coercive forms of leadership than had prevailed before. The movement from coercion to persuasion accelerated in the United States when the draft was abolished in 1973 and the services had to rely entirely on volunteers.

MORALE AND MOTIVATION

From the time when the first group of hunters drew on their supportive habits to collaborate in a successful warband raid on their neighbors or in the defense of their village, the small-group camaraderie in military units has influenced the effectiveness of skirmishes, naval engagements, and pitched battles. Anything that disrupted that camaraderie was suspected of damaging military effectiveness. French revolutionary leaders in the Committee of Public Safety knew how to organize small squads of about fifteen men. When those men received their portions of stew in the evening, they often were provided with revolutionary broadsides or songs that they were expected to learn by the evening campfire. French revolutionaries understood the importance of patriotic fervor as well as

what modern sociologists call the primary group (Lynn 1990). That induced bonding generally was successful. "A new comradeship and unity blossomed in our young lives," Emlyn Davies recalled of his early days in the Seventeenth Royal Welsh Fusiliers in 1914 (Simkins 1988, p. 302). The Canadian major George Pearkes wrote home in 1917 that "it always seems to me that I'm not fighting for King and Country but just for [my] company, which seems to be everything to me these days" (Pearkes).

In the 1950s U.S. Army researchers concluded that in battles between German and American units in World War II the German units generally appeared to have bested comparable American groups. In 1983 Martin van Creveld argued that this was the case in part because American policies with regard to unit formation and casualty replacement practices resulted in a fighting force with lower small group cohesion and trust than German units, in which cohesion was the conscious objective of commanders. Other research offers an additional explanation for German morale: the strength and depth of Nazi ideology and indoctrination (Van Creveld 1983; Bartov 1991).

Many Americans entered Vietnam with confidence in the rightness of their cause and the effectiveness of their weapons and leaders. That confidence often was reduced after months of heavy combat in steaming-hot terrain to what one veteran called "a war waged for survival in which each soldier fought for his own life and the lives of the men beside him, not caring who we killed … or how many or in what manner" (Lewis 1985, p. 118). Their plight was made more perilous by the high command's practice of cycling career officers through brief combat command tours of duty.

THE CONSEQUENCES OF MILITARY SERVICE

As the rate, range, and lethality of fire and the duration of exposure to it rose over five centuries, combatants experienced increasing stress (Keegan 1976). After prolonged periods of combat, the din of battle and the sight of dying friends produced "the shakes" and other symptoms of mental distress in many soldiers. In World War I their reaction was called shell shock; in World War II, battle fatigue. This phenomenon appears to have affected men in the American Civil War as well (Dean 1997).

The increasing lethality of combat might have been expected to lead to greater unwillingness to respond to orders under fire. However, although there is clear evidence of this among French forces in World War I (Smith 1994) and some evidence in other armies in the twentieth century, most troops have obeyed orders that placed them in "the killing zone." Most mutinies involve matters of pay or living and working conditions (Bushnell 1985; Rose 1982). Many combat veterans who suffered post-traumatic stress disorder (PTSD) long after their years of service owed their distress to the trauma of combat, but not every veteran of heavy combat became a victim of PTSD (Card 1985).

Military service has both temporary and long-term effects. Some who appear to have been transformed by the experience are better understood to have possessed those propensities before entering the service or to have entered the service with traits or personalities that made them especially prone to experience the change. West German recruits who were given an "authoritarianism" questionnaire before entering basic training, again after completing eighteen months of service, and again two years after the completion of their service were found to have undergone a decline in their level of authoritarianism while experiencing it firsthand in the *Bundeswehr*. However, they then drifted back to the original higher level after they had put that experience behind them (Roghmann and Sodeur 1972). The process of self-selection into American airborne training and Green Beret service as a result of already possessed values proved to be more important than the training or duty assignments afterward in explaining post-training or post-service attitudes and values (Cockerham 1973; Mantell 1975). Thus the impact of training and efforts on transforming attitudes can be overstated. Militarization, if and when it occurs, often has been confused with the reinforcement of established values.

In some modern cases mobility opportunities in subsequent occupations improved as a result of military service, as was the case for minorities in the U.S. military in the 1950s and afterward (Browning, Lopreato, and Poston 1973). One's perspective on the world could be altered as well. Certain American Revolutionary War soldiers seem to have experienced a change in political perspective. Officers who served outside their own states tended to adopt more cosmopolitan political positions after the Revolution, as did some enlisted men. Others who had not left their state but were similar in age, nativity, religion, social class, and county affiliation (the sum total of these characteristics constitutes "background") to those who had left their state exhibited no such change. One group had seen more of the Confederation and its plight and had seen the need for stronger bonds in the form of a new Constitution (Benton 1964; Burrows 1974). Similarly French soldiers who had served in America during the war were more actively involved than others in attacks on the homes and records of French nobility during the early stages of their revolution (McDonald 1951). Service in the Prussian/German armies and navies appears to have made militarists of many veterans (Ward and Diehl 1975). In analyzing the interactions of the military and society, future scholars will continue to ask how military service may have affected those who served as well as how some military institutions have affected the societies they belonged to whereas others simply have reflected those societies.

SEE ALSO *American Revolution; Civil-Military Relation; Democracy; Feudalism; French Revolution; Gulf War of 1991; Iraq-U.S. War; Militarism; Military Regimes; Military-Industrial Complex; Monarchy; Motivation; Nationalism and Nationality; Nation-State; Nazism; Patriotism; Personality, Cult of; Post-Traumatic Stress; Selective Service; State, The; Subsistence Agriculture; Technological Progress, Economic Growth; Technological Progress, Skill Bias; Volunteerism; War; Weapons Industry; World War I; World War II*

BIBLIOGRAPHY

Alpern, Stanley B. 1998. *Amazons of Black Sparta: The Warrior Women of Dahomey*. New York: New York University Press.

Anderson, Fred. 1984. *A People's Army: Massachusetts Soldiers and Society in the Seven Years War*. Chapel Hill: University of North Carolina Press.

Andrzejewski, Stanislaw. 1954. *Military Organization and Society*. London: Routledge and Paul.

Bartov, Omer. 1991. *Hitler's Army: Soldiers, Nazis, and War in the Third Reich*. New York: Oxford University Press.

Ben-Ari, Eyal. 1998. *Mastering Soldiers: Conflict, Emotions, and the Enemy in an Israeli Military Unit*. New York: Berghahn Books.

Benton, William. 1964. Pennsylvania Revolutionary Officers and the Federal Constitution. *Pennsylvania History* 31 (4): 419–435.

Bigelow, Robert. 1969. *The Dawn Warriors: Man's Evolution toward Peace*. Boston: Little, Brown.

Black, Jeremy. 1998. *War and the World: Military Power and the Fate of Continents, 1450–2000*. New Haven, CT: Yale University Press.

Bowen, Don. 1977. Guerilla War in Western Missouri, 1862–1865: Historical Extensions of the Relative Deprivation Hypothesis. *Comparative Studies in Society and History* 19 (1): 30–51.

Browning, Harley L., Sally C. Lopreato, and Dudley L. Poston Jr. 1973. Income and Veteran Status: Variations among Mexican Americans, Blacks, and Anglos. *American Sociological Review* 38 (1): 74–85.

Burroughs, Edwin. 1974. Military Experience and the Origins of Federalism. In *Aspects of Early New York Society and Politics*, eds. Jacob Judd and Irwin H. Polishook, 83–92. Tarrytown, NY: Sleepy Hollow Restorations.

Bushnell, John. 1985. *Mutiny amid Repression: Russian Soldiers in the Revolution of 1905–1906*. Bloomington: Indiana University Press.

Card, Josephina J. 1985. *Lives after Vietnam: The Personal Impact of Military Service*. Lexington, MA: Lexington Books.

Cockerham, William. 1973. Selective Socialization: Airborne Training as Status Passage. *Journal of Political and Military Sociology* 1–2: 215–229.

Cohen, Stephen P. 1990. *The Indian Army: Its Contribution to the Development of a Nation*. Delhi, India, and New York: Oxford University Press.

Cortright, David, and Max Watts. 1991. *Left Face: Soldier Unions and Resistance Movements in Modern Armies*. New York: Greenwood.

Cronin, Christopher, ed. 1998. *Military Psychology: An Introduction*. Needham, MA: Simon and Schuster.

Dalfiume, Richard M. 1969. *Desegregation of the U.S. Armed Forces: Fighting on Two Fronts, 1939–1953*. Columbia: University of Missouri Press.

Dawson, Doyne, 1986. The Origins of War: Biological and Anthropological Theories. *History and Theory* 35 (1): 1–28.

Dean, Eric T. 1997. *Shook over Hell: Post-Traumatic Stress, Vietnam, and the Civil War*. Cambridge, MA: Harvard University Press.

Divale, William Tulio. 1973. *Warfare in Primitive Societies: A Bibliography*. Santa Barbara, CA: ABC-CLIO.

Dunlay, Thomas W. 1982. *Wolves for the Blue Soldiers: Indian Scouts and Auxiliaries with the U.S. Army, 1860–1890*. Lincoln: University of Nebraska Press.

Enloe, Cynthia H. 1980. *Ethnic Soldiers: State Security in Divided Societies*. Athens: University of Georgia Press.

Feaver, Peter, and Richard H. Kohn. 2001. *Soldiers and Civilians: The Civil-Military Gap and American National Security*. Cambridge, MA: MIT Press.

Feld, Maury. 1975. Middle Class Society and the Rise of Military Professionalism: The Dutch Army, 1589–1609. *Armed Forces and Society* 1 (2): 419–442.

Finer, Samuel E. 1988. *The Man on Horseback: The Role of the Military in Politics*. 2nd ed. Boulder, CO: Westview.

Fleming, Keith. 1990. *The U.S. Marine Corps in Crisis: Ribbon Creek and Recruit Training*. Columbia: University of South Carolina Press.

Fuller, J. F. C. 1961. *The Conduct of War, 1789–1961*. New Brunswick, NJ: Rutgers University Press.

Fussell, Paul. 1975. *The Great War and Modern Memory*. New York: Oxford University Press.

Fussell, Paul. 1989. *Wartime: Understanding and Behavior in the Second World War*. New York: Oxford University Press.

Gal, Reuven, and A. David Mangelsdorff, eds. 1991. *Handbook of Military Psychology*. Chichester, NY: Wiley.

Gelfand, H. Michael. 2006. *Sea Change at Annapolis: The United States Naval Academy, 1949–2000*. Chapel Hill: University of North Carolina Press.

Goldman, Emily O. 2006. Cultural Foundations of Military Diffusion. *Review of International Studies* 32: 69–91.

Hemingway, Mark. 2006. Warriors for Hire. *Weekly Standard*, December 18, pp. 23–28.

Huntington, Samuel P. 1957. *The Soldier and the State: The Theory and Politics of Civil-Military Relations*. Cambridge, MA: Belknap Press of Harvard University Press.

Janowitz, Morris. 1960. *The Professional Soldier: A Social and Political Portrait*. Glencoe, IL: Free Press.

Karsten, Peter. 1972. *The Naval Aristocracy: The Golden Age of Annapolis and the Emergence of Modern American Navalism*. New York: Free Press.

Karsten, Peter. 1982. Consent and the American Soldier: Theory versus Reality. *Parameters* 12: 42–49.

Karsten, Peter. 1983. Irish Soldiers in the British Army, 1792–1922: Suborned or Subordinate? *Journal of Social History* 17: 31–64.

Karsten, Peter. 1997. The Coup d'Etat and Control of the Military in Competitive Democracies. In *To Sheathe the Sword: Civil-Military Relations in the Quest for Democracy*, ed. John Lovell, 149–163. Westport, CT: Greenwood.

Keegan, John. 1976. *The Face of Battle*. London: J. Cape.

Keeley, Lawrence H. 1996. *War before Civilization*. New York: Oxford University Press.

Kindsvatter, Peter S. 2003. *American Soldiers: Ground Combat in the World Wars, Korea, and Vietnam*. Lawrence: University Press of Kansas.

Kirby, Andrew, ed. 1992. *The Pentagon and the Cities*. Newbury Park, CA: Sage Publications.

Knorr, Klaus Eugen. 1956. *The War Potential of Nations*. Princeton, NJ: Princeton University Press.

Lender, Mark. 1986. The Social Structure of the New Jersey Brigade. In *The Military in America from the Colonial Era to the Present*, ed. Peter Karsten, 65–78. New York: Free Press.

Levi, Margaret. 1996. The Institution of Conscription. *Social Science History* 20 (1): 133–167.

Lewis, Lloyd B. 1985. *The Tainted War: Culture and Identity in Vietnam War Narratives*. Westport, CT: Greenwood.

Lynn, John A. 1984. *The Bayonets of the Republic: Motivation and Tactics in the Army of Revolutionary France, 1791–94*. Urbana: University of Illinois Press.

Lynn, John, ed. 1990. *Tools of War: Instruments, Ideas, and Institutions of Warfare, 1445–1871*. Urbana: University of Illinois Press.

Mandelbaum, David Goodman. 1952. *Soldier Groups and Negro Soldiers*. Berkeley: University of California Press.

Mann, Michael. 1986. *The Sources of Social Power*. Vol. 1, *A History of Power to 1760*. Cambridge, U.K.: Cambridge University Press.

Mantell, David Mark. 1975. *True Americanism: Green Berets and War Resisters: A Study of Commitment*. New York: Teachers College Press.

McDonald, Forrest. 1951. The Relationship of the French Peasant Veterans of the American Revolution to the Fall of Feudalism in France, 1789–1792. *Agricultural History* 25 (4): 151–161.

McNeill, William H. 1982. *The Pursuit of Power: Technology, Armed Force, and Society since AD 1000*. Chicago: University of Chicago Press.

Melman, Seymour. 1985. *The Permanent War Economy: American Capitalism in Decline*. New York: Simon and Schuster.

Moskos, Charles C., John Allen Williams, and David R. Segal, eds. 2000. *The Postmodern Military: Armed Forces after the Cold War*. New York: Oxford University Press.

Mosse, George L. 1990. *Fallen Soldiers: Reshaping the Memory of the World Wars*. New York: Oxford University Press.

Mumford, Lewis. 1961. *The City in History: Its Origins, Its Transformations, Its Prospects*. New York: Harcourt, Brace, and World.

Nef, John U. 1950. *War and Human Progress: An Essay on the Rise of Industrial Civilization*. Cambridge, MA: Harvard University Press.

O'Connell, Robert L. 1995. *Ride of the Second Horseman: The Birth and Death of War*. New York: Oxford University Press.

Pearkes, George. George Pearkes Papers. Imperial War Museum, London.

Peri, Yoram. 1983. *Between Battles and Ballots: The Israeli Military in Politics*. Cambridge, U.K., and New York: Cambridge University Press.

Perrin, Noel. 1979. *Giving up the Gun: Japan's Reversion to the Sword, 1543–1879*. Boston: G. K. Hall.

Redlich, Fritz. 1964–1965. *The German Military Enterpriser and His Workforce: A Study in European Economic and Social History*. Wiesbaden, Germany: F. Steiner.

Rockoff, Hugh. 2005. War and the Economy. In *The Encyclopedia of War and American Society*, vol. 3, ed. Peter Karsten, 235–247. Thousand Oaks, CA: Sage Publications.

Roghmann, Klaus, and Wolfgang Sodeur. 1972. The Impact of Military Service on Authoritarian Attitudes: Evidence from West Germany. *American Journal of Sociology* 78 (2): 418–433.

Rose, Elihu. 1982. The Anatomy of a Mutiny. *Armed Forces and Society* 8: 561–574.

Russett, Bruce M. 1970. *What Price Vigilance? The Burdens of National Defense*. New Haven, CT: Yale University Press.

Sherrow, Victoria. 1996. *Women and the Military: An Encyclopedia*. Santa Barbara, CA: ABC-CLIO.

Simkins, Peter. 1988. *Kitchener's Army: The Raising of the New Armies, 1914–16*. Manchester, U.K., and New York: Manchester University Press.

Smethurst, Richard J. 1974. *A Social Basis for Prewar Japanese Militarism: The Army and the Rural Community*. Berkeley: University of California Press.

Smith, Adam. 1937. *An Inquiry into the Nature and Cause of the Wealth of Nations*. New York: Modern Library.

Smith, Leonard V. 1994. *Between Mutiny and Obedience: The Case of the French Fifth Infantry Division during World War I*. Princeton, NJ: Princeton University Press.

Stepan, Alfred C. 1971. *The Military in Politics: Changing Patterns in Brazil*. Princeton, NJ: Princeton University Press.

Stone, John. 2004. Technology, Society, and the Infantry Revolution of the Fourteenth Century. *Journal of Military History* 68: 361–380.

Stouffer, Samuel A. 1949. Studies in Social Psychology during World War II. In *The American Soldier*, 4 vols. Princeton, NJ: Princeton University Press.

Thompson, William R. 1973. *The Grievances of Military Coup-Makers*. Beverly Hills, CA: Sage Publications.

Tilly, Charles. 1992. *Coercion, Capital, and European States, AD 990–1992*. Cambridge, MA: Blackwell.

Vagts, Alfred. 1959. *A History of Militarism: Civilian and Military*. New York: Meridien Books.

Van Creveld, Martin. 1983. *Fighting Power: German and U.S. Army Performance, 1939–1945*. Westport, CT: Greenwood.

Vasillopulos, Christopher. 1995. The Nature of Athenian Hoplite Democracy. *Armed Forces and Society* 20: 49–63.

Ward, Stephen, and James Diehl, eds. 1975. *The War Generation: Veterans of the First World War*. Port Washington, NY: Kennikat.

Wilson, Edmund. 1962. *Patriotic Gore: Studies in the Literature of the American Civil War*. New York: Oxford University Press.

Wool, Harold. 1968. *The Military Specialist: Skilled Manpower for the Armed Forces*. Baltimore, MD: Johns Hopkins University Press.

Peter Karsten

MILITARY-INDUSTRIAL COMPLEX

In his January 17, 1961, farewell address to the nation, departing president Dwight D. Eisenhower warned his fellow Americans of what he termed the "military-industrial complex." According to historian Stephen E. Ambrose, Malcolm Moos, a speechwriter for Eisenhower, invented the term when he helped the president prepare his speech. In the middle of his televised speech, Eisenhower stated, "In the councils of government, we must guard against the acquisition of unwarranted influence, whether sought or unsought, by the military-industrial complex. The potential for the disastrous rise of misplaced power exists and will persist."

During his presidency from 1953 to 1961, Eisenhower was irritated and troubled by the increasingly strident demands of Democrats in Congress that he approve higher defense spending, especially for bomber planes, missiles, and nuclear submarines after the Soviets launched their *Sputnik* satellite in 1957. Eisenhower believed that these Democratic demands were politically motivated, fiscally irresponsible, and unnecessary for a strong national defense in the days of the cold war. Some of the most outspoken Democratic advocates of higher defense spending represented states that especially depended on defense spending for their economies. One of them was Senator Stuart Symington of Missouri, a state that included McDonnell-Douglas, a major airplane manufacturer. Symington unsuccessfully sought the Democratic presidential nomination of 1960. Another was Senator Henry "Scoop" Jackson of Washington, a state that included Boeing, an aerospace manufacturer. Both Symington and Jackson were seriously considered for the vice presidential nomination of 1960.

As the 1960 presidential campaign progressed, Eisenhower was angered by Democratic presidential nominee John F. Kennedy's frequent contention that a "missile gap" existed to the advantage of the Soviet Union and that the Republican president had allowed this missile gap to develop. According to Kennedy's rhetoric, the missile gap was the most serious example of how the United States had fallen dangerously behind the Soviet Union in the cold war struggle during the Eisenhower administration. For Eisenhower and his supporters, it was unfair and absurd that liberal Democrats implied that a Republican president who was a retired general was weak on defense and oblivious to the military threat of the Soviet Union. Actually, it was Eisenhower who had previously emphasized nuclear deterrence, commonly known as "a bigger bang for the buck," as a way to reduce the size and expense of conventional military forces and the possibility of future "limited wars" like the Korean War.

The concept of a military-industrial complex was not commonly used until the late 1960s. By then, liberal and New Left opponents of the Vietnam War claimed that since World War II the United States had developed and become dependent on a warfare state, a permanent war economy, or a national security state. According to this perspective, both major political parties, every president, Congress, labor unions, corporations, Wall Street, the Pentagon, and elite research universities benefited from high defense spending and justified it by emphasizing militant anti-Communism in foreign policy, violating civil liberties in the name of national security, and supporting regular "limited wars" like those in Korea and Vietnam. These left-wing critics presented a more sinister, conspiratorial portrayal of the military-industrial complex than that conveyed by Eisenhower.

The idea of a military-industrial complex ruthlessly determined to permanently control American politics, government, economics, and foreign policy has also influenced American popular culture, especially political dramas in films and novels. In the novel and 1964 film *Seven Days in May*, an American president prepares to sign a nuclear disarmament treaty with the Soviet Union. After the economy plunges into a recession because of the expected drop in defense spending, the president becomes unpopular and controversial. A famous, right-wing general organizes a conspiracy to overthrow the president in order to reject the treaty. The 1991 film *JFK*, a fictional movie about John F. Kennedy's assassination in 1963, implies that Vice President Lyndon B. Johnson conspired with the Central Intelligence Agency and the Joint Chiefs of Staff to assassinate Kennedy so that Johnson as the new

president could expand the American military effort in Vietnam.

In analyzing sharp increases in defense spending during the presidency of Ronald W. Reagan (1981–1989), journalist Hedrick Smith explained the existence of "iron triangles." For every new weapons system, such as the B-1 bomber and Divad anti-aircraft gun, there was a symbiotic, three-way relationship of Pentagon officials, defense contracts, and members of Congress who supported its development, authorization, and funding. Regardless of how excessively expensive, unnecessary, or ineffective a weapons system was, it was continued because of the economic, political, and career interests of the participants in each iron triangle.

The military-industrial complex perspective was updated and revived for the post–cold war era by critics and opponents of President George W. Bush's foreign and defense policies in Afghanistan and Iraq. They claim that long before the terrorist attacks of September 11, 2001, the Bush administration was planning to invade Iraq and overthrow its dictator, Saddam Hussein, partially for the purpose of protecting American oil interests in the Middle East, and was seeking a pretext for doing this. They also contend that it was no coincidence that Halliburton and other corporations associated with Bush administration officials, especially Vice President Richard Cheney, received major government contracts in Bush's global war on terrorism. These criticisms and perceptions of Bush's foreign and defense policies based on the assumption of a military-industrial complex are evident in the documentaries *Fahrenheit 9/11* (2004) and *Why We Fight* (2005). Like the fictional movie *JFK*, *Why We Fight* includes film footage of Eisenhower's farewell address.

BIBLIOGRAPHY

Ambrose, Stephen E. 1990. *Eisenhower: Soldier and President.* New York: Simon and Schuster.

Higgs, Robert. 2005. *Resurgence of the Warfare State: The Crisis Since 9/11.* Oakland, CA: The Independent Institute.

Leebaert, Derek. 2002. *The Fifty-Year Wound: The True Price of America's Cold War Victory.* Boston: Little, Brown.

Smith, Hedrick. 1988. *The Power Game: How Washington Works.* New York: Ballantine.

Sean J. Savage

MILITARY REGIMES

The study of military regimes rose to prominence within the social sciences during the latter half of the twentieth century, thanks in part to the presence during the 1960s,

1970s, and 1980s of a large number of military regimes around the globe. In 1979, fourteen military regimes held power in sub-Saharan Africa, nine in Latin America, five in the Arab states and North Africa, three in Southeast Asia, one in South Asia, and one in East Asia. No single social science discipline dominated the research into military regimes. Political scientists, economists, sociologists, and historians all devoted much time and energy to studying this form of government.

A military regime is a form of government wherein the political power resides with the armed forces. The military is the legitimate power-holding group that centralizes political and legal authority. Military regimes, however, cannot simply be classified as governments dominated by the military, because they are seldom purely military in composition. Civilian bureaucrats and politicians generally play a role in the government, but the military always has the final say. The presence of civilians in military governments shows that military elites do not necessarily organize military regimes. Nevertheless, a military regime is always governed by a military officer, active or retired, with the support of the military establishment, and the political structure includes routine mechanisms for high-level military officers to influence policy and political appointments.

Military regimes are generally held together by their egalitarian belief in equal political, economic, social, and civil rights for all people. Thus, military regimes emerge most often as products of political, economic, and societal crises to replace weak executives and governments. The most popular mechanism used to achieve this is the military *coup d'état*, wherein members of the armed forces remove a state's chief executive through the use or threat of force. Once the military regime is firmly in place, characteristic features of this form of government include an intact military hierarchy, and a militarily controlled security apparatus. Military regimes also include features that would characterize governments more generally. These include institutions for deciding questions of succession, and routine consultation between the leader and the rest of the officer corps.

Despite the fact that military regimes are generally egalitarian, historically a variety of ideologies have held them together. Military regimes have practiced authoritarianism and free market liberalism, for example, in the military government of Augusto Pinochet in Chile from 1973 to 1990. Avowedly socialist military regimes held power in Haiti from 1957 to 1994 and also in Peru for a short period. These variations can occur because military rule is fundamentally undemocratic. Democracies require self-expression and the questioning of authority. Thus, the ideology that holds democracies together is inherently antiauthoritarian. However, military regimes are grounded in the military model of giving and taking orders and absolute obedience. Therefore, depending on the ideology of the armed forces, variations among military regimes are inevitable.

Military regimes require unquestioned obedience to the leadership, which holds absolute power, to stabilize the government. This makes military regimes both authoritarian and autocratic, but the degree of authoritarianism varies from regime to regime. Once power is established, variations abound. Military regimes are shaped by a mixture of variables derived from specific conditions peculiar to particular countries, which complicates conceptualization even further. In the Middle East and Africa, for example, military regimes have often been autocracies led by a single military officer, whereas Latin American military regimes have frequently been ruled by a junta, a committee composed of several officers.

Despite these differences, however, most military regimes are variations on one of four basic types, described by Christopher Clapham and George Philip in *The Political Dilemmas of Military Regimes* (1985). The first is known as a veto regime, which pits the military against strongly organized civilian political structures. Veto regimes support the existing social order and their aim is to defend it. Consequently, these regimes are highly repressive. The second type, the breakthrough regime, seeks to attack a social order that threatens its plans for modernization. Breakthrough regimes attempt to radically reform government. As with veto regimes, a high degree of repression is likely.

A third type is the moderator regime. Highly professional militaries make up these regimes, which aim to clean up the mess made by civilian governments and then return power to the civilians. Found in societies at varying levels of social and economic development, moderator regimes tend to be highly unstable due to internal disputes over exactly when to relinquish power. Moderator regimes are not particularly authoritarian or repressive. The fourth type, factional regimes, are formed when military officers align themselves with civilian political actors and groups based on shared traits such as ethnicity or ideology. Like moderator regimes, factional regimes tend to be highly unstable and are not particularly repressive.

THE EMERGENCE OF MILITARY REGIMES

Although military regimes certainly existed prior to World War II, the modern military regime is distinctly and analytically a new phenomenon restricted to the developing and modernizing world. The impetus for military regimes is found in the changing nature of the military itself and in its role in the development and modernization of the society within which it exists. Protection against communist or revolutionary takeover was historically the most common objective of military regimes, especially during the 1960s and 1970s.

The early 1960s saw a rapid rise in military regimes, which led many scholars to conduct theoretical analyses of the phenomenon. These studies focused on military intervention in politics as an exceptional and negative departure from the norm of an elected civilian government. Analysts had previously assumed that economic and social modernization in developing countries would lead militaries to become more professional and modern. The hope was that this would prevent them from meddling in politics in favor of defending their countries against internal and external attack.

In practice, however, as John Johnson argued in *The Military and Society in Latin America* (1964), the military was frequently the most modernized and technically advanced sector of the middle class, which allowed it to make a special contribution to development, and especially democratization. His theory was validated by the mid-1960s, when militaries overthrew one government after another, especially where decolonization was in progress in Africa and Latin America. The research argues that in turbulent modernizing societies the armed forces are best suited to promote order, making them highly likely to intervene in politics.

Marxism heavily influenced a second set of analyses that emerged during this period. Scholars in this camp utilized dependency theory, which suggests that the wealthy nations of the world need a peripheral group of poorer states in order to remain wealthy. These scholars argued that that the dependency of poor states on wealthier states led to close ties between their militaries. This led to the premise that the armed forces were willing instruments of capitalism and its domestic class allies. In turn, the militaries of poorer states would do as wealthier states pleased. Consequently, wealthier nations advocated military intervention to safeguard their control over essential economic materials.

The theory of bureaucratic authoritarianism was also used to explain the abundance of military takeovers during the 1960s. This highly influential theory combines elements of modernization, dependency, and Marxist theory to argue that military takeovers may occur as one of the stages of industrialization. The theory posits that populist democracy initially fosters urbanization, popular participation in government, and trade union development. This is followed by a stage in which industrialization needs to deepen, and governmental control over the popular sector is seen as the way to maintain order and pursue policies that will attract foreign investors. Military takeover can be an efficient way to achieve this.

THE DECLINE OF MILITARY REGIMES

Beginning in the mid-1970s, many military regimes started to hand power back to civilians. In turn, theoretical analyses of military regimes began to ask why. In *The Military and the State in Latin America* (1987), Alain Rouquié argues that the military's lack of legitimacy due to unfulfilled promises of democratization precipitated the change. The disillusionment of the economic elite and the middle class due to the repressiveness and economic incompetence of military regimes was another contributing factor.

Policy performance also helps explain why military regimes declined in number. Early research failed to find lower levels of economic development or performance in countries with military regimes compared to countries with other forms of government; these studies, however, failed to establish any strong relationship between regime type and public policy performance. Karen Remmer, in her *Military Rule in Latin America* (1989), convincingly shows that the military is in fact not generally very successful as modernizers or as promoters of economic development. As far as social policy goes, the principle difference between military and civilian regimes is that the military spends more money on weapons and the civilians spend more money on social welfare. This inhibits public support for military regimes and ultimately forces them to turn power back over to civilians.

The number of military regimes around the globe decreased dramatically beginning in the 1990s. Their lack of international legitimacy and inability to rule successfully even when they were robust were the prominent factors in their decline. The end of the cold war and the collapse of the Soviet Union also made it more difficult for military regimes to use the threat of communism as a justification for their actions. Nevertheless, military regimes continue to hold power around the globe. Military regimes came into power in countries such as Fiji, Thailand, and Mauritania at the beginning of the twenty-first century. Military regimes in Libya and Myanmar, which came to power during the 1960s, are still thriving. In the end, although the number of military regimes has decreased dramatically around the globe, it appears unlikely that they will become extinct anytime soon. Understanding why is the challenge that social scientists now face.

SEE ALSO *Authoritarianism; Coup d'Etat; Democratization; Militarism; Military*

BIBLIOGRAPHY

Clapham, Christopher, and George Philip. 1985. *The Political Dilemmas of Military Regimes.* London: Croom Helm.

Danopoulos, Constantine. 1988. *The Decline of Military Regimes: The Civilian Influence*. Boulder, CO: Westview.

Johnson, John J. 1964. *The Military and Society in Latin America*. Stanford, CA: Stanford University Press.

Odetola, Theophilus Olatunde. 1982. *Military Regimes and Development: A Comparative Analysis of African States*. Boston: Allen and Unwin.

Perlmutter, Amos. 1980. The Comparative Analysis of Military Regimes. *World Politics* 33 (1): 96–120.

Remmer, Karen L. 1989. *Military Rule in Latin America*. Boston: Unwin Hyman.

Rouquié, Alain. 1987. *The Military and the State in Latin America*. Trans. Paul E. Sigmund. Berkeley: University of California Press.

Sigmund, Paul E. 1993. Approaches to the Study of the Military in Latin America. *Comparative Politics* 26 (1): 111–122.

David Mastro

MILL, JAMES
1773–1836

James Mill was a British political philosopher, economist, and historian. Born in Scotland, he was educated at the University of Edinburgh through the patronage of Sir John Stuart, where he attended the lectures of the philosopher Dugald Stewart (1753–1828) and specialized in philosophy, according to Alexander Bain's 1882 *James Mill: A Biography*. Mill moved to London in 1802 to pursue a career as a journalist, writing for several periodicals. He became closely associated with Jeremy Bentham (1748–1832) and was an ardent advocate of utilitarianism and of the Benthamite objective of achieving "the greatest happiness of the greater number" (Stephen [1900] 1968). The group of radicals around Bentham and Mill shared a set of policy objectives that included the abolition of Britain's Poor and Corn Laws, the extension of the franchise, and religious tolerance.

Mill wrote a pamphlet in 1804 in which he reviewed the history of the Corn Laws, calling for the removal of all export bounties and import duties on grains and criticizing Thomas Robert Malthus (1766–1834), among others, for defending them. As noted in Thomas Sowell's *Say's Law: An Historical Analysis* (1972), Mill's *Commerce Defended* (1808) reiterated his arguments against the Corn Laws and is credited with providing the first version in English of Jean-Baptiste Say's (1767–1832) law of markets, which states that "supply creates its own demand." In 1977 William Baumol pointed out that, for Mill, Say's law was not fundamentally about the impossibility of overproduction, but rather about the notion that productive consumption (investment), rather than consumption of luxuries, was the effective means to promote growth. David Ricardo (1772–1823), who became Mill's close friend, adopted Say's law in part as a result of Mill's influence.

Mill extended the utility principle to the science of politics in his essay titled "On Government" ([1820] 1967). For Mill, the aim of government was to increase human happiness, and only individuals could make the utilitarian calculation of pleasure and pain. Thus, Mill concluded that only representative democracy was compatible with the principle of utility, since it would prevent those in power from acting for their own advantage. According to Murray Milgate and Shannon Stimson, in a 1993 article in the *American Political Science Review*, the requirement for voting was the capacity to judge one's own interest; that is, knowledge, rather than birth or property, was at the center of Mill's political theory. In his *History of British India* (1817), which helped him secure a permanent position with the East India Company, Mill defended British rule in India, contradicting his own theory of political representation. In addition, his Eurocentric views on colonial rule reveal contempt for other cultures and societies.

Mill's 1821 book, *Elements of Political Economy*—written as lessons for his son John Stuart Mill (1806–1873)—were central in popularizing a certain version of Ricardian economics that included elements like the "wage fund" theory, which were extraneous to Ricardo's ideas, according to a 2004 article in *European Journal of the History of Economic Thought* by Sergio Cremaschi. Neil De Marchi (1983) contrasts the dogmatic Mill of the *Elements*, which simplifies and deduces everything from first principles, with the more open-minded thinker of previous works. Mill's defense of Ricardian economics and his commitment to utilitarianism led to a confluence of both strands of his thought, which would eventually come together within the marginalist school.

SEE ALSO *Corn Laws; Say's Law; Utilitarianism*

BIBLIOGRAPHY

Bain, Alexander. [1882] 1967. *James Mill: A Biography*. New York: Kelley.

Baumol, William. 1977. Say's (at Least) Eight Laws, or What Say and James Mill May Really Have Meant. *Economica* 44: 145–162.

Cremaschi, Sergio. 2004. Ricardo and the Utilitarians. *European Journal of the History of Economic Thought* 11 (3): 377–403.

De Marchi, Neil. 1983. The Case for James Mill. In *Methodological Controversy in Economics: Historical Essays in Honor of T. W. Hutchison*, ed. A. W. Coats, 155–184. New York: JAI Press.

Milgate, Murray, and Shannon Stimson. 1993. Utility, Property, and Political Participation: James Mill on Democratic Reform. *American Political Science Review* 87 (4): 901–911.

Mill, James. [1804] 1966. *An Essay of the Impolicy of a Bounty on the Exportation of Grain, and on the Principles which Ought to Regulate the Commerce of Grain.* New York: Kelley.

Mill, James. [1808] 1965. *Commerce Defended.* New York: Kelley.

Mill, James. [1817] 1968. *The History of British India.* New York: Chelsea House.

Mill, James. [1820] 1967. On Government. In *Essays on Government, Jurisprudence, Liberty of the Press and Law of Nations.* New York: Kelley.

Mill, James. [1821] 1963. *Elements of Political Economy.* New York: Kelley.

Sowell, Thomas. 1972. *Say's Law: An Historical Analysis.* Princeton, NJ: Princeton University Press.

Stephen, Leslie. [1900] 1968. *The English Utilitarians.* Vol. 2: *James Mill.* New York: Kelley.

Matías Vernengo

MILL, JOHN STUART
1806–1873

Defining the social sciences as encompassing "mental or cultural sciences that deal with the activities of the individual as a member or group" ("Social Science," *Merriam-Webster's Medical Dictionary* 2007) provides space for interpreting which subjects are appropriate for social scientific inquiry. However, in the case of John Stuart Mill, the British economist, moral and political philosopher, and administrator, it is difficult to argue that he is not the quintessential social scientist. Additionally he is someone others attempt to emulate in their intellectual work and philosophical beliefs.

During the early nineteenth century, Mill sought philosophical enlightenment, focusing on the common person. His investigations of moral and ethical thought began early, although they were published later in his life. Some believe that Mill did not fully explore some of his more radical beliefs, yet he left an indelible mark on democracy and law, economic trade, feminism and women's rights, labor theory, mathematics, political theory, poverty and welfare concerns, psychology, religion and theology, and scientific method and empiricism.

It is clear that Mill influenced African American economists, such as Abram Lincoln Harris Jr. (1899–1963). Harris, who chaired Howard University's Economics Department (1936–1945) and also served on the University of Chicago faculty (1946–1963), began as a Marxist but was influenced during the Great Depression

by the moderately socialist—or at the very least liberal—writings of Mill. Harris finds his beliefs at home with Mill because both men believed that "justice would come from a class-based solution generated by social science objectivity and expertise" (Holloway 2002, p. xiv).

Harris suggested that a unified militant worker effort, organized along racial lines, could alleviate African American social and economic inequality. The racially and economically entrenched working class had historical and social reasons for continued divisive operations, but Harris and Sterling Spero, in *The Black Worker* (1931), argued that the problems were solvable through time and higher academic achievement by the next generation of African Americans. The historical basis for worker problems spawned from slavery and the fact that many African Americans led agrarian lifestyles prior to moving to urban, industrialized areas meant that they were unfamiliar with unions and organized worker movements. In addition the leadership of groups such as the National Urban League proffered an antiunion sentiment that appealed to many African Americans but led to additional racial stratification for the working class. Harris's book *The Negro as Capitalist* (1936) launches a savage attack on the impact of African American business people on the African American masses.

As a child John Stuart Mill, who was born in the London suburb of Pentonville, the eldest son of James Mill and Harriet Barrow, flourished and delved into classical writings. He was educated only by his father, who served as a leading member of philosophical radicals strongly linked to the utilitarian teachings of Jeremy Bentham (1748–1832). Though James Mill served as an East India Company administrator, he used Bentham's associationalist psychology to educate his eldest son, who knew both Greek and Latin by the time he was eight years old. Learning these languages allowed John Stuart Mill to read most of the classics by the age of fourteen. In addition he had a wide understanding of history, logic, mathematics, and economic theory.

Influenced by his reading of the philosophical radicals, Mill began to think of himself as a person seeking to improve the human condition but at the same time focusing on the interest of the individual. In 1826 Mill suffered a lengthy depression, which perhaps strengthened and elevated his philosophical convictions. He found some solace for his feelings in the poetry of William Wordsworth (1770–1850).

After his recovery, Mill began to question and revise his utilitarian views. Originally he worked from three defining characteristics of Bentham's teachings: the greatest happiness principle, universal egoism, and the artificial identification of one's interests with those of others. In 1828 he met Gustave d'Eichtahl (1804–1882), a follower of Henri de Saint-Simon (1760–1825), and began to consider how social and cultural institutions shaped history and overall human development. Influenced by thinkers such as Auguste Comte (1798–1857) and Samuel Taylor Coleridge (1772–1834), Mill came to believe that British society was on the cusp of an organic period, when society would replace inefficient and bureaucratic institutions with better organizations. He also believed that British society needed him as a catalyst for change; otherwise society would stagnate.

Exploring Wordsworth's poetry was crucial also in Mill's relationship with Harriet Taylor (1807–1858), whom he met in 1830. Though Taylor was married at the time, Mill and Taylor formed a close friendship. In 1851, two years after the death of Taylor's husband, Mill and Taylor married, against the wishes of Mill's family, especially his father. James Mill supported Epicurean principles but practiced Scots Calvinism. In this sense Mill surpasses his father to have a richer understanding of the role of pleasure in human development and attributes that philosophical growth to Harriet Taylor. She convinced Mill that individuals were not maximizing the benefits in their lives and that a new theory of the human condition was necessary. Taylor died in 1858; however, one can see her influence over Mill's later works.

Although Mill still believed in utility and positivism, his position on how to present and implement social change differed from that of most of Bentham's followers. For Mill, new philosophical proclamations that demanded quick modifications must be avoided, and slow, gradual delivery of new thoughts were necessary for acceptance and integration with existing values. Examples of how Mill introduced new ideas slowly come from *On Liberty* (1859) and *The Subjection of Women* (1869). In *On Liberty*, Mill examined government formation and proclaimed that the success of government organization depends on "utility in the largest sense, grounded on the permanent interest of man as a progressive being" (Mill 2005 [1859], p. 224). A sharp criticism of government came from Mill in *The Subjection of Women*, where he stated: "Stupidity is much the same the world over. A stupid person's notions and feelings may confidently be inferred from those which prevail in the circle by which the person is surrounded. Not so those whose opinions and feelings are emanations from their own nature and faculties" (Mill 2004 [1869], p. 273). Each individual is responsible for his or her own happiness, but government is responsible for helping each person develop a path to happiness. Thus in his fight for suffrage rights for women, Mill felt that the Conservative Party was foolish in not responding to the will of the people in a manner that improved utility.

Mill reached beyond his roots in conventional politics to comment on the connection between logic and economic theory and political and social life. After declining to study at Oxford or Cambridge University, he worked for the British East India Company until 1858, then he was an independent member of Parliament from 1865 to 1868 and served as the lord rector of the University of St. Andrews during the same period. Trade and growth theory received particular attention from Mill, who at an early age had read the complete works of Thomas Malthus (1766–1834), David Ricardo (1772–1823), and Adam Smith (1723–1790). Much influenced by Ricardo and his father, Mill investigated taxation, wages and profit, competition, and the division of factors of production. In *Analysis of the Phenomena of the Human Mind*, published in 1869, Mill, accepting the human mind's importance to good decision making, revised and corrected his father's work, *Analysis of the Phaenomena of the Human Mind* (1829). James Mill believed that one derives an idea, no matter how complex, from its associated parts. Mill took his father's *associationism* conception one step forward and proposed that when considering pleasure one can have lower levels of pleasure that make up higher levels of pleasure. As a person builds pleasure upon pleasure, a new whole comes into being.

In political economy, researchers attribute social scientific investigative methodology to Mill. In later revisions of his text *Principles of Political Economy* (1848), Mill argued, rather radically, that progressive taxation was bad and akin to stealing, that the wage system needed to be abolished because it lacked equality, and that production was closely linked to social networks, thus making competition difficult. Maximizing human development and pleasure required freedom for the person to grow. Freedom in the economic marketplace, laissez faire economic policies and principles, framed only one part of the picture. Individuals must also have political freedom. His text is still used at Oxford University in the early twentieth century and continues to influence thought. For example, John Rawls, Robert Nozick, Bertrand Russell, Karl Popper, and Peter Singer have produced controversial yet honest social commentary similar to Mill's.

SEE ALSO *Bentham, Jeremy; Economics; Ethics; Harris, Abram L., Jr.; Liberalism; Mill, James; Morality; Philosophy; Radicalism; Social Science; Utilitarianism; Women and Politics*

BIBLIOGRAPHY

PRIMARY WORKS

Mill, John Stuart. 1963. *Collected Works of John Stuart Mill.* Ed. John M. Robson. Toronto: University of Toronto Press.

Mill, John Stuart. 1998. *Utilitarianism.* New York: Oxford University Press.

Mill, John Stuart. [1848] 1999. *Principles of Political Economy.* New York: Oxford University Press.

Mill, John Stuart. [1869] 2004. *The Subjection of Women.* Kila, MT: Kessinger.

Mill, John Stuart. [1859] 2005. *On Liberty.* London: Longman.

SECONDARY WORKS

Donner, Wendy. 1993. John Stuart Mill's Liberal Feminism. *Philosophical Studies* 69 (2–3): 155–166.

Halévy, Elie. *La formation du radicalisme philosophique.* 3 vols. Paris: F. Alcon, 1904. *The Growth of Philosophic Radicalism.* Trans. Mary Morris. London: Faber and Faber, 1928.

Hamburger, Joseph. 1999. *John Stuart Mill on Liberty and Control.* Princeton, NJ: Princeton University Press.

Harris, Abram Lincoln, Jr. 1936. *The Negro as Capitalist: A Study of Banking and Business among American Negroes.* New York: Negro University Press.

Holloway, Jonathan S. 2002. *Confronting the Veil: Abram Harris Jr., E. Franklin Frazier, and Ralph Bunche, 1919–1994.* Chapel Hill: University of North Carolina Press.

Mackie, John L. 1974. *The Cement of the Universe.* Oxford: Oxford University Press.

Sen, Amartya. 1970. *Collective Choice and Social Welfare.* San Francisco: Holden-Day.

Social Science. In Dictionary.com. 2007. *Merriam-Webster's Medical Dictionary.* Merriam-Webster, Inc. http://dictionary.reference.com/browse/social science, June 11.

Spero, Sterling, and Abram Lincoln Harris, Jr. 1931. *The Black Worker.* New York: Columbia University Press.

Raymonda Burgman

MILLENNIUM DEVELOPMENT GOALS
SEE *World Bank, The.*

MILLENNIUM ECOSYSTEM ASSESSMENT
SEE *Deforestation.*

MILLER, MERTON H.
SEE *Finance; Modigliani-Miller Theorems.*

MILLER, WARREN
1924–1999

Warren Edward Miller was a pioneering survey researcher and institution builder who helped transform the study of elections in political science.

Miller, who earned his doctorate at Syracuse University in New York in 1954, taught at the University of California, Berkeley, before arriving at the University of Michigan at Ann Arbor in 1956. At Michigan, Miller founded the Center for Political Studies (CPS) at the Institute for Social Research. The CPS's biennial election surveys, which began in 1948, created the first longitudinal source of scientific data on public opinion. In 1960 Miller published *The American Voter*, written with social scientists Angus Campbell (1910–1980), Philip Converse, and Donald Stokes (1927–1997), an instant classic that drew on CPS data to offer the first systematic analysis of electoral behavior. Miller and his coauthors then produced an acclaimed follow-up titled *Elections and the Political Order* (1966).

In 1962 Miller founded and began serving as director of the Inter-University Consortium for Political and Social Research (ICPSR), which was created in part to meet demand for scholarly access to CPS data. ICPSR subsequently became a central archive for quantitative social science data and methodological training, helping to further transform political science and its sister disciplines. Miller later served as director of CPS (1970–1981) and helped secure long-term support from the National Science Foundation for the biennial CPS election survey, which was renamed the National Election Studies (NES) in 1977.

During the 1960s and 1970s, Miller lent his expertise to the television networks as a consultant for their election coverage. He also served as president of both the American Political Science Association (1979–1980) and the Social Science History Association (1979). In 1982 Miller moved to Arizona State University in Tempe, where he continued to publish scholarly books and articles until late in his life, including *The New American Voter* (1996), cowritten with J. Miller Shanks.

Miller's work on the CPS/NES helped launch the "behavioral revolution" in political science, a movement that revolutionized the field. By creating the first nationally representative survey datasets, Miller and his colleagues allowed researchers to study the correlates of vote choice and political opinion. In addition, by repeating a common set of questions in each study, they made it possible for researchers to study changes in public opinion and voting behavior over time. A vast literature quickly emerged on both topics.

Over time, however, this approach to voting research faced criticism for its theoretical and methodological weaknesses. Its proposed model of voting behavior, which was known as the "funnel of causality," fell apart as researchers realized that the variables that were thought to influence vote choice were themselves affected by voter's preferences toward candidates—a problem known as endogeneity. As a result, political scientists later shifted toward mathematical models and experiments, two techniques that many think provide additional leverage for understanding political behavior.

Nonetheless, Miller will be remembered as a trendsetting quantitative researcher who revolutionized the field of election studies. In the introduction to their 1994 edited volume in his honor, M. Kent Jennings and Thomas E. Mann write, "Warren Miller and the study of elections are synonymous. It is impossible to account for the institutional and intellectual developments that have shaped post-World War II scholarship on voting without acknowledging his crucial role" (p. 3).

SEE ALSO *American National Election Studies (ANES); Divisia Monetary Index; Interest Rates; Monetary Base; Money; Money, Demand for; Policy, Monetary*

BIBLIOGRAPHY

Campbell, Angus, Philip Converse, Warren Miller, and Donald Stokes. 1960. *The American Voter.* New York: Wiley.

Jennings, M. Kent, and Thomas E. Mann. 1994. Warren Miller and the Study of Elections. In *Elections at Home and Abroad: Essays in Honor of Warren E. Miller,* eds. M. Kent Jennings and Thomas E. Mann, 3–13. Ann Arbor: University of Michigan Press.

Traugott, Michael. 1999. In Memoriam: Warren E. Miller, 1924–1999. *Public Opinion Quarterly* 63 (4): 590–591.

The University Record (University of Michigan News Service). 1999. Obituary: Warren E. Miller. 54 (18): February 8.

Brendan Nyhan

MILLER, WILLIAM

SEE *Sanitation.*

MILLS, C. WRIGHT

1916–1963

The American sociologist Charles Wright Mills wrote about the growth in the size and scope of bureaucracies in the modern era. The resulting concentration of authority, he maintained, has dramatic effects upon such institutions as family, democratic government, science, education, and the economy. It also profoundly affects individuals, both those who wield the power and those who are subject to it. Mills forcefully chastised his colleagues about the proper role of social science in exploring and clarifying these and other central issues of the time.

EARLY LIFE AND EDUCATION

Mills was born on August 28, 1916, in Waco, Texas. His father was an insurance salesman and his mother a homemaker. From the age of seven the family began moving around Texas, and Mills experienced what he later described as a childhood of loneliness and isolation. He attended Texas A&M University in 1934–1935, but found the required regimentation and demands for deference toward professors and upperclassmen to be intolerable. In later years, Mills reflected on how these childhood and adolescent experiences caused him to focus on work as his "salvation," taught him to demand intellectual and social independence, and gave him both a tolerance and a preference for being a loner.

After a disastrous freshman year Mills transferred to the University of Texas, where he received a bachelor's degree in sociology and a master's degree in philosophy in 1939. He then went on to the University of Wisconsin, where he received his doctorate in sociology. By all accounts he was a brilliant though difficult student. His relations with his professors were often stormy; he was looked upon as arrogant and exceedingly ambitious. When defending his dissertation he refused to make revisions demanded by his committee; the dissertation was later quietly accepted without formal committee approval.

In 1941 Mills accepted his first academic appointment at the University of Maryland. It was here that Mills finished his dissertation on American pragmatism and collaborated with Hans Gerth, one of his professors at Wisconsin, on *From Max Weber: Essays in Sociology* (1946). This book has since become a classic, interpreting the German sociologist Max Weber as far more of a radical conflict theorist than the prevailing American view of the time. In 1945 Mills joined Columbia University where he taught and wrote for the remainder of his career.

In all of his writings, Mills interpreted the world through a theoretical perspective very much influenced by Weber. Like Weber, Mills's vision comprised a holistic view of entire sociocultural systems. His main body of work centers upon the theme of rationalization, the practical application of knowledge to achieve a desired end. Rationalization is a method of thought focused on total coordination and control over processes needed to attain whatever goal the individual or organization has set. It is the thought process behind the application of science, observation, and reason in the development of technology to manipulate the environment. It is the thought process behind bureaucracy, social organizations specifically designed for the attainment of goals. It was Mills's contention that rationalization was increasing with modernity. Mills believed that because the social system is interdependent, the rationalization process has profound effects on human behavior, values, and thought.

WHITE COLLAR

Mills's first breakthrough came with the publication of *White Collar: The American Middle Classes* in 1951. According to Mills, the rise of white-collar work was due to the era's growth in bureaucracy caused by technological change and the increasing need to market the goods and services of an industrial society. The central characteristic of white-collar workers is that they are unorganized and dependent upon large bureaucracies for their existence. By their mass existence and dependence, Mills maintained, they have changed the character and feel of American life.

With the automation of the office and the increase in the division of labor, the number of routine jobs is increased, while authority and job autonomy become attributes of only the top positions. There is an ever greater distinction made in terms of power, prestige, and income between managers and staff. The routinized worker is discouraged from using his or her own independent judgment; decision making is in accordance with strict rules handed down by others. Job performance and promotion become based on following the bureaucratic rules and dictates of others, not on critical intelligence. The aim of schooling shifts from the creation of the "good citizen" to one of creating the "successful specialist."

In white collar society there is also a shift of social power from force and coercion to authority and manipulation. This form of power is founded upon the ever more sophisticated methods of control given elites by mass communication and the social sciences. This shift is from the overt to the covert, from the obvious to the subtle. Exploitation becomes the rule, depriving the oppressed from identifying the oppressor. This form of power effectively removes the check of reason and conscience of the ruled on the ruler.

THE POWER ELITE

In *The Power Elite* (1956) Mills demonstrated that the bureaucracies of state, corporations, and military have become enlarged and centralized, and are a means of power never before equaled in human history. These hierarchies of power, Mills argued, are the key to understanding modern industrial societies. Major national power resides almost exclusively at the top of these bureaucracies; all other institutions have diminished in scope and been pushed to the side of modern history or made subordinate to the big three.

The elite who run these organizations are closely related through intermarriage. Some of their coordination comes from an interchange of personnel between the three elite hierarchies, but a good deal of coordination also comes from a growing structural integration of the dominant institutions. As each of the elite domains becomes larger, its integration with the other spheres becomes more pronounced. But the major source of unity of the elite, Mills stated, is their common background—they are all from the upper social class, they attended the same preparatory schools and Ivy League universities, and belong to the same exclusive clubs and organizations.

The positions of the elite give them access to power that make their decisions (as well as their failure to act) extremely consequential. Mills believed these leaders are acting (or failing to act) with irresponsibility, thus leading the nation and the world to disaster. But this does not always need to be so; the enlargement and concentration of power into so few hands now makes it imperative to hold these men responsible for the course of events.

SOCIOLOGICAL IMAGINATION

Mills believed it is the task of social scientists to address how the concentration of power, and the resulting structural and historical issues, affect human values and behaviors. Mills's *Sociological Imagination* (1959) was a call to arms for social scientists to focus upon these substantive problems, to bring reason to bear on human affairs.

In this work, like Weber before him, Mills cautioned that a society dominated by rational social organization is not based on reason, intelligence, and good will toward all. Further, it is through rational social organization that modern-day tyrants (as well as more mundane bureaucratic managers) exercise their authority and manipulation, often denying the opportunity to their subjects to exercise their own judgment. One then has "rationality without reason. Such rationality is not commensurate with freedom," Mills said, "but the destroyer of it" (1976, p. 170).

Because of his abrasive personality, his insistence upon writing polemics for a broader audience, and his increasingly strident and critical views of the status quo and of the work of his colleagues, Mills became increasingly isolated as a sociologist. His personal manners and dress were far removed from the buttoned-down professional academics of Columbia. In 1963 Mills died of heart disease at the age of forty-five, virtually excommunicated from the mainstream of his profession. However, over the years his reputation has grown among those who take a critical view of modernity and its drift.

SEE ALSO *Blue Collar and White Collar; Bureaucracy; Bureaucrat; Military-Industrial Complex; Power; Power Elite*

BIBLIOGRAPHY

Horowitz, Irving L. 1983. *C. Wright Mills: An American Utopian.* New York: Free Press.

Mills, C. Wright. [1951] 1956. *White Collar: The American Middle Classes.* New York: Oxford University Press.

Mills, C. Wright. [1956] 1970. *The Power Elite.* New York: Oxford University Press.

Mills, C. Wright. 1958. *The Causes of World War Three.* London: Secker and Warburg.

Mills, C. Wright. [1959] 1976. *The Sociological Imagination.* New York: Oxford University Press.

Mills, C. Wright. [1963] 1967. *Power, Politics, and People: The Collected Essays of C. Wright Mills.* Ed. Irving L. Horowitz. New York: Oxford University Press.

Mills, C. Wright. 2000. *Letters and Autobiographical Writings.* Ed. Kathryn Mills with Pamela Mills. Berkeley: University of California Press.

Frank Elwell

MILLS, EDWIN
1928–

Edwin Smith Mills is an emeritus professor of real estate and finance at Northwestern University in Evanston, Illinois. He was born on June 25, 1928, in Collingswood, New Jersey. After graduating from Collingswood High School in 1946, he served two years in the U.S. Army and was commissioned a second lieutenant in the Corps of Engineers. After obtaining his undergraduate degree from Brown University in 1951 and his PhD in 1956 from the University of Birmingham in England, he held faculty positions at Massachusetts Institute of Technology, Johns Hopkins University, Princeton University, and Northwestern University. Over almost five decades of teaching and research focused on real estate and urban economic development, Mills authored fifteen books and more than one hundred papers, served as an adviser to numerous domestic and foreign governments, and was a member of many national committees seeking solutions to urban and environmental problems.

Mills is best known for his undergraduate textbook *Urban Economics*, first published in 1972, as well as for founding and editing the premier academic journal in urban economics (*Journal of Urban Economics*) and for his research treatise on urban spatial structure (*Studies in the Structure of the Urban Economy*). The latter book, which was published in 1972, is considered to be one of three classics (the other two are William Alonso's *Location and Land Use* [1964] and Richard Muth's *Cities and Housing* [1969]) that established the core of what today is identified as the field of urban economics. This core consists of a model, commonly referred to as the *standard urban land-use model*, that explains urban spatial structure and how this structure has changed over time. Urban spatial structure refers to the location of alternative land uses (such as apartments, houses, offices, and manufacturing plants) within cities, as well as to the locations of alternative income groups. The usefulness of the model is multifold, providing answers to such questions as why offices are concentrated within the center of metropolitan areas, why high-income households tend to live farther from the center than low-income households, and why many households and firms have moved from the central city to the suburbs.

Besides his contributions to the theoretical development of the standard urban model, Mills has provided many of the most important empirical tests of the model. Within *Studies in the Structure of the Urban Economy*, he developed methods for estimating population density gradients, which show how population per square mile changes as distance increases from the center of the metropolitan area. These techniques were used by Mills in a series of papers and by other urban economists to study population suburbanization, which continues to be a major focus of urban scholars in light of recent concerns related to urban sprawl. Mills's research has shown that suburbanization is the result of both a natural evolutionary process resulting from higher real incomes and urban population growth and a flight from blight, as households and firms move from the central city to the suburbs to escape social and fiscal problems that are more severe within central cities.

While Mills is best known for his development and testing of the standard urban model, his writings have also expanded understanding of numerous urban problems (such as air and water pollution, housing segregation, and urban decay) and what might be done to solve them. His policy prescriptions have stressed the importance of allowing markets to work more efficiently without excessive government intervention.

SEE ALSO *Economics, Urban; Pollution; Pollution, Air; Pollution, Water; Segregation, Residential; Spatial Theory*

BIBLIOGRAPHY

Alonso, William. 1964. *Location and Land Use: Toward a General Theory of Land Rent.* Cambridge, MA: Harvard University Press.

Mills, Edwin S. 1972. *Studies in the Structure of the Urban Economy.* Baltimore, MD: Johns Hopkins University Press.

Mills, Edwin S., and Bruce W. Hamilton. 1994. *Urban Economics.* 5th ed. New York: Harper Collins.

Muth, Richard F. 1969. *Cities and Housing: The Spatial Pattern of Urban Residential Land Use.* Chicago: University of Chicago Press.

Keith R. Ihlanfeldt

MILOSEVIC, SLOBODAN
1941–2006

Slobodan Milosevic was the president of Serbia from 1989 to 1997, and president of the Federated Republic of Yugoslavia from 1997 to 2000. Milosevic was born in Pozarevac, Serbia, the second son of a former Orthodox priest and a Serbian schoolteacher; both parents later committed suicide. In high school Milosevic met Mirjana Markovic, the daughter of prominent Yugoslav Communist Party members. They married in 1965 and had two children, Marija and Marko. Milosevic completed college at the University of Belgrade, studied law, and then became head of Technogas, the state-owned gas company, and, later, president of Beobanka, the United Bank of Belgrade.

In 1984 Milosevic entered politics as leader of the Belgrade Communist Party. Calling for a centralized federal political and economic system, Milosevic became a spokesperson for Serbian nationalist sentiments and the long-standing desire for the creation of a Serbian republic throughout former Yugoslavia. In 1987, while in the Albanian providence of Kosovo, Milosevic assured the Serbian minority population that Yugoslavia's non-Serbian populations would not extract concessions from the Serbians as they sought greater autonomy from the once-powerful Yugoslavian confederation. Soon afterward, Yugoslavia's fragile, multiethnic coalitions disintegrated into regional enclaves at war. In 1988, in a wave of Serbian nationalism, Milosevic was elected president of Serbia. By 1992–1993, Slovenia, Croatia, and Bosnia sought to secede from Yugoslavia to form autonomous governments. Milosevic directed the Serbian-dominated Yugoslav Army to wage war against these movements and protect the Serbian minority population from its non-Serbian secessionists. By arming Serbia's minority populations in the provinces, the goal of the war changed from a preservation of the Yugoslav confederation to an ethnic civil war, taking the lives of more than 250,000 people and displacing more than 2 million.

In 1995, in its first military operation against a European nation, the North Atlantic Treaty Organization (NATO) commenced air strikes against Serb targets in Croatia, bringing Milosevic into negotiations, which became known as the Dayton Peace Accord. In 1996 Milosevic was elected president of Yugoslavia and in 1997 Serbia was at war in Kosovo. In 1999 NATO again bombed targets inside Serbia, including Belgrade, until Serbian forces withdrew from Kosovo. In 2000 economic and international isolation created enough popular unrest in Belgrade to force Milosevic from power. In June 2001 Milosevic was arrested and extradited to The Hague for trial in the United Nations Criminal Tribunal. Milosevic was charged with three indictments: for his role in atrocities committed by Serbian forces during the Kosovo campaign, including the murder of more than 600 people and the deportation of 700,000; for breaches of the Geneva Conventions in Croatia, including the forced removal of 200,000 non-Serbians; and for crimes against humanity and genocide in Bosnia, namely the killing of thousands of Bosnian Muslims and Bosnian Croats.

The court held that as president of the Republic of Serbia, Milosevic exercised control over the participants in the conflict. After refusing to enter a plea or accept assistance from lawyers provided by the court, Milosevic elected to defend himself. The trial lasted five years and, with less than one month of deliberations remaining, Milosevic was found dead in his cell at the age of sixty-four. On March 14, 2006, his trial was officially terminated, without a verdict. Historians regard Milosevic's war of nationalism and ethnic cleansing as one of Europe's most destructive conflicts and human rights atrocities since World War II.

SEE ALSO *Genocide; Tito (Josip Broz)*

BIBLIOGRAPHY

Brkic, Courtney. 2005. The Wages of Denial. *New York Times*, July 11.

Gutman, Roy. 1993. *Witness to Genocide.* New York: Macmillan.

Traynor, Ian. 2006. Slobodan Milosevic (obituary). *Guardian Unlimited Special Reports*, March 13. http://www.guardian.co.uk/obituaries/story/0,,1729460,00.html.

Vulliamy, Ed. 1994. *Seasons in Hell: Understanding Bosnia's War.* New York: St. Martin's Press.

Wood, Nicolas, and Judy Dempsey. 2006. Death Poses Challenges as Serbia Faces Past and Future. *New York Times*, March 13.

James Freeman

MIMESIS

SEE *Representation.*

MIND-BODY DICHOTOMY

SEE *Knowledge; Psychoanalytic Theory.*

MINIMAX THEOREM

SEE *Zero-sum Game.*

MINIMIZATION

In his influential 1784 essay "Idea for a Universal History with a Cosmopolitan Intent," Immanuel Kant (1724–1804) defends his third thesis in the following terms:

> Nature does nothing unnecessary and is not prodigal in the use of means to her ends. Nature seems here to have taken delight in the greatest frugality and to have calculated her animal endowments so closely—so precisely to the most pressing needs of a primitive existence—that she seems to have willed that if man should ever work himself up … he alone would have the entire credit for it and would have only himself to thank. (Kant [1784] 1983, p. 31.)

This Leibnizian key to how Nature plans and attains its ends and objectives—approaches the principal-agent problem, if not a game, that it is confronted with—had already been identified by Leonhard Euler (1707–1783) at least forty years earlier:

> Namely, because the shape of the whole universe is most perfect and, in fact, designed by the wisest creator, nothing in all of the world will occur in which no maximum or minimum rule is somehow shining forth [nihil omnino in mundo contingit, in quo non maximi minimive ratio quapiam eluciat] (Euler [1744] 1952, p. 411).

It is in Paul Samuelson's 1947 *Foundations of Economic Analysis* that Lionel Robbins's (1898–1984) redefinition of economics as the "science which studies human behavior as a relationship between ends and scarce means which have alternative uses" (Robbins 1932, p. 16) is taken and squarely rooted into the "general properties of minimum systems" (the latter being one of the two section headings of Samuelson's 1964 foreward to the reprint

of his book). The trajectory of the notion of *minimization*, and its mirror-image *maximization*, in the evolution of economic science and of the social sciences, insofar as they submit to the analytical lead of the former, is so well charted that the paired terms do not merit an entry in *The New Palgrave* (Eatwell et al. 1987; also see Samuelson 1971). Thus V. M. Tikhomirov begins *Stories about Maxima and Minima* with the blasé statement that in "daily life it is constantly necessary to choose the best possible (optimal) solution [and] a tremendous number of such problems arise in economics and in technology" (Tikhomirov [1986] 1990, p. ix). Pareto-optimal and core allocations, to take only two solution concepts pertaining to the collective level, can be seen, respectively, as the outcomes at the individual level of expenditure-minimization and of preference maximization problems at some suitably chosen set of prices. (For the precise definitions and assumptions underlying these results, see Lange 1942; Arrow 1951; and Debreu 1959 for the former; and Edgeworth 1881; Debreu and Scarf 1963; and Aumann 1964 for the latter.)

In conclusion, two points need flagging: an unfortunate tendency to single out calculus as the only key to problems involving minimization and maximization (Koopmans 1957; Dorfman et al. 1958; Debreu 1959; and Niven 1981 are vigorous antidotes) and, more controversially perhaps, a tendency (as in Euler, this entry and also possibly in Kant) to single out the principle of minimization (and maximization), and the consequent submission to quantification that it implies, as the only explanatory key to social science phenomena. A fuller elaboration of these postmodern demurrals is best left to longer entries.

SEE ALSO *Kant, Immanuel; Mathematical Economics; Mathematics in the Social Sciences; Maximization; Methods, Quantitative; Models and Modeling; Optimizing Behavior; Quantification; Rationality; Samuelson, Paul A.*

BIBLIOGRAPHY

Arrow, Kenneth J. 1951. An Extension of the Basic Theorems of Classical Welfare Economics. In *Proceedings of the Second Berkeley Symposium on Mathematical Statistics and Probability*, ed. Jerzy Neyman, 507–532. Berkeley: University of California Press.

Aumann, Robert J. 1964. Markets with a Continuum of Traders. *Econometrica* 32: 39–50.

Debreu, Gerard. 1959. *Theory of Value: An Axiomatic Analysis of Economic Equilibrium.* New York: Wiley.

Debreu, Gerard, and Herbert Scarf. 1963. A Limit Theorem on the Core of an Economy. *International Economic Review* 4: 235–246.

Dorfman, Robert, Paul A. Samuelson, and Robert M. Solow. 1958. *Linear Programming and Economic Analysis*. New York: McGraw-Hill.

Eatwell, John, Murray Milgate, and Peter K. Newman, eds. 1987. *The New Palgrave: A Dictionary of Economics*. London: Macmillan.

Edgeworth, Francis Y. 1881. *Mathematical Psychics*. London: Kegan-Paul.

Euler, Leonhard. [1744] 1952. *Methodus inveniendi curvas lineas maximi minimive proprietate gaudentes: Sive solution problematis viso isoperimetrici latissimo sense accepti*. In *Opera Omnia*, series 1, vol. 24. Leipzig, Germany: Tuebner.

Kant, Immanuel. [1784] 1983. Idea for a Universal History with a Cosmopolitan Intent. In *Perpetual Peace and Other Essays on Politics, History, and Morals*. Trans. Ted Humphrey, 29–40. Indianapolis, IN: Hackett.

Koopmans, Tjalling C. 1957. *Three Essays on the State of Economic Science*. New York: McGraw-Hill.

Lange, Oskar. 1942. The Foundations of Welfare Economics. *Econometrica* 10: 215–228.

Mordukhovich, Boris S. 2006. *Variational Analysis and Generalized Differentiation*. Berlin: Springer.

Niven, Ivan. 1981. *Maxima and Minima without Calculus*. Washington, DC: Mathematical Association of America.

Robbins, Lionel. 1932. *An Essay on the Nature and Significance of Economic Science*. London: Macmillan.

Samuelson, Paul A. 1947. *Foundations of Economic Analysis*. Cambridge, MA: Harvard University Press.

Samuelson, Paul A. 1971. Maximum Principles in Analytical Economics. In *Les Prix Nobel en 1970*, 273–288. Stockholm: The Nobel Foundation.

Tikhomirov, V. M. [1986] 1990. *Stories about Maxima and Minima*. Trans. Abe Shenitzer. Providence, RI: American Mathematical Society.

M. Ali Khan

MINIMUM WAGE

Historically, the idea of a minimum wage was to allow a full-time worker to earn enough to buy the basic necessities of life. Following the Great Depression of the 1930s and World War II, watershed legislation established minimum wages around the world, most notably the Fair Labor Standards Act (FALSA) of 1938 in the United States and the Wage Council Act of 1945 in the United Kingdom. FALSA, for instance, established a minimum wage of 25 cents per hour when it was formed; that became $5.85 in 2007, and will increase to $7.25 by 2009. The value of this minimum, however, declines over time due to inflation or productivity growth. The problem with the minimum wage is its interference with the labor-market mechanism, creating ambiguous influences on employers, workers, and teenagers (and even more so

on nonwhite teenagers) for whom the market-clearing wage is lower than the minimum wage. In the case of extreme poverty, the argument that policy authorities should pass a legal minimum wage through legislation is not in dispute, but disagreement over a minimum wage abounds in the areas of efficient allocation of resources, full employment, effect on income, and alternative ways to combat poverty (Stigler 1946).

Economists study the effect of minimum wages relative to the market equilibrium wages. If the demand for labor, N_d, is not equal to the supply of labor, N_s, then wages change. At equilibrium, the change in the wage rates, w, over time, t, is $dw / dt = f(N_d - N_s) = 0$. One implication of the equilibrium is that a laborer is paid a wage, w, equal to the marginal product of labor (MPL). If a minimum wage is binding, such as for the unskilled, young, less educated, and part-time workers, then the minimum wage would exceed the equilibrium wage, creating unemployment. The unemployed may transfer to industries that are not covered by the minimum wage, thus decreasing wage and productivity there. One possibility is that employers may then substitute more automation, or skilled labor for low-skilled labor as wages increase. Another factor is that competition between the covered and the uncovered sectors of the labor market tends to equilibrate the wages between the two sectors. Thus, the MPL of workers still employed in the covered industry will tend to rise to where $w = MPL$ (Hicks 1948, p. 179). As Martin Bronfenbrenner asserts: "If they were better fed and clothed and housed, and better cheered as well, by higher wages, their physical efficiency might rise in the same proportion as the wage rate" (Bronfenbrenner 1943, p. 82).

Economists emphasize empirical work to assess the net possible effect of minimum wages. Several studies by David Card and Alan Krueger held that minimum wages increase the employment in fast-food firms such as Burger King, KFC, Roy Rogers, and Wendy's. At the firm level, Card and Krueger (1994) studied the increase in minimum wages in New Jersey, the highest minimum wage in the nation as of April 1, 1992, against no change in the minimum wage in Pennsylvania. They found that employment increased in New Jersey by 0.6 workers, and declined in Pennsylvania by 2.1 workers, a difference-in-differences of 2.7 workers. Similar findings were made for firm-level data in Texas, and for state data in California (Card and Krueger 1995). An attempt by David Neumark and William Wascher (2000) to replicate the Card and Krueger finding used employment data reported by establishments rather than survey data. They found that the job gain in New Jersey could be zero or slightly negative. The technology of the fast-food firms suggests that employers may need a fixed number of employees per grill or cash register, and therefore will not reduce employment when minimum wages increase, but that they may be discouraged from opening new franchises, thus lowering potential employment.

The analysis of the amount of the unemployment can be stated in elasticity of demand terms. If the elasticity is less than one, increase in wages will increase payroll, enhancing benefits to workers. The elasticity of −1 is the standard labor market assumption, which leads to the expectation that unemployment will fall in equal proportion to wage increases. Earlier empirical studies by Charles Brown, Curtis Gilroy, and Andrew Kohen (1982; 1983) indicated that the effect of minimum wages on employment was slightly negative or insignificant, indicating an elasticity of demand close to zero.

In the Keynesian world, "the customary treatment of involuntary unemployment and unemployment equilibrium frequently is based upon rigidity of money wage rate" (Darity and Horn 1983, p. 725). The post-Keynesians are well known for defending the wage-rigidity assumption. John Maynard Keynes's (1973, p. 54) correspondence with the classical economist Arthur Cecil Pigou revealed a rigid labor supply curve, indicating rigid wages for some level of employment. Keynes, however, eased up on the wage-rigidity assumption in chapter 19 of his *General Theory of Employment, Interest, and Money* (1936). According to Axel Leijonhufvud (1968, p. 37) the assumption of a minimum wage is maintained by Keynesians, who assume competitive conditions make wage rigidity into a special case for this model. Don Patinkin (1948, p. 545) argued that rigidity in the Keynesian system is possible under static modeling of Keynesian economics, but rigidity is not an essential Keynesian element in a more dynamic setting.

Modern macroeconomic discussion involves models dealing with wage-setting, where wages are set as a markup on expected price, and with price-setting, where prices are set as a markup on expected wages. Unemployment then depends on the solution of the joint equations Price Setter: $p - w^e = \beta_0 - \beta_1 u$, $(\beta_1 \geq 0)$, and Wage Setter: $w^e - p = \gamma_0 - \gamma_1 u$, $(\gamma_1 > 0)$, where w is money wage, u is unemployment, p is price, e is expected, and the Greek letters are parameters to be estimated (Layard, Neckell, and Jackman 1994, pp. 19–20). When price and wage expectations materialize, real wages can be analyzed against employment. Any factors that contribute to wage push, γ_0, such as the minimum wage, raise the unemployment rate.

SEE ALSO *Economics, Labor; Expectations; Markup Pricing; Poverty; Sticky Wages; Unemployment; Unemployment Rate; Wages*

BIBLIOGRAPHY

Bronfenbrenner, Martin. 1943. Minimum Wages, Unemployability, and Relief: A Theoretical Note. *Southern Economic Journal* 10 (July): 52–59.

Brown, Charles, Curtis Gilroy, and Andrew Kohen. 1982. The Effect of the Minimum Wage on Employment and Unemployment. *Journal of Economic Literature* 20 (June): 487–529.

Brown, Charles, Curtis Gilroy, and Andrew Kohen. 1983. Time-Series Evidence on the Effect of the Minimum Wage on Youth Employment and Unemployment. *Journal of Human Resources* 18 (Winter): 3–31.

Card, David, and Alan B. Krueger. 1994. Minimum Wages and Employment: A Case Study of the Fast-Food Industry in New Jersey and Pennsylvania. *American Economic Review* 84 (September): 772–793.

Card, David, and Alan B. Krueger. 1997. *Myth and Measurement: The New Economics of the Minimum Wage.* Princeton, NJ: Princeton University Press.

Darity, William A., and Bobbie L. Horn. 1983. Involuntary Unemployment Reconsidered. *Southern Economic Journal* 49, no. 3 (January): 717–733.

Hicks, John. [1932] 1948. *The Theory of Wages.* New York: Peter Smith.

Keynes, John Maynard. 1936. *The General Theory of Employment, Interest, and Money.* London: Macmillan.

Keynes, John Maynard. [1973] 1987. *The General Theory and After, Part II: Defence and Development,* ed. Donald Moggridge. London: Macmillan.

Layard, Richard, Stephen Nickell, and Richard Jackman. 1994. *The Unemployment Crisis.* Oxford: Oxford University Press.

Leijonhufvud, Axel. 1968. *On Keynesian Economics and the Economics of Keynes: A Study in Monetary Theory.* Oxford: Oxford University Press.

Modigliani, Franco. 1980. *Collected Papers of Franco Modigliani.* Vol. 1, ed. Andrew Abel. Cambridge, MA: MIT Press.

Neumark, David, and William Wascher. 2000. Minimum Wages and Employment: A Case Study of the Fast-Food Industry in New Jersey and Pennsylvania, Comment. *American Economic Review* 90 (December): 1362–1269.

Patinkin, Don. 1948. Price Flexibility and Full Employment. *American Economic Review* 38 (September): 543–564.

Stigler, George J. 1946. Economics of Minimum Wage Legislation. *American Economic Review* 36, no. 3. (June): 358–365.

Lall Ramrattan
Michael Szenberg

MINING INDUSTRY

Mining is a site-specific economic activity creating wealth from the extraction of nonrenewable resources from land and sea. The boundaries of the mining industry are imprecise. It conventionally excludes oil, gas, and water, but coal and uranium are normally included. Bulk construction materials and stone are extracted in the same fashion as other minerals, and the volume of their output exceeds that of most other minerals, but they are usually excluded from definitions of the industry. The downstream boundaries are somewhat indeterminate, depending on processes, corporate structure and end uses. Mines usually produce ores that require further processing rather than finished products and the ores may contain one or several economic products. The usable materials are often a small proportion of the ore mined. There are various methods of mining, each suited to the specific circumstances of each mineral deposit, and each with different cost structures. Most minerals are either extracted from open workings in which the overburden is first stripped away to expose the economic ore, or from underground workings that access the ore through shafts or tunnels. Substantial volumes of waste are mined as well as ores, particularly in open pit mines producing base and precious metals.

GLOBAL FEATURES

Ore deposits are not evenly distributed around the globe, with different minerals concentrated in specific geological environments. Typically, deposits located near major centers of industry and population have been depleted and mines are increasingly concentrated in more remote regions. Transport costs are a major determinant of competitiveness, and reductions in shipping costs since the mid-twentieth century have internationalized the markets for many products, like coal and iron ore, that formerly served regional or local markets. The European Union, Japan, and the United States have become increasingly dependent on imports, either of mineral raw materials, or of semi-processed products, to supply their requirements. The fast developing countries of the Asian Pacific Rim are also heavily reliant on imports of minerals. Economic growth in the latter region, combined with rapidly rising demand from China, is putting renewed pressure on mineral supplies. China has by far the world's largest minerals industry, accounting for about 12 percent of global minerals turnover, excluding coal, and nearly 18 percent, including coal. Many, but by no means all, of its mines are antiquated, undercapitalized, small-scale operations with poor environmental and health and safety records.

Most minerals and their first-stage products are traded internationally at prices determined in global markets. Shifts in exchange rates and domestic economic policies thus influence an individual mine's ability to compete. The amount of usable product contained in ore, its ease of processing, and accessibility are the main endogenous determinants of competitiveness. Energy is a large element of costs, so that rising oil prices have an adverse impact. Economies of scale are important, and the typical scale of operations has risen considerably over the past fifteen years. Many small mines have closed down, and larger mines have expanded, so that the number of mining operations has contracted. Technical change and rising productivity have also driven down costs.

Labor costs are relatively unimportant in many mines, although U.S. companies are often burdened by large legacy costs. Organized mining accounts for much less than 1 percent of the world's workforce—fewer than 15 million people, with a further 11.5 to 13 million people working in small-scale mines. According to the International Labor Office, the total number of people relying on mining, both large and small, for a living, taking dependents into account, is about 300 million, of which up to one-third depend on small-scale mining. The numbers have fallen markedly since the 1980s with the closure of many small mines and improving productivity, especially in China. There is a growing global shortage of skilled and professional labor, because of a rundown in mining education and a lack of new entrants.

LABOR CONDITIONS AND STATE OF THE INDUSTRY

Mines are only located where there are viable ore deposits, and these are often in physically remote areas, far from major population centers. The modern tendency is for workers to commute to mine sites for extended shift periods of up to a month, from well-established communities with good infrastructure and social amenities. Before the development of low-cost air travel such commuting was seldom possible and dedicated mining camps were often established to house the workers, not always with their families. Such communities were natural breeding grounds for the social ills of alcohol abuse and prostitution. They also insulated workers from outside influences and fostered their solidarity. That was enhanced by the arduous and dangerous nature of mining, particularly when underground. Even minor grievances, real or imagined, could be blown up out of proportion. The conditions were ideal for periodic labor unrest and trade union militancy. Moreover, miners in rural areas could live cheaply, especially in the summer months when there were alternative agricultural, hunting, or fishing opportunities. That remains true in some regions, such as parts of Canada.

In practice union membership and militancy have not been significantly greater in most of the mining industry than in other sectors of economic activity. According to the Bureau of Labor Statistics, in the United States, for example, the 8 percent of workers in the mining industry that belong to a union compare with 7.8 percent for the private sector as a whole, 13 percent in manufacturing, and 36.5 percent in government. When strikes did occur, however, they were often longer and more acrimonious than elsewhere. The cyclical nature of most mineral markets contributed in that regard, as it still does. Workers naturally seek to increase their earnings when markets are buoyant, as in 2005 and 2006, and are more prepared to strike than when markets are depressed. At such periods employers aim to reduce their labor costs. Today that will be achieved mainly through agreed redundancies. Historically, however, wages were cut, with or without prior consultation with employees. Some of the most bitter and most prolonged strikes resulted from such actions, for example in the U.S. and U.K. coal industries during the late 1920s and 1930s. In North America a tradition of labor contracts covering three- to five-year periods even today may prompt strikes at their renewal, in the copper and nickel industries for example. In neither sector has there been any to compare in recent years with those of the 1960s. Elsewhere, as in parts of Latin America, strikes may be used as a political weapon to achieve broad social and community goals that are more properly within the purview of governments than of the companies affected.

Mechanization and modern capital-intensive mining methods, often in open-pit mines, have greatly reduced the mining industry's historic need to attract a large pool of unskilled or semi-skilled workers. That has in turn altered the nature of the relationship between mining companies and their employees in many sectors of the industry. In South Africa the progressive abolition of apartheid from 1990 greatly enhanced this global process. Previously racial discrimination was legally enforced in the mines. Migrant workers, both from neighboring countries and from within South Africa, were subject to repressive labor laws. They were unable to live with their families but were housed in single men's hostels with their attendant social problems. Wages for unskilled workers were held very close to the poverty line. Over the past decade changing economic conditions have led to the closure of many mines and a substantial reduction in the numbers employed. The living standards and opportunities of the remaining workers have greatly improved. Legislation on black empowerment is also fast changing patterns of ownership.

Mining is a relatively small contributor to global output as well as employment. The world's minerals production was worth some $375 billion ex mine in 2004, excluding bulk construction materials, but including coal. This equalled around 0.7 percent of global gross domestic product (GDP). U.S. minerals output was $40 billion or 0.3 percent of U.S. GDP, with coal making up half the total. Mining is a much more important source of income in a few countries and of exports in many more. It provides over 8 percent of Chile's GDP, 5.7 percent of Australia's, and 1.7 percent of Canada's. In some small

countries it is the major economic activity. In Namibia, for example it makes up 15 percent of GDP, and in Botswana 35 percent. Shares of total output understate the mining industry's true importance, as it provides the essential raw materials for most forms of economic activity. Mineral-based products include metals, ceramics, construction goods, and many chemicals and plastics. The total output of the mineral industries is growing, although many of its prices have been on a declining trend. Demand moves cyclically with economic activity. Prices, and to a lesser extent output, are consequently volatile. Individual mines are depleting even as total output grows. Different products have experienced different growth rates.

The industry's corporate structure has evolved with global political and economic change. There is a wide range of different types of organization involved in the industry. Multinational mining companies are less important than is suggested by the attention they receive. The concentration of ownership varies markedly from product to product. Foreign-owned mining companies were effectively unable to operate in most developing and centrally planned economies during much of the period since World War II. During the 1990s most countries liberalized their mining codes, privatized state-owned mineral projects, and became receptive to foreign investment. Some countries, particularly in Latin America, attracted a wave of foreign investment in export-based mineral projects. Political risk nonetheless remains high in many mineral-rich areas, limiting foreign involvement to high unit value products like gold and gemstones. In many countries there remains strong opposition to foreign exploitation of natural resources and this tends to emerge most strongly at the local level. Mining companies can then become a focus for popular discontent with national governments.

Mining necessarily has an impact on the local environment, and some mineral products, like asbestos and lead, create hazards to human health. Although the standards of modern large-scale mining are infinitely higher than those of earlier times, the scars and environmental blight of historic mining and a few well-publicized lapses and accidents influence public perceptions. Whereas mining was once universally treated as having a preeminent claim on land use, that is no longer the case. Tracts of land have been debarred to mining in many countries, and increasingly onerous environmental requirements have been imposed. Larger international companies tend to follow best practice, but the costs of meeting higher standards have risen. Where capital-intensive large-scale projects are developed in rural areas they can upset the social fabric, especially of indigenous peoples. Mines are no different in that regard from other modern industries, except that their location is dictated by the availability of ore. Preserving good community relations is a major challenge for all mining companies.

Coal output of roughly 5 billion tonnes accounts for $105 billion of global turnover, with production for domestic sale in China, India, the United States and Russia accounting for the greater part. U.S. output was almost 1 billion tonnes, with a value approaching $20 billion. Some mines serve both domestic and export markets, but world trade is dominated by Australia, Indonesia, South Africa, Canada, and Colombia. Production for export from large-scale, mainly open-cast, modern mines makes up less than 15 percent of total coal output. Thermal coal for power stations comprises about 60 percent of world trade. The main export markets for coal are in Europe and Pacific Asia whose domestic output has become increasingly uncompetitive, and is often only sustained through subsidies and protection.

The value of global turnover of metal mining varies with prices. The bulk ferrous metals, led by iron ore, made up one eighth of 2004's sales. Domestic production in China and the United States contrasts with large-scale export-oriented output in countries like Australia and Brazil. The major nonferrous ores, of which copper is the most important, account for 15 percent of turnover. As the metal content of many ores is often low, metal mines are responsible for a much greater share of the world's ore and waste extracted than of turnover. Mines shipping concentrates for processing in industrial centers coexist with mines serving domestic smelters and refineries that produce metal for export or domestic use. Large international companies operate alongside state-owned companies like Chile's Codelco, and smaller domestic firms. Other metallic products, including uranium, make up 10 percent of turnover. Often they are produced as by-products of the major metals, being extracted at the smelting stage. Precious metals (gold, silver, and platinum group products) contribute one-ninth of turnover, and gem diamonds a further one-tenth. Platinum output is highly concentrated in Russia and South Africa but output of gold and silver is widely distributed. Large-scale modern mines, controlled by international companies, coexist with small-scale operations and artisanal workings. The bulk of diamonds is extracted by major companies in Australia, Botswana, Canada, Russia and South Africa, but small-scale workings persist in many developing countries. The health and safety and environmental conditions of the small-scale workings for gold and gems are often very poor. The remaining one-eighth of turnover comes from fertilizer and industrial minerals. Many are mined for domestic markets by local companies, or by companies from downstream sectors like chemicals or building products. In some instances, where only a few deposits are known globally, production tends to be dominated by large international companies.

SEE ALSO *Bauxite Industry; Copper Industry; Diamond Industry; Gold Industry; Industry; Natural Resources, Nonrenewable; Petroleum Industry; Silver Industry; Steel Industry*

BIBLIOGRAPHY

Breaking New Ground, Mining, Minerals, and Sustainable Development. 2002. The Report of the MMSD Project. London and Sterling, VA: Earthscan Publications.

International Labour Office, Geneva. 2002. http://www.ilo.org/public/english/dialogue/sector/sectors/mining/emp/htm.

Mineral Commodity Summaries 2005, United States Geological Survey. http://minerals.usgs.gov/minerals.

Mining Journal's State of the Industry Report. January 2004. London: Raw Materials Group and Mining Journal.

Taylor, L. E., J. A. Hillier, and A. J. Benham. 2005. *World Mineral Production 1999–2003, British Geological Survey.* Nottingham, U.K.: Keyworth.

World Economic Outlook Database, September 2005, International Monetary Fund. http://www.imf.org.

Phillip Crowson

MINORITIES

The term *minority* and how it is used and defined has changed over time. Typically, social scientists use the term to define a group's social, political, and economic power in a society. Historically, in society, the term has also been used to focus on physical traits such as phenotype in African Americans and other people of color (Parrillo 2006).

According to Joe Feagin and Clairece Booher Feagin, Louis Wirth defined minorities as "a group of people who, because of their physical or cultural characteristics, are singled out from others in the society in which they live for differential and unequal treatment and who therefore regard themselves as objects of collective discrimination" (Feagin and Feagin 2003, pp. 10–11). Vincent N. Parrillo explains that not everyone agrees with Wirth's definition:

> Richard Schermerhorn, for example, notes that this "victimlogical" approach does not adequately explain the similarities and differences among groups or analyze relationships between majority and minority groups. A third attempt to define minority groups rests on examining relationships between groups in terms of each group's position in the social hierarchy. This approach stresses a group's social power, which may vary from one country to another, as, for example, does that of the Jews in Russia and in Israel. The emphasis on

stratification instead of population size explains situations in which a relatively small group subjugates a larger number of people (e.g., the European colonization of African and Asian populations). Schermerhorn adopts a variation on this viewpoint. He also viewed social power as an important variable in determining a group's position in the hierarchy, but he believes that other factors are equally important. Size (a minority group must be less than half the population), ethnicity (as defined by Wirth's physical and cultural traits), and group consciousness also help to define a minority group. (Parrillo 2006, pp. 15–16)

Social scientists hold a variety of views about what it means to be a minority. The anthropologists Charles Wagley and Marvin Harris listed five defining characteristics shared by minority groups throughout the world (Parillo 2006, p. 16):

minority groups receive "unequal treatment";

they are "easily identifiable because of physical or cultural characteristics," as in, for example, the phenotype of African Americans and other minorities of color;

they tend to "share a sense of peoplehood—that each of them shares something in common with other members";

"membership in the minority group has an ascribed status; a person who is considered a member of a particular minority group is born into it"; and

they have a tendency to marry within their own minority group, either by choice or by necessity, because of the social isolation that they experience in their lives.

The term *minority* often is used to describe people who have "less power, are oppressed, or are a subordinate segment within a political unit" (Myers 2007, p. 42). A person can be classified as a minority based on his or her religious affiliation, age, disabilities, sexual orientation, or gender. And a person can belong to both a minority group and the majority group. For example, "An American Roman Catholic who is white belongs to a prominent religious minority group but also is a member of the racially dominant group" (Parrillo 2006, p. 17). Women are considered a minority group based on their gender and because they have been oppressed and controlled (Myers 2007), and women of color are often considered a minority within a minority. One can be born a member of a majority group and later become a member of a minority group (e.g., the elderly). People can be born with disabilities such as polio, blindness, and missing limbs, or dis-

abilities can occur over the course of a person's life (Parrillo 2006).

Contemporary scholars hold that it is not accurate to classify a group as a minority based on the numerical representation of that group. "Scholars today consider it more accurate to use the term dominant group for the majority group and the term subordinate group for a minority group. This usage is appropriate because a majority group in this sense can be numerically a minority.… [I]f current trends continue, the white majority, in population terms, is likely to become a statistical minority in the United States by the middle of the twenty-first century" (Feagin and Feagin 2003, p. 11). But whites will still constitute the majority based on their economic and political power.

CIVIL RIGHTS

The struggle for equal rights has been an ongoing challenge for minority groups, which historically have been discriminated against in the United States. They have also been subject to stereotypes that are psychologically harmful and deny a people their humanity. Along with racial discrimination, the belief in stereotypes can affect the physical, economic, and life chances of minority groups (Feagin and Feagin 2003). "Negative stereotypes and images of African Americans and other Americans of color are constantly used, refurbished, played with, amended, and passed along in millions of white kinship and friendship networks, from one community to the next and one generation to the next" (Feagin 2006, p. 44). These "racial stereotypes and prejudices are useful for whites in explaining why certain people of color do not have as much or do as well as whites across multiple areas of the society" (Feagin and Vera 2001, p. 8). The stereotypes applied to different minority groups are remarkably similar. African Americans are depicted as lazy, violent, criminal, untrustworthy, and unintelligent. Latinos have been viewed as inferior, criminal, and uninterested in education or their families (Suarez-Orozco and Paez 2002). In contrast, Asian Americans have been stereotyped as the *model minority*, a term created by whites as an example of what other minorities groups should become—hardworking, intelligent, and docile (Feagin and Feagin 2003). Some might view this stereotype as positive, but others contend that "the model minority myth hurts Asian Americans" (Wu 2002, p. 67). It is a stereotype that pits other minorities and Asian Americans against each other, implying to African Americans, Latinos, and Native Americans that they too can have the American dream if they model themselves after Asian Americans. Native Americans have struggled for years with the stereotypes and racist images that portray them as savages; currently they are fighting the use of racist Native American images that are used for sports mascots. Since the attacks of September 11th, 2001, Arab Americans have been battling stereotypes that depict them as terrorists, treacherous, and cruel (Feagin and Feagin 2003).

Minority groups, specifically African Americans, have been instrumental in fighting for the equal rights of all citizens in the United States. In the 1960s the Voting Rights Act and the civil rights movement led the way for minority groups of all ethnicities to receive equal rights in the United States. The success of the movement prompted other movements, such as the women's rights movement and, more recently, a movement to secure rights for undocumented immigrants in the United States.

MINORITIES IN POLITICS

The political voice of minority groups has changed over time. In the U.S. Senate in 2007 there was one African American, Barack Obama from Illinois; two Asian Americans, Daniel K. Inouye and Daniel K. Akaka, both from Hawaii; three Hispanic Americans, Ken L. Salazar from Colorado, Melquiades R. Martinez from Florida, and Robert Menendez from New Jersey; and no Native Americans (though Ben Nighthorse Campbell from Colorado served in the Senate from 1993 to 2005). In 2007 sixteen Senate seats were held by women.

In the United States, African Americans, Native Americans, Asian Americans, and Latino Americans are all considered minorities in society, based on their economic and political standing. Presently, these minority groups are still underrepresented in politics. However, in South Africa, black South Africans are the statistical majority but white South Africans, the statistical minority, control a majority of the land and much of the economic power. Some scholars would say that black South Africans are the minority group because they are the subordinate group. Furthermore, white South Africans are the majority group in this sense, even though they are numerically the minority, because they are the dominant group and control all of the economic power.

WHITES THE NEW MINORITY?

According to Marcelo Suarez-Orozco and Mariela Paez, "in a widely cited report, scientists at the U.S. Bureau of the Census concluded that by the year 2050, some 50 percent of the U.S. population would be members of ethnic minorities" (2002, p. 1). According to Dale Maharidge, "By 2050 Hispanics will make up about 21 percent of the American population, blacks 15 percent, and Asians and Pacific Islanders 10 percent" (Maharidge 1996, p. 13). According to a May 2007 U.S. Census Bureau press release, the minority population in the United States surpassed the 100 million mark in 2006. The report noted, "Hispanic remained the largest minority group, with 44.3

million on July 1, 2006—14.8 percent of the total population. [African-American] was the second-largest minority group, totaling 40.2 million. They were followed by Asian (14.9 million), American Indian and Alaska Native (4.5 million), and Native Hawaiian and other Pacific Islander (1 million).... [N]on-Hispanic whites who indicated no other race totaled 198.7 million in 2006." The U.S. census report also indicated that the District of Columbia, California, New Mexico, Hawaii, and Texas are "majority-minority." However, unless minorities gain additional political and economic power, they will remain minorities.

The report stated that the minority population is growing, but will this pattern continue as younger generations of Hispanic groups self-identify as *white* and racial boundaries shift? According to Jonathan W. Warren and France Winddance Twine, "In the 1990 census, more than half of the Hispanic population racially self-identified as white ... and in 1992 that about 95 percent of Latinos self-identified as white" (Warren and Twine 1997, p. 213). According to Clara E. Rodriguez, "what Latinos say they are in standard U.S. racial terms is not necessarily what they are perceived to be by others" (Rodriguez 2000, p. 136). Ethnic minorities self-identify as white based on their age, education, socioeconomic status, citizenship, length of time in the U.S., and language (Rodriguez 2000). As immigrants self-identify as white, the white population will grow and they will most likely remain the dominant majority numerically, economically, and politically.

SEE ALSO *Affirmative Action; Ethnicity; Ethnocentrism; Intergroup Relations; Jingoism; Majorities; Model Minority; Nationalism and Nationality; Other, The; Racism; Subaltern; Whiteness*

BIBLIOGRAPHY

Feagin, Joe R. 2006. *Systemic Racism: A Theory of Oppression.* New York: Routledge.

Feagin, Joe R., and Clairece Booher Feagin. 2003. *Racial and Ethnic Relations.* Upper Saddle River, NJ: Prentice Hall.

Feagin, Joe R., and Hernan Vera. 2001. *White Racism.* New York: Routledge.

Maharidge, Dale. 1996. *The Coming White Minority.* New York: Vintage.

Myers, John P. 2007. *Dominant-Minority Relations in America: Convergence in the New World.* New York: Pearson Education.

Parrillo, Vincent N. 2006. *Strangers to These Shores: Race and Ethnic Relations in the United States.* New York: Pearson Education.

Rodriguez, Clara E. 2000. *Changing Race: Latinos, the Census, and the History of Ethnicity in the United States.* New York: New York University Press.

Suarez-Orozco, Marcelo M., and Mariela M. Paez. 2002. *Latinos: Remaking America*. Berkeley: University of California Press.

United States Census Bureau. 2007. Minority Population Tops 100 Million. http://www.census.gov/Press-Release/www/releases/archives/population/010048.html.

United States Senate. Minorities in the Senate. http://www.senate.gov/reference/reference_index_subjects/Minorities_vrd.htm.

Warren, Jonathan W., and France Winddance Twine. 1997. White Americans, the New Minority? Non-Blacks and the Ever-Expanding Boundaries of Whiteness. *Journal of Black Studies* 28 (2): 200–218.

Wu, Frank H. 2002. *Yellow: Race in America Beyond Black and White*. New York: Basic Books.

Ruth Thompson-Miller

MINORITY ENTERPRISE SMALL BUSINESS INVESTMENT CORPORATION (MESBIC)

SEE *Capitalism, Black.*

MINSKY, HYMAN
1919–1996

A dissenter from mainstream macroeconomics, Hyman ("Hy") Minsky became intellectually prepared from the University of Chicago's undergraduate teachings of Oscar Lange, Paul Douglas, Jacob Viner, Frank Knight, and Henry Simmons rather than the Harvard Keynesians. Minsky was born in Chicago in 1919 and attended public schools in Lima, Ohio, Chicago, and New York City before entering the University of Chicago in 1937 to study mathematics. He was drawn to economics, his BS degree in mathematics notwithstanding, after attending the integrated social science sequence course and the seminars taught by Lange, Knight, and Simmons at Chicago. Strongly influenced by his working-class family with its active involvement in the American socialist movement and his close relationship with Gerhard Meyer at Chicago, he decided to pursue graduate studies in economics. His graduate work at Harvard, where he was awarded the MPA (1947) and PhD (1954), was interrupted by a number of years in the U.S. Army with assignments in New York City and overseas during the mid-1940s. The interrelationships between market structure, financing investment, survival

of firms, aggregate demand, and business cycles, advanced in his PhD dissertation in 1954 (published in 2005), were further sharpened and became the focus of his lifelong research agenda (Papadimitriou 1992).

After an initial appointment to the faculty at Brown University (1949–1955), Minsky moved to the University of California at Berkeley (1956–1965) and then to Washington University in St. Louis, where he remained until his retirement in 1990. He was then appointed Distinguished Scholar at the Levy Economics Institute of Bard College, a post he held until his death in 1996.

Minsky's earliest writings centered on the endogeneity of financial innovation that was dependent on profit-seeking behavior, the institutional prerequisites of ceilings and floors to the multiplier-accelerator model, and the importance of the initial conditions of financial positions that would determine the future of the economy—whether stable or unstable—beginning with robust balance sheets that over time would become fragile, resulting in economic conditions that might make a debt deflation such as that of the 1930s happen again (Minsky 1957a; 1957b; 1959). Addressing endogenous money, financial innovation that "stretched liquidity," behavioral changes induced by government policy, lender-of-last-resort activity, and market-driven, instability-enhancing behavior over the course of the business cycle, Minsky broke away from conventional macroeconomic canons (Papadimitriou and Wray 1998). These were all issues that occupied his research program during the 1960s. These issues helped him develop his financial instability hypothesis and focus on the examination of the workings of financial markets and institutions.

Minsky's main contribution in *John Maynard Keynes* (1975) is the "financial theory of investment" arising from the realization that in an advanced capitalist economy, there are two price levels determined from different relations and variables—one for "current output," the second for "financial and real assets." The price level of current output—dependent mainly on labor costs and a markup—ensures that production and distribution take place and that costs are recovered. The price level of "capital assets" is based on demand price—integrating uncertainty and prospective returns from ownership, and supply price—relating to production and finance costs of capital goods. In Minsky's words, expected returns "present views about the future, and therefore are prone to change as views about the future change" (Minsky 1975, p. 95). Thus, for investment to take place the demand price must exceed the supply price. Using Keynes's concepts of "borrower's risk" and "lender's risk," Minsky built into his model of "Financial Keynesianism" the concept that the demand price is downwardly adjusted to reflect the risk to the borrower of exceeding internal funds (borrower's risk) while the supply price is upwardly adjusted to account for the increased risk to the lender (lender's risk) as the borrower assumes greater debt. When expectations are high, the demand price is also high in relation to the supply price, engendering investment and generating growth. Undertaking investment, in turn, is the main determinant of aggregate profit flows that at the end validate the optimistic expectations. Euphoria then sets in, decreasing lenders' and borrowers' risks, bringing about the lowering of margins of safety until expectations are revised or fall short. When aggregate investment falls, so do profit flows, thus invalidating past investment decisions. "A fundamental characteristic of our economy," Minsky wrote in 1975, "is that the financial system swings between robustness and fragility and these swings are an integral part of the process that generates business cycles."

Minsky's *Stabilizing an Unstable Economy* (1986) suggested a framework within which policy interventions could ameliorate this inherent instability. His agenda for policy reform addressed four areas—"big government (size, spending, and taxing), an employment strategy (employment of last resort), financial reform, and market power"(Minsky 1986, p. 295).

Hyman Minsky was an independent thinker, a real-world economist, and a persuasive policy advocate.

SEE ALSO *Bubbles; Business Cycles, Empirical Literature; Business Cycles, Political; Business Cycles, Real; Business Cycles, Theories; Casino Capitalism; Economic Crises; Economics, Post Keynesian; Financial Instability Hypothesis; Financial Markets; Keynes, John Maynard; Loan Pushing; Ponzi Scheme*

BIBLIOGRAPHY

Minsky, Hyman P. 1957a. Central Banking and Money Market Changes. *The Quarterly Journal of Economics* 71: 171–187.

Minsky, Hyman P. 1957b. Monetary Systems and Accelerator Models. *American Economic Review* 47: 859–883.

Minsky, Hyman P. 1959. A Linear Model of Cyclical Growth. *Review of Economics and Statistics* 41: 133–145.

Minsky, Hyman P. 1963. Can "It" Happen Again? In *Banking and Monetary Studies*, ed. Dean Carson. Homewood, IL: Richard D. Irwin.

Minsky, Hyman P. 1965. The Role of Employment Policy. In *Poverty in America*, ed. Margaret S. Gordon. San Francisco: Chandler.

Minsky, Hyman P. 1969. Private Sector Asset Management and the Effectiveness of Monetary Policy: Theory and Practice. *Journal of Finance* 24: 223–238.

Minsky, Hyman P. 1972. Financial Instability Revisited: The Economics of Disaster. In *Reappraisal of the Federal Reserve Discount Mechanism*, Board of Governors, Federal Reserve System.

Minsky, Hyman P. 1975. *John Maynard Keynes*. New York: Columbia University Press.

Minsky, Hyman P. 1986. *Stabilizing an Unstable Economy*. Connecticut: Yale University Press.

Minsky, Hyman P. 2005. *Induced Investment and Business Cycles*, ed. Dimitri B. Papadimitriou. United Kingdom: Edward Elgar.

Papadimitriou, Dimitri B. 1992. Minsky on Himself. In *Financial Conditions and Macroeconomic Performance: Essays in Honor of Hyman P. Minsky*, eds. Steven Fazzari and Dimitri B. Papadimitriou. New York: M.E. Sharpe.

Papadimitriou, Dimitri B., and L. Randall Wray. 1998. The Economic Contributions of Hyman P. Minsky: Varieties of Capitalism and Institutional Reform. *Review of Political Economy* 10 (2): 199–225.

Dimitri B. Papadimitriou

MINSTRELSY

The twelfth-century term *minstrelsy* designated a form of local entertainment originally performed by professionals paid by European lords. Later, these professionals became traveling entertainers, and the male roving minstrel connoted either a local or an itinerant performer. Minstrels often were hounded by church officials and town authorities during minstrelsy's heyday in Europe during the eleventh to fifteenth centuries. Walking from town to town with a harp or viol on their backs, the minstrels' brightly colored clothes, dance slippers, nonbearded faces, and close-shorn hair are said to be vestiges of the Teutonic bard and the mime of the Roman theater. An integral part of many gatherings, including those occurring in noblemen's halls, marketplaces, and along pilgrim pathways, minstrels sang stories about the Christian saints, the scriptures, and heroes. They accompanied themselves instrumentally and also danced and performed acrobatic stunts to further the entertainment value.

Some scholars believe medieval minstrels transmuted Roman theatrical practice into liturgical drama. This transfer of form and aesthetic occurred primarily in France. High-born minstrels (*trouvères* and *troubadours*) were said to practice a "gay science," and their poetry was considered the product of nobility. With this heightened social status, minstrels in Paris incorporated themselves, building their own church and hospital. However, as soon as the minstrels were economically successful and accepted by society, they came to be imitated by a lower class of performers. The low-culture minstrels in the medieval period imitated the high-culture minstrels through exaggeration. In the lower-culture version of European minstrelsy, the traditional bright costumes became garish, clever lyrics became bawdy, and the music was less lyrical.

Minstrelsy experienced a renaissance in the United States when, in a northern city around 1828, the white actor Thomas Dartmouth Rice (1808–1860) imitated an African American slave whom he had seen dancing to a song known as "Jumpin' Jim Crow." Rice either bought or stole the black man's clothes. He performed the song and dance as an entr'acte, and legend has it that Rice became an overnight sensation. Rice performed the Jim Crow character for the rest of his career. His costume—a tattered coat and too-short pants, oversized shoes, and a felt hat, along with blackface makeup—became the look of the early American minstrel until 1840. At that time, the Virginia Minstrels formed in New York City. Made up of Dan Emmett, Billy Whitlock, Dick Pelham, and Frank Brower, the Virginia Minstrels' costumes and songs, accompanied by fiddle, tambourine, bones, and banjo, were more refined than those of Rice. The Virginia Minstrels began composing songs still familiar to this day, including "Old Dan Tucker" and "Jimmy Crack Corn." Blackface minstrelsy was extremely popular in the Bowery and the Five Points districts of New York City, particularly among young, recently urbanized men, and minstrel troupes began performing primarily in northern cities, eventually traveling to the West to mining camps and then into Australia and New Zealand. American blackface minstrels also traveled east to England, Scotland, Ireland, and even to parts of Africa.

Blackface minstrelsy in America became embroiled in local and national politics during the 1850s after performers found fault with the women's suffrage and antislavery movements. It was at this time that the well-known stereotypes of African Americans were cultivated and refined: the loud-mouthed plantation mammy, the overdressed male dandy, the sexually promiscuous light-skinned woman, and the compliant Uncle Tom. In the years after the Civil War (1861–1865), African Americans flooded the minstrel stage, creating a rivalry between white men who claimed authenticity as minstrel performers and black men who stated they were the more "legitimately" black and therefore better performers than the imitative blacks. Women, both black and white, also began performing in the 1870s, and they too had rivals from the ranks of female impersonators who had performed as part of the minstrel shows since the 1840s. By 1890 American minstrelsy became a primarily amateur activity on the popular stage, though vestiges of minstrelsy can be easily identified in vaudeville, musical revues, and American musical theater.

Minstrelsy did continue professionally in the United States on radio and in early television. The radio show *Amos 'n' Andy*, performed by two white men, Freeman Gosden (1899–1982) and Charles Correll (1890–1972), premiered in 1928. Gosden and Correll created two African American characters that based much of their situational humor on sketches born in the minstrel shows. In 1951 CBS introduced a television version of *Amos 'n'*

Andy featuring African American actors—the first of its kind on American television. Though popular with white and black audiences, *Amos 'n' Andy*'s dependency on minstrelsy stereotypes and the NAACP's campaign against their perpetuation on television led to the canceling of the show in 1953, though it ran in reruns until 1966.

SEE ALSO *Blackface; Entertainment Industry; Jim Crow; Race; Racism*

BIBLIOGRAPHY

Bates, Alfred, ed. 1906. *The Drama: Its History, Literature, and Influence on Civilization.* Vol. 7. London: Historical Publishing Company.

Bean, Annemarie, James V. Hatch, and Brooks McNamara, eds. 1996. *Inside the Minstrel Mask: Readings in Nineteenth-Century Blackface Minstrelsy.* Hanover, NH: Wesleyan University Press and University Press of New England.

Annemarie Bean

MINTZ, SIDNEY W.
1922–

Sidney Mintz earned his bachelor's degree in psychology from Brooklyn College in 1943 and his PhD in anthropology from Columbia University in 1951. Starting in 1948 in Puerto Rico on a now-famous collaborative research project directed by Julian Steward, Mintz's historical ethnographic research in the Caribbean laid the foundation for significant contributions in anthropology and history. His wide-ranging oeuvre addresses and helped to stimulate research and debate in various topical areas, including plantation societies, slavery and rural proletarianization, race and colonialism, peasantries and internal market systems, life history, and the anthropology of food and eating. Writing against the habitual tendency to view social systems as relatively self-contained and internally coherent, Mintz's anthropology—influenced by the German political philosopher Karl Marx and global in its implications—underscores the dialectical interconnections between seemingly distinct regions and peoples in the modern world; between the rich and the impoverished. With ethnographic data from the Caribbean, Mintz has examined sociocultural dimensions of European colonial capitalist expansion and its consequences for both regions.

Mintz's study of sugar plantation agriculture in Puerto Rico, and the changes brought about by the consolidation of family-owned estates into capital-intensive, corporate-owned latifundia, contributed to shifting anthropology away from its near-exclusive focus on so-called traditional societies and, correspondingly, helped establish the compelling need for the discipline to attend to the impact of European and North American power. One product of this research, *Worker in the Cane* (1960), is also celebrated as an early example showing the value of the life history in ethnographic writing.

Insistently comparative and historical in his approach, Mintz followed upon his Puerto Rico research with fieldwork in Jamaica and Haiti in the 1950s and early 1960s. His studies of rural small farmers and market women who traded these farmers' produce in local marketplaces led to various seminal contributions. Among them was the notion of the "proto-peasantry," a term Mintz coined to characterize the informal agricultural and marketing economy that grew up in the very teeth of slavery, laying the foundation for vibrant rural communities that developed after slavery ended in many Caribbean societies. A few of Mintz's choicest essays based on research in Puerto Rico, Jamaica, and Haiti are collected in his *Caribbean Transformations* (1974).

A hallmark of Mintz's scholarship, then, is its relational quality, that ability to show how seemingly distinct, sometimes distant, social worlds shape one another. For example, in *The Birth of African American Culture* (coauthored with Richard Price, 1992), the authors eschew conventional models prevailing at the time that posit relatively monolithic "African" and "European" cultures coming into contact, and the primacy of these prior cultural traditions in shaping their descendants' adaptations to the New World. Instead, Mintz and Price proposed a more dynamic model that emphasized the formative role social conditions in the Americas played in shaping complex processes of amalgamation and change Africans and Europeans underwent, with their vastly different access to power. Through their everyday, sometimes intimate interactions, blacks and whites *remade* each other. This and others of Mintz's generative contributions to the study of New World slavery relied on his grasp of the contradictions in the institution of plantation slavery itself, and his ethnographic appreciation for the determined inventiveness with which slaves exploited those systemic paradoxes to assert their dignity and humanity.

In his benchmark study, *Sweetness and Power* (1985), Mintz provided an expanded view of the complex, centuries-long, fundamentally transforming processes of capitalist globalization. There, the view from Caribbean cane fields that shaped Mintz's earlier work is joined with a corresponding examination of European workers, consumers, and owners who were mollified by and profited from the labor of Caribbean plantation workers. As one follows the profound changes that the colonial sugar economy brought about in diet, consumption habits, and social/cultural meaning in England and the Western world, cus-

tomary antimonies between production and consumption, plantation slaves in the Americas and the European working class, the "West" and its Caribbean "Others" are called into question and undermined.

SEE ALSO *Anthropology, U.S.; Caribbean, The*

BIBLIOGRAPHY

Guisti Cordero, Juan A. 1996. Para leer a Mintz … en Puertorriqueño: Una Approximación bibliográfica y crítica. *Fundamentos* 3–4.

Mintz, Sidney W. 1960. *Worker in the Cane: A Puerto Rican Life History.* New Haven, CT: Yale University Press.

Mintz, Sidney W. 1974. *Caribbean Transformations.* Chicago: Aldine.

Mintz, Sidney W. 1985. *Sweetness and Power: The Place of Sugar in Modern History.* New York: Penguin.

Mintz, Sidney W. 1996. *Tasting Food, Tasting Freedom: Excursions into Eating, Culture, and the Past.* Boston: Beacon.

Mintz, Sidney W., and Richard Price. 1992. *The Birth of African American Culture: An Anthropological Approach.* Boston: Beacon.

Scott, David. 2004. Modernity That Predated the Modern: Sidney Mintz's Caribbean. *History Workshop Journal* 58.

Charles V. Carnegie

MIRABEAU, MARQUIS DE

SEE *Quesnay, Francois.*

MIRACLES

The idea of miracles was not invented by Christians; the terminology is endemic to theism and has always formed part of the language of religious discourse, in other religions and in paganism, meaning the wonder caused in man by events beyond his understanding. Since the Gospels contain accounts of miracles, an understanding of the miraculous is central to Christianity, but because of its use in other theistic contexts, it has always been a point of discussion. In the early twenty-first century the word "miracle" is given a limited meaning by dictionaries which generally describe a "miracle" as: "an event exceeding the known powers of nature owing to special intervention by a deity or of some supernatural agency." This is to stress the etymology of the English word "miracle," which derives its meaning from the Latin *mirare*, meaning "to wonder." Exclusive stress is thereby laid on that which causes wonder and amazement. Popular use of the word unfortunately suggests that the more that is known about the laws of nature the less room there is for intervention by God. Miracle is then seen as opposed to nature, in terms of inexplicable wonder, but that is not the basic understanding of miracle within the Christian church. In the ancient world, the statement "the world is full of miracles" would not have meant "the constant infraction of the course of this world" principally because the notion of the law of nature was not used; it would have meant "everything created is a wonder issuing from the hand of God."

The ideas underlying the English word "miracle" are complex. In the Bible it translates more than one synonym in Hebrew, Greek, and Latin. In the New Testament, certain words and actions of Christ are called "miracles," and the same word is used at times in English translations of the Old Testament. But in Hebrew the words translated by "miracle" are *mopet* (a prodigy), *ot* (a sign), and *nipla* (a marvel), and in Greek these events are called by other names, such as *dunamis* (an act of power) and, most often of all, *semeon* (a sign). The Latin Bible did not use *miraculum* for any of these; they were rendered mainly as *signum*, though *virtus*, *mirabilia*, *prodigia*, or *portentum* were also used. The word *miraculum* entered Christian vocabulary from another source; its root, *miror*, "I marvel," was widely used in classical literature in describing any event that gave rise to this reaction, but the main word used both in Scripture and in the writings of the early church fathers was *signa*, "a sign," stressing theological meaning rather than psychological reaction. For the early church there is only one miracle, that of creation, with its corollary of re-creation by the resurrection of Christ. God, they held, created the world out of nothing in six days, and within that initial creation he planted all the possibilities for the future. All creation was, therefore, both "natural" and "miraculous." Everyday events—the birth of children, the growth of plants, rainfall—were all "daily miracles," signs of the mysterious creative power of God at work in the universe. But it was always possible that people would become so accustomed to these daily miracles that they would no longer be moved to awe by them and would need to be provoked to reverence by unusual manifestations of God's power. Such events were also within the original creation, hidden within the nature and appearance of things, which at times caused "miracles" that seemed to be contrary to nature but were in fact inherent in it. The most usual channel for these "hidden causes" to be made manifest was the prayers of the saints, living and dead, through whom the re-creating work of Christ was revealed. Events happened in nature or miraculously, but both were equally the work of God.

To pose only the question "How does this happen?" to any event need not exclude the older question "Why does this happen, what does it mean?" The "why" and the "how" questions about miracles can be equally useful.

Miracles and nature were for centuries put on an equal footing as signs from God to man. However, in the twelfth century a distinction was found possible in the relationship between miracles and events of other kinds. While miracles were an accepted way in which Christians were in touch with the supernatural, other modes of supernatural contact to some extent were distinguished from miracles. Most of all, a distinction was made between miracle and magic. The "arts of magic" were consistently forbidden in the Christian church as being a manipulation and distortion of creation by mankind. Edicts of church councils and disciplinary directions in penitentials alike forbade magical practices to Christians throughout the Middle Ages. The church's teachings on magic did not change, nor did the disregard for those teachings at a popular level decrease. In fact, in the twelfth century the revival of learning, and the interest in how things happened rather than why, led to an increase in the amount of magic practiced, and discussion of the question of the mechanics of events began to predominate over the question of their significance.

Modern-day miracles are often connected with the saints, those who are thought to have most clearly embodied the love and power of God in their lives. Miracles are recognized as signs that God is able to work uniquely through those nearest to Him in charity, especially in healing sickness; such signs of this work of God will be seen both in the lives of saints and also after their deaths. This view is connected with the theology of Christ as the Second Adam, re-creating all the world in a redeemed form so that a new relationship is set up between redeemed humanity and God's mercy. Such a perspective is often seen in the stories about the new relationship of love and respect between the saints and the four elements of air, earth, fire, and water; the life of plants, animals and birds, as well as humans, were then seen to be miracles in both senses of the word. Miracles can then be understood as both natural and significant, as a normal part of redeemed creation.

SEE ALSO *Roman Catholic Church*

BIBLIOGRAPHY

Cavadini, John C., ed. 1999. *Miracles in Jewish and Christian Antiquity: Imagining Truth.* Notre Dame, IN: University of Notre Dame Press.

Chenu, M. D. 1968. *Nature, Man, and Society in the Twelfth Century.* Eds. and trans. Jerome Taylor and Lester K. Little. Chicago: University of Chicago Press.

Lewis, C. S. 1950. *Miracles: A Preliminary Study.* London: Geoffrey Bles.

Ward, Benedicta. 1982. *Miracles and the Medieval Mind: Theory, Record, and Event, 1000–1215.* London: Scholar Press.

Benedicta Ward

MIRANDA RIGHTS

SEE *Interrogation.*

MIRROR REPRESENTATION

SEE *Constituency.*

MISANTHROPY

Misanthropy refers to the tendency in people to focus on others' negative rather than positive characteristics and qualities. In social psychology, the tendency is reflected in people's inclinations to regard the positive behaviors of others as being caused by the circumstances a person is in (e.g., abiding by prosocial norms or as a result of ulterior motives), but to see others' negative behaviors as being caused by an individual's own personality. Thus, when one is misanthropic, one credits others for their bad behavior but explains away and does not credit others for their good behavior. This also has implications for how much information one is willing to take in before judging others (more for supposed positive qualities).

The word *misanthropy* has also been used to refer to a belief that people in general are not to be trusted because they are driven by selfish motives with little concern for the group or the greater society. The misanthropic theme can be seen in related constructs, such as anomie and alienation, in the sociology literature, and it is also reflected in social science research that deals with the study of negative attitudes, such as prejudice toward people from different cultural groups. However, *misanthropy* is generally used to refer to a dislike of all humans, not just those who are members of groups to which one does not belong.

The concept of misanthropy is also reflected in many classics in political and social philosophy—for example, Machiavelli (1469–1527) and Thomas Hobbes (1588–1679)—and in literature. A widely recognized example is the character Alceste from the comedic play *Le Misanthrope* (1666) by the French writer Molière (1622–1673). In the play, which takes place in seventeenth-century Paris, Alceste is disgusted by the corrupt and socially manipulative nature of human life. The play provides many details as to how Alceste has arrived at such attitudes and beliefs—namely, by being embroiled in lawsuits that are not judged in unbiased fashion and by his romantic interest, Célimène, a young widow who entices various suitors in addition to Alceste.

In Molière's play, Alceste's misanthropic attitude is the result of his negative life circumstances. In addition to such precipitating factors, a misanthropic attitude is usually thought to result from a person's inadequacies or insecurities or his or her negative mood or outlook. For example, research has shown that people who are temporarily led to feel good about themselves before learning about a person they do not know, remember more positive and less negative things about the person. However, control participants nevertheless display a misanthropic outlook in their perceptions of others.

Thus, based on recent scientific research in social cognition, it can be said that misanthropes are not necessarily unusual or rare. In a sense, most people have the capacity for negative and ungenerous perceptions about others. What may distinguish this general sense of misanthropy from that ascribed to specific, individual misanthropes is that misanthropes become known for their misanthropy. Most people, though, may not want to be known for having such thoughts or feelings about their fellow human beings. The question then is, why should most people have a tendency to be misanthropic?

Social cognition research has provided an answer to this perplexing question. In modern times, most societies and the smaller social systems within them are relatively stable, in that most of the behavior people enact tends to be neutral or of a *prosocial* nature. Given that there is a norm for behavior that supports the group or society, most people when trying to make sense of others around them cannot assume that others behave prosocially because of the type of people they are. Other people might be behaving as they are because they are conforming to the established prosocial norm. Consequently, this leaves people, as social perceivers, with a sense of social uncertainty about others' motives, thus laying the foundation for social vigilance and misanthropy. Thus, misanthropy may be taken to reflect a basic mental framework people use to make sense of others, with an eye to reducing interpersonal costs (i.e., assuming others are good and they turn out not to be). However, it is not impossible to change such views toward any one individual. People's suspicions of another's motives can be assuaged through more extended and positive social contact with that person. It might be that part of the basis for friendship rests in this process through which suspicions eventually give way to greater trust in others.

SEE ALSO *Misogyny*

BIBLIOGRAPHY

Ybarra, Oscar, 1999. Misanthropic Person Memory When the Need to Self-enhance Is Absent. *Personality and Social Psychology Bulletin* 25 (2): 261–269.

Ybarra, Oscar. 2002. Naive Causal Understanding of Valenced Behaviors and Its Implications for Social Information Processing. *Psychological Bulletin* 128 (3): 421–441.

Ybarra, Oscar, and Walter G. Stephan. 1996. Misanthropic Person Memory. *Journal of Personality and Social Psychology* 70 (4): 691–700.

Ybarra, Oscar, and Walter G. Stephan. 1999. Attributional Orientations and the Prediction of Behavior: The Attribution-Prediction Bias. *Journal of Personality and Social Psychology* 76 (5): 718–727.

Oscar Ybarra

MISCEGENATION

Miscegenation is generally defined as an intimate sexual relationship between individuals of different races. In practice, however, it has mostly referred to relationships between whites and people of color. Because of its pejorative connotation, the word is not generally used today to refer to interracial relationships.

While the term *miscegenation* did not exist until the late nineteenth century, interracial sexual intimacy was a matter for concern soon after the first Europeans and Africans settled permanently in the Americas in the 1500s and 1600s. In North America, English colonists founded Jamestown, Virginia, in 1607. It was only seven years later that Pocahontas and John Rolfe celebrated their marriage, which was unusual and sensational but not legally questionable. The growing presence of African slaves, however, generated significant legal questions about status, family, and heredity. In 1662, Virginia's colonial assembly declared that a child's status as slave or free was based on the status of the mother, and in 1691 it passed the first law against sexual relations between free English or other white women and nonwhites (including both Native Americans and "negroes" or "mulattoes"). The 1691 statute also provided for the banishment of any white who contracted a marriage across the racial line. While Virginia was the first colony to act comprehensively to bar interracial marriage and control interracial sex, other colonies followed. Of the thirteen original colonies, nine had laws against interracial marriage in effect at the time of the Revolution. Racial categorization in the colonial era and early history of the United States increasingly moved toward a black-white dichotomy, and policymakers as well as the general white populace came to see individuals with significant African ancestry as black.

Chattel slavery was also prevalent in colonial Latin America, though Spanish and Portuguese colonies initially enslaved Native Americans. The use of Native Americans as slaves, however, was quickly overshadowed by the importation of Africans, particularly as the Native American population declined due to intentional extermination and widespread disease. In the mid-1500s, the Brazilian economy shifted away from reliance on forced Native American labor and toward black chattel slavery, and Portugal began to import slaves to Brazil in 1549. The Catholic Church opposed interracial marriage and procreation early in the colonial period, and European states echoed this condemnation in Brazil and elsewhere. Nonetheless, interracial sexual relations between Portuguese and Spanish men and African and Native American women, which was often coerced, took place extensively in the colonial period and produced a significant mixed-race demographic. During the 1700s and early 1800s, a complex racial hierarchy developed in Latin America, with mixed-race populations increasingly gaining specific recognition as distinct groups. The cultural permissiveness toward interracial sexual contact transitioned toward legal and institutional support during these years as well.

The term *miscegenation* was coined in 1863 in the United States in the context of the critical 1864 election. Editors of a New York-based Democratic newspaper secretly produced a pamphlet advocating the immediate legalization of interracial marriage as a natural and proper implication of emancipating the slaves. They created the word *miscegenation* to describe such relationships, combining the Latin words *miscere*, meaning "to mix," and *genus*, or "race." Though the Democrats certainly did not support the idea of interracial marriage, they planned to lure Republicans into openly agreeing with the ideas in the pamphlet. Thus, they sent copies of the pamphlet to prominent Republicans, hoping that some would endorse it and provide the Democrats with a campaign issue, but the Republicans ignored the pamphlet. While their gambit failed to link the Republican Party to a controversial endorsement of racial equality, it did ignite a national discussion among white elites about the dangers of interracial procreation. At the height of Reconstruction, a few individuals challenged emerging criminal prohibitions on interracial marriage, and they even secured a short-lived court victory in Alabama. Ultimately, however, the U.S. Supreme Court allowed the states to regulate freely against interracial relationships, and most southern and western states took up the invitation. While the southeastern states primarily focused on relationships between African Americans and whites, southwestern and western states also identified Mexicans, Malays, Hawaiians, Asians, and Native Americans as unsuitable marriage partners for whites. In the late nineteenth and early twentieth centuries, blackness increasingly became defined strictly in legal terms, and several southern states moved toward the position that any African ancestry rendered an individual black. Several states actively prosecuted men and women, both white and nonwhite, for crossing the racial boundary. Legal penalties ranged from defining interracial cohabitation as a more serious misdemeanor than intraracial cohabitation to Alabama's two-to-seven year terms in the state penitentiary for interracial marriage, adultery, or fornication.

With the exceptions of Brazil and Cuba, most Latin American nations eliminated slavery in the mid-nineteenth century; Brazil and Cuba emancipated their slaves in the 1880s. Brazil sought to change its national racial complexion by actively soliciting white immigrants and banning black immigration in 1890. In conjunction with this policy, the state endorsed a policy of "whitening" that actively encouraged individuals of mixed racial ancestry to intermarry with whites. Social, legal, and cultural incentives led to increasing proportions of the population choosing to identify themselves as mixed race or white. While informal and social modes of discrimination persisted, Brazil and other Latin American nations largely eschewed the legal-formalistic path of racial domination that the United States embraced, and race was largely understood more as a continuum than as a binary in formal terms. Even in the United States, however, the emerging legal binary masked a finer-grained racial hierarchy based upon the greater social and economic advancements available to individuals with lighter skin colors, even if these individuals were not able to "pass" for white.

The first steps to dismantling the modern formal prohibitions against interracial intimacy in the United States took place in the courts. California's high court invalidated the state's ban on interracial marriage in *Perez v. Sharp* in 1948, claiming that the main state interest that the ban served was the reinforcement of the illegitimate doctrine of white supremacy. A few western states removed their bans through legislative action in the 1950s, but the legal prohibitions in the South remained until the U.S. Supreme Court first struck down Florida's stricter punishments for interracial cohabitation in *McLaughlin v. Florida* in 1964. The Court finally invalidated Virginia's antimiscegenation law in *Loving v. Virginia* in 1967. Scattered litigation, however, was required in the late 1960s and 1970s to ensure that *Loving*'s rule was respected throughout the nation by justices of the peace and other governmental officials asked to provide marriage licenses to mixed-race couples.

Despite these rulings, a core of social opposition to interracial marriage persists in the United States. As recently as November 2000, 40 percent of Alabama's voters rejected a symbolic amendment to Alabama's constitution that removed the ban on interracial marriage, which had been legally unenforceable since the Supreme Court's ruling in *Loving*. Some evidence also suggests that even in the contemporary United States, many individuals with interracial backgrounds conceal or downplay their black ancestry, despite the emergence of a greater social and political consciousness among mixed-race people.

Recent studies of Brazil and Cuba have challenged the myth of racial democracy, a general impression that racial discrimination was never a core element in either nation's political development. In reality, racial hierarchies remained deeply embedded in Brazilian and Cuban economy and society throughout the twentieth century. While interracial relationships did not have to be legitimized as they did in the United States, mixed-race individuals remained in subordinated systems supported by governmental institutions that refused to acknowledge the social and economic meaning of color. In recent years, movements seeking racial solidarity and empowerment have begun the hard work of dismantling these hierarchies, with mixed-race individuals and groups playing important roles in the process.

SEE ALSO *Marriage, Interracial; Race Mixing; Race Relations; Racism*

BIBLIOGRAPHY

Butler, Kim. 1997. *Freedoms Given, Freedoms Won: Afro-Brazilians in Post-Abolition São Paulo and Salvador.* New Brunswick, NJ: Rutgers University Press.

Helg, Aline. 1995. *Our Rightful Share: The Afro-Cuban Struggle for Equality, 1886–1912.* Chapel Hill: University of North Carolina Press.

Marx, Anthony. 1998. *Making Race and Nation: A Comparison of the United States, South Africa, and Brazil.* New York: Cambridge University Press.

Novkov, Julie. 2002. Racial Constructions: The Legal Regulation of Miscegenation in Alabama, 1890–1934. *Law and History Review* 20: 225–277.

Romano, Renee. 2003. *Race Mixing: Black-White Marriage in Postwar America.* Cambridge, MA: Harvard University Press.

Sawyer, Mark. 2005. *Racial Politics in Post-Revolutionary Cuba.* New York: Cambridge University Press.

Wallenstein, Peter. 2002. *Tell the Court I Love My Wife: Race, Marriage, and Law—an American History.* New York: Palgrave.

Julie Novkov

MISERY INDEX

The *Misery Index* is a simple objective measure of the economic condition obtained by summing the unemployment rate plus the annual rate of inflation.

Misery Index = Unemployment Rate + Annual Inflation Rate

This measure, initially known as the Economic Discomfort Index, was devised by Arthur Okun, who served as President Lyndon Johnson's chief economic adviser. As columnist Richard F. Janssen explained in

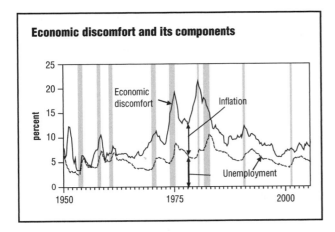

Figure 1

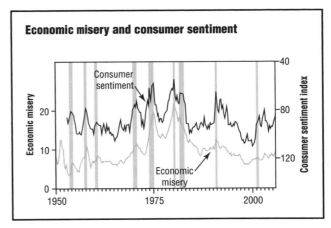

Figure 2

introducing the concept to readers of the *Wall Street Journal* in 1971:

> It is derived by simply lumping together the unemployment rate and the annual rate of change in consumer prices—apples and oranges, surely, but it is those two bitter fruits which feed much of our economic condition. The higher the index the greater the discomfort—we're less pained by inflation if the job market is jumping, and less sensitive to others' unemployment if a placid price level is widely enjoyed ... (p. 1).

The dramatic way in which the index has fluctuated since the mid-twentieth century is revealed by Figure 1 (the vertical bands indicate recessions).

Politicians, in particular, have found the index useful. George McGovern invoked the Economic Discomfort Index in scorning opponent Richard Nixon's economic record during the 1972 presidential campaign. Jimmy Carter used it in disparaging Gerald Ford in 1976. Ronald Reagan, who renamed it the Economic Misery Index, employed it in castigating Carter in 1980. Walter Mondale invoked the index in deriding Reagan, and Bill Clinton used it in successfully unseating George H. W. Bush in 1992. Speech writers drop the term from their vocabulary when the index is low, as they did during the Clinton administration.

Although the Misery Index ignores the poverty rate, the degree of income inequality, and both the government and the balance of payments deficits, there is evidence that it captures much of the public's feelings about the level of economic wellbeing. As Figure 2 shows, it tracks fairly closely the path of the University of Michigan's Index of Consumer Sentiment, which is based on the answers provided by telephone respondents to several questions, including:

"Would you say that you and your family are better off or worse off financially than you were a year ago?"

"Now looking ahead—do you think that a year from now you will be better off financially, or worse off, or just about the same as now?" (University of Michigan Surveys of Consumers Questionnaire, p. 2)

Note from the graph's right-hand scale that the Index of Consumer Sentiment is plotted inversely because a high level of the index indicates that the public is thinking positively about the economy. A casual inspection of the graph suggests a rather remarkable link between the two measures, although the survey evidence suggests that in the early 1980s and 1990s the Consumer Sentiment declined more dramatically than the Misery Index.

Okun relied on his intuition in deciding that unemployment and inflation would receive equal weight in constructing his Economic Discomfort Index. The fact that the correlation between his index and the Index of Consumer Sentiment is r = −0.74 reveals that his index does better than he had any right to expect. However, the following regression suggests that inflation deserves a somewhat higher weight than unemployment:

Consumer Sentiment = 109 − 2.49 Inflation Rate
(1.95) (0.17)

− 1.87 Unemployment Rate + e
(0.35)

1953:1 − 2005:4 $\bar{R}^2 = 0.607$

With the aid of hindsight, this regression implies that giving a 57% = 2.49/(2.49 + 1.87) weight to inflation and 42% = 1.87/(2.49 + 1.87) to unemployment might provide a slightly better measure of Economic Misery:

Economic Misery Revised = 42% Unemployment + 57% inflation

In their 2002 research Michael Lovell and Pao-Lin Tien provided more detail. It is reasonable to conclude that Okun's decision to give equal weight to unemployment and inflation was remarkably close to matching this retrospective regression.

BIBLIOGRAPHY

Janssen, Richard F. 1971. Appraisal of Current Trends in Business and Finance. *Wall Street Journal*, January 4.

Lovell, Michael. 1975. Why Is the Consumer Feeling So Sad? *Brookings Papers on Economic Activity*: 473–479.

Lovell, Michael, and Pao-Lin Tien. 2002. Economic Discomfort and Consumer Sentiment. *Eastern Economic Journal* 26 (1): 1–8.

University of Michigan Surveys of Consumers Questionnaire. http://www.sca.isr.umich.edu.

Michael C. Lovell

MISES, LUDWIG EDLER VON
1881–1973

The economist Ludwig Edler von Mises was born in Lemberg, Austria-Hungary (now L'viv, Ukraine). He entered the University of Vienna in 1900 and received a doctoral degree in law and economics in 1906. Appalled by the rise of more legislation governing capitalist economics, and of socialism and Marxism, Mises dedicated his life to a defense of freedom by integrating his version of Austrian economic theory into an imposing system of social philosophy that elucidates classical liberalism, socialism, and interventionism (a policy steering between liberalism and socialism).

From 1934 to 1940 in the storm haven of Geneva, Mises consolidated and added to the ideas in his earlier publications, producing his treatise *Nationalökonomie* (*Political Economy*) (1940). That year he fled Europe to New York City, where he revised the treatise, creating in English his magnum opus, *Human Action* (1949), and elaborated upon his system in books and essays until his death in New York in 1973.

Mises sought to ground his system in an epistemology based upon a physical-mental dualism, individualism, teleology, libertarianism, and subjectivism, and in rationality that flows perfectly into human action supporting a method able to yield *apodictic* truth. His method involves deduction from professedly a priori terms and proposi-

tions; methodological individualism to explain all social phenomena as unplanned outcomes of autonomous individuals' choices; abstraction from causal forces to create "imaginary constructions" used to explain "a contrario" the effects of that which has been abstracted; avoidance of mechanical analogies; and rejection of mathematical techniques. Empirical data, he contended, can neither confirm nor disconfirm his theory. His arguments that the empirical method and mathematical techniques are inappropriate in the field of social science conflicted with the trend of beliefs within the economics profession.

Liberalism, socialism, and interventionism agree on freedom, material prosperity, and peace as ends, differing only over the means to achieving them, Mises believed. He began with classical liberalism, reconstructing its foundations in sociology (which he renamed *praxeology*) and in economics (renamed *catallactics*). Starting with one isolated, egoistic individual, Mises's sociology explains that individuals choose to enter society: it is more profitable due to the greater productivity of division of labor and exchange, workable only, Mises insisted, given private ownership of the means of production. Social order arises because individuals choose to obey moral rules derived from human nature and the requirements of preserving social cooperation; named *praxeological laws* by Mises, they require private ownership, private contract without fraud, and pursuit of one's rational, "rightly-understood," long-run self-interest. Because not all people obey such laws, a state is necessary. Practicing laissez-faire by enacting only juristic laws to enforce the praxeological laws constitutes the pure, "unhampered," case of capitalism (renamed the *free market economy*).

Upon this sociology, Mises explicitly based his economic theory—which is more than a partial social science, he held—and his task was to work out the consequences of the praxeological laws. To construct his theory he at first abstracted from the influences of barter; exchange using money; entrepreneurs and the "market process;" savings, investment and capital accumulation; money credit, interest, and banking; and international trade in order to explain the economy of one isolated individual. He then built up his theory by restoring seriatim the influences he had abstracted from at first. His theory allowed him to reach several conclusions. Transitory monopoly may rarely arise, but generally no economic power exists; "financial pressure" occurs in markets, but not coercion (defined as deliberate human compulsion), hence freedom in the negative sense of absence of coercion is maximized, constrained only by juristic laws that enforce the praxeological laws. Harmony of interests exists because all interests are subordinated to "consumer sovereignty," effectuated by entrepreneurs (the consumers' "virtual mandataries") and by catallactic (not anticompetitive) competition. Efficiency and material prosperity are maximized. Under the gold standard and free banking, only small self-correcting trade cycles disturb stability. Eternal peace prevails.

Socialism establishes social ownership of the means of production, and from 1920 onward Mises defended his thesis that without private ownership of the means of production and without competition, market prices cannot come about, rendering rational economic calculation impossible. Socialist planning entails commands overriding consumer sovereignty, curtailing freedom and resulting in a loss of efficiency and material prosperity. Socialism does not promise peace.

Interventionism signifies a state that formally upholds private ownership, but intervenes in markets with the aim of curing short-run economic problems. All such policies, Mises demonstrated, are counterproductive. For example, interest rate policies to alleviate unemployment generate malinvestment and serious trade cycles. Persistent interventionism over the long run leads to a burgeoning state that broadens and deepens its controls, inexorably leading to socialism.

Thus, the only long-run policy alternatives, Mises concluded, are either laissez-faire liberalism or socialism. He argued that since the consequences of the former best satisfy ends sought by all, liberalism and its demands for private ownership and freedom are justified on utilitarian grounds.

Mises's work has stirred controversy over economic and philosophical issues. How, in precise philosophical terms, should his epistemology be classified? Can his method yield empirical truth? Can his praxeological laws be considered natural laws? Is his economic theory value-free? Mises's work remains an imposing system, a defense of freedom, and a riposte to socialism, Marxism, and interventionism.

BIBLIOGRAPHY

Gonce, Richard A. 2003. Review of *Ludwig von Mises: The Man and His Economics,* by Israel M. Kirzner. *American Journal of Economics and Sociology* 62 (3): 633–636.

Hutchison, T. W. 1964. *'Positive' Economics and Policy Objectives.* London: Allen and Unwin.

Meek, Ronald L. 1977. *Smith, Marx, and After: Ten Essays in the Development of Economic Thought.* London: Chapman and Hall.

Mises, Ludwig E. von. 1966. *Human Action: A Treatise on Economics.* 3rd rev. ed. Chicago: Regnery.

Myrdal, Gunnar K. [1920] 1953. *The Political Element in the Development of Economic Theory.* Trans. by Paul Streeten. London: Routledge.

Rothbard, Murray N. 1988. *Ludwig von Mises: Scholar, Creator, Hero.* Auburn, AL: Ludwig von Mises Institute.

Smith, Barry. 1990. Aristotle, Menger, Mises: An Essay in the Metaphysics of Economics. In *Carl Menger and His Legacy in Economics,* ed. Bruce J. Caldwell. Durham, NC: Duke University Press.

Richard A. Gonce

MISOGYNY

Deriving from the Greek *misogynia* (antiwoman), misogyny is an unreasonable fear or hatred of women. Misogyny differs from *male chauvinism*. The latter supports male political privileges and favors female subjugation in law; misogyny is an emotional prejudice based on phobia or dislike. Without specific political ends, misogyny has no formal ideological position other than to denigrate females.

Misogyny is by no means limited to modern Western civilizations. It occurs in many kinds of societies and at all levels of human social organization, including Stone Age cultures, and at all times in history. Studies by anthropologists and historians show that misogyny is, and always has been, widespread. Some examples of this prejudice among contemporary preindustrial peoples are described below.

In the highlands of New Guinea (Langness 1999), many tribesmen sleep apart from their wives, believing that women's bodies are, especially when menstruating, contaminating and even poisonous to males. In the Amazon rain forest of South America, many Native American men regard women as the work of the devil—not only intellectually inferior to men, but also scheming, destructive, even demonic (Gregor 1985). In many areas of sub-Saharan Africa, women's monthly flow is viewed with horror, and menstruating women are not allowed to appear in public. Many East African peoples practice clitoridectomy (surgical removal of the clitoris), a painful operation specifically designed to diminish a woman's sexual pleasure, which is considered immoral (unlike a man's).

In ancient Europe, the Greeks displayed an ingrained misogyny, often describing woman as one of the plagues inflicted upon man by the gods. Some Attic poets proposed that women were the source of *kakon* (evil) in the world. The ancient world was indeed populated with nefarious she-demons and sorceresses, such as the sinister Circe, who turned men into pigs, not to mention the Furies and the Harpies, foul-smelling half-human hags who persecuted men and boys. Classical antiquity was full of female monsters: sirens, maenads, nymphs, lamias, and the sea viragoes Scylla and Charybdis who drowned sailors off the coast of Sicily. The snake-haired gargoyle Medusa turned men to stone with a look. One of the earliest Greek poems,

"Woman" by Semonides (eighth century BCE), reviled females as being as stubborn as mules, as smelly as pigs, and as perilous to men as the untamed sea (see Coole 1988).

Many organized religions are highly misogynistic. The Christian Bible, the Muslim Koran, the Hebrew Torah, and the sacred Buddhist and Hindu texts frequently criticize women for various moral defects and condemn woman's body for the lust it inspires in men. Most religions blame woman for licentiousness and depravity and for committing original sin or its theological equivalent. In the Bible, for example, it is Eve, not Adam, who brings about the expulsion from paradise. Like the Greek Pandora, it is a woman who lets evil into the world. Many early Christian theologians—Thomas Aquinas (c. 1225–1274), Tertullian (fl. c. 200 CE), and Jerome (c. 347–419/20)—derided Eve and her descendants, calling woman "the devil's gateway" (Bloch 1989). The great writers of European literature, even William Shakespeare (1564–1616), bemoan woman's supposed tendency to gossip, to be shrewish, to dance with the devil, and to sway men from righteousness (Dijkstra 1996).

Many misogynists appear to be obsessed with female sexual anatomy, their fears centering on the vagina. In many cultures, women are even said to wear sharp teeth or knives in their sex organs, giving rise to the widespread motif of *vagina dentata*, the gnashing vulva. And wherever people believe in them, witches are primarily women (Brain 1996), and thousands of innocent women and girls have been burned at the stake as a result of this near-universal myth. Cultures throughout the world are full of pejorative mother-in-law and bad-wife jokes, but negative humor about fathers-in-law and husbands is rare. The evil-stepmother is a stock character in folktales around the world (e.g., Snow White), but evil stepfathers hardly appear.

As a sexual dogma or prejudice, misogyny appears to be virtually universal. Oddly, this gratuitous sex hostility was largely unreciprocated by institutionalized male-hatred among women until recent fulminations of a few radical feminists. For example, there is no word in English to describe female revulsion about men—no lexical obverse of misogyny. *Misanthropy*, which would be the semantic equivalent, simply means a dislike of humanity, not of males specifically. The one-sidedness of this prejudice is no less salient in preliterate cultures, and this fact in itself poses many questions about why so many men think so negatively about women in so many places. It also raises questions about the underlying ambivalence of male sexual desire, which seems so wedded to shame and guilt and thus with the need to scapegoat women. There seems to be something about being a human male that produces a conundrum in relating to women (as in the complaint, "can't live with 'em, can't live without 'em").

Misogyny then, is a frequent component of male psychology and of subsequent cultural representations, what might be called a male gender neurosis.

Can we identify the causes of misogyny? There are numerous theories, none totally convincing, as recent reviews (Gilmore 2001) show. Many theories rely upon the psychological concepts of ambivalence (contradictory love/hate feelings). One theory (Spiro 1997) holds that men are ambivalent about their own sexual impulses. They therefore experience mental stress, which is alleviated by denigrating the source of their desire—women. A second theory argues that men are conflicted about their powerful nonsexual needs for women (for food, caretaking, comforting, mothering). Thus, many men feel inferior to women and dependent upon them; many men cannot tolerate such imagined weakness in themselves, so they attack women as a way of restoring their damaged self esteem. Yet another theory (see Chodorow 1994) holds that all people are essentially bisexual and that many men are deeply disturbed by their own feminine side. Such conflicted men attack women as a way of denying or distancing their inner female. In various writings, Freud explained the universal male fear and disgust of menstrual blood as a product of castration anxiety: the flow of blood reminding men of the cut penis. Probably all of these factors play a role in misogyny, the causes of which are both cultural and psychological.

SEE ALSO *Gender; Inequality, Gender; Inequality, Political; Misanthropy*

BIBLIOGRAPHY

Bloch, R. Howard. 1989. Medieval Misogyny. In *Misogyny, Misandry, and Misanthropy*, eds. R. Howard Bloch and Frances Ferguson, 1–24. Berkeley: University of California Press.

Brain, James L. 1996. Witches and Wizards: A Male/Female Dichotomy? In *Denying Biology: Essays on Gender and Pseudo-Procreation*, eds. Warren Shapiro and Uli Linke, 75–88. Lanham, MD.: University Press of America.

Chodorow, Nancy. 1994. *Femininities, Masculinities, Sexualities: Freud and Beyond.* Lexington: University Press of Kentucky.

Coole, Diana. 1988. *Women in Political Theory: From Ancient Misogyny to Contemporary Feminism.* Sussex, U.K.: Wheatsheaf.

Dijkstra, Bram. 1996. *Evil Sisters: The Threat of Female Sexuality and the Cult of Manhood.* New York: Knopf.

Gilmore, David D. 2001. *Misogyny: The Male Malady.* Philadelphia: University of Pennsylvania Press.

Gregor, Thomas. 1985. *Anxious Pleasures: The Sexual Lives of an Amazonian People.* Chicago: University of Chicago Press.

Langness, Lewis L. 1999. *Men and "Woman" in New Guinea.* Novato, CA: Chandler and Sharpe.

Spiro, Melford. 1997. *Gender Ideology and Psychological Reality: An Essay on Cultural Reproduction.* New Haven, CT: Yale University Press.

David D. Gilmore

MISSIONARIES

Missionaries are individuals sent out as representatives of their particular religious group to proselytize, teach, and preach among nonadherents. Though often associated specifically with Christian missions, throughout history a wide variety of religious traditions have utilized missionaries to spread their religious visions and religious practices. Although missionaries usually attempt to attract converts by means of persuasion and through philanthropic endeavors, coercive methods have also been used at times. Criticism of traditional missionary practices has grown especially since the early twentieth century, leading some religious leaders to redefine missionary activity solely in terms of social service or political activity.

Though not frequently associated with missionary activity, Eastern religious traditions produced some of the earliest known missionaries. Ancient tradition holds that the Buddha himself instructed his followers to spread the Noble Truths of Buddhism. By the beginning of the Common Era, Buddhist missionaries entered China and spread their message through the efforts of figures such as Bodhidharma (c. early fifth century) and Kumārajīva (350–409/413). During this same period, Hindus accompanied traders and merchants and helped spread Hinduism to Southeast Asia. Buddhism in particular possessed key traits that aided missionary efforts. For example, Buddhism moved away from Hinduism's emphasis on the caste system, which in turn gave its followers greater freedom in their interactions with others from different social classes.

Since the late nineteenth century, Hindu and Buddhist missionary activity has increased. Hindu missionaries have gained a significant number of converts in Western nations, especially the United States. Swami Vivekananda, for example, established the Ramakrishna Mission and famously introduced many Americans to Hindu beliefs and practices at the World Parliament of Religions in Chicago in 1893. Other key Hindu mission movements during the twentieth century include the International Society for Krishna Consciousness (ISKCON) as well as Paramahansa Yogananda's Self Realization Fellowship, which combined Hindu beliefs and practices with scientific and psychological concepts. Nichiren Shōshū, a particularly mission-oriented form of Buddhism, developed during the thirteenth century and has been reinvigorated during the twentieth century through the Sōka Gakkai organization. Similarly, in the mid-twentieth century the Indian politician Bhīmrāo Rām Ambedkar (1891–1956) established the Bharatiya Buddha Mahasabha organization in order to encourage Hindus to convert to Buddhism. Ambedkar viewed Buddhism as a solution to the social inequality associated with the Hindu caste system, and he gained a large following among fellow Dalits ("untouchables") who represented the lowest stratum of the caste system.

Judaism also is not usually associated with proselytism, yet there is evidence to suggest extensive Jewish missionary activity in the Roman Empire, especially during the first century CE. Following the Jewish revolts in 66–73 and 132–135, however, laws were passed prohibiting conversion to Judaism, which greatly diminished the number of converts. Since that time converts have entered Judaism mainly through marriage, though there is significant debate within contemporary Judaism over whether or not active proselytism should be encouraged to counter the impact of the increasing number of marriages of Jews to non-Jews.

From its inception, Christianity has demonstrated a strong missionary impulse based on Jesus' command that his disciples spread the Christian message to nonbelievers. Carried out initially by figures such as Saint Paul, missionary activity eventually was linked to territorial expansion and official state policy beginning in the fourth century, when Christianity became the official religion of the Roman Empire. Throughout the next several centuries church leaders of the Roman West and the Orthodox East encouraged missionary activity throughout Europe among Germanic and Slavic peoples. These efforts eventually reached as far east as China, and often were led by monks such as Boniface and members of religious orders such as the Dominicans and the Franciscans beginning in the thirteenth century.

Beginning in the sixteenth century Christian missionary activity spread rapidly with the colonial expansion of modern nation-states into the Americas, Africa, and Asia; during this same period missionary efforts were reinitiated in regions including China, Persia, India, and parts of Africa. Among Catholics, the Jesuits were especially well known for their missionary zeal and discipline. The Jesuits often adapted their message to the cultural symbols and practices of the host culture (*inculturation*); the efforts of Matteo Ricci (1552–1610) in China are a good example. This contrasted sharply with the mission practices of other groups, such as the Spanish Franciscans in the Americas, who saw Christianity as inexorably tied to Spanish customs and civilization. Missionary activity by Protestants accelerated beginning in the eighteenth century with the spread of evangelical forms of piety in Britain and the American colonies. Women also began to play a much more visible role by the 1800s, accounting for half of the U.S. missionaries by the mid-nineteenth century.

Protestant and Catholic missionaries often brought with them knowledge of modern technical innovations and Western educational and medical ideas. By the twentieth century, in fact, some mission endeavors took on a solely philanthropic function as various twentieth-century religious leaders linked previous missionary efforts with cultural imperialism. But more conservative approaches that emphasized conversion continued to grow, as seen in the rapid global spread of Pentecostal forms of Christianity beginning in the twentieth century, as well as the growth of new religious movements such as Mormonism.

Historically, Islam also has had a strong missionary impulse. Although few Muslims throughout history have identified themselves specifically as missionaries, traditional Islam calls for the steady expansion of Islamic rule into non-Muslim regions, and indeed after the death of the Prophet Muhammad in 632 it spread rapidly across the Arabian Peninsula, Northern Africa, Spain, Persia, and Central Asia. Nevertheless, non-Muslims who are "peoples of the Book" (i.e., Jews and Christians) often have been allowed to maintain their faiths within Muslim societies, as was frequently the case during the Middle Ages—this despite the fact that Muslims believe the Jewish and Christian scriptures to have been corrupted over the years. Whereas traditional Islamic teachings enjoin Muslims to help spread Islam for the benefit of humanity, the Prophet Muhammad specifically repudiated conversion by force. Pagan groups usually did not have the same protected status as Jews and Christians in Muslim societies during the Middle Ages, and all non-Muslim subjects were expected to recognize Muslims' final authority in society.

In general, missionary activity has been criticized for its sometimes complicit role in the oppression of subjugated peoples and for its contribution to religious conflict. A sharp delineation between religious believers and nonbelievers, for example, often has served as an underlying justification for imperialistic colonial endeavors. Other critics insist that a focus on conversion distracts from the need for more practical reforms in social and political spheres, but missionaries often have often been at the forefront of educational and philanthropic efforts, and have sought to alleviate human suffering. Furthermore, their cross-cultural endeavors have initiated contact between different religious traditions and helped generate religious change and innovation.

SEE ALSO *Protestantism; Roman Catholic Church*

BIBLIOGRAPHY

Feldman, Louis H. 1993. *Jew and Gentile in the Ancient World: Attitudes and Interactions from Alexander to Justinian.* Princeton, NJ: Princeton University Press.

Hodgson, Marshall G. S. 1977. *The Venture of Islam: Conscience and History in a World Civilization.* 3 vols. Chicago: University of Chicago Press.

Jenkins, Philip. 2002. *The Next Christendom: The Coming of Global Christianity.* New York: Oxford University Press.

Tweed, Thomas A., and Stephen R. Prothero. 1999. *Asian Religions in America: A Documentary History.* New York: Oxford University Press.

Walls, Andrew F. 1996. *The Missionary Movement in Christian History: Studies in the Transmission of Faith.* Maryknoll, NY: Orbis.

Joseph W. Williams

MISSPECIFICATION TESTS

SEE *Specification Tests.*

MITCHELL, WESLEY CLAIR
1874–1948

Wesley Mitchell pioneered the empirical study of business cycles. A founder of the National Bureau of Economic Research, he was one of the major figures within the institutionalist movement in American economics.

Mitchell was born in Rushville, Illinois, and brought up in Decatur, Illinois. He entered the new University of Chicago in 1892, obtaining his AB degree in 1896 and his PhD in 1899. At Chicago he came under the influence of Thorstein Veblen and John Dewey, but it was J. Laurence Laughlin who supervised his PhD dissertation, published in 1903 as *A History of the Greenbacks.* In that year Mitchell moved to the University of California at Berkeley and then to Columbia University in New York in 1913. Except for a brief period at the New School for Social Research (1919–1922), which he helped to found, he remained at Columbia until his retirement in 1944. He was also director of research for the National Bureau of Economic Research (NBER) from its founding in 1920 until 1945 and a major figure in the founding of the Social Science Research Council (SSRC).

Mitchell wrote on many subjects, including rationality and economic activity (Mitchell 1910), the economics of the household (1912), the history of economics (1918), the distinction between making money and making goods (1923), and the links he saw between institutional and quantitative economics (1925), but Mitchell's major work was his 1913 book *Business Cycles.* Here Mitchell provided an "analytic description" of the course of business cycles consisting of four stages, with each stage setting the conditions for the next, and the cycle as a whole growing out of the institutions of the "money economy" in the form of the interaction of business decisions based on profit expectations, the behavior of the banking system, and the leads and lags in the movement of wages and prices. The book also commented on the shortcomings of many of the existing theories of the cycle.

After 1922 Mitchell continued his own work on cycles through the NBER. The original plan was for two books, later expanded to three. The first, *Business Cycles: The Problem and Its Setting* (1927), discussed existing theories and statistics and laid out the research agenda. The project grew, and with it a vast number of studies of particular aspects of the cycle and an array of measurement issues relating to timing, amplitude, and rates of change across successive cycles. This eventually resulted in the development of the "NBER method" of specific and reference cycles (Morgan 1990, pp. 44–56), presented in detail in the second book, *Measuring Business Cycles* (1946), coauthored with Arthur F. Burns. The final volume, which was supposed to be a theoretical volume, was never completed, although a part was published after Mitchell's death as *What Happens during Business Cycles* (1951).

Measuring Business Cycles was sharply attacked by Tjalling Koopmans of the Cowles Commission for engaging in "measurement without theory" (Koopmans 1947, p. 161). Mitchell did of course use theories as a guide to what data should be collected and examined, but he was not enthusiastic about enamored econometric methods.

Mitchell's great contribution was in the development of empirical research in economics, not only through his own work but also through the work he promoted via the NBER and SSRC. As Jeff Biddle pointed out in 1998, for Mitchell, it was only through such research that economics could become a useful tool in the solution of economic problems.

SEE ALSO *Business Cycles, Real; Koopmans, Tjalling*

BIBLIOGRAPHY

PRIMARY WORKS

Mitchell, Wesley Clair. 1903. *A History of the Greenbacks, with Special Reference to the Economic Consequences of Their Issue, 1862–65.* Chicago: University of Chicago Press.

Mitchell, Wesley Clair. 1910. The Rationality of Economic Activity. Pts. 1 and 2. *Journal of Political Economy* 18 (February): 97–113; (March): 197–216.

Mitchell, Wesley Clair. 1912. The Backward Art of Spending Money. *American Economic Review* 2 (June): 269–281.

Mitchell, Wesley Clair. 1913. *Business Cycles.* Berkeley: University of California Press.

Mitchell, Wesley C. 1918. Bentham's Felicific Calculus. *Political Science Quarterly* 33 (June): 161–183.

Mitchell, Wesley C. 1923. Making Goods and Making Money. Reprinted in *The Backward Art of Spending Money.* 1950. New York: Augustus M. Kelley.

Mitchell, Wesley C. 1925. Quantitative Analysis in Economic Theory. *American Economic Review* 15 (March): 1–12.

Mitchell, Wesley Clair. 1927. *Business Cycles: The Problem and Its Setting.* New York: National Bureau of Economic Research.

Mitchell, Wesley Clair. 1951. *What Happens during Business Cycles: A Progress Report.* New York: National Bureau of Economic Research.

Mitchell, Wesley Clair, and Arthur F. Burns. 1947. *Measuring Business Cycles.* New York: National Bureau of Economic Research.

SECONDARY WORKS

Biddle, Jeff. 1998. Social Science and the Making of Social Policy: Wesley Mitchell's Vision. In *The Economic Mind in America: Essays in the History of American Economics.* Ed. Malcolm Rutherford, 43–79. London: Routledge.

Koopmans, Tjalling C. 1947. Measurement without Theory. *Review of Economic Statistics* 29 (August): 161–172.

Mitchell, Lucy Sprague. 1953. *Two Lives: The Story of Wesley Clair Mitchell and Myself.* New York: Simon and Schuster.

Morgan, Mary S. 1990. *The History of Econometric Ideas.* Cambridge U.K.: Cambridge University Press.

Malcolm Rutherford

MIXED STRATEGY

In the theory of games a player is said to use a mixed strategy whenever he or she chooses to randomize over the set of available actions. Formally, a mixed strategy is a probability distribution that assigns to each available action a likelihood of being selected. If only one action has a positive probability of being selected, the player is said to use a pure strategy.

A mixed strategy profile is a list of strategies, one for each player in the game. A mixed strategy profile induces a probability distribution or lottery over the possible outcomes of the game. A (mixed strategy) Nash equilibrium is a strategy profile with the property that no single player can, by deviating unilaterally to another strategy, induce a lottery that he or she finds strictly preferable. In 1950 the mathematician John Nash proved that every game with a finite set of players and actions has at least one equilibrium.

To illustrate, one can consider the children's game Matching Pennies, in which each of two players can choose either heads (*H*) or tails (*T*); player 1 wins a dollar from player 2 if their choices match and loses a dollar to player 2 if they do not. This game can be represented as follows:

	H	T
H	(1, −1)	(−1, 1)
T	(−1, 1)	(1, −1)

Here player 1's choice determines a row, player 2's choice determines a column, and the corresponding cell indicates the payoffs to players 1 and 2 in that order. This game has a unique Nash equilibrium that requires each player to choose each action with probability one-half.

Another example is provided by the Hawk-Dove game, which has been used by evolutionary biologists to model animal conflicts:

	H	D
H	(0, 0)	(4, 1)
D	(1, 4)	(2, 2)

In this game any strategy profile in which one player chooses *H* and the other picks *D* is in equilibrium. Hence, there are two pure strategy equilibria, (*H,D*) and (*D,H*). In addition, there is a mixed strategy equilibrium in which each player selects *H* with probability 2/3.

One feature of a mixed strategy equilibrium is that given the strategies chosen by the other players, each player is indifferent among all the actions that he or she selects with positive probability. Hence, in the Matching Pennies game, given that player 2 chooses each action with probability one-half, player 1 is indifferent among choosing *H*, choosing *T*, and randomizing in any way between the two. Because randomization is more complex and cognitively demanding than is the deterministic selection of a single action, this raises the question of how mixed strategy equilibria can be sustained and, more fundamentally, how mixed strategies should be interpreted.

In an interpretation advanced in 1973 by John Harsanyi, a mixed strategy equilibrium of a game with perfect information is viewed as the limit point of a sequence of pure strategy equilibria of games with imperfect information. Specifically, starting from a game with perfect information, one can obtain a family of games with imperfect information by allowing for the possibility that there are small random variations in payoffs and that each player is not fully informed of the payoff functions of the other players. Harsanyi showed that the frequency with which the various pure strategies are chosen in these perturbed games approaches the frequency with which they are chosen in the mixed strategy equilibrium of the

original game as the magnitude of the perturbation becomes vanishingly small.

A very different interpretation of mixed strategy equilibria comes from evolutionary biology. To illustrate this, consider a large population in which each individual is programmed to play a particular pure strategy. Individuals are drawn at random from that population and are matched in pairs to play the game. The payoff that results from the adoption of any specific pure strategy will depend on the frequencies with which the various strategies are represented in the population. Suppose that those frequencies change over time in response to payoff differentials, with the population share of more highly rewarded strategies increasing at the expense of strategies that yield lower payoffs. Any rest point of this dynamic process must be a Nash equilibrium. In the special case of the Hawk-Dove game any trajectory that begins at a state in which both strategies are present converges to the unique mixed strategy equilibrium of the game. In other words, the long-run population share of each strategy corresponds exactly to the likelihood with which it is played in the mixed strategy equilibrium.

SEE ALSO *Evolutionary Games; Game Theory; Nash Equilibrium; Nash, John*

BIBLIOGRAPHY

Harsanyi, John C. 1973. Games with Randomly Disturbed Payoffs: A New Rationale for Mixed Strategy Equilibrium Points. *International Journal of Game Theory* 2: 1–23.

Maynard Smith, John. 1982. *Evolution and the Theory of Games.* Cambridge, U.K., and New York: Cambridge University Press.

Maynard Smith, John, and G. R. Price. 1973. The Logic of Animal Conflict. *Nature* 246: 15–18.

Nash, John F. 1950. Equilibrium Points in N-Person Games. *Proceedings of the National Academy of Sciences* 36 (1): 48–49.

Osborne, Martin J., and Ariel Rubinstein. 1994. *A Course in Game Theory.* Cambridge, MA: MIT Press.

Taylor, Peter D., and Leo B. Jonker. 1978). Evolutionarily Stable Strategies and Game Dynamics. *Mathematical Biosciences* 40: 145–156.

Rajiv Sethi

MOBILITY

Social mobility describes the fluidity or rigidity of a stratified system, or the degree of openness of a society that determines the extent to which individuals or groups can and do change their relative position or social status within that society. An analysis of social mobility examines the extent to which an individual's life chances or social position is a function of his or her social origin (i.e., the social status of the individual's parents). Nineteenth-century theorists of social mobility grappled with the emergence of industrial societies whose social organization and social relationships were qualitatively different than their feudal and agrarian predecessors. Questions of modernity that were prominent at the time animated much of this inquiry as well.

The underlying logic rested on the idea that the social organization of preindustrial societies, where an individual's location in the social structure was almost entirely determined by birth (often by ascribed characteristics), would give way to a more open system in which an individual's abilities and characteristics would determine his or her fortunes. The increasing bureaucratization and rationalism characteristic of newly industrializing societies were expected to give rise to meritocracy, in which individual merit would dictate outcomes more so than social origin. With increasing education and technological developments, intergenerational mobility should increase. Furthermore, as success becomes more focused at the individual level, the impetus for class solidarity should decrease.

RESEARCH TRADITIONS

Early social mobility research can be divided along several dimensions. One of these encompasses two distinct threads: *intragenerational mobility* (class mobility during the life course, typically occurring during one's career years) and *intergenerational mobility* (a change in class status between parents and offspring from one generation to the next). In both threads the focus was on explaining the likelihood of a difference in one's destination (or outcome) compared to one's origin. Another distinction in early mobility research was an emphasis on either individual mobility (e.g., status attainment research) or class mobility and formation (e.g., the position and change in relative power of specific strata or classes). Karl Marx's (1818–1883) theory of class formation and power and Max Weber's (1864–1920) notion of class and status groups were central influences in the latter line of inquiry.

Social theorists of mobility contrasted the rigid mobility structures characteristic of social systems organized by castes and those under feudalism with the "new" social and economic structure emerging in nineteenth-century industrializing nations. Feudalism and caste social systems, which were marked by little social mobility, were archetypes against which newly emerging social systems, which were marked by increasing mobility, were compared. A *caste* is a "hierarchy of endogamous divisions in which membership is hereditary and permanent" (Berreman 1960, p. 120). Contact between members of

different castes is limited and allocation to occupations is determined by an individual's caste membership. India's caste system was one of the most widely documented during the first half of the twentieth century. Though the subject of considerable debate, India's caste system was considered the most rigid of stratification systems, marked by its stability as the divisions were justified on religious principles to which almost everyone in the society subscribed.

From the eleventh through fifteenth centuries, feudalism, the chief social system explored in early writings about stratification, was the dominant mode of production in Europe that preceded capitalism. It was a hierarchical system with few strata, in which control of land and property granted social status and legal rights to rule. Power and social status were founded on ownership of land and control of peasants; membership in the noble class of lords, which was achieved primarily through birth or marriage, was necessary in order to exercise power. Feudalism was a relatively closed social system in which the distribution of goods and services was closely integrated with the hierarchy of the social status.

Following feudalism, the emergence of industrialization in the mid-eighteenth century and the changing economic and social system embodied in early capitalism allowed individuals in the merchant class to experience mobility not through birth or marriage but through their fortuitous role in creating markets for goods. Merchants played a key role in the expansion of markets for goods and in the production of goods that ushered in industrialization and early capitalism. They carried this out by developing and managing consumer markets, and by acquiring knowledge of consumer tastes, which allowed them to manage, fulfill, and profit from growing consumer demand. This class was a crucial force in shaping early capitalism, and merchants profited from their propitious position as the new economic system flourished.

As industrialization progressed during the first half of the twentieth century, social theorists such as Gerhard Lenski (1966) observed that mobility opportunities were beginning to increase steadily for a larger segment of society, namely workers in the industrial sector of the economy. This was especially true for those who had access to opportunities to become skilled at using emerging technology in the rapidly changing production process. European immigrants were absorbed rapidly into growing industries. Lenski argued that stratification (which he called a distributive system) was a function of the complexity and degree of technological sophistication of a society. The extent of inequality in a society varies with the amount of surplus in that society. Goods and services are distributed according to need when there is no surplus.

Within this framework, those who have control of the surplus of goods have more power.

A recurring theme throughout the mobility theories predominant at this time was the increasing role of technological advances in stratifying workers, allowing mobility for some and limiting it for others. Skilled workers were in an advantaged position relative to other workers to benefit from the new strata of higher-paying jobs created by these new technologies. Thus, mobility for certain groups of workers increased substantially during this period. Moreover, historians and social scientists document the strategies that both employers and white workers used to limit competition for these premium jobs by excluding blacks, Chinese, other racial and ethnic minorities, and white women from these burgeoning opportunities. Government subsidies aimed at increasing the education and training of workers (e.g., the GI Bill) were largely reserved for white men who took advantage of and benefited from these opportunities in substantial numbers, entrenching the widening gap between these workers and other marginalized workers.

Status attainment research became the chief lens with which to view this new opportunity structure during the 1950s. The principle assumption in status attainment research was that individual investments in education would allow for mobility of any worker, regardless of his social origins (many of these studies only involved men). In this tradition, status attainment research was concerned with the *allocation* of individuals into jobs or social positions (also referred to as *selection* in earlier work). Status attainment research examined an individual's position along a scale of occupational status. The emphasis was on determining the level of parental influence on the child's eventual occupational outcomes. The underlying idea was that parents with higher social status and good jobs can pass on to their children resources that aid them in the labor market—resources such as information about jobs and how to attain them, and access to networks, opportunities, and cultural capital.

Related to the status attainment paradigm is *human capital theory*, or its more recent variant, the *skills mismatch hypothesis*. Underlying all of these theories is the notion that the United States is largely an achievement-based society characterized by an open opportunity structure. The center of analysis in these theoretical frameworks is the individual and his or her corresponding traits; this focal shift stood in contrast to early stratification research in which the social structure of the society itself was the central focus. A critique of the status attainment and human capital approaches posits that they do not take into account important structural factors that may have an impact on the opportunity structure, and commensurately, the likelihood of mobility.

Proponents of a structural analysis of mobility turned their attention to assessing the influence of economic, political, and social forces on the opportunity structure and mobility opportunities. These contrasting approaches have also been situated within a supply/demand framework in which both the attributes individuals bring to the market and the demands of market institutions (e.g., which industries are experiencing growth or decline, which skills employers are seeking) are considered important factors bearing on opportunities for workers.

MOBILITY IN POSTINDUSTRIAL SOCIETIES

A large segment of social mobility research relies on comparative analyses of different countries, typically Western countries, because a society's stratification system is the implied unit of analysis in the paradigm's core theories (i.e., a central question is whether certain stratification systems enable more or less mobility). Robert Erikson and John Goldthorpe (1992) conducted an extensive cross-national comparison to address whether or not mobility was increasing in postindustrial nations. They found that the United States and Western European countries are not markedly different in mobility and that patterns of mobility were common over time, a pattern they described as a *trendless fluctuation*.

Large-scale structural changes of the later twentieth century, primarily deindustrialization and globalization, vastly changed the factors that mediate access to work and opportunity. Deindustrialization and the accompanying shift to a service, information, and technology-based economy created an increased demand both for higher-educated and skilled workers and for low-wage workers to fill the increasing number of service jobs that proliferated in the economy. An increasingly bifurcated workforce resulted. Higher-educated workers fared and continue to fare better in the labor market by all accounts. Thus, access to higher education became a determinative factor in an individual's labor market outcomes. Marked group differences (class, race, ethnicity) in access to education have always existed, but these disparities have greater consequence in the contemporary economy as the currency of education grows.

This inequality is further exacerbated by the dismantling of policies designed to enable equal access to higher education. Both lower-income and minority individuals have lower rates of college attendance and graduation; of those that do enroll in college, a smaller percentage actually finishes compared to white or middle-class students. The effect of school status on employment outcomes also contributes to this inequality given the difference in status of the schools that whites and minorities attend. This difference has been shown to contribute to differences in earnings, occupational attainment, and so on among workers with college degrees. Furthermore, education explains only 25 percent of the race gap in wages. Although different studies reveal different numbers, none has entirely removed the effect of race. Education plays a determinative role and improves the relative position of everyone who is able to access it; however, increasing evidence reveals that it has not been realized as the equalizing force that had been anticipated.

Another structural change that figures prominently in questions of mobility in postindustrial societies is the emergence of a globalizing economy. The globalization of labor has tightened and changed opportunities for workers. As companies reduced their workforces, moved production overseas, and instituted flexible work arrangements to remain competitive, job stability and wages fell and advancement opportunities diminished for many workers, particularly for lower-wage and lower-status workers at the bottom of the scale.

LIMITED SOCIAL MOBILITY FOR RACIAL AND ETHNIC GROUPS

Mobility chances vary significantly across different social groups in the contemporary United States. Ample evidence demonstrates that access to opportunity continues to be mediated by race and immigrant status, among other factors. Given the ongoing currency of education and skills in the postindustrial economy, group differences in access to quality education play a sizable role in this inequality. Persistent patterns of school segregation resulting from residential segregation are a key factor underlying continuing labor market disparities between white and minority workers. School segregation among primary and secondary schools has regressed to the levels that existed at the time of the desegregation order resulting from the 1954 *Brown v. Board of Education of Topeka* decision by the U.S. Supreme Court. Minorities are segregated into schools with substantially fewer resources, and consequently they receive a poorer education. Poor white children, on the other hand, do not face significant class-based school segregation, and in fact are more likely to attend schools with middle-class children than are black middle-class children. In addition, the decentralization of companies from urban centers to outlying suburbs, a development that followed the mass suburbanization of most large cities beginning in the 1950s, created what some theorists call a *spatial mismatch* between jobs and minority communities. This further decreased access to work and to attendant mobility opportunities.

Another explanatory factor for racial mobility disparities is access to information about jobs. Researchers have found that job seekers tend to find out about and pursue jobs through social networks. The quality of the informa-

tion in these networks varies widely; access to networks with higher-status individuals with better jobs yields better information and thus increased access to better jobs. Because the networks of most individuals are made up of the people with whom they regularly interact, these networks tend to be segregated by race. Additionally, mounting evidence points to the role of discrimination in the hiring process. Discrimination audit studies, in which equally qualified job applicants of different races apply for the same job, consistently reveal that employers are more likely to hire white applicants over equally qualified black or Latino applicants.

Even in the early years of the twenty-first century, the evidence supports the conclusion that an individual's origin continues to play a significant role in his or her eventual socioeconomic status. The expectation that this influence would decline in postindustrial nations has seemingly not come to bear to the extent that was anticipated; there does not seem to be a trend toward increasing mobility. There is an enormous debate over the subject; however, it has shifted to why and to what extent mobility has or has not increased. As societies and their economies evolve, transform, and become more complex, the number of factors to consider when determining an individual's chances of moving beyond his or her origins will continue to increase, demanding more complex models for understanding mobility.

SEE ALSO *Caste; Education, Unequal; Mobility, Lateral; Upward Mobility*

BIBLIOGRAPHY

Berreman, Gerald. 1960. Caste in India and the United States. *American Journal of Sociology* 66 (2): 120–127.

Blau, Peter, and Otis Duncan. 1967. *The American Occupational Structure.* New York: Wiley.

Dickerson, Niki T. 2002. Is Racial Exclusion Gendered? The Role of Residential Segregation in the Employment Status of Black Women and Men in the US. *Feminist Economics* 8 (2): 199–208.

Erikson, Robert, and John H. Goldthorpe. 1992. *The Constant Flux: A Study of Class Mobility in Industrial Societies.* Oxford and New York: Oxford University Press.

Fix, Michael, and Raymond J. Struyk, eds. 1993. *Clear and Convincing Evidence: Measurement of Discrimination in America.* Washington, DC: Urban Institute Press.

Glasmeier, Amy. 1990. The Role of Merchant Wholesalers in Industrial Agglomeration Formation. *Annals of the Association of American Geographers* 80: 394–417.

Green, Gary, Leann Tigges, and Daniel Diaz. 1999. Racial and Ethnic Differences in Job-Search Strategies in Atlanta, Boston, and Los Angeles. *Social Science Quarterly* 80 (2): 263–278.

Hearn, James C. 1991. Academic and Non-academic Influences on the College Destinations of 1980 High-School Graduates. *Sociology of Education* 64: 171–195

Kozol, Jonathan. 2005. *The Shame of the Nation: The Restoration of Apartheid Schooling in America.* New York: Crown.

Lenski, Gerhard. 1966. *Power and Privilege: A Theory of Social Stratification.* New York: McGraw-Hill.

Marx, Karl. [1852] 1973. The Eighteenth Brumaire of Louis Bonaparte. In *Karl Marx and Friedrich Engels: Selected Works.* Vol. 1, 394–487. Moscow: Progress Publishers.

Marx, Karl. [1894] 1959. *Capital.* Vol. 3. Moscow: Foreign Language Publications.

Orfield, Gary. 1993. School Desegregation after Two Generations: Race, Schools, and Opportunity in Urban Society. In *Race in America: The Struggle for Equality*, eds. Herbert Hill and James E. Jones, 234–262. Madison: University of Wisconsin Press.

Orfield, Gary, Erica D. Frankenberg, and Chungmei Lee. 2003. The Resurgence of School Segregation. *Educational Leadership* 60 (4): 26–30.

Pager, Devah. 2003. The Mark of a Criminal Record. *American Journal of Sociology* 108 (5): 937–975.

Sorokin, Pitirim. 1927. *Social Mobility.* New York: Harper.

Weber, Max. 1968. *Economy and Society: An Outline of Interpretive Sociology.* Eds. Guenther Roth and Claus Wittich, trans. Ephraim Fischoff et al. New York: Bedminster.

Wilson, William J. 1987. *The Truly Disadvantaged: The Inner City, the Underclass, and Public Policy.* Chicago: University Chicago Press.

Wilson, William J. 1996. *When Work Disappears: The World of the New Urban Poor.* New York: Knopf.

Niki T. Dickerson

MOBILITY, LATERAL

The term *lateral mobility* refers to movement among occupational categories that does not result in an improvement in occupational status. An occupational category is a set of jobs that comprise essentially the same list of skills and activities—examples are waiter, computer programmer, and college professor. These detailed occupations are also grouped into broader, more generalized occupational categories. For example, a waiter is in the service category, a computer programmer is in the technical category, and a professor is in the professional category.

Occupational mobility is significant because movement among occupations can be a strategy to improve economic position, whether over a lifetime or from generation to generation. A worker starting out in a relatively low-skilled, low-paid occupation may acquire work experience, develop skills, or use the earnings to invest in further education or training in order to move to a better-paid occupation. Low-paid workers may also invest in their children's educations and training, allowing for improvement in occupational status over generations.

However, not all occupational mobility results in improved status. Occupational mobility may be vertical—either upward or downward—or it may be lateral. Upward mobility would indicate improving economic prospects, while downward mobility would indicate the opposite. Lateral mobility occurs when workers change occupations without substantially improving their economic prospects, or when succeeding generations of a cohort remain at the same occupational status. While this might be a benign state of affairs for well-paid occupations, it constitutes a serious quandary for workers—or for families generationally—who become mired in a low-wage job market in which change of occupation leads to no significant economic improvement. Workers may fail to achieve upward occupational mobility if the jobs they have access to provide limited development of marketable skills or lack well-established promotional ladders—both problems that have been observed, for example, for jobs in fast food restaurants.

Further, not all workers achieve the same level of mobility from a given occupation, nor do all families, generationally. Several empirical studies suggest that the experience of lateral, as opposed to upward, mobility may be affected by the class and racial-ethnic background of previous generations, as well as current workers' class and racial-ethnic profiles. William Darity Jr., Jason Dietrich, and David K. Guilkey (2001) introduced the concept of lateral mobility over generations in a study of the *intergenerational drag hypothesis*. This hypothesis suggests that past generations' experiences of discrimination and disadvantage may significantly impede the ability of subsequent generations to improve their economic position. Using data from the available U.S. decennial censuses between 1880 and 1990, Darity and his colleagues inquired whether the degree of economic advantage or disadvantage of different ethnic and racial groups affects the occupational mobility of their descendants. They posit the lateral mobility hypothesis: that the social status attained by the majority of first-generation migrants to the United States from a specific ethnic group will critically influence the social status of their children and grandchildren. Measuring social status by mobility among occupations, ranked by their median earnings, Darity, Dietrich, and Guilkey use various measures to show that mobility within immigrant groups over generations has a strong lateral element. They conclude that "turn-of-the-century, group-specific variables appear to have lasting effects on individual level economic outcomes a century later, even after important individual level socioeconomic characteristics are taken into account" (2001, p. 466).

Another study, by Marilyn Power and Sam Rosenberg (1995), uses data from the National Longitudinal Survey to compare occupational mobility by race for a cohort of black and white U.S. women who began their work lives as service workers, a relatively low-wage occupational category. Measuring occupational status by mean earnings for women who worked full time in the 1970 census, the study compares the women's occupational statuses in 1972 and 1988, and finds a significant difference in the experience of mobility. While a substantial majority of the white women experienced upward mobility, leaving service jobs for higher-paying clerical and professional occupations (albeit in the traditionally female professions), the majority of the black women experienced only lateral mobility, moving among service occupations or into similarly ranked blue-collar jobs. Power and Rosenberg conclude, "service jobs, even low-paid ones, may be more of a bridge to better positions for young white women and more of a trap for young black women" (1995, p. 46).

Starting in the last few decades of the twentieth century, the number of full-time, contract manufacturing jobs began to decline in the United States, while employment in low-skilled, often part-time service occupations increased. At the same time, the use of temporary or contingent (off-contract) workers grew across the economy. As a result of these changes, the possibilities for the development of job skills and seniority that could lead toward upward mobility have declined, particularly for low-skilled workers in service and operative jobs, who are disproportionately racial-ethnic minorities. The implication of these changes is that lateral mobility may be replacing upward mobility for an increasing number of the most vulnerable workers, leading to widening inequality of income and prospects across the labor force. This trend creates a serious challenge for public policies that emphasize labor market experience as the key route out of poverty.

SEE ALSO *Immigrants to North America; Intergenerational Transmission; Migration; Mobility; Occupational Status; Upward Mobility*

BIBLIOGRAPHY

Appelbaum, Eileen, Annette Bernhardt, and Richard J. Murnane, eds. 2003. *Low-Wage America: How Employers Are Reshaping Opportunity in the Workplace.* New York: Russell Sage Foundation.

Barker, Kathleen, and Kathleen Christensen. 1998. *Contingent Work: American Employment Relations in Transition.* Ithaca, NY: ILR Press.

Darity, William, Jr., Jason Dietrich, and David K. Guilkey. 2001. Persistent Advantage or Disadvantage? Evidence in Support of the Intergenerational Drag Hypothesis. *American Journal of Economics and Sociology* 60 (2): 435–470.

Power, Marilyn, and Sam Rosenberg. 1995. Race, Class, and Occupational Mobility: Black and White Women in Service Work in the United States. *Feminist Economics* 1 (2): 40–59.

Marilyn Power

MOBILIZATION

Mobilization refers to the deployment of resources for purposeful action to achieve a specific political or social goal. Important resources include people (e.g., troops and security forces, voters, social movements), shared identities (e.g., partisanship, class, ideology, religion), material support (e.g., money to maintain a standing army and weaponry, campaign donations), information (intelligence and strategic plans, campaign and movement issue statements), and organization (level of military professionalism, networks with other social or political groups, campaign volunteers).

Charles Tilly explained how revolutions and similar collective actions are an outcome of mobilization, which is "the process by which a group acquires collective control over the resources needed for action" (Tilly 1978, p 7). Mobilization flows from organization and determines the level and success of collection action. This basic process also applies to political and military mobilization. Political scientists analyze voting and interstate war, whereas sociologists place greater emphasis on the social qualities of mobilization through social movements and protest.

SOCIAL AND POLITICAL MOBILIZATION

The level of institutional involvement distinguishes social from political mobilization. Mass social mobilization includes protest that pressures a government to institute or reverse a course of action. Rebellions, revolutions, and nationalist movements lie at the extreme end of popular social mobilization and seek comprehensive social and political change that usually is accompanied by violence (Snyder 2000). Those actions often are responded to with countermobilization efforts by government security forces and the military (Tilly 1978, Skocpol 1988). In contrast, political mobilization occurs in accordance with prescribed institutional rules (see Table 1).

Electoral mobilization refers to the basic process of popular participation in democratic politics or in some cases staged elections, as in the former Soviet Union. Partisans organize citizens into institutionalized actions to reelect or change political leaders. Political parties serve as conduits for providing voters with information about

Types of political and social mobilization	Institutional	Extrainstitutional
Government (military and security forces)	War, domestic security actions (martial law, protest policing)	Coup d' etat, counterinsurgency
Popular (citizens, mass)	Electoral campaign, voting	Protest, rebellion, ethnic nationalism, revolution

SOURCE: Adapted from Claudia Dahlerus, *Do Targets Matter? Repressive Targeting in East Central Europe*, unpublished Ph.D. dissertation (University of Colorado, Boulder, 2001).

Table 1

where a party and its candidates stand on a range of issues. Parties are most active in the campaign stage of elections, recruiting supporters, disseminating information, and contacting voters to ensure that loyal and potential supporters turn out on election day (Verba, Schlozman, and Brady 1995).

Costs often are attached to electoral and protest mobilization. Thus, the dilemma for social scientists lies in explaining what influences mass mobilization in the first place. There are behavioral, structural, and cultural arguments that explain the causes of mobilization. For example, behavioral theories explain how political parties and interest groups are the main vehicles of voter mobilization because they minimize information costs. The role of social movements in mobilizing support for minor parties is also important, especially in times of heightened polarization. Although voting has costs (time, acquiring information about candidates and parties), protest adds the costs and risks of being injured, arrested, or labeled a dissident and a threat to the political status quo. These reasons are highlighted to explain the challenges of mobilizing people into social movement actions such as protests and demonstrations as opposed to electoral mobilization.

High levels of popular involvement in campaigns are associated with electoral success at the polls (Rosenstone and Hansen 1993, McCann, Rapaport, and Stone 1999). Recruiting supporters through phone banks, door-to-door campaigning, and, increasingly, the Internet is important in mobilizing people to support a party and get them to vote on election day. E-mail listservs and campaign Web sites have come to play a role in electoral mobilization in industrialized democracies such as the United States. Presidential candidate Howard Dean represented a major shift in campaigning in the 2004 U.S. presidential election. Much of his support was generated through his cam-

paign Web site, which became an efficient and low-cost method for disseminating information, acquiring donations, and persuading people to get involved in the campaign.

Social movements are equally successful in using the Internet for getting their messages to the public, building networks, and mobilizing supporters. The continued growth of the Internet in developing countries increasingly allows parties and movements to exploit the low cost and expansive reach of the Internet for political and social mobilization.

MILITARY MOBILIZATION

Distinct from political and social mobilization, military mobilization involves actions directed externally in an offensive or defensive manner against other countries or occupying powers. War mobilization, for example, occurs when a government prepares to engage in hostilities with another country, as in the cases of World Wars I (1914–1918) and II (1939–1945). Internal military mobilization involves the use of security forces to bring about domestic order, as in martial law, and is used when the military stages a coup d'état and assumes the role of government, usually through a junta.

Military mobilization is often explained by reference to rational choice models such as expected utility models to predict whether a government will decide to mobilize its armed forces for outright war (Small and Singer 1982, Huth and Russett 1984). The initial onset of mobilization may be used as a deterrent tactic, as in the case of saber rattling.

Rationalist explanations of military mobilization privilege the role of elite decision makers, in particular a chief executive such as a president, prime minister, or monarch and that leader's close circle of military advisors. The decision to mobilize entails a cost-benefit analysis of the presence or absence of factors that predict the likelihood of a successful strike or invasion. Material resources such as troop size and weaponry figure prominently, as do support from allies and others in the international community (e.g., the United Nations) and domestic support in democracies.

ANALYSES OF MOBILIZATION

Social scientists interested in popular social mobilization approach military and government mobilization from a different analytical perspective. Theda Skocpol (1988) and Charles Tilly (1978), for example, explain government mobilization as a response or preemptive action that is an obstacle to social and political mobilization. In other words, mobilization of the police against protestors and counterinsurgency actions by security and military forces are types of government mobilization that commonly are referred to as repression. In this sense mobilization is interactive. The military mobilizes against the populace, which may continue its protest and insurgency or curtail its mass mobilization. In some cases the military moves to thwart elections (popular political mobilization).

Mobilization also can be analyzed by tracing the chronological evolution of different emphases on key actors and actions. Analyses of World Wars I and II focus on specific qualities of troop mobilization and the weapons arsenals of the major adversaries, including Germany, the United States, and Great Britain (Small and Singer 1982). This practice continued through the beginning of the cold war between the Soviet Union and the United States, in which mobilization also included proxy wars in Korea and Vietnam and border skirmishes. Internal military mobilization received greater attention as civilian and postcolonial governments in Latin America and Africa were toppled by military coups from the 1950s through the 1970s.

Interest in electoral mobilization developed in the 1950s with the rise of the behavioral revolution in the social sciences and studies of democratic participation in the United States and Europe. At about the same time attention to popular mass mobilization was prompted by protests in democracies such as the United States and France and insurgencies in states beset by military coups in Latin America and many postcolonial states. Beginning in the 1990s, there were attempts to explain the sources of the democratic revolutions in Eastern Europe and the former Soviet Union, along with the outcome of the first elections in those fledgling democracies.

As democracies have continued to emerge, popular mobilization is used more frequently in the social sciences to describe movements that are intended to accomplish internal political change through protest along with voting. Increasingly, social movements are vehicles that press for change through both extrainstitutional and institutional collective action (Tarrow 1994). The broader term *collective action* may come to supplant *mobilization* in electoral and social mobilization studies.

Mobilization refers to a fluid set of social and political behaviors. Mobilization may be violent (war, insurgency) or nonviolent (demonstrations) and institutionalized (voting and formal military action) or extrainstitutional (rebellions). Social, political, and military mobilization takes place in these different manifestations in both democracies and authoritarian states.

SEE ALSO *Campaigning; Cold War; Collective Action; Democracy; Military; Political Parties; Protest; Resistance; Revolution; Social Movements; Social Science; Voting*

BIBLIOGRAPHY

Dahlerus, Claudia. 2001. *Do Targets Matter? Repressive Targeting in East Central Europe.* Unpublished PhD dissertation. University of Colorado, Boulder.

Huth, Paul, and Bruce Russett. 1984. What Makes Deterrence Work? Cases from 1900 to 1980. *World Politics* 36: 496–526.

McCann, James A., Ronald B. Rapaport, and Walter J. Stone. 1999. Heeding the Call: An Assessment of Mobilization into H. Ross Perot's 1992 Presidential Campaign. *American Journal of Political Science* 43 (1): 1–28.

Rosenstone, Steven J., and John Mark Hansen. 1993. *Mobilization, Participation, and Democracy in America.* New York: Macmillan.

Skocpol, Theda. 1988. Social Revolutions and Mass Military Mobilization. *World Politics* 40 (2): 147–168.

Small, Melvin, and J. David Singer. 1982. *Resort to Arms: International and Civil Wars, 1816–1980.* Beverly Hills, CA: Sage Publications.

Snyder, Jack. 2000. *From Voting to Violence: Democratization and Nationalist Conflict.* New York: Norton.

Tarrow, Sidney. 1994. *Power in Movement: Social Movements, Collective Action, and Politics.* Cambridge, U.K.: Cambridge University Press.

Tilly, Charles. 1978. *From Mobilization to Revolution.* Reading, MA: Addison-Wesley.

Verba, Sidney, Kay Lehman Schlozman, and Henry E. Brady. 1995. *Voice and Equality: Civic Voluntarism in American Politics.* Cambridge, MA: Harvard University Press.

Claudia Dahlerus

MOBUTU, JOSEPH
1930–1997

Mobutu Sese Seko Kuku Ngbendu Waza Banga (Joseph-Désiré) was born on October 14, 1930, at Lisala in the Mongala region, located in the province of Equateur, in what was then called the Belgian Congo. The child of Alberic Gbemani and Marie Madeleine Yemo, he belonged to a family that included three sons. He was baptized on December 2, 1930, and christened Joseph-Désiré. He began study at the Primary School of Saint-Anne in Léopoldville (Kinshasa) in 1937 but was forced to leave the school after the death of his father in 1938. He recommenced his elementary and intermediary studies at the School of the Christian Brothers in Coquilathville in 1946. He was dropped from this school in 1948 for having prolonged his scholastic vacations to Léopoldville without authorization.

This expulsion marked Mobutu's departure from school and the beginning of his career in the colonial army. Colonial rule required that students dismissed from school be incorporated into the colonial army, and

Mobutu entered the army in February 1950. He was sent to the École des Cadres in Luluabourg, where he was trained as a typist. He obtained his secretarial certificate in 1952 and joined the general staff of the colonial army in Léopoldville in 1953. He was promoted to sergeant in April 1954 but quit the army in 1955. He debuted in the journalism community in 1956 as a member of the editorial committee for the journal *Actualités africaines* and became the editor-in-chief several months later. In 1958 he made his first trip to Belgium, acting as a newspaperman at the Universal Exposition of Brussels. He returned to Belgium in 1959 as a professional apprentice to the Office of Information and Public Relations for the Belgian Congo and the Inforcongo. Mobutu also took classes at the Press House and at the Institut Supérieur d'Études Sociales, both in Brussels. Numerous observers have suggested that it was during this stay in Belgium that the Belgian secret service and the U.S. Central Intelligence Agency (CIA) first recruited him.

As a former sergeant in the colonial army, Mobutu was promoted to colonel and chief of staff of the new Congolese army in July 1960 by Patrice Lumumba. In January 1961 Mobutu was promoted to general major and major chief of state of the National Congolese Army. He became lieutenant general in November 1965, then marshal in December 1982. Despite his military achievements and the legend around the battle of Kamanyola, Mobutu and the Congolese army never achieved major military victories without the help of foreign troops. This was the case with the two wars of Shaba in 1977 and 1978, won with the combined help of Morocco, Belgium, and France. Abandoned by his allies in 1996, Mobutu was unable to stop the advance of rebel troops led by Laurent Désiré Kabila with the help of Rwanda and Uganda. As a result in May 1997 Mobutu was forced to flee to Morocco, where he later died of prostate cancer.

Mobutu's adherence to the Mouvement National Congolais (MNC; National Congolese Movement) in December 1958 marked the beginning of his political career. Starting in 1960 he was charged with the MNC-Lumumba in Belgium and represented this political party from April through May 1960 at the Conference of the Economic Round Table, charged with studying the economic terms of independence in the Congo. Named major chief of state in the new Congolese army in July 1960, he attempted his first military coup with a group of Congolese university students. This takeover not only removed Lumumba from power but also provided the impetus for his eventual assassination. Mobutu's motivations for seeking to overthrow and eliminate Lumumba were twofold. In 1960 Mobutu was considered a part of the *évolués*, that is, the Congolese elite who occupied an intermediary social position between the Belgians and the majority of the Congolese people. During this period each of the Congolese évolués vied for leadership. Second, it is important to place this conflict within the context of the cold war. The Europeans and Americans accused Lumumba of being a communist, and as an agent of both the Belgian and the American secret services, Mobutu contributed to his elimination. However, Mobutu did not take supreme control but instead left power in the hands of Joseph Kasa-Vubu as head of state. On November 24, 1965, Mobutu attempted his second overthrow and became president of the republic, establishing a military dictatorship. On May 20, 1967, Mobutu created the Mouvement Populaire de la Révolution (MPR; Popular Revolutionary Movement), the state party. Starting in October 1971 a new type of nationalism was implemented to purge the country of colonialist traces. The name of the country was changed from Democratic Republic of the Congo to Zaire, and the names of the cities, avenues, and former colonial places were rechristened with African names. In 1972 the people of Zaire were invited to reject their Christian first names and adopt authentically African names. Mobutu himself rejected his Christian first name (Joseph-Désiré) and took the name of Mobutu Sese Seko Kuku Ngbendu Waza Banga.

In a demonstration of his political agenda of authenticity and for his own personal prestige, Mobutu welcomed the Muhammad Ali–George Foreman heavyweight fight or "Rumble in the Jungle" in 1974. For African Americans, this fight in Africa symbolized a type of return to their roots. According to Ali, his trip to Kinshasa established a relationship between African Americans and Africans. In preparation for this fight, Kinshasa was embellished with new public works, most notably public lighting along the capital's major avenues. The MPR declared its nationalism "authentic," that is to say, "returning" to African cultural values. It proclaimed Zaire's nonaffiliation and rejected imported ideologies, capitalism as much as communism. In the course of its evolution, the MPR agenda was systematized. Its doctrine was "authentic Zairian nationalism;" its ideology, authenticity; its platform, the return to authenticity. Together these elements constituted "Mobutism," which was defined as the teachings, the thoughts, and the actions of the president-founder. This ideological construct made Mobutu the "inventor" of society. In his function as president of the republic, he was the "manager" of the entire Congolese state. This political schematic made the president-founder the primary organ of the party and thus of the republic as a whole. In keeping with this postulate, he became the living symbol for the nation's viability and the guarantor of its continuation. His was a lifetime mandate that could not be breached except in the event of insanity. Thus the concept of a "return to authenticity" furnished sufficient basis for the legitimization of Mobutu's power.

Mobutu's reign was characterized by a systematic pillaging of the country and a lack of any infrastructure developments, such as schools, hospitals, or viable roads. According to one estimate from the World Bank, Mobutu exploited about $15 billion in public funds for family and personal expenses. He placed this money in foreign accounts, and upon his death the new Congolese authorities attempted to reclaim the money. Some banks declared that there was nothing left in any of the accounts, and other banks claimed that there had been millions of dollars rather than billions. In truth the country had become weakened by a long civil war, and the government that succeeded Mobutu was neither strong enough nor organized enough to reclaim the money. Thus when Mobutu relinquished power in 1997, he left his country in enormous debt to the International Monetary Fund and the World Bank.

SEE ALSO Ali, Muhammad (USA); Central Intelligence Agency, U.S.; Corruption; Decolonization; Liberation Movements; Lumumba, Patrice; Neocolonialism

BIBLIOGRAPHY

Gondola, Charles Didier. 2002. *The History of Congo.* Westport, CT: Greenwood.

Mutamba Makombo and Mabi Mulumba. 1986. *Cadres et dirigeants au Zaire, qui sont-ils?* Kinshasa: Éditions du Centre Recherches Pédagogiques.

Ndaywel è Nziem, Isidore. 1998. *Histoire générale du Congo: De l'héritage ancien à la République Démocratique.* Brussels: Duculot.

Charles Tshimanga

MODE

SEE Descriptive Statistics.

MODE, THE

Of the three measures of central tendency, the mode is the simplest to calculate but is used less often than either the mean or the median. The concept of central tendency is widely used in everyday life as well as in academic research. For any kind of information, it is important to know what describes the typical case as well as the range of variation. The mode is the only measure of central tendency appropriate for nominal or discrete variables such as gender, ethnicity, or language. *The mode* can be defined as the category with the largest number, frequency, or percentage. The mode is not the frequency but the category.

So, for example, the U.S. Census Bureau data for the year 2000 indicate that approximately twenty-eight million people in the United States speak Spanish, followed by approximately two million Chinese speakers and fewer numbers who speak other languages. Thus in this example, the mode of distribution of foreign-language speakers in the United States is "Spanish." To compute the mode, list all the values (or categories) in the distribution and tally the frequencies for each value or category. The category with the most is the mode.

If a distribution has two categories with equal numbers or proportions in it, then the distribution is said to be bimodal. Suppose that, in a survey of a group of 100 college students about their political views and party affiliations, it turns out that 20 of them are Independents, 10 are Green Party affiliates, 10 are Libertarians, 30 are Democrats, and 30 are Republicans. This distribution is bimodal, with Democrats and Republicans both being modes (figure 1).

The mode can also be used for other types of variables: ordinal, interval, and ratio. However, it has a limitation that other measures of central tendency do not. It takes into account only one or two categories, the biggest ones. The median, or fiftieth percentile, cuts in half a distribution that is ordered from low to high or high to low, but extreme values at either end of the distribution do not affect the median. The mean takes each and every value into consideration. Extreme values will affect the mean, making it higher than the median if the extreme values are at the high end of the distribution (such as Bill Gates's income in a distribution of average Americans) or lower than the median if the values are on the low end (perhaps a homeless person) of the distribution. The mode may be located anywhere in the distribution.

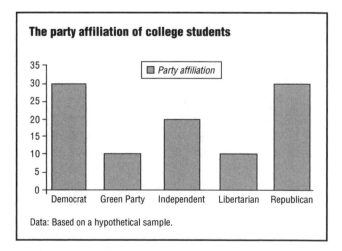

The party affiliation of college students

Data: Based on a hypothetical sample.

Figure 1

Occasionally researchers report a mode for grouped frequency distributions or for variables that may be collected at the ratio level, such as years of education, and collapsed into categories such as less than high school, high school, some college, and so on. If a researcher were to ask eleven people how many years of schooling they completed and got the following results, here is how the researcher could proceed.

Jaime	14
Gina	20
Jorge	10
Susana	11
Carlos	16
Angela	9
Cindy	12
Roberto	12
Gabby	13
Mando	16
Diana	16

First, the data indicate that there are three people with 16 years of education. There are more respondents in that educational category, so 16 years is the mode. Next, if the years are arranged in order, the result is: 9, 10, 11, 12, 12, 13, 14, 16, 16, 16, 20. The sixth number (13, corresponding to Gabby) is the median, because there are five cases on either side. To obtain the mean, all the years are added up (149) and divided by 11. That gives a mean of 13.5. If the years of education were collapsed into a table that showed categories, some information would be lost, but it would present the data in a way most people think about education.

Education Level	Frequency
< High School	3
High School	2
Some College	2
College or Higher	4

Judgments would have to be made, though, and in some cases that might be tricky. One would have to assume that people who reported fewer than 12 years of education did not skip any grades and that all people who reported 12 years actually received a high school diploma. Unless the question were asked, one would not know if someone obtained a GED. Similarly, one would have to assume that those people who listed 16 years of education received a college degree. The mode in this case would be college or higher.

SEE ALSO *Central Tendencies, Measures of; Mean, The; Standard Deviation; Statistics*

BIBLIOGRAPHY

U.S. Census Bureau. 2003. Language Use and English-Speaking Ability: 2000. Census 2000 Brief. Washington, DC.

M. Cristina Morales
Cheryl Howard

MODE OF PRODUCTION

The term *mode of production* derives from the work of Karl Marx (1818–1883), and the concept has played a significant role in subsequent Marxist theory. Mode of production refers to the varied ways that human beings collectively produce the means of subsistence in order to survive and enhance social being. Marx believed that human history could be characterized by the dominant modes of production. In this sense the term refers to a specific economic system. Marx was interested in doing two things: providing an analytical framework for defining specific modes of production and locating those modes in terms of a theory of historical development. That being said, he never developed these two points in a consistent or systematic manner, and thus there are both ambiguities and contradictions contained in his writings (not unlike his treatment of social class). Nonetheless, the basic contours of what he was getting at are clear.

RELATIONS AND FORCES OF PRODUCTION

Any particular mode of production is the result of the distinctive articulation of a system that involves specific relations of production and forces of production. The relations of production define specific social relations predicated on the mode of appropriation of surplus labor and a specific institutionalized practice concerned with the distribution of the means of production. Social relations are primarily defined in terms of social classes, which form the basis of the structural system that regulates human relationships. These relations become codified in law and in more general terms legitimated by the hegemonic ideology. Forces of production define the labor process itself wherein raw materials are transformed into determinate products. Factors that affect the forces of production include raw materials, the personal activity of people (labor), and the instruments used to transform raw materials into products. Of particular note in assessing the level of development of the forces of production is the nature of the technologies, machines, and scientific advances being deployed in the productive process.

While the forces of production and relations of production together constitute the economic structural base of a particular mode of production, the political and ideological institutional apparatus shapes its superstructure. One of the enduring problems in deciphering Marx's understanding of the relationship between the economic base and the superstructure is that at times he lends credence to both those who positively depict his theory of economic determinism and those who critically accuse it. These internal contradictions are reflected in the subsequent historical development of Western Marxism, where, for example, the leaders of the Third International offer a decidedly economistic version of Marxism while Antonio Gramsci (1891–1937), Georg Lukács (1885–1971), and members of the Frankfurt School accord considerable autonomy to culture. Marx devoted considerably more attention throughout his work to the economic base and comparatively less attention to the superstructure, which accounts in part for the difficulty in deciphering how he understood the relationship between the two. Despite these rather different emphases, few would object to Louis Althusser's (1918–1990) position, which accords relative autonomy to the superstructure while arguing that in the last instance it is economic factors that are most determinative in either perpetuating any particular mode of production or setting the stage for the emergence of a new mode of production.

HISTORY AND STAGES OF DEVELOPMENT

Marx used the concept of modes of production as a classificatory tool to describe and differentiate various economic systems in historical terms. He also used it, problematically as it turns out, to account for historical materialism's dialectical stages of development. As with his analyses of class structure, he did not offer a consistent portrait of the number of modes of production that can be found throughout human history. He employs different terminology in different passages and it is not always clear whether some terms are meant to be synonyms for, subsets of, or qualitatively distinct from other terms. Thus, one can find the following adjectives used at various places to describe modes of production: communal, simple property, independent peasant, state, slave, ancient, feudal, capitalist, socialist, and communist. That being said, most subsequent commentators have identified four modes of production that are the most developed in Marxist thought: Asiatic, slavery/ancient, feudalism, and capitalism. These are examples of class societies and as such need to be located in terms of Marx's threefold schema of history, which involves the movement from the

pre-class societies characteristic of the earliest human societies that existed before recorded history to the class societies of which these four are the most significant, and leading in the future (whether Marx thought this was inevitable or merely a potentiality is open for debate) to a post-class society that was variously identified as socialism or communism. Of particular note is the fact that the Asiatic mode of production stands not simply geographically apart from the other types, which can be identified with stages of European history, but as a distinct civilization. Marx thought that the Asiatic mode existed in societies that were historically static, lacking the class consciousness and conflict necessary for development to occur. External factors would be required to effect change.

Marx's primary focus was on class societies, and in particular on capitalism. Indeed, it is fair to say that his major preoccupation, certainly during the mature period of his life that commenced when he settled in London, was on understanding the particular characteristics and contradictions of the capitalist mode of production. On the other hand, he had comparatively little to say about pre-class and post-class societies. Although both modes of production can be characterized as communistic, he differentiated them, referring to the former as primitive communism. The post-class mode of production he wished for did not entail a return to the former state of communism; rather, it represented a qualitatively new mode of production, but one that was indebted to the unleashing of industrial productive forces brought about by capitalism. In other words, in the general thrust of his work, it was clear that communism was only possible once the productive forces of capitalism had been unleashed and developed. For Marx, the difference between the two was that pre-class societies were defined in terms of an undifferentiated unity, while the communism of the future would find a new form of societal unity predicated on differentiation. What he had in mind was something akin to Émile Durkheim's (1858–1917) portrayal of the division of labor in society, with pre-class society being an instance of mechanical solidarity and post-class society a case of organic solidarity.

Marx, the advocate of communism, wrote very little about what such a mode of production would look like, contending that its particular contours would be the product of those who create it. His unwillingness to describe communism, aside from stressing that it entailed abolishing private ownership of the means of production, was in part intended to contrast his work to that of those he dubbed "utopian socialists." He faulted them for failing to see the historical connections between capitalism and communism and for simultaneously being inattentive to the significance of social classes and to class conflict.

In various works, Marx discusses the importance of class divisions in the Asiatic, ancient, and feudal modes of production. Marx accorded a privileged role to social classes, and in so doing downplayed the significance of other key divisions, such as gender and race. While any specific mode of production would be characterized by an ensemble of different social classes, in all class societies, two would be central: the economically dominant class that wields control and ownership of the means of production, and the class that most directly confronts the dominant class in an antagonistic relationship. Thus, at the introduction to *The Communist Manifesto* (1848) Marx and Engels depict all of (recorded) history as entailing class conflict, pitting master against slave in the ancient mode of production, lord against serf in the feudal mode, and capitalist or bourgeoisie against the worker or proletariat in capitalism.

Marx attempted, with rather limited success, to explain the transition from one mode of production to another. He saw two factors at work—the development of the forces of production and class conflict—but they are not adequately integrated into a coherent theory of social change. This is evident in his treatment of the transition from feudalism to capitalism, which generally fails to take into account the class struggle between the two key classes involved. Instead, he discusses such matters as population growth, the advent of European colonialism, and new techniques of warfare. Quite correctly, peasant revolts are not seen as a significant factor in the demise of feudalism. Neither is the development of productive forces.

CAPITALISM

The primary focus for Marx was capitalism itself, and he was less interested in explaining its rise than in offering an account of how it worked and where it was headed. In this regard, he argued that built into capitalist economies is a necessity on the part of capitalists to constantly revolutionize the means of production. In this regard, he viewed capitalism as a progressive, and indeed revolutionary, economic system. At the same time, however, it could only function by exploiting and alienating the worker, thereby creating an inherently conflict-ridden relationship. In this mode of production, the worker was not only perceived as oppressed by the capitalist, but was also seen as an agent of the social change that could lead to the emergence of the communist mode of production. This would occur only if a class-conscious proletariat organized successfully to challenge and overthrow the domination of capital.

As with his understanding of the dialectical character of historical change, Marx's claim that the proletariat was a universal class derived from his reinterpretation of Hegelian theory. According to Marx, what made the proletariat a universal class was that it had no interest in preserving itself as a class, and as such it had the capacity to act in the interests of society as a whole. When the proletariat acts in its own self-interest in challenging the capitalist class, it is not to strengthen its position within capitalism, but to eliminate itself as a class by eliminating the socially antagonistic or contradictory class relations that characterize capitalism.

More than a century after Marx's death, the emergence of a classless society has not been realized. Attempts to forge classless economic systems that arose out of societies that at the moment of revolution were not capitalist—Russia and China—failed in that attempt. Whether this means that Marx, despite his own efforts to resist it, actually succumbed to utopianism is an open question. What is clear is that at this particular historical juncture capitalism remains hegemonic. That being said, it is too early to determine whether the "new class" (composed of managers, professionals, and the intelligentsia) will challenge its hegemony and whether capitalism's crisis tendencies can in the long run be overcome.

SEE ALSO *Althusser, Louis; Anderson, Perry; Bourgeoisie; Capitalist Mode of Production; Class; Class Conflict; Conjunctures, Transitional; Exploitation; Feudal Mode of Production; Forces of Production; Frankfurt School; Gramsci, Antonio; Lukacs, Georg; Managerial Class; Marx, Karl; Marxism; New Class, The; Slave Mode of Production*

BIBLIOGRAPHY

Elster, Jon. 1986. *An Introduction to Karl Marx.* Cambridge, U.K.: Cambridge University Press.

Marx, Karl. 1965. *Pre-Capitalist Economic Formations.* Trans. Jack Cohen; ed. E. J. Hobsbawm. New York: International Publishers. (Orig. pub. 1857–1958.)

Marx, Karl, and Friedrich Engels. 1967. *The Communist Manifesto.* Trans. Samuel Moore. Harmondsworth, U.K.: Penguin. (Orig. pub. 1848.)

Richards, Alan. 1986. *Development and Modes of Production in Marxian Economics: A Critical Evaluation.* London: Harwood Academic Publishers.

Russell, James W. 1989. *Modes of Production in World History.* London: Routledge.

Wolpe, Harold, ed. 1980. *The Articulation of Modes of Production: Essays from Economy and Society.* London: Routledge and Kegan Paul.

Peter Kivisto

MODEL MINORITY

On January 9, 1966, sociologist William Petersen published "Success Story: Japanese American Style" in the

New York Times Magazine. Petersen asserted that by dint of their cultural resilience, Japanese Americans had saved themselves from the fate of "problem minorities." A few months later, *US News and World Report* weighed in with an article about Chinese Americans entitled "Success Story of One Minority in the US" (December 26, 1966). This latter article opened with an explicit comparison between different minority groups: "At a time when it is being proposed that hundreds of billions be spent to uplift Negroes and other minorities, the nation's 300,000 Chinese Americans are moving ahead on their own." As with Petersen's article, this one pointed to the importance of family values and Chinese cultural traditions, for "[s]till being taught in Chinatown is the old idea that people should depend on their own efforts—not a welfare check—in order to reach America's 'Promised Land.'" In 1971 *Newsweek* published "Success Story: Outwhiting the Whites" (June 21), which called to task not only non-Asian minorities, but also white Americans for their failure to keep up with Asian immigrants into the United States, whose cultural traditions more closely matched those that had historically pushed Northwestern Europe into world dominance. Not for nothing did *Fortune* label Asian Americans a "Super Minority" (November 1986).

In the century that preceded Petersen's article little augured the birth of the "model minority" stereotype. White supremacists routinely reviled Asians, who were seen alternatively as deviant (opium smokers and sexual predators) or as coolies (who would lower the wages of white Free Labor). In sum, as Lothrop Stoddard, the author of *The Rising Tide of Color against White Supremacy*, put it in 1920, the "obviously dangerous Oriental" had to be barred from entry into the United States because Asians posed "the greatest threat to Western Civilization and the White Race." This view was held not only by white supremacist elites, it was also the position of the leading trade union association (the American Federation of Labor or AFL) and its leader (Samuel Gompers). In 1882 the U.S. Congress passed the Chinese Exclusion Act, which was defended in 1902 by Gompers in a coauthored book, *Some Reasons for Chinese Exclusion: Meat vs. Rice; American Manhood against Asiatic Coolieism: Which Shall Survive?* Originally published by the AFL, the book was republished a few years later by the Asiatic Exclusion League. In 1905, at its 25th Annual Convention, the AFL argued that the "American working-man" had enough to deal with "without being required to meet the enervating, killing, underselling and under-living competition of that nerveless, wantless people, the Chinese." Such being the historical attitude toward the Chinese and Japanese, it is not a surprise that both peoples faced immense immigration restrictions after 1924 and that the latter were interned during World War II. From the birth of the American Republic to 1966, Asia's

people represented a Yellow Peril, needed for its labor, but reviled.

What changed, then, in the mid-1960s? Between 1964 and 1965, the U.S. Congress passed three central pieces of legislation. After a century-long struggle, the civil rights movement achieved partial victories with the passage of the Civil Rights Act (1964) and the Voting Rights Act (1965). Both laws cut down Jim Crow segregation, but neither promised the fullness of freedom demanded by the movement. In his important *Report on the Black Family* (1965), President Johnson's assistant Daniel Patrick Moynihan registered the manner in which the movement digested its victory. Quoting the sociologist and Moynihan associate Nathan Glazer, the report asserted that the "demand for economic equality is now not the demand for equal opportunities for the equally qualified; it is now the demand for equality of economic results." Rather than simply seeking equality of opportunity, the disenfranchised had begun to demand "equality of results, of outcomes." A move in this direction threatened to undermine the hierarchy of class and the justification for its persistence in a liberal democracy. It would inevitably lead to uncomfortable questions: What makes some rich families remain rich, and why is it that the bulk of rich families are also white?

The third Congressional bill, the Immigration Act of 1965, enabled the emergence of a novel theory of persistent inequality. The U.S. Congress reversed the prohibitions against Asian immigration, and now welcomed thousands of people who had received advanced technical training in places such as India and China. The "state selection" of the 1965 Act that allowed only highly educated migrants to enter the country provoked a reconsideration of Asians on "natural selection" lines: If it was state policy that transformed the demography of Asian America, it was a stereotype of their culture that was used to account for their success. The new "model minority," the Asians, became a useful bludgeon against the "problem minorities." Inequalities within the Asian American community and racism faced by Asians disappeared from the frame of reference, just as the putative recalcitrance of Latinos and blacks became part of the Asian American story. In this way the myth of the "model minority" aided the perpetuation of racism in the post–civil rights era.

Asians were not the only ones represented as a "model minority." In December 1964 Nathan Glazer published an essay in *Commentary* entitled "Negroes and Jews: The New Challenge to Pluralism." Noting the "shift of Negro demands from abstract equality to group consideration, from color-blind to color-conscious," Glazer argued that the new demands of the civil rights movement are anathema not only to American values, but also to "model minorities" like the American Jews. Long reviled by the

U.S. power structure, Jews, like Asians, became acceptable as beneficiaries of the post–civil rights form of racism that lifted up the "model minorities" as a weapon against the "problem minorities." When conflict over community schools erupted in New York City in 1967, the concept of the exemplary Jewish American was used in much the same way as notions of the Asian model minority would later be used. Black and Puerto Rican students demanded to be taught not only by "white" teachers, but also by black and Puerto Rican teachers. As it turned out the "white" teachers in Ocean Hill-Brownsville were Jewish Americans, who in turn became pawns in a reconfiguration of Jewish liberalism that saw it shift toward neoconservatism.

In his 1964 article, Glazer argued that Jewish Americans benefit as the "model minority" because their interests "coincide with the new rational approaches to the distribution of rewards." In other words, so long as educational institutions are equally endowed, justice can be achieved through a color-blind system based on merit. Those minorities that can do well in such a system, because of family cultures that promote educational achievement, are model. In this conception, all historical advantages and disadvantages (such as those derived from immigration policy) are ignored.

Three ideological streams work together to absolve U.S. society from the perpetuation of inequality: multiculturalism (which promotes bureaucratic diversity and claims to value all "cultures" equally), colorblindness (which promotes individual advancement through merit), and the notion of the "model minority" (which demonstrates that some cultures are superior after all, and it is for this reason that certain "races" succeed in a colorblind merit system). Together these enable the reproduction of inequality and the perpetuation of the American ideology of "fairness" and "justice." The "model minority" myth, therefore, plays a crucial role in post–civil rights racism.

Of course, the social power of the "model minority" myth was strengthened when upwardly mobile Asians and Jews adopted its tenets to further their own advancement. As opportunities opened up, those with saleable skills and with modest amounts of capital mobilized the constellation of ideas around the myth to gain some leverage over a political economy still shaped by white supremacist cultural expectations. In other words, the myth was largely adopted by upwardly mobile sections of minority groups, who found it valuable in gaining entry into the higher rungs of the class structure. Scholars of those who are not able to ascend the ladder afford us with empirical proof of the fallacy of the model minority myth. They also demonstrate the ways in which the myth occludes the existence of working class Asians and Jews (Stacey J. Lee 1996). The myth also prevents us from fully grasping the interaction

between Asian and Jewish small merchants and the African American and Latino working poor (Jennifer Lee 2002; Kim 2000; Prashad 2001).

SEE ALSO *African Americans; Assimilation; Civil Rights Movement, U.S.; Equal Opportunity; Equality; Glazer, Nathan; Hierarchy; Immigration; Jews; Jingoism; Migration; Minorities; Mobility; Mobility, Lateral; Moynihan Report; Moynihan, Daniel Patrick; Multiculturalism; Nativism; Orientalism; Race-Blind Policies; Racism; Stereotypes; Stratification*

BIBLIOGRAPHY

Brodkin, Karen. 1998. *How Jews Became White Folks and What That Says about Race in America*. New Brunswick, NJ: Rutgers University Press.

Cho, Sumi K. 1997. Converging Stereotypes in Racialized Sexual Harassment: Where the Model Minority Meets Suzie Wong. In *Critical Race Feminism: A Reader*, ed. Adrien Katherine Wing, 203–220. New York: New York University Press.

Fong, Timothy P. 1998. *The Contemporary Asian American Experience: Beyond the Model Minority Myth*. Upper Saddle River, NJ: Prentice-Hall.

Kim, Claire Jean. 2000. *Bitter Fruit: The Politics of Black-Korean Conflict in New York City*. New Haven, CT: Yale University Press.

Lee, Jennifer. 2002. *Civility in the City: Blacks, Jews, and Koreans in Urban America*. Cambridge, MA: Harvard University Press.

Lee, Robert G. 1999. *Orientals: Asian Americans in Popular Culture*. Philadelphia: Temple University Press.

Lee, Stacey J. 1996. *Unraveling the "Model Minority" Stereotype: Listening to Asian American Youth*. New York: Teachers College Press.

Lowe, Lisa. 1996. *Immigrant Acts: On Asian American Cultural Politics*. Durham, NC: Duke University Press.

Prashad, Vijay. 2000. *Karma of Brown Folk*. Minneapolis: University of Minnesota Press.

Prashad, Vijay. 2001. *Everybody Was Kung Fu Fighting: Afro-Asian Connections and the Myth of Cultural Purity*. Boston: Beacon Press.

Vijay Prashad

MODEL SELECTION TESTS

Statistical inference and forecasting, widely used in all of the sciences, are usually based on a statistical model. Yet, the specification of an appropriate statistical model is a difficult problem that has yet to be satisfactorily solved. Model building is as much an art as a science. All statistical models are necessarily false, and their usefulness is their ability to provide the best approximation to the "true" model. A summary of the complementary approaches used in this important problem of model specification is provided below.

THEORY AND SAMPLE DATA

The *conceptual approach* is based on the use of subject matter theory in the specification of a model. However, there may be many competing theories leading to many alternative models. The many different macroeconomic models are an example. In other situations, theory may provide little, if any, information on model specification. For example, dynamic modeling theory typically provides little information on the dynamic relations among variables.

Another source of model specification is the data. Previously unknown relations between variables can be suggested from the data. An example is given by the Phillips curve relation in macroeconomics.

STATISTICAL APPROACHES: HYPOTHESIS TESTING

The problem of model specification can also be addressed using statistical hypothesis testing. In this approach, the comparisons are generally between two competing models. If the two models are nested—that is, one model can be obtained as a special case of the other by specifying appropriate restrictions—standard hypothesis tests can be used to choose between the two models. Although easy to implement, this approach can be problematic. First, the significance level of the test is an arbitrary choice that can affect the conclusion. Also, using the conventional 5 percent level of significance, the null hypothesis has an advantage over the alternative hypothesis.

In situations where two models are nonnested, an artificial compound model can be formulated that includes both rival models as special cases, and then the above nested testing procedure can be applied. Common examples include the *J*-test of Russell Davidson and James MacKinnon (1981) and the D. R. Cox test (1961). Both the *J* and Cox tests can be generalized to situations where there are more than two models. However, these tests include the additional possibility that one accepts or rejects both models. In the hypothesis testing approaches, the order of testing is important and can and usually does affect the final outcome. Thus, two different researchers with exactly the same models and data can arrive at different conclusions based on different orders of testing and significance levels.

SELECTION CRITERIA

An alternative statistical approach to model specification is to construct a metric M, which measures the deviation of the data from the model. Model selection criteria have been devised to help choose the "best" model among a number of alternative models on the basis of the sample information. Both nested and nonnested models can be compared, and all models are treated symmetrically. Model simplicity and goodness of fit are both taken into account in choosing a "best" model. The principle of parsimony is an important requirement in modeling and forecasting. It is only worthwhile to adopt a more complex model if that model does a substantially better job of explaining the data than some simpler model.

The most commonly used selection criteria are the *Akaike information criteria* (AIC) introduced by Hirotugu Akaike (1969); the *Schwarz information criteria,* also known as the *Bayesian information criteria* (BIC), introduced by Gideon Schwarz (1978); and the *final prediction error criteria* (FPE), introduced by Akaike (1970). All three criteria, along with the conventional adjusted R-squared criteria (written as a function of the S^2), can be written as;

$$(1) \quad S^2 = \left(\frac{SSE}{T}\right)\left(\frac{T}{T-k}\right)$$

$$(2) \quad AIC = \left(\frac{SSE}{T}\right)e^{2k/T}$$

$$(3) \quad BIC = \left(\frac{SSE}{T}\right)T^{k/T}$$

$$(4) \quad FPE = \left(\frac{SSE}{T}\right)\left(\frac{T+k}{T-k}\right)$$

$$(5) \quad \bar{R}^2 = 1 - ((T-1)(S^2)/TSS)$$

where SSE = the sum of squared residuals in the sample, TSS = the total sum of squares of the dependent variable Y, T = the sample size, and K = the number of parameters in the model.

The goal is to choose the model that minimizes the chosen criteria. The difference among the criteria is in the penalty factor, which multiplies the common goodness-of-fit term SSE/T. This penalty factor for model complexity is a function of the number of parameters k and sample size T. These criteria can be used for all data types; however, the sample period T must be the same for all models considered. In realistic samples ($T > 8$), the ranking of these criteria is $S^2 < FPE < AIC < BIC$. Thus, BIC penalizes complex models the most, while the adjusted R-squared statistic penalizes complex models the least. Unlike the other three criteria, the adjusted R-squared statistic is not based on the explicit consideration of a loss function and is a poor choice, leading to models that are too complex.

Other selection criteria are available based on similar theoretical arguments, and in theory one can go on inventing new criteria indefinitely using this approach. If all the criteria achieve a minimum for the same model, then we have a unique choice for the "best" model. In situations where the criteria choose different models, one must proceed with caution. Of the four criteria described above, only the BIC criterion is consistent. For the BIC criteria, the probability of choosing the best approximation to the true model approaches 1 as the sample size becomes infinitely large. The other criteria will tend to choose models that are too complex in large samples. However, small sample property considerations imply that the BIC criterion tends to choose models that are overly simplistic in small samples. Both Monte Carlo evidence and small sample considerations have shown that the AIC is a better choice than the SIC. The amount by which the model selection criterion differs across models has no meaning, thus any monotonic transformation can also be used. A common choice is the logarithmic transformation. Generalized versions of these selection criteria are also available to compare multivariate models.

An alternative approach is to split the data into an in-sample and out-of-sample period and evaluate and compare the out-of-sample forecasting performance of the different models. This approach provides an independent check on the specification of the model suggested by the in-sample period. These different approaches to model selection serve only as an aid. Recall that one is choosing the best model in the set of models considered; thus a better model may exist outside of those considered. Also, in some situations it may be advisable to carry more than one model forward.

SEE ALSO *Distribution, Normal; Hypothesis and Hypothesis Testing; Instrumental Variables Regression; Loss Functions; Monte Carlo Experiments; Properties of Estimators (Asymptotic and Exact); Regression; Specification Error*

BIBLIOGRAPHY

Akaike, Hirotugu. 1969. Fitting Autoregressive Models for Prediction. *Annals of the Institute of Statistical Mathematics* 21: 243–247.

Akaike, Hirotugu. 1970. Statistical Predictor Identification. *Annals of the Institute of Statistical Mathematics* 22: 203–217.

Cox, D. R. 1961. *Tests of Separate Families of Hypothesis.* Vol. 1: *Proceedings of the Fourth Berkeley Symposium on Mathematical Statistics and Probability.* Berkeley: University of California Press.

Davidson, Russell, and James G. MacKinnon. 1981. Several Tests for Model Specification in the Presence of Alternative Hypotheses. *Econometrica* 49: 781–793.

Kennedy, Peter. 2003. *A Guide to Econometrics.* 5th ed. Cambridge, MA: MIT Press.

Schwarz, Gideon. 1978. Estimating the Dimension of a Model. *Annals of Statistics* 6 (2): 461–464.

William Veloce

MODELS AND MODELING

Social sciences rely increasingly on modeling as a result of their mathematization, the overall computerization of science, and the increase of available data. Once dubbed the "hermeneutic sciences," the social sciences now resemble more than before the natural sciences, in which model building, testing, and comparison occupy a central role. In this development, economists have undoubtedly been pioneers among the social scientists: Since World War II, model building has become the main practice of economists. What is more, the various modeling methods adopted and developed by economists have disseminated to other social sciences. Especially, political scientists have been inspired by the rational-choice style of modeling and the associated mathematical techniques used by economists (see Morton 1999). Sociologists have, however, preferred statistical modeling, being rather skeptical about modeling social phenomena in abstract mathematical terms (Edling 2002).

Interestingly, although social scientists use in their modeling activities the same kinds of mathematical and statistical tools that natural scientists use, they often see models in a different light than do natural scientists. Whereas for social scientists models tend to be highly abstract and even unrealistic depictions of their target systems, both natural scientists and philosophers have tended to appreciate the concreteness of models as opposed to the theory. This contrast between the attitudes of social and natural scientists is partly explained by the fact that with models, social scientists often refer to what they call "formal" or "mathematical models," which seem hopelessly plain and simple in comparison to the social phenomena they aim to explain. Although by "formal models" social scientists usually mean "mathematical models," a model need not be mathematical to be formal. Any model that is presented symbolically or diagrammatically, allowing one to manipulate the model in order to obtain different results or predictions, can be regarded as formal. A good example of formal but not mathematical models is provided by chemical formulas (such as H_2O for water).

Several philosophers, especially adherents to the semantic conception of theories (see below), distinguish between "abstract models" and the mathematical means used to express them. From their point of view, a set of mathematical equations, that is, what frequently is called a "mathematical model" by social scientists, actually should not be regarded as a model, but rather the abstract entity to which these equations refer.

Generally speaking, the most conspicuous feature of scientific models is perhaps the variety of the forms and functions they may take in scientific endeavors. The things called "models" in science make up a truly heterogeneous group: They can be diagrams, physical three-dimensional things, mathematical equations, computer simulations, model organisms, or even laboratory populations. Apart from explanation and prediction, models are used for heuristic purposes and as a tool for theory construction. Moreover, it is typical of modeling that models are often employed to explore the implications, dynamics, or internal consistency of multiple theoretical assumptions. Models can also be used as "proofs" of various theoretical possibilities.

Examples of well-known theoretical models in economics and political science include the Heckscher-Ohlin-Samuelson model, which is a general equilibrium mathematical model of international trade; the Hicks-Hansen IS-LM model, which summarizes some major features of Keynesian macroeconomics with the help of two curves; the Edgeworth-Bowley diagram, which is a geometric device defining efficient allocations in exchange situations; and the Hotelling-Downs model of two-party competition, which predicts that candidates converge to the policy preferred by the median voter. What is remarkable about these models (and is reflected, in fact, by their names) are the long histories during which they have been developed and extended by several authors. These examples exemplify also other typical features of models: their didactic value, for which the IS-LM model is especially famous, and the applicability of models as general templates to very different kinds of problems. For instance, the Edgeworth-Bowley diagram has been used for analyzing various kinds of situations in economics: consumers in exchange, production decisions of firms, welfare questions, and so on. The Hotelling-Downs model has in turn traveled from economics to political science, in which instance the original geographical dimension of the model has become merely metaphoric.

Theoretical models in the social sciences are tested either through experimentation or by estimating them by statistical methods. Often, though, the empirical models in the social sciences are based on informal theoretical reasoning, not having a formal model as a starting point. Apart from testing, integrating data, and guiding further

observation and theory construction, empirical quantitative models are also constructed for predictive purposes. The statistical techniques used for predictive analysis can be grouped into different regression techniques widely used by econometrics and machine-learning approaches that originate from the research on artificial intelligence. Sharing characteristics of both theory and experiment, computer simulation offers an alternative to traditional mathematical modeling in that it allows theoreticians to experiment with more complex theoretical models than what is possible if the models are required to be analytically solvable. Moreover, the possibility provided by multiagent simulation models of exploring the emergence of macro-level behaviors from the interactions of micro-level entities in some environmental contexts seems attractive from the social science point of view.

Given the multiplicity of models and their uses in science, it has been difficult to explicate what kind of entities models are and how they give us knowledge. Two different philosophical approaches to models can be discerned in the literature. On one hand, there have been attempts to establish, within a formal framework, what scientific models are: The earlier, syntactic view of theories and the prevailing semantic approach to models are both attempts of this kind. According to the syntactic view, the task of a model was to provide an interpretation to a skeletal axiomatized theory "in terms of more or less familiar conceptual or visualizable materials" (Nagel 1961, p. 90). The syntactic view was contested by the semantic conception of theories, which replaced the syntactic formulation of a theory with a theory's models. According to the semantic conception, theories are not assemblages of propositions or statements, but rather assemblages of models, which are taken to be structures that are defined by the use of suitable logico-mathematical language.

On the other hand, issues such as scientific reasoning, scientific discovery, and theory change have prompted philosophers to focus on the role and place of models in scientific practice (see Hesse 1966). Continuing this line of work, Margaret Morrison and Mary Morgan (1999) have suggested that models should be understood as investigative instruments that mediate between theory and data because of their autonomous nature. The autonomousness of models is due to their heterogeneous construction: Apart from theoretical notions and empirical data, they may contain also analogies, mathematical techniques, stylized facts, and policy views (Boumans 1999). As Morrison and Morgan stress that through the work of constructing and manipulating models we learn from them, their approach provides a starting point for treating models also as productive things, instead of attributing their cognitive value only to representation (Knuuttila 2005).

Indeed, the epistemic value of models has traditionally been assigned to representation. It has been claimed that models give us knowledge to the extent that they represent accurately their target phenomena. This has proven problematical, especially for the social sciences, because we usually already have some kind of preunderstanding of the social reality—which may not match with the theoretical representations of it. Of all the social sciences, economics, whose mathematization started already in the nineteenth century, has been most ridden with this problem. The most persistent philosophical problem of economics has concerned the "realisticness" of economic theories and their basic assumptions. The issue has been whether such assumptions as utility maximization, perfect information, and perfectly competitive markets "are ('too') unrealistic or ('sufficiently') realistic," or whether that should matter at all (Mäki 1994, p. 236). Famously, the 1974 Nobel prize winner in economics, Milton Friedman, has claimed that the "unrealism" of the assumptions of economics does not matter because the goal of science is the development of hypotheses that give "valid and meaningful" predictions about phenomena (Friedman 1953). To economists themselves, however, the basic assumptions do seem to matter—being a subject of continued discussion—and thus the question is how to defend them.

Uskali Mäki has suggested that economists practice a "method of isolation," in which a set of elements is theoretically removed from the influence of other elements in a given situation with the help of idealizing assumptions (Mäki 1992). Consequently, a theory may be true even if it is partial and involves idealizations, if it has succeeded in representing the workings of the isolated causal factors in a right way. Robert Sugden (2002) denies that economic models are made by abstracting key features of the real world. He treats economic models as (more or less) "credible worlds" whose relation to the real world is established by inferential reasoning. Moreover, he claims that we compare model systems to real systems in much the same way as we compare two real systems to each other. What the two approaches have in common is that they both conceive of economic modeling as devising plausible causal mechanisms that might produce the observable phenomena.

SEE ALSO *Economics; Friedman, Milton; Game Theory; Heckscher-Ohlin-Samuelson Model; Ideal Type; IS-LM Model; Mathematics in the Social Sciences; Mundell-Fleming Model; Philosophy of Science; Positivism; Realism; Samuelson, Paul A.; Social Science*

BIBLIOGRAPHY

Boumans, Marcel. 1999. Built-In Justification. In *Models as Mediators: Perspectives on Natural and Social Science*, ed. Mary S. Morgan and Margaret Morrison, 66–96. Cambridge, U.K.: Cambridge University Press.

Edling, Cristofer R. 2002. Mathematics in Sociology. *Annual Review of Sociology* 28: 197–220.

Friedman, Milton. 1953. *Essays in Positive Economics*. Chicago: University of Chicago Press.

Hesse, Mary. 1966. *Models and Analogies in Science*. Notre Dame, IN: University of Notre Dame Press.

Knuuttila, Tarja. 2005. Models, Representation, and Mediation. *Philosophy of Science* 72: 1260–1271.

Mäki, Uskali. 1992. On the Method of Isolation in Economics. *Poznań Studies in the Philosophy of Science and Humanities* 26: 316–351.

Mäki, Uskali. 1994. Reorienting the Assumptions Issue. In *New Directions in Economic Methodology*, ed. Roger Backhouse, 236–256. London: Routledge.

Morrison, Margaret, and Mary S. Morgan. 1999. Models as Mediating Instruments. In *Models as Mediators: Perspectives on Natural and Social Science*, ed. Mary S. Morgan and Margaret Morrison, 10–37. Cambridge, U.K.: Cambridge University Press.

Morton, Rebecca M. 1999. *Methods and Models: A Guide to the Empirical Analysis of Formal Models in Political Science*. Cambridge, U.K.: Cambridge University Press.

Nagel, Ernest. 1961. *The Structure of Science*. New York: Harcourt, Brace.

Sugden, Robert. 2002. Credible Worlds: The Status of the Theoretical Models in Economics. In *Fact and Fiction in Economics: Models, Realism, and Social Construction*, ed. Uskali Mäki, 107–136. Cambridge, U.K.: Cambridge University Press.

Tarja Knuuttila

MODERATES

In the broadest and most general usage, moderates are defined by their opposition to radicalism, extremism, and fanaticism. Moderates value calm, continuity, consensus, tolerance, and stability. They are satisfied with the present condition of society but may agree that specific areas are in need of improvement. Proposals for change disruptive to society, though, are to be avoided. Persons who take the middle position in politics do not consider themselves to be either left or right on the political spectrum, although some may identify themselves as either moderate conservatives or moderate liberals.

Called variously the political center, the middle-of-the-road, the mainstream, the middling way, or the *juste milieu*, moderation is an inherently provisional and problematical category of thought. Moderates profess no specific body of philosophical principles and pride themselves on making decisions based solely on pragmatic considerations. Their political positions, hence, tend to follow the shifts in the political culture. A moderate stance on universal health care in socialist Sweden, for example, may be rejected as extreme in the more free market–oriented United States. Complicating even further the problem of definition is the fact that no intellectual histories of moderate thought, comparable to Russell Kirk's *The Conservative Mind* (1953) or Kenneth Minogue's *The Liberal Mind* (1963), have been written.

In moral thought, the moderate pursuit of one's pleasures is generally hailed as a virtue. Since Homeric times, the axiom "everything in moderation, nothing in excess" was a cardinal principle in Greek moral thinking. The "golden mean," Aristotle (384–322 BCE) taught, should be the guiding standard for one's conduct. The ethical life, he explained in his *Nicomachean Ethics*, "is a mean between two vices, the one involving excess, the other deficiency" ([c. 350 BCE] 1908, bk. 2, chap. 9). He did not believe, it must be stressed, that the individual should be average or mediocre nor split the difference between two competing vices. Nor did he imply that the mean is always the best. In calculating the mean, persons must consider what is appropriate for them within a particular situation. For example, a ten-dollar donation to a worthy cause might be considered too much for a poor person, but not enough for a wealthy individual. To achieve "what is intermediate in passions and in actions," Aristotle admitted, "is no easy task." Any person "can get angry—that is easy—or give or spend money; but to do this to the right person, to the right extent, at the right time, with the right motive, and in the right way, that is not for every one, nor is it easy; wherefore goodness is both rare and laudable and noble" (bk. 2, chap. 9). Moral virtues are not so much taught or learned as acquired by proper upbringing. Society itself amounts to a vast education project to teach its members how to live lives in the middle. Encouraged by the presence of good models and shared expectations, the *Spoudaios*, Aristotle's person of moral excellence, habitually chooses to pursue his or her pleasures in moderation.

Moderation in politics, on the other hand, is not always universally praised nor rewarded with success. Political parties attempting to stake out moderate positions during times of revolutionary upheaval often suffer at the hands of extremist groups. The Girondins and Feuillants, for example, voiced moderate republican views during the French Revolution (1789–1799) but were brutally suppressed during the bloody Reign of Terror by their more radical adversaries, the Jacobins. The Mensheviks envisioned a moderate bourgeois democratic revolution in Russia in which they would take part in a democratically elected socialist government. They were opposed by the more radical V. I. Lenin (1870–1924) and the Bolsheviks, who imposed the "dictatorship of the proletariat." After losing a power struggle for control of the

party, the Mensheviks were declared illegal in 1921. Its members either fled Russia or were liquidated. As Vincent E. Starzinger notes in his *The Politics of the Center*, the politics of moderation "is least realistic where it is most relevant, and most realistic where it is least relevant." In societies torn by extreme political divisions, "the center will very likely be pulverized from both sides and driven to futile negativism. On the other hand, commitment to the center is likely to be a fairly realistic enterprise where the political left and right both stand within the same value consensus" (1991, p. 16).

Moderates are often condemned by their critics as trimmers, opportunists, or persons who lack the courage of their convictions. Leftists denounce moderates as defenders of the status quo who impede beneficial reforms for the poor and oppressed. Right-wingers, for their part, think that moderates and liberals are ideologically indistinguishable. Stung by relentless accusations of extremism during his campaign for the Republican presidential nomination, Senator Barry Goldwater (1909–1998) questioned whether moderation is always the best policy: "Extremism in the defense of liberty is no vice," the conservative candidate famously declared in his nomination speech to the 1964 Republican National Convention, "and let me remind you also that moderation in the pursuit of justice is no virtue."

Embracing extremism, though, is not generally regarded as a winning strategy in American politics. Especially in national and statewide elections, successful candidates typically tack toward the political middle. The Framers consciously designed the American Constitution to favor moderate outcomes. After noting in "Federalist No. 10" (1787) that the greatest danger to stability and order is "the violence of faction," James Madison (1751–1836) argued that among the many advantages of the Constitution were the institutional mechanisms it provides for controlling the harmful effects of factional strife. Madison hailed a system of functional checks and balances, federalism, and representative government as salutary remedies "for the diseases most incident to republican government." Madison favored an extended commercial republic covering a vast territory and population. "Extend the sphere," he argued, "and you take in a greater variety of parties and interests; you make it less probable that a majority of the whole will have a common motive to invade the rights of other citizens," or, in the event that such a motive exists, sufficient impediments would exist to block its realization.

Moderation, then, is not an ideology but a mentality, a temperament, a frame of mind, a strategy that one brings to the theory and practice of politics.

SEE ALSO *Left and Right; Philosophy, Political*

BIBLIOGRAPHY

Aristotle. [c. 350 BCE] 1908. *Nicomachean Ethics*. Trans. W. D. Ross. Oxford: Clarendon. http://etext.library.adelaide.edu.au/a/aristotle/nicomachean/.

Madison, James. 1787. Federalist No. 10: The Union as a Safeguard Against Domestic Faction and Insurrection. *The Federalist Papers*, 1787–1788, by Alexander Hamilton, John Jay, and James Madison. http://thomas.loc.gov/home/histdox/fedpapers.html.

Starzinger, Vincent E. 1991. *The Politics of the Center: The Just Mileu in Theory and Practice, France and England, 1815–1848*. New Brunswick, NJ: Transaction.

W. Wesley McDonald

MODERNISM

It is helpful to distinguish between "modernism" and that which is "modern." What is known as "modern" is that which is in step with the times, or not so far out of step as to have vanished from cultural memory. A list of what is "modern" would surely include automobiles and paved roads, photography, electric lights, travel by rail and by air, mass transit and mass production, the telegraph and telephone and television, motion pictures, recorded sound, and so on, whereas a butter churn or reading by candlelight would not qualify.

Most of what is known as "modern" today had its beginnings in one brief historical period of Western culture. Although there is some dispute over exact dates, the "modern" period is generally held to extend from the third quarter of the nineteenth century to the beginning of World War II. During this timeframe there were overwhelming changes in American lifestyles. From the landing at Plymouth Rock until the 1920s, for instance, a majority of Americans had taken their living in one form or another from the land. By 1920 this had changed as American society became more industrialized and moved away from agrarian culture, changing into a mercantile and commercial society, not to mention a metropolitan one. The 1920 census reported that for the first time in history, more Americans were living in urban environments than were living beyond them. The census suggested as well that a new strata of society was well along in its making. A "modern" middle class was developing as people left the land and came to work in the industries of major metropolitan areas, and this was an important modification economically because they were one and all consumers. The majority of Americans were earning their livings from some form of mass manufacture, and their buying power was likely to increase because higher wages were available to those able to acquire the greatest industrial skills. This, in turn, provided the chance to rise out of the circumstances in which one was born, not just for a few, but for the majority. Never before had a promise of upward mobility been so widely extended. Never had the American Dream seemed so American.

But it was coming at a price. Urban life was isolating. Factory work was unfulfilling. Nothing seemed sacred anymore. The result was a greater level of unhappiness.

The term *modernism* refers to the responses to this period of turbulence and change. T. S. Eliot's essay "Tradition and the Individual Talent" (1919), for instance, articulated the central challenges for those setting foot in the modern era. Eliot warned the poets of his generation they would have to put aside traditional poetic forms and long-standing poetic techniques. Modern life was so far removed from what earlier generations had experienced, poets would have to abstract what was best from the past, then find new forms of their own making in which to articulate what it now meant to be human. Most immediately, Eliot was calling for a break with the nineteenth-century notion of metrics and rhyme. Still, the implications of his call are far-reaching, for "Tradition and the Individual Talent" also served as a challenge to verities about human experience that dated back to the seventeenth century, or, more specifically, to the Age of Enlightenment, when thinkers such as René Descartes (1596–1650) broke with the mysticism and superstition of the Dark and Middle Ages and held out the possibility that human reason could, over time, gain a full understanding of our world and our lives. Foregrounding the human capacity for reason—particularly the human capacity for inductive and deductive thought—the Age of Enlightenment posited a world that was subject to a matrix of fixed principles, many of which remain the core of the sciences today. If there were fixed principles to be found at the core of the sciences, it stood to reason that this was also true of all of human experience. Surely life was comprehensible if only we could grasp the causal relationships at its center, properly sequence related events, and so on.

But what if the world was not "fixed"? The modernists were suspicious. What if it was fluid, contiguous, ever-changing, always a step or two ahead of what anyone might grasp? What if we were losing our way? What if this overriding faith in ourselves had left us now with nothing to believe in? These were the questions modernist writers were posing in their novels, particularly Marcel Proust (1871–1922), James Joyce (1882–1941), and Virginia Woolf (1882–1941) in Europe, as well as Ernest Hemingway (1899–1961), William Faulkner (1897–1962), and F. Scott Fitzgerald (1896–1940) in the United States. None of these novelists rejected out of hand what Enlightenment thought had achieved. The periodic tables developed in the 1890s were valuable; clearly there were ways in which the world was fixed and stable. What modern experience was proving was just that being alive was a more intricate matter than the Enlightenment had allowed, the powers of science be hanged; to draw from the Irish poet William Butler Yeats's famous "The Second Coming" (1920):

> Things fall apart; the centre cannot hold;
> mere anarchy is loosed upon the world …

The greatest novels of the modernist period are concerned with remembrance and reconstruction. Work as otherwise diverse as Proust's *Á la recherche du temps perdu* (1913–1927), Hemingway's *A Farewell to Arms* (1929), and Fitzgerald's *The Great Gatsby* (1925) all deal with protagonists who are trying to organize the confusion of their pasts into a coherent, viable text. They are doing their best to take fragments of experience and place them in a meaningful, causal sequence. That they can only make sense of their lives through a process sure to falsify or otherwise misrepresent some of what actually happened is a "given," but, for the modernist novel, that is the best one can do. Everything is approximate. Everything is relative. Meaning is in a constant state of flux, so, to make meaning out of our experience is to reconfigure life into forms simple enough to make sense of.

Proust's novel is best known in English by its earliest translated title, *Remembrance of Things Past*, but "In Search of Lost Time" is a closer approximation to what Proust seems to have had in mind. Both titles, though, speak to the modernist experience, a concern with organizing experience into spatial, temporal patterns so that they might be understood and appreciated. This is literally the case in Woolf's *To the Lighthouse* (1927), in which one of her protagonists, Lily Brisco, discovers that the ocean scene she means to paint is so mutable it alters before she can fix it on her canvas. To complicate matters, her perspective is mutable as well, she discovers. One can apprehend the scene, but never quite comprehend it before it changes, or, a more daunting thought still, before Lily changes herself.

For such modernists, this is true not just in art but in all of life. The human mind is no match for a world so contiguous and contradictory, so replete with fleeting images, sounds, and sensations. In an attempt to affix meaning, we actually *make* meaning. We are constantly recapitulating our experiences, making them simpler than we know them to be, forever fitting them into patterns of our own very personal design.

When Henry Ford (1863–1947) introduced the $5, 8-hour workday in 1914 for the workers on his assembly line in Michigan, he was recognizing the changes taking place in the social fabric of the country. This was to be an era of mass production, one in which more goods would be made available to more people than had ever been known throughout human history. But mass production meant that the aesthetics of what was desired would have to be carefully adjusted. For one thing, standardization of a product would have to be accepted in the marketplace as a virtue. Ford recognized that mass production was dependent upon mass consumption bringing about "mass taste." Modern business practice would have to create a consumer with predictable spending habits; it would have to find ways to compensate those it employed and socialize them to both the boredom and rigors of "routinized" labor, and a delicate balance would have to be struck between the nation-state, large capital, and labor organizations.

Modernist architects such as the Dutch Ludwig Mies van der Rohe (1886–1969) and the French Le Corbusier (1887–1965) realized that creating living and working space in the cities of their day meant accommodating the need for flexibility and easy modification. Architecture had to be responsive to an incredible variety of diverse experiences and ever-changing catalysts. But this would have to be balanced against a host of conflicting demands. Architects were being called upon by a powerful capitalist agenda to design in ways that signaled permanence, that were highly functional. If the freedoms and opportunities of urban living often made life seem formless, even chaotic, it was up to them to find new forms that might bring order to bear. The more fragmented and fractured and unstable life came to seem, the more they would have to design with an eye toward historical continuity and collective memory.

The French painter Marcel Duchamp (1887–1968) rocked the art world in 1913 when his painting *Nude Descending a Staircase* was displayed at the Armory Show in New York City. One saw neither a nude nor a staircase, but rather a dizzying series of fragments, one atop the other, suggesting body parts in sequential motion—yet, somehow, in no particular order. Other painters such as Georges Braque (1882–1963), Paul Klee (1879–1940), and Pablo Picasso (1881–1973) were working in a similar vein, defying convention, thwarting long-standing aesthetics of artistic representation. It would be a mistake to equate this with a rejection of the past, however. Much of this modernist avant garde actually owed a significant debt to "primitive" work from Egypt, Sumeria, China, and, in Picasso's case, to African art in general. Was it meaningful to speak any longer of divisions between the modern and the ancient, the East and the West, the avant garde and primitive?

Surely it is not coincidental that at much the same time Albert Einstein (1879–1955) was challenging Euclidian geometry, James Joyce was challenging how a novel should be written with his dizzying tour de force

Finnegans Wake (1939). Neither is it coincidental that in this same period, Béla Bartók (1881–1945), Alban Berg (1885–1935), and Arnold Schoenberg (1874–1951) were creating atonal musical scores that were calling into question precisely what "music" was in general, and a "modern" music in particular. Nor is it coincidental that in this same period economists such as John Maynard Keynes were creating new economic models to fit the peculiar demands brought about in the modern era as compromises were being struck between fixity and stability on the one hand, and the flux of global capitalism on the other.

All found themselves facing the overriding question of modernism itself: How does one respond to an era so unlike any other in the history of all humankind?

SEE ALSO *Alienation; Alienation-Anomie; Architecture; Colonialism; Critical Theory; Culture; Decolonization; Development; Keynes, John Maynard; Literature; Metropolis; Modernity; Modernization; Postcolonialism; Postmodernism; Relativism; Technological Progress, Economic Growth; Urbanization; Visual Arts; Work Day*

BIBLIOGRAPHY

Calinescu, Matei. 1987. *Five Faces of Modernity: Modernism, Avant-Garde, Decadence, Kitsch, Postmodernism.* Durham, NC: Duke University Press.

Eliot, T. S. [1919] 1950. Tradition and the Individual Talent. *Selected Essays.* New York: Harcourt, Brace.

Fussell, Paul. 1975. *The Gender of Modernity.* Cambridge, MA: Harvard University Press.

Harvey, David. 1990. *The Condition of Postmodernity.* Oxford, U.K.: Blackwell.

Kern, Stephen. 1983. *The Culture of Time and Space, 1880–1918.* Cambridge, MA: Harvard University Press.

Nicholls, Peter. 1995. *Modernisms: A Literary Guide.* London: Macmillan.

Jay Boyer

MODERNITY

When Niccolò Machiavelli (1469–1527) undertook to promote "new modes and orders" unlike those that had previously existed, he was expressing a historical vision that came to define *modernity* (from the late Latin *modernus*, derivative of the classical Latin *modo*, meaning "just now" or "in a certain manner"). This vision was one shared in diverse ways by other founders of modernity such as Francis Bacon (1561–1626), Galileo Galilei (1564–1642), and René Descartes (1596–1650), as well as world explorers of the period and leaders of the Protestant Reformation. From politics and science to phi-

losophy and religion, an influential cadre argued for the possibility of introducing an historical break as significant as any that had preceded it, although they also often made the case for this break as a kind of return to lost traditions of antiquity.

That Machiavelli is considered a founder of a new form of political science indicates the significance of this vision for the social sciences. Indeed, modernity gave rise both to the kinds of societies or social relations studied by the field as well as to widespread notions about what it means to practice science. Yet it is an ambivalent term. Modernity can denote different historical periods and phenomena, and it is celebrated and reviled for a variety of reasons. It has multiple meanings that inform debates about the human condition and the nature of the social sciences. This is especially true at the dawn of what many theorists describe as the "postmodern age."

GENERAL FEATURES OF MODERNITY

Three essential features of the modern era set it apart from premodern ways of life. First, modernity refers to radical societal changes, including the rise of democracies, the spread of religious pluralism and secularization, the European colonization of other parts of the world, the formation of the bureaucratic nation-state and market economies, increased social mobility and literacy, and the growth of industrial society with all the attendant changes in working conditions. Modernity is characterized by advanced technoindustrial society, which has brought gains in material well-being primarily to the developed (or modernized) parts of the world. Indeed, a central motif of modernity is the notion of unlimited progress. Yet it is also characterized by uniquely modern problems such as the environmental risks associated with technologies. Many social theorists argue that the emerging knowledge or information age constitutes a novel, postmodern society.

Second, modernity is characterized by a growing emphasis on reason and experience, which speaks to the rise of modern science and technology. Most importantly, modern science altered what it means to *know*. In the prologue to the never-completed work *The Great Instauration*, Bacon first made the radical argument that "human knowledge and human power meet in one." Complaining of the vain speculations of earlier philosophers, Bacon argued that knowledge should lead to "the conquest of nature for the relief of man's estate" (*Novum Organum*, 1620, LII). Unlike the ancients, for whom theory was about things eternal, modern thinkers promoted a more practical science concerned with altering the changeable. This alliance between knowing and changing the world is rooted in the modern subject/object dualism first articulated by Descartes.

Third, modernity ushered in new understandings of the human self and political community, which reflected and conditioned these social and cultural changes. Modern theorists such as Thomas Hobbes (1588–1679) and Immanuel Kant (1724–1804) conceptualized the self as a reflexive, autonomous, and rational will, freely choosing its ends and projecting its values onto an indifferent nature that is void of purpose. Political association is cast less as the common pursuit for higher ends (the "perfectionism" of ancient political theorists) than as procedures for adjudicating demands within a framework of individual rights and freedoms. C. B. Macpherson named this political aspect of modernity "possessive individualism" (1962).

SPECIFIC MEANINGS OF MODERNITY

Modernity should be set within specific contexts, insofar as it is used to describe different periods of history and aspects of life. Indeed, there are numerous features associated with "being modern," which have been developed in several fields of study. For example, "modern art" refers to works produced in the period from the late nineteenth century to the 1970s, a time characterized in part by the abandonment of earlier emphases on representationalism and religious iconography. A related term is *modernism*, which also has multiple meanings, but is often used to refer to cultural movements composed of "modernists" who embrace the features of modern life identified above. Bruce Lawrence, for example, characterizes many religious fundamentalists as modern because they take advantage of technological advances (Lawrence 1989). But they are not modernists, because they reject the fundamental philosophical underpinnings of modernity and refuse to wholly adapt their personal identities and social lives to the dictates of the modern world. At its extreme, this rejection of modernity has led to terrorist acts.

A few prominent uses of modernity from philosophy and social science indicate its multiplicity. Karl Marx (1818–1883) emphasized the alienation of humankind under modern capitalist systems and envisioned communism as an emancipating force. Indeed, alienation is one predominant motif in critical theories of modernity. For example, Friedrich Nietzsche (1844–1900) suggested that the essence of modernity is "the death of God." For Nietzsche, the modern worldview necessitates that "*the highest values devaluate themselves. The aim is lacking: 'why?' finds no answer*" (Nietzsche [1901] 1967, p. 9). He argued that each individual should mold his or her own values as the pure expression of selfhood, ignoring traditions about good and evil. In modernity, what was once thought of as transcendent and given becomes the unstable product of the human will. Marx summarized this rad-

ical historical contingency: "all that is solid melts into air" ([1848] 1994). Critical approaches to modern society thus often focus on securing personal orientation and meaning, frequently through spiritual or communal practices.

Auguste Comte (1798–1857) described the modern era as the culmination of a three-stage historical process, which is itself a characteristically modern interpretation of history in its linear, progressive outlook. The scientific or "positive" stage transcends the earlier "theological" and "metaphysical" stages. For Comte, the methods of the natural sciences provide the only route to certain knowledge. In a more pessimistic account, Max Weber (1864–1920) argued that the rationalization of life in modern society traps individuals in an "iron cage" of rule-based control. Similarly, Jürgen Habermas (b. 1929) criticized the modern notion of subject-centered reason by developing theories of communicative rationality. Peter Wagner explained such conflicting interpretations by arguing that modernity is ambiguous in presenting two counterposed metanarratives—liberation and disciplinization (1994). Michel Foucault (1926–1984) did much to highlight the latter dimension of modernity by arguing that modern society involves pervasive systems of control and surveillance, which has informed many theories critical of development and globalization. He argued that modernity possesses certain underlying conditions of rationality that constitute an understanding of the world and define what counts as truth. Similarly, Martin Heidegger (1899–1976) argued that modernity is a unique way of revealing and being in the world, which he called *Gestell* ("enframing"). For Heidegger, modern human existence is constituted by a technological approach to the world.

Work in feminist epistemology and the sociology of science has further refined critiques of modern rationality. Thomas Kuhn (1922–1996), for example, argued that scientific advance is not the steady polishing of the mirror of nature leading to a correspondence with reality "in itself." Rather, science is a community endeavor in which groups define common problems and standards. Kuhn's work ushered in a variety of postmodern approaches to science and theories of our linguistically mediated existence. Indeed, all of the thinkers mentioned here have spurred thought about various alternatives to modernity. In one of the most provocative of such accounts, Bruno Latour (b. 1947) argued that "we have never been modern," meaning that we have never been able to sustain the conceptual categories or the binary types, especially those of "nature" and "culture," posited by the modern worldview. The harder we try to purify our world into distinct, bounded domains, the more intermediary forms proliferate.

SEE ALSO *Comte, Auguste; Foucault, Michel; Globalization, Social and Economic Aspects of; Habermas, Jürgen; Kuhn, Thomas; Marx, Karl;*

Modernism; Modernization; Nietzsche, Friedrich; Postmodernism; Rationality; Science

BIBLIOGRAPHY

Bacon, Francis. [c. 1620] 1994. *Novum Organum; with Other Parts of the Great Instauration.* Chicago: Open Court.

Bauman, Zygmunt. 1991. *Modernity and Ambivalence.* Ithaca, NY: Cornell University Press.

Giddens, Anthony. 1991. *Modernity and Self-Identity: Self and Society in the Late Modern Age.* Stanford, CA: Stanford University Press.

Hirschman, Albert. 1977. *The Passions and the Interests: Political Arguments for Capitalism Before Its Triumph.* Princeton, NJ: Princeton University Press.

Latour, Bruno. 1993. *We Have Never Been Modern.* Cambridge, MA: Harvard University Press.

Lawrence, Bruce. 1989. *Defenders of God: The Fundamentalist Revolt Against the Modern Age.* San Francisco: Harper and Row.

Macpherson, C. B. 1962. *The Political Theory of Possessive Individualism: Hobbes to Locke.* Oxford: Clarendon.

Marx, Karl, and Frederick Engels. [1848] 1948. *Manifesto of the Communist Party.* New York: International Publishers.

Nietzsche, Friedrich. [1901] 1967. *The Will to Power.* Ed. Walter Kaufman. New York: Vintage Books.

Taylor, Charles. 1989. *Sources of the Self: The Making of the Modern Identity.* Cambridge, MA: Harvard University Press.

Turner, Bryan S., ed. 1990. *Theories of Modernity and Postmodernity.* London: Sage.

Wagner, Peter. 1994. *A Sociology of Modernity: Liberty and Discipline.* London: Routledge.

Adam Briggle

MODERNIZATION

Modernization was a theory of global social change, as well as an American political project. Articulated across several disciplines by American social scientists from the 1950s through the 1970s, the concept of modernization defined a universal, historical process through which *traditional* societies became *modern*. It proposed to map a global, evolutionary pattern in which cultural values, economic systems, and political institutions moved along an incremental, linear path toward the rational economy, liberal society, and democratic order that theorists identified most clearly with countries like the United States. In this approach, *tradition* and *modernity* marked endpoints of a common, historical scale. All societies, considered as integrated, organic wholes, moved from one point of historical equilibrium to another as they systematically abandoned institutions shaped by fatalism, family author-

ity, local affinity, and religious constraints in favor of activist orientations, market economies, and liberal political institutions. Theorists believed, moreover, that this natural process could be decisively accelerated. Through a careful study of the traditional world, proponents of modernization hoped to identify the essential levers of social change. They also aspired to promote the diffusion of the advanced forms of knowledge, technology, and financial assistance necessary to promote a destabilizing yet necessary transition toward a democratic, capitalist endpoint. At the peak of the cold war, modernization embodied the highest aspirations of American liberalism. In addition to defining the historical course of global change, modernization also promised the tools necessary to direct it.

Rooted in Enlightenment models of progress, modernization theory first appeared in the work of American sociologists. Talcott Parsons (1902–1979) and Edward Shils (1911–1995) provided much of the inspiration for the concept by framing a holistic view of social systems. As they argued, values and cultural norms, transmitted through social institutions, played vital roles in regulating human behavior and ensuring individual action consistent with the social order. Societies, therefore, were integrated, functioning units. When institutions and cultural values distributed resources and mediated conflict in harmony with the needs of individuals, societies rested at points of balanced consensus. Different historical points of equilibrium, moreover, could be identified in the form of "pattern variables" that defined the dichotomy between "primitive" and "advanced" societies. "Primitive" societies functioned to meet individual needs, but they did so through institutions characterized by a reverence for ascribed status, particularism, diffuse roles, and an orientation toward the collective. "Advanced" societies, however, reflected values of achieved status, universalism, specific social roles, and self-orientation. In books like *The Social System* (1951) and *Structure and Process in Modern Societies* (1960), Parsons argued that if a society were under enough strain, then it would make the dramatic shift from one historical pole to the other. Modernization, sociologists insisted, was a global force, transcending all lines of culture or history. As Daniel Lerner (1917–1980) claimed in *The Passing of Traditional Society: Modernizing the Middle East*: "The same basic model appears on all continents of the world, regardless of variations in race, color, or creed" (1958, p. viii).

Modernization also proved attractive to political scientists searching for an overarching theory to analyze the changes of the postwar world. Scholars like Gabriel Almond (1911–2002), Myron Weiner (1931–1999), and Lucian Pye all adapted Parsons's functionalist assumptions. As they argued, specialists studying diverse regions could contribute to a more integrative approach by positing universal functions that all political systems needed to fulfill. By correlating functions with specific political structures, they could map the overall, universal patterns of transformation. By applying that model, as Pye did in *Politics, Personality, and Nation Building: Burma's Search for Identity* (1962), political scientists sought to analyze the way that modern markets, values, and technologies awakened new aspirations among previously fatalistic, traditional peoples and spurred them to create new political forms.

Modernization also took hold among economists concerned with "development." For many scholars, poverty, high population growth, and lack of infrastructure made the problems of "emerging" countries so different from "advanced" ones that standard macroeconomic theory had to be modified by an approach stressing behavioral and cultural obstacles as well as structural ones. Walt W. Rostow (1916–2003), author of *The Stages of Economic Growth: A Non-Communist Manifesto* (1960), argued that compound interest and investment remained the primary engines for change, but he also emphasized that the passage from traditional fatalism and "pre-Newtonian science" through a "take-off" to the "age of high mass consumption" required new, activist attitudes toward the natural world, as well as habits of efficiency and advances in transportation and communications.

Theories of modernization were profoundly shaped by the cold war context. Many American policymakers and social scientists viewed the post–World War II (1939–1945) collapse of European empires with profound anxiety. Decolonization opened doors for progressive change, but it also appeared to accelerate what many theorists and policymakers called a "revolution of rising expectations" in the "emerging nations" of the world. Destitution, violence, and anticolonial politics, U.S. officials feared, created opportunities for Soviet expansion and subversion. Communists, Rostow and others warned, were "scavengers of the transitional process," opportunists that sought to derail the natural course of change. It was imperative, therefore, for the United States to accelerate the process of modernization and drive decolonizing societies through the dangerous window of instability toward progress. As the cold war moved into the "third world," theorists and policymakers began a symbiotic relationship. Many scholars moved from academia into government service to promote the use of foreign aid, technical assistance, propaganda, civil-service training, and military advising as key tools for managing the future of the "developing world." Rostow, for example, joined the State Department of President John F. Kennedy (1917–1963) and later became Lyndon Johnson's (1908–1973) national security adviser, while Pye advised the Agency for International Development. Government funding, in turn, flowed into social scientific research. The Central Intelligence Agency provided support for Massachusetts

Institute of Technology's Center for International Studies, and the National Defense Education Act (1958) channeled federal funds into research on human behavior, area studies, and language programs.

In practice, however, modernization largely failed. Poverty turned out to be far more intractable than modernizers expected, and neither U.S. aid nor World Bank loans produced decisive economic "take-offs" in the 1960s. Agencies like the Peace Corps did promote gains in literacy, but because modernization tended to fold all matters of local politics and culture into its universal, linear model, theorists often ignored problems created by oligarchies that had little intention of promoting liberal reforms. From the mid-1950s through the final American withdrawal, the Vietnam War (1957–1975) was understood as a project in modernization. U.S. advisers aspired to create a new, modern South Vietnamese nation-state where one had never existed before, yet despite massive investments in economic aid, administrative training, and promises to build a Tennessee Valley Authority on the Mekong River, repressive regimes continued to alienate much of South Vietnam's population. Vietnamese culture also mattered in ways that the linear model of modernization failed to take into account as the historically rooted vision of an independent, united Vietnam prevailed over a government that, in the eyes of many, was simply the latest manifestation of foreign, imperial control. While modernization won few "hearts and minds" in Vietnam, its failure provided striking evidence that the "traditional" world was not so easily malleable after all.

By the early 1970s, modernization had largely collapsed as a scholarly paradigm. Conservatives like Robert Nisbet (1913–1996) and Samuel Huntington rejected it as a failed liberal dream, a naive vision of consensual reform. From the political Left, scholars like André Gunder Frank (1929–2005) and Immanuel Wallerstein challenged modernization with dependency and world-systems models. Instead of linear progress, they argued that contact between Western metropoles and Southern Hemisphere satellites produced patterns of exploitation and impoverishment. Other scholars attacked the ethnocentric tone of modernization, its resonance with imperial claims, its universal assumptions, and its tendency to favor consensus, authority, and order in ways that precluded a serious consideration of class conflict and power relations.

Many of modernization's underlying assumptions and aspirations, however, have continued to thrive in public policy and popular debate. The collapse of the Soviet Union in 1991 stimulated renewed claims that the world was indeed converging on a liberal, capitalist, democratic endpoint. After the attacks of September 11, 2001, calls for the United States to promote transformative "nation building" as part of a global "war on terror" also reflected the durability of assumptions that America might chart the future of a "traditional" world.

SEE ALSO *Developing Countries; Development Economics; Liberalism; Modernity*

BIBLIOGRAPHY

Cooper, Frederick, and Randall Packard, eds. 1997. *International Development and the Social Sciences: Essays on the History and Politics of Knowledge.* Berkeley: University of California Press.

Eisenstadt, S. N. 1974. Studies of Modernization and Sociological Theory. *History and Theory* 13 (3): 225–252.

Gilman, Nils. 2003. *Mandarins of the Future: Modernization Theory in Cold War America.* Baltimore, MD: Johns Hopkins University Press.

Latham, Michael. 2000. *Modernization as Ideology: American Social Science and "Nation Building" in the Kennedy Era.* Chapel Hill: University of North Carolina Press.

Lerner, Daniel. 1958. *Passing of Traditional Society: Modernizing the Middle East.* Glencoe, IL: Free Press.

Rostow, W. W. 1960. *The Stages of Economic Growth: A Non-Communist Manifesto.* Cambridge, U.K.: Cambridge University Press.

Tipps, Dean C. 1973. Modernization Theory and the Comparative Study of Societies: A Critical Perspective. *Comparative Studies in Society and History* 15 (2): 199–226.

Michael E. Latham

MODIGLIANI, FRANCO
1918–2003

Franco Modigliani was an Italian-born Jewish-American economist. He fled the fascist and anti-Semitic regime of Benito Mussolini (1883–1945) in 1939 and migrated to the United States with a doctor of law degree (1939) from the University of Rome. He earned a doctorate in economics from the New School University in New York in 1944, writing his dissertation on the Keynesian liquidity preference. In his dissertation, he reworked the Hicksian IS and LM curves to present a new version of Keynesian economics. His Keynesian paradigm laid the foundation for the Federal Reserve Bank econometric model. In 1962 Modigliani joined the economics department of the Massachusetts Institute of Technology, where he stayed for the rest of his career.

Liquidity preference explains unemployment without wage rigidity. It posits a relationship of money to prices. The price of money is anything that can be exchanged for it. Money in the future is also a price with a discount rate $R_t = (1 + r_t)^{-1}$. Being flexible, the rate of interest will rise in tight money situations. People will raise cash by liquidating money instruments or through borrowing. Investment and savings will fall and be subsequently followed by a fall of income and employment. The demand for money will then fall to equal its supply. Essentially, Modigliani argued for a "rate of interest" to "output" adjustment consequent to a tight monetary policy, in contrast to classical economists, who argued for a "rate of interest" to "price of all goods" adjustment. By keeping policymakers on guard to supply an adequate quantity of money or to fix an appropriate interest rate, Modigliani made unemployment an equilibrating mechanism.

Modigliani rid the investment concept in corporate finance of its traditional utility and production analyses. The Modigliani-Miller hypothesis first argued that a firm trying to increase its value by moving from only equity to a mixture of debt and equity positions will encourage arbitrage among individual investors that would undo its actions, making value invariant to the debt/equity ratio. Second, the rate of return on equity is linearly dependent on the debt/equity ratio. If a firm's stock is $1,000, debt is $400, interest on debt is 0.05, and the expected rate of return is 0.1, then its return on equity will be $0.1 + (0.1 - 0.05)\frac{400}{600} = 0.1333$. Third, new investment opportunities are also independent of the debt/equity ratio. This three-part hypothesis abstracted from the effects of taxes and bankruptcy. The discussion was extended to a dividend invariance value model.

In Modigliani's second best-known hypothesis, the *life-cycle hypothesis of saving* (LCH), consumers receive income, Y, up to the end of their working life, N. They accumulate savings during their working year, and consume, C, uniformly during their lifetime, $L > N$. Since lifetime consumption must equal lifetime income, assuming no bequest, we can express $CL = NY$, or $C = (N \mid L)Y$, in which case the terms in parentheses represent the marginal propensity to consume. Fitting the LCH to labor income and net assets, A, the equation $C = .766Y + .073A$ reconciled some anomalies of the post–World War II (1939–1945) period.

For his contributions to investment and consumption theories, Modigliani received the Nobel Prize in economics in 1985. He also contributed to economic policy debates, evolving the NIRU (noninflationary rate of unemployment) concept through the Phillips curve, and Okun's unemployment versus the gross domestic product gap relationship, public deficits, and reinstated personal savings into the post-Keynesian debate on the equilibrium profit rate, creating the dual or anti-Pasinetti theorem.

SEE ALSO *Life-Cycle Hypothesis; Modigliani-Miller Theorems*

BIBLIOGRAPHY

Ando, Albert, and Franco Modigliani. 1963. The "Life Cycle" Hypothesis of Saving: Aggregate Implications and Tests. *American Economic Review* 53 (1): 55–84.

Modigliani, Franco. 1944. Liquidity Preference and the Theory of Interest and Money. *Econometrica* 12: 45–88.

Modigliani, Franco. 1949. *Studies in Income and Wealth.* Vol. 11: *Fluctuations in the Saving-Income Ratio: A Problem in Economic Forecasting.* New York: National Bureau of Economic Research.

Modigliani, Franco. 1963. The Monetary Mechanism and Its Interaction with Real Phenomena. *Review of Economics and Statistics* 45: 79–107.

Modigliani, Franco. 1986. Life Cycle, Individual Thrift, and the Wealth of Nations. *American Economic Review* 76 (3): 297–313.

Modigliani, Franco. 1988. MM-Past, Present, Future. *Journal of Economic Perspectives* 2 (4): 149–158.

Modigliani, Franco. 2003. The Keynesian Gospel According to Modigliani. *American Economist* 47 (1): 2–24.

Modigliani, Franco, and Richard Brumberg. 1954. Utility Analysis and the Consumption Function: An Interpretation of Cross-Section Data. In *Post-Keynesian Economics,* ed. Kenneth K. Kurihara, 388–436. New Brunswick, NJ: Rutgers University Press.

Ramrattan, Lall, and Michael Szenberg. 2004. Franco Modigliani, 1918–2003: In Memoriam. *American Economist* 43 (1): 3–8.

Ramrattan, Lall, and Michael Szenberg. 2007. *Franco Modigliani, A Mind That Never Rests: An Intellectual Biography.* Houndmills, U.K.: Palgrave Macmillan.

Lall Ramrattan
Michael Szenberg

MODIGLIANI-MILLER THEOREMS

The Modigliani-Miller (M&M) theorems, developed by economists Franco Modigliani (1918–2003) and Merton Miller (1923–2000) in a series of papers, represent a major milestone in corporate finance theory. Modigliani and Miller won Nobel prizes in economics in 1985 and 1990, respectively, in part for their contributions to what are often referred to as the *capital structure irrelevance* and *dividend irrelevance* theorems.

Contrary to financial theory of the time, which focused on institutions, the M&M theorems were among the first efforts by economists to bring rigorous analysis to the understanding of corporate finance issues. Corporate financial capital, the funds invested in a firm, consists of money borrowed from others (bonds and loans) and business owners' own money (stock). Lenders receive a stated rate of interest and have the first claim on corporate assets. Stockholders receive all remaining current and future profits of the company. Leverage represents the proportion of debt (bonds and loans) to stock. Modigliani and Miller (1958) presented the idea that, assuming perfect financial markets and in the absence of taxes, the value of a levered firm is the same as that of an unlevered firm if both firms represent the same investment opportunities. In other words, change in capital structure (the mixture of debt and stock) alone does not affect a firm's value. Their no-arbitrage proof stated that, if these firms have different values, investors will be able to replicate the higher-valued firm with the lower-valued firm plus their own borrowing or lending. Alternatively, management of the firm can change the capital structure of the firm to achieve its highest value. In a later paper, Modigliani and Miller argued that a firm's value is not affected by its dividend policy (payment to stockholders) because increased return in the form of dividends is offset by the reduction in the firm's assets.

The M&M framework and methodology had a major impact in shaping future research. In the decades that followed, the corporate finance literature was significantly enriched by attempts to relax various original M&M assumptions, such as no taxation and no bankruptcy costs. The no-arbitrage proof has also become part of financial economists' standard toolkit and was applied in many prominent works, such as the development of the put-call parity in option pricing theory.

Introducing corporate income tax into the model leads to the naive result that the firm should depend on debt financing alone to maximize the benefit of the tax shield. The reason that this is not observed in the business world is because the tax benefit for debt financing at the firm level is counterbalanced by unfavorable tax treatment at the household level. Dividends and bond returns are taxed annually, while taxes on unrealized equity returns can be indefinitely deferred. In most jurisdictions, corporations and households are subject to different tax rates. The risk of bankruptcy also limits the amount of debt a firm should use, since the cost of equity increases with leverage. Consequently, different tax situations and risk preferences demand firms with different kinds of capital structures. The fact that firms choose different tax structures attests to the validity of the capital structure irrelevance theorem, rather than discrediting it.

Relaxing the assumption that managers and shareholders have the same information about a firm's cash flow, researchers developed the signaling theory of dividends. Because managers tend to have information not yet available to shareholders, their action to increase or decrease dividends often reflects information not yet embedded in the stock price. This extension of the M&M

theorems explains why stock prices often react to changes in dividends.

SEE ALSO *Capital; Expectations; Expectations, Rational; Finance; Leverage; Market Fundamentals; Modigliani, Franco; Wealth*

BIBLIOGRAPHY

Miller, Merton. 1988. The Modigliani-Miller Propositions after Thirty Years. *Journal of Economic Perspectives* 2 (4): 99–120.

Miller, Merton, and Franco Modigliani. 1961. Dividend Policy, Growth, and the Valuation of Shares. *Journal of Business* 34: 411–433.

Modigliani, Franco, and Merton Miller. 1958. The Cost of Capital, Corporation Finance, and the Theory of Investment. *American Economic Review* 48: 261–297.

Shi Larry Cao

MOHAMMED

SEE *Muhammad.*

MOMENT GENERATING FUNCTION

The moment generating function of the random variable X, provided it exists, is $M_x(t) = E[e^{tX}]$ where $E[g(X)]$ denotes the expectation of the function $g(X)$. For example, if the random variable X follows the normal distribution with mean μ and variance σ^2, the moment generating function of X is $M_X(t) = e^{\mu t + \sigma^2 t^2 / 2}$.

The moment generating function has two main uses. First, as the name implies, it can be used to obtain the moments of a random variable. Specifically, the kth moment of the random variable X, $\alpha_k = E[X^k]$, is given by $\alpha_k = M_X^{(k)}(0)$ where $M_X^{(k)}(0)$ is the kth derivative of $M_X(t)$ evaluated at $t = 0$. For example, if X is normally distributed with mean μ and variance σ^2, and hence moment generating function $M_X(t) = e^{\mu t + \sigma^2 t^2 / 2}$, it follows that

$$M_X^{(1)}(t) = [\mu + t\sigma^2] e^{\mu t + \sigma^2 t^2 / 2}$$

and

$$M_X^{(2)}(t) = (\sigma^2 + [\mu + t\sigma^2]^2) e^{\mu t + \sigma^2 t^2 / 2}.$$

It follows that the first moment of X is μ and the second moment of X is $\mu^2 + \sigma^2$.

The second, and perhaps more important, use of the moment generating function derives from the fact that the moment generating function uniquely identifies the distribution function of a random variable. Thus, if $M_{X_1}(t) = M_{X_2}(t)$, then $Pr(X_1 \leq x) = Pr(X_2 \leq x)$. For example, if the random variable X has the moment generating function $M_X(t) = e^{\mu t + \sigma^2 t^2 / 2}$, then X necessarily follows the normal distribution. This property of the moment generating function can sometimes be used to determine the distribution of the limit of a sequence of random variables. Consider, for example, a sequence of random variables $\{Y_n; n = 1, 2, \ldots\}$ with distribution functions $\{F_n(y); n = 1, 2, \ldots\}$ and corresponding moment generating functions $\{M_n(t); n = 1, 2, \ldots\}$. If $\lim_{n \to \infty} M_n(t) = M(t)$, where $M(t)$ is the moment generating function of a random variable Y with distribution function $F(y) = Pr(Y \leq y)$, then $\lim_{n \to \infty} F_n(y) = F(y)$. $F(y)$ is called the limiting distribution of the sequence $\{Y_n; n = 1, 2, \ldots\}$ and Y_n is said to converge in distribution to Y. For n sufficiently large, $F(y)$ provides a good approximation to the distribution of Y_n. For example, consider the sequence of sample means $\{\bar{X}_n; n = 1, 2, \ldots\}$ obtained from random samples of size n from a population with mean μ and variance σ^2. Under certain conditions, the standardized sequence $\{Y_n = \sqrt{n}(\bar{X}_n - \mu) / \sigma; n = 1, 2, ..\}$ converges in distribution to a standard normal random variable. This result, referred to as a central limit theorem for the sample mean, is typically obtained by showing that the sequence of corresponding moment generating functions $\{M_{\bar{X}_n}(t)\}$ converges to $M(t) = e^{t^2 / 2}$, the moment generating function of a normal random variable with mean zero and variance 1, that is, a standard normal random variable.

Closely related to the moment generating function is the so-called characteristic function. The characteristic function of the random variable X is $C_X(t) = E[e^{itX}]$ where $i = \sqrt{-1}$ and $e^{itX} = \cos(tX) + i\sin(tX)$. The advantage of the characteristic function is that it always exists whereas the moment generating function may not. If the moment generating function exists, the characteristic function is related to it by $C_X(t) = M_X(it)$. Thus, for example, the characteristic function of a normally distributed random variable with mean μ and variance σ^2 is $C_X(t) = e^{it\mu - \sigma^2 t^2 / 2}$. Like the moment generating function, the characteristic function can be used to obtain moments of the random variable. And since it uniquely identifies the distribution of the random variable, it can be used to obtain the limiting distribution of sequences of random variables.

Elementary mathematical treatments of the moment generating function are given in Donald A. Berry and Bernard W. Lindgren and John E. Freund. Intermediate treatments may be found in Robert V. Hogg and Allen T. Craig, and Lindgren and advanced mathematical discussion can be found in Harald Cramér and M. Loève. David attributes the first occurrences in print of the term *moment generating function* to Henri Poincaré (1912 in French) and Cecil C. Craig (1936 in English).

BIBLIOGRAPHY

Berry, Donald A., and Bernard W. Lindgren. 1996. *Statistics: Theory and Methods*. 2nd ed. Belmont, CA: Duxbury Press at Wadsworth Publishing.

Cramér, Harald. 1946. *Mathematical Methods of Statistics*. Princeton, NJ: Princeton University Press.

David, H. A. 1995. First (?) Occurrence of Common Terms in Mathematical Statistics. *American Statistician* 49 (2): 121–133.

Freund, John E. 1992. *Mathematical Statistics*. 5th ed. Englewood Cliffs, NJ: Prentice Hall.

Hogg, Robert V., and Allen T. Craig. 1995. *Introduction to Mathematical Statistics*. 5th ed. Englewood Cliffs, NJ: Prentice Hall.

Lindgren, Bernard W. 1976. *Statistical Theory*. 3rd ed. New York: Macmillan.

Loève, M. 1977. *Probability Theory I*. 4th ed. New York: Springer-Verlag.

E. Philip Howrey

MOMENTS

SEE *Descriptive Statistics.*

MONARCHISM

Monarchism is a belief in and advocacy of monarchy, one of the oldest forms of government, which typically consists of a single head of state who reigns over a sovereign territory and its people for life. Monarchism embodies the traditional values of heredity, class and clericalism, concepts antithetical to modern notions of popular sovereignty, egalitarianism, and secularism.

HISTORICAL BACKGROUND

Some of the earliest monarchs were well-known Hebrew kings of the Bible—Saul and Solomon—whose power derived from divine authority. These early monarchs often came from the ranks of judges, and in addition to ruling at the pleasure of the deity, served as guardians and interpreters of law and justice. The rulers of the Roman Empire were monarchs who derived their authority from the warrior and upper classes by acclamation and ruled over nearly every aspect of Roman society. Rome's emperors from Augustus (27 BCE–14 CE) to Constantine XI Palaeologus (1449–1453) ruled over vast swaths of land in Europe, Africa, and the Middle East for several centuries.

Throughout the Middle Ages, absolute monarchy was the dominant form of government in Europe, giving rise to a number of influential figures including Charlemagne (768–814), William the Conqueror (1066–1087), and King John of England (1199–1216). One of the earliest efforts to limit the monarch's power and establish a constitutional monarchy occurred with the signing of the Magna Carta in 1215. In 1649 King Charles I was overthrown and beheaded during the English Revolution, marking the first time in history that a monarch had ever been publicly executed. Despite these efforts to curtail the monarch's authority, absolute monarchy continued to be the dominant form of government in Europe until the French Revolution in 1789.

In France, the concept of popular sovereignty arose from the ashes of the French Revolution and the overthrow of the monarch, Louis XVI. The demise of the monarchy led to the emergence of imperial rule under Napoléon Bonaparte (Napoléon I) and the Napoleonic Wars throughout Europe. The French eventually restored the Bourbon Dynasty (Louis XVIII) to the throne following the abdication of Napoléon I. The ouster of Louis-Philippe in 1848 paved the way for the Second Republic and the ascendency of Napoléon III. Since then, royalists have attempted to restore the monarchy of France, but with little success. The entanglement of the French monarchy and the Catholic Church—the long-standing alliance between the "Throne and the Altar"—is largely to blame for the demise of monarchism in France and the development of the modern secular French state.

Since the mid-nineteenth century, monarchies have been dismantled in Russia, Germany, Italy, and Austria-Hungary, among other nations. Most monarchies have retained their royal families for traditional or symbolic reasons, as in the United Kingdom, Belgium, Luxembourg, Denmark, Norway, and Japan. Today, forty-five nations are considered to be monarchies in one form or another; sixteen of them fall under the common monarch of the United Kingdom. Those Commonwealth nations that continue to recognize the British monarch include Antigua and Barbuda, Australia, the Bahamas, Barbados, Belize, Canada, Grenada, Jamaica, New Zealand, Papua New Guinea, Saint Kitts and Nevis, Saint Lucia, the Soloman Islands, and Tuvalu.

FORMS OF MONARCHY

Monarchy can take a variety of forms, including absolute monarchy, elected monarchy, hereditary monarchy, and constitutional monarchy. In an absolute monarchy, the monarch possesses total power over the land and its inhabitants, and there is no authority or body of law above the monarch. Bhutan, Brunei, Kuwait, Saudi Arabia, and Swaziland are considered to be absolute monarchies today.

An elected monarchy is a form of government in which the king or queen is elected by the people or a select body of individuals. In this system, succession to the throne is determined by election, usually by a small group of people or a council. In the Holy Roman Empire (800–1806) kings were elected by a council of nobles. Between the seventh and eleventh centuries the *Witenagemot* consisted of noblemen charged with the task of approving the succession of monarchs in Anglo-Saxon England. The twentieth century saw the election of monarchs to the thrones of Norway, Greece, Romania, and Bulgaria. At present, elective monarchies exist in Andorra, Cambodia, Kuwait, Malaysia, and Vatican City, where the pope is elected to a life term by the College of Cardinals. Most elective monarchies have been succeeded by hereditary monarchies.

In a hereditary monarchy the succeeding monarch comes from the same family or bloodline. A major advantage of this form of monarchy is that it ensures predictability and stability in the transition to power from one monarch to the next. Typically, an order of succession is established beforehand so that when a monarch dies or abdicates the throne, the crown is usually passed to a son or daughter, based on seniority. Throughout history, disputes over hereditary succession to the throne have led to numerous wars. Most of the world's existing monarchies today are hereditary monarchies in which the order of succession is determined by primogeniture. In most of these, the royal families act in a primarily ceremonial capacity, serving a symbolic role in society.

A constitutional monarchy is a form of government in which the monarch's power is limited by a separate branch of government. In this system, a parliament or legislative body usually acts on behalf of the state, and the constitutional monarch has little power in government, generally playing a symbolic role as the figurehead representing the nation and doing charitable work. Modern constitutional monarchies usually incorporate the separation of powers concept, with the monarch serving as the head of the executive branch in a purely ceremonial role, the parliament or legislature serving as the lawmaking body, and a high court interpreting and enforcing the law. Today, most constitutional monarchies are representative democracies. The English monarchy is the oldest continuous constitutional monarchy.

MONARCHIST GROUPS

Monarchism is defended and supported by a variety of groups who believe that monarchies serve an important symbolic role in society and provide an important link to a nation's past. For example, promonarchist movements in France support the revitalization of monarchy as the best way to reestablish cultural and religious ties to the Catholic Church. Moreover, debates over the relevance of monarchy in Australia, Canada, and New Zealand serve as a driving force for these governments to maintain cultural ties to the United Kingdom. The traditional values of heredity, class, and clericalism embued in monarchical systems tend to

clash with the more modern notions of democracy, egalitarianism, and secularism in different parts of the world.

Some of the more prominent organizations and political groups that support the retention or restoration of monarchy as a form of government include Action Française, the Monarchist League of Canada, the Monarchist League of New Zealand, Australians for Constitutional Monarchy, the National Alignment (Greece), the People's Monarchist Party (Portugal), the Legitimists and Orléanists (France), the Iraqi Constitutional Monarchy, the Vietnamese Constitutional Monarchist League, the Iranian Monarchists, the Southeast Asia Imperial and Royal League, and the International Monarchist League. These groups believe in the values and traditions embedded in the monarchical system of government and are committed to preserving these values and traditions in society.

SEE ALSO *Democracy; French Revolution; Monarchy; Monarchy, Constitutional; Sovereignty; Tradition*

BIBLIOGRAPHY

Dower, John. 2000. *Embracing Defeat: Japan in the Wake of World War II.* New York: W. W. Norton.

Downes, Paul. 2002. *Democracy, Revolution, and Monarchism in Early American Literature.* Cambridge, U.K.: Cambridge University Press.

Falk, Ze'ev W. 1964. *Hebrew Law in Biblical Times.* Jerusalem: Wahrmann Books.

Griffiths, Ralph Alan, and John Ashton Cannon. 1998. *The Oxford Illustrated History of the British Monarchy.* Oxford: Oxford University Press.

Harvey, Robert. 2006. *The War of Wars: The Great European Conflict, 1793–1815.* New York: Carroll and Graf.

Hastings, Adrian. 2000. *A World History of Christianity.* Grand Rapids, MI: Eerdmans.

Hobsbawm, Eric J. 1992. *Nations and Nationalism Since 1780: Programme, Myth, Reality.* Cambridge, U.K.: Canto.

Kaufmann, Walter. 1953. *Monarchism in the Weimar Republic.* New York: Bookman Associates.

Pearsall, Ronald. 1998. *Kings and Queens: A History of British Monarchy.* New York: New Line Books.

Said, Edward. 1979. *Orientalism.* New York: Vintage.

Taylor, Antony. 1999. *'Down with the Crown': British Antimonarchism and Debates About Royalty Since 1790.* London: Reaktion Books.

Klint W. Alexander

MONARCHY

Monarchy literally means "rule by one," and comes from the combination of the Greek words for "alone" (*mono*) and "to rule" (*archein*). It is a form of government in which supreme authority is vested in a single person, the monarch, who is consecrated in office and whose right to rule is generally hereditary and lifelong. By contrast, a republic is a form of government that does not have a monarch. All but a few countries in the world are republics, as there were only twenty-nine sovereign monarchies at the beginning of the twenty-first century (Lesotho, Morocco, and Swaziland in Africa; Bhutan, Brunei, Cambodia, Japan, Malaysia, Nepal, and Thailand in Asia; Belgium, Denmark, Holland, Liechtenstein, Luxembourg, Monaco, Norway, Spain, Sweden, and the United Kingdom in Europe; Bahrain, Jordan, Kuwait, Oman, Qatar, Saudi Arabia, and the United Arab Emirates in the Middle East; and Samoa and Tonga in the Pacific). A monarch typically reigns as a permanent head of state with varying formal and ceremonial powers. If the monarch is only a nominal ruler, then a regent will govern in his or her name. In contrast, the head of state in a republic is usually an elected president, who is chosen for only a limited period of time.

Monarchs have traditionally based their claim to the throne in terms of blood descent from a reigning or dynastic family, or even from a god (e.g., the kings of ancient Sparta claimed to be descended from the mythical Greek hero and demigod Hercules). Some European monarchs were originally elected by the ruling nobility (e.g., the Holy Roman Emperors), but in the early Middle Ages the elective principle was replaced by the purely hereditary principle and the ecclesiastical consecretion of the monarch as proof of godly sanction. Legitimacy was formally conferred by a solemn religious ceremony, the coronation, in which the monarch was given a crown as a symbol of office upon his or her succession to the throne. Hereditary monarchy was justified on the grounds of royal birthright, religion, history, and tradition. Today monarchy is more likely to serve as a symbol of national unity and continuity—with powers ranging from nominal to absolute. Most modern monarchies are constituted by tradition or are codified by law so that the crowned sovereign has little real practical authority, but in others the monarch holds considerable or even absolute power. But even where the monarch's will is law and the royal court is the acme of political power and prestige, the king or queen must still rule by custom.

In ancient Greece, the philosopher Plato (428–347 BCE) believed that a monarchy ruled by a sagacious philosopher-king was the best form of government. For Plato's pupil Aristotle (384–322 BCE), monarchy was a benevolent dictatorship, under which power is vested in a person of exceptional virtue and wisdom who rules for the benefit of the entire people. But Aristotle admitted that monarchy can degenerate into tyranny, a corrupt and unstable form of government, under which rulers exercise undivided power for the benefit of themselves alone, ignoring the will of the people.

Monarchy is the oldest form of government, whose origins can be traced to the primitive kingship of early tribal chiefs. The kingdoms of antiquity claimed divine descent for their monarch, who—as the embodiment or descendant of God—could do no wrong. The king of Babylon and the pharaoh of Egypt were each considered a living god with supernatural powers, and the pharaohs even married their sisters or daughters so that royal authority could remain within the sacred family. Other ancient monarchs, such as the "celestial" emperor of China or the Achaemenid "king of kings" in Persia, claimed to be the temporal representatives of God, ruling on Earth on behalf of the omnipotent deity. Later monarchs, such as the tyrants of ancient Greece, the Roman emperors, or the kings of the Franks, also claimed to be God's annointed, but derived their authority from the consent of the warrior aristocracy. As the chosen agents of God's will and defenders of the Christian faith, the medieval European monarchs were crowned by the church, but their power was still dependent on the nobles. Later European monarchs, such as Henry VIII of England (1491–1547), Louis XIV of France (1638–1715), Frederick II of Prussia (1712–1786), and Catherine the Great of Russia (1729–1796), became increasingly absolutist at a time when centralized nation-states were formed. They justified their total power with the doctrine of the "divine right of kings," developed in the sixteenth and seventeenth centuries, which claimed that the monarch was responsible not to the governed, including the church, but to God alone. The essence of monarchical absolutism was epitomized by the famous words of Louis XIV: "L'état c'est moi!" ("I am the state!").

With the democratic revolutions of the eighteenth and nineteenth centuries, absolute monarchy began to decline, and although many monarchs kept their life tenure and remained symbols of national unity and statehood, real power gradually passed to representative assemblies. Many of the countries retaining monarchy as a form of government turned into limited or constitutional monarchies—that is, a monarchy in which the central authority of the sovereign is limited by the provisions of a constitution and the acts of a legislature. The figurehead monarch is legally obligated to follow the advice of his or her government ministers and is always politically neutral. The first step in the movement toward constitutional monarchy was the incremental rise of parliamentary supremacy ("the king-in-parliament") in England, which imposed significant legal and political limitations on monarchical authority, and as a result of which no British monarch has challenged an act of Parliament since 1703.

After the French Revolution of 1789 most countries eventually abolished their monarchies and became instead presidential or parliamentary republics. Today many remaining monarchies are figurehead constitutional monarchies in which the monarchs have a largely symbolic and ceremonial role, such as those found in Europe. For example, although King Juan Carlos I has played an active political role since 1975, especially in restoring democracy in his country, Spain is officially a "parliamentary monarchy" under the constitution of November 1978. A popular referendum in 2003 empowered the regnant prince of Liechtenstein to dismiss the cabinet government at will, making him by far the most powerful constitutional monarch in Europe, but this probably temporary shift in constitutional authority could be easily reversed by another referendum. The British queen, Elizabeth II, also holds significant potential power as head of state, nominal head of the Anglican Church, and leader of the British Commonwealth of Nations, but like all titular heads of state, she only symbolically represents her nation—mostly by receiving foreign dignitaries, giving speeches on ceremonial occasions, and formally approving decisions made by elected officials. As in most limited monarchies, the head of government—the British prime minister, who is elected by parliament—is the real working executive responsible for the day-to-day operation of the cabinet government. But many constitutional monarchs retain certain important residual powers, under which they could potentially exercise considerable political influence. These so-called prerogative powers, which could be used in a political emergency to protect the constitution from abuse and partisan manipulation, include formally nominating the head of government, convening or dissolving the legislature, and signing enacted legislation into law.

In absolute monarchies, by contrast, there are no constitutional restrictions on the prerogatives of the autocratic ruler, who is theoretically above the law. Among the few remaining absolute monarchies at the beginning of the twenty-first century were Kuwait, Saudi Arabia, Oman, Qatar, Bahrain, the United Arab Emirates, Brunei, Bhutan, and Swaziland. In Jordan and Morocco, the king still wields substantial despotic power independently of his formal role within the constitutional framework. The traditional monarchies that survive today are probably doomed unless they can eventually transform themselves into limited monarchies. Failure to do so led to the overthrow of traditional monarchies and their replacement by radical revolutionary regimes in Egypt, Iraq, Libya, Ethiopia, Cambodia, and Iran during the second half of the twentieth century. After failing to crush a stubborn Maoist insurgency, the king of Nepal was forced to give up absolute rule and surrender all his powers as head of state to the prime minister in December 2006.

The monarchical institution is believed to have performed an integrative function, holding together diverse social groups during the difficult period of democratization. The traditional sectors of society—the clergy, the aristocracy, army officers, and big landowners—usually oppose democracy and may be tempted to carry out coups d'état to derail the process of democratization. But these sectors are also monarchist in orientation, and if the king or queen is seen to support democracy, the traditional sectors of society will also go along with it. The monarchy thus facilitated the transition from the traditional political system of the late Middle Ages to the democratic political system of today (Lipset 1981, pp. 65–66). For instance, King Juan Carlos I of Spain defeated an attempted military coup in 1981 when he went on national television to declare that he was defending democracy and expected the armed forces to do the same. Following his public rebuke, the rebellion collapsed for lack of military backing; even the staunchly antimonarchist Spanish Communist Party announced its support for the monarch. By proclaiming his loyalty to the new democratic institutions, the king united the fractious sectors of Spanish society in defense of democracy, including those that had previously been revolutionary and antimonarchist.

SEE ALSO *Aristocracy; Authoritarianism; Democracy; Divine Right; Monarchism; Monarchy, Constitutional; Nation-State; Referendum*

BIBLIOGRAPHY

Bendix, Reinhard. 1978. *Kings or People: Power and the Mandate to Rule.* Berkeley: University of California Press.

Lipset, Seymour Martin. [1960] 1981. *Political Man: The Social Bases of Politics.* Baltimore, MD: Johns Hopkins University Press.

Pine, Leslie Gilbert. 1958. *The Twilight of Monarchy.* London: Burke.

Slavin, Arthur Joseph. 1964. *The "New Monarchies" and Representative Assemblies: Medieval Constitutionalism or Modern Absolutism?* Boston: Heath.

Tames, Richard. 2003. *Monarchy.* Chicago: Heinemann Library.

Tomlinson, Richard. 1995. *Divine Right: The Inglorious Survival of British Royalty.* Boston: Little, Brown.

Rossen Vassilev

MONARCHY, CONSTITUTIONAL

Constitutional monarchy is a system of government in which a monarch serves as the titular head of state but not the head of government and the monarch's powers are strictly limited by the constitution. Constitutional monarchies emerged in seventeenth-century Europe as the outcome of the struggle of the landed aristocracy and merchant class to limit the power of absolute monarchs. A leading example is the Glorious Revolution of 1689 that made Parliament supreme in the English system of government but retained a significant role for the crown. These efforts to curb royal absolutism were inspired by the liberal political philosophy of the Enlightenment. In the nineteenth and early twentieth centuries, as monarchical liberal democracies became more fully democratic, kings and queens came to play primarily a symbolic, ceremonial role in government.

Constitutional monarchy is a feature of many, but not all, parliamentary democracies. In parliamentary democracies that are constitutional monarchies, the king or queen retains nominally very large powers as the titular head of state. Acts of government are carried out in the crown's name. The monarch is the head of the armed forces. Acts of parliament require the monarch's signature, and the monarch summons and dissolves parliament. But the monarch exercises all these powers on the advice of ministers who have a majority in the elected house of parliament.

In parliamentary democracies, the government is headed by a prime minister and cabinet ministers who are members of the parliamentary party or coalition of parties that have a majority in the elected house of parliament. In monarchical parliamentary democracies, the monarch formally appoints the prime minister. Normally, the monarch has no choice as to who should be appointed prime minister: the leader of the political party or coalition of parties that has a majority in the elected house of parliament must be appointed. However, in the unusual circumstances of a "hung parliament," when it is not clear which party or combination of parties has a majority, the monarch (or in Commonwealth countries, the governor-general who represents the queen) may play a more significant and discretionary role.

In exceptional situations where discretionary judgment is required, the monarchical head of state's objective is to ensure that it is the parliament elected by the people that is supreme, not the prime minister. This principle may mean that it is constitutionally appropriate for a monarch to reject a prime minister's advice and act independently. For example, if an incumbent prime minister refuses to accept the result of a general election that produces a parliament in which his or her party no longer has a majority, and if the prime minister refuses to resign or allow any other party leader to try to form a government, and instead asks the monarch to dissolve parliament and call another election, the monarch would be justified in rejecting the prime minister's advice. In these circum-

stances, it would be constitutionally correct for the monarchical head of state to dismiss the prime minister and invite another party leader to test the will of parliament.

Some parliamentary systems are republican rather than monarchical. In a republican parliamentary system, the head of state is a president elected directly by the people or indirectly by parliament. In republican parliamentary systems, presidential heads of state tend to have greater powers than monarchical heads of state in parliamentary systems. The powers of presidents in republican parliamentary systems are carefully delineated in written constitutions, whereas the position of constitutional monarchs is more the product of historical evolution and is largely governed by unwritten constitutional conventions.

Belgium, Denmark, the Netherlands, Norway, Spain, and Sweden are leading examples of constitutional monarchies in Western Europe. Most of the world's constitutional monarchies are member states of the Commonwealth of Nations. Queen Elizabeth II is either sovereign or head of state of sixteen of these states. Besides the United Kingdom, these states include Australia, Bahamas, Barbados, Belize, Canada, Grenada, Jamaica, New Zealand, Papua New Guinea, and the Solomon Islands. Five other Commonwealth countries—Brunei, Lesotho, Malaysia, Swaziland, and Tonga—have their own indigenous monarchies. Only in the United Kingdom are the powers and responsibilities of the crown exercised by the queen herself. In the other Commonwealth constitutional monarchies whose queen is Elizabeth II, a governor-general representing the queen discharges the crown's responsibilities. In most of these Commonwealth monarchies, the office of governor-general has been indigenized by having the queen appoint the governor-general on the advice of the prime minister of the country in which the governor-general will serve and by having a citizen of that country fill the office.

SEE ALSO *Aristocracy; Democracy; Government; Monarchy; Parliaments and Parliamentary Systems*

BIBLIOGRAPHY

Blake, Lord. 1977. The Queen and the Constitution. *The Queen: a Penguin Special.* New York: Penguin Books.

Bogdanor, Vernon. 2003. The Monarchy. *The British Constitution in the Twentieth Century*, ed. Vernon Bogdanor. Oxford: Oxford University Press.

Smith, David. 1995. *The Invisible Crown.* Toronto: University of Toronto Press.

Peter H. Russell

MONARCHY, HEREDITARY

SEE *Monarchism.*

MONETARISM

Monetarism is an economic school of thought that emphasizes minimal government intervention into the marketplace and the importance of the money supply in explaining economic fluctuations. Modern-day monetarism, as advanced by the American economist Milton Friedman in the late 1940s and 1950s, was presented as a theoretical challenge to the emerging Keynesian paradigm that began to gain popularity in the aftermath of the Great Depression and World War II. Keynesians viewed the Great Depression as evidence that the prevailing classical school of thought in which all unemployment was voluntary and markets self-correct was considered seriously flawed. With the unemployment rate in the United States reaching a peak of 25 percent during the Great Depression, it became painfully obvious there was insufficient demand and involuntary unemployment was an issue for policymakers to address. Upon the recommendation of the English economist John Maynard Keynes in 1936, the Roosevelt administration undertook an aggressive expansionary fiscal policy approach in the implementation of the New Deal programs to promote spending in the United States. While Keynesians viewed the decline in consumption and investment as the cause of the Great Depression, Friedman thought it could be attributed to the Federal Reserve's inability to provide enough liquidity to the economy. Rather than restrict the money supply, the Federal Reserve should have increased the money supply especially given the deflationary environment.

In light of the Keynesian focus on the role of fiscal policy to remedy insufficient demand in the private sector, monetarism reestablished the importance of the quantity theory in explaining economic fluctuations. The monetarist position rests on several fundamental propositions with respect to the role of money and economic activity. First, the money supply is the most important factor in the determination of nominal income. In particular, changes in the money supply cause changes in nominal income whereby the money supply is determined largely by the central bank. Second, in the long run changes in the money supply only influence the price level and nominal variables whereas real variables are determined by labor, capital, and the level of technology with the economy operating at or near full employment output. Third, contrary to the long run impact of the money supply, changes in the money supply can influence real variables in the short run. Fourth, monetarists view the economy as relatively stable with government policies destabilizing the economy rather than stabilizing it.

QUANTITY THEORY OF MONEY

The quantity theory of money provides the theoretical underpinnings for the proposition that the money supply is the most important factor in the determination of nominal income. The basis of the monetarist approach begins with the equation of exchange $M \times V = P \times Y$, where M is the money supply, V is velocity of money (the turnover rate of the money supply), P is the price level, and Y is real output. As it stands, the equation of exchange is an identity; however, monetarists assume that velocity is stable in the short run and if this assumption is taken to the extreme fixed (stable) as well.

Hence, the equation of exchange is transformed to the quantity theory of money as follows: $M \times \bar{V} = P \times Y$, where $\bar{V}$ denotes velocity as fixed. The above equation states that changes in the money supply will affect nominal income, $P \times Y$. Moreover, monetarists would contend that changes in the money supply cause changes in nominal income.

With respect to the long run consequences associated with changes in the money supply, monetarists believe that the economy is always operating near or at full employment determined by the markets for labor, capital, and technology. Indeed, if the economy is operating at its potential, the quantity theory of money in the long run can be stated as follows: $M \times \bar{V} = P \times Y_p$, where Y_p denotes potential real output. Thus, the long run changes in the money supply will only affect the price level.

While the changes in the money supply will only affect the price level in the long run, changes in the money supply in the short run can have real effects. Monetarists assert that in the short run, changes in the money supply can influence real variables such as output and employment. The rationale stems from the rigidities in prices and wages. Prices and wages may not fully adjust in the short run due to the presence of wage and price controls, implicit contracting, and the degree of unionization. Therefore, changes in the money supply will affect both prices and real output in the short run.

FISCAL AND MONETARY POLICY

Unlike the Keynesian position that the private sector is inherently unstable, monetarists view the private sector as inherently stable. Well functioning markets in the private sector serve as a stabilizer, self-adjusting in response to the instability created by the destabilizing forces associated with government intervention. The instability generated by government intervention could be the result of discretionary monetary policy actions, wage and price controls, or excessive bureaucratic costs and social programs, in which the price mechanism in the allocation of resources is disrupted. Thus, unlike the Keynesian view, monetarists do not look upon fiscal policy as a viable stabilizing force in the economy.

Contrary to the Keynesian view that both discretionary monetary and fiscal policies are useful in stabilizing the economy, the policy recommendations advocated by monetarists are rules oriented with minimal government interference. First, because monetarists believe that the money supply is the main factor in explaining nominal output in the short run and the price level in the long run, monetarists argue that monetary authorities should follow a rules oriented policy approach rather than a discretionary policy approach. This policy stance stems from the monetarist assertion that the economy is inherently stable, always adjusting toward full employment, and that discretionary monetary policy actions by the central bank will often times destabilize the economy. The money growth rate rule would have the central bank target the growth rate of money to equal the growth rate of real output. This rules oriented policy would ensure that the money supply would grow at the rate of real output and prevent inflationary pressures in the economy. With respect to fiscal policy, monetarists do not advocate government intervention in the marketplace, trusting instead the functioning of free markets and the operation of automatic stabilizers within the economy to minimize the impact of spending shocks on the economy.

LATE TWENTIETH-CENTURY EMPIRICAL EVIDENCE ON MONETARISM

The empirical support for the monetarist position has been rather mixed. In an attempt to control the accelerating inflation rate throughout the 1970s, the Federal Reserve embarked on what some economists called the "monetarist experiment" in targeting money growth from 1979 to 1982 under Federal Reserve chairman Paul Volcker. However, during the 1980s and into the 1990s the velocity of money became unstable. The instability in velocity severed the relationship between the money supply and nominal income. This instability was largely attributed to the deregulation of the banking industry and the increase in financial innovations, which induced instability in the demand for money. The stability of velocity was the cornerstone to monetarism's reliance on the quantity theory to argue that changes in the money supply explain movements in nominal output in the short run and the price level in the long run. Once the stability of velocity came into question, the monetarist paradigm also came under greater scrutiny.

Though monetarism has not regained its popularity, the monetarist view that the money supply is an important factor in explaining economic fluctuations has had an impact on the economics discipline. Rapid money growth beyond what is sustainable at full employment will lead to price instability and inflation. This observation is substantiated, for example, by the hyperinflation episodes in several European countries in the 1920s and the ongoing battle with inflation in several Latin American countries.

SEE ALSO *Banking; Economics, New Classical; Expectations; Expectations, Rational; Friedman, Milton; Inflation; Interest Rates; Money; Phillips Curve; Policy, Monetary*

BIBLIOGRAPHY

Edwards, Sebastian. 1995. *Crisis and Economic Reform in Latin America.* New York: Oxford University Press.

Friedman, Milton. 1948. A Monetary and Fiscal Framework for Economic Stability. *American Economic Review* 38: 245–264.

Friedman, Milton. 1956. The Quantity Theory of Money: A Restatement. In *Studies in the Quantity Theory of Money*, ed. Milton Friedman. Chicago: University of Chicago Press.

Friedman, Milton. 1968. The Role of Monetary Policy. *American Economic Review* 58: 1–17.

Friedman, Milton, and Anna J. Schwartz. 1963. *A Monetary History of the United States, 1867–1960.* Princeton, NJ: Princeton University Press.

Hicks, James. 1937. Mr. Keynes and the Classics: A Suggested Interpretation. *Econometrica* 5: 147–159.

Judd, John P., and John L. Scadding. 1982. The Search for a Stable Money Demand Function: A Survey of the Post-1973 Literature. *Journal of Economic Literature* 20: 993–1023.

Keynes, John M. 1936. *A General Theory of Income and Employment, Interest, and Money.* Cambridge, U.K.: Cambridge University Press.

Sargent, Thomas J. 1982. The Ends of Four Big Inflations. In *Inflation: Causes and Effects*, ed. Robert E. Hall. Chicago: University of Chicago Press.

James E. Payne

MONETARY BASE

In monetary economics, the *monetary base* is defined and measured as the sum of currency in circulation outside a nation's central bank and its treasury, plus deposits held by deposit-taking financial institutions (hereafter referred to as "banks") at the central bank. More generally, the monetary base consists of whatever government liabilities are used by the public to purchase and sell goods and services, plus those assets used by banks to settle interbank transactions. During certain specific historical periods, measures of the monetary base have also included commodity monies such as gold and silver coin and bullion. The components—currency and deposits at the central bank held by banks—are often referred to as *base money*.

Some authors have defined the monetary base as currency held by the public plus the cash reserves of banks. This definition can lead to confusion and should be avoided, however. A correct definition must include all base money held by banks, not solely the portion held to satisfy regulatory reserve requirements.

MONETARY ECONOMICS

In monetary economics, the monetary base has several unique characteristics. First, its components include the assets issued directly by a nation's monetary authorities (the treasury and central bank) that are used by the private sector (the public and banks) to settle transactions. Transactions, of course, may also be settled through the exchange of privately issued bank deposits, but these have risk characteristics that differ from those of base money. Second, the size of the monetary base changes only if the monetary authorities take actions, actively or passively, to permit the change—the private sector cannot change the size of the monetary base without the cooperation of, and participation by, the monetary authorities. Hence, in monetary theory, the monetary base is the direct link between monetary policy actions and economic activity, including subsequent inflation. As a practical matter, no central bank seeks to control closely the size of its monetary base day-to-day, fearing that so doing would sharply increase the volatility of market interest rates.

SUPPLY AND DEMAND

Central banks control the supply of the monetary base by buying and selling assets. Purchases of assets, of any type, increase the monetary base when the central bank pays for such assets with currency or increased central-bank deposit liabilities. Similarly, central-bank sales of assets, of any type, reduce the monetary base when the purchaser surrenders currency or central-bank deposit liabilities in payment. So long as the public willingly holds additional base money, the central bank is able to purchase assets and expand its size. Historically, this has tempted governments with weak fiscal discipline to utilize the central bank as a purchaser-of-last-resort for government debt when private capital markets are unreceptive, often leading to hyper-inflation.

Demand for the monetary base includes the public's transaction demand for currency and banks' demand for base money to be used in their usual banking business and to satisfy statutory reserve requirements imposed on them by regulatory agencies.

Cross-country comparisons of monetary-base growth occasionally have appeared in international economics because central-bank interventions to affect exchange rates necessarily are conducted by the purchase and sale of assets, altering the size of the monetary base. When a central bank sterilizes the effects of its actions on the monetary base by offsetting the purchase or sale of one asset with the sale or purchase of another (buying, perhaps, a foreign-issued bond while simultaneously selling from its portfolio a domestically issued bond), such that the size of the monetary base remains unchanged, most studies have found little effect on exchange rates.

MONETARY POLICY

In all current economies, the growth of the monetary base is an endogenous variable—that is, it is a variable determined simultaneously with other variables, such as employment, output, prices, and market interest rates. In modern times, only the Swiss National Bank has included among its monetary policy objectives a growth rate for the monetary base, although the Bank of England maintained a monitoring range during the latter half of the 1980s. Most of the world's central banks conduct monetary policy by setting and manipulating the level of a short-term interest rate. In the United States, the Federal Open Market Committee implements policy by choosing a target level for the overnight federal funds rate (the interest rate charged by banks to each other for overnight loans of deposits at the Federal Reserve). The federal funds rate is maintained close to the target rate each day by increasing or decreasing the supply of base money.

Many empirical studies have examined linkages among the growth of the monetary base, the growth of broader monetary aggregates, and an economy's inflation rate. Over long periods of time, there is a clear positive relationship: absent significant structural or regulatory changes, prolonged inflation (especially hyperinflation) cannot continue without increases in the monetary base. In most historical cases, excessive growth of the monetary base has reflected a lack of fiscal discipline, not a failure of monetary policy. Sharp reductions in inflation such as occurred in the United States during 1979–1980, are typically accompanied by, and probably require, sharp reductions in the monetary base. There is substantive disagreement, however, regarding short-run relationships. While some studies claim to have found direct linkages between the growth of the inflation-adjusted monetary base and inflation-adjusted economic activity, other studies have found no reliable shorter-run connections. In 1988 the economist Bennet McCallum proposed a monetary policy rule in which the level of the federal-funds-rate target would be adjusted in response to the growth of the monetary base. After initial widespread attention, the rule's impact on monetary policy has diminished in recent years.

U.S. CURRENCY HELD ABROAD

In some countries outside the United States, large amounts of U.S. currency circulate freely and are used for the purchase and sale of goods and services. The question then arises as to whether measures of the monetary base in those countries should include the circulating U.S. currency. Common practice is to exclude it, including only domestically issued base money. It is common practice, however, for measures of the monetary base to exclude foreign-issued currency. This practice is not without controversy. To the extent that inflation is driven by total aggregate demand, the foreign currency that is used in transactions matters. To the extent that a country's long-run inflation is caused primarily, or perhaps exclusively, by increases in its own monetary base, however, foreign currency is properly excluded. Current empirical studies provide little guidance as to which is the more appropriate measure in these cases.

For the United States, one additional issue arises. Alone among the world's nations, a large proportion of U.S. currency (more than half, and perhaps as much as two-thirds) is held outside the United States. Should this currency be excluded from measures of the U.S. monetary base? While experimental measures have been constructed that do so, no such measure has gained wide acceptance, and none is currently published, despite Edward Nelson's finding in 2002 that such a measure of the domestically held U.S. monetary base has been more closely connected to economic activity than other monetary aggregates.

CHANGES IN RESERVE REQUIREMENTS

To be used as a longer-run measure of the stance of monetary policy, measures of the monetary base must be adjusted for the effect of changes in statutory reserve requirements. The resulting series is referred to as the *adjusted monetary base*. Increases in statutory reserve requirements, for example, tend to increase the quantity of base money demanded by depository institutions to satisfy the requirements, conditional on their level of deposits. If no offsetting action is taken by the central bank, this increase is economically equivalent to the central bank reducing the monetary base itself. To avoid sudden jumps in market interest rates due to changes in statutory reserve requirements, central banks have tended to match such increases in demand with increases in supply. (For a further discussion of this, see Anderson and Rasche 2003.)

THE FUTURE

Two developments that began during the 1990s portend a reduced future for the monetary base and a reduced demand for base money. First, central banks worldwide have reduced regulatory reserve requirements to very low levels, attenuating banks' demand for central-bank deposits. In the United States, although regulatory reserve requirements have not changed, banks have used retail deposit sweep programs to sharply reduce their holdings of base money. (In a retail deposit sweep program, a bank reclassifies a transaction-oriented deposit subject to a high reserve requirement as a savings-oriented deposit subject to a low requirement.) Most banks that have implemented such automated sweep systems have reduced their required reserves to a level small enough to be satisfied by the amounts of vault cash and deposits at Federal Reserve Banks that they hold for use in their ordinary business of making and receiving payments. In this case, regulatory reserve requirements cease to be a determinant of the demand for the monetary base. In other countries, regulatory reserve requirements have been replaced with payments-oriented requirements that generally allow banks to hold zero deposits overnight at the central bank. The European Central Bank (ECB) imposes a broad regulatory reserve requirement on most bank deposits at a 3 percent rate. This requirement must be satisfied solely with deposits held at the ECB; vault cash is not eligible.

The second continuing development is the growth of electronic payments. In the absence of binding regulatory reserve requirements, demand for base money is driven by the need of households, firms, and governments to initiate and settle payments. If electronic payments displace most currency and paper checks, then the demand for base money might fall to such a low level that central banks would find that the control of its supply was a weak lever with which to implement policy. The solution to this problem remains uncertain, but many economists have noted that tax payments play a central role. Most governments require that taxes be paid in base money. In the United States, for example, tax payments to the U.S. Treasury must be settled in deposits at the Federal Reserve Banks—payments from households and firms drawn on banks are accepted only to the extent that such payments are later settled by the banks on behalf of their customers in deposits at the Federal Reserve Banks. Economists as diverse as Sir John Hicks and Michael Woodford have argued that this tax-payment function will assure a long-term role for base money in the economy.

DATA AVAILABILITY

In the United States, both the Board of Governors of the Federal Reserve System in Washington, D.C., and the Federal Reserve Bank of St. Louis publish monetary-base data with and without adjustments for the effects of changes in statutory reserve requirements. Data and details of the calculations and adjustments are available from those institutions.

SEE ALSO *Monetarism; Money; Money, Demand for; Money, Supply of*

BIBLIOGRAPHY

Anderson, Richard G., and Robert H. Rasche. 2003. A Reconstruction of the Federal Reserve Bank of St. Louis Adjusted Monetary Base and Reserves. *Federal Reserve Bank of St. Louis Review.* 85 (3): 39–70.

Anderson, Richard G., Michael J. Bordo, Hugh Rockoff, et al. 2006. Monetary Aggregates. In *Historical Statistics of the United States: Millennial Edition*, ed. Susan B. Carter. Vol. 3. New York: Cambridge University Press.

Borio, Claudio E. V. 1997. *The Implementation of Monetary Policy in Industrial Countries: A Survey.* Bank for International Settlement Economic Papers No. 47, July.

Fischer, Stanley, Ratna Sahay, and Carlos A. Vegh. 2002. Modern Hyper- and High Inflations. *Journal of Economic Literature* 40 (3): 837–880.

Goodhart, Charles A. E. 1989. The Conduct of Monetary Policy. *The Economic Journal* 99: 293–346.

Hicks, John R. 1973. *A Theory of Economic History.* Oxford: Oxford University Press.

McCallum, Bennett T. 1988. Robustness Properties of a Rule for Monetary Policy. *Carnegie-Rochester Conference Series on Public Policy* 29: 173–203.

Nelson, Edward. 2002. Direct Effects of Base Money on Aggregate Demand: Theory and Evidence. *Journal of Monetary Economics* 49 (4): 687–708.

Rich, Georg. 1997. Monetary Targets as a Policy Rule: Lessons from the Swiss Experience. *Journal of Monetary Economics* 39 (1): 113–141.

Woodford, Michael. 2003. *Interest and Prices: Foundations of a Theory of Monetary Policy.* Princeton, NJ: Princeton University Press.

Richard G. Anderson

MONETARY POLICY
SEE *Policy, Monetary.*

MONETARY PRODUCTION ECONOMY
SEE *Production.*

MONETARY THEORY

Money in some form has been around for at least five thousand years, with the earliest evidence of its use in the Fertile Crescent in Mesopotamia. In contrast even after three hundred years a theory of money has scarcely been developed.

There are several basic reasons why a theory of money has been long in coming. The number of properties that ideal money needs to possess is so large that it is easy for any author to develop a theory omitting several functions. Thus we have seen the development of many partially correct theories, each one emphasizing different properties relevant to the context of the times. The blending of history, context, and institutional understanding with abstraction and analysis is one that is rarely congenial to either institutionally or mathematically oriented scholars. Furthermore, because money and financial institutions are at the center of practical affairs, theory and practice, advocacy and understanding, have been dangerously mixed.

PRECURSORS

Although Plato noted in passing the use of money as a means of exchange, possibly the first person known to have considered seriously the meaning of money was Aristotle. He identified the uses of money as a means of exchange, a store of value and a numeraire. However, considerable damage persists even today from Aristotle's misunderstanding of the subtlety of the basic properties of economic systems utilizing money. Utilizing an unfortunate and simplistic analogy between the fecundity of the living and the sterility of inanimate objects, Aristotle's comments helped to lay the philosophical foundation for opposition to the charging of any rate of interest whatsoever on loans by the Catholic Church and by the Moslems.

The Romans had an advanced business economy and legal system that included the development of the corporation, but there is little evidence of an interest in economic theory. Nor is there any clear evidence of it in Chinese thought or elsewhere. Possibly the next glimmerings on theorizing about money and interest were the Catholic scholastic doctors as exemplified by Saint Thomas Aquinas (1225–1274).

Key themes developed from Jean Bodin (1530–1596) and Richard Cantillon (1680?–1734) onward have been the quantity theory of money and the credit or "bills only" view of financing. Another basic division in the development of monetary theory has been the development of microeconomic theory, where the control role of government is hardly alluded to, as contrasted with the macroeconomic approaches, where government and the control aspects of the economy are central. The work of John Maynard Keynes (1883–1946), his followers James Tobin (1918–2002) and Don Patinkin (1922–1995), and competitors such as Milton Friedman (1912–2006) exemplify a joining of theoretical studies and advocacy of policy.

TWENTIETH-CENTURY DEVELOPMENTS

Prior to the great work of Keynes, the early twentieth century produced significant works by Ludwig Edler von Mises (1881–1973), Joseph A. Schumpeter (1883–1950), and Knut Wicksell (1851–1926) that set the stage for the developments to come. In a class of its own, but of considerable importance to those who wish to appreciate the subtlety of money and financial institutions, is the work of Georg Simmel (1858–1918) dealing with the philosophy of money.

In the debate on macroeconomic control of the economy, Friedman and his followers, in contrast with Keynes and his intellectual successors, have stressed the importance of the quantity of money as key to control of the economy. Simon Newcomb (1835–1909) first wrote down the explicit equation to describe the quantity theory as $MV = PT$, where P is the average price level, M is the amount of money in the system, V is the velocity of circulation, and T is the number of transactions in the economy. Irving Fisher (1867–1947) provided the more sophisticated analysis. In its simplest form it is assumed that V and T are constants, thereby giving an equation where a change in the money supply directly changes the price level.

The observations by William Stanley Jevons (1835–1882) concerning the failure of the double coincidence of wants may be regarded as a precursor to much formal mathematical work on the microeconomic theory of money. The failure of the double coincidence of wants can be illustrated by three individuals trading in three commodities where no pair can improve directly by trade but all can benefit from monetary intermediation that enables pairs to trade.

The work of John Hicks (1904–1989) straddled general equilibrium theory and the macroeconomic theory of money. He also introduced the idea of calculating adjustments in multistage general equilibrium models with sticky or fixed prices. This was taken up by Jean-Michel Grandmont (1983) and Jean-Pascal Bénassy (1982).

Work on the microeconomic theory of money has grown considerably since 1960, perhaps given impulse by Gerard Debreu's *Theory of Value; An Axiomatic Analysis of Economic Equilibrium* (1959). This work, which established the general mathematical conditions for the existence of efficient market prices, was presented as an extension of the work of Léon Walras (1834–1910). Yet paradoxically it does not involve money except in the sense that the mathematical observation that prices are homogeneous of order zero implies the classical dichotomy that a homogeneous increase of money merely changes the price level.

Search and sequential binary trade models have been utilized as mathematical economic anthropology models to consider pre-market mechanisms of exchange that might lead to the emergence of markets and money. This includes the works of Ross M. Starr, Ariel Rubinstein, Douglas Gale, and others.

Frank H. Hahn raised the basic question of what supports the value of a paper money in any economy with a finite existence. Because all know the paper will be worthless at the end, by backward induction it can be shown that no one will take it at the start. How can this backward argument be avoided? It turns out that there are many different solutions to this problem depending on institutional and technical detail, such as terminal conditions, transactions costs, costs of producing money, policing trade, handling default, and enforcing contract.

Hahn, Mordecai Kurz, Duncan Foley, and several others have considered transactions costs. Seignorage and cost of production have been considered by Martin Shubik and Dimitri Tsomocos. Nobuhiro Kiyotaki and Randall Wright offered a formal model of three individuals producing and trading three commodities where the failure of the double coincidence of wants is overcome endogenously at equilibrium by consistent expectations that support intrinsically worthless money. Per Bak, Simon Norrelykke, and Shubik utilized a somewhat related model to consider the dynamics of adjustment.

David Cass and Karl Shell note that the presence of outside or exogenous uncertainties which would appear to have nothing to do with the functioning of a monetary economy can have a correlating influence on behavior generating what they term "sunspot equilibrium." In a monetary economy with many different independent agents the obtaining of coordination is critical for efficient behavior.

Maurice Allais (1946) and Paul A. Samuelson (1958) recognized the importance of the overlapping generation aspects of a human economy. Real property and financial assets are transferred across the generations as individuals are born and die. Samuelson showed the important role played by money acting as a store of value in this process.

A game theoretic approach to the theory of money and financial institutions has been developed by Martin Shubik (1999) and others. In particular the set of models known as Strategic Market Games (see Lloyd Shapley and Shubik [1977], Pradeep Dubey and Shubik, [1978], and Sylvain Sorin [1996]) make it possible to devise full process models that can be studied for their noncooperative equilibriums. A noncooperative equilibrium is an outcome that satisfies mutually consistent expectations; if all individuals expect that all others are going to take certain actions, there are some actions for which everyone's expectations will turn out to be correct. These expectations are also known as *rational expectations*.

The key stress is on the game theory and the experimental gaming concept of a playable game as a device to make sure that a full process model is constructed. There are so many institutional possibilities in constructing process models that a concept of *minimal institution* is called for.

Parallel stochastic dynamic programs to study monetary phenomena was first introduced by Robert Lucas (1972); Lucas and colleagues have laid out a considerable program linking primarily representative agent, cash-in-advance microeconomic optimizing models to macroeconomic models utilizing solutions with rational expectations. They have utilized these models to address several of the major problems in macroeconomics. Some believe that it is premature to try to draw policy conclusions from models at this level of aggregation and low dimension.

In contrast Ioannis Karatzas, Shubik, and William Sudderth (1994) primarily have considered the behavior of individual agents. These models lead to the existence of equilibriums showing nonsymmetric income and wealth distributions caused by the random elements.

DEBATE ON THE NEUTRALITY OR NON-NEUTRALITY OF MONEY

Although new methods of parallel dynamic programming have been introduced and the mathematical models of process have evolved considerably since the writings of David Hume (1711–1776), the debate on the neutrality or non-neutrality of money is still present among economists in the early twenty-first century, although in a form somewhat different from the debate of the previous 250 years. Basically the argument has been that if money is of no intrinsic value, a doubling or halving of its supply will merely influence the price level and not the distribution of real resources. But if it does not influence the distribution of real resources it can be said to be neutral in its effect. This is a virtual tautology when comparing equilibrium states. However, when issue or withdrawal of money by the government is considered as a potential dynamic control variable, what may be a tautology in equilibrium may be false in a dynamic process.

Friedman offers a thought experiment in which a helicopter drops banknotes on a city. How do the prices and distribution of money change during this exercise? Patinkin discusses the classical separation of the monetary sector from the real economy. All of these writings deal with the same empirical problem. The key question is exactly how much the monetary and financial control mechanism actually controls the real economy. The followers of Schumpeter who are concerned with this equi-

librium and uncertainty would say a great deal. The Keynesians, neo-Keynesians, Friedmanites, and neo-Friedmanites all perceive the same question but differ in the answer.

The microeconomists viewing the economy from the assumptions of general equilibrium theory can prove rigorously that the price system is homogeneous of order zero. This means, in plain English, that a doubling or halving of prices makes no difference to the real economy. The mathematics is rigorous, but the model is incomplete for the problem at hand. Modifications such as Hicks's temporary equilibrium studied by individuals such as Grandmont arrive at different conclusions. Other microeconomic theorists such as Pradeep Dubey, John Geanakoplos, Shubik, Charles Wilson, and William R. Zame introduce bankruptcy. The bankruptcy penalty links the value of paper money to the utility function, and if there are any limits to the supply of money and its velocity this implies that money is no longer neutral. Prices are defined on a finite closed interval.

The difficulties in defining and measuring near monies or other money substitutes and the empirical problems in measuring velocity make the forceful statements of Hume and the attractive simple price quantity equation of Newcombe and Fisher no longer generally tenable. We can say, "Given the assumptions of general equilibrium theory and its macroeconomic equivalents, in equilibrium, money is neutral in the economy." It is a matter of the appropriate modeling. In reality, with incomplete markets and time lags in reaction, money is not neutral in disequilibrium. It influences the distribution of real goods. How heavily non-neutral it is and how useful it is as a control mechanism over the economy is a matter of judgment concerning detailed economic observations and measurements. No matter what the economist's persuasion, the consensus in the early twenty-first century appears to be that the control mechanism of money over the economy is weakened by the growth of modern communications and the proliferation of money substitutes.

In spite of the considerable developments since the early twentieth century, many problems, especially those concerning the measurement of velocity and the understanding of how it changes, remain to be dealt with. A satisfactory theory of money must deal with financial institutions and with the nature and the relationship of government fiscal and monetary control. Much of the mathematical analysis of the theory of money leaves out innovation, expertise, and heterogeneous expectations. The straitjacket of the dynamic programming format together with representative agents with rational expectations forces a fixed velocity on most models. In contrast, the nonmathematical models of Keynes, Schumpeter, and

Hyman Minsky present a world with innovation and differentiation in both expertise and expectations. This gives room for a dynamics of control based not on the smooth noncooperative equilibrium of the dynamic programming approach but one with the government, banks, and financiers directing parts of the money supply selectively across the economy.

SEE ALSO *Finance; Macroeconomics; Money; Neutrality of Money; Policy, Monetary*

BIBLIOGRAPHY

Allais, Maurice. 1946. *Économie et intérêt.* Paris: Commission des Annales des mines et des carburants.

Bénassy, Jean-Pascal. 1982. *The Economics of Market Disequilibrium.* New York: Academic Press.

Debreu, Gerard. 1959. *Theory of Value; An Axiomatic Analysis of Economic Equilibrium.* New York: Wiley.

Dubey, Pradeep, and Martin Shubik. 1978. The Noncooperative Equilibria of a Closed Trading Economy with Market Supply and Bidding Strategies. *Journal of Economic Theory* 17 (1): 1–20.

Fisher, Irving. 1931. *The Purchasing Power of Money.* 2nd ed. New York: Macmillan.

Friedman, Milton. 1969. *The Optimum Quantity of Money, and Other Essays.* Chicago: Aldine.

Grandmont, Jean-Michel. 1983. *Money and Value: A Reconsideration of Classical and Neoclassical Monetary Theories.* Cambridge, U.K. and New York: Cambridge University Press.

Hicks, J. R. [1939] 1946. *Value and Capital: An Inquiry into Some Fundamental Principles of Economic Theory.* 2nd ed. Oxford: Oxford University Press.

Jevons, W. Stanley. 1875. *Money and the Mechanism of Exchange.* London: Macmillan.

Karatzas, Ioannis, Martin Shubik, and William D. Sudderth. 1994. Construction of Stationary Markov Equilibria on a Strategic Market Game. *Mathematics of Operations Research* 19 (4): 975.

Keynes, John Maynard. [1936] 1957. *The General Theory of Employment, Interest, and Money.* London: Macmillan.

Lucas, Robert E. Expectations and the Neutrality of Money. 1972. *Journal of Economic Theory* 4 (2): 103–124.

Samuelson, Paul A. 1958. An Exact Consumption-Loan Model of Interest with or without the Social Contrivance of Money. *Journal of Political Economy* 66 (6): 467–482.

Shapley, Lloyd, and Martin Shubik. 1977. Trade Using One Commodity as a Means of Payment. *Journal of Political Economy* 85 (5): 937–968.

Shubik, Martin. 1999. *The Theory of Money and Financial Institutions.* 2 vols. Cambridge, MA: MIT Press.

Simmel, Georg. 1978. *The Philosophy of Money.* London: Routledge and Kegan Paul. (Trans. 1907 by Tom Bottamore and David Frisby.)

Sorin, Sylvain. 1996. Strategic Market Games with Exchange Rates. *Journal of Economic Theory* 69 (2): 431–446.

Tobin, James. 1956. The Interest Elasticity of the Transactions Demand for Cash. *Review of Economics and Statistics* 38 (3): 241–247.

Tobin, James. 1961. Money Capital and Other Stores of Value. *American Economic Review* 51 (2): 26–37. (Papers and Proceedings of the Seventy-third Annual Meeting of the American Economic Association, May 1961.)

Wicksell, Knut. [1935] 1962. *Lectures on Political Economy.* Vol. 2: *Money.* London: Routledge and Kegan Paul.

Martin Shubik

MONEY

Money can only be defined adequately in the context of a dynamic economy with markets and other financial institutions existing in a society complete with its laws and customs. It is a network or system of public good of considerable complexity. Even if money is privately produced, in the sense that it always depends on network acceptance it is a public good.

A quick perusal of any standard textbook immediately specifies the key economic properties of money as: (1) a means of payment; (2) a store of value; and (3) a numeraire. There are also a host of physical properties that are desirable for an item that serves as money. A partial list includes: (1) transportability; (2) durability; and (3) cognizability.

Left off these two lists is the strategic and informational properties of money. In particular the rules of operation with money distinguish among economic agents. The powers of an individual with respect to the creation and destruction of money are different from those of commercial banks, the central bank, and the treasury.

Part of the basic financial control mechanism of any society is the ability of some institutions to control the money supply and influence the money rate of interest. Although it can be shown at a high level of abstraction that with a perfect clearing system all individuals could issue their own currencies, the degree of reputation, trust, and memory required for such a system to work is unreasonable. The financial institutions that have been invented have been designed to provide a viable system for imperfect individuals.

The informational aspects of the use of money are critical to a modern complex economy. Money is an information aggregating, disaggregating device. Given prices, any collection of diverse assets can be valued by a single number. Bets of almost any variety on the future deal not only with the changes in uncertain bundles of assets, but with how they will be evaluated in monetary terms.

Because people are almost always concerned with a dynamic economy in disequilibrium, money does not provide a constant standard of measure like a carefully measured standard meter. It is a somewhat flexible, crude, and changing store of value. The conditions required to guarantee that a unit of money is of the same value in each period are rarely if ever encountered. A strict specification of all of the conditions that must be specified to guarantee no inflation or deflation is such that it is rarely met in reality. However in a dynamic economy the fact is that money does not maintain a precise value throughout time but permits prices to change in a flexible manner. And, up to a point, this is a desirable property.

Given that there are many desirable properties for ideal money, the institutional manifestation of the ideal money is hard to come by as most actual financial instruments called money miss some of the properties.

ON THE ALLOCATION OF RESOURCES

Precisely when in history individuals switched over from direct trade, where commodity *A* was exchanged for commodity *B* with no intervening means of payment, is not known. The open market with prices is by no means the only way that society distributes its resources. Among the ways extant today are direct bargaining, bidding, the free market with a price system, the dictates of higher authority, force, fraud and deceit, custom including inheritance and other gifts, and last, but not least, chance. Most of these, like society itself, preceded the development of an organized law-enforcing economy utilizing money.

A dynamic economy is a living organism with many ways of achieving some of its goals. Even the most advanced economy will not transfer many of its resources only through markets. Government, alone, at its many levels will account for 20 to 40 percent of the reported monetary income of any society. Gifts will still be made; housewives, husbands, handymen, and gardeners will still produce a considerable nonmarket produce; bribes and theft are all present to contribute to the nonmarket or only obliquely market parts of the economy.

A BRIEF HISTORY OF MONEY

It is not clear whether the development of money preceded, succeeded, or happened simultaneously with the evolution of markets. Their functions are deeply intertwined. The knowledge of the existence of markets makes it easier for individuals to find what they want to buy and where they should go to sell. The existence of money and other financial instruments makes it easier for them to trade. Among the earliest known monies were barley and silver, both of which were used in Mesopotamia over four

thousand years ago. A considerable variety of substances have been used as money. They can be usefully divided into storable consumables, such as barley, and durables such as silver. Consumable monies have included barley, rice, cocoa beans, salt, bricks of tea, and cigarettes. Durables have included cowrie shells, wampum, furs, and many metals, including gold, silver, copper, tin and platinum, as well as alloys.

Among the earliest portrayals of the use of a metal as money is a painting from the tomb of Mereruka at Saqqara, Egypt, dating around 2300 BCE, showing gold being weighed in a transaction. Before the invention of coinage, payments utilizing metals were made in dust or ingot form. The invention of coinage is attributed to King Andrys of Lydia around 630 BCE. When one views money and financial institutions it is helpful to adopt the viewpoint of an engineer. This dispels much of the mystery often associated with finance. In particular, the transactions technology is seen to be a part of the economic production process. The switch to coinage contrasts with using metal by weight as a means of exchange. Coinage provided standardization of both the weight and quality of the metal and came with the stamp of authority, providing for law and its enforcement.

In return for the services rendered by coinage the king took a payment termed a seignorage fee estimated at 3 percent. As is evinced by the association of Croesus with wealth, coinage by the king was a source of revenue. In the subsequent history of coinage permission for the operation of mints has often been granted to private entities, although the government has always played a role. The technology of the production of coins has progressed from slow crude hand striking to vast automation where machines can produce coins at the rate of 45,000 per hour. Coining is still a profitable occupation as is evinced by the profits that the U.S. Mint turns over to the U.S. Treasury. It is also an art form as is illustrated by the design by the renowned sculptor Saint-Gaudens of the double eagle gold coin.

Within a few hundred years the use of coinage stretched from England to China. Although historians are not certain, it appears that the Chinese might have invented coinage independently a little later than the West. The mere fact that coinage was quickly and broadly accepted, providing many services that payment in bullion did not provide, does not imply that all coins are accepted even if the issuer is trusted. Mixtures of law, custom, and even aesthetic appeal all come into play. An example is provided by the livre tournois in the thirteenth century, which dominated the use of the livre parisis of Paris, the official coin of the central government.

NOTES ON GOLD AND OTHER METALS

Gold is malleable, ornamental, inert, and easily alloyed. It is estimated that at the end of 2005, the stock of mined gold was approximately 171,000 tons, of which 64 percent had been mined since 1950. World production in 2005 was 2,770 tons. There is a considerable amount of gold in the ocean, but retrieval costs are prohibitive.

Various countries have employed gold, silver, and copper as currency simultaneously. A reason for doing so is to provide a fit for different levels of consumption: coppers for a glass of beer or newspaper; silver for a pair of shoes; and gold to buy a house. The size of a gold coin to buy a beer is too small and as Sweden's experiment with a copper currency demonstrated, buying a house with copper currency required cartloads of copper.

When one country bases its currency on gold and another on silver, any attempt by a country to fix an internal price between gold and silver will cause an influx or outflow of one of the metals. When the English physicist and mathematician Sir Isaac Newton (1642–1727) was master of the mint, in 1717 he overvalued gold in terms of silver sufficiently that silver went out of circulation as it could be sold for gold and the proceeds repatriated and converted at a profit.

PAPER MONIES, NEAR MONIES, AND THE MONEY SUPPLY

From the late seventeenth century onward starting with the formation of the Bank of England in 1694, the world switched more and more to the use of paper currencies. Each currency represents a claim by a national government that it can use its monetary strategic powers to help to control its economy. Monetary consolidations such as the introduction of the euro must be viewed in terms of politics as well as economics. Viewed purely from economics the currency union offers a considerable saving in transactions costs, but from the viewpoint of international politics it marks a considerable change in the strategic powers of individual nation-states.

The mixture of law, custom, and logic that produces a viable monetary system is sufficiently subtle that it is extremely difficult to produce formal models that adequately reflect the many functions of money and near monies. The phrase "near money" refers to an instrument that has many but not all of the properties of a money. For example, confining the observations to the transactions use of money, it should be acceptable in all markets. Nevertheless there may be financial instruments in existence, such as bank checks, which are accepted in almost all markets. For many purposes of analysis it makes sense to lump bank money with the issue of the government.

Because other financial instruments and real assets may have some, but not all, of the properties of money there is a considerable problem in defining a single simple measure of the amount of money there exists in any country. For example the property of being a store of value is present for assets such as land or houses as well as gold.

If a single number is required to measure the amount of money, the United States produces three different measures with many components. The three measures are aggregations called M1, M2, and M3. M1 is the sum of paper currency and coin that is held outside banks, traveler's checks, and checking accounts (but not demand deposits), minus the amount of money in the Federal Reserve float. M2 is the sum of M1, plus savings deposits, including money market accounts from which no checks can be written, time deposits less than $100,000, and retirement accounts. M3 is the sum of M2 plus the large time deposits, Eurodollar deposits, dollars held at foreign offices of U.S. banks, and institutional money market funds.

In the twenty-first century with the proliferation of computers and cheap communication together with data banks on credit evaluation, many new forms of payment, credit cards, debit cards, and e-money are coming into being. Groups of individuals who trade frequently and are well known to each other can set up their own clearing and credit systems without using banks.

MONEY AND CREDIT AND THE QUANTITY THEORY

One of the mysteries of fiat money and national income accounting is what backs fiat or paper money. Is it custom, the power of government, trust in the government, gold reserves and other government assets, the presence of taxation, expectations, the negative incentives of default punishment, or factors associated with insurance and inheritance? A tentative answer is all of the above, in part. The mix may vary through time and place. The ideal money is a symbol that serves as a substitute for trust. It is an abstract "trust pill." This ideal currency does not exist, but the currency of a stable noninflationary economy is hopefully an approximation to this trust pill. Fiat money is an asset like gold but it is an artificial or societally created virtual gold. Treating it as an asset has some paradoxical features. What does one receive on surrendering a one dollar bill to the Federal Reserve? One gets another new bill. Currently the average life of a dollar bill is estimated at twenty-two months; hence this activity is not merely symbolic but relevant. In their work *Money in a Theory of Finance* (1960), Jack Gurley and Edward Shaw made a distinction between "outside money" and inside money that stresses the role of government. Outside money is government fiat money against which a government debt exists. Inside money is fiat money held as an unencumbered asset by a private individual. A way in which the government can adjust the overall supply of fiat money held by private individuals is by selling to or buying from them, public debt. The basic difference between fiat money and credit is that money is a virtual commodity. It is a fictitious gold. It is the only financial instrument for which there is no operationally meaningful offsetting instrument on the other side of the balance sheet. The government maintains a fiction that it owes something to the individual who owns a dollar bill, but apart from obtaining a newer piece of paper from the bank it has no operational meaning. From the mid-eighteenth century until today there has been considerable interest in what has become known as the quantity theory of money. In his essay "Of Interest" (1752) the Scottish philosopher and historian David Hume (1711–1776) noted, "All augmentation has no other effect than to heighten the price of labor and commodities; and even this variation is little more than that of a name.... Money having chiefly a fictitious value, the greater or less plenty of it is of no consequence if we consider a nation within itself" ([1752] 1985, pp. 296–297).

In the modern terminology of Don Patinkin, Hume's concept of money shows a classical dichotomy illustrating that the amount of money does not matter. More money merely raises the level of prices. The classical dichotomy means that the structure of real economy in equilibrium is independent of the amount of money in the system. The latter only fixes the price level.

The conditions for the classical dichotomy between money and other goods are that there are absolutely no frictions in the speed of adjustment of the economy to the introduction of more money. This is counterfactual as can be seen by trying to build a playable game of the system.

EQUILIBRIUM OR DISEQUILIBRIUM

In the 2000s there are at least two major schools of thought, one deriving from Hume, the monetarists, exemplified by Milton Friedman and the other modern followers, and modifiers of the work of the English economist John Maynard Keynes. Both schools have skilled analysts. The key distinctions lie in basic assumptions and different interpretations of unclear evidence. Those following variants of the quantity theory appear to stress long-run equilibrium conditions playing down the influence of short-term adjustments and coordination problems as well as ignoring nonsymmetries in wealth, expertise, and decision-making abilities. The neo-Keynesians are more concerned with the influence of monetary policy on short-run adjustments and on problems in economic coordination. They tend to be more concerned with nonsymmetries among industry, the workforce, consumers, and government. More than the monetarists they appreciate the constant disequilibrium in the economic system.

A strategic and more biological view of money and financial institutions is that they represent the neural network and control system over the economic body of society. The government and the private financial establishment form a considerable segment of the economy. They are large enough to have considerable influence on the overall supply of money and credit. This alone places an upper bound on prices. The presence of default penalties and bankruptcy laws places a lower bound on prices. If there is enough deflation it pays a debtor to default unless the bankruptcy laws are changed at the same speed as the money supply. The laws of contract and the bankruptcy laws reflect a society's attitude toward risk. In a highly innovative society in constant disequilibrium, the laws of default and bankruptcy control the innovation rate or the speed of mutation of that society. Furthermore the ability of the government and banks to create money and the other parts of the financial system to direct where credit goes gives government and the financial system considerable control in directing the disequilibrium dynamics of a modern economy. In this structure money matters considerably. In a static equilibrium of a society without innovation the classic dichotomy appears and the importance of money and financial institutions is diminished.

The financial system and money provide the interfacing mechanisms between the economy and the polity. Human society, like an individual's body, is not an undifferentiated mass of independent individuals or cells. There is a complex organization, which in both instances requires a flow of information, control instructions, and nourishment to differentiated organisms that require coordination. The financial system provides for the flow of information and control and the economy provides the various physical forms of nourishment needed by the society.

SEE ALSO *Balance of Payments; Currency; Divisia Monetary Index; Exchange Rates; Monetary Theory; Money, Endogenous; Money, Exogenous; Policy, Monetary; Quantity Theory of Money; Trade*

BIBLIOGRAPHY

Bagehot, Walter. [1873] 1962. *Lombard Street*. Homewood, IL: Irwin.

Fisher, Irving. [1930] 1977. *The Theory of Interest*. Philadelphia: Porcupine Press.

Fisher, Irving. 1931. *The Purchasing Power of Money*. 2nd ed. New York: Macmillan.

Gurley, John G., and Edward Shaw. 1960. *Money in a Theory of Finance*. Washington, DC: Brookings Institution.

Friedman, Milton. 1969. *The Optimum Quantity of Money and Other Essays*. Chicago: Aldine.

Hume, David. [1752] 1985. Of Interest. In *Essays: Moral, Political and Literary*, ed. E. F. Miller, 296–297. Indianapolis, IN: Liberty Classics.

Jevons, William S. 1875. *Money and the Mechanism of Exchange*. London: MacMillan.

Keynes, John M. [1936] 1957. *The General Theory of Employment, Interest and Money*. London: Macmillan.

Lejonhufvud, Axel. 1968. *On Keynesian Economics and the Economics of Keynes*. New York: Oxford University Press.

Simmel, Georg. [1907] 1978. *The Philosophy of Money*. London: Routledge and Kegan Paul.

Schumpeter, Joseph A. 1934. *The Theory of Economic Development*. Cambridge: MA: Harvard University Press.

Schumpeter, Joseph A., ed. 1954. *History of Economic Analysis*. London: Allen and Unwin.

Shubik, Martin. 1999. *The Theory of Money and Financial Institutions*. 2 vols. Cambridge, MA: MIT Press.

Tobin, J. 1961. Money Capital and Other Stores of Value. *American Economic Review* 51: 26–37.

Von Mises, Ludwig. 1935. *The Theory of Money and Credit*. New York: Harcourt Brace.

Wicksell, Knut. [1935] 1962. *Lectures on Political Economy*. Vol. 2. London: Routledge and Kegan Paul.

Martin Shubik

MONEY, DEMAND FOR

Money exists because there is a demand for it, and that demand creates its own value (like any other asset). The intrinsic value of money may be zero; still, the nominal value of money is equal to its face value. An intrinsically worthless paper acquires value because it performs the role of the medium of trade. People demand money because they believe that most people demand it. In other words, they know that they can exchange money for goods and services or other assets now or in the future. If people know that there will be no demand for money in the future, then nobody will demand it now, so there must be a belief system that money will be demanded in future for indefinite periods. Hence a medium of exchange necessarily becomes a store of value, though not every store of value is a medium of exchange. The liquidity of an asset makes it money. The degree of liquidity is defined as the easiness with which the asset is converted to any other commodity or service. If an asset can be exchanged seamlessly for another asset, then it fulfills the ideal definition of money. Similarly, if money is exchanged for another asset or goods or services and if no transaction cost is involved, then the money is perfectly liquid.

WHAT IS DEMAND FOR MONEY?

Demand for money is not exactly like demand for any other commodity. Money does not give any direct utility to a consumer, nor is it used as an intermediate good in the production process. However, it facilitates transactions in the processes of production, consumption, and distribution. Money has purchasing power whereby one can purchase any marketable good or service. Further in a sense money gives more utility than a set of goods or services of the same value because it provides a generalized purchasing power. An infinite set of choices of goods and services are possible if money exists. Hence demand for money is an indirect demand for goods and services, both in current and in future periods. If more money is chasing the same amount of goods or services, then value of money goes down; this is an inflationary situation. For the holders of money, it is the purchasing power—that is, the real money balances—that matters.

According to John Maynard Keynes, an asset possesses three properties: a yield, a liquidity premium, and a carrying cost. He defined money as an asset that has zero yield but a positive liquidity premium in excess of its carrying cost.

The most common form of money in the early twenty-first century world is the liabilities of central banks. The almost universal requirement that taxes be paid to the governments in the form of liabilities of a central bank ensures that there is a demand for such liabilities (see Jordan 2006).

THEORETICAL SIGNIFICANCE

Demand for money arises from medium of exchange and store of value functions. Because people need money to smooth transactions, they hold it for future needs. Money as a medium of exchange is a facilitator of transactions and hence an essential lubricant to the mechanism of exchange. In fact these two roles of money are interrelated. Unless money is a store of value, it cannot be a medium of exchange and vice versa. However, the transaction demand is more fundamental. There are other assets besides money that are competing and even better stores of value but no better medium of exchange. In developing countries, though, money's store of value role is particularly significant. Money generally serves as the unit of account and the standard of deferred payment because it is convenient as well as efficient. However, the medium-of-account role is not logically tied to the medium of exchange (Wicksell 1906).

Keynes in *The General Theory of Employment, Interest, and Money* (1936) identified three motives for holding money: the transaction motive, the precautionary motive, and the speculative motive. The transaction motive and precautionary motive relate to money's role as the medium of exchange, whereas the speculative motive relates to money's role as a store of value. The transaction motive arises for exchanging money for goods and services, as it is extremely unlikely to have double coincidence of "wants," especially in a modern economy. It may not be possible for me to exchange a few pages of my research paper for a meal in a restaurant because my "want" and the "want" of the restaurant owner need not coincide. Holding money involves a trade-off between forgoing the interest that can accumulate with savings and bearing the inconvenience of not holding money for transaction purposes. People may hold money to meet future payments, which are uncertain; this is the precautionary motive for holding money (see Whalen 1966). Money is also held for speculative purposes, that is, to avoid the risk inherent in other assets, which may pay higher returns (see Tobin 1958).

Demand for money varies between developed and developing countries because the former have relatively advanced financial systems, states of technology, and degrees of enforceability of contracts. The volume of transactions also influences demand for money. In less developed countries cash is used more often for transactions; in more developed nations the use of credit cards reduces the demand for cash.

There are several economic variables that affect the demand for money, including gross domestic product (GDP), interest rates, inflation rates, financial innovations in the economy, degree of monetization in the economy, exchange rates, structure and level of external trade, and so on. Various theories explain the relationships between these variables and money. The original quantity theory of money (Fisher 1911) was followed by the Keynesian theory of liquidity preference (Keynes 1936) and later by more modern variants of both (Friedman 1956; Tobin 1956, 1958; Baumol 1952). The Keynsian approach makes interest rate an explicit determinant of the demand for money.

Technical progress in the financial sector introduces two competing influences on the trend behavior of velocity, each of which dominates a different stage of development in a particular country. During the first stage of development, the economy is characterized by increasing monetization and expansion of bank branches. Cash and demand deposits are increasingly used for transactions, replacing earlier reliance on barter trade. The income velocity of money falls. In the second phase of development, new securities are introduced as an alternative store of value. The change in technology and regulatory mechanisms in the financial sector and the resultant rapid transfer of funds across time, space, and economic agents economizes on money balances. This results in a rise in velocity, giving rise to a U-shaped function for the veloc-

ity with respect to time. Money has an inherent tendency to instability through the development process as the velocity varies (see Bordo and Jonung 1987).

EMPIRICAL SIGNIFICANCE

Money demand is one of the most extensively studied relationships in economic literature. Innumerable articles were published in the last decades of the twentieth century on empirical money demand estimations for numerous countries and time periods. Empirical research on the demand for money progressed as theory evolved, and econometric techniques improved in order to posit a plausible validation for the theoretical relationships (or lack thereof). The growing arsenal of time-series econometric techniques, such as cointegration and error correction, has permitted more sophisticated examinations of demand for money functions.

There is a vast amount of empirical literature examining the stability of demand for money. This is explained by the ever-changing technology, innovations, and regulatory mechanisms in the financial markets. Further the large fluctuations in the interest rates can render a large amount of instability to the velocity of circulation of money.

Markus Knell and Helmut Stix (2003) performed a meta-analysis of almost 500 empirical money demand studies to investigate whether different study characteristics might play a role in variations. They showed that the estimations for the income elasticity of money demand are systematically and significantly higher if broader definitions for monetary aggregates are used; the inclusion of variables such as wealth and financial innovation tend to be associated with lower estimates. The results for the use of different scale variables, the use of different econometric methods, and various additional details of the specification are less clear-cut. Surprisingly they also found that some of these results are similar to observations made in previous surveys, despite the facts that they use a completely different sample of papers and that in their sample most studies use modern cointegration techniques, whereas older surveys (see Laidler 1993) were dominated by partial adjustment models, and so on.

In an international sample of studies, income elasticities between −14.11 and 44.79 (or corrected for outliers between .01 and 2.46) were observed; sometimes substantial differences can be found even within the same country and time period (Knell and Stix 2003). Most surveys show divergence of empirical findings in terms of coefficient values. However, this is to be expected because macroeconomic environment varies across countries and across sample periods.

During the 1970s and 1980s most studies looked at Organization for Economic Cooperation and Development (OECD) countries and particularly the United States and the United Kingdom, but since the 1990s a number of papers on developing countries have become available. The literature on developing countries suggests that the models on narrow money work better, reflecting weak banking systems and low financial sector development (Pradhan and Subramanian 2003). Automatic teller machines, for example, allow withdrawals from savings accounts, so the narrow money changes but not the broad money. Hence financial innovation has made narrow money relatively more unstable in advanced economies (see Hetzel and Mehra 1989; Hafer and Jansen 1991). Generally currency, demand deposits, and other checkable deposits constitutes the "narrow money"; "broad money" includes some more financial assets in addition to the narrow money.

Despite the numerous efforts to estimate the demand for money functions, there is little agreement among the authors of this literature. The range of estimated income and interest-rate elasticities is wide, and although some papers maintain that money demand is stable, others come to the opposite conclusion.

POLICY SIGNIFICANCE

The long-run relationship between real money balances, real output, and interest rate has immense policy implications. If demand for money is stable, then output and price level are predictable to a given supply of money. A monetary policy that seeks to limit the supply of money to its demand facilitates the task of macroeconomic management and tries to ensure price stability in the economy. The rate of growth of money supply should be in conformity to the expected growth rate of output in order to constrain the price level from rising to an unacceptable level. The relation between the demand for money balances and its determinants is a fundamental building block in most theories of macroeconomic behavior and is a crucial component in the formulation of monetary policy. This requires a stable demand for money. Furthermore if the growth of money supply increases at a much faster rate than the real GDP, then the currency becomes unstable; this works against the Hayekian requirement of a stable currency for a proper market economy (Jordan 2006). If the demand function itself is not stable, then generally the interest rate rather than the money supply is targeted.

We saw that stability of demand for money has implications for policy. One can see this through the famed IS-LM framework as well. An unstable money demand function generates an unstable LM curve, which renders the IS-LM equilibrium unstable, making the policy impact on income and interest rates unpredictable.

SHORTCOMINGS AND CRITICISMS OF THE CONCEPT

Stability of demand for money is one of the most important issues in macroeconomic policy analysis. However, money demand functions are found to be not robust. Stability and reliability of estimates of parameters of demand functions of money for many countries have been found wanting for various time periods. Unusual economic conditions, including severe bouts of inflation, record-high interest rates, and deep recessions, are responsible for instability of money demand function. This happens across countries due to business cycles. Also the adoption of floating exchange rates and substantial institutional changes brought about by financial innovation and financial deregulation create instability. These changes, which occurred earlier in developed countries, are now affecting many emerging market economies, such as India and China.

There are measurement problems relating to the determinants, such as transaction variable, opportunity cost variable, and wealth variable. In fact measurement and definition problems arise with respect to the money variable itself. What we call "money" also keeps changing across time and geography. Improving the specifications and/or using improved econometric techniques helps matters to an extent. In fact these developments provide opportunities to explore new relationships and to use modern time-series techniques of cointegration and error correction and beyond.

However, statistical techniques are only tools to summarize data; therefore, they cannot always answer difficult questions that need deeper economic insights. More explorations are needed on the conceptual aspects of demand for money.

SEE ALSO *Friedman, Milton; Interest Rates; Keynes, John Maynard; Liquidity; Liquidity Premium; Liquidity Trap; Money; Neutrality of Money; Quantity Theory of Money; Tobin, James*

BIBLIOGRAPHY

Ball, Laurence. 2002. Short-Run Demand for Money. National Bureau of Economic Research Working Paper W9235.

Baumol, William J. 1952. The Transactions Demand for Cash: An Inventory Theoretic Approach. *Quarterly Journal of Economics* 66: 545–556.

Bordo, Michael D., and Lars Jonung. 1987. *Long-Run Behaviour of the Velocity of Circulation: The International Evidence.* Cambridge, U.K.: Cambridge University Press.

Cagan, Phillip. 1956. The Monetary Dynamics of Hyperinflation. In *Studies in the Quantity Theory of Money,* ed. Milton Friedman, 25–117. Chicago: University of Chicago Press.

Dornbusch, Rudiger, Stanley Fischer, and Richard Startz. 2004. *Macroeconomics.* New Delhi: Tata McGraw-Hill.

Duca, John V., and David D. VanHoose. 2004. Recent Developments in Understanding the Demand for Money. *Journal of Economics and Business* 56: 247–272.

Fase, Martin. 1994. In Search for Stability: An Empirical Appraisal of the Demand for Money in the G7 and EC Countries. *De Economist* 142 (4): 421–454.

Fisher, Irving. 1911. *The Purchasing Power of Money.* New York: Macmillan.

Friedman, Milton. 1956. The Quantity Theory of Money: A Restatement. In *Studies in the Quantity of Theory of Money,* 3–21. Chicago: University of Chicago Press.

Friedman, Milton. 1959. The Demand for Money: Some Theoretical and Empirical Results. *Journal of Political Economy* 67: 327–351.

Friedman, Milton, and Anna J. Schwartz. 1963. *A Monetary History of the United States: 1867–1960.* National Bureau of Economic Research Studies in Business Cycles 12. Princeton, NJ: Princeton University Press.

Goldfeld, Stephen M., and Daniel E. Sichel. 1990. Demand for Money. In *Handbook of Monetary Economics,* vol. 1, eds. Benjamin M. Friedman and Frank H. Hahn, 299–356. Amsterdam: North-Holland.

Hafer, Rik W., and Dennis Jansen. 1991. The Demand for Money in the United States: Evidence from Cointegration Tests. *Journal of Money, Credit, and Banking* 23: 155–168.

Hetzel, Robert, and Yash Mehra. 1989. The Behavior of Money Demand in the 1980s. *Journal of Money, Credit, and Banking* 21: 455–463.

Hicks, John R. [1935] 1951. A Suggestion for Simplifying the Theory of Money. *American Economic Association, Readings in Monetary Theory,* 13–32. Philadelphia: Blakiston.

Jordan, Jerry L. 2006. Money and Monetary Policy for the Twenty-First Century. *Federal Reserve Bank of St. Louis Review,* November–December, 485–510.

Keynes, John Maynard. [1930] 1958–1960. *A Treatise on Money.* 2 vols. London: Macmillan.

Keynes, John Maynard. 1936. *The General Theory of Employment, Interest, and Money.* London: Macmillan.

Knell, Markus, and Helmut Stix. 2003. How Robust Are Money Demand Estimations? A Meta-Analytic Approach. Austrian Central Bank Working Paper.

Laidler, David E. W. 1993. *The Demand for Money: Theories, Evidence, and Problems.* 4th ed. New York: HarperCollins College.

Marshall, Alfred. [1923] 1960. *Money, Credit, and Commerce.* New York: Kelley.

Meltzer, Allan H. 1963a. The Demand for Money: A Cross-section Study of Business Firms. *Quarterly Journal of Economics* 77: 405–422.

Meltzer, Allan H. 1963b. The Demand for Money: The Evidence from the Time Series. *Journal of Political Economy* 71: 219–246.

Miller, Merton H., and Daniel Orr. 1966. A Model of the Demand for Money by Firms. *Quarterly Journal of Economics* 80 (August): 413–435.

Pigou, Arthur C. [1917] 1951. The Value of Money. In *American Economic Association, Readings in Monetary Theory,* 162–183. Philadelphia: Blakiston.

Pradhan, Basanta K., and A. Subramanian. 2003. On the Stability of Demand for Money in a Developing Economy: Some Empirical Issues. *Journal of Development Economics* 72: 335–351.

Tobin, James. 1956. The Interest-Elasticity of Transactions Demand for Cash. *Review of Economics and Statistics* 38: 241–247.

Tobin, James. 1958. Liquidity Preference as Behavior toward Risk. *Review of Economic Studies* 25: 65–86.

Whalen, Edward H. 1966. A Rationalisation of the Precautionary Demand for Cash. *Quarterly Journal of Economics* 80: 314–324.

Wicksell, Knut. [1906] 1935. *Money.* Vol. 2 of *Lectures on Political Economy.* London: Routledge.

Basanta Kumar Pradhan

MONEY, ENDOGENOUS

Economists have disputed the nature of money since the dawn of capitalism. Two polar positions have evolved: the quantity theory (also known as *monetarism*) and endogenous money. The former emphasizes money's role as a means of exchange, and argues that the money supply is primarily controlled by the government. The latter emphasizes money as a unit of account, and argues that the supply of money is determined primarily by the credit operations of commercial banks. Each theory acknowledges that the total money supply is the sum of *fiat money* produced by the government and *credit money* produced by commercial banks, but the theories differ in their views of the hypothesized causal sequence.

The well-known quantity theory sees causation as running from fiat to credit money. The government determines the volume of *base money* (M_0) by printing currency and borrowing from the central bank. This is deposited with commercial banks, which then create credit money $(M_2$ minus $M_0)$ via *fractional banking*, where they retain a fraction m (the money multiplier) of the deposits, and lend the remainder. The redepositing of this loaned fraction by borrowers amplifies the initial creation of fiat money, so that the total money supply (M_2) ultimately equals m times M_0. Deposits are thus needed to create loans, and credit money is created from fiat money via a time-lagged process. The quantity theory puts primary responsibility for the rate of inflation on the government, since it can manipulate the quantity of money via changes to M_0 and m. The ratio between the money supply and the volume of output in turn determines the price level.

In contrast, endogenous money asserts that credit money is created by commercial banks in response to the needs of predominantly large companies for working capital and investment finance. To ensure an adequate supply of working capital, large companies arrange lines of credit with banks that function rather like individual credit cards—in that the extent to which the line of credit is utilized is determined by the borrower, not the bank. Investment finance is only forthcoming if banks agree to issue loans, which enables them to ration credit to borrowers with poor credit ratings. However, banks compete to provide investment finance to highly rated corporations, so that in general the demand for money by corporations determines the supply of credit money by banks.

When a corporation utilizes its line of credit to pay a supplier, the firm's recorded debt to the bank increases, and simultaneously the supplier's account is credited with newly created credit money. When the corporation negotiates an investment finance loan, its debt to the bank increases and simultaneously an identical sum of credit money is deposited in its account with the bank. In either case, the bank loan instantly creates an identical deposit—the reverse of the causal relation between loans and deposits of the quantity theory, with no time lag.

Instead, there is a lag between the creation of new credit money by the commercial banks and the generation of new fiat money by the government. According to endogenous money theorist Basil Moore, the government's primary role is to ensure that the financial system does not experience crises like those that periodically racked the largely credit money system of nineteenth-century America—culminating in the Great Depression. It does this by providing sufficient currency to meet the public's need for "cash in hand," and by modifying the regulatory requirements on any bank that experiences a run to ensure that depositors' demands for cash can be met.

Endogenous money theory thus sees the government as largely captive to the needs of the corporate and finance sectors, and only able to influence the rate of credit creation at the expense of serious disruptions to economic activity by causing liquidity crises. The one aspect of the financial system that the government does control is the interbank interest rate, which then sets the floor for short-term commercial interest rates.

The quantity theory still dominates economics pedagogy in the form of the exogenous money supply of the IS-LM model, and economic theory in the form of rational expectations macroeconomics. However, the world's central banks subscribe to endogenous money theory, implicitly if not explicitly, in that they abandoned any attempt to control the supply of money after the monetarist-inspired experiments by the U.S. and British governments in the 1980s. While inflation was gradually reduced, economic activity was severely disrupted, and the central banks consistently failed to meet their money creation targets—normally by large margins.

These failed practical experiments were reinforced by empirical research in the 1990s, which found that changes in $M_2 - M_0$ preceded changes in M_0 by up to a year—a result that is consistent with endogenous money and contradicts the quantity theory. Though empirically confirmed, the theory of endogenous money is less well developed than its quantity/monetarist rival, and is still undergoing development.

Augusto Graziani's proposition that all exchanges in a monetary economy involve a single commodity and three parties—a seller, a buyer, and a bank that records payment as a transfer from the buyer's account to the seller's—clarified John Maynard Keynes's (1883–1946) argument that a monetary economy is fundamentally different from a barter economy, and therefore that the neoclassical model of a barter economy cannot adequately describe its behavior. However Graziani's attempt to analyze monetary circulation confused the issue of how monetary profits are generated from borrowed money. Endogenous money theorists also have yet to resolve how much influence banks have vis-à-vis firms in determining the money supply, with the subhypothesis that banks are completely passive being labeled *horizontalism* or *accommodationism*, while the alternative that banks have some control over the quantity and terms of money supply is known as *structuralism*. Other contributors to the debate argue that current disputes in endogenous money emanate from a confusion of stocks with flows, an argument made by Keynes in 1937 when outlining a distinctly endogenous view of money creation, in contrast to the predominantly exogenous perspective that dominated his *General Theory of Employment, Interest, and Money* (1936).

SEE ALSO *Banking; Central Banks; Money; Money, Exogenous; Money, Supply of*

BIBLIOGRAPHY

Dow, Sheila, 1989. Endogenous Money. In *A "Second Edition" of the* General Theory, eds. Geoffrey C. Harcourt and P. A. Riach, Vol. 2, 61–78. London: Routledge.

Graziani, Augusto. 2003. *The Monetary Theory of Production.* Cambridge, U.K.: Cambridge University Press.

Keen, Steve. 2006. The Need and Some Methods for Dynamic Modelling in Post Keynesian Economics. In *Complexity, Endogenous Money, and Macroeconomic Theory: Essays in Honour of Basil J. Moore,* ed. Mark Setterfield, 36–59. Aldershot, U.K.: Edward Elgar.

Keynes, John Maynard 1937. Alternative Theories of the Rate of Interest. *Economic Journal* 47: 241–252.

Kydland, Finn E., and Edward C. Prescott. 1990. Business Cycles: Real Facts and a Monetary Myth. *Federal Reserve Bank of Minneapolis Quarterly Review* 14 (2): 1–17.

Moore, Basil. 1983. Unpacking the Post-Keynesian Black Box: Bank Lending and the Money Supply. *Journal of Post Keynesian Economics* 5: 537–556.

Steve Keen

MONEY, EXOGENOUS

Money is considered exogenous or endogenous depending on its relationship to the economy. If its existence and quantity are determined by the economy alone, money is considered endogenous. Conversely, if the existence and quantity of money are determined by forces outside the economy—most often by the state—money is considered exogenous. Since the inception of recorded monetary thinking, there has been an ongoing debate about whether money should be treated as endogenous or exogenous.

Much of this debate centers around the issues of (1) whether a royal or state authority should have the right to interfere in the monetary mechanism, and (2) whether the economy is better off with a growing money stock. For much of the medieval, Renaissance, and early modern periods, many writers argued that rulers should not be allowed to exercise their power over the monetary mechanism. This position was influenced by writers like Nicholas Oresme (c. 1320–1382), a French clergyman, mathematician, and economist, who argued that money belongs to the community and debasement was a violation of the people's rights, and the English merchant and financier Thomas Gresham (c. 1519–1579), who famously proclaimed that debased coins will drive out full-bodied coins—or more generally that bad money drives out good money.

During the sixteenth and seventeenth centuries, a general consensus emerged that the quantity of money was a significant factor in determining the amount of domestic commerce. This conjecture was based on the observation that the gold and silver inflow from the Americas coincided with the general economic prosperity of the sixteenth century, while the economic depression of the seventeenth century commenced around the same time that the flow of precious metals across the Atlantic began to abate. The formulation of the quantity theory of money as a conceptual framework, often credited to the French political philosopher Jean Bodin (c. 1529–1596), further clarified the relationship between the money stock, prices, and economic activity. As a result, many theorists proclaimed that the key to national economic prosperity was to find a way to expand the money supply.

Hence, while many writers opposed royal manipulations of the money stock, in particular debasements, this position was problematized by the conviction that an increase in the money supply would generate economic prosperity. The question that was passed on to the next generation of monetary thinkers was whether the money supply should be increased from the inside or from the outside.

Before turning to the eighteenth-century view on this question, the perspective of these theorists on the broader relationship between money and the polity must be considered. One of the key debates among early modern thinkers concerned the role that money played in the formation of modern society. For the English philosopher John Locke (1632–1704), money served as an external force that sparked the transition from a state of nature to modern society, while for the Scottish philosopher and historian David Hume (1711–1776), money developed in conjunction with private property and markets. Hence, for some writers, money had an independent outside existence with the potential to transform the rest of society, while for others, money could only exist as an institution embedded inside society's social and economic configuration.

John Locke also engaged in two long-lasting arguments regarding the relationship between the state and money. One of these debates centered around whether money had to be composed of a commodity with intrinsic value or whether it was possible for the government to use its authority to create money through fiat. Locke suggested that it was indeed semiotically necessary for money to be composed of a precious metal because people would only trust a currency that was grounded in something outside the authority of the state. By anchoring money to something incorruptible, like silver, people could trust money without having to rely on the state to behave responsibly. Others, such as Locke's contemporary Nicholas Barbon (c. 1640–1698), argued the contrary position that the state can turn any object into money by its stamp of authority, as long as it is fully committed to keeping the money stock sufficiently scarce. Hence, for some writers, money functions best when it operates independently of the state, while for others, the state is responsible for the very existence of money.

The other debate that Locke was actively engaged in concerned whether the quantity of money should be determined by the economy or by the state—endogenously or exogenously. Locke opined, in agreement with some of his seventeenth-century mercantilist predecessors, that the quantity of money circulating in a nation should be dictated by the bullion flows between countries. That is, the only way to expand the nation's money supply was to engineer a favorable balance of trade, either by producing tradable goods more efficiently or by imposing trade restrictions. Under such circumstances, the state had limited independent power over the quantity of money.

Others, such as the Scottish banker and monetary theorist John Law (1671–1729), proposed the establishment of a credit currency that could expand and contract in response to the amount of economic activity. Law proposed a credit currency backed by a tangible commodity, such as land, and administered by a bank that would only issue credit money to borrowers intending to use the money for legitimate investment projects. Law argued that a credit currency of this kind would allow the market to determine the proper amount of money—when the economy was prospering and the demand for money was high, the bank would be able to expand the money supply and thus facilitate the growth of the economy. As such, the quantity of money would be determined inside, or endogenously to, the economy.

The reality of the early eighteenth-century credit currencies, however, differed from Law's proposal. Over time, the issuance of credit money by state-chartered banks, such as the Bank of England and the Bank Générale, was determined more by the interest of the state than by the demands of the economy. Hence, the emergence of a credit currency increasingly allowed the state to control the quantity of money in the economy. However, since the note-issuing bank was forced to redeem its paper notes with silver or gold on demand, states did not yet have complete control over the amount of money issued. Toward the end of the eighteenth century, however, when the state-chartered banks started issuing fiat money—paper money that was no longer redeemable for gold or silver—the state acquired a more direct method to control the money supply. A fully exogenous form of money had now developed.

David Hume provided one of the eighteenth-century's most complete reflections on the difference between inside and outside, or endogenous and exogenous, money. He argued that money should always be organized and theorized as endogenous to the economy. Firstly, the origins of money occurred as part of an organic development of the economy, fully independent of the state. Secondly, the quantity of metallic money should always be determined by the specie-flow mechanism between countries, and the amount of credit money should be determined by the liquidity needs of the merchants and not the fiscal advantage of the state. Phrased within the quantity theory of money, Hume believed that the quantity of money was determined by the nation's price level and its level of output—when output was increasing the price level would fall, encouraging exports and an inflow of specie to the country. Any attempt by the state to try to expand the money supply and thus treat money as if it were exogenous would only lead to inflation and possibly even a destabilization of the economy.

Hume did not have the final word on the issue of endogeneity and exogeneity. The conversation continued throughout the nineteenth century between bullionists and antibullionists, the currency school and the banking school. Once Keynesian ideas on countercyclical monetary policy were implemented systematically after World War II (1939–1945) and the state consistently treated the money supply as exogenous, the debate over the actual and proper relationship between money and the economy resurfaced, continuing to this day. These debates have centered around the extent to which the money stock is determined by the price level, interest rate, and output level (endogeneity) or whether the causality runs in the opposite direction with the money stock controlling prices, interest rates, and output (exogeneity). Part of this controversy is sustained by an inability to agree on a definition of money: whether the money stock is primarily composed of money with intrinsic value, credit money, or fiat money.

This issue has become even more complicated in the post–Bretton Woods era, when the U.S. dollar ceased to be redeemable for gold at a fixed price. This period has also witnessed rapid financial developments that have further blurred the definition of money. Add to this the tendencies toward transnational currencies, most prominently exemplified by the European euro, and the adoption of other nation's currencies, such as the dollarization of Ecuador, and the issue of exogeneity and endogeneity becomes all the more complex. For example, the notion that the state is able to control exogenous money no longer holds. Nations that eliminate their own national currency in favor of the U.S. dollar clearly have an exogenously determined money stock, but one over which their own state cannot exercise any control.

In an economic world comprising many different forms of money and near-money, what dictates whether money is exogenous or endogenous is the level of abstraction of the inquiry. If the time horizon is long and the global economy is considered the unit of analysis, most forms of money appear to be endogenous. But if the time span is reduced and the focus is on a particular region, certain forms of money will be found to operate either with weak exogeneity or strong exogeneity. Hence, it is not just institutional features that determine whether money functions endogenously or exogenously; as important is the theoretical framework from which money is viewed.

SEE ALSO *Central Banks; Money; Money, Endogenous; Money, Supply of*

BIBLIOGRAPHY

Desai, Meghnad. 1992. Endogenous and Exogenous Money. In *The New Palgrave Dictionary of Money*, eds. John Eatwell, Murray Milgate, and Peter Newman, 146–150. London: Macmillan.

Wennerlind, Carl. 2005. David Hume's Monetary Theory Revisited: Was He Really a Quantity Theorist and an Inflationist? *Journal of Political Economy* 113 (1): 223–237.

Carl Wennerlind

MONEY, HIGH-POWERED

SEE *Monetary Base.*

MONEY, HOT

SEE *Hot Money.*

MONEY, NEUTRAL

SEE *Neutrality of Money.*

MONEY, SUPPLY OF

Central bank policy influences the supply of monetary services. The transmission mechanism is not the same in all countries, but commonly the procedure operates through open market operations, by which the central bank buys or sells domestic Treasury securities. Such purchases and sales alter the central bank's balance sheet and thereby *high-powered money*, also called the *monetary base*, defined to be the sum of currency and bank reserves. The resulting changes in interest rates and in bank balance sheets alter *inside money*, defined to be monetary services produced by banks and other financial intermediaries. How to measure the resulting change in the supplied monetary-service flow in the economy is a complicated matter that has been the subject of much debate.

The conventional measurement procedure is to add up the nominal balances of monetary assets. The resulting sum is called the *money supply*. Subtracting the monetary base from that sum produces what is commonly treated as inside money. Much of the modern literature on business cycles revolves around empirical work on the relative effects of inside money and outside money. But the usual measurement of inside money is unrelated to the theory of production and the ways in which that theory determines the output services produced by financial intermediaries.

HIGH-POWERED MONEY

During the Great Depression of the 1930s, the monetary base continued to rise in a normal manner as the supply of money in the economy collapsed. Why did this happen? Currency is dollar-for-dollar pure money. But reserves back demand deposits with a multiplier, k. For every dollar removed from demand deposits as the banking system crashed, currency increased by one dollar, while reserves declined by $1/k$ dollars, so that the monetary base changed by $1 - 1/k$, which is positive. Hence, runs on banks increased the monetary base at the same time that demand deposits were declining and banks were failing. As an instrument or indicator of policy, the monetary base is defective, since it adds together currency and reserves, which have very different effects on the economy.

INSIDE MONEY

According to the theory of production, there are two ways to measure the output of a firm. One way is to measure the gross value of the output *aggregator function, g*. The other way is to measure the net *value added* by the firm's production. By the most conventional and simplest accounting convention, called *double deflation*, value added subtracts from aggregate output the aggregate over intermediate factor inputs. Value added then depends only upon primary inputs, such as capital, land, and labor. In the obsolete labor theory of value, only the one labor factor was needed, since inputs were assumed to be employed in fixed proportions.

Consider the case of a bank that produces a vector of n monetary-asset balances, $m_t = (m_{1t}, m_{2t}, …, m_{nt})'$, during period t and pays on those assets the nominal interest rates $r_t = (r_{1t}, r_{2t}, …, r_{nt})'$, by employing the vectors of primary inputs, x_{1t}, and intermediate inputs, x_{2t}. If the bank's technology is described by the production function, f, with outputs separable from inputs, we can write $g(m_t) = f(x_{1t}, x_{2t})$, where the value of the output aggregator function is $M_t = g(m_t)$. For the most general procedure to measure value added in banking, see William Barnett (2000, pp. 92–93).

The special case of double deflation accounting requires two further assumptions. The first is the existence of aggregator functions, f_1 and f_2, over primary and intermediate inputs, so that $M_t = g(m_t) = f(f_1(x_{1t}), f_2(x_{2t}))$. The second is strong separability between primary and intermediary inputs, so that $M_t = g(m_t) = f_1(x_{1t}) + f_2(x_{2t})$. Value added then becomes $f_1(x_{1t}) = g(m_t) - f_2(x_{2t})$.

Under those assumptions, production theory tells us that the supply of inside money produced by a bank can be measured by, $M_t = g(m_t)$, while value added in banking is $f_1(x_{1t}) = g(m_t) - f_2(x_{2t})$. Neither theoretical concept has any known relationship with the simple sum monetary aggregate, $\sum_{i=1}^{n} m_{it}$, provided by most central banks, or with inside money, as measured by the simple sum monetary aggregate minus the monetary base. In contrast, it has been shown in Barnett (2000) that total inside money services, $M_t = g(m_t)$, can be measured from the Divisia index over m_t, and that value added in banking, $g(m_t) - f_2(x_{2t})$, can be measured by subtracting from M_t the Divisia index over x_{2t}.

THE DIVISIA INDEX

The Divisia Monetary Index has user-costs as prices within the formula, since monetary assets are durable. So long as required reserves do not exist, the formula for the user-cost price of a monetary-asset supplied is the same as the formula for the user-cost price of a monetary-asset demanded. That formula is

$$\pi_{it} = \frac{R_t - r_{it}}{1 + R_t},$$

where the benchmark asset rate of return, R_t, for a financial firm on the supply side of money markets, is the rate of return on loans by the financial intermediary. But if noninterest-bearing required reserves exist, there is a regulatory wedge, requiring subtraction of the implicit tax on banks out of the formula. As shown in Barnett (2000, p. 57), the corrected user cost price becomes

$$\pi_{it} = \frac{(1 - k_i)R_t - r_{it}}{1 + R_t},$$

where k_I is the required reserve ratio on monetary asset i.

THE ECONOMIC STOCK OF MONEY

The Divisia demand-side index and the Divisia supply-side index both measure flows. Since the transmission mechanism of money is sometimes viewed as operating through a wealth effect, it is useful to know how to discount the present value of the service flow to find the economic capital stock of money. Because of the dependency of that capital stock on future expectations, measurement of that capital stock is one of the most challenging areas of this field of research. Since money is now a joint product producing both monetary services and investment yield, wealth effects must untangle the discounted present value of the monetary services flow from the discounted present value of the investment yield (see, for example, Barnett, Chae, and Keating 2006).

CONCLUSION

There is reason to be concerned about conclusions regarding policy reached using conventional monetary aggregates and conventional measures of inside versus outside money. The data provided by many central banks is unrelated to the relevant economic theory, unless all financial assets are perfect substitutes. With different interest rates being paid on different monetary assets, that implied assumption has been unreasonable for over a half century.

Although little research has been done using the relevant theory to measure aggregate money on the supply side, a few such empirical studies have been published and reprinted in Barnett and Jane Binner (2004, pp. 351–434) and Barnett, Melvin Hinich, and Warren Weber (1986).

SEE ALSO *Central Banks; Divisia Monetary Index; Federal Reserve System, U.S.; Friedman, Milton; Interest Rates; Keynes, John Maynard; Monetary Base; Money; Money, Demand for; Money, Endogenous; Money, Exogenous; Policy, Monetary*

BIBLIOGRAPHY

Barnett, William A. 2000. The Microeconomic Theory of Monetary Aggregation. In *The Theory of Monetary Aggregation*, eds. William A. Barnett and Apostolos Serletis, 49–99. Amsterdam: North Holland.

Barnett, William A., and Apostolos Serletis, eds. 2000. *The Theory of Monetary Aggregation*. Amsterdam: North Holland.

Barnett, William A., and Jane M. Binner, eds. 2004. *Functional Structure and Approximation in Econometrics*. Amsterdam and Boston: Elsevier.

Barnett, William A., Melvin J. Hinich, and Warren E. Weber. 1986. The Regulatory Wedge between the Demand-Side and Supply-Side Aggregation-Theoretic Monetary Aggregates. *Journal of Econometrics* 33: 165–185. Reprinted in Barnett and Serletis (2000), 433–453.

Barnett, William A., Unja Chae, and John Keating. 2006. The Discounted Economic Stock of Money with VAR Forecasting. *Annals of Finance* 2 (2): 229–258.

William A. Barnett

MONEY ILLUSION

The term *money illusion* was coined in the 1920s by Irving Fisher, who defined it as "the failure to perceive that the dollar, or any other unit of money, expands or shrinks in value" (1928, p. 4). As a matter of fact, *money illusion* refers to individual or aggregate economic behavior that consists in failing to distinguish transactions in terms of either nominal or real monetary values. This odd tendency is a direct consequence of the fact that money as a measure of value or unit of account, such as the dollar or the euro, differs fundamentally from physical yardsticks such as miles, kilos, and ohms in that it is not an intrinsically fixed measure over time.

This failure of the public to recognize real and nominal monetary changes is primarily a psychological phenomenon. In economic theory, with its bias toward monetary neutrality, this often has been assumed away, so money illusion has been regarded with some suspicion because the basic assumption of its absence underlies the long-run neutrality property embraced by the quantity theory of money.

Authors such as Leontief (1936) and Haberler (1964) consider money illusion to be a violation of the homogeneity postulate of economic theory. This theory hypothesizes that the demand and supply functions are homogeneous of degree zero in all nominal prices; that is, that demand and supply depend on relative rather than absolute prices and thus are insensitive to relative price changes. Patinkin (1949, 1965) extended this to include monetary assets as cash balances. Consequently, Patinkin postulates the absence of money illusion on the basis of the zero-homogeneity property of net-demand functions in all money prices and the money value of initial holdings of assets. Operationally, this is equivalent to the assumption of rational behavior that predicts that a proportional change in all prices and monetary balances would leave money's purchasing power unaffected. It is this property that offers a yardstick for the assessment of money illusion in practice.

The absence of money illusion is the main assumption underlying neoclassical economic theory that cherishes David Hume's famous "money veil," denoting that money is only useful to exchange for other things which are unlike money of direct significance for economic welfare because, following Pigou (1941, pp. 20–27), money does not comprise any of the essentials of real economic life. Nevertheless, recognition of money illusion has a long tradition among economic heterodox and monetary economists. With his 1928 monograph *Money Illusion* Irving Fisher devoted an entire book to this topic, attempting to discredit the absence of money illusion in the real world on the basis of historical and statistical evidence from all over the world. To him, money illusion was an important explanation for business cycle fluctuations.

Nowadays, interest in the empirical validity of the assumption of money illusion is no longer anathema to the economics profession, firstly because the absence of money illusion helps to account for price stickiness and less than perfect economic adjustment processes, and secondly, because a lot of empirical or quasi-empirical evidence seems to support the occurrence of money illusion. Two kinds of evidence dominate. On the one hand, several well-designed psychological experiments at the individual level show a convincing bias toward nominal rather than real magnitudes, which according to these experiments results in considerable inertia (see Shafir et al. 1997; Fehr and Tyran 1997). On the other hand, recent experience also seems to provide clear-cut evidence for the existence of money illusion at the individual and aggregate levels. The most notable evidence is associated with the introduction of the euro in 2002. This operation offered a splendid opportunity for a real-life experiment to examine the occurrence of money illusion in the main western European countries. From a purely monetary point of view, the replacement of the national currencies of the Euro zone countries by a single currency merely amounted to a redefinition of prices through multiplication by a given and fixed number, for example 0.45 for the Dutch guilder. According to the homogeneity postulate—that is, the absence of money illusion—demand and supply conditions remain unchanged. However, this purely nominal operation resulted in an upward pressure of prices for particular commodities and especially services, affecting household expenditure, as national account statistics of Euro zone countries unambiguously show. This statistical observation, combined with ad hoc information on expenditure in several sectors of the economy in the relevant countries, point to some degree of money illusion. So, both economic experiments (with questionnaires on hypothetical situations allowing either nominal or volume variations) and actually observed expenditure behavior seem to violate the neutrality property of money. Hence, the empirical evidence indicates the existence of money illusion. Moreover, the difficulty of distinguishing between real and nominal exchange rates in daily economic activity provides additional empirical support for this conclusion.

Taken together, the occurrence of money illusion is quite likely in the real world and is, in fact, nothing but a particular manifestation of incomplete knowledge or economic frictions. These findings discredit monetary neutrality of neoclassical economic theory and the innocence of a nominal monetary reform in purchasing power such as the introduction of the euro in 2002.

SEE ALSO *Keynes, John Maynard; Sticky Prices; Unemployment; Wages*

BIBLIOGRAPHY

Fehr, Ernst, and John-Robert Tyran. 1997. Does Money Illusion Matter? *American Economic Review* 112: 1239–1262.

Fisher, Irving. 1928. *The Money Illusion.* New York: Adelphi.

Haberler, Gottfried. 1964. *Prosperity and Depression: A Theoretical Analysis of Cyclical Movements.* 4th ed. Cambridge, MA: Harvard University Press. Note that the relevant footnote has disappeared in later editions.

Leontief, Wassily. 1936. The Fundamental Assumptions of Mr. Keynes' Monetary Theory of Unemployment. *Quarterly Journal of Economics* 51: 192–197.

Patinkin, Don. 1949. The Indeterminacy of Absolute Prices in Classical Economic Theory. *Econometrica* 17: 1–27.

Patinkin, Don. 1965. *Money, Interest, and Prices*. 2nd ed. New York: Harper and Row.

Pigou, Arthur Cecil. 1941. *The Veil of Money*. London: Macmillan.

Shafir, Eldar, Peter Diamond, and Amos Tversky. 1997. Money Illusion. *Quarterly Journal of Economics* 112: 341–374.

Martin M. G. Fase

MONEY LAUNDERING

Money laundering, also known as "cleaning of money," is the practice of engaging in specific financial transactions in order to conceal the identity, source, or destination of money. Money laundering is a main operation of the underground economy. "Dirty money" is useless to organized crime because it leaves a trail of incriminating evidence. Criminals who wish to benefit from the proceeds of crime have to disguise their illegal revenues without implicating themselves. Therefore, money laundering is a process whereby the origin of funds generated by illegal means such as drug trafficking, gun smuggling, corruption, bribery, embezzlement, fraud, and extortion is concealed. The objective of the operation, which usually takes places in several stages, is to make illegally gained assets appear as though they are derived from a legitimate source. Money laundering is a dynamic process that requires three stages: *placement*, or moving the funds from direct association with the crime; *layering*, or disguising the trail to foil pursuit; and *integration*, or making the money available to the criminal once again with its occupational and geographic origins hidden from view. The consequences of money laundering are detrimental to business, economic development, government, and the rule of law. Money laundering increases the demand for cash, makes interest and exchange rates more volatile, and causes high inflation. The drainage of financial resources from ordinary economic growth is detrimental for the whole economy. Most importantly, money laundering empowers corruption and organized crime.

Money laundering is not a new phenomenon; it is as old as crime itself. However, the forms and dimensions of this type of crime have evolved and have become more sophisticated as a result of the rapid growth of globalization, integration, and economic liberalization, as well as dramatic developments in the provision of financial information, in technology, and in communications. Illegal money can be moved anywhere in the world with speed and ease. Tax havens (offshore centers) that offer stability, quality of service, and bank secrecy allow criminals to shield money in complex networks of shell companies. At the same time, the escalation of the drug market and the globalization of organized crime have led to an increased international awareness of the problem of money laundering. The International Monetary Fund (IMF) estimates that money laundering accounts for between 2 and 5 percent of the world's Gross Domestic Product (GDP), or about $600 billion annually.

While the term *money laundering* was once only applied to financial transactions related to organized crime, its definition has expanded. The term today covers any financial transaction that generates an asset or value as the result of an illegal act, including tax evasion or false accounting. Accordingly, in addition to members of organized crime, individuals, small and large businesses, government officials, and even national governments can be considered money launderers. However, the authorities have reacted primarily to the danger of abuse of the financial market by criminal organizations. Over the years, national and international agencies have created a new relationship between law enforcement authorities and those involved in the financial sector, allowing for a united fight against money laundering. In addition, since September 11, 2001, there has been a coordinated attempt, especially in the United States, to cut off terrorist financing. Through the aggressive pursuit of money trails, law enforcement hopes to identify and capture criminals and terrorists and to deny terrorist entities the funds necessary to finance further acts of terror.

SEE ALSO *Capital Flight; Corruption; Drug Traffic; Finance*

BIBLIOGRAPHY

Alldridge, Peter. 2003. *Money Laundering Law: Forfeiture, Confiscation, Civil Recovery, Criminal Laundering, and Taxation of the Proceeds of Crime*. Oxford: Hart Publishing.

Beare, Margaret E., ed. 2003. *Critical Reflections on Transnational Organized Crime, Money Laundering, and Corruption*. Toronto: University of Toronto Press.

Camdessus, Michel. 1998. *Money Laundering: The Importance of International Countermeasures*. Washington, DC: International Monetary Fund.

Jain, Arvind K., ed. 1998. *Economics of Corruption*. Boston: Kluwer Academic Publishers.

Jain, Arvind K., ed. 2001. *The Political Economy of Corruption*. London and New York: Routledge.

Naylor, R. T. 1987. *Hot Money and the Politics of Debt*. New York: Linden Press/Simon and Schuster.

Aristidis Bitzenis
John Marangos

MONEY MULTIPLIER
SEE *Multiplier, The.*

MONIZ, ANTONIO EGAS
SEE *Lobotomy.*

MONKEY TRIAL
SEE *Scopes Trial.*

MONOCENTRIC MODELS
SEE *Spatial Theory.*

MONOPOLY

Monopoly in its pure form is an extreme market form with complete lack of competition. A monopoly firm, or a monopolist, is the only seller, facing no competition in the marketplace for the good or service it is selling. The product in question is unique and has no close substitutes. An example is a single ferry service between two islands, or a pharmaceutical firm that is the sole manufacturer of a particular drug.

Pure monopolies, where there are no close substitutes for the product or service offered, are uncommon in the modern world due to the availability of substitute products and/or government mandates, but monopoly power is exercised by producers in various markets. *Monopoly power* is a broad term that refers to the ability of sellers to hike prices above costs. For instance, although the seller of a famous clothing label is not considered to be a pure monopolist, it has monopoly power to charge prices above those of less popular labels. Conversely, sellers facing many competitors (e.g., newspaper vendors) must price at or very close to costs, and have little monopoly power.

Less common variants of a monopoly include monopsony and a bilateral monopoly. A monopsonist is a single buyer facing many sellers: for example, the Department of Defense is the sole buyer of the wares of various defense equipment manufacturers. A bilateral monopoly is the special scenario where a single buyer faces a single seller. Exchange in a bilateral monopoly takes place depending upon the relative bargaining strengths of the buyer and seller. In the case of a natural monopoly structurally there is room for only one firm in a market.

In such cases, a single firm's costs decline as it serves more customers. Hence, one firm can continue to lower costs by producing more, and competitors with small market shares are unable to survive due to higher costs. Public utility companies such as power and water companies are prime examples of natural monopolies.

The primary reason for the emergence and long-term viability of a monopoly is the presence of entry restrictions, or entry barriers, for new competitors (see Bain 1956). These entry restrictions include exclusive ownership of raw materials, patents, franchises (both public and private), and so on. Some entry restrictions may be natural or independent of the monopolist's efforts, whereas others may be deliberately created by the monopolist (e.g., lobbying to make entry more difficult for firms that follow by having them satisfy stricter environmental restrictions). Governments sometimes create artificial monopolies for limited periods by mandating entry restrictions. Patents are a principal example of this. A patent confers a monopoly upon the patent holder until its expiry. In certain instances, governments enter into business by themselves to ensure service and reliability, or for national security considerations.

The longevity of a monopoly depends on the strength and the height of entry barriers. A monopolist can continue to earn supernormal profits over the long term if entry barriers are successful at preventing the entry of competitors. A monopolist ferry operator can continue to earn supernormal profits if the transit authority does not award another ferry license over the foreseeable future. On the other hand, a monopoly will be eroded as competitors are able to circumvent entry restrictions over time. For example, successful innovations are often copied as time passes.

The measurement of monopoly power is essential before any government action can be undertaken to dismantle monopolies to promote competition. A common (and easy to calculate) measure is the concentration ratio. The concentration ratio is the percentage of industry sales accounted for by the largest firm(s) in question. A pure monopoly has the concentration ratio of 100 percent. Thus, the farther away (less than) the concentration ratio is from 100 percent, the more competitive (or less like a monopoly) a market is. Although concentration ratios have the advantage of ease of computation, their primary drawback lies in their inability to reveal the actual behavior of firms (e.g., are firms aggressive or passive competitors?). There are other measures of monopoly power that overcome these shortcomings, but they are relatively difficult to compute.

There are some common misperceptions about monopolies. First, it is not true that a monopolist can charge whatever price it pleases, including the highest possible price, because at the highest price for most goods, consumers either buy poor substitutes or do not buy at all. Second, a monopolist does not always make profits. In reality, monopolists initially might have to take losses as consumers are educated about their new product(s). This explains the losses of some Internet startup companies.

Economists have shown that compared to a competitive firm, a monopolist's price is higher and production is smaller (Intriligator, 1971). For example, a single airline serving a town will have higher fares and a less frequent schedule than if there were numerous airlines serving the same route. The monopolist's behavior with regard to other strategic variables such as advertising and research and development (R&D) is less clear; that is, it is not clear whether a monopolist would advertise more (or conduct more R&D) than would a competitive counterpart. On the one hand, a monopolist might not have an incentive to advertise because it has no competitors to take customers from; on the other hand, a monopolist might advertise if advertising were to expand the total market by bringing in new buyers. With respect to R&D, a monopolist has the resources to innovate but might not have the desire to introduce new products (Goel 1999).

Public policy in most countries is driven by a pro-competitive, antimonopoly stance. Government regulators try to break up monopolies and make markets more competitive, though government tolerance of monopolies varies across nations. The recent antitrust proceedings against Microsoft Corporation and the earlier breakup of American Telegraph and Telephone (also known as AT&T or the "Bell System") are examples. The main criticism against monopoly is that it deliberately reduces production to raise prices. This quantity restriction shuts out some buyers who otherwise would have benefited from buying the product at the (lower) competitive price. Less significant criticisms of monopoly are that it promotes corruption (potential monopolists might be willing to bribe public officials to obtain exclusive contracts) and organizational waste (due to a lack of competition, a monopolist is likely to have a "fatter" organization than is essential to successfully conduct business). Taxation of a monopolist might also pose problems. Given a captive market, a monopolist might see a higher excise tax as an opportunity to raise the price of the product by more than the amount of the tax. This is in contrast to the behavior of a competitive firm, whose post-tax price increase is equal to or less than the amount of the tax.

Joseph Schumpeter (1942) provided the main redeeming grounds for a monopoly in arguing that monopolies were perhaps better at producing innovations because of their deep pockets (resources). Competitive firms with rather limited resources, in contrast, are less willing to undertake risky research projects. Empirical evi-

dence on the advantage of monopoly firms over other (competitive) firms in producing innovations is inconclusive, however. The state-run patent programs in various countries are driven by the recognition that state-sanctioned monopolies granted by patents will spur innovation. Technology, therefore, has the potential to create as well as to dismantle monopolies. A successful new inventor receives a patent and establishes a monopoly. On the other hand, some technologies might create substitutes for existing monopoly products or services; an example of this is Internet companies creating online travel agents to compete with conventional travel agents.

Even for sellers, having a monopoly might not be such a desirable scenario when pricing decisions for a durable good are being considered (see Coase 1972). Durable goods are goods such as cars and washing machines that last a number of years. The dilemma facing monopolist sellers of durable goods is whether to lease them or sell them, and at what level of longevity (durability) to market the durable product. Relatively low initial prices for durable goods do not generate repeat business because the customers use durable goods for such long periods, and high selling prices encourage second-hand (used goods) markets that do not make any money for the monopolist. In contrast, there are no resale markets when a good is leased rather than sold, but complex lease clauses might scare some buyers away.

In sum, although monopolies are not very common in their pure form, monopoly power exists in many markets. Whereas government policy across the world continues to generally favor competitive markets, there are some redeeming features of monopolies. However, as new technologies emerge, we can expect more monopolies (at least in the short term) and destruction of existing ones.

SEE ALSO *Competition, Perfect*

BIBLIOGRAPHY

Bain, Joe S. 1956. *Barriers to New Competition.* Cambridge, MA: Harvard University Press.

Coase, Ronald H. 1972. Durability and Monopoly. *Journal of Law and Economics* 15: 143–149.

Goel, Rajeev K. 1999. *Economic Models of Technological Change.* Westport, CT: Quorum Books.

Intriligator, Michael D. 1971. *Mathematical Optimization and Economic Theory.* Englewood Cliffs, NJ: Prentice-Hall.

Leibenstein, Harvey. 1966. Allocative Efficiency vs. X-Efficiency. *American Economic Review* 56: 392–415.

Schumpeter, Joseph A. 1942. *Capitalism, Socialism, and Democracy.* New York: Harper and Brothers.

Tirole, Jean. 1988. *The Theory of Industrial Organization.* Cambridge, MA: MIT Press.

Rajeev K. Goel

MONOPOLY CAPITALISM

Monopoly capital theory states that capitalism undergoes phases of evolution and transformation when some of its dominant institutions change significantly over time. It also states that historical changes toward greater concentration of industry need to be incorporated into the edifice of economic theory. It is not sufficient to simply assume high levels of competition, as the degree of monopoly is critical to the performance of capitalism in many ways.

Much of the debate about monopoly capitalism concerns the degree of concentration of industry; what forces control the large corporation; whether a tendency exists for stagnation due to effective demand failure; and whether a large amount of so-called waste is necessary for capitalism to periodically minimize demand problems.

THEORETICAL ORIGINS

The theoretical origins of monopoly capitalism include certain Marxist writers, and later post-Keynesians and institutionalists joined the debate. Karl Marx in volume one of *Capital* (1867) discussed the tendency for greater centralization and concentration of capital. Rudolf Hilferding in *Finance Capital* (1900) scrutinized an era of conglomerates along with the financial domination of industry. Paul Baran and Paul Sweezy in *Monopoly Capital* (1966) believed that managers of large corporations were often the largest shareholders and held control. Harry Braverman extended the analysis of monopoly capital to the labor process in *Labor and Monopoly Capital* (1974). Keith Cowling and Roger Sugden analyzed the implications of late-twentieth-century globalization and corporate expansion to monopoly capital theory in *Transnational Monopoly Capital* (1986).

CHANGING TRENDS

Up until the late 1800s relatively high levels of competition were characteristic of capitalism. Degrees of competition changed, however, over the business cycle and long waves of growth. With the development of the joint stock company in advanced nations, firms grew in size during the mid- to late 1800s. During the late 1870s to the 1890s overproduction led to periodic deep recessions and depressions. In response to this, around the turn of the twentieth century a major merger movement stimulated greater concentration, along with selling costs such as advertising, while globalization and imperialism expanded the market. This all led to higher profit and accumulation until World War I, as Thorstein Veblen showed in *Absentee Ownership* (1923).

By the 1930s a serious level of oligopoly and monopolistic competition became institutionalized in the major capitalist economies. Through the postwar boom of the 1950s until the early 1970s the dominant oligopoly sector controlled the major industries, while the weaker competitive sector survived through contracts and agreements with the dominant sector. During this time, monopoly capitalism was seen as based on big business, big unions, and big government.

TENDENCY TO STAGNATION

The term *monopoly capitalism* did not become popular until the publication of Baran and Sweezy's *Monopoly Capital*. The authors drew attention to the tendency for the potential economic surplus over necessary costs to rise as big companies benefit from economies of scale, research and development, and profit mark-ups. Problems exist, though, especially the tendency to periodic stagnation through insufficient effective demand or inadequate markets.

In 1965 Michel Kalecki published his *Theory of Economic Dynamics*, which explains that when the commanding heights of industry are controlled by oligopolies, the profit mark-up can increase through time. Those who receive income from profit have a higher propensity to save, leading to lower aggregate demand, unless investment rises, which is unlikely as investment depends on consumption. As productivity is greater than demand, capacity output utilization declines, leading to the tendency toward insufficient demand.

The tendency to stagnation creates anomalous solutions such as wasteful advertising and other selling expenses; destructive military spending; and global corporate dominance of the culture. Under monopoly capitalism, billions of dollars are wasted on conspicuous consumption and fashion to reinforce social distinction. Escalating managerial bonuses heighten class distinctions and expand inequality. Monopoly capital enterprises promote the degradation of work through skill fragmentation into tiny compartments of minor skills, according to Braverman. Workers are less master craftspeople and more mere appendages to the technical apparatus.

Credit creation may potentially enhance consumption to lessen aggregate demand problems. But without higher real wages this may stimulate excess debt and escalating speculative bubbles that lead to periodic deep recession, such as during the 2001–2003 recession in the United States. The problem of realizing the surplus continues while the needs of business and privilege outweigh the potential for egalitarian reform.

In *Transnational Monopoly Capital*, Cowling and Sugden detailed problems associated with transnationals spreading stagnation tendencies to the global economy.

Demand problems are worse when the power of labor is declining and governments are reducing productive social investments. While greater globalization seemingly raises competition, it can enhance the power of large corporations through lower costs and larger markets. They also emphasize the distributional conflict between managers and shareholders, and how managerial salaries are part of the economic surplus (rather than being a necessary cost).

CRITICAL QUESTIONS

Three critical questions can be raised about monopoly capital. The first is historical. The origins of monopoly capital were from 1900 to the 1940s, while the 1950s to early 1970s represent the Fordist long boom. Globalization from the 1980s to the 2000s has seen the emergence of many East Asian nations (especially China) as serious players in the world economy. New competitors in the global system also engage in cooperation through strategic alliances, joint ventures, and mergers and acquisitions. Although monopoly capital tendencies remain, a competitive-innovation dynamic has been actively at work. How this affects monopoly capital tendencies needs to be further researched.

Second, is stagnation linked purely to effective demand problems? Have changes in capitalism created new anomalous tendencies? For instance, outside of East Asia and a few other nations, long-term profitability, productivity, and gross domestic product (GDP) growth per capita have all been below par from the mid-1970s to the early 2000s (despite business cycle upswings). Perhaps excess competition, neoliberal governments, and financial dominance of industry have been the major players in this anomalous performance, along with inadequate demand, as Phillip O'Hara suggested in his *Growth and Development in the Global Political Economy* (2005).

Third, a central concept to emerge from monopoly capital theory is the economic surplus. The production, distribution, and reproduction of economic surplus are critical to the long-term performance of capitalism. And, as James Stanfield has suggested, it provides a potential (surplus) fund for democratic social change out of which a more progressive system may emerge.

SEE ALSO *Competition, Marxist; Economics, Post Keynesian; Institutionalism; Marxism; Primitive Accumulation*

BIBLIOGRAPHY

Braverman, Harry. 1974. *Labor and Monopoly Capital.* New York: Monthly Review.

Cowling, Keith, and Roger Sugden. 1987. *Transnational Monopoly Capital.* Sussex, U.K.: Wheatsheaf.

Foster, John Bellamy. 1986. *The Theory of Monopoly Capital: An Elaboration of Marxian Political Economy.* New York: Monthly Review Press.

Kalecki, Michal. 1969. *Theory of Economic Dynamics: An Essay on Cyclical and Long-Run Changes in Capitalist Economy.* Rev. ed. New York: Kelley.

O'Hara, Phillip Anthony. 2005. *Growth and Development in the Global Political Economy.* London and New York: Routledge.

Stanfield, James Ronald. 1992. The Fund for Social Change. In *The Economic Surplus in Advanced Economies*, ed. John Davis, 130–148. Aldershot, U.K.: Edward Elgar.

Steindl, Josef. 1976. *Maturity and Stagnation in American Capitalism.* Rev. ed. New York: Monthly Review Press.

Phillip Anthony O'Hara

MONOPSONY

A competitive market has many buyers and sellers, none of whom can influence market price. By contrast, a market with many buyers and one seller who can influence price is termed a *monopoly*, whereas if there is only one buyer and many sellers we say that the buyer is a *monopsonist*. For example, a government may effectively compel farmers to sell to a state monopsonist (marketing board). Because the latter is the sole buyer, it may use this dominant position to lower the price it pays to sellers, thus generating monopsony profits (see Bonner 1988). A market with a small number of large buyers who have some monopsony power is known as an *oligopsony*, whereas a market with many buyers and sellers but where each buyer still has some monopsony power is said to have *monopsonistic competition* (see Bhaskar, Manning, and To 2002 for a discussion).

Joan Robinson (1932) first used the term *monopsony* in a discussion of the labor market (see Thornton 2004 for a discussion of the origin of the term). While there may be monopsony power in any market, its application to the labor market has dominated the literature. The standard early monopsony model was the "company town model." The idea is as follows: In a relatively isolated town, an employer may be large enough to affect the market wage in that town. If the employer lowers/raises employment, the market wage will fall/rise. If the town is relatively isolated, travel costs will prevent other companies from competing for workers. However, in recent decades, as both labor and capital have become more mobile, it has become less credible that an employer could pay less than the competitive wage without other firms moving to town and competing away the lower wage, or workers availing themselves of higher wages elsewhere.

More recent models such as Burdett and Mortensen (1998) or Bhaskar and To (1999) can be used to rationalize monopsony power in modern labor markets. If there are search costs associated with either workers finding jobs or employers finding workers, or if workers have preferences for particular employers, firms may have some monopsony power that allows them to pay a wage below the competitive wage. The source of monopsony power here is that a worker may accept a relatively low wage offer from an employer if continuing to search for a better offer is costly. In these models, there is monopsonistic competition in that there may be many employers, but each has some monopsony power.

Manning (2003) discusses the implications of such models for a wide range of important labor market topics. For example, in a monopsony model, the impact of minimum wages or trade unions on employment and efficiency are ambiguous, in contrast to more traditional competitive models of the labor market where minimum wage or unions typically lower employment and are inefficient. Monopsony/search models also provide a rationale for frictional unemployment and wage discrimination against women if women are less mobile across jobs than men.

Monopsony models, such as the job-search models referred to earlier, also provide a plausible way of understanding observed features of labor markets that are difficult to rationalize in other models. For example, if it is costly and time-consuming for workers to search for jobs, a search model predicts that there will always be some frictional unemployment even when the economy is doing well. Another long-standing puzzle in labor economics is the large differences in observed wages between similar workers doing similar jobs. Monopsony models provide a rationale for these observed wage differences. More traditional competitive models of the labor market, on the other hand, deal inconsistently with these differences in wages (see Mortensen 2003 for a discussion of this issue).

SEE ALSO *Competition, Imperfect; Discrimination, Price; Monopoly; Robinson, Joan*

BIBLIOGRAPHY

Bhaskar, V., Alan Manning, and Ted To. 2002. Oligopsony and Monopsonistic Competition in Labor Markets. *Journal of Economic Perspectives* 16 (2): 155–174.

Bhaskar, V., and Ted To. 1999. Minimum Wages for Ronald McDonald Monopsonies: A Theory of Monopsonistic Competition. *Economic Journal* 109 (455): 190–203.

Bonner, Raymond. 1988. A Reporter at Large: Indonesia. *The New Yorker*, June 13: 72–91.

Burdett, Kenneth, and Dale T. Mortensen. 1998. Wage Differentials, Employer Size, and Unemployment. *International Economic Review* 39 (2): 257–273.

Manning, Alan. 2003. *Monopsony in Motion: Imperfect Competition in Labor Markets.* Princeton, NJ: Princeton University Press.

Mortensen, Dale T. 2003. *Wage Dispersion: Why Are Similar Workers Paid Differently?* Cambridge, MA: MIT Press.

Robinson, Joan. 1932. *The Economics of Imperfect Competition.* London: Macmillan.

Thornton, Robert J. 2004. How Joan Robinson and B. L. Hallward Named Monopsony. *Journal of Economic Perspectives* 18 (2): 257–261.

Frank Walsh

MONOTHEISM

The term *monotheism* derives from the Greek words *monos* ("single," "only") and *theos* ("god"). It refers to the belief that there is only one God. Although various forms of monotheism can be traced to ancient times, the term itself is relatively modern. After the Irish freethinker John Toland (1670–1722) published *Christianity Not Mysterious* (1696), the term *pantheism* was applied to his concept of the divine. Eventually, it became necessary to distinguish traditional monotheism, which understands God as transcendent or distinct from the universe, from pantheism and other forms of theism.

VARIETIES OF MONOTHEISM

As the study of religions developed in the 1800s and 1900s, further distinctions were made between traditional *monotheism* (belief in a single, transcendent God who communicates by revelation), *polytheism* (belief in multiple or many gods), *deism* (belief in God as a transcendent being or power who does not intervene in history), *henotheism* (exclusive adherence to one God without denying the existence of other gods), and *pantheism/monism* (affirmation of an identity between the universe and God or the affirmation of a single, ultimate reality of which the multiple existing things are only parts or extensions).

Traditional monotheism, as developed principally within Judaism, Christianity, and Islam, understands the one divine being not only as transcendent but also as the almighty creator and sustainer of all things, and, therefore, as distinct from and exalted above the created universe. Because everything that exists has been created by and depends on the one God, human beings owe this sublime being complete obedience, submission, and adoration. Moreover, God is understood as infinite, omnipotent, and endowed with all perfections. Although God is transcendent and mysterious, human beings know the divine will by means of supernatural revelation, mediated variously through God's interventions in human history (e.g., sacred covenants, inspired writings, prophets, and, in the case of Christianity, the incarnation of God's Word). Traditional monotheism, therefore, looks upon God as a personal being who oversees and guides human affairs.

Various types of monotheism can be found in the world. *Deism*, as developed during the 1600s to 1700s, understands God within the bounds of reason rather than revelation. Deists see the divine as the ultimate source of creation and order in the universe rather than a personal God who intervenes in history with prophecies and miracles. Many scholars consider *pantheism*, insofar as it affirms one divine reality, to be a form of monotheism—even though it does not distinguish God from the universe. *Pan-en-theism*—which believes God is both above the universe and within it (as a dynamic principle or life-force)—is another type of monotheism. Some even believe that monotheism can incorporate polytheism when the multiple gods are conceived as manifestations of an underlying divine unity (as in many forms of Hinduism).

ORIGINS OF MONOTHEISM

Scholars differ as to when monotheism first emerged. The German anthropologist and Catholic priest Wilhelm Schmidt (1868–1954) maintained that monotheism was the primordial belief of human beings. In his twelve-volume work *Ursprung der Gottesidee* (Origin of the Idea of God, 1912–1954), Schmidt argued that the "High God" found in many primitive cultures pointed to an original monotheism (subsequently obscured by devotions to lower spirits and gods). Many anthropologists, however, believe polytheism is more primordial and monotheism the result of a higher cultural development.

The origins of monotheism often have been linked to Judaism and the biblical tradition. Abraham (c. 1800 BCE) is understood as the unifying figure of the three monotheistic or *Abrahamic* religions of Judaism, Christianity, and Islam. Some scholars, however, believe Abraham was not a full-fledged monotheist but a henotheist (i.e., one who pledges exclusive devotion to one God without denying the existence of other gods; from the Greek, *heis* [one] *theos* [god]). Exegetes point to the use of the plural, "gods" (*elohim*; see Gen. 1:26; Exod. 12:12), and to several biblical names (e.g., *el-elyon*, Gen. 14:19; *el shaddai*, Gen. 17:1) that might have referred to distinct gods worshipped by the early Hebrews.

Some, however, argue that the plural, *elohim*, is used in a royal sense or as an intensive use of the plural to show that the one God embodies all the qualities of the divine. These same scholars maintain that names such as *el shaddai* refer exclusively to the one God; thus, for them, there is no evidence of biblical polytheism or henotheism.

Other biblical exegetes find layers of tradition in the Pentateuch or Torah (the first five biblical books), which manifest a gradual move from henotheism to true monotheism. By the time the Pentateuch acquired its final edited form (c. fifth century BCE), authentic monotheism was certainly in force (see Deut. 32:39: "See now that I, even I, am he, and there is no god beside me"). In chapter 45 of Isaiah (c. 539 BCE), the God of Israel proclaims: "I am the Lord, and there is no other" (Isa. 45:6) and: "There is no other god besides me" (Isa. 45:21).

Many scholars, though, find evidence for early forms of monotheism not influenced by the Hebrew biblical tradition. The consensus, therefore, is that monotheism cannot be traced, in a unilinear manner, to a single historic source. Instead, the concept of a single God emerges from an underlying perception of unity or the postulation of an original cause of the cosmos. Monotheism, therefore, is understood as a natural structuring of reality by the human mind rather than a concept demanding supernatural revelation.

THE ABRAHAMIC RELIGIONS

The monotheism of the Abrahamic religions (Judaism, Christianity, and Islam) requires the exclusive worship of the one God. Thus, the Jewish sage Maimonides (c. 1135–1204 CE) numbered among the basic articles of Judaism the necessity of worshiping God alone who is the one, eternal, and incorporeal Creator.

Although some contemporary Jewish scholars acknowledge strands of early biblical polytheism, Judaism, as a whole, has been tenacious in affirming authentic monotheism. Thus, references to the Lord's dominion over the "gods" (see, for example, Prov. 58:1–2 and 82:1) are rarely interpreted in a polytheistic manner. Instead, such passages are read either as a statement of God's power over all pretenders to divinity or as an affirmation of the Lord's authority over created spirits or angels. Similarly, the "Angel of the Lord" (see Gen. 16:7 and 22:11 and Exod. 3:2,6, and 13) is perceived as a manifestation of God's own self and not a separate divinity. The other angels mentioned in the Bible are understood as messengers and servants of God; they are not in any way thought of as separate "gods."

Christianity emerged out of Jewish monotheism, but its belief in the divinity of Jesus and the Holy Spirit led to the doctrine of the Trinity: three eternal Persons (Father, Son, and Holy Spirit) as hypostases or subsistences of the one divine essence. Although some see the Trinity as a compromise of authentic monotheism, Christian creeds and councils reject the view of the Trinity as "three gods" and affirm the unity of the divine essence. The Christian councils of the fourth and fifth centuries proclaimed Jesus as the eternal Word of God who assumed a human nature and not a creature to whom divinity was subsequently ascribed.

Some people regard the devotion to the saints in Catholic and Orthodox Christianity as a form of "functional polytheism." In Catholic and Orthodox theology, however, the saints are not considered deities; instead, they are sanctified human beings who pray for the living from heaven (see, for example, Rev. 5:8). The saints are "divinized" in the sense that they come to share in the divine nature (see 2 Pet. 1:4). They are sometimes called "gods" (John 10:34; Prov. 82:6)—not because they are uncreated deities—but because they participate in the grace of divine life bestowed upon them by God.

Various Protestant Christians likewise consider devotion to images of the Blessed Virgin Mary, the angels, and saints as a form of "idolatry." Catholics and Orthodox, however—following the teaching of the Second Council of Nicea (787 CE)—distinguish between the worship (*latreia* or *latria*) due to God alone and the veneration (*dulia, proskunesis*) given to the holy images (ikons) of Mary, the angels, and the saints.

There is, though, evidence of crypto-polytheism in Afro-Caribbean religions such as Santeria that blend the Yoruba deities of Africa with the Catholic saints. Also, the Mormons (the members of the Church of Jesus Christ of Latter-Day Saints) are sometimes considered polytheists because of their understanding of the Trinity and other doctrines. In spite of these examples, Christianity, as a whole, has been strictly monotheistic.

Islam claims to be the primordial religion of humankind, because all the prophets, since the time of Adam, have taught the same doctrine of God's unity proclaimed by Muhammad (570–632 CE). The Qur'an, revealed through Muhammad, is seen as the final revelation of God (Allah), which corrects the corruptions that had entered into earlier revelations (such as the Torah, revealed through Moses, and the Gospel, revealed through Jesus).

Islam rejects the Christian doctrines of the Trinity and the divinity of Jesus. Allah is the one and only God, who "begets not, nor is He begotten, and there is none like unto Him" (Qur'an 112:3–4). For Muslims, the greatest sin is *shirk*, the idolatry of associating something other than Allah with Allah.

Islamic monotheism influenced the religion of Sikhism, which emerged in India under the guru, Nanak (1469–1538). The Sikhs incorporate certain Hindu teachings, but their concept of God is completely monotheistic. Bahai, which originated in Iran in the nineteenth century, likewise grew out of Islam, and is entirely monotheistic.

MONOTHEISM IN THE NON-ABRAHAMIC RELIGIONS OF THE WORLD

The religion of ancient Egypt was polytheistic, but in the fourteenth century BCE the pharaoh, Amenhotep IV (reigned c. 1364–1347 BCE), changed his name to Akhenaten (servant of Aten) and affirmed Aten (or Aton) as the one true God, symbolized by the solar disk. Akhenaten suppressed the cults of other Egyptian gods, and he referred to Aten as the "sole God, other than whom there is no other."

Akhenaten's endorsement of monotheism, though, did not persist. After his death, devotion to the other Egyptian gods was restored. In his 1939 book *Moses and Monotheism*, Sigmund Freud (1856–1939) theorized that Moses (c. 1300–1200 BCE) borrowed his monotheism from Akhenaten. Most scholars, though, dispute this claim.

The religions of ancient Greece and Rome were polytheistic, but some signs of monotheism emerged. Plato (427–347 BCE) referred to a supreme spirit (*psyche*) as the source of motion and order in the universe (see Book 10 of the *Laws*), but he seemed to believe that universal Ideas, like the Good, actually transcend the cosmos governed by the supreme Spirit. Aristotle (384–322 BCE) affirmed the existence of an eternal and immutable "unmoved" or "prime mover" who is "self-thinking thought" and "pure act." This concept of the divine, however, was closer to deism than traditional monotheism because the "prime mover" is completely transcendent and not concerned with the affairs of human beings or the universe.

The Greek and Roman Stoics affirmed a supreme ordering principle in the universe known as Reason (*Logos*). For the most part, however, this Reason was not distinct from the material universe but an active principle within it. This was a form of pan-en-theism or pantheism rather than traditional monotheism.

Plotinus (c. 205–269 CE) developed a mystical-philosophical form of monotheism. He believed in a supreme, transcendent reality known as the One out of which all other things emanate in descending, hierarchical order: from the Intellect (*nous*), to the Soul (*psyche*), and finally to matter.

The Persian religion of Zoroastrianism, named after the prophet Zoroaster (or Zarathustra; c. 900s–800s BCE), was monotheistic in its original form. Ahura Mazda, the Wise Lord, is the supreme Creator of the material world, and from him came forth the twin spirits: Spenta Mainyu (the Holy Spirit who chose the good) and Angra Mainyu (the Evil Spirit who chose "the lie"). The "Holy Immortals" (e.g., Good Thought, Immortality, etc.) are not other gods but eternal forms or attributes of Ahura Mazda.

The original monotheism of Zoroastrianism, however, was obscured by the rise of the cult of Mithra (c. second century BCE) and by the later tendency to depict Ahura Mazda and Angra Mainyu as competing gods. Zoroastrianism, however, completely rejected the matter/spirit dualism taught by Mani (c. 216–276 CE).

Hinduism originated as a polytheistic religion with virtually millions of gods (*devas*). As the tradition developed, some hints of monotheism or monism emerged. Even in the early Hindu scriptures known as the Vedas (c. 1200–900 BCE), there was the recognition that: "The real is one, though the sages name it variously" (Rig-Veda I, 169). By the time of the mystical writings called the Upanishads (c. 800–500 BCE), some Hindu thinkers began to understand the many gods as expressions or manifestations of the one supreme reality known as *Brahman*. When the Hindu sage Yājñavalkya (c. 800s BCE) was asked how many gods there really are, he answered, "One."

Hindu monotheism, however, sometimes lapsed into monism when *Brahman* was considered the only true and permanent reality. By contrast, devotional Hinduism tended to concentrate all the attributes of the divine into one personal manifestation of *Brahman*. Thus, in the Bhagavad Gita (c. 200s BCE), Krishna states: "By me, unmanifest in form, this whole universe was spun: in me subsist all beings, I do not subsist in them" (IX, 4).

Although differing forms of monotheism or monism can be found in Hinduism, the many gods mentioned in the Vedas could never be denied without repudiating the authority of the Vedas themselves. Thus, in Hinduism, polytheism on a popular and mythological level has continued to coexist with various forms of mystical monism and philosophical monotheism.

In original Buddhism, the focus was on achieving detachment from craving in order to reach a state of liberation called *nirvāna*. In later Mahayana Buddhism, the ultimate reality was identified variously as emptiness (*śūnyatā*), consciousness, or the Buddha-nature. There was, therefore, a single absolute reality.

In some forms of devotional Buddhism, the Buddha became deified, and there emerged the doctrine of the three "bodies" or aspects of the Buddha: (1) the *Transformation Body*, which was the body of the Buddha on earth; (2) the *Bliss* or *Enjoyment Body* assumed by the various celestial Buddhas; and, (3) the *Truth-Body*, which is the ultimate reality of the Buddha-essence. Devotional Buddhism, therefore, developed a belief in a unified supreme reality behind all things, which can be understood, at least analogously, as a form of monotheism.

Ancient China was originally polytheistic, but aspects of monotheism emerged in the concept of Heaven (*T'ien*), taught by Confucius (c. 551–479 BCE), and in the *Tao* of the Tao Te Ching, the mystical treatise attributed to Lao-Tzu (c. sixth–fifth century, BCE). In his Analects, Confucius speaks of Heaven as the transcendent source of order and morality, a reality somewhat analogous to a personal God.

The *Tao* also is analogous to God, because it is "the mother of the myriad creatures" (I, 2) and "the genesis of all things" (I, 4). As the all-pervasive source of things, the *Tao* is like a divine principle guiding the universe (i.e., a type of pan-en-theism).

Native American religion is multifaceted, and various gods or spirits are acknowledged. There is, however, a deep sense of a "Great Spirit" who pervades nature and is expressed in the numerous powers of animal and human life. In a certain sense, the universe is the dwelling place or body of the Great Spirit, and, therefore, a form of pan-en-theism is present.

CONCLUSION

The religions of the world incorporate different forms of monotheism: from the strict monotheism of Islam to the mystical monotheism of Hinduism (coexisting with popular polytheism). Because Christians and Muslims combine to make up over half of the world's population, a case can be made that monotheism resonates well with basic human needs for order, meaning, and direction.

SEE ALSO *Atheism; Christianity; Church, The; Hinduism; Islam, Shia and Sunni; Judaism; Polytheism; Religion; Roman Catholic Church; Theism*

BIBLIOGRAPHY

Armstrong, Karen. 1993. *A History of God: The 4,000-Year Quest of Judaism, Christianity, and Islam.* New York: Ballantine Books.

Ellwood, Robert S., Jr. 1977. *Words of the World's Religions: An Anthology.* Englewood Cliffs, NJ: Prentice-Hall.

Kramer, Kenneth. 1986. *World Scriptures: An Introduction to Comparative Religion.* Mahwah, NJ: Paulist Press.

Ludwig, Theodore M. 2005. In *The Encyclopedia of Religion*, 2nd ed., Vol. 9, ed. Lindsay Jones, 6155–6163. Detroit, MI: Thomson Gale.

Pereira, José, ed. 1991. *Hindu Theology: Themes, Texts, and Structures.* Delhi: Motilal Banarsidass Publishers.

Smart, Ninian. 1989. *The World's Religions.* Englewood Cliffs, NJ: Prentice-Hall.

Smart, Ninian. 1991. *The Religious Experience.* 4th ed. New York: Macmillan.

Smith, Huston. 1991. *The World's Religions: Our Great Wisdom Traditions.* San Francisco: HarperCollins.

Smith, Mark S. 2002. *The Early History of God: Yahweh and the Other Deities in Ancient Israel.* 2nd ed. Grand Rapids, MI: William B. Eerdmans.

Robert Fastiggi

MONROE, JAMES

SEE *Monroe Doctrine*.

MONROE DOCTRINE

The Monroe Doctrine is a principle of American foreign policy in the Western Hemisphere that was announced by President James Monroe (1758–1831) on December 2, 1823, in his annual message to Congress. The Monroe Doctrine was intended to discourage and prevent further colonialism and military intervention by European powers, especially Britain and Russia, in the Western Hemisphere and any attempts by European powers to exploit or endanger the growing independence of Latin American countries from the Spanish empire. The major tenets of the Monroe Doctrine are that, first, the Western Hemisphere has a political existence that is separate from Europe. Second, the United States would regard further European efforts to colonize or extend political and military influence in the Western Hemisphere as hostile actions against American national security. Third, the United States would not interfere with existing European colonies or political matters.

The Monroe Doctrine was particularly influential in American foreign policy toward Latin America during the late nineteenth and early twentieth centuries. In 1895, the United States cited the Monroe Doctrine in a boundary dispute between Venezuela and Britain. In 1898, the United States relied on the Monroe Doctrine to justify its war against Spain in Cuba and its later intervention in Puerto Rico and the Dominican Republic. The application of the Monroe Doctrine to Cuba was strengthened by the Platt Amendment of 1902. This amendment to the Cuban constitution specified that the United States retained the right to intervene militarily and politically in Cuba. In 1904, President Theodore Roosevelt (1858–1919) announced the Roosevelt Corollary to the Monroe Doctrine. The Roosevelt Corollary stated that the United States has an obligation to prevent political and economic instability in Caribbean nations.

Until 1934, the Monroe Doctrine was used to justify American military intervention in Haiti, Nicaragua, and the Dominican Republic. In 1934, however, President Franklin D. Roosevelt (1882–1945) rejected the Roosevelt Corollary in announcing his Good Neighbor policy toward Latin America. The principles of this policy included that the United States would respect Latin American governments as diplomatic equals, that the Platt Amendment would be repealed, and that the United States would refrain from intervening in Latin American domestic affairs. The Good Neighbor policy improved cooperation and diplomatic understanding between the United States and most Latin American governments during the 1930s and 1940s, but American economic domination and exploitation of Latin America continued.

During the cold war, the United States revived the use of the Monroe Doctrine to legitimize military intervention because of its concern that communism would develop and expand in Latin America, especially after Cuba became a Soviet ally. American presidents made public or private references to the Monroe Doctrine to justify the U.S. naval blockade of Cuba in 1962 and the American invasions of the Dominican Republic in 1965 and Grenada in 1983. The end of the cold war and greater economic development and democratization in Latin America made it less likely that the United States would invoke the Monroe Doctrine.

SEE ALSO *Cold War; Colonialism; Communism; Cuban Revolution; Foreign Policy; Imperialism; National Security*

BIBLIOGRAPHY

Dallek, Robert. 1983. *The American Style of Foreign Policy: Cultural Politics and Foreign Affairs.* New York: Oxford University Press.

Smith, Gaddis. 1994. *The Last Years of the Monroe Doctrine, 1945–1993.* New York: Hill and Wang.

Sean J. Savage

MONT PELERIN SOCIETY

Directly after World War II (1939–1945), a group of thirty-six scholars—mostly economists, with some historians and philosophers as well—were invited by the economist Friedrich von Hayek to Mont Pelerin, a Swiss Mountain resort, to discuss the state of classical liberalism. They feared that Western society was in danger and liberty was being threatened by totalitarianism and other forces. After ten days of deliberations, the Mont Pelerin Society was founded on April 10, 1947.

Hayek's hope in founding the Society was to create "an international academy of political philosophy" with the aim of "regenerating the ideas of classical liberalism in order to refute socialism" (Hartwell 1995). His aim was educational, and he hoped to influence political structures through ideas, not through direct political involvement. Because of this, the organization does not form or align itself with any political party or parties, nor does it conduct propaganda. Instead, the Mont Pelerin Society is a forum for free discussion aiming "not to spread a given doctrine, but to work out in continuous effort, a philosophy of freedom" (Hartwell 1995).

The Mont Pelerin Society is decentralized. It has no office, no paid staff, nor any central organization other than a Web site. All discourse and discussion of ideas occurs through meetings, which are organized, funded, and run by local ad-hoc committees. Since 1947 the Society has held thirty-three General Meetings, twenty-seven Regional Meetings, and a number of Special Meetings. These have occurred in Europe, Central and South America, the United States, Asia, Australia, and Africa. Because of its decentralization, and because it does not act as one body, the Society's influence is difficult to quantify.

The Society is composed of persons who see dangers in the expansion of government, not least when it leads to the welfare state, in the power of trade unions and business monopolies, and in the continuing threat and reality of inflation. Membership is exclusive and anyone seeking to join must be nominated by current members. Current and past members include eight Nobel Prize winners in economics, various heads of state and other high-ranking government officials, business leaders, and established scholars. The membership of the Society has risen from under 50 members in 1947 to over 550 members in 2007, representing more than fifty countries. Some of the most well-known current and former members include Friedrich Hayek, Ludwig von Mises, Milton Friedman, George Stigler, Ronald Coase, Karl Popper, Ralph Harris, Vernon Smith, Gary Becker, Vaclav Klaus, and Mart Laar.

SEE ALSO *Austrian Economics; Freedom; Friedman, Milton; Hayek, Friedrich August von; Liberty; Smith, Vernon L.; Welfare State*

BIBLIOGRAPHY

Freedom House. 2006. Freedom in the World 2006. http://www.freedomhouse.org/template.cfm?page=15.

Hartwell, R. M. 1995. *A History of the Mont Pelerin Society*. Indianapolis, IN: Liberty Fund.

Miles, Mark A., Kim R. Holmes, and Mary Anastasia O'Grady. 2006. *2006 Index of Economic Freedom*. Washington, DC: Heritage Foundation; New York: *Wall Street Journal*.

Mont Pelerin Society Website. http://www.montpelerin.org/.

Ed Feulner

MONTAGU, ASHLEY
1905–1999

The anthropologist Ashley Montagu was born as Israel Ehrenberg into a poor Russian Jewish immigrant family in the East End of London. He was a precocious schoolboy, and with the encouragement of a kind schoolteacher, he took a skull found on the banks of the Thames to the anthropologist Sir Arthur Keith (1866–1955), and peppered the great man with questions. As a result of Keith's encouragement, he was admitted as a diploma student to University College London at the age of seventeen, and studied physical anthropology with Grafton Elliot Smith (1871–1937) and statistics and psychology with Karl Pearson (1857–1936) and C. E. Spearman (1863–1945). He was, at the same time, Bronislaw Malinowski's (1884–1942) first student in social anthropology at the London School of Economics.

Israel Ehrenberg immigrated in 1927 to the United States, where he changed his name to Montague Francis Ashley-Montagu (he was an admirer of Lady Mary Wortley Montagu [1689–1762]). He explained that this name opened doors that were at that time closed by anti-Semitic prejudice. He completed a PhD with Franz Boas (1858–1942) and Ruth Benedict (1887–1948) at Columbia University (1937) and taught at various universities and medical colleges, but he largely supported himself independently through writing and lecturing. He became, with Margaret Mead (1901–1978), one of the most effective communicators in anthropology, becoming a regular guest on *The Tonight Show*.

Montagu's sixty books cover an enormous range and vary from technical tracts on human genetics and Australian Aboriginal reproductive beliefs, to more popular accounts such as *The Elephant Man* (1971), which became the basis for the play and film of that name. In all his work he emphasized the interplay of genetic and environmental factors in producing human behavior. Two books in particular had tremendous influence: *Man's Most Dangerous Myth: The Fallacy of Race* (1942) and *The Natural Superiority of Women* (1953). The former stemmed from his work for UNESCO in its "Statement on Race" (1950), but he had long opposed the orthodox view of the existence of discrete races, and his position that "race" was not a scientific category but a "social construction" has become, in turn, its own orthodoxy. The matter is still in dispute however, and proponents of the "reality" of racial differences are making a comeback. His position on women was prescient, but his argument that their superiority was based on their quality as nurturers of the young caused him to be attacked by early feminists.

Montagu saw himself as carrying out the Malinowskian program of understanding culture in terms of human needs, and this required a detailed knowledge both of culture and of human evolutionary biology. He championed the idea of *neoteny*—the retention of infant traits into adulthood—as the basis of human sociability, with a consequent stress on playfulness, creativity, curiosity, and love. Love he saw as the basic human attribute, rooted in the mother-child relationship, and our failure to capitalize on it as our greatest danger. Human neoteny was biologically rooted, but it gave us an astonishing flexibility and the opportunity to create cooperative societies. Montagu's vision of a unified anthropology that would use knowledge of our evolutionary past to illuminate the possibilities of a peaceful future was perhaps his greatest gift to science and to humankind.

SEE ALSO *Anthropology; Race*

BIBLIOGRAPHY

Montagu, Ashley. 1942. *Man's Most Dangerous Myth: The Fallacy of Race.* New York: Columbia University Press.

Montagu, Ashley. 1953. *The Natural Superiority of Women.* New York: Macmillan.

Montagu, Ashley. 1996. *The Elephant Man: A Study in Human Dignity.* 3rd ed. Lafayette, LA: Acadian House.

Robin Fox

MONTE CARLO EXPERIMENTS

Monte Carlo experiments consist of statistical resampling techniques usually employed on computers to provide approximate solutions to a variety of mathematical problems. These techniques apply both to deterministic as well as to stochastic problems. The resampling methodology was first introduced in 1908 by William S. Gosset, who used the pseudonym Student in his publications. It was Stanislaw Ulam who thought of automating the procedure by means of the first fast electronic calculators in 1946. Subsequent work with Nicholas C. Metropolis and John von Neumann produced the first algorithms for computer implementations. The technique is named after the city of Monte Carlo, renowned for its casino, because it is based on a random number generator, as in the game of roulette.

A typical example of the application of Monte Carlo techniques in statistics concerns the evaluation of the properties of an estimator in cases when the exact distribution is difficult or impossible to calculate, or when the asymptotic approximations are either not very good or not applicable (i.e., in small samples). For example, the analyst may be interested in evaluating the bias of an estimator $\hat{\theta}$ when estimating a parameter vector θ_0, or the efficiency of an estimator $\hat{\theta}$ compared to alternative estimators of θ_0.

The methodology is based on resampling, that is, on replicating the real world M times, calculating M different estimates, one for each replication. The empirical distri-

bution of these estimates approximates the true distribution of the estimator object of the study.

The implementation of a Monte Carlo experiment is intuitive, although generally computationally intensive. First, the investigator has to choose a distribution for the variables included in the model characterized by the vector of parameters θ_0. Once the artificial values for θ_0 are set, an N-dimensional sample is drawn and an estimator computed from the sample. This procedure is iterated M times, obtaining a set of estimates $\hat{\theta}_m$ with $m = 1,\ldots, M$. At that stage it is possible to assess the properties of the estimator, for example, calculating the sample mean and variance.

Good practice suggests varying the value of θ_0, the sample size N, and the number of iterations M. The methodology is then computationally expensive, for it requires calculations in different scenarios, all possibly characterized by a large N and a large M.

One limitation of Monte Carlo studies is that the analyst must completely specify the statistical model. This includes making assumptions about the form and parameters of the distribution of the error term, usually assumed independent of the explanatory variables. The results of the experiment depend, therefore, on these assumptions, with a great deal of loss of generality.

In constructing a Monte Carlo experiment, the analyst faces strategic issues such as the choice of a distribution, the degree of variation of the parameters of interest, a trade-off between accuracy and flexibility, the choice of the number of iterations M, and the sample size N. In addition, the results usually involve the production of a large number of tables that need to be well organized for the experiment to be meaningful for the reader.

The standard error of a Monte Carlo analysis decreases with the square root of N. However, a larger N may require increasing computational complexity. Less computationally expensive methods are variance-reducing techniques. These involve, for example, the use of common random numbers, that is, the use of the same pseudo–random numbers when evaluating different strategic choices. This is likely to induce positive correlations between the estimators compared in the experiment, and therefore to reduce the variance of estimated differences.

Given the nature of the typical Monte Carlo experiment, it may be unclear to the analyst if the results apply to a specific population of interest. In that case, the bootstrapping methodology helps in refining the inference on a particular sample in alternative to asymptotic approximations. It simply consists of a Monte Carlo experiment where a specific data set is considered as the population. In each iteration b, with $b = 1,\ldots, B$, a random sample is drawn with replacement from the data set. Then, an estimate is computed on each iteration and the usual Monte Carlo procedures apply.

Applications of Monte Carlo techniques in economics include the investigation of the properties of stochastic models, for example, in the real business cycle literature. An example of applications of Monte Carlo methods to deterministic problems is the computation of multidimensional finite integrals. In this case, the integral can be interpreted as the expected value of the integrand function applied to a random vector uniformly distributed on the region of integration. This can be approximated by means of the usual resampling technique.

SEE ALSO *Properties of Estimators (Asymptotic and Exact); Student's T-Statistic*

BIBLIOGRAPHY

Davidson, Russell, and James G. MacKinnon. 1993. *Estimation and Inference in Econometrics.* New York: Oxford University Press.

Greene, William H. 2003. *Econometric Analysis,* 5th ed. Upper Saddle River, NJ: Prentice Hall.

Judd, Kenneth L. 1998. *Numerical Methods in Economics.* Cambridge, MA: MIT Press.

Metropolis, Nicholas, and Stanislaw Ulam. 1949. The Monte Carlo Method. *Journal of the American Statistical Association* 44 (247): 335–341.

Student. 1908. The Probable Error of a Mean. *Biometrika* 6: 1–25.

Luca Nunziata

MOOD

The systematic study of mood has received attention from a broad variety of social scientists. For example, social, personality, cognitive, and clinical psychologists have reasons for working to understand how people develop, experience, and respond to certain moods. Social psychologists may be interested in investigating how good or bad moods influence social interaction patterns. Personality psychologists may be interested in investigating how certain personality types may predict people's tendencies to experience certain moods. Alternately, cognitive psychologists may be more interested in examining how mood influences decision-making processes. Clinical psychologists may, in turn, be more interested in studying how mood disorders are manifest. Due to the wide appeal of investigation of people's moods, the study of mood has enjoyed a long and productive history. The subdomains of psychology approach the study of mood as well as its causes, effects, and correlates in different ways. Social psychologists have typically studied moods through laboratory manipulations, which induce short-term state changes. Personality and clinical psychologists typically explore mood-related phenomena through the use of self-report instruments, interviews, and observational methods designed to assess both state variations and trait-anchored propensities.

Mood may be conceptualized along several dimensions: dimensions of valence, negative to positive; strength, weak to strong; and arousal, not aroused to aroused. Examples of moods include happiness, sadness, excitement, nervousness, and calmness. A given mood may persist for short amounts of time (e.g., a few hours) to relatively long amounts of time (e.g., a few weeks). Mood differs from related psychological experiences, such as affect, attitude, emotion, and temperament, in several key ways. Affect refers to people's "good" or "bad" cognitive appraisals of attitude objects. Emotion and mood both exist as affective states, "by-products" of positive or negative appraisals of experiences or objects. However, mood differs from emotion in that mood is usually experienced as a diffuse state that is often not readily perceived as attributable to any given attitude object. In contrast, emotion is most often perceived as the result of a discrete experience. For example, a person might not be aware that he or she is in a good mood because the person anticipates receiving a paycheck the following day. This same person might also be acutely aware that he or she is, potentially at the same time, experiencing the emotion of happiness due to a recent engagement for marriage.

Whereas emotion and mood are most often the results of affective responses, attitude and temperament influence affective response patterns. That is, attitude and temperament play a role in how people evaluate events or objects whereas emotion and mood result from these evaluations. Though attitude is more readily distinguished from mood, how people evaluate attitude objects most assuredly differs from the mood that they may experience as a result, the distinction between mood and temperament is less clear. For example, it may be difficult to determine whether or not a person is merely in a sad mood or whether he or she is clinically depressed. Both the mood and temperament of depression, or dysphoria, may have similar symptoms to the observer (i.e., lethargy, crying, irritability). Accordingly, the most useful rule of thumb may be to conceptualize temperament as a lasting, relatively stable personality trait and mood as a shorter-lived, more dynamic psychological state.

MOOD AND COGNITION

Though a given mood might not persist for a very long time, it influences how people perceive and make sense of the world around them. An impressive body of research suggests that people who are in positive moods may be more likely to use cognitive shortcuts, relying on general and idiographic heuristics, than people who are in negative moods. Alternately people who are in negative moods may be more likely to use information in their environment rather than rely on heuristics to make their decisions. Interestingly, as a result, people in positive moods may be more susceptible to persuasive appeals and more likely to engage in stereotyping than people in negative moods.

Additionally mood may influence people's memories for certain situations. More specifically, being in a particular mood (e.g., surprised) may prompt a person to recall other times during which he or she experienced the relevant mood strongly (e.g., a surprise birthday party). Correspondingly, being in or recalling a situation that evoked strong affective responses (e.g., watching the September 11, 2001, terrorist attacks on television) may evoke associated moods, such as fear.

Furthermore mood may provide people with information concerning how they should manage or respond to cues in their environments. For example, a popular theory of self-esteem, sociometer theory, posits that negative mood may signal to a person that he or she is being excluded or rejected. An increase in negative mood may alert the rejected person that he or she is being devalued in a social interaction and that he or she should do something interpersonally (e.g., flatter the rejector) or intrapersonally (e.g., artificially inflate reported self-evaluations) in order to maintain positive self-worth.

MOOD, PHYSIOLOGY, AND BEHAVIOR

In addition to its influences on cognition, mood is also associated with certain patterns of physiological responding. Brain imaging studies have revealed that, though affective and nonaffective centers in the brain share common components, differences between these areas exist, indicating that structures associated with affective responding are distinct from those not associated with affective responding. Moreover, positive affect and negative affect may share neural processes indicating that people may have the capacity to experience both positive and negative affect at the same time.

Although the possibility that one can simultaneously experience, for example, pleasure and pain, exists, the bulk of research examining the influence of mood on physiology and vice versa suggests that positive and negative moods are associated with distinct patterns of brain activation and corresponding arousal and behavior patterns. More specifically, good mood is associated with varying levels of positive arousal whereas bad mood is associated with varying levels of negative arousal. Stated differently, positive mood fosters approach behaviors, whereas negative mood fosters withdrawal behaviors.

The experience of negative mood may be so aversive that, not only do people seek to avoid it, they may also take potentially harmful behaviors in an attempt to overcome it. People who are in bad moods are more likely to make decisions that are self-serving in the present rather than the future, making riskier decisions than people in better moods.

In contrast, being in a good mood is associated with a variety of more positive behaviors. For example, people in positive moods are more inclined to help others. They are also more likely to respond to tasks and problems with more creative approaches than people who are in bad moods.

SUMMARY

Mood exists as a response to the processing of internal and external affective stimuli. The study of mood draws the intellectual attention of a variety of social scientists. Correspondingly, research has revealed that mood influences both cognition and behavior. Moreover, there are both biological and neurobiological correlates of mood. In general, people in good moods evidence a variety of positive outcomes and behaviors relative to those who are in bad moods. Being in a good mood may come with some costs, however. Most centrally, people who are in good moods may be less likely than those who are in bad moods to critically process persuasive information.

SEE ALSO *Attitudes; Emotion; Temperament*

BIBLIOGRAPHY

Cacioppo, John T., and Gary G. Bernston. 1994. Relationship between Attitudes and Evaluative Space: A Critical Review, with Emphasis on the Separability of Positive and Negative Substrates. *Psychological Bulletin* 115: 401–423.

Cacioppo, John T., Stephen L. Crites, and Wendi L. Gardner. 1996. Bioelectrical Echoes from Evaluative Categorizations: I. A Late Positive Brain Potential that Varies as a Function of Trait Negativity and Extremity. *Journal of Personality and Social Psychology* 67: 115–125.

Clore, Gerald L., et al. 2000. Affective Feelings as Feedback: Some Cognitive Consequences. In *Theories of Mood and Cognition*, ed. Leonard L. Martin and Gerald L. Clore, 27–62. Mahwah, NJ: Erlbaum.

Isen, Alice M. 1970. Success, Failure, Attention, and Reactions to Others: The Warm Glow of Success. *Journal of Personality and Social Psychology* 1: 17–27.

Janis, Irving L., Donald Kaye, and Paul Kirschner. 1965. Facilitating Effects of "Eating While Reading" on Responsiveness to Persuasive Communications. *Journal of Personality and Social Psychology* 15: 294–301.

Leary, Mark R., et al. 1995. Self-Esteem as an Interpersonal Monitor: The Sociometer Hypothesis. *Journal of Personality and Social Psychology* 68: 518–530.

Leith, Karen P., and Roy F. Baumeister. Why Do Bad Moods Increase Self-Defeating Behavior? Emotion, Risk-Taking, and Self-Regulation. *Journal of Personality and Social Psychology* 71: 1250–1267.

Petty, Richard E., and Daniel T. Wegener. 1998. Attitude Change: Multiple Roles for Persuasion Variables. In *The Handbook of Social Psychology*, ed. Daniel Gilbert, Susan Fiske, and Gardner Lindzey, 323–390. New York: McGraw Hill.

Russell, James A., and James M. Carroll. 1999. On the Bipolarity of Positive and Negative Affect. *Psychological Bulletin* 98: 219–235.

Watson, David, and Auke Tellegen. 1985. Toward a Consensual Structure of Mood. *Psychological Bulletin* 98: 219–235.

Jorgianne Civey Robinson

MOOD CONGRUENT RECALL

Mood congruent recall refers to the observation that people tend to remember more information that is consistent or congruent with their mood at the time that they were exposed to that information. Being in a particular mood can cause people to pay more attention to information that matches their mood and to think more about or elaborate that information (Bower and Forgas 2000). These cognitive processes lead to better memory for the information. For example, a person in a happy mood may pay more attention to the happy scenes of a movie and elaborate the scenes by relating them to happy events in his or her life. As a result, weeks after seeing the movie, the person may remember more of the happy scenes than the sad scenes.

Mood congruent recall differs from *mood dependent recall*—the observation that the information a person attends to while in one mood is better recalled later if the person is in the same mood (regardless of its emotional quality). For example, Eric Eich, Dawn Macaulay, and Lee Ryan (1994) directed university students to read familiar nouns (e.g., ship, street), then describe an autobiographical event that came to mind for each noun. A happy (or sad) mood was induced in students by having them entertain elating (or depressing) thoughts while listening to lively (or languid) music. Participants described a range of happy, sad, and neutral events in response to the nouns. Later, they recalled the autobiographical events either in the same or opposite mood. Participants recalled more positive, negative, and neutral events when they were in the same mood than in the opposite mood.

Several approaches have been proposed to explain mood congruent recall (see Eich and Forgas [2003] for a review of these approaches). Gordon Bower (1981) suggested that a person's long-term memory is characterized by an associative network of concepts whereby emotions become associated with thought processes and concepts of things and situations encountered in daily life. When an emotion is aroused, it spreads activation to concepts and thought processes that are associated with the emotion. This knowledge guides a person's interpretation of the current context in a way that is congruent with the emotion.

According to the *affect as information* view, people make judgments by implicitly asking themselves, "How do I feel about it?" (Clore et al. 2000). For example, when people were asked about their reaction to a happy or sad film that they had just watched, they showed strong mood congruence, with happy filmgoers recalling the film to be much more positive than the sad filmgoers (Schwarz and Clore 1983).

The *affect infusion model* attempts to explain the conditions under which mood congruence occurs or fails to occur by examining the different kinds of cognitive processes that are involved (Forgas 1995). For example, people may be *motivated* not to act in a mood congruent way (as when a person really wants a job at a company and ignores negative feelings toward some of the interviewers). However, mood congruence occurs when people engage in relatively elaborate processing, such as trying to form an impression of someone with an unusual combination of attributes—for example, a surfer who likes Italian opera.

Research on mood congruence highlights the important interplay between emotions and cognition. For many years, scholars tended to neglect emotion or consider it detrimental to judgment and decision-making. However, the interplay between emotions and cognition appears to be ubiquitous, and can even be beneficial.

SEE ALSO *Cognition; Decision-making; Emotion; Memory; Mood; Motivation*

BIBLIOGRAPHY

Bower, Gordon H. 1981. Mood and Memory. *American Psychologist* 36: 129–148.

Bower, Gordon H., and Joseph P. Forgas. 2000. Mood and Social Memory. In *Handbook of Affect and Social Cognition*, ed. Joseph P. Forgas, 96–120. Mahwah, NJ: Erlbaum.

Clore, Gerald L., Karen Gasper, and Erika Garvin. 2000. Affect as Information. In *Handbook of Affect and Social Cognition*, ed. Joseph P. Forgas, 121–144. Mahwah, NJ: Erlbaum.

Eich, Eric, and Joseph P. Forgas. 2003. Mood, Cognition, and Memory. In *Handbook of Psychology*, Vol. 4: *Experimental Psychology*, eds. Alice F. Healy and Robert W. Proctor, 61–83. Hoboken, NJ: Wiley.

Eich, Eric, Dawn Macaulay, and Lee Ryan. 1994. Mood Dependent Memory for Events of the Personal Past. *Journal of Experimental Psychology: General* 123: 201–215.

Forgas, Joseph P. 1995. Mood and Judgment: The Affect Infusion Model (AIM). *Psychological Bulletin* 117: 39–66.

Schwarz, Norbert, and Gerald L. Clore. 1983. Mood, Misattribution, and Judgments of Well-being: Informative and Directive Functions of Affective States. *Journal of Personality and Social Psychology* 45: 513–523.

Edward Wisniewski

MOOD DEPENDENT RECALL

SEE *Mood Congruent Recall.*

MOORE, BARRINGTON
1913–2003

Barrington Moore was a major sociologist who used history to wrestle with the philosophical dilemmas of justice and liberty. He saw all society and the maintenance of all values as inherently repressive, and he thought gradualism was far too accepting of the pain and death associated with injustice. Yet, he was convinced that those dedicated to drastic transformation were highly intolerant and repressive.

Moore built on the work of three great scholars—Max Weber, Karl Marx, and Sigmund Freud. He agreed with Marx about the inequality in modern democratic society, with Weber about the restrictions on freedom created by bureaucracy and rational-technical values, and with Freud about restrictions imposed by all societies on individual spontaneity, especially in the sexual realm.

After World War II (1939–1945) Moore focused on the Soviet Union and the impact of the pressures of efficiency emphasized by Weber. His *Soviet Politics: The Dilemmas of Power* (1950) examined how the imperatives of successful industrialization had led Josef Stalin to repudiate many central tenets of Marxist and Leninist ideology, particularly the values of equality and a nonhierarchical society. In *Terror and Progress USSR* (1954), published immediately after Stalin's death, Moore looked to the future and discussed how bureaucratization and governance through rules could and probably would limit the power of party leaders in the post-Stalin society. These two books influenced a generation of scholars and graduate scholars at the Russian Research Center at Harvard University to see the Soviet Union in terms of long-term

social forces rather than simply the ideology of those at the top. Yet, Moore himself never studied the post-Stalin period.

Instead, Moore spent a decade exploring why some countries become more or less democratic and others adopt various types of dictatorship, studying particularly the histories of Britain, France, Germany, Japan, India, and China. This type of comparative work became his most enduring contribution to sociological methodology. The result was Moore's most famous book, *Social Origins of Democracy and Dictatorship: Lord and Peasant in the Making of the Modern World* (1966), which was published during the Vietnam era. The book's focus on peasant revolutions, its negative treatment of bureaucracy, its pessimism about gradualism and the repression of modern society, and its use of many Marxist categories but without Marx's universal pattern of history spoke directly to a generation of students.

Moore saw democracy as dependent on a vigorous bourgeoisie and on landlords being ready to accept commercialization of agriculture. He believed commercialization of agriculture was necessary both to break up traditional peasant organizations and to set the stage for a landlord-bourgeoisie alliance against the bureaucracy. The absence of that alliance doomed democracy. But without commercialization of agriculture, the traditional peasant organizations were not destroyed. Moore believed that this left dictatorships highly susceptible to peasant revolt, except in rare cases such as Japan, where these organizations were coopted. He explained the Communist revolutions in China and Russia as this type of peasant revolt. Yet, Moore thought peasants were attracted to doctrinaire and intolerant leaders who were highly repressive. Tragically, these leaders were perhaps most repressive of the peasants themselves.

Moore wrote seven books in the last thirty years of his life. The titles of six of them reflect the moral dilemmas that obsessed him: *Reflections on the Causes of Human Misery* (1972), *Injustice: The Social Bases of Obedience and Revolt* (1978), *Privacy: Studies in Social and Cultural History* (1984), *Authority and Inequality under Capitalism and Socialism* (1987), *Moral Aspects of Economic Growth and Other Essays* (1995), and *Moral Purity and Persecution in History* (2000). Many of them were based on detailed comparative work of diverse societies that included preliterate society, the peoples of the Old Testament, Greece, and India.

The last phase of Moore's work was not as influential as the earlier two. He continued to believe that informal norms and values are inevitable but restrictive of freedom, that the prospects for a free and natural society are bleak in the world's leading societies, and that radical solutions are usually the most intolerant and repressive of all. He called only for a more tolerant and egalitarian society. Most of the time, this combination of views is not psychologically satisfying. Yet, anyone desiring to explore the moral dilemmas of, for example, the current Middle East in broad historical perspective can find no place better to begin than Moore's work.

SEE ALSO *Authoritarianism; Bureaucracy; Democracy; Dictatorship; Egalitarianism; Freud, Sigmund; Justice; Liberty; Marx, Karl; Peasantry; Revolution; Sociology; Stalin, Joseph; Tolerance, Political; Totalitarianism; Union of Soviet Socialist Republics; Weber, Max*

BIBLIOGRAPHY

Moore, Barrington. 1950. *Soviet Politics: The Dilemmas of Power.* New York: Harper.

Moore, Barrington. 1954. *Terror and Progress USSR: Some Sources of Change and Stability in the Soviet Dictatorship.* Cambridge, MA: Harvard University Press.

Moore, Barrington. 1966. *Social Origins of Democracy and Dictatorship: Lord and Peasant in the Making of the Modern World.* Boston: Beacon Press.

Moore, Barrington. 1972. *Reflections on the Causes of Human Misery and Upon Certain Proposals to Eliminate Them.* Boston: Beacon Press.

Moore, Barrington. 1978. *Injustice: The Social Bases of Obedience and Revolt.* New York: Random House.

Moore, Barrington. 1984. *Privacy: Studies in Social and Cultural History.* Armonk, NY: M. E. Sharpe.

Moore, Barrington. 1987. *Authority and Inequality under Capitalism and Socialism.* New York: Oxford University Press.

Moore, Barrington. 1995. *Moral Aspects of Economic Growth, and Other Essays.* Ithaca, NY: Cornell University Press.

Moore, Barrington. 2000. *Moral Purity and Persecution in History.* Princeton, NJ: Princeton University Press.

Skocpol, Theda, ed. 1998. *Democracy, Revolution, and History.* Ithaca, NY: Cornell University Press.

Smith, Dennis. 1893. *Barrington Moore: Violence, Morality, and Political Change.* London: Macmillan.

Jerry Hough

MORAL DOMAIN THEORY

Moral domain theory has proposed that individuals acquire moral concepts about fairness, others' welfare, and rights (the "moral" domain) beginning in early childhood, and that this knowledge develops during childhood and adolescence. In contrast to global stage theories outlined by Lawrence Kohlberg, in which morality is viewed as a series of hierarchical stages, moral domain theory pro-

poses that moral reasoning is distinct from other forms of social knowledge, such as societal and psychological knowledge. In his book *The Development of Social Knowledge: Morality and Convention* (1983), Elliot Turiel outlined three domains of knowledge: the moral (principles of how individuals ought to treat one another), the societal (regulations designed to promote the smooth functioning of social groups and institutions), and the psychological (an understanding of self, others, and beliefs about autonomy and individuality). Beginning in early childhood, children construct moral, societal, and psychological concepts in parallel, rather than in succession, as is proposed by global stage theory (in which children are first selfish, then oriented to familial and societal regulation, and then formulating principled morality in adolescence). According to moral domain theory, the morality includes concepts of physical harm, psychological harm, the distribution of resources, freedoms, and rights.

Since the 1980s extensive empirical research has demonstrated the multiple ways in which children, adolescents, and adults evaluate social events using these categories of knowledge. Researchers have identified social knowledge domains using a set of criteria that define each domain and justifications that reveal the underlying reasoning about issues within the domain. For the moral domain, for example, for the issue of physical harm, an interviewer could ask a child whether it would be okay to hit if a teacher did not have a rule against hitting (authority jurisdiction), whether the rule could be changed (alterability), whether the rule applies in other settings (generalizability), whether it is wrong to hit someone if there is no punishment (punishment avoidance), and whether the act was wrong if there was no rule about it (rule contingency). Children as young as three and a half years of age use these criteria to evaluate moral transgressions. In addition, moral domain methodology involves analyzing the types of reasons individuals give for their evaluations of acts and transgressions. Extensive empirical observations have been conducted to examine the types of responses children, peers, and adults use in response to transgressions.

Studies have demonstrated how individuals apply the moral domain to complex issues, such as those involving cultural expectations, rights, exclusion, parent-adolescent conflict, autonomy, environmental issues, bullying, and emotions. In straightforward situations, children and adolescents give priority to morality; in complex situations, individuals weigh a number of considerations that take different priority depending on the salience and associated informational assumptions.

In her review chapter in the *Handbook of Moral Development* in 2006, Judith Smetana reports the types of age-related changes within the moral domain that researchers have documented. Very young children understand that hitting is wrong because this act involves negative intrinsic consequences to others. This is a concrete, observable concept that children acquire through a process of experience, abstraction, and evaluation. By the preschool years, children understand why it is important to share objects (toys), referred to as the fair distribution of resources. Distribution of resources is more complex than issues about physical harm because there are a number of factors to weigh, such as legitimate claims, ownership, and methods of distribution. During middle childhood, children understand the wrongfulness of teasing and exclusion. By early adolescence, exclusion, fairness, and rights take on a more elaborated form, in which issues surrounding the intergroup context as well as governmental and societal laws become quite salient.

Culture is influential in how individuals acquire moral concepts and the types of experiences that lead them to make moral judgments. There is extensive research documenting that individuals in many cultures use the same criteria to identify moral issues (justice, others' welfare, and rights), and that these concerns are distinct from conventional regulations and traditions. While cultural traditions and customs may embody moral codes (e.g., "Do not harm others"), moral principles are not defined by consensus or agreement but by reference to an independent set of maxims about how individuals ought to treat one another. Understanding cultural and moral norms is essential for children to achieve the goal of becoming full members of communities and societies.

BIBLIOGRAPHY

Arsenio, William F., and Elizabeth A. Lemerise. 2004. Aggression and Moral Development: Integrating Social Information Processing and Moral Domain Models. *Child Development* 75: 987–1002.

Helwig, Charles C. 2006. Rights, Civil Liberties, and Democracy Across Cultures. In *Handbook of Moral Development*, ed. Melanie Killen and Judith G. Smetana, 185–210. Mahwah, NJ: Erlbaum.

Kahn, Peter H. 1999. *The Human Relationship with Nature.* Cambridge, MA: MIT Press.

Killen, Melanie, Jennie Lee-Kim, Heidi McGlothlin, and Charles Stangor. 2002. How Children and Adolescents Evaluate Gender and Racial Exclusion. *Monographs of the Society for Research in Child Development* 67 (4): 1–132.

Killen, Melanie, Nancy G. Margie, and Stefanie Sinno. 2006. Morality in the Context of Intergroup Relationships. In *Handbook of Moral Development*, ed. Melanie Killen and Judith G. Smetana, 155–184. Mahwah, NJ: Erlbaum.

Killen, Melanie, and Judith G. Smetana. 1999. Social Interactions in Preschool Classrooms and the Development of Young Children's Conceptions of the Personal. *Child Development.* 70: 486–501.

Kohlberg, Lawrence. 1984. *Essays on Moral Development.* Vol. 2 of *The Psychology of Moral Development: The Nature and Validity of Moral Stages.* San Francisco: Harper and Row.

Nucci, Larry, C. Camino, and Clarice Milnitsky-Sapiro. 1996. Social Class Effects on Northeastern Brazilian Children's Conceptions of Areas of Personal Choice and Social Regulation. *Child Development* 67: 1223–1242.

Smetana, Judith G. 1995. Morality in Context: Abstractions, Ambiguities, and Applications. In *Annals of Child Development*, vol. 10, ed. R. Vasta, 83–130. London: Jessica Kingsley.

Smetana, Judith G. 2006. Social Domain Theory: Consistencies and Variations in Children's Moral and Social Judgements. In *Handbook of Moral Development*, ed. Melanie Killen and Judith G. Smetana, 119–154. Mahwah, NJ: Erlbaum.

Smetana, Judith G., and Elliot Turiel. 2003. Morality During Adolescence. In *The Blackwell Handbook of Adolescence*, ed. Gerald R. Adams and Michael D. Berzonsky, 247–268. Oxford: Blackwell.

Tisak, Marie S. 1995. Domains of Social Reasoning and Beyond. In *Annals of Child Development*, vol. 11, ed. R. Vasta, 95–130. London: Jessica Kingsley.

Turiel, Elliot. 1983. *The Development of Social Knowledge: Morality and Convention.* Cambridge, U.K.: Cambridge University Press.

Wainryb, C., and Elliot Turiel. 1994. Dominance, Subordination, and Concepts of Personal Entitlements in Cultural Contexts. *Child Development* 65: 1701–1722.

Melanie Killen

MORAL HAZARD

The term *moral hazard* describes a situation in which two or more parties voluntarily interact, but the value of this interaction to one or more of the parties can be adversely affected by actions the other party may take for personal benefit. This phenomenon is particularly troublesome in instances in which the affected party can neither (contractually) control nor perfectly monitor these actions (directly or indirectly).

While many examples exist, perhaps the most common and compelling ones come from the insurance industry. Consider, for example, theft insurance, in which the owner of some valuable items contracts with an insurance carrier that in the event of the theft of the property, the insurance company will pay the owner the entire value of the property. The insured party, in most instances, can carry out actions that will lower the probability that the property will be stolen—for example, installation of a security system, hiring guards to protect the property, installing better locks on doors and windows, and so on. Each of these actions is costly, but some of them are likely to nonetheless be worthwhile investments. Specifically, if the decrease in the expected loss from theft is greater than the cost of the action, then the investment is socially desirable (not taking into account the utility of the thief). However, if the lost property is fully covered by the insurance policy, the owner has little reason to expend these resources. What triggers the problem is the shifting of the risk from the party that can most efficiently protect the property to a party that cannot. If this problem cannot be overcome, the cost of the insurance policy will be such that the insurance company can cover its expected cost given that the desired precautions will not be taken, and there may even be market failure, whereby the insurance premium is so high that the parties cannot reach agreement.

The theoretical underpinnings of this problem are attributed largely to a series of articles written by J. A. Mirrlees in the early to mid-1970s, with one of the most influential not being actually published until 1999 (although completed in 1975). Recognition of the problem predates these writings, going back to Mark Pauly (1968), Kenneth Arrow (1971), and Richard Zeckhauser (1970), who was the first to model the phenomenon. The idea of moral hazard has been shown to have implications for a large variety of fields in economics, including banking, environmental economics, health economics, international trade and lending, regulation, and growth. Most central, however, is the development of optimal-contracts literature, which has its roots in the moral hazard literature.

To this end, consider, once again, the insurance problem. In some instances, steps can be taken, either contractual or other, to attempt to overcome the moral hazard problem. For instance, the insurance company may try to control the problem by refusing to insure the property unless some of the steps mentioned are taken, or the insurer can condition payment of a claim on proof that the steps were carried out. Unfortunately, such contracts are unlikely to guarantee optimal behavior on the insured party's part. This is because: (1) theft can occur even if the desired steps are taken, so there is no (indirect) way to be sure that the desired precautions were not taken; and (2) it is unlikely that the company will be able to (directly) perfectly check the level of security given by the system, the number and quality of guards hired, or the quality of the locks installed, and even if it can, it is likely to face difficulties in proving these things in a court of law.

Alternatively, the insurance company may try to shift some of the risk back to the property owner by, for example, selling a policy with a large deductible or only paying a percentage of the loss, thus better aligning the interests of the insured party with those of the insurance company. This, however, lowers the value of the insurance policy, and does not allow for the pooling of risks that are at the base of the insurance industry. As another possibility, the insurance company could provide its own security (and charge for it), but the insurance company is almost certainly not as well situated as the insured party to provide such services or to ensure that they are carried out as desired. Thus, it seems almost inevitable that the moral hazard problem will persist in such markets.

The issue of optimal contracts has been well developed in *principal-agent* settings, of particular importance in the accounting literature. Consider a situation with two parties—a principal (the owner of a firm or manager) and an agent (worker). The agent is hired to carry out some task, and the level of success depends upon the level of effort invested by the agent. The agent prefers to exert himself as little as possible, but the principal desires that the agent put in a large amount of effort in order to maximize the principal's expected return. The agent, left to his own, is likely to exert as little effort as he feels he can get away with, and the principal, therefore, is interested in finding a way to align the worker's interests with his own. If the effort can be observed directly, either through observation of the agent's working habits or by the fact that there is a one-to-one relationship between effort and output, then the principal can write an employment contract that will have the effect of causing the agent to choose to exert effort (assuming there are no other problems with this solution, such as a requirement to prove the effort level in court). However, if effort cannot be directly observed, and the outcome of the worker's effort is uncertain, so that the output level can be low even in the face of great effort, then the principal is faced with a more difficult situation because the worker can always say that he exerted effort, but was unlucky.

In some circumstances, writing a contract that shifts the risk from the principal to the agent can eliminate this problem. If successful, such a contract has the effect of making the agent take direct consideration of the effects of his effort, and causes him to exert the optimal amount of effort. However, this is not always possible; if, for instance, the agent is risk-averse and the principal is risk-neutral, it may be the case that the worker will be unwilling to bear risk that is actuarially worthwhile for the principal.

There are those who feel that the importance of the moral hazard concern is overstated. Specifically, they feel that in instances in which the interaction between the principal and the agent is of a repeated game nature (long-term employment), this problem may disappear. Even if not, if reputation is important to the agent, he is unlikely to slack even when the principal cannot prove bad faith.

SEE ALSO *Information, Asymmetric; Insurance; Insurance Industry; Principal-Agent Models*

BIBLIOGRAPHY

Arrow, Kenneth J. 1971. The Economics of Moral Hazard: Further Comment. In *Essays in the Theory of Risk Bearing.* Amsterdam: North Holland.

Kreps, David M. 1990. *A Course in Microeconomic Theory.* Princeton, NJ: Princeton University Press.

Mirrlees, J. A. 1999. The Theory of Moral Hazard and Unobservable Behavior: Part I. *Review of Economic Studies* 6 (1): 3–21.

Pauly, Mark V. 1968. The Economics of Moral Hazard. *American Economic Review* 58: 531–537.

Zeckhauser, Richard. 1970. Medical Insurance: A Case Study of the Tradeoff Between Risk Spreading and Appropriate Incentives. *Journal of Economic Theory* 2 (1): 10–26.

Avi Weiss

MORAL PHILOSOPHY

SEE *Philosophy, Moral.*

MORAL SENTIMENTS

The field of economics developed out of political economy, which in the early twenty-first century would be thought of as an interdisciplinary combination of economics, political science, sociology, history, and moral philosophy. Prior to that evolution, political economy was part of the curriculum of "expediency," a subfield of moral philosophy. Adam Smith, for example, was a professor of moral philosophy, and not until Thomas Malthus is political economy itself deemed worthy of a sole professorship. Smith, often considered the "father of economics," was the author not only of *The Wealth of Nations* (1776) but also of *The Theory of Moral Sentiments* (1769). While there was long a debate over whether the two works were consistent with one another, the consensus in the early twenty-first century is that the two works are generally (if not entirely) compatible.

In the *Theory of Moral Sentiments* (TMS), Smith addressed the question of whether a society of perfect liberty, in other words, a society freed from the fetters of feudal and ecclesiastic authority, could attain moral order. In the *Wealth of Nations* (WN), Smith asked the same question but about economic order. The link was to be a third work on the institutional and legal framework ensuring this perfect society, which Smith never was able to complete but which is outlined in his *Lectures on Jurisprudence* (LJ). TMS is about the socialization of the individual, and WN is about the economic outcomes of the behavior of socialized individuals in the legal and institutional context of LJ (Macfie 1967; Heilbroner 1982).

In TMS, Smith introduces "sympathy" (what in the early twenty-first century would be called *empathy*) as the social cement of society. Sympathy is not pity but is rather fellow feeling of any kind. Our approval or disapproval of the behavior of others is determined by our imagining how we would feel and how we would respond if we were in a like situation—thus the importance in Smith of the role of the imagination. We ask whether the person's response is appropriate to the situation and then about the effects of the response. If we sympathize, we approve; if not, we disapprove. We judge our own behavior in a similar way. Here Smith introduces his idea of the "impartial spectator"—we imagine ourselves in someone else's shoes observing our own behavior and evaluating it in a like manner. The judgment of the impartial spectator requires more than sympathy—it also requires reason. Sympathy, when joined with reason, becomes "sympathetic reason" or "rational sympathy," the "best head joined to the best heart." Over time the many judgments we are all making result in social codes of conduct, some of which may become law, others unwritten but no less strict codes of morality. Self-deceit or excessive self-regard can intrude, however, and if untamed may result in us justifying or rationalizing behavior we know to be wrong. Here Smith looks to "self-command" (self-control) and a "sense of duty" (commitment to society) to ensure individuals will generally obey the social rules of society.

Interestingly in TMS Smith identifies two levels of prudence. The lower level includes what we think of as economic activities, whereas the higher level concerns valor, benevolence, justice, and the like. The former is only worthy of "a certain cold esteem," and it is only the latter, higher level that is truly and properly called *prudence.* Thus it can be said that, in Smith, *proper* self-regard—self-interested behavior moderated by self-command and a sense of duty as well as the socially responsible adherence to social rules and obligations—can be socially beneficial under certain conditions. It is not the higher level of prudence, but it is a kind of prudence. In no way can it be said that Smith subscribed to the notion that "greed is good." Economic order requires not only the proper institutions but also the moral sentiments, without which Smith's society of perfect liberty would be impossible (Rothschild 2001, pp. 236–246 and *passim*).

SEE ALSO *Liberty; Philosophy, Moral; Smith, Adam*

BIBLIOGRAPHY

Heilbroner, Robert L. 1982. The Socialization of the Individual in Adam Smith. *History of Political Economy* 14 (3): 427–439.

Macfie, A. L. 1967 *The Individual in Society.* London: Allen and Unwin.

Rothschild, Emma. 2001. *Economic Sentiments: Adam Smith, Condorcet, and the Enlightenment.* Cambridge, MA: Harvard University Press.

Mathew Forstater

MORAL SUASION

Moral suasion is a discursive strategy that references a set of principles to pressure individuals, groups, or nation-states to change their policies. Moral suasion strategies have been used by various actors and organizations for diverse purposes throughout history. It tacitly assumes that most (but not all) humans are reasonable, flexible, and have capacities for conceiving an agreed-upon sense of justice. It therefore takes a rather progressive view of human history, in that barriers to human freedom can be "broken down" through persuasive dialogue that uses universal principles as the basis for its truth claims. Moral suasion is a nonviolent form of influence, and therefore the groups and organizations that use it have themselves prohibited the use of violence to further their political goals. For instance, the King Center, a nonprofit organization founded by Coretta Scott King, lists *moral suasion* in its "Glossary of Nonviolence." Moral suasion strategies historically have been and continue to be used by a myriad of organizations.

In the late eighteenth and early nineteenth centuries certain U.S. abolitionist organizations used moral suasion to seek an end to slavery. Abolitionists such as William Lloyd Garrison (1805–1879) used this strategy in their published writings and public speeches. These groups based their discourse in a faith in (what they viewed as) universal values of human equality and freedom. The scholar Tunde Adeleke wrote that "moral suasion … reflected the enduring character and impact of … the Enlightenment. Late eighteenth-century Enlightenment culture prioritized rationalism, secularism and a utilitarian conception of government" (Adeleke 1998, p. 128).

Certain U.S. civil rights organizations, beginning especially in the 1950s and 1960s, used moral suasion for purposes similar to those of the abolitionists: Leaders such as Martin Luther King Jr., along with both secular and religious organizations, sought to bring about desegregation in the U.S. South. These movements combined moral suasion with other tactics, such as nonviolent resistance and civil disobedience, to secure the rights of African Americans during this time.

Economists have recently used the term *moral suasion* to reference the tactic used by financial authorities (such as the Federal Reserve and the International Monetary Fund) to pressure financial institutions to adhere to mon-etary or fiscal guidelines. It is driven morally by the assumption that these guidelines will improve the economic well-being of a regional, national, or international society, including their individual members.

Most recently, humanitarian nongovernmental organizations such as Human Rights Watch and Amnesty International have used moral suasion to criticize global human rights abuses and to pressure the international community to systematically act to stop these abuses. These groups legitimate their moral language by referring to conventions that have been ratified by a majority of the international community (e.g., the Convention on the Prevention and Punishment of the Crime of Genocide, and the Geneva Convention), but they also seek to effect action from influential nation-states by referencing those nation-states' traditions of human rights: "The moral arguing here is mainly about identity politics, that is, Western governments and their societies are reminded of their own values as liberal democracies and of the need to act upon them in their foreign policies" (Risse and Ropp 1999, p. 251).

SEE ALSO *Civil Disobedience; Desegregation; Enlightenment; Gandhi, Mohandas K.; Human Rights; King, Martin Luther, Jr.; Passive Resistance; Persuasion; Slavery*

BIBLIOGRAPHY

Adeleke, Tunde. 1998. Afro-Americans and Moral Suasion: The Debate in the 1830s. *The Journal of Negro History* 83 (2): 127–142.

King Center. 2004. Glossary of Nonviolence. http://www.thekingcenter.org/prog/non/glossary.html.

Risse, Thomas, and Stephen C. Ropp. 1999. International Human Rights Norms and Domestic Change: Conclusions. In *The Power of Human Rights*, ed. Thomas Risse, Stephen Ropp, and Kathryn Sikkink, 234–278. Cambridge, U.K.: Cambridge University Press.

Brent J. Steele

MORALITY

Morality (Latin neuter plural: *moralia*) is a multifaceted term. It is commonly used to describe the behavioral teaching and practical lessons of literary and artistic works. As a descriptive term about the cultural and social realms, *morality* signifies the habits and norms of behavior that establish right and wrong conduct for individuals in particular societies. Normatively, morality is the system-atic and principled reflection concerned with determining what ought to be the standards of conduct and duties for particular agents and communities and how these standards are reproduced in members of society. In this sense, morality thus specifies the proper practice of individual and communal life and prescribes what constitutes the "good life" and how it is to be attained. In doing so, moral reflection draws upon the cultural, religious, and theoretical worldviews and values of particular societies in determining the proper standards of behavior.

MORALITY AS A DESCRIPTIVE CATEGORY

Morality is a term of social theory used to "describe" the range of acceptable human behaviors, that is, the norms that structure and guide proper, intentional behavior for a particular community. In this sense, morality describes the customs and principles that particular societies use to determine what is right or wrong for behavior in that social order. At the external level, morality can merely signify the customs and common practices that tell a member of society how to act within interpersonal relationships and social circumstances. These practices and customs generally rest upon a theoretical and ideal foundation, sometimes called a *worldview*, that expresses the internal beliefs and values of the society. Émile Durkheim (1858–1917) called this the "collective or common consciousness" and defined it by stating, "The totality of beliefs and sentiments common to the average members of society forms a determinate system with a life of its own" ([1893] 1984, pp. 38–39). Such a worldview system provides the horizon of values and stock of norms and duties within which individuals and social groups determine courses of intentional action. Individual and communal actions are judged according to their conformity with or deviation from these duties. This horizon of beliefs and values functions to reinforce desired behaviors, reproduce norms in succeeding generations, and impose implicit and explicit sanctions for deviant behavior.

MORALITY AS A NORMATIVE CATEGORY

Morality also describes the process of judgment whereby people determine what actions to undertake. As opposed to anthropological descriptions of social and individual behaviors (e.g., what *is* the behavior of this set of peoples?) or judgments that are narrowly *customary* (e.g., should I send a thank-you note to the host of the dinner?), *aesthetic* (e.g., does this new building fit into the city skyline?), or *political* (e.g., how do we shape the democratic will of the people to adopt this particular policy?), *moral* judgments specifically inquire into what behavior or action one *ought* to undertake. This view of morality, most commonly studied in moral philosophy and moral theology, denotes a set of inquiries that purport to describe and analyze

human behavior through determining "what ought to be the case" from some "objective" perspective that goes beyond descriptive accounts of actual behavior or mere instrumental achievement of prudential goals. How do humans learn these norms and standards of behavior that specify what duties and obligations they must respond to?

Moral judgments draw upon the *mores* of a social group to specify proper behavior. Moral norms are based upon the stock of principles and values contained in the worldview that set duties and obligations for human action and behavior. These standards may come to be known by means of external revelation; by referring to the traditions, practices, and behaviors determined by protocol or exemplars in one's community; by reference to internal emotional sentiments shaped through character development and habituation; or by rational determinations carried out through the agent's own cognitive capacities.

Many early societies (e.g., Hebrews, Babylonians) believed that norms were revealed by divine beings through a special dispensation of knowledge by the deity. This tradition continues today in some religious moral reflection, commonly called *divine-command ethics*, wherein the norms of behavior for the religious group are thought to emerge through revelation (i.e., through the text of the Bible or the law given through a religious authority) that shapes the authoritative traditions and rituals of religious communities.

The customs, habits, and traditions of social groups can also serve as the primary source of norms for setting standards of behavior. The authority of the norms rests on their continuity with the community's past practices and its own standards of the ideal member. The customs might be implicit and known to the individual only through informal means. For instance, communal and familial expectations can place pressure on individuals to act in certain ways or follow a particular life course. These customs may also be codified in formal codes, such as moral proverbs, narratives, or codes of conduct. While communal customs still inform and undergird positive laws in many modern social orders, modern legal systems have increasingly divorced the legitimacy of law from mere custom or historical practice.

Some accounts of the role of custom and habit in the moral life (i.e., those by Scottish philosophers Francis Hutcheson [1694–1746] and David Hume [1711–1776]) hold that the knowledge of right and wrong arises from sensorily perceiving that an action produces sentiments of moral pleasure or displeasure. In this view, humans are constitutively feeling creatures, and right or wrong action gives rise to distinctively *moral* pleasure or displeasure. Reason, while helping to discern what ought to be done, cannot motivate an agent to act on its own. The motivating force, rather, is the pleasure produced through the moral action. The moral norms of a community are customs and habits that reflect these moral sentiments, reproducing proper character of community members by rewarding proper actions and sanctioning illicit behavior.

The utilitarian theories of Jeremy Bentham (1748–1832) and John Stuart Mill (1806–1873) extend this view of seeking pleasure but require a duty for the human to maximize societal benefit. While humans are motivated to action by the desire for pleasure and avoidance of pain, reason is used to determine what course of action will maximize pleasure. This calculus is based on the principle of utility—the agent must always act so as to maximize the greatest happiness for the greatest number in society. Utilitarians thus submerge the individual's moral desires under the overall outcome of the well-being of the community.

Some moral theory privileges the role of reason as the source of the moral norms. The Stoic philosophers, as well as thinkers in the Christian natural law tradition, held that rational capacities allow human beings to discern the purpose of life from perceiving the order of nature and rationally comprehending the role and structure of human life within the cosmos. The modern emphasis on the autonomy of the will, shaped by the Protestant emphasis on individual conscience and unmediated relation to the divine, was articulated by modern philosophers like John Locke (1632–1704) and Immanuel Kant (1724–1804). In this strand of moral thought, the human is thought to be a rational agent who reflectively engages in determining what should be the proper course for his or her action. For Kant, the freedom of individuals using their own reason to determine the best course of action and set ends for themselves is the basis of the possibility of the moral life. The norms of action are determined through universalizing the proposed action and determining whether the action, if it were to become a universal law, could be rationally consistent as a duty for all agents. The "good will" is not, therefore, merely one that *acts* in a way that conforms to the custom of the society. Rather, the "good will" is one that is motivated by pure respect for the moral law: to act upon one's rationally prescribed duty, not merely to achieve instrumental outcomes or gain advantage. The moral life is self-imposed, not derived from obedience to external sources. In this way, Kant thought that humans stood out from their natural, animalistic aspects, and at the same time the individual could never legitimately be made subject to another's arbitrary will. This sentiment reflected and heralded the liberal, democratic political ideals of his age.

In general the moral life is the process of applying these norms in practical circumstances to achieve desirable—or good—ends, thereby fulfilling one's duties and obligations. What constitutes these good ends, and the corresponding moral obligation that thereby arises, depends upon the source of the norms applied. The agent who lives in a manner that is responsive to these moral obligations acts over time in ways that inculcate good habits. These habits are said to produce a virtuous agent if the moral actions cause the agent to develop predispositions to act in ways that fulfill his or her duties. Likewise, those who fail to respond to obligations, and develop predispositions to act contrary to moral duty, are said to act immorally and may, over time, develop vicious character traits.

Ethics in the Greco-Roman and early Christian traditions tended to focus on the agent's character in relation to society. The moral life revolved around shaping character so as to develop habits of virtue that led to the good life, a state of happiness, or well-being (*eudaimonia*). Thinkers in the Aristotelian tradition conceived of moral education as a process of transforming the agent's character so that his or her desires were inclined toward the virtuous "mean" of possible courses of action. If one's habits inclined the agent to flee a dangerous situation where one's assistance was required to save another (cowardice) or to wantonly intervene without regarding the complexity of the situation (recklessness), virtuous agents, instead, would be properly habituated so their instincts, emotions, and habits would allow them to intervene in a cool and calculated way, not withering in the face of the danger (courage).

Under pressures from modernization, the traditional patterns and norms of the moral life have become more disoriented in contemporary society. Industrialization and urbanization have upended small-scale communities and transformed social bonds; historical, scientific, and technological understanding is more predominant, disrupting traditional explanations for value origins and compromising their explanatory legitimacy (disenchantment); globalization has decentered community and national identity through a growing recognition of the basic diversity of worldviews; and the social and political order is increasingly instrumentalized and bureaucratized, leading to coordination and steering problems for building political will. In the wake of the upheaval of traditional societies, professional ethics (especially in law, business, and medicine) have arisen as a mode of moral regulation that set standards of behavior whose legitimacy derives from consensus among members of the profession. In society at large, traditional moral norms are felt to be decreasingly persuasive or authoritative, and the charge is often levied that contemporary society has become increasingly individualistic and relativistic. In reaction to this decentering, some thinkers such as Alasdair MacIntyre have charged that traditional moral categories, while still commonly used, are uncoupled from their worldview contexts and their resulting use is often considered to be confused, shallow, and contingent.

BIBLIOGRAPHY

Aristotle. 1962. *Nicomachean Ethics*. Trans. Martin Ostwald. New York: Macmillan.

Bentham, Jeremy. [1789] 1948. *The Principles of Morals and Legislation*. New York: Hafner.

Durkheim, Émile. [1893] 1984. *The Division of Labor in Society*. Trans. W. D. Halls. New York: Free Press.

Habermas, Jürgen. 1975. *Legitimation Crisis*. Trans. Thomas McCarthy. Boston: Beacon.

Hadot, Pierre. 1995. *Philosophy as a Way of Life: Spiritual Exercises from Socrates to Foucault*. Trans. Michael Chase. Oxford: Blackwell.

Hume, David. [1739] 1969. *A Treatise of Human Nature*. New York: Penguin.

Hutcheson, Francis. [1728] 2002. *An Essay on the Nature and Conduct of Passions and Affections, with Illustrations on the Moral Sense*. Indianapolis, IN: Liberty Fund.

Kant, Immanuel. [1785] 1991. *The Metaphysics of Morals*. Ed. Mary Gregor. Cambridge, U.K.: Cambridge University Press.

Kant, Immanuel. [1788] 1997. *The Critique of Practical Reason*. Ed. Mary Gregor. Cambridge, U.K.: Cambridge University Press.

Locke, John. [1690] 1997. *An Essay Concerning Human Understanding*. New York and London: Penguin.

MacIntyre, Alasdair. 1984. *After Virtue: A Study in Moral Theory*. 2nd ed. Notre Dame, IN: University of Notre Dame Press.

Mill, John Stuart. 1969. *Utilitarianism* (1861). In *The Collected Works of John Stuart Mill*, ed. J. M. Robinson, vol. 10, 203–259. London and Toronto: Routledge and University of Toronto Press.

Michael Kessler

MORALITY AND INEQUALITY

Often public discourse on class and racial inequality is reduced to discussions of the lack of morality among minorities and the poor. The disadvantaged social position of these frequently demonized groups is blamed on their immorality. This essay will challenge this tendency by presenting the argument—consistent with research findings of Michelle Lamont, Eduardo Bonilla-Silva and others—that political and racial contestation creates not one static morality but rather multiple and fluid moralities. The emphasis here is that minorities and the poor often are embedded in structural contexts that shape their moralities. Before examining how the process of moral development takes place in various contexts and institutions, the meaning of morality must first be considered.

DEFINITIONS OF MORALITY

For some, morality has a religious base and is therefore a static concept emphasizing the "moral community." In this view, political reform is "occasionally equivalent to moral reform in accord with God's law" (Williams 1995, p. 130). Others believe the definition of morality depends on the context in which individuals live. Lamont states that "vice is not defined in clear opposition to virtue when 'decent' and 'street' people live side-to-side and have to learn to accommodate each other" (Lamont 1999, p. 7). Some definitions of morality emphasize collective elements such as solidarity and generosity, while others focus on individualistic characteristics such as responsibility, hard work, self-reliance, and protection of the family. Researchers have found that whites tend to stress the latter and minorities the former (Lamont 1999; Richardson 1999). The difference likely contributes to the demonization of minorities and the poor in a public discourse shaped by the dominant ideology of whites. The evolution of mainstream explanations for racial inequalities reflects the impact of this dominant ideology.

OPPOSITIONAL CULTURE THEORY

When explaining educational inequality, consider the "culture of poverty" thesis that argued that the poor, and therefore minorities, had a flawed culture characterized by a propensity toward violence, lack of deferred gratification and general immorality. As Oscar Lewis pointed out in 1966, the relative educational failure of these groups was seen as inevitable because of their immoral culture, regardless of exposure to greater educational and occupational opportunity. This highly individualistic view of educational inequality was refined in the 1970s with the development of oppositional culture theory. As laid out by John U. Ogbu in 1978, this theory argues that involuntary minorities, or racial groups incorporated as a result of slavery, colonization, or conquest—such as blacks, Mexicans, Native Americans and Puerto Ricans—perceive limited occupational opportunity relative to whites. This promotes pessimism and resistance to school values: Schooling is associated with whiteness and is therefore viewed as inappropriate for these minorities. Oppositional culture theory assumes that high-achieving individuals are put-down, or sanctioned, by their minority peers when they achieve school success (Fordham and Ogbu 1986).

Despite the acknowledgment of structural causes of student resistance, Lundy has criticized oppositional culture theory for essentially reverting to the culture of poverty position by emphasizing improvements in school-related attitudes and behaviors of involuntary minorities rather than addressing the limited opportunities they face (Lundy 2003). In 2000 John McWhorter stripped the oppositional culture position of its structural foundation and focused on the immorality of blacks as the root cause of their educational failure. He argued that blacks adhere to cults of victimology, separatism, and anti-intellectualism. Therefore they are solely responsible for their plight. Such emphases on blacks' immorality as the cause of their educational failure ignores James Ainsworth-Darnell's and Douglas Downey's research showing that blacks actually have more positive school-related attitudes than do whites (1998). In fact, subsequent responses to oppositional culture theory—including those of Karolyn Tyson, William Darity Jr., and Domini R. Castellino in 2005 and Prudence L. Carter the same year—argue that blacks highly value education. Rather than explaining poor educational performance as an immoral cultural response, these researchers emphasize structural disadvantages and discrimination.

NEGATIVE MORAL JUDGMENTS VERSUS STRUCTURAL INEQUITY

This pattern of mainstream ideology pointing to the immorality of blacks and the poor as the main cause of inequality (with social researchers responding by emphasizing structural disadvantages and discrimination) is repeated in literatures discussing several institutions, including the judicial system and the family.

Specifically, high crime rates among the poor and minorities are often explained by their "poor work habits, inadequate skills, and a preference for joining predatory gangs to accepting low-wage jobs" (Wilson 1992, p. 92). Many researchers, including Rachel Gordon, Benjamin B. Lahey, and Eriko Kawai, simply conclude that poor minorities join gangs and commit crimes without consideration of the structural causes of such choices (2004). Likewise, Bill Bush and Max Neutze view drug use and addiction as morally sinful, without the discussion of the broader context in which drug use takes place (2000). Alternatively, Suhir Alladi Venketesh argued in 1997 that gang activity must be viewed in relation to the structural context and social organization of the larger community. He found that economic success often leads gangs to embrace the community in a moral way. That is, gangs provide informal social services in impoverished communities. This calls into question the moral judgments often made of poor and minority criminals.

Other research shows that the widespread emphasis on the immorality of minorities and the poor can have profound effects on the treatment and outcomes they face in the justice system. George S. Bridges and Sara Steen found in 1998 that parole officers were more likely to explain crimes committed by blacks as a result of intrinsic personal characteristics of the offender. Similar crimes committed by whites were explained away as young men caught up in the wrong situation. Similarly, Steen, Rodney L. Engen, and Randy R. Gainey found in 2005 that white drug offenders faced harsh treatment only when they closely resembled the stereotypical dangerous drug offender. In contrast, black offenders avoided harsh treatment only when they clearly did not resemble minority or poor stereotypes. Several other studies echo this pattern of blacks facing harsher punishments (Graham and Lowery 2004), lower likelihood that judges withhold the adjudication of guilt (Bontrager, Bales, and Chiricos 2005), greater likelihood of being drug tested (Gee et al. 2005), and a greater likelihood of being confined in a secure detention facility (Leiber and Fox 2005).

Negative moral judgments are also used to make sense of the high teen pregnancy rates and common single-parent family structure among minority populations and the poor. Patricia K. Jennings claimed in 2004 that the dominant imagery suggests that welfare dependency leads to out-of-wedlock births and that both are major characteristics of the "underclass" culture. According to this view, single mothers are seen as lacking the "appropriate" orientation toward work and mainstream family values. Contrary to this dominant ideology, Jennings found that having children seemed to spark a desire to participate in socially valued roles and encouraged responsibility. In short, young black mothers acknowledged the negative, welfare queen image and acted against being labeled as such. In Carolyn E. Cocca's view (2002), the conflation of nonmarital adolescent reproduction and poverty and the definition of this relationship as a moral affront to "traditional" American values furthers a conservative political agenda that limits broader discussion of social inequalities. In short, a focus on morality limits the scope of the debate and pushes structural considerations to the background, a point also discussed by Judith Stacey in 1996.

Overall, minorities and the poor are often vilified in the dominant public discourse and blamed for their own failures. The mainstream ideology compares them to the rest of society without consideration of their structural disadvantages and concludes that they have family lives and work habits that do not conform to mainstream morals, norms, and values. Many researchers turn to the moral development of these classes of people as the appropriate focus for policy reform. But this perspective addresses symptoms or a mirage rather than the true structural causes of racial and class inequality. Until policy makers and researchers stop focusing on the moral decay of the minority poor and start considering structural causes, such as poverty, residential segregation, and discrimination, discussion of class and racial inequality is destined to remain flawed and fruitless.

SEE ALSO *Benign Neglect; Culture of Poverty; Norms, Social; Values*

BIBLIOGRAPHY

Ainsworth-Darnell, James, and Douglas Downey. 1998. Assessing the Oppositional Culture Explanation for Racial/Ethnic Differences in School Performance. *American Sociological Review* 63 (4): 536–553.

Bonilla-Silva, Eduardo. 1997. Rethinking Racism: Toward a Structural Interpretation. *American Sociological Review* 62 (3): 465–480.

Bontrager, Stephanie, William Bales, and Ted Chiricos. 2005. Race, Ethnicity, Threat and the Labeling of Convicted Felons. *Criminology* 43 (3): 589–622.

Bridges, George S., and Sara Steen. 1998. Racial Disparities in Official Assessments of Juvenile Offenders: Attributional Stereotypes as Mediating Mechanisms. *American Sociological Review* 63 (4): 554–570.

Bush, Bill, and Max Neutze. 2000. In Search of What Is Right: The Moral Dimensions of the Drug Debate. *Australian Journal of Social Issues* 35: 129–144.

Carter, Prudence L. 2005. *Keepin' It Real: School Success beyond Black and White.* Oxford: Oxford University Press.

Cocca, Carolyn E. 2002. From "Welfare Queen" to "Exploited Teen": Welfare Dependency, Statutory Rape, and Moral Panic. *NWSA Journal* 14 (2): 56–79.

Fordham, Signithia, and John U. Ogbu. 1986. Black Students' School Success: Coping with the Burden of "Acting White." *Urban Review* 18: 176–206.

Gee, Gilbert C., Barbara Curbow, Margaret E. Ensminger et al. 2005. Are You Positive? The Relationship of Minority Composition to Workplace Drug and Alcohol Testing. *Journal of Drug Issues* 35 (4): 755–778.

Gordon, Rachel, Benjamin B. Lahey, Eriko Kawai et al. 2004. Antisocial Behavior and Youth Gang Membership: Selection and Socialization. *Criminology* 42 (1): 55–87.

Graham, Sandra, and Brian S. Lowery. 2004. Priming Unconscious Racial Stereotypes about Adolescent Offenders. *Law and Human Behavior* 28 (5): 483–504.

Jennings, Patricia K. 2004. What Mothers Want: Welfare Reform and Maternal Desire. *Journal of Sociology and Social Welfare* 31: 33, 113–130.

Lamont, Michele. 1999. Schudson, Wolfe, and Universal Morality. Paper presented at conference on "The Transformation of Civic Life." Middle Tennessee State University, Nov. 12–13, Murfreesboro and Nashville, TN.

Leiber, Michael J., and Kristan C. Fox. 2005. Race and the Impact of Detention on Juvenile Justice Decision Making. *Crime and Delinquency* 51 (4): 470–497.

Lewis, Oscar. 1966. *La Vida: A Puerto Rican Family in the Culture of Poverty.* San Juan, PR, and New York: Random House.

Lundy, Garvey F. 2003. The Myths of Oppositional Culture. *Journal of Black Studies* 33 (4): 450–467.

McWhorter, John H. 2000. *Losing the Race: Self-Sabotage in Black America.* New York: Perennial Publishing.

Ogbu, John U. 1978. *Minority Education and Caste: The American System in Cross-Cultural Perspective.* New York: Academic Press.

Richardson, Chad. 1999. *Batos, Bolillos, Pochos, and Pelados: Class and Culture on the South Texas Border.* Austin: University of Texas Press.

Stacey, Judith. 1996. *In the Name of the Family: Rethinking Family Values in the Postmodern Age.* Boston: Beacon Press.

Steen, Sara, Rodney L. Engen, and Randy R. Gainey. 2005. Images of Danger and Culpability: Racial Stereotyping, Case Processing, and Criminal Sentencing. *Criminology* 43 (2): 435–468.

Tyson, Karolyn, William Darity Jr., and Domini R. Castellino. 2005. It's Not a Black Thing: Understanding the Burden of Acting White and Other Dilemmas of High Achievement. *American Sociological Review* 70 (4): 582–605.

Venkatesh, Suhir Alladi. 1997. The Social Organization of the Street Gang Activity in an Urban Ghetto. *American Journal of Sociology* 103 (1): 82–111.

Williams, Rhys H. 1995. Constructing the Public Good: Social Movements and Cultural Resources. *Social Problems* 42 (1): 124–144.

Wilson, James Q. 1992. Crime, Race, and Values. *Society* 30 (1): 90–93.

James W. Ainsworth
Johanna Boers

MORBIDITY AND MORTALITY

Morbidity, meaning illness or frailty, is currently defined as a diagnosis with a specific disease listed in the International Classification of Diseases, Tenth Revision (ICD-10). The language of ICD-10 was adopted by the World Health Organization (WHO) so that disease and mortality data could be compared globally. Morbidity rates are measured as the number of cases of a disease divided by the midyear population times 100,000. Morbidity reporting of specific contagious diseases is an important aspect of public health. The WHO and the U.S. Centers for Disease Control and Prevention (CDC) require the reporting of infectious diseases (e.g., AIDS, bubonic plague, malaria) in order for localities to contain and manage these diseases. Morbidity may be further delineated by a measure of adaptive functioning, or the ability of a person to take care of personal needs or live independently.

Mortality, or death, is usually defined by cause of death. Similar to morbidity, the WHO recommends using the ICD-10 as the diagnostic nomenclature for cause of mortality. Internationally, vital statistics include death certificates with standardized information, such as date of birth, date of death, and cause of death.

Mortality is measured by the crude death rate (CDR), which is defined as the number of persons in a population who died in a specific year per one thousand members of the midyear population. The age-specific death rate (ASDR), which measures the number of persons in a specified age group (typically given in five-year intervals) within a population who died in a one-year period, is another useful rate, since persons of all ages do not die at the same rate. Sex-specific death rates and disease-specific death rates can also be calculated. Since those at the most advanced ages have greater risks of mortality, nations with younger populations tend to use crude death rates. International comparisons of the crude death rate must therefore take the age structure of the countries into consideration, converting each country's CDR into a standardized death rate by comparing both populations to the age structure of a standardized population.

Another method of measuring mortality is through the use of life tables. The Englishman John Graunt (1620–1674) began the scientific study of mortality by analyzing published lists of those who died in London and noting that mortality followed definite patterns. Some of his observations, such as the longevity of females over males, continue to be true today. He used these analyses to develop life tables, used today to determine life expectancies. Life tables begin with a population of 100,000 at age 0, and then subject the population to the mortality probabilities of each age group up until all the members of the population have died. Life tables are used to determine either life expectancy at birth or life expectancy at a specific age. Life expectancies have increased dramatically in the modern era. "In 2001 the average life expectancy at birth in the United States was 77 years. Japan had the world's highest expectancy—81 years. The lowest life expectancy estimates for the early 2000's were in HIV/AIDS-plagued countries in sub-Saharan Africa: 34 years for Mozambique and 37 years for Botswana and Lesotho" (McFalls 2003, p. 11).

HISTORICAL TRAJECTORY OF MORBIDITY AND MORTALITY

Historically, humans evolved around 200,000 years ago in Africa. Early humans were hunter-gatherers, and they lived as nomads with high fertility and high mortality. Estimates for most of human history give the life expectancy at birth at approximately ten to twelve years of age. Infant mortality (the number of infants who die prior to one year of age), stood at around 500 per 1,000 live births (Haub 1995). Multiple factors contributed to high mortality, including infanticide (infants were a liability for nomads); a scarcity of food; and the risks involved in

hunting large mammals with primitive weapons. By about 8,000 years ago, just prior to the development of horticulture or agriculture, the human population of the Earth was approximately 5 million. According to the evolutionary biologist Jared Diamond, by the time agricultural development began, nomadic humankind had migrated to all of the globe's continents.

Agriculture occurred independently in nine areas through the domestication of wild plants and animals: Southwest Asia, China, Mesoamerica, the Andes of South America, the Eastern United States, the Sahel zone of Africa, West Africa, Ethiopia, and New Guinea. Agricultural societies had decreased mortality and increased fertility because they increased their food availability. Humans could now remain in a stable location and store food, leading to a decrease in starvation. Agriculture was also less risky than hunting large mammals. In an agricultural society, children were valued as laborers, so there was greater fertility. However, this was matched with high mortality, and population growth was slow. Agriculture also allowed for the development of permanent settlements. Initially, the move to settlements, and later to cities, led to higher mortality because concentrations of humans allowed diseases to be spread more easily. Yet improved nutrition in agricultural societies led to increased life expectancies, so that by the time of the Roman Empire life expectancy had increased to around twenty-two years. By the Middle Ages it had grown to over thirty. In the first approximately 10,000 years of agriculture, the population of the world grew from 4 million to 629 million in 1750.

Infectious diseases were a primary cause of mortality in premodern times. Epidemics caused the mortality to ebb and flow, thus maintaining minimum population growth. Livi-Bacci (1992) noted that infectious diseases are continually evolving. Three forms of the plague—bubonic, septicemic, and pneumonic—became pandemic, causing millions of deaths. The bubonic form of the disease—the most common type and spread by fleas—has symptoms of high fever, swollen lymph glands, and cardiac failure, with a 67 to 75 percent mortality rate. The septicemic form also has symptoms of fever, chills, headache, and gastrointestinal issues with a 30 to 50 percent mortality rate. The pneumonic form, spread by coughing or sneezing, has symptoms of spitting blood and is usually lethal (Dohl 1979). "The epidemic may have begun about 542 A.D. in Western Asia, spreading from there. It is believed that half the Byzantine Empire was destroyed in the sixth century, a total of 100 million deaths" (Habu 2006). Perry and Fetherston (1997) described three pandemics. The first was the Justinian Plague, which occurred in cycles, about every decade, from 541 to 622 CE. It began in Ethiopia and spread through North Africa, Europe, and most of Asia, killing an estimated 50 to 60 percent of the population. The second pandemic, called the Black Death, began in Central Asia and spread along trade routes, in two- to five-year cycles, killing 10 to 40 percent of the population (mortality was increased by the co-occurrence of epidemics of other diseases such as smallpox, influenza, and syphilis). The third pandemic started in China in 1855 and spread through Africa, Australia, Europe, India, Japan, and North and South America. Although declining, this third pandemic continues. "WHO reported an average of 1,666 plague cases per year worldwide" (Perry and Fetherston 1997, p. 56).

Throughout the world, infectious diseases became endemic, with cycles of reoccurrence. Survivors became resistant, however, so that the severity of reoccurrence lessened in the next generation. This cycling continued until there was an eventual adaptation of the disease to a less virulent strain. Yet infectious diseases, which were benign in an area where the population had adapted to the pathogens, could devastate a virgin population. This was evident when diseases such as measles, smallpox, and influenza, which had transformed into less virulent strains in Europe, reached America and caused widespread mortality. From 1500 to 1800, the population of Native Americans in what is now the continental United States decreased from 5 million to 60,000. Similar declines occurred among the inhabitants of other lands explored by Europeans, including Tasmania, Australia, and Tierra del Fuego.

Although decreases in mortality occurred with modernity, there is a debate as to whether these were due to medical advances or public health measures. The argument for public health is that mortality declines began prior to the development of medical advances. There is agreement that the effects of modernity led to rapid decreases in mortality in the eighteenth century. By the 1800s, life expectancy in the United States was about forty years. Food supplies increased with advances in technology. But diseases such as malaria, dysentery, smallpox, and typhoid fever could spread rapidly, especially in closely confined settlements, and effectively kill off a local population. In Europe, Louis Villermé (1782–1863) proved that crowding and unsanitary conditions led to the spreading of diseases. In the eighteenth century, medical advances, such as inoculations against smallpox, combined with widespread public health vaccinations and inoculations, led to the management and containment of lethal diseases. Public health measures, such as safe water supplies and sewage systems to dispose of waste products, controlled disease and immediately improved infant survival rates. Other public health measures designed to confine and contain the spread of diseases aided in controlling pandemics that followed trade and immigrants routes. Life expectancies continued to improve: In the United

States, the life expectancy increased from 47 in 1900 to 77 in 2001 (McFalls 2003).

"Doubling time," the number of years it will take a population to double its size, is used to describe population growth. In 1,000 CE, the population was 311 million and the doubling time was 1,000 years (Weeks 2005). In modernity, the population grew rapidly with doubling times decreasing. Joseph McFalls summarizes the historical population growth in increments of billions. Globally, the human population was under one billion from the Stone Age, one million years ago, until 1800. Two billion was reached in 1930, three billion in 1960, four billion in 1975, five billion in 1987, and six billion in 1999. A population of seven billion is projected for 2015.

KEY DETERMINANTS OF MORBIDITY AND MORTALITY

Morbidity and mortality are caused by a combination of factors, including disease, senescence (the physical deterioration that leads to increased vulnerability and susceptibility to diseases), and socioeconomic and political conditions. Mortality by infectious and parasitic diseases was the primary cause of mortality and morbidity in premodern societies. In modernity, the leading causes of mortality and morbidity are chronic and degenerative diseases such as cancer, cardiovascular disease, and diabetes. However, infectious diseases such as pneumonia, influenza, and HIV/AIDS, along with homicide, suicide, and accidental death, all rank high on the list of leading causes of death. The leading causes of mortality in the United States, Mexico, and Canada in 2001 were cardiovascular disease and cancer; but accidents, pneumonia, and influenza ranked in the top ten causes of mortality (Weeks 2005).

Morbidity and mortality are affected by biological, social, and socioeconomic conditions. In their 2005 article "Adult Mortality," Richard Rogers and colleagues break these causes down into three categories: demographic characteristics (age, sex, and race and ethnicity); distal causes (socioeconomic status, social relationships, geographic factors, and environmental or human hazards); and proximate factors (health behaviors such as smoking and drinking, health condition, and physiological influences such as height and genetic markers).

Age is perhaps the factor most closely associated with mortality: The youngest and the oldest are the most likely to die. In 2005, Japan had the lowest infant mortality rate (IMR), 3 per 1,000, and Afghanistan had the highest, 154 per 1,000 (Weeks 2005). Infant mortality is also influenced by race and ethnicity: The higher socioeconomic segments of society have lower IMRs. The exception, known as the "Hispanic Paradox," is that Hispanics in the United States, who have a generally lower socioeconomic status, have IMRs similar to non-Hispanic whites and Asians, revealing that family social support and lifestyles issues influence IMR. Humans are more likely to die as they age due to senescence. In 1825, Benjamin Gompertz presented a mathematical formula demonstrating the relationship between aging and death.

Gender has an effect on mortality, with females generally living longer than males. James Carey notes in his book *Longevity* (2003) that although females hold the longevity records across species, female mortality advantages are contextual. Females face greater risks during reproduction, especially in premodern societies. Females at the oldest ages also experience greater morbidity from chronic and degenerative diseases. With modernity, the gender gap in mortality is decreasing. In the United States, the greatest difference in death rates between sexes is for males aged fifteen to twenty-four, who are three times more likely to die than females of the same age. This increased mortality is due to accidents from risky behaviors, suicides, and homicides.

Socioeconomic status affects mortality in numerous ways. Minorities with lower socioeconomic status generally have higher mortality, and education level is inversely related to mortality. Infant mortality is greatly influenced by basic education about hygiene, eating a nutritious diet, and drinking unpolluted water. A higher level of educational attainment is generally indicative of higher socioeconomic functioning, and those with higher education attain higher income, have access to better housing, and have healthier lifestyles. Combining the effects of education and minority status, in the United States, black males with low educational attainment have a 19.9-year lower life expectancy than more educated whites (Seeman and Crimmins 2001).

Lifestyle choices, including physical fitness, exercise, limiting alcohol use, and maintaining a balanced diet, are related to lower morbidity and mortality. A pioneer longitudinal study begun in 1965 identified seven health habits, commonly called the "Alameda 7" that can improve morbidity and decrease mortality due to chronic diseases. The identified habits are: "engaging in regular physical activity, never smoking, drinking less than five drinks at one sitting, sleeping 7 to 8 hours a night, maintaining desirable body mass, avoiding snacks, and eating breakfast regularly" (Rogers et al. 2005, p. 271).

Sociopolitical causes of mortality include war, terrorism, and starvation. According to James Riley, the author of *Rising Life Expectancy* (2001), the leading causes of mortality in the twentieth century were war, famine, and disease. World War I led to an estimated 19 million deaths; the influenza epidemic of 1918–1919 caused over 40 million deaths; World War II caused about 52 million deaths; China's Great Leap Forward in 1959–1961, which

resulted in a politically caused famine, led to between 14 million and 26 million deaths, and UNAIDS reported in 2006 that the AIDS epidemic had caused 25 million deaths since 1981.

MORTALITY THEORIES

Malthusian theory represents one of the initial explanations of mortality and population growth. In 1798, Thomas Robert Malthus suggested that because population increased geometrically while the food supply could only increase arithmetically, population would be stabilized by positive checks, such as war, disease, and starvation, and preventive checks, such as controlling births (with the preferred method being moral restraint or abstinence, rather than contraception and abortion). Karl Marx and Freiderich Engels challenged this theory. While they agreed that the population was growing, they asserted that population growth was good, and that science could increase food supplies to such an extent that, at least in a socialistic society, poverty and starvation could be eliminated.

Changing conditions of modernity have also challenged Malthusian theory. While rapid global population growth has occurred, the stable food supply has increased along with the population base. The current Malthusian position, as presented by Paul and Anne Ehrlich in *The Population Explosion* (1990), is neo-Malthusian, for it accepts the use of abortion and birth control to control population size, contrary to Malthus. Neo-Malthusians argue that continued population growth will be catastrophic. They argue that the dramatic increases in food production that occurred in the past, through the use of chemicals and new technologies, cannot continue. The earth's resources are finite, nonrenewable, and being depleted by continuing population growth, placing mankind at risk of annihilation.

Demographic transition theory explains the mortality changes that have occurred with modernity. In a premodern society there is high infant mortality and a short life expectancy with high mortality. Modernity drastically improved life expectancy through changes in public health practices, the most important being the availability of fresh sanitary water, sewerage systems, adequate diets, and modern medicine. Prior to the development of modern medicine, public health practices also managed the spread of contagious diseases through containment and isolation. The most dramatic improvements in mortality rates were made initially through decreasing infant mortality. In the transition phase, the sharp drop in mortality rates precipitated an immediate rapid increase in the population, as those who would previously have died in infancy survived and lived an extended life span (Weeks 2005).

The epidemiological transition theory, hypothesized by Abdel Omran in 1971, suggests there were three stages of epidemiological modernization. The first stage was the Age of Pestilence and Famine, which lasted from premodern times until around 1875 in developed societies. The primary causes of mortality in this stage were influenza, pneumonia, smallpox, tuberculosis, and other related diseases, resulting in high infant and childhood mortality and a life expectancy averaging between twenty and forty years. The second stage was the Age of Receding Pandemics, which lasted from around 1875 to 1930 in developed countries. In this second stage there was a decline in mortality due to improved standards of living, sanitation, and public health. The third, current, stage is the Age of Chronic and Degenerative Illnesses. In this stage the causes of mortality are the chronic degenerative diseases (heart disease, cancer, and stroke), and life expectancy at birth exceeds seventy years.

S. Jay Olshansky and A. Brian Ault (1986) have proposed a fourth stage—the Stage of Delayed Degenerative Diseases. In this stage, diseases are influenced by individual behavior or lifestyle choices, and deaths are due to social pathologies such as accidents, alcoholism, suicide, and homicide, as well as lifestyle issues such as smoking and diet. Jean-Marie Robine (2001) suggests a fifth stage, called the Age of the Conquest of the Extent of Life, as it is now possible for humans to live between 110 and 120 years. James Vaupel notes that after about the age of 95, mortality decelerates and actually plateaus. This would support a compression of mortality, with those surviving to be the "oldest old" having either lesser or later onset of chronic and degenerative diseases.

Another theoretical explanation for mortality is the "rectangularization of the mortality curve" that occurred with modern health practices. In 1825 Benjamin Gompertz developed a mathematical formula, which he called a "law of mortality," depicting mortality rates as a sloped graph, with rates of mortality increasing with age. He argued that there is a biological limit to the human life span, with a life expectancy of around age eighty-five or ninety due to senescence. So even if there are medical advances in curing cancer or treating heart disease, those who survive one specific disease will be frail, raising the risk of morbidity through other disease processes. Although there have been dramatic increases in life expectancy during demographic transitions, the greatest strides were in mortality in infancy, childhood, and early adult life. Olshansky and colleagues (2001) argue that the only way to have another similar increase in life expectancy would be to increase the life span of those over age seventy, which will be more difficult than the earlier reduction of infant mortality.

THE HUMAN LIFE SPAN

Longevity experts question the existence of a definite human life span. The longest known life span is 122 years and 5 months, based on the life span of a single human, Jeanne Calment, who died in 1997. This record could be broken by one person who lives to 122 years and 6 months. Vaupel notes that prior to the nineteenth century only a few scattered individuals survived past 100. There were countries where over one million people live but that had no documented centurions or supercenturions (aged 110 and over). However, at the beginning of the twentieth century, there were over 100,000 documented centurions. Beginning with the first documented supercenturion, Katherine Plunket, who died at age 111 in 1932 in Northern Ireland, experts began to verify the age validity of supercenturions, which requires collaborative documentation (see Vaupel 2001; Vaupel et al. 1998).

Dennis Ahlburg and James Vaupel (1990) argue that current projections for life expectancy are based on conservative forecasting. They argue that mortality rates have declined at a rate of 1 percent to 2 percent per year in developed countries, especially the mortality rates of those age 65 and over. They assume that if this mortality decrease continues at a 2 percent progression, in 2080 the expected life expectancy would be 100 years for females and 96 for males.

If life expectancy was approaching a biological limit, one would assume that the mortality rates of the oldest old would tend to be higher in countries with higher rates of the oldest old. However, Vaupel has found that countries with the oldest old, such as France, Japan, and Sweden, show a slowing of the mortality rates in the oldest old. Vaupel, the director of the Max Planck Institute for Demographic Research, argues that life expectancy has been rising at a linear pace over the last 160 years at a rate of almost three months per year. Shiro Horiuchi and John Wilmoth reported in 1998 that mortality in the elderly goes through three stages: a deceleration of mortality after age 80, a mortality plateau between ages 80 to 105, and an actual decline in mortality in the highest ages (over 110). Manton and colleagues argued in 1991 that even with the interdependence of diseases, as we progress in treating specific diseases we are altering senescence.

SEE ALSO *AIDS; Death and Dying; Demographic Transition; Demography; Disease; Population Studies; Psychosomatics, Social; Public Health; Sanitation; Suicide*

BIBLIOGRAPHY

Ahlburg, Dennis, and James W. Vaupel. 1990. Alternative Projections of the U.S. Population. *Demography* 27 (4): 639–652.

Campion, H. 1949. International Statistics. *Journal of the Royal Statistical Society, Series A* 112 (2): 105–143.

Carey, James R. 2003. *Longevity: The Biology and Demography of Life Span.* Princeton, NJ: Princeton University Press.

Diamond, Jared. 1997. *Guns, Germs and Steel: The Fates of Human Societies.* New York: Norton.

Dols, Michael W. 1974. Plague in Early Islamic History. *Journal of the American Oriental Society* 94 (3): 371–383.

Ehrlich, Paul R., and Anne H. Ehrlich. 1990. *The Population Explosion.* New York: Simon and Schuster.

Haub, Carl. 1995. *How Many People Have Ever Lived on Earth?* Washington, DC: Population Reference Bureau. http://www.prb.org.

Hetzel, A. M. 1997. *History and Organization of the Vital Statistics System.* Hyattsville, MD: National Center for Health Statistics.

Horiuchi, Shiro, and John R. Wilmoth. 1998. Deceleration in the Age Pattern of Mortality at Older Ages. *Demography* 35 (4): 391–412.

Livi-Bacci, Massimo. 1992. *A Concise History of World Population.* Trans. Carl Ispen. Cambridge, MA: Blackwell.

Manton, Kenneth G. 1982. Changing Concepts of Morbidity and Mortality in the Elderly Population. *Milbank Memorial Fund Quarterly, Health and Society* 60 (2): 183–244.

Manton, Kenneth G., Michael J. Wrigley, Harvey J. Cohen, et al. 1991. Cancer Mortality, Aging, and Patterns of Comorbidity in the United States: 1968–1986. *Journal of Gerontology* 46, no. 4 (July 1991): S225.

McFalls, Joseph. 2003. *Population: A Lively Introduction.* 4th ed. Washington, DC: Population Reference Bureau. http://www.prb.org/pdf/populationlivelyintro.

Olshansky, S. Jay, and A. Brian Ault. 1986. The Fourth Stage of the Epidemiologic Transition: The Age of Delayed Degenerative Diseases. *Milbank Quarterly* 64 (3): 355–391.

Olshansky, S. Jay, B. A. Carnes, and A. Desesquelles. 2001. Demography: Prospects for Human Longevity. *Science* 291(5508): 1491–1492.

Omran, Abdel R. 1971. The Epidemiologic Transition. *Milbank Quarterly* 49: 509–538.

Perry, Robert D., and J. D. Fetherston. 1997. Yersinia Pestis–Etiologic Agent of Plague. *Clinical Microbiology Review* 10: 35–66.

Poston, Dudley L., Jr., Mary Ann Davis, and Chris Lewinski. 2006. Mortality. In *The Cambridge Dictionary of Sociology,* ed. Bryan Turner, 403–405. Cambridge, U.K.: Cambridge University Press.

Riley, J. C. 2001. *Rising Life Expectancy: A Global History.* Cambridge, U.K.: Cambridge University Press.

Robine, Jean-Marie. 2001. Redefining the Stages of the Epidemiological Transition by a Study of the Dispersion of Life Spans: The Case of France. *Population: An English Selection* 13 (1): 173–193.

Rogers, Richard G., and Robert Hackenberg. 1987. Extending Epidemiologic Transition Theory: A New Stage. *Social Biology* 34 (3–4): 234–243.

Rogers, Richard G., Robert A. Hummer, and Patrick M. Krueger. 2005. Adult Mortality. In *Handbook of Population,* ed. Dudley L. Poston Jr. and Mike Micklin. New York: Springer.

Rogers, Richard G., Robert A. Hummer, and Charles B. Nam. 2000. *Living and Dying in the USA: Behavioral, Health, and Social Differentials of Adult Mortality.* San Diego, CA: Academic Press.

Seeman, Teresa E., and Eileen Crimmins. 2001. Social Environmental Effects on Health and Aging: Integrating Epidemiological and Demographic Approaches and Perspectives. *Annals of the New York Academy of Sciences* 954: 88–117.

United Nations Programme on HIV/AIDS. 2006. UNAIDS/WHO AIDS Epidemic Update: December 2006. http://www.unaids.org/en/HIV_data/epi2006/default.asp.

U.S. Census Bureau. *Historical Estimates of World Population 2006.* http://www.census.gov/ipc/www/worldhis.html.

Vaupel, James. 1997. The Remarkable Improvements in Survival at Older Ages. *Philosophical Transactions: Biological Sciences* 352 (1363): 1799–1804.

Vaupel, James. 2001. Demographic Insights into Longevity. *Population: An English Selection* 13: (1) 245–259.

Weeks, J. R. 2005. *Population: An Introduction to Concepts and Issues.* 9th ed. Belmont, CA: Thompson Wadsworth.

World Health Organization. 2006. International Statistical Classification of Diseases and Related Health Problems. 10th Revision, Geneva: WHO. http://www.who.int/classifications/apps/icd/icd10online/.

Mary Ann Davis

MORENO/A

Racial classifications in Latin American and Caribbean countries are complex and inevitably reflect relations to skin color, or colorism, which were established and are maintained as a result of structured racial hierarchies. Throughout the Americas there are variations in racial terminology and a certain amount of fluidity in the identification of racial categories. The variations in racial identifiers in these societies are a product of colonialism and the relations among persons of white European, African, and indigenous ancestries. One commonly used racial term in Latin American and Caribbean societies is moreno/a.

Moreno, and morena, the grammatical feminine form of the term, is frequently used in colloquial speech throughout Latin America and the Caribbean. The term denotes skin color and literally means brown or brunette. Moreno/a's connotation to skin color unavoidably designates placement in recognized racial hierarchies within societies that were established as a result of colonization by white Europeans. The term's bond to African ancestry, and its close association to the term *negro*, or black, also points to this relationship. The term has a historical connection to whiteness and white supremacy in societies throughout the Americas, which reflects its use by some people as a racial identifier. Some people, for instance, use moreno/a as a form of whitening if they are "on the dark end of the racial continuum" (Telles 2004, p. 98). Edward Telles notes in *Race in Another America* that in Brazil, "The ambiguity with the term moreno allows persons who might not have the option of calling themselves white to escape the more stigmatized nonwhite categories" (2004, p. 98).

Moreno/a is used to indicate connections to whiteness and blackness, as well as relations to indigenous ancestry. The term is used in several ways to denote nonwhite racial categories throughout Latin America and the Caribbean. For instance, moreno/a often denotes brown-skinned or black-skinned individuals as well as dark-haired individuals (Twine 1998; Stephens 1999). Several studies indicate that differences in the use of the term occur according to locality (Stephens 1999). Historically, the term referred to a subcaste of free blacks, for example, in Puerto Rico (Kinsbruner 1996). In addition, moreno/a has been used in recognizing persons of mixed ancestry. This is reflected in the use of the term in identifying people of mestizo origin in Mexico (Stephens 1999). Moreno/a has also identified the progeny of mulatto and white European or white Spanish individuals (Stephens 1999). In addition, the term's racial ambiguity is further evidenced by its use for identifying white individuals. Moreno/a is used in Brazil in identifying sunburned Europeans. Likewise, white individuals use the term for referencing brunettes of predominate European and/or indigenous descent (Twine 1998). The term is also often coupled with adjectives that identify hair texture (Stephens 1999). This is the case in the use of *morena alisada*, which translates into "smooth brunette" and is used in identifying women who use straightening agents in their hair (Stephens 1999).

There remains particular ambiguity in the use of the term as a racial identifier because people use the term fluidly, and identification often depends on individual observers (Telles 1995). Overall, the term's racial evasiveness reflects racial consciousness and issues of racial hierarchy influenced by colonialism and white supremacy. People may make distinctions in their use of moreno/a by using a light-to-dark continuum. For example, within the racial continuum are light or fair, medium, and dark qualifiers used with the term in referencing varying degrees of pigmentation. This is the case with *morena/o clara/o* for light brown, *morena/o oscura/o* for dark brown, or *morena/o escura/o* for dark brown, which is used in Brazil.

Furthermore, augmentative and diminutive forms of the term are frequently used in everyday discourse. The augmentative form is *morenote*, meaning "big, dark one." The common use of the diminutive suffixes *-ito* or *-ita* may also be used for affective purposes. The terms *morenito* and *morenita* refer to people as "little" or "small, dark one." The all-encompassing use of the term is also reflected in its use as a euphemism. Since the term Negro, in reference to black, is recognized as demeaning in some Latin American countries, moreno/a offers individuals what would be considered a polite substitution for dark-skinned or black as a racial identifier (Kany 1960; Telles 2004). Moreover, the historic use of *moreno/a esclavo/a* for black slave and *moreno/a libre* for free black or mulatto (Stephens 1999) reference the subjugation of enslaved blacks by whites in the Americas. This historic association to the enslavement of blacks by whites may, in some instances, facilitate the use of the term as a pejorative.

The use of racially stigmatized terms may challenge established racial ideologies and assist in the efforts toward reclaiming blackness, or negritude, in the Americas. For instance, this is illustrated by the actions of black social movements in Brazil that have sought to reclaim the long-stigmatized term *negro* (Telles 2004). As a result, in some cases the use of moreno/a may challenge the established history of white supremacy in societies throughout the Americas because it embraces diverse ancestries. However, moreno/a may also prove symbolic of the traditional views of racial democracy, which fail to defy established racial ideologies and colorism in Latin America and the Caribbean (Telles 2004).

Moreno/a demonstrates the complexity of racial identification and categorization in Latin American and Caribbean societies. Its many uses provide evidence of the association between racial categorization and skin color, or colorism, within these societies. Likewise, the permanence and evasiveness in racial terminology, whether state sanctioned or informal, reflects an established legacy of colonialism throughout these societies.

SEE ALSO *Blackness; Colorism; Hierarchy; Identification, Racial; Latinos; Mulattos; Negro; Pardo; Race; Racial Classification; Stratification; Whiteness*

BIBLIOGRAPHY

Kany, Charles E. 1960. *American-Spanish Euphemisms.* Berkeley and Los Angeles: University of California Press.

Kinsbruner, Jay. 1996. *Not of Pure Blood: The Free People of Color and Racial Prejudice in Nineteenth-Century Puerto Rico.* Durham, NC: Duke University Press.

Stephens, Thomas M. 1999. *Dictionary of Latin American Racial and Ethnic Terminology,* 2nd ed. Gainesville: University Press of Florida.

Telles, Edward E. 2001. Racial Ambiguity among the Brazilian Population. *California Center for Population Research On-line*

Working Paper Series, 1-46.
http://www.ccpr.ucla.edu/ccprwpseries/ccpr_012_01.pdf.

Telles, Edward E. 2004. *Race in Another America: The Significance of Skin Color in Brazil.* Princeton, NJ: Princeton University Press.

Twine, France W. 1998. *Racism in a Racial Democracy: The Maintenance of White Supremacy in Brazil.* New Brunswick, NJ: Rutgers University Press.

Aurelia Lorena Murga

MORGAN, LEWIS H.
SEE *Communism, Primitive.*

MORGENTHAU, HANS
1904–1980

Born in Coburg, Germany, in 1904, Hans Joachim Morgenthau became the greatest contributor to the theory of realism in the field of international relations. Until his death in New York in 1980, Morgenthau actively influenced generations of scholars and policymakers, and his writings continue to do so today. Morgenthau's writings reflect his antipathy toward liberalism and idealism, arguing that the influence of international law, norms, and organizations were minimal at best. Along with E. H. Carr (1892–1982) and George F. Kennan (1904–2005), Morgenthau is known as a founder of the field of international relations.

Before immigrating to the United States, Morgenthau studied law and diplomacy at the universities of Frankfurt and Munich and taught public law at the University of Geneva. In 1937 he fled to the United States due to his Jewish identity and the growing Nazi power in Germany. Morgenthau taught at several universities for short periods before ending up at the University of Chicago, where he taught political science from 1943 to 1971. After his retirement, he taught at City College of New York and the New School for Social Research. In addition to teaching and writing, Morgenthau worked as an adviser and consultant to the U.S. departments of State and Defense in the 1940s and 1960s.

Morgenthau's first book, *Scientific Man versus Power Politics*, published in 1946, outlined his belief that human nature is truly selfish and humans have a natural longing to dominate each other through power. By applying his realist philosophy of human nature to politics, Morgenthau argued that all politics was merely a struggle for power. His most seminal work, *Politics among Nations:*

The Struggle for Power and Peace, published in 1948, provided an empirical basis for the theory of realism, the most influential theory in international relations. The theory of realism argues that power is the primary interest of all states in the international community and therefore, policies and actions taken by governments are merely means to achieve or maintain power relative to other states.

Politics among Nations argued that all states in the international community would pursue foreign policies that sought to maintain or achieve relative levels of power and that international politics was therefore about the competition of states to seek power. A major contribution to realist theory was the idea of balance of power, in which Morgenthau claimed that the most powerful states would attempt to balance each other by pursuing certain foreign policies to either gain more relative power or suppress the relative power of another state. Unlike political scientist Kenneth Waltz, who later argued that bipolarity was the most stable type of power balance, Morgenthau was skeptical that the balance of power between the United States and the Soviet Union was stable. Rather, Morgenthau argued that there should be a larger number of great powers in order to achieve stability in the international system. In addition to *Politics among Nations*, Morgenthau published many other books and hundreds of articles about power politics, diplomacy, U.S. foreign policy, cold war politics, and U.S. relations with the Soviet Union.

SEE ALSO *Cold War; Diplomacy; Realism; Realism, Political; Waltz, Kenneth*

BIBLIOGRAPHY

Bucklin, Steven. 2001. *Realism and American Foreign Policy: Wilsonians and Kennan-Morgenthau Thesis.* Westport, CT: Praeger.

Griffiths, Martin. 1999. *Fifty Key Thinkers in International Relations.* London: Routledge.

Morgenthau, Hans. 1985. *Politics among Nations: The Struggle for Power and Peace.* 6th ed. New York: Knopf.

Russell, Greg. 1990. *Hans J. Morgenthau and the Ethics of American Statecraft.* Baton Rouge: Louisiana State University Press.

Thompson, Kenneth, and Robert J. Myers, eds. 1977. *A Tribute to Hans Morgenthau (Truth and Tragedy): With an Intellectual Autobiography by Hans J. Morgenthau.* Washington, DC: New Republic.

Krista E. Wiegand

MORTALITY
SEE *Morbidity and Mortality.*

MORTALITY SALIENCE

SEE *Salience, Mortality.*

MOSES, ROBERT
1888–1981

Robert Moses is known as the "master builder" of New York. After receiving his BA from Yale, MA from Oxford, and PhD from Columbia, Moses officially began an extraordinary career in public service in 1924. His career ended in 1968 after he had served under seven governors and five mayors. He held several city and state offices, often simultaneously, including commissioner of the New York City Department of Parks and coordinator of construction, as well as chairman of the New York State Power Authority and chairman of the State Council of Parks. His close friend and mentor was the legendary Al Smith, Democrat and four-term governor of New York. Moses never held elected office, although in 1934 he ran unsuccessfully as a Republican for governor.

Moses's public projects in New York City include seven major bridges, 658 playgrounds, seventeen public swimming pools, 416 miles of highway, and over two million acres of parkland and other works throughout the state. He was also an important force in the construction of 1,082 public-housing buildings. The cost of only those projects for which he was directly responsible, from conception to completion, was roughly equivalent to what NASA spent in the 1960s to land a man on the moon. Moses mastered the art of using federal funds and was a pioneer in the development of the "public authority," in particular the Triborough Bridge and Tunnel Authority, the financial base of his planning empire.

Author of 102 articles in national and regional publications, Moses published little of a theoretical nature. Yet there are parallels between his planning philosophy and that of Le Corbusier, the hypermodernist urban designer (although there is no entry for Le Corbusier in either Robert Caro's 1974 *The Power Broker* or Hilary Ballon and Kenneth T. Jackson's 2007 *Robert Moses and the Modern City*). Both viewed averages and aggregates as starting points for understanding cities. Both discounted the role of face-to-face, street-level interactions and the complex social orders that spontaneously emerge from them that for urbanist Jane Jacobs, Moses's great nemesis, are the life of a city. And both promoted "efficient" cities and massive urban reconstruction, especially for the automobile, at the expense of traditional neighborhoods. Unlike Le Corbusier, however, Moses acquired the political clout to "get things done."

Both supporters and detractors describe him as visionary, brilliant, tireless, driven, and ruthless. Thanks largely to Caro's 1974 book, the latter have tended to outnumber the former, although over time the pendulum will swing surely in both directions.

Many believe that Jacobs is chiefly responsible for Moses's decline from power, but other factors are also important. First, Moses was approaching his eighties when his defeats began to accumulate in the 1960s. Second, this was also when New York City began facing chronic economic and financial problems that for long afterward soured public opinion against expensive large-scale public projects. Third, the status of Le Corbusier–style modernism was waning among influential intellectuals. His decline coincided with, and probably helped hasten, the rise of so-called "participatory planning," in which formal public hearings are an essential part of the planning process.

Thus, not only at his height but also in the wake of his fall, Moses exerted a deep and lasting influence on urban planning.

SEE ALSO *Architecture; Cities; Jacobs, Jane; Metropolis; Modernism; Planning; Public Goods; Regions, Metropolitan*

BIBLIOGRAPHY

Ballon, Hilary, and Kenneth T. Jackson, eds. 2007. *Robert Moses and the Modern City: The Transformation of New York.* New York: Norton.

Caro, Robert. 1974. *The Power Broker: Robert Moses and the Fall of New York.* New York: Knopf.

Sanford Ikeda

MOSSADEGH, MOHAMMAD
1882–1967

Born in Tehran in 1882 into a prominent family of notables, Mossadegh was educated in Tehran, France, and Switzerland, where he gained a doctorate in law. Returning to Iran in 1914, he taught at the School of Political Science, wrote on significant legal, financial and political issues, and engaged in party political activity. He opposed the abortive Anglo-Iranian Agreement of 1919, aimed at formalizing British tutelage over Iran. Assuming various high-ranking, including ministerial, positions, he gained prominence as a nationalist and constitutionalist member of the 5th and 6th Parliaments (1924–1928). His opposition to the autocracy of Reza Khan (later Shah)

Pahlavi resulted in his exclusion from political life and virtual house arrest from 1936 onward.

Following the Anglo-Soviet occupation of Iran in 1941 and Reza Shah's abdication, Mossadegh returned to the political scene to represent Tehran twice in the Parliament, receiving the highest number of votes cast in the capital. He advocated a neutralist foreign policy, and in the wake of aggressive Soviet demands for an oil concession, sponsored a bill banning the granting of concessions to foreigners. He also advocated reform of the electoral laws. The National Front, formed in October 1949 and led by Mossadegh, advocated free and fair elections, freedom of the press, and an end to martial law. It also challenged Britain's entrenched position in Iran, which rested on its control over Iranian oil. The failure of negotiations to revise the British oil concession eventually resulted in the nationalization of the Anglo-Iranian Oil Company. The oil issue became the rallying cry for a popular movement that linked national self-determination—as symbolized by the nationalization of oil—with popular sovereignty. The leadership of Mossadegh in this process led to his premiership in late April 1951.

Determined to subvert the government of Mossadegh, the British imposed an embargo on the sale of Iranian oil and resorted to extensive covert activities. The shah also quietly sought to undermine him, refusing to embrace the role of a constitutional monarch as demanded by Mossadegh. The machinations of pro-British and royalist elements and the shah's attitude resulted in Mossadegh's resignation in July 1952, but a popular uprising returned him to power a few days later. Mossadegh's difficulties persisted, however; the Tudeh (Communist) Party continued to harass his government, while enabling its opponents to invoke a communist threat. The army and security forces would not readily accept prime-ministerial control, and some of Mossadegh's less committed supporters joined his active opponents. Despite Iranian willingness to pay equitable compensation, the British and the Americans refused to accept the nationalization of the oil industry in Iran. From early 1953, the Anglo-American secret services, aided by Mossadegh's domestic opponents, intensified their efforts to engineer his downfall, eventually succeeding through a coup d'etat in August 1953.

Following the coup, which established royal autocracy, committed Iran to the West, and revoked the substance of oil nationalization, Mossadegh was tried by a military tribunal, accused of having violated the constitution, and condemned to three years of imprisonment. Subsequently, he was confined to his country home away from the capital until his death in 1967. He did not abandon his opposition to autocracy or efforts to galvanize his supporters, whose endeavors were thwarted by the royalist

government. A secular democrat and a civic nationalist, dedicated to promoting representative democracy and national sovereignty, Mossadegh enacted many reforms, did not lose faith in democratic values, was averse to violence, and relied on international law to further Iran's case against British imperialism. He also maintained an enduring reputation as a man of conviction and integrity.

SEE ALSO *Anticolonial Movements; Central Intelligence Agency, U.S.; Coup d'Etat; Nationalization; Neutral States; Petroleum Industry; Sovereignty*

BIBLIOGRAPHY

Azimi, Fakhreddin. 1989. *Iran: The Crisis of Democracy, 1941–1953.* London and New York: St. Martin's Press.

Gasiorowski, Mark J., and Malcolm Byrne, eds. 2004. *Mohammad Mosaddeq and the Coup of 1953 in Iran.* Syracuse, NY: Syracuse University Press.

Fakhreddin Azimi

MOTHERHOOD

The term *motherhood*, which began to be used at the end of the nineteenth century, refers to the state or condition of being a mother. Motherhood is usually distinguished from the term *mothering* in that mothering is the set of activities or practices concerned with nurturing and caring for children. While mothering entails a focus on the everyday practices associated with being a mother and looking after children, motherhood is a social institution and is thus characterized by specific meanings and ideologies. The two terms are, however, inextricably linked in that the practices of mothering in any society are performed and experienced in the context of the meanings and ideologies of motherhood.

The difference between mothering and motherhood has consequences for understandings of both mothering and motherhood. For example, the focus on mothering as performance of the tasks essential to child rearing meant that those who studied child development in the 1970s and 1980s extended the term *mothering* to include child rearing done by men who nurture children. This usage of mothering has diminished as the importance of fathering and the need to understand better what fathers do with children gained increased emphasis beginning in the 1990s. In contrast, motherhood is associated only with women since the state of motherhood has a direct impact on women's lives, regardless of whether or not they become mothers. In most societies a central feature of motherhood is that it should ideally occur within a heterosexual relationship where a man and a woman are cohabiting (and preferably legally married). The rearing of children is supposed to be the major task of this unit, which is idealized as bound together through mutual ties of affection, common identity, and relationships of care and support. This model is often assumed to be the natural and normal (as well as ideal) form of social organization and to be stable over time.

A focus on motherhood arose from feminist work on gender relations as a key aspect of recognition that motherhood is central to women's lives—whether or not they become mothers. For example, in 1975 the sociologist Jesse Bernard suggested (in *The Future of Motherhood*) that there is a tension between the idealized image of the selfless mother and many mothers' experiences of hard, repetitive work that is socially devalued and unfulfilling. In the 1970s Bernard and other feminists in Europe and North America, such as Adrienne Rich, argued that the institution of motherhood was oppressive in making most women feel that they should become mothers and stay at home in segregated gender roles rather than, for example, pursuing employment and careers. At the same time researchers such as the sociologist Ann Oakley pointed out (in *Becoming a Mother*) that the idealized image of motherhood is unattainable and causes women to feel guilt, unhappiness, and anxiety about their failure to measure up to the ideal in their everyday practices.

MOTHERHOOD IS CHANGING

While it is often assumed that motherhood is historically stable, it has changed a great deal. For example, Linda Nicholson, a historian of ideas, suggests that it was only in the economic boom of the 1950s that it became possible for working-class women in Western countries to stay at home with their children as many more privileged women had been doing (although working-class mothers did not have servants to do the housework and look after the children). As the technology for housework and cooking became more sophisticated, motherhood came to be idealized as the institution responsible for entertaining and ensuring the optimal development of children—morally and academically. Ann Dally argues in *Inventing Motherhood* that also in the 1950s women in the affluent Europe and North America could be relatively confident each pregnancy would lead to a live birth and to the baby's survival. As researchers have pointed out, this situation still does not pertain for poorer women in countries where there continue to be high rates of maternal and child mortality as well as higher birthrates. Access to efficient contraception and abortion in the more affluent countries led to markedly decreased birthrates from the late 1950s, with a few exceptions, and mothers have been expected to

devote more time and effort to caring for and developing their children.

Since the 1950s, motherhood—the condition in which women mother—has changed markedly and become more complex in many societies. In particular, as Fiona Williams makes clear in *Rethinking Families*, demographic changes in many societies mean that women in the early twenty-first century are more likely to be single mothers than previously and to live in reconstituted, blended families or stepparent families with children sometimes being shared across households. Mothers in European and North American society and affluent mothers in any society are likely to be older when they have their first child and to have fewer children. There has also been an increase in the number of affluent women who have only one child or no children and an increasing number who give birth through assisted reproduction techniques or as surrogates for other women. In addition governments frequently intervene (directly or indirectly) in motherhood to limit or increase population size or to attempt to guarantee the quality of the population. Examples include the Chinese one-child policy instituted in the twentieth century and pronatalist policies designed to encourage reproduction (e.g., in France and the former Soviet Union).

In modern times it is common for mothers to be employed outside the home, and there is ideological commitment to equality between women and men with expectations that child care and housework will be shared between employed parents. Motherhood within one society is therefore as differentiated as is motherhood between societies. Idealized images of motherhood have adjusted to accept that women may be employed outside the home and even that they may cohabit without being married. Images of motherhood have not, however, changed sufficiently to accommodate the demographic and social changes. As Estella Tincknell points out in *Mediating the Family*, media representations frequently accommodate some changes but reassert the ideal of the white, middle-class nuclear family. Ideologies of motherhood continue to suggest implicit disapproval of many categories of mothers, including those who are single, aged under twenty, and either out at work for long hours each day or unable to make economic provision for their children. In practice there is often less sharing of household and child care work between mothers and fathers than might be expected. As a consequence there is a marked discrepancy between the expectations of motherhood and the experiences of mothering, with the result that motherhood is painful and disappointing for many women. This discrepancy points to the fact that motherhood is not naturally occurring but is socially constructed in ways that suggest that there is an essence to motherhood.

EXPECTATIONS AND EXPERIENCES OF MOTHERHOOD

Despite the changes in motherhood, most women in all societies still become mothers. The oft-reported unhappiness of those who find that they cannot have children provides an indication of how psychologically important it can be for women to become mothers. To some extent this is because motherhood is socially constructed as an essential part of adult femininity so that women who do not become mothers (for whatever reason) can be made to feel that they are not proper women. In addition many women share the idealized view of motherhood common in many societies so it is not the case that they are coerced into having children. Many women choose to become mothers, and whether or not they do, their identities are partly negotiated in relation to motherhood. It is therefore important to consider women's desires in relation to motherhood (conscious and unconscious) as well as the contexts in which they mother. In other words, motherhood requires psychosocial (both psychological and social) understandings.

One benefit of feminist work on motherhood has been its focus on women's expectations and experiences of it. While many women want to become mothers and subscribe to social constructions of motherhood as natural, blissful, and something with which they should be able to cope, women frequently feel conflicted about how they will be able to manage as mothers. In the early twenty-first century the sociologist Tina Miller conducted a study of motherhood that used cultural scripts from Bangladesh and the Solomon Islands to contextualize experiences of motherhood in the United Kingdom. Miller found that women often said they were worried and frightened about becoming mothers. Miller suggests that this is related to cultural messages about the right way to be a good mother and the moral context within which motherhood occurs.

After birth, almost all women learn the tasks associated with successful mothering. However, it can take time for women to feel comfortable with their identities as mothers. The British sociologist Stephanie Lawler suggests that this is partly because women have to negotiate a contradiction between a belief in autonomy as a central part of adulthood and a perception that autonomy is lost with motherhood. Women therefore have to develop practices and narratives that allow them to inhabit identities as mothers. Experience of the contradictions of motherhood do not, however, lead mothers to feel solidarity with other mothers. The psychologist and anthropologist Meryle Kaplan points out: "Instead of questioning what has been called an institution of motherhood, these modern women most frequently question other mothers and resist affiliating themselves with other women" (Kaplan 1992,

p. 202). This self-differentiation between mothers is one reason why motherhood is differentiated among mothers.

Motherhood is also expressed differently over time and varies by social class, race, ethnicity, and culture. For example, in *Janani: Mothers, Daughters, Motherhood*, Maitreyi Chatterji says:

> Motherhood may have been pitched to an exalted position, but the ground reality for Indian mothers is an entirely different matter. India's maternal mortality rate and chronic malnutrition makes a mockery of motherhood myths … yet we find women legitimize motherhood through acts of immense sacrifice. Indian mothers eat last or not at all.… Women go through multiple pregnancies to continue the male family line or risk abortions if the fetus is female. (*Bhattacharya* 2006, pp. 36–37)

It is important, however, to recognize that there are marked differences between mothers within each country because social class, ethnicity, and culture all intersect to position women in different ways. Yet as the sociologist Terry Arendell reported in 2000 after a decennial review of U.S. literature, although the United States is diverse, little is known about the meanings and practices of motherhood for minority ethnic women, who are frequently used only as comparisons when white U.S. motherhood is being reified. This is also the case within other European and North American societies.

The enormous changes in the conditions under which motherhood occur demonstrate that motherhood is not an essentialist concept. Instead, it is diverse and practiced in different ways according to the social, economic, and psychological contexts in which women live. Nonetheless, ideologies of motherhood continue to idealize and romanticize motherhood in ways that make ideal motherhood unattainable and a source of anxiety for most women as they forge motherhood identities. For this reason, many motherhood researchers argue that it is important to expand the range of narratives around mothering and to challenge the pervasive myths of motherhood.

SEE ALSO *Children; Family; Family Structure; Fatherhood; Feminism; Gender Gap; Inequality, Gender; Parent-Child Relationships; Parenthood, Transition to; Parenting Styles; Work and Women*

BIBLIOGRAPHY

Arendell, Terry. 2000. Conceiving and Investigating Motherhood: The Decade's Scholarship. *Journal of Marriage and Family* 62 (4): 1192–1207.

Bernard, Jesse. 1975. *The Future of Motherhood.* New York: Penguin Books.

Chatterji, Maitreyi. 2006. My Mother, My Daughter. In *Janani: Mothers, Daughters, Motherhood*, ed. Rinki Bhattacharya. New Delhi: Sage.

Dally, Ann. 1982. *Inventing Motherhood: The Consequences of an Ideal.* London: Burnett.

Hollway, Wendy. 2006. *The Capacity to Care: Gender and Ethical Subjectivity.* London: Routledge.

Kaplan, Meryle. 1992. *Mothers' Images of Motherhood.* New York: Routledge.

Lawler, Stephanie. 2000. *Mothering the Self: Mothers, Daughters, Subjects.* London: Routledge.

Macfarlane, Alison, Miranda Mugford, Jane Henderson, et al. 2000. *Birth Counts: Statistics of Pregnancy and Childbirth*, vol. 1. London: Stationery Office.

Miller, Tina. 2005. *Making Sense of Motherhood: A Narrative Approach.* Cambridge, U.K.: Cambridge University Press.

Nicholson, Linda. 1997. The Myth of the Traditional Family. In *Feminism and Families*, ed. Hilde Lindemann Nelson. London: Routledge.

Oakley, Ann. 1979. *Becoming a Mother.* Oxford: Martin Robertson.

Orbach, Susie. 1997. Family Life. In *Living Together*, eds. David Kennard and Neil Small. London: Quartet Books.

O'Reilly, Andrea, ed. 2004. *Mother Matters: Motherhood as Discourse and Practice.* Toronto: Association for Research on Mothering.

Phoenix, Ann, Anne Woollett, and Eva Lloyd. 1991. *Motherhood: Meanings, Practices and Ideologies.* London: Sage.

Rich, Adrienne. 1976. *Of Woman Born: Motherhood as Experience and Institution.* New York: Norton.

Tincknell, Estella. 2005. *Mediating the Family: Gender, Culture, and Representation.* London: Hodder Arnold.

Williams, Fiona. 2004. *Rethinking Families.* London: Calouste Gulbenkian Foundation.

Ann Phoenix

MOTIVATION

The history of motivation research from the prescientific era to the present has seen a radical diversity in conceptualizations of motivation, and subsequently a vast range of perspectives on the domain of motivational explanation (Bolles 1967). Perhaps the most comprehensive way of characterizing motivation is as a state or process that determines the direction, intensity, and persistence of behavior and thought. Motivational states generally have distinctive activation and deactivation conditions (e.g., hunger and satiety), but their duration can range broadly from a momentary urge to the drive of a super-marathon runner to the indefinite toiling of an author in the completion of a novel. Some motivational states express one's capacity for self-control, whereas others are seen as lapses of will or compulsions. Across the social sciences, motivated beings have been regarded as agents with needs to control themselves and their environments, as agents with motivational dispositions constitutive of their personality profiles, and as agents with preferences governed by the temporal proximity of benefits.

Substantial effort has been devoted to understanding the relationship between beliefs about one's capacity for control and the motivation to control a given phenomenon, be it the self, other people, or some environmental process. One assumption underlying research into personal control is that humans are intrinsically motivated to explore their capacities and master their environments (Gecas 1989). Common tools for measuring personal control include the Rotter I-E scale and the Pearlin personal mastery scale.

The Rotter I-E scale consists of twenty-three questions used to determine where an individual locates the causes responsible for experienced reinforcements and outcomes. An internal locus of control is a source of causal efficacy within an individual, whereas an external locus of control is attributed to social and environmental forces, including luck. Each question on the Rotter I-E scale consists of two generalizations. One statement suggests that a person or group's circumstances are to be explained via an appeal to an external locus of control, the other an internal locus of control. The respondent is instructed to pick the most agreeable statement. Higher scores suggest that a respondent is a more external individual. Effective applications of the Rotter I-E scale account for individual differences in risk-taking behavior, where lower scores signal lower risk aversion. Several variations on the Rotter I-E scale have been proposed (Lefcourt 1991).

The Pearlin personal mastery scale was developed to study coping strategies in commonplace stressful situations (Pearlin and Schooler 1978). Mastery is the extent to which one judges that opportunities fall under one's own control, a concept Leonard Pearlin and Carmi Schooler contrasted with fatalism (which is comparable to external control). Coping in this framework is construed as any behavior aimed at reducing, avoiding, or controlling emotionally distressing environmental circumstances (often social situations in particular). A higher self-rating of personal mastery was found to predict a lower rating of emotional distress in a personally meaningful circumstance.

The scale itself consists of seven statements with four response categories specifying how strongly the respondent agrees or disagrees. Such statements include "There is really no way I can solve some of the problems I have" and "I can do just about anything I really set my mind to." Higher scores indicate that the respondent has greater confidence in having mastered an environment. Pearlin and colleagues (1981) found that challenges in the workplace affect job stress through personal mastery.

Questions linger concerning the relation between locus of control, personal mastery, and related concepts such as self-efficacy (Bandura 1980), all of which generally fall under the heading of personal control. It may be that the locus-of-control concept subsumes personal mastery (Lefcourt 1991), but this point is debatable (see Pearlin and Pioli 2003).

Research suggests that the connection between personal control and stress is culturally variable. Jaya Sastry and Catherine Ross (1989) studied the relation between personal mastery self-assessments and stress in Asian (Japanese, South Korean, Chinese, and Indian) and Asian American populations. Their finding was that Asians and Asian Americans report lower levels of perceived control than non-Asians. However, lower perceived control has less of an effect on distress. The authors attribute the difference to contrasting individualistic and collectivist value systems. Other work on self-efficacy suggests significant differences between Asian and European or North American populations. For example, Hazel Markus and Shinobu Kitayama (1991) found that subjects in the United States attribute poor academic performance to lack of ability, whereas Japanese subjects attribute such performance to lack of effort. Markus and Kitayama suggest that such differences stem from divergences between Asian and Western self-conceptions.

Setting aside cultural differences, individual differences in motivation may be attributable generally to trait differences beyond personal control. For example, the five-factor model defines distinct dimensions of affective tendencies, such as openness, conscientiousness, extraversion, agreeableness, and neuroticism. In the model, neuroticism is constituted by a spectrum leading from a calm, contented, and unemotional disposition to an anxious, emotional, and moody disposition (John 1989). The actualizations of these affective tendencies are sensibly regarded as responses toward the status of one's goals (see Lazarus 2001). Goals, the direction-determining component of motivational states, are then related to action selection and persistence via traits. For example, Gerald Matthews (1999) notes that nonanxious individuals maintain task performance better when lack of environmental controllability and severity of threat otherwise tend to discourage task focus (see also Lazarus and Folkman 1984). Thus the perceived capacity for control interacts with personality in determining task motivation within an individual.

Research on personal control largely assumes that beliefs concerning one's capacities combine with needs in order to determine behavior. Such needs may be regarded as the determinants of a preference ranking over plans for action. Abraham Maslow (1954) famously proposed a hierarchy of needs, where needs themselves were prioritized. In a related vein, goal theory countenances an explicit ranking of goals, where a goal whose achievement has a higher perceived difficulty tends to outrank a goal whose attainment poses a lesser challenge. One explanation of the ranking is that such goals are associated with more profitable outcomes (Locke and Latham 1990). How to taxonomize the goals that figure into a hierarchy remains a contentious issue (see Chulef, Read, and Walsh 2001).

In assessing needs and goals, we recognize greater and lesser urgency modulating action preferences. In learning theory, the matter is framed in terms of the balance between preferences for smaller, temporally proximal rewards and preferences for greater but temporally distant rewards. The classic economic representation of these aspects of motivation is found in the discounted utility (DU) model of intertemporal choice. In the DU model, agents are expected to employ the same discount factor consistently when weighing future benefits at varying temporal intervals from the present. Appeal to an agent's discount factor has been used to explain addictive consumption and self-defeating behavior. For example, when an agent selects an action with a low short-term expected benefit and high long-term expected cost (e.g., indulging a cocaine addiction), the choice of the indulgence over abstinence is attributed to the agent's setting immediate benefits (e.g., withdrawal relief) at a much higher priority than distant benefits (e.g., the greater net benefits from sobriety). Both this kind of explanation and the DU model have undergone sustained attack regarding agents' consistency in temporal discounting (Bickel and Marsch 2001; Ainslee 2001).

Researchers have attempted to coordinate economic and psychological approaches to motivation with the methods of neuroscience in a field called "neuroeconomics" (Camerer, Lowenstein, and Prelec 2005). Early results indicate that distinct neural circuits encode estimated value functions, that is, contingencies between actions and benefits summed over a temporal interval (Montague and Berns 2002). Neuroeconomics synthesizes the optimization assumptions of expected utility models and self-regulation approaches to motivation with the parallel processing concepts of computational neuroscience and the attention to bounded rationality prominent in behavioral decision theory (see Carver and Scheier 1998). Greater cross-disciplinary collaboration in motivation research can be expected in the future.

SEE ALSO *Diathesis-Stress Model; Guttman Scale; Locus of Control; Maslow, Abraham; Neuroeconomics; Overachievers; Rationality; Rotter's Internal-External*

Locus of Control Scale; Scales; Stress; Stress-Buffering Model; Underachievers

BIBLIOGRAPHY

Ainslie, George. 2001. *Breakdown of Will.* New York: Cambridge University Press.

Bandura, Albert. 1980. Gauging the Relationship between Self-Efficacy Judgment and Action. *Cognitive Therapy and Research* 4: 263–268.

Bickel, Warren K., and Lisa A. Marsch. 2001. Toward a Behavioral Economic Understanding of Drug Dependence: Delay Discounting Processes. *Addiction* 96: 73–86.

Bolles, Robert C. 1967. *Theory of Motivation.* New York: Harper and Row.

Camerer, Colin F., George Loewenstein, and Drazen Prelec. 2005. Neuroeconomics: How Neuroscience Can Inform Economics. *Journal of Economic Literature* 43: 9–64.

Carver, Charles S., and Michael F. Scheier. 1998. *On the Self-Regulation of Behavior.* New York: Cambridge University Press.

Chulef, Ada S., Stephen J. Read, and David A. Walsh. 2001. A Hierarchical Taxonomy of Human Goals. *Motivation and Emotion* 25 (3): 191–232.

Gecas, Viktor. 1989. The Social Psychology of Self-Efficacy. *Annual Review of Sociology* 15: 291–316.

John, O. P. 1989. Towards a Taxonomy of Personality Descriptors. In *Personality Psychology: Recent Trends and Emerging Directions*, ed. David M. Buss and Nancy Cantor, 246–260. New York: Springer Verlag.

Lazarus, Richard S. 2001. Relational Meaning and Discrete Emotions. In *Appraisal Processes in Emotion*, ed. Klaus R. Scherer, Angela Schorr, and Tom Johnstone, 37–68. New York: Oxford University Press.

Lazarus, Richard S., and Susan Folkman. 1984. *Stress, Appraisal, and Coping.* New York: Springer.

Lefcourt, Herbert M. 1991. Locus of Control. In *Measures of Personality and Social Psychological Attitudes*, vol. 1, ed. John P. Robinson, Phillip R. Shaver, and Lawrence S. Wrightsman, 413–499. San Diego, CA: Academic.

Locke, Edwin A., and Gary P. Latham. 1990. *A Theory of Goal Setting and Task Performance.* Englewood Cliffs, NJ: Prentice Hall.

Markus, Hazel, and Shinobu Kitayama. 1991. Culture and the Self: Implications for Cognition, Emotion, and Motivation. *Psychological Review* 98: 224–253.

Maslow, Abraham. 1954. *Motivation and Personality.* New York: Harper.

Matthews, Gerald. 1999. Personality and Skill: A Cognitive-Adaptive Framework. In *Learning and Individual Differences: Process, Trait, and Content Determinants*, ed. Phillip L. Ackerman, Patrick C. Kyllonen, Richard D. Roberts, 251–275. Washington, DC: American Psychological Association.

Montague, Read P., and Gregory Berns. 2002. Neural Economics and the Biological Substrate of Valuation. *Neuron* 36: 265–284.

Pearlin, Leonard I., and Mark F. Pioli. 2003. Personal Control: Some Conceptual Turf and Future Directions. In *Personal Control in Social and Life Course Contexts*, ed. Steven H. Zarit, Leonard I. Pearlin, and K. Warner Schaie. New York: Springer.

Pearlin, Leonard I., and Carmi Schooler. 1978. The Structure of Coping. *Journal of Health and Social Behavior* 18: 2–21.

Pearlin, Leonard I., Morton A. Lieberman, Elizabeth G. Menaghan, and Joseph T. Mullan. 1981. The Stress Process. *Journal of Health and Social Behavior* 22: 337–356.

Sastry, Jaya, and Catherine E. Ross. 1989. Asian Ethnicity and the Sense of Personal Control. *Social Psychology Quarterly* 61 (2): 101–120.

Anthony Landreth

MOVEMENTS, ANTICOLONIAL

SEE *Anticolonial Movements.*

MOVING AVERAGE MODEL

SEE *Autoregressive Models.*

MOVING EQUILIBRIA

SEE *Social System.*

MOVING TO OPPORTUNITY

The U.S. Department of Housing and Urban Development's (HUD) Moving to Opportunity (MTO) for Fair Housing Demonstration was intended to rigorously explore the ways that neighborhood environments affect the life chances of very poor families, by testing the effects of helping public housing families who lived in areas of *concentrated poverty* (neighborhoods where more than 40% of the households are poor) to move to better neighborhoods. Researchers and policy makers hoped that these moves would enable these residents to find jobs and their children to succeed in school.

The MTO demonstration grew out of a body of research on how neighborhood environments affect life chances (c.f. Wilson 1987). There was increasing evidence that living in high-poverty neighborhoods was related to a range of problems such as poor school performance, teen pregnancy, delinquency, drug use, weak labor-force attachment, and poor health (Ellen and Turner 1997; Ellen, Mijanovich, and Dillman 2001; Leventhal and Brooks-Gunn 2000). Among the most destructive communities were central-city public-housing developments, where residents endured miserable living conditions and horrific rates of violent crime and drug trafficking (Popkin et al. 2000a).

THE GAUTREAUX PROGRAM

MTO was modeled on Chicago's Gautreaux program, which was the result of a landmark desegregation lawsuit filed against the Chicago Housing Authority (CHA) and HUD. In *Hills v. Gautreaux* (1976) the courts found that the CHA and HUD had discriminated against black tenants, concentrating them in large-scale developments located in poor, black neighborhoods. The court ordered relief in the form of 7,100 Section 8 vouchers—subsidies that were to be provided to current and former CHA residents to use in neighborhoods *that were less than 30 percent black* (Polikoff 2006). Section 8 (Housing Choice) vouchers permit low-income households to rent private market units; recipients pay up to 30 percent of their income for rent and the local housing authority pays the rest. The Gautreaux program also provided mobility counseling to participants to help them find housing in predominantly white communities.

Research on the program seemed to indicate big gains for participants who succeeded in moving to predominantly white suburbs. Adults were more likely to be employed (Popkin, Rosenbaum, and Meaden 1993) and children more likely to stay in school, to be employed after graduation, and to go on to four-year colleges or universities (Kaufman and Rosenbaum 1992; Rubinowitz and Rosenbaum 2000). But Gautreaux participants self-selected into the program and were heavily screened, undergoing home visits and credit checks; most of the families (about 80%) that came through the program never moved; and the research relied on a retrospective design (Popkin et al. 2000b).

MTO DESIGN

The MTO demonstration was designed as a true random experiment. There was a critical difference between Gautreaux and MTO: MTO used poverty rather than race to define "opportunity neighborhoods." Between 1994 and 1998 more than 4,600 low-income families from high-poverty (more than 40% poor) public housing developments enrolled in MTO in Baltimore, Boston, Chicago, Los Angeles, and New York. Participants were randomly assigned to one of three groups: (1) an experimental treatment group that received counseling and received vouchers they could only use in a low-poverty (less than 10% poor) census tract; (2) a "regular" Section 8 comparison group that received vouchers with no special counseling and no neighborhood restrictions; and (3) an in-place control group that continued to live in public housing (Goering and Feins 2003).

MTO families were surveyed at baseline, before random assignment. HUD then funded several single-site studies one to three years after families moved to get preliminary data on how families were faring (Goering and Feins 2003). An interim evaluation was conducted in 2002, including analysis of administrative data on employment, welfare recipiency, and arrests; in-depth qualitative interviews of parents and youth; surveys of parents, children, and youth; blood pressure measurement for adults; and educational testing of youth.

Findings from the interim evaluation showed dramatic gains in quality of life for MTO participants, especially in terms of neighborhood safety and sense of security; these gains persisted, even though many families made subsequent moves to higher poverty communities (Orr et al. 2003). Adult women and adolescent girls experienced significant improvements in mental health; adult women also experienced declines in obesity relative to the control group. Boys did not experience these improvements in mental health; and boys in the experimental group had higher arrest rates for any crime, especially property crimes, and significant increases in smoking, although not in other types of risky behavior. Finally, there were no measured effects on employment or academic achievement for either adults or adolescents.

There are a number of possible explanations for these findings. First, unlike Gautreaux families, most MTO families did not move to white suburban neighborhoods, but to predominantly minority city neighborhoods that grew poorer between 1990 and 2000; few MTO families moved out of their original urban school districts. Second, because of welfare reform and the booming economy of the 1990s, employment rates increased dramatically for all three treatment groups; these trends may have masked any smaller treatment effects. Third, MTO families were significantly more disadvantaged than the Gautreaux families, and may not have been as able to take advantage of new opportunities. Fourth, MTO was a housing assistance program; it did not include any job training or other employment services; further, expectations that neighbors in low poverty would serve as role models and provide information about jobs may have been unrealistic. Finally, it simply may be that not enough time had elapsed to see significant effects on employment and education. The final evaluation, scheduled for 2007, will address the long-term effects of MTO.

MTO has shown that it is possible to use housing mobility as a tool for improving poor families' life circumstances. The improvements, including a sense of security and mental health for adult women and girls, are substantial, and may well have long-term implications for families' economic well-being. But the MTO findings also highlight the limitations of using poverty rather than race to define opportunity communities, as well as the need for more supports to help profoundly disadvantaged public housing families.

SEE ALSO *Gautreaux Residential Mobility Program; Poverty; Social Experiment*

BIBLIOGRAPHY

Ellen, Ingrid Gould, and Margery A. Turner. 1997. Does Neighborhood Matter? Assessing Recent Evidence. *Housing Policy Debate* 8: 833–866.

Ellen, Ingrid Gould, Tod Mijanovich, and Keri-Nicole Dillman. 2001. Neighborhood Effects on Health: Exploring the Links and Assessing the Evidence. *Journal of Urban Affairs* 23 (3–4): 391–408.

Goering, John, and Judith Feins. 2003. *Choosing a Better Life? Evaluating the Moving to Opportunity Social Experiment.* Washington, DC: Urban Institute Press.

Kaufman, Julie E., and James E. Rosenbaum. 1992. The Education and Employment of Low-Income Black Youth in White Suburbs. *Educational Evaluation and Policy Analysis* 14 (3): 229–240.

Leventhal, Tama, and Jeanne Brooks-Gunn. 2000. The Neighborhoods They Live In: Effects of Neighborhood Residence upon Child and Adolescent Outcomes. *Psychological Bulletin* 126: 309–337.

Orr, Larry, Judith D. Feins, Robin Jacob, et al. 2003. *Moving to Opportunity Interim Impacts Evaluation.* Washington, DC: U.S. Department of Housing and Urban Development.

Polikoff, Alexander. 2006. *Waiting for Gautreaux: A Story of Segregation, Housing, and the Black Ghetto.* Evanston, IL: Northwestern University Press.

Popkin, Susan Judith, Larry F. Buron, Diane K. Levy, and Mary K. Cunningham. 2000b. The Gautreaux Legacy: What Might Mixed-Income and Dispersal Strategies Mean for the Poorest Public Housing Tenants? *Housing Policy Debate* 11: 911–942.

Popkin, Susan Judith, Victoria E. Gwiasda, Lynn M. Olson, et al. 2000a. *The Hidden War: Crime and The Tragedy of Public Housing in Chicago.* New Brunswick, NJ: Rutgers University Press.

Popkin, Susan Judith, James E. Rosenbaum, and Patricia M. Meaden. 1993. Labor Market Experiences of Low-Income Black Women in Middle-Class Suburbs: Evidence from a Survey of Gautreaux Program Participants. *Journal of Policy Analysis and Management* 12(3): 556–573.

Rubinowitz, Leonard S., and James E. Rosenbaum. 2000. *Crossing the Class and Color Lines: From Public Housing to White Suburbia.* Chicago: University of Chicago Press.

Wilson, William Julius. 1987. *The Truly Disadvantaged: The Inner City, the Underclass, and Public Policy.* Chicago: University of Chicago Press.

Susan J. Popkin

MOYNIHAN, DANIEL PATRICK
1927–2003

Born in Tulsa, Oklahoma, Moynihan grew up in a poor neighborhood in New York City, shining shoes to earn money. He served on active duty as a gunnery officer on the USS *Quirinus*. He went on to graduate from Tufts University, receiving three graduate degrees from the Fletcher School of Law and Diplomacy. He was a Fulbright fellow at the London School of Economics. A member of Averell Harriman's New York gubernatorial campaign in 1954, he served for four years on the governor's staff and became a Kennedy delegate at the 1960 Democratic National Convention. During the Kennedy and Johnson administrations he was an assistant secretary of labor and was influential in formulating national policy that came to be known as the War on Poverty.

In developing his views on the position of the black community in American society, Moynihan was influenced by Stanley Elkins's *Slavery: A Problem in American Institutional and Intellectual Life* (1959), which argued that the dependency of black Americans on society was produced by slavery and that slavery had, like the Nazi concentration camps, produced a psychological infantilism. Moynihan supported the idea of affirmative action to counteract the historical legacy of slavery. Moynihan was impressed by the fact that, while unemployment was declining, more people were joining the welfare rolls, and these welfare recipients were typically families with children with a lone parent (invariably the mother).

In 1963 he coauthored *Beyond the Melting Pot* with Nathan Glazer, claiming that intermarriage was not common and that ethnic divisions were resulting not in a "melting pot" but a "salad bowl." His internal memorandum with regard to black families was leaked to the press. Subsequently known as the Moynihan Report, it identified a "tangle of pathology" in the dysfunctional black family, resulting in welfare dependency. Critics saw the report as a case of "blaming the victim"—the title of William Ryan's 1971 book taking issue with white liberalism in general and Moynihan in particular. Moynihan's views were appropriated by racists who seized upon press coverage, focusing on the fact that many black children were being born out of wedlock. In the Aid to Families

INTERNATIONAL ENCYCLOPEDIA OF THE SOCIAL SCIENCES, 2ND EDITION with Dependent Children program, the "man out of the house rule" was said to encourage lone parents not to cohabit because otherwise their welfare entitlements would be jeopardized. Joining Richard Nixon's White House staff, Moynihan supported Nixon's commitment to a guaranteed annual income, which he discussed in *The Politics of a Guaranteed Income* (1973). He became notorious for a memo to Nixon in 1969 recommending that "the issue of race could benefit from a period of benign neglect" (DeWitt 2005). Moynihan's critics have argued that his influence on the Nixon administration meant that the cause of black emancipation was curtailed by lack of attention to the social and economic issues confronting black Americans.

After a brief spell as director of the Joint Center for Urban Studies at Harvard University and the Massachusetts Institute for Technology, he had major appointments as ambassador to India (1973–1975) and as U.S. representative to the United Nations. He controversially ensured that the UN Security Council took no action against the illegal annexation of East Timor by Indonesia in 1975 on the grounds that Indonesia was a cold war ally of the United States.

Moynihan remained a controversial figure by opposing President Bill Clinton's proposal to expand health care coverage to all American citizens. Moynihan took the view that there was no health care crisis, and he supported a ban on partial-birth abortions, which he saw as close to infanticide. Having chaired the Commission on Government Secrecy, he published *Secrecy: The American Experience* in 1998, arguing that suspicion and lack of information created unnecessary political schisms.

While the *Almanac of American Politics* described him in 1994 as "the nation's best thinker among politicians since Lincoln and the best politician among thinkers since Jefferson," his critics have argued that his views on the black family had damaging consequences for black Americans, that his opposition to health care coverage was regressive, and that his strategy toward East Timor resulted in thousands of civilian deaths.

SEE ALSO *Benign Neglect; Culture of Poverty; Glazer, Nathan; Moynihan Report*

BIBLIOGRAPHY

Barker, Lucius Jefferson, Mack H. Jones, and Katherine Tate. 1999. *African Americans and the American Political System.* 4th ed. Upper Saddle River, NJ: Prentice Hall.

DeWitt, Larry. 2005. Moynihan, Welfare Reform, and the Myth of "Benign Neglect." http://www.larrydewitt.net/Essays/Moynihan.htm.

Hodgson, Godfrey. 2000. *The Gentleman from New York: Daniel Patrick Moynihan: A Biography.* Boston: Houghton Mifflin.

Katzmann, Robert A., ed. 1998. *Daniel Patrick Moynihan. The Intellectual in Public Life.* Washington DC: The Woodrow Wilson Center Press.

Moynihan, Daniel Patrick. 1965. *The Negro Family: The Case for National Action.* Washington, DC: Office of Policy Planning and Research, U.S. Department of Labor.

Moynihan, Daniel Patrick, and Nathan Glazer. 1963. *Beyond the Melting Pot: The Negroes, Puerto Ricans, Jews, Italians, and Irish of New York City.* Cambridge, MA: MIT Press.

Ryan, William. 1971. *Blaming the Victim.* New York: Pantheon.

Bryan S. Turner

MOYNIHAN REPORT

In early 1965 Daniel Patrick Moynihan (1927–2003), then assistant secretary for policy planning and research at the Department of Labor, completed a report that was eventually published as *The Negro Family*. In the report Moynihan had identified certain anomalies in U.S. employment data; for example, by the early 1960s the unemployment rate for minorities was going down while the dependency rate (or rate of welfare payments) was going up. This paradox came to be known as "Moynihan's scissors." He also observed that the black out-of-wedlock birth rate was climbing steeply. Moynihan's departmental paper on these empirical findings on the black family came to be known as the Moynihan Report. It argued that the single-parent family in the ghetto was becoming more common, and that these single-mother families were not the product of unemployment, but the legacy of black slavery. A similar argument had been put forward by the black sociologist E. Franklin Frazier (1894–1962) in his *The Negro Family in the United States* (1939). Moynihan described the crisis (what he called the "tangle of pathology") in the urban ghetto in terms of criminality, unemployment, educational failure, and fatherlessness. The unraveling of the black family was associated with the fact that with growing rates of teenage pregnancy, young parents failed to complete school and find employment. Fathers were largely absent from the home, and single mothers often became welfare dependents.

There were in fact two components to Moynihan's argument. One was the presence of cultural norms (of dependency, family organization, and crime) in the black community that were the long-term legacy of slavery. The second was the high incidence of unemployment among black men that reduced their desirability and practicability in the marriage market. This second feature received relatively little attention in the public debate about female-headed households.

The substance of Moynihan's report was influential in U.S. politics. Lyndon Johnson referred to it in his commencement address at Howard University in June 1965, focusing on the alleged dysfunctions of the black family and ignoring the issue of male unemployment. The empirical basis of the report also influenced academic research. James Coleman (1926–1996) published with several colleagues *Equality and Educational Opportunity* (1966) in which they demonstrated that the best predictor of a child's educational achievement is not the material conditions within schools but the family background of the child. Welfare dependency and child poverty in black ghettoes remained stubbornly high, and by 1990 around 65 percent of all black children were born to unmarried mothers.

Moynihan's report became an important aspect of "the politics of controversy" in postwar America. Some days after the report was leaked to *Newsweek*, riots broke out in Los Angeles's Watts ghetto on August 11, 1965, and Moynihan's critics argued that the report was used by the administration as an explanation for the riots. William Ryan, an activist in the Congress of Racial Equality and a clinical psychologist at Boston College, published his *Blaming the Victim* (1971), which claimed that the Moynihan report was racist in suggesting that the problems of the ghetto were the consequence of black male promiscuity: Because whites had better access to contraception, abortion, and adoption, their behavior was not regarded as licentious. Attacking black sexuality masked the failure of American society to deliver social justice. The report also was criticized by the black feminist and academic Joyce Ladner, who claimed in *Tomorrow's Tomorrow: The Black Woman* (1971) that the report did not challenge the myths surrounding the white middle-class family. Feminists criticized the nuclear family as oppressive and defended the black single-parent family as a foundation for the socialization of children.

On joining President Richard Nixon's White House staff, Moynihan supported Nixon's commitment to a guaranteed annual income, which he analyzed in *The Politics of a Guaranteed Income* (1973). Moynihan subsequently became notorious for a memorandum to Nixon recommending that the question of race could benefit from a period of benign neglect. However, the issue of racial injustice remained on the social science agenda. In 1987 William Julius Wilson published *The Truly Disadvantaged*, in which he described the social pathology of the ghetto, criticizing liberals for failing to address black social problems. Sara McLanahan and Gary Sandefur in *Growing Up with a Single Parent* (1994), summarizing the social science data on family life, concluded that children in single-parent homes did not do as well as other children on a range of indicators. Kay Hymowitz argued in *Liberation's Children* (2003) that opposition to Moynihan has to be seen in the context of the rebellious climate of the 1960s.

There are other, substantive criticisms of the report. Firstly, although Moynihan praised the Nation of Islam ("black Muslims"), he ignored the extensive network of black churches, the Urban League, black fraternities and sororities, the Masons, the National Association for the Advancement of Colored People, and black colleges, all of which contribute significantly to civil society. Secondly, the historical evidence from 1915 to 1960 showed that the rate of black births out of wedlock remained relatively unchanged, and that from the early 1960s the African American birth rate began to decline, especially among married women. Thirdly, the real "family issue" is not the number of unmarried women having too many children, but the declining prevalence of marriage as such. Clearly, female marriage rates are closely associated with male marriageability. The decline in marriage rates is in part a consequence of the dramatic increase in the educational achievement of African Americans. In 1940 African Americans in the age group 25 to 34 years had a median of 6.9 years of completed schooling; by 1960 this had increased to 10.3 years; and by the 1970s the figure was over 12 years. The gap between white and black Americans in terms of education declined steadily during this period. As high school graduation and postsecondary education became the norm between 1960 and 1975, African American men and women delayed entry into marriage, and there was a corresponding decline in fertility. In addition, adverse labor market conditions—declining real wages and labor force participation, and earnings instability—resulted in male marginalization, further contributing to the decline in marriage rate.

The critical response to the Moynihan Report essentially revolved around the idea of the pathological family in which men are absent and lone mothers dominate. This view is not unrelated to Frazier's earlier description of these families as a "matriarchate." An alternative explanation, which was pioneered by researchers such as Andrew Billingsley in 1968, is that the extended, matriarchal black family was an effective adaptation to the socioeconomic difficulties that African Americans confronted in racially divided society. The black family was in fact an appropriate structural response rather than a social pathology.

SEE ALSO *Black Middle Class; Female-Headed Families; Moynihan, Daniel Patrick; Slavery; Unemployment*

BIBLIOGRAPHY

Billingsley, Andrew. 1968. *Black Families in White America.* Englewood Cliffs, NJ: Prentice Hall.

Coleman, James, et al. 1966. *Equality and Educational Opportunity.* Washington, DC: Office of Education, U.S. Government Printing Office.

Frazier, E. Franklin. 1939. *The Negro Family in the United States.* Chicago: University of Chicago Press.

Hymowitz, Kay S. 2003. *Liberation's Children: Parents and Kids in a Postmodern Age.* Chicago: Ivan R. Dee.

Ladner, Joyce. 1971. *Tomorrow's Tomorrow: The Black Woman.* Garden City, NY: Doubleday.

McLanahan, Sara, and Gary Sandefur. 1994. *Growing Up with a Single Parent: What Hurts, What Helps.* Cambridge, MA: Harvard University Press.

Moynihan, Daniel Patrick. 1965. *The Negro Family: The Case for National Action.* Washington, DC: Office of Policy Planning and Research, U.S. Department of Labor.

Moynihan, Daniel Patrick. 1973. *The Politics of a Guaranteed Income: The Nixon Administration and the Family Assistance Plan.* New York: Random House.

Rainwater, Lee, and Martin Yancey. 1967. *The Moynihan Report and the Politics of Controversy.* Cambridge, MA: MIT Press.

Ryan, William. 1976. *Blaming the Victim.* Rev. ed. New York: Vintage.

Wilson, William Julius. 1987. *The Truly Disadvantaged: The Inner City, the Underclass, and Public Policy.* Chicago: University of Chicago Press.

Bryan S. Turner

MUGABE, ROBERT
1924–

Robert Mugabe, the president of Zimbabwe, was born in rural Rhodesia (the country's earlier colonial name), and spent his adult life struggling for the independence of Zimbabwe. He has led the country since 1980, first as prime minister and then as president. The son of Gabriel and Bona Mugabe, he managed to gain admission to South Africa's Fort Hare University, which was then one of the few institutions reserved for non-white higher education in apartheid South Africa. He began to develop his political consciousness at the university and returned to Rhodesia in 1960, immediately joining Joshua Nkomo's Zimbabwe African People's Union (ZAPU), but he deserted Nkomo three years later to help establish the rival Zimbabwe African National Union (ZANU). The two men conducted an uneasy rivalry, with periods of conditional cooperation, right up to Nkomo's death in 1999.

This sort of political maneuvering characterized Mugabe's rise to pre-eminence within ZANU itself, and rivals were either eclipsed or mysteriously died. At the foundation of ZANU, however, the radical demeanour of the party so alarmed Ian Smith's white minority government that Mugabe was imprisoned without trial in 1964 and remained incarcerated for ten years. When, a year later in 1965, Smith declared unilateral independence from Britain rather than permit black majority rule, it was

a sign to the imprisoned Mugabe that democracy and black rights would require armed struggle.

Mugabe studied intensely while in prison and acquired a list of degrees from the universities of London and South Africa, including two master's degrees. His intellectual acuity has always been one of his hallmarks.

Mugabe was released from prison in 1974 and went to Zambia. While there he became president of ZANU, deposing another of his veteran rivals, Ndabaningi Sithole, and in 1975 the predominant figure in ZANU, Herbert Chitepo, was assassinated. Mugabe and many of his allies were immediately arrested in Zambia, but they were released a month later and made their way to Mozambique, where they fostered the armed insurrection against the Smith regime, using Mozambique as a base for their operations into Rhodesia. The war became sufficiently fierce and bloody for a series of international peace efforts to be launched from both Britain and the United States.

In 1979 the pressures of both war and international diplomacy led to negotiations among all parties under the chairmanship of the British foreign and commonwealth secretary in London, and it was agreed that a British governor would take charge of Rhodesia and conduct elections leading to independence under the name of Zimbabwe. Mugabe's ZANU scored a comprehensive electoral victory. He increased the sense of surprise by immediately issuing a call for reconciliation and cooperation. Although he and Nkomo had negotiated jointly in London, Mugabe declined to form a coalition with Nkomo, but did provide him with a place in government.

The early years of rule astounded the international community with its moderation and liberalism, although it was only in the 1990s that full appreciation was gained of a secretive conflict in western Zimbabwe from 1982 to 1987. There, dissident supporters of Nkomo were ruthlessly crushed by Mugabe's armed forces, with tens of thousands of innocent civilians killed. His pride and political capacity crushed, Nkomo was thereafter fully subordinate to Mugabe, but the outside world was prepared to turn a blind eye to a protracted episode where violence had replaced democracy.

Beginning in 1992, however, Mugabe began speaking intensely of land reform and redistribution. By far the majority of Zimbabwe's arable land was still in white ownership, and political independence had not been accompanied by majority ownership of land. Even so, it took until 1997 when, after a bitter quarrel with British prime minister Tony Blair, Mugabe began to speak violently about seizing land without compensation.

Mugabe had won all of the elections held after independence. Although the 1990 elections occurred with much violence in the east of the country, Mugabe garnered legitimate electoral victories in all of them. In 1999, however, a formidable opposition party, the Movement for Democratic Change (MDC) emerged under Morgan Tsvangirai. The MDC inflicted a first defeat on Mugabe in February 2000, at a referendum over constitutional changes. In March, Mugabe unleashed the veterans of the liberation war to invade and take over the land of white farmers and to reassert violence into the political landscape. Since then, the economic and political travails of Zimbabwe have spiralled out of control.

Without a productive agri-industrial base, inflation in Zimbabwe had soared to 1600 percent by February 2007. The MDC suffered defeat at successive elections, and it is clear that Mugabe had resorted to rigging in order to ensure his victories. Political suppression increased as the economic meltdown of the 2000s continued.

Mugabe is now in his eighties and there is a debate as to his posterity. In the West, he is seen as the violent guerrilla leader who merely cloaked his ruthlessness for many of the years of his rule, but who has shown his true character in deliberately plunging his country into turmoil. Some view him as reasserting his early Maoist ideology in a Zimbabwean Cultural Revolution. Many in Africa, however, see him as the last great nationalist who, perhaps belatedly, was determined to assert the meaning of black majority rule in terms of ownership of land. Here he takes his place alongside such intellectual nationalist leaders as Amilcar Cabral and Kwame Nkrumah. This more sympathetic view suggests that, in the long term, Mugabe's accomplishment will be recognized as a final, if messy, breakthrough to full nationalism. In the meantime, the messiness has gripped Mugabe's land and people with catastrophe and deprivation.

SEE ALSO *Autocracy; Cabral, Amilcar; Colonialism; Decolonization; Guerrilla Warfare; Land Claims; Land Reform; Liberation Movements; Nkrumah, Kwame*

BIBLIOGRAPHY

Chan, Stephen. 2003. *Robert Mugabe: A Life of Power and Violence.* Ann Arbor: University of Michigan Press.

Raftopoulos, Brian, and Tyrone Savage, eds. 2004. *Zimbabwe: Injustice and Political Reconciliation.* Cape Town, South Africa: Institute of Justice and Reconcilation.

Stephen Chan

MUHAMMAD
c. 569–632

In the Islamic tradition, Muhammad is a messenger of God and the "seal of the prophets." Muslims consider the prophethood of Muhammad as the final act of a monotheistic God's revelations to humanity, which had earlier been transmitted through the biblical prophets, including Jesus and Moses.

According to classical Islamic sources, Muhammad was born in Mecca around 569. His family belonged to the Hashemite branch of Quraysh, the dominant tribe in Mecca, then a major site of pagan pilgrimage in Arabia as well as a major center of caravan routes. The city's dominant religion was Arab paganism, although some monotheists influenced by Abrahamic traditions also resided there. His father, 'Abdullah, died before Muhammad was born, so the infant was placed primarily in the care of a foster mother in addition to his grandfather and his mother, Amina, both of whom died within his eighth year, leaving the care of the orphan to his uncle.

Muhammad's first forty years of life were relatively undistinguished. He reportedly made a living as a merchant and participant in Mecca's long-distance caravans, and his most profitable missions were carried out on behalf of an older female employer, Khadija, whom he eventually married. While before the revelations he was never recognized as anything but an ordinary member of the community, as a merchant he developed a reputation for honesty and integrity. At age forty, following years of periodic seclusion and meditation, Muhammad received his first revelations from God through the archangel Gabriel, the medium through which, according to Muslim tradition, the entire Qur'an was revealed to Muhammad.

Several years of proselytizing in Mecca generated a small number of recruits to the new faith, but Muhammad's claim to being a messenger of God was rejected by the city's larger pagan community. Muhammad's teachings had a clear affinity to Jewish and Christian ideas permeating Arabia at that time, his main nemesis being the dominant pagan religion. Around 622 Muhammad and his band of followers, seeing no more prospects in Mecca and being subject to increasing harassment, migrated to Medina (then Yathrib), where they established the first self-governing Muslim community. That community consisted at first of two distinct groups: the Meccan Muslims who came with Muhammad, or *al-muhajirun* (the emigrants); and a larger group of local Medinian faithful who had been Islamized before Muhammad's migration to the city, known as *al-ansar* (the backers). Medina became Muhammad's headquarters until his death. The mosque of Medina, built around his tomb, is the second-holiest shrine for Muslims worldwide.

Muhammad's migration (*Hijra*) to Medina allowed him not only to establish an independent Muslim community but also to elaborate further features of such a community. In Medina it became increasingly evident that Islam was becoming a trans-tribal religion, and Muhammad frequently found himself acting as a trans-tribal statesman and arbitrator as well as prophet. Hostility to Mecca is evident in that part of his biography, since his home city had, according to the Qur'an, rejected a faith that was intended to safeguard it from danger in the world. Many skirmishes and battles are recorded throughout that period between the Muslims of Medina and the pagans of Mecca. Under Muhammad, the Muslims, especially *al-muhajirun*, sought to undermine Mecca's trade routes and also gain access to Mecca's *haram* (sanctuary), which was holy to all pagan Arabs but also to Muslims, who traced its construction to Abraham and saw it as integral to the history of monotheism.

During the Medinian part of Muhammad's life Islam was spreading in Arabia, but Muhammad remained focused on Mecca until he conquered the city in 630 in a bloodless campaign. He confirmed the holy status of the now-Islamized city. The originally pagan *haram* of Mecca was sanctified as a Muslim sanctuary and a Muslim pilgrimage site, and the pagan objects of worship within it were destroyed.

Muhammad died in Medina in 632, shortly after performing his last pilgrimage to Mecca, and at a time when Muslim communities had sprung up throughout Arabia. He left no instructions as to how the community should be ruled after him, leaving the task to the elders of the community. After deliberations they chose Abu Bakr, Muhammad's close companion and one of the earliest believers, as the first caliph in Islam.

Muhammad counts as one of the most influential men in history. In the Qur'an he is presented as a mere human person with no divine qualities and no supernatural powers, and he is not credited with miracles. His role is presented as one of bearing witness to his people and as a conveyor of God's final and true revelation; with the teachings of Muhammad, God acquires a highly abstract character. The tradition further highlights Muhammad's illiteracy, which in the context of the highly refined, poetic language of the Qur'an establishes all the more the book's divine origin.

Muhammad combined in his career several roles—prophet, statesman, warrior, legislator—and through that combination managed to establish an enduring trans-tribal community in Arabia that, after his death, became the model for a universal Muslim community. The corpus of sayings attributed to him, or hadith, along with the traditions around his life, constitute the sunnah, which is generally considered second to the Qur'an as source of Muslim tradition and also provides Muslims with an exemplary model of proper Muslim life and composure.

The basic teachings of Muhammad emphasized Islam as a trans-tribal fellowship, a harmonious community whose inner peace was safeguarded through regulated legal relations that closely mirrored the contractual outlook of the merchant class. Muhammad also mandated and expanded earlier techniques of wealth redistribution through elevating almsgiving to a religious duty. While presenting Islam as the last chapter in the history of monotheism, Muhammad also operated in a territory that was far removed from imperial or great power centers. Central western Arabia in Muhammad's time was becoming increasingly connected to world trade routes, but being situated deep in the desert, remained independent of the great powers of the time. The context in which Muhammad operated, therefore, provided for the emergence of a new type of political community, one that was not based on imperial politics but rather on overcoming and reworking Arab tribal traditions and integrating various classes and social groups under the banner of a new religion that gave them a sense of common and universal identity, binding contractual relations, and solidaristic practices and attitudes.

SEE ALSO *Islam, Shia and Sunni; Muslims*

BIBLIOGRAPHY

Bamyeh, Mohammed A. 1999. *The Social Origins of Islam: Mind, Economy, Discourse*. Minneapolis: University of Minnesota Press.

Rodinson, Maxime. 1980. *Muhammad*. Trans. Anne Carter. New York: Pantheon.

Watt, W. Montgomery. 1980. *Muhammad, Prophet and Statesman*. London and New York: Oxford University Press.

Mohammed A. Bamyeh

MUHAMMAD, ELIJAH
1879–1975

Elijah Muhammad was born on or about October 7, 1879, in Sandersville, Georgia, as Elijah Poole into a family with thirteen siblings. In his late teens or very early twenties he married Clara Evans, with whom he had eight children. He moved to Detroit, Michigan, in 1929 or 1930 to find employment, as did many blacks during the Great Migration from the South to the North during and after the stock market crash of 1929. In Detroit Clara Poole first heard of a "peddler/preacher" named Master Fard Muhammad who was preaching a different religious message—"the oneness of God," and that "blacks needed to embrace the religion of their ancestors"—Islam. Intrigued, Elijah went to investigate both the man and the message, and soon was Fard Muhammad's favored student. The community the Poole family joined was recorded as the Nation of Islam (NOI), founded by Fard Muhammad.

An ardent and trustworthy student, Poole was first given the surname Karriem and then Muhammad as he matured from student to minister to Supreme Minister. By 1934 Fard Muhammad had left active participation in the NOI and Elijah Muhammad was appointed its leader, which enabled him to put what he had learned into action. His enduring task was to teach black people that their history written by white people was not true, to enlighten them about who they actually were in creation and the civilization of the world, and to maximize their potential as productive human beings working to better their spiritual, moral, and economic lives in a hostile, evil society. With a truncated U.S. education (ended at about the fourth grade) and a highly developed intellect accompanied by firm belief, Elijah Muhammad built a small but concrete empire. The Nation owned land, farms, schools, grocery stores, a national newspaper, clothing factories, and an international fish shipping company.

Muhammad used a multipronged, basic approach in his community. This was to engender moral and spiritual cleanliness (inwardly and outwardly); to instill the notion of seeking knowledge; to understand the command to work for self and the betterment of the black community by building and sustaining an economy, eating right, and nurturing strong families; and to avoid those things that would hamper any of the above, such as drinking alcohol, eating pork, gambling, and so on. This approach resulted in greater land and building ownership and the establishment of import-export businesses, clothing and grocery stores, and savings plans, and the publication of numerous texts as well as a newspaper that is now more than seventy years old.

The "Muslim Program" of the Nation of Islam has always been characterized as being divided between what Muslims want and what they believe. Simply summarized, Muhammad recognized that the United States had engineered a genocidal program against its ex-slaves that included regular lynchings, beatings, segregation, and racial discrimination. His response was to call for the establishment of a separate state where blacks could prosper. Members of his community believe in the oneness of God (Allah), the Holy Qur'an, and all the revealed scriptures—the Torah, the Bible—with the same qualifications as Sunni and Shi'a Muslims (for example, they do not believe that Jesus is God). They also believe that the so-called "Negroes" in America are God's chosen people.

The main goal for this community has always been the same: to uplift the black community to take a place in world leadership, moving away from dominion over others to cooperative living. With this in mind, members of this community have conscientiously objected to military service through several European wars and the United States's aggressions overseas. Their points were most ardently made by one of the most outspoken of the NOI's members, El-Hajj Malik Shabazz (Malcolm X). Shabazz was introduced to the teachings of the Nation of Islam while in prison in the 1950s, and upon his release he met Muhammad and became his student. Shabazz's intellect and charisma propelled him quickly through the ranks of the NOI to become one of its most visible spokespersons, until his assassination in 1963. Shabazz had publicly questioned the integrity of Muhammad, revealing that he had affairs with several of his secretaries, producing children. It is widely suspected that these public revelations, as well as jealousy engendered by Shabazz's high public profile, provoked his assassination; the men arrested for the murder were associated with the Nation of Islam. Muhammad lived until 1975, when leadership of the Nation of Islam passed to another student, Louis Farrakhan, until 2006; the leadership at that point transferred to a board.

SEE ALSO *Black Nationalism; Islam, Shia and Sunni; Malcolm X; Nation of Islam; Nationalism and Nationality; Religion; Rituals*

BIBLIOGRAPHY

Lincoln, C. Eric. 1991. *The Black Muslims in America.* Queens, NY: Kayode Publications.

Muhammad, Elijah. 1965. *Message to the Black Man in America.* Chicago: Muhammad Mosque of Islam No. 2.

Muhammad, Elijah. 1967. *How to Eat to Live.* Chicago: Muhammad Mosque of Islam No. 2.

Aminah Beverly McCloud

MULATTO ESCAPE HATCH

Brazil and the United States were the two largest slave-holding societies of the New World. However, differing racial dynamics characterized each context during those years and continue to do so. Carl Degler offered an explanation for the contrasts in his 1971 book *Neither Black nor White: Slavery and Race Relations in Brazil and the United States.* He posited the existence of a "mulatto escape hatch" in Brazil, or a space ceded to mulattos amounting to an intermediate social position between whites and blacks. In his words, "In Brazil the mulatto is not a Negro, whereas in the United States he is" (p. xviii), a distinction that provides "an escape from the disabilities of blackness for some colored people" (p. 178). This position challenges traditional views of Brazil as a racial democracy, that is, where there is no discrimination against persons of any degree of African ancestry. On what historical grounds did Degler base his theory of the mulatto difference in Brazil and what were and are its supposed consequences?

The possible existence of an escape hatch in Brazil rested on the recognition of intermediate categorization for persons of mixed racial heritage, in contrast to the gradual adoption of the "one-drop rule" in the United States (i.e., where any "noticeable" African ancestry means assignment to the black race category). Degler's explanation for these diverging developments included more frequent racial intermixing in Portuguese America. This dynamic resulted from both the imbalanced sex ratios among Europeans in Portuguese America (where European women were scarce) in comparison to British America (where many early settlers came as families) and the higher social position of European women in British America that afforded them more control over the sexual exploits of their husbands. In addition, Degler noted that manumission rates were higher in Brazil than in the United States, especially for mulattos. These factors meant that whereas in the United States the boundary between free and slave populations was more generally coterminous with that between whites and blacks, in Brazil the free versus slave distinction was crosscut more significantly by skin tone. Hence, the all-encompassing and caste-like definition of blackness in the United States was made more difficult in Brazil.

The contrasting definitions of blackness were further strengthened in the nineteenth and twentieth centuries. Whereas both colonial societies practiced slavery, de jure racial discrimination ended in Brazil with slavery's abolition in 1888. In contrast, in the United States, after the abolition of slavery in 1865, the nation moved toward a re-entrenchment of de jure race-based discrimination that lasted into the 1960s. Color distinctions gradually became obsolete in a U.S. society ruled by black codes and Jim Crow segregation. The all-encompassing one-drop rule strengthened its hold as the twentieth century progressed and was even officially adopted by the U.S. census at least from 1930 to that century's end. In contrast, the Brazilian census has employed intermediate or mixed-race categorization since its inception in 1872.

As to the consequences of a racially intermediate category in Brazil, Degler presents evidence that there may have been some mulatto advantage in colonial years (e.g., higher manumission rates). Some research also suggests a modest amount of advantage for lighter-skinned individuals among those of African ancestry in contemporary Brazil in terms of select socioeconomic indicators (Telles 2004), although others argue that there are no real differences among Afro-Brazilians (Silva 1985). If a space of relative privilege does characterize some mulattos in Brazil,

however, it is a space much closer to that occupied by blacks than by whites (Telles 2004). Interestingly, Edward Telles further argues that the advantage of lighter skin tone for persons of African ancestry is much more clearly the case in contemporary U.S. society than in Brazil. Earlier, Verna Keith and Cedric Herring revealed the same, positing that lighter-skinned blacks in the United States not only received some relative privilege compared to darker-skinned blacks during the years of slavery (e.g., higher manumission rates), but that patterns of relative advantage continue today in terms of education and income. Importantly, they claim that the present-day disadvantage of darker-skinned blacks is not a historical artifact, but results from continuing "greater discrimination against darker blacks" (Keith and Herring 1991, p. 775).

Despite some findings of a lack of evidence for significant mulatto advantage in Brazil, a preference for intermediate categorization continues among a large majority of Brazilians of some African ancestry. That preference may reflect a symbolic escape from the stigma of blackness. That is, the *actual* existence of the mulatto escape hatch may be less important in Brazil than the *belief* in its existence.

As to other consequences of intermediate categorization in Brazil, researchers hold that it hampers the construction of ethnic consciousness and solidarity among Brazilians of varying degrees of African ancestry that might otherwise be mobilized against racialized inequality. The U.S. African American community is surely the counterexample. An emphasis on individual strategies for social mobility (as opposed to collective) may further condition that solidarity in Brazil. Additionally, class identities in Brazil may be more central in the minds of poor Brazilians of all colors, further challenging the mobilization of clear racial divisions. Lastly, intermediate categorization may be implicated in the continuing stigma that is attached to blackness, resulting in a type of psychological trauma for mulattos whose disadvantage flows in part from their nonwhiteness but who adopt nonblack identities.

Traditions of intermediate categorization (and perhaps many of their consequences) are predominant in other countries of Latin America that have significant African-descent populations, including Venezuela, Colombia, Cuba, and the Dominican Republic. As Degler and others have pointed out, the United States may be the exceptional case in terms of its historic adoption of the "one-drop rule" for categorizing individuals of African ancestry. However, racial classification patterns are in flux in both the United States and Brazil. Ironically, for example, the United States institutionalized a type of multiracialism in its 2000 census with the "mark one or more races" option, while Brazil is discarding multiracial categorization for the identification of Afro-Brazilian beneficiaries of its new affirmative action strategies in higher education.

SEE ALSO *Democracy, Racial; Mulattos*

BIBLIOGRAPHY

Degler, Carl N. 1971. *Neither Black nor White: Slavery and Race Relations in Brazil and the United States.* Madison: University of Wisconsin Press.

Keith, Verna M., and Cedric Herring. 1991. Skin Tone and Stratification in the Black Community. *American Journal of Sociology* 97 (3): 760–778.

Silva, Nelson do Valle. 1985. Updating the Cost of Not Being White in Brazil. In *Race, Class, and Power in Brazil*, ed. Pierre-Michel Fontaine, 42–55. Los Angeles: Center for Afro-American Studies.

Telles, Edward E. 2004. *Race in Another America: The Significance of Skin Color in Brazil.* Princeton, NJ: Princeton University Press.

Stanley R. Bailey

MULATTOS

The term *mulatto*, referring to an individual of mixed white and black ancestry, has been in use for centuries. The sociologist Edward B. Reuter (1918) and the historian Joel Williamson (1995) generally use the term to include all people of mixed "white blood" and "black blood," without consideration for the degree of mixture. Early twenty-first-century social scientists of course view such notions of "blood" and "race" as social constructions, not as biological realities. However, an important issue related to the social construction of the term *mulatto* is its racist basis. The historian Patricia Morton argues that "mulatto is a Latin term for the mule and in a popular 'muleology' linked the mule and the mixed 'blood.' The mule was the hybrid product of the mating of a horse and a donkey, and, supposedly like the mulattos, had no parents of its own breed and no descendants since it could not produce offspring. Similarly, mulattoes were perceived as the product of an unnatural union" (Morton 1985, p. 111). The tragic mulatto character that frequently appears in American media and literature depicts "mixed-bloods as a visible symbol of lust and what the culture deemed, pejoratively, miscegenation" (Morton 1985, p. 111).

THE EMERGENCE OF THE MULATTO

From the inception of the continental slave trade through the era of legal segregation, mulattos have been a constant reminder of the historical raping and coercion of black women. In some instances the unions between white men and black women, as well as those between white women and black men, were thought to be consensual. However, the majority of unions were a result of violent sexual coercion by whites in an effort to enforce the racial oppression of blacks. The raping and sexual coercion of black women by white men prompted governments to enact antimiscegenation laws throughout the southern United States. These laws were not constructed to protect black women from rape or to discourage white men from having sexual relations with black women; rather, the laws ensured that the children of these forced unions could not claim rights to inheritance or freedom. Antimiscegenation laws varied from state to state, but the main objective was to protect the institution of slavery and wealthy landowners' inheritance.

According to Stephan Talty (2003), enslaved black women were regularly raped and then witnessed the selling of their mulatto children who, in most instances, looked too much like their masters to keep them on the plantations. However, there were instances when "wealthy landowners freed their … mulatto children" (Talty 2003, p. 63). The mulatto population grew rapidly during the slavery era; in the 1860 census mulattos in the South represented over 10 percent of the slave population and nearly 37 percent of the free black population (Toplin 1979). It became increasingly difficult for white slave owners to sell slaves who looked as white as or whiter than the person purchasing them. However, because of their lighter complexions, when mulattos were sold, they were purchased for a higher price than that paid for dark-skinned slaves.

In addition to the mixed race population that resulted from the raping of African women in the United States, there was a large infusion of mixed-race people from Haiti into southern Louisiana. The connection between Haiti and Louisiana became reinforced "in the 1790's when the French, driven out of Haiti by mulatto revolutionaries, transplanted island culture to lower Louisiana …. There also rose a free mulatto population of some size and, at the top, of impressive wealth…. Nowhere in America did mulattoes rise so high as in lower Louisiana" (Williamson 1995, pp. 20–21).

In New Orleans free mulatto women and white men frequently engaged in interracial relations that became "institutionalized in quadroon balls" (Williamson 1995, p. 23). In New Orleans white men would choose a mulatto woman and seek permission from her parents to establish *placage*, an arrangement in which the man agreed to establish a house for the woman, provide for her economically, and care for any children she conceived with him without the benefit and security of marriage. In some *placage* situations, the man would eventually marry a white woman who understood that he had a concubine (Williamson 1995).

Enslaved mulatto women were frequently purchased as concubines for single, married, and widowed white men. According to Williamson, mulatto women were often referred to as "fancy girls" (Williamson 1995, p. 69), and it was understood that though they were trained for domestic work, they were primarily used as concubines. There was a great demand for mulatto women in New Orleans, and some of these women were sold on the auction block to prominent men. White women hated the competition presented by mulatto women: "It was not, after all, the lower classes—the laborers, the plain farmers and tradesman—who paid fancy prices," it was prominent men in the community who did so (Williamson 1995, p. 70). However, these mulatto women were still enslaved, and many suffered the same deplorable and harsh treatment as darker-skinned men and women. This was particularly true because many southern white women failed to acknowledge the power and responsibility of white men in these relationships and held great animosity toward mulatto women who engaged in sexual relations with white men.

During the slavery period, a growing number of mulatto men and women became educated, were granted inheritances from their rich landowner fathers, and were freed. Many whites in both the South and the North gave preferential treatment to mulattos over darker-skinned blacks, whether they were slaves or not. According to the historian Robert Toplin, "whites frequently made invidious comparisons between Negroes and mulattoes and claimed that the admixture of white blood gave mulattoes special qualities" (Toplin 1979, p. 194).

Indeed mulattos often held leadership positions and were trusted by both whites and blacks. As a result some mulattos internalized this attitude of superiority, buying into the white racist structure that privileged whiteness. Many newly freed mulattos moved to the North, and abolitionists used them to gain white support against slavery by noting the physical similarities between mulattos and whites to invoke outrage at the institution of slavery. Some mulattos relied on their white features to win inheritance cases in court. According to Charles Robinson, "petitions for freedom actually came before the county magistrates from biracial offspring prior to … 1662" (Robinson 2003, p. 3). Mulattos would buy their freedom and the freedom of their family members. During the Reconstruction era in the United States, after slaves had been freed, the majority of black leaders in politics, economics, and education were mulattos.

PASSING FOR WHITE

After slavery ended, the need to discourage interracial unions increased as concerns about maintaining racial purity moved to the forefront for southern whites. Robinson argues that "mixed-race people could and did pass as white and successfully join white society by dint of marriage. Southern whites became increasingly alarmed about the potential of 'invisible' blackness to infiltrate white society" (Robinson 2003, p. 102). Robinson further notes that "in 1924, the state of Virginia passed the first anti-miscegenation statute that firmly embraced the one-drop rule" (Robinson 2003, p. 101): Citizens of the state were required to register their racial identities, and anyone with any degree of black ancestry was required to register as black.

The United States was not alone in providing special privileges for mulattos. In Brazil, which had a large mulatto population, mulattos were advantaged because there were so many of them. The historian Carl Degler argues for the importance of examining universal attitudes in reference to mulattos: "There are only two qualities in the United States racial pattern: black and white. A person is one or the other; there is no intermediate position" (Degler [1971] 1986, p. 102). However, others argue that in the United States, as in many other parts of the world, including Brazil, there are a variety of degrees for what people consider to constitute white, black, and mulatto.

In the United States research provides compelling data that the darker the skin hue of an African American, the more racism and discrimination he or she will experience in economic life, health care, and sentencing outcomes for criminal punishment (Goldsmith et al. 2006; Eberhardt et al. 2006; Carter 2007). Elizabeth Klonoff and Hope Landrine found that "67% of subjects who experience frequent discrimination were dark-skinned and only 8.5% were light-skinned. Dark-skinned Blacks were 11 times more likely to be in the high discrimination group than their light-skinned counterparts" (Klonoff and Landrine 2000, p. 336).

Arthur Goldsmith, Darrick Hamilton, and William Darity Jr. found that "among black males there was a substantial wage advantage (on the order of 7 percent) for having light skin" (Goldsmith, Hamilton, and Darity 2006, p. 245). In cases where black defendants are accused of killing whites, Eberhardt and colleagues suggest that "jurors are influenced not simply by the knowledge that the defendant is Black, but also by the extent to which the defendant appears stereotypically Black" (Eberhardt et al. 2006, p. 385). In Mississippi and some other states the darker the skin hue, the broader the nose, and the fuller the lips, the more likely a defendant will be convicted of a crime and, when applicable, sentenced to death (Eberhardt et al. 2006; Gyimah-Brempong and Price 2006).

SEE ALSO *Colorism; Moreno/a; Pardo; Passing; Phenotype; Race; Race Mixing; Racism; Rape; Slave Trade; Slavery; Whiteness*

BIBLIOGRAPHY

Carter, Robert T. 2007. Racism and Psychological and Emotional Injury: Recognizing and Assessing Race-Based Traumatic Stress. *Counseling Psychologist* 35 (1): 13–105.

Darity, William A., Jr. 2003. Employment Discrimination, Segregation, and Health. *American Journal of Public Health* 93 (2): 226–231.

Degler, Carl N. [1971] 1986. *Neither Black nor White: Slavery and Race Relations in Brazil and the United States.* Madison: University of Wisconsin Press.

Eberhardt, Jennifer L., Paul G. Davies, Valerie J. Purdie-Vaughns, and Sheri Lynn Johnson. 2006. Looking Deathworthy: Perceived Stereotypicality of Black Defendants Predicts Capital-Sentencing Outcomes. *Psychological Science* 17 (5): 383–386.

Goldsmith, Arthur H., Darrick Hamilton, and William A. Darity Jr. 2006. Shades of Discrimination: Skin Tone and Wages. *American Economic Review* 96 (2): 242–245.

Gyimah-Brempong, Kwabena, and Gregory N. Price. 2006. Crime and Punishment: And Skin Hue Too? *American Economic Review* 96 (2): 246–248.

Klonoff, Elizabeth A., and Hope Landrine. 2000. Is Skin Color a Marker for Racial Discrimination? Explaining the Skin Color–Hypertension Relationship. *Journal of Behavioral Medicine* 23 (4): 329–338.

Morton, Patricia. 1985. From Invisible Man to "New People": The Recent Discovery of American Mulattoes. *Phylon* 46 (2): 106–122.

Reuter, Edward B. 1918. *The Mulatto in the United States: Including a Study of the Role of Mixed-blood Races throughout the World.* Boston: Badger.

Robinson, Charles Frank. 2003. *Dangerous Liaisons: Sex and Love in the Segregated South.* Fayetteville: University of Arkansas Press.

Talty, Stephan. 2003. *Mulatto America: At the Crossroads of Black and White Culture: A Social History.* New York: HarperCollins.

Toplin, Robert B. 1979. Between Black and White: Attitudes toward Southern Mulattoes, 1830–1861. *Journal of Southern History* 45 (2): 185–200.

Williamson, Joel. 1995. *New People: Miscegenation and Mulattoes in the United States.* Baton Rouge: Louisiana State University Press.

Ruth Thompson-Miller

MULTI-CITY STUDY OF URBAN INEQUALITY

The Multi-City Study of Urban Inequality (MCSUI) is composed of a set of related surveys, funded by the Russell Sage Foundation and Ford Foundation and available from the Inter-university Consortium for Political and Social Research, that focus on how the relationship between race, employment, and housing generate and perpetuate urban poverty and racial inequality. Four household surveys, using standardized sampling frameworks and similar questions, were conducted between April 1992 and August 1994 in four metropolitan areas: Atlanta, Boston, Detroit, and Los Angeles. Complementing these surveys were thirty-minute phone interviews of about nine hundred business establishments in each of the four metropolitan areas. Almost 1,200 of the employer surveys were conducted with employers identified in the household survey as the current or last employer of the respondent. In addition, in-depth, face-to-face follow-up interviews were conducted in each city with about forty-five employers identified by household respondents holding jobs requiring no more than a high school education.

The MCSUI is the work of a large interdisciplinary team of researchers. It started with conversations among researchers at the University of California Los Angeles and the University of Michigan who had written on various aspects of urban inequality. The original plan was to conduct a two-city comparative survey expanding on the 1976 Detroit Area Study, which addressed racial attitudes and residential segregation. The objective of the MCSUI project was to create a database that could be used to explore how racial attitudes and stereotypes, labor market dynamics, and residential segregation interact to create urban inequality. The project expanded to four metropolitan areas, the household surveys adopted a much broader focus, and employer surveys were added. (Alice O'Connor [2001] provides a detailed history of the development of the MCSUI.)

The MCSUI has many unique features. First, the surveys are very extensive, both in terms of the number of households interviewed and the breadth of the interviews. Completed household interviews number 1,529 in Atlanta, 4,025 in Los Angeles, 1,543 in Detroit, and 1,820 in Boston. These in-person interviews averaged about ninety minutes, with approximately six hundred questions being asked. The number of completed employer interviews is 3,510. Second, the household sample includes approximately an equal number of each racial-ethnic group and an oversampling of low-income households, which provides for more detailed analysis than allowed for by most surveys. Third, linking the household and employer surveys is a unique and perhaps unprecedented feature, allowing analysis of both the supply and the demand side of the labor market. Fourth, the surveys contain much more detailed information than most social and labor market surveys. The household survey gathered information well beyond a standard set of demographic characteristics to include the respondents' views about neighborhood and community issues; attitudes about integration, racial stereotypes, and discrimination; and the nature of social networks.

Questions on labor market dynamics incorporate a standard set of variables, as well as more nuanced variables such as length of time on job, size of employer, instances of harassment and discrimination, use of networks, requirements regarding wage levels and commute times, access to knowledge about job opportunities, and job search activities. Employers were queried about characteristics of their firm, including composition of the firm's labor force, vacant positions, the person most recently hired, educational qualifications, and the firm's recruiting methods, as well as demographic information for the respondent, job applicants, customers, and labor force.

Fifth, while the MCSUI provides for much finer detail than can be found using typical national-level data, it still allows for comparative analysis across metropolitan areas. Household survey questions were asked in at least two of the four survey cities, and most questions were asked in all four cities. Comparisons are aided by the contrast between the four metropolitan areas, which represent different regions of the country, different economic conditions, different population growth rates, and different racial/ethnic makeup.

Six books that rely on the MCSUI were published by the Russell Sage Foundation. The first book explored issues that were informed by the employer surveys. Each of the metropolitan areas was the focus of a book, while a sixth book used the surveys to explore issues in a multimetropolitan framework. The MCSUI has also been the basis for a number of dissertations and dozens of journal articles.

Given the richness of the MCSUI, the research that has used the data spans a wide range of topics across many disciplines. The following provides a flavor of what has been learned. Several papers explore how the mismatch between residential location and employment opportunities results in negative labor market outcomes for low-skilled minorities. The role of information about jobs, access to job opportunities, job discrimination in the suburbs, fear of being poorly treated in suburban locations, and job search strategies have been found to be associated with worse employment outcomes for central-city minorities. Using questions concerning the specific skills required for jobs, it was determined that jobs requiring lower levels of skill are more likely to be found in the suburbs. A comparison of the results from MCSUI with the 1976 Detroit Area Study found a substantial increase in willingness of whites to live in integrated neighborhoods.

Racial stereotypes are widespread and influence the way minorities view one another, and the factors that determine perceptions of discrimination differ by race. Researchers have found that racial discrimination, stereotypes, and economic disparities all contribute to maintaining residential segregation. The employer survey shows that employers use an applicant's neighborhood as a signal that affects the employer's hiring decision, and that new jobs require not only "hard" skills (i.e., those associated with computers, math, and writing) but also "soft" skills (those involving behavioral and personal interactions). Researchers have found that job search methods are bundled differently by race and ethnicity and that reliance on different social networks leads nonwhites to lower-status, lower-wage, racially segregated jobs.

The MCSUI can be used to explore many of the existing single-factor explanations of urban inequality, but the richness of the MCSUI data allows for investigations of more complex explanations and of alternative hypotheses and for research that delves beneath what other data, such as census data, can tell us. The MCSUI has advanced urban poverty research and has the capacity to further our understanding of how urban poverty and racial inequality are generated and perpetuated.

BIBLIOGRAPHY

Bluestone, Barry, and Mary Huff Stevenson, eds. 2000. *The Boston Renaissance: Race, Space, and Economic Change in an American Metropolis.* New York: Russell Sage Foundation.

Bobo, Lawrence D., Melvin L. Oliver, James H. Johnson Jr., and Abel Valenzuela Jr., eds. 2000. *Prismatic Metropolis: Inequality in Los Angeles.* New York: Russell Sage Foundation.

Danziger, Sheldon H., Reynolds Farley, and Harry J. Holzer. 2000. *Detroit Divided.* New York: Russell Sage Foundation.

Holzer, Harry J. 1999. *What Employers Want: Job Prospects for Less-Educated Workers.* New York: Russell Sage Foundation.

O'Connor, Alice. 2001. Understanding Inequality in the Late Twentieth-Century Metropolis: New Perspectives on the Enduring Racial Divide. In *Urban Inequality: Evidence from Four Cities*, ed. Alice O'Connor, Chris Tilly, and Lawrence D. Bobo, 1–33. New York: Russell Sage Foundation.

O'Connor, Alice, Chris Tilly, and Lawrence D. Bobo, eds. 2001. *Urban Inequality: Evidence from Four Cities.* New York: Russell Sage Foundation.

Sjoquist, David L., ed. 2000. *The Atlanta Paradox.* New York: Russell Sage Foundation.

David L. Sjoquist

MULTICOLLINEARITY

A multiple regression is said to exhibit multicollinearity when the explanatory variables are correlated with one another. Almost all multiple regressions have some degree of multicollinearity. The extent to which multicollinearity is a problem is widely misunderstood. Multicollinearity is not a violation of the classical statistical assumptions underlying multiple regression. Specifically, multicollinearity does not cause either biased coefficients or incorrect standard errors. For this reason, while identifying multicollinearity can be helpful in understanding the outcome of a regression, "corrections" to reduce multicollinearity are rarely appropriate.

In the regression model

$$y_i = b_1 x_{i1} + b_2 x_{i2} + \dots + b_k x_{ik} + e_i$$

there is multicollinearity if the x variables are correlated with one another, as is usually the case. The consequence of such correlation is that the estimates of regression coefficients are less precise than they would be absent such correlation. For example, in the regression $y_i = a + b_1 x_{i1} + b_2 x_{i1} + e_i$ with n observations, the variance of the estimated coefficient $\hat{b}_1$ can be thought of as

$$\mathrm{var}(\hat{b}_1) = \frac{\mathrm{var}(e)}{n \cdot \mathrm{var}(x_1)} \times \frac{1}{1 - \mathrm{corr}(x_1, x_2)^2}.$$

When x_1 and x_2 have a high correlation, $\mathrm{corr}(x_1, x_2)$, the uncertainty about b_1 will be large. Because the formulas for reporting standard errors reflect this, such uncertainty will be correctly reflected in the reported regression statistics.

Fundamentally, a regression estimates the effect of one explanatory variable holding constant the other explanatory variables. If one or more variables tended to move together in the available data, in which case the data will be *multicollinear*, then very little evidence is available about the effect of a single variable, as is reflected in the variance formula above.

The only "cures" for multicollinearity are (1) to find data with less correlation among the explanatory variables, or (2) to use a priori information to specify a value for the coefficient of one of the correlated variables, and by so doing avoid the need to separately estimate the effect of each variable.

If one explanatory variable equals a linear combination of other explanatory variables (for example, if $x_1 = x_2 + x_3$) the regression has *perfect multicollinearity*. Perfect multicollinearity makes it impossible to estimate the regression model, as indicated by the infinite variance in the formula above. However, perfect multicollinearity almost always indicates an error in specifying the model. One common error is the *dummy variable trap*, in which a complete set of dummy variables and an intercept, or more than one complete set of dummy variables, are included in a regression. For example, including a variable for female gender (coded 1/0), a variable for male gender, and an intercept would cause the regression to fail.

Because of limits on the numerical accuracy of computer arithmetic, a high degree of multicollinearity can lead to numerical, as opposed to statistical, errors in computing regression results. This is rarely a problem with modern software, which typically includes internal checks for such errors.

One indication of significant multicollinearity is that individual coefficients are insignificant but sets of coefficients are jointly significant. For example, a set of indicators of underlying socioeconomic status (e.g., mother's education and father's education) may be jointly significant even though no single indicator is significant. In such situations, investigators sometimes drop all but one indicator. While not strictly rigorous, such a procedure is not harmful so long as the coefficient on the retained variable is interpreted as a proxy for the entire set of socioeconomic indicators rather than being the effect of the specific variable that was retained. (One might retain only mother's education, but interpret the effect loosely as "parent's education.")

Another indication of multicollinearity that is sometimes used is a high *variance inflation factor* (VIF), which measures the increase in variance of $\hat{b}_i$ due to correlation between x_i and the other explanatory variables. In the example above, the VIF is $1/(1 - \mathrm{corr}(x_1, x_2)^2)$.

SEE ALSO *Least Squares, Ordinary; Principal Components; Properties of Estimators (Asymptotic and Exact)*

BIBLIOGRAPHY

Goldberger, Arthur S. 1991. *A Course in Econometrics.* Cambridge, MA: Harvard University Press.

Richard Startz

MULTICULTURALISM

Multiculturalism is the notion that people in a given society should coexist with one another, without having to fear or resent that their cultural identity will be not be accepted if it does not fit in with the normative cultural climate of that society. Scholars have also defined multiculturalism as an attempt to preserve a "cultural mosaic" of separate ethnic groups. While the term *multiculturalism* originated in Sweden in 1957, Canada was the first country to recognize that multiculturalism was integral to its national identity and adopted it as its national policy in 1960. Originally the term made explicit reference to racial and ethnic groups living within a particular nation. Soon the term spread to most of the Western world, as democracies grappled with increasing competition along racial, ethnic, linguistic, and religious lines. With time, and increasing awareness of difference, gender and sexual orientation, age, and disability, issues of geographic origin and immigration were also folded into the general construct of multiculturalism. As such, multiculturalism came to be seen as an official policy to manage and ensure diversity.

Multiculturalism emphasizes diversity and social cohesiveness by recognizing that previous programs of assimilation or absorption not only distorted but also in many ways served to destroy individuality. Therefore diversity, rather then being perceived as problematical, is presented as the model. The notion of strength through diversity is in direct contrast to previous assimilation or absorption models that held sway in countries such as Canada, the United States, Australia, and England. Multiculturalism encourages all to fully participate in the social processes of a nation while being free to maintain and perpetuate individual group identities. Therefore multiculturalism fostered concerns for race relations, social justice, and civic participation. Multiculturalism as a social movement aims at minimizing conflict, encouraging inclusion, and celebrating the differences, which are represented by various identity groups that comprise a pluralist society. Multiculturalism, so defined, can be discussed in terms of historical (factual), ideology, policy, and critical discourse.

MULTICULTURAL IDEOLOGY

Ideologically, multiculturalism refers to a set of ideas, which attempt to explain, justify, or promote diversity, cultural awareness, and inclusiveness. As a consequence associated with multicultural ideology are values, attitudes, and perspectives that are intended to define interaction among diverse populations.

Within the United States, the growth and spread of multicultural ideology is associated with the increased agitation for civil rights of African Americans and the increased immigration of Asian and Hispanic Americans during the mid- to late 1960s. In the 1970s and 1980s feminists provided the necessary critical mass to which the intellectual and educational elite responded. As magazine articles and books began exposing the multicultural ideology the media and political elite began discussing the issue as well. By the mid-1980s, the ideology of multiculturalism became the dominant expression of liberal values, and the target for conservative attacks.

MULTICULTURAL POLICY

Multicultural policy refers to the political apparatus established to institutionalize and normalize cultural diversity within a multicultural society. Such policy attempts to create environments that value cultural diversity, encourage tolerance for difference, promote cultural awareness, and create systems of inclusion. Within such a framework, cultural groups are encouraged to preserve their distinctiveness by asserting their right to be different. While mul-

ticultural policies vary across nations, several distinctive features seem universal to include: official acceptance of linguistic differences in the media, schools, and public conveyances; support of cultural festivals and holidays; support of religious and cultural differences in the military, schools, and other major institutions; support of alternative artistic expressions; and support of cultural diversity in political offices, business practices, and educational offerings.

MULTICULTURALISM AS CRITICAL DISCOURSE

Challenging a historical past dominated by "dead white men" in almost every avenue of education represents the critical discourse of multiculturalism. Prior to this discourse, few educators challenged the dominance of white males in classics, theory, music, art, literature, and politics. Beginning in the late twentieth century, the critical discourse of multiculturalism argued for a more inclusive academic canon that looks at history from a female and multicultural perspective. Educational institutions have witnessed the creation of academic departments in women's, gender, and queer studies, African American and black studies, Latin and Hispanic studies, and Jewish and Muslim studies, to name a few. Even with this proliferation and othering of the academic discourse many argue that rather than encouraging inclusion these academic programs have fostered divisiveness and balkanization.

MULTICULTURAL PROBLEMS AND THE CONSERVATIVE BACKLASH

Many on the Right, both in politics and education, perceived the advance of multiculturalism as a direct threat to Western values, history, and culture. Even before author Nathan Glazer declared "we are all multiculturalists now" in 1997, a full-scale assault was levied. Ignoring that this book represented Glazer's personal misgivings regarding multiculturalism, there has been a constant assault upon multiculturalism. This assault, taking both scholarly presentations and political movements, has been vociferous and constant since the mid-twentieth century. Under the rubric of political correctness, attacks made in the early twenty-first century utilize the arguments of freedom and inclusiveness to attack multiculturalism. Accordingly, multiculturalism is described as a misguided policy and ideology, which victimizes cultural, gendered, racial, and ethnic groups while demonizing primarily white males. Thus, it is argued that rather than leading to greater individuality and freedom, multiculturalism has become another vicious form of bias. Critics of multiculturalism, citing such movements as black English, bilingualism, affirmative action, feminism, and gay marriages, point to what they perceive as the ethnic and racial balkanization of American society into identity groups, riots, and increased conflict, and the advancement of extreme liberal/homosexual/feminist agendas at odds with the core values of America.

The debate over multicultural education engenders such passion because it is about more than adding other voices to a reading list or determining whether waving a confederate flag is deemed hate speech. At the center of the issue of inclusiveness are questions of what constitutes knowledge and whose knowledge should be valued. Allan Bloom's *Closing of the American Mind* (1987) eloquently speaks to these issues. Bloom blamed technology, the sexual revolution, and the introduction of cultural diversity into the curriculum at the expense of classics for producing students without wisdom, values, or morality. In an academic universe where multicultural perspectives are explored the question of whose voice is heard becomes more difficult to decide.

SEE ALSO *Diversity; Ethnicity*

BIBLIOGRAPHY

Bloom, Allan. 1987. *The Closing of the American Mind: How Higher Education Has Failed Democracy and Impoverished the Souls of Today's Students.* New York: Simon and Schuster.

Duster, Troy. 1991. Myths about Multiculturalism. *Mother Jones.* http://www.motherjones.com/commentary/columns/1991/09/affirm.html.

Fleras, Augie, and Jean Leonard Elliott. 2002. *Engaging Diversity: Multiculturalism in Canada.* Toronto: Nelson Thomson.

Glazer, Nathan. 1997. *We Are All Multiculturalists Now.* Cambridge, MA: Harvard University Press.

Rodney D. Coates

MULTIDIMENSIONAL INVENTORY OF BLACK IDENTITY

As defined by Robert M. Sellers and colleagues in the Multidimensional Model of Racial Identity (MMRI), racial identity is the significance and qualitative meaning that individuals attribute to being black in their conceptualizations of self (Sellers, Smith, Shelton, et al. 1998). The significance component of racial identity is referred to as *racial centrality*, and the qualitative meaning of racial identity is referred to as *racial ideology* and *racial regard*. The MMRI outlines four ideologies that reflect African Americans' views on what it means to be black: (1) a nationalist ideology; (2) an oppressed minority ideology; (3) an assimilationist ideology; and (4) a humanist ideol-

ogy. Additionally, African Americans vary in their affective and evaluative judgments of their racial group (private regard) and in their beliefs about others' affective and evaluative judgments of African Americans (public regard).

The Multidimensional Inventory of Black Identity (MIBI) is a measure that assesses the dimensions of racial identity outlined by the MMRI (Sellers, Rowley, Chavous, et al. 1997). Participants indicate their agreement with various statements on a scale from 1 (strongly disagree) to 7 (strongly agree). The MIBI is composed of seven subscales. The centrality scale consists of items measuring the extent to which being African American is central to the respondents' definition of himself or herself (e.g., "Being black is important to my self-image"). The regard scale is composed of two subscales, private and public regard. The private regard subscale consists of items measuring the extent to which respondents have positive feelings toward African Americans in general (e.g., "I feel good about black people"). The public regard subscale consists of items measuring the extent to which respondents feel that other groups have positive feelings toward African Americans (e.g., "Overall, blacks are considered good by others"). The ideology scale of the MIBI has four subscales. The assimilation subscale consists of items measuring the extent to which respondents emphasize the relationship between African Americans and mainstream America ("Blacks should try to work within the system to achieve their political and economic goals"). The humanist subscale consists of items measuring the extent to which respondents emphasize the similarities among individuals of all races ("Blacks would be better off if they were more concerned with the problems facing all people rather than just focusing on black issues"). The minority subscale consists of items measuring the extent to which respondents emphasize the similarities between African Americans and other minority groups ("The same forces which have led to the oppression of blacks have also led to the oppression of other groups"). Finally, the nationalist subscale consists of items measuring the extent to which respondents emphasize the uniqueness of being African American ("White people can never be trusted where blacks are concerned"). The factor structure and convergent validity have been established in samples of college students (Sellers, Chavous, and Cooke 1998), and all subscales of the MIBI have been shown to have adequate internal consistency in studies with adults (Rowley, Sellers, and Smith 1998; Sellers, Chavous, and Cooke 1998) and older adolescents (Chavous, Bernat, Schmeelk-Cone, et al. 2003).

The MIBI differs from other widely used measures of racial or ethnic identity in that it does not assess mechanisms for identity development. Jean S. Phinney's 1992 model assesses the extent to which the individual has searched for information regarding their ethnic group and the extent to which he or she has committed to that identity. Thomas A. Parham and Janet E. Helms's Racial Identity Attitude Scale (1981) measures individuals' movement from problack, antiwhite beliefs to an achieved identity that includes tolerance for other groups and in-group pride. In contrast to these other models, the MMRI is primarily concerned with the significance and content of an individual's identity at a specific point in time.

The MMRI has made significant contributions to research on African Americans. The MMRI and MIBI have been used in research regarding African American adults' and adolescents' experiences with discrimination (Sellers and Shelton 2003; Sellers, Caldwell, Schmeelk-Cone, et al. 2003), adolescents' academic beliefs and achievement (Rowley 2000; Sellers, Chavous, and Cooke 1998), and family dynamics and substance abuse (Caldwell, Sellers, Bernat, et al. 2004). The MMRI provides a vehicle for understanding the diverse experiences of African Americans in the United States.

SEE ALSO *Identity; Ideology; Race*

BIBLIOGRAPHY

Caldwell, Cleopatra H., Robert M. Sellers, Debra Hilkene Bernat, et al. 2004. Racial Identity, Parental Support, and Alcohol Use in a Sample of Academically At-risk African American High School Students. *American Journal of Community Psychology* 34 (1–2): 71–82.

Chavous, Tabbye M., Debra Hilkene Bernat, Karen Schmeelk-Cone, et al. 2003. Racial Identity and Academic Attainment among African American Adolescents. *Child Development* 74 (4): 1076–1090.

Parham, Thomas A., and Janet E. Helms. 1981. The Influences of a Black Student's Racial Identity Attitudes on Preferences for Counselor's Race. *Journal of Counseling Psychology* 28: 250–256.

Phinney, Jean S. 1992. The Multigroup Ethnic Identity Measure: A New Scale for Use with Diverse Groups. *Journal of Adolescent Research* 7 (2) 156–176.

Rowley, Stephanie Johnson. 2000. Profiles of African American College Students' Educational Utility and Performance: A Cluster Analysis. *Journal of Black Psychology* 26 (1): 3–26.

Rowley, Stephanie Johnson, Robert M. Sellers, Mia A. Smith, et al. 1998. The Relationship between Racial Identity and Self-esteem in African American High School and College Students. *Journal of Personality and Social Psychology* 74 (3): 715–724.

Sellers, Robert M., Cleopatra H. Caldwell, Karen H. Schmeelk-Cone, et al. 2003. Racial Identity, Racial Discrimination, Perceived Stress, and Psychological Distress among African American Young Adults. *Journal of Health and Social Behavior* 44 (3): 302–317.

Sellers, Robert M., Tabbye M. Chavous, and Deanna Y. Cooke. 1998. Racial Ideology and Racial Centrality as Predictors of African American College Students' Academic Performance. *Journal of Black Psychology* 24 (1): 8–27.

Sellers, Robert M., Stephanie Johnson Rowley, J. Nicole Shelton, et al. 1997. Multidimensional Inventory of Black Identity: Preliminary Investigation of Reliability and Construct Validity. *Journal of Personality and Social Psychology* 73 (4): 805–815.

Sellers, Robert M., and J. Nicole Shelton. 2003. The Role of Racial Identity in Perceived Discrimination. *Journal of Personality and Social Psychology* 84 (5): 1079–1092.

Sellers, Robert M., Mia A. Smith, J. Nicole Shelton, et al. 1998. Multidimensional Model of Racial Identity: A Reconceptualization of African American Racial Identity. *Personality and Social Psychology Review* 2: 18–36.

J. Nicole Shelton
Stephanie Johnson Rowley

MULTIDISCIPLINARY RESEARCH

SEE *Research, Trans-disciplinary.*

MULTIFINALITY

The term *multifinality* refers to a condition in which the same cause leads to different outcomes. Although the concept of multifinality may seem trivial at first glance, it has posed serious challenges to the concept of causality that happens to lie at the heart of science. In fact, the concept of causality is so important that scientists work tirelessly throughout their lives to identify the causes of important outcomes (conflict, aggression, anger, etc.). Of course, scientists are not unique in their preoccupation with causal relationships. Indeed, most people work tirelessly throughout their lives trying to figure out the factors that cause a range of important outcomes, from the desired affection of a potential love interest to success in the boardroom. From a practical standpoint, the ability to understand causal relationships carries enormous benefits because knowing the factors that cause important outcomes provides the key to predicting and controlling those outcomes. For example, the knowledge that X (parenting skills) causes the outcome Y (childhood achievement) can be used to manipulate X (through training in parenting skills) to cause changes in the outcome of Y (increased childhood achievement).

Although the exact criteria for assuming a causal relationship between two variables has long been a subject of debate, most scholars agree that at least three important criteria must be met to assume that one variable causes another. First, the two variables must covary such that changes in the first variable correlate with changes in the second variable. Second, the variable assumed to be the cause (e.g., poor parenting skills) must precede in time the observation of the outcome or effect variable (e.g., low childhood achievement). Third, all alternative explanations (e.g., low socioeconomic status, unstable home environment, genetic factors, etc.) must be ruled out before concluding that the proposed causal variable X (poor parenting skills) did cause the outcome Y (low childhood achievement). Assuming these criteria are satisfied, one can tentatively assume that X causes Y.

Although the concept of causality may appear straightforward, closer inspection reveals that what may seem to be a straightforward causal relationship can actually be quite complex in real life. Particularly in the social and behavioral sciences, multifinality and the related concept of equifinality qualify the ability to assume a direct causal relationship between a single cause (X) and a single effect (Y): Multifinality recognizes that sometimes the same cause (X) produces many different outcomes (Y_1, Y_2, Y_3), whereas equifinality recognizes that, at other times, different causes (X_1, X_2, X_3) produce the same outcome (Y).

More specifically, equifinality recognizes that different causes may, nevertheless, arrive at a common outcome. Stated otherwise, many roads lead to the same end. For example, in developmental psychology, research suggests that the different developmental experiences (poor parenting skills versus low socioeconomic status) can lead to the same outcome (low childhood achievement). As noted earlier, multifinality is unique in its recognition that similar, or even seemingly identical, causes may lead to different outcomes. In developmental psychology, research suggests that sometimes the same developmental experiences (child abuse) can lead to different outcomes (high childhood achievement versus low childhood achievement). In addition, goal psychologists have shown that the same behavior (working out at the gym) can result in the satisfaction of many different goals (goal 1: improve fitness; goal 2: meet new people). As these examples illustrate, the concept of multifinality describes a case in which a single road can lead to many different destinations.

So, what does the concept of multifinality mean for the goal of identifying causal relationships between variables? Multifinality (as well as the sister concept of equifinality) poses a serious challenge to science because it reduces the ability to confidently conclude that one causal variable (X) always leads to a second outcome variable (Y). That is, multifinality ultimately makes it difficult to confidently conclude that a particular outcome (Y) is, and always is, the result of a particular causal condition (X). Although adding complication, the awareness of multifinality has enriched rather than invalidated the sci-

entific pursuit of identifying causal relationships. Scientists have simply had to adjust the discourse and terminology they use when addressing the concept of causality to account for multifinality. Specifically, multifinality (and the sister concept of equifinality) has forced scientists to abandon attempts to discuss causal relationships between variables as statements of fact. Instead, scientists have refined their claims to present and discuss proposed causal relationships in the language of probability rather than fact. That is, scientists realistically incorporate a measure of error into their causal statements to account for multifinality, and to suggest that X is *likely* to cause rather than *always* causes Y, and that Y is *likely* rather than *always* caused by X. In this sense, the concept of multifinality has only prompted scientists to face the cold hard fact that, however probable, there is no such thing, including a causal relationship, that is absolutely certain in life.

SEE ALSO *Causality; Regression; Regression Analysis; Social Science*

BIBLIOGRAPHY

Cicchetti, Dante, and Fred A. Rogosch. 1996. Equifinality and Multifinality in Developmental Psychopathology. *Development and Psychopathology* 8: 597–600.

Kruglanski, Arie W., and Shira Fishman. 2006. Terrorism between "Syndrome" and "Tool." *Current Directions in Psychological Science* 15: 45–48.

Patrick J. Carroll

MULTILATERALISM

The simplest definition of *multilateralism* focuses on numbers: that is, an agreement or alliance among three or more members. Yet multilateralism also has a qualitative dimension. In this sense, it refers to rule-governed behavior in which states restrain their pursuit of immediate goals, presumably in order to achieve long-run interests through cooperation. As John Ruggie writes, "multilateralism is an institutional form which coordinates relations among three or more states on the basis of 'generalized' principles of conduct … without regard to the particularistic interests of the parties or the strategic exigencies that may exist in any specific occurrence" (1992, p. 571).

In particular, three normative principles constitute the institution of multilateralism. First, *indivisibility* refers to the notion that all actors are equal participants in the cooperative endeavor. It is illustrated by the concept of *collective security*, where an attack on any state is seen as an attack on everyone. Second, *nondiscrimination* implies that any benefit received by one state must be available to all, as exemplified in the most-favored-nation principle of the World Trade Organization. Finally, *diffuse reciprocity* refers to the idea that concessions and rewards balance out over the long run and states do not need to insist upon a strict tit-for-tat exchange (specific reciprocity).

While multilateral cooperation often occurs through formal organizations, it need not. Kenneth Abbot and Duncan Snidal (1998) have pointed out the efficiency and legitimacy that such organizations can bestow, though Charles Lipson (1991) has argued that the flexibility and low political profile of informal cooperation may sometimes make this a preferable means of acting multilaterally.

The concept of multilateralism is not new. An early example was the Concert of Europe, in which the great powers of nineteenth-century Europe coordinated their management of the international system by moderating their own behavior and consulting with one another over any territorial changes. Alliances such as the North Atlantic Treaty Organization and collective security organizations such as the United Nations represent other examples of multilateral cooperation designed to protect security.

Multilateralism is also prominent in economic relations. Much of the controversy over regional trade agreements stems from the conflict between the principle of multilateralism (and especially its nondiscrimination norm) and the preferential treatment that members of regional trade blocs receive from one another. In this context, multilateralism is seen as valuable not only because it facilitates liberalization, but also because it prevents political rivalries and alignments from interfering with economic exchange and thus diminishing both the economic effects and the political benefits of interdependence.

While multilateralism provides states with many advantages, it raises challenges as well. This is particularly true when states with differing levels of power coordinate their behavior. Large states often accuse small states of free-riding, while the latter see powerful states as undermining the principles of multilateralism by seeking to further narrow interests. Yet, states still see multilateralism as an effective way to achieve their interests. Very often, it is simply too costly or even impossible for states to go it alone.

This is true even for a hegemon like the United States, which rediscovered the value of multilateral institutions during the second term of President George W. Bush when Washington sought the legitimacy provided by UN approval in order to advance its goals in such places as Iraq, Iran, and North Korea.

SEE ALSO *Bilateralism; Internationalism; Napoleonic Wars; Trilateralism; Unilateralism; United Nations; World Trade Organization; World War I; World War II*

BIBLIOGRAPHY

Abbot, Kenneth W., and Duncan Snidal. 1998. Why States Act Through Formal Organizations. *Journal of Conflict Resolution* 42 (1): 3–32.

Frankel, Jeffrey A. 1997. *Regional Trading Blocs in the World Economic System.* Washington, DC: Institute for International Economics.

Jervis, Robert. 1985. From Balance to Concert: A Study of International Security Cooperation. *World Politics* 38 (1): 58–79.

Lipson, Charles. 1991. Why Are Some International Agreements Informal? *International Organization* 45 (4): 495–538.

Ruggie, John Gerard. 1992. Multilateralism: The Anatomy of an Institution. *International Organization* 46 (3): 561–598.

Jonathan Crystal

MULTIPARTY SYSTEMS

Electoral competition among a high number of parties and the formation of multiparty coalition governments are typical features of most democratic regimes. In contrast, two-party systems producing single-party governments are characteristic of a few of the oldest, institutionally frozen democracies, including the United Kingdom of Britain and the United States of America. In the past, two-party systems were considered a sound formula for effective and stable government. But the expansion of suffrage rights and the diffusion of democratic regimes, not only in continental Europe but also across the rest of the world, has confirmed Robert Dahl's early intuition: "It might be reasonable to consider multiparty systems as the natural way for government and opposition to manage their conflicts in democracies, while two-party systems, whether resembling the British pattern or the American, are the deviant cases" (1966, p. 334).

The degree of multipartyism can be measured not only by the absolute number of parties in the system, but also by their relative size. For this purpose, several indices of fractionalization, including the "effective number" of parties, have been proposed in which each party is weighed by its proportion of either votes or seats (depending on the electoral or legislative focus of the analysis). A conventional estimate is that multiparty systems exist when there are at least three *effective* parties. In other words, there is still a two-party system, even if there are more than two parties in the assembly, if two of the parties are sufficiently large (as happens, for instance, in the British House of Commons). About three-fourths of more than eighty democratic countries with more than one million inhabitants at the beginning of the twenty-first century have multiparty systems, that is, more than three effective electoral parties.

MULTIPARTY ELECTIONS

In any complex society, multiple parties can be formed on the basis of the politicization of new issues if political entrepreneurs take the initiative to introduce policy proposals alternative to the status quo. Potential issues to be politicized include defense, security, taxes, freedom, trade, school, property, family, welfare, the environment, race, and so on. The corresponding parties raising new policy alternatives have historically been called conservatives, liberals, radicals, socialists, Christians, agrarians, greens, ethnic, regionalists, and many other labels. In two-party systems, the agenda can be manipulated by shifting salience to only one or a few issues at a time, which usually produces high polarization between the two parties. In multiparty systems, by contrast, multiple policy issues can be given salience by different parties at the same time, thus broadening the public agenda and the opportunities for citizens' choice.

There has been some discussion over the propensity of multiparty systems to promote either "moderate" or "polarized" electoral competition. Polarization indices capture the degree of party concentration of votes or seats and the relative distance between various parties' policy positions. Obviously, polarization is minimal when there is only one, internally compact party—that is, when all voters prefer the same policy, which is indeed a rare occurrence in a democratic regime. But polarization is maximal when the number of parties is two, they have similar size, and are located at a great distance from each other. In countries with more than two parties, the higher the number of parties, the lower their relative distances (because intermediate, relatively close positions emerge), and the lower the degree of polarization in electoral competition among them.

A traditionally illustrative case is Switzerland, where there are a high number of parties and a high degree of policy consensus among them. Systematic analyses have shown that, in general, high fractionalization, that is, a high number of parties, is associated with low polarization.

In fact, most democratic party systems have moderate degrees of both party fractionalization and party polarization. At the beginning of the twenty-first century, multiparty systems exist in democratic countries such as Argentina, Belgium, Brazil, Costa Rica, the Czech Republic, Denmark, Finland, France, Germany, Indonesia, Israel, Japan, the Netherlands, New Zealand, Norway, Poland, Sweden, Switzerland, as well as in the European Parliament and many other institutions.

MULTIPARTY COALITIONS

In multiparty assemblies, decision-making usually requires the formation of majority multiparty coalitions. In most parliamentary regimes, cabinets are formed with more than one party. In regimes with separate powers, multiparty coalitions are also frequently formed both for legislative decisions and in support of presidential cabinets.

When parties form coalitions, they usually prefer partners with relatively close policy and ideology positions in order to maintain consistency with their own positions and win voters' credibility. As a consequence, majority coalitions typically include the median legislator's party, which can be located around a centrist, moderate position. If there is proportional representation, the median party corresponds to the median voter's choice. As the median voter's position minimizes the sum of distances from all the voters, this outcome can be considered relatively socially efficient. In contrast, in a two-party system with a majoritarian electoral rule, a single party may receive a majority of seats in the parliament on the basis of a minority of popular votes, which does not necessarily include the median voter. On average, multiparty coalition cabinets based on proportional representation are substantially closer to the median voter's position than are single-party cabinets based on plurality or majority rules.

In multiparty cabinets, the distribution of offices among parties may follow two criteria. On some issues of general interest, such as economic policy and interior and foreign affairs, the parties in the coalition tend to compromise on intermediate and moderate policies. Over time, even if some partners of the successive governmental coalitions change, there is a significant degree of consensus and continuity on major policies, in contrast to frequent policy reversals when single-party governments alternate. On other issues, separate portfolios are allocated to different parties according to the issue on which they are most prominently defined—such as finance for liberals, education for Christians, labor for socialists, agriculture for agrarians, environment for greens, culture for regionalists, etc.— which may satisfy people with intense issue preferences.

LARGE ELECTORAL RULES

The formation of multiple parties promotes the choice of inclusive political and electoral institutions. In general, if there are only one or two large parties they prefer small assemblies and single-member electoral districts with plurality rule, that is, institutions able to exclude others from competition. In contrast, multiple small parties prefer large assemblies and large electoral district magnitudes (that is, high numbers of seats per district), the latter using proportional representation rules, able to include them in the system.

But the pressures from multiparty systems to adopt inclusive electoral rules work differently in countries of different size. In large countries, a large assembly with the number of seats positively correlated to the country's population can be sufficiently inclusive. In the United States, for instance, the ideological range of Congress members, in spite of belonging formally to only two parties, is similar to that of typical multiparty systems in Europe, including conservative, Christian-democratic, liberal, and social-democratic positions. This derives from the fact that each representative is elected by the rather homogeneous population of a small territory in a very large and heterogeneous country. The two parties are large umbrellas for varied representation.

By contrast, in small countries in which small assemblies do not create large room for political variety, the development of multiple parties favors more strongly the adoption of inclusive, large multimember districts with proportional representation rules. A relevant development is that the average size of democratic countries decreases as a consequence of the fact that the number of countries and the number of democracies in the world increase. As the number of parties also increases within each democratic country, more and more countries tend, thus, to adopt electoral systems with rules of proportional representation.

All in all, traditional two-party systems, which reflected early political developments in relatively simple societies with limited suffrage rights, have been associated in recent times with high electoral polarization, adversarial politics, socially biased, minority governments, and policy instability. In contrast, multiparty systems, which result from widespread and continuing initiatives for policy and ideology innovation in democratic countries, are associated with inter-party competition and cooperation, broad public agendas, coalition governments with majority social support, consensual and relatively stable policy-making, and inclusive political institutions.

SEE ALSO *Democracy; First-past-the-post; Party Systems, Competitive; Plurality*

BIBLIOGRAPHY

Colomer, Josep M. 2001. *Political Institutions.* New York and Oxford: Oxford University Press.

Dahl, Robert, ed. 1966. *Political Oppositions in Western Democracies.* New Haven, CT, and London: Yale University Press.

Laver, Michael, and Norman Schofield. 1990. *Multiparty Government.* New York and Oxford: Oxford University Press.

Lijphart, Arend. 1999. *Patterns of Democracy.* New Haven, CT, and London: Yale University Press.

Powell, G. Bingham. 2000. *Elections as Instruments of Democracy.* New Haven, CT, and London: Yale University Press.

Sartori, Giovanni. 1976. *Parties and Party Systems.* Cambridge, U.K., and New York: Cambridge University Press.

Shepsle, Kenneth. 1991. *Models of Multiparty Electoral Competition.* London: Harwood.

Josep M. Colomer

MULTIPLE BIRTHS

Aristotle long ago aptly noted that multiple births are "*praeter naturam,*" that is, "outside nature's normal course." Being outside the normal, their reception in society is also different than that afforded to the single child. In many parts of the world, they are seen as good luck and have become absorbed into the local mythology. This was the case in ancient Rome and Greece, for example, and also in Mesoamerica. In other parts of the world, as was often the case in some but not all parts of Africa, they were not welcomed, being seen as evidence of maternal marital infidelity.

The fact that Aristotle's dictum remains correct centuries later is based on two inescapable facts: First, all multiple births are high-risk pregnancies in contrast to singletons (single births), and second, as the human female is genetically programmed to have a single child, both mother and child suffer these risks. This latter statement relates to the facts that under normal circumstances 98 percent of human pregnancies deliver one child only and that the distensibility of the human uterus is clearly limited. This reality is probably the greatest reason that higher-order multiples deliver preterm.

Twins are the most common form of multiple pregnancies, followed by triplets and then the rare occurrences of quadruplets and quintuplets. Prior to modern technologies for assisted reproduction, the incidence of twins was 1 in 89 deliveries, of triplets 1 in 89^2, and of quadruplets 1 in 89^3. All that changed after 1975 when clomiphene citrate became available; even more drastic changes followed post-1985 with the introduction of in vitro fertilization and embryo transfer. The rate of twin births has more than doubled, while that of triplets has tripled. U.S. trends were duplicated in many other localities that have access to modern treatments for infertility.

Twins are either *identical* or *fraternal*, though neither term is correct in that identical twins, derived from a single fertilized ovum, are never truly identical at the molecular genetic level, and fraternal twins, derived from two fertilized ova, may be female as well as male. More precise terms are *monozygotic* (MZ), meaning "one-egg," and *dizygotic* (DZ), meaning "two-egg," which both refer to embryological origins. Natural twins, the most frequent form of multiples, occur most commonly in Africans and least commonly in Asians, with the Euro-American Caucasian population in-between. The exact reasons for this have never been clarified, but it is known that the majority of twins in African populations are dizygotic, whereas the majority in Asian populations are monozygotic. In Caucasians, approximately two-thirds of naturally occurring twins are DZ and one third are MZ. In Africans, DZs far outnumber the MZs, presumably because of frequent double ovulation. In Asians, MZs predominate due to the relative scarcity of double ovulation. These racial variations have always been regarded as fact within the literature on multiples and have never been interpreted as signs of racial superiority/inferiority.

A third type of twins is the so-called Siamese or conjoined variety, named after the twins Eng and Chang, from Siam (now Thailand). These occur in somewhere between 1 in 50,000 and 1 in 100,000 births. Their cause is due to partial division of one zygote after thirteen days post fertilization. Female conjoined twins are more common than males in a ratio of 1.6:1, for reasons that are not entirely clear. It has been suggested that when conjoined twinning occurs at the embryonic plate, it is more lethal in males, though this has not been proven.

The prime cause of morbidity and mortality among all multiples is preterm delivery and low birth weight, which go hand in hand. Whereas the normal gestational length for singletons is forty weeks, the median gestational length is thirty-seven weeks for twins, thirty-three weeks for triplets, thirty-one for quadruplets, and twenty-nine for quintuplets. The increased numbers of preterm multiples raises U.S. rates of cerebral palsy by at least 7 percent. Mothers of multiples face five risks: anemia, postpartum bleeding, PIH (high blood pressure), polyhydraminos (excess water in one of the amniotic sacs), and preterm labor.

SEE ALSO *Twin Studies*

BIBLIOGRAPHY

Blickstein, Isaac, and Louis G. Keith, eds. 2001. *Iatrogenic Multiple Pregnancy*. London: Parthenon.

Blickstein, Isaac, and Louis G. Keith, eds. 2005. *Multiple Pregnancy: Epidemiology, Gestation, and Perinatal Outcome*. 2nd ed. London: Parthenon.

Keith, Louis G., and Isaac Blickstein, eds. 2002. *Triplet Pregnancies and Their Consequences*. London: Parthenon.

Louis Keith

MULTIPLE EQUILIBRIA

Derived from the Latin, the word *equilibrium* means "equal weight" or "balance" as illustrated by an equal-armed scale. Physically, a body acted upon by two or more forces in a state of equilibrium maintains a stationary position. This state is known as *static equilibrium*, as distinct from *dynamic equilibrium*, in which the body's position may change over time but maintains a state of static equilibrium at any given instant. The orbital motion of planets exemplifies dynamic equilibrium. Along with the notion of equilibrium comes that of *stability*, the tendency of a system to return to an equilibrium position after experiencing small perturbations of parameters influencing its prior equilibrium state. In the late nineteenth century, these concepts were adapted to economics and later game theory. In economics, the aim was, in part, to address the central question of prices that coordinate supply and demand.

DEFINITION OF MULTIPLE EQUILIBRIA

For the most part, economic equilibria are studied through the development, analysis, and application of mathematical models. The values of interest are solutions of systems of equations and inequalities. Economists distinguish between *general* and *partial* equilibrium theory. Partial equilibrium theory differs from general equilibrium theory by having a specific set of variables held constant for the analysis. The French economist Léon Walras (1834–1910) is credited with being the father of general equilibrium theory. His great seminal work, *Elements of Pure Economics* (1874), sets forth his conception of the subject in increasing levels of completeness and detail. In dealing with a pure exchange economy with multiple markets, he developed a mathematical model in the form of a system of simultaneous equations having exactly as many unknowns as equations; a solution of the system would presumably yield an equilibrium. As it happens, neither the existence nor the uniqueness of a solution to the formulated system is guaranteed on the grounds of having as many equations as variables. Moreover, even if a solution exists, there is no guarantee it will be nonnegative (or even real).

Walras's system was first rigorously addressed in the mid-1930s by Abraham Wald (1902–1950), a doctoral student (and participant in the Mathematical Colloquium) of Karl Menger (1902–1985). Between the work of Walras and Wald there appeared a series of significant contributions. Gustav Cassel (1866–1945) simplified some of Walras's writings. Independently, Frederik Zeuthen (1888–1959), Hans Neisser (1895–1975), and Heinrich von Stackelberg (1905–1946) emphasized the importance of modeling some or all constraints with inequalities rather than equations. Around this time, Karl Schlesinger (1902–1985) introduced the notion of *complementary slackness*, which says that if a resource is not fully utilized, then its price must be zero, and if a price is positive, then the corresponding inequality constraint must hold as an equation. These advances culminated in Wald's existence proof of competitive equilibrium. This, however, was to be superseded almost twenty years later by the work of Kenneth Arrow and Gerard Debreu (1921–2004).

ORIGIN AND STATUS OF THIS CONCEPT

It is difficult to pinpoint the discovery of multiple equilibria. On the history of general equilibrium analysis, Arrow and F. H. Hahn remark, "in general, there is no need that equilibrium be unique, and examples of non-uniqueness have been known since Marshall" (1971, p.15). In fact, in section 64 of his *Elements*, Walras points out that in a two-commodity exchange problem there could be no solution, and in section 65 he notes that there could be multiple equilibria. Irving Fisher's (1867–1947) 1891 PhD thesis contains an equilibrium model for an exchange economy and an ingenious hydraulic physical model for computing equilibrium prices and the resulting distribution of endowments. More recently, William Brainard and Herbert Scarf have elaborated this work and simulated the capability of Fisher's device to compute equilibrium prices and even to find multiple equilibria.

If an economy has multiple equilibria, their number may be finite or infinite. Debreu argues that "such economies still seem to provide a satisfactory explanation of equilibrium as well as a satisfactory foundation for the study of stability provided that all the equilibria of the economy are locally unique. But if the set of equilibria is compact (a common situation), local uniqueness is equivalent to finiteness" (1970, p. 387). He gives sufficient mathematical conditions for the existence of finitely many equilibria. This line of investigation employs the concept of a *regular economy*, a detailed exposition of which is beyond the scope of this entry. The key concept involves the rank of the Jacobian matrix of the excess supply mapping. An economy is *regular* if this Jacobian is of full rank at every equilibrium point. Taking this a step further, if the determinant of the Jacobian at an equilibrium point p is positive (negative), define $i(p) = 1$ ($i(p) = -1$). The sum of $i(p)$ over all the finitely many equilibria is 1. This implies that the number of equilibria of a regular economy is finite odd. Hence if $i(p) = 1$ for every equilibrium point p, then there can be only one of them. Conditions for local uniqueness have received considerable attention in literature. Michael Allingham (1989) gives a readable account of the subject.

THE SIGNIFICANCE OF MULTIPLE EQUILIBRIA

The possibility that a general equilibrium model can have multiple equilibria presents challenges on a variety of fronts. Timothy Kehoe (1998) gives necessary and sufficient conditions for uniqueness of equilibrium. But, as he concedes, "useful conditions that guarantee uniqueness of equilibrium are very restrictive.... The problem is that translating these mathematical conditions into easy-to-check and interpretable economic conditions, they lose their necessity" (1998, p. 38). Kehoe identifies the crux of the matter saying "it may be the case that most applied models have unique equilibria. Unfortunately, however, these models seldom satisfy analytical conditions that are known to guarantee uniqueness, and are often too large and complex to allow exhaustive searches to numerically verify uniqueness" (1998, p. 39).

The size of models can require aggregation and therein lies another problem. A type of result separately discovered by Hugo Sonnenschein, Rolf Mantel, and Debreu implies that aggregate excess-demand functions do not inherit all the properties known to be sufficient for proving uniqueness of equilibrium. In short, there could be more than one price vector at which excess demand is zero. This finding is sometimes called the *anything goes theorem*.

Franklin Fisher (1983), among many others, has emphasized the importance of *disequilibrium analysis*, the study of the process by which prices change when the economy is not in equilibrium. This is made all the more complicated by the presence of multiple equilibria.

In addition to dynamics, critiques of the Arrow-Debreu general equilibrium theory have signaled the need to consider features such as uncertainty, (asymmetric) information, money, and taxes. Some of this is addressed in Stephen Morris and Hyun Song Shin (2001) and Fabio Petri (2004). It has been said that there is a role for public policy in the reconciliation of cases where there are multiple equilibria in applied problems.

SEE ALSO *Equilibrium in Economics; General Equilibrium; Jacobian Matrix; Nash Equilibrium; Partial Equilibrium; Prisoner's Dilemma (Economics); Walras, Léon*

BIBLIOGRAPHY

Allingham, Michael. 1989. Uniqueness of Equilibrium. In *General Equilibrium: The New Palgrave*. eds. John Eatwell, Murray Milgate, and Peter Newman. 324–327. New York: Norton.

Arrow, Kenneth J., and Gerard Debreu. 1954. Existence of Equilibrium for a Competitive Economy. *Econometrica* 22: 265–290.

Arrow, Kenneth J., and F. H. Hahn. 1971. *General Competitive Analysis*. San Francisco: Holden-Day.

Debreu, Gerard. 1970. Economies with a Finite Set of Equilibria. *Econometrica* 38: 387–392.

Eatwell, John, Murray Milgate, and Peter Newman, eds. 1989. *General Equilibrium: The New Palgrave*. New York: Norton.

Fisher, Franklin M. 1983. *Disequilibrium Foundations of Equilibrium Economics.* Cambridge, U.K.: Cambridge University Press.

Kehoe, Timothy J. 1998. Uniqueness and Stability. In *Elements of General Equilibrium Analysis,* ed. Alan Kirman, 38–87. Malden, MA: Blackwell.

Morris, Stephen, and Hyun Song Shin. 2001. Rethinking Multiple Equilibria in Macroeconomic Modeling. In *NBER Macroeconomics Annual 2000*, 139–161. Cambridge, MA: MIT Press.

Petri, Fabio. 2004. *General Equilibrium, Capital, and Macroeconomics: A Key to Recent Controversies in Equilibrium Theory.* Cheltenham, U.K.: Edward Elgar.

Richard W. Cottle

MULTIPLE GENDERS

SEE *Gender, Alternatives to Binary.*

MULTIPLE INTELLIGENCES THEORY

Among various theories of intelligence are some that view intelligence as a system. The overarching assumption in these theories is that intelligence is not a single entity but a multifaceted structure. Correspondingly, traditional definitions of intelligence were called excessively narrow, and the quest for definitions and theories reflecting the variety of ways humans think, learn, and adapt to their environments began in the early 1980s in the United States. Among such systemic theories of intelligence are, most notably, Howard Gardner's theory of multiple intelligences and Robert Sternberg's triarchic theory of intelligence. Another relevant example is the theory of emotional intelligence, initially presented in the scientific literature in 1900 by Peter Salovey and Jack Mayer and popularized by Daniel Goleman in his 1995 best-selling book.

Gardner's theory of multiple intelligences (also referred to as MI theory) assumes the presence of a number of distinct forms of intelligence. Individuals possess these types of intelligence in varying degrees, which establishes their unique cognitive profiles. The theory arose based on the argument that traditional definitions of intelligence do not capture the wide variety of abilities humans display. While presenting and defending this argument, Gardner analyzed cases of individuals with unusual talents, neuropsychological evidence supporting the idea of specialization of certain brain areas on processing particular types of information, evolutionary evidence, and psychological studies of intelligence. According to Gardner, there are eight primary forms of intelligence:

linguistic (manifested in dealing with spoken or written words);

musical (demonstrated in dealing with rhythm, music, and hearing);

logical–mathematical (invoked while reasoning inductively or deductively and dealing with abstractions and numbers);

spatial (engaged in vision and spatial judgment);

bodily-kinesthetic (required for movement and doing);

interpersonal (needed for interactions with others);

intrapersonal (manifested in dealing with self);

naturalistic (demonstrated in dealing with nature, nurturing, and classification).

The addition of a ninth type—existential (descriptive of the capacity to raise and consider existential questions) intelligence—is under consideration. Because of its humanistic approach to acknowledging and promoting the value and contributions of each and every student, the MI theory has been embraced and supported by the educational community around the world.

A number of schools and many teachers claim to use MI theory as the fundamental framework for their pedagogies. Yet the theory has been widely criticized as well. It has been argued that the theory is based primarily on Gardner's intuition and observations rather than evidence, that there are no or limited empirical data to support the evidence, that the separation between the constructs of multiple intelligences and personality types is blurry, that the assumption that all students are gifted in something might lead to intellectual relativism, and that there has been no systematic evaluation of the value of the theory in the classroom.

The MI theory has many implications, among which the following four are stressed. First, because individuals possess different degrees of varying intelligence, it is important to identify "dominant" intelligences early and try to enhance these intelligences. Yet teaching for all types of intelligence is important because students need help developing the intelligences in which they demonstrate weaknesses. Second, dominant intelligences also represent dominant learning modalities, and teaching should match the pattern of dominant abilities. Thus schools should offer education that is centered on individuals and their profiles of intelligence. Third, because many intelligences exist, there should be many assessments, not only those that traditionally focus on linguistic and logical-mathematical intelligences. Fourth, of importance is the realization that different cultures differentially treat various intelligences. Thus what might be viewed as "preferred" intelligence in one culture might not be such in another culture.

Sternberg's theory of triarchic intelligence was developed at the same time as Gardner's theory of multiple intelligences. Being a part of the same quest against traditional narrow definitions of intelligence, Sternberg defined intelligence as mental activity central to one's life in real-world environments and aimed at adaptation to, selection, and shaping of these environments; thus the main premise is that this mental activity is relevant to success in real life. Correspondingly, in the late 1990s Sternberg changed the name of the theory to the *theory of successful intelligence*. As per its original name, the theory consists of three parts: *analytical* (also referred to as componential), *practical* (also referred to as contextual), and *creative* (also referred to as experiential). Analytical intelligence is evoked while analyzing, evaluating, criticizing, reasoning, and judging. Practical intelligence is used while implying, implementing, and using. Creative intelligence is manifested while discovering, inventing, dealing with novelty, and creating. Based on the prediction of the theory, intelligent people are expected to identify their strengths and weaknesses and make the most of their strengths and compensate for their weaknesses. Individuals are not restricted to excelling in only one of the three intelligences; both integrated and uneven profiles of intelligences are possible. This theory has also been widely accepted by both educators and psychologists. Unlike the MI theory, Sternberg's theory has a large body of empirical research associated with it. From a practical point of view, it has influenced U.S.-based practices of college admission, pedagogies across all levels of schooling, and the identification of gifted and talented students. Although the theory has numerous critics, over the years of its existence it has strengthened its empirical and theoretical grounds.

Intellectually, the theory of emotional intelligence is associated with Gardner's (through intra- and interpersonal intelligences) and Sternberg's (through practical intelligence) theories. Emotional intelligence is typically referred to as an ability, capacity, or skill to perceive and register, judge and assess, and manage and act on the emotions of self and others, yet there is currently no consensus definition for this term. The roots of the theory are in the use of the term *social intelligence* by the American psychologist Edward Thorndike, who used this term to refer to the skill of getting along with other people. The term *emotional intelligence* is associated with the PhD dissertation work of Wayne Payne (1986). The field of emotional intelligence is relatively new, and a number of psycholo-

gists and educators are continuing to work on the definition, assessment, and predictive power of this concept.

SEE ALSO *Creativity; Cultural Relativism; Intelligence; Intelligence, Social; IQ Controversy; Personality*

BIBLIOGRAPHY

Gardner, Howard. 1993. *Multiple Intelligences: The Theory in Practice.* New York: Basic Books.

Goleman, Daniel. 1995. *Emotional Intelligence.* New York: Bantam.

Salovey, Peter, and Jack D. Mayer. 1990. Emotional Intelligence. *Imagination, Cognition, and Personality* 9: 185–211.

Sternberg, Robert J. 1996. *Successful Intelligence.* New York: Simon and Schuster.

Elena L. Grigorenko

MULTIPLE PERSONALITIES

Multiple personality disorder, now labeled "dissociative identity disorder" (DID), is a psychological condition characterized by the presence of two or more distinct personality states that reflect an inability to integrate various aspects of identity, memory, and consciousness into a single coherent identity. The latest edition of the *Diagnostic and Statistical Manual of Mental Disorders* requires the following conditions for diagnosis:

1. multiple distinct identities

2. recurrent control of the person's behavior by at least two identities

3. an inability to recall important personal information

4. the absence of a general medical condition or substance use that could otherwise explain the dissociative symptoms (American Psychiatric Association 2000)

According to publications by Frank W. Putnam (1989) and Richard P. Kluft (1984), identities are considered entities with a coherent sense of self that respond to certain stimuli with a consistent pattern of behavior and feelings. Many argue, pointed out Colin A. Ross in *Dissociative Identity Disorder: Diagnosis, Clinical Features, and Treatment of Multiple Personality* (1997), that the distinct identities—"alters," "subpersonalities," or "personality states"—that characterize DID are not separate personality states per se but "fragmented parts of one personality" that individuals create to adapt to painful life experiences (Ross 1997, p. 144). Reports on the number of alternate identities vary considerably from two to several hundred with the average between thirteen and fifteen. The most common alters reported, according to Ross, are those of children, "protectors," "persecutors," and alters of the opposite sex. In addition often a host alter appears to control the body the majority of the time. Support for the notion of distinct personality states come from research suggestion differences in vocal patterns, handedness, respiration, and brain wave activity between alters; however, Scott O. Lilienfeld and Steven Jay Lynn (2003) have criticized this work because of naturally occurring variability among these factors and lack of controlled studies.

Epidemiological studies estimate that 6 to 12 percent of the U.S. inpatient psychiatric population and 1 to 3 percent of the general population meet DID criteria (Ross 1997). DID is consistently reported to occur more often in females, perhaps due to the increased rate of females seeking inpatient treatment. Individuals diagnosed with DID often meet criteria for mood and anxiety disorders. In particular there is a high comorbidity between posttraumatic stress disorder and DID (Ross 1997). J. Douglas Bremner and Elizabeth Brett confirmed this in their 1997 study when they found that dissociative symptoms occur more often in individuals with post-traumatic stress disorder.

Reports of DID in the United States have increased since the mid-1980s, although the cause of the increase is subject to speculation. Some, such as David Gleaves in his 1996 article "The Sociocognitive Model of Dissociative Identity Disorder: A Reexamination of the Evidence," attribute the rise in reported cases to increased awareness and understanding of the disorder. Others, like Nicholas Spanos in his 1994 article "Multiple Identity Enactment and Multiple Personality Disorder: A Sociocognitive Perspective," claim the rise in DID is the result of misdiagnosis, fabrication, or suggestibility through the use of questionable therapeutic techniques and media portrayal of DID. Nonetheless, research demonstrates that DID is reliably diagnosed across clinicians and settings (Ross, Duffy, and Ellason 2002; Latz, Kramer, and Hughes 1996). However critics question this reliability claiming that DID is reported by a small number of specialized clinicians.

The cause of DID is debated. The posttraumatic model was articulated by David Gleaves (1996), although several predecessors had connected DID and trauma by the early 1980s (Coons 1980; Greaves 1980; Spiegel 1984). Gleaves hypothesizes that DID is a posttraumatic condition in which dissociation functions as a coping strategy in response to overwhelming psychological pain brought about by childhood maltreatment. The high rates of self-reported physical and sexual abuse and/or post-

traumatic stress disorder among those diagnosed with DID support this theory. Conversely the sociocognitive model introduced by Spanos (1994) posits that DID is a socially derived condition produced by therapeutic suggestion and sociocultural influences, such as the media. It is hypothesized that DID can occur in the absence of childhood abuse and that alters are role enactments created and maintained by social reinforcement. For example, role-playing studies, such as the 1985 report conducted by Nicholas P. Spanos, John R. Weekes, and Lorne D. Bertrand, demonstrate that features of DID can be elicited from participants without the disorder through subtle cues or suggestions. This evidence supports arguments that features of DID are known to the public and may be easily induced (Lilienfeld et al. 2003). Finally, some theorists combine these two positions, proposing that the cause of DID cannot be entirely iatrogenic or trauma induced and that multiple pathways should be considered (Ross 1997, p. 92).

Regardless of the cause, DID continues to be categorized as a major psychological disorder. Most agree that DID symptoms exist and cause significant distress regardless of origin. Continued research may provide clarification regarding factors that contribute to the development of DID, prevention, and intervention. Further it may be essential to consider that both models provide important information about the development and maintenance of DID that could lead to a more complex conceptualization of the disorder in the future.

SEE ALSO *Anxiety; Mental Illness; Mood; Neuroticism; Personality; Post-Traumatic Stress; Psychotherapy*

BIBLIOGRAPHY

American Psychiatric Association. 2000. *Diagnostic and Statistical Manual of Mental Disorders: DSM-IV-TR.* 4th ed., text revision. Washington, DC: Author.

Bremner, J. Douglas, and Elizabeth Brett. 1997. Trauma-Related Dissociative States and Long-Term Psychopathology in Posttraumatic Stress Disorder. *Journal of Traumatic Stress* 10 (1): 37–49.

Coons, P. M. 1980. Multiple Personality: Diagnostic Considerations. *Journal of Clinical Psychiatry* 41 (10): 330–336.

Gleaves, David H. 1996. The Sociocognitive Model of Dissociative Identity Disorder: A Reexamination of the Evidence. *Psychological Bulletin* 120 (1): 42–59.

Greaves, G. B. 1980. Multiple Personality Disorder: 165 Years after Mary Reynolds. *Journal of Nervous and Mental Disease* 168: 577–596.

Kluft, Richard P. 1984. An Introduction to Multiple Personality Disorder. *Psychiatric Annals* 14: 19–24.

Latz, Tracy, Stephen I. Kramer, and Doreen L. Hughes. 1995. Multiple Personality Disorder among Female Inpatients in a

State Hospital. *American Journal of Psychiatry* 152: 1343–1348.

Lilienfeld, Scott O., and Steven Jay Lynn. 2003. Dissociative Identity Disorder: Multiple Personalities, Multiple Controversies. In *Science and Pseudoscience in Clinical Psychology*, eds. Scott O. Lilienfeld et al., 109–142. New York: Guilford.

Lilienfeld, Scott O., Steven Jay Lynn, Irving Kirsch, et al. 1999. Dissociative Identity Disorder and the Sociocognitive Model: Recalling the Lessons of the Past. *Psychological Bulletin* 125 (5): 507–523.

Putnam, Frank W. 1989. *Diagnosis and Treatment of Multiple Personality Disorder*. New York: Guilford.

Ross, Colin A. 1997. *Dissociative Identity Disorder: Diagnosis, Clinical Features, and Treatment of Multiple Personality*. 2nd ed. New York: Wiley.

Ross, Colin A., Colleen M. M. Duffy, and Joan W. Ellason. 2002. Prevalence, Reliability, and Validity of Dissociative Disorders in an Inpatient Setting. *Journal of Trauma and Dissociation* 3 (1): 7–17.

Spanos, Nicholas. 1994. Multiple Identity Enactment and Multiple Personality Disorder: A Sociocognitive Perspective. *Psychological Bulletin* 116: 143–165.

Spanos, Nicholas P., John R. Weekes, and Lorne D. Bertrand. 1985. Multiple Personality: A Social Psychological Perspective. *Journal of Abnormal Psychology* 94: 362–378.

Spiegel, David. 1984. Multiple Personality as a Post-Traumatic Stress Disorder. *Psychiatric Clinics of North America* 7 (1): 101–110.

River J. Smith
Elana Newman

MULTIPLEX

SEE *Symbols.*

MULTIPLIER, THE

In macroeconomics, the multiplier is the ratio of a change in the equilibrium level of national income (or of aggregate employment) to the change in autonomous spending (or in employment on public-works projects) that brought it about. As early as Walter Bagehot's *Lombard Street* in 1871 and Alfred and Mary Marshall's *Economics of Industry* in 1879 (and arguably even in an oration by Pericles, as reported by Plutarch), it has been recognized that an initial round of spending in one sector caused successive rounds of spending as the recipients of each round of income spent that increase in their income in ways that created more income for others.

John Maynard Keynes and Hubert Henderson invoked this long-held belief in their 1929 pamphlet *Can Lloyd George Do It?*, in which they endorsed the pledge by Liberal leader (and former prime minister) David Lloyd George to eliminate Britain's interwar unemployment through public-works spending that would indirectly generate more jobs than just the direct employment on public works. The problem with winning acceptance for that argument was that it was unclear why the process would be finite, why employing one person on public works would not push the whole economy to full employment. The crucial advance was not recognition of successive rounds of spending but the analysis of the leakages from each round of spending that led to the multiplier having a finite value. If a fraction of each round of income is not spent on domestic output, the geometric series of rounds of spending sums to a finite value (just as, about the same time, it was shown that in a fractional-reserve banking system, a change in the monetary base leads to a finite change in the money supply because of leakages into currency and required reserves).

The successive contributions to this analysis by Ralph G. Hawtrey, Lyndhurst F. Giblin, Richard Kahn, Jens Warming, J. M. Keynes, Michal Kalecki, and John Maurice Clark from 1928 to 1935 are reprinted in Dimand (2002) (see Hegeland 1954; Wright 1956; Davis 1980; Kahn 1984; Dimand 1988, 1994). Keynes's 1933 pamphlet *The Means to Prosperity* and his *General Theory* (1936), crediting Kahn (1931), used such a finite-valued spending multiplier to analyze how expansionary fiscal policy could increase output and employment in an economy operating below full employment, with the difference that while Kahn (1931) analyzed successive rounds of employment, Keynes (1933, 1936) considered successive rounds of spending. Davis (1980) argues that, in addition to the influence of Kahn (1931), Keynes was also influenced by correspondence with Hawtrey. Translated from changes in income and autonomous spending to their levels, the multiplier analysis led to the IS goods market equilibrium condition of the IS-LM model. However, understanding of the multiplier process and the goods market equilibrium condition need not imply support for activist fiscal policy. Hawtrey, the British Treasury economist who provided early numerical examples and algebraic analysis of the finite-valued multiplier, held that fiscal expansion would simply crowd out private investment because he considered the demand for money not responsive to the interest rate (in later terminology, a vertical LM curve).

The Keynesian spending multiplier k represents the change in equilibrium income and expenditure (Y) resulting from a change in autonomous investment (I) or government spending (G), $\Delta Y = k \, \Delta I$ or $\Delta Y = k \, \Delta G$, assuming that the price level, money wage rate, and interest rate do not change. It can thus be best viewed as the amount by which the IS curve (the goods market equilibrium condition) shifts horizontally at a given interest rate in the Hicks-Hansen IS-LM diagram (which is drawn for given prices and money wages) rather than as a change in the ultimate equilibrium of a complete model. The aggregate demand curve, on an aggregate demand/aggregate supply diagram with the price level and income on the two axes, would shift by as much as the IS/LM intersection shifted. In a footnote at the start of the very first multiplier article, Kahn (1931) promised a second article showing the results carried through even if fiscal expansion increased money wages, but that article never appeared and the footnote is not in the reprint in Kahn (1972). The Keynesian spending multiplier k, long the workhorse of introductory macroeconomics courses, is $1/(1 - z)$, where z is the marginal propensity to spend. If there were no taxes or imports, the marginal propensity to spend would equal the marginal propensity to consume out of disposable income, c. With an income tax rate, t, and a marginal propensity to import, m, the marginal propensity to spend $z = (1 - t) c - m$. Since the marginal propensities to consume and save out of disposable income add to 1 ($s + c = 1$), the denominator of the multiplier, $1 - z$, is equal to $s (1 - t) + t + m$. The larger the leakages from spending on domestic output into taxes, saving, and imports, the smaller the multiplier for a small open economy. (The multiplier for a large open economy would have to recognize that an increase in imports has a multiplier effect on equilibrium income in the rest of the world, which causes the rest of the world to import more from the home country.)

Because a change in taxes affects disposable income rather than spending in the first round, its effect will be proportionally smaller than that of a change in government spending. If there were only lump-sum taxes, with (for simplicity) no proportional taxes and no marginal propensity to import, the multiplier for a change in government spending would be $1/(1 - c)$ and that for a change in taxes would be $c/(1 - c)$. Notice that for a balanced budget increase in government spending, with lump-sum taxes increased by as much as government spending, the balanced budget multiplier would $(1 - c)/(1 - c)$, which is 1.

The empirical importance of the simple Keynesian multiplier was diminished by the permanent income and life-cycle theories of consumption, which argued that the marginal propensity to consume out of a change in current income (and hence also the value of the multiplier) is much smaller than had been assumed. The importance, and presumed size, of the multiplier was further diminished by the theory of Ricardian equivalence or debt neutrality, which argued that a deficit-financed increase in government spending causes consumers to save in anticipation of the future tax liabilities implied by the government borrowing, so that any change in government spending, whether financed by current taxes or by borrowing against future taxes, will only shift the IS curve by the amount of the balanced budget multiplier effect. The multiplier continues to be a central feature of introductory macroeconomics courses but in more advanced courses is subsumed in the goods market equilibrium condition represented by the IS curve. The multiplier is used in regional and urban policy analysis to analyze the effects on a local economy of a public-works project such as a new sports stadium.

SEE ALSO *Economic Growth; Economics, Keynesian; Full Employment; Involuntary Unemployment; Kahn, Richard F.; Keynes, John Maynard; Macroeconomics; Propensity to Consume, Marginal; Propensity to Import, Marginal; Underemployment; Unemployment*

BIBLIOGRAPHY

Davis, Eric G. 1980. The Correspondence between R. G. Hawtrey and J. M. Keynes on the *Treatise*: The Genesis of Output Adjustment Models. *Canadian Journal of Economics* 13: 716–724.

Dimand, Robert W. 1988. *The Origins of the Keynesian Revolution.* Aldershot, U.K.: Edward Elgar, and Stanford, CA: Stanford University Press.

Dimand, Robert W. 1994. Mr. Meade's Relation, Kahn's Multiplier, and the Chronology of the General Theory. *Economic Journal* 104: 1139–1142.

Dimand, Robert W., ed. 2002. *The Origins of Macroeconomics*, 10 vols. London and New York: Routledge.

Hegeland, Hugo. 1954. *The Multiplier Theory.* New York: Augustus M. Kelley Reprints of Economic Classics, 1966.

Kahn, Richard F. 1931. The Relation of Home Investment to Unemployment. *Economic Journal* 41: 173–198.

Kahn, Richard F. 1972. *Selected Essays on Employment and Growth.* Cambridge, U.K.: Cambridge University Press.

Kahn, Richard F. 1984. *The Making of Keynes's General Theory.* Cambridge, U.K.: Cambridge University Press.

Keynes, John Maynard. 1936. *The General Theory of Employment, Interest and Money.* London: Macmillan.

Wright, A. Llewellyn. 1956. The Genesis of the Multiplier Theory. *Oxford Economic Papers*, n.s. 8: 181–193.

Robert W. Dimand

MULTIRACIAL MERITOCRACY

SEE *Meritocracy, Multiracial.*

MULTIRACIAL MOVEMENT

The American multiracial movement is best known for its advocates' efforts throughout the 1990s to add a "multiracial" category to the 2000 census. By the end of that decade, the federal government, along with a number of state governments, had not only devoted substantial resources to investigating the issue; eventually it also agreed to document race in a new way. Although a multiracial category was *not* added to the census in 2000, for the first time ever a "mark one or more" (MOOM) option—allowing individuals to identify officially with as many groups as they saw fit—appeared on the form.

The Office of Management and Budget (OMB) is responsible for coordinating the activities of all federal statistical agencies, including the Census Bureau. Responding to ongoing criticism of the census and to rapid change in the racial and ethnic makeup of the country, the OMB conducted a comprehensive review of the racial categorization system from 1993 to 1997. While a variety of issues were considered, the review eventually focused on the multiracial category proposal. Before the review, identification with more than one race was not allowed. After the review, the OMB gave everyone the option to identify with as many races as they wished.

The experience of parents registering children from the growing number of interracial unions for school loomed large in the OMB decision. Many of these parents felt that a monoracial census forced unacceptable and avoidable decisions on individuals and families to identify with one parent and deny the other. The issue of multiracial recognition on government forms helped to galvanize the multiracial movement, which started with a handful of groups that formed on the West Coast in the late 1970s and early 1980s. In 1988 a number of these local adult organizations joined forces to create the Association of MultiEthnic Americans (AMEA), whose political objective was to push the OMB to add a multiracial category on government forms.

Soon after the establishment of the AMEA, two other organizations claiming national memberships and networks also came to the fore: Project RACE (Reclassify All Children Equally) and A Place For Us (APFU). The three groups' orientations and goals were divergent from the beginning; however, they shared the conviction that it was inaccurate and improper to force multiracial Americans into monoracial categories. On this basis, the groups often worked together during the 1990s. AMEA took the position that multiracial people should have the right to claim their entire heritage and embrace their total identity. One means to that end, AMEA maintained, was multiracial recognition on the census. For Project RACE, the main objective was to get a multiracial classification on all school, employment, state, federal, local, census, and medical forms requiring racial data so that multiracial children would not have to suffer the adverse consequences of being regarded as "Other." Finally, APFU viewed the "support and encouragement of interaction between anyone involved with interracial relationships" as their purpose and a "color-blind society" as their goal. Together the three represented the backbone of the multiracial category effort. In the mid-1990s, during the height of the movement's activity, there were thirty active adult-based multiracial organizations across the United States and approximately the same number of student organizations on college campuses.

Over the course of that decade, civil rights groups increasingly came to perceive the multiracial movement as a threat. The civil rights community feared that a multiracial category would dilute the count of minority populations, and—although in actuality this prospect triggered different concerns for different civil rights organizations—their shared position was that a multiracial identifier would undercut existing civil rights safeguards. Multiracial advocates, however, saw compulsory single-race categories as an outdated response to a growing multiracial reality and maintained that their recognition would come at no adverse civil rights cost.

In MOOM and related stipulations, the OMB tried to strike a balance between capturing increasing diversity and providing the statistics necessary to measure discrimination and enforce the nation's civil rights laws. Even so, the implications of MOOM remain unclear and the circumstances invite further challenge. For instance, in order to distinguish those persons who selected a single race—say Asian—from those who selected Asian and another race, groups were reported in ranges from minimum to maximum sizes: This created alternate—yet official—counts of racial groups. As a result, the denominator is debatable. Moreover, allowing people to mark more than one race resulted in a total of fifty-seven possible multiple-race combinations in 2000. Add to that the five official single-race categories plus a sixth option, "Some Other Race," and the tally increases to sixty-three racial categories. Because each racial category is also divided by a question asking respondents if they are Hispanic, the constellation of race/ethnic mixtures swells to a universe of 126 possibilities. As a result, the proliferation of categories could itself complicate civil rights enforcement efforts. The decision to allow people to identify with multiple racial heritages has introduced new data, questions, and controversies into an already volatile debate on race-conscious public policy.

SEE ALSO *Civil Rights Movement, U.S.; Identification, Racial; Marriage, Interracial; Minorities; Mulattos;*

Multiracials; Politics, Identity; Race; Race Mixing; Race-Conscious Policies; Racial Classification

BIBLIOGRAPHY

Alonso, William, and Paul Starr, eds. 1987. *The Politics of Numbers.* New York: Russell Sage Foundation.

Perlmann, Joel, and Mary Waters, eds. 2002. *The New Race Question: How the Census Counts Multiracial Individuals.* New York: Russell Sage Foundation.

Skerry, Peter. 2000. *Counting on the Census? Race, Group Identity, and the Evasion of Politics.* Washington, DC: Brookings Institution Press.

Williams, Kim M. 2006. *Mark One or More: Civil Rights in Multiracial America.* Ann Arbor: University of Michigan Press.

Kim M. Williams

MULTIRACIALS IN THE UNITED STATES

The 2000 U.S. Census provided the first opportunity for persons to self-identify with more than one race. More than 6.8 million Americans, representing 2.4 percent of the U.S. population, marked two or more races in the 2000 Census. Of these self-identified persons of multiple races, 2.2 million reported just two categories: white and "some other race," representing the largest category, or 32.32 percent of multiple-race combinations; and white and American Indian, 15.86 percent of the multiracial population. The next largest categories reported combinations of white and Asian, or 12.72 percent of the multiracial population, and white and black, or 11.50 percent of the multiracial population. In other words, nearly three-quarters of the multiracial population reported two races, combining white with something else (Social Science Data Analysis Network 2000). Hawaii and Alaska are the states with the largest multiracial populations (21.4 percent and 5.4 percent, respectively). In the continental United States, California and Texas have the largest number of counties with multirace populations that exceed 5 percent (Besl 2001).

The 2000 Census method of counting multiracial populations may yield under estimates of the total numbers of persons who identify as multiracial. Analysis of the National Longitudinal Study of Adolescent Health, a panel that includes multiple indicators of race, shows that contextual factors influence responses to the multirace question. For example, whereas 3.6 percent of all (non-Hispanic) respondents reported multirace identification when interviewed in a home setting, 6.8 percent reported multirace identification in a self-administered school interview (Harris and Sim 2002).

Alternative methods of counting multiracials would permit persons to identify as multiracial or biracial, a position advocated by multiracial advocacy groups such as Project RACE and the Association of MultiEthnic Americans (Rockquemore and Brunsma 2002), groups that have mobilized various constituencies to identify persons of mixed race as a separate category (Farley 2002; Childs 2004). Some believe that this method of counting multiracials would result in a larger count of multiracials and a lower count of single-race persons, particularly blacks (Farley 2002).

At various points in U.S. history, persons of mixed racial heritage have been documented and counted within single racial categories. In early censuses racial categories included free whites, slaves, free colored (nonwhites), and all other persons, excluding Indians not taxed (see U.S. Census Bureau 1821, p. 14). Persons of multiple races were included as slaves, free colored, or "all other persons." Rules evolved to assign mixed-race persons to specific single-race categories; a common one in most U.S. states was the "one-drop rule," whereby persons with even a small amount of black blood were assigned to the Negro category (Hunter 2005). American Indians of mixed heritage were classified by a different rule. In the 1870 census Francis A. Walker, superintendent of the census, reported that "[T]he principle that has governed in the classification of persons of part-Indian blood in the present census has been as follows: Where persons reported as 'Half-breeds' are found residing with whites, adopting their habits and life and methods of industry, such persons are to be treated as belonging to the white population" (U.S. Census Bureau 1871, p. xiii).

In the 1850 census Negroes were designated for the first time as either black or mulatto (Daniel 2002, p. 40). Mulattos accounted for 24.8 percent of the black population in the North and 11.2 percent of the black population overall (Daniel 2002, p. 40). The 1890 census categorized mixed-race Negroes into further groups. Of the 62,622,250 persons counted in the 1890 census, 7,638,366 were reported to be colored, and of those, 7,470,049 were classified as "of Negro descent." Persons of Negro descent were further classified as Negroes, mulattos (one-half black), quadroons (one-quarter black), and octoroons (one-eighth black). Negroes accounted for 6,337,980 of those classified as persons of Negro descent, and mixed-race persons of Negro descent represented about 15 percent of the black population.

In New Orleans and Charleston, mixed-race persons were middlemen between the black and white communities, justifying a codification that made a distinction between Negroes determined by the one-drop rule and multiracial persons with separate identities, social organizations, and networks (Daniel 2002, pp. 55–60). However, this status was threatened by *Plessy v. Ferguson* (1896), which solidified the one-drop rule and denied octoroons rights held by whites (Daniel 2002, p. 79). The allegation that persons of mixed race have social and economic advantages has been challenged in recent research, although lighter skin color seems to confer educational and income advantages to African American women (Hunter 2005, p. 48).

In 1977 the Office of Management and Budget (OMB) Statistical Policy Directive 15 established four racial classifications for use in federal statistics and administrative reporting: (1) white, (2) black, (3) Asian or Pacific Islander, and (4) American Indian or Alaskan Native. These classifications, along with two ethnicity categories and the category "some other race," provided the basis for reporting and data collection. After considerable lobbying by multiracial groups and following public hearings and a workshop hosted by the National Academy of Sciences, the OMB issued new regulations in 1997. The revised standards stated that the minimum categories for racial classification would be: American Indian or Alaska Native; Asian; black or African American; Native Hawaiian or other Pacific Islander; and white. Respondents to federal questionnaires or surveys would be able to select one or more races. The 2000 census included a sixth racial category, "some other race" (U.S. Census Bureau 2000), and the OMB provided further clarification on collecting and reporting multiracial data for federal civil rights monitoring and enforcement (Office of Management and Budget 2000).

During the 1990s a vocal group of multirace advocates unsuccessfully lobbied for the inclusion of a specific Census category called multiracial. Although such a category can be inferred from the 1997 OMB standards, it did not achieve the political ends its advocates desired. Kim Williams, a leading analyst of the multirace political movement, concluded that advocates want the multiracial designation to help improve the self-esteem of children of mixed race backgrounds. The multirace political movement is seen as an alternative to traditional civil-rights approaches focusing on single races (Williams 2005; 2006).

SEE ALSO *Marriage, Interracial; Miscegenation; Multiracial Movement; Race Mixing*

BIBLIOGRAPHY

Besl, John. 2001. Diversity on a Personal Level: A First Look at Multiple Race Population. *Indiana Business Review* (June). http://www.ibrc.indiana.edu/ibr/2001/summer01/02.pdf.

Campbell, Mary, and Jennifer Eggering-Boeck. 2006. What about the Children? The Psychological and Social Well-Being of Multiracial Adolescents. *The Sociological Quarterly* 47: 147–173.

Childs, Erica Chito. 2004. Multirace.com: Multiracial Cyberspace. In *The Politics of Multiracialism: Challenging Racial Thinking*, ed. Heather Dalmage, 143–160. Albany: State University of New York Press.

Daniel, G. Reginald. 2002. *More Than Black? Multiracial Identity and the New Racial Order.* Philadelphia: Temple University Press.

Farley, Reynolds. 2002. Racial Identities in 2000. In *The New Race Question*, eds. Joel Perlmann and Mary Waters, 33–37. New York: Russell Sage Foundation.

Harris, David, and Jeremiah Sim. 2002. Who Is Multiracial? Assessing the Complexity of Lived Race. *American Sociological Review* 67 (4): 614–627.

Hunter, Margaret. 2005. *Race, Gender, and the Politics of Skin Tone.* New York: Routledge.

Office of Management and Budget. 2000. Guidance on Aggregation and Allocation of Data on Race for Use in Civil Rights Monitoring and Enforcement. http://www.whitehouse.gov/omb/bulletins/b00-02.html.

Rockquemore, Kerry Ann, and David Brunsma. 2002. *Beyond Black: Biracial Identity in America.* Thousand Oaks, CA: Sage Publications.

Snipp, C. Matthew. 2002. American Indians: Clues to the Future of Other Racial Groups. In *The New Race Question: How the Census Counts Multiracial Individuals*, eds. Joel Perlmann and Mary Waters, 189–214. New York: Russell Sage Foundation.

Social Science Data Analysis Network. 2000. U.S. Multiracial Profile. CensusScope Web Site. http://www.censusscope.org/us/chart_multi.html.

U.S. Census Bureau. 1821. Census for 1820. Washington, DC: Gales and Seaton. http://www2.census.gov/prod2/decennial/documents/1820a-01.pdf.

U.S. Census Bureau. 1871. Report of the Superintendent of the Ninth Census. Washington, DC: Government Printing Office.

U.S. Census Bureau. 2000. Racial and Ethnic Classifications Used in Census 2000 and Beyond. http://www.census.gov/population/www/socdemo/race/racefactcb.html.

Williams, Kim M. 2005. Multiracialism & The Civil Rights Future. *Daedalus* 134 (winter): 53–60.

Williams, Kim M. 2006. *Mark One or More: Civil Rights in Multiracial America.* Ann Arbor: University of Michigan Press.

Samuel L. Myers Jr.

MULTISECTOR MODELS

Economists use models to understand different aspects of the economy. A *multisector model* is used primarily to study the allocation of resources across different economic activities. A multisector model, however, has more uses than simply the study of the distribution of resources. Some of the most exciting work being done with multisector models is in the economic theory of growth and development. This work originates in the observation that as an economy grows its production activities and employment shares move from agriculture to industry and services, with services eventually claiming the vast majority of the country's employment potential. So, if economists can understand what causes these shifts in sectoral employment shares, they might understand what makes countries grow; conversely, if they can understand what makes countries grow, they might understand how the workforce allocates its time across economic sectors.

What is an economic sector? The United Nations has produced a system of activity classifications—the ISIC (International Standard Industrial Classifications), designed to help classify economic sectors across countries in a comparable way. Using the ISIC, one can define sectors as one-digit, two-digit, three-digit, and so on, depending on the detail required. For example, agriculture, industry, and services are one-digit sectors, whereas textiles and vehicle manufacture are two of the many two-digit sectors within manufacturing.

Economists, however, find that a more useful way of defining a sector draws from the objectives of the multisector model in hand. Examples of multisector models can be found in the fields of economic growth, development economics, labor economics, international trade, spatial (geography) economics, business cycles, and others. In each case, the definition of the sector may differ, and the challenge facing the applied economist is to find the correspondence between the way the sector is defined in the model and the ISIC classification. For example, a multisector model may define sectors according to whether the goods produced within a sector are primary, secondary, or tertiary; agricultural, industrial, or service goods; tradable or nontradable; and public or private. In addition to matching the sectors in the model to the ISIC classification, for other purposes a multisector model may define sectors according to whether the goods are traditional or modern, rural or urban, produced in a formal or informal business environment, and produced at home or in the market.

Multisector models in economic development have added to our knowledge of how an economy leaves the stagnant agricultural state and enters modern growth. An important example is the multisector model by Gary Hansen and Edward Prescott (2002). Their model has a traditional sector and a modern sector. Both sectors produce the same goods but with different technologies. Land is a fixed factor that is used only in the traditional sector but not in the modern sector. Modern technology has a higher rate of productivity growth than traditional technology. Both technologies have diminishing marginal return to their inputs. Hansen and Prescott show that, initially, resources are devoted only into the traditional sec-

tor, but as the technology of the modern sector improves, more resources shift into it.

A related class of multisector models has enriched our understanding of the declining share of agriculture, the rise and fall of industry, and the rising share of services observed in most countries that have experienced modern growth. L. Rachel Ngai and Christopher Pissarides (2007) show that when sectors produce goods that are complements of each other, resources move from the sector with high productivity growth to the sector with low productivity growth. Since agricultural and manufacturing sectors experience, on average, faster productivity growth than the services sector, resources are shifted away from agriculture and into manufacturing and services. As the agriculture sector shrinks, eventually resources also shift away from manufacturing and into service production.

So far, the examples of what defines a multisector model are based mainly on *technology*, but there are other definitions, such as those that are based on *preferences* and *institutions*. Addressing the same issue of the decline in agriculture and the rise of services, Piyabha Kongsamut, Sergio Rebelo, and Danyang Xie (2001) present a multisector model that is based on preferences. In their model, agriculture produces an inferior good and services a luxury good; then, as incomes rise, demand shifts from agriculture to services. As a result, resources shift from agricultural to service production.

A third class of multisector models relies on an institutional definition. One class of institution-based multisector models is motivated by the fact that official statistics only report formal market activities. However, there are plenty of studies that show that a large fraction of resources is allocated to informal activities and activities at home. These studies are based on the time-use surveys conducted by individual countries, such as the United Kingdom and the United States, and on a cross-country survey conducted by the World Bank. The production activities at home and in the informal sector can all potentially be produced in the formal market sector, which will then enter the official statistics. The economic activities at home include child care, cooking, cleaning, and so on. If the child is sent to a day-care center, its care will be recorded as part of GDP (gross domestic product). Home production is substantial in most of the time-use surveys. For example, it took up as much time as market production in the United States during the 1990s. The economic activities in the informal sector in general refer to activities that evade government regulation, including tax evasion. This is a more common phenomenon in developing countries.

There are many reasons why economists care about whether a certain activity is done in the formal market sector or in the informal or home sector. Two intuitive and important reasons concern accurate measurement of economic activity and the formulation and implementation of public policies that will increase social welfare. Knowing what fraction of the economy's resources are devoted to the formal market sector is important for understanding and interpreting measured GDP, especially when comparisons are made across countries. Second and perhaps more importantly, it might have different policy implications not only for welfare but also for measured economic activities.

A good example is the multisector model by Stephen Parente, Richard Rogerson, and Randall Wright (2000). In their model, goods can be produced in the nonmarket sector or in the market sector. They show that distortionary policy that affects capital accumulation has a larger impact on measured GDP in their multisector model than in the usual one-sector model. This improves our understanding of the reasons that cross-country income differences are so large. Models with home and market sectors are also used for explaining the dynamics of labor supply. Taxes on the market sector play an important role in these models as they shift production from the formal market to the home or informal sector.

SEE ALSO *Economic Model; Input-Output Matrix; Models and Modeling; Social Accounting Matrix; Structural Transformation; Two-Sector Models*

BIBLIOGRAPHY

Hansen, Gary D., and Edward C. Prescott. 2002. Malthus to Solow. *American Economic Review* 92 (4): 1205–1217.

Kongsamut, Piyabha, Sergio Rebelo, and Danyang Xie. 2001. Beyond Balanced Growth. *Review of Economic Studies* 68 (4): 869–882.

Ngai, L. Rachel, and Christopher A. Pissarides. 2007. Structural Change in a Multisector Model of Growth. *American Economic Review* 97 (1): 429–443.

Parente, Stephen L., Richard Rogerson, and Randall Wright. 2000. Homework in Development Economics: Household Production and the Wealth of Nations. *Journal of Political Economy* 108 (4): 680–687.

Liwa Rachel Ngai

MULTIVOCALITY
SEE *Symbols.*

MUNDELL-FLEMING MODEL

The Mundell-Fleming model integrates international trade and finance into macroeconomic theory. This approach was developed in the early 1960s by the Canadian economist Robert Mundell (winner of the 1999 Nobel Prize in economics) and the British economist J. Marcus Fleming (1911–1976). In this period, both authors were members of the International Monetary Fund's Research Department, where they independently extended the traditional Keynesian model to an open economy setup in which the capital and goods markets are internationally integrated. The resulting research constitutes the original version of the Mundell-Fleming model (Mundell 1963; Fleming 1962).

The Mundell-Fleming model shows that, under a flexible exchange rate regime, fiscal policy does not have any power to affect output, while monetary policy is very effective. The opposite is true if the exchange rate is fixed. The assumption that international capital markets are completely integrated plays a crucial role in determining these results.

FLEXIBLE EXCHANGE RATE CASE

Since a monetary expansion tends to decrease the interest rate, this policy also encourages an outflow of financial capital as domestic investors seek higher returns by purchasing foreign bonds. Investors need to buy foreign currency to acquire foreign bonds. Accordingly, the supply of domestic currency increases to purchase the foreign currency needed to acquire foreign bonds. The domestic exchange rate depreciates; that is, more units of domestic currency must be exchanged for each unit of foreign currency. This makes domestic goods cheaper compared to foreign goods, thus improving the trade balance (purchases of imports decline and sales of exports increase) and stimulating domestic output and employment. The domestic money demand therefore increases, bringing the domestic interest rate back in line with the world interest rate. In the equilibrium that emerges after the monetary expansion, the interest rate is unaltered while output is increased proportionally to the increase in the money supply.

In the case of a fiscal expansion, the initial increase in domestic government spending creates an excess demand for goods and tends to raise output, employment, and income. This, in turn, raises the demand for money and the level of the interest rate. The fact that the domestic interest rate is now higher than the world interest rate causes an inflow of capital, which causes an appreciation of the domestic exchange rate (fewer units of domestic currency must be provided for each unit of foreign currency). In this case, therefore, domestic goods become more expensive compared to foreign goods, and the trade balance deteriorates (more imports are purchased and fewer exports are sold), depressing domestic output, employment, and income. A new equilibrium is reached in which the trade balance is worsened while output and the interest rate are restored to their original levels.

Free capital mobility and trade integration therefore determine the ability of monetary policy to stimulate the domestic economy but frustrate the effects of fiscal policy when the exchange rate is flexible.

FIXED EXCHANGE RATE CASE

The results illustrated above are reversed in a pegged exchange rate regime. With pegged interest rates, the central bank increases or decreases the money supply as necessary so as to maintain a fixed rate of exchange of domestic currency for foreign currency. In this case, the pressure for exchange rate depreciation that follows a monetary expansion is neutralized by central bank intervention in the foreign exchange market, with no final effect on domestic output. Similarly, the central bank intervenes to neutralize the domestic exchange rate appreciation that follows a fiscal expansion. This allows the fiscal policy shock to raise the level of domestic output. The central bank commitment to a given exchange-rate level therefore implies high effectiveness of fiscal policy.

REAL WORLD RELEVANCE OF THE MODEL

Some of the underlying assumptions and policy options of the Mundell-Fleming model, such as international capital market integration and the possibility of permitting the fluctuation of the exchange rate, were not predominant features of the world economy in the early 1960s. Restrictions to trade assets and foreign exchange were widespread, and the majority of currencies were fixed within the Bretton Woods system. In this regard, the Mundell-Fleming model is, to a large extent, more appropriate for describing the global economy as it developed after the collapse of the Bretton Woods system, which is characterized by high financial integration and floating exchange rates, than the economic reality of the times in which the model was originally developed. This prophetic trait of the analysis, as well as the success of the theoretical predictions in matching empirical facts (such as the effects of U.S. macroeconomic policies in the 1980s), help explain the influence of the Mundell-Fleming model among both academics and policymakers. The model has nevertheless not been immune to criticisms, some of which have stimulated further research.

CRITICISMS AND EXTENSIONS

One important criticism of the model is that the assumption of perfect capital mobility might be extreme. Mundell (1963) was well aware of this limitation and recognized that the assumption should not be taken literally.

Introducing imperfect capital mobility into the model implies that a fiscal expansion can play a role in affecting output under a flexible exchange rate and monetary policy can have a role under a fixed exchange rate, but the results on the relative effectiveness of the two policy instruments still hold.

Several other shortcomings of the Mundell-Fleming model have also been emphasized. In particular, the model is completely static and therefore not able to address issues related to the long run, as well as to the transitional dynamics of private wealth and government finance. In order to address this limitation, Rudiger Dornbusch (1976) introduced more sophisticated, "rational" (rather than static) private agents' expectations into the model. This extension implies an "overshooting" result: following a monetary expansion, the exchange rate depreciates more in the short run than in the long run.

Furthermore, in the Mundell-Fleming model the relations between economic variables are not explicitly derived from a microfoundation of agents' behavior. This prevents an analysis of the welfare impact of macroeconomic policies based on a utility measure. Because of this, any welfare consideration in the Mundell-Fleming model is necessarily limited to the effects of output movements, neglecting the welfare implications of such variables as consumption and leisure time. Several researchers are therefore attempting to move beyond the Mundell-Fleming model (see Obstfeld 2001) by developing a new framework for the analysis of macroeconomic interdependence, which is explicitly based on microeconomic foundations and intertemporal optimizing behavior. This field of research aims at introducing a more rigorous analysis of the welfare impact of macroeconomic policies. Whether the new framework will ultimately succeed in supplanting the Mundell-Fleming model remains to be seen. The fact that the researchers active in this area still consider the Mundell-Fleming model as the relevant benchmark against which to compare their results is, in any case, a testimony to the model's lasting influence.

SEE ALSO *Balance of Payments; Exchange Rates; IS-LM Model; Macroeconomics; Trade*

BIBLIOGRAPHY

Dornbusch, Rudiger. 1976. Expectations and Exchange Rate Dynamics. *Journal of Political Economy* 84: 1161–1176.

Fleming, J. Marcus. 1962. Domestic Financial Policies under Fixed and under Floating Exchange Rates. *International Monetary Fund Staff Papers* 9: 369–379

Mundell, Robert A. 1963. Capital Mobility and Stabilization Policy under Fixed and Flexible Exchange Rates. *Canadian Journal of Economics and Political Science* 29: 475–485

Obstfeld, Maurice. 2001. International Macroeconomics: Beyond the Mundell-Fleming Model. *International Monetary Fund Staff Papers* 47: 1–39

Giovanni Ganelli

The opinions expressed are personal and should not be interpreted as reflecting any view of the International Monetary Fund.

MUNDIAL UPHEAVAL SOCIETY

SEE *Wolf, Eric.*

MÜNSTERBERG, HUGO
1863–1916

The science of psychology in the United States dates from the early laboratories of the 1880s, yet it quickly spread beyond the laboratory into several applied fields in the early twentieth century. Arguably, no figure in American psychology was more identified with the promotion of applied psychology than Hugo Münsterberg. By 1916 he had published influential books on forensic psychology, educational psychology, psychotherapy, industrial psychology, and the psychology of motion pictures. Münsterberg was born June 1, 1863, in Danzig, Germany. According to biographer Matthew Hale Jr., when Münsterberg died on December 16, 1916, in Cambridge, Massachusetts, "he was arguably the best-known psychologist in America and the most prominent member of America's largest minority, the German-Americans" (1980, p. 3).

Münsterberg's roles as public psychologist and German nationalist defined his years in the United States. He earned his PhD in psychology in 1885 at the University of Leipzig under Wilhelm Wundt (1832–1920), usually acknowledged as the founder of scientific psychology. Münsterberg's experimental work there was principally on the subject of the will. In 1887 he earned a medical degree from the University of Heidelberg, and then began his academic career in that same year at the University of Freiberg. Münsterberg's research showed that the will was not directly experienced, but was the result of the perception of changes in muscles, joints, and tendons. That finding was in opposition to Wundt's ideas about voluntary control, a controversy that brought attention to Münsterberg's work. One admirer was William James (1842–1910), who invited him to come to Harvard University in 1892 to direct the psychology laboratory.

Münsterberg accepted Harvard's invitation for a three-year period, but then returned to Germany. He hoped to secure a position in one of Germany's more prestigious universities, but when that was not forthcoming he returned to Harvard in 1897. He remained there for the rest of his career.

The laboratory did not hold Münsterberg's interest for long. His first book in English, *Psychology and Life* (1899), was based on a series of articles in the popular press. It gave him a taste of the role of psychological expert and seemed to lure him into a greater public presence. *On the Witness Stand* (1908), also based on popular articles, delved into the accuracy of memory, eyewitness testimony, false confessions, lie detection, and jury deliberations. It is considered the pioneering book in forensic psychology. In 1913 he published his most influential work, *Psychology and Industrial Efficiency*, a book that was popular with American managers seeking to increase efficiency. Münsterberg was interested in matching worker abilities to job requirements. He believed that psychology possessed the tools to create that match by determining the psychological traits required for any job and using mental tests to identify suitable workers. In a time in which efficiency was the watchword for American business, Münsterberg's book promoted opportunities for psychologists in the business world, especially in advertising and employee selection.

Münsterberg also served as a spokesperson for German culture in the United States, a task he carried out in books, magazine articles, letters to editors, and public speeches. His defense of Germany's aggression in the early years of World War I (1914–1918) made him despised by most Americans, including his Harvard colleagues. He lived the last few years of his life as a social outcast, the stress of which perhaps contributed to his death at age fifty-three.

BIBLIOGRAPHY

Benjamin, Ludy T., Jr. 2006. Hugo Münsterberg's Attack on the Application of Scientific Psychology. *Journal of Applied Psychology* 91 (2): 414–425.

Hale, Matthew, Jr. 1980. *Human Science and Social Order: Hugo Münsterberg and the Origins of Applied Psychology.* Philadelphia: Temple University Press.

Münsterberg, Hugo. 1899. *Psychology and Life.* Boston: Houghton Mifflin.

Münsterberg, Hugo. 1908. *On the Witness Stand: Essays on Psychology and Crime.* New York: Doubleday, Page.

Münsterberg, Hugo. 1913. *Psychology and Industrial Efficiency.* Boston: Houghton Mifflin.

Ludy T. Benjamin Jr.

MURDER

Roughly 1 in 15,000 people is murdered in the United States each year (Stolinsky and Stolinsky 2000). Computed over a seventy-five year life span, this equates to a 1 in 200 chance of being murdered at some point in an American's lifetime (Ghiglieri 1999). Homicide rates vary predictably from culture to culture (Wilson and Daly 1997). In the United States the rates of killing are much higher than in many industrialized nations, exceeding those in Canada, many western European nations, and Japan. In many other countries, including Venezuela, Colombia, and South Africa, homicide rates exceed those in the United States by as much as a factor of ten (United Nations 1998). Among those nations that currently exhibit low homicide rates, murder rates were much higher in the recent past, suggesting that the relative absence of homicide is a fairly new societal invention (Ruff 2001; Dower and George 1995). All of these within-culture rates of homicide do not include casualties of warfare or genocide.

The homicide rates in industrialized nations are much lower than in many non-industrialized cultures. Homicides account for roughly one in ten deaths of adult men among the Huli of Papua New Guinea; one in four deaths among the Mae Enga also of Papua New Guinea; and one in three deaths among the Dugum Dani of the Highlands of West New Guinea and the Yanomamo of central Brazil (Chagnon 1988). In a 1993 study Douglas T. Kenrick and Virgil Sheets found that homicidal fantasies among people in the general population are even more frequent than actual killings.

Despite the fact that tens of thousands of murders are committed worldwide each year, the psychology of homicide is not well understood. For our understanding of homicide to be complete, we must explain, for example: (1) why men are vastly overrepresented among murderers (87 percent); (2) why men are also overrepresented among murder victims (75 percent); (3) why women commit some kinds of homicide more than men (e.g., infanticide of own children); (4) why people kill in qualitatively distinct conditions, leading to predictable motives for murder; and (5) why people experience murder fantasies in circumstances that turn out to correspond closely to the contexts in which people actually commit murder.

The majority of theories that have been used to explain homicide were not designed specifically for that purpose. They are general theories of behavior regarding all crimes, or all violent crimes. For this entry these explanations will be considered as they apply to murder specifically. Unfortunately space limitations prevent an exploration of all relevant theories of murder.

CULTURAL AND SOCIAL THEORIES OF HOMICIDE

Different theories of homicide need not be competing. They often address different levels of explanation and are often complementary, capable of contributing unique insight to the explanation of why a person commits murder.

According to 1973 and 1977 studies by Albert Bandura cultural and social theories of homicide rely on fundamental principles of learning theory. These theories propose that learning from the social environment is responsible for differences in homicide rates between groups, including differences in men's and women's propensities to kill. The specific environmental source identified as the causal force behind murder differs from theory to theory (Cullen and Agnew 2006; Walsh and Ellis 2006). For example some theorists suggest disorganized communities lead to crime (Bursik and Grasmick 1993; Sampson 1993; Shaw and McKay 1969); others argue that crime is learned through differential association with deviant peers (Akers 1973; Sutherland and Cressey 1978; Sykes and Matza 1957); while others argue that the gap between desires for a better lifestyle and lack of legitimate means to fulfill them creates strain that fuels crime (Cohen 1965; Cloward and Ohlin 1960; Merton 1938; Messner and Rosenfeld 1994). Each of these theories argues that murder is the product of learning by normal people. Other theories propose that homicide is the result of psychological dysfunction.

PATHOLOGICAL THEORIES OF MURDER

Pathology theories of murder propose that people commit murder when their thinking is abnormal. The causes of cognitive malfunctions vary, as do the forms of abnormal cognition they produce. For example suboptimal arousal theory is based on the observation that some people have a preference for intense environmental stimulation. Those who feel most starved for arousal are presumed to be more likely to engage in highly arousing thrill seeking and risk taking activities (Ellis 1987). Criminal behaviors including murder may be committed more often by those who are suboptimally aroused.

Seizuring theories of crime are based on research into the causes of epilepsy. Not all seizures lead to convulsions. If subconvulsive seizures are located in the limbic system, argued Dan Mungas in his 1983 article "An Empirical Analysis of Specific Syndromes of Violent Behavior," they may have significant effects on emotions, sometimes resulting in criminal behavior.

Other pathology explanations, such as the one offered by R. J. Lueger and K. J. Gill in their 1990 study "Frontal-Lobe Cognitive Dysfunction in Conduct

Disorder Adolescents," have argued that failure of the frontal lobes to function properly may disinhibit violent behavior. Frontal lobe damage is associated with increased impulsivity and lack of planning ability that may contribute to some murders.

Another pathology theory is rooted in the observation that one male out of every 700 to 1,000 is born with an extra Y-chromosome, and one male out of every 500 is born with an extra X-chromosome (Hoffman 1977). Both genetic abnormalities result in males who score lower on standard intelligence tests (Horgan 1993) and show an increased likelihood of criminal behavior, including murder. However these genetic abnormalities are likely to explain only a tiny fraction of the homicides committed, since males with an extra chromosome only constitute 1 to 2 percent of the total prison population (Witkin, Mednick, Schulsinger, et al. 1976).

PERSONALITY DIFFERENCES AND MURDER

Explanations of murder have not been limited to individual differences so extreme they are considered disordered. Individual differences in personality also have been proposed to contribute to the likelihood that an individual will commit murder. For example people who score high on measures of antisocial personality, low in conscientiousness, high in neuroticism, and low in intelligence have been shown to be more likely to engage in criminal activities, including murder (Plomin, DeFries, McGuffin, and McClearn 2000; Hodgins 1992; Monahan, Steadman, Silver, et al. 2001).

Individual differences in personality may also lead to the differential activation of cognitive mechanisms that produce homicidal tendencies in other ways. Personality leads people to experience the same environments differently, seek out different environments, and be excluded from a certain subset of social environments (Rowe 1994; 1996). People with personalities that lead them to occupy environments characterized by high levels of interpersonal conflict may be more likely to encounter contexts that predictably lead to murder.

Another group of explanations for murder propose that individual differences may make homicide more adaptive for some people in terms of evolutionary fitness. Cheater theory argues that two alternative reproductive strategies have evolved in human males. One type of male is law abiding and loyal. Male cheaters, conversely, are argued to adopt strategies of criminality, including murder, in contexts of social exchange to obtain resources and short-term mating strategies in mating relationships.

David Rowe's alternative adaptation theory points out that criminals typically devote more effort to mating than they do to parenting (Rowe, Vazsonyi, and Figueredo 1997; Rowe, Vazsonyi, and Flannery 1995). Furthermore Rowe argued that criminality is a strategy that can only thrive when there are others to exploit. As the number of criminals in a population increases, the effectiveness of criminal strategies like murder will decrease.

Conditional adaptation theory attempts to integrate adaptive individual difference theories and learning theories. It proposes that everyone has the same genetic potential to exhibit criminal behavior at birth, and early life experiences cause individuals' potentials to change. Children who witness poor, unstable relationships between their parents and live in relatively resource-scarce environments are argued to be more likely to adopt short-term, opportunistic mating strategies as adults and riskier strategies for obtaining resources, including theft, violence, and murder (Belsky 1997). While the preceding adaptive individual difference theories suggest that murder may be adaptive for some people, other explanations propose that homicide is not evolutionarily adaptive for anyone.

According to Martin Daly and Margo Wilson in their 1988 publication *Homicide*, homicide may be considered an over-reactive mistake, the by-product of evolved, functional psychological mechanisms (adaptations) designed for nonlethal outcomes. For example the behavior of a teenage mother who abandons her newborn in a dumpster to die may be explained by the failure of her psychological mechanisms for parenting to engage. Despite their contention that murder is a maladaptive by-product of psychological adaptations, Daly and Wilson did emphasize that an evolutionary account of homicidal behavior is extremely important.

The previous explanations of homicide are able to predict some characteristics of who is likely to become a criminal and identify some broad features of situations that may trigger criminal behavior. However they share many of the same weaknesses, including: (1) no comprehensive explanation of the patterns of homicide; (2) no predictions about when homicide, instead of some other criminal behavior, is likely to occur; (3) no explanation for a large number of the observed patterns of homicide; (4) failure to provide an explanation for why people who are not pursuing a general strategy of criminality would ever commit homicide; (5) an inability to explain why the majority of ordinary people report experiencing homicidal fantasies; and (6) failure to explain the prevalence and patterns of people's homicidal fantasies.

David M. Buss and Joshua D. Duntley proposed a new theory that humans possess adaptations for murder that addresses these weaknesses. Although some researchers have suggested the possibility of adaptations for homicide (Ghiglieri 1999; Pinker 1997) and others, such as Napoleon A. Chagnon in his 1988 article "Life

Histories, Blood Revenge, and Warfare in a Tribal Population," have argued that humans may have an instinct to kill, no other theorists have gone into depth in exploring the likely design of adaptations for homicide (see a notable exception dealing with warfare entitled *The Evolution of War and Its Cognitive Foundations* by John Tooby and Leda Cosmides).

Homicide adaptation theory (HAT) proposes that natural selection could have favored murder to solve some of the ancestrally recurrent problems that lead to conflict with others. Homicide is unique from nonlethal solutions to conflict because a dead competitor cannot inflict costs on or influence the environment of his killer in the future. According to HAT, natural selection has built in psychological processes that lead us to fantasize about murder and, rarely, kill others when we encounter contexts of conflict that were successfully won by homicide in the evolutionary past.

Homicide adaptation theory does *not* imply that homicide would have evolved to be the preferred strategy for each or any adaptive problem in all situations. In most sets of circumstances the extremely high costs of committing murder would have outweighed its benefits. The theory does propose that homicidal behavior was sometimes the best of available solutions for rare *combinations* of adaptive problems and circumstances, which provided selection pressure for the evolution of homicide adaptations.

SEE ALSO *Bandura, Albert; Crime and Criminology; Culture; Death and Dying; Morbidity and Mortality; Neuroscience; Punishment*

BIBLIOGRAPHY

Akers, Ronald L. 1973. *Deviant Behavior: A Social Learning Approach.* Belmont, CA: Wadsworth.

Bandura, Albert. 1973. *Aggression: A Social Learning Analysis.* Englewood Cliffs, NJ: Prentice-Hall.

Bandura, Albert. 1977. *Social Learning Theory.* Englewood Cliffs, NJ: Prentice-Hall.

Beccaria, Cesare. 1983. *An Essay on Crimes and Punishments.* Brookline Village, MA: Branden. (Orig. pub. 1775.)

Belsky, Jay. 1997. Attachment, Mating, and Parenting: An Evolutionary Interpretation. *Human Nature* 8: 361–381.

Bursik, Robert J., and Harold G. Grasmick. 1993. *Neighborhoods and Crime: The Dimensions of Effective Community Control.* New York: Lexington.

Buss, David M., and Joshua D. Duntley. 1998. Evolved Homicide Modules. Paper presented to the Annual Meeting of the Human Behavior and Evolution Society, Davis, CA.

Buss, David M., and Joshua D. Duntley. 1999. Killer Psychology: The Evolution of Intrasexual Homicide. Paper presented to the Annual Meeting of the Human Behavior and Evolution Society, Salt Lake City, UT.

Buss, David M., and Joshua D. Duntley. 2003. Homicide: An Evolutionary Perspective and Implications for Public Policy. In *Violence and Public Policy,* ed. N. E. Dess. Westport, CT: Greenwood.

Caspi, Avshalom, Terrie E. Moffitt, Phil A. Silva, et al. 1994. Are Some People Crime-Prone: The Personality-Crime Relationship Across Countries, Genders, Races, and Methods. *Criminology* 32 (2): 163–195.

Chagnon, Napoleon A. 1988. Life Histories, Blood Revenge, and Warfare in a Tribal Population. *Science* 239 (4843): 985–992.

Cloward, Richard A., and Lloyd E. Ohlin. 1960. *Delinquency and Opportunity: A Theory of Delinquent Gangs.* Glencoe, IL: Free Press.

Cohen, Albert K. 1965. The Sociology of the Deviant Act: Anomie Theory and Beyond. *American Sociological Review* 30 (1): 5–14.

Cohen, Lawrence E., and Marcus Felson. 1979. Social Change and Crime Rate Trends: A Routine Activity Approach. *American Sociological Review* 44 (4): 588–608.

Cornish, Derek B., and Ronald V. Clarke, eds. 1986. Introduction. In *The Reasoning Criminal: Rational Choice Perspectives on Offending,* 1–16. New York: Springer-Verlag.

Cullen, Francis T., and Robert Agnew, eds. 2006. *Criminological Theory: Past to Present.* 3rd ed. Los Angeles: Roxbury.

Daly, Martin, and Margo Wilson. 1988. *Homicide.* New York: de Gruyter.

Dower, John W., and Timothy S. George. 1995. *Japanese History and Culture from Ancient to Modern Times.* 2nd ed. Princeton, NJ: Markus Wiener.

Ellis, Lee. 1987. Relationships of Criminality and Psychopathy with Eight Other Apparent Behavioral Manifestations of Sub-Optimal Arousal. *Personality and Individual Differences* 8 (6): 905–925.

Ghiglieri, Michael Partick. 1999. *The Dark Side of Man: Tracing the Origins of Violence.* Reading, MA: Perseus.

Glueck, Sheldon, and Eleanor Glueck. 1950. *Unraveling Juvenile Delinquency.* New York: Commonwealth Fund.

Hodgins, Sheilagh. 1992. Mental Disorder, Intellectual Deficiency, and Crime. Evidence from a Birth Cohort. *Archives of General Psychiatry* 49 (6): 476–483.

Hoffman, B. F. 1977. Two New Cases of XYY Chromosome Complement and a Review of the Literature. *Journal of the Canadian Psychiatric Association* 22: 447–455.

Horgan, John. 1993. Eugenics Revisited. *Scientific American* 268: 122–131.

Kenrick, Douglas T., and Virgil Sheets. 1993. Homicidal Fantasies. *Ethology and Sociobiology* 14: 231–246.

Lombroso-Ferrero, Gina. 1911. *Criminal Man.* New York: Putnam's.

Lueger, R. J., and K. J. Gill. 1990. Frontal-Lobe Cognitive Dysfunction in Conduct Disorder Adolescents. *Journal of Clinical Psychology* 46: 696–706.

Merton, Robert. 1938. Social Structure and Anomie. *American Sociological Review* 3: 672–682.

Messner, Steven F., and Richard Rosenfeld. 1994. *Crime and the American Dream.* Belmont, CA: Wadsworth.

Monahan, John, Henry J. Steadman, Eric Silver, et al. 2001. *Rethinking Risk Assessment: The MacArthur Study of Mental Disorder and Violence.* New York: Oxford University Press.

Mungas, Dan. 1983. An Empirical Analysis of Specific Syndromes of Violent Behavior. *Journal of Nervous and Mental Disease* 171 (6): 354–361.

Paternoster, Raymond, and Alex Piquero. 1995. Reconceptualizing Deterrence: An Empirical Test of Personal and Vicarious Experiences. *Journal of Research in Crime and Delinquency* 32 (3): 251–286.

Pinker, Steven. 1997. Why They Kill Their Newborns. *New York Times,* November 2.

Plomin, Robert, John C. DeFries, Peter McGuffin, and Gerald E. McClearn. 2001. *Behavioral Genetics.* 4th ed. New York: Worth.

Rowe, David C. 1994. *The Limits of Family Influence.* New York: Guilford.

Rowe, David C. 1996. An Adaptive Strategy Theory of Crime and Delinquency. In *Delinquency and Crime: Current Theories,* ed. J. David Hawkins, 268–314. Cambridge, U.K.: Cambridge University Press.

Rowe, David C., Alexander T. Vazsonyi, and Aurelio Jose Figueredo. 1997. Mating-Effort in Adolescence: A Conditional or Alternative Strategy. *Personality and Individual Differences* 23 (1): 105–115.

Rowe, David C., Alexander T. Vazsonyi, and Daniel J. Flannery. 1995. Sex Differences in Crime: Do Means and Within-Sex Variation Have Similar Causes? *Journal of Research in Crime and Delinquency* 32: 84–100.

Ruff, Julius R. 2001. *Violence in Early Modern Europe 1500–1800.* New York: Cambridge University Press.

Sampson, Robert J. 1993. The Community Context of Violent Crime. In *Sociology and the Public Agenda,* ed. William Julius Wilson, 274–279. Newbury Park, CA: Sage.

Shaw, Clifford R., and Henry D. McKay. 1969. *Juvenile Delinquency and Urban Areas: A Study of Rates of Delinquency in Relation to Differential Characteristics of Local Communities in American Cities.* Chicago: University of Chicago Press.

Stafford, Mark, and Mark Warr. 1993. A Reconceptualization of General and Specific Deterrence. *Journal of Research in Crime and Delinquency* 30 (2): 123–135.

Stolinsky, S. A., and D. C. Stolinsky. 2000. Homicide and Suicide Rates Do Not Covary. *Journal of Trauma, Injury, Infection, and Critical Care* 48: 1168–1169.

Sutherland, Edwin H., and Donald R. Cressey. 1978. *Criminology.* Philadelphia: Lippincott.

Sykes, Gresham, and David Matza. 1957. Techniques of Neutralization: A Theory of Delinquency. *American Sociological Review* 22 (6): 664–670.

Tooby, John, and Leda Cosmides. 1988. *The Evolution of War and Its Cognitive Foundations.* Institute for Evolutionary Studies, Technical Report #88-1.

United Nations. 1998. *United Nations 1996 Demographic Yearbook.* New York: United Nations.

Walsh, Anthony, and Lee Ellis. 2006. *Criminology: An Interdisciplinary Perspective.* Thousand Oaks, CA: Sage.

Wilson, Margo, and Martin Daly. 1997. Life Expectancy, Economic Inequality, Homicide, and Reproductive Timing in Chicago Neighbourhoods. *British Medical Journal* 314: 1271–1274.

Witkin, Herman A., S. A. Mednick, F. Schulsinger, et al. 1976. XYY and XXY Men: Criminality and Aggression. *Science* 193 (4253): 547–555.

Joshua Duntley

MURRAY, CHARLES
SEE *Underclass.*

MUSEVENI, YOWERI
1944–

Yoweri Kaguta Museveni, president of Uganda, was born "among the Banyankore Bahima nomads of south-western Uganda in about the year 1944" (Museveni 1997, p. 1). In 1970 he graduated with a BA in political science from Tanzania's University of Dar-es-Salaam. While there, Museveni enjoyed the tutelage of the pan-Africanist scholar Walter Rodney (1942–1980) and the Trinidadian American civil rights leader Stokely Carmichael (1941–1998). Museveni's early Marxist inclinations evolved during this period, although he is more of a nationalist cum pragmatist than an ideologue. When the dictator Idi Amin (c. 1924–2003) took power in Uganda in 1971, Museveni joined the anti-Amin movement. After Amin was overthrown in 1979, Museveni occupied several ministerial portfolios in two interim governments in Uganda before a rigged general election in 1981 resulted in a second government for Milton Obote (1924–2005). Museveni and his National Resistance Movement (NRM) and National Resistance Army (NRA) then launched a protracted guerrilla war against Obote that ended in 1986 with Museveni's takeover as president.

Upon assuming power Museveni was faced with two daunting challenges: a collapsed state and a subsistence-level economy. The NRM initiated several reforms geared toward the reconstruction of the state: the institutionalization of local councils (LCs), general elections for parliament and president, constitutional reform, the construction of a national army, the resuscitation of civil society, and a crusade against the HIV/AIDS pandemic. By 1996 Museveni had reestablished statehood, security, and relative peace, but his nineteen-year ban on political party activity and his role in the constitutional repeal of presidential term limits have constrained political competition and blocked the much-heralded transition to democracy. Political corruption among top government officials including cabinet ministers has tarnished the image of the NRM government at home and abroad. Most notably, scandals such as the "ghost soldiers" debacle, through which military officers were paid for nonexistent staff, and the importation of defective helicopters from Belarus in 1997 earned Uganda the ignominious rank of 113 in the Transparency International's corruption index. Finally, Uganda has received a lot of criticism for its counterinsurgency tactics against the Lords Resistance Army (LRA), a rebel group that has destabilized northern Uganda and brutally massacred thousands.

Museveni revolutionized Uganda's economy by enacting liberal reforms in monetary and fiscal policy and paving the way for a free-market economy; in particular, the Uganda shilling was devalued and floated against other currencies, and forex bureaus facilitated foreign exchange. Government subsidies and state controls were removed. Through privatization, parastatals were sold and social expenditures cut. Finally, trade was liberalized, deficits minimized, and inflation kept in check. However, over 50 percent of Uganda's recurrent expenditure is serviced by donors, and notwithstanding the poverty-reduction programs such as *Entandikwa, Bonna Baggaggawale* and Universal Primary Education (UPE), unequal wealth distribution and poverty continue to be major challenges. A small, politically well-connected clique has emerged that is adept at rent-seeking and wealth accumulation, and with a per capita income of about $170, in 2007 Uganda ranks among the poorest countries in the world.

In the mid-1990s Museveni was hailed as one of a new breed of African leaders, but his exploits in neighboring Democratic Republic of Congo (DRC), Rwanda, and Sudan have harmed his status. Uganda's incursion into the DRC in 1998, ostensibly conducted to rout out anti-Uganda rebels, became a pretext for exploiting Congo's wealth. In December 2005 the International Commission of Jurists ruled that Uganda had violated Congo's sovereignty and plundered its natural resources, and it identified top Ugandan military officers, including the president's brother, Salim Saleh, as culprits. Relations between Uganda and Rwanda deteriorated as the two sought control over the mineral-rich area of eastern Congo. Until recently, Uganda has perennially accused Sudan of providing safe haven to the LRA. Sudan in turn has blamed Uganda for supporting the Sudan Peoples Liberation Army (SPLA). Thus the off-and-on relations between Kampala and Khartoum have been shaped by these cross-border conflicts.

Museveni has been at the vanguard of reestablishing the East African Community (EAC). Although the EAC is still in its infancy, he can be credited for providing strong leadership by speaking to the virtues of an expanded and integrated regional market. The jury is still out with regard to the success of the EAC, and only history will determine the achievement of Museveni's statesmanship in the region.

SEE ALSO *Amin, Idi*

BIBLIOGRAPHY

Bussey, Erica. 2005. Constitutional Dialogue in Uganda. *Journal of African Law* 49 (1): 1–23.

Hansen, Holger B., and Michael Twaddle, eds. 1998. *Developing Uganda*. Kampala, Uganda: Fountain.

Kassimir, Ronald. 1996. Reading Museveni: Structure, Agency, and Pedagogy in Ugandan Politics. *Canadian Journal of African Studies* 33 (2–3): 649–673.

Mugaju, Justus, and J. Oloka-Onyango, eds. 2000. *No-Party Democracy in Uganda: Myths and Realities*. Kampala, Uganda: Fountain.

Museveni, Yoweri K. 1997. *Sowing the Mustard Seed: The Struggle for Freedom and Democracy in Uganda*. London: Macmillan.

Rubongoya, Joshua B. 2004. Political Leadership. In *Democratic Transitions in East Africa*, ed. Paul Kaiser and F. Wafula Okumu, 64–82. Aldershot, U.K.: Ashgate.

Joshua B. Rubongoya

MUSIC

The study of music from a modern social scientific perspective has a distinguished history, reaching back to Jean-Jacques Rousseau's 1781 *Essay on the Origin of Language* (1998). Major advances include the development of comparative musicology by nineteenth- and early-twentieth-century scholars such as Erich von Hornbostel, Alexander Ellis, Carl Stumpf, and Curt Sachs; Max Weber's path-breaking work on musical "rationalization" during the emergence of European capitalism in *The Rational and Social Foundations of Music* (1921); the close attention paid to music (both "classical" and "popular") and to the mass mediation of music by Theodor Adorno and other associates of the Frankfurt School of critical theory; and the development of ethnographic musical anthropology (often wrongly subsumed under the history of ethnomusicology in contemporary intellectual histories) by George Herzog, Melville Herskovits, David McAllester, John Blacking, Alan Merriam, and Steven Feld from the mid-twentieth century onward. Sociological approaches to music have proliferated in many national traditions in the twentieth century, and include such distinctive disciplines as ethnomusicology, ethnographic musical anthropology, the sociology of music, folkloristics, the psychology of music, popular cultural studies, and so-called "new" (historical) musicology; even the discipline of music theory has begun to grapple with cultural and social perspectives on sound structure and musical meaning. And music has become an important focus for cultural analysis in disciplines such as comparative literature, working-class studies, sociology, media studies, performance studies, gender and sexuality studies, race and ethnic studies, and many area studies traditions.

Given the heterogeneity of these approaches and disciplines, it is challenging to summarize a paradigmatic contemporary view of music as such—that is, as an object of specifically sociological inquiry. Even limiting consideration to the approaches prevalent in the Euro-American academy in the early twenty-first century would require separate considerations of approaches from anthropology (see Feld and Fox 1994), ethnomusicology (see Ellingson 1992), popular cultural studies, historical musicology, and psychology. A survey of the broad claims and premises of these approaches, however, suggests important points of consensus.

Chief among these is that music is not only, or even primarily, a sonic phenomenon that can be considered apart from human social action. Most modern approaches to music as an object of social inquiry begin with the premise that the object of such inquiry must be what musicologist Christopher Small (1998) calls *musicking*— that is, the active making of musical sound and interpretation by socially situated agents. Whether this active process is viewed as a behavioral or mental phenomenon, or as primarily mediated by language, the sociological study of music broadly rejects a central principle of elite Western musical aesthetics that long dominated the humanistic study of music. This principle asserts the autonomy of (specifically, "art" or "classical") music from social life, and typically entails the hypostatization of the "work" of musical art, often represented by a written text ("score") that describes a phenomenologically specific sonic musical "structure," unrelated to the social organization of its creators' lifeworlds, or the music's social "context," and distinctive from any actual instantiation of the musical work in performance. In the traditionally humanistic music disciplines, as in the traditionally natural scientific ones, musical structure has been primarily explained in terms of principles of human neurobiology and cognition, or abstract mathematical models of formal systems, or histories of stylistic influence that are described as largely independent of social or cultural determinations, or in terms of particular individualistic (or conversely, aculturally universal) psychological characterizations of composers, performers, and listeners.

In contrast, the core premise of almost all sociomusical approaches is the claim that there must be *determinate relationships* between music as sound structure and the "social structure" of musical activity in particular, or more generally the social structure of the human communities in which particular idioms and genres of musicking take place. The anthropologist John Blacking famously and influentially described this relationship as one between "humanly organized sound" and "soundly organized humanity" ([1974] 1995), while anthropologist Alan Merriam offered a succinct and widely cited model for the sociological study of music as the mediation of "concept, behavior, and sound," with all three abstractions rooted in a "cultural context" of community-specific functional values (1964). Merriam described the aims of musical anthropology as "the study of music *in* its cultural context," which he later revised to become "the study of music *as* cultural context" (1964, 1977). Alan Lomax developed a systematic approach to the study of formal patterns of relationship between "folk" music "song structure" (broken down into codified descriptions of performance techniques and aesthetic ideals) and social structure (defined as a bundle of functional traits characteristic of particular forms of social organization, such as egalitarian or hierarchical political structures) (1962).

Interpretive and phenomenological traditions of theorizing "culture" reshaped Euro-American sociomusical scholarship in the 1970s and 1980s, influenced by developments in cultural Marxism and popular cultural studies, interpretive anthropology, semiotics, folkloristics, and linguistic anthropology. Most contemporary sociomusical scholars tend to describe principled relationships between abstracted sonic and social structures in terms of *mediation* rather than in terms of *correspondence, homology*, or *determination*. Steven Feld (1984a, 1984b, 1988) and Thomas Turino (2001), among others, have stressed the complexity of this mediation, applying semiotic and communication theory to characterize the principled relationships that might obtain between sonic and social structures.

But despite this diversity of approaches, the key problem in sociomusical scholarship has been, and remains, the question of music's social essence: How does musical practice, understood as comprising sonic, conceptual, and behavioral dimensions, either reflect, determine, or mediate social life? What kind of analytic purchase does music provide on "sociality" or "culture" that is not provided by analyzing language or other modalities of human practice and communication? And how might the social functions, meanings, and values enacted in specific forms of musical practice be understood as providing the basis for a general social theory that would explain why it is a fact that *all* humans make music? These are ultimately comparative questions that presume a universal basis for a diverse range of human practices, the boundaries of which remain poorly understood or even described, especially when compared with the massive advances in addressing these same questions for language in linguistic theory.

Several major empirical and methodological foci have been central to the efforts of ethnomusicologists, musical anthropologists, and other sociomusical scholars to address such questions systematically. Among these foci, the most important have been the mutual embeddedness of music and language in *song* (see Feld and Fox 1994); the inextricable association between music and emotional or affective dimensions of culture; and the nexus of music and ritual (also generally understood to include dance, poetic language, and other forms of the patterned communicative embodiment of social experience and ideology). A final major focus that has emerged as central in recent years is a questioning of the adequacy of conceptual distinctions between "folk," "art," and "popular" musics, with the last category grounding an increasingly forceful critique of the investment of Western musical disciplines in an ideologically narrow conception of musical meaning and value. Beyond that, the turn to popular music as not only a legitimate object of sociomusical inquiry, but as perhaps the most important musical expression of "modern" societies has reshaped contemporary sociomusical thought profoundly.

Many contemporary sociomusical scholars challenge the longstanding ideological and analytic delimitation of "folk" musics as functional and communal and fundamentally face-to-face and oral forms of expression detached from the political and economic logics of capitalist modernity, a delimitation bound up in the nationalist projects of nineteenth-century folkloristics (an important ancestor of contemporary ethnomusicology, which remains very much concerned with questions of culture as a symbol of political identity, rather than culture in the anthropological sense of a way of life or system of values). Increasingly, many sociomusical scholars also challenge the delimitation of "art" musics—and their partial exemption from sociomusical study—as autonomous and individualistic idioms unrelated to the functions of folk and popular musics. Many contemporary sociomusical scholars, including an increasing number of musicologists concerned primarily with interpreting the Western "art" musical canon, as well as ethnomusicologists and anthropologists who write about non-Western "art" musical traditions such as Hindustani music (Neuman 1990), increasingly describe "art" musics not in terms of their transcendence of mere social function or cultural symbolism, but in terms of specific systems of elite patronage and labor organization that arise when wealthy and cosmopolitan classes and societies are able to support music as a specialized form of economic activity and leisure practice, and thus to support the making of music as a profession. Such a characterization, which eschews the idea that "art" musics are distinguished from other musics by their degree of autonomy from social life, makes the dis-

tinction between "art" musics and "popular" musics largely one of degree, because "popular" musics are generally understood primarily as products of a commercial process of mass mediation and economic exchange in the service of such non-aesthetic social functions as symbolizing ethnic, generational, and nationalistic political identities, earning a profit (the industrial apparatus of popular music production has been extensively studied since by sociologists in recent years), and providing a pleasurable leisure experience.

Conversely, many sociomusical scholars have been concerned to show the high levels of artistry and individual expressive genius characteristic of "folk" and "popular" musics, increasingly with the aid of music theorists now attempting to describe the particular dimensions of complexity and aesthetic significance in "popular" musics, which are often refractory to theoretical models designed to elucidate the structural complexity of (especially Western) "art" musics. But the overwhelming thrust of contemporary sociomusical scholarship has been to breach the wall separating the study of music as an elite "art" and the study of music as a fundamental human activity, which in modern societies has come to mean an activity imbricated with commerce and modern social functions.

Recent developments in sociomusical scholarship, heavily influenced by popular music studies, have advanced the enormous significance of modern musical and communications technologies for a vast range of contemporary musical practices, focusing on the diverse ways technological mediation shapes and is shaped by commercial, aesthetic, political, and cultural imperatives. Ethnomusicology in particular has focused on the emergent category of *world music* and, in turn, the central modern social scientific subject of cultural, economic, and political globalization, a focus that brings together perspectives on "art," "folk," and "popular" musics under the umbrella of a broader theory of cultural modernity and the global circulation of musical commodities and styles (see Stokes 2004). This turn has engendered a strong critique of the ideological history of established *sociomusical* concepts (as much as musicological ones), such as the premise of a universal human musicality or the premise of an "authentic" or "unmediated" mode of human musical experience that is not determined by particular social histories and cultural systems.

Inarguably, the sociological study of music, despite a long history of systematic work, is still in its theoretical infancy, and remains a less widely institutionalized tradition of thought than parallel humanistic and natural scientific traditions. However, the influence of sociomusical theory on those traditions has grown substantially since the mid-twentieth century, and increasingly it has become fundamental to contemporary interdisciplinary musical thought, in the process sharply revising many deeply entrenched ideologies of musical value and assumptions about music's essential sociality.

SEE ALSO *Bluegrass; Blues; Calypso; Classical Music; Distinctions, Social and Cultural; Ethnology and Folklore; Ethnomusicology; Hip Hop; Jazz; Music, Psychology of; Popular Culture; Popular Music; Reggae; Rock 'n' Roll; Rousseau, Jean-Jacques; World Music*

BIBLIOGRAPHY

Blacking, John. [1974] 1995. *How Musical Is Man?* Seattle: University of Washington Press.

Ellingson, Ter. 1992. Transcription. In *Ethnomusicology: An Introduction*, ed. Helen Myers, 110–152. New York: W. W. Norton.

Feld, Steven. 1984a. Sound Structure as Social Structure. *Ethnomusicology* 28 (3): 383–409.

Feld, Steven. 1984b. Communication, Music, and Speech about Music. *Yearbook for Traditional Music* 16: 1–18.

Feld, Steven. 1988. Aesthetics as Iconicity of Style, or "Lift-up-over Sounding": Getting into the Kaluli Groove. *Yearbook for Traditional Music* 20: 74–113.

Feld, Steven, and Aaron Fox. 1994. Music and Language. *Annual Review of Anthropology* 23: 25–53.

Lomax, Alan. 1962. Song Structure and Social Structure. *Ethnology* 1 (4): 425–451.

Merriam, Alan P. 1964. *The Anthropology of Music.* Evanston: University of Illinois Press.

Merriam, Alan P. 1977. Definitions of "Comparative Musicology" and "Ethnomusicology": An Historical-Theoretical Perspective. *Ethnomusicology* 21 (2): 189–204.

Neuman, Daniel M. [1980] 1990. *The Life of Music in North India: The Organization of an Artistic Tradition.* Chicago: University of Chicago Press.

Rousseau, Jean-Jacques. [1781] 1998. *Essay on the Origin of Languages and Writings Related to Music*, ed. and trans. John T. Scott. Hanover, NH: Dartmouth College and University Press of New England.

Small, Christopher. 1998. *Musicking: The Meanings of Performing and Listening.* Hanover, NH: University Press of New England.

Stokes, Martin. 2004. Music and the Global Order. *Annual Review of Anthropology* 33: 47–72.

Turino, Thomas. 2001. Signs of Imagination, Identity, and Experience: A Peircian Semiotic Theory for Music. *Ethnomusicology* 43 (2): 221–255.

Weber, Max. [1921] 1958. *The Rational and Social Foundations of Music*, ed. and trans. Don Martindale, Johannes Riedel, and Gertrude Neuwirth. Carbondale: Southern Illinois University Press.

Aaron A. Fox

MUSIC, PSYCHOLOGY OF

The psychology of music is a field of scientific inquiry studying the mental operations underlying music listening, music-making, dancing (moving to music), and composing. The field draws from the core disciplines of psychology, cognitive science, and music, and music-related work in the natural, life, and social sciences. The most prominent subdiscipline is music cognition, in which controlled experiments examine how listeners and performers perceive, interpret, and remember various aspects of music.

The field traces its origins to experimentation with musical instruments in ancient Greece and China. Aristoxenus (364–304 BCE) argued that one should study the *mind* of the listener, not merely the collection of sounds impinging on the ear. Descartes, Galileo, and the eighteenth-century French composer Jean-Philippe Rameau, among others, were interested in musical scales and questions of consonance and dissonance (i.e., pleasant/unpleasant sound combinations). In the late 1800s, the German physicists Hermann von Helmholtz and Gustav Fechner, and the German psychologist Wilhelm Wundt, applied modern scientific methods to study musical experience. The Gestalt psychologists (e.g., Christian von Ehrenfels and Max Wertheimer) asked how a melody retains its identity under transposition, that is, with all component pitch or duration values changed but their relations preserved. In the early twenty-first century, music psychology is experiencing a renaissance, with an exponential increase in scholarly activity over the preceding century (700 papers were published in 2006). This surge of interest follows increasing communication across scholarly disciplines, the emergence of cognitive psychology in the 1960s, and new technologies that facilitate the preservation, presentation, and manipulation of sound (e.g., magnetic tape, hard disks, computers, digital signal processing).

Prominent lines of research include: (1) perception and cognition (e.g., perceptual thresholds—the smallest perceptible differences in pitch, loudness, etc.; memory for musical attributes such as melody, rhythm, timbre, etc.; attention and perceptual organization including fusion/separation of voices and instruments); (2) development (how music behaviors change across the life span); (3) performance, motor planning, and the attainment of expertise; (4) assessment and predictors of musical ability; (5) the role of music in everyday life; (6) disorders of music processing; (7) cross-cultural similarities and differences; (8) the impact of music training on nonmusical domains; (9) education (how best to teach music); and (10) the biological and evolutionary basis of music. Scholars in the field have taken increased interest in musical emotion, music-language comparisons, and neural substrates of musical behaviors, the assessment of the latter in particular having been made possible by advances in neuroimaging.

The media-promoted notion that passive exposure to classical music (especially Mozart) enhances intelligence is exaggerated. The original research suffered from inadequate controls, with the effect being attributed to arousal; and equal short-term benefits have been seen from listening to books on tape or performing any mentally stimulating task prior to taking cognitive tests. Modest long-term benefits on academic performance have been linked to systematic or formal music training, perhaps because such training incorporates components of school-based learning. Some studies—and some anesthesiologists—have noted that listening to music reduces pain and stress (probably by distraction effects or by increasing endorphins and dopamine) and increases feelings of well-being and social relatedness.

A central controversy is music's historical and neuroanatomical relationship to language. Some cross-cultural similarities in the structure of music (e.g., octaves, scales) and in music processing probably arise from cognitive constraints; these remain to be identified, but cross-species studies are revealing innate constraints.

A long-standing problem affecting public policy (and the distribution of educational opportunities) is how to identify musical aptitude, or the potential to acquire musical expertise. Some scholars contend that genetic variations primarily underlie musical ability or talent, whereas others dispute this, arguing instead that high levels of music achievement are primarily attributable to the combined effects of motivation and effort. Impediments to progress on this issue include difficulties defining musical talent, quantifying performance for component skills (rhythm, pitch, melody, harmony), and their manifestations in complex domains such as performance, interpretation, and composition.

Much of the neural basis for music perception and cognition remains obscure, particularly at the level of the cerebral cortex. The stability of pitch over large dynamic ranges, how multiple instruments and voices are separated, the creation and violation of musical expectancies, and how melodies are recognized under transposition, remain unsolved.

Comparatively little work has been conducted outside of Western musical contexts. The relation between music and culture, and the evolutionary origins of music, remain relatively understudied. Prominent ongoing inquiries concern the social psychology of music—the influence of peer groups, music and ritual, trance states, and automatic (machine) recognition of music and style; and identifying the neural substrates of musical behaviors.

SEE ALSO *Classical Music; Cognition; Culture; Education, USA; Music; Neuroscience; Popular Music; Social Psychology*

BIBLIOGRAPHY

Aiello, Rita, and John A. Sloboda, eds. 1994. *Musical Perceptions.* New York: Oxford University Press.

Bamberger, Jeanne. 1991. *The Mind behind the Musical Ear: How Children Develop Musical Intelligence.* Cambridge, MA: Harvard University Press.

Clarke, Eric. F. 2005. *Ways of Listening: An Ecological Approach to the Perception of Musical Meaning.* New York and Oxford: Oxford University Press.

Deutsch, Diana, ed. 1999. *The Psychology of Music.* 2nd ed. San Diego, CA: Academic Press.

Juslin, Patrik N., and John A. Sloboda, eds. 2001. *Music and Emotion.* Oxford and New York: Oxford University Press.

Lerdahl, Fred, and Ray Jackendoff. 1983. *A Generative Theory of Tonal Music.* Cambridge: MIT Press.

Levitin, Daniel J. 2006. *This Is Your Brain on Music: The Science of a Human Obsession.* New York: Dutton.

London, Justin. 2004. *Hearing in Time: Psychological Aspects of Musical Meter.* Oxford and New York: Oxford University Press.

Miell, Dorothy, Raymond MacDonald, and Donald J. Hargreaves. 2005. *Musical Communication.* Oxford and New York: Oxford University Press.

Peretz, Isabelle, and Robert J. Zatorre, eds. 2003. *The Cognitive Neuroscience of Music.* Oxford and New York: Oxford University Press.

Trehub, Sandra E. 2003. The Developmental Origins of Musicality. *Nature Neuroscience* 6 (7): 669–673.

Daniel J. Levitin

MUSLIMS

Muslims are the second-largest religious group in the world, after Catholics (Saenz 2005). The group is racially and ethnically diverse, but the Muslim identity has taken on racial connotations at various points in U.S. history, most recently after the terrorist attacks on the World Trade Center in New York City and the Pentagon building near Washington, D.C., on September 11, 2001. Although the racialization of a religious identity is not a new phenomenon—for example, Jews experienced an identity change during and after the Holocaust—the impact of this transformation and increased "otherization" of Muslims and Muslim Americans has profound implications for a group that is seen as both a religious and a cultural threat to the mostly white, Christian U.S. population.

BELIEFS AND PRACTICES

Currently, over a billion Muslims live in Europe, Asia, Africa, and North America. There are roughly forty-four Islamic countries in the world today. Although Muslims vary in their particular religious practices and cultural beliefs from region to region, the majority follow the same basic tenets of Islam (Esposito 1998).

Islam is one of three Abrahamic religions, along with Christianity and Judaism, that trace their communities back to the biblical Abraham. The basic teachings of Islam were said to have been revealed to Muhammad (c. 570–632), the final prophet, and collected and recorded in the Qur'an. Muslims rely on the Qur'an for the fundamental Islamic teachings and guidelines for their lives. Aside from the teachings in the Qur'an, Muslims also believe that Muhammad led an exemplary life that all Muslims should attempt to emulate. These examples can be found in the hadith, the documented reports of the prophet's life, which Muslims also rely on for spiritual and practical direction.

In addition, every Muslim is required to follow the five pillars of Islam—obligatory practices outlined in the Qur'an (Nasr 2003). The first of these is the profession of faith, where a Muslim declares, "There is no god but God and Muhammad is the messenger of God," emphasizing the monotheistic nature of the religion (Esposito 1998, p. 68). In making this declaration, a person becomes a Muslim. The second pillar is prayer, or *salat*. Muslims are instructed to pray at specific times, five times a day. Prayers begin with the *azan*, the call to prayer, followed by an ordered series of recitations from the Qur'an in conjunction with bowing and prostrations toward the direction of Mecca. *Zakat*, the third pillar of Islam, is a religious tax required of those who have enough money to give to the poor and needy. Giving of alms is not voluntary, but rather a duty defined by *sharia*, or Islamic law. Fasting during Ramadan is the fourth pillar of Islam. Every year, Muslims are required to fast from sunrise to sunset during the Islamic month of Ramadan, based on the lunar calendar. According to John Esposito (1998), this is a time for Muslims to reflect on their spiritual beliefs and gratitude for good health and wealth, and to remember their duties toward those who are less fortunate than themselves. The final pillar of Islam is pilgrimage, or hajj. During the twelfth month of the Islamic calendar, Muslims who are physically and financially able are required to perform the pilgrimage to Mecca; this needs to be done only once in a person's lifetime. Once in Mecca, Muslims perform a series of rituals such as circling the Ka'ba (House of God) while reciting verses from the Qur'an. According to Seyyed Nasr "hajj signifies a return both to the spatial center of the Islamic universe and to

the temporal origin of the human state itself" (Nasr 2003, p. 95).

ISLAMIC CIVILIZATIONS

Islamic civilization grew rapidly after the death of Muhammad in 632. Over the course of the century beginning around 600 CE, an Islamic Empire spread to occupy what was once known as Arabia, Central Asia, North Africa, and parts of Europe. Throughout the next few centuries, Islamic imperialism had a profound effect on the arts, sciences, and philosophy. Many scholars note that during this time Islam advanced beyond predominantly Christian Europe in many areas, including trade and commerce, exemplified by the urban centers that popped up all across the Islamic Empire (Turner 1995; Esposito 1998; Nasr 2003). Islamic scholars greatly contributed to the progress of math and science, expanding on Greco-Roman geometry and advancing algebra and trigonometry. Universities and academies flourished in Islamic countries. Nonetheless, although Islamic contributions were significant, they are often overlooked in Western cultures. The Enlightenment brought about a positivist view of the world that refuted religious explanations, ignoring the contributions of Islamic civilizations while promoting eurocentric scientists and artists.

SECTS OF ISLAM

Islam has never been a homogenous or unified religion. During the era of Islamic imperialism there were vast differences in Islamic practices and the development of Islamic cultures. The best known sects today are Sunni Islam, Shiism, Sufism, and the Nation of Islam.

Sunni and Shiite Islam Sunni Muslims constitute the majority of the roughly one billion Muslims in the world today; Shia comprise the second-largest Islamic sect. After Muhammad's death a schism occurred over who should be the next caliphate, or leader of the Muslims. Abu-Bakr became the first caliphate after Muhammad, followed by Umar, Uthman, and then Ali (the son-in-law and cousin of Muhammad). The Shia believe that Ali should have been the first caliphate because of his blood relation to Muhammad. Sunnis practice a more decentralized version of Islam than the Shia, which does not require one religious authority, but relies instead on a community of learned religious scholars and the standard religious texts. Thus, Sunnis are more literalist than Shia when interpreting the Qur'an and hadith. Shia follow the Qur'an too, but they rely on imams, religious leaders, who they see as divinely guided by God to help them interpret the Qur'an. Thus, they follow a more authoritarian form of Islam compared to Sunnis, who are more communitarian in their practice.

Sufism Sufis follow a very different version of Islam than Sunnis and Shia. Whereas Sunnis are more literalist in their interpretation of the Qur'an, the Sufis' interpretation is more symbolic and allegorical, and their religious practices are often described as mystic. Sufism developed out of a desire to return to a purer and more spiritual version of Islam as a reaction to the corruption that Sufis felt had became rampant during imperialist Islam. Hence, Sufis embrace an ascetic way of life and reject materialism in an attempt to return to the lifestyle of Muhammad's time. Sufism focuses particularly on God's love and meditation.

The Nation of Islam The Nation of Islam is a newer sect of Islam, introduced to African Americans in the 1930s through Wallace D. Fard (1891?–1934?) and then made popular in the United States by Elijah Muhammad (1897–1975). Fard took passages from both the Bible and the Qur'an and preached a religion that encouraged black liberation, using messages from Islam about brotherhood and social justice to encourage African Americans to reject the domination of their white oppressors. Elijah Muhammad took over leadership of the Nation of Islam after Fard disappeared in 1934. He claimed that Fard was Allah (the Arabic word for "God"), and that he was his messenger. It was during Muhammad's leadership of the Nation of Islam that the sect welcomed the most conversions, due to the popularity of one of Elijah's disciples, Malcolm Little, or Malcolm X (1925–1965), and the racially charged climate of the 1960s in the United States. As the civil rights movement gained momentum, the Nation of Islam offered an alternative to African Americans who lived in mostly poor urban areas and who felt that their immediate issues and needs were not being addressed by the leaders of the mainstream movement. The Nation of Islam lost members in 1964 after the split with Malcolm X and the passage of the Civil Rights Act, and suffered a further decline in membership after the death of Elijah Muhammad in 1975. Elijah Muhammad's son Warith Deen Muhammad (b. 1933) succeeded him and converted to Sunni Islam, taking many leaders with him and leaving the Nation of Islam under the leadership of Louis Farrakhan (b. 1933).

MUSLIMS AFTER SEPTEMBER 11, 2001

The events of September 11, 2001, had an impact on Muslims around the world. Since then, both Afghanistan and Iraq have been invaded by the United States with the support of a number of allies. In the Euro-American media, anti-Muslim rhetoric demonstrates a simplified and reductionistic understanding of Islam and its followers rather than depicting the various political and cultural particularities of Muslims from different Muslim countries. Moreover, Muslims are often portrayed as a homogenous group fanatical in their religious beliefs, and either participants in, or supporters of, terrorism. Muslims in the United States face increasing racism through racial profiling and the perpetuation of negative stereotypes in the media. Jack Shaheen's *Reel Bad Arabs* (2001) identified roughly 900 American movies from the 1900s through the early 1990s in which Muslims and Arabs have been negatively stereotyped. Because these images are so long-standing, they seem to Americans to be "normal," "natural" attributes of Muslims, and this has led to public and political support for the creation and implementation of racist laws and policies such as the U.S. Patriot Act, which has curbed the civil rights of Muslims in the United States and spurred military action against Muslim-majority countries.

The United States is not the only country where Muslims face racism and persecution due to misunderstanding of their culture and religious beliefs. In France, Muslim girls are forbidden from wearing the *hijab* (headscarf), and in 2005 a Danish newspaper published a political cartoon that depicted Muhammad as a terrorist. Acts of violence by Muslims are stripped of their political motivations and reduced to religious fanaticism; images of Muslims as violent terrorists perpetuate an already anti-Muslim ideology that Islam is a threat to both modernity and a democratic world. In truth, Islam is not a monolithic religion; Muslims vary in their cultural makeup, political views, level of religiosity, and in the type of Islam that they choose to practice.

SEE ALSO *Enlightenment; Fundamentalism, Islamic; Islam, Shia and Sunni; Jihad; Muhammad; Mysticism; Orientalism; Pan-Arabism; Racialization; Racism; Religion; September 11, 2001; Stereotypes; Terrorism*

BIBLIOGRAPHY

Armstrong, Karen. 2000. *Islam: A Short History.* New York: Modern Library.

Bloom, Jonathan, and Sheila Blair. 2000. *Islam: A Thousand Years of Faith and Power.* New York: TV Books.

Curtis, Edward E. 2006. *Black Muslim Religion in the Nation of Islam, 1960–1975.* Chapel Hill: University of North Carolina Press.

Denny, Frederick Mathewson. 2006. *An Introduction to Islam.* 3rd ed. Upper Saddle River, NJ: Prentice Hall.

Esposito, John. 1998. *Islam the Straight Path.* 3rd ed. Oxford, U.K.: Oxford University Press.

Nasr, Seyyed Hossein. 2003. *Islam: Religion, History, and Civilization.* San Francisco: HarperSanFrancisco.

Saenz, Rogelio. 2005. The Changing Demographics of Roman Catholics. Population Reference Bureau. http://www.prb.org/Articles/2005/ TheChangingDemographicsofRomanCatholics.aspx.

Shaheen, Jack. 2001. *Reel Bad Arabs: How Hollywood Vilifies a People*. New York: Olive Branch Press.

Turner, Howard R. 1995. *Science in Medieval Islam*. Austin: University of Texas Press.

Saher Selod
David G. Embrick

MUSSOLINI, BENITO
1903–1945

Universally recognized as the founder of fascism, Benito Mussolini remains an enigmatic figure about whom historical interpretations differ. He was born in Predappio, Italy, on July 29, 1883, and died in Mezzegra on April 28, 1945. Before 1935 world opinion viewed him as the person who had saved his country from communism and revived its fortunes, and Italian fascism had many imitators. After World War II Mussolini's reputation changed from that of a savior to that of an inept and brutal dictator, if not a clownlike figure. From the historiographical viewpoint it took until the 1970s for more serious interpretations to emerge.

THE EARLY YEARS

The son of a socialist blacksmith and a devout Catholic schoolteacher, Benito Mussolini was born in the Romagna. He exhibited violent tendencies as a youth and alternated between social interaction and withdrawal. In an attempt to impart discipline to her son his mother sent him to a Catholic boarding school, but Mussolini rebelled against the harsh discipline and resented the discrimination against the poorer students.

Even at that early age Mussolini called himself a socialist, and it was through his socialist contacts that he found a teaching position in 1902, which he had to leave because of a scandalous love affair. He spent time in Switzerland and Trent writing for Italian socialist newspapers. He avoided the draft at first but later fulfilled his military obligations and spent several years teaching.

Between 1906 and 1912 Mussolini established a national reputation as the leader of the Socialist Party in Forlì and as a journalist. During that period the Italian Socialist Party was split between reformists and revolutionaries such as Mussolini who believed in violence. In 1911 Italy declared war on Turkey over Libya. Mussolini was arrested and jailed for blocking troop transports. At the Congress of Reggio Emilia in 1912 he successfully proposed the expulsion of old and respected reformists. He later became editor of *Avanti!*, the socialist daily newspaper, infusing it with a violent tone, greatly expanding its

circulation, and increasing party membership. In June 1914 his calls for revolution seemed to come true with a serious revolt in the Romagna known as Red Week. However, when the movement collapsed, Mussolini lost his belief in a revolution driven by Marxist principles but retained his faith in revolution as a goal in itself.

POLITICAL ASCENDANCY

When World War I broke out, Mussolini supported the Italian Socialist Party position favoring neutrality but soon changed his mind because he thought the war would produce a revolution. The party expelled him, and Mussolini accepted financial support from industrialists to found his own newspaper, *Il Popolo d'Italia*, leading socialists to charge that he had betrayed their cause.

Mussolini participated in the conflict as a corporal and was wounded. After the war he created a movement that he considered both socialist and nationalist. The new movement took the name *fascist* from a meeting of his supporters organized as the *fasci di combattimento* in Milan on March 23, 1919.

The fascists presented themselves in the 1919 elections with a radical program but did not elect anyone. In 1919 and 1920 violence by leftists advocating a revolution divided Italy. Nationalist groups fought the leftists in the streets, and fascist squads, known as the Black Shirts because of their distinctive uniform, distinguished themselves for their violence. They gained support in rural areas, where returning peasant soldiers who had been promised land threatened large landholders. In the cities strikes and fighting raged as the country struggled to return to a peacetime economy amid unemployment and business crises. The fascists received support from moneyed interests and abandoned their 1919 program.

In 1921 and 1922, leftist influence in the country declined and the Socialist Party split into three major groups—revolutionaries, reformists, and communists—that were unable to resist the fascists. In that situation of political instability traditional politicians refused to lead the country. On October 28, 1922, the fascists marched on Rome and King Victor Emanuel III refused to sanction martial law because he feared civil war. He offered the post of prime minister to Mussolini, who promised to bring stability and peace to the country.

Mussolini's first government included fascists in the most important posts and received a vote of confidence even though the parliament included only thirty-five fascist deputies; the majority assumed that it could vote the government out. In the 1924 elections the fascists received a majority as a result of widespread intimidation. Giacomo Matteotti, a socialist deputy, denounced the violence and called for new elections but was murdered. That event caused a crisis in the country that the opposition could not exploit because Mussolini retained the king's support. Between 1925 and 1929 Mussolini altered Italian institutions and successfully set up a dictatorship.

Known as the Duce, Mussolini established a one-party state, brooked no political opposition, and created a secret police, although he controlled the country through the established police forces. Many Jews supported his regime, and there was no official anti-Semitism until 1938, when, to the surprise of many people, racial laws were enacted. In the economic sphere Mussolini followed traditional policies until the Great Depression. Later he worked through nonfascist economists to establish an innovative state holding company (IRI) that rescued failing companies to save the economy. The fascists also established a corporate state, which divided the national economy into sectors run by institutions in which employers and employees were represented; in practice, however, employers had control. Both strikes and lockouts were prohibited.

In foreign policy Mussolini talked tough but was too weak to act unilaterally. In 1934 he stopped Hitler from absorbing Austria. The failure of the Allies to provide what he considered a proper reward led him gradually to support Hitler because he believed that he could exploit the balance of power that was emerging in the interwar period. His invasion of Ethiopia and intervention in the Spanish Civil War enmeshed him with Hitler, and he later proved unable to resist Hitler's embrace. Under Mussolini's leadership and against the advice of his foreign minister, Italy entered into the "pact of steel" with Germany on May 22, 1939. This agreement assumed that war would break out in three years and obliged both countries to coordinate their military action and economic production.

THE OVERTHROW

When World War II broke out before three years had passed, Mussolini declared Italian neutrality but then, convinced that Germany would win, entered the war on its side despite Italian military unpreparedness. The poor performance of his nation in the conflict and the invasion of Sicily in 1943 led to the overthrow of the Duce. Mussolini was imprisoned but freed in a daring German rescue. The Germans brought him to northern Italy to head the Italian Social Republic as the Allies fought their way up the Italian peninsula. He tried to flee with the retreating Germans at the end of the war but was recognized by Italian resistance fighters, handed over by the Germans, and shot. His body, along with that of his mistress, was hung by its heels at a gas station in Milan and exposed to mob violence.

A small Italian neofascist party survived the war. That movement later became more moderate, shed its extremist elements, and participated in the parliamentary structure of the Italian republic that replaced Mussolini's regime.

SEE ALSO *Authoritarianism; Colonialism; Dictatorship; Fascism; Hitler, Adolf; Left and Right; Personality, Cult of; Revolution; Socialism; Spanish Civil War; World War I; World War II*

BIBLIOGRAPHY

Bosworth, R. J. B. 2002. *Mussolini.* New York: Oxford University Press.

Cardoza, Anthony L. 2006. *Benito Mussolini: The First Fascist.* New York: Pearson Longman.

Mack Smith, Denis. 1983. *Mussolini.* New York: Vintage.

Mussolini, Benito. 1998. *My Rise and Fall.* Ed. Max Ascoli. New York: Da Capo.

Spencer M. Di Scala

MUTH, JOHN
SEE *Efficient Market Hypothesis; Expectations, Rational.*

MUTUALLY ASSURED DESTRUCTION
SEE *Retaliation; Deterrence, Mutual.*

MYERS-BRIGGS TYPE INVENTORY
SEE *Equilibrium in Psychology; Jung, Carl.*

MYOPIA
SEE *Farsightedness.*

MYRDAL, GUNNAR
1898–1987

Gunnar Myrdal, a Swedish economist and 1973 Nobel Prize winner for his early work on monetary theory, made major contributions to macroeconomic theory, international economics, development economics, economic methodology, and social and economic policy. He was a critic of mainstream neoclassical economics and a proponent of institutionalist economics.

Myrdal's early work on money was theoretical in nature. As a leading contributor to the Stockholm school, he followed Knut Wicksell's (1851–1926) cumulative process analysis, in which cumulative inflation occurs when banks hold the loan rate of interest below the natural rate of interest (at which saving out of full-employment income is equal to investment), resulting in a high level of investment demand. In a 1931 work (published in English in 1939 as *Monetary Equilibrium*), Myrdal examined the implications of banks maintaining a high loan rate, which results in low investment, low aggregate demand, and unemployment. This analysis is sometimes seen as a precursor of Keynesian analysis. However, it focuses more on expectational issues and dynamics rather than on equilibrium with unemployment, which is arguably central to Keynesian analysis.

Following this, Myrdal and his wife, Alva, became actively involved with politics and policymaking, playing a major role in the creation of the Swedish welfare state in the 1930s. In the 1940s Myrdal served in the Swedish parliament, as chairman of the Planning Commission, as minister of Trade and Commerce, and as executive secretary of the United Nations Economic Commission for Europe.

Following his purely theoretical work on money, his scholarly contributions became increasingly critical of mainstream neoclassical economics, leading him to adopt what may be called the institutionalist approach. In addition to giving real-world institutions a central role in his analysis, Myrdal's approach emphasized the role of values and the importance of noneconomic factors. He saw an interdependence between economic and noneconomic factors, and criticized the neglect of noneconomic factors by most economists. In addition, he was critical of the tendency of many economists to hide their values under the guise of objectivity, and he argued that economists should make their value premises explicit; his own values emphasized equity and concern for the poor and the underprivileged, in addition to efficiency. Although these aspects of his writings mark a departure from his earlier work, his emphasis on cumulative processes and dynamics, in contrast to the static equilibrium analysis of neoclassical economics, reveal continuity.

In his *An American Dilemma* (1944), Myrdal applied the cumulative causation approach to the study of race relations in the United States, explaining discrimination and the poor conditions of African Americans in terms of the interplay of low opportunities, low incentives, and hence low effort (for instance, in obtaining a better education). In *Economic Theory and Under-developed Regions* (1957), he examined the problem of inequality among nations, and explained increasing international inequality in terms of cumulative causation. He pointed out that although there are spread effects from rich to poor countries—due, for example, to economic expansion in the former increasing the demand for products from the latter—backwash effects, involving increasing returns and external economies leading to a high level of profitability in rich countries and the siphoning of capital from poor countries, tend to outweigh them. While the cumulative causation concept provides a fruitful approach to analyzing vicious circles and rising inequality, it is problematic because it does not distinguish between unstable cases and situations in which the cumulative process converges to a stable equilibrium.

Myrdal's monumental three-volume *Asian Drama* (1967) provides an excellent example of the institutionalist, interdisciplinary approach to the study of the problems of less-developed countries. Among the many contributions of this work are: the analysis of the implications of dysfunctional land tenure systems, such as sharecropping, on agricultural productivity and growth; the crisscrossing of interest groups based on caste, religion, and economic status, which stands in the way of organizing the poor in favor of land reforms; and the concept of the "soft" state that is unwilling to employ coercion to implement its declared policy goals, reflecting the power structure and the gap between the declared and real intentions of the state (rather than its gentleness).

Myrdal's analysis of economic problems caused him to question the ability of the market to produce equitable growth and development. This view, and his concern for economic and social justice, made him a strong advocate of interventionist government policies and planning. He was also in favor of applying the concept of the welfare state to the world as a whole, for instance, through increases in foreign aid to poor nations. However, his discussion of soft states and his criticism of foreign aid because of its diversion to corrupt politicians suggest that he was not blind to the problems of the interventionist approach.

SEE ALSO *American Dilemma; Cumulative Causation; Stockholm School*

BIBLIOGRAPHY

Appelqvist, Orjan, and Stellan Andersson, eds. 2005. *The Essential Gunnar Myrdal.* New York and London: The New Press.

Myrdal, Gunnar. [1931] 1939. *Monetary Equilibrium.* London: Hodge.

Myrdal, Gunnar. 1944. *An American Dilemma: The Negro Problem and Modern Democracy.* New York: Harper.

Myrdal, Gunnar. 1957. *Economic Theory and Under-developed Regions.* London: Duckworth.

Myrdal, Gunnar. 1968. *Asian Drama: An Inquiry into the Poverty of Nations.* 3 vols. New York: Twentieth Century Fund.

Streeten, Paul. 1990. Gunnar Myrdal, *World Development*, July, 1031–1037.

Amitava Krishna Dutt

MYSTICISM

It is a major premise of the mystical traditions that it is possible for humanity to come into direct contact with the one God, the one Goddess. These traditions can be found in many places and in many eras. This entry provides a brief introduction to this profound area of human experience.

One such tradition can be found in the Holy Kabbalah, which embodies the mystical, esoteric teachings of the Jewish faith. Its primary glyph is the tree of life, which is a complex symbol that represents both the microcosm and the macrocosm (the symbol of which is the Star of David—a hexagram uniting two triangles). The tree is composed of ten emanations of God, called *sephira*, and twenty-two connecting paths that correspond to the twenty-two letters of the Hebrew alphabet. Each *sephiroth* is associated with a different vision experience. The two greatest of these visions are the vision of God face-to-face and the vision of union with God. It is interesting to note that even Moses, who received the Ten Commandments on Mount Sinai, was denied the vision of God face-to-face. He was only allowed to see his "hind parts." The vision of union with God was experienced by several prophets in the Old Testament, including Elijah. Christians refer to this experience as being "translated." Once one experiences this vision, in accord with Kabbalistic teachings, one is taken from the earth. A relatively modern manifestation of these teachings can be found in the writings of the Hermetic Order of the Golden Dawn, an organization that only lasted about twenty years but was composed of such important figures as William Butler Yeats (1865–1939), Dion Fortune (1890–1946), and Israel Regardie (1907–1985). Offshoots of this group can be found today.

The Holy Kabbalah is the centerpiece of a larger body of knowledge referred to as the Western esoteric tradition. It included such people as the Swiss physician Paracelsus (c. 1493–1541), Nostradamus (1503–1566), and Isaac Newton (1642–1727). These alchemists, in their search for the philosopher's stone, sought the hidden truths by which they could successfully engage in a process called the *great work*. This process entails transforming all that is lead or dross within one's nature into pure gold. These transformational processes allow one to transcend ordinary human limitations and bring one into contact with the higher powers and the beings through whom these powers flow. This approach is referred to as *process theology*, which is in close harmony with mystical traditions. This process is often described as being "on the path" or as one's "personal journey." Perhaps the best known example of this is the story of Saul who was blinded for three days and nights on the road to Damascus. There he met a holy man by the name of Ananias who aided him in his spiritual transformation by which he became Paul, the Apostle.

The mystical tradition exists within Christianity as well, although it has been historically suppressed. The founding fathers, such as Origen (c. 185–254 CE), placed much more emphasis on the inner Christ than is true of most of Christendom today. The Gnostic movement in the early church promoted this approach by developing practices by which one could experience the Christ principle found deep within the consciousness of all people. This gave it a universalistic thrust that would appeal to mystics of all ages. Mahatma Gandhi (1869–1948) stated, when asked what religion he was, that in his true essence he was a Christian, in his true essence he was a Hindu, in his true essence he was a Buddhist. Implied in this answer, is that all world religions flow from the same source. It is their concrete expressions that give rise to dogmatism and social conflict. Were all people to adopt this perspective, religious strife, bigotry, and arrogance would come to an end.

The centerpiece of Buddhism is the achievement of nirvana or enlightenment. That experience is so powerful that it releases one from the wheel of rebirth. This event happened in the life of Prince Siddhartha (who became an enlightened one) when he sat under the banyan tree 2,500 years ago and declared unto humanity that all is sorrow. He had what the Kabbalah describes as the vision of the sorrow of the world. He then gave us the noble eightfold path by which one can experience the ineffable bliss. This process entails the raising of the kundalini fire up the spinal chord, vivifying each chakra along the way until it reaches the thousand-petal lotus located within the crown chakra. Each petal of the lotus represents a different spiritual power. Thus, an enlightened one is born. Successful completion of this process frees one from the wheel of rebirth.

Native American spiritualism provides yet another fine example of mysticism. Wankan Tanka, the Lakota term for the Great Spirit, suggests the awe one experiences when one draws near these primal forces. Lakota culture, like many Indian tribal cultures, emphasizes the harmony ethos in which tribal members are encouraged to place their lives in harmony with these powerful forces found in nature. Such rites as sweats, crying for a vision, and the most sacred of all Lakota rituals, the sun dance, aid one in this process, termed the *medicine path*. The focus here is to come into an understanding of who one is and the spiritual purpose for which one has been placed on earth. Native culture is about being. Anglo culture is about doing.

Modern psychology also contains traditions that speak to these exalted states of consciousness. William James (1842–1910), the father of psychology, wrote *The Varieties of Religious Experience* (1902), which provides descriptions of these experiences. More recently, transpersonal psychologists have devoted considerable effort to better understand these phenomena. The American psychologist Abraham Maslow (1908–1970), a forerunner of this tradition, described these events as peak experiences that can have great meaning for those who experience them. Regardless of the tradition to which one subscribes, all agree on the premise that it is possible to come into contact with God.

SEE ALSO *American Dilemma; Buddhism; Christianity; Cox, Oliver C.; Gramsci, Antonio; Hegel, Georg Wilhelm Friedrich; Ideology; Judaism; Lukacs, Gyorgy; Marx, Karl; Marxism; Myrdal, Gunnar*

BIBLIOGRAPHY

Black Elk. 1961. *Black Elk Speaks: Being the Life Story of a Holy Man of the Ogalala Sioux.* As told to John G. Neihardt. Lincoln: University of Nebraska Press.

Fortune, Dion (Violet Firth). [1935] 1998. *The Mystical Qabalah.* Boston: Weiser.

James, William. [1902] 1963. *The Varieties of Religious Experience: A Study in Human Nature.* Hyde Park, NY: University Books.

Maslow, Abraham. 1971. *The Farther Reaches of Human Nature.* New York: Viking.

Regardie, Israel. [1932] 2004. *A Garden of Pomegranates: Skrying on the Tree of Life.* St. Paul, MN: Llewellyn.

Paul R. Newcomb

MYSTIFICATION

The obfuscatory dimension of human reason has been a subject of Western philosophical investigation since Aristotle, and the term *mystification* has been deployed in various ways to explain how deception, disguise, and dissimulation play a role in driving human behavior. It has relevance throughout the social sciences—for example, in experimental psychology, with game theory in political science and economics, and in sociological analyses of propaganda and mass action—as both a methodological approach for testing behavioral subjects and as an explanatory paradigm for rationalizing human action. For the purposes of this article, discussion is principally limited to the most developed employment of mystification as a category of theoretical analysis originating in the Marxian political economic tradition. When reference is made to mystification in Marx, one of three processes is potentially being referenced: a mystification of the consumptive and productive processes that underlie the commodity; a mystification of historical truth through the promulgation of narratives sympathetic to the structural position of dominant classes; or a philosophical mystification of the important role practice plays in driving history through the relativization of ideological positions over material reality.

MYSTIFICATION OF THE COMMODITY

Karl Marx's discussion of commodities in volume 1, part 1, of *Capital* famously differentiates between use and exchange values, where

> as use-values, commodities differ above all in quality, while as exchange-values they can only differ in quantity.... if we make abstraction from its use-value, we abstract also from the material constituents and forms which make it a use-value [in particular, the labor embodied in its construction]. It is no longer a table, a house, a piece of yarn or any other useful thing. *All its sensuous characteristics are extinguished* (Marx 1990a, p. 128; emphasis supplied).

He suggests that labor time expenditures, though obscured in the exchange of its product, are calculable, while value in exchange derives socially, thus making the commodity more "mystical," "abounding in metaphysical subtleties and theological niceties" (p. 163). Thus through their exchange, commodities "appear as autonomous figures endowed with a life of their own, which enter into relations both with each other and with the human race," a process Marx regards as "fetishism which attaches itself to the products of labour as soon as they are produced as commodities, and is therefore inseparable from the production of commodities" (p. 165). Marx's writings concerning fetishism have been extensively referenced and syncretized with other categories of analysis within the social sciences and humanities, particularly with respect to the concept of consumption (not only of commodities, but also of ideas, literature, art, and so on). In Marx and his more orthodox interpretation, however, fetishism's meaning (with respect to the production commodities on the one hand and capital on the other) is quite specifically economistic.

Volume 3 of *Capital* contains an exhaustive cost accounting of the mystification of the productive process, in which Marx provides a very thorough econometric differentiation between profit and surplus value and differentiates his method from that of classical economics. Marx concludes the volume with a critique of the classical economic "Trinity Formula" of "capital-profit (or better still capital interest), land-ground-rent, and labour-wages," wherein he argues that

> this economic trinity [and its itinerant] connection between the components of value and wealth in general and its sources completes the mystification of the capitalist mode of production, the reification of social relations, and the immediate coalescence of the material relations of production with their historical and social specificity: the bewitched, distorted and upside-down world haunted by Monsieur le Capital and Madame la Terre, who are at the same time social characters and mere things (Marx 1990b, pp. 968–969).

While this cost-accounting antidote to mystification continues to enjoy some popularity among Marxist economists, the thrust of this intervention in contemporary social science can largely be found in the proliferation of commodity studies increasingly popular since the mid-1980s. There is also an extensive body of work in cultural studies, beginning most prominently with the critical theory of the Frankfurt School, which, rather than focusing on an accounting or analysis of production, theorizes the commodity principally in terms of consumption, through studies of media such as advertising, art, and literature. The contemporary literature on fetishization (of everything from commodity fetishization to the fetishization of the state) in fact stems very much from these particular theoretical developments.

HISTORICAL MYSTIFICATION

Capital, volume 1, part 8, on "So-Called Primitive Accumulation," presents an alternative history of the rise of capitalism focused on political economic inequities arising out of a history of exploration and conquest by the West. In it, Marx argues that the bourgeoisie has mystified the development of capitalism by reifying the birth of capitalism as a story about the saving and hard work of Europeans. "So-called primitive accumulation" is thus simply "the historical process of divorcing the producer from the means of production" (1990a, p. 875). He argues here that in fact the resources accumulated in the West for its massive capitalist expansion emerged from centuries of brutally extractive and exploitative relationships with the non-West, particularly with expedition and colonialism in the Americas.

Marx's intervention inspired a large body of work in the social sciences and economic history devoted to discussing the dominance of capitalism in world historical terms and the matrices of its relationship with the non-West, most conspicuously with the work of Andre Gunder Frank, Samir Amin, Immanuel Wallerstein, and Walter

Rodney. At the same time, reactions against Marx's theory of capitalist development have emphasized its cultural dimensions, beginning notoriously with Max Weber's *The Protestant Ethic and the Spirit of Capitalism*, which argues the success of modern capitalism as having derived from the asceticism of European Protestantism and the moral values placed on saving and accumulation.

While the Marxian analysis of historical mystification provides a useful backdrop for understanding how knowledge is produced and politicized, claims of mystification in historical representation more generally have had an active scholarly life outside the Marxian tradition. This is evident in the historical debates about the emergence and development of modern racism. Denying any connection to Marx, the sociologist Oliver C. Cox criticized many of his peers, such as Robert Park and Gunnar Myrdal, as well as anthropologists (notably Ruth Benedict), for suggesting that racial inequality was based on institutionalized marginalization or ethnocentrism. He argued conversely that racism was historically contingent upon class inequalities and programs of global capitalist expropriation and colonialism that prompted racial antagonisms. Cox even suggested that Myrdal's famous Carnegie studies of race (which, following W. Lloyd Warner, suggested an analogy between race and caste) were "mystical." Critics maintained Cox's assertions were mystical themselves, ignoring a long history of racial antagonisms that predated capitalism. The debate highlights competing concerns about the predominance of global capital institutions against charges that economic reductionism inheres in such an approach.

PHILOSOPHICAL MYSTIFICATION

The final dimension of Marx's discussion of mystification relates to his insistence on developing a materialist theory of praxis. A student of Georg F. W. Hegel, Marx was concerned with adapting Hegel's *Grundilinien der Philosophie des Rechts* (1821; Eng. trans., *Elements of the Philosophy of Right*, 1991) for a historical approach grounded less in thoughts and ideas and more in the reality in which they are performed. The postface to the second edition (1873) of *Capital* contains Marx's most relevant criticism of the obfuscatory power of philosophy as complicit in the practical building of power relationships:

> the mystification which dialectic suffers in Hegel's hands by no means prevents him from being the first to present its general form of motion in a comprehensive and conscious manner. With him it is standing on its head. It must be turned right side up again, if you would discover the rational kernel within the mystical shell. (Marx 1990a, p. 103)

Marx's tempered criticism of Hegel (he refers to him in the same breath as a "mighty thinker") sees his own dialectical method as "exactly opposite," where "the ideal is nothing but the material world reflected in the mind of man" (1990a, p. 102). Marx thus sees himself standing steadfast against the complicity of a German idealist legacy that abetted the legitimacy of the state and empire: "in its mystified form, the dialectic became the fashion in Germany, because it seemed to transfigure and glorify what exists" (1990a, p. 103).

Marx's materialist legacy continues to be a subject of much debate in the social sciences. Regardless of its merits or shortcomings, there is an extensive tradition of scholars (beginning prominently with György Lukács, Antonio Gramsci, and here also with elements of the Frankfurt School) concerned methodologically with outlining the development of ideology through theories of practice. Scholars such as Gramsci (and later Michel Foucault) maintain that mystification enables forms of domination based on social and cultural institutions that inculcate and naturalize inequitable social relations, rather than domination legitimated by force. Of course, such works tend to be more critical and radical in their approach but nonetheless recall writings by Émile Durkheim, Weber, and others on religion and the origination and maintenance of social order. Others are unabashed in their appreciation of the benefits of mystification. The American political-philosophical movement known as neoconservatism (fomented mostly through the work of Leo Strauss) extols the virtues of mystifying a self-destructive public through articulated deception (a "noble lie") by a vanguard elite. Still, among the vast majority of social scientists, mystification remains a troublesome social process around which conversations about deception, hegemony, and social justice occur.

SEE ALSO *American Dilemma; Cox, Oliver C.; Gramsci, Antonio; Hegel, Georg Wilhelm Friedrich; Ideology; Lukacs, Gyorgy; Marx, Karl; Marx, Karl: Impact on Anthropology; Marxism; Myrdal, Gunnar*

BIBLIOGRAPHY

Mantz, Jeffrey W., and James H. Smith. 2006. Do Cellular Phones Dream of Civil War? The Mystification of Production and the Consequences of Technology Fetishism in the Eastern Congo. In *Inclusion and Exclusion in the Global Arena*, ed. Max Kirsch. New York: Routledge.

Marx, Karl. 1990a. *Capital: A Critique of Political Economy.* Trans. Ben Fowkes. Vol. 1. New York: Penguin Books in association with New Left Review. (Orig. pub. 1867.)

Marx, Karl. 1990b. *Capital: A Critique of Political Economy.* Trans. Ben Fowkes. Vol. 3. New York: Penguin Books. (Orig. pub. 1894.)

Robinson, Guy. 1998. *Philosophy and Mystification: A Reflection on Nonsense and Clarity.* New York: Routledge.

Jeffrey Mantz

MYTH AND MYTHOLOGY

In educated circles, myths or mythical materials can be concepts, images, symbols, and narratives. They may be regarded variously by different persons, within specific sociohistorical contexts, as being more or less important at different stages of biosocial development. Accordingly, adolescents may deconstruct mythic heroes during the transitions from the sixth to the twelfth grade.

Myths have often been labeled as "sacred," or at least as essential parts of the religio-ritual-scriptural complexes of religious institutions. This has been the dominant position within myth studies, as represented in the title of a collection of essays edited by the American folklorist Alan Dundes (1934–2005), *Sacred Narrative: Readings in the Theory of Myth* (1984). Dundes begins his introduction on page one of this collection: "A myth is a sacred narrative explaining how the world and man came to be in their present form," which now seems as at least a doubly limiting definition, linking the sacred to a creation myth.

The concept of "the secular" is established precisely as "the profane" (literally *outside* the temple walls) in highly religious societies. Yet increasingly, less-religious Western peoples have begun to notice that "the religious" actually represents, at most, some selective enclaves, and that "the secular" (the term means, etymologically, only "of this age, contemporary") is the primary source of experience for most people in our era. And it has become all too obvious that quite apart from holding "sacred" status, hundreds of hardly religious mythic figures and images are more influential today than traditional religious ones: Pop culture has become the major source of experience in our societies, one in which the ironically self-named singer Madonna or rappers such as Eminem are referred to far more frequently than figures and stories from traditional religious repertoires.

Of course, myths remain "sacred" within explicitly religious organizations. Recent decades have witnessed strong growth of fundamentally restrictive puritanisms, and there, to be sure, "mythical" connotes false, sacrilegious, or heathen. Even highly educated persons may equate myth with any religious institution's attitude that they oppose. Demonstrations of the problems that primitive Christians had with their Jewish compatriots and forebears (the New Testament has several equations of "myth" with "Jewish concepts") generally help more neutral audiences to understand some of the hostility that led to early-Christian burning of the great Alexandrian collection of all remaining Greek manuscripts because they were mythic and hence "anti-Christian."

OTHER CLASSIFICATIONS OF MYTH

Modern and contemporary anthropological evaluations of the mythic include Bronislaw Malinowski's (1884–1942) emphasis upon myth as an active social force and Claude Lévi-Strauss's proposals that myths represent attempts to resolve philosophical dialectics between—ultimately—being and nonbeing. Yet it is perhaps an open question whether or not myths really resolve the ancient Zoroastrian dichotomies reflected in the Hebraic prophetic contrast between human inclinations toward good or evil. The issue was posed by the Talmud no less than in the Christian Didache's ethical teaching about the "Two Ways"—itself an echo of the Greek image of Herakles at the crossroad having to choose between plain-Jane virtue and gorgeous vice. What is more obvious than resolving this particular ethical-intellectual dichotomy is that mythic orientations can be understood as ultimately responsible for long-range positions that can lead to military aggression and racism or, on the other hand, to utopian planning, multiculturalism, and pacifism.

At some point in the development of mythological studies (mythography), issues of form/structure versus content/ideological dimension appeared. Formally, many myths (although certainly not all, as assumed repeatedly) seemed to be strongly related to rituals, especially those associated with life transitions and communal festivals. And likewise it has become evident that myths ought to be less readily regarded as coherent narratives than as fragments, whether in ordinary discourse or in displayed works of art (see especially Danser 2005, pp. ix–x, p. 14, and chap. 3).

Alive within a mythological universe, then, myths are less scriptural monoliths than segments of memories, portions of wholes that may or may not cohere as "religious" systems, yet have a flavor of mythicity that identifies "the American dream," the Western hero monomyth, rock and roll, or a political plank. "Mythicity" usually seems naively natural, although it is certainly difficult to parse in technical language; we may be least aware of those mythological perspectives through which we cipher importance and significance in culture.

Myths reinforce ancient educative values, as Plato (c. 427–347 BCE) notably realized. But one might look also at contemporary Navajo myths that, in their entirety, project an amazingly exact geographical gazetteer of their native nation's boundaries. Such mythological performances (and later texts) are also evocative scenarios—the

metaphors by which societies elect to follow this or that projected sociopolitical choice as well as various hermeneutical-interpretive-moral alternatives.

Here the mythological and the ideological-political spheres overlap, because myths model moral choices (positively or negatively). They are often ways the individual learns how to adjust to social roles and statuses—one's own and those of peers with whom one chooses to associate. Mythological materials can be seedbeds of new metaphors for comprehending and changing societies, providing perspectival ways of seeing that are constantly changing images of possible realizations of communal, artistic, and individual growth and fulfillment. Martin Luther King's 1963 "I have a dream!" speech, for example, had a powerful mythico-political force.

FORWARD-LOOKING MYTH

Notably, myths can fund prospects for the future derived from the traditions of the past, as they lubricate the transitions and initiations that fine-tune social interactions and provide the symbols of communication. It is easy to note their afterlife in language, as is seen in English-language adjectives originating from the Greeks: hermetic, mercurial, Apollonian, Dionysian, narcissistic, oedipal.

Many of these figures reflect the central roles of creativity and development that somehow always recur as an important dimension of the mythological. Such a dimension represents various options in cultures that are seldom still regarded today as formative and revisionary, yet continue to ferment like dreams and visions, revolutionary modes of imaging. Hence, there are so many instances of mythical stories of transformations and changes, metamorphoses and apocalyptic endings, as well as recourses to originary energies of beginnings, the recountings of which still have the affective-effective power to motivate and stimulate change.

TRADITIONAL CATEGORIES OF MYTHS

Two important categories of myths that remain very much alive in American schools are those from classical Greece and Rome, and world mythologies. The former were simply part of the worldview and diction of antiquity, not at all a matter of coherent pantheons, as it would appear from modern textbooks and lists of mythical symbols, but instead a situation where deities and heroes were respected primarily as the powerful figures of specific cities or locales. Any one of them had various ritual epithets, according to how the figure had manifested locally (the Zeus of such and such a town). Later handbooks and catalogues appeared only as earlier Greek culture was waning and Roman adaptations of many of the Greek figures threatened to replace them. The polished, famous accounts of Apollodoros (c. second or first century BCE and Ovid (c. 43 BCE – 17 CE) become the models for medieval and Renaissance rediscoveries of long-latent mythological resources.

Thanks to Plato and then subsequent movements within Greek thought, the two basically identical terms for "word, saying"—*logos* and *mythos*—were differentiated. The "mythical" came to be considered less important than the "logical," and the history of Western science was off and running with Aristotle (384–322 BCE). In the Roman period, largely due to excesses of allegorical interpretation, *mythos* had become so disdained that the Latin equivalent of the Greek *mythos*, *fabula* (as in *fabula fictiva*), named such traditional mythological stories—and then later the Christian apologists sought to show that the Christ myths were superior to the traditional Western stories (even though their artists repeatedly created early Christian images using the traditional heroic models).

Certainly biblical folklore and mythology presents a third most important source of Western mythological traditions, but today "world mythology" has become yet more central in most educational contexts, even at the United States Military Academy in West Point, New York, where the English department is responsible for the humanities education of the plebes. The Academy has found world mythology to be an excellent way to inculcate tolerance and receptivity to other world cultures (primarily using one of the many widely available collections, such as Donna Rosenberg's *World Mythology* [1999]).

NEW MULTIDISCIPLINARY FOCUS

Mythological studies in itself provides a convenient canvass of the history of scholarship: the study of myths and rituals has become a focus of many analyses in literature, anthropology, and religious studies. Attitudes toward the mythological today are less "monotheistic" than in the past—but few scholars would argue for earlier models that presumed that myths merely constituted primitive attempts at science, or reflected interpretations of astrological models. Rather, a multidisciplinary approach acknowledging several factors is widely accepted: psychological functions, sociological applications, even philosophical dimensions are now considered relevant.

Myths and mythologies are like the lenses in our now variously tinted spectacles: we see through them. Even today, we code our universe with mythic figures and stories, and our psyches still echo them at night. In popular culture, ideological implications arise when myths are reified in such ways as to reinforce political or religious values, or when certain sets of mythological figures are considered a society's primary models for gender or power relationships.

In such monocultures, whole bodies of mythology may be suppressed or ignored; it is remarkable how few of the general U.S. population today are aware of the complexity of American Indian or African American mythologies, or how uncritically people regard stories about or from other times and cultures.

COMMUNICATING AND INCULCATING CULTURE

Yet, beyond the aesthetic beauty of stories, myths have important communicative functions as they are put to corporate use in shaping communities or individually in forming self-identity. Hence Plato's concern that the primary stories (myths) told to young Greeks were told by their uneducated childhood nurses; but, on the other hand, he was quick to devise his own mythical stories to convey sophisticated philosophical teachings (Brisson 1998 and 2004 are exhaustive in their scope).

Particularly when myth is employed in politics or for inculcating religious moralities, it readily assumes claims of being a "truth" that would never be attributed to other types of stories. While secondary or tertiary mythical influences may not excite the faithful, the primary myths soon attain canonical or scriptural force, and may even be considered absolute, closed to analysis or criticism. Monotheistic "literal" interpretations have become suspect in a postmodernist world, due to the fact that they are naïve and untheorized.

Beyond romantic effusions of admiration, contemporary appreciations of myth can at last include ancient appropriations while realizing that they garner ancient wisdoms at their own risks—even while developing contemporary realizations and reapplications of what seem to remain long-lasting (one may no longer say "eternal" or "universal") cultural inheritances. Myths and mythologies resurface repeatedly because of the long history they trail as representing important sociocultural values, seldom figured explicitly in popular culture expressions, yet all too often lodged beneath the glitz and glamour of popular films, television shows, and advertisements.

SEE ALSO *Magic; Religion*

BIBLIOGRAPHY

Brisson, Luc. 1998. *Plato the Myth Maker*. Trans. and ed. Gerard Naddaf. Chicago: University of Chicago Press.

Brisson, Luc. 2004. *How Philosophers Saved Myths: Allegorical Interpretation and Classical Mythology*. Trans. Catherine Tihanyi. Chicago: University of Chicago Press.

Danser, Simon. 2005. *The Myths of Reality*. Loughborough, U.K.: Alternative Albion.

Doty, William G. 2000. *Mythography: The Study of Myths and Rituals*. 2nd ed. Tuscaloosa: University of Alabama Press.

Doty, William G. 2004. *Myth: A Handbook.* Westport, CT: Greenwood.

Dundes, Alan, ed. 1984. *Sacred Narrative: Readings in the Theory of Myth.* Berkeley: University of California Press.

Rosenberg, Donna. 1999. *World Mythology: An Anthology of the Great Myths and Epics.* 3rd ed. Lincolnwood, IL: NTC.

William G. Doty

N

NADER, RALPH
1934–

Ralph Nader has been one of the most important and enduring figures of the American Left since his emergence on the national stage in 1965 with the publication of *Unsafe at Any Speed*. In this work, Nader argued that the American automobile industry paid insufficient attention to safety. The book sparked public outrage and congressional action, including the creation in 1966 of the National Highway Safety Bureau (now the National Highway Traffic Safety Administration) and passage of many car safety regulations. Perhaps more enduringly, Nader persuaded the public to give more weight to safety concerns when purchasing cars. With his far-reaching advocacy work over the decades, Nader has firmly established his place in the radical American tradition as a critic of the concentration of corporate power. Nader views corporate power as a threat to consumer rights and health, the environment, government integrity, and, most importantly, a well-functioning democracy.

The son of immigrant parents from Lebanon who owned a modest restaurant in a small Connecticut town, Nader earned his undergraduate degree at Princeton University and a law degree at Harvard. His years after law school were spent traveling, dabbling in journalism, and practicing law in Connecticut. He relocated to Washington, D.C., when his work on auto safety caught the attention of policymakers, and he quickly established himself as the most effective "policy entrepreneur" of his generation.

The 1966 to 1976 period marks the height of Nader's influence in American politics. With an innate talent for conducting exhaustive policy research, generating public attention, and manipulating the press, Nader's advocacy pushed such legislation as the Wholesale Meat Act, the Wholesale Poultry Products Act, the National Gas Pipeline Safety Act, and the Radiation Control for Health and Safety Act through to passage in the late 1960s. His stature in Washington grew to such proportions that Democratic presidential nominee George McGovern invited Nader to consider joining his ticket in the 1972 election.

Building on his successes and public acclaim, Nader established a consumer advocacy group in Washington, the Center for the Study of Responsive Law, in 1968. Staff lawyers, publicists, and grassroots activists, dubbed "Nader's Raiders" for their proclivity to challenge the Washington and corporate establishment, investigated patronage practices at the Federal Trade Commission, special interest pressure in Congress, and the safety of the nuclear power industry, among other issues. Over the years, Nader would create a long list of not-for-profit advocacy groups, including the Public Interest Research Group, Public Citizen, and Democracy Rising.

Nader's career, however, has been marred by his inability to accept compromise as the price of democratic politics. His intransigence derailed the effort to create a federal department of consumer affairs. He also turned against many of his protégés who served in the Jimmy Carter administration (1977–1981) because, in Nader's view, they were too quick to compromise on matters of corporate regulation. Nader lost battles, allies, and influence as a consequence of his ideological purity.

By 1980 a concerted effort by American business to counter Nader's consumer rights movement by increasing corporate lobbying paid off. Conservative Ronald Reagan (1911–2004) won election as president, and Congress and the country moved in a more conservative direction. Throughout the 1980s and 1990s, Nader and his allies fought to hold the advances in regulatory policy that they had made in the 1960s and 1970s.

Locked out of the newly conservative Washington establishment, Nader traveled and lectured throughout the country, seeding small citizen projects at the state and local level. Unhappy with the centrism of the Bill Clinton Democrats in the 1990s, Nader ran for U.S. president four times: in 1992 as a write-in candidate for the Democratic nomination in the early primary states; in 1996 as the Green Party nominee; in 2000 as the candidate of the Association of State Green Parties; and in 2004 as an independent candidate. Nader argued that both major parties were beholden to corporations, and he promised to enact campaign finance reform, limit free trade agreements, and extend government regulation of the environment and the economy. In all of his runs, Nader would win no more than 3 percent of the popular vote (in 2000).

The move into electoral politics embittered many former Nader's Raiders, who thought that Nader's run for the presidency jeopardized the Democratic Party's chances. In 2000 these critics were proved right when Nader siphoned likely voters for the Democratic nominee, giving Republican candidate George W. Bush a narrow margin of victory in the state of Florida, a victory that provided Bush with enough electoral votes to win the presidency.

BIBLIOGRAPHY

Martin, Justin. 2002. *Nader: Crusader, Spoiler, Icon.* Cambridge, MA: Perseus.

Nader, Ralph. 1965. *Unsafe at Any Speed: The Designed-in Dangers of the American Automobile.* New York: Grossman. Expanded ed., 1972.

Nader, Ralph. 2002. *Crashing the Party: Taking on the Corporate Government in an Age of Surrender.* New York: St. Martin's.

Richard M. Flanagan

NADER'S RAIDERS

The first Nader's Raiders were seven law students and recent graduates assembled by the consumer advocate Ralph Nader in the summer of 1968 to undertake a study of the Federal Trade Commission (FTC). The group investigated the agency's activities with great thoroughness. The journalist William Greider, then a *Washington Post* reporter, gave the group its name, and the label stuck.

Although Nader initially complained that the name rang of the "cult of personality," he later admitted that it brought the group valuable publicity.

The Raiders' 185-page report issued in January 1969 spared no one. It called for a total revamping of FTC practices and personnel and received extensive press coverage. President Richard Nixon asked the American Bar Association (ABA) to appraise the performance of the FTC; ultimately the students' report—and the ABA appraisal that followed—sparked a congressional investigation and a major overhaul of the agency.

The success of the group established a pattern for subsequent teams that would work with Nader on similar projects. In 1969 about a hundred undergraduate and law students, most from Ivy League schools and many from affluent families, were hired to investigate an array of areas of government and corporate abuse, including mine safety, the health hazards of air pollution, and the oversight of the food industry by the Food and Drug Administration.

Although the Raiders earned only modest pay, competition for those jobs quickly grew fierce. By 1970 more than three thousand students had applied for two hundred summer jobs. In subsequent summers new investigations examined worsening water pollution and the lack of an effective response from the federal government, the indignities and frauds practiced by nursing homes, the dangerous use of pesticides in agriculture, and bureaucratic mismanagement under the Community Mental Health Centers Act.

Charged with researching the performance of key government agencies and previously ignored social problems, those task forces produced reports that forced the federal power structure to take notice. The Raiders' impact can be measured by the fact that their first four reports had combined sales of over 450,000. By 1972 the Raiders had completed seventeen books. Their practice of providing both particulars and meticulous documentation made their reports hot copy. The fact that they were largely students exposing instances of government footdragging, special-interest collusion, corporate malfeasance, and outright corruption made the reports compelling. Reflecting later on revelations of environmental pollution and government scandal in the Nixon and Reagan administrations, Nader commented that in hindsight the reports were "quite understated" (Bollier 1991, Chap. 1).

Nader used the proceeds from the settlement of an invasion of privacy lawsuit he filed against General Motors in 1970 to extend the Raiders' size and reach. He funded a network of consumer groups that provided training grounds for political activists and lawyers. After their work with Nader some Raiders went into private law practice, where they represented the interests of injured consumers and workers, helping to generate an increase in tort lawsuits in the 1970s and 1980s. Many of those lawsuits redressed real wrongs, for example, by recovering damages for victims of the Ford Pinto, which became notorious for exploding and burning when rear-ended. Businesses claimed, however, that many of those lawsuits were filed on unjustifiable grounds, clogging the courts and leading to outrageous verdicts, particularly when they involved punitive damages.

SEE ALSO *Consumer Protection; General Motors; Interest Groups and Interests; Nader, Ralph; Privacy*

BIBLIOGRAPHY

Bollier, David. 1991. *Citizen Action and Other Big Ideas: A History of Ralph Nader*. Washington, DC: Center for Study of Responsive Law. http://www.nader.org/template.php?/archives/7-Citizen-Action-and-Other-Big-Ideas-By-David-Bollier.html.

Bowen, Nancy. 2002. *Ralph Nader: Man with a Mission*. Brookfield, CT: Twenty-First Century Books.

Graham, Kevin. 2000. *Ralph Nader: Battling for Democracy*. Denver, CO: Windom Press.

Martin, Justin. 2002. *Nader: Crusader, Spoiler, Icon*. Cambridge, MA: Perseus.

Alexandra Cooper

NAEP, THE

SEE *National Assessment of Educational Progress.*

NAFTA

SEE *North American Free Trade Agreement.*

NANOTECHNOLOGY

Nanotechnology, or nanotech, is a collective term for several dozen related techniques that manipulate and manufacture molecules that are measured by the nanometer (one-billionth of a meter, or 10^{-9}m, in scientific notation). Instruments invented in the early 1980s now enable scientists to observe and rearrange molecules and atoms as never before, thereby enriching our knowledge of the world of the nanoscale. Viruses and atomic surfaces, for example, are understood much better than before, while carbon atoms are arranged into new shapes, including spheres and tubes. Because of its ability to rearrange the building blocks of matter, nanotech has great potential to affect medicine, information technology, materials science, the environment, and other areas. Developments in medical diagnostics and therapeutics, along with smaller, faster computers, are especially exciting, while toxicity and threats to privacy are uncertain but worrisome. Social scientists are interested in nanotech because it also affects economic, cultural, social, and political conditions.

While the scientific basis of nanotech is many decades old, the policy framework emerged in the late 1990s and early 2000s as governments organized public-sector funding and encouraged private-sector investments. Some social scientists began to study nanotech at that time. Many had previously studied biotechnology or information technology, so they brought mature research methods and sophisticated insights to nanotech. Their work consisted not only of observing the emergence of a new technology, but also of trying to influence its direction before society became locked into an unfortunate trajectory of technological determinism. Furthermore, the status of the scholarly literature has been dynamic. Commentaries on nanotech in the sciences, the humanities, or the social sciences become outdated very quickly.

HISTORY AND HYPERBOLE

Four kinds of issues are especially prominent in social science research on nanotech. First there are several contested histories of nanotechnology. One version says that nanotech began with a prescient talk in 1959 by Richard P. Feynman (1918–1988), the 1965 Nobel laureate in physics. Another points to the invention of the scanning tunneling microscope by IBM scientists Gerd Binnig and Heinrich Rohrer in 1981. A third narrative emphasizes the vision popularized by K. Eric Drexler in his 1986 book *Engines of Creation*. A fourth indicates that the underlying science was well established but intellectually diffuse until January 2000 when President Bill Clinton gathered many strands into one agenda called the National Nanotechnology Initiative (NNI).

In weighing these narratives, the critical perspectives of the social sciences reveal an ideological landscape of explicit and implicit discourses, with much competition to establish definitions, iconic images, and authoritative meanings, not to mention priorities for government funding. The Feynman origin theory appeals to quantum physicists and some people in the California Institute of Technology community, where Feynman taught for more than thirty years. The account that begins with the scanning tunneling microscope is preferred by the IBM community and most nanoscientists other than quantum physicists. The Drexler story is more credible outside of scientific circles than within because it delivers limitless promises of technological salvation, although several scientists credit Drexler for inspiring their scientific work. Finally, the NNI version demands that nanotechnology produce tangible products quickly, which justifies generous government support for science and technology, plus government cheerleading for private-sector developments. It also draws upon a sense of economic nationalism: The NNI is a way for the United States to maintain economic and technological leadership. This story has parallel versions elsewhere, particularly in a series of European Union plans to unify European nanotechnology.

A second set of issues involves the power and consequences of hyperbole, both for and against nanotechnology. Nanotech evokes some intense interpretations of culture and technology: The so-called nano visionaries describe a magical set of tools that will transmute matter, end death, and perform other amazing changes, while their counterparts on the other end of the ideological spectrum preach that nanotech leads to the end of humanity, the end of our environment, and other evils.

These forms of hyperbole cause one to wonder whether they are grounded in the scientific and technical realities of nanotech. Or, do they express hopes and fears unrelated to nanotech reality, but gratuitously superimposed on nanotech? Another question is the changing relation between the technology and the hyperbole. Is the antinano hype discredited when beneficial applications come into our lives? Is there a nanophobic backlash: Do policymakers and nonexperts feel deceived by extravagant promises that turn out to be unrealistic? Social scientists have been tracking these questions of hope and trust. Furthermore, changes in relations between the technology and the hyperbole do not necessarily constitute a victory of one form of hype over another. They can also take the form of centrist positions displacing either form of hype.

DEMOCRATIC AND MORAL RESEARCH

The third cluster of questions appeals to the conscience of the social sciences, for these are the issues of justice and the common good. Nanotechnology has consequences for power, wealth, privacy, trust, discrimination, and other moral questions that animate social scientists. One topic is especially salient, namely, the longstanding problem of how a democratic society uses democratic processes to make science policy. The philosopher and educator John Dewey (1859–1952) argued that when a democratic society makes science policy, it needs many citizens who are well informed about science. Jon D. Miller pursued this by measuring civic scientific literacy beginning in the early 1980s, and he found consistently that it was dreadfully low. In a parallel development in the United Kingdom in 1985, a program for public understanding of science took the form of a simplistic agenda in which scientists talked and nonscientists listened and then passively internalized what they had been told. This is entirely unrealistic.

At the same time, however, social scientists in the United States observed stakeholder democracy in which the general population may be uninterested and inert about scientific policy, but those who see themselves as being affected by a given policy will take an active interest. Participatory democracy is the label for the activism of nonexperts who take part in making science policy. Case studies include AIDS activists playing constructive roles in clinical trials, or environmental disputes in which nonexperts become important actors, or laypersons serving on advisory committees for the National Institutes of Health. The ideas of stakeholder democracy and participatory democracy are corroborated by observations that show that nonexperts can acquire, understand, and deploy technical information when they have to. Meanwhile, social scientists in the United Kingdom advocate something similar called *upstream public engagement* in nanotechnology policy. This is meant to be an antidote to the simplistic plan of public understanding of science.

Nanotech is not necessarily more suitable to participatory democracy and upstream engagement than other technologies, but it gained attention among nonexperts at the same time that these discourses matured. And so, by historical coincidence, nanotechnology became a platform for experimenting with mechanisms and processes by which nonexperts have active and constructive roles in the creation of science policy. This is likely to be among the most important forms of social science activity concerning nanotechnology.

The fourth area of interest is a soul-searching debate about the moral value of a program named SEIN, which stands for "societal and ethical implications of nanotechnology." This is a priori problematic. *Implications* usually suggests that when the new technology arrives, it changes the society, and the consequences are understood after the fact. But if one wants to advocate one policy or another before nanotech causes major disruptions, it is necessary to revise the meaning of SEIN. Societal interactions with nanotech suggests that society coevolves with the technology, in which case stakeholders can make decisions about nanotech before technological change becomes a fait accompli.

This leads to an argument about the connection between SEIN and ELSI, the program to study the "ethical, legal, and societal implications" of the Human Genome Project. ELSI was generally recognized as a successful effort to describe and communicate those topics from the Human Genome Project, but many social scientists felt that ELSI constituted an uncritical acceptance of the agenda of the project. If SEIN is a child of ELSI, does this mean that social scientists are censoring themselves when they receive government funding to do SEIN research?

The U.S. Congress had ELSI in mind as a model when it included a program for SEIN in the Twenty-first Century Nanotechnology Research and Development Act of 2003. For this reason, some social scientists conclude that SEIN is not meant to raise social or ethical questions in government-funded nanotechnology research. They say that SEIN is intended to lubricate popular acceptance of nanotech, that is, to eliminate the social frictions that frustrate technological determinism.

The U.S. government's programmatic documents on nanotechnology often reveal a spirit of technological determinism, but that does not necessarily mean that there is a coherent plan for SEIN that conforms to that spirit. SEIN is very vaguely described in the 2003 act and related documents. Furthermore, the idea of participatory democracy for nanotech—that nonexperts will have active and constructive roles in nanotech policy—is at least as credible among those who are doing government-funded SEIN work as the manipulative view of SEIN. One reason is because much of nanotech is meant to lead to tangible consumer products, and it would be a major disaster for industry and government to misread consumer concerns and values, especially after investing billions of dollars to create those products.

This is not to claim that government science bureaucrats have become leftists. The point rather is that the future and the value of SEIN research are far from determined. There is neither documentation nor experience to conclude that SEIN is intrinsically corrupt for social scientists.

Nanotechnology derives from multiple strands of scientific work, some of which are many decades old. It also evokes numerous everyday issues concerning economy, culture, society, and power, and it is strongly shaped by visions of what will happen in the near future. To a social scientist, this is worth noting: a culture whose past, present, and future are interesting and problematic.

SEE ALSO *Microelectronics Industry*

BIBLIOGRAPHY

Baird, Davis, and Tom Vogt. 2004. Societal and Ethical Interactions with Nanotechnology. *Nanotechnology Law and Business* 1 (4): 391–396.

Binnig, Gerd, and Heinrich Rohrer. 1987. Scanning Tunneling Microscopy: From Birth to Adolescence. *Reviews of Modern Physics* pt. 1, 59 (3): 615–625.

Drexler, K. Eric. 1986. *Engines of Creation: The Coming Era of Nanotechnology*. Garden City, NY: Anchor.

Feynman, Richard P. 1960. There's Plenty of Room at the Bottom. *Engineering and Science* 23: 22–36.

Fisher, Erik. 2005. Lessons Learned from the Ethical, Legal, and Social Implications Program (ELSI): Planning Societal Implications Research for the National Nanotechnology Program. *Technology in Society* 27: 321–328.

Guston, David, and Daniel Sarewitz. 2002. Real-time Technology Assessment. *Technology in Society* 24: 93–109.

Macnaghten, Phil, Matthew Kearnes, and Brian Wynne. 2005. Nanotechnology, Governance, and Public Deliberation: What Role for the Social Sciences? *Science Communication* 27 (2): 268–291.

Munn Sanchez, Edward. 2004. The Expert's Role in Nanoscience and Technology. In *Discovering the Nanoscale*, eds. Davis Baird, Alfred Nordmann, and Joachim Schummer, 257–266. Amsterdam: IOS.

Royal Society and Royal Academy of Engineering. 2004. *Nanoscience and Nanotechnologies: Opportunities and Uncertainties*. London: Royal Society.

Toumey, Chris. 2005. Apostolic Succession: Does Nanotechnology Descend from Richard Feynman's 1959 Talk? *Engineering and Science* 68 (1): 16–23.

Chris Toumey

NAPOLÉON BONAPARTE
1769–1821

Napoléon Bonaparte was born in Ajaccio, Corsica, to a noble family of modest means, the second of eight children of Carlo and Letizia Buonaparte. He studied at a military school at Brienne in France, then at the École Militaire in Paris, and became a second lieutenant in an artillery regiment (1785). Following the outbreak of the French Revolution, he returned to Corsica and served in the Corsican National Guard. Sharp disagreements with Pasquale Paoli, the elder Corsican leader, forced him to flee to France with his family in 1793. The revolution opened the higher military ranks to talent, allowing Napoléon to advance rapidly. France also needed new officers to fight the revolutionary wars after numerous noble officers had fled the country. In 1793, Napoléon participated in the siege of the port of Toulon, which had revolted against the Republic with the help of the British fleet. Napoléon's artillery expelled the enemy fleet, and he was promoted to general. In 1795, his guns dispersed a royalist insurrection against the government in Paris; subsequently, he rose to major-general and was appointed commander of the interior. In March 1796, Napoléon married Josephine de Beauharnais.

Soon, Napoléon invaded northern Italy, where he defeated the Austrians in numerous battles, including Lodi, Arcole, and Rivoli (1796–1797), and forced them beyond the Alps. He then negotiated the Treaty of Campo Formio with Austria, which left most of northern Italy under France and ended the War of the First Coalition. Only Britain remained at war, and so Napoléon sailed to Egypt to strike at British trade. He defeated the Mamelukes and occupied Egypt (1798) but was left stranded after the British admiral Nelson destroyed his fleet at Abukir. Meanwhile, scholars who accompanied him explored Egypt and in effect launched the field of Egyptology. Napoléon returned to France, and with the help of Abbé Sieyès and Lucien Bonaparte, he overthrew the corrupt and unpopular Directory in the coup of Brumaire (November 9–10, 1799) and became First Consul.

The new Constitution of Year VIII, approved by a plebiscite, endowed Napoléon with extensive power. In 1800, he secured his position by defeating Austria at Marengo and signing the Treaty of Luneville (1801), thereby ending the War of the Second Coalition. In 1802, he signed the Treaty of Amiens with Britain. Soon, he became consul for life.

Napoléon betrayed the original ideals of the French Revolution by establishing a dictatorship. He eliminated free speech and outlawed any form of opposition. He created the first modern police state, forming a powerful police force under Joseph Fouché to secure law and order and suppress criticism of his government. Fouché set up a network of spies to suppress dissent. An attempt on Napoléon's life in December 1800, the "machine infernal," gave him an excuse to crush the remaining Jacobins. Pro-Bourbon royalist revolts were also suppressed and their leaders executed. Napoléon purged the legislative branch of liberal critics and emptied it of any power. He established strict censorship, closing down numerous newspapers.

During the same years, Napoléon also launched significant reforms designed to consolidate his power and create a more efficient state. He established a more effective state bureaucracy and appointed the prefects, subprefects, and mayors who ran its eighty-three departments and cities. He continued the revolution's principle of making careers "open to talent" by appointing officials based on merit rather than birth. Napoléon increased public revenues by adding new taxes and improving tax collection.

Napoléon signed the Concordat of 1801 with Pope Pius VII, which shored up Catholic support and sanctioned continuing state control over the French church. Catholicism was recognized as "the religion of the vast majority of French citizens" but not as the state religion. Napoléon nominated new bishops, while the pope invested them with spiritual authority. The pope also acknowledged the new owners of pre-1789 church properties.

In 1804, Napoléon's most important legacy, the Civil Code, known also as the Code Napoléon, took effect. Possessing a simple, concise, and coherent style, it laid the foundations of France's legal unity. It confirmed important revolutionary principles, such as legal equality, freedom of occupation, and the right of private property. It also sanctioned a strong, patriarchal family structure and subordinated the wife to the husband. Napoléon believed that obedience to the father would extend to submission to the head of state. The code allowed divorce on three grounds: ill treatment, criminal conviction, and adultery.

Napoléon constructed a system of national education characterized by uniformity, hierarchy, and state control. He aimed at turning students into loyal citizens and training them as efficient bureaucrats. His most lasting legacy was a system of secondary schools, the *lycées*, with a standardized curriculum and strong discipline. A new administrative body, the Imperial University, ran the national education system and licensed teachers.

In 1804, Napoléon crowned himself emperor at the Notre Dame Cathedral, with Pope Pius VII present, thus terminating the Republic. He created an imperial court and nobility, appointed his relatives as top military officers and civil servants as nobles, and endowed them with fiefs and privileges, although most of his nobility was based on merit. Napoléon wished to imitate great Greek and Roman leaders such as Alexander, Caesar, and Augustus. Imperial Rome fascinated him and was his point of reference. He assumed the title of consul, adopted the eagle as one of his symbols, built the Arc de Triomphe to celebrate his victories, and gave his son the title of King of Rome. Jacques-Louis David, the main exponent of neoclassical art and Napoléon's court painter, glorified him in some unforgettable paintings, most notably *Napoléon Crossing the Great Saint Bernard* and *Sacre de Joséphine*, which recorded the coronation ceremony.

Napoléon also reversed the revolutionary laws on slavery. In 1794, the Convention had ended slavery, following a massive slave insurrection in Saint-Domingue (Haiti), France's most profitable colony. Toussaint Louverture, an ex-slave, emerged as the leader of that revolt. Following emancipation, he joined the French army and, in 1801, became the colony's governor. In 1802, however, in response to demands of plantation owners, Napoléon restored slavery and dispatched General Charles Leclerc to reoccupy Saint-Domingue. The French faced stiff resistance, however. Leclerc summoned Toussaint to a meeting, arrested him, and dispatched him to France, where he died in jail in April 1803. Still, the French failed to defeat the rebels, and in January 1804, leaders of the rebellion established an independent state, which they named Haiti. The loss of Haiti convinced Napoléon to abandon his colonial plans and sell Louisiana to the United States (1803).

While his colonial plans failed, Napoléon repeatedly defeated his enemies in Europe and established a large empire there. He achieved these goals by means of a formidable Grande Armée based on an improved conscription system initiated by the revolutionary regime and introduced throughout his empire. The Grande Armée was, in effect, a European army, consisting of Poles, Italians, Germans, and people of other nationalities aside from French. The emperor stressed effective organization, training, discipline, morale, and good use of weapons, most notably artillery, and he promoted officers on the basis of merit. Napoléon introduced no innovations in weapons and tactics, inheriting these from the Old Regime and the revolution, respectively. Napoléon's principal military innovation was making the corps the standard unit, replacing the division, which became subordinate to the corps. A corps numbered 20,000–30,000 troops, comprising infantry, cavalry, artillery, engineers, and support units. It was usually commanded by a marshal and able to wage a battle on its own.

Napoléon's aggressive foreign policy caused the resumption of hostilities with Britain in 1803. At Boulogne, he prepared an army to invade his archenemy but never carried out that attack. In 1805, Russia and Austria joined Britain, forming the Third Coalition. However, Napoléon defeated the Austrians at Ulm and an Austrian-Russian army at Austerlitz, his greatest victory, later that year. In the Treaty of Pressburg, Austria ceded substantial territories to France and her German allies. In early 1806, the French occupied southern Italy and expelled the Bourbons from Naples; they then routed Prussia at Jena and Auerstädt. In Berlin Napoléon declared the Continental Blockade, intended to seal off Britain from trade with Europe and force its surrender. In 1807, he inflicted a severe defeat on the Russian army at the Battle of Friedland. In the subsequent Treaty of Tilsit, Tsar Alexander I recognized Napoléon's domination in western and central Europe and the newly created Duchy of Warsaw, and agreed to join the blockade. Napoléon's only defeat during these years came at sea, when the British navy under Nelson destroyed the French navy at Trafalgar (October 1805), eliminating any hopes Napoléon had of invading Britain.

In 1807, Napoléon occupied Portugal briefly before being expelled by the British. In 1808, he toppled the Spanish Bourbons, replacing them with his brother Joseph. The Spanish revolted, and Napoléon led an army to quell it. But Spanish armies and guerrillas, with sizable British military support, persisted in their resistance, and after five years forced Joseph to evacuate Iberia. The "Spanish Ulcer" exacted a huge price in human lives and expense, contributing to Napoléon's downfall.

In 1809, the Austrians suffered their fourth defeat by Napoléon, this time at Wagram. In the Treaty of Schönbrunn, they surrendered still more lands, which became the Illyrian Provinces. In 1810, Napoléon married Marie-Louise, an Austrian princess, after divorcing Joséphine, who had borne him no heir. Marie-Louise soon gave birth to a son, who never rose to power, however. Meanwhile, Pope Pius VII refused to join the blockade of Britain, and Napoléon annexed Rome and the Papal State to his empire and exiled him to France (1809).

Napoléon expanded his empire continuously. Aside from his imperial title, he assumed other titles: the Mediator of the Swiss Confederation (1803), the King of Italy (1805), and the Protector of the Confederation of the Rhine (1806). He appointed his brothers as rulers of his satellite kingdoms: Joseph in Naples and later Spain, Louis in Holland, and Jerome in Westphalia. Eugène de Beauharnais, his stepson, became viceroy of the Kingdom of Italy, and Murat, his brother-in-law, received the Kingdom of Naples after Joseph left. Napoléon also annexed lands to France, which by the end of 1810 spread over an area of 293,000 square miles and consisted of 130 departments. Among these territories were Piedmont, Liguria, Tuscany, Rome, the Rhineland, the Netherlands, Hamburg, and Lübeck.

Napoléon's imperial rule possessed a Janus face, combining reforms, modeled on the French system, with exploitation. In his subject states he introduced constitutions, efficient bureaucracies based on merit, legal equality, property rights, termination of the seigneurial system, reduction of church power, and an advanced school system. At the same time, Napoléon exploited the fiscal resources of these lands and drafted their young men into his army.

The Continental Blockade failed to force the British to capitulate, and in 1810 Russia resumed trade with Britain. Napoléon's Grande Armée, 600,000 strong and comprising at least ten nationalities, invaded Russia to force Alexander I to return to the blockade. Napoléon reached Moscow, but the tsar refused to negotiate with him. Napoléon had no choice but to retreat in disarray, losing most of his troops.

He now faced a formidable European coalition as Austria and Prussia resumed hostilities. His defeat at the Battle of the Nations at Leipzig in October 1813 forced him out of Germany; shortly thereafter, he lost the rest of his empire. In April 1814, he abdicated and was exiled to Elba, while Louis XVIII assumed the throne.

In March 1815, Napoléon escaped from Elba, landed in southern France, and marched unopposed to Paris. This time he ruled for only 100 days, proclaiming a new constitution and gathering a new army to fight against the European powers. In June 1815, his last campaign ended at Waterloo, where he was defeated by the British and Prussian armies led by Wellington and Blücher.

Waterloo marked the end of the Napoleonic Era. The British exiled Napoléon to the remote island of St. Helena in the south Atlantic. At St. Helena, Napoléon dictated his memoirs to Emmanuel de Las Cases and talked with other persons who recorded their conversations, thereby helping to create the myth of an emperor who governed for the benefit of the French and other European nationalities. Napoléon died in May 1821.

SEE ALSO *Authoritarianism; Constitutions; Dictatorship; French Revolution; Haitian Revolution; Militarism; Napoleonic Wars; Toussaint Louverture; War*

BIBLIOGRAPHY

Broers, Michael. 1996. *Europe under Napoléon. 1799–1815.* London: Arnold.

Chandler, David G. 1966. *The Campaigns of Napoléon: The Mind and Method of History's Greatest Soldier.* New York: Macmillan.

Connelly, Owen. 1987. *Blundering to Glory: Napoléon's Military Campaigns.* Wilmington, DE: Scholarly Resources.

Ellis, Geoffrey. 1996. *Napoléon.* London and New York: Longman.

Englund, Steven. 2004. *Napoléon: A Political Life.* New York: Scribner.

Fremont-Barnes, Gregory, ed. 2006. *The Encyclopedia of the French Revolutionary and Napoléonic Wars: A Political, Social, and Military History.* 3 vols. Santa Barbara, CA: ABC-CLIO.

Grab, Alexander. 2003. *Napoléon and the Transformation of Europe.* London and New York: Palgrave Macmillan.

Lefebvre, Georges. 1969–1974. *Napoléon.* 2 vols. Trans. J. E. Anderson. London: Routledge and Kegan Paul.

Lyons, Martyn. 1994. *Napoléon Bonaparte and the Legacy of the French Revolution.* New York: St. Martin's Press.

Alexander Grab

NAPOLEON COMPLEX

As a colloquial term used occasionally in psychology, psychiatry, and psychoanalysis, the Napoleon complex refers to a specific type of inferiority complex associated with short people, and especially with short men. It is also sometimes called the "Napoleon syndrome" or the "shortman complex." Individuals with this disposition are claimed to overcompensate for their short stature by being excessively belligerent, hostile, or quarrelsome in their interpersonal relationships. A fictional example is depicted in John Steinbeck's *Of Mice and Men*: The character Curley was a "shorty" who always felt obliged to prove his worth by picking fights with bigger men. However, the Napoleon complex is said to motivate other forms of behavior besides interpersonal violence and aggression. Most innocuously, a short male might make himself feel taller by placing home wall hangings a little lower than normal. Or he might wear shoes with slightly thicker heels.

In contrast, such persons may be driven to ameliorate their supposed low self-esteem by pursuing highly ambitious goals. In fact, the eponymic source for the term is Napoléon Bonaparte, whose military and amorous conquests have been attributed to the desire to compensate for his diminutive size. Nevertheless, this attribution lacks merit insofar as Napoléon was actually a bit taller than the average Frenchman of his day. His alleged shortness derived from a commonplace misunderstanding of the contemporary French inch (which was 7 percent longer than the modern English inch) as well as a mistranslation of his nickname *le petit caporal* into "little corporal" (when *petit* indicates affection rather than dimension). Thus, ironically, Napoléon is not a genuine example of the Napoleon complex. Indeed, the fact that he surrounded himself with an elite guard of soldiers who were all at least six feet tall suggests that he was not at all defensive about his own height.

The Napoleon complex is often associated with the name of Alfred Adler, a former associate of Sigmund Freud and the founder of Individual Psychology. A key concept in Adler's theory was the *inferiority complex*. Although this psychological condition may take many forms, an especially crucial one is the sense of *organ inferiority* with respect to some physical trait. This conception may have been partially inspired by Adler's own experiences as a sickly child, including a bout with rickets that prevented him from walking until he was four. Under special circumstances, the individual may respond to organ inferiority by directly overcompensating for the disability. An illustration is Wilma Rudolph, a victim of debilitating childhood polio who later became the first American woman to win three track-and-field gold medals at the Olympic Games. Other times overcompensation will adopt a more oblique or symbolic form. Hence, because short persons cannot easily make themselves physically taller, they may act to appear psychologically taller—more dominant, assertive, even antagonistic or arrogant. For some individuals of potential genius, the solution may be an extraordinary need for power that takes the guise of military conquest. Accordingly, the Napoleon complex can be viewed as a particular implication of Adlerian psychology.

Even so, Adler himself did not invent the term. Despite identifying numerous "complexes" of various kinds, the Napoleon complex was not included among them, nor was Napoléon used to illustrate overcompensation. Moreover, the complex does not constitute a recognized personality disorder in the *Diagnostic and Statistical Manual of Mental Disorders* published by the American Psychiatric Association, and the term is seldom granted an entry in encyclopedias and dictionaries devoted to psychological science and practice. In addition, the Napoleon complex is almost never the explicit subject of scientific research in the professional journals of psychology, psychoanalysis, or psychiatry. In the main, it represents a pseudoscientific term that is popular among journalists who want to provide an apparent explanation for the behavior of politicians, entrepreneurs, and other celebrities who happen to be shorter than average. It has also become a mainstay of folk psychology, the expression at times being evoked to explicate the odd behavior of a friend or acquaintance.

Yet, somewhat surprisingly, the Napoleon complex has recently been introduced as a scientific concept in a totally unexpected discipline, namely, evolutionary biology. In animal species that feature male competition for reproductive opportunities and resources, it is sometimes the smaller rather than the larger male who most likely initiates aggressive behavior. This phenomenon has been subjected to cost-benefit analyses that indicate the conditions under which such seemingly maladaptive behavior is most likely to be selected. Nonetheless, it is clear that this usage departs significantly from the original meaning of the term. This novel application may therefore not revive the Napoleon complex as a technical term in the social sciences.

SEE ALSO *Inferiority Complex; Overachievers; Personality; Personality, Authoritarian; Psychoanalytic Theory; Psychology; Self-Esteem*

BIBLIOGRAPHY

Adler, Alfred. 1956. *The Individual Psychology of Alfred Adler*, eds. Heinz L. Ansbacher and Rowena R. Ansbacher. New York: Basic Books.

Just, Winfried, and Molly R. Morris. 2003. The Napoleon Complex: Why Smaller Males Pick Fights. *Evolutionary Ecology* 17: 509–522.

Dean Keith Simonton

NAPOLEONIC WARS

The Napoleonic Wars (1803–1815) were fought between the French emperor, Napoléon Bonaparte (Napoléon I; 1769–1821) and the European powers of Britain, Austria, Russia, and Prussia. Ultimately, the wars extended to all corners of the European continent, profoundly affecting European politics, society, and culture. The wars encompassed eight separate military campaigns divided into three broader periods: 1803 to 1807, the ascendancy of Napoleonic power in Europe; 1807 to 1812, the height of Napoléon's Grand Empire; and 1812 to 1815, the decline and fall of Napoléon's empire.

Napoléon became ruler of France in November 1799 when he participated in a coup d'etat, overthrowing the Directory. He immediately inherited the war of the Second Coalition, the last of the wars of the French Revolution. Within months of coming to power he declared the French Revolution ended, and defeated the Second Coalition led by Austria and England. Napoléon concluded the Peace of Lunèville with Austria in 1801. He created satellite republics in Italy (the Cispadane and Cisalpine Republics) in 1796 and 1797, but consolidated them into the Italian Republic in 1802. England signed the Peace of Amiens in 1802 after losing their continental allies. The peace was an expedient, and neither Britain nor Napoléon trusted the other. In May 1803 Britain declared war on France, inaugurating the Napoleonic Wars.

In January 1805 Spain joined France in an anti-British alliance. Napoléon prepared an invasion force to be ferried and protected by a combined Franco-Spanish fleet. Britain sought allies to tie the French to the continent. By summer 1805 England, Russia, and Austria formed a Third Coalition against France. Napoléon's policies in Germany and Italy prior to 1805 alienated Austria and Russia, leading to the formation of the Third Coalition in July 1805. Napoléon, however, capitalized upon his favorable relations with the princes of Germany to gain their support against Austria. The campaign of 1805 was Napoléon's most successful. In October he achieved a dramatic victory over the Austrian army at Ulm in Bavaria. Napoléon invaded Austria, taking Vienna by the end of November. At Austerlitz on December 2, 1805, Napoléon soundly defeated the combined Russo-Austrian army under the eyes of Tsar Alexander I and Kaiser Franz I.

Victory over the Third Coalition enabled Napoléon to make sweeping changes to the map of Europe. The Holy Roman Empire (Germany) was abolished in the summer 1806 and replaced by the Confederation of the Rhine, with France as its protector. Austria and Prussia were excluded from this new German entity. The number of German territories was substantially reduced through secularization and mediatization from 120 to 37. The Italian Republic, a kingdom after 1804, annexed Venetia, nearly doubling its size.

In February 1806 a French army occupied the Kingdom of the Two Sicilies, giving Napoléon the entire peninsula. He then isolated Great Britain by instituting an economic blockade embodied in the Milan and Berlin decrees, often referred to as the "Continental System."

Tensions between Prussia and France culminated in September 1806 in the second campaign of the Napoleonic Wars. The Prussian army was destroyed in two battles, Jena and Auerstadt (October 14, 1806), and the kingdom was overrun. The belated arrival of a Russian army in Poland extended the war into the winter and spring of 1807. Napoléon fought the Russians to a draw at Eylau in February, but decisively defeated them in June at Friedland. The victory over Russia virtually completed Napoléon's conquest of Europe. Tsar Alexander I met the French emperor at Tilsit and agreed to a continental alliance.

Shortly after Tilsit, Napoléon authorized the invasion of Portugal, a British ally. Spanish support for Napoléon's endeavors was lukewarm after the destruction of its fleet at Trafalgar in October 1805. The Spanish king, Carlos IV, and his first minister, Manuel de Godoy, wanted to extricate themselves from the French alliance. Napoléon distrusted the Spanish and in spring 1808 overthrew the Spanish monarchy and occupied Spain. He placed his elder brother Joseph on the throne, which generated enormous popular resistance. The Spanish feared the revolutionary anticlericalism of France, and the imposition of a foreign king. Formal Spanish military resistance gave way to a guerilla war that continued until 1814. Napoléon led a second army into Spain in October 1808, reestablishing French control, but Portugal was lost to the British earlier in the year. Napoléon kept more than 250,000 French and allied troops in the Iberian Peninsula for the next four years. The Peninsular War tied down military resources, and provided Britain with a theater of war on the European continent.

The British army in Portugal in 1809 was led by General Arthur Wellesley, later the Duke of Wellington. He used the small kingdom to conduct offensive operations into Spain, and played a "cat and mouse" game with King Joseph and the French army through 1810. French military power, tied down by Spanish guerillas, was insufficient to retake Portugal. In 1812, as Napoléon invaded Russia, Wellington launched an invasion of Spain supported by the Portuguese and Spanish. Between 1812 and 1813 Joseph and the French Imperial army were forced back to the Pyrenees, and in 1814 Wellington crossed into southern France, finally ending the Peninsular War.

Napoléon returned to Paris in January 1809 to face a new threat from Austria. The Austrians believed that with Napoléon occupied in Spain they stood in a good position to regain control of the German and Italian states. In April 1809 Austrian armies invaded the Confederation of the Rhine, the Kingdom of Italy, and the Grand Duchy of Warsaw—the Napoleonic satellite state of Poland. A combination of Napoléon's military skill, and more signifi-

cantly the strength of his alliances with the German princes and Russia, enabled him to defeat Austria. By mid-May Napoléon sat in Vienna. Although he was repulsed at Aspern-Essling, he attacked again in July and defeated Archduke Charles at Wagram.

Napoléon extended the borders of imperial France in 1810 to include Holland, northwest Germany, Tuscany, and the Papal States. The expanding imperium led to confrontation with Tsar Alexander I of Russia. In June 1812 Napoléon invaded Russia with a French Imperial army of 500,000 men. By the end of September Napoléon had defeated the Russians at Borodino and captured Moscow. Tsar Alexander and his generals evacuated the capital and withdrew east of the city, refusing to surrender or negotiate. Napoléon withdrew from Moscow in the middle of October with no prospect of a clear victory. During both the advance and retreat, his army suffered far more from desertions and disease than from battle casualties. In December the army that returned to central Europe was reduced to 120,000 men. The enormity of the French losses led Tsar Alexander to continue the pursuit and liberate Europe. In March 1813 Frederick William III, the king of Prussia, joined the coalition against France.

Napoléon had rebuilt the French army by the spring 1813 and defeated the Russians and Prussians at Lutzen and Bautzen in Saxony. All sides agreed to a temporary armistice through the summer. During this time Austria joined the coalition against France. The armistice expired in August, and Napoléon found himself under attack from three directions—Prussia, Poland, and Austria. German princes defected from their French alliances, and in October Napoléon was soundly beaten at Leipzig, forcing him to abandon Germany.

Prussian forces crossed the Rhine at the end of December. Coalition armies moved into France from Spain, Germany, and Belgium. Napoléon initially held the Prussians and Russians at bay, but was ultimately overwhelmed by numbers. Napoléon abdicated in April 1814, and went into exile on the island of Elba. Louis XVIII, the brother of the former French king, was restored to the throne.

Napoléon returned to France in February 1815 and was welcomed by the army and the French population, who had lost their taste for kings. The coalition, meeting in Vienna, committed itself to his utter defeat. Napoléon assembled an army and invaded Belgium. In June 1815 he was defeated at Waterloo by British and Prussian armies. He abdicated a second time and was taken prisoner by the English. The former French emperor spent his remaining days on the island of St. Helena in the south Atlantic. He died in 1821.

The Napoleonic Wars transformed the European continent, reshaping the borders of Germany and Italy.

Napoléon purposely fostered Italian nationalism in order to strengthen his satellite states, but in Germany and Spain, nationalism emerged in reaction to French military occupation. Liberalism, the desire for constitutional government, also manifested in Western and Central Europe. The Napoleonic Wars also led to the creation of a European international system established at the Congress of Vienna (1814–1815), which was based upon the principles of balance of power and territorial compensation. The congress system called upon the monarchical powers to suppress revolutions to prevent another crisis like the one that had affected Europe for the previous twenty-five years.

SEE ALSO *Borders; Constitutions; Empire; Imperialism; Liberalism; Monarchy; Monarchy, Constitutional; Napoléon Bonaparte; Nationalism and Nationality; Revolution; War*

BIBLIOGRAPHY

Connelly, Owen. 2006. *The Wars of the French Revolution and Napoleon, 1792–1815.* London: Routledge.

Dwyer, Philip, ed. 2001. *Napoleon and Europe.* Harlow, U.K.: Longman.

Esdaile, Charles. 1995. *The Wars of Napoleon.* Harlow, U.K.: Longman.

Rothenberg, Gunther E. 1978. *The Art of Warfare in the Age of Napoleon.* Bloomington: Indiana University Press.

Schneid, Frederick C. 2005. *Napoleon's Conquest of Europe.* Westport, CT: Praeger.

Schroeder, Paul. 1994. *The Transformation of European Politics, 1763–1848.* Oxford: Clarendon Press.

Frederick C. Schneid

NARCISSISM

Narcissism refers to a personality trait that includes grandiosity, vanity, and self-love. Narcissistic individuals are often described with such adjectives as arrogant, self-centered, cocky, or conceited. The term *narcissism* is derived from the ancient Greek myth of Narcissus. According to the myth, Narcissus was a handsome young man who was in search of his ideal romantic partner. One day he fell in love with his own reflection in a pool of water. Narcissus died while gazing at his reflection, and on that spot a flower (a narcissus or daffodil) grew.

The British sexologist Havelock Ellis (1859–1939) was the first to suggest the character of Narcissus for describing a psychological state. It was Sigmund Freud (1856–1939), however, who made narcissism into a central concept in psychology. In the early twenty-first century the concept of narcissism can be found in several branches of the social sciences. Most frequently narcissism is used in psychology, where it refers to both a personality trait and a personality disorder. Narcissism is also used in fields such as sociology, political science, and criminology.

In personality psychology narcissism is considered to be a continuously distributed, "normal" personality trait. Narcissism appears to have three core characteristics: First, narcissism is associated with an inflated view of the self. Narcissists see themselves and their actions in an overly positive light. This often includes a sense of uniqueness and entitlement (e.g., "I deserve special treatment"). Second, narcissism is associated with interpersonal relationships that lack warmth and emotional intimacy. Third, narcissism is associated with a pattern of behaviors that maintain the inflated, grandiose view of the self. Examples of such behaviors include bragging, showing off, and blaming others when things go wrong. Narcissism and high self-esteem are often confused. Both traits are associated with feeling positively toward oneself. With narcissism, however, those positive feelings are linked specifically to their perceived standing on so-called *agentic* traits, such as social status, intelligence, confidence, and physical attractiveness. Narcissism is not associated with positive feelings on what are called *communal* traits, such as caring, warmth, and compassion. In contrast, individuals with self-esteem feel positively about themselves on both agentic and communal traits.

In clinical psychology and psychiatry narcissism is described as a personality disorder (i.e., *narcissistic personality disorder*, or NPD). A personality disorder is a relatively stable and fixed pattern of thinking, feeling, and behaving that leads to emotional suffering and functional impairment (e.g., problems in love or at work). According to the *Diagnostic and Statistical Manual of Mental Disorders* (1994), NPD involves a pattern of grandiosity, a need to be admired, and a lack of empathy; the disorder is assessed using nine specific criteria, including arrogant behavior, a sense of entitlement, and fantasies of success and brilliance.

In sociology and social history narcissism has been used to describe culture or a cultural movement. A narcissistic culture is one where values like self-promotion, individualism, and self-centeredness are central and where narcissistic individuals are common. The most well-known example of this cultural perspective on narcissism is the historian Christopher Lasch's *The Culture of Narcissism* (1978). Lasch argues that American culture is becoming increasingly narcissistic.

In political science the concept of narcissism is used in the study of leadership. Some leaders, especially dictators and despots (e.g., Adolf Hitler, Joseph Stalin), have been described as narcissistic. In addition narcissism has been examined as a potential factor in political terrorism.

In criminology narcissistic personality traits are thought to predict criminal behavior, including murder, rape, assault, spousal abuse, and white-collar crime. Narcissism is also a key feature of a psychopathic personality, which is perhaps the most important personality profile for predicting serious criminal behavior.

Several significant issues remain unresolved in the scientific study of narcissism. First, there remains debate over the definition of narcissism. While there is strong agreement on key features of narcissism like grandiosity and low empathy, there is disagreement about the link between narcissism and feelings of depression or unhappiness. Some theorists argue that narcissism contains a component of depression or low self-esteem; others argue that narcissism is related to positive emotions. Still others argue that narcissism is linked to negative emotions and self-perceptions but that these feelings are experienced only at an unconscious level. Second, while there are several theories about the development of narcissism in individuals, there is no firm conclusion about its etiology. Some researchers argue that narcissism results from permissive parenting, while others argue that narcissism is a reaction to cold, controlling parents. Finally, the role of culture in maintaining narcissism is not well understood. Some researchers and theorists have identified a rising tide of narcissism, but the cause of this remains unclear.

SEE ALSO *Freud, Sigmund; Individualism; Leadership; Neuroticism; Obsession; Personality; Political Science; Psychology*

BIBLIOGRAPHY

American Psychiatric Association. 1994. *Diagnostic and Statistical Manual of Mental Disorders*. 4th rev. ed. Washington, DC: Author.

Freud, Sigmund. [1914] 1957. On Narcissism: An Introduction. In *The Standard Edition of the Complete Psychological Works of Sigmund Freud*, ed. and trans. James Strachey, vol. 14, 67–104. London: Hogarth.

Lasch, Christopher. 1978. *The Culture of Narcissism: American Life in an Age of Diminishing Expectations*. New York: Norton.

Morf, Carolyn C., and Frederick Rhodewalt. 2001. Unraveling the Paradoxes of Narcissism: A Dynamic Self-regulatory Processing Model. *Psychological Inquiry* 12 (4): 177–196.

W. Keith Campbell
Joshua D. Miller

NARRATIVES

Whether defined in literature, law, philosophy, or the social sciences, narrative has generally been understood as a form of accounting or representing events in language, whether these are real or fictitious, and in a manner that suggests a causal relation between each event. Two of the earliest theories of narrative occur in Plato's *Republic* and Aristotle's *Poetics*, both philosophers being concerned with the role of narrative in mimesis. Where Plato (c. 427–347 BCE) distinguishes between mimesis and diegesis, with the latter requiring the poet to speak in his own name rather than in another's voice, Aristotle (c. 384–322 BCE) identifies narrative itself as a mode of mimesis—the other mode being direct representation, as in drama.

At the heart of both philosophers' discussion is the relationship of narrative to actuality. Plato condemns mimesis in poetic and visual art. However, he also asserts the necessity of tales that model virtuous thought, as opposed to those that invite the imitation of others' emotions. Plato thus turns to a narrative form, allegory, to explicate the relationship between language and the things it ostensibly names.

Aristotle, by contrast, treats mimesis as a faculty natural to humans. According to Aristotle, we learn through imitation because it affords observation and inference. More importantly, the vehicle of this learning is catharsis. Plato condemns mimesis and narrative catharsis on the grounds that they invite false and dangerous emotion in an observer.

Aristotle's emphasis on the affective function of narrative has been a persistent theme throughout Western philosophy. In the twentieth century, it was taken up most notably in the work of Sigmund Freud (1856–1939), who defined catharsis as the release of abnormal affect, and deployed it in trauma therapy while defining trauma as a state characterized by an incapacity to narrate. He thereby normalized narrative in psychological terms.

The tension between an impulse to narrate and the effect of narrative has continued to play itself out, not only in psychology, but also in the social sciences. Thus, one hears the echo of Aristotle when Hannah Arendt (1906–1975) remarks that the distinguishing characteristic of the human is not only the capacity to discern events in history, but also to narrate these events. Arendt emphasizes the political element of storytelling in a manner that anticipates Jürgen Habermas. She stresses the communicative and deliberative processes essential to the formation of a public sphere through speech and action.

Walter Benjamin (1892–1940) likewise writes of the "art of storytelling" as that which enables intergenerational social relations. Benjamin's focus on the immediacy of traditional storytelling as opposed to the information-bearing function of the novel or newspaper has been criticized for its nostalgia. However, it resonates strongly with those theories of sociality in eras and contexts that have not been dominated by technologized forms of print and electronic media. Moreover, his emphasis on the ethics of listening has found sympathy in the fields of anthropology, sociology, folklore studies, and the like, which have taken as their primary object of analysis the speech of others.

In their analysis of the difference between myth and novelistic narrative, Theodor Adorno (1903–1969) and Max Horkheimer (1895–1973) arrive at a theory of the latter's relation to the development of bourgeois modernity's self-mythologizing impulses. This conclusion is outlined in *Dialectic of Enlightenment* (*Dialektik der Aufklärung*, 1947), where they engage the political consequences of a shift from the atemporality of myth to the novelistic narrative that accompanies the rise of capitalism. They thus see the temporalizing effect of narrative as the basis of individuation and the cultural ground of bourgeois subjectivity.

The development of narrative studies was nonetheless interrupted by structuralism and its focus on binary oppositions. In this, structuralism tended to elide both the Aristotelian and the Platonic emphases on sequentiality, temporality, and causality. By the mid-twentieth century, however, counterdiscourses had emerged. Their proponents were historians led by Hayden White, Carlo Ginzberg, and Natalie Zemon Davis. Informed by Northrop Frye's (1912–1991) analysis of narrative structure, White argues that historians employ the same strategies of emplotment as fiction, the exception being chronicles and annals that are not concerned with emplotment and are therefore, for White, nonnarrative. The task of metahistory is, then, to interrogate the presuppositions within which these narratives are produced.

Much of the turn to narrative studies was inspired by a rereading of Mikhail Bakhtin (1895–1975). In conversation with Georg Lukács (1885–1971), Bakhtin identifies the novel form as the space characterized by the reciprocity and simultaneity of many voices and discourses. Their interplay suggests, for Bakhtin, a resistance to formula. Lukács's Marxist reading posited the novel as a bourgeois form of narrative and an antithesis to the closed atmosphere of the heroic Greek epic world. For Bakhtin, the novel is heteroglossic. It resists the drive to totalization because its language bears the history of use by people of different classes and origins. The imperative in his work becomes an ethical one, and insists upon attending to those voices that have yet to be heard by the dominant. Underpinning this theory is a concept of historical time that rolls forward incessantly as each unheard voice comes to be heard.

In their approach to narrative, the twentieth century can be understood in part as a conflict between materialists and structuralists. Among the most influential structuralists, along with Roland Barthes (1915–1980) and Tzvetan Todorov, Gérard Genette drew upon linguistics to analyze the underlying structures of narrative, and to ask what we mean by the term *narrative*, and, thereby, to engage discourse embedded within discourse. Narratology, as he practices it, addresses the typology of narrators—here, continuing questions about who or what narrates and at what level—to identify classes of narrators according to their points of view or their diegetic or extra-diegetic roles. Accordingly, Genette considers narrative time in terms of duration and frequency (that which is iterative).

This question of time is taken up by Paul Ricoeur's (1913–2005) three-volume interdisciplinary *Time and Narrative* (*Temps et Récit*, 1984/1988). Ricoeur argues that all human experience is temporal and that narrative, being more than the mere creation of the individual, is the understanding and orderly mimesis of this lived time. He thereby liberates the study of narrative from purely literary considerations. For this reason, his work has exercised enormous influence on Hayden White, Clifford Geertz (1926–2006), and others. White draws upon Ricoeur in his arguments on mimesis and claims that narrative coherence is far more imaginary than actual. As an interpretivist anthropologist, White argued that story—as the irreducibly mediated text within which experience becomes available to the analyst—must be treated in its narrativity and not merely as the receptacle of information.

Mieke Bal extended the work of Genette and Ricoeur by introducing the question of point of view as part of her argument against the extreme formalism of structuralism. She revisits narratological structure, offering a theory of focalization. Her reading of biblical texts returns to them the narrative elements that structuralists such as Mary Douglas had explained away in the interest of finding such primal oppositions as those between the pure and the impure, the clean and defiled. In renarrating these biblical myths, Bal also insists that the traditions of reading narrative perform ideological work and that the reading of any given story tends to be conducted within the terms of socially privileged metanarratives. It was this analysis that resonated so well within social sciences.

Renewed and wider interest in narrative grew in the social sciences in the mid-1980s. Reasons for this interest came from different spheres, including postcolonial, gender, and critical race theorists. Among formalist analysts of narrative, feminist critic and film theorist Teresa de Lauretis returns to Russian formalism—particularly to semiotician Yuri Lotman (1922–1993)—to analyze metanarrative structure in terms of patriarchal logics, noting that the climax/catharsis in most Western literature and cultural texts is achieved in the moment that a masculine subject possesses or traverses or passes through a feminine obstacle. De Lauretis's feminist critique of the viewing structures in cinematic texts asks—like such theorists as Barbara Johnson, Annette Kolodny, Shoshana Felman, and Mary Ann Doane—questions of point of view. Doane, Johnson, Felman, and Kolodny question metanarratives within psychoanalysis.

In postcolonial and subaltern studies, for example, Edward Said (1935–2003) took up narrative theory to consider the discursive possibilities for third-world subjects vis-à-vis the Western philosophical and ideological hegemonies. Linked to anticolonial and postcolonial assertions of narrative forms and voices that had been discredited by hegemonic master narratives, critical race theory also draws upon anthropology, sociology, history, philosophy, and politics. In critical legal studies, legal scholar Patricia Williams announced in *The Alchemy of Race and Rights*, "My words are my only valuables" (1991, p. 211) thus signaling the manner in which critical race theory would distance itself from mainstream legal discourse. Williams, Richard Delgado, Derrick Bell, Mari Matsuda, Kimberlé Crenshaw, Kendall Thomas, William Tate, and others challenged the neutrality of the law, particularly with regard to race. Bell's direct, narrative criticism epitomized the stylistics of critical race theorists, although Crenshaw, Thomas, and others retained their legalistic styles. All assert the value of a narrated personal experience in tandem with the principles and precedents of legal thought.

The notions of social construction and the reality of race and discrimination are ever-present in the writings of contemporary critical race theorists, who also draw upon pioneers in the field, including W. E. B. Du Bois (1868–1963), Frantz Fanon (1925–1961), and Max Weber (1864–1920). In *Black Skin, White Masks* (1952), Fanon—a student of Aimé Césaire, founder of the négritude movement—gave a first-person account of experiencing the embedded mechanisms of racism. This insertion of direct experience would be found in the narrative critique of colonialism and its legacies in the work of fiction writers as well as theorists of colonialism and anticolonialism. Fanon, like Du Bois at the turn of the twentieth century, showed how one's *weltanschauung* was shaped by social and ideological factors. Interest in Fanon was renewed in the late 1980s and 1990s as postcolonial theorists like Homi Bhabha sought a language that would enable a more effective understanding of the legacies of colonization. Cultural anthropologists, having collected narratives and treated them as signifiers of the world, joined literary theorists in attending to narrative's role in pointing to more than a simple pattern of oppressive/oppositional violence between colonizer and colonized.

SEE ALSO *Arendt, Hannah; Aristotle; Du Bois, W. E. B.; Ethnography; Ethnology and Folklore; Fanon, Frantz; Fiction; Freud, Sigmund; Habermas, Jürgen; Linguistic Turn; Lying; Plato; Postcolonialism; Psychoanalytic Theory; Racism; Reality; Said, Edward; Storytelling; Structuralism*

BIBLIOGRAPHY

Abu-Lughod, Lila. 1993. *Writing Women's Worlds: Bedouin Stories.* Berkeley: University of California Press.

Arendt, Hannah. 1958. *The Human Condition.* New York: Doubleday.

Bakhtin, Mikhail M. 1981. *The Dialogic Imagination: Four Essays,* ed. Michael Holquist; trans. Caryl Emerson and Michael Holquist. Austin: University of Texas Press.

Bakhtin, Mikhail M. 1986. *Speech Genres and Other Late Essays,* eds. Caryl Emerson and Michael Holquist, trans. Vern W. McGee. Austin: University of Texas Press.

Benjamin, Walter. [1968] 1969. The Storyteller: Observations on the Works of Nikolai Leskov. In *Illuminations,* trans. Harry Zohn, 83–109. New York: Schocken.

Bruner, Edward M. 1986. Ethnography as Narrative. In *The Anthropology of Experience,* eds. Victor W. Turner and Edward Bruner, 139–155. Urbana: University of Illinois Press.

Christian, Barbara. 1987. The Race for Theory. *Cultural Critique* 6: 51–63.

Delgado, Richard. 1989. Storytelling for Oppositionists and Others: A Plea for Narrative. *Michigan Law Review* 87 (8): 2411–2441.

De Lauretis, Teresa. 1984. *Alice Doesn't: Feminism, Semiotics, Cinema.* Bloomington: Indiana University Press.

Doane, Mary Ann. 1991. Dark Continents: Epistemologies of Race and Sexual Difference in Psychoanalysis and the Cinema. In *Femmes Fatales: Feminism, Film Theory, Psychoanalysis,* 209–248. New York: Routledge.

Douglas, Mary. 1966. *Purity and Danger: An Analysis of Concepts of Pollution and Taboo.* London: Routledge.

Fanon, Frantz. [1952] 1967. *Black Skin, White Masks.* Trans. Charles Lam Markmann. New York: Grove.

Freud, Sigmund. 1920. *Selected Papers on Hysteria and Other Psychoneuroses.* Trans. Abraham Arden Brill. 3rd ed. New York: Nervous and Mental Disease Publishing.

Genette, Gérard. 1980. *Narrative Discourse: An Essay in Method.* Trans. Jane E. Lewin. Ithaca, NY: Cornell University Press.

Plato. [1927] 1979. *Charmides.* In *Charmides. Alcibiades I and II. Hipparchus. The Lovers. Theages. Minos. Epinomis.* Trans. W. R. M. Lamb. Cambridge, MA: Harvard University Press.

Polkinghorne, Donald. 1988. *Narrative Knowing, and the Human Sciences.* Albany: State University of New York Press.

Ricoeur, Paul. 1984–1988. *Time and Narrative.* Vols. 1–3. Trans. Kathleen McLaughlin and David Pellauer. Chicago: University of Chicago Press.

Riffaterre, Michael. 1990. *Fictional Truth.* Baltimore, MD: Johns Hopkins University Press.

Taussig, Michael. 1993. *Mimesis and Alterity: A Particular History of the Senses.* New York and London: Routledge.

White, Hayden. 1973. *Metahistory: The Historical Imagination in Nineteenth-century Europe.* Baltimore, MD: Johns Hopkins Press.

Williams, Patricia. 1991. *The Alchemy of Race and Rights.* Cambridge, MA: Harvard University Press.

Yvette Christiansë

NASH, JOHN
1928–

In a few short papers between 1950 and 1953, John F. Nash Jr. formulated two major concepts of game theory: the Nash bargaining solution and Nash equilibrium. His formulation of noncooperative equilibrium was one of the greatest conceptual breakthroughs in social science. Nash then turned his focus to mathematical analysis and made important contributions to the theory of manifolds. His work was tragically interrupted by mental illness after 1960. Decades later, his recovery and return to active work was widely celebrated in the field of economics, where his ideas had triumphed even in his absence. (See Sylvia Nasar's biography *A Beautiful Mind: A Biography of John Forbes Nash Jr.* published in 1998. A popular movie in 2001 presented a fictional version of Nash's life.)

The Nash bargaining solution (1950a, 1953) is a general theory of efficient and equitable outcomes for two-person bargaining problems. A bargaining problem is characterized by a convex set of allocations that are feasible for the players, where each allocation is a pair of numerical payoffs, one for each player. Letting 0 represent the payoff that a player could get without any cooperative agreement, we assume that the allocation (0,0) is in the feasible set.

In simple examples where both players' payoffs are measured in transferable units of money, a reasonable solution would divide equally the amount that they can earn by cooperating. But Nash argued that when payoffs are not transferable, a reasonable solution should remain invariant when the scale in which a player's payoffs are measured is multiplied by a positive constant or when feasible alternatives other than the solution are eliminated. Remarkably, Nash proved that these properties are satisfied by a unique solution, which maximizes the multiplicative product of the players' gains. Nash's bargaining solution has become the cornerstone of the theory of cooperative games without transferable utility.

Nash equilibrium is a general solution concept for games in strategic form. A strategic-form game is defined by specifying the set of players, the set of strategies for each player, and the payoff that each player would get from every possible combination of strategies that the players could choose. A Nash equilibrium is a combination of strategies such that no player can increase his or her expected payoff by choosing a different strategy, when the other players' strategies are held fixed. Nash (1950b, 1951) proved that any finite game has such noncooperative equilibria, when randomized strategies are admitted, and he argued that noncooperative equilibrium analysis should be a general methodology for analyzing games of any kind. In 1953 he worked to show how his cooperative bargaining theory could be based on equilibrium analysis of noncooperative games in which players independently choose their bargaining strategies.

The importance of Nash equilibrium is manifested when we consider any question about reforming any economic, political, or social institution. To reform an institution is to change the rules of the game that people play in this institution. A case for reform must depend on some predictions about how people would behave in this institution, with or without the reform. If a case for reform depended on a prediction that was not a Nash equilibrium, it could be undermined by an individual who recognizes that behaving differently would earn a better payoff. Such difficulties are avoided by analyzing and comparing Nash equilibria of different institutions.

Nash equilibrium formalizes basic economic assumptions concerning the intelligence and rationality of individuals. The assumption of payoff-maximizing individual behavior has been common in economic analysis since Augustin A. Cournot (1838). But Nash equilibrium also assumes the independence of individual decision-making, which was viewed as a restrictive assumption until John von Neumann (1928) presented a broader concept of strategic decision-making, in which a strategy is a complete plan of actions for a player in all possible contingencies (Myerson 1999). This concept of strategy was used in Nash's argument that any dynamic bargaining process can be studied as a noncooperative game in which players plan their strategies independently before bargaining begins.

Later work in noncooperative game theory has refined and extended the equilibrium concept to take fuller account of sequential decision-making and communication in games. These developments broadened the analytical power of noncooperative game theory, which has transformed the scope of economics. Before Nash, many economists accepted a narrow definition of economics as being principally concerned with production and allocation of material goods. But noncooperative game theory provides a general framework for studying competition in any arena, and so economists have come to define their field more broadly, as being concerned with analysis of incentives in all social institutions. Thus by accepting game theory as a core analytical methodology alongside price theory, economic analysis has returned to the breadth of vision that characterized the ancient Greek social philosophers who gave economics its name.

SEE ALSO *Equilibrium in Economics; Game Theory; Nash Equilibrium; Noncooperative Games; Strategic Games*

BIBLIOGRAPHY

PRIMARY WORKS

Nash, John F. 1950a. The Bargaining Problem. *Econometrica* 18 (2): 155–162.

Nash, John F. 1950b. Equilibrium Points in N-Person Games. *Proceedings of the National Academy of Sciences U.S.A.* 36 (1): 48–49.

Nash, John F. 1951. Noncooperative Games. *Annals of Mathematics* 54 (2): 289–295.

Nash, John F. 1953. Two-Person Cooperative Games. *Econometrica* 21 (1): 128–140.

SECONDARY WORKS

Cournot, Augustin A. 1838. *Recherches sur les principes mathématiquess de la théorie des richesses.* Paris: Hachette. Published in an English translation by Nathaniel T. Bacon as *Researches into the Mathematical Principles of the Theory of Wealth* (New York: Macmillan, 1927).

Myerson, Roger B. 1999. Nash Equilibrium and the History of Economic Theory. *Journal of Economic Literature* 37 (3): 1067–1082.

Von Neumann, John. 1959. On the Theory of Games of Strategy. In *Contributions to the Theory of Games IV*, trans. S. Bargmann, ed. R. D. Luce and A. W. Tucker, 13–42. Princeton, NJ: Princeton University Press. Originally published in German in 1928 as "Zur Theorie der Gesellschaftsspiele" (*Mathematische Annalen* 100: 295–320).

Roger B. Myerson

NASH EQUILIBRIUM

Nash equilibrium is a fundamental concept in the theory of games and the most widely used method of predicting the outcome of a strategic interaction in the social sciences. A game (in strategic or normal form) consists of the following three elements: a set of players, a set of actions (or pure-strategies) available to each player, and a payoff (or utility) function for each player. The payoff functions represent each player's preferences over action profiles, where an action profile is simply a list of actions, one for each player. A *pure-strategy Nash equilibrium* is an action profile with the property that no single player can obtain a higher payoff by deviating unilaterally from this profile.

This concept can best be understood by looking at some examples. Consider first a game involving two players, each of whom has two available actions, which we call *A* and *B*. If the players choose different actions, they each get a payoff of 0. If they both choose *A*, they each get 2, and if they both choose *B*, they each get 1. This "coordination" game may be represented as in Figure 1, where player 1 chooses a row, player 2 chooses a column, and the resulting payoffs are listed in parentheses, with the first component corresponding to player 1's payoff. The action profile (*B*,*B*) is an equilibrium, since a unilateral deviation to *A* by any one player would result in a lower payoff for the deviating player. Similarly, the action profile (*A*,*A*) is also an equilibrium.

As another example, consider the game "matching pennies," which again involves two players, each with two actions. Each player can choose either heads (*H*) or tails (*T*); player 1 wins a dollar from player 2 if their choices are the same, and loses a dollar to player 2 if they are not. This game is shown in Figure 2 and has no pure-strategy Nash equilibria.

In some cases, instead of simply choosing an action, players may be able to choose probability distributions over the set of actions available to them. Such randomizations over the set of actions are referred to as *mixed strategies*. Any profile of mixed strategies induces a probability distribution over action profiles in the game. Under certain assumptions, a player's preferences over all such lotteries can be represented by a function (called a *von Neumann-Morgenstern utility function*) that assigns a real number to each action profile. One lottery is preferred to another if and only if it results in a higher expected value of this utility function, or expected utility. A mixed strategy Nash-equilibrium is then a mixed strategy profile with the property that no single player can obtain a higher value of expected utility by deviating unilaterally from this profile.

The American mathematician John Nash (1950) showed that every game in which the set of actions available to each player is finite has at least one mixed-strategy

	A	B
A	(2,2)	(0,0)
B	(0,0)	(1,1)

Figure 1

	H	T
H	(1,−1)	(−1,1)
T	(−1,1)	(1,−1)

Figure 2

	C	D
C	(2,2)	(0,3)
D	(3,0)	(1,1)

Figure 3

equilibrium. In the matching pennies game, there is a mixed-strategy equilibrium in which each player chooses heads with probability 1/2. Similarly, in the coordination game of the above example, there is a third equilibrium in which each player chooses action *A* with probability 1/3 and *B* with probability 2/3. Such multiplicity of equilibria arises in many economically important games, and has prompted a large literature on equilibrium refinements with the purpose of identifying criteria on the basis of which a single equilibrium might be selected.

Nash equilibria can sometimes correspond to outcomes that are inefficient, in the sense that there exist alternative outcomes that are both feasible and preferred by all players. This is the case, for instance, with the equilibrium (*B,B*) in the coordination game above. An even more striking example arises in the prisoner's dilemma game, in which each player can either "cooperate" or "defect," and payoffs are as shown in Figure 3.

The *unique Nash equilibrium* is mutual defection, an outcome that is worse for both players than mutual cooperation. Now consider the game that involves a repetition of the prisoner's dilemma for *n* periods, where *n* is commonly known to the two players. A pure strategy in this repeated game is a plan that prescribes which action is to be taken at each stage, contingent on every possible history of the game to that point. Clearly the set of pure strategies is very large. Nevertheless, all Nash equilibria of this finitely repeated game involve defection at every stage. When the number of stages *n* is large, equilibrium payoffs lie far below the payoffs that could have been attained under mutual cooperation.

It has sometimes been argued that the Nash prediction in the finitely repeated prisoner's dilemma (and in many other environments) is counterintuitive and at odds with experimental evidence. However, experimental tests of the equilibrium hypothesis are typically conducted with monetary payoffs, which need not reflect the preferences of subjects over action profiles. In other words, individual preferences over the distribution of monetary payoffs may not be exclusively self-interested. Furthermore, the equilibrium prediction relies on the hypothesis that these preferences are commonly known to all subjects, which is also unlikely to hold in practice.

To address this latter concern, the concept of Nash equilibrium has been generalized to allow for situations in which players are faced with incomplete information. If each player is drawn from some set of types, such that the probability distribution governing the likelihood of each type is itself commonly known to all players, then we have a *Bayesian game*. A pure strategy in this game is a function that associates with each type a particular action. A *Bayes-Nash equilibrium* is then a strategy profile such that no player can obtain greater expected utility by deviating to a different strategy, given his or her beliefs about the distribution of types from which other players are drawn.

Allowing for incomplete information can have dramatic effects on the predictions of the Nash equilibrium concept. Consider, for example, the finitely repeated prisoner's dilemma, and suppose that each player believes that there is some possibility, perhaps very small, that his or her opponent will cooperate in all periods provided that no defection has yet been observed, and defect otherwise. If the number of stages *n* is sufficiently large, it can be shown that mutual defection in all stages is inconsistent with equilibrium behavior, and that, in a well-defined sense, the players will cooperate in most periods. Hence, in applying the concept of Nash equilibrium to practical situations, it is important to pay close attention to the information that individuals have about the preferences, beliefs, and rationality of those with whom they are strategically interacting.

SEE ALSO *Game Theory; Multiple Equilibria; Noncooperative Games; Prisoner's Dilemma (Economics)*

BIBLIOGRAPHY

Cournot, A. A. 1838. *Recherches sur les principes mathématiques de la théorie des richesses.* Paris: L. Hachette.

Fudenberg, Drew, and Jean Tirole. 1991. *Game Theory.* Cambridge, MA: MIT Press.

Harsanyi, John C. 1967–1968. Games with Incomplete Information Played by Bayesian Players. *Management Science* 14 (3): 159–182, 320–334, 486–502.

Harsanyi, John C., and Reinhard Selten. 1998. *A General Theory of Equilibrium Selection in Games.* Cambridge, MA: MIT Press.

Kreps, David, Paul Milgrom, John Roberts, and Robert Wilson. 1982. Rational Cooperation in the Finitely Repeated Prisoner's Dilemma. *Journal of Economic Theory* 27: 245–252.

Nash, John F. 1950. Equilibrium Points in N-Person Games. *Proceedings of the National Academy of Sciences* 36 (1): 48–49.

Osborne, Martin J., and Ariel Rubinstein. 1994. *A Course in Game Theory.* Cambridge, MA: MIT Press.

von Neumann, John, and Oskar Morgenstern. 1944. *Theory of Games and Economic Behavior.* Princeton, NJ: Princeton University Press.

Rajiv Sethi

NASSER, GAMAL ABDEL
1918–1970

Gamal Abdel Nasser, who served as president of Egypt from 1956 to 1970, was born on January 15, 1918, in the small village of Bani Mor in the Egyptian province of

Assiut, where he lived for eight years. He came from a humble and poor background to become one of the most prominent and influential leaders in the Middle East and the third world. His father worked as a mail carrier in the Egyptian Ministry of Communication, a position that required him to move with his family from Bani Mor to Alexandria and finally Cairo, where Nasser lived for ten years. In his memoirs, Nasser spoke proudly of his humble origin. His poor background might have been behind his socialist tendencies and his commitment to improve the living conditions of Egyptian peasants and workers.

During his high school years, Nasser participated in student demonstrations against the British occupying forces. After receiving his high school diploma in 1937, Nasser entered the Egyptian Royal Military Academy, which started admitting sons of lower-income families in 1936. A year later, he joined the Egyptian army, where he met several of his future colleagues, including Anwar el-Sadat (1918–1981) and Zakaria Mohyi El Deen, both of whom served as his vice presidents, and Abdul Hakeem Amer, who became a minister of defense. In 1942 Nasser was transferred to Sudan, where he and other officers founded the Free Officers, a secret revolutionary organization. The Free Officers was a secular nationalist movement that was opposed to the British occupation of Egypt, the "corrupt" royal family, and the domination of Egypt's economy and parliament by a small landowning class. In 1948 Nasser was a member of the Egyptian army that along with other Arab armies was sent to Palestine to thwart the establishment of Israel. The humiliating defeat of the Arab armies in the 1948 war raised his awareness of the Palestinian problem and the inefficacy of the existing Arab governments.

On July 23, 1952, Nasser and his Free Officers seized power and deposed the king. A year later, the Revolutionary Command Council of the Free Officers promulgated a new constitution, abolished the monarchy, and declared Egypt a republic. Though General Mohammad Naguib (1901–1984) served as the head of the government from 1952 to 1954, Nasser held the real power through his control of the Revolutionary Command Council. In November 1954 Nasser placed Naguib under house arrest, accusing him of knowing about an attempt by a member of the Muslim Brotherhood to assassinate Nasser.

In 1956 Nasser was elected president of Egypt, a position he held until his death in 1970. As president, Nasser created an authoritarian police state, banning political parties and suppressing political opposition, including the local communists and members of the Muslim Brotherhood. He ruled the country through the Arab Socialist Union, a government-controlled party.

Between 1956 and 1966, Nasser introduced several socialist measures, including the nationalization of various industries, private companies, and banks, and he expanded the public sector significantly. He also introduced agrarian reform, including the confiscation of 2,000 square miles of cultivable land from wealthy landowners, which he distributed to Egypt's poor peasants. The aim of these socialist measures was to improve the living conditions of the country's peasants and workers. Nasser contended in his book *The Philosophy of the Revolution* (1955) that Arab socialism was a prerequisite for Arab unity and freedom and for surmounting the social and economic legacy of colonialism.

In addition to his domestic socialist reforms, Nasser adopted an anti-Western and anticolonial foreign policy. Initially however, he tried to secure arms from Britain and the United States, and it was only after the two countries declined his request that he acquired such weapons from the Soviet Union and Eastern Europe. Along with Prime Minister Jawaharlal Nehru (1889–1964) of India and President Sukarno (1901–1970) of Indonesia, Nasser also founded the nonaligned movement.

Nasser tried to obtain Western funding to build a dam on the Nile (the Aswân Dam) that would provide electricity to neighboring villages and towns and increase the amount of cultivable land available to peasant farmers. Though at first the administration of U.S. president Dwight D. Eisenhower (1890–1969) expressed an interest in financing the construction of the Aswân Dam, it rescinded its offer to protest Nasser's anti-Western policies and his rapprochement with the Soviet Union, Eastern Europe, and Communist China, as well as his nonalignment policy. In reaction, Nasser nationalized the Suez Canal Company with the hope of using the income generated from tolls levied on ships crossing the canal to finance the construction of the dam. The Suez Canal Company was seen as a symbol of Western colonialism and hegemony.

In response to the nationalization of the Suez Canal Company, Britain, France, and Israel invaded Egypt and occupied Sinai in late 1956. Under pressure from the United Nations and the United States, however, the invading armies were forced to withdraw and UN peacekeeping troops were deployed into the Sinai. The invasion of Egypt intensified Nasser's opposition to Western influence and military alliances in the Middle East, and made him a strong advocate of Arab nationalism and freedom from colonial control. The Suez crisis also significantly increased Nasser's popularity in the Arab world. Likewise, his message of social justice at home and anticolonialism abroad inspired millions of Arabs, who formed political parties to bring about Arab unity and socialism.

In response to a request from the Syrian military and civilian leaders for a merging of Syria and Egypt, Nasser created in 1958 the United Arab Republic as the first step toward Arab unity. The union ended in 1961; Syrian military officers and civilians resented Egyptian domination of Syrian politics, the secret police's harsh repression of Syrian opposition, and nationalization of the Syrian private sector. In 1962 Nasser sent his army to Yemen in support of the military coup that overthrew the monarchy. Egyptian military intervention in Yemen, which lasted for five years, was costly.

In May 1967 Nasser incited the June War (the Six-Day War) when he requested the withdrawal of the UN Emergency Force from Sinai and closed the Gulf of Aqaba to Israeli ships. In reaction, Israel launched a surprise attack on Egypt and occupied the Sinai Peninsula. In the aftermath of the humiliating defeat of his army, Nasser resigned from office, but he rescinded his decision in the wake of massive popular support for his rule. However, Nasser never regained his previous stature, and his government became increasingly dependent on military and economic aid from the Soviet Union.

Nasser died of a heart attack on September 28, 1970. Five million Egyptians attended his funeral, making it the largest funeral in history. His legacy has been the subject of intense debate. Some criticize his autocratic rule and his suppression of political opposition. Others criticize his aggressive and militaristic foreign policies, including his incitement of the 1967 June War and his military involvement in Yemen. Such military ventures tainted his legacy and caused severe difficulties for Egypt and the Arab countries. In contrast, others commend his struggle against Western colonialism, his restoration of Arab dignity, and his embodiment of the dream of Arab unity and nationalism. Still others commend Nasser's role in modernizing Egypt's educational system and making it free to the poor, as well as his strong support of the arts, theater, film, music, and literature.

SEE ALSO *Arab League, The; Arab-Israeli War of 1967; Arabs; Nationalism and Nationality; Pan-Arabism; Suez Crisis; United Arab Republic*

BIBLIOGRAPHY

Gordon, Joel. 1992. *Nasser's Blessed Movement: Egypt's Free Officers and the July Revolution.* New York: Oxford University Press.

Mikdadi, Faysal. 1991. *Gamal Abdel Nasser: A Bibliography.* Westport, CT: Greenwood.

Nasser, Gamal Abdel. 1959. *The Philosophy of the Revolution.* Intro. John S. Badeau and bio. John Gunther. Buffalo, NY: Smith, Keynes & Marshall.

Emile Sahliyeh

NAST, THOMAS
1840–1902

Thomas Nast both drove and commented on the most pressing questions of his age through evocative engravings and cartoons. Highlighting nationalism, political corruption, and urban poverty, Nast launched a new means of communication that appealed to and touched an entire nation.

Nast gained fame with *Harper's Weekly* magazine, where he worked from 1859 until 1886. Reflecting his emotional responses to the carnage he saw as a war correspondent, Nast's engravings went beyond reporting and into the realm of the visual editorial. Vivid engravings of the battles of the Civil War (1861–1865), the patriotic sacrifice needed to preserve the Union, and the harsh realities of slavery made the war real to the average citizen and inspired them to service. One of his most representative images shows Columbia weeping as a tattered Union amputee shakes the hand of a refined Southern soldier. Called "Compromise with the South," this use of allegory and warnings against the sacrifice of right in the name of expediency became a powerful tool for the Republican campaign to re-elect President Abraham Lincoln.

As the war ended, Nast turned to immigration, political corruption, and free silver as ripe ground for his images. Moving from commentary to activism, Nast's work unmasked the political corruption behind the "party boss" system and helped imprison New York's infamous Boss Tweed. In a series of cartoons from 1869 to 1872, the artist openly accused Tweed of rigging elections and accepting bribes, all while giving a moral slant to the subject that turned the public against the iron-fisted leader. The power of Nast's imagery is best expressed by a quote attributed to Tweed himself: "Stop the damned pictures … my constituents can't read, but, damn it, they can see pictures" (Fischer 1996, p. 2). In this age of immigration, emotional images appealed to an urban citizenry that was often illiterate yet anxious to make their way in a new country.

Nast aptly demonstrated the role of political cartoons in electoral campaigns. In 1872 his visual barrage of cartoons contributed to the defeat of Horace Greeley's run against Ulysses S. Grant. By 1876, his support for Rutherford B. Hayes propelled the candidate to the presidency. The power of Nast's aura is undeniable: His candidates won seven consecutive presidential elections and his images of the elephant and donkey battles have currency in the twenty-first century.

Depicting a clear line between good and evil, Nast's style was pedantic, explicit, and expressed a definitive right-wing stance. His harsh black-and-white lines and crosshatchings for *Harper's Weekly* stood in stark contrast to the more subtle irony in his competitors' illustrations for *Puck* magazine. Nevertheless, Nast's methods redefined the political cartoon medium. Instead of relying on the talking bubbles of the eighteenth century, he liberally incorporated labels and allegory to emphasize the character and ideas of his subjects. His ultrarealistic style instantly made a point without requiring lengthy analysis from his audience, a quality still admired in cartoonists in the early twenty-first century. Through Nast's efforts, the political cartoon stepped out of the shadow of commentary and into the realm of activism, where it remains today.

SEE ALSO *Cartoons, Political; Media; U.S. Civil War*

BIBLIOGRAPHY

Fischer, Roger A. 1996. *Them Damned Pictures: Exploration in American Political Cartoon Art.* North Haven, CT: Archon Book.

Keller, Morton. 1975. *The Art and Politics of Thomas Nast.* New York: Oxford University Press.

Paine, Albert Bigelow. 1974. *Thomas Nast: His Period and His Pictures.* Princeton, NJ: Pyne Press.

Starr, Roger. Thomas Nast: America's Premier Political Cartoonist. http://www.city-journal.org/article02.php?aid=1417.

Rita B. Trivedi

NATION

The term *nation* connotes a broad community of individuals, whose members consider themselves linked on the basis of shared long-standing cultural practices, ethnicity, history, memories, or traditions, who are typically associated with a specific geographical homeland, and who are predisposed to make political claims of autonomy, sovereignty, or other assertions of rights on the basis of their membership. Though nations are abstractions, in practice they are quite real to those who believe they belong to one. The idea that nations are real and legitimate forms of social organization is a fundamental assumption in ideologies of nationalism and national self-determination.

While in vernacular and economic use *nation* is often synonymous with *country* or *state*, the historical and sociological understanding of the term does not demand the existence of government or recognized statehood. Despite this difference, *nation* and *state* are often used interchangeably. For example, the United Nations is in fact an assembly of states, not nations, much as *international relations* actually refers to relations between *states*. To further confuse matters, citizens of states are often described as having that state's *nationality*. However, states grant citizenship to recognize rights in the political community of the state, whereas nationality solely describes one's membership in the nation. *Nation* is also commonly used as a synonym for an *ethnic group*, which may in some cases overlap in practice, though the term is analytically distinct.

Core disputes in theories of the nation include the very nature of nations' existence: Are they real? Is it natural for humans to organize themselves into nations? Are these organizations based on natural differences, or are these differences social constructions? How long have people felt themselves part of nations? Is membership voluntary or ascribed?

Eighteenth- and nineteenth-century theorists believed that all people were born as members of a nation, with an inherent national character endemic to their group. Philosophers such as Johann Gottfried Herder (1744–1803) argued that nations were naturally occurring linguistic and cultural communities, real and hereditary expressions of an eternal essence, generally unchanging over time, which deserved self-determination due to their differences from other groups. This school of thought has come to be known as *primordialism*. While contemporary scholarship has generally rejected this view, it lives on in the rhetoric of nationalist leaders, and in some representations of nations in popular media, particularly during times of war, when conflicts may be portrayed as ancient hatreds with no identifiable beginning and no possibility for resolution.

Refining the primordialists' belief that nations are natural and real, *perennialist* scholars emerged in the mid-twentieth century to describe the robustness of nations without reliance on nature. Authors such as Anthony D. Smith suggested that nations may have a birth moment in the past, rooted in unique cultural practices and traditions that could be described as *ethnic*. However, once established, these characteristics of the nation become entrenched to the point of permanence, perennially reiterated in subsequent generations. Tales of "golden ages" or ancient battles with other national groups are passed down to younger generations, told and retold to cement the new generation's links with its past.

Against this view of nations as ancient or eternal, so-called *modernist* theorists such as Ernest Gellner and Benedict Anderson examined the process of nation formation and argued that nations resulted from economic advances and industrialization. These authors grow out of a social constructivist tradition, which argues that no human enterprise can be understood as innately natural or "real." From this perspective, nations are invented or imagined, and only gain legitimacy through broad public acceptance, not a priori existence. Anderson, perhaps the most famous representative of the modernist or *constructivist* school, argued that nations were "imagined political

INTERNATIONAL ENCYCLOPEDIA OF THE SOCIAL SCIENCES, 2ND EDITION communities," in which individuals came to believe that they were connected through cultural and political bonds to others whom they had never met, even the dead or not-yet-born. According to Anderson, these beliefs were disseminated as a byproduct of modern inventions such as the printing press, which, in combination with the capitalist desire to sell books and newspapers, helped standardize language and information dissemination across wide territories. "Print-capitalism" increased the scope of communities, but also defined their boundaries. As information spread, images of both the in-group and the out-group were constructed.

Modernists also highlight the role of the state in constructing the nation, through common symbols such as flags and holidays, common institutions such as public education and national museums, and through activities that cemented the community's boundaries and limits, such as maps and censuses. The modernist paradigm has created a vast research program into the history of nations, asking how particular nations developed and how belief in these nations was manifested. Furthermore, it has opened up new perspectives: Once a nation is seen as imagined or constructed, it becomes possible to conceive of alternatives. This raises the questions of whether membership in the nation is a choice, either at the individual or the group level, and whether nations can be based on civic values, such as political principles, rather than ethnic traditions. In turn, *postmodernists*, writing since the mid-1990s, have argued that nations can never be fully constructed, that their content is subject to "discursive" redefinition and change, and that nations continually undergo reconstruction and reproduction.

As their name suggests, modernists also argue that the nation is a recent phenomenon. Many authors point to the French Revolution as a critical historical moment in the spread of the idea. When revolutionaries called for government to represent the people, they referred to the nation, instead of a particular class, religion, or region. This arguably had the effect of making illegitimate those forms of government that did not claim to represent the nation. Simultaneously, the ideology that states should represent nations, and that nations should have their own states, potentially hides other divisions that might exist within a society, for example, gender or class disparities. Postmodern and Marxist scholars have critiqued the "hegemony" of the nation as an organizing principle of political life.

A country whose borders coincide with a perceived national homeland is called a *nation-state*. However, this is an ideal type, and with the growth of immigration and globalization the idea of a homogeneous nation-state is arguably losing relevance. On the other hand, political leaders may nonetheless rule as if their state were an uncontested nation-state, and accordingly may enact policies on behalf of "their" nation, thereby keeping the nation a part of political life. As Rogers Brubaker suggests, the nation cannot be written off; even if its meaning cannot be pinned down, the idea of a nation remains useful as a "category of practice."

SEE ALSO *Citizenship; Ethnicity; Identity; Nationalism and Nationality; Revolution; Society; Sovereignty; State, The*

BIBLIOGRAPHY

Anderson, Benedict. 1991. *Imagined Communities: Reflections on the Origin and Spread of Nationalism.* Rev. ed. London: Verso.

Brubaker, Rogers. 1996. *Nationalism Reframed: Nationhood and the National Question in the New Europe.* Cambridge, U.K.: Cambridge University Press.

Gellner, Ernest. 1983. *Nations and Nationalism.* Ithaca, NY: Cornell University Press.

Herder, Johann Gottfried. [1803] 1997. *Auch eine Philosophie der Geschichte zur Bildung des Menschheit.* Stuttgart, Germany: Reclam.

Kohn, Hans. 1944. *The Idea of Nationalism: A Study in Its Origins and Background.* New York: Macmillan.

Renan, Ernst. [1882] 1990. "Qu'est-ce qu'une nation?" [What Is a Nation?] Trans. Martin Thom. In *Nation and Narration*, ed. Homi K. Bhabha, 8–22. London: Routledge.

Smith, Anthony D. 1986. *The Ethnic Origins of Nations.* Oxford: B. Blackwell.

Mark Ashley

NATION OF ISLAM

In his classic work *The Black Muslims in America* (1961), religion scholar C. Eric Lincoln (1924–2000) argued that originally the Nation of Islam was less a religious movement than a protest movement against centuries of racial oppression. Founded in 1930 by W. D. Fard (pronounced *Far-rod*), the Nation of Islam borrowed heavily from the teachings of Marcus Garvey's (1887–1940) United Negro Improvement Association and Noble Drew Ali's (1886–1929) Moorish Science Temple. Built around Islamic symbolism and a philosophy that challenged white supremacy, the Nation of Islam encouraged members to work toward economic and social independence from the white community. Far more radical than protest organizations including the National Association for the Advancement of Colored People (NAACP), the Urban League, the Southern Christian Leadership Conference (SCLC), the Congress of Racial Equality (CORE), and the Student Nonviolent Coordinating Committee

(SNCC), the Nation of Islam espoused racial segregation as a solution to institutional racism.

The Nation of Islam began in Detroit, Michigan. W. D. Fard, a peddler possibly of Arab descent, began teaching small gatherings of "so-called Negroes" about the glorious history of "Afro-Asia." Fard warned his followers that ignorance of their past weakened them to the "tricknology" of whites, namely white supremacy. Fard argued that ignorance of history produced in the "Asiatic" community a sense of intellectual and moral inferiority. Education, he reasoned, preceded liberation, and therefore it is the responsibility of black men and women to seek knowledge and then to use that knowledge to inform daily practices. Fard, for example, admonished blacks to live and eat as their ancestors had in order to reclaim their birthright and to reestablish a system of equality, justice, and freedom. Fard also instituted Muslim Girls Training Classes, which taught girls and women the domestic arts, and the Fruit of Islam, which was a form of military training for men. These gender-segregated programs were designed to promote a sense of dignity, self-discipline, and social order.

Fard chose Elijah Muhammad (1897–1975), formerly Elijah Poole, as his lieutenant in the Nation of Islam. Born in Sandersville, Georgia, Poole was the son of William, a pastor, and Mariah, a domestic servant. With his wife Clara, Elijah Poole joined the great migration north in 1923 to flee the racial violence, poverty, and the boll weevil infestation that had destroyed crops in the South. The Pooles settled in Detroit with their two children (three more children would follow). In Detroit, Elijah Poole became a devoted follower of Fard, and eventually cast away his "slave name" to become Elijah Karriem and eventually Elijah Muhammad in 1933. Following Fard's disappearance from Detroit in 1934, Elijah Muhammad fought to maintain his position as *the* Minister of Islam. In his capacity as leader, Elijah Muhammad deified Fard as the embodiment of Allah. This decision effectively positioned Fard as the last Prophet of Allah, a heretical notion for Sunni and Shiite Muslims. After serving three years at MCI Prison for failure to register for selective service during World War II (1939–1945), Elijah Muhammad resumed leadership of the Nation of Islam in 1946. Following his release, Muhammad continued to reach out to black prisoners.

While serving time at Norfolk Prison Colony in Massachusetts, Malcolm Little (1925–1965) was introduced to the teachings of Elijah Muhammad. Malcolm Little identified strongly with the idea that his past behavior was the result of having been brainwashed by white supremacy. In response, Little spent his time in prison studying history, philosophy, and religion. He also maintained an ongoing correspondence with Elijah Muhammad, and eventually converted and changed his name to Malcolm X. Following his release from prison in 1952, Malcolm X began a journey that would eventually lead to his becoming the most articulate, powerful, and controversial spokesman for the Nation of Islam.

Unlike the other protest organizations at the turn of the century that fought for the full benefits of citizenship in an integrated United States, the Nation of Islam espoused a philosophy that whites were "blue-eyed devils" created by an evil black scientist named Yacub. Slavery, de jure segregation, the epidemic of lynchings, and institutional racism were offered as proof by followers that even if whites were not devils, they acted like devils. The militant and antiwhite rhetoric of the Nation of Islam made the organization unpopular even within the black community, and until the 1960s the philosophy appealed almost exclusively to southern migrants living in the urban Northeast and Midwest. Membership levels grew and shrank from 1930 to 1942, probably never rising above one thousand. In the 1950s, membership in the Nation was possibly as high as five thousand. With a large recruitment drive in the 1960s, Nation membership most likely reached its highest level of about twenty thousand. The number of members is not, however, indicative of the influence of Elijah Muhammad's and Malcolm X's teachings. There were thousands of African-Americans who sympathized with the Nation's philosophy of self-sufficiency and Afrocentrism, and with the Nation's declared willingness to physically defend their community.

There were two major tensions within the Nation of Islam following Malcolm X's rise as the organization's most charismatic spokesman. The first tension surrounded the relationship between Nation of Islam philosophy and "orthodox" Islam. With greater media attention came greater scrutiny, and a number of Sunni Muslims were more than willing to highlight the differences between Nation teachings and traditional Islam. In the press, Elijah Muhammad was characterized as a phony by Sunni Muslims who knew that the leader's beliefs were a syncretic blend of Christianity and black nationalism layered with Islamic symbolism. By the 1960s, Elijah Muhammad's son Wallace Muhammad and Malcolm X were pushing their leader to adopt traditional Islam, but Elijah Muhammad held firm to the original tenets of his organization. The second tension had to do with the question of race. The Nation of Islam was characterized in the press as a black supremacist organization that preached hate. Black leaders including Martin Luther King Jr. (1929–1968) and NAACP attorney Thurgood Marshall (1908–1993) castigated the organization. The Nation's anti-integration stance and tolerance of self-defense was seen as a threat to the current gains of the civil rights movement. Beyond the political repercussions, many blacks thought that the philosophy of the nation was cynical and untenable.

Major changes occurred in the Nation of Islam in the 1960s. Scandals surrounding Elijah Muhammad, integration following civil rights legislation, and the assassination of Malcolm X (renamed El-Hajj Malik El-Shabazz before his death) all contributed to the slow delegitimization of some of the beliefs and practices of the Nation of Islam. When Elijah Muhammad died in 1975, he passed leadership to his son Wallace Muhammad. Wallace Muhammad subsequently dismantled the Nation of Islam and built the World Community of Islam in the West, now the American Muslim Mission. The American Muslim Mission continues to promote Sunni Islam within the African American community. In 1977 Minister Louis Farrakhan rejected the leadership of Wallace Muhammad and rebuilt the Nation of Islam in order to continue the teachings of Elijah Muhammad. While still focused on the mission of black empowerment, Louis Farrakhan's Nation of Islam continues to incorporate traditional Islamic practices.

SEE ALSO *Black Power; Civil Rights Movement, U.S.; Islam, Shia and Sunni; King, Martin Luther, Jr.; Malcolm X; Muhammad, Elijah; National Association for the Advancement of Colored People (NAACP)*

BIBLIOGRAPHY

Clegg, Claude Andrew. 1997. *An Original Man: The Life and Times of Elijah Muhammad.* New York: St. Martin's.

Curtis, Edward E. 2002. *Islam in Black America: Identity, Liberation, and Difference in African-American Islamic Thought.* Albany: State University of New York Press.

Evanzz, Karl. 1999. *The Messenger: The Rise and Fall of Elijah Muhammad.* New York: Pantheon.

Lincoln, C. Eric. 1993. *The Black Muslims in America.* 3rd ed. Grand Rapids, MI: Eerdmans; Trenton, NJ: Africa World Press.

Malcolm X. 1965. *The Autobiography of Malcolm X.* Ed. Alex Haley. New York: Grove.

Tate, Sonsyrea. 1997. *Little X: Growing Up in the Nation of Islam.* San Francisco: Harper.

Carolyn M. Rouse

NATIONAL ADVISORY COMMISSION ON CIVIL DISORDERS

SEE *Kerner Commission Report.*

NATIONAL ASSESSMENT OF EDUCATIONAL PROGRESS

The National Assessment of Educational Progress (NAEP) was mandated by Congress in 1969 to provide accurate measurement and reporting of levels and trends in academic achievement of U.S. elementary and secondary students. NAEP has met this goal through regular testing of students in selected subjects and most often at the fourth, eighth, and twelfth grades. For most NAEP reporting, student achievement in the most recent assessment is compared with student achievement in previous years in the same subject and grade to identify changes and trends.

NAEP provides a continuing assessment of the core subjects of reading, mathematics, writing, and science. National and state assessments in reading and mathematics are conducted every other year, and every four years in science and writing. NAEP also tests achievement in other subjects that are widely taught in the schools, such as U.S. history, civics, geography, economics, and the arts, but they are assessed less often and sometimes at only one grade. In addition NAEP conducts special studies on topics such as long-term achievement trends, the influence of course-taking on outcomes, assessment results in urban schools, and the effects of educational technology.

NAEP policy setting, administration, and implementation are conducted by several organizations. NAEP policy is set by the National Assessment Governing Board (NAGB), whose members are appointed by the secretary of education. Members include governors, educators, school administrators, state legislators, and the public. NAGB selects the subject areas for assessment, develops the general objectives and specifications for the assessment, prepares guidelines for reporting, and is responsible for making all policy decisions. NAEP administration is the responsibility of the National Center for Education Statistics (NCES), which oversees assessment development and scoring. NAEP implementation is carried out through contracts, grants, and cooperative agreements with qualified organizations and individuals. They define the material to be assessed within each subject and at each grade level, prepare the assessment instruments, select the school and student samples, score student responses, analyze the data, and write the NAEP reports.

The most important part of the assessment process is the development of a content framework. It defines what students should know and be able to do at each assessed grade level, how assessment items should be written to address that content, and what should be reported. The framework is prepared from the work of many content experts, teachers, curriculum specialists, policymakers, and public representatives. It is then given final review and approval by NAGB.

The assessments include multiple-choice items and constructed-response items that require students to give short or extended written responses. NAEP also collects background data through questionnaires completed by the students, their teachers, and school administrators. Some data, for example student demographics such as gender, race and ethnicity, and region, are standard for all NAEP assessments. Background information is also obtained on factors that may influence academic performance, such as time spent on homework, instructional practices, and teacher background. Additional questions may directly relate to the subject being assessed. For example, in economics, students might be queried about whether they have had a course in economics in their high school careers.

NAEP uses probability sampling to select a representative group of students to participate in the assessment. The sample size for each state averages one hundred schools and three thousand students at each grade level and within each subject. The sample is sufficiently large so it can produce reliable and valid results at the national level at each grade level and for subgroups of students defined by specified characteristics such as gender, race and ethnicity, eligibility for a lunch subsidy, and region. State-level results are also reported for reading, mathematics, writing, and science.

NAEP assessments also use item sampling of subject matter content. In item sampling, each student is only given a sample of all the test items. This design means that NAEP can administer a large number of items, and because the assessment blocks are linked, valid and reliable achievement results can be constructed for representative samples of students in each subject area and grade level. By law, only the overall results for a representative sample of students are reported. Given this sampling, it is impossible to report individual student results.

Subject-matter results are reported by averages and percentiles and by achievement levels. The primary means of reporting are three achievement levels defined by NAGB. Students at the *basic* level "demonstrate partial mastery of prerequisite knowledge and skills that are fundamental for proficient work at each grade." Students at the *proficient* level "demonstrate solid academic performance for each grade assessed. These students demonstrate competency over challenging subject matter, including subject-matter knowledge, application of such knowledge to real-world situations, and analytical skills appropriate to the subject matter." Students at the *advanced* level "demonstrate superior performance."

The scores and achievement levels are developed independently for each subject; thus the results cannot be compared across subjects. In general, however, the results for subjects show that most students score either below or at the basic level, far fewer score at the proficient level, and very few score at the advanced level. For example, the 2005 twelfth-grade science assessment reported the following results for students: below basic, 32 percent; basic, 39 percent; proficient, 26 percent; and advanced, 3 percent.

NAEP results, including scale scores and achievement levels for subgroups of students as well as background data that relate to student achievement, are used for research in a wide variety of studies. The NCES provides training on their use for primary or secondary education analysis and, in combination with other student and school data sets, makes the NAEP data available to researchers. Studies have been conducted on how student achievement is affected by the prior academic work of students, student experiences outside of school, class size, and teacher characteristics. In addition, student, teacher, and school factors have been investigated to identify their effects on achievement levels of ethnic, gender, and regional groups.

NAEP is not without critics despite the money and effort expended to develop accurate measures of achievement. Levels of understanding, but not trends, may be understated because of the voluntary nature of the assessment and the lack of student motivation to score well, especially when it is administered to graduating seniors. The measures are aggregate ones for the national or state level; no individual or school-specific results are reported. NAEP may also create incentives for establishing a national curriculum in the schools.

SEE ALSO *National Family Health Surveys; National Longitudinal Study of Adolescent Health; National Longitudinal Survey of Youth; Panel Study of Income Dynamics; Surveys, Sample*

BIBLIOGRAPHY

National Center for Education Statistics. 2005. *The Nation's Report Card: An Introduction to the National Assessment of Educational Progress (NAEP)*. Washington, DC: U.S. Government Printing Office.

Stephen Buckles
William B. Walstad

NATIONAL ASSOCIATION FOR THE ADVANCEMENT OF COLORED PEOPLE (NAACP)

The National Association for the Advancement of Colored People (NAACP) was incorporated in 1910 as an organization dedicated to mobilization on behalf of racial justice. The founding of the organization occurred through the discourse and several meetings among black and white intellectuals, business persons, educators, and professionals who, over a number of years prior to the NAACP's founding, laid the groundwork to mobilize efforts to fight racial discrimination against African Americans. Many of the leaders and participants of these precursory efforts reached a consensus on developing a major organization that would fight racial discrimination, and eventually, the NAACP was established.

One meeting that contributed to the development of the NAACP was held in Niagara Falls, New York, in 1905; this meeting marked the founding of the Niagara Movement. At the meeting, the participants discussed their opposition to the accommodationist policies of Booker T. Washington (1856–1915). They supported black progress by way of higher education in cultural and scientific studies, economic development, and integration within the formal political structures with full citizenship rights, the franchise, and civil rights.

By the time of the second annual Niagara Movement meeting in 1906, several members were alarmed by the continuing brutality, lynching, and loss of property, among other oppressive conditions, facing blacks at that time. This led white leaders Mary White Ovington (1865–1951) and Oswald Garrison Villard (1872–1949), grandson of abolitionist William Lloyd Garrison (1805–1879), along with W. E. B. Du Bois (1868–1963), to convene a meeting, referred to as The Call, to discuss the "Negro question." On February 12, 1909, the one-hundredth anniversary of the birthday of Abraham Lincoln (1809–1865), fifty-three signatories (who comprised the membership of the National Negro Committee) called for a national conference to be held on May 30, 1909.

By the time the second national conference was held in May 1910, the National Association for the Advancement of Colored People was incorporated by five people: Du Bois, Villard, Ovington, Walter E. Sachs (1884–1980), and John Haynes Holmes (1879–1964). The Niagara Movement, from which the NAACP was an outgrowth, eventually dissolved. Many of the movement's members, however, were also members of the NAACP. Continuing many of the concerns of the Niagara Movement, the NAACP proposed to address the social and political equality of African Americans. A 1911 NAACP program declared that its objectives were to sponsor meetings and lectures on questions about race, political representation, foreign affairs, antilynching policy, disfranchisement, educational inequities, discrimination in employment, crime, and public accommodations.

THE ORGANIZATIONAL STRUCTURE

The organization's leadership consisted of a National Board of Directors that was elected from a slate of candidates chosen by the NAACP Nominating Committee. Members of the National Board of Directors had the power to establish committees, departments, bureaus, branches, and college chapters. The National Board of Directors consisted of the president (an ex officio member), vice president, treasurer, chairman of the board (the most powerful officer of the association), and the executive secretary. Other NAACP members made up youth councils, college chapters, and various branches within states.

Some notable former members of the NAACP Board of Directors include the political scientist Ralph Bunche (1904–1971) and Eleanor Roosevelt (1884–1962), wife of President Franklin D. Roosevelt (1882–1945). Other famous members include Du Bois, who acted as the director of publicity and research and who, for a number of years, acted as editor of the association's chief publication, *The Crisis.* Ida B. Wells-Barnett (1862–1931), a strong advocate of antilynching policy in the early twentieth century, was also a member. James Weldon Johnson (1871–1938), known for writing the lyrics to "Lift Every Voice and Sing," the "Negro national anthem," was a national organizer of membership, and he later became executive secretary of the organization.

NAACP membership was (and continues to be) open to all people, regardless of race. Much of the leadership in the early organization consisted of whites. Since 1932, when Louis T. Wright (1891–1952), a black man, was appointed to the Board of Directors, African Americans have been more central to the association's leadership. Today, the organization is structured similarly to its past organization, comprising a National Board of Directors, several departments, state branches with regional offices, youth councils, and college chapters. Julian Bond, a longtime civil rights activist, became chair of the Board of Directors in 1998. In 2005 Bruce S. Gordon became NAACP president, replacing Kweisi Mfume, a civil rights activist and former Maryland representative of the U.S. House of Representative who had served as NAACP president since 1996.

Despite its sound leadership, strong following, and prior financial stability, the NAACP faced both financial difficulties and leadership woes during the early 1990s. During this time, the NAACP experienced alleged financial malfeasance, a budget deficit, and a sex scandal that involved its president, Benjamin F. Chavis Jr. (now known as Benjamin F. Chavis Muhammad). The controversy surrounding Chavis's leadership led to his being asked by the National Board of Directors to resign from the presidency.

Mfume is credited with leading the organization out of its troubled period.

In 2006 the NAACP comprised over two thousand local chapters and more than 500,000 members. It faces the challenge of increasing its membership among a younger generation of political activists. Financial support comes mostly from individuals and corporate donors. Prior to the separation of the NAACP Legal Defense and Educational Fund, Inc. (LDF, also known as the "Inc. Fund") from the main organization, the association benefited financially from tax-exempt donations made to the Inc. Fund. The NAACP also has tax-exempt charitable status, which was initiated via the NAACP Special Contribution Fund in 1964.

POLITICAL INVOLVEMENTS

NAACP political activism consists of policy reviews, political lobbying, political protests, political mobilization, and legal challenges. The organization's early policy concerns were related to African Americans acquiring civil rights. The NAACP compiled and disseminated information to members and other blacks about senators' and representatives' votes on policies that affected civil rights. This information served as a public record of official support for antiblack policies and as a means by which support could be galvanized for NAACP policy concerns.

The NAACP lobbied U.S. presidents and members of Congress for support of civil rights policies, and openly opposed President Woodrow Wilson's (1856–1924) initiation of segregation in the federal government. Early pressure from the NAACP in the 1940s contributed to President Franklin Roosevelt's implementation of Executive Order 8802, which desegregated the American defense industry. Such pressure on the executive branch also resulted in President Harry S Truman (1884–1972) implementing Executive Order 10308, which created a committee to enforce the prohibition of racial discrimination in employment.

In 1930 the NAACP successfully galvanized support in Congress to block the confirmation of Judge Robert Parker of North Carolina (an opponent of black rights) to the U.S. Supreme Court. Similar tactics have been used by the association in more recent years to acknowledge support or nonsupport of various nominations to government posts.

In the early twentieth century, Walter White (1893–1955), former NAACP executive secretary, and James Weldon Johnson lobbied Congress to secure the passage of the Dyer Anti-Lynching Bill, but the bill failed due to a lack of support in the Senate, despite its passage in the House of Representatives. Thereafter, the NAACP decreased its attention to antilynching policy and adopted a focus on other policy interests. Important legislative vic-

tories—the Civil Rights Act of 1964, the Voting Rights Act of 1965, and the Fair Housing Act of 1968—occurred as a result of the efforts of NAACP leaders Roy Wilkins (1901–1981) and Clarence Mitchell (1911–1984).

In international affairs, the NAACP denounced African colonization, calling international conferences on the subject in 1919, 1921, 1923, 1927, and 1944. The Pan-African Congress (under the direction of DuBois) specifically asked the U.S. president to take a stand against colonialism and the exploitation of black people around the world.

Political protests by NAACP members also challenged segregated environments. Rosa Parks (1913–2005), an NAACP member, ignited protests across the South when she refused to give up her seat on a segregated bus in 1955 in Montgomery, Alabama. Moreover, sit-ins by NAACP Youth Council members in Greensboro, North Carolina, in 1960 led to nonviolent protest strategies that challenged and eventually desegregated lunch counters.

One of the most effective strategies for fighting racial discrimination consisted of the NAACP litigating Jim Crow laws in the South and eventually in other regions of the country. Charles Hamilton Houston (1895–1950), special counsel for the NAACP and dean of Howard University Law School, launched the NAACP's litigation campaign.

In 1939 Thurgood Marshall (1908–1993), an NAACP attorney who was later appointed to the U.S. Supreme Court, formalized the litigation strategy within the NAACP when he developed the NAACP Legal Defense and Educational Fund (LDF). Becoming a formal entity within the NAACP in 1940, the LDF fought cases that challenged restrictions against blacks voting in primary elections (*Smith v. Allwright*, 1944); restrictive covenants (*Shelley v. Kraemer*, 1948); and educational segregation and discrimination (*Brown v. Board of Education of Topeka*, 1954). These LDF efforts effectively changed the second-class citizenship status of African Americans. The landmark decision in *Brown* declared that the "separate but equal" doctrine established in *Plessy v. Ferguson* (1896) was unconstitutional.

Upon the separation of the LDF from the NAACP in 1957, Robert Carter (NAACP general counsel) continued the NAACP's litigation strategies through the NAACP Legal Department. Under Carter's counsel, the NAACP won a decision in *Gomillion v. Lightfoot* (1960), in which the Supreme Court acknowledged the concept of "one person, one vote."

The NAACP was one of the leading civil rights organizations of the modern civil rights movement, along with the Congress of Racial Equality (CORE, founded in 1942), the Student Nonviolent Coordinating Committee

(SNCC, founded in 1960), the Southern Christian Leadership Conference (SCLC, founded in 1956), and the National Urban League (founded in 1910). These organizations mostly supported nonviolent, direct action strategies (sit-ins, marches, picketing, and especially litigation) to protest racial discrimination.

By the mid-1960s SNCC (whose membership comprised many of the black youth in the movement) and CORE became more radical and militant as members became frustrated with the violent and mostly unmoved opposition of many white Americans to black progress. SNCC leader Stokely Carmichael (1941–1998) expressly supported the notion of "Black Power" as a new objective of black protest. The commitment of the NAACP and other organizations to integrationism (integrating blacks in white society) contrasted with the increasingly nationalistic sentiments of activists like Carmichael and other black youth, as Black Power and black nationalism garnered more support among the black masses.

The national executive director at that time, Roy Wilkins, publicly denounced what he perceived to be the racially separatist and antiwhite orientation of Black Power ideology. The Black Panther Party, at that time a prominent black nationalist organization and a leading proponent of Black Power, disagreed with a political strategy that focused on integrating blacks with whites in society. Instead, the Black Panthers emphasized building the black community (without white resources or integration) to address race and poverty. The party supported building a "black nation."

The Black Panther Party criticized the NAACP as being a mainstream, passive, and bourgeois civil rights organization that represented older, outmoded views about the position of blacks in American society. Moreover, the Black Panthers disagreed with the NAACP's strategy to address racial discrimination without self-defense and without critical opposition to class oppression. In contrast, the Black Panther Party supported more militaristic tactics to protest racial discrimination and violence by whites, and it focused on implementing programs that addressed the overwhelming poverty of black Americans. Although the NAACP supported pacifist resistance and protest movements on a national level, some local chapters and members—in particular, Robert F. Williams (1925–1966), president of the Monroe, North Carolina, chapter of the NAACP—supported self-defense tactics that were akin to the black nationalist tenets of the Black Panther Party.

The vanguard leadership of the NAACP also differed generationally and ideologically from the Black Panther Party, which was comprised mostly of black youth. This generational difference translated into what members of the Black Panther Party perceived to be the desire of older activists to assimilate into white society, as opposed to appreciating black culture as distinct from white influence. The Black Panther Party ushered in an increasing embrace of black pride among black youth and the black masses—a transformation of African American identity that also emphasized less reliance on white resources and more appreciation for black self-determination. As support for black pride became more popular among the black masses, the NAACP became more supportive of black consciousness and black community-building. As always, however, the NAACP was prejudicial about racial separatism.

Over the years, the NAACP has continued to address issues related to race and discrimination. It has also incorporated into its political agenda more programs focusing on economic inequality. Such issues as disparities in education, redistricting and vote dilution, fair housing, criminal justice, and environmental racism now form part of the NAACP's commitment to fighting racial discrimination. The NAACP has also protested apartheid in South Africa, sponsored voter registration drives, encouraged increased voter turnout, challenged negative images of blacks in the media, promoted economic empowerment, and advocated improved healthcare regardless of race. NAACP activism has been extended to address the discrimination of various racial and ethnic minorities, while still focusing on the conditions of African Americans.

SEE ALSO *African American Studies; African Americans; Black Panthers; Black Power;* Brown v. Board of Education, 1954; *Civil Rights; Civil Rights Movement, U.S.; Du Bois, W. E. B.; Integration; Jim Crow; Race; Segregation*

BIBLIOGRAPHY

Cose, Ellis, and Vern E. Smith. 1994. The Fall of Benjamin Chavis: Civil Rights: How the NAACP's Controversial Leader Did Himself In. *Newsweek* 124 (9): 27.

Greenberg, Jack. 1994. *Crusaders in the Courts: How a Dedicated Band of Lawyers Fought for the Civil Rights Revolution.* New York: Basic Books.

Hosenhall, Mark, and Vern E. Smith. 1994. Trial by Fire at the NAACP: Civil Rights, the Scandal Engulfing Director Ben Chavis Could Threaten the Entire Organization. *Newsweek* 124 (8): 24.

Janken, Kenneth Robert. 2003. *White: The Biography of Walter White, Mr. NAACP.* New York: New Press.

Jonas, Gilbert. 2005. *Freedom's Sword: The NAACP and the Struggle against Racism in America, 1909–1969.* New York: Routledge.

Kellogg, Charles Flint. 1967. *NAACP: A History of the National Association for the Advancement of Colored People.* Baltimore, MD: John Hopkins University Press.

Kweisi Mfume Takes the NAACP Out of the Recovery Room. *Journal of Blacks in Higher Education* 29: 40–41.

Marger, Martin N. 1984. Social Movement Organizations and Response to Environmental Change: The NAACP, 1960–1973. *Social Problems* 32 (1): 16–30.

Miller, Jake C. 2002. The NAACP and Global Human Rights. *The Western Journal of Black Studies* 26 (1): 22–31.

National Association for the Advancement of Colored People. http://www.naacp.org.

Ogbar, Jeffrey O. G. 2004. *Black Power: Radical Politics and African American Identity.* Baltimore, MD: John Hopkins University Press.

Ovington, Mary White. 1947. *The Walls Came Tumbling Down.* New York: Harcourt Brace.

St. James, Warren D. 1958. *The National Association for the Advancement of Colored People: A Case Study in Pressure Groups.* New York: Exposition Press.

Topping, Simon. 2004. Supporting Our Friends and Defeating Our Enemies: Militancy and Nonpartisanship in the NAACP, 1936–1948. *Journal of African American History* 9 (1): 17–35.

Tyson, Timothy B. 1999. *Radio Free Dixie: Robert F. Williams and the Roots of Black Power.* Chapel Hill: University of North Carolina Press.

Ware, Gilbert. 1994. The NAACP-Inc. Fund Alliance: Its Strategy, Power, and Destruction. *Journal of Negro Education* 63 (3): 323–335.

Wickham, DeWayne. 2004. Troubling Exit for NAACP's Mfume. *USA Today* (November 30).

Shayla C. Nunnally

NATIONAL CENTER ON FATHERS AND FAMILIES

SEE *Fatherhood.*

NATIONAL COMORBIDITY SURVEY

SEE *Smoking.*

NATIONAL DEBT

A national debt is generated when a government runs a budget deficit for consecutive fiscal years; hence its expenditures (for administration, defense, welfare programs, and so forth) exceed its revenues (taxes). In such cases, the government seeks to finance its deficit by borrowing money either from internal sources or from abroad. The "national debt" is the sum total of all the outstanding obligations (bonds, bills, and notes) issued by the Treasury.

Consequently, much of the concern about public deficits arises from their cumulative effect on the national debt.

Nowadays, most countries, regardless of their level of development, face persistent deficits and increasing national debts, which in many economies (such as Latin America, Southeast Asia, and Europe) have reached alarming proportions in relation to their GDP, which is the basis for appraising the size and the safety of national debts. To cite examples, for the United States this ratio is approximately 65 percent; for Italy, 120 percent; for France, 75 percent; and for Belgium, 100 percent. Most contemporary economic policies have as a major target the reduction of the national debt, and most governments follow stabilization policies that reduce their public deficits through cutting their expenditures. But what is the burden of a public deficit and by extension of a national debt?

A major burden of national debt on an economy comes from interest payments, which, however, should not burden an economy if the payment does not involve a leakage of income to foreign holders of the debt (external debt) or if it does not impose severe distortions in the way income is distributed among various groups. In general, as long as growth continues and the debt's relation to GDP remains the same, there is no reason why a national debt cannot increase indefinitely. Is there, then, no burden to a debt? If debt remains a constant fraction of the GDP, we should experience no burden because tax revenues would provide the needed interest. If debt increases, it should still pose no burden as long as the economy grows fast enough to provide the additional tax revenues needed for additional interest.

Critics of budget deficits often argue that the burden of deficits eventually falls on future generations because deficits cause the "crowding-out effect" that results from the intense competition for capital funds between private and public investors. The outcome of this search for funds is an increase in interest rates, which eventually reduces growth in the business sector and the income stream of future generations. Furthermore, the increase in interest rates attracts foreign investors and leads to foreign indebtedness; as a result, the externality of the debt creates increasing leakages from the domestic income stream.

Is the debt too large? Is the deficit a danger to an economy? These questions cannot be answered without taking into consideration many aspects of the economic policy a government is pursuing. Deficits can be useful in promoting growth by generating demand (the Keynesian perspective), or they can be dangerous as they generate excess demand (the monetarist and new classical perspectives). The general consensus among economists and policy makers, however, is that there is no absolute magnitude that separates a useful debt from a dangerous one. A deficit that is mainly incurred to promote public growth-producing services such as education, health, and infrastructure (productive activities) will definitely have an impact on the development process of an economy that is different from a deficit incurred to promote activities such as administration and defense (nonproductive activities). The reason is that growth-promoting state activities generate future income activities and tax revenues to repay the debt, whereas the second case is just a form of income leakage.

SEE ALSO *Aggregate Demand; Government; Macroeconomics; Policy, Fiscal*

BIBLIOGRAPHY

Eisner, Robert. 1994. *The Misunderstood Economy: What Counts and How to Count It.* Boston: Harvard Business School Press.

Heilbroner, Robert, and Peter Bernstein. 1989. *The Debt and the Deficit: False Alarms/Real Possibilities.* New York: Norton.

Lipsey, Richard G., Paul N. Courant, and Christopher T. S. Ragan. 1998. *Economics,* 12th ed. New York: Addison-Wesley.

Persefoni V. Tsaliki

NATIONAL DEFICIT

SEE *National Debt.*

NATIONAL ECONOMIC ASSOCIATION

The National Economic Association was founded in 1969 as the Caucus of Black Economists (CBE). At that time, fewer than three score African Americans in the United States were identified as holding a PhD in economics. Most were employed as faculty or administrators in historically black colleges and universities (HBCU). A small number held faculty positions at major research universities throughout the country. Others held professional positions in the federal government in agencies including the Department of Labor, Agriculture, Treasury, and Housing and Urban Development, and in the Federal Reserve system. The great majority of black economists were men, but the first African American known to earn a PhD in economics was a woman, Sadie T. M. Alexander, a member of an old Philadelphia family. She received her degree from the University of Pennsylvania in 1921. The most prominent African American woman in economics in 1969 was Phyllis A. Wallace, who had earned her PhD from Yale University in 1948 and was then director of technical studies at the U.S. Equal Employment Opportunity Commission.

Given the gender mix of African American economists when the NEA was founded, it is important to note that an increasing number of African American women have completed doctoral degree programs and entered the field since 1969. The narrowing gender gap among black economists might reflect the black female/male imbalance in higher education, where many institutions show a ratio of two or more black women enrolled for every black man. (A similar gender gap is seen in the greater proportion of African American women than men entering the medical and legal professions in recent years.)

GENESIS OF THE NEA

Economists are organized around fields of topical interest, such as the American Economic Association (AEA), American Finance Association (AFA), Econometric Society (ES), Labor and Employment Relations Association (LERA), and others. In 1969 there were seven such organizations; by the end of the twentieth century there were fifty-one. Most economists hold membership in two or more such groups. Each year, economists from the various fields gather together at the Allied Social Sciences Association (ASSA) meetings to present and discuss new research, debate economic policy issues, and address other matters of interest to the profession. Many African American economists hold memberships in the organizations, and attend the annual meetings. But in 1969, few African Americans were invited to present papers or act as discussants on research panels and in policy forums.

The 1960s was a period of increased black assertiveness, as reflected in the emergence of the civil rights movement, the black power movement, and organizations like the Black Panther Party and the Nation of Islam. Black members in mainstream professional organizations began to organize affinity groups to address issues of particular interest to black people in those fields. In that climate, a group of black economists gathered together during the 1969 ASSA meetings in New York City to organize the Caucus of Black Economists.

Leading the organizational effort was a group of black economists who were affiliated with major academic institutions. The key organizers were Charles Z. Wilson, professor of economics and vice chancellor of UCLA, and Professor Marcus A. Alexis, University of Rochester. Joining them were Professor Thaddeus Spratlen, University of Washington; Professor Karl Gregory, Oakland University, Michigan; Richard F. America, lecturer, the Business School, University of California, Berkeley; Robert S. Browne, president of the Black Economic Research Center in Harlem, New York; and

Assistant Professor Bernard E. Anderson, the Wharton School, University of Pennsylvania.

The purpose of the Caucus, as expressed in its mission statement, was to "increase the supply of black economists, and to promote research and publication on economic issues of importance to the black community." The consensus view among the organizers was that the economics profession suffered from both the paucity of black people in the profession and the lack of research and analysis by black economists on economic issues affecting the black community. The new organization was committed to encouraging black college students to study economics and choose economics as a career, and to supporting research and publication by black economists and gaining recognition for their work.

Members of the dues-paying organization selected a twelve-person executive board to serve three-year staggered terms. Officers are the president, president-elect, immediate past president, secretary, and treasurer. Membership is open to all who support the mission of the organization. While most members are African American, Caribbean, or African, all racial and ethnic groups are welcome to join, and some white economists have done so.

One of the goals of the CBE was to gain recognition by ASSA as an affinity group authorized to sponsor panels at the annual ASSA meetings. Groups like AEA, AFA, and LERA are allocated a number of time slots for panel sessions they organize on topics of interest to their members. Additional time slots and other accommodations are granted for organizational events such as luncheons, business meetings, and receptions.

In 1971, ASSA recognized the Caucus, and granted time and space for two sessions. That allocation was later expanded to six, including a joint session with AEA. Under the rules of the ASSA, however, only the papers presented in joint AEA sessions were published. The Caucus acquired a publication vehicle of its own when Robert S. Browne, founder of the *Review of Black Political Economy*, transferred its ownership to the new organization. Papers presented at the annual meetings and other research on race and economics is regularly published in the *Review*, a refereed journal published continuously since 1970.

By 1974, the spirit of protest expressed by black professionals in the 1960s receded as mainstream organizations became more sensitive to the importance of racial concerns within the social and behavioral sciences. In response, the CBE leadership agreed to change the name of the organization to the National Economic Association.

The major professional associations had dropped their racially exclusionary membership requirements by the mid-1970s and admitted black members. The American Economic Association had never barred black economists from membership, but few other than those with appointments to the economics departments of research universities joined. When racial exclusion ended, black professionals saw much value in maintaining dual membership in both the mainstream and race-oriented groups in order to assure that the special interests of the African American community continued to receive appropriate attention.

EDUCATIONAL PROGRAMS

In 1970 the NEA sponsored a summer workshop on economics at Washington University in St. Louis in an effort to promote African American students' interest in economics. A small group of black undergraduates and first-year graduate students met with faculty members for a week to discuss economic affairs and recent economic research, as well as the challenges and opportunities for graduate study in the field. The NEA's goal of increasing the supply of black economists was advanced significantly when the American Economic Association organized the Committee on the Status of Minorities in the Economics Professions. The committee was charged with promoting minority students' interest in economics as a profession and enhancing opportunities for graduate study. That goal was pursued in part through support for the AEA's Summer Program in Economics for Minority Students.

The AEA Summer Program was designed and organized by Professor Marcus Alexis, one of the founders of the NEA. The program was hosted by Northwestern University, where Professor Alexis held an appointment in the Economics Department. Supported by a three-year grant from the Rockefeller Foundation, the five-week program included courses in price theory, macro theory, quantitative methods, and public policy. Guest lectures by prominent black and other economists explained what economists do, how they do it, and the impact economists have on public policy and economic affairs. Participants in the Summer Program who chose to continue on toward graduate studies in economics were eligible to apply for a doctoral fellowship/internship program developed by the Federal Reserve Board.

The Summer Program has continued in regular session since 1974, and in addition to Northwestern has been hosted by Temple University, Philadelphia; the University of Texas, Austin; and Stanford University, Palo Alto, California. Since 2003 it has been hosted by Duke University in Durham, North Carolina. In response to national developments in affirmative action policy, participation in the program has been broadened beyond African American students to include Hispanics, Native Americans, and others, including a small number of white students.

Many of the students who have participated in the Summer Program since its inception have gone on to earn graduate degrees in economics, including doctorates from some of the elite graduate programs in the field. Some completed graduate and professional studies in other fields, including business and finance, law, and public administration. A few became entrepreneurs. Most who remain in the economics profession now hold faculty positions at a variety of colleges and universities. But as a matter of fact and concern, 90 percent of university economics departments in the United States do not have and have never appointed an African American to their faculty.

PROMOTING RESEARCH

In 1969, black economists had produced little published research on race and economics. Swedish economist Gunnar Myrdal had published the major work on the subject, *The American Dilemma*, in 1944. Other relevant work in the field included a theoretical analysis by Professor Gary Becker of the University of Chicago, *The Economics of Discrimination*, published in 1957.

Most studies of black economic conditions by black scholars were conducted by non-economists. Notable among that work was W. E. B. Du Bois's classic 1899 study *The Philadelphia Negro*. Du Bois also conducted a series of studies while he was affiliated with Atlanta University. Other black scholars, including historians Carter G. Woodson and Charles Wesley, wrote books on black business and black labor. The most prominent work by a black economist in the first half of the twentieth century was a study coauthored by University of Chicago professor Abram Harris, *The Black Worker* (1931).

In addition to the scholarly work, there were occasional studies of local economic conditions in the black community conducted by the staff of advocacy organizations like the National Urban League and the NAACP. Overall, however, there was little published work by professional black economists before 1970. In that year, under the leadership of Charles Z. Wilson, the Caucus of Black Economists obtained a Ford Foundation grant to organize a research collaborative which would provide financial support through competitive grants to encourage black economists to conduct research on topics related to the economic status of the black community.

The Research Collaborative awarded grants to a team of agricultural economists at Virginia State University to study land loss among black farmers in the South and to the Black Economic Research Center to support studies on the economics of discrimination. The grant was also used to support workshops and seminars where black economists and others discussed their research. Faculty from the historically black institutions were especially encouraged to participate. The goal was to promote cross-fertilization among scholars in the major research universities and others in smaller institutions who shared a mutual interest in race and economics. Meetings were held in Washington, D.C., New York City, and at Virginia State University. In 1972, a conference on economic development in Africa was cohosted by the NEA, and held at Atlanta University.

Overall, however, the Research Collaborative proved to be an ineffective device for promoting economic research by black economists. Several institutional factors explain the difficulty. Because only small awards could be made, most of the applications received by the Collaborative were for funds to "top off" research that was already underway. Also, in the early 1970s many black economists were faculty members at historically black colleges and universities (HBCUs), where the emphasis was on teaching and not research. Only a few HBCUs, including Howard University, the Atlanta University complex, North Carolina A&T, and one or two others had economics departments where faculty were regularly engaged in economic research.

Black economists affiliated with non-HBCU research universities typically received research support through those institutions. The leadership of the Collaborative preferred not to use the limited resources from the Ford Foundation four-year grant to embellish support for those who, in their view, had access to other funds. In short, the Research Collaborative, while an innovative initiative, was a flawed device for promoting academic research by black economists. Support for the Collaborative was not renewed by the Ford Foundation when the grant expired in 1974 and the NEA never attempted to revive the project.

RECOGNITION AND HONORS

Over the years, the NEA developed several initiatives to recognize and celebrate the achievements of black economists, including the Samuel Z. Westerfield Award, the Rhonda M. Williams Doctoral Dissertation Award, and the Sir Arthur Lewis Memorial Lecture. They are conferred only when a suitable and appropriate candidate is identified to receive the honors.

The Westerfield Award The first award developed by the NEA was the Samuel Z. Westerfield Award, which is conferred periodically on an economist with a distinguished record of scholarship, teaching, and public service. The award is named in honor of Samuel Z. Westerfield (1919–1972), who earned a PhD in economics at Harvard, taught economics and was dean of the School of Business at Atlanta University, and served as deputy assistant secretary of the U. S. Treasury Department, assistant secretary of state for Africa, and U.S. ambassador to Liberia.

The first Samuel Z. Westerfield Award was conferred posthumously upon Westerfield in 1972. Since that time, seven economists have received the Westerfield Award, the NEA's highest honor: Marcus A. Alexis, Phyllis A. Wallace, Andrew F. Brimmer, Clifton R. Wharton Jr., Samuel L. Myers Sr., Bernard E. Anderson, and David H. Swinton.

The Rhonda M. Williams Doctoral Dissertation Award
To encourage and recognize excellence in graduate study, the NEA established the NEA Doctoral Dissertation Award in 1992 to recognize outstanding dissertations written by minority doctoral candidates, selected by a committee of NEA scholars. In addition to receiving the award, the recipient is given the opportunity to publish a revised version of the dissertation in the *Review of Black Political Economy*.

In 2001, the award was renamed in honor of Rhonda Williams, a black economist and professor at the University of Maryland, who succumbed to cancer in 2000. Professor Williams earned her PhD in economics at the Massachusetts Institute of Technology, and held faculty positions at Yale and the University of Texas, Austin, before her appointment at Maryland. She was widely recognized as one of the brightest young economic theorists in the field. The first dissertation award was presented to William Rodgers of Harvard in 1993, who went on to hold a full professorship at Rutgers University.

The Sir Arthur Lewis Memorial Lecture One of the most celebrated members of the NEA was Sir W. Arthur Lewis, a Nobel laureate in economics and professor of economics at Princeton University. Professor Lewis was a world-renowned scholar on economic development theory and practice. To recognize and encourage work on that topic, the NEA initiated the Sir Arthur Lewis Memorial Lecture, which is presented during the ASSA annual meeting. An economist who has produced seminal research on economic development or made a significant contribution to economic development through public service may be selected to present the Lewis Lecture. Since 1985, Lewis Lectures have been presented by Lance Taylor, Donald Harris, Charles Kindelberger, Ronald Findlay, Irma Adelman, and Paul Streeten.

SEE ALSO *American Economic Association; Black Sociologists; Discrimination; Lewis, W. Arthur; National Association for the Advancement of Colored People (NAACP); Professionalization; Race; Racism*

BIBLIOGRAPHY

Anderson, Bernard E. 1970. *Negro Employment in Public Utilities*. Philadelphia: University of Pennsylvania Press.

Becker, Gary S. 1957. *The Economics of Discrimination*. Chicago: University of Chicago Press.

Darity, William R., and Samuel L. Myers. 1998. *Persistent Disparity: Race and Economic Inequality in the United States since 1945*. Northampton, MA: Elgar Publishing.

Du Bois, W. E. B. 1899. *The Philadelphia Negro*. Philadelphia: University of Pennsylvania.

Greene, Lorenzo J., and Carter G. Woodson. 1930. *The Negro Wage Earner*. Washington, DC: Association for the Study of Negro Life and History.

Myrdal, Gunnar. 1944. *An American Dilemma: The Negro Problem and Modern Democracy*. New York: Harper.

National Economic Association. http://www.neaecon.org.

Review of Black Political Economy. Published by Transaction Publishers for the National Economic Association and the Southern Center for Studies in Public Policy of Clark Atlanta University. Published continuously since 1970.

Sowell, Thomas. 1983. *The Economics and Politics of Race: An International Perspective*. New York: W. Morrow.

Spero, Sterling D., and Abram L. Harris. 1931. *The Black Worker: A Study of the Negro and the Labor Movement*. New York: Columbia University Press.

Wesley, Charles H. 1925. *Negro Labor in the United States, 1850–1923: A Study of American Economic History*. PhD diss., Harvard University.

Bernard E. Anderson

NATIONAL EDUCATION LONGITUDINAL STUDY

The National Center for Education Statistics (NCES) sponsored the National Education Longitudinal Study (NELS). The purpose of the NELS was to collect information that would help social scientists to determine the factors that affect the educational, social, and personal outcomes of children. The NELS is known for having exceptional measures of family background, characteristics of schools, and measures of educational attainment.

The study started with the survey of a nationally representative sample of eighth-graders in 1988. The survey was made nationally representative by first choosing a representative sample of schools (1,052) and then by randomly sampling students in each of the schools. One of the advantages of the NELS versus other social science datasets is that the NELS contains information from student questionnaires, teacher questionnaires, parent or guardian questionnaires, and school administrator questionnaires. The original survey contained information from 24,599 students, 5,193 teachers, 22,651 parents, and 1,052 schools (Curtin, Ingels, Wu, et al. 2002). Follow-up surveys of the students in the original survey were conducted in 1990, 1992, 1994, and 2000. Since there was attrition in the follow-up surveys, the NELS also surveyed some new students who were not in the original survey in order to maintain a nationally representative sample of students in each of the years. In addition to the information contained in the questionnaires, the NELS also contains transcript information, test scores, and zip code information.

Prior to the NELS, the NCES conducted the National Longitudinal Study of the High School Class of 1972 (NLS-72) and the High School and Beyond Survey (HS&B). Many of the components of the NELS were designed to facilitate comparisons between the surveys.

MAJOR STUDIES AND FINDINGS

Hundreds of social science studies have used the NELS to evaluate educational outcomes, social outcomes, and personal outcomes. What follows is a discussion of a few strands of research where the NELS has proven to be extremely beneficial.

The literature on school choice has benefited a great deal from the availability of the NELS. Caroline Hoxby (2000) used the NELS to evaluate whether school choice improves school quality. She evaluates the effects of school choice by measuring the effects of Tiebout choice. Tiebout choice is the process by which individuals choose where to live based on the public-good characteristics of the area. She finds that increases in the amount of Tiebout choice leads to increased productivity, higher achievement, and less spending. Her results have recently been criticized by Jesse Rothstein (2005). She replied to these criticisms in Hoxby (2005).

The NELS has also been used as a resource for evaluating private-school enrollment. Robert Fairlie and Alexandra Resch (2002) use the NELS to evaluate enrollment in private schools and test whether private-school enrollment is related to the fraction of minority students enrolled in the local public school. They use several unique features of the NELS, in particular the information on the student's zip code and information on the racial attitudes of the respondents. The authors find some evidence of "white flight" from public schools to private schools when the public schools enroll a large proportion of minority students.

Given the rich amount of information available on family background in the NELS, several studies have measured the effects of particular family characteristics on educational outcomes. Gary Painter and David Levine (2000) use the NELS to test whether divorce or remarriage of the student's parents affects educational attainment. The authors found that divorce increased high school dropout rates and also affected out-of-wedlock births for young women.

The NELS has also been used to evaluate whether teacher characteristics affect student learning outcomes and student evaluations. Ronald G. Ehrenberg, Daniel D.

Goldhaber, and Dominic J. Brewer (1995) used the information in the teacher questionnaires to analyze whether the match between the teacher's demographic information and the student's demographic information influenced the amount the student learned in the classroom or the teacher's evaluation of the student. The authors found that there was little correspondence between the teacher's demographics and learning outcomes but that there appeared to be a relationship between the teacher's demographics and the teacher's evaluations of demographically dissimilar students. Thomas Dee (2005) revisited the information in the teacher questionnaires and found that teachers who were demographically dissimilar to the student being evaluated were more likely to rate the student unfavorably.

The NELS has also been used to document the extent of drug usage by teenagers. Philip DeCicca, Donald Kenkel, and Alan Mathios (2002) used the NELS to evaluate the extent of teenage smoking and the effects of cigarette taxes on teenage smoking. After utilizing the panel nature of the NELS, they found that taxes were not strongly related to teenage smoking. Thomas Dee and William Evans (2003) used the information contained in the NELS to document the amount of teenage drinking and the correlation of teenage drinking to educational attainment.

FUTURE STUDIES

The most recent and final wave of the NELS was conducted in 2000. The 2000 data include information on family formation, educational attainment, and earnings. Future studies will most likely analyze the data included in the most recent follow-up and compare the outcomes of respondents of the NELS to the outcomes of the respondents to the HS&B survey and the NLS-72 survey.

Future studies may also use the large amount of information on educational outcomes available in the NELS. In particular, studies will most likely consider the determinants of whether a student attends college, whether the student persists in college, whether the student graduates from college, and what types of curriculum the student chooses to study in college. In addition, these studies will also most likely analyze the effects of these educational attainment measures on earnings.

In the future, we might also see studies that investigate how characteristics of the student's family and area where the student grew up affect where the student chooses to live and work as a young adult. The one limitation of the NELS is that there are no other planned follow-ups, so the ability to measure the effects of factors during childhood on outcomes in adulthood will be limited to only those outcomes that are observed when the individual is approximately twenty-five years old.

SEE ALSO *Acting White; Data, Longitudinal; Drugs of Abuse; Education, USA; Public Goods; Research, Longitudinal; Sample Attrition; School Vouchers; Schooling; Social Science; Surveys, Sample*

BIBLIOGRAPHY

Curtin, Thomas R., Steven J. Ingels, Shiying Wu, et al. 2002. User's Manual National Education Longitudinal Study of 1988 Base-Year to Fourth Follow-Up Data File User's Manual. U.S. Department of Education. Office of Educational Research and Improvement. NCES 2002-323.

DeCicca, Philip, Donald Kenkel, and Alan Mathios. 2002. Putting Out the Fires: Will Higher Taxes Reduce the Onset of Youth Smoking? *Journal of Political Economy* 110 (1): 144–169.

Dee, Thomas S. 2005. A Teacher Like Me: Does Race, Ethnicity or Gender Matter? *American Economic Review* 95 (2): 158–165.

Dee, Thomas S., and William N. Evans. 2003. Teen Drinking and Educational Attainment: Evidence from Two-Sample Instrumental Variables Estimates. *Journal of Labor Economics* 21 (1): 178–209.

Ehrenberg, Ronald G., Daniel D. Goldhaber, and Dominic J. Brewer. 1995. Do Teachers' Race, Gender, and Ethnicity Matter? Evidence from the National Education Longitudinal Study of 1988. *Industrial and Labor Relations Review* 48 (3): 547–561.

Fairlie, Robert W., and Alexandra M. Resch. 2002. Is There "White Flight" into Private Schools? Evidence from the National Education Longitudinal Survey. *Review of Economics and Statistics* 84 (1): 21–33.

Hoxby, Caroline. 2000. Does Competition Among Public Schools Benefit Students and Taxpayers? *American Economic Review* 90 (5): 1209–1238.

Hoxby, Caroline. 2005. Competition Among Public Schools: A Reply to Rothstein (2004). *National Bureau of Economic Research Working Paper* No. 11216. http://www.nber.org/papers/W11216.

Painter, Gary, and David I. Levine. 2000. Family Structure and Youths' Outcomes: Which Correlations Are Causal? *Journal of Human Resources* 35 (3): 524–549.

Rothstein, Jesse. 2005. Does Competition Among Public Schools Benefit Students and Taxpayers? A Comment on Hoxby (2000). *National Bureau of Economic Research Working Paper* No. 11215. http://www.nber.org/papers/w11215.

Lisa M. Dickson

NATIONAL ELECTION STUDIES

SEE *Pollsters.*

NATIONAL FAMILY HEALTH SURVEYS

India's National Family Health Surveys (NFHS) are designed to provide key information about population and health conditions and the needs of the country's women, men, and children. Information is collected from nationally representative samples of households throughout the country. The surveys, which are part of the global Demographic and Health Surveys program, collect information on such topics as reproductive health, child health, immunizations, family planning, HIV/AIDS, nutritional status, women's status, population growth, and household living conditions.

Since the early 1990s, India has conducted two National Family Health Surveys and a third is being implemented in 2005–2006. The surveys are conducted under the stewardship of India's Ministry of Health and Family Welfare (MOHFW). The International Institute for Population Sciences in Mumbai (formerly Bombay) has been the coordinating agency for all three surveys. The first two surveys were funded by the United States Agency for International Development (USAID), with additional funding from the government of India, and with some supplementary funds from the United Nations Children's Fund (UNICEF) for the second survey. Macro International, USA, and the East-West Center, USA, provided technical assistance to the first two surveys. The third survey is funded by USAID, the U.K. Department for International Development, the Bill and Melinda Gates Foundation, UNICEF, the United Nations Population Fund, and the government of India. Macro International is again providing technical assistance to the third survey.

The NFHS surveys collect individual, household, and community-level information by conducting face-to-face interviews and by measuring key biomarkers. The interviews and measurements are conducted using well-developed and tested survey instruments and rigorously trained survey personnel. Survey questionnaires have been translated into more than twenty languages, and interviews are conducted in the predominant local language of the respondents. Participation in the surveys is completely voluntary. Informed consent is obtained from all survey respondents before questions are asked and before blood specimens are collected. Stringent quality control measures are employed in all aspects of survey planning and implementation, including sample design, the development and field-testing of survey instruments, the training of survey personnel, and the supervision of data collection and data processing.

The first National Family Health Survey (NFHS-1) was conducted in 1992–1993 in about 90,000 households and covered all states of India except Sikkim. The first survey was aimed at strengthening the research capabilities of

India's network of eighteen population research centers (located mainly in universities and semiautonomous research institutions throughout the country), which is supported by the MOHFW. India had resisted conducting a World Fertility Survey or a Demographic and Health Survey for many years, but became interested in the NFHS when it was suggested that this would be the ideal mechanism through which to upgrade the survey capabilities of its population research centers. The first survey proved to be a major landmark in the development of a comprehensive demographic and health database for India.

The second National Family Health Survey (NFHS-2), conducted in 1998–1999 in about 90,000 households in all Indian states, expanded this database by providing time-trend information and including additional information on postpartum care, the quality of health and family-planning services, reproductive health problems, and domestic violence. The second survey also tested hemoglobin levels in the blood of women and young children and tested household salt to see if the salt was iodized.

The third National Family Health Survey (NFHS-3), which is being implemented in 2005–2006, builds on the strengths and successes of NFHS-1 and NFHS-2 by maintaining continuity in core content and coverage, while adding new dimensions. In response to new and emerging health and demographic data needs, NFHS-3 has an extended size and scope. In addition to ever-married women age fifteen to forty-nine, NFHS-3 is collecting data for the first time from never married women age fifteen to forty-nine, and both married and unmarried men age fifteen to fifty-four throughout India. NFHS-3 is additionally collecting blood samples from adult women and men for HIV testing. NFHS-3 aims to interview about 240,000 women and men and to take blood specimens for about 280,000 anemia tests and 135,000 HIV tests.

The findings from the NFHS surveys have been used extensively for evidence-based decision-making. The information gathered in the surveys has been instrumental in bringing about a number of major policy and program changes in India, and the survey data are being used to monitor the progress of various population and health programs.

NFHS data have been used extensively in the development and implementation of India's Five-Year Plans. For example, the Tenth Plan (2002–2007) has set national and state goals of increasing exclusive breastfeeding, achieving timely complementary feeding of children, and reducing severe undernutrition based primarily on the findings of NFHS-2. The survey findings of serious health conditions among scheduled castes, scheduled tribes, and other disadvantaged groups formed the basis for revising and refocusing India's National Health Policy in 2002 to better address the health needs of the poorest segments of society. The survey findings on unmet need for contraception were instrumental in facilitating a complete overhaul of the country's family welfare program.

The NFHS data have also been used extensively for policy and program purposes at the state level. For example, based on the NFHS findings of serious nutritional deficiencies among very young children, the government of Gujarat developed an action plan to refocus its nutrition programs on children under three years of age. NFHS data were also instrumental in galvanizing the Tamil Nadu state government to mount a more aggressive campaign to deal with the spread of HIV/AIDS.

The NFHS surveys have also greatly increased India's capacity to undertake and analyze first-rate demographic and health surveys. The surveys are considered the "gold standard" in survey-taking and a source of the most reliable information on major population and health indicators in India. Data gathered in the surveys have resulted in hundreds of research and policy publications in professional and scientific journals and have been the subject of numerous Ph.D. dissertations around the world. In addition, the results of the surveys have received extensive media coverage. In response to NFHS-2 alone, there were some three hundred newspaper articles, TV broadcasts, radio shows, and Internet articles based solely on the survey findings.

Important limitations of these surveys should also be recognized, however. First, the survey samples are not large enough to collect reliable information on certain important but relatively rare health conditions or events, such as maternal mortality. Second, the surveys do not provide the much needed district-level population and health indicators, again due to inadequate sample sizes. Third, the data collected on several health indicators in the surveys are self-reported, making them not as reliable as clinical data. And finally, the cross-sectional designs of the surveys limit their usefulness for causal analysis and understanding reasons for change.

In spite of these inherent limitations, there is overwhelming evidence that the NFHS surveys have provided valuable information on key population and health issues, and have been instrumental in building India's research capacity.

SEE ALSO *National Assessment of Educational Progress; National Longitudinal Study of Adolescent Health; National Longitudinal Survey of Youth; Panel Study of Income Dynamics; Survey; Surveys, Sample*

BIBLIOGRAPHY

International Institute for Population Sciences (IIPS). 1995. *National Family Health Survey (MCH and Family Planning), India 1992–93.* Bombay: IIPS.

International Institute for Population Sciences (IIPS) and ORC Macro. 2000. *National Family Health Survey (NFHS-2), 1998-99: India.* Mumbai, India: IIPS.

National Family Health Survey, India Web site. http://www. nfhsindia.org.

Vinod Mishra
Fred Arnold

NATIONAL GEOGRAPHIC

The National Geographic Society was founded in January 1888 in Washington, D.C., to support "the increase and diffusion of geographical knowledge." In October of that year, the society published the first issue of what was originally called *The National Geographic Magazine*, which was considered a way to fulfill the society's educational mission. The generally bland and often technical articles that characterized the magazine's early issues (which contained no photographs) scarcely hinted at the style that was to transform the journal into one of the most widely read magazines in the United States.

The National Geographic Magazine, issued erratically for its first eight years, became a monthly in January 1896. In this era, the magazine was edited by committee and had limited appeal, but November 1896 marked the appearance of something that would later become a hallmark of the magazine: a photograph of a bare-breasted ("native") woman.

Frustrated by the magazine's struggles to gain readership, the society turned to a young Gilbert H. Grosvenor (1875–1966), who joined the magazine's staff in 1899 as its first full-time employee at the rank of assistant editor. Under Grosvenor's leadership, the magazine's circulation grew to more than five million by the time of his death in 1966. The keys to the popularization of the magazine were to be found partly in Grosvenor's editorial principles, which included timelines, "absolute accuracy," "permanent value," an "abundance of beautiful, instructive, and artistic illustrations," eschewing topics of a "partisan or controversial character," and steering clear of anything "unpleasant or unduly critical" (Pauly 1979, p. 528). But most of all, it was the magazine's visual presentation that cemented its status in American popular culture.

It was through the magazine's famous photographs that Grosvenor achieved the goal of combining scholarship and entertainment. Public response to the images was strong, and an unprecedented eleven-page layout of photos from Tibet in 1905 helped to increase society membership from 3,400 to 11,000 by the end of the year.

National Geographic photographs were intended to present an unproblematic, unmediated view of reality, readily accessible to the average reader. In the 1930s, natural color photographs came to dominate its pages, enhancing the magazine's realism; as a result, the photographs served as both evidence and spectacle. The color photographs boosted the magazine's entertainment value at the same time that they reinforced the sense that it was truly delivering the world as it really was to its readers.

The assumptions about the production and dissemination of visual representations that underlie the magazine's approach would later be criticized by scholars. Those who view the production of knowledge as fundamentally shaped by power relations have argued that *National Geographic*'s articles reinforce a sense of Western superiority through the juxtaposition of "backward," timeless, native cultures with a more "advanced," progressive Western civilization. The photos and text do not simply and unproblematically convey geographic information; rather, they create geographic knowledge according to an identifiable set of cultural norms. Likewise, the regular appearance of bare-breasted "native" women in the magazine encourages a masculinized sense of access and control to "exotic" cultures that depends on and reproduces unequal power relations between those being represented and those consuming the representations.

Such criticisms have not diminished *National Geographic*'s global appeal; in addition to its millions of readers in the United States, the society publishes international editions in about two dozen languages. Well into its second century of publication, the magazine is still a cultural force with few, if any, peers.

BIBLIOGRAPHY

Bryan, C. D. B. 1997. *The National Geographic Society: 100 Years of Adventure and Discovery.* Updated and enlarged ed. New York: Abrams.

Lutz, Catherine A., and Jane L. Collins. 1993. *Reading National Geographic.* Chicago: University of Chicago Press.

Pauly, Philip J. 1979. The World and All That Is in It: The National Geographic Society, 1888–1918. *American Quarterly* 31 (4): 517–532.

David R. Jansson

NATIONAL HEALTH AND NUTRITION EXAMINATION SURVEY

SEE *Research, Cross-Sectional.*

NATIONAL HEALTH INSURANCE

Health is described as a state of complete physical, social, and mental wellbeing. In order to ensure that the population of a given nation remains at or achieves a good health status, health expenditures must be financed. Health care expenditures are the total amount of spending for personal health care, administration, research, construction, and other expenses that are directly related to patient care. Although insurance coverage is not the sole determinant of health, timely access to quality care does play a key role in maintaining and improving health. Many developed nations have a system of national health insurance to finance health care for their citizens. Though these plans vary, all provide national health insurance and take into account the political, historical, and social factors of the given society. Variations in national health insurance plans may relate to the organization of the health care system in a given country, or to the provisions of the plan. Many plans guarantee minimal national health insurance to all constituents; others provide insurance to all who meet low income standards, and yet others provide national health insurance with provisions that allow citizens to purchase supplemental private insurance. Countries that have national health insurance plans include Australia, Japan, China, Sweden, Russia, the United Kingdom, Germany, the Netherlands, Austria, Sri Lanka, Chile, and Canada, to name a few.

These national health insurance plans have limitations and differing levels of effectiveness. The Canadian national health insurance plan is one of the most impressive and historically established plans among developed nations. Initially developed in 1968, this plan is funded by federal and provincial tax revenues, as well as insurance premiums paid by all taxpaying citizens. Consequently, Canada ranks high on indicators that suggest the health of a society. Infant mortality, for example, is low in Canada, and the life expectancy of Canada's citizens is high. Despite this success, some have criticized Canada's system for a decrease in the professional authority of physicians and the rationing of health care. Critics of Canada's national health care system argue that in theory the system provides everyone with health care, but not necessarily superior health care.

In contrast, Sri Lanka, a peripheral or developing nation, instituted a national health insurance plan in 1992. The Sri Lankan government provides health care to its civilians mostly free of cost. The Sri Lankan government split the management of health care between provinces and administrative divisions. Provincial levels of government are responsible for the management of all health care institutions; divisions, which include medical officers, are responsible for administering health care. Though the national health insurance plan of Sri Lanka is not as well established as Canada's, health indicators for this country are good. Like Canada, Sri Lanka boasts a relatively low infant mortality rate (59.6 per 100,000 births), and life expectancy has been increasing. Although it is too early to assess the limitations of Sri Lanka's national health insurance plan, the plan includes provisions for development and change. The Sri Lankan Ministry of Health is responsible for the formulation of health policy; the ministry monitors the performance of the country's health organizations, and moderates and changes policy when necessary.

The United States stands as one of the world's developed nations that does not have a comprehensive national health insurance plan. Despite the lack of such a plan, the United States spends a larger percentage of its gross domestic product (the nation's total economic output) on health care expenditures than any other country, including countries that provide national health insurance coverage. Many American citizens have no insurance. The American health care system can be characterized as heavily influenced by such political action committees (PACs) as the American Medical Association (AMA), the American Hospital Association (AHA), the American Pharmacists Association (formerly the American Pharmaceutical Association, APA), and other special interest groups. The American health care system is also based upon a profit incentive, and health care expenditures are funded through numerous sources. These factors have contributed to vast inequalities in who receives health insurance and health care. These factors also explain why there is no national health insurance system in the United States, and the emergence of categories of Americans who are characterized as *underinsured* and *uninsured*.

The U.S. medical-industrial complex—the rapidly growing industry that supplies health care services for profit—is the result of the AMA's and APA's professional and political efforts during the nineteenth century to establish accredited medical training and unfavorable views of holistic medical practices. These historical efforts led to a great increase in the power of these and other special interest groups associated with American health care. While changes to existing insurance standards and policies are the responsibility of the U.S. government, the corporations that make up the medical-industrial complex employ PACs to influence congressional decisions regarding health care. Failures in efforts during the 1990s to implement a national health insurance system illustrate the strength of the influence of the medical industry. In November 1993 the administration of President Bill Clinton announced a national health insurance plan called *managed competition*. This plan would have provided national health coverage and was designed to account for problems related to both access to and the cost of health care. But the aforementioned special interest groups opposed this plan, voicing reservations about new forms of bureaucracy and cost controls. The AMA and AHA opposed the proposed limits placed on physician fees and hospital charges, while the APA opposed cost controls on the production of drugs. Ultimately, the Clinton plan was not implemented.

Corporate managed care represents an evolutionary process in the American health industry that started in the 1970s when prepaid *health maintenance organizations* (HMOs) were introduced. Ideally, the purpose of managed care is to provide appropriate health care, including preventive services, thereby reducing costs while maintaining, even improving, quality. In practice, such plans typically compete for subscribers by offering the lowest possible cost for health care. Health care is generally organized into plans that consist of an insurer who administers the plan and who has numerous contracts with physician groups, clinics, laboratories, and so on. Since the inception of corporate managed care, *preferred provider organizations* (PPOs) and *point-of-service* (POS) plans have been developed in addition to HMOs. However, many contemporary managed care corporations operate on a for-profit basis, which can lead to controversy. The primary issue is that the provision of health care is pitted against the pressure on corporations to make profits; the mission of offering access to care runs contrary to the incentive of financial gain.

Health insurance in the United States is provided through a mixture of private (individual, employers, family) and public (federal, state, and local government) insurance programs. In 1965 Title XVIII of the Social Security Act created both the Medicare and the Medicaid insurance programs. These programs were the first and remain among the few federal insurance programs established in the United States. Medicare is designed to provide health insurance to persons over the age of sixty-five, permanently disabled workers and their dependents, and persons with end-stage renal disease. Medicaid is a jointly funded federal and state program that is designed to provide health insurance to the poor, with stringent eligibility requirements. State Child Health Insurance Programs (SCHIPs) are a more recent initiative to provide public health insurance in the United States. These programs allow states flexibility in planning and implementing health insurance for low-income children under the age of eighteen.

Most U.S. health care expenditures are covered through private insurance programs. Private insurance is funded largely by employers with employee subsidies. In addition, many Americans own family or individual policies. Nonetheless, in 2004 approximately forty-five million Americans were uninsured and did not have any private or public health care coverage. Many of the unin-sured are poor working-class Americans who may work only part-time. There are others who are considered *underinsured.* They have jobs that provide minimal health care coverage, or insurance policies with major loopholes that are often costly to the consumer.

The profit motive and the influence of the medical-industrial complex are not solely responsible for the lack of national health insurance in the United States. The culture of the United States is based heavily on the principles of individualism, capitalism, and laissez-faire. For many Americans, the notion of government-run national health insurance seems un-American. Alternative versions of national health insurance that are being promoted in the United States include *single-payer* and *pay-or-play* insurance plans. Proponents argue that these alternatives are less socialistic and would promote capitalism. Although Americans do not agree on the solution, most public health officials, health care providers, and U.S. citizens agree that a more inclusive type of health insurance should be developed.

SEE ALSO *Health Economics; Insurance; Insurance Industry; Medicaid; Medicare; Mental Health*

BIBLIOGRAPHY

Alistair, Woodward, and Ichiro Kawachi. 2000. Why Reduce Health Inequalities? *Journal of Epidemiology and Community Health* 54: 923–929.

Blendon, John, and John M. Benson. 1998. Whatever Happened to Politicians? Concerns about the Nation's Uninsured? *American Journal of Public Health* 88 (3): 345–346.

Hoffman, Earl D., Barbara S. Klees, and Catherine A. Curtis. 2000. Overview of the Medicare and Medicaid Programs. *Health Care Financing Review* 22: 175–193.

Relman, Arnold S. 1980. The New Medical Industrial Complex. *New England Journal of Medicine* 303: 963–970.

Weiss, Gregory L., and Lynne E. Lonnquist. 2006. *The Sociology of Health, Healing, and Illness.* 5th ed. Upper Saddle River, NJ: Pearson Prentice Hall.

World Health Organization: Regional Office of South-East Asia. Country Health Profile: Sri Lanka. http://w3.whosea.org/ LinkFiles/Sri_lanka_srilanka.pdf.

La Fleur F. Small

NATIONAL HEALTH SERVICE

SEE *Competition, Managed; National Health Insurance.*

NATIONAL INCOME ACCOUNTS

The national income accounts are an internally-consistent matrix of statistics on a national economy's income, consumption, production, foreign trade and asset accumulation. National income accounts have two central roles: the measurement of economic activity and the measurement of economic well-being, or progress. In an important sense, these two roles are one, as economic activity derives its rationale from its social benefit.

According to British economist A. C. Pigou (1877–1959), whose work set forth the basic framework for welfare analysis in economics, national income is a measure of the part of social welfare that can be "brought directly or indirectly into relation with a money measure" (1932, p. 31). Pigou's definition is limited to those elements of welfare that can be measured by money, but it does not draw a fixed line between what can and cannot be measured. In practice, that boundary has evolved over time.

The limited but highly practical achievement of this measurement task has been one of the great accomplishments of economics, and supports the claim that economics is an empirical science. A nation's national income accounts have grown to include analytical detail on consumption, production, income, and foreign trade, as well as integrated statistics on saving and investment and their relation to stocks of physical capital and financial assets and liabilities. These statistics are central to economic and political evaluation and planning throughout the world.

The British economist Richard Stone (1913–1991) received the 1984 Nobel Prize in Economics for establishing the framework for the United Nations' System of National Accounts (SNA), which is the international standard for national income accounting. Its principles are subscribed to by virtually all nations. Indeed, almost all countries now prepare national income accounts; more than two hundred countries have accounts published in the United Nations' national accounts statistics.

Why are national income accounts so important to economies and to governments? First, they provide an excellent approximation of a nation's available economic resources and actual output. This is invaluable for setting government fiscal and monetary policy, and for evaluating the impact of governmental policies. Second, national income accounts provide a precise understanding of the current state of national economic demand, supply, and inflation. This creates a sound basis for current business and financial decisionmaking. Third, the national income framework has proved to be a useful basis for long-term forecasting of economic activity for business and government planning at multiyear horizons. Finally, the statistics are used for international and interregional cost sharing and aid agreements.

National income accounts can only fulfill these roles because they have been widely accepted as good measures of economic activity and well-being. They are not now and are unlikely ever to be ideal measures of either. Economists and national income accountants persistently attempt to widen and sharpen national income measurement, including creating *satellite accounts* (statistics provided by national income accountants but not included in the official accounts) that provide data on additional items not yet of high enough quality or on the same theoretical footing as those already measured.

MEASURING WELFARE WITH MONEY MEASURES

In accepting the measuring rod of money, we accept limitations on our welfare measure both in concept and in scope. The measure is largely plutocratic, as wealthy households command more consumption than poor ones. As such, it is a measure that is comfortable with the existing structures of economic power. As the American economist and 1971 Nobel laureate Simon Kuznets (1901–1985) stressed, changes in income distribution across households should be a crucial component of the evaluation of national income, but as of 2006 income distribution was not included in national income accounts.

Monetized activity sets the general boundary for national income measurement. Household production—the use of household time and energy in tasks such as studying, cooking, and cleaning—is generally not included in consumption because it is unpriced. One exception is that owner-occupied housing is treated as if the household were renting from itself; otherwise the shift from tenancy to owner-occupation in many countries would appear as a decline in consumption of shelter services. Another exception, important in many countries, is owner-consumption of farm products.

Production has two objects: consumption and accumulation. This entry will turn first to consumption expenditures, which form the core of measured welfare benefits.

Consumption Comparisons Over Time As prices and money, or *nominal* expenditures, change, is it possible to quantify the degree to which consumers are better off in one period compared to another? Within limits, yes. In two periods, the consumer buys two different baskets of goods and services. Now suppose the items bought in the first period could have been purchased in the second period for less than the items actually purchased in the second period. Then we can argue that the consumer must be better off, for the alternative was freely chosen. If the second-period consumer pays 2 percent more than the first-period basket would have cost, *real consumption* *expenditures* are said to have risen by (at least) 2 percent. While this does not amount to 2 percent more happiness, it does imply that the consumer could have remained as well off using 2 percent less of the products and thus 2 percent less work and capital (assuming constant returns to scale), so it is a meaningful quantification.

So one measure of price increase, or the *inflation rate*, between two periods can be constructed by pricing out the first period's basket in both periods. This price index, called a *Laspeyres* price index, gives, if anything, an overestimate of the rate of inflation. We can go the other way around. A price index constructed by pricing out the second basket in both periods, called a *Paasche* price index, creates an underestimate of inflation.

Before the 1980s, which of the two methods was used did not make a great deal of difference. However, very rapid declines in the prices of computers and other electronics caused large gaps between the two methods. The solution was to construct *Fisher ideal indexes* averaging the two inflation rates over each pair of consecutive quarters (precisely, the two price index ratios are multiplied and the square root is taken).

Subtracting the inflation rate from the nominal growth rate, a process called *deflation*, gives the real growth rate of output. Similarly, we can calculate real output at disaggregated levels by final product or by industry. Unfortunately, these subindexes do not sum up exactly to their aggregate counterparts, because the averaging of growth rates has a nonlinear impact on levels. National accounts often include tables that show the contributions of final product components to the movement of total gross domestic product in a way that does add up.

These price index methods assume that there are no new goods or services (products that cannot be found in the earlier period). As the rate of new-product introduction has accelerated, price statisticians have turned to methods (called *hedonic methods*) that attempt to price product *characteristics*, so that a new product can be evaluated as a new bundle of existing characteristics whose prices can be found in the previous period. The notion is roughly that if consumers are willing to pay 10 percent more for a computer that operates 20 percent faster, we can use that fact to estimate what a 20-percent-faster computer would have cost last period, even if it was not sold then.

When consumption expenditures are made by governments or nonprofit institutions on behalf of consumers, the Fisher ideal method does not apply, because there is no market price paid by the consumer. Instead, we can deflate output using the average cost of the inputs (for example, labor costs by wage inflation) or by the prices of similar products sold privately.

Cross-Border Comparisons When we compare the consumption of two countries, we face the problem that they have different currencies. One solution would be to compare the incomes based on the currencies' exchange rates. However, many countries control the exchange rates of their currencies, so that the exchange rate is not market-based. Where the exchange rate is not controlled, it is often highly volatile, rendering these comparisons unreliable.

To solve this difficulty, national statisticians construct measures of *purchasing power* by pricing similar baskets of goods in different countries. This is inevitably a cruder calculation than intertemporal comparisons, because there are two worse problems: (1) the location of consumption affects its desirability, and (2) many products are available in some countries and not in others.

MEASURING OVERALL ECONOMIC PROGRESS: PRODUCTIVITY MEASURES

To consumption, we now add investment. To capture overall economic progress, the rate of *net investment*—gross investment less the loss of existing capital due to depreciation, called *capital consumption*—provides an idea of how much more production could have been devoted to consumption without running down the capital stock, and at the same time of how rapidly the economy is likely to grow, since more net investment today implies more capital input for tomorrow's production.

Mainly for historical reasons, gross domestic product (GDP, product without deducting capital consumption) has been the featured measure of real economic activity. Consumption of fixed capital is about 10 percent of net domestic product in countries as different as the United States and India. *Net domestic product*, GDP less capital consumption, would be more exact as a measure of progress, but GDP is easier to measure in detail.

One way to measure real investment in terms comparable to real consumption could be to deflate nominal investment growth by the consumption inflation rate, a measure showing the quantity of consumption that is given up to provide investment. The alternative, the method actually employed in national income accounting, is to measure the change of prices of these investment goods themselves, combining them into Fisher ideal indexes. This measure is the appropriate one for measuring the contribution of the new investment to the stock of capital assets.

More recently, it has been recognized that *intangible* assets can also be accumulated and have been rising in importance. The 1993 revision of the United Nations' System of National Accounts called for the recognition of investment in software, mineral exploration (such as drilling and surveys), and the creation of expressions, such as entertainment, literary works, and original art. Deliberately omitted were firm research and development expenditures, which were relegated to a satellite account, although the long-term value of these expenditures, about 2 percent of U.S. GDP, has been well documented. When long-lived investments are misclassified as expenses, output is underestimated, as are assets. As a consequence, future measured output growth and profitability may be underestimated. Investments in human capital—education and on-the-job experience—are also omitted from national income accounts.

Output Per Person and Productivity For many comparative purposes, it is sensible to measure economic progress relative to growth in population, hours worked, or total input of labor and capital services. Angus Maddison (1995) used *real gross domestic product per capita* (following in Kuznets's footsteps) to assess total world economic growth and inequality between regions. His statistics showed that between 1500 and 1820, world real GDP per capita rose only about 15 percent, while from 1920 to 1992, it rose 700 percent. His statistics also showed that the richest regions had roughly three times as much per capita income in 1820 as the poorest, while in 1992 the richest regions had fifteen times as much income per capita, so that this period of industrialization was one of substantial income divergence overall.

The main household time cost of economic activity is employment. For this reason, an alternative measure of economic efficiency is output per hour worked, also called *labor productivity*. Because Europeans work fewer hours per year than Americans, the U.S. economy fares better on GDP per capita measures, while Europe looks better on labor productivity measures.

The American economist and 1987 Nobel laureate Robert Solow (1957), noting that from 1909 to 1949 output per hour in the United States expanded 1.5 percent annually, argued that roughly one-eighth of this growth was due to increased capital per worker, and the remainder was due to overall advances in the techniques of production, or *total factor productivity*.

Solow used rather crude measures of labor and capital. Labor hours are not equal in economic value due to differentials in talent and training (formal or informal) reflected in differences in compensation rates. The services available from capital also vary; computers and fiber optics, for example, are more efficient than mechanical calculators and copper cable. The current state of the art in national income is to carefully adjust capital and labor for these quality differences when constructing measures of total factor productivity.

Dale W. Jorgenson, J. Steven Landefeld, and William D. Nordhaus (2005) have argued that gross domestic *income* should be deflated so as to reflect these real input services. That is, labor income would be deflated by the change in compensation for a given quality of labor services, averaged over the various types of labor in the economy. Similarly, capital income would be deflated to reflect the cost of capital services of various qualities. Under their proposal, *nominal* income and expenditure would remain equal, but *real income*, deflated by input prices, and *real expenditure*, deflated by output prices, would grow at different rates, with the difference being the growth of total factor productivity. The growth rate of quality-adjusted labor depends on demographics and on measures of human capital production and accumulation that are not yet in the national accounts.

A BRIEF HISTORY OF THE DEVELOPMENT OF THE NATIONAL INCOME ACCOUNTS

The first estimates of national income were made in England by the politician and economist Sir William Petty (1623–1687) in the seventeenth century. Petty, whose aim was tax reform, estimated total expenditure as 40 million British pounds. He estimated capital income as 15 million pounds, obtaining labor income as a residual 25 million pounds. Towards the end of that century, Gregory King (1648–1712) made more systematic estimates for the income, saving, and expense of England for the year 1688. In the late seventeenth and early eighteenth century, the French economist Pierre de Boisguillebert (1646–1714), also a tax reformer, developed crude estimates of income and consumption in France, followed by more careful estimates by Sébastien Le Prestre de Vauban (1633–1707), a military engineer and advisor to the king, in 1707.

These early isolated estimates were based on comprehensive notions of production and output without the benefit of formal economic theorizing. As economic theory emerged, it unfortunately advocated overly limited estimates. The French physiocrats believed that only land produced net output over and above costs, which influenced the chemist Antoine-Laurent Lavoisier's (1743–1794) estimates of France's income in the late eighteenth century, made while a commissioner of the public treasury. The classical economists, beginning with Adam Smith (1723–1790) and continuing through Karl Marx (1818–1883), distinguished the potential for labor to produce material wealth and thus emphasized the production of goods as opposed to services. National income estimates in much of the nineteenth century placed their main reliance on commodity production data, which also dominated the material product accounting of the Soviet-bloc countries in the twentieth century.

In 1921 it was possible to count nine countries that had comprehensive national income estimates for the year 1914, almost all prepared by scholars rather than government officials; of these only four could be judged to be within a probable error of 10 percent. Since that was the year World War I (1914–1918) broke out, governments often did not know their economic ability to mobilize for total war.

Official Estimates National income estimates, it became clear, were useful in anticipating the potential for income taxation and for estimating the potential for national defense production in times of war. The interwar depression offered new reasons for national income estimation: gauging the course of the economic crisis and measuring the relative "pump-priming" impact of government expenditure.

Beginning in 1925 in Canada and Russia, national governments began to support ongoing production of official estimates of national income. Simon Kuznets, whose article on "National Income" in the 1933 edition of the *Encyclopedia of the Social Sciences* set forth a highly influential conceptual framework and justification for national income accounting, inaugurated the U.S. official annual estimates in 1934 with the publication of *National Income, 1929–1932*. This publication included not only careful definitions of the concepts used but also line-by-line derivations of the text tables, with sources and methods.

The publication of *General Theory of Employment, Interest, and Money* (1936) by the British economist John Maynard Keynes (1883–1946), which emphasized the relationships among consumption, investment, and employment, added further impetus to the development of national income statistics, particularly given Keynes's active role in government. In England, Colin Clark's (1905–1989) *National Income and Outlay* (1937) laid the statistical foundations for the modern manifold accounting framework by bringing together estimates of income, output, consumption, government revenue and expenditure, capital formation, saving, foreign trade, and the balance of payments. By 1939 official estimates were prepared in nine countries. Richard Stone in the 1940s put together the integrated system of accounts much as we have them today.

THE CIRCULAR FLOW OF ECONOMIC ACTIVITY AND THE LOGIC OF THE SNA

This entry will now explore the underlying logic that Stone brought to bear in constructing the SNA, beginning from the long-recognized fact that monetized economic activity is essentially both circular and two-sided, as illustrated in the highly simplified economy depicted in Figure 1.

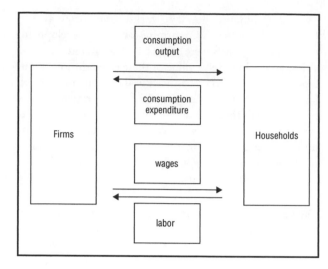

Figure 1. The circular flow of economic activity, as adapted from Hulten (2005).

The Circular Flow Once monetized, economic activity is necessarily circular. Households, in their role as employees, supply labor to firms who demand it, and receive wages. Firms use labor to supply consumption goods and services, which households buy using their wages.

Two-sided Flow The fact that each transaction has two equal sides—a purchase and a sale—is a fundamental source of the interlocking character of the national accounts. Wages appear as an *expense* of firms and as an *income* of households. Consumption expenditures are an income of *firms* and an expense of *households*.

Were there no other economic actors or activities, we would have the simple accounts in Table 1. Because entries appear twice in the table, each set of accounts appears as a check on the other. Each of these tables matches *resources* (also called income or supply) and *uses* (also called expenses).

Now let us add capital to the firm's accounting framework, arriving at Tables 2a and 2b, still highly simplified. The production of investment goods takes its place alongside consumption goods in firm resources. The portion of investment goods used up in production, that is, capital consumption, appears as a use. The expenditure on investment is instead an immediate contribution to capital and appears in the change-of-capital account. Given these definitions, the firm's resources and uses table is balanced by *operating surplus*.

The change-of-capital account resources are firm income (called *operating surplus* or, in the corporate account, retained earnings after deducting payouts to shareholders) and capital consumption, and the *use* is capital investment. Capital investment may not equal

Firm income and expense

Firm	Uses	Resources
	Employee compensation	Consumption expenditure

Table 1a.

Household income and expense table

Household	Uses	Resources
	Consumption expenditure	Employee compensation

Table 1b.

Firm income and expenses	Uses	Resources
	Employee compensation	Revenues
	Capital consumption	
	Corporate income taxes	
Balancing item	Operating surplus	

Table 2a.

Change-of-Capital account	Uses	Resources
	Gross capital investment	Operating surplus
		Capital consumption
Balancing item	Net lending (or *less* net borrowing)	

Table 2b.

internal funds, and the item *balancing* the account is net lending or borrowing. The change-of-capital account links to the capital stock account because gross investment less capital consumption equals the increase in capital stock. Net borrowing or lending similarly equals the change in net financial assets. (Both these statements hold in principle rather than fully in practice, due to revaluations of assets.)

The national income accounts track all these transactions, not only for domestic firms and households, but also for governments, nonprofit institutions, and the rest of the world (foreigners as they interact with nationals through trade, investment, or transfers, such as foreign aid). Taxes and transfers, transportation costs, interest and

dividend payments, and a host of the messy details of actual economies must be carefully inserted and measured. Each of these five groups of transactors has a current income and expense account (labeled *resources* and *uses* in the SNA), change-of-capital accounts, capital stocks, and financial assets and liabilities. This entry will not cover all these details, but their flavor can be discerned from the following account of gross domestic product.

THE FORMAL CONSTRUCTION OF GROSS DOMESTIC PRODUCT

The SNA begins from the broader concepts of *total supply* and *uses* of goods and services in the economy. Total supply can be produced domestically (domestic output) or purchased from abroad (imports). Domestic output, in turn, includes both *final products* and *intermediate products* that are consumed in production, such as flour baked into bread. Uses include intermediate consumption (equal to intermediate production), final consumption, gross capital investment, and exports. The two sides of the accounts form an equation: Supply (total output plus imports) equals uses (intermediate consumption plus final consumption plus gross capital investment plus exports). Included in final consumption are expenditures of governments and nonprofits on behalf of households.

Total supply is a consistent, measurable aggregate of economic activity, but it is not as good a measure of domestic economic activity because it includes imports (produced by foreigners) and because it counts activities that are early in the supply chain more than once. Subtracting imports and intermediate consumption from both sides, we arrive at gross domestic product as defined from the product side.

Nominal gross domestic product (Table 3) is defined as the market value of all *final* goods and services produced within a country in a given period of time (typically a year or a quarter year) measured in units of currency. From the expenditure side, as we have just shown, this includes consumption, investment, net exports (exports less imports), and government expenditures. Real gross domestic product is this quantity made comparable over time by adjusting for inflation.

THREE APPROACHES TO CONSTRUCTING GROSS DOMESTIC PRODUCT

Gross domestic product can be measured from three aspects: by expenditure on final product, by industrial origin, and by income. Under good statistical practice, the three sides are measured in large part independently and the closeness of the independent estimates forms a measure of the size of statistical errors and omissions.

Three measures of gross domestic product

1. Output	*defined as*		
	Output of all units gross of intermediate production		
Less	*defined as*		
2. Intermediates	Materials and services consumed during production		
Equals	*defined as*	*also equal to:*	*and equal to:*
3. Gross Domestic Product	4. Expenditure on final product equals sum of:	5. Output by industrial origin equals sum of:	6. Gross domestic income equals sum of:
	4a. Private Consumption plus	5a. Gross value added by industry plus	6a. Compensation of employees
	4b. Government expenditure plus	5b. Net taxes on product	6b. Taxes, less subsidies, on production and imports plus
	4c. Gross Investment plus		6d. Operating surplus and mixed income, gross
	4d. Net exports		

Table 3.

Expenditures on Final Products To obtain estimates of final products, government statisticians survey firms that sell final products: retailers, service providers such as hotels, equipment manufacturers, and construction companies. Government expenditures are obtained from governmental budget statistics and net exports from customs data.

Industrial Origin The contribution of an industry to gross domestic product is its gross value added, that is, the industry's output less purchases of products and services from other industries (Table 3, column 3). These data are typically obtained from establishments, defined as units that produce output at a given location (a farm, a factory, a store) rather than firms, the legal entities that control establishments, which supply income data.

Input-output tables that show which industry supplies inputs to each industry enable analysts to calculate the ultimate resources—raw materials, labor, and capital—required in each industry's final products. Such tables, developed by the 1973 Nobel laureate Wassily Leontief (1906–1999), a Russian-born American economist, permit the forecasting of the impacts of large fiscal projects on the nation's and the world's resources.

The revenues of establishments do not include taxes applied to the product. A consumer might spend 10 euros, but if sales tax is 5 percent, the store's revenues are only 9.50 euros. Thus when output is measured as *industry gross value added at basic prices*, the government's share, *taxes less subsidies on products*, must be also added in.

For a complex, industrial society, measuring industry value added is harder than measuring expenditures on final products because it requires data on intermediate inputs as well as revenue, and on all establishments, not just those selling final products. On the other hand, this estimate is not dependent on the accuracy of foreign trade statistics. And in developing countries where agriculture remains a large part of the economy, farm surveys are a means of measuring output with reasonable accuracy. In such countries, wholesale prices (called *basic* prices) may be used to evaluate this output.

Income When we turn to measuring income, we can no longer ignore the possibility that foreigners may own part or all of firms located domestically, or may have lent money to nationals. *Domestic product* measures output from activities located within the borders of a nation, regardless of whether the income accrues to nationals or foreigners. Gross *national* income measures the income of nationals, and must be adjusted for income earned abroad on foreign investment, less income foreigners earn domestically (Table 3, column 4). Converting to this basis permits us to calculate domestic income and saving.

In principle, the national accounts make a sharp distinction between firm capital income and household employment income, but in practice, such business units as sole proprietorships and partnerships mix employment and capital income, and are called *mixed income*. The precise treatment of this boundary necessarily varies from country to country.

Although households, nonprofits, and governments are clearly domestic, there are many income transfers among them, and with foreign entities. These include social welfare, education, medicine, and foreign aid. Determining exactly where to place such payments is to a certain extent arbitrary. The SNA includes a secondary income account to accommodate most of these transfers.

Included in the income account, for example, are government expenditures on behalf of consumers, which become final consumption of households in the secondary account.

The data obtained from tax filings on individuals and businesses are natural sources for estimates of income. These data are available with some lag, so they are supplemented by employment surveys, corporate reports, and sales data. Moreover, taxed income may be underreported. For example, in the United States, the bulk of proprietors and partnership income is estimated to go unreported in tax records.

Reconciliation There are inevitably discrepancies between the three measures of gross domestic product arising from their separate sources of data. Some countries, such as the United Kingdom, produce a final measure by averaging the three. Others, such as the United States, anoint one side of the accounts as being likely the most accurate (final product), and show a statistical discrepancy in the others.

National income accountants often produce tables that provide the details of how they transform the underlying data (say, corporate reports) in preparing their national income counterparts. These sectoral reconciliation tables help analysts understand the precise meaning of the national income statistics, and also can help in forecasting tax reports or corporate earnings reports.

Accuracy, Timeliness, and Revisions National income account statistics are revised as new data become available, and as new theory and empirical analysis improve our understanding of how to measure economic activity.

Initial official estimates of a given quarter's economic activity in advanced economies are made available within a few weeks of the quarter's end, when economic reports for the quarter are incomplete. National accountants generally prepare one or two revisions in the months immediately following, then annual revisions as tax statistics become available, and *benchmark* multiyear revisions when economic census or other occasional data become available. It is usually during benchmark revisions that new concepts and different methods are incorporated.

Because economic decisions are taken in the light of available statistics, some economic theories need to be tested in the light of national income statistics as they appeared when the decisions were taken. In the wake of work by Dean Croushore and Tom Stark (2001), the collection of *real-time* data—the preservation of economic statistics as they appeared at different dates, referred to as *vintages* of data—has become a responsibility accepted by some national income accountants.

CAPITAL AND FINANCIAL ACCOUNTS

This entry will not discuss the many complexities of capital and financial accounts, beyond a few important limitations to their measures.

In principle, net investment in domestic assets should equal the increase in domestic wealth. However, these book values of assets may differ widely from their market values. National income accountants have agreed not to include capital gains on assets—for example, increases in market value of corporations that are not reflected in retained earnings—as part of income. Doing so would make income highly volatile, and would largely separate movements in income from movements in economic activity. Excluding capital gains creates difficulties in measuring the output of financial institutions. Changes in capital gains are reflected in the financial asset accounts as changes in assets, but are not otherwise linked to the accounts.

Capital assets in the national accounts are divided into produced and nonproduced assets. In particular, land and mineral rights are considered nonproduced assets that do not change over time in real terms. Statistically, real additions to residential land have been small; in the United States they have been estimated to be less than 1 percent of GDP annually. Mineral depletion is not deducted from net domestic product.

CRITIQUES AND SATELLITE ACCOUNTS

The large gap between ideal national income accounts and actual income accounts has been partially filled by scholarly studies that fashion alternative measures, and by satellite accounts prepared by national accountants but considered too inaccurate, too controversial, or insufficiently important to be included in the standard accounts. The literature here is too vast to be cited, but the pioneering work of American economist Gary Becker, the 1992 Nobel laureate, must be acknowledged.

Household Production Accounts A longstanding concern about the valuation of the national income accounts is the productive activity that occurs within the household. To fill this void, nations are increasingly engaging in surveys of household time use, in which individuals diarize a day in five- to fifteen-minute intervals. By adding how the diarists feel during these activities, worklike activity might be differentiated from leisure activity.

Worklike activities can be priced either by opportunity cost (the wage the individual is foregoing) or by replacement cost (the cost to hire someone else to do the activity or to buy the output). Diaries also supply a measure of study time (to measure the creation of human capital).

Human Capital Accounts What are our investments in labor quality? In the national accounts, the costs of private and public education are considered household- and government-consumption expenditures, respectively. An unrecorded input is the time cost of the student or the worker. Reclassifying education as investment would involve both a reclassification of consumption items as investment and an addition to output due to inclusion of student work time and on-the-job training.

Health Accounts Health is produced through a combination of household production, environmental impacts, and medical production. One such quantification is quality-of-life years, where the average effect on the quality of life of a given disease is measured either based on capability or subjective reports.

Relative to labor, health can be linked to human capital, evaluating the cost of disease as a diminution of human capital. Or, more directly, health may be evaluated when law courts value loss of life or pain and suffering in civil trials.

Environmental Accounts Economists have long been aware that economic activity can have externalities, byproducts—either desirable or undesirable—that affect other economic agents. Economic impacts may be quantifiable, for example, as costs incurred, when one firm's pollution raises the cost of another firm's activity or reduces the value of another firm's land. Or a price may be placed on the type of pollution either directly via a tax (an SO_2 tax) or through a market in which polluters must buy the right to pollute a certain amount (SO_2 rights). More broadly, environmental satellite accounts can include the land, mineral rights, biota, and so forth.

Distribution The distribution of consumption and income is part of the economic welfare of a nation. Some of this difference may be due to economic choices, reflecting differing preferences and talents. Yet most observers believe that for a given level of average per capita income, a more even distribution of incomes is preferable to a less even one.

In principle, it is possible to estimate how much consumers are willing to pay to avoid declines in wealth, and therefore to provide a direct measure of consumer valuation of income distributions. This is an active and controversial area of research. As Kuznets suggested, it would be desirable at a minimum for national income accounts to include estimates of income distribution to aid in evaluating economic welfare.

SEE ALSO *Gross Domestic Product; Gross National Income*

BIBLIOGRAPHY

Becker, Gary S. 1993. *Human Capital: A Theoretical and Empirical Analysis, with Special Reference to Education*, 3rd ed. Chicago: University of Chicago Press.

Clark, Colin. 1937. *National Income and Outlay*. London: Macmillan.

Croushore, Dean, and Tom Stark. 2001. A Real-Time Data Set for Macroeconomists. *Journal of Econometrics* 105: 111–130.

Hulten, Charles R. 2005. The "Architecture" of Capital Accounting: Basic Design Principles. In *A New Architecture for the U.S. National Accounts*, eds. Dale W. Jorgenson, J. Steven Landefeld, and William D. Nordhaus. Chicago: University of Chicago Press.

Jorgenson, Dale W., J. Steven Landefeld, and William D. Nordhaus, eds. 2005. *A New Architecture for the U.S. National Accounts*. Chicago: University of Chicago Press.

Keynes, John Maynard. 1936. *The General Theory of Employment, Interest, and Money*. London: Macmillan.

King, Gregory. [1696] 1936. *Two Tracts*. Ed. George E. Barnett. Baltimore, MD: Johns Hopkins University Press.

Kuznets, Simon A. 1933. National Income. In *Encyclopedia of the Social Sciences*. New York: Macmillan. Reprinted in *Readings in the Theory of Income Distribution*. 1946. Eds. William Fellner and Bernard F. Haley, 3-43. Philadelphia and Toronto, Ontario: Blakiston.

Maddison, Angus. 1995. *Monitoring the World Economy, 1820-1992*. Paris: Development Centre of the Organization for Economic Co-operation and Development.

Petty, William. 1899. *The Economic Writings of Sir William Petty*. Ed. Charles Hull. Cambridge, U.K.: Cambridge University Press.

Pigou, A. C. 1932. *The Economics of Welfare*, 4th ed. London: Macmillan.

Solow, Robert M. 1957. Technical Change and the Aggregate Production Function. *Review of Economics and Statistics* 39: 312–320.

Stone, Richard A. 1986. Nobel Lecture: The Accounts of Society. *Journal of Applied Econometrics* 1: 5–28. http://nobelprize.org/economics/laureates/1984/stone-lecture.html.

United Kingdom Office for National Statistics. National Statistics Online. http://www.statistics.gov.uk/.

United Kingdom Office for National Statistics. 1998. *United Kingdom National Accounts Concepts, Sources, and Methods*. London: Stationery Office. http://www.statistics.gov.uk/downloads/theme_economy/Concepts_Sources_&_Methods.pdf.

United Nations Department of Economic and Social Affairs, Statistics Division, National Accounts Section. http://unstats.un.org/unsd/nationalaccount/nadefault.htm.

United Nations Department of Economic and Social Affairs, Statistics Division, National Accounts Section. 1993. *1993 System of National Accounts*. http://unstats.un.org/unsd/sna1993/introduction.asp.

United Nations Department of Economic and Social Affairs, Statistics Division, National Accounts Section. 2004. *National Accounts: A Practical Introduction*. New York: United

Nations. http://unstats.un.org/unsd/publication/SeriesF/seriesF_85.pdf.

United States Bureau of Foreign and Domestic Commerce. 1934. *National Income, 1929–1932: Letter from the Acting Secretary of Commerce Transmitting in Response to Senate Resolution No. 220 (72nd Cong.) a Report on National Income, 1929–32.* Washington, DC: U.S. Government Printing Office.

United States Department of Commerce. Bureau of Economic Analysis. http://www.bea.gov/.

Leonard Nakamura

The views expressed here are those of the author and do not necessarily reflect those of the Federal Reserve Bank of Philadelphia or of the Federal Reserve System.

NATIONAL INSTITUTES OF MENTAL HEALTH
SEE *Ginzberg, Eli.*

NATIONAL LABOR RELATIONS ACT
SEE *Labor Law.*

NATIONAL LABOR RELATIONS BOARD
SEE *Labor Law.*

NATIONAL LIBERATION MOVEMENTS
SEE *Liberation Movements.*

NATIONAL LONGITUDINAL STUDY OF ADOLESCENT HEALTH

The National Longitudinal Study of Adolescent Health (Add Health) is an ongoing study of a nationally representative sample of more than 20,000 individuals that began with in-school questionnaires administered to adolescents in grades seven to twelve in the United States in 1994 and 1995. The in-school survey was followed by three waves of in-home interviews in 1995, 1996, and 2001–2002, with a fourth wave planned for 2007–2008 when the sample will be aged twenty-four to thirty-two.

Add Health was developed in response to a mandate from the U.S. Congress to fund a study of adolescent health and was designed by a nationwide team of multidisciplinary investigators from the social, behavioral, and health sciences. The original purpose of Add Health was to understand adolescent health and health-related behavior with special emphasis on the forces that reside in the multiple contexts of adolescent life. Toward that goal, innovative features of the research design provided independent measurements of the social environments of adolescents, including contextual data on the family, neighborhood, community, school, friendships, peer groups, and romantic relationships.

The Add Health cohort has been followed over time as research questions turned to how adolescent experiences and behaviors were related to social, behavioral, and health outcomes in early adulthood. Across all interview waves, comprehensive data on health and health-related behavior were collected, including diet, physical activity, health service use, morbidity, injury, violence, sexual behavior, contraception, sexually transmitted infections, pregnancy and childbearing, suicidal intentions and thoughts, substance use and abuse, and delinquency. Data were also collected on such attributes as height, weight, pubertal development, mental health status, and chronic and disabling conditions. Achievement and academic progress were updated in each wave, including school performance, school problems, relationships with students and teachers, self-esteem, self-confidence, and future expectations for education, health, and family formation.

STUDY DESIGN AND DATA

Add Health used a school-based design in which a stratified sample of eighty high schools was selected from a sampling frame of all high schools in the United States. Schools were stratified by region, urbanicity, school type, ethnic mix, and size. For each high school selected, a feeder school was identified and recruited with probability proportional to its student contribution to the high school, yielding one school pair in each of eighty different communities. Overall, 79 percent of the schools contacted agreed to participate in the study.

During the 1994–1995 school year, in-school questionnaires were administered to over 90,000 students in selected schools. The in-school questionnaire provided measurement on the school context, friendship networks, school activities, future expectations, and a variety of health conditions. An additional purpose of the in-school questionnaire was to identify and select special supplementary samples of individuals in rare but theoretically crucial categories. School administrators also completed a questionnaire in the first and second waves of the study.

In a second stage of sampling using the school rosters of selected schools, adolescents and their parents were selected for in-home interviews constituting the Wave I (WI) in-home sample. To form a core sample, students were stratified in each school by grade and sex, and approximately 200 adolescents were sampled from each pair of schools. From answers provided on the in-school survey, supplemental samples were drawn based on ethnicity (Cuban, Chinese, and Puerto Rican adolescents), genetic relatedness to siblings (twins, full sibs, half sibs, and unrelated adolescents living in the same household), adoption status, and disability. Add Health also oversampled African American adolescents with highly educated parents. Finally, a special "saturated" sample was included in WI by selecting all enrolled students from two large schools and fourteen small schools for in-home interviews. Complete social network data were collected in the saturated field settings by generating a large number of romantic and friendship pairs for which both members of the pair have in-home interviews. The core sample plus the special samples produced a sample size of 20,745 adolescents in WI. The WI in-home sample is the basis for all subsequent longitudinal follow-up interviews. A parent also completed an interviewer-assisted interview at WI. Over 85 percent of the parents completed the parental interview.

In 1996 all adolescents in grades seven through eleven in WI (plus twelfth graders who were part of the genetic sample and the adopted sample) were followed up one year later for the Wave II (WII) in-home interview (N=14,738). Response rates for the in-home interviews are 79 percent for WI and 88 percent at WII.

The in-school and Waves I and II in-home interviews constitute the adolescent period in Add Health and contain unique data about family context, school context, peer networks, spatial networks, community context, and genetic pairs. School context data come from the in-school surveys based on the census of students in each school, as well as from school administrator questionnaires. Peer network data are obtained from the in-school questionnaire where adolescents nominated their five best male and five best female friends from the school roster such that links to friends' survey responses can be made. Spatial data indicating the exact location of all households were collected using Global Positioning System (GPS) devices, and used to merge with extant data describing the neighborhood and community contexts in which adolescents are embedded. Finally, the "genetic pairs data," based on more than 3,000 pairs of adolescents who have varying degrees of genetic relatedness, represent a fully articulated behavioral genetic design and are unprecedented for a national study of this magnitude.

At Wave III (WIII), all original WI in-home adolescent respondents were reinterviewed from 2001 to 2002 with a response rate of 77 percent. This interview captured the Add Health cohort during their transition to adulthood when they were aged eighteen to twenty-six. In WIII, quota samples of 500 partners each in married, cohabiting, and dating couples were recruited by Add Health respondents, resulting in the partner sample of 1,507. Spatial data were again attached to the WIII individual-level data using the geocodes of the home residence. New data on family formation, college attendance and context, mentoring, and civic participation were collected at WIII. Also new at WIII was the collection of several biospecimens. Urine and saliva were collected to test for STDs and HIV, and buccal cell DNA was collected from the twins and full siblings in the genetic sample. The Web site supported by the Carolina Population Center of the University of North Carolina provides information about Add Health's design and data availability.

Add Health has been funded over the period 1994–2010 by the National Institutes of Child Health and Human Development (P01 HD031921), with co-funding from seventeen other federal agencies. Add Health has an enlightened dissemination policy in that the scientific community is given access to the data at the same time as are project investigators. As a result, Add Health has become a national data resource for over 3,000 Add Health researchers who have obtained more than 200 independently funded research grants and have produced hundreds of research articles published in multidisciplinary journals and research outlets.

ADD HEALTH RESEARCH

Add Health research has exploited its unique design to explore the role of social contexts in the lives of adolescents, including the importance of family, peer, school, and neighborhood context as factors influencing adolescent development, behavior, health and well-being, and outcomes in the transition to adulthood. Ground-breaking research is identifying the social contexts that facilitate genetic expression in health behaviors, including substance use, sexual behavior, and delinquency and violence. Add Health has also made possible important new research on the health status and health behaviors of special populations such as disabled youth, adopted youth, youth living with surrogate parents or relatives, multiracial youth, youth with same-sex romantic attractions or relationships, and adolescents in immigrant families.

Add Health has also been an ideal data set for conducting health disparities research. Large and persistent racial, ethnic, and socioeconomic disparities in health exist across the life course in the United States. The reduction and ultimate elimination of health disparities has been identified as a major public health goal, exemplified by *Healthy People 2010*, the nation's promotion and disease prevention strategy for the first decade of the twenty-first century. Add Health tracks longitudinal trends in race and ethnic disparities in the leading health indicators from *Healthy People 2010* across multiple domains from adolescence to young adulthood. The interdisciplinary design of Add Health has resulted in a multidisciplinary user base of researchers in sociology, economics, human development, public health, biomedical sciences, and related fields who are exploring social, behavioral, and biological factors in developmental and health trajectories from adolescence into young adulthood.

LIMITATIONS OF ADD HEALTH

The school-based design of Add Health misses high school dropouts in the initial in-school survey, although dropouts after this point are followed in all subsequent interviews. Research from 2003 by J. R. Udry and Kim Chantala, examining the impact of this potential bias of missing high school dropouts, reports minimal impact. In addition, because Add Health is an omnibus study, many standard sociometric scales for various measures are included in shortened forms. Thus, although the breadth of topics covered in the Add Health instruments is comprehensive, the depth may not be present for all topics.

SEE ALSO *National Family Health Surveys; National Longitudinal Survey of Youth; Panel Study of Income Dynamics; Sample Attrition; Sampling; Survey; Surveys, Sample*

BIBLIOGRAPHY

Add Health. The National Longitudinal Study of Adolescent Health. University of North Carolina, Carolina Population Center. http://www.cpc.unc.edu/addhealth.

Udry, J. R., and Kim Chantala. 2003. Missing School Dropouts in Surveys Does Not Bias Risk Estimates. *Social Science Research* 32 (2): 294–311.

Kathleen Mullan Harris
Hedwig Lee

NATIONAL LONGITUDINAL SURVEY OF YOUTH

The National Longitudinal Survey of Youth (NLSY) is a set of panel surveys in which the same respondents are interviewed periodically about various aspects of their life experiences. Sponsored and largely funded by the U.S. Bureau of Labor Statistics, the NLSY data do not primarily contribute to official government statistics; instead the microdata are available to researchers for basic research on the life course. By 2006 the bibliography of publications from these data included over four thousand items on topics such as transition from school to work, job mobility, youth unemployment, educational attainment and the returns to education, welfare recipiency, the impact of training, and retirement decisions. The Center for Human Resource Research at Ohio State University carries out much of the content planning, and the National Opinion Research Center at the University of Chicago carries out the interviewing, either in person or by telephone.

The precursors of the NLSY are two cohorts of the National Longitudinal Survey of Labor Market Experience (NLS), 5,000 each in the Young Men cohort, aged fourteen to twenty-four in 1966, and the Young Women, aged fourteen to twenty-four in 1968. The young men were interviewed biennially until 1981; the young women continue to be interviewed as of 2006.

Interviewing of a new cohort comprising a 12,686-member probability sample of the age-specific U.S. population of young men and young women aged fourteen to twenty-two started in 1979 with broadly expanded survey instruments. Interviews with the NLSY79 cohort were annual through 1994 and biennial thereafter. This sample originally included military members (dropped in 1985) and an oversample of disadvantaged youths (dropped in 1991). So the eligible sample after 1991 consisted of just fewer than 10,000 respondents. The twenty-second round of interviewing took place in 2006. Interviewing of a further cohort of 8,984 young men and young women aged twelve to sixteen at the time started in 1997 and continues biennially as NLSY97.

All children born to the women in NLSY79 become members of the cohort called Children of the NLSY79, from which data have been collected biennially since 1986; as these children reach age fifteen they graduate into a separate young adult sample, begun in 1994 and also fielded biennially. The child sample and the young adult sample do not represent probability samples of their age groups in the United States, as children born to women who immigrated after 1979 and children born to women not in the age cohort fourteen to twenty-two in 1979 are excluded from the sampling frame; but they do represent a sample of all children born to women in the age cohort.

Data (without identifiers) are available as public use files, either for analysis online or for downloading, at the Web site supported by the Bureau of Labor Statistics. NLSY questions concentrate on labor force behavior but also ask about education and training, income and assets, health conditions, alcohol and substance abuse, and marital and fertility histories. There are also linked data of scores on the Armed Services Vocational Aptitude Battery, which includes measures of cognitive development. Also linked are data on the secondary schools attended by respondents. In the child sample, mothers are asked about pregnancy and prenatal care; children are given cognitive assessments at ages four and fourteen and are interviewed about family life between ages ten and fourteen. Members of the young adult sample are administered interviews similar to the NLSY79 interview itself.

Because of the longitudinal nature of the data, analyses are possible on a wide variety of topics in economics, sociology, and other areas. For example, one can trace not only entrances into and exits from the labor force, but also marital history, family formation, and the impact of such changes on labor force participation. The cognitive test information is useful for controlling for varying inputs in investigations of individual attainment. The longitudinal nature of the data also assures that the first criterion of causality—that the putative cause be temporally prior to the putative effect—has been met, in a way that cannot be achieved in a cross-sectional survey.

As in all longitudinal data, attrition from the sample can detract from the value of the data. In the original cohorts, if a respondent missed two consecutive interviews, that person was dropped from further follow-up. Hence the sample became less representative as time went on. In the 1979 cohort, however, efforts are made to contact all respondents at each round, with some success in recovering lost respondents (a response rate of 80 percent of the living original respondents for the 2002 round [Pierret 2005]). Further, a major innovation of the 1979 and 1997 cohorts is the elicitation of life histories. Respondents not only report about their current status on such variables as employment and marital status, but also report and date any changes in these statuses since the previous interview. Thus if a respondent misses one or more biennial interviews, longitudinal data for that respondent are nevertheless available from the retrospective reports given in the life history. This further ameliorates the problem of attrition, although possibly at some cost in accuracy if respondents' memories are faulty.

SEE ALSO *National Assessment of Educational Progress; National Family Health Surveys; National Longitudinal Study of Adolescent Health; Panel Study of Income Dynamics; Research, Longitudinal; Sample Attrition; Survey; Surveys, Sample*

BIBLIOGRAPHY

National Longitudinal Surveys of Youth. Bibliography of work using NLSY data, http://www.nlsbibliography.org. Overview, Bureau of Labor Statistics, http://www.bls.gov/nls/ nlsview.htm. Detailed documentation, http://www.nlsinfo. org/web-investigator/docs.php.

Pierret, Charles. 2005. The National Longitudinal Survey of Youth: 1979 Cohort at 25. *Monthly Labor Review* 128 (2): 3–7. http://www.bls.gov/opub/mlr/2005/02/art1exc.htm.

Judith M. Tanur

NATIONAL ORGANIZATION FOR WOMEN

Founded in 1966, the National Organization for Women (NOW) has approximately 500,000 contributing members and roughly 550 chapters across the United States. NOW maintains a diverse policy agenda and tactical repertoire. It has employed legal, legislative lobbying, electoral, and protest tactics, leading campaigns not only for the legal equality of women and for the equal rights amendment but also against sexual harassment, for the maintenance of women's access to abortion clinics and against clinic violence, against domestic violence and rape, and for poor women's rights.

Many individuals contributed to the organization's founding, including activists in the union movement and the civil rights movement as well as men and women working within the federal bureaucracy. They shared a common concern that the newly created Equal Employment Opportunity Commission (EEOC) was refusing to enforce Title VII of the Civil Rights Act of 1964, which prohibited discrimination against women in the workplace. Women's rights advocates like Richard Graham and Aileen Hernandez, both EEOC commissioners, sought a spokesperson to lead an organization similar to the NAACP, an advocacy organization for African Americans, that would be dedicated to women's equality issues.

Betty Friedan was one individual recruited to take on this role. A freelance writer who often wrote on women's and labor issues, Friedan had gained significant media attention as a result of *The Feminine Mystique*, published in 1963. NOW was formed after members of the National Conference of the Commission on the Status of Women (and Friedan, who attended with a press pass) attended a frustrating annual meeting in 1966 where attendees were stymied in their attempts to pass resolutions demanding changes at the EEOC. Twenty-eight women and men constituted the original founders, and Friedan became NOW's first president. She and Pauli Murray wrote the organization's original statement of purpose, which said in part that the purpose of NOW was "to take action to bring women into full participation in the mainstream of American society now, exercising all the privileges and responsibilities thereof in truly equal partnership with men" (Carabillo, Meuli, and Bundy Csida 1993, p. 47). From NOW's inception its leaders were determined that the organization would operate independently from established political institutions, such as political parties, which they believed had paid only lip service to women's equality. They also insisted that the group must be an activist rather than an educational organization. Organizationally speaking, NOW is among the most democratic of progressive social organizations. All members are eligible to become voting delegates to vote for national board members and officers at national conventions and to vote on resolutions pertaining to NOW's goals and strategies.

NOW's earliest actions centered on pressuring the EEOC to uphold Title VII. Drawing largely on the resources and talents of the organization's founders, NOW initially focused on attracting media attention and on lobbying executive agencies and legislators on this issue. Soon, however, the group's members (now including members of the women's liberation movement) and some leaders argued that these tactics—long used by organizations like the NAACP—had failed to produce results. Consequently over the course of its founding period (1966–1971), NOW began to incorporate mass mobilization and protest activities into its tactical repertoire along with legislative lobbying, the campaign to ratify the equal rights amendment, and electoral activism. NOW also began to focus on broader goals, including abortion rights and lesbian rights.

The campaign to ratify the equal rights amendment (ERA) is one of NOW's best-known endeavors. NOW's leaders were not immediately successful in convincing members to participate in this challenge, however, and as a result the organization did not focus intently on the measure until 1978. The ERA was not ratified by its 1982 deadline, falling short by only three states. The campaign nevertheless proved a potent mobilizing force, swelling NOW's ranks to over 200,000 members and exposing members and leaders to multiple tactics, including lobbying, protest, state-level politics, electoral politics, mobilization, and fund-raising, that for many were their first experience in politics.

Among the longest-serving of NOW's presidents is Eleanor Smeal, who was elected three times and presided from 1977 to 1982 and from 1985 to 1987. Smeal led the organization during the latter stages of the equal rights amendment campaign and spearheaded NOW's increased investment in electoral politics, coining the term *gender gap*. She founded the Feminist Majority Foundation in 1987. Patricia Ireland led NOW for ten years (1991–2001) and extended the organization's involve-

ment in elections, most notably during the 1992 Year of the Woman. She also led campaigns against sexual harassment and in 1996 worked against the revocation of welfare benefits for poor women. Ireland's priorities also included lesbian and gay rights. In 2001 Kim Gandy became president of NOW.

SEE ALSO *Friedan, Betty; Women and Politics; Women's Liberation; Women's Movement*

BIBLIOGRAPHY

Barakso, Maryann. 2004. *Governing NOW: Grassroots Activism in the National Organization for Women*. Ithaca, NY: Cornell University Press.

Carabillo, Toni, Judith Meuli, and June Bundy Csida. 1993. *Feminist Chronicles, 1953–1993*. Los Angeles: Women's Graphics.

Freeman, Jo. 1975. *The Politics of Women's Liberation: A Case Study of an Emerging Social Movement and Its Relation to the Policy Process*. New York: David McKay.

Mansbridge, Jane J. 1986. *Why We Lost the ERA*. Chicago: University of Chicago Press.

Maryann Barakso

NATIONAL SAMPLE SURVEY (INDIA)

The National Sample Survey (NSS) is one of the oldest continuing household sample surveys in the developing world. The survey is conducted on a regular basis by the National Sample Survey Organisation (NSSO), India's premier data collection agency. Since 1972, the NSSO has fallen under the Ministry of Statistics and Program Implementation of the Government of India (GOI).

The role of the NSS must be seen in the broader context of Indian economic development. At independence and through much of its early development, the country was faced with a subsistence production structure (mainly in agriculture) characterized by mass poverty and hunger. Systematic data on the extent, magnitude, and patterns of poverty, as well as on household consumption patterns and trends, were not readily available for informed policy interventions. To remedy this, the GOI launched the NSS to gather nationally representative information on household structure, consumption, and production.

The first NSS round was conducted in 1950–1951 and included information on land utilization, prices of essential commodities, and daily wages of skilled and unskilled laborers at the village level. At the household level, data was obtained on demographic characteristics as well as land ownership, cultivation, and utilization. In addition, detailed data was gathered on monthly and weekly consumption, as well as on entrepreneurial activities, from a subset of the sampled households. The first round was based on a random sample of only 1,833 villages out of a total of 560,000.

Since that first round, more than sixty NSS rounds have been conducted. Naturally, both the organization and the surveys have undergone many changes since then. At the organizational level, the technical wing of the NSSO was divested from the Indian Statistical Institute and placed under the direct control of the GOI. The field operations group was placed under the guidance of a governing council headed by an eminent academic and members drawn both from government and academia since 1970; it now functions as a full-fledged wing of the GOI.

Important changes also occurred in the surveys themselves. With increased demand for more disaggregated information, the sample size of the rounds has expanded significantly, from 1,833 villages in the first round to more than 14,000 rural villages and urban blocks in more recent rounds. With the large increase in sample size, a decision was made (beginning with the 1973–1974 round) to split the rounds into two: quinquennial (or "thick") rounds done at approximately five-year intervals on a large sample of households (about 120,000) and "thin" rounds undertaken during intervening periods on smaller samples (approximately 35 to 40 percent of the thick-round samples). The expansion of the sample size, especially for the collection of data on consumption expenditure and employment, has allowed NSS estimates to be representative at the below-state (but not district) level. The NSSO is representative at the level of regions— collections of several districts grouped together on the basis of broadly similar agro-climatic conditions. Regions are not administrative units. The NSS has delineated a total of seventy-eight regions in the country.

The coverage of the NSS varies over the different rounds. Each round always obtains information on consumption and employment; however, the rounds also cover other subjects, such as health, schooling, or disability, in the form of additional modules. Thus, for instance, the fifty-eighth round focused on disability, housing conditions, village facilities, and urban slums, while the sixtieth round covered morbidity, health care, and conditions of the elderly. Since its inception, the NSS has covered some fifty different subjects in its surveys, such as household debt and investment, literacy and culture, health, schooling, and village-level infrastructure.

Until 1998 the unit record data from the NSS was not available to the public. This restricted considerably the wider use of the surveys by researchers. Indeed, only a few studies were based on the NSS data, including the measurement of poverty and unemployment and the construction of price indices, such as those by Ahluwalia (1978), Bhattacharya et al. (1980), Jain and Tendulkar (1989, 1990), and Minhas et al. (1987, 1988). In 1998 the GOI made the NSS unit record data, retrospectively from the thirty-eighth round of 1983, available in the public domain at a modest fee. Since that time, numerous researchers have used the data to address a number of issues, such as health, nutrition, schooling, disability, small-scale industry, and food subsidies (Borah 2006; Deolalikar 2005; Gupta 2003; Subramanian and Deaton 1996). Poverty and, to a smaller extent, unemployment remain the two top issues that are explored by researchers with the NSS data (e.g., Datt 1999; Deaton and Dreze 2002; Dubey and Gangopadhyay 1998; Sen 2000; Sundaram 2001a, 2001b; Sundaram and Tendulkar 2001).

The NSS has sometimes changed its data collection methodology midstream, and this has affected the comparability of NSS estimates over time. This was particularly the case in the fifty-fifth round, when the NSS adopted a different reporting period for certain types of consumption expenditures, rendering consumption and poverty estimates from that survey noncomparable to those from earlier periods. Another weakness of the data is that, unlike some other national socioeconomic surveys (notably the National Socio-Economic Household Survey, or SUSENAS, of Indonesia), there is no fixed rotation schedule for the special-interest modules that are attached to the core consumption-employment module of the NSS. As a result, it is difficult to obtain nationally representative data on important topics such as health and education on a regular, ongoing basis. For instance, the NSS included a health-care module in the fifty-second round conducted in 1995–1996, but this was not repeated until the sixtieth round in 2004. Likewise, the topic of rural assets and indebtedness was covered in the forty-eighth round in 1992 and only revisited in 2003 in the fifty-ninth round. It would be helpful if a regular rotation schedule were established whereby important topics such as health, schooling, and assets could be covered every three or four years.

SEE ALSO *National Family Health Surveys; National Longitudinal Survey of Youth; Panel Study of Income Dynamics*

BIBLIOGRAPHY

Ahluwalia, Montek S. 1978. Rural Poverty and Agricultural Performance in India. *Journal of Development Studies* 14 (3): 298–323.

Bardhan, Pranab K. 1974. The Pattern of Income Distribution in India: A Review. *Sankhya* C-36 (2): 103–138.

Bhattacharya, N., P.D. Joshi, and A.B. Roychoudhury. 1980. Regional Price Indices Based on NSS 25th Round Consumer Expenditure Data. *Sarvekshana* 3 (4): 107–121.

Borah, Bijan J. 2006. A Mixed Logit Model of Health Care Provider Choice: Analysis of NSS Data for Rural India. *Health Economics* 15 (9): 915–932.

Datt, Gaurav. 1999. Has Poverty Declined since Economic Reforms? *Economic and Political Weekly*, 34 (50): 3516–3518.

Deaton, Angus, and Jean Dreze. 2002. Poverty and Inequality in India: A Reexamination, *Economic and Political Weekly*, September 7: 3729–3748.

Deolalikar, Anil B. 2005. *Attaining the Millennium Development Goals in India: Reducing Infant Mortality, Child Malnutrition, Gender Disparities and Hunger-Poverty and Increasing School Enrollment and Completion?* New Delhi: Oxford University Press.

Dubey, Amaresh, and S. Gangopadhyay. 1998. *Counting the Poor: Where Are the Poor in India? Sarvekshana* Analytical Report No. 1. New Delhi, India: Ministry of Statistics and Program Implementation, National Sample Survey Organisation.

Government of India. 1952. *General Report No. 1 on First Round: October 1950–March 1951.* New Delhi, India: Ministry of Finance, Department of Economic Affairs.

Government of India. 1980. *Report of the Task Force on Projections of Minimum Needs and Effective Consumption Demand.* New Delhi, India: Planning Commission, Perspective Planning Division.

Government of India. 1993. *Report of the Expert Group on Estimation of Proportion and Number of Poor.* New Delhi, India: Planning Commission, Perspective Planning Division.

Government of India. 1994. *NSSO, 50th Round: Note on Sample Design and Estimation Procedure.* Kolkata, India: Ministry of Statistics and Program Implementation, Survey Design and Research Division.

Government of India. 2000. *National Sample Survey: Fifty Years in the Service of the Nation (1950–2000).* New Delhi, India: Ministry of Statistics and Program Implementation, National Sample Survey Organisation.

Gupta, Indrani. 2003. Inequities in Health and Health Care in India: Can the Poor Hope for a Respite? Mimeo. New Delhi, India: Institute of Economic Growth.

Jain, L. R., and Suresh D. Tendulkar. 1989. Intertemporal and Interfractile-Group Movements in Real Levels of Living for Rural and Urban Population of India: 1970–1971 to 1983. *Journal of Indian School of Political Economy* 1: 313–334.

Jain, L. R., and Suresh D. Tendulkar. 1990. Role of Growth and Distribution in the Observed Change in Headcount Ratio Measure of Poverty: A Decomposition Exercise for India. *Indian Economic Review* 25 (2): 165–205.

Minhas, B. S., L. R. Jain, S. M. Kansal, and M. R. Saluja. 1987. On the Choice of Appropriate Consumer Price Indices and Data Sets for Estimating the Incidence of Poverty in India. *Indian Economic Review* 22 (1): 19–49.

Minhas, B. S., L. R. Jain, S. M. Kansal, and M. R. Saluja. 1988. Measurement of General Cost of Living for Urban India. *Sarvekshana* 12 (1): 1–23.

Sen, Abhijit. 2000. Estimates of Consumer Expenditure and Its Distribution. *Economic and Political Weekly*, December 16: 4499–4518.

Subramanian, Shankar, and Angus Deaton. 1996. The Demand for Food and Calories. *Journal of Political Economy* 104 (1): 133–162.

Sundaram, Krishnamurthy. 2001a. The Employment-Unemployment Situation in India in the 1990s: Some Results from the NSS 55th Round Survey. *Economic and Political Weekly*, March 17: 931–940.

Sundaram, Krishnamurthy. 2001b. Employment and Poverty in 1990s: Further Results from NSS 55th Round Employment-Unemployment Survey, 1999–2000. *Economic and Political Weekly*, August 11: 3039–3049.

Sundaram, Krishnamurthy, and Suresh Tendulkar. 2001. NAS-NSS Estimates of Private Consumption for Poverty Estimation: A Disaggregated Comparison for 1993–1994. *Economic and Political Weekly*, 36 (2): 119–129.

Sundaram, Krishnamurthy, and Suresh Tendulkar. 2003. Poverty *Has* Declined in the 1990s: A Resolution of the Comparability Problems in NSS Consumer Expenditure Data. *Economic and Political Weekly*, 38 (4): 327–337.

Anil B. Deolalikar
Amaresh Dubey

NATIONAL SECURITY

Although central to studies across social science disciplines like political science, national security is a dynamic and contested concept. This entry surveys its history, definition, and entailments.

National security seems a simple concept with familiar resonance and clear articulations through history. Nation-states from their inception have sought security from external and internal threats and employed many means to survive. As the English philosopher Thomas Hobbes wrote in *The Leviathan* (1660), security is the raison d'être of the Westphalian state: keeping domestic peace and safeguarding people and property against civil and foreign threats. Traditionally, external threats are highlighted, including those involving other states and matters of territory, population, and military/economic/political competition. Interstate wars, grand strategies, armaments, and alliances are emphasized. However, the internal dimension is also important; whether the time or place was early modern Europe, colonial America, Imperial Japan, or postcolonial Africa, Asia, and Latin America, issues of taxation, conscription, constitutional design, royal succession, class relations, religion, rights and liberties, food supply, and public health have all to varying degrees affected domestic stability and probabilities of conflict internally and externally.

Despite ordinary usage, the term *national security* is difficult to define. National security is security of the nation-state, but this means little without defining the terms *nation-state* and *security*. While there are competing conceptions, the nation-state is commonly understood as a political-legal entity possessing a monopoly on legitimate use of force within its territory. The state includes—in political scientist Barry Buzan's formulation—physical (territory, population), institutional (rules, norms, governing apparatus), and ideational (nationalism, state legitimacy) elements. The state also possesses varying types and degrees of sovereignty. Security is more ambiguous. The scholar David Baldwin suggested the concept is "confused or inadequately specified" (2000, p. 12), and Buzan concluded security is "essentially contested," eluding general definition (1991, p. 7). The problem, Baldwin argued, is not positing a general definition but the many particular specifications of that definition possible. For example, most definitions of security center on the idea of freedom from threat. This is vague and requires further specification: What constitutes freedom? How much is necessary? Who and what constitute threats? Who and what need to be protected? Is threat subjective, objective, or both; what does this mean for security? Depending on answers, widely different specifications result. Moreover, most specifications include other contested terms. Political scientist Arnold Wolfers's classic definition of security as "absence of threats to acquired values … [and] absence of fear … such values will be attacked" (2000, p. 485) and Baldwin's modification, "[L]ow probability of damage to acquired values" (2000, p. 13), both rely on acquired values. However, as scholar Bernard Brodie argued, values and vital interests are fundamentally debatable with no single, objective meaning.

What then is national security? National security is freedom from threat to the nation-state. Because national security absorbs confusion from the term *security*, it requires further specification. If the nation-state involves physical/institutional/ideational components, which components need to be secured? If trade-offs are involved in securing different components, how are preferences over components determined? How do variations along different components (e.g., different regime types or cultural-historical backgrounds) alter conceptions of national security? Who and what threaten the nation-state? If absolute security is unattainable, how much security is necessary? Without specifying these dimensions, national security is ambiguous and subject to political manipulation.

Selected definitions show possible variations. The influential journalist and political commentator Walter Lippmann said national security means a state need not sacrifice core values in avoiding war and can maintain them by winning in war. Scholars Frank Trager and Frank Simonie maintain national security is policy seeking favorable national and international political conditions for protecting and extending vital interests. Professor Richard Ullman finds national security is threatened by anything that can drastically and quickly degrade citizen quality of life or significantly narrow state or nongovernmental entity policy choices. Scholar David Lake said national security is the ability to use wealth as a polity sees fit. Most definitions include policy objectives like providing defense, preserving sovereignty over population and territory, protecting citizens' lives and property, preventing external interference, maximizing wealth and/or power, protecting economic opportunities and quality of life, promoting national values, seeking international prestige, and securing policy flexibility and leverage. Interestingly, state survival in the strictest sense of maintaining Westphalian statehood is mostly a consideration only for weak or failed states. Overall, each specification of national security, knowingly or not, imply different worldviews about the meaning of security and the nature of world politics and, therein, different understanding of threats to be guarded against and values to be maximized.

Different definitions of national security preference different strategies and policy instruments. Traditional views emphasize maintaining national defenses; ensuring resilience/redundancy of critical infrastructure; gathering accurate intelligence to assess threats; and skillfully using diplomacy and cryptodiplomacy to protect against military threats from other states (conventional and unconventional weaponry delivered via land, sea, air, or space). Domestic threats are downplayed. External strategies may vary. Realism identifies national security with state power and ability to secure national interest, however defined. Security is achieved by maintaining self-reliance through internal balancing (strengthening national resources and military might). External balancing (alliances) is used to maintain a balance of power among states (e.g., nineteenth-century Europe) so no hegemony or coalition can predominate. Liberalism identifies national security with states applying reason and ethics to collectively and peacefully lead international relations. National security is not just state security but individual and global empowerment. Liberalism advocates international law and institutions, collective security arrangements, and disarmament (e.g., League of Nations, Kellogg-Briand Pact). Neoliberalism also sees global strategies like promotion of free markets, international law/institutions, and transnational relations as key to national (and international) security. Neorealism, traditionally the dominant perspective on national security, identifies security (especially military security) as the prime motivation of states. Like realism, neorealism advocates internal and external balancing. Developing during the cold war, though, neorealism takes international structure into greater account. Understanding that efforts to increase security might paradoxically decrease it (e.g., arms race), neorealism developed more nuanced theories of coercion, or the limited or threatened use of force to induce an adversary to behave in some way. Coercion includes deterrence (discouraging actions detrimental to coercer's interests by making perceived costs outweigh benefits) and compellence (changing target behavior by manipulating costs and benefits). Conventional and nuclear coercion and coercion short of force (e.g., sanctions) are thus key policy instruments. Last, nontraditional views of national security broaden and deepen the concept to put greater emphasis on third world security, the constructed nature of security, non military issues (e.g., human rights, economic/political development, the environment, demographics, public health, gender), nonstate actors, and nonmilitary policy instruments.

SEE ALSO *Arms Control and Arms Race; Defense; Defense, National; Deterrence; Intelligence*

BIBLIOGRAPHY

Baldwin, David A. 2000. The Concept of Security. In *National and International Security*, ed. Michael Sheehan. Burlington, VT: Ashgate Publishing.

Brodie, Bernard. 1973. *War and Politics*. New York: Macmillan.

Buzan, Barry. 1991. *People, States and Fear: An Agenda for International Security Studies in the Post-Cold War Era*. 2nd ed. New York: Harvester Wheatsheaf.

Hobbes, Thomas. [1660] 1985. *The Leviathan*. Edited with an introduction by C. B. MacPherson. Harmondsworth, U.K.: Penguin.

Schultz, Richard H. Jr., Roy Godson, and George H. Quester, eds. 1997. *Security Studies for the Twenty-First Century*. Washington, DC: Brassey's.

Ullman, Richard H. 1983. Redefining Security. *International Security* 8 (1): 129–153.

Walt, Stephen M. 1991. The Renaissance of Security Studies. *International Studies Quarterly* 35 (2): 211–239.

Wolfers, Arnold. 2000. "National Security" as an Ambiguous Symbol. In *National and International Security*, ed. Michael Sheehan. Burlington, VT: Ashgate Publishing.

Erika Seeler

NATIONAL SERVICE PROGRAMS

In his 2002 State of the Union address, President George W. Bush called on American citizens to donate four thousand hours to community service—the equivalent of two working years—over their lifetime. The U.S. government has supported volunteering and community service in various ways since the 1930s. One of the ways is to establish national service programs that engage citizens in helping other people. The term *national service* traditionally refers to a nationwide program of public/community work in which citizens, mostly young people, serve for one or two years at a subminimum wage to help the community as well as themselves (Gorham 1992; Moskos 1988). In countries such as Israel, Korea, Austria, Singapore, and Turkey, young people (mostly male) are required to serve in the military. In other countries, for example, Germany, (male) citizens may choose whether they want to serve in the armed forces or participate in alternative national service programs. In the mid-1960s, many programs in the United States began to engage a broader array of the population, including students and senior citizens, in a variety of activities.

HISTORY OF NATIONAL SERVICE

The first large-scale national service program in the United States was developed during the Great Depression of the 1930s. In March 1933 President Franklin D. Roosevelt created the Civilian Conservation Corps (CCC). The CCC essentially was an employment/welfare program that provided basic education and income for young, unemployed people. The program employed over three million participants until 1942, when capable young men were no longer available because of the advent of World War II (1939–1945) (Perry 2004). The Roosevelt Administration also created the Works Progress Administration in May 1935, offering work to more than 3.4 million of the unemployed by the next year (Indiana University 2006).

National service in the United States reached an early peak under the administrations of Presidents John F. Kennedy and Lyndon B. Johnson in the 1960s. The early success of the Peace Corps in rallying support for public service contributed significantly to the development of later service programs, such as Volunteers in Service to America (VISTA; the so-called domestic Peace Corps), as well as Foster Grandparents, Senior Companions, and the Retired Senior Volunteer Program, the latter three of which have been administered by the Corporation for National and Community Service (CNCS) since 1993. The goal of all of these programs was to enact changes in the ways institutions addressed issues of poverty and community empowerment.

In the 1970s, the focus of national service programs shifted from institutions to individuals. New programs, such as the Youth Conservation Corps in President Richard M. Nixon's administration, sought to change individuals, rather than to alter institutions (Perry 2004). However, the efforts of President Ronald Reagan's administration to shrink the size and breadth of the federal government also led to the downsizing of federal support for many national service programs (Perry 2004).

The 1990s witnessed renewed interest in national service in the United States. President Bill Clinton's National and Community Service Trust Act of 1993 expanded the National and Community Service Act of 1990 by creating a new agency called the Corporation for National and Community Service (CNCS) to house all domestic national service programs. The Clinton administration also established AmeriCorps, which provides full- and part-time community service opportunities to individuals in education, public safety, the environment, and human needs. In the wake of the tragic events of September 11, 2001, the second Bush administration launched the USA Freedom Corps, an umbrella agency with responsibility for coordinating volunteer programs across all federal agencies, and increased AmeriCorps programs, sponsored by CNCS.

NATIONAL SERVICE PROGRAMS, POST-2005

As mentioned, CNCS houses all domestic national service programs: national and state AmeriCorps programs, AmeriCorps VISTA, AmeriCorps NCCC (National Civilian Community Corps), Senior Corps, and Learn and Serve America. In 2005 the CNCS sponsored and managed about 3.7 million volunteers, with a budget of about $927 million. Citizen Corps, a vital component of Freedom Corps administered by the Department of Homeland Security, represents five programs that provide opportunities for Americans to participate directly in security efforts: Citizen Corps Councils, Community Emergency Response Teams, Medical Reserve Corps, Neighborhood Watch, the Fire Corps, and Volunteers in Police Service. In 2006 the Peace Corps program enrolled 7,810 volunteers in seventy-five countries, with a budget of $318.8 million (Peace Corps 2006).

CHALLENGES

National service programs in the United States face difficult challenges, including financial, social, and legitimacy.

Funding Challenge Funding national service programs has been a continual and critical issue. For example, many AmeriCorps programs have undergone budget cuts. Continuing concern about the management of the National Service Trust Fund, which is dedicated for educational awards to AmeriCorps participants, and budgetary cutbacks by the federal government have forced the program to decrease the number of enrollments (Schwinn 2003; Wilhelm 2003).

Social Challenge National service programs can impose a social challenge by widening the split between the middle class and the underprivileged, rather than narrowing it. As

Charles C. Moskos argued in his 1988 book, *A Call to Civic Service,* American national service can be seen as having a "two-tier" system: Elite programs such as the Peace Corps attract highly educated college graduates. Ninety-six percent of Peace Corps volunteers have at least an undergraduate degree, and 13 percent have earned graduate credits or degrees. By contrast, the large national service programs such as AmeriCorps attract primarily entry-level workers by offering a stipend and college education awards to participants.

Legitimacy Challenge A third issue confronting national service is the legitimacy challenge. In this case, legitimacy means that the overall benefits of these programs must exceed their costs, or that the benefits would not occur in the absence of the program. For example, if as survey research demonstrates, a sizable percentage of Americans (26.7 percent in 2006) volunteer apparently on their own volition (Bureau of Labor Statistics 2007), the justification for subsidizing these efforts through national service appears suspect. William F. Buckley Jr. (1990) maintains that there is no point in taxing citizens if the purpose is to give back the same amount. Of course, national service programs offer a variety of nonmonetary benefits, for instance, skill development, civic responsibility, and greater knowledge and awareness. These benefits, however, are not readily measurable, and consequently, demonstrating the legitimacy of these programs remains critical.

PROSPECTS

Despite the promotion by recent presidents of voluntary national service, marshalling sufficient monetary resources for this purpose is likely to remain an issue. One way to augment funds for national service is through partnering with private and nonprofit organizations, as well as attempting to recover a portion of related costs from them, a strategy pursued increasingly by AmeriCorps.

One of the significant changes in national service programs is increased inclusiveness. Traditionally, national service programs mainly targeted youth; more programs have been created to engage diverse populations, such as older people. These efforts can help to alleviate the socioeconomic gap in national and community service.

Finally, studies of broader scope can be conducted to address the legitimacy challenge confronting national service. Analysis of costs and impacts of these programs—not only for affected communities but also for national service participants—may demonstrate greater benefits, improve current programs, and increase public support.

SEE ALSO *Great Society, The; Johnson, Lyndon B; Kennedy, John F.; Military; New Deal, The; Volunteer Programs; Volunteerism*

BIBLIOGRAPHY

Buckley, William F., Jr. 1990. *Gratitude: Reflections on What We Owe to Our Country.* New York: Random House.

Bureau of Labor Statistics (BLS). 2007. Volunteering in the United States, 2006. http://www.bls.gov/news.release/volun.nr0.htm.

Corporation for National and Community Service. 2005. Fiscal Year 2005 Performance and Accountability Report. http://www.nationalservice.gov/about/role_impact/strategic_plan.asp.

Corporation for National and Community Service. The Role of the Federal Government. http://www.nationalservice.gov/about/volunteering/federal.asp.

Gorham, Eric B. 1992. *National Service, Citizenship, and Political Education.* Albany: State University of New York Press.

Indiana University Lilly Library. More about the WPA. http://www.indiana.edu/~liblilly/wpa/wpa_info.html.

Moskos, Charles C. 1988. *A Call to Civic Service: National Service for Country and Community.* New York: Free Press.

Peace Corps. Fast Facts. http://www.peacecorps.gov/index.cfm?shell=learn.whatispc.fastfacts.

Perry, James L., and Ann Marie Thomson. 2004. *Civil Service: What Difference Does It Make?* Armonk, NY: M.E. Sharpe.

Schwinn, Elizabeth. 2003. A Dwindling Corps: Anticipated Slash in AmeriCorps Enrollment Could Prove Dire for Charities That Rely on the Program. *Chronicle of Philanthropy*, June 26. http://www.philanthropy.com/free/articles/v15/i18/18003501.htm.

Wilhelm, Ian. 2003. AmeriCorps Expects to Cut Number of Participants in Half This Year. *Chronicle of Philanthropy*, May 23. http://www.philanthropy.com/free/update/2003/05/2003052301.htm.

Jeffrey L. Brudney
Young-joo Lee

NATIONAL SOCIALISM

SEE *Nazism.*

NATIONAL SURVEY OF BLACK AMERICANS

The Program for Research on Black Americans (PRBA) at the University of Michigan's Institute for Social Research is the longest-running social science research project devoted to the collection, analysis, and interpretation of survey data based on international, national, and regional probability samples of black populations. The findings from analyses of the original 1980 National Survey of Black Americans (NSBA) and over twenty subsequent studies continue to be of major scientific value and relevance to public policy. Both the quality and the precision of the original national cross-section, panel, and three-generation family samples, as well as the numerous subsequent studies, make the results of immense importance to social scientists and policymakers.

The 1980 NSBA adult cross-section study is notable because, using novel sampling techniques, it permitted for the first time national estimates of the statuses and life situations of black Americans across the entire range of socioeconomic and other demographic groupings in the population. The inclusion of policy-relevant questions revealed individual and group opinions and feelings that fully represented the breadth and diversity of black people located in all walks of life across the entire United States.

One more recent national study, the 2003 National Survey of American Life (NSAL), includes a very large, nationally representative sample of African Americans (3,600), permitting an examination of the heterogeneity of experience across groups. The NSAL also includes the first nationally representative sample of Caribbean blacks (1,650). As a result, the data from this project permit the identification of differences among various important demographic groups often lumped together within the black American population. A related international study of black multigeneration family members in the United States and the Caribbean, as well as large regional adult samples in Jamaica and Guyana, was completed in 2006.

These types of data are critical due to changing immigration patterns and the major changes in living patterns and conditions, family structure, and social circumstances that have occurred among black populations since 1980. The NSAL successfully employed new methods to ascertain the methodological and substantive influences of structurally missing members of black households (e.g., young men in prisons and lockups) on sampling and social, psychological, and health estimates. Finally, all respondents (including the 1,006 whites) in the NSAL were selected from the targeted geographic segments in proportion to the African American and Afro-Caribbean population. Thus, questions related to neighborhood characteristics, service use, and risk and protective factors, for example, will make for important and novel comparisons not possible with prior studies.

In sum, nearly thirty years of PRBA's large probability studies of political participation, perceived and reported discrimination, religion, physical and mental health, and life-course development in population-based black samples have emanated from the original, pathbreaking 1980 NSBA thirteen-year, four-wave, longitudinal panel survey. PRBA research continues to make major contributions to understanding how social, cultural, and other contextual factors relate to the ways in which racial status and racialized treatment affect the behaviors, physical and mental health, attitudes, and values of blacks in the United States and the larger African diasporas.

SEE ALSO *African Americans; Demography; Discrimination; Employment; Inequality, Racial; Occupational Status; Race; Racism; Unemployment; Wages*

BIBLIOGRAPHY

Jackson, James S. ed. 1991. *Life in Black America.* Newbury Park, CA: Sage.

Jackson, James S., Harold W. Neighbors, Randolph M. Nesse, et al. 2004. Methodological Innovations in the National Survey of American Life. *International Journal of Methods in Psychiatric Research* 13 (4): 289–298.

Jackson, James S., Myriam Torres, Cleopatra H. Caldwell, et al. 2004. The National Survey of American Life: A Study of Racial, Ethnic, and Cultural Influences on Mental Disorders and Mental Health. *International Journal of Methods in Psychiatric Research* 13 (4): 196–207.

Jackson, James S., and David R. Williams. 2004. Surveying the Black American Population. In *A Telescope on Society: Survey Research and Social Science at the University of Michigan and Beyond*, eds. James S. House, F. Thomas Juster, Robert L. Kahn, et al., 393–438. Ann Arbor: University of Michigan Press.

James S. Jackson

NATIONALISM AND NATIONALITY

Nationalism is one of the most potent political forces on the world stage today. Fusing the intractability of cultural politics with the power of the state, nationalism organizes individuals into cohesive political communities that are unique, exclusionary, and wedded to mythologized histories. Nationalism sometimes inspires violence and xenophobia, but it also supplies the wellspring for sentiments such as patriotism and self-sacrifice. The deep emotions that nationalism taps into make it a powerful tool in the hands of demagogues, who manipulate nationalist sentiments for political gain. Scholars offer several competing explanations of nationalism and nationality; this entry highlights where they overlap while indicating some of the range of scholarship that exists on the topic.

DEFINITIONS AND ORIGINS OF NATIONALISM

To understand nationalism and nationality, one must first have a working definition of the terms *nation* and *state*. A *nation* is a self-identified cultural group that regards itself as distinctive in some fundamental and significant way. There is no particular attribute that a group must have in order to qualify as a nation, but language, ethnicity, and religion are the three most common bases of national identity. *Nationality* is the aspect of identity that derives from one's membership in a nation. Typically, members of a nation imagine themselves to share a common history that binds them both to one another and to a given territory, and this sense of mutual attachment feels natural even if its objective bases are sometimes exaggerated or even invented. Despite the subjective origins of national identities, they possess an objective status that shapes how individuals regard themselves and are treated by others. Most scholars regard nationalism as a modern phenomenon due to its explicit association with states, which are a product of modern European history. *States* are the territorially based political units that structure global politics today; their provenance is conventionally attributed to the Peace of Westphalia (1648). During the period spanning the age of imperialism in the latter half of the nineteenth century through the years of decolonization in the mid-twentieth century, all of the world's territory and peoples came to be organized politically as states. As statehood emerged as the fundamental mode of political organization during these years, nationalism became the standard means of legitimating state authority, with extant political communities reconceived as nationalities.

Nationalism exists when a nation seeks to fuse its identity with the administrative apparatus of a state. Ideally, coordinating the boundaries of a nation and a state will yield a neatly delineated nation-state, but this outcome is almost impossible as a practical matter and is rarely approached in reality. All states are to some degree multinational, and most states also include segments of their populations that could one day evolve from subcultures into nationalities. Throughout the world, nationalism influences social and political relations in important ways for three related reasons. First, nationality has become a universal component of identity; everyone belongs to a nation. Second, nationalist sentiments are emotional and thus less amenable to rational compromise than are most other political interests. For example, disputes over land that is deemed to possess nationalist significance, as in Israel/Palestine, cannot be solved easily through bargaining, because the nations involved regard their identities to be tied deeply to the land itself. Third, the way that state boundaries were historically drawn often resulted in the division of nations into multiple states, the aggregation of several nations within a single state, or, most commonly, some combination of the two. Insofar as nationality issues are politically salient in these circumstances, the possibility for violence is increased, as demonstrated for example in the numerous conflicts that plague central Africa. Taken together, these three factors promise a pervasive and often disruptive role for nationalism in world politics for the foreseeable future.

Nationalism originated in Europe. Its roots are most commonly traced to the Napoleonic Wars of the late eighteenth century, although some identify Henrician England or even the medieval era as the actual period when nationalism first emerged. Scholars who focus on the way groups have described themselves or others using the vocabulary of nationality tend to place the origins of nationalism in the earlier periods, whereas those who stress its role in political mobilization and legitimation point to the Napoleonic era as marking the true birth of nationalism. Either way, the widespread acceptance of nationality as a marker of identity and of nationalism as a mode of political legitimation depended on the existence of technological and administrative capacities that could enable geographically dispersed individuals to imagine themselves as belonging to a community larger than the village or town; the invention of the printing press and the gradual consolidation of Europe into unified states thus provided essential foundations for the spread of the national idea.

Nationalism as a social construct has thrived by giving meaningful form to the basic human tendencies to categorize and to distinguish the self from others. The positive and negative features of nationality both issue from this source. On the one hand, nationality confers status on the self by defining an individual as belonging to a higher, meaning-bearing collectivity, which in turn inspires loyalty and pride in one's national identity. On the other hand, nationality is an essentialist characteristic—you either have it or you don't, and the status of minority nationalities within states is often one of vulnerability and marginalization. By asserting its special nature and history, in other words, each nation implicitly provides a rationale for excluding those who are not full members of the national community.

Nationalism legitimates political authority by grounding it in the will or "essence" of the community over whom sovereignty is exercised. As a result, when rulers do not share the national identity of a territory's population, as with colonialism or cases of one group's domination of a multinational state, nationalism provides a way for the population to articulate why it regards the rule of the community by "others" as being illegitimate. It is not coincidental that nationalism and democracy took root together, because both reflect variations on the theme of popular sovereignty. Despite their similar foundations

in the primacy of the people, however, democracy and nationalism follow very different logics and are often mutually exclusive in practice, because democracy is blind to the cultural characteristics of the individuals who participate in its processes. Nationalism, by contrast, seeks to empower the group—the nation—without necessary regard for either the individuality of its members or the rights and interests of individuals of different nationalities.

Within Europe, the blossoming of nationalism as a political force was spurred by resistance to Napoleon's imperial ambitions—hence the widespread identification of his reign with the birth of nationalism. Because Napoleon was clearly an "other" in the eyes of the populations in the territories that he conquered, leaders of those states, particularly in Central Europe, rallied their people partly on this basis. In addition, the Napoleonic Wars also marked the start of the modern era, when the creation of citizen armies first gave ordinary people a perceived stake in the chessboard warfare of their rulers. After Europe subsequently conquered the rest of the world, nationalism in turn supplied a rationale that the world's peoples could hold against the Europeans themselves. Although nationalism was not necessary to challenge the Europeans as being illegitimate exercisers of sovereign authority in their colonial possessions, its vocabulary was adopted by political entrepreneurs among the colonized. These leaders, including Mohandas K. Gandhi in India and Kwame Nkrumah in Ghana, recognized that nationalism was a construct that could inspire their conationals to pursue independence, even as it provided a justification for their efforts that Europeans could understand. A growing consensus holds that the colonial era ended only after Europeans accepted that the norm of self-determination trumped their own interests.

CONTEMPORARY MANIFESTATIONS OF NATIONALISM

As a political force, nationalism can take several forms. First, as just described, nationalist sentiment can lead a nation to seek control of a government that is dominated by nonmembers of the nation. This process was most obvious during the decolonization period of the mid-twentieth century, when the peoples living in what are now the states of Africa and Asia gained independence from European imperialism, and it was repeated in the 1990s, during the most recent wave of nationalist awakening, after the Soviet Empire relinquished control of many of its subject nations, which became states such as Ukraine and Kazakhstan. During these episodes, nationalism seems to be a positive force—who can argue against decolonization?—but the fissiparous tendencies thereby unleashed can sometimes spiral out of control. For example, after Georgia separated from the USSR and became an independent state, the South Ossetians almost immediately sought to gain independence from Georgia, and the Abkhazians achieved autonomy within Georgia that they have since sought to convert into sovereign independence. Considerable bloodshed has accompanied both efforts, and neither situation appears to be close to resolution. This sort of fractiousness, and the impossibility of distinguishing legitimate from illegitimate cases of nationalist aspirations, has made self-determination on the basis of national identity deeply problematic.

A second common manifestation of nationalism occurs when one segment of a state's population seeks to align the state's policies and identity with the nation's values or cultural preferences, without regard for the values of minority nationalities. For example, after Yugoslavia split into smaller states during the 1990s, Serbian nationalists and Bosnian nationalists fought a vicious civil war whose purpose was to establish the identity of the emerging Bosnian state as "belonging" to one or the other nation. This episode was extreme in several respects, including the efforts of the Serbs to "ethnically cleanse" the territory of non-Serbs in order to create a nationally homogenous territory that could then be united with Serbia. A less dramatic example is the reassertion of Russian national identity after the fall of the Soviet Union. Among the manifestations of renewed Russian nationalism during this period were the renaming of Soviet cities according to their original Russian designations, with Leningrad becoming Saint Petersburg once again, and the reestablishment of the Russian Orthodox Church as the state religion of Russia. (The church had been marginalized under Communism's official policy of atheism, but it always remained a potent source of identity and pride for the Russian people.)

A third expression of nationalism is irredentism, which relates to the relationship between a nation-state and the members of the nation who live in other states. A currently prominent example is the status of ethnic Germans who live in Poland. After World War II, when the eastern border of Germany was moved westward for geopolitical reasons, the German population living in the ceded territory were simply transferred to Poland along with the land on which they lived. So far, no major problems have resulted from the status of the German minority community in Poland, but both states seem to agree that the situation calls for a neater resolution than is realistically possible. Like many nationalist issues, this case reflects how rarely political line-drawing has historically taken account of the distribution of the national populations within the territories. The lack of fit between national identities and state borders has been the cause of considerable tensions, and is currently responsible for instability in, for example, China, central Africa, and Kashmir, among other places.

Other representative examples of nationalism shaping politics in the world include: whether Northern Ireland will remain a province of the United Kingdom or rejoin with the Republic of Ireland; the recurring debates in the United States over immigration, which have always included clear ethnic overtones, especially during the late nineteenth century, when Chinese nationals specifically were prohibited from coming to the United States; the hyper-nationalism of Nazism and Italian fascism; the failed efforts of Gamel Abdel Nasser to unite the Arabs of the Middle East under a pan-Arabic umbrella; the dispersion of Kurds in Turkey, Iraq, Syria, and Iran; and intermittent efforts of Basques in Spain to establish themselves as an independent state. All of these examples, which can be multiplied practically without end, demonstrate how nationalism evokes fundamental questions about who is, should be, or can be a member of a political community. Insofar as this question is answered on the basis of nationality, one should expect the recurrence of inter-national tensions and conflict, both within and between states. Then again, it is not clear that the underlying function that nationalism serves in constructing political identities can be replaced with a less conflict-inducing alternative. In the final analysis, the central role of nationalism in modernity's cognitive structure guarantees it a long life in social and political affairs, for good or ill.

SEE ALSO *Borders; Colonialism; Culture; Ethnocentrism; Fascism; Gandhi, Mohandas K.; Identity; Ideology; Immigration; Jingoism; Land Claims; Nasser, Gamal Abdel; Nation; Nation-State; Nativism; Nazism; Nkrumah, Kwame; Other, The; Pan-Arabism; Patriotism; Self-Determination; Sovereignty*

BIBLIOGRAPHY

Anderson, Benedict. 1991. *Imagined Communities.* Rev. ed. New York: Verso.

Breuilly, John. 1994. *Nationalism and the State.* 2nd ed. Chicago: University of Chicago Press.

Greenfeld, Liah. 1992. *Nationalism: Five Roads to Modernity.* Cambridge, MA: Harvard University Press.

Hastings, Adrian. 1997. *The Construction of Nationhood: Ethnicity, Religion, and Nationalism.* New York: Cambridge University Press.

Kedourie, Elie. 1993. *Nationalism.* 4th ed. Cambridge, U.K.: Blackwell.

Paul T. McCartney

NATIONALIZATION

Goods and services can be provided by private or by publicly owned producers. Some, such as the postal service or defense, have historically, though not invariably, been provided by states. The concept of expropriating other forms of wealth or activity from private hands into common ownership began to appear in the eighteenth century. The idea that private ownership of land—then still the main source of wealth—vested both economic and political power in a narrow elite led the English radical Thomas Spence (1750–1814) to call for land to be owned by local parishes instead. This was, however, a form of municipalization, not nationalization. In the later nineteenth century calls for state ownership of land, as the most obvious of natural monopolies, were heard in socialist circles. Land nationalization also appealed as an apparent means of coping with the periodic bouts of unemployment experienced in maturing industrial societies. However, land's diminishing economic importance and the rivalry of Henry George's (1839–1897) concept of taxing land values ensured that this idea—notwithstanding continuing practice in communist societies—faded in western Europe and North America by the early twentieth century.

Meanwhile the idea of common ownership of other forms of economic capital or activity was gaining support. Earlier it had been assumed that competition was sufficient to secure the public interest. The high fixed costs of new utility industries, however, meant that in some places, such as Belgium, the very development of railways was from the beginning a state activity. In France private unwillingness to invest meant that the state built and maintained the rail network, while private companies ran the trains until the entire system was nationalized in the 1930s. Nationalization was thus a means of providing public goods when the market failed to do so. But it was not just in utilities that nationalization was felt to be beneficial. In a number of countries perceived market failure in investment also led to bank nationalizations in the twentieth century.

Nationalization could thus be seen either as a way of directing investment or of ensuring uniform provision of services. Some utilities were seen as natural monopolies, and nationalization was felt to be both more efficient and less susceptible to private rationing of services to maximize profits. Private telegraphy providers in Britain before nationalization in 1868, for instance, were accused of restricting services and charging excessive prices. It was also argued that competition was itself wasteful. Nationalization could rationalize assets to achieve economies of scale in the coal industry, for instance, that markets had failed to deliver. In other cases the decision was forced upon sometimes reluctant governments, as in the creation of the Canadian National Railways after World War I (1914–1918), when the government of Canada took over a variety of struggling companies in order to save the service from bankruptcy.

Nationalization was promoted as much for political as economic reasons. In Communist countries, the nationalization of a wide range of assets was seen as a way of controlling the means of production and securing a fairer distribution of social goods. Nationalization of some industries—notably the drink trade—was widely seen as desirable on moral or health grounds in the early twentieth century, and parts of this industry remain nationalized in Finland. And cultural nationalism was a key factor in the development of broadcasting along nationalized lines in interwar Europe. Similar considerations, as well as strategic communications, were to influence the development of European airlines as nationalized "flag carriers" in the middle years of the twentieth century. Security concerns have meanwhile led to the nationalization of a range of industries, from oil to the Transportation Security Administration in the United States in the wake of 9/11.

State control reached its greatest extent in Europe in the years following World War II (1939–1945). This did not stop angry reactions when European assets were taken over by third countries, as occurred, for instance, with the nationalization of the Suez Canal by Egypt in 1956. For Egypt, this was a way of accessing ready revenues for the state.

By the 1970s and 1980s, however, criticisms of nationalization were growing. The failure of state control in Communist systems to distribute goods efficiently was apparent. Evidence in the mixed economies of western Europe was more varied. A plethora of nationalized airlines undoubtedly contributed to overcapacity and inefficiency in that market. Political interference could, though it by no means invariably did, lead to overmanning or inappropriate investment by nationalized industries. More importantly at the popular level these industries could be portrayed as huge faceless organizations more responsive to their unions than to public demand. The rising cost of maintaining subsidies to nationalized industries by the 1980s also made states increasingly unwilling to shoulder this burden.

Privatization, popularized in Margaret Thatcher's Britain in the 1980s, had two significant consequences. The rhetoric may have been about competition; in practice most of the privatized entities remained monopolistic. The result was the development of a network of regulatory authorities. Meanwhile financial liability for those industries has been transferred. So has the political pressure to use that control to, for instance, mop up unemployment by expanding the jobs available in the nationalized industries. Both the financial risk and the political opprobrium have been shifted to the private sector, while a degree of control has been maintained through regulation.

Some countries, like Britain, Germany, and various eastern European states, have undergone large-scale privatization; the process has been less marked in other countries, such as France. In some cases privatization has been reversed, not least in Vladimir Putin's Russia, where the state has reacquired a number of assets in, for instance, the oil industry since 2000. Meanwhile in Latin America privatization has failed to fulfill expectations either in terms of economic growth or of poverty reduction. Instead, it was felt to leave major assets, such as the oil industry, largely in foreign hands. It is to tackle this, in the hope that it will prevent capital extraction in an increasingly globalized world economy, that nationalization has made a comeback as a political panacea since 2000 in Latin America.

SEE ALSO *Communism; Dependency Theory; Monopoly; Nationalism and Nationality; Planning; Privatization; Public Goods; Railway Industry; Revolutions, Latin American; Socialism; State Enterprise; State, The; Washington Consensus*

BIBLIOGRAPHY

Foreman-Peck, James, and Robert Millward. 1994. *Public and Private Ownership of British Industry, 1820–1990.* Oxford: Oxford University Press.

Foster, Christopher D. 1992. *Privatization, Public Ownership, and the Regulation of Natural Monopoly.* Oxford: Blackwell.

Fournier, Leslie T. 1935. *Railway Nationalization in Canada: The Problem of the Canadian National Railways.* Toronto: Macmillan.

Peter Catterall

NATION-STATE

The term *nation-state* is frequently used but less often carefully defined or theorized, and conceptual confusion is exacerbated by the fact that social scientists use the word in quite varied ways. Agreement is limited to general observations such as that it describes at least some modern states that claim to represent a distinct people called a nation. Indeed, it is possible to identify at least three more or less distinct meanings of the term, the first of which is associated with long-dominant theories of international relations (IR) where it typically denotes any sovereign state. A narrower view of the nation-state as a particular type of sovereign state characterizes the other two uses of the term, one of which focuses on the historical processes by which this type of polity is created and maintained and a second that emphasizes the distinct ethno-national composition of its population.

A VIEW FROM ABOVE: THE MODERN SOVEREIGN STATE

A widespread assumption that the terms *nation* and *state* are practically synonymous underlies much of the popular discourse about the nation-state in world politics and interstate relations. Names of intergovernmental organizations like the League of Nations and the United Nations suggest that their member states are all nations, and phenomena like terrorism or environmental pollution are labeled transnational because they cut across state borders. Not even the academic study of relations between states has been immune to this conceptual ambiguity, as the very name of the discipline *international relations* reveals. This may in part be explained by the influence of IR scholars in the realist tradition, who often used the terms *nation* and *state* interchangeably, to set the research agenda for the U.S. leg of the discipline in particular.

Despite the title of Hans J. Morgenthau's canonical realist text, *Politics among Nations* (1948) primarily discussed politics among states, not nations. While acknowledging that the two are distinct, Morgenthau justified the practice of treating them as synonyms with the observation that in modern international relations "a nation pursues foreign policies as a legal organization called a state" (p. 116). By implication, the term nation-state simply describes the coincidence of nations and states as actors in modern world politics. Accordingly, later realists would frequently use the term synonymously with words like state, nation, and—colloquially—country. Indeed, neorealist or structural realist writers like Kenneth Waltz were even less inclined to use terms such as *nation-state* to differentiate between types of state, given the neorealist assumption that the anarchical structure of the international system—that is, the lack of a world government—socializes sovereign states into becoming functionally similar units.

A dramatic resurgence of substate separatist nationalism and intra-state ethnic conflict in the decade after the end of the cold war prompted some neorealists to revisit the question of the relationship between nation and state. Few ultimately severed the ties between the two, as illustrated by John Mearsheimer's analysis of what he called hypernationalism, which echoed Morgenthau's argument that nationalism primarily functions to strengthen citizens' identification with and support for the state. These reconsiderations thus generally did not result in any major changes in how the term nation-state is used in neorealist writing.

Much of the work in IR since Morgenthau can be seen as contributing to an enduring debate about core realist and neorealist assumptions regarding the primacy of the sovereign state and the inadmissibility of its domestic characteristics in explanations of interstate conflicts. Nevertheless, even realism's opponents usually accept the basic connotation of the term *nation-state* as it is used in the realist tradition. David Held and other scholars have argued that the increasing interdependence brought on by globalization may be causing the decline or even death of the nation-state, a development that would be incompatible with the key realist assumption of the sovereign state as the primary actor in world politics. In these debates, however, critics of realist theory usually accept their opponents' use of the term nation-state to denote all modern sovereign states, and like Held primarily focus their critique on the supposition that the latter is actually sovereign.

However, the preoccupation with the state as nation-state in IR has come under fire by the growing number of IR scholars who—like the contributors in Yosef Lapid and Friedrich Kratochwil's appropriately titled edited volume—advocate *The Return of Culture and Identity in IR Theory* (1996). Lapid and Kratochwil insist that "a serious reengagement with the 'national' is imperative" considering "how costly the failure of a clear analytical distinction between 'nation' and 'state' is for studies of contemporary world politics" (pp. 105, 123). In *National Collective Identity* (1999), Rodney Bruce Hall agrees and asserts that "a more coherent theory of international politics must be predicated, in part, on an adequate theory of the nation-state." Hall's historical examination of the emergence of nation-states represents one of two major alternatives to the traditional view of the nation-state in IR.

A HISTORICAL PERSPECTIVE: THE NATION-BUILDING-STATE

Historical studies of nationalism and the formation of modern states typically distinguish nation-states from other contemporary types of state and from premodern forms of sociopolitical organizations such as empires, medieval fiefdoms, dynastic states, and the territorial-sovereign states in Europe after the Treaty of Westphalia (1648). Rodney Bruce Hall focuses on the unique legitimizing principles of earlier types of polities as their defining and distinctive features. Hall's account of the emergence of what he called "national-sovereign states" in nineteenth-century Europe reflects a view common among students of nationalism, according to which enlightenment ideas championing the people as the only legitimate source of a state's power gradually replaced earlier dynastic legitimizing principles. Unable to adapt in the face of the popular and nationalist revolts that followed the French and American revolutions, the auto-

cratic European states were ultimately transformed into states whose regimes appealed to the new legitimizing concept of popular sovereignty.

However, the notion that rulers were legitimate only to the extent that they represented the people raised an explosive question: Who were the people? Traditional practices of defining the people from above—for example, as the ruler's subjects—were clearly incompatible with the idea that the power of the ruler emanated from below, from the people. Popular sovereignty was based on the assumption that the people were prior to the ruler, not the other way around. In the end, nationalism provided the definitive answer to the question: The people—as a single, unified entity—was the nation. Popular sovereignty thus implied national self-determination, most famously championed in Woodrow Wilson's Fourteen Points. There are many variations of this historical narrative but to most students of the history of nationalism and state formation, the emergence of nation-states is intimately associated with the spread of nationalist ideas of self-determination across Europe and the Americas from the late eighteenth to the early nineteenth centuries and across Africa, the Middle East, and Asia during the anticolonial movements of the twentieth century.

The definitions of the terms *nationalism* and *nation* are also hotly contested, but a common view among experts holds that the former is an ideology premised on the belief that, as Johan Gottfried Herder put it in *Outlines of a Philosophy of the History of Man*, "[t]he most natural state ... is *one* nation, with one national character," which sees national self-rule as the only legitimate form of governance (1966, p. 249). A nation is often described as a politically mobilized people whose members are conscious of their unity as a nation and of their distinctiveness from other nations on the basis of cultural, historical/mythical, linguistic, and/or ethnic criteria. Whereas nationalists aim to create the complete concordance between state and nation boundaries, most students of nationalism and state formation heed the advice of scholars like Hugh Seton-Watson and Walker Conner to clearly distinguish between the two entities, understanding a state as the legal, territorial polities in which nations reside. Only by keeping the two concepts analytically separate, they argue, can we properly understand the dynamics of nationalism and its most important institutional manifestation: the nation-state.

In *The Nation-State and Nationalism in the Twentieth Century* (1996), Montserrat Guibernau defined the nation-state by situating it in its historical context as:

> a modern phenomenon, characterized by the formation of a kind of state which ... seeks to unite the people subjected to its rule by means of homogenization, creating a common culture,

symbols, values, reviving traditions and myths of origin, and sometimes inventing them. (p. 47)

On this historicized view, the nation-state is a nation-building state—one pursuing the nationalist and therefore necessarily modern goal of creating a nation that coincides with its borders. An important additional element of such nation-building projects is captured in Hall's criteria that a "national-sovereign" state seeks legitimacy by claiming to represent a single nation that is presumed to include the people living within its territory. Considering Guibernau's processual definition, such a project does not have to be fully and successfully completed—it seldom is—or the claim entirely justified for the state to qualify as a nation-state. In the eyes of most students of nationalism and state formation, however, the existence and persistence of sizeable or numerous minority groups that resist and loudly contest such nation-building policies may so undermine a regime's claim to represent the nation that it can no longer legitimately portray itself as a nation-state.

In a variation on this view, the term nation-state denotes any state that with some success promotes a common national identity among its citizens, even if the latter is based only on solidarity toward shared political symbols, institutions, or ideals. This use potentially defines most if not all modern states as nation-states, including many culturally and ethnically diverse states that are said to have created a unified civic or contractual—as opposed to ethnic or cultural—nation, a distinction inspired by Hans Kohl's analysis of differences in the historical development of Western and Eastern nationalisms. This view is embraced by proponents of liberal nationalism, such as Ross Poole, who in his article "The Nation-State and Aboriginal Self-Determination" advocates the creation of what he calls "multi-nation nation-states" (Seymour 2004, p. 95). Poole reconciles the seemingly contradictory elements of this notion with the presumption that a multicultural/multiethnic state can forge a stable, unified civic nation while respecting the diversity and integrity of its cultural or ethnic nations.

Scholars like Bernard Yack have criticized this distinction on the basis that, as Rogers Smith argued in *Stories of Peoplehood* (2003), "[m]ost if not all senses of nationhood or peoplehood invoke an account of unchosen, inherited, usually quasi-ethnic identity" (p. 65). Even someone as sympathetic to the broader aspirations of liberal nationalists as Will Kymlicka has pointed out that many states pursuing supposedly civic nation-building projects are in fact imposing a dominant culture on national minorities in the manner described by Guibernau. Hence, while they may be (actual or aspiring) nation-states, they are seldom civic nation-states. On the other hand, these critics argue, if states like Switzerland do explicitly recognize and respect different cultural/ethnic nations within its borders, they ought not to be described as nation-states. Leaders of such multinational states may speak of the "national interest" or "national unity" and refer to the state rather than any one of its nations when doing so, but the pervasive terminological confusion of state with nation is merely evidence of the extraordinary success of nationalist rhetoric portraying the nation-state as the ideal form of political organization. It does not mean that all states are nation-states.

A VIEW FROM BELOW: THE SINGLE-NATION-STATE

In fact, students of ethnic conflict maintain that an underlying source of many violent conflicts in modern history is the fact that, despite the power and prevalence of the one nation—one state ideal, few nations are in reality coterminous with state borders. This suggests a third major view of the nation-state that is also evident among nationalism scholars who, like Anthony D. Smith, emphasize the durable quality of nations and the ethnic and cultural ties that underlie them. Smith prefers to call the type of nation-building state described by Guibernau's processual criteria national state, and his own definition of a nation-state in *Nations and Nationalism in a Global Era* (1996) focuses on the actual concordance of boundaries between given entities:

> Strictly speaking, we may term a state a 'nation-state' only if and when a single ethnic and cultural population inhabits the boundaries of a state, and the boundaries of that state are coextensive with the boundaries of that ethnic and cultural population. (p. 86)

The most important element in Smith's definition is the first criteria, which demands that nation-states are ethnically and culturally homogenous internally. (Not all writers in this third group embrace the second criteria as it would exclude internally homogenous states like the two Koreas, given that the Korean nation is dispersed over two states.) The nation-state is here distinguished not from premodern forms of state, but from contemporary states populated either by multiple nations or by a single nation that also extends into other states. Studies of ethnic conflict typically focus on the latter two types of states because they tend to be more unstable than the ethnically homogenous nation-states, which therefore often figure in these studies mainly as part of a typology of states or as the exception that proves the rule of its more numerous and potentially volatile multinational counterparts.

Research by students of ethnic conflict like Ted Gurr suggests that conflict in multinational states is often associated with an erosion of the legitimacy of the state in the eyes of marginalized nations, which may have been precipitated by a dominant nation's use of state institutions to impose its culture on all citizens. Members of nations who do not perceive that the state represents the interests of their nation are likely to make demands for greater autonomy or even secession, and sometimes take up arms to achieve such goals. In light of the fact that so many of the world's national groups straddle state boundaries, these kinds of international dynamics within states often cause neighboring states to get involved and are therefore important for a proper understanding of world politics as interstate relations.

The reverse is also true: Interstate politics may affect intra-state relations between national groups, and rules and norms of the world state-system such as a sovereign state's right to freedom from outside interference in domestic affairs, define the conditions under which, for example, secessionist movements have to operate. In light of these observations, a natural conclusion suggests itself: A more complete understanding of the nation-state would combine insights from theories of interstate relations with knowledge from studies of intra-state ethnic relations, and the tendencies of both to reify either state or nation could be mitigated by adopting the processual focus of historical approaches to nationalism and state formation.

SEE ALSO *Nation; Nationalism and Nationality; Sovereignty; State, The*

BIBLIOGRAPHY

Breuilly, John. 1994. *Nationalism and the State.* 2nd ed. Chicago: University of Chicago Press.

Connor, Walker. 1978. A Nation Is a Nation, Is a State, Is an Ethnic Group Is a … *Ethnic and Racial Studies* 1 (4): 378–400.

Guibernau, Montserrat. 1996. *The Nation-State and Nationalism in the Twentieth Century.* Cambridge, MA: Blackwell Publishers.

Hall, Rodney Bruce. 1999. *National Collective Identity: Social Constructs and International Systems.* New York: Columbia University Press.

Herder, Johann Gottfried. 1966. *Outlines of a Philosophy of the History of Man.* Trans. T. Churchill. New York: Bergman Publishers.

Lapid, Yosef and Friedrich Kratochwil. 1996. The Return of Culture and Identity in IR Theory. Boulder, CO: Lynne Rienner.

Morgenthau, Hans J. 1948. *Politics among Nations: Struggle for Power and Peace.* Boston: McGraw Hill Higher Education, 2006.

Seymour, Michael, ed. 2004. *The Fate of the Nation-State.* Ithaca, NY: McGill-Queen's University Press.

Smith, Rogers M. 2003. *Stories of Peoplehood: The Politics and Morals of Political Membership.* New York: Cambridge University Press.

Paul T. Levin

NATIVE AMERICANS

Though referring properly to anyone born in America, the term *Native Americans* has referred to American indigenous peoples since the eighteenth century. Its use became popular in the 1970s as part of a movement to advance indigenous political and legal rights by emphasizing the aboriginal status of pre-Columbian peoples. The choice to use *Native American* rather than *Indian*, the term Christopher Columbus (1451–1506) gave and the other term commonly used in the United States, remains a matter of political debate in some indigenous communities. *Aboriginal peoples of the Americas* is more accurate, but unfamiliar. Further, it does not, strictly speaking, refer to Arctic peoples, sometimes known as *Eskimo*, *Inuit*, and other names pertaining to particular geographic groups, since the ancestors of these peoples arrived millennia after the ancestors of the people known as *Indians*. *Indigenous* has been criticized on the grounds that it means "originating in," and all human beings originated in the Old World. *Native American* finds wide usage only in the United States, and for this reason this entry focuses on the United States. Moreover, *Native American* usually does not include aboriginal Alaskans, widely and officially known as *Alaska Natives*. Canadians usually use the term *First Nations Peoples* (French: *première nations*), *aboriginal peoples* (French: *autochtone*), *Inuit*, *Native Canadians*, *natives*, or *Indians*. In Latin America, the terms *indigenous peoples* (Spanish: *pueblos indígenas*; Portuguese: *povos indígenas*), *Indians* (Spanish: *indios*; Portuguese: *índios*), and sometimes *aborigine* (Spanish: *aborigen*) are used. There, the term *pre-Columbian peoples* (Spanish: *pueblos precolumbinos*; Portuguese: *povos pré-colombianos*) refers to aboriginal people prior to 1492, not to anyone alive today. Most autonyms simply mean "(the) people."

ORIGINS

Archaeological data suggest that the first people probably arrived in North America from Asia approximately 15,000 years ago, although this date remains controversial. Numerous physical features are common to American Indians and East Asians, and unknown or unusual among Europeans and Africans: a brachycephalic (relatively wide) skull; Mongoloid spot (a greenish-blue birthmark above the coccyx which disappears within a few years); shovel-shaped incisors; dark, coarse, straight hair; little body hair; dry earwax; and others.

Prehistory The ancestors of modern American Indians spread out over the Americas rapidly. About 11,200 to 10,900 years ago, hunters developed the beautiful fluted Clovis point and played an important role in the extinction of many animal species, including mammoths, mastodons, giant sloths, horses, and several species of camel. The Ice Age ended 11,600 years ago, and with it the Paleolithic life of large-game hunting. Neolithic peoples hunted smaller animals and gathered wild plant foods. One exception includes the Maritime Archaic peoples in the extreme Northeast, who subsisted on deep-sea fish. With the exception of the alpaca, vicuña, and llama in South America, the turkey in Central America, and the dog everywhere, pre-Columbians had no domesticated animals. Beans, squash, and most importantly maize for the energy it supplies were all domesticated in Central America before 7,000 years ago. Maize probably originated from selective breeding of a grass called *teosinte.* Maize first arrived in the southwestern United States around 3,500 to 3,000 years ago. Around 1,300 years ago, a new variety called *northern flint* or *maiz de ocho* appeared, and with its larger kernels and much shorter growing season it spread throughout eastern North America, occasionally as far north as southern Canada.

Cultures The cultures and societies of the original peoples of North America represent an astonishing range of diversity. While some lived in a city of tens of thousands (Cahokia, in present-day Illinois), others living in parts of the Great Basin and subarctic regions never met more than two hundred people their entire lives. People who adopted maize tended to become sedentary and developed food surpluses, concentrations of wealth and political power, and larger, denser populations. In North America, maize production frequently correlates with matrilineality and matrilocal residence, whereas primary dependence on hunting often correlates with patrilineality and patrilocal residence. When maize first arrived in an area, women probably cultivated it, since women already gathered plant foods while men hunted. As maize became more important in the diet over time, women's increasing contribution to the economy brought them greater political power and the most valuable types of property, in some cases including the society's political offices, often descended from mother to daughter. Even where men later ended up doing most or all of the farming, matrilineal social structure and inheritance often remained. An example of this latter case is the Hopi, arguably the most matrilineal people on earth—so much so that what we think of as "normal" sex roles are sometimes reversed: men traditionally wove and women did most of the house construction. The Crow, once matrilineal farmers, later moved out onto the plains, where men provided most of the food through bison hunting. Crow men after a time began to argue for patrilineal social structure.

Some two hundred to five hundred different languages were spoken in North America, and there were at least sixty-two language families and isolates. While immense differences exist between the various languages of North America, they all share the characteristics of polysynthesis and agglutination, meaning that they can bring together subject, object, verb, tense, adjective, adverb, mood, and so on in one word. For example, the Micmac word *ketulmieyap* means "I wanted to go home."

CULTURE AREAS

It has long been recognized that peoples in various parts of North America share more cultural similarities with peoples of the same geographic area than with peoples of other geographic areas. Although controversy persists in identifying exact culture area boundaries, one can say much about the general locations of these areas and the general characteristics of the peoples inhabiting each area.

California Most California peoples subsisted on fish and game, but especially on acorns, an abundant food that made them, like the peoples of the Northwest Coast, capable of sedentary life in permanent villages, and thus nearly unique among all hunting-and-gathering peoples. Here, great wealth meant concentrations of both wealth and power, and peoples such as the Yurok developed a sharply defined nobility. Yurok *pegerks* owned great wealth, especially money, heirlooms, and even prehistoric antiquities. They lived at named elevated locations, served as priests and judges, wore distinctive clothing, ate foreign foods, employed aides, gave gifts and feasts at ceremonies, spoke foreign languages, traveled extensively, and used ornate speech. Most societies have moieties, and some have ambilateral social structure in which each individual had the choice to join the father's group or the mother's group; often individuals chose the group with the most resources. Some southern California people also raised maize, beans, and squash.

Great Basin This intermontane region of Nevada, Utah, and adjoining areas was home to some of the most mobile and dispersed populations of hunters and gatherers in the world. Due to the difficulty of survival, which affected all parts of life, bands were small, often the size of a nuclear family, with fluid membership, and kinship was largely bilateral with little or no emphasis on lineages, which would confer no benefits to such dispersed people. People hunted and collected seeds and roots. Because of the rigorous conditions and sexual division of labor, marriage was essential to survival; people married early, and they married people living at a distance to create kinship links over a wider area. In some places, the sororate and levirate were legally required and both polygyny and polyandry were practiced. Warfare was almost unknown, cooperation was so essential for survival. In places, giving birth to twins was considered unlucky—in a few places, one of the pair was killed.

Northeast From Maine to Wisconsin and south to Virginia and Kentucky, people depended partially on maize, beans, and squash, which the Iroquois named "the three sisters," but also upon hunting, gathering, and fishing. As swidden horticulturalists, people had to move their villages every decade or so as soil lost fertility, weeds encroached, and firewood and game became scarce. The Iroquoisian peoples are matrilineal; elsewhere social organization is patrilineal. Warfare for the purpose of revenge occurred frequently, and villages were often palisaded.

Northwest Coast The coastal region of Oregon to southern Alaska has some of the most distinctive cultures in the world. These people traditionally subsisted on the immensely abundant salmon, making them the wealthiest in North America and leading them to build permanent villages. Their cultures reflected this: fine arts and theater were developed, people (slaves) were considered a measure of wealth, and the rich gave lavish feasts known as *potlatches*, which because of the wealth acquired through trade with Europeans, grew to titanic proportions in the nineteenth century, involving the giving away and destruction of what would be millions of dollars in today's money. Warfare, including raiding for slaves, was common, and many villages were palisaded. Many groups had an elaborate system for ranking individuals, and for those in high positions, marriage to someone of equal rank was the only possibility. Both men and women were wealthy, owning various types of corporeal and incorporeal property, which was inherited both matrilineally and patrilineally.

Plains The Plains consists of two smaller areas, the high plains (short-grass prairie) to the west of the hundredth meridian where mobile people hunted, and the prairie-plains (tall-grass prairie) to the east where people lived as horticulturalists and hunters. Though many associate the High Plains culture with that of North American Indians generally, High Plains culture is unique in most respects in North America. What we have come to know as High Plains culture did not exist until recent times, because few people could manage to live on the high plains: the region is dry, inhospitable to agriculture without a steel plow, and the prolific denizen of the plains, the bison, was very difficult to find and kill reliably. But the European introduction of the horse allowed people to find and kill sufficient quantities of bison so that entire societies could live by hunting alone on the high plains, encouraging people from all surrounding culture areas to live there, developing within two hundred years what we know as Plains culture. Due to Euro-American hunger for land, this culture disappeared even more quickly. The High Plains Indian culture represents an almost unique case in human history of people leaving farming to become hunters. Because of the extreme mobility of high plains life in which individuals and families moved from one band to another, lineal groups were rare.

Plateau From southeastern British Columbia and eastern Washington and Oregon, east to Montana, were people who, like the peoples of the Northwest Coast, subsisted primarily on salmon. However, the fish sometimes did not migrate in large numbers so far inland, and thus the people of the plateau region had to depend upon other foods, particularly various roots such as the camas bulb. Therefore, semipermanent villages were usually located at prime fishing spots, but the populations of those villages tended to be fluid as resources determined. Some groups took to raiding Plains peoples after the horse came, and combined into confederacies to repel Plains raiders. Kinship structure is bilateral, sometimes with emphasis on the patriline, and the kindred was important.

Southeast In the Southeast, warm temperatures, abundant rainfall, fertile soil, and maize all combined to produce far more food than was necessary, and commonly large and fast-growing populations, concentrations of wealth in the hands of a few in stable classes, cities (often palisaded), priestly classes, large armies frequently built by conscription, fine arts, monumental earthworks, leaders holding the power of life and death over followers, celebration of the annual Green Corn Ceremony (emphasizing renewal), playing of the ball game (a lacrosse-like game with two sticks), and wars often due to rivalries between leaders. Many villages and cities were permanent, since maize fields were planted on floodplains that were refertilized each spring with silt. Probably because of the importance of maize, all the peoples here are matrilineal. This is the one part of North America for which arguments have been made for the existence of state societies. In many of these societies, male leaders held offices, but which because of the matrilineal social structure were passed through the female line.

Southwest The Southwest is a complex area because its range of environment supported a number of subsistence strategies. The area was dominated on the one hand by the Puebloan peoples, sedentary matrilineal maize farmers who live in permanent villages and who sometimes had to run for dozens of miles to tend distant maize fields. The other dominant peoples are the Apache and Navajo, two closely related matrilineal Athabaskan-speaking migratory peoples who hunted, gathered, raided, and farmed and whose ancestors arrived in the Southwest from the western subarctic in the 1400s. Numerous other populations include the patrilineal Piman and bilateral Yuman peoples.

Subarctic Stretching from Alaska to eastern Canada lies a territory too far north to grow any kind of crops in premodern times. In this cold and wet land, small groups of people had to depend almost entirely on the large game and fish that men acquired. Thus, a patrilinealizing influence pervaded this region, fully evident among the Algonquian speakers of the eastern half. In the western half, the traditionally matrilineal culture of the Athabaskans competes with this influence, to produce cultures that are nominally matrilineal or have bilateral kinship. Mostly migratory, most groups had summer gathering places. Here, people sought the hardest workers as spouses.

INDIAN-EUROPEAN RELATIONS

Major European colonial powers differed in their relationships with Native Americans. Britain and the United States sought a more formal legal relationship, and used treaties recognizing American Indian groups as politically independent entities, while maintaining social and cultural separation. The Spanish and French did not recognize Indians as separate legal entities, but rather intermarried with and assimilated them to a greater degree. Both the English and the Spanish sought control over conquered territories, whereas the French had more interest in establishing strategic trading venues than in controlling territories.

European invasion brought alcohol, increased warfare, and diseases (including typhoid, cholera, typhus, smallpox, measles, influenza, and malaria) to which aboriginals had little resistance, killing 10 to 80 percent of each population, and destroying entire societies. We shall never know about the cultures of many peoples or even the size of the population of the Americas before Columbus.

Initial aboriginal reactions to the European invasion varied greatly. The Iroquois, for example, had long dominated their political environment by warring with other Indian peoples, walking as far as Wisconsin, Georgia, and Nova Scotia to do so. The Iroquois for a time cooperated with the Dutch and later the English to control the fur trade in the Northeast, benefitting both parties at the expense of their neighbors, Indian and European.

Having endured military losses, alcohol, and disease, as well as the loss of land, freedom, and game, many native peoples became dispirited. When conditions change and people feel that their culture no longer serves them ideally in their new circumstances, it often happens that a leader with an idea for cultural revitalization appears. This occurred numerous times among native North Americans, and one of the most famous of these cultural revivals took place in the latter half of the nineteenth century in the West. A Paviotso man named Wovoka (c. 1856–1932) had a vision—a direct connection with a supernatural being in which many American Indians place great faith—taking him to the other world, where he saw a great spirit, and there all the people who had died were young and happily engaging in traditional pursuits. The great spirit's message was that he go back and tell his people that they must dance, be good, live in peace with white people, work, be honest, and give up war. If they obeyed him they would be reunited with those who had died and no one would grow old or die; from this resurrection of the dead came the name *Ghost Dance.* As time went on, many Indian people in much of the West accepted this message as a ray of hope. But as the Ghost Dance traveled orally, it began to change. A new message arose stating that white people would vanish, while the technological advancements they brought would remain.

Still later, the idea of the Ghost Dance shirt, allegedly providing invulnerability to the white man's bullets, was added. The altered message became popular among some of the Sioux of South Dakota in 1890. The Sioux had been militarily defeated, crowded into guarded camps, largely disarmed of their rifles (though not revolvers or clubs), experienced the assassination of their leader Sitting Bull (c. 1831–1890) by hostile Indian police, and suffered violations of every treaty that they had signed, most importantly the one guaranteeing them sufficient food (beef) to survive the winter. One irate adherent of the Ghost Dance, perhaps believing the message of invulnerability, fired on the U.S. cavalry, igniting a melee that killed the Sioux warriors present as well as a number of cavalrymen, and enraging the remaining cavalrymen, who themselves were still angry over the cavalry's obliteration at Little Bighorn in 1876, to the point that they then retaliated against any Sioux they could find, including women and children. This fight became known as the Sioux outbreak of 1890 and later as the Wounded Knee massacre. Following the demonstrated ineffectiveness of the Ghost Dance shirt, many Sioux became interested, temporarily at least, in Christianity.

Although rarely by design, European influences have sometimes benefited aboriginal peoples. Pacification, for example, ended indigenous warfare. The United States freed Hopi from the attacks of the Navajo, and the United States, by defeating the raiding Apache and purchasing their wheat and cotton crops, helped the Pimas (Akimel O'odham, "river people") become wealthy farmers in the second half of the eighteenth century. Technological introductions eased many of life's difficulties, and the imposition of the English language provided Indians with their first true lingua franca.

In 1969 Vine Deloria Jr. (1933–2005) published *Custer Died for Your Sins*, which argued that most of the types of information about Indians that interested scholars were unimportant. Deloria called upon scholars, particularly anthropologists, as well as missionaries, government workers, and others, to work toward the betterment of the living conditions of North American Indian people. His message was well heeded in academia, where two important effects can be noted. The first was a multiplication of programs of American Indian and Native American studies at North American universities, a development intended to increase the numbers of Native American college students. Another effect has been to discourage American Indian students from pursuing academic interests in anthropology, something that American Indian anthropologists have decried.

LEGISLATION

Although often framed in terms positive to Indian interests, most significant nineteenth-century U.S. legislation aimed to dispossess Indians of their lands for the benefit of non-Indians. For example, the 1830 Indian Removal Act promised southeastern Indians ownership of land in Indian Territory (now Oklahoma), but those who did not accede to its terms were rounded up (some escaped) and forced to walk to Indian Territory, causing thousands of deaths. Even when aboriginal peoples agreed to cede lands, it was usually under intense pressure from non-Indians, often including both a military presence and payments to treaty signers. Moreover, the resulting reservation lands were often whittled away by official measures and encroachment. In addition, treaty provisions for food and medicine were often poorly enforced. As one-sided, deceptive, and coercive as the treaty process was, it at least recognized indigenous peoples as separate and capable of making their own decisions, and therefore gave them power to negotiate terms. The 1871 Indian Appropriation Act ended the power of Indians to make treaties, although it did give legal protection to those already made. In the same year, rules preventing Indians from leaving reservations ended.

In 1887 the U.S. Congress passed the General Allotment Act (also known as the Dawes Act), breaking up 118 reservations into individual parcels allotted to each family. The primary goal was to free up land for white settlers, since lands above and beyond those needed for each family allotment were considered "surplus" and were taken from the Indians and sold off. Native Americans lost 34,800,000 hectares, or 62 percent of reservation lands. The secondary goal was to assimilate Indians and acculturate them as farmers. Predictably, the first goal was met admirably, since in addition to the taking of lands, many Indians sold their lands or lost them due to their inability to pay the taxes on them. The second goal was rarely met. Indian poverty and misery both increased, due in part to the allotments' effects on social unity and the loss of resources. Because the Dawes Act made no provision for later generations, many people had no land of their own.

The 1934 Indian Reorganization Act encouraged U.S. Indians to adopt a federally prescribed means of choosing leaders and forming governments to ensure democratic elections and governments where sometimes none had previously existed. This arrangement was accepted by approximately three-quarters of all U.S. Indian groups. Although representing an advance in democracy, it must be said that this measure also represented a change of the culture and a step back from independence. The question of what is best for a people is not clear-cut, and often this exact question divides communities. This legislation and other rules also created administrative units for American Indian governments based upon the concept of a tribe, a concept that despite popular opinion applies to few Amerindians. What people think of as a "tribe" is usually only a class of people speaking the same language. To call these "tribes" is comparable to thinking of all U.S. citizens, New Zealanders, South Africans, and so on as a single group because they all speak English. Traditional means of dealing with social frictions became useless in these new larger "tribes." Nowadays, these groups possess more political power as a result of their greater size.

In 1953 and 1954 the U.S. Congress voted to terminate federal controls over many American Indians, prompting considerable outcry from Native Americans and others. As much as Native Americans dislike and distrust the federal government, they realize that they benefit from its oversight, financial assistance, and protections, and many groups split apart as a result of this program.

The Native American Graves Protection and Repatriation Act of 1990 (NAGPRA) grants Indians in the United States rights over some human remains of ancestors and religious and culturally central objects. This legislation has allowed Indian peoples to reacquire many of these objects from federally funded institutions such as museums, as well as to gain legal standing to do such things as challenge the treatment of Kennewick Man, an ancient skeleton found in 1996 near the Columbia River in Kennewick, Washington.

From the 1970s onward, Congress chose to support tribal autonomy by encouraging and financing tribal courts. For many types of offenses, both the federal government and the tribal government have jurisdiction. Tribal courts decide many issues pertaining to disputes between Indians on the reservation, but cannot deal with the most serious crimes. These courts also have jurisdiction over disputes involving contracts between Indians and non-Indians on the reservation, which has led many non-Indian entrepreneurs to avoid doing business with

Indians on reservations, and which therefore must be considered a reason for poor economic development there. Unfortunately, the Bureau of Indian Affairs, which is accountable for the operation of these courts, has not always ensured that the courts operate according to the principles of procedure and justice upheld elsewhere in the United States.

The 1990s began to see U.S. courts interpret treaty rights liberally in favor of Indians. In *Minnesota et al. v. Mille Lacs Band of Chippewa Indians et al.*, 526 U.S. 172 (1999), the U.S. Supreme Court decided that even though the Mille Lacs Chippewa in their 1855 treaty with the United States relinquished "all" of their interests in Minnesota lands, this did not include their rights to hunt, fish, and gather.

Although American Indians are among the poorest people in the United States, conditions are improving. Unemployment, domestic crowding, and poverty rates are dropping, educational levels are rising, and incomes are increasing at three times the rate of the general U.S. population. And whereas more than half of the American Indian population in the United States lived in cities in the 1980s, by 2000 people were moving back to the reservations in large numbers. Even Shannon County, one of the country's poorest, which lies in Pine Ridge Reservation in South Dakota, saw its population rise by more than a fourth between 1990 and 2000. One of several reasons for this growth is the employment opportunities accompanying newfound wealth deriving from the more than four hundred Indian casinos in twenty-eight states. In 2005 these casinos earned profits of $20 billion. While some Native American communities have become very wealthy because of their casinos, many other American Indian groups, particularly the poorest rural ones, have lost money with their casinos, and many of these have closed. And despite the fact that Indians acquired the right to operate casinos because of their "limited sovereignty," states can still prevent and regulate casinos within their borders. Utah, for this reason, has no Indian casinos. Those groups with profitable casinos have used the money to build houses, fund education, create employment, and buy influence; in 2004 Indians gave $8.6 million to political candidates.

Cultural retention remains important to many Indians. Partly for reasons of pride in themselves, their people, and their history, many Indians are careful to teach their children about their traditions, language, and values both at home and in some reservation schools, partly as a way to counter the influences of Euro-American culture in schools, off the reservations, and especially on television. Others wish to retain culture for political reasons, now that most aboriginal North Americans dress the same way other Americans do, live in

the same kinds of houses, and so on. Some worry that non-Indian Americans will argue that Indians do not differ from other Americans, and therefore do not deserve special rights. But on this matter, like all matters pertaining to the future of Indian people in North America, there are as many opinions as there are Native American individuals. Some Indian parents, even ones whose first languages are indigenous, go out of their way to speak to their children in English, believing that success in English is paramount to economic success in the United States and that knowledge of an Indian language represents an impediment. Although culture loss is lamentable, the fact that aboriginal peoples are attempting in myriad ways to succeed in this changing modern world must be viewed positively.

SEE ALSO *American Indian Movement; Burial Grounds, Native American; Cherokees; Indigenous Rights; Inuit; Iroquois; Navajos; Sitting Bull; Trail of Tears*

BIBLIOGRAPHY

Deloria, Vine, Jr. 1969. *Custer Died for Your Sins: An Indian Manifesto.* New York: Macmillan.

Fagan, Brian. 2005. *Ancient North America: The Archaeology of a Continent.* 4th ed. New York: Thames & Hudson.

Fenton, William N. 1998. *The Great Law and the Longhouse: A Political History of the Iroquois Confederacy.* Norman: University of Oklahoma Press.

Krech, Shepard, III. 1999. *The Ecological Indian: Myth and History.* New York: Norton.

Kroeber, Alfred Louis. 1925. *Handbook of the Indians of California.* Washington, DC: Government Printing Office.

Llewellyn, Karl N., and E. Adamson Hoebel. 1941. *The Cheyenne Way: Conflict and Case Law in Primitive Jurisprudence.* Norman: University of Oklahoma Press.

Mooney, James. [1896] 1965. *The Ghost-Dance Religion and the Sioux Outbreak of 1890.* Chicago: University of Chicago Press.

O'Brien, Sharon. 1989. *American Indian Tribal Governments.* Norman: University of Oklahoma Press.

Spicer, Edward H. 1962. *Cycles of Conquest: The Impact of Spain, Mexico, and the United States on the Indians of the Southwest, 1533–1960.* Tucson: University of Arizona Press.

Sturtevant, William C., et al., eds. 1978–2004. *Handbook of North American Indians.* 20 vols. Washington, DC: Smithsonian Institution Press.

Swanton, John Reed. 1911. *Indian Tribes of the Lower Mississippi Valley and Adjacent Coast of the Gulf of Mexico.* Washington, DC: Government Printing Office.

Daniel P. Strouthes

NATIVES

The term *native* refers to "a person … by nature, innate, inherent, [and] natural to" a place, an environment, or condition (*Concise Oxford Dictionary* 1982, p. 674). One meaning is "of one's birth, where one was born; [and] belonging to one by right of birth"; another "found in a pure or uncombined state"; and another "born in a place (esp. of non-Europeans), indigenous, not exotic; of the natives of a place …" (*Concise Oxford Dictionary* 1982, p. 674). The term developed in tandem with the historic rise of colonialism and colonialism's incumbent discourse, and was shaped by a system of regulation set to incorporate those native people within boundaries and jurisdictions rather than forcing them into diaspora. *Native* carried a pejorative meaning in the Americas, New Zealand, and Australia—especially in former colonies of the British Empire when colonist settlers spoke of and to indigenous populations. A variety of terms arise from the concept of native: *Indian* came into use within the context of Spanish imperialism, *savage* in New France, and *aborigine* specifically in the Australian context. Any indigenous person who became a colonial subject was often referred to as a "native" by colonial settlers, and slavery was simply another dimension of control, but for indigenous peoples in the Americas this had only limited effectiveness. (See Forbes 1988 for extensive discussion of the language Europeans have historically used to designate shades of skin color and other constructed racial markers.)

Prior to the popularization of the term *indigenous* in the 1980s, *native* was often used to describe peoples who claimed to originate from a particular geographic location. Two basic perspectives, often contrasted with each other, are primordial and contructionist orientations (Lawrence 2004, p. 1–16).

When a society has occupied a territory for a period before the subsequent arrival of others, the first group, conscious of its primordial claim that they are native to a region, perceives its historic occupation as centrally tied to its identity as a native people. This nativity concept, "from birth," contributes to the group's understanding of its origins. Residing on the same lands as one's ancestors gives the group an understanding of its origins and nativity similar to that of previous generations. Boundaries for these regions are either delimited or undefined, but the group locates its nativity as a fixed place, and this nativity is often chartered by a rich oral tradition or written history that has a specific ethnographical knowledge of how a people are native.

In contrast, a constructionist orientation of nativity is based upon a group's perception and assertion that its claim is an original or immemorial right. Such claims often emerge when groups are threatened by new immigrant populations competing for resources and survival.

In these cases, the historic sources for a consistent and continuous heritage of occupation, be they archaeological, ethnographic, or textual, are often incomplete, or may be open to competing interpretations. This "nativism" or "indigenism" becomes as much a political as a cultural construct. This reality means that claims being made are open to scrutiny based upon a wider range of considerations. The United Nations Declaration on the Rights of Indigenous Peoples (1994), and the decades-long political struggle to see its adoption, epitomizes this fact.

The geographic connection of a people to their homeland is strengthened when a group either seeks or achieves sovereignty. Often, sovereignty is conceptualized in terms of a group's origins and the maintenance of the group's identity over time. The identity of many groups is not straightforward; rather, it is complicated by vagaries of a given group's cultural history. Consequently, the degrees of recognition that any identity receives is often either affirmed or denied as much as it is asserted by outsiders. State-sanctioned status for native groups may even be extended from the recognition of a group as a minority to a denial of a specific identity in exchange for another.

For example, the term *native* in Canada has been applied to the Métis—who, before the 1982 Constitution of Canada, had no recognition—as well as to nonstatus Indians, non-Métis mixed-bloods, and other aboriginals living off-reservation, often in cities. The term *native* often has been used by these unrecognized, unofficial aboriginals to refer to themselves, but also by outsiders to refer to them. With the introduction of the term *aboriginal* in the Canadian Constitution as an all-encompassing term for Indian, Métis, and Inuit, *native* has been replaced in many contexts in favor of *aboriginal*. However, many aboriginal groups prefer their ethnocultural names for themselves. And although a number of academic programs are still called "Native Studies," the parlance has shifted in favor of *indigenous* instead of *native*.

In the United States, recognition is accorded to the members of federally recognized Indian tribes, and then specifically to members who are minimally one-quarter in blood quantum; no recognition is accorded to others of native heritage, nor to anyone not a member of a recognized tribe. The term *Native American* was in use for several decades, but because of its confusion with native-born Americans as opposed to immigrant Americans, the term is rarely used, having been dropped in favor of *American Indians*; most American Indian groups prefer to call themselves by tribal designations. In Australia, the term *native* is used in the larger society to refer to anyone descended from Aborigines or Torres Strait Islanders. Most groups refer to themselves by their own names for themselves, reflecting their linguistic or geographical location names, and the use of "native" is also made in reference to their struggle for legal title to their traditional territories.

SEE ALSO *Colonialism; Gaze, Colonial; Indigenismo; Indigenous Rights; Native Americans; Nativism; Other, The; Racism; Self-Determination; Sovereignty*

BIBLIOGRAPHY

Banton, Michael. 1996. Native Peoples. *Dictionary of Race and Ethnic Relations*, 4th ed., ed. Ellis Cashmore, 256–257. London and New York: Routledge.

Dombrowski, Kirk. 2004. The Politics of Native Culture. *A Companion to the Anthropology of American Indians*, ed. Thomas Biolsi, 360–382. Malden, MA: Blackwell Publishing.

Forbes, Jack. 1988. *Black Africans and Native Americans: Color, Race, and Caste in the Evolution of Red-Black Peoples.* Oxford: Blackwell.

Lawrence, Bonita. 2004. *"Real" Indians and Others: Mixed-Blood Urban Native Peoples and Indigenous Nationhood.* Vancouver: University of British Columbia Press.

Niezen, Ronald. 2003. *The Origins of Indigenism: Human Rights and the Politics of Identity.* Berkeley: University of California Press.

David Reed Miller

NATIVISM

Nativism is a recurring social and political movement characterized principally by hostility to supposed foreigners. While the attitudes and dynamics that distinguish nativism have developed and continue to develop in many countries, the term itself has been elaborated primarily by sociologists and historians in studies of nineteenth- and twentieth-century American politics and social relations. Nativism, as a form of ethnic discrimination, is closely related to racism but may be distinguished by its emphasis on language and the privileges of citizenship as the bases of its politicized rhetoric.

In the United States nativism led to the formation of influential political parties beginning in the 1830s and declining in the years before the Civil War, when slavery became virtually the exclusive issue of political contention. The most important of these parties was the Know-Nothing Party of the 1850s. The Know-Nothings began as the Order of the Star-Spangled Banner, a secret fraternal organization whose members allegedly claimed to "know-nothing" whenever queried about the group. The efforts of the members were directed toward stopping the immigration of Catholics who were arriving principally from Germany and Ireland. Officially registered as the American Party, the Know-Nothings asserted in their party platform of 1856 that *"Americans must rule America"* (emphasis in original); that is, naturalized citizens—whose national allegiance and devotion to the principal of the separation of church and state were considered suspect—were not considered eligible to hold government office.

As John Higham described in his seminal study of American nativism, *Strangers in the Land* (1955), during the periods of economic crises in the late nineteenth century nativists became increasingly concerned with the political rather than the religious beliefs of recent immigrants. It was deemed that American institutions were imminently threatened by radical socialist ideas and movements that had periodically toppled European regimes. Elements of economic nativism also characterized nationalist labor unions, where leaders such as Samuel Gompers argued that open immigration policies lowered wages and degraded the condition of the native-born American worker.

Nativism surged again in the early decades of the twentieth century, when the retrospectively pseudoscience of eugenics manifested widespread fears of racial degeneration. This most explicitly racialized nativism embraced simplified notions drawn from evolutionary science to elaborate a paranoid vision of imminent national and even human catastrophe. These nativists—well represented by Madison Grant, author of *The Passing of a Great Race* (1933)—argued that Anglo-Saxons were the pinnacle of human evolution. Open immigration, particularly of what were described as the degraded peoples of southern and eastern Europe, threatened Anglo-Saxon racial purity and thus the very future of the American nation. It was in fact such racial nativism that led to the passage of National Origins Act of 1924; the act severely limited immigration of people from southern and eastern European countries.

Nativism is again a force in American politics and society. After the September 11, 2001, terrorist attacks, it became increasingly difficult for Arabs to immigrate to the United States, and anti-Arab sentiments and policies were employed with virtual impunity for political gain. However, ethnic Arabs are a small minority population in the United States; nativists in the early twenty-first century contended over the matter of the status of legal and illegal Hispanic immigrants.

In 1994 the passage of Proposition 187 in California marked a watershed moment in American nativism. No longer was it possible to consider nativism a movement of the past; furthermore Proposition 187 clearly demonstrated that the principal issues around which nativists rallied had once again shifted, though arguably to a refined form of economic nativism focused on social services. Proposition 187 called for the denial of public education, health care, and other social services to illegal immigrants, most of whom, in California, came from Mexico and other parts of Latin America. Nativists, such as the members of Americans for Immigration Reform, consider social services for illegal immigrants an unreasonable cost burden for taxpayers. Though Proposition 187 was eventually overruled in federal courts, efforts to pass restrictive legislation persisted, including President George W. Bush's 2006 immigration reform bill.

Exclusivist movements that share the dynamics of nativism have grown rather than ebbed throughout the world alongside increasing globalization, which many scholars once thought would put an end to such movements and conflicts. Versions of nativists' attitudes have achieved (sometimes violent) social and political expression in virtually every European nation since the late twentieth century, and what might fairly be called nativist policies are taken for granted in many Asian and African countries. In the United States nativism endures as a remarkable contradiction to the powerful myths of American egalitarianism and opportunity, including the notions that the United States embraces and prospers from the diversity of its peoples.

SEE ALSO *Citizenship; Identity; Immigration; Nationalism and Nationality; Natives; Naturalization; Other, The; Race Relations; Racism; September 11, 2001; Social Exclusion; Xenophobia*

BIBLIOGRAPHY

Anbinder, Tyler G. 1994. *Nativism and Slavery: The Northern Know Nothings and the Politics of the 1850s.* New York: Oxford University Press.

Bennett, David H. 1995. *The Party of Fear: From Nativist Movement to the New Right in American History.* New York: Vintage.

Higham, John. [1955] 1974. *Strangers in the Land: Patterns of American Nativism, 1860–1925.* New York: Atheneum.

Stephen Germic

NATO

SEE *North American Free Trade Agreement.*

NATURAL CHILDBIRTH

The term *natural childbirth* refers to a group of approaches to managing childbirth that share the common aim of facilitating childbirth without medical intervention. A variety of techniques may be used to achieve this aim. Although there have been, and there still are, wide variations in cultural practices surrounding childbirth, the dominant trend in Western industrialized societies has been to medicalize birth. This means that birth has become increasingly attended and managed by medical professionals in medical settings such as hospitals. Natural childbirth approaches stand in contrast to the medicalization of childbirth, and indeed developed in response to it. From early in the twentieth century there was concern amongst obstetricians that Western civilization had impeded women's ability to labor with the brevity and ease of their less "civilized" sisters. One response was to treat childbirth as a risky, pathological process requiring medical intervention and management: in particular, to anesthetize the birthing woman and to use episiotomy and operative delivery such as with forceps. Hence the popularity in the United States from 1914, when the New England Twilight Sleep Association was formed, into the 1940s of administering scopolamine and morphine to induce "twilight sleep," which meant that women were barely conscious through their deliveries, and had no memory of the event. Proponents of natural childbirth took the opposite view, arguing that obstetrics was becoming too mechanistic, indeed "veterinary," and that its orientation needed to broaden to include psychological, social, and spiritual aspects of childbirth as well as the biomechanical. One means of achieving this was to involve women in antenatal physiotherapy and exercises to prepare for childbirth. The most influential response, however, came from Dr. Grantly Dick-Read in his 1933 analysis of labor pain, *Natural Childbirth*. In it he argued that fear of childbirth in Western society had produced physiological responses in birthing women that prolong labor and make it more painful. He developed an approach to foster the active involvement and conscious cooperation of birthing women that empowers them and makes them less fearful of birthing. The potential advantages of minimizing medical intervention and maximizing women's control over their bodies in natural childbirth included shorter labor, less pain, a more satisfying birth experience, and a more alert (and hence healthier) baby because of lack of exposure to morphine and other drugs in utero. As a result of both mother and baby being conscious and alert at delivery, affective bonds between mother and child could also develop immediately and naturally from the moment of birth. Opponents of natural childbirth cite the risks associated with birthing, including maternal and neonatal mortality, as justification for using medical interventions preventatively or in immediate response to potential problems.

A number of different techniques for natural childbirth have evolved in Europe, the United States, and elsewhere. They are associated with practitioners such as

Fernand Lamaze, Frederick Leboyer, Michel Odent, and Frances Vaughan, who stress different aspects of childbirth such as the setting (e.g., quiet, dark, water births) or positions that facilitate natural childbirth (e.g., squatting). In the United States, Robert A. Bradley developed Dick-Read's approach and expanded it from the 1960s to include fathers in the antenatal preparation and the coaching of their partners through childbirth (the "Bradley method"). In more recent years this has been further expanded to include other support persons for the birthing woman; these may include friends or family members, or a paid "doula." In most Western societies birth attendants must be licensed to practice and generally include only doctors and midwives. The practice of most midwifery, particularly for autonomous or independent midwives, is premised on the understanding of birth as a normal, holistic, physiological, emotional, and social process, and hence encourages natural childbirth approaches. Many women's and consumer groups are also supportive of natural childbirth approaches.

SEE ALSO *Children; Midwifery; Motherhood*

BIBLIOGRAPHY

Dick-Read, Grantly. 1933. *Natural Childbirth*. London: William Heinemann.

Leavitt, Judith Walzer. 1986. *Brought to Bed: Childbearing in America, 1850–1950*. New York: Oxford University Press.

Moscucci, Ornella. 2003. Holistic Obstetrics: The Origins of "Natural Childbirth" in Britain. *Postgraduate Medical Journal* 79: 168–173.

Reiger, Kerreen. 2001. *Our Bodies, Our Babies*. Melbourne: Melbourne University Press.

Maria Zadoroznyj

NATURAL DISASTERS

A natural hazard is an extreme natural phenomenon that threatens human lives, activities or property, or the environment of life. Natural disasters are the destructive consequence of extreme natural hazards, and globally there are more than 700 of them each year. Floods are the most common natural disaster. Together with earthquakes and cyclonic storms they are the most destructive of such manifestations.

Natural phenomena may be transformed into hazards either by excess or by dearth. For example, too great a discharge of water may give rise to flooding, whereas too little may cause a drought. A situation becomes hazardous when the physical forces or environmental stresses at work exceed the ability of human social, economic, cultural, or health systems to absorb, resist, or avoid the resulting negative impact. In this respect, natural hazards are defined not only by the natural forces that induce them, but also by the vulnerability of human systems. Vulnerability is defined here as the susceptibility of people or things to harm.

The threat of a natural hazard is either constantly present or is subject to fluctuations. Many hazards are cyclical; for example, earthquakes of a certain size will occur on a given fault when enough tectonic stress has been accumulated to overcome the frictional resistance of the rock mass to slipping, a process which will probably occur with a definable time interval because of the gradual build-up of strain on the fault. Other hazards, especially meteorological ones, may be seasonal.

Generally, the vast majority of hazards are subject to a rule of magnitude and frequency in which the higher the magnitude, the lower the frequency of occurrence. Some hazards, such as volcanic eruptions, may operate on a geological timescale that is much longer than the scale of human lives. In such cases it can be very difficult to justify the allocation of resources to prepare effectively for events that have a low probability of occurrence during a single human lifetime.

In other cases, the repetitiveness of a hazard may be a problem. For instance, the solvency of the U.S. National Flood Insurance Program (NFIP) depends as much on reducing the instance of repeated claims as it does on anticipating and reducing the impact of large, infrequent events. In a small number of cases, claims have been made for reimbursing damage to a single property up to five times in a decade. Such problems must be abated by reducing either the hazard or the vulnerability to it.

In everyday situations the product of hazard and vulnerability is risk, which can be defined as the probability or likelihood that an event of a given kind and size will occur in a given interval of time and with an anticipated set of negative consequences. Engineers tend to define risk by calculating numerical values of the probability, while social scientists may be more interested in how risk is perceived and how some of the intangible features of human behavior affect it. In any event, paradoxically, risk is a hypothetical quantity (though no less important for that). It materializes as impact, which should lead to an emergency response that reduces the harm done as much as possible. Hence:

Hazard × Vulnerability [× Exposure] = Risk → Impact → Emergency Response

Exposure to natural hazards becomes an issue when an item (such as a person, a community, a building, or an economic activity) is not constantly at risk. Despite temporal variations in strain upon Earth's crust, to all intents and purposes we may consider earthquake risk to be fairly constant, especially as it cannot accurately be predicted in the short term. However, predictable hazards such as hurricanes, which can be monitored and tracked before they make landfall (i.e., arrive at a coast), may allow a forecast to be turned into a warning that stimulates an organized response on the part of the threatened community. Generally, where it is feasible, evacuation is the most effective means of reducing the exposure of people to death or injury in high magnitude events.

The question of exactly what phenomena should be classified as natural hazards has long been debated by students of the field. The core phenomena consist of geophysical events from the atmosphere, hydrosphere, and geosphere (the lithosphere), and to a lesser extent from the biosphere. Earthquakes, landslides, and subsidence of the ground are geospheric hazards of the first order; tropical cyclones (also known as hurricanes and typhoons), tornadoes, and windstorms are the leading examples of meteorological hazards; and drought and floods are the principal threats from the hydrosphere, with subdivision of the latter into riverine, rain-fed, coastal, and glacial outburst forms.

By convention, though not necessarily on the basis of any very robust theoretical reasoning, disease outbreaks in humans, animals, and plants (i.e., epidemics, epizootics, and epiphytotics) are not usually classified as natural hazards. However, locust infestations are often included.

A further definitional problem occurs when disasters have mixed natural and human-induced (anthropogenic) causes. For example, destructive floods can result from dam bursts, which can in turn result from excessive river flows, earthquakes, or rapid landslides or snow avalanches that cause water waves in the reservoir, if not from failure of the materials or design of the dam itself. In point of fact, *natural hazard* and *natural disaster* are convenience terms. Whatever one's religious convictions, responsibility for damage and destruction cannot be shrugged off by referring to unpredictable "acts of God," as they stem from failure to mitigate forms of human and environmental vulnerability that are well known and understood.

In conceptual terms, serious study of natural hazards began in the 1920s with the development of the "human ecology" field. From 1945 onward the Chicago school founded by Harlan Barrows (1877–1960) and taken forward by Gilbert Fowler White (1911–2006) gradually revealed the human perceptual and social processes of adjusting to hazards. White and his students found a rich source of study in the struggles of U.S. Great Plains farmers to adapt to varying patterns of drought and flood. By and large, research in many other parts of the world has confirmed the findings of the U.S. human ecologists and geographers, despite some variations due to cultural differences. Thus, the "hazardousness of place" is tempered by the choice of adjustments that people who inhabit zones of hazard are able to employ.

The Chicago school was motivated to explain why structural responses had not solved the problem of natural hazards. For example, a century of canalization and levee building by the U.S. Army Corps of Engineers on the Mississippi River ended in 1993 with the worst and most prolonged flood on record. Clearly residents, developers, and planners on the floodplain had made some false assumptions about the infallibility of structural flood defenses.

With some success White and his colleagues advocated an approach based on a mixture of structural and nonstructural protection. It may still be necessary to build barriers to stop flooding, or to strengthen buildings so that they resist earthquakes, but it is equally necessary to tackle such hazards with organizational methods. Hence the nonstructural solutions include evacuation (where feasible), emergency planning, land-use control, and public awareness campaigns.

Unfortunately, despite the best efforts of mitigation specialists, the world has not become less susceptible to hazards over the last half-century. For example, Hurricane Katrina, which made landfall in Louisiana and Mississippi on August 29, 2005, killed 1,848 people, seriously damaged or destroyed 78,000 homes, and left more than half of the population of New Orleans without shelter. As Hurricane Ivan had narrowly missed crossing the city a year previously, the scenario for a major storm impact was well known. Despite this, the heights and state of maintenance of levees were insufficient, as were evacuation and recovery plans. Failures of coordination between local, state, and federal levels of government led to a relief debacle. Rebuilding will probably take eight to eleven years and, due to the phenomenon of geographical inertia (the reluctance of long-term residents to relocate their homes and businesses), will necessarily require considerable investment in major yet fallible structural defenses.

The relentless rise in global population, polarization of wealth between rich and poor, marginalization of vulnerable communities, and the prevalence of about twenty-five complex humanitarian emergencies have all contributed to the increasing toll of natural disasters. So has the increasing complexity and interdependence of modern society, and so, no doubt, will global warming and climate change, as more extreme, if not more frequent, meteorological phenomena are likely to occur.

The average annual death toll in natural disasters is about 140,000, but there is very considerable variation from one year to another. In fact, after five years in which the death toll averaged about 58,000, the Asian tsunami of December 26, 2004, took at least 230,000 lives. Despite the irregularities, there are discernible upward trends in the number of people directly affected by natural disasters (at least 250 million a year) and the cost of disasters (well in excess of US$100 billion a year), although improved protection has had some effect in stemming the rise in mortality.

Despite much debate and many good intentions, global vulnerability to natural hazards remains unacceptably high. Critical facilities—schools, hospitals, essential lifelines—remain heavily at risk in many countries (for example, in the Kashmir earthquake of October 5, 2005, schools frequented by 48,000 children collapsed). More money continues to be spent on responding to disasters than on reducing the risks of future ones. Although vulnerability and poverty are not precisely synonymous, in both rich and poor countries they are very closely linked. Hence natural disaster impacts involve serious questions of equity. Natural hazard impacts need to be mitigated by a mixture of prevention, avoidance, and sustainable development: In short, sustainable disaster reduction is required.

SEE ALSO *Disaster Management; Shocks*

BIBLIOGRAPHY

Abbott, Patrick L. 2004 *Natural Disasters.* 4th ed. New York: McGraw-Hill.

Alexander, David E. 1993. *Natural Disasters.* London and New York: Routledge.

Burton, Ian, Robert W. Kates, and Gilbert F. White. 1993. *The Environment as Hazard.* 2nd ed. New York: Guilford.

Perry, Ronald W., and Enrico L. Quarantelli, eds. 2005. *What Is a Disaster? New Answers to Old Questions.* Philadelphia: Xlibris.

David Alexander

NATURAL EXPERIMENTS

Most empirical tests in the social sciences are motivated by the desire to estimate a potentially causal effect of an independent variable on a dependent outcome. For example, one might want to know whether a policy intervention, such as a training program for unemployed individuals or an additional year of schooling, has an effect on the outcome of interest, such as earnings or the likelihood of finding a job. To make any causal inference, a researcher must compare the outcome of individuals in a treatment condition with the outcome of individuals in a control condition. The two groups should differ only in that the former group has been subjected to an intervention and the latter has not. This is particularly important if one is concerned that a third, omitted factor may influence the outcome, or that the treatment group is a special selection of people.

Controlled experiments in which people are randomly assigned by the researcher to be part of a treatment condition are rarely possible in the social sciences. Natural experiments represent a second-best way to make causal inferences. A natural experiment does not rely on randomization initiated and controlled by the researcher; instead, it uses observational data involving transparent, naturally occurring random or pseudo-random variations in the treatment and control condition assignments. The treatment group and the control sample should be equivalent before the treatment. The randomization can then take care of any confounding factors (e.g., omitted variables or selection issues). For the natural experiment to be valid, the assignment must be uncorrelated with the measured outcome.

Previous studies have relied on various types of natural experiments. One group of studies uses random changes in public policy. These studies might analyze, for example, how the introduction of a higher minimum wage affects state-level employment, by comparing employment in one U.S. state that has raised the minimum wage with employment in a neighboring state that has not and is (assumed to be) otherwise equal. A second group of studies uses random biological or climate-related events, such as birth dates or weather conditions. These natural experiments are appealing, because the assignments are more plausibly seen as being uncorrelated with the outcomes to be explained than are the assignments in the first group. A third group uses naturally occurring random assignments to treatment and control groups. For example, a lottery might determine—randomly—whether people receive a sudden boost to their disposable income, are eligible to participate in a program, or are required to enter military service. The outcomes of individuals who "win" (treatment condition) can then be compared with those of individuals who participate but do not win (control condition).

Though controlled experiments have a long tradition in medicine and psychology, in the late twentieth century natural experiments became more prominent in the social sciences as a means of increasing the internal validity of empirical research. Indeed, the use of natural experiments has been extended to empirically test hypotheses where causality may be initially confusing. For example, it is not clear whether additional education leads to higher earnings or whether individuals who will earn a lot in the future seek additional education for other reasons. Natural experiments can disentangle these two lines of causality. One could measure the effect of schooling on earnings more generally by using the variation in years of schooling that is not directly correlated with earning but comes from the variation in the natural experiment, for example the date of birth or winning of a lottery.

Natural experiments, however, have limitations with respect to both internal and external validity. In experiments driven by policy changes, for example, the randomness of the intervention is often questionable, but hard to test. Changes in policy may be driven by political factors associated with the outcome. If this is the case, the change in policy is not independent of the outcome and cannot be assumed to be exogenous. What is labeled a natural experiment may then yield results no closer to true causal inference than would a simple observational study. Further, the source of the natural experiment may make it difficult to judge its external validity. The winning of a lottery to participate in a particular program may affect both the losers and the winners. The former may substitute another activity if they fail to win. This would bias the estimated effect of the treatment, even though assignment had been random. Nevertheless, natural experiments are still the best, and often the only, method available to obtain causal inferences in empirical studies in the social sciences when the researcher cannot control treatment assignment.

SEE ALSO *Case Method; Experiments; Social Experiment*

BIBLIOGRAPHY

Campbell, Donald T., and Julian C. Stanley. 1963. *Experimental and Quasi-Experimental Designs for Research.* Boston: Houghton Mifflin.

Meyer, Bruce D. 1995. Natural and Quasi-Experiments in Economics. *Journal of Business and Economic Statistics* 13 (2): 151–162.

Rosenzweig, Mark R., and Kenneth I. Wolpin. 2000. Natural "Natural Experiments" in Economics. *Journal of Economic Literature* 38 (4): 827–874.

Winship, Christopher, and Stephen L. Morgan. 1999. The Estimation of Causal Effects from Observational Data. *Annual Review of Sociology* 25: 659–706.

Stephan Meier

NATURAL PRICE

SEE *Exchange Value; Long Run.*

NATURAL RATE OF UNEMPLOYMENT

The natural rate of unemployment is a concept that was developed by the economists Milton Friedman and Edmund Phelps in the late 1960s, and it has been extremely influential in shaping the way that the economics profession views the economy. The notion of a natural rate of unemployment represents a return to the classical pre-Keynesian economics that ruled before and during the Great Depression, and many of the arguments are clearly anticipated in David Champernowne's 1936 discussion of monetary unemployment. The theory was especially influential on policy in the 1970s and 1980s. However, its influence began to wane in the 1990s for a variety of reasons, including the emergence of new ideas and the recognition that the theory has significant operational difficulties when used for policy.

The natural rate is also referred to as the NAIRU (nonaccelerating inflation rate of unemployment). According to the theory, inflation will be steady at the NAIRU, but attempts to lower the unemployment rate further will ignite ever-accelerating inflation. The policy implication is straightforward: do not push unemployment below the natural rate.

The core idea is that the levels of employment and unemployment in an economy are determined by the supply of and demand for labor, which also jointly determine the real value (i.e., purchasing power) of wages. Unemployment arises because of "frictions" and "rigidities" in the economy that prevent the smooth operation of labor markets. How much so-called natural unemployment there is depends on the extent of labor-market frictions and rigidities.

Examples of frictions are imperfect information among workers as to where jobs are, and imperfect information among firms as to which workers want jobs. This gives rise to "search" unemployment, whereby unemployed workers seeking jobs are unable to match up with job vacancies. Examples of rigidities are the minimum wage and trade unions, which are argued to cause unemployment by setting wages too high, thereby reducing labor demand and employment.

According to Friedman and Phelps, the minimum wage and trade unions raise the natural rate of unemployment. This conclusion follows from their description of the labor market in terms of supply and demand. As such, natural rate theory has provided political conservatives with a justification for opposition to the minimum wage and trade unions on the grounds that they prevent the labor market from operating efficiently. From a natural rate perspective, the only way to lower the equilibrium rate of unemployment is to eliminate wage protections, improve matching arrangements between employers with vacancies and unemployed workers, change incentives and attitudes toward work, and change the demographic composition of the workforce. That is fundamentally different from Keynesian economics, which also emphasizes aggregate demand management.

A second important implication concerns policy toward inflation. In the 1960s economic policy was dominated by the idea of the Phillips curve, which claimed that there was a negative relationship between inflation and unemployment. That implied that policymakers could lower unemployment by slightly increasing inflation. The theory of the natural rate of unemployment challenged this claim, and argued that increasing inflation would have no effect on the long-run rate of unemployment. Any increase in the rate of inflation would just be matched by an increase in wage inflation.

Once again, the economic logic follows from the supply-and-demand model of labor markets. Workers supply labor in return for real wages that determine how much they can purchase. Likewise, firms hire workers because of the output they produce, and they pay workers a wage based on the value of that output. The implication is that labor supply and demand are unaffected by inflation. If prices double, then wages will also double, leaving employment and real wages unchanged.

One caveat to this conclusion is so-called unexpected or surprise inflation. Suppose workers see wages rising, but they are unaware that prices are also rising. In this case, they will think the real value (purchasing power) of wages has gone up and workers searching for jobs will accept jobs they would not previously have taken. Employment will therefore rise and unemployment will fall. However, workers will soon learn that prices are also rising so that real wages have not increased. When that happens, they will quit these jobs, and employment will fall back again and unemployment will rise.

This conclusion has had a major impact on monetary policy. In the 1960s and early 1970s, central banks (such as the Federal Reserve) thought that if they kept interest rates low and allowed a little higher inflation, they would lower unemployment. The theory of the natural rate of unemployment contradicted this belief, and instead said there would be no long-run effect. This has ushered in a new era in which policy emphasizes low inflation. The argument is that since inflation cannot reduce unemployment, the Federal Reserve should aim to keep inflation low.

Additionally, the Federal Reserve should aim to keep inflation predictable and stable. Though surprise inflation can temporarily reduce unemployment, such surprises are undesirable. The argument is that workers are being tricked into accepting jobs because they do not realize that prices have also gone up. Workers are therefore making decisions based on incorrect information, and this is a form of economic inefficiency.

The theory of the natural rate is now being challenged. With regard to the relationship between inflation and unemployment, some economists believe that low inflation acts as a form of "grease" that helps adjustment in labor markets, giving rise to a Phillips curve. The economic logic is as follows. Workers will always accept wage increases from their employers, but they will resist wage cuts. This is because workers cannot distinguish whether a wage cut is warranted because business conditions have deteriorated or the firm is just trying to exploit them. Under these conditions, inflation can help reduce unemployment. Prices and money wages will rise at firms where business conditions remain healthy. However, they will remain unchanged at firms where business conditions are weak. Consequently, relative prices and the purchasing power of wages at these weaker firms will fall, thereby shifting demand to them and raising employment at them. The net result is that higher inflation will raise employment and lower unemployment, as predicted by the Phillips curve.

Another reason for the diminished influence of natural rate theory concerns operational policy difficulties. The natural rate is not an observed unemployment rate. Instead, it must be estimated. However, empirical estimates have proven highly variable, and for the U.S. economy they have varied between 4 and 8 percent. This makes it of little use for guiding policy.

When it comes to the minimum wage and unions, these institutions may be needed to correct imbalances of power in labor markets. The supply-and-demand model of labor markets assumes that neither firms nor workers have any labor-market power. When it comes to jobs and the employment relation, power is assumed to be completely absent. However, if this is not the case, the supply-and-demand model is wrong. If the labor market naturally favors firms (since they have greater financial backing and do not have families to feed), then firms will have greater wage-bargaining power. In this case, workers may need minimum-wage laws and trade unions to equalize bargaining power and prevent exploitation.

The equalization of bargaining power can improve the distribution of income and thereby create demand for firms' output. A mass production economy needs mass consumption. Keynesian economics maintains that free market economies may not automatically generate enough demand to ensure full employment, as exemplified by the experience of the Great Depression in the 1930s. In this case, unions and minimum wages can be seen as economic institutions that create a pattern of income distribution that generates sufficient consumption demand to ensure full employment. This Keynesian view of the economy contrasts with the natural rate's labor supply-and-demand model that claims the economy automatically reaches full employment via wage adjustment.

If the natural rate of unemployment is so problematic, why did it become so popular in the 1970s and 1980s? Here, politics and history are important. Natural rate theory is a revival of classical laissez-faire economics that opposes institutions such as the minimum wage and trade unions. Classical laissez-faire economics also opposes Phillips curve policies that encourage a little inflation to stimulate higher employment. Political conservatives never accepted these institutions and policies, and natural rate theory gave them new grounds for opposition. When the national political climate became more conservative in the 1970s, this created a favorable environment for the spread of natural rate thinking.

Additionally, the 1970s were a period of great economic disruption owing to OPEC (Organization of Petroleum Exporting Countries) oil shocks. This disruption caused the economy to underperform, and it also created a new type of energy price inflation in which inflation rose but unemployment did not fall. Conservatives opportunistically interpreted this oil shock inflation as evidence confirming natural rate theory and rejecting Phillips curve theory.

The history of the natural rate of unemployment provides two critical lessons. The first is that theories depend on their assumptions. In the case of natural rate theory, its conclusions about unions, minimum wages, and the employment effects of inflation stem from its description of labor markets in terms of demand and supply. If this is an inappropriate description of how labor markets operate in the real world, then the theory of the natural rate of unemployment is wrong. The second lesson is that the spread of economic ideas is influenced by what is happening in society. When society drifts left, economic ideas will likely drift left. And when society drifts right, economic ideas will likely drift right. Like everyone else, economists live in society. That means they too are influenced by what is happening in society.

SEE ALSO *Adaptive Expectations; Economics, New Classical; Expectations; Expectations, Rational; Friedman, Milton; Long Run; Market Clearing; Monetarism; Phillips Curve; Sticky Wages; Unemployment; Wages*

BIBLIOGRAPHY

Champernowne, David G. 1936. Unemployment, Basic and Monetary: The Classical Analysis and the Keynesian. *Review of Economic Studies* 3 (3): 201–216.

Friedman, Milton. 1968. The Role of Monetary Policy. *American Economic Review* 58: 1–17.

Galbraith, John Kenneth. 1997. Test the Limit. *Challenge* 34: 66.

Palley, Thomas I. 1998 Zero is Not the Optimal Rate of Inflation. *Challenge* 41: 7–18.

Palley, Thomas I. 1999 The Structural Unemployment Policy Trap: How the NAIRU Can Mislead Policymakers. *New Economy* 6: 79–83.

Staiger, Douglas, James H. Stock, and Mark W. Watson. 1997. The NAIRU, Unemployment, and Monetary Policy. *Journal of Economic Perspectives* 11 (1): 33–50.

Tobin, James. 1972. Inflation and Unemployment. *American Economic Review* 62: 1–18.

Thomas I. Palley

NATURAL RESOURCES, NONRENEWABLE

It is common to subdivide natural resources into the nonrenewable and renewable categories, respectively. The former, predominantly metals and fossil fuels, are derived from a limited stock, whose ultimate size is unknown. The supply of the latter, primarily of biological origin, relies on regeneration that can be repeated in perpetuity. This difference leads to frequent assertions that sustainability requires more reliance on renewables, to avoid, or at least delay, an impending and unavoidable depletion of nonrenewable resources.

The differences in the conditions of long-term supply between the two categories are often exaggerated. Everything being equal, the supply of both tends to become more costly with expanded use, for that necessitates the employment of more meager mineral deposits and more marginal soils. Everything is not equal, however, and technological progress has more than compensated for this upward push, so that the real cost of mineral as well as agricultural output has tended to fall over time. Furthermore, examples of dramatic exhaustion are easier to quote from the renewable category. Witness how the forests disappeared in antique Italy and in seventeenth-century England, or the virtual extinction of cod in the world's oceans in the late twentieth century.

The fear of depletion of exhaustible resources is almost as old as humankind, but the available experience suggests that painful scarcity is less of an immediate threat than ever in history. Despite impressive growth rates in usage, which have raised present world consumption to many times that of the early or mid-twentieth century, the reserves of virtually all metal minerals and fossil fuels have expanded at even faster rates, through a combination of discovery and subsequent appreciation of the newfound deposits. Extraction costs show a falling trend in real terms, and the prices of most exhaustible resources have declined in parallel. All this is counter to the predictions of a dire future made by the Club of Rome in the early 1970s. These predictions completely missed the point, primarily because they neglected technological progress in exhaustible resource exploration and exploitation. There are no indications that the benign trends caused by technological innovation are in the process of reversal.

Though in most cases, declining costs have resulted in falling prices, there are important exceptions. The price of oil has followed an upward trend in real terms ever since the Organization of Petroleum Exporting Countries (OPEC) took effective command of the oil market in the early 1970s. The cartel has been able to exercise market management to its advantage because its members control the world's largest and most economical reserves, those in the Middle East. The most potent tool for maintaining monopolistic pricing in the oil market has been a virtual arrest since the late 1970s in the cartel's expansion of capacity to exploit this resource wealth. The prices of petroleum have spilled over to other fossil fuels, since the latter can substitute for oil in many cases. Monopolistic market conditions are likely to be maintained so long as the cartel remains in charge.

The prices of virtually all primary materials, exhaustible as well as renewable, rose impressively in the first half of the 2000s. The price of oranges and rice increased by 50 percent between 2002 and 2005, coffee went up by 68 percent, and rubber by 95 percent. The price of oil doubled while the prices of nickel and copper increased by even more. This was the third powerful and general commodity boom since World War II (1939–1945). As was the case with commodity booms during the time periods between 1950 and 1951 and between 1973 and 1974, this boom was triggered by a sudden and sizable demand expansion at a time when inventories were small and no slack capacity existed to satisfy the surge. As on previous occasions, the rising prices were temporarily decoupled from the costs of production.

The demand shock centered on 2004 was primarily due to a very fast growth in world gross domestic product (GDP). The new phenomenon was that the economies of several large developing countries, notably China and India but also Brazil and Indonesia, expanded at voracious rates, and contributed strongly to the global boom. The successful growth performance in those nations was primarily due to the economic liberalization measures implemented during preceding decades. An intensified participation in the integration of the global economy was a key factor behind these countries' impressive growth rates. At the present stage of their economic development, involving industrialization, urbanization, and the build-up of infrastructure, these economies are very intensive resource users. This accentuated the demand shock in the raw materials markets.

Normality will likely return to these markets before the end of the 2000s, just as it did a few years after the outbreak of the earlier commodity booms. The year 2004 was exceptional in terms of global growth, unlikely to be repeated in the near future. The profitability of the natural resource industries at the prevailing prices is exceedingly high, so the incentive to invest in capacity expansion is strong. Sizable investment efforts are also under implementation. Building new capacity will take several years to complete, but once that capacity becomes operational, and the supply can increase, prices are bound to fall, to reflect once more the cost of production. Oil is an exception in this regard. The cartel's efforts to keep capacity constrained may permit it to continue extracting monopolistic prices.

Successful globalization could well result in higher world economic growth than was attained in past decades. But there is no reason to believe that this will compromise the nonrenewable natural resources availability. The world is still very far from the bottom of the barrel of the resource wealth, and with continued cost-reducing technological progress, it is uncertain whether that bottom will ever be seen. Faster growth in the demand for natural resource commodities can easily be accommodated by a more speedy supply expansion, but producers must be given a sufficiently early warning of what to expect in order to adjust their production capacity. Successful globalization brings prospects for a speedier increase in the incomes of the poor in this world, which should be seen as a blessing and not a resource threat.

BIBLIOGRAPHY

Radetzki, Marian. 2002. Is Resource Depletion a Threat to Human Progress? Oil and Other Critical Exhaustible Materials. *Energy Sustainable Development: A Challenge for the New Century (Energex2002).* Krakow: Mineral and Energy Economy Research Institute, Polish Academy of Sciences.

Tilton, John. 2003. *On Borrowed Time? Assessing the Threat of Mineral Depletion.* Washington, DC: Resources for the Future.

Marian Radetzki

NATURAL RESOURCES, RENEWABLE

SEE *Natural Resources, Nonrenewable; Resources.*

NATURAL RIGHTS

John Locke's natural rights theory is derived from what is called *natural law.* It maintains that individuals enter society with basic rights, such as the right to life and liberty, which cannot be abrogated by government. According to this ethical theory, the moral standards that govern human behavior are, in some sense, objectively derived from the *nature* of human beings. *Naturalism* is thus a philosophical position that attempts to explain all phenomena and account for all values by means of strictly natural categories, as opposed to supernatural categories (i.e., God).

According to Locke, the state of nature can be understood properly as men living together according to reason. This differs from Thomas Hobbes's conception of the state of nature, which is characterized in *Leviathan* (1651) as chaos and "war of all against all." For Locke, "reason, which is the law, teaches all mankind who will but consult it, that, being all equal and independent, no one ought to harm another in his life, health, liberty or possessions" (1690). This natural moral law is the recognition of individuals' value and their virtue as God's creatures.

The philosophical implication of Locke's state of nature is a set of natural laws—the law of opinion, civil law, and divine law. The law of opinion is society's reflection of natural standards for happiness. As Locke outlines in *Two Treatises of Government* (1690), through nature or reason we discover moral rules mirroring God's law. Because the natural world is created by God, and because God associates actions with pleasure ("good") or pain ("evil")—touching fire, for example, causes pain—the study of nature allows us to learn morality and to understand "the good." Through an analysis of *a priori* morality and of "justice," the commonwealth sets civil law, enforced by police and courts, and supplements nature with a rational law-based social theory. Locke defines ethics as involving voluntary conformity to or disagreement with rational rules or moral law; conformity is known as *virtue*. Divine law reveals what to do, or avoid doing, to achieve success in the afterlife. It is the standard for all law, and is revealed through reason or revelation. Its importance is that unlike the law of opinion or civil law, it provides a basis for individual morality.

Locke's natural law implies natural rights with associated duties. Individuals have rights, and their duties are defined as protecting these rights, as well as the rights of others. One natural right that concerned Locke was the right to own private property, a right grounded in moral law. Here, Locke was concerned with relations of body (self), labor, and property. Locke's position, derived from Hobbes, was that private ownership's jurisdiction was granted through labor, as property is conceived of as the self in its extended form in the material world. When labor is applied to common property, the laborer came to own this property via their labor. Through this mixing of self and its interactions with the environment (i.e., a plowed field), the body's acts are revealed, leaving traces on the material world. Through the combination of labor and common property, private property emerges. Consequently, property comes to include lives, liberty, and estates.

Moreover, Locke was concerned with freedom to worship and to have one's voice heard in the government. Locke wrote about human rights' inalienable character and argued that a political society rests on the individual's consent to having laws made and enforced by society, as ruled by the majority. Through consent we assume the responsibilities and duties of citizenship. Additionally, Locke located the sovereign in the legislature—the representatives of the majority of people—and in a system based on divisions of power. Thus, property's preservation and inalienable human rights become the impetus behind social laws and government, and subsequently, civil government and political society.

One of the main natural-rights arguments made today is the argument for a "right to life." This holds that at a minimum level, the individual should be free from any coercion (or "harm") that might hinder this right (such as murder). The position is based on both beneficence and a respect for human worth and dignity. Additionally, the right to control one's property is invoked, especially when property rights are defined as including the right to one's own body. However, the "right to life" and the "right to property" can be seen as contradictory, particularly when the latter is used to justify abortion.

Critiques of natural rights are found within discussions of individual liberty. The argument that a right exists that coincides with the nature of human beings to be free was challenged by utilitarian theories, which advocate that individuals should be free because their freedom is somehow useful for society. Émile Durkheim also presents a critique of natural rights, arguing that rights are granted by society.

SEE ALSO *Civil Rights; Human Rights; Locke, John; Naturalism; Property Rights*

BIBLIOGRAPHY

Beauchamp, Tom L., and LeRoy Walters. 1994. *Contemporary Issues in Bioethics.* 4th ed. Belmont, CA: Wadsworth.

Bentham, Jeremy. [1789] 1970. *An Introduction to the Principles of Morals and Legislation*, eds. J. H. Burns and H. L. A. Hart. Oxford: Oxford University Press.

Hobbes, Thomas. [1651] 1982. *Leviathan*, ed. C. B. MacPherson. London: Penguin Group.

Locke, John. [1690] 1952. *Second Treatise of Government*, ed. Thomas P. Peardon. New York: Liberal Arts Press.

Locke, John. [1690] 1988. *Two Treatises of Government*, ed. Peter Laslett. Cambridge, U.K.: Cambridge University Press.

Ryan Ashley Caldwell

NATURAL SELECTION

Natural selection is the central process of evolutionary theory, presented by Charles Darwin (1809–1882) in his 1859 book *The Origin of Species*. Darwin's theory of natural selection is really a simple idea. It states that (1) if there is variation among members of a species in their hereditary traits and (2) some of those traits are more conducive to survival and reproduction than others, then (3) the frequency of individuals carrying those traits will gradually increase in the population. The result is that the species' total pool of hereditary traits will gradually change over generations, so long as environmental conditions do not dramatically change. Thus, natural selection is crucial to how a species adapts to its environment. Evolutionary theory describes how these functional, problem-solving adaptations originate and are maintained.

Theorists and researchers in the social sciences have increasingly applied the concept of natural selection to their explanations of human individual and social behaviors. A major impetus was the writings of twentieth-century evolutionary biologists and sociobiologists such as George Williams, Robert Trivers, Edward O. Wilson, and Richard Dawkins. The 1980s and 1990s saw many social scientists, particularly psychologists, incorporating the theory of natural selection into accounts of human behavior. This effort has led to a new approach in psychology, called evolutionary psychology (EP).

NATURAL SELECTION APPLIED TO HUMAN BEHAVIOR

Unlike sociobiologists, who use natural selection to explain the behavior of social animals, evolutionary psychologists (EPs) focus primarily on how certain human behaviors may have evolved, how they are interrelated, and how or why they survive in the population. Whereas behavior geneticists are interested in how individual differences in human behavior can be explained by differences in genes, EPs are more interested in the evolved neural architecture that is shared by all humans, much of which may be outside of conscious awareness.

In 1992 anthropologist Jerome Barkow, psychologist Leda Cosmides, and anthropologist John Tooby edited *The Adapted Mind: Evolutionary Psychology and the Generation of Culture*. This book energized the EP field. It helped to popularize the idea that humans evolved distinct brain circuitry or information processing modules adapted to solve problems faced by our hunter-gatherer ancestors. Researchers have proposed brain modules for speech and language, facial recognition, the recognition of emotional expressions, social reasoning, and many other aspects of information processing. A popular EP description of the brain is that it is analogous to a Swiss Army knife with its various specialized modules, a reflection of successful problem-solving adaptations during human evolutionary history.

EPs have applied the theory of natural selection to human behavior in several ways. These scientists argue that the majority of human "cultural universals," including social traditions, laws, religions, and ethical positions arose out of the "reproductive imperative" to reproduce and leave behind as many offspring as possible. EPs argue that humans are neurologically predisposed to develop certain phobias (e.g., snakes, enclosed spaces, heights) that were presumably tied to the greatest dangers present in ancient ancestral environments, rather than developing fears toward the dangers of current technologically advanced society (e.g., guns, automobiles, electric sockets).

A good example of the EP application of selection is in the controversial area of gender differences. EPs have suggested that sexual selection (processes relating to how males and females compete for mates) has played an important role in human patterns of mate selection and jealousy. With regard to mate selection, these researchers argue that men have lower overall parental investment in offspring than women. If men are more interested in reproducing than in investing parental resources, then they will tend to find the reproductive potential of a prospective partner to be particularly attractive. Because they have greater parental investment, women will find a partner's potential for providing resources and protection for offspring to be relatively more attractive. This analysis has been used to account for men's greater emphasis on their resources, such as occupation or income, and women's greater emphasis on factors related to their ability to reproduce, such as their age or appearance, when trying to attract a prospective mate.

With regard to jealousy, EPs argue that whereas women are always sure they are the mothers of their offspring (due to internal gestation), men can have doubts about fathering offspring. The implication of such differences in "parental certainty" is that males are more likely to take steps to make sure their investment of resources is legitimate. Thus, they will be more concerned with possible sexual rivals and place a high value on the chastity of a prospective mate. Male "parental uncertainty" predicts that men will attempt to coercively control female reproductive capacity by showing vigilance, mate concealment, violence, derogation of competitors, and threats to others.

CRITIQUES OF NATURAL SELECTION IN HUMAN BEHAVIOR

There are many criticisms of the application of the theory of natural selection to human behavior. One of the main criticisms is that EP is overly deterministic in its focus on biological or genetic "destiny." Much human social, group, and cultural behavior is thought to have emergent properties that cannot be traced back to the evolved structure of individual brains. Thus, culture and socialization may be better explanations for gender differences than natural selection.

Critics argue that natural selection did not necessarily create human brain specialization for any adaptive purpose. Many aspects of modern human behavior can be described as non-adaptive side consequences of natural selection. Critics of the EP approach also argue that empirical evidence is not only lacking but is often impossible to obtain for many of its claims. Because researchers cannot recreate the evolutionary forces that affected ancient human ancestors (what EPs call the "environment of evolutionary adaptation"), these claims become nothing more than "just-so stories" telling us that "people are this way because they are this way."

Another area of controversy concerns the rate and extent of natural selection when applied to humans. Several lines of research suggest that natural selection in humans can occur quite rapidly. For example, researchers have identified increases in recent gene variants related to brain development and size, resistance to HIV infection in parts of Africa, lactose tolerance (i.e., the ability for humans to digest milk sugars), intelligence increases among certain ethnic groups (such as Ashkenazi Jews), and salt retention and hypertension among African slave descendants. In these cases advocates of rapid selection propose a relatively recent appearance of genetic changes or rapid proliferation of those changes throughout the human population. However, the possibility of rapid selection has been questioned by epidemiologists and evolutionary biologists. Critics argue that in many cases the relevant genetic mechanisms or variants that can account for such rapid evolutionary changes have not been identified. Rather, environmental, cultural, or more complicated biocultural influences may account for the observed changes.

Some social scientists argue that natural selection has decreased in importance for humans. Rapid cultural, medical, and technological changes are thought to be more strongly linked to contemporary human survival and reproduction than genetic factors. For example, improvements in public health mean that newborns are much more likely to survive to reproductive age today than they were 500 years ago. Such improvements are thought to neutralize the process by which less adaptive genes are removed from the population. In addition, successful scientific efforts to manipulate the human genome are likely to replace or compete with natural or sexual selection pressures in the future.

The application of the theory of natural selection to the social sciences has made great strides since the 1980s. A good deal of social, political, and scientific controversy and criticism has accompanied social scientists' efforts. Establishing whether and to what extent natural selection applies to human behavior is an ongoing and difficult process. Whether the criticisms will hold up or merely reflect the growing pains of a new discipline remains to be seen.

SEE ALSO *Darwin, Charles; Darwinism, Social; Determinism; Determinism, Biological; Durkheim, Émile; Enlightenment; Evolutionary Psychology; Functionalism; Hypertension; Nature vs. Nurture; Popper, Karl; Racism; Slavery; Sociobiology; Teleology; Weber, Max*

BIBLIOGRAPHY

Barkow, Jerome H., Leda Cosmides, and John Tooby, eds. 1992. *The Adapted Mind: Evolutionary Psychology and the Generation of Culture.* New York: Oxford University Press.

Cosmides, Leda, and John Tooby. 1997. Evolutionary Psychology: A Primer. Center for Evolutionary Psychology. http://www.psych.ucsb.edu/research/cep/primer.html.

Darwin, Charles. 1859. *On the Origin of Species by Means of Natural Selection.* London: John Murray.

Rose, Hilary, and Steven Rose, eds. 2000. *Alas Poor Darwin: Arguments Against Evolutionary Psychology.* New York: Harmony Books.

Wilson, Edward O. 1998. *Consilience: The Unity of Knowledge.* New York: Knopf.

Thomas M. Brinthaupt

NATURALISM

Naturalism is a term that stands for a family of positions that endorse the general idea of being true to, or guided by, "nature," an idea as old as philosophy itself (e.g., Aristotle is often called a "naturalist") and as various and open-ended as interpretations of "nature." Since the rise of the modern scientific revolution in the seventeenth century, nature has come to be identified increasingly with the-world-as-studied-by-the-sciences. Consequently, naturalism has come to refer to a set of positions defined in terms of the scientific image of nature or the methods of scientific inquiry. This brief article focuses upon explicating three versions of this modern *scientific* naturalism: (1) naturalism in the arts, especially literature; (2) philosophical naturalism; and (3) naturalism in the social sciences. These different naturalisms involve different ways of appealing to science, whether it be adopting a scientific stance toward human and social life, or a broadly empirical approach to inquiry in some area, or a scientific worldview, or some combination of these.

NATURALISM IN THE ARTS

Naturalism in the field of the arts refers to art that depicts everyday subjects in a "realistic" manner, free from stylization, idealization, and academic convention. Although naturalism has been used to describe a style of painting since the late seventeenth century (e.g., Caravaggio's), it only became an important term of art criticism in the nineteenth century when it was applied to painters such as Gustave Courbet (1819–1877). Naturalism as a literary category was first applied to a genre of French fiction exemplified by the writings of Émile Zola (1840–1902), which built on the antiromantic "realist" fiction of Gustave Flaubert (1821–1880) and Honoré de Balzac (1799–1850), writers who deliberately adopted a scientific—that is, detached and objective—approach to human life. The vision of the human depicted in naturalist literature owed much to a picture of the world suggested by Charles Darwin's theory of evolution: a purposeless, Godless world of competitive striving where free will is an illusion. Under these historical and ideological influences, American literary naturalism arose in the 1890s as a reaction to the "realist" fiction of middle- and upper-class life of the 1870s and 1880s—for example, the novels of Henry James (1811–1882). Its chief exemplars include Stephen Crane (1871–1900), Theodore Dreiser (1871–1945), Jack London (1876–1916), and Frank Norris (1870–1902). The American school is typified by an anti-individualist view of humans as largely determined by environmental forces, frank and animalistic depictions of sex and violence, and an unflinching treatment of the harsh realities faced by immigrants and the working-class in modern industrialized U.S. cities.

It is important to note, however, that not all appeals to nature are to be understood in terms of an allegiance to naturalism. For example, the writings of Ralph Waldo Emerson (1803–1882) and Henry David Thoreau (1817–1862)—memorably, Thoreau's *Walden* (1854)—reveal a vision of nature that challenges the assumptions of naturalism, particularly the idea that the objective is a matter of excluding the subjective. Although Emerson and Thoreau accepted that nature is everything that is distinct from one's own consciousness, they were interested in a larger reciprocity and interdependence of mind and nature that bears the influence of German philosophers such as Immanuel Kant (1724–1804) and F. W. von Schelling (1775–1854). Another example of an antinaturalist appeal to nature is the tradition of thinking about human conduct and law in terms of natural rights, or the related, but older, idea of natural law. Here the appeal to nature refers to principles or rules of conduct that are given as opposed to humanly constructed. In this tradition what is naturally given is typically understood as a matter of God's law. Naturalism, of course, is strongly opposed to theism.

PHILOSOPHICAL NATURALISM

Modern philosophy recognizes two basic strains of naturalism: ontological naturalism and methodological naturalism. Ontological naturalism takes the subject matter of the natural sciences as its model of the genuinely real. A leading advocate, David Armstrong, holds "that reality consists of nothing but a single all-embracing spatiotemporal system" (1980, p. 149). He is representative in thinking that this implies a conception of nature as a single unified causal order. This ontological outlook is primarily meant to exclude supernatural entities such as the Christian God, demons, spirits, and souls—none of which are the subject matter of a natural science. Naturalism can accommodate religion, however, but only to the extent that it is interpreted as a certain kind of experience which can be understood without any commitment to the existence of supernatural entities or events (e.g., angels, miracles).

It is important to note that ontological naturalism comes in more or less reductive forms depending upon one's attitude to the social (or human) sciences. Typically, naturalists favor a reductive form—because they tend to share a skeptical attitude to the social (or human) sciences—claiming that the natural world is nothing but the world posited by the explanations of the natural sciences exclusively (e.g., physics, chemistry, and biology). This, in turn, leads to a sharp contrast between the scientific image of the world and the manifest image of everyday human experience. Consequently, contemporary metaphysicians ask how we can "place" items in the manifest image (e.g., reasons, meanings, moral goodness, and aesthetic values) within the scientific image. Such debates within naturalism are often conducted in a semantic key. That is, the question is one about how we are to interpret the core concepts of a target nonscientific discourse given a scientific view of nature. For instance, how are we to account for or refer to anything in nature? If not, are the sentences in which it occurs true or false, for our thought and talk about moral goodness? Does the term *good* refer to anything in nature? If not, are the sentences in which it occurs true or false, or do they play a nonfactual role? The semantic project of accounting for the function of nonscientific concepts in this way is called naturalization. Just how revisionary of ordinary ways of thinking this project is depends upon two important questions: whether there are irreducible and indispensable nonscientific forms of understanding, and whether one accepts the legitimacy and distinctiveness of the social sciences.

The second strain of philosophical naturalism is methodological naturalism, which takes scientific methods of inquiry as its model. It holds that nature as a whole is properly studied by the same empirical methods as those employed by the natural sciences. Because human beings are a part of nature, this implies that the study of human nature is continuous with the study of nonhuman nature. It also implies that knowledge is, properly speaking, scientific knowledge. W. V. Quine draws the radical conclusion that there is no a priori knowledge, thereby undermining traditional philosophy (see especially Quine 1964 and 1969). The question whether philosophy has any autonomy in relation to science has subsequently become an important topic of dispute.

NATURALISM IN THE SOCIAL SCIENCES

Naturalism in the social sciences is usually understood as a form of skepticism about the legitimacy of the social sciences or, less drastically, the doctrine that the posits of these sciences are reducible in principle to the posits of paradigmatic natural sciences such as physics. However, there is nothing in naturalism itself that requires this dismissive or reductive approach to the ontology of the social sciences, and not all naturalists share it (e.g., pragmatists such as John Dewey). Notwithstanding, most writers in the social sciences understand naturalism primarily as a methodological doctrine: the view that the methods of inquiry of the natural sciences (e.g., the attempt to discover laws or law-like regularities, empirical testing and corroboration, a clear distinction between facts and values) are no less applicable to man than to nature—that is, to the study of people, society, morality, politics, and culture. Such methodological naturalism is often coupled with a rejection of the influential idea defended by Wilhelm Dilthey (1833–1911), Max Weber (1864–1920), and others that there is a fundamental difference between the scientific understanding of nature (*Erklären*) and the sort of empathetic understanding of human beings that involves seeing things from the subject's point of view (*Verstehen*).

An important debate in philosophy and the social sciences is whether we should follow the naturalistic identification of nature with the scientific image of the world. John McDowell, for example, has argued that it is a metaphysical prejudice to treat the "disenchanted" world of the natural and social sciences as exhausting our conception of nature. What it arguably leaves out of account is a richer conception of the world revealed to critical human thought and experience, one that includes sui generis normative phenomena such as reasons, meanings, and values.

SEE ALSO *Atheism; Industrialization; Kant, Immanuel; Modernization; Natural Rights; Philosophy; Realism; Science; Scientific Method; Secular, Secularism, Secularization; Theism; Thoreau, Henry David*

BIBLIOGRAPHY

Armstrong, David M. 1980. Naturalism, Materialism, and First Philosophy. In *The Nature of Mind and Other Essays*. St. Lucia, Australia: University of Queensland Press.

Danto, Arthur. 1967. Naturalism. In *The Encyclopaedia of Philosophy*, vol. 5, ed. Paul Edwards, 448–450. New York: Macmillan.

Dewey, John. 1944. Antinaturalism in Extremis. In *Naturalism and the Human Spirit*, ed. Yervant H. Krikorian, 1–16. New York: Columbia University Press.

Dilthey, Wilhelm. [1883] 1988. *Introduction to the Human Sciences*. Trans. Ramón J. Betanzos. Hemel Hempstead, U.K.: Harvester.

Emerson, Ralph Waldo. 1983. *Emerson: Essays and Lectures*. Ed. Joel Porte. New York: Library of America Press.

Jones, Peter. 2006. Human Rights. In *Routledge Encyclopedia of Philosophy*, ed. Edward Craig. London: Routledge.

Macarthur, David, and Mario De Caro, eds. 2004. *Naturalism in Question*. Cambridge, MA: Harvard University Press.

McDowell, John. 1995. Two Sorts of Naturalism. In *Virtues and Reasons: Philippa Foot and Moral Theory*, eds. Rosalind Hursthouse, Gavin Lawrence, and Warren Quinn, 149–179. Oxford: Clarendon Press.

Michaels, Walter Benn. 1987. *The Gold Standard and the Logic of Naturalism: American Literature at the Turn of the Century*. Berkeley: University of California Press.

Pizer, Donald, ed. 1995. *The Cambridge Companion to American Realism and Naturalism: Howells to London*. Cambridge, U.K.: Cambridge University Press.

Quine, W. V. [1953] 1969. Epistemology Naturalized. In *Ontological Relativity and Other Essays*, 69–89. New York: Columbia University Press.

Quine, W. V. 1964. Two Dogmas of Empiricism. In *From a Logical Point of View*, 2nd edition, 20–46. Cambridge, Mass.: Harvard University Press.

Quine, W. V. 1981. *Theories and Things*. Cambridge, MA: Harvard University Press.

Richardson, Robert D., Jr. 1999. Emerson and Nature. In *Cambridge Companion to Ralph Waldo Emerson*, eds. Joel Porte and Saundra Morris, 97–105. Cambridge, U.K.: Cambridge University Press.

Thoreau, Henry David. [1854] 2004. *Walden: A Fully Annotated Edition*, ed. Jeffrey S. Cramer. New Haven, CT: Yale University Press.

David Macarthur

NATURALIST VS. NOMINALIST PERSPECTIVES

SEE *Disease.*

NATURALIZATION

Naturalization is the means by which a person of foreign birth is made a full citizen. Naturalization is a process always complicated by race, gender and sexuality, religion, ethnicity, class, and the structural and political choices societies and their members make with regard to assimilation, acculturation, and boundary making.

Neither *jus soli* (citizenship by birth in a particular place) nor *jus sanquinis* (citizenship by descent) encompass purposeful choice-driven naturalization by an individual. The seemingly sharp demarcation between natural events and naturalization is actually fuzzy as official procedures for denoting citizenship can divest membership from those with a natal/descent claim, and invest it in those most recent arrivals deemed most worthy of citizenship status. Several historical and contemporary examples bear this out.

In the United States, the process of naturalization was explicitly set out in the 1790 Naturalization Act, and the caveats of gender, class, and race were made more or less explicit. For example, naturalization was limited to those defined as "free white person[s]." One could claim natural citizenship if one was born to U.S. citizens outside the geographic limits of the nation, "Provided, That the right of citizenship shall not descend to persons whose fathers have never been resident in the United States" (Takaki 1993, p. 80).

In the United States, the caveats of race and ethnicity with regard to naturalization were complicated by various combinations of birth, descent, and residence. Members of indigenous groups were not covered by the Naturalization Acts, as they were not white—however, "taking on the habits of white men" and leaving the reservation could suffice to entitle an Indian to citizenship (Cohen 1971, p. 24). Although African Americans were quite purposefully naturalized in practical terms by the Fourteenth Amendment, they had up to that point been systematically denied both *jus soli* and *jus sanquinis*, and this state of affairs would continue in both cultural understanding and law to varying degrees at least through the 1960s.

For non-white voluntary immigrants and their descendants, the lines between race, ethnicity, birth, residence, and naturalization have been murky and addressed through a variety of Supreme Court decisions on a piecemeal basis, most often on the impetus of these nascent citizens themselves, with widely varying outcomes (*U.S. v. Bhagat Singh Thind*, 1923; *U.S. v. Wong Kim Ark*, 1898; and *In re Halladjian*, 1909). The 1965 Immigration and Nationality Act dismantled the United States' older racial/ethnic/nationality-based quota system, but the preference for family members of current U.S. citizens preserved an extant preference for those groups already in the country ("An Act to Amend the Immigration and Naturalization Act," 1965). However, the migration patterns had by that time drastically shifted from Europe, and new migrant groups could then put their citizenship to work for their family ties.

Gendered understandings of naturalization have also been quite prominent. Until 1922 in the United States, only women who married noncitizens lost their citizenship, and the equalization of citizenship (vis-à-vis nationality, not specific areas of rights) was not completed until the 1930s (Freeman 1989). According to several scholarly works documenting naturalization procedures in the late twentieth century, such gendered naturalization practices continue to be widespread (Cook 1994; Beyani 1994; Al Nuaimi 2001).

In the United States, class was far more explicit in the discussion leading up to the implementation of the 1790 Act than in its final product; read, for example, the discussion of "those likely to become chargeable," and "the common class of vagrants [and] paupers," and those who worried about the merchant class who would "remain so long as will enable them to acquire a fortune, and then they will leave" (*Gales and Seaton's History of Debates in Congress* 1790, pp. 1148, 1152, 1156). Class is of course implicated when workers are invited in to fill economic vacancies, but explicitly not invited to take part in the process of immigrant-to-citizen (Walzer 1983). This is shown in early Chinese immigration to the United States, the Bracero Program for Mexican workers in the United States, and the guest worker system in several European nations (Walzer 1983).

Practices that incorporate *jus sanquinus* far beyond one's parents raise the question of just what counts as "natural" in terms of membership. In Ireland one may have preference in applying for citizenship if, for example, at least one grandparent was Irish-born (termed "Citizenship by Application"). Israel's Law of Return extends the offer of naturalized citizenship to "every Jew who has expressed his desire to settle in Israel" (as expressed in its Law of Return and "Acquisition of Israeli Nationality"). Although others eligible to naturalization must wait from two to five years, for Jews under the Law of Return the naturalization is instantaneous upon arrival ("Acquisition"). In 1970 this law was extended to "include the child and the grandchild of a Jew, the spouse of a Jew, the spouse of a child of a Jew, and the spouse of a grandchild of a Jew. The purpose of this amendment is to ensure the unity of families where intermarriage had occurred." These sorts of practices highlight a perspective that understands all citizenship as a process of naturalization because the concept is a human one based upon stories of belonging. Denaturalization is the flip side of the process.

BIBLIOGRAPHY

Acquisition of Israeli Nationality. 2001. Israel Ministry of Foreign Affairs. http://www.mfa.gov.il/MFA/MFAArchive/ 2000_2009/2001/8/Acquisition%20of%20Israeli%20 Nationality.

Al Nuaimi, Wadha. 2001. This Is the Price We Pay: A Study of Divorce in the United Arab Emirates from Women's Perspectives. Master's thesis, Western Michigan University, Kalamazoo.

Beyani, Chaloka. 1994. Toward a More Effective Guarantee of Women's Rights in the African Human Rights System. In *Human Rights of Women: National and International Perspectives*, ed. Rebecca J. Cook. Philadelphia: University of Pennsylvania Press.

Citizenship by Application—Citizenship by Descent. 2005. Embassy of Ireland. http://www.irelandemb.org/living.html#three.

Cohen, Felix S. 1971. *Handbook of Federal Indian Law*. Albuquerque: University of New Mexico Press.

Cook, Rebecca J. 1994. State Accountability under the Convention on the Elimination of All Forms of Discrimination against Women. In *Human Rights of Women: National and International Perspectives*, ed. Rebecca J. Cook. Philadelphia: University of Pennsylvania Press.

Freeman, Jo. 1989. The Legal Revolution. In *Women: A Feminist Perspective*, ed. Jo Freeman. Mountain View, CA: Mayfield Publishing.

Gales and Seaton's History of Debates in Congress (microfilm edition). 1790. Washington, DC: Gales and Seaton.

Law of Return 5710-1950. 1950. Israel Ministry of Foreign Affairs. http://www.mfa.gov.il/MFA/MFAArchive/ 1950_1959/Law%20of%20Return%205710-1950.

Takaki, Ronald. 1993. *A Different Mirror: A History of Multicultural America*. Boston: Little, Brown.

U.S. Circuit Court of Massachusetts. 1909. *In re Halladjian*. 174 F. 834; 1909 U.S. App. Lexis 5266.

U.S. Congress. 1790. *Naturalization Act of 1790*. 1 Stat 103-104.

U.S. Congress. 1965. *An Act to Amend the Immigration and Nationality Act*. Public Law 89-236. Washington, DC: U.S. Government Printing Office.

U.S. Supreme Court. 1856. *Dred Scott v. Sandford*. 60 U.S. 393.

U.S. Supreme Court. 1896. *Plessy v. Ferguson*. 163 U.S. 537.

U.S. Supreme Court. 1898. *U.S. v. Wong Kim Ark*. 169 U.S. 649; 18 S. Ct. 456; 42 L. Ed. 890; 1898 U.S. Lexis 1515.

U.S. Supreme Court. 1923. *U.S. v. Bhagat Singh Thind*. 261 U.S. 204; 43 S. Ct. 338; 67 L. Ed. 616; 1923 U.S. Lexis 2544.

U.S. Supreme Court. 1971. *Rogers v. Bellei*. 401 U.S. 815; 91 S. Ct. 1060; 28 L. Ed. 2d 499; 1971 U.S. Lexis 61; 27 A.F.T.R.2d (RIA) 1006.

Walzer, Michael. 1983. *Spheres of Justice: A Defense of Pluralism and Equality*. New York: Basic Books.

Sarah N. Gatson

NATURE, HUMAN
SEE *Nature vs. Nurture.*

NATURE VS. NURTURE

One of the goals of the social sciences is to explain human behavior. Nature, which may be defined in terms of inheritance, biological background, and genetic makeup, must be taken into account, along with nurture, which may be defined in terms of experience and learning.

Historically, nature and nurture represented a dichotomy. The ancient Greeks, for example, debated the role of nature and nurture as influences on character and human nature. Since that time, nativists have argued that human personality, intelligence, and capabilities are tied to a person's biological background. Empiricists have countered with arguments that each person is a *tabula rasa*, or a blank slate, and experience determines who humans are and what they can do. Learning theories that developed during the 1950s through the 1970s were sometimes radically empiricist; some theories suggested that any individual is capable of just about anything, if the experience is optimal.

In the first half of the twentieth century, the nature and nurture debate focused on personality and intelligence. Scientific methods were brought to bear on the topic, and there was a shift away from "nature or nurture" to a discussion over the role played by each. One of the key concepts resulting from this work, known as a range of reaction, captures the possible interaction between nature and nurture. In particular, a range of possibilities is genetically determined, and environment and experience determine how much of the potential is fulfilled. For example, certain individuals might have the genetic potential to be anywhere from 5 feet 6 inches to 5 feet 11 inches tall, but their experience (for example, exercise, nutrition) determines the height within that range to which they eventually grow.

A genotype is defined as the genetic constitution (and potential) of an individual. A phenotype, in contrast, is the observable characteristics resulting from the interaction of nature and nurture. Nature and nurture may interact such that experience operates within the potentials set by the genotype, as implied by the range of reaction. But nature and nurture may also interact such that genetic potentials influence the environment. In simple terms, a child may inherit a particular talent, but the talent is immature; it is mere potential. Parents, teachers, or coaches may recognize the potential and do what they can to support it. In this case, the genetic potential actually determines which experiences will be provided. Nature and nurture interact in a bidirectional fashion.

The interplay of nature and nurture has been studied extensively in behavioral genetics. Twins are often studied by behavioral geneticists. Monozygotic twins are genetically identical; they developed in utero from one fertilized egg cell. Fraternal or dizygotic twins, in contrast, developed from two egg cells and are consequently only 50 percent similar genetically. Knowing the precise genetic contributions allows researchers to make inferences about the impact of nature and nurture. In the clearest case, monozygotic twins who have been reared apart (for instance, separated before the age of six months) are, later in life, compared in terms of IQ or various personality traits. If genes play a significant role, the twins should be very similar, even though they had different experiences. The magnitude of the genetic contribution is calculated with a correlation, known as the heritability index. Empirical results suggest that monozygotic twins have the highest heritability, sometimes as high as .70, even when reared apart. Other siblings, including dizygotic twins, have much lower heritability indices (usually below .50).

Similar support for a genetic contribution to IQ comes from adoption studies. The logic parallels that of twin studies, only here the comparisons are between biological parents and their children (who share 50 percent of their genetic makeup) and foster or adoptive parents (who are dissimilar genetically to their adopted children but share the same environment with them). As with twin studies, the genetic contribution is quite apparent in adoption studies. Biological parents tend more often to have IQs that are similar to their children than do foster or adoptive parents.

The most ambitious investigation into the nature/nurture debate is the U.S. Human Genome Project. The project started in 1990 with the general objective of identifying all the genes in human DNA. There may be 25,000 such genes, with literally billions of chemical sequences. In addition to investigations of human DNA, the project examined mice, fruit flies, and even bacteria. The project was considered to have been completed in 2003 although research of the data is ongoing.

There are numerous political ramifications to the study of nature and nurture. Francis Galton (1822–1911), a cousin of Charles Darwin (1809–1882), believed strongly in the inheritance of ability and promoted the advantages of eugenics, or the strengthening of desirable characteristics using selective mating. Although eugenics is contrary to an appreciation of diversity and equality, various factions nonetheless support it. There is, for example, one well-known sperm bank in California that only deals with highly able donors and recipients. The implications of genetic research for medicine and clinical treatments are likely to have more practical importance.

In most cases, traits and capabilities are polygenetic; that is, more than one gene is responsible for them. Great headway has been made with the identification and even engineering of various genes and gene combinations. Modern genetics is increasingly precise about the contributions of nature and the biological influences on human behavior, and the inferences of behavioral genetics are no longer necessary. Alcoholism, autism, creative potential, and many other human tendencies have been examined and the influence of specific genes determined. Addiction, for example, seems to be strongly tied to the presence of a gene allele called D2R2, which is responsible for dopamine reception. Only about 20 percent of the population has that allele, and thus a proclivity toward addiction. Clearly, some of the most important implications of research on genetics are those within medicine.

SEE ALSO *Determinism, Biological; Determinism, Genetic; Flynn Effect; Heredity; IQ Controversy*

BIBLIOGRAPHY

Rutter, Michael. 2006. *Genes and Behavior: Nature–Nurture Interplay Explained.* Malden, MA: Blackwell.

Scarr, Sandra, and Kathleen McCartney. 1983. How People Make Their Own Environments. *Child Development* 54 (2): 424–435.

Mark A. Runco

NAVAJO-HOPI LAND DISPUTE

SEE *Navajos.*

NAVAJOS

The Navajo, who in 2007 numbered approximately 290,000 people, the majority of whom occupy a thirteen-million-acre reservation that spans parts of Arizona, New Mexico, and Utah, understand themselves to be a chosen people living within a sacred geography. A rich oral tradition documents the travails of their ancestors as they traverse a series of three or four underworlds, each of which is portrayed in some state of chaos and disorder resulting in the need for migration upward into the next world. The oral tradition also documents the preparation of this world and the creation of the Navajo people and establishes tenets for living. In the last underworld, First Man and First Woman—the first beings with humanlike form—were created; they and their progeny flourished until lust led to a conflict between First Man and First

Woman, which resulted in an event now referred to as the "separation of the sexes." While men and women lived apart, libidinous desires led women to masturbate with quills, cacti, antlers, stones, and bones. The men relieved their longing with mud or the flesh of freshly slain game animals. Eventually the men and women agreed to rejoin and live as one group.

Shortly after the reunion, circumstances necessitated their escaping upward through a great female reed. Their journey culminated on the earth's surface at the Hajiináí, or "the place of emergence." There First Man and First Woman built a sweat house in which to think and sing the Navajo universe into existence. By some accounts, this world was first conceived in thought, after which its form was projected onto primordial substance through the compulsive power of speech and song. The newly created world was said to be in a state of "natural order" in which all living things were in their proper relationships with all other living things. This orderliness was disrupted as a result of the sexual aberrations and excesses of the last underworld. The women who had masturbated with foreign objects gave birth to twelve misshapen creatures that grew into monsters and preyed on healthy children, pushing Navajo ancestors to the brink of extinction. The Holy People resolved this dilemma by arranging for Changing Woman to be found, grow in a miraculous way, and give birth to warrior sons who slew the monsters. It is she who created the original Navajo matrilineal clans and turned the world over to them.

As with Native Americans across North America, complex changes have occurred in Navajo society since their initial contact with Spaniards, Mexicans, and Americans. At the time of European contact, the Navajo subsisted on hunting and gathering supplemented by some agriculture. Extended family units, generally centered on matrilocal residence and the strength of their clan system, lived in widely dispersed settlements. Spanish Franciscans first attempted to convert Navajo people when they built a mission along the Rio Grande in 1627; it was soon abandoned. Subsequent efforts over the next two centuries met with little success.

Upon the introduction of livestock into the region, a herding economy based on sheep and goats developed. The Navajo population and their area of settlement gradually expanded as new crops, animals, and technological innovations were added to their subsistence base during the Spanish and American periods. In 1848 the United States defeated Mexico in war and through the Treaty of Guadalupe Hidalgo assumed political jurisdiction over most of what is known as the American Southwest. Members of an 1849 American military expedition into Navajo country were impressed by the size of the Navajo sheep and goat herds as well as the well-nourished and healthy condition of tribal members.

Westward expansion resulted in frequent clashes between Navajos and outsiders, leading to American military intervention. The general good health noted in the 1840s was undermined when Kit Carson (1809–1868) and his troops, with scorched-earth tactics, rousted nearly 9,000 Navajos from their homeland and forced them to walk several hundred miles to Hweeldi, "the place of suffering," where they were incarcerated from 1863 to 1868. At Fort Sumner in New Mexico, the Navajo suffered under difficult living conditions, some of which hastened or exacerbated the spread of disease. In addition unfamiliar foods and alkaline water led to gastric upset and other problems.

Since their capture and internment at Hweeldi and the establishment of a reservation on a portion of their homelands in 1868, the Navajo have been in a relationship of constant domination and control by the larger American society. The colonial assault was repeated at different points in time through repression of the native language and traditions, enforcement of boarding school attendance, impediments to religious freedom, and threats to Navajo land and resources by stock reduction in the 1930s and 1940s, timber harvesting, and coal and uranium mining. These concerns developed alongside a gradual shift to wage-work economics among the Navajo, a recession in the 1970s and 1980s, resource depletion, unsuccessful attempts to preserve sacred sites, Navajo job-preference problems, deaths from improperly regulated uranium mining, radioactive waste spills, continuing poverty for many, and land disputes.

In what is known as the Navajo-Hopi land dispute, Navajo individuals were forced to move off land partitioned by the Navajo-Hopi Land Settlement Act of 1974. This political drama stems from President Chester A. Arthur's (1829–1886) executive order of 1882, which granted 2.5 million acres of land around the Hopi mesas to the Hopis and "such other Indians as the Secretary of the Interior may see fit to settle thereon," ignoring the Navajo families who had lived in this area for centuries. Attempts were made to reconcile boundary conflicts between Navajo and Hopi families by legal means on numerous occasions between 1891 and 1962, when a federal court ruled that 1.8 million acres of the 1882 reservation were jointly owned. This legislation led to mandatory livestock reductions beginning in 1972 and land partition in 1974. The latter mandated the relocation of all members of either tribe living in the area granted to the other, slating over 10,000 Navajos and 100 Hopis for compulsory relocation. Despite the commitment of enormous amounts of time and money toward resolution by all parties, this dispute remains unresolved.

By the last decades of the twentieth century, the Navajo had moved toward political self-determination and cultural renewal. But many Navajo families have been shattered due to complex social and health problems, including economic underdevelopment and chronic unemployment. Thousands of Navajos are gainfully employed in the fields of health care, education, government service, and commercial farming or resource-extraction industries. Yet reservation unemployment rates far exceed national norms, resulting in the need for many Navajos to work off the reservation in construction or other fields to support their families.

Changes in mode of production and diet have had grave consequences on Navajo health. Diabetes mellitus is more prevalent among Navajos than in the general U.S. population, and clinical diagnoses are rising. As a consequence, the Navajo have the highest lower-extremity amputation rate in the world. American Indians and Alaskan Natives have a 3.5 times higher prevalence of end-stage renal disease (ESRD) than white Americans, and due to its skyrocketing rate of diabetes mellitus, the Navajo population has an even higher rate of ESRD. Alcohol abuse contributes to these complex health concerns. It is within this context of rapid cultural change, health crises, and fragmentation that members of the Navajo Nation have searched out new sources of spiritual and curative powers, including those available from biomedical technologies and Christianity, especially fundamentalist forms and the Native American Church.

SEE ALSO *Confiscation; Land Claims; Native Americans; Religion; Spirituality*

BIBLIOGRAPHY

Aberle, David. 1993. The Navajo-Hopi Land Dispute and Navajo Relocation. In *Anthropological Approaches to Resettlement: Policy, Practice, and Theory*, ed. Michael Cernea and Scott Guggenheim, 153–200. Boulder, CO: Westview.

Frisbie, Charlotte. 1992. Temporal Change in Navajo Religion: 1868–1990. *Journal of the Southwest* 34 (4): 457–514.

Hodge, Frederick, George Hammond, and Agapito Rey, eds. 1945. *Fray Alonso de Benavides' Revised Memorial of 1634, with Numerous Supplementary Documents Elaborately Annotated*. Albuquerque: University of New Mexico Press.

Iverson, Peter. 2002. *Diné: A History of the Navajos*. Albuquerque: University of New Mexico Press.

Johnson, Broderick, ed. 1973. *Navajo Stories of the Long Walk Period*. Tsaile, AZ: Navajo Community College Press.

Kunitz, Stephen, and Jerrold Levy, with K. Ruben Gabriel et al. 2000. *Drinking, Conduct Disorder, and Social Change: Navajo Experiences*. New York: Oxford University Press.

Narva, Andrew. 2003. Pathophysiology and Etiology of Chronic Renal Disease. *Kidney International* 63: S738–S742.

O'Bryan, Aileen. 1956. *The Diné: Origin Myths of the Navaho Indians*. Washington, DC: Government Printing Office.

Reichard, Gladys. 1950. *Navaho Religion: A Study of Symbolism*. New York: Pantheon.

Schwarz, Maureen Trudelle. 1997. *Molded in the Image of Changing Woman: Navajo Views on the Human Body and Personhood*. Tucson: University of Arizona Press.

Schwarz, Maureen Trudelle. 2001. *Navajo Lifeways: Contemporary Issues, Ancient Knowledge*. Norman: University of Oklahoma Press.

Trennert, Robert. 1998. *White Man's Medicine: Government Doctors and the Navajo, 1863–1955*. Albuquerque: University of New Mexico Press.

Unwin, Nigel. 1998. Epidemiology of Lower Extremity Amputation in Centers in Europe, North America, and East Asia. *British Journal of Surgery* 87 (3): 328–337.

Wilkins, David. Governance within the Navajo Nation: Have Democratic Traditions Taken Hold? *Wicazo Sa Review* 17 (1): 91–129.

Yazzie, Ethelou. 1971. *Navajo History*. Vol. 1. Navajo Curriculum Center. Rough Rock, AZ: Rough Rock Demonstration School.

Maureen Trudelle Schwarz

NAZISM

Nazism is a convenient abbreviation for the ideology of National Socialism, which flourished, principally in Germany, in the period 1920 to 1945. In this context, *National* meant "nationalist," and *Socialism* a doctrine that preached equality between all members of the nation. The National Socialist German Workers' Party was founded on January 5, 1919, in Munich, Bavaria, as the German Workers' Party. Its official program, adopted on February 24, 1920, signaled the change of name and announced its aims: uniting all ethnic Germans in a single state; acquiring new land, or "living space," for Germans to rule; revoking the 1919 peace settlement that had reduced Germany's territory, restricted its armed forces in size and equipment, and imposed a huge financial penalty on Germany; replacing democratic institutions by a dictatorship; and denying Jewish Germans fundamental civil rights.

ORIGINS

The Nazis synthesized a variety of strands of extremist political thought that had developed in Germany and Austria in the late nineteenth century. Racist anti-Semitism had evolved out of old traditions of Christian anti-Semitism during the economic depression of the 1870s, as demagogues drew upon new racial theories to argue that supposedly Jewish characteristics were racially inherited, independently of religious adherence. In this view, the Jews were a parasitic, conspiratorial race that undermined German civilization. In the 1890s extreme nationalists in Germany began to argue that the unification of the country achieved in 1871 under Otto von Bismarck (1815–1898) was incomplete. These "pan-Germans" demanded the annexation of other German-speaking areas of Europe and the conquest of a colonial empire both within Europe and without. At the same time, Social Darwinists and eugenicists in Germany began to argue that the German, "Aryan," race had to be strengthened for this task by improvements in health, an increase in the birth rate (which was starting to decline), and the elimination—by forced sterilization or even killing—of the weak, the criminal, the hereditarily unfit, and the disabled.

These ideas were brought together in 1919 by Adolf Hitler (1889–1945), a former frontline soldier born in Austria. Hitler believed, like other ultranationalists, that Germany's defeat in World War I had been caused by Jewish-led revolutionaries within Germany who had administered a "stab in the back" to the supposedly undefeated German armies. For Hitler, war and revolution legitimized the use of violence for political ends. The threat of communism, seen by the Nazis as part of the worldwide Jewish conspiracy against Germany, justified for them the use of extreme force in the defense of German racial interests. In 1920 members of the Nazi movement founded a paramilitary wing, which by 1924 had become the Stormtrooper Organization. It was designed to inflict maximum violence on the Nazis' opponents. By the mid-1920s the Nazi movement had adopted the "leadership principle" by which the commands of Hitler, known as the *Führer* ("Leader"), were transmitted down through the ranks and had to be obeyed without question.

RISE AND TRIUMPH TO 1933

Nazism owed a good deal to the example and inspiration of Italian Fascism, from which it borrowed the Fascist salute, the cult of the "leader," the use of violence, the glorification of youth, and the relegation of women to the primary function of childbearing. Imitating Benito Mussolini's mythical "March on Rome" in 1922, which had led to the appointment of the Italian Fascist leader as Italy's prime minister, Hitler staged a putsch in the Bavarian capital, Munich, on November 9, 1923, the anniversary of the outbreak of the 1918 German Revolution. He marched on the city center with the intention of taking it over and then marching on the German capital, Berlin, but he had failed to win the support of the army, the police, or business and political elites, and the putsch was dispelled in a hail of gunfire. Hitler was tried for treason and briefly imprisoned.

On his release, Hitler reorganized the Nazi movement and gained new supporters. The movement now focused on winning votes. In the national election of 1928, however, it won only 2.6 percent of the vote. In 1929 the Wall Street crash caused the withdrawal of U.S. loans to German businesses, leading to bank failures and bankruptcies on a huge scale. By July 1932 over a third of the German workforce was unemployed. Those without jobs flocked to the Communist Party, which rapidly increased in strength. Alarmed, the middle classes turned to the Nazis, who seemed the only party ruthless enough to stop a revolution. Campaigning with ceaseless energy, the Nazis also won over many first-time voters, many previously unorganized workers, and numerous Protestant peasants. In the elections of July 1932 the Nazis won 37.4 percent of the vote, becoming Germany's largest party. Only the Catholic Centre Party, the Social Democrats, and the Communists retained significant electoral support in the face of the Nazis' popularity.

THE NAZI SEIZURE OF POWER

By this time, democratic government in Germany had collapsed under the strain of social conflict during the Depression, and the country was being led by a succession of men who wanted to destroy the democratic system and impose authoritarian rule in order to defeat the Communists and revive Germany's international fortunes. But they needed popular support. On January 20, 1933, the Nazis were co-opted into a national government headed by Hitler but with a majority of non-Nazi conservatives who hoped to use them for their own ends.

Over the following months Hitler outmaneuvered them completely. On February 28, 1933, following the burning down of the Reichstag (the national parliament building), Hitler persuaded President Paul von Hindenburg to issue a decree suspending civil liberties. Thousands of Communists were arrested and thrown into hastily erected concentration camps, where they were soon joined by many Social Democrats and trade unionists. On March 23, 1933, Hitler persuaded members of the Reichstag by a mixture of threats and promises to pass the Enabling Law, which allowed the cabinet to pass laws without parliamentary or presidential approval. Murder and intimidation forced the remaining political parties to dissolve themselves by the summer of that same year.

NAZISM AND WAR

Hitler called his state the *Third Reich*, connecting it to the First Reich (*the Holy Roman Empire*), founded by Charlemagne in the year 800 and lasting a thousand years, and the Second Reich (*the German Empire*), founded by Bismarck in 1871. Many new laws were introduced, making opposition a capital offense, "coordinating" the media under the new propaganda ministry, dismissing political opponents and dissenters, and above all, depriving Jewish Germans of their rights and their livelihoods. Hitler began immediately preparing Germany for a war of conquest in the east. In 1936 German troops marched into the Rhineland, an area established as a demilitarized zone by the 1919 peace settlement. In March 1938 Germany annexed the German-speaking state of Austria. Then, in September 1938, using the threat of war, Hitler secured an international agreement to annex the German-speaking part of Czechoslovakia. In March 1939 German troops marched into the rest of the country, making it clear to all that the Nazis were aiming not just to revise the peace settlement, but also to conquer eastern Europe and achieve European domination. When the German army invaded Poland in September 1939, Britain and France declared war.

Nazism had sought before 1939 to drive German Jews out of the country to prevent a repeat of the "stab-in-the-back" of 1918. After invading Poland, the Nazi administration forced the country's large Jewish population into ghettos, where many starved. Following the invasion of the Soviet Union, further emigration of Jews from Germany was banned. The Nazi belief in a world-wide Jewish conspiracy to undermine Germany culminated in the conviction that the United States—which entered the war informally in summer 1941 with its decision to supply Germany's enemies with raw materials and armaments—was working with the Soviet Union and Britain to destroy the Third Reich.

By the end of 1941 the decision had been made to transport all European Jews to specially created camps in the occupied parts of eastern Europe where they would be killed, thus inaugurating what later became known as the *Holocaust*. Many people thought to be undermining the German war effort or the values of Nazism—including homosexuals, gypsies, Jehovah's Witnesses, African Germans, petty criminals, and "asocials"—were also exterminated. In addition, up to 200,000 German inmates of mental hospitals and institutions were killed, nearly half of them by gassing, the rest by starvation or lethal injections. Finally, a "General Plan for the East" envisaged the death by starvation of up to 30 million Slavs, and as a start, at least 3.3 million Soviet prisoners of war were left to die of hunger and disease in German camps.

DEFEAT AND AFTERMATH

Nazism's ambition for the racial reordering of Europe could not be fulfilled. The combined strength of the Soviet Union, the British Empire, and the United States inflicted total defeat on Germany, many of whose towns and cities had been destroyed by bombing by the time peace was signed on May 8, 1945. Hitler and many other leading Nazis committed suicide. The others were tried for war crimes by the International Military Tribunal at Nuremberg, setting an important precedent. Many were found guilty and executed or sentenced to long terms of imprisonment.

There was no serious resistance to the Allied occupation of Germany; Nazism's support, dependent on the charismatic force of Hitler and seduced by the belief that might is right, vanished when Hitler died and Germany was defeated. The genocidal crimes of Nazism were widely publicized. Since 1945, neo-Nazism has everywhere been a fringe, extremist movement, despite gaining some support in times of economic depression, and neo-Nazis have been forced to deny the reality of the Holocaust, even while claiming that Jews have too much influence in the modern world. Neo-Nazi movements are illegal in many countries, and the major focus of racist extremism today is against racial minorities in postcolonial Europe. White supremacists in the United States and neo-Nazis in Eastern Europe often express admiration for Hitler, but they have to confront the fact that Nazism led to the extermination of millions of Slavs and other Europeans.

SEE ALSO *Anti-Semitism; Aryans; Authoritarianism; Civilizations, Clash of; Concentration Camps; Ethnocentrism; Eugenics; Fascism; Genocide; Great Depression; Hitler, Adolf; Holocaust, The; Mussolini, Benito; Nationalism and Nationality; Personality, Cult of; Racism; Totalitarianism; White Supremacy; World War I; World War II*

BIBLIOGRAPHY

Burleigh, Michael, and Wolfgang Wipperman. 1991. *The Racial State: Germany 1933–1945*. Cambridge, U.K.: Cambridge University Press.

Evans, Richard J. 2003. *The Coming of the Third Reich*. New York: Penguin.

Evans, Richard J. 2005. *The Third Reich in Power*. New York: Penguin.

Evans, Richard J. 2008. *The Third Reich at War*. New York: Penguin.

Kershaw, Ian. 2000. *The Nazi Dictatorship: Problems and Perspectives of Interpretation*. 4th ed. London: Arnold.

Kershaw, Ian. 2002. *Hitler*. 2 vols. New York: Penguin.

Richard J. Evans

NDEMBU, THE

SEE *Turner, Victor.*

NECESSITIES

Necessities may be defined as imperative needs that motivate wants and desires. Survival necessities such as food and water motivate intense wants and desires, so intense that people may struggle to the death to satisfy them. However, humans live "not by bread alone," and they may go on hunger strikes for what they see as higher imperatives than survival. This essay deals with both survival necessities and "higher" necessities.

Survival necessities may be divided into physical, social, and psychological. *Physical necessities* include air, food, water, shelter, warmth, excretion, and exercise.

Social necessities include sex, reproduction, and caretaking of children. Reciprocally, children must have caretakers and require constant attachment figures. Sexual and caretaking necessities require families, and families have been the core of evolutionary survival groups. Such groups comprised clans and tribes consisting of up to hundreds of people. These survival groups in turn had two necessities: territory and organization. Territory provided a defensive perimeter and sources of shelter and food. Organization provided specialization of roles and a hierarchy of leaders and followers. A well-functioning group could now compensate for human biological vulnerability to predators and natural disasters. It could coordinate hunting and defense, distribute resources down a hierarchical line, regulate sexuality, and care for its offspring.

Psychological necessities are sensations and emotions of satisfaction and pleasure that signal and regulate fulfilment of physical and social necessities. Dissatisfactions and displeasures signal lack of fulfilment of such necessities. Examples of pleasurable and unpleasurable opposites are satiety and hunger, security and fear, sexual satisfaction and frustration, and belonging and being alone. The intensity of the quest for satisfactions and avoidance of displeasures reflects the importance of the necessities that sensations and emotions regulate.

Humans share with other social animals the necessities examined thus far. "Higher," exclusively human, necessities reflect evolution of ever-newer platforms of organization in the human brain and within the mind. Once basic survival necessities are satisfied, fulfilments of ever-higher levels of necessities take over the insistent motivation of earlier necessities. Though higher necessities appear to fulfill purely human desires and motivations, they are ultimately connected to survival needs, and assume their urgency.

Aristotle noted progression of human desires from the body to reason or soul. In modern times, Abraham Maslow described a hierarchy of human needs, ranging from physiological needs through needs for safety, love and esteem, to actualization of potentials. Both Aristotle

and Maslow maintained that once basic needs were satisfied, higher needs took over their urgency.

Divergence from animal necessities to purely human ones may be seen in moral necessities. Some animals, such as dogs, exhibit primitive guilt, but only humans have complex moral necessities that align individual and group survival needs. Moral necessities include positive external judgments (of virtue, worth, and justice) and a corresponding praiseworthy conscience (that one is good, lovable, and righteous). Negative judgments of badness, worthlessness, and injustice evoke guilt, shame, and a sense of wrongdoing.

The level above morality is that of ethics. It includes ideals of proper behavior and codes of conduct, values such as honor and human dignity, and principles of justice such as human rights. These concepts subsume survival needs such as space, territory, and distribution of resources, but go beyond them. Even so, the abstract concepts and ideas maintain the original motivations and urgency. For instance, people may risk survival in struggles for justice, freedom, and dignity, or kill themselves if they feel that they have lost their honor.

The level of beliefs, religions, and ideologies encompasses all prior levels and in addition provides theories of causation of the world and its disasters, and blueprints for action that bring imminent earthly solutions, or resolutions in the next world. This level also includes evolution of symbols that stand for complex issues. For instance, a flag may symbolize patriotism, which itself symbolizes the whole path back to tribe and territory and defense against enemies. Symbols can assume the intensity of their precursors. People may die for the flag or the cross, or an idea such as democracy. This level and subsequent ones fulfill necessities that have been called spiritual.

The next level contains the necessity to be part of a sensible universe in which one has a significant niche. Such a universe provides answers to questions of life and death, order and chaos, good and evil, beginnings and endings, times and connections. It provides a sense of awe and sacredness, of mystical consciousness, of the numinous and the sublime.

With the evolution of self-consciousness, humans developed a need to see themselves as significant identities who subsumed all prior levels, but now in addition to those levels required existential meanings and purpose. Without them, people could feel that their lives were pointless. It became necessary for people to be self-consciously content and happy, fulfilling their human capacities at all levels and in all forms of loving and satisfying relationships. In addition, meaningful self-awareness involved creativity, ranging from procreation to creation within different art forms and in science. Helping others to feel secure and fulfilled and providing comfort and beauty for others could also be existentially meaningful.

Finally, humans have a need to know and understand the truth about themselves and their universe. This necessity is expressed variably as the need to discover the face of God, the human soul, beauty, reason, wisdom, or truth. They may be necessities for the completion of a full, wholesome life.

Because fulfilment necessities derive from survival ones, and because survival necessities may vary and be contradictory according to circumstances, fulfilments at higher evolutionary levels may also display conflicts and contradictions. For instance, sometimes it is noble to kill; at other times it is evil. Even wisdom can reflect contradictory survival experiences, as seen in the sayings "You reap what you sow" and "The good die young." Understanding strategies of survival (caretaking, attachment, goal achievement, goal surrender, fight, flight, competition, cooperation) and their ramifications may provide a framework for understanding the intricacies of necessities at different levels. Understanding survival necessities may help people both to survive better and to fulfill their higher human necessities.

SEE ALSO *Competition; Cooperation; Ethics; Food; Homelessness; Maslow, Abraham; Morality; Needs; Needs, Basic; Nutrition; Symbols*

BIBLIOGRAPHY

Koestler, Arthur. 1983. *Janus: A Summing Up.* London: Picador.

Maslow, Abraham H. 1970. *Motivation and Personality.* 2nd ed. New York: Harper and Row.

Scott, John P. 1989. *The Evolution of Social Systems.* New York: Gordon and Breach Science.

Valent, Paul. 1998. *From Survival to Fulfilment: A Framework for the Life-Trauma Dialectic.* Philadelphia: Brunner/Mazel.

Paul Valent

NEED FOR COGNITION

In 1982 the American psychologists John T. Cacioppo and Richard E. Petty proposed that people differ with respect to their tendency to engage in and enjoy effortful cognitive activity. People high in need for cognition are characterized as having a propensity toward seeking out, acquiring, and thinking critically and carefully about information in order to make sense of the world around them. In comparison, people low in need for cognition are characterized as being more likely to rely on low-effort heuristics or rules of thumb (e.g., "what do the experts say?") to achieve such understanding.

Considerable research attests to the validity of this distinction between individuals high and low in need for cognition. It has been repeatedly found that people higher in need for cognition (as measured by the Need for Cognition Scale) remember more of the information to which they are exposed. This result is consistent with the basic memory literature, which demonstrates that thinking about and elaborating on information improves its subsequent recall. When they encounter events that are unexpected, individuals high in need for cognition tend to spontaneously generate explanations to account for such events. Individuals low in need for cognition, on the other hand, generally lack the motivation to engage in such effortful explanatory processing.

Their willingness to exert themselves cognitively can often help people high in need for cognition avoid some common judgmental biases. Research indicates that a higher need for cognition can assist individuals in overcoming the fundamental attribution error—the tendency to attribute another's behavior to dispositional causes (i.e., to his or her unique qualities) even when clear situational factors were present that would have caused most people to behave similarly. The fundamental attribution error is known to be most severe when people fail to deliberately and effortfully consider the role of the situation in generating explanations for the behavior of others. Because they are more disposed to engage in this kind of processing, those high, as compared to low, in need for cognition will make attributions that more appropriately reflect the influence of situational variables.

The factors that lead people to change their attitudes seem to depend heavily on their need for cognition. Individuals high in need for cognition respond best to strong arguments that are cogent and backed up with compelling evidence. They scrutinize and reflect carefully on the presented arguments, and to the extent that their thoughts about the message are on balance favorable, they will modify their attitude in accordance with the message. Because assessing argument quality requires considerable cognitive effort, people low in need for cognition rely instead on more heuristic cues, such as the expertise of the communicator or the source of the message, to help them decide whether to agree or disagree with the message.

It should be noted that these differences in need for cognition can be moderated by the demands of the situation. When a situation strongly calls for effortful cognitive processing, people low in need for cognition are quite capable of matching the quality and quantity of thinking exhibited by people high in need for cognition. Similarly, some situations require minimal cognitive engagement to negotiate; in such instances, even individuals high in need for cognition may refrain from cognitively exerting themselves.

SEE ALSO *Attitudes; Persuasion*

BIBLIOGRAPHY

Cacioppo, John T., and Richard E. Petty. 1982. The Need for Cognition. *Journal of Personality and Social Psychology* 42 (1): 116–131.

Cacioppo, John T., Richard E. Petty, Jeffery A. Feinstein, and W. Blair G. Jarvis. 1996. Dispositional Differences in Cognitive Motivation: The Life and Times of Individuals Varying in Need for Cognition. *Psychological Bulletin* 119 (2): 197–253.

G. Daniel Lassiter

NEEDS

Human needs are advocated, rejected, or problematized by different groups of scholars. This essay deals only with the first group. For surveys of "rejectors" and "problematizers" see Doyal and Gough (1991) and Springborg (1981), respectively. Human needs are grounded in human nature as Williams (1987, p. 101) and Gasper (2002, section 6.3) argue. Márkus (1978) systematizes Marx's views: Human beings distinguish themselves from animals as their vital activity, work, is oriented toward need satisfaction through mediations (*tool-making animal*), a view confirmed by modern paleoanthropologists (e.g., Leakey 2001). Through work humans become *universal natural-historical beings* capable of transforming all natural elements into objects of their needs and activities and of developing their *human essential forces* (needs and capacities) and creating themselves. Through work, which breaks the animal subject/needs-object fusion and makes human conscience and self-conscience possible, humans become a *universal conscientious being*, as conscience expands with work objects. In work the conditions of humans as *social universal beings* are given. Work is always social: Men and women work for each other using inherited means and capacities. Lastly, human beings are *free beings* who can actualize, by their conscious decision, the objective possibilities created by social evolution.

According to Maslow ([1954] 1987, chapter 4), human needs are *instinctoid* as men and women only inherit the impulse but have to learn the other two elements of instincts (object, activity). Fromm ([1955] 1990, p. 23) argues that at a certain point of evolution, life became self-aware and action ceased to be determined by instincts. This rupture in the dominion of life by instincts is the same implied in work as a mediated activity, as tool making is not instinctual and means a huge liberty leap.

Marx ([1857] 1973) conceives needs (except biological original needs) as produced in a similar sense as products and capacities are produced. Production creates not only consumption objects but also consumption modes, consumption impulses, and the consumer himself. The historical character of human needs expresses itself in the *humanization of biological needs* and in the *creation of new needs devoid of biological roots* : for example, aesthetic and cognitive needs. Marx's conception contrasts with neoclassical economics' instrumentalist view of production at the service of the sovereign consumer and his preexistent preferences, not needs (Rothenberg 1974).

Wiggins (1998) distinguishes needs from desires/wants and defines rigorously needs and the needed object. In the following three paragraphs his ideas are explained and other viewpoints are incorporated.

Distinguishing needs from desires/wants. Needs are not strong or unconscious desires (or preferences):

> Unlike desire, or want, then need *is not evidently an intentional verb.* What I need depends not on thought or the workings of my mind (or not only on this) but on the way the world is. Again, if one wants something because it is F, one believes or suspects that it is F. But if one needs something because it is F, it must really be F, whether or not one believes that it is. (Wiggins 1998, p. 6)

Doyal and Gough (1991, p. 42) distinguish between *objective needs* conceived as goals universally associated with *prevention of serious harm* and *subjective wants*, which are not.

Need and human harm. The special force of the term *need* and the normative character of noninstrumental but categorical/absolute needs come from the *noncontroversial character of its purpose, avoiding human harm or human flourishing* (Wiggins 1998, pp. 9, 13). Doyal and Gough (1991, pp. 2, 39) adopt the similar concept of serious harm ("significantly impaired pursuit of goals") or flourishing but also define needs as *universal,* with which Fromm ([1955] 1990, chapter 3) and Max-Neef, Elizalde, and Hopenhayn (1986, p. 27) agree: If all human beings have the same capacity to suffer serious harm or to flourish, all have human objective basic needs conceived as universalizable goals, Doyal and Gough argue. Fromm and Maslow identify the serious consequences of unsatisfied needs as physical or mental disease: For example, Fromm ([1955] 1990, pp. 30–36) identifies *narcissism* (which in its extreme forms is equivalent to insanity) as the consequence of the insatisfaction of the need for intimate relations.

On the definition of the needed object and needs. Wiggins defines the object needed: "A person needs *x* (absolutely) if and only if, whatever morally and socially acceptable variation it is … possible to envisage occurring within the relevant time span, he will be harmed if he goes without *x*" (1998, p. 14). He also defines needs as *states of dependency (in respect of not being harmed), which have as their proper objects things needed*" (1998, p. 16). This distinction of satisfiers and needs is made by many authors, and Max-Neef et al. (1986, pp. 41–43) also distinguish satisfiers from goods as different analytical spaces in the sense of spaces developed by Amartya Sen (1983, p. 335). Orthodox economists, and paradoxically Sen (1985), usually restrict satisfiers to goods and services, whereas Lederer (1980) identifies objects, relations, and activities as satisfiers and Boltvinik (2007), on the base of Márkus's description of Marx's conception of human nature and of Max-Neef's satisfiers and needs matrix, has identified seven types of satisfiers: goods; services; activities; relations; information, knowledge and theories; capacities; and institutions.

Needs constitute what is called "thick ethical concepts," speaking of which "factual description and valuation can and must be entangled" (Putnam 2002, p. 39). To use this term "with any discrimination one has to be able to identify imaginatively with an evaluative point of view." Needs, poverty, and Sen's capabilities are entangled terms in which description depends on evaluation (Putnam 2002, pp. 62–63). The entanglement thesis defeats many frequent criticisms addressed to scholars on the grounds that they incorporate values, and we can illustrate this with Fitzgerald's criticism of Maslow. When Fitzgerald (1977, p. 49) states, "Speaking on the need of self-actualisation is either tautological or unequivocally normative" (that is, it is not synthetic or falsifiable), he adopts the logical positivists tripartite classification of all judgments, which constitutes the expression of the fact/value dichotomy: (1) synthetic or falsifiable; (2) analytical (false or true by the rules of logic only, and thus tautological); (3) without cognitive meaning (ethical, metaphysical, and aesthetic judgments). He thus states that speech on the need for self-actualization is located in categories 2 or 3.

Poverty (usually defined as economic incapacity to satisfy needs) is a central field of application of the concept of needs and is dominated by economists who are advocates of the fact/value dichotomy and rejectors of the concept of needs. As they conceive that rationality cannot be present in matters of values, they assume, and insist on it all the time, that the definition of the poverty threshold (highly charged with values) is an arbitrary act by the researcher, promoting a total void on this topic and making it easy for all those who want to minimize the extent of poverty to use thresholds that deny most human needs. They are impoverishing poverty studies in the same way that they impoverished welfare economics, as Putnam (2002, chapter 3) describes.

SEE ALSO *Development Economics; Ethics; Fromm, Erich; Functionings; Marx, Karl; Maslow, Abraham; Needs, Basic; Poverty; Sen, Amartya Kumar; Universalism; Want Creation; Wants; Welfare; Welfare Economics*

BIBLIOGRAPHY

Boltvinik, Julio. 2007. Elementos para la crítica de la economía política de la pobreza. *Desacatos. Revista de antropología social* 23 (January–April): 53–86.

Doyal, Len, and Ian Gough. 1991. *A Theory of Human Need.* New York: Guilford Press.

Fitzgerald, Ross. 1977. Abraham Maslow's Hierarchy of Needs— An Exposition and Evaluation. In *Human Needs and Politics*, ed. R. Fitzgerald, 36–51. Sydney, Australia: Pergamon Press.

Fromm, Erich. 1955. *The Sane Society.* New York: Holt, 1990.

Gasper, Des. 2004. *The Ethics of Development.* Edinburgh: Edinburgh University Press.

Heller, Agnes. 1976. *The Theory of Need in Marx.* London: Allison and Busby.

Leakey, Richard. 1994. *The History of Humankind: Unearthing Our Family Tree.* London: Phoenix, 2001.

Lederer, K. 1980. Introduction. In *Human Needs: A Contribution to the Debate*, eds. K. Lederer, J. Galtung, and D. Antal, 3–14. Cambridge, MA: Oelgeschlager, Gunn and Hain.

Márkus, György. 1978. *Marxism and Anthropology: The Concept of "Human Essence" in the Philosophy of Marx.* Trans. E. de Laczay and G. Márkus. Assen, Netherlands: Van Gorcum.

Marx, Karl. 1857. Introduction to the *Critique of Political Economy.* In *Grundrisse: Foundations of the Critique of Political Economy.* Trans. Martin Nicolaus, 81–111. Harmondsworth, U.K.: Penguin, 1973.

Maslow, Abraham. 1954. *Motivation and Personality*, 3rd ed. New York: Addison-Wesley, 1987.

Max-Neef, Manfred, Antonio Elizalde, and Martín Hopenhayn. 1986. *Desarrollo a escala humana. Una opción para el futuro*, *Development Dialogue*, Special Issue, Santiago de Chile and Uppsala, Sweden: Cepaur and Dag Hammarskjöld Foundation, 1986. English version: Max-Neef, Manfred, Antonio Elizalde, and Martín Hopenhayn. 1989. Human-Scale Development: An Option for the Future. In *Development Dialogue* 1: 5–81. Expanded as *Human-Scale Development: Conception, Application and Further Reflections.* New York and London: Apex Press, 1991.

Putnam, Hilary. 2002. *The Collapse of the Fact: Value Dichotomy and Other Essays.* Cambridge, MA: Harvard University Press.

Rothenberg, Jerome. 1974. Soberanía del consumidor. *Enciclopedia Internacional de las Ciencias Sociales.* Vol. 3, ed. David L. Sills. Madrid: Aguilar.

Sen, Amartya. 1984. Poor, Relatively Speaking. In *Resources, Values and Development*, ed. Amartya Sen, 325–345. Cambridge, MA: Harvard University Press.

Sen, Amartya. 1985. *Commodities and Capabilities.* Amsterdam and New York: North-Holland.

Springborg, Patricia. 1981. *The Problem of Human Needs and the Critique of Civilisation.* London and Boston: Allen & Unwin.

Wiggins, David. 1998. *Needs, Values, Truth: Essays in the Philosophy of Value*, 3rd ed. Oxford: Clarendon Press.

Williams, Bernard. 1987. The Standard of Living: Interests and Capabilities. In *The Standard of Living. The Tanner Lectures*, ed. Amartya Sen, 94–102. Cambridge, UK: Cambridge University Press.

Julio Boltvinik

NEEDS, BASIC

People's basic needs include the requirements for survival, health, and fulfilment: food, water, warmth and, shelter at one extreme and self-expression and self-actualization at the other. However, questions of how to understand, identify, and meet basic needs remain somewhat contested.

Sigmund Freud (1856–1939) proposed two primal, biologically based instincts: self-preservation and fulfilling the sexual drive to procreate (Rickman 1937, p. 85), distinguishing the need for life from the death wish, or the aggressive drive to destroy or even self-destruct (Freud 1933, pp. 133–144). Carl Jung (1875–1961) transcended Freud's individualistic notion of instinct, incorporating historical and cultural factors that externally impel the person (Progoff 1953, pp. 33–39). Jung proposed that in later life a psychologically healthy person shifts from fulfilling more basic needs to a focus on self-realization, and this informed Henry Murray's ideas about self-actualization (1938).

Abraham Maslow (1908–1970), influenced by Murray, developed his hierarchy of needs in the early 1940s (Maslow 1943), based on a five-level pyramid from people's most basic physical "deficiency" needs to the most fulfilling "growth" needs, the satisfaction of each making possible the progression to the next. While deficiency needs leave the individual at rest when met, growth needs persist, continuing to motivate the person. The pyramid includes: (1) biological and physiological needs, for air, food, drink, sleep, shelter, warmth, and sex; (2) safety needs, for protection and security boundaries; (3) affection and belonging needs, for loving relationships in the family and satisfaction at work; (4) esteem needs, for appreciation by others, status, reputation, and recognition of achievements; and (5) self-actualization needs, for personal development and fulfilment. Three more levels of growth needs were added in the late 1960s (Maslow 1999), their precise origins being uncertain, however. These included (6) cognitive needs, for knowledge and understanding; (7) aesthetic needs, to create or appreciate beauty and harmony; and (8) transcendence needs, enabling other people to achieve self-actualization.

Maslow drew on anthropologist Ruth Benedict's application of the concept of synergy in cultures where cooperation was rewarded to everybody's benefit, applying this concept to work organizations to increase motivation, functioning, and production. He studied how to achieve synergy—that is, convergence—between the interests of the commercial organization and its employees through enlightened management based on humanistic theories about meeting people's needs.

Maslow's optimistic view of human nature and the satisfaction of needs informed Douglas McGregor's Theory Y (1960). McGregor proposed two contrasting managerial theories about human nature: theory X, that people meet their basic needs by expressing their fundamental selfishness and laziness; and theory Y, that they meet their needs by expressing fundamental tendencies toward being cooperative, hardworking, and productive.

From an economic perspective, John Maynard Keynes (1930) distinguished basic or absolute needs—for food and drink, for example—which are limited because they disappear once a person is satisfied, from relative needs—for advancement and superiority over other people—which are insatiable. However, more affluent people's needs to enjoy eating and drinking beyond satisfying basic appetites are widely recognized. Also, there are many further reasons why both absolute and relative needs are insatiable, such as the desire to improve one's quality of life.

Perspectives on responding to basic needs have widespread application beyond psychological work with people, including social policy, counseling, health care, social care, and education. Jonathan Bradshaw (1972) distinguishes four categories of social need: *normative*, judged according to a predetermined norm or standard; *comparative*, specified in relation to the needs of other people; *felt*, or wants experienced by people rather than judged by others; and *expressed*, as stated by people in the light of their experience. The strengths perspective developed by Dennis Saleeby (2002), involves assessing people's needs from their strengths and potential rather than simply deficits, building on their existing knowledge, skills, and resources to enable them to cope with challenges and difficulties. Person-centered assessment involves keeping individual needs at the center throughout the process of assessment and ensuring that the person's perception of his or her basic needs is always taken into consideration at every stage. In these terms, analysis of basic needs is more holistic, assessing the needs of whole person: the stage of the life course reached, the capacity of relatives, partners, and careers to respond to needs, and the resources available in the family, neighborhood, and wider environment.

Conceptions of basic needs not only cross disciplinary boundaries but also have transnational currency, although the ways these are presented may foster an illusion of global consensus rather than reflecting the reality of the contested nature of proposed responses, including those based on human rights. Basic needs derive not just from what are held to be physical or psychological imperatives but also from socially and politically constructed statements, some of which cross cultural and national boundaries. The 1948 UN Declaration of Human Rights asserts that all people share rights and freedoms, irrespective of their age, race, birth, or other differences. Many such statements of rights translate directly into statements of human need. Thus, in Article 3, "Everyone has the right to life, liberty and security of person," the words "basic need for" could be substituted for "right to." Similarly, the 1990 UN Convention on the Rights of the Child implies that children, from prebirth to adulthood, have needs and rights over and above those of adults. Many children are more vulnerable to their basic needs not being met through poverty, homelessness, neglect, abuse, their own or their parents' disease or poor health, and lack of access to education and justice.

Needs are often presented as though they are absolute, whereas in reality their social construction differs according to countries and cultures. In the late 1970s, Frances Stewart (1985) and Paul Streeten et al. (1981) developed the Basic Needs Approach (BNA) adopted by the World Bank, aiming to benefit developing countries, conditional on introducing fiscal policy changes and tax reforms—the principle of conditionality. The Capability Approach to understanding poverty has much in common with the BNA, both going beyond the possession of commodities and acknowledging that subjective experience may be at variance with people's physical circumstances (Sen 1985, pp. 82–83).

SEE ALSO *Benedict, Ruth; Conditionality; Culture; Development; Functionings; Keynes, John Maynard; Maslow, Abraham; Needs; Want Creation; Wants; World Bank, The*

BIBLIOGRAPHY

Bradshaw, Jonathan. 1972. A Taxonomy of Social Need. *New Society* 30 (March): 640–643.

Freud, Sigmund. 1933. Anxiety and Instinctual Life, Lecture 32. *New Introductory Lectures on Psycho-Analysis.* 107–143. London: Hogarth Press.

Keynes, John Maynard. 1930. Economic Possibilities for Our Grandchildren. *Essays in Persuasion*, 321–332. Vol. 11 of *The Collected Writings of John Maynard Keynes.* London: Macmillan.

Maslow, Abraham. 1943. A Theory of Human Motivation. *Psychological Review* 50: 370–396.

Maslow, Abraham. 1999. *Toward a Psychology of Being*, 3rd ed. New York: Wiley. (Originally published in 1968.)

McGregor, Douglas. 1960. *The Human Side of Enterprise.* New York: McGraw-Hill.

Murray, Henry, et al. 1938. *Explorations in Personality : A Clinical and Experimental Study of Fifty Men of College Age, by the Workers at the Harvard Psychological Clinic.* New York: Oxford University Press.

Progoff, Ira. 1953. *Jung's Psychology and Its Social Meaning.* London: Routledge and Kegan Paul.

Rickman, John, ed. and trans. 1937. Instincts and Their Vicissitudes (1915). *A General Selection from the Works of Sigmund Freud. Psycho-Analytical Epitomes No. 1*, 79–98. London: Hogarth Press and Institute of Psycho-Analysis.

Saleeby, Dennis, ed. 2002. *The Strengths Perspective in Social Work Practice*, 3rd ed. Boston: Allyn and Bacon.

Sen, Amartya K. 1985. *Commodities and Capabilities.* Oxford: Elsevier Science.

Stewart, Frances. 1985. *Planning to Meet Basic Needs.* London: Macmillan.

Streeten, Paul, S. J. Burki, Mahbub ul Haq, et al. 1981. *First Things First, Meeting Basic Human Needs in the Developing Countries.* New York: Oxford University Press.

Robert Adams

NEGATIVE INCOME TAX

A negative income tax (NIT) provides an income guarantee to families without other sources of income, but taxes away that guarantee as the family's earnings increase. An NIT is thus usually specified in two parts: (1) the guaranteed income for families with no other income; and (2) the marginal tax rate on earnings. It is a negative tax in the sense that low-income families receive a tax credit from the government rather than paying taxes to the government.

The idea of an NIT is often credited to Milton Friedman and James Tobin, who conceived it in the 1960s as a unified alternative to the complex array of means-tested cash and in-kind assistance programs that were available (and continue to be available) in the United States. They envisioned an NIT that would be administered by the U.S. Treasury as part of the overall tax system, thus eliminating much governmental bureaucracy in providing assistance to low-income families. The NIT was intended to ensure that families had adequate income regardless of their earnings while encouraging work with a lower marginal tax rate than under other means-tested programs.

Versions of the NIT were studied in four large-scale randomized experiments in the United States and one in Canada beginning in 1968. The experiments were conducted because of concerns that the income guarantee would discourage some adults from working and because of concerns about the costs of an NIT. The findings generally confirmed the expectations that higher levels of guaranteed income would reduce work effort and that lower marginal tax rates would encourage work. The results were especially strong among married women. However, the labor supply response in the NIT experiments was modest compared to prior nonexperimental estimates. Perhaps the most surprising result—and one of the most controversial and disputed—was that the NIT encouraged married couples in Seattle and Denver to break up.

Although the NIT in its original form has not become policy, the idea and the randomized experiments inspired a number of similar policy changes and additional randomized experiments. The Earned Income Credit in the United States is similar to the NIT but aims to reduce work disincentives by providing a refundable income tax credit only to families with earnings and by increasing the tax credit with earnings up to a certain point. Two Canadian provinces tested what was essentially an NIT with a work requirement that subsidized only those who worked 30 hours or more per week. Earned income disregards in many welfare and other systems use the NIT's basic notion that reduced tax rates will encourage work by slowly reducing means-tested benefits when earnings increase. In Germany a Targeted Negative Income Tax has been designed to encourage work among the long-term unemployed.

SEE ALSO *Income Maintenance Experiments*

BIBLIOGRAPHY

Hum, Derek, and Wayne Simpson. 2001. A Guaranteed Annual Income? From Mincome to Millennium. *Policy Options* (January–February): 78–82.

Munnell, Alice, ed. 1987. *Lessons from the Income Maintenance Experiments.* Boston: Federal Reserve Bank of Boston.

Charles Michalopoulos

NEGATIVE REINFORCEMENT

SEE *Reinforcement Theories.*

NEGOTIATION

Resolving a family dispute, concluding a business deal, settling a lawsuit, or agreeing to end hostilities all involve negotiation. Negotiation is a common technique for resolving disagreements and conflicts that arise between individuals, businesses, or nation-states. It is particularly important in the political arena, where violence has been and continues to be used as a way to reconcile competing values and interests. Negotiation is a nonviolent method of regulating political competition and resolving conflicts that competition inevitably creates. It is a prominent feature of democratic political systems and the democratic norm of bounded competition. Likewise, negotiation in international politics is a technique of regulated argument between nation-states seeking to arrive at a mutually acceptable outcome on an issue or issues of common concern. It is an important function of diplomacy and central to the functioning of the international system.

Negotiation is a process of communication between two or more parties whose interests in an issue or issues overlap or conflict. As a process, it provides a channel for identifying common or conflicting interests and reaching agreement on collective action or compromise. The negotiation process can be either competitive (there are winners and losers as a result of negotiations) or collaborative (the outcome of a negotiation is one of mutual gain or "win-win"). Negotiations that are primarily competitive in approach are often conceptualized as a game or strategic contest like chess or checkers. The fundamental objective of the participants in this kind of negotiation is to prevail over their opponent within mutually accepted rules and procedures. Positional bargaining is the tactic commonly associated with this approach. Negotiations that are collaborative in approach emphasize common interests as the basis for a dialogue. The goal of the participants in this kind of negotiation is to achieve a result that is minimally acceptable to all involved. The tactic identified with this approach is called interest-based bargaining. While the competitive approach to negotiations is the most prevalent, the collaborative approach is considered to produce better and more lasting outcomes. Whether a negotiation is competitive or collaborative depends on a number of contextual and situational factors, such as the negotiation environment or setting, the issues and actors involved, and the strategies or bargaining tactics employed.

It is common to think of the negotiation process in terms of stages or phases. There are a variety of ways of dividing the negotiation process into its component parts. One popular framework divides the process into three stages—the prenegotiation stage, the formula stage, and the detail stage. Another divides the process into five phases—preparation, beginning, middle, end, and implementation. In any case, negotiations are predicated on recognition that an issue under contention is negotiable. For negotiations to take place, the parties in conflict must agree on the possibility that a negotiated settlement may prove advantageous to all concerned. This aspect of the preparatory or prenegotiation stage is perhaps the most difficult, particularly in conflicts where the stakes are high. Once the need and willingness to negotiate is established, two other matters are then taken up—the agenda and the procedures. Setting an agenda and establishing the procedures for talks can also be very difficult and contentious though less so in matters of low importance or if the stakes are low. After the agenda (what issues are to be discussed and in what order) and the procedures (the format, venue, the level and composition of delegations, and timing) have been settled, the formal negotiations commence. In this stage of the process, the parties through designated negotiators engage in the give-and-take of the negotiation process. In many cases, negotiators will initially try to agree on the broad principles of a settlement (the formula stage) followed by negotiations on the details of the agreement (the details stage). Ostensibly the negotiation process ends when an agreement (e.g., a contract, treaty, protocol) is signed, though it is argued that the process often extends to a postnegotiation or implementation stage.

Although the negotiation process in the international arena displays many of the same characteristics and operates according to many of the same rules developed 300 years ago, it has become much more complex as the international system has evolved. Today, international negotiations, which are predominantly multilateral and conducted within established international institutions, such as the United Nations, the World Trade Organization, and the International Monetary Fund, address a host of contentious global issues (e.g., climate change, human rights, HIV/AIDS) beyond the traditional military-security concerns (e.g., arms control, Arab-Israeli conflict) and involve a vast number of nonstate actors (e.g., nongovernmental organizations, networks of experts or specialists—so-called epistemic communities, multinational or transnational corporations) active in the international arena. These and other situational factors have altered the dynamics of international negotiations, making an already complicated, arduous, and time-consuming process even more so. At the same time, new and innovative negotiation forums have developed—so-called track two negotiations in which individuals or nongovernmental organizations rather than government officials are the negotiators—that supplement or complement traditional "official" international negotiations.

SEE ALSO *Civil Society; Conflict; Diplomacy; Foreign Policy; Game Theory; Government; International Monetary Fund; International Relations; Legal Systems; Nation; Nongovernmental Organizations (NGOs); North Atlantic Treaty Organization; Partition; Peace; Peace Process; Secession; Settlement, Negotiated; United Nations; World Trade Organization*

BIBLIOGRAPHY

Berridge, Geoffrey R. 2005. *Diplomacy: Theory and Practice*, 3rd ed. London: Palgrave.

Cohen, Raymond. 1997. *Negotiating Across Cultures: Communication Obstacles in International Diplomacy*, revised ed. Washington, DC: United States Institute of Peace Press.

Dixon, William J., and Paul D. Senese. 2002. Democracy, Disputes, and Negotiated Settlements. *The Journal of Conflict Resolution* 46 (4): 547–571.

Muldoon, James P., Jr., JoAnn Fagot Aviel, Richard Reitano, and Earl Sullivan, eds. 2005. *Multilateral Diplomacy and the United Nations Today*, 2nd ed. Boulder, CO: Westview Press.

Starkey, Brigid, Mark A. Boyer, and Jonathan Wilkenfeld. 1999. *Negotiating a Complex World: An Introduction to International Negotiation*. Lanham, MD: Rowman & Littlefield.

James P. Muldoon Jr.

NEGRITUDE

SEE *Pan-Africanism; Socialism, African.*

NEGRO

The term *Negro* emerged as a social and political marker for Africans south of the Sahara in the fifteenth century. In its earliest usage it generally referred only to color and could be applied to anyone viewed as black, nonwhite, or non-European. *Negro* derives from the Latin *niger*, meaning "black," and became *Negro/a* in Spanish and Portuguese. (The letter *a* signifies the grammatical feminine form of the word.) When the Portuguese began to enslave Africans in Portugal in the 1440s, the term became synonymous with "slave" and was used by the Spanish as they carried slaves from West Africa to New World societies at the beginning of the sixteenth century.

The meaning of the term was modified by the histories of slavery in the New World, and as it entered other languages its meanings percolated through the social realities of each society. That is to say, while the denotations were similar, the connotations varied over time and space. However, the creation of mixed-race populations through miscegenation required new labels that connoted different statuses, particularly for those who were free.

By the beginning of the seventeenth century, *Negro* was synonymous with "slave" in Latin America. By the nineteenth century, however, the number of free blacks and mixed-race groups was so great that a *régimen de castas* (caste regime) was enacted to govern blacks and mixed-race groups. These laws restricted them to an inferior legal status, reserving social and economic mobility for whites. New terms allowed different groups to distance themselves from the negative implications of *Negro/a*, which came to signify poverty, crime, and many forms of degeneration. The term *prado/a* referred to mixed-race or brownness. There was also a long list of other terms such as *mulatto, mestizo,* or *moreno* that identified a nonwhite heritage but in a diluted form.

The meanings of these terms cannot be uncoupled from the struggle over citizenship that came to most of these societies in the late nineteenth century and early twentieth century. However, the leaders and intellectuals in these countries believed fervently in racial determinism and "had no doubts that the historical trajectories of individuals, nations, and peoples were irrevocably determined by their 'racial' ancestry" (Andrews 2004, p. 118). In spite of the claims of universal citizenship that took hold after slavery, the *Negro/a* or black had to either disappear or be transformed into an insignificant entity. Most of these nations therefore embarked on a campaign of whitening through immigration to create "white republics" rather than mixed-raced ones. These campaigns failed, but the effort to dilute blackness through narratives of brownness or *mestizaje* ("race mixing") continues. But for the black population, the effort to claim racial identity and push for acceptance into the larger society found expression in labor struggles but also resulted in an ambivalent relationship to the term *Negro/a* or blackness. For example, in Brazil and Colombia organizations have emerged that celebrate blackness, and efforts are in place to develop political representation based on race. Yet blacks struggle over their desire to be accepted as citizens, and as blacks some embrace *mestizaje* as a way to avoid dilemmas associated with the term *Negro/a*. One example of the tensions that remain over blackness is in the use of the diminutive form *negrito/a*. This is a term of endearment and affection in societies where the term *Negro/a* is a pejorative label.

In North America the term *Negro* migrated into English from Spanish and Portuguese and was used to identify African people both slave and free. By the mid-eighteenth century the term was synonymous with "slavery" even though many blacks were free. By the nineteenth century *Negro* was corrupted to the even more sinister slur *nigger*. According to the historian Michael Gomez, the term *Negro* was not accepted by Africans, who generally continued to use the term *African* or their memory of specific ethnic terms such as Ibo or Yoruba. Though these practices varied in degree from place to place, evidence suggests that blacks effectively resisted a racial classification until around 1830, when a black consciousness emerged in response to the continued degradation of slavery and the attempt to send free blacks back to Africa. At this moment of history blacks embraced the term *colored* or *Negro* instead of *African* as an effort to claim their citizenship and push their demand for an end to slavery.

By the latter half of the century, after slavery's demise, the term *Afro-American* competed with *Negro* for most blacks as a term of both citizenship and a global identity. The debate over naming was shaped by the massive deni-

gration of African people and the poverty and powerlessness of Africa in the colonial age. The term *colored* was rejected in favor of *Negro*, which was a term of validation for many. Alexander Crummell, his political pupil W. E. B. Du Bois, and the intellectuals in the American Negro Academy campaigned to have the term capitalized. Black nationalists pushed for the term *Anglo-American*, while many women's organization registered a preference for *Afro-American*.

In the first half of the twentieth century disenfranchisement, lynchings, and segregation became codified in law and in practice. In the context of the apartheid system of the South known as Jim Crow, other nonwhites were also labeled as *Negro*. These included Chinese, Native Americans, Asian Indians, and Japanese, all of whom were subjected to the same Jim Crow laws as African Americans. These practices were challenged in the courts and in the culture.

By mid-century the political climate shifted with the rise of the civil rights movement, and with this shift the term *Negro* fell out of favor. For the postwar generations it became a term of conservatism and complacency. The civil rights movement embodied a sense of black pride, and with the rise of decolonization in Africa, the desire to claim both blackness and an African identity shaped the battle over name. In the early twenty-first century *Negro* is generally used by blacks to reference a person who is politically unacceptable, and most, though not all, insist upon *African American*, rejecting the more racially charged *Negro*. But ambivalence over hyphenated terms remains as well as discomfort and confusion over the term *African*. An increasing minority rejects the African designation and insists on only the term *American*. Almost no one uses the term *Negro*.

SEE ALSO *Blackness; Civil Rights Movement, U.S.; Jim Crow; Moreno/a; Mulattos; Racial Slurs; Racism; Slavery; Whiteness*

BIBLIOGRAPHY

Andrews, George Reid. 2004. *Afro-Latin America, 1800–2000.* New York: Oxford University Press.

Gomez, Michael A. 1998. *Exchanging Our Country Marks: The Transformation of African Identities in the Colonial and Antebellum South.* Chapel Hill: University of North Carolina Press.

Hanchard, Michael George. 1994. *Orpheus and Power: The Movimento Negro of Rio de Janeiro and São Paulo, Brazil, 1945–1988.* Princeton, NJ: Princeton University Press.

Stuckey, Sterling. 1987. *Slave Culture: Nationalist Theory and the Foundations of Black America.* New York: Oxford University Press.

Tiffany Ruby Patterson

NEHRU, JAWAHARLAL
1889–1964

Born in November 1889, Jawaharlal Nehru would become India's first prime minister.

Nehru's ancestors were Kashmiri Brahmins who had settled in Allahabad, in northern India. His father, Motilal Nehru, was a successful barrister and a prominent figure in the Indian National Congress (INC), which was established in 1885.

In 1905 Nehru was sent to England, studying first at Harrow, then at Cambridge University, and finally joining the Inner Temple and passing the Bar examinations. By 1905 the INC had begun to shift from a gradualist "moderate" politics to a more "extremist" anti-colonial stance as evinced by Bal Gangadhar Tilak (1856–1920) among others. Jawaharlal, unlike his father, found himself more in sympathy with this militant position. Nevertheless, during the years following his return to India in 1912, Nehru entered the legal profession through his father's chambers. By 1917 he joined the Home Rule League movement guided by the "extremist" Tilak and the theosophist Annie Besant (1847–1933).

But it was events in 1919 that drove Nehru into deeper political involvement with congress's politics under the leadership of Mohandas Karamchand Gandhi (1869–1948). First, the colonial government decided to continue wartime ordinances into peacetime under the Rowlatt Act, which would allow the British to hold Indian political agitators without trial. Gandhi launched an all-India civil disobedience campaign in protest. Second, while support for the campaign was uneven, General Reginald Dyer's orders on April 13 to fire without warning upon an unarmed crowd of villagers galvanized Indian opposition. The villagers, ignorant of martial law regulations, had assembled to hear speeches in the city of Amritsar. Although Dyer was dismissed from the army, the House of Lords virtually exonerated him when it passed a motion in his favor. For Nehru, this was a sign that it was time for a more assertive struggle to achieve freedom.

Nehru became an avid supporter of Gandhi and joined the non-cooperation movement launched by him in 1920. In February 1927, on a personal visit to Europe, Nehru attended the International Congress against Colonial Oppression and Imperialism held in Brussels. Here he encountered the Marxist and socialist ideas of other delegates and a few months later he was invited to the Soviet Union to join in the tenth anniversary celebration of the Bolshevik Revolution. The socialist reforms Nehru witnessed left a profound impression on him and convinced him that as another largely agrarian country with an impoverished and mostly illiterate population, India could usefully emulate the Soviet experiment.

Returning with an arsenal of ideas, Nehru urged a more comprehensive struggle against the British. His ideas involved supporting an increasingly radical peasant agitation; a distancing from the conservative landlord and industrial supporters of the congress; and reforms such as the abolition of landlordism, socialization of the land, planned economic development, and state acquisition of key industries for the future. These ideas, however, brought Nehru into disagreement with Gandhi, who feared the class struggle they would provoke might fracture Indian unity. While they continued to diverge on many of these issues, Nehru desisted from openly challenging Gandhi's political leadership in the interests of maintaining a consolidated anti-colonial movement.

With the British "transfer of power" on August 15, 1947, Nehru became India's prime minister. Assuming power amid the devastating violence of the partition of British India into the nation-states of India and Pakistan, Nehru left the imprint of his political ideals as he sought to steer the new country into calmer political seas. Among Nehru's most significant legacies was to set India on the path of democracy in that elections rather than military coups produced changes of governments. Another of Nehru's bequests was the Indian state's adoption of the ideal of secularism, defined not as a "separation of church and state" but as the commitment by the government to treat every religion equally. There was little resistance to this principle in the aftermath of the religious violence surrounding partition and Gandhi's assassination at the hands of a Hindu supremacist on January 30, 1948.

However, Nehru is also credited with perpetuating the colonial government's over-centralized state structure that he had so vociferously criticized. Nearly 200 articles of the British-instituted Government of India Act of 1935 passed into the constitution of independent India. The imbalance of power between the central and provincial (called states in independent India) governments, in favor of the former, was retained as was the bureaucracy, the empire's "steel frame." The Gandhian ideal of a non-party government with a weak center and power devolved to "village republics" was discarded in substance.

On the economic front, although Nehru had compromised earlier with Gandhi, he now sought to apply many of his socialist ideas. However, as prime minister, he also had to take into account the wide variety of demands on the state as well as India's pre-existing capitalist economic framework. While still adhering to his principle of planned development Nehru opted for a mixed economy in which the government would only control its capital goods and strategic industries. Through a series of five-year plans, heavy industry was given priority over consumer goods manufacture, and import substitution policies were pushed to attain self-sufficiency. But these measures took their toll in that the drive for self-sufficiency further isolated India's economy and pushed up consumer prices. State-owned industries were maintained despite their often demonstrated inefficiency while large Indian capitalists, although firmly regulated, monopolized the domestic market, often dumping substandard consumer goods on it.

With regard to land reform too, Nehru's success is ambivalent. Among his first measures was to abolish landlordism and set land ceilings in the early 1950s. Yet the large dispossessed landlords were given compensation, and although land reforms were administered not from the center but by the states, prosperous peasant groups who dominated the Congress party at the provincial level increased the maximum acreage that could be held, to their advantage in many instances. Moreover, by exploiting loopholes in the legislations, many landlords transferred portions of their estates into the hands of family members or retainers. In the end, landless laborers benefited little from the agrarian reforms despite Nehru's commitment to removing the economic inequity of the colonial era.

The new nation-state of India was also pulled into a world of other nation-states. Nehru's achievements here, gaining him international renown, lay in steering India between the Scylla and Charybdis of the cold war blocs led by the United States and the Union of Soviet Socialist Republics through the principle of "Non-Alignment." A term coined by Nehru, non-alignment was a principle put into international play along with leaders such as Gamal Abdel Nasser (1918–1970) of Egypt and Josip Broz Tito (1892–1980) of the former Yugoslavia. However, although advocating principled neutrality, Nehru's policies were often viewed with suspicion by many political leaders and observers, especially those aligned with the Western bloc—and especially when he refused to condemn the Soviet invasion of Hungary in 1956.

Perhaps Nehru's gravest political crisis was his country's defeat in the 1962 Sino-Indian war provoked by border disputes emanating from the colonial past. The conflict itself was an embarrassing repudiation of a "friendship" that purportedly began when India became the first country to recognize Mao Zedong's People's Republic of China established in 1949. Nehru was not only brutally disappointed by China's "aggression," but for the remaining two years of his life some of Nehru's domestic policies produced challenges to his leadership in parliament until his death on May 27, 1964.

SEE ALSO *Anticolonial Movements; Chinese Revolution; Cold War; Congress Party, India; Decolonization; Democracy; Gandhi, Indira; Gandhi, Mohandas K.;*

Indian National Congress; Industrialization; Land Reform; Landlords; Mao Zedong; Neutral States; Partition; Planning; Secular, Secularism, Secularization; Socialism

BIBLIOGRAPHY

PRIMARY WORKS

Nehru, Jawaharlal. 1936. *An Autobiography.* London: Lane.

Nehru, Jawaharlal. 1941. *Towards Freedom.* New York: John Day.

Nehru, Jawaharlal. 1946. *The Discovery of India.* Calcutta: Signet Press.

Nehru, Jawaharlal. 1961. *India's Foreign Policy.* Delhi: Government of India Publications Division.

SECONDARY WORKS

Akbar, M. J. 1988. *Nehru: the Making of India.* London: Viking.

Chatterjee, Partha. 1993. *Nationalist Thought and the Colonial World: A Derivative Discourse.* Minneapolis: University of Minnesota.

Gopal, Sarvepalli. 1975–1984. *Jawaharlal Nehru: A Biography.* 3 vols. London: J. Cape.

Khilnani, Sunil. 1999. *The Idea of India.* New York: Farrar Straus Giroux.

Nanda, B. R. 1995. *Jawaharlal Nehru: Rebel and Statesman.* New Delhi; New York: Oxford University Press.

Mridu Rai

NEIGHBORHOOD EFFECTS

Researchers employ the concept of neighborhood effects to explore the causes of social pathology among the urban poor and minorities in terms of the spatial dynamics caused by segregation, deindustrialization, and government neglect. In its various forms, including the "culture of poverty" (Lewis 1961), "the urban underclass" (Wilson 1987), and "culture of segregation" (Massey and Denton 1993), research on neighborhood effects demonstrates (1) how structural factors and racism explain the formation of poor neighborhoods, and (2) how these neighborhoods become the basis for an urban subculture that further marginalizes the poor. This research makes assumptions about the interrelations of structural factors (e.g., jobs and housing markets) and culture that under closer scrutiny raise more questions than answers. In addition, this research tends to homogenize the "culture" of urban poverty rather than exploring its complexities and constitutive role in producing both popular and dominant cultures.

As Catherine Garner and Stephen Raudenbush (1991) note, the first question that one must ask when looking at neighborhood effects is, "What constitutes a neighborhood?" How does one compare a vibrant "neighborhood" such as Harlem with a marginalized African American community in another city (Newman 1991)? In developing statistical analyses of segregation many researchers, such as Douglas Massey and Nancy Denton (1993), rely mainly on census tract data. Massey and Denton are careful to mention the limitations of analysis based on census tract information. However, in terms of defining the impacts of neighborhood on "culture," a qualitative approach that takes into account the specific history, politics, and race relations that define neighborhoods is needed. This does not mean, however, that qualitative research alone can provide an accurate understanding of urban culture.

Based on research in Mexico, Puerto Rico, and Cuba (primarily during the 1950s and 1960s), Oscar Lewis sought to understand how urban poverty generated a series of social pathologies among the poor, including sexism, fatalism, and an inability to plan for the future. In their well-known 1970 refutation of the application of the culture of poverty theory, Edwin Eames and Judith Goode argued that many of the characteristics Lewis associated with poverty, including matrifocal families and mutual aid, are rational adaptations. The continuing prevalence of poverty, they stated, must be understood in terms of restricted access to and attainment of job skills. Studies that pathologize the poor have received justified criticism for privileging middle-class values, being vague about the overall characteristics of poverty and their interrelations, and viewing matrifocal households as a cause rather than a result of poverty. As Katherine S. Newman (1991) pointed out, matrifocal households also may be seen as part of a larger strategy of maintaining large networks of kinship ties in order to alleviate economic insecurity. Following the lead of Carol Stack's path-breaking book *All Our Kin* (1974), Newman emphasized how social actors are not only adapting but also creating notions of family and community that both alter and reproduce traditional middle-class ideals of the nuclear family.

This point about family structure is crucial because William Julius Wilson (1987) attributed many of the characteristics of the culture of the "urban underclass" to the prevalence of female-headed households. These households, according to Wilson, are in turn the result of the lack of job opportunities for African American men. Their high rate of unemployment due to deindustrialization, combined with the departure of the African American middle class from the inner city, has created a subculture of poverty that generates single-parent families with no middle-class role models. Poor African American neighborhoods are now "hermetically sealed" from the middle-class values that can lead to prosperity. This argument, however, must be subject to closer scrutiny that questions

the mechanical relationship between economics and culture (again, compare Harlem to a more "isolated" neighborhood). Does the presence of middle-class families, for example, provide positive role models? Indeed, studies have shown that in many cases the middle-class disdain their poorer neighbors. And what about the kinship, work, recreational, educational, and other ties that connect urban neighborhoods? How do we account for the strength of churches in many poor neighborhoods?

In another statistically based analysis, Massey and Denton (1993) argued that segregation has led to a subculture of linguistic isolation (black English), low school achievement, and an overall oppositional stance towards the dominant culture. The authors critiqued Wilson's work by arguing that segregation, not joblessness, is a stronger causal factor in the creation of an urban underclass. For example, Wilson emphasized that between 1967 and 1987 Chicago lost about 60 percent of its manufacturing jobs. Massey and Denton argued that deindustrialization alone does not explain residential patterns. The authors showed that the spatial aspects of poverty must be understood in terms of the increase, from 1970 to 1980, in African Americans living in geographically concentrated neighborhoods. Massey and Denton's study is powerful in demonstrating how housing discrimination, poor job opportunities, and the lack of public services has severely affected the urban poor. Like Wilson, they then attempted to show a causal relationship between these factors and the formation of an urban subculture. However, one could argue that the formation of an oppositional culture (a common feature among youth of any class) is a response to a number of factors, including the production of popular cultures. Indeed, many elements of inner-city culture, including music and dance, exist in a complex relationship with dominant cultures.

Research by Wilson, Massey, and Denton is persuasive in exploring the structural factors that lead to joblessness and segregation. For all of these authors, however, the notion of culture is undertheorized. Like Lewis with his "culture of poverty" theory, these authors attempt to articulate a mechanical relationship between economics and poverty that does not do justice to the richness of the urban experience. What is needed is fine-tuned ethnographic research that can better understand the variety of ways in which the urban poor have survived and thrived in U.S. cities.

SEE ALSO *Anthropology, Urban; Culture; Culture of Poverty; Economics, Urban; Ethnography; Female-Headed Families; Industrialization; Lewis, Oscar; Oppositionality; Pathology, Social; Popular Culture; Poverty; Role Models; Segregation, Residential; Sociology, Urban; Underclass; Urban Studies*

BIBLIOGRAPHY

Eames, Edwin, and Judith Goode. 1970. On Lewis' Culture of Poverty Concept. *Current Anthropology*, 11(4): 479-482.

Garner, Catherine L., and Stephen W. Raudenbush. 1991. Neighborhood Effects on Educational Attainment: A Multilevel Analysis. *Sociology of Education* 64 (4): 251–262.

Lewis, Oscar. 1961. *The Children of Sanchez.* New York: Random House.

Massey, Douglas S., and Nancy A. Denton. 1993. *American Apartheid: Segregation and the Making of the Urban Underclass.* Cambridge, MA: Harvard University Press.

Newman, Katherine S. 1991. Culture and Structure. *City and Society* 6 (1): 3–25.

Stack, Carol. 1974. *All Our Kin.* New York: Harper and Row.

Wilson, William J. 1980. *The Declining Significance of Race: Blacks and Changing American Institutions.* Chicago: University of Chicago Press.

Wilson, William J. 1987. *The Truly Disadvantaged.* Chicago: University of Chicago Press.

Miguel Diaz-Barriga

NEIGHBORHOODS

The concept of neighborhood is widely used throughout the social sciences as a geographical unit of analysis, and internationally as a planning concept. Neighborhoods can be diverse, containing a mix of ethnic and socioeconomic status groups; or they can be extremely homogenous, ranging from low-income minority areas to gated communities denying entry to undesired visitors.

Neighborhoods are residential districts located in urban areas. Historically, neighborhoods tended to have developed in an unplanned fashion. Throughout the twentieth century there have been increasing efforts to plan neighborhoods as cohesive residential areas that contain basic services, parks, shops, schools, and other amenities. Although the term *neighborhood* is typically used to identify self-contained or socially cohesive areas, it is often difficult to determine neighborhood boundaries for the purposes of research. Residents themselves often harbor very different ideas about the precise boundaries of their neighborhood, and the character of their neighborhood. In the U.S. and Canadian census, units that approximate neighborhoods are called census tracts.

Much contemporary thinking about neighborhoods in the social sciences is shaped by and offers criticism of the Chicago school, a group of sociologists who worked at the University of Chicago during the early twentieth century; earlier work, by Friedrich Engels (1892 [1845]) on working-class slums in England, has also been influential. In North America social scientists have traditionally focused on the segregation between neighborhoods according to race, ethnicity, and socioeconomic status. In 1988 the sociologists Nancy A. Denton and Douglas S. Massey illustrated that segregation can be statistically measured across five different dimensions: evenness, exposure, concentration, centralization, and clustering. Each dimension emphasizes a different characteristic of segregation. Today, countless international studies exist that examine segregation across neighborhoods by race, ethnicity, class, language, religion, and other categories.

Social scientists have mixed perspectives on segregation. Ceris Peach (1996), for example, uses the terms *good* and *bad segregation* to distinguish between processes of discrimination and violence against minorities, and voluntary residential association. On the one hand, discrimination by real estate agents and financial institutions can segregate minorities into neighborhoods with inferior schools, housing stock, infrastructure, public services, and shopping opportunities. In addition, more affluent residents and members of the majority population sometimes decide to move out of the neighborhood once a critical mass of minority population has moved in—a phenomenon known in the United States as "white flight." The so-called spatial mismatch hypothesis further suggests that living in inner-city neighborhoods denies many members of racial minorities access to an increasingly suburban job market, resulting in high levels of unemployment. On the other hand, their concentration in particular neighborhoods can offer social and emotional support for minorities, facilitating the establishment of ethnic and institutional networks. Sometimes these positive developments are the result of people, living in segregated conditions, making the best of those circumstances. Compared to the classical model described by the Chicago school, segregation of African American and Latino minorities in the United States after around 1950 tends to be more permanent. In the case of newly arriving immigrants, spatial concentrations can help newcomers integrate into society. In North American cities of the twentieth century such immigrant reception areas were typically located in inner cities. Today, an increasing number of immigrant neighborhoods are located in the suburbs of large metropolitan areas.

In North American cities, neighborhoods tend to undergo a typical life cycle. When initially established they contain new housing stock, state-of-the-art infrastructure, and high-level services, and are inhabited by relatively well-off families. As housing stock and infrastructure age, the socioeconomic status of neighborhoods also declines. At the low point of the cycle there is severe decay and property abandonment, at which point some neighborhoods gentrify, that is, they regenerate through the investments made by relatively affluent groups. Gentrification usually is initiated by individuals (often artists) who renovate cheap housing stock, give their neighborhood a fashionable image, and thereby attract more wealthy groups. Recent scholarship has recognized, however, that gentrification is not part of a natural cycle, as implied by some research that followed the Chicago school, but rather a social process. Over the last few decades, governments and development agencies have attempted to actively facilitate and plan the gentrification of inner-city neighborhoods. A consequence of gentrification can be the displacement of poorer residents, the homeless, and other vulnerable groups. Processes of gentrification also assume very different characteristics and have different social and economic consequences in different parts of the world.

A body of research suggests that the social contexts of neighborhoods themselves shape the behavioral norms and attitudes of the residents. These so-called "neighborhood effects" are responsible for the persistence of inner-city social problems, including crime, drug abuse, teenage pregnancy, dropping out of school, and poor labor-market performance among youths. Researchers theorize that negative neighborhood effects operate through three distinct mechanisms: local teenage peer groups, negative adult role models, and local schools and other institutions that fail to provide adequate support to residents. To diminish negative neighborhood effects, social scientists have advocated mixed-income housing and housing-dispersal policies, which enable poor and minority families to locate outside of segregated neighborhoods. However, the neighborhood effects theory has been criticized for neglecting processes of social and cultural exclusion that affect individuals and neighborhoods alike. It may be that dispersal and mixed-income policies diminish social isolation only because they stimulate social assimilation to "mainstream" cultural practices. In addition, quantitative research on neighborhood effects has been criticized for making speculative inferences of causality based on statistical correlations, whereas qualitative research has been criticized for making unsubstantiated cultural claims based on specific cases and few actors.

Recent work by social scientists has emphasized the cultural construction of neighborhood identity. Kay Anderson's pathbreaking work *Vancouver's Chinatown* (1991) illustrates how that neighborhood has assumed different cultural identities throughout history based on the changing role and status of the Chinese minority in Canadian society. Contemporary research shows how struggles between social groups over the space and the aesthetical appearance of a neighborhood can facilitate the racialization of social groups and inflame ethnic tension and social conflict. Cultural representations of neighborhoods can also lead to the social exclusion or privileging of residents. According to this research, the construction of race, ethnicity, and other cultural identities are deeply entangled with neighborhood processes.

SEE ALSO *Lewis, Oscar*

BIBLIOGRAPHY

Anderson, Kay. 1991. *Vancouver's Chinatown: Racial Discourse in Canada, 1875–1980.* Montreal: McGill-Queen's University Press.

Denton, Nancy A., and Douglas S. Massey. 1988. Residential Segregation of Blacks, Hispanics, and Asians by Socioeconomic Status and Generation. *Social Science Quarterly* 69 (4): 797–817.

Engels, Friedrich. [1845] 1892. *The Condition of the Working-Class in England in 1844.* London: Swan Sonnenschein.

Peach, Ceris. 1996. Good Segregation, Bad Segregation. *Transactions of the Institute of British Geographers* 21: 216–235.

Harald Bauder

NEOBEHAVIORISM
SEE *Tolman, Edward.*

NEOCLASSICAL GROWTH MODEL

The neoclassical model of long-run economic growth, introduced by Robert Solow (b. 1924) and Trevor Swan (1918–1989) in 1956, analyzes the convergence of an economy to a growth rate set by exogenous population increase and, as added the following year by Solow (1957), an exogenous rate of technical change. Earlier growth models by R. F. Harrod (1900–1978) in 1939 and Evsey Domar (1914–1997) in 1946 (both reprinted in Stiglitz and Uzawa 1969) had assumed fixed coefficients in products, which the Solow-Swan neoclassical model generalized to allow for substitution between capital and labor. The term *neoclassical* reflected the model's concern with long-run equilibrium growth of potential output in a fully employed economy, abstracting from short-run Keynesian issues of effective demand.

The neoclassical growth model assumes the existence of an aggregate production function $Y = F(K, N)$, where Y is aggregate output, K is the capital stock, and N is the number of workers. The production function has constant returns to scale (if K and N change in the same proportion, Y will also change in that proportion), with positive but diminishing marginal products of capital and labor. Dividing by the number of workers N, output per capita $y = Y/N$ is a function of the capital/labor ratio $k = K/N$:

$$y = f(k)$$

and y = c + i, where c = C/N is consumption per capita and i = I/N is investment per capita. The per capita consumption function is assumed to be c = (1–s)y, where s is the marginal propensity to save and (1–s) is the marginal propensity to consume. In equilibrium, (desired) investment is equal to saving, i = sy = sf(k).

In the steady-state equilibrium, per capita output (y) and the capital/labor ratio (k) do not change, and total output Y grows at the rate n, the exogenous growth rate of the population and labor force (N). Required gross investment in the steady state will be just enough to cover depreciation (replacement investment) and to equip each new worker with the same amount of capital that existing workers have. Required investment per capita in the steady state is thus (n + d)k, where n is the rate of population growth and d is the depreciation rate. The steady state equilibrium capital/labor ratio k* will be given by sf(k*) = (n + d)k* and steady state output per capita will be y* = f(k*). Because f, the rate of change of output per capita with respect to a change in the capital/labor ratio, is positive but decreasing (an increase in the capital/labor ratio raises output per worker, but not by as much as the previous increase of the same size), if k is initially less than k*, investment and saving will exceed the investment needed to keep k constant, and the capital/labor ratio k will increase until it reaches k*. If k is initially greater than k*, investment and saving will be less than the investment needed to keep k constant, and k will decrease until it is equal to k*.

Solow allowed for neutral technical change by writing the production function as Y = A(t)F(K, N), where A(t) is an index of total factor productivity at time t. By calculating how much growth was due to growth of capital and labor inputs, and subtracting these estimates from the observed growth rate, Solow (1957) obtained a measure of the rate of change of A (the Solow residual), an implicit measure of technical change. Later studies adjusted for improvements in the quality of capital and labor inputs (such as better educated and trained workers), and thus reduced Solow's high original estimates of how much economic growth was due to technical change.

In the neoclassical growth model, the growth rate is independent of the savings rate, and depends only on population growth and technical change, both taken as determined exogenously outside the model. A higher propensity to save leads to a higher level of output per capita in the steady state, but not a higher steady state growth rate. Faster population growth reduces per capita output and consumption in the steady state.

Neoclassical growth theory was sharply criticized by the Cambridge school, building on works on capital accumulation and income distribution by Joan Robinson (1903–1983) and Nicholas Kaldor (1908–1986), both

published in 1956 (see Harcourt 1972 on the Cambridge capital controversies between Post-Keynesians at Cambridge University and neoclassical economists, such as Solow, at Massachusetts Institute of Technology). The Cambridge theorists objected to explaining the return on capital by differentiating an aggregate production function with respect to the capital stock K, measured as so many identical machines. They denied the existence of an aggregate production function, and argued that since capital goods are heterogeneous, there is no physical measure of aggregate capital that is independent of prices and rates of return, hence of income distribution (see papers by Robinson, Kaldor, Richard Kahn, and David Champernowne reprinted in Stiglitz and Uzawa 1969).

Beginning with Kaldor's and James Mirrlees's technical progress function and with Kenneth Arrow's "learning by doing," which makes total factor productivity depend on cumulative past investment (both reprinted in Stiglitz and Uzawa 1969), economists have tried to dispense with the exogeneity of technical change in neoclassical growth theory. Unlike the neoclassical growth model, endogenous growth theory ("new growth theory"), pioneered by Paul Romer, models improvements in productivity as depending on investment in research and development and, through education and health care, in human capital.

The neoclassical growth model implies that, if the same technology is available to all countries, every country will converge to a growth rate that differs from that of any other country only by the difference in their rates of population growth. Whether such convergence of growth rates has been observed is controversial. Endogenous growth theory, by dropping the assumption of diminishing returns to investment, does not follow the neoclassical growth model in predicting convergence (see the symposium by Romer et al. 1994).

Criticisms of the Solow-Swan neoclassical growth model, whether directed at the aggregate production function with a single capital good or at the exogeneity of technical change, view the model as an oversimplified parable. It was, however, the simplicity of the neoclassical growth model that kept it tractable, and made it so useful and influential as a framework for organizing thinking about economic growth.

SEE ALSO *Cambridge Capital Controversy; Golden Rule in Growth Models; Growth Accounting; Immiserizing Growth; Optimal Growth; Saving Rate; Solow Residual, The; Solow, Robert M.; Technological Progress, Economic Growth*

BIBLIOGRAPHY

Harcourt, Geoffrey C. 1972. *Some Cambridge Controversies in the Theory of Capital.* Cambridge, U.K.: Cambridge University Press.

Romer, Paul M., Gene M. Grossman and Elhanan Helpman, et al. 1994. Symposium: New Growth Theory. *Journal of Economic Perspectives* 8 (1): 3–72.

Solow, Robert M. 1956. A Contribution to the Theory of Economic Growth. *Quarterly Journal of Economics* 70: 65–94 (reprinted in Stiglitz and Uzawa 1969).

Solow, Robert M. 1957. Technical Change and the Aggregate Production Function. *Review of Economics and Statistics* 39: 312–320.

Solow, Robert M. 2000. *Growth Theory: An Exposition.* 2nd ed. New York: Oxford University Press.

Stiglitz, Joseph E., and Hirofumi Uzawa, eds. 1969. *Readings in the Modern Theory of Economic Growth.* Cambridge, MA: MIT Press.

Swan, Trevor W. 1956. Economic Growth and Capital Accumulation. *Economic Record* 32: 334–361 (reprinted in Stiglitz and Uzawa 1969).

Robert W. Dimand

NEOCOLONIALISM

The term *neocolonialism* came into use in the 1960s as former European colonies in Africa were gaining their independence. It describes a continuing relationship between Western countries and former colonies that is said to offer the Western world many of the advantages of colonial rule without many of the costs. Kwame Nkrumah (1909–1972), the first president of Ghana, was apparently the first person to use the term in print, in his 1965 study *Neo-colonialism: The Last Stage of Imperialism.* Nkrumah was particularly concerned about the economic relationship between former colonial masters and their African dependencies, and focused on the role of the mining industry. Nkrumah's analysis is also more frankly Marxist than other, later critics who use the term.

The term has come to cover a broad range of relationships—for example, those between the United States and Latin American countries and those between regional powers, such as France, in Africa and countries that were never their colonies. It also has come to be used by analysts from a wide range of theoretical backgrounds, though at its core the idea owes a great deal to Marx. The historian Immanuel Wallerstein, for example, gave the idea a broad theoretical basis in his book *The Modern World System*, first published in 1974. Wallerstein offered a general theoretical structure governing both the rise of colonialism and its decline and replacement with new, but still exploitative, forms of international relationships. Wallerstein's ideas were drawn from neo-Marxist theory and were also influenced by the French Annales school and its foremost proponent, Fernand Braudel. Wallerstein has in turn stimulated a series of collaborators and followers, including Andre Gunder Frank and Charles Tilly. Another strand of neocolonial theory comes from the Latin American Dependency school economists, also somewhat influenced by neo-Marxist ideas. The Egyptian political scientist Samir Amin has updated the concept in his work since the turn of the twenty-first century, focusing on the political economy of international relations between wealthy and poor nations.

Neocolonialism is a controversial term, implying that the objective of the wealthier partner is to keep the poorer country dependent and poor. Generally used by people on the political Left, the term has also enjoyed a vogue among far-right critics of internationalism in the United States. Use of the alternative term *neoimperialism* makes clear that the speaker believes that the wealthy nation intends to establish an empire through economic means, whereas *neocolonialism* leaves open a more classical Marxist dialectical interpretation of the process.

ECONOMIC RELATIONSHIPS BETWEEN NATIONS

Neocolonialism as a concept focuses on economic relationships between wealthier and poorer countries. Wealthier countries are said to use various mechanisms—political and military as well as strictly economic—to keep within their national economies as much as possible of the value added in any productive process with international components, while relegating the more laborious and less valuable parts of the productive process to poorer countries. Wallerstein suggests that the world (or that part of it in regular, economically significant contact) at any point in time is divided into three zones: a core zone, in which the most profitable production takes place and where control over the whole system resides; the semi-periphery, where valuable forms of production take place under the supervision of the core; and the periphery, where less valuable forms of production take place. The peripheral areas under the control of any given core increase; the exploitation and even force that marks the relationship between the core and the peripheral areas grow, as the core gets more efficient at production and at governing itself. Semi-peripheral areas share more in the fruits of their labor and are a reasonably favored class of countries. Indeed, when the system changes and a new set of core countries come to power, they generally come from the semi-periphery (as, for example, when the United States supplanted or joined the United Kingdom in the early twentieth century).

The relationship between countries can be seen as an analogy to the relationship between people in classical Marxist economic analysis. The core countries are like the capitalists: They do not generally produce much themselves (though they might have some productive functions), but they exercise control over production by controlling money. The semi-peripheral countries are like the professional or technical elite of an industrial society: They produce very valuable things, and are pampered as a result, though they have little control. The peripheral countries are like the working class: They are exploited as aggressively as possible. Some development theorists have noted that many areas in the periphery are actually for the most part outside the world system and equate these "fourth world" countries or failed states to Marx's *lumpenproletariat*. Other writers following up on Wallerstein's ideas have suggested that subdividing the world beyond the level of the nation-state might be more productive. Regions or cities may be better units of analysis. New York, London, Berlin, and Tokyo are the core cities of the modern world economy, whereas, say, Seattle, Canberra, Bangalore, Dubai, Singapore, and Beijing are semi-peripheries and rural West Virginia might be nearly as peripheral to the world economy as rural Inner Mongolia (though perhaps not quite so far away from the core as rural Congo).

CLASS DIVISIONS

Wallerstein points out that the societies of core and peripheral countries are marked by very sharp class divisions, with a few very wealthy people ruling over many poor. Meanwhile, the semi-peripheries are often places of relative class harmony. One sign that a country (or region) has moved out of the semi-periphery and into the core is the rise in class tensions there. Wallerstein detects this pattern at work in Renaissance Europe; similar changes have taken place in American society since World War I. In the peripheral countries, the class divisions often result in the creation of a ruling class tied to the interests of foreign capitalists. The dependency school economists in Latin America made this point when describing the economic relationship between their countries and the United States in the mid-twentieth century. Their signal contribution to the understanding of neocolonialism was to show not only what happened but also how it happened.

Even though in most cases Latin American countries (outside the Caribbean) had ceased being formal colonies by the middle of the nineteenth century, they had not evolved toward greater economic independence but instead toward greater dependence on the core countries of the world-economy—Britain until World War I and then the United States. British and American business interests either owned most of the means of production or controlled the terms of trade such that local owners had to do business on their terms. Country after country found its mineral or agricultural products moving into a world market at a price just barely above that which producers needed to stay in business, with the ensuing profits and well-paying jobs in transformation industries remaining

in North America and Europe. Latin American observers felt the local ruling class was acting in the interests of North American and European capitalists rather than their own countrymen. They deduced from this that, as Marx had suggested, class solidarity trumps national identity. Just as the German and American worker have more in common with each other than either has with their own country's capitalists, the Venezuelan oil magnate or Argentine rancher has more in common with the New York banker or Texas oilman than he does with Venezuelan or Argentine workers. Thus it was the "enemy within the gates" who ensured that the relationship between poor and wealthy countries was exploitative.

MECHANISMS OF CONTROL

The mechanisms by which the core exerts control over its peripheries have changed over time. In classical colonial rule in the nineteenth century, the colonial masters ruled with the assistance of a large cadre of local officials, recruited through an elitist educational system and often made more loyal by careful exploitation of ethnic loyalties. France ruled its huge west African colony, comprising seven modern nations with tens of millions of inhabitants, with about fifty thousand French civilians of all descriptions and a few thousand French soldiers. They employed more than a million African officials who fulfilled functions from the most humble to some very prestigious positions. When formal colonial rule ended in Africa and Asia after World War II, these local elites became the ruling class of their new countries. As Nkrumah pointed out, in country after country the educational systems and ethnic political divisions continued to alienate the ruling classes from their own people and give them a sense of common identity with the international business and development bureaucratic class from the core countries. The sharp distinction between the lifestyle, attitudes, skills, and ambitions of the ruling classes of developing countries and those of their humbler countrymen stands in sharp contrast to the relatively homogenous societies of semi-peripheral countries such as Sweden, Singapore, or Dubai. (In the latter two cases, natives of peripheral countries are brought in as an oppressed and permanently alienated servant class so that social equality between citizens can be maintained.) On the other hand, an increasing distinction exists between the lifestyle, outlook on life, attitudes, ambitions, and values of the wealthiest Americans and those of ordinary people.

Military force was the final buttress of traditional colonialism. Neocolonialism cannot rely as much on force but has not abandoned it entirely. France still maintains significant garrisons in its former colonies in Africa, and those troops intervene regularly in such places as Rwanda, Ivory Coast, Chad, and Congo to defend French interests.

U.S. interventions have been legion since the end of the nineteenth century. When an intervention goes badly, neocolonial interests around the world suffer. For example, when the U.S. intervention in Somalia in 1993 ended in failure, Haitian opponents of the American-led peace process were emboldened to attack the American election monitor mission and drive them out of the country.

Political means have been used to strengthen the control of wealthy countries over poor ones. One of the best-known and most controversial in the first decade of the twenty-first century is the use of international financial institutions, particularly the International Monetary Fund (IMF) and the World Trade Organization (WTO), to force peripheral countries to grant favorable terms of trade on primary products. They do this by requiring privatization of state enterprises and free trade in primary products, which strengthens the control of core-country capital over the most productive sectors of the peripheral-country economy. Another effect of IMF-mandated economic restructuring has been to sharpen class divisions in the peripheral countries by forcing governments to reduce investment in rural development and education. Peripheral country elites have cooperated because continued contact with the world economy is essential for them to preserve their lifestyle; that contact would be imperiled if their country lost its IMF certification and could not be a member of the WTO. In countries where IMF coercion has been less successful, like Mexico, bilateral free-trade agreements with core countries, which bring substantial benefits for the peripheral country's bourgeois, have served as the key to chain those economies to their dominant partners.

SEE ALSO *Amin, Samir; Anticolonial Movements; Apartheid; Colonialism; Decolonization; Dependency; Dependency Theory; Empire; Exploitation; Frank, Andre Gunder; Imperialism; International Monetary Fund; Liberation Movements; Neoimperialism; Nkrumah, Kwame; Postcolonialism; Wallerstein, Immanuel; World Trade Organization; World-System*

BIBLIOGRAPHY

Amin, Samir. 2006. *Obsolescent Capitalism: Contemporary Politics and Global Disorder*. London: Zed Books.

Cardoso, Fernando Henrique, and Enzo Faletto. 1979. *Dependency and Development in Latin America*. Trans. Marjory Mattingly Urquidi. Berkeley: University of California Press.

Gunder Frank, Andre, and B. K. Gills, eds. 1993. *The World System: Five Hundred Years or Five Thousand?* London and New York: Routledge.

Nkrumah, Kwame. 1965. *Neo-colonialism: The Last Stage of Imperialism*. London: Nelson. http://www.marxists.org/subject/africa/nkrumah/neo-colonialism.

Tilly, Charles. 2003. *Contention and Democracy in Europe, 1650–2000*. Cambridge: Cambridge University Press.

Wallerstein, Immanuel. 2004. *World-Systems Analysis: An Introduction*. Durham, NC: Duke University Press.

Stewart R. King

NEOCONSERVATISM

Neoconservatism is a term that emerged in the 1970s to describe a set of positions on U.S. domestic and foreign policy developed by a somewhat amorphous but identifiable group of political journalists and social scientists who previously had identified with the political left, often with the Trotskyist left, but had subsequently moved to the right as a reaction to the political and cultural struggles of the 1960s. The conversion of many of these figures from left to right is one of the senses of *neo*. By the time of the presidency of George W. Bush (2001–2009), neoconservatism, by then into its second generation and detached from its leftist origins, had become identified primarily with foreign policy, particularly with respect to the administration's response to the terrorist attacks of September 11, 2001, and to the motivations behind the decision to go to war with Iraq.

Although the label is said to have originated with the American social democrat Michael Harrington, who used it as a term of opprobrium, the first prominent self-described neoconservative was Irving Kristol, who had been the cofounder, with the English poet Stephen Spender, of the liberal anti-Communist (and, it turned out, surreptitiously Central Intelligence Agency–funded) journal *Encounter*. Along with the sociologist Daniel Bell, Kristol in 1965 founded the journal the *Public Interest*, which established what would become the neoconservative tone on domestic politics. This consisted largely of empirical and theoretical criticisms of government programs, grouped under the heading of President Lyndon Johnson's Great Society, aimed at alleviating racial discrimination and poverty. In 1985 Kristol founded another journal, the *National Interest*, which signaled the increasing neoconservative interest in and influence upon foreign policy. Over time neoconservatives also became well entrenched in Washington, D.C., think tanks, most notably the American Enterprise Institute, where Kristol became a fellow in 1988.

The budding neoconservatives first distinguished themselves from traditional conservatives by their application of social science methods to the criticism of government policies that they deemed partly misguided in intent and wholly detrimental in consequence. Their principal themes were determined by reactions to the turmoil, and increasing militancy, of the civil rights movement in American society at large and campus unrest over civil rights, educational policies, and the Vietnam War in particular. Neoconservatives came to see the U.S. system as on the cusp of a crisis generated by the affluence produced by a successful capitalism. That affluence threatened to undermine itself by eroding its implicit, generally overlooked moral foundations, including the virtues of deferred gratification and self-discipline. Predominantly the products of immigrant families and of public education, the neoconservatives balked at the perceived decline in individual initiative born of strong family encouragement and what they saw as the loss of civic consciousness and civilized behavior in a self-indulgent, permissive culture. Government programs aiming at economic redistribution through such practices as minority quotas, preferential hiring, and welfare payments only aggravated the problems where they did not directly contribute to them.

Whereas traditional conservatives and libertarians emphasized the need to cut back on government programs in general and to exercise fiscal responsibility in balancing the federal budget, the neoconservatives tended to support expansive government action on two fronts: domestically, in an aggressive assault on what they deemed to be the pernicious moral decline in the United States; and externally, in a muscular foreign policy predicated upon the expansion of U.S. military power and ideological warfare. Moral values, as they understood them, thus stood at the center of both policy dimensions and tended to overshadow, where they did not replace, specific policy proposals. While they shared conservatives' demands for tax cuts, neoconservatives were much more tolerant of budget deficits than their predecessors. They also categorically rejected traditional American conservatism's disdain for foreign involvements, pushing instead for an aggressive foreign policy previously associated with anti-Communist liberals. These differences constitute the second sense of *neo*. Neoconservative thought, with its emphasis on social morality, is thus distinguished from Thatcherism as well as the broader trend in neoliberalism to extend market relations into all aspects of political and social life. It is also obviously opposed to libertarianism, with its "anything goes" attitude toward individual desires. But these differences also explain how neoconservatives, who were predominantly of Jewish origin, found common cause with Christian fundamentalists on some issues such as marriage and pornography, because the two groups shared the view that government should place morality at the center of its purposes and programs.

The first notable political evidence of neoconservative influence could be seen in the administration of Ronald Reagan (1981–1989), particularly in Reagan's rejection of the policy of détente with the Soviet Union

and emphasis on challenging the USSR through a military buildup and the promotion of anti-Communist insurgencies worldwide. Most famously, Reagan's characterization of the Soviet Union as an "evil empire" often has been ascribed to the neoconservative emphasis upon introducing moral language into foreign policy. It was the alleged success of Reagan's foreign policy in bringing the Soviet Union to its knees that inspired the second generation of neoconservatives, led by Irving Kristol's son, William Kristol, founder and editor of the *Weekly Standard*, to challenge the foreign policy positions taken by George H. W. Bush and Bill Clinton for embracing a form of moral relativism and realism rather than the forceful assertion of American values as a fundamental aspect of U.S. national interests. Underlying the neoconservative challenge was the idea that reviving a moral language in foreign policy would reverberate domestically. This challenge bore fruit in the younger Bush's policies and rhetoric after September 11.

By time of the 2006 midterm elections, the neoconservative project of asserting American values in the Middle East had been seen largely as a disaster because of the war in Iraq, though various neoconservative figures who had been in or around the administration blamed the failures on the execution of the war by others, including President Bush and his secretary of defense, Donald Rumsfeld, rather than on the merits of the neoconservative policy behind it. But the identification of neoconservatism with a failed moralizing foreign policy may ultimately prove to be neoconservatism's Achilles's heel.

SEE ALSO *Bush, George W.; Central Intelligence Agency, U.S.; Conservatism; Foreign Policy; Fundamentalism; Fundamentalism, Christian; Great Society, The; Iraq-U.S. War; Liberalism; Militarism; Neoliberalism; Reagan, Ronald; September 11, 2001; Terrorism; Thatcher, Margaret; Union of Soviet Socialist Republics; Welfare State*

BIBLIOGRAPHY

Fukuyama, Francis. 2006. *America at the Crossroads: Democracy, Power, and the Neoconservative Legacy.* New Haven, CT, and London: Yale University Press.

Kristol, Irving. 2003. The Neoconservative Persuasion. *Weekly Standard* 8 (August 25).

Kristol, William, and Robert Kagan. 1996. Toward a Neo-Reaganite Foreign Policy. *Foreign Affairs* 75 (4): 18–32.

Thompson, Michael J., ed. 2007. *Confronting the New Conservatism: The Rise of the Right in America.* New York: New York University Press.

Nicholas Xenos

NEOIMPERIALISM

Whereas imperialism is typically characterized by conquest and rule, and colonialism by migration and residence in the conquered territory, *neoimperialism* is domination and sometimes even hegemony over others primarily by way of formally free legal agreements, economic power, and cultural influence. One of many designations for the form taken by U.S. political power and economic domination in the twentieth century, especially during and after World War II, *neoimperialism* is a name with serious faults. Other, clearer, and more vivid designations include *informal empire, imperialism without empire, empire of liberty,* and *Pax Americana.* But *neoimperialism* is the most common term, and therefore will be used here. The United States is not history's only neoimperialist power, and neoimperialism is not exclusively a phenomenon of the twentieth and twenty-first centuries. However, the United States is history's most predominant and creative deployer of neoimperial power strategies, as opposed to directly colonial or imperial strategies. And the second half of the twentieth century is the period in which neoimperialism became the predominant mode of global political power.

Neoimperialism became a significant topic of discussion after the end of the cold war. Journalists and opinion-makers, poets and scholars, made efforts to measure and evaluate neoimperialism, and to advise the United States in its role as the world's "indispensable nation" (as U.S. Secretary of State Madeleine Albright once put it). In the wake of the attacks of September 11, 2001, discussion of the ways and means of U.S. power intensified and took new turns as the United States became far more explicitly aggressive militarily, and returned to doctrines of nation-building and democratization through military intervention. But U.S. neoimperialism is not merely about use of military force, and did not begin after the cold war.

In fact, to understand U.S. neoimperialism, it might even be necessary to reconsider the foundations of the United States itself, as a republic in a world increasingly dominated by European empires. The British public first embraced the idea of a British Empire, an empire to rival or even exceed Rome's famous empire, after victory in the Seven Years' War in 1763. When the rebellion that began in 1776 freed the British Atlantic colonies from royal rule, the former colonists used a Roman and Whig political vocabulary to form a republic that emphasized democracy, equality, citizenship, freedoms, and strict legal limitations on governmental power. The new United States built a military apparatus primed more for intervention than conquest. This was partly out of weakness and necessity, rather than principle, and the United States showed little hesitation in using force to take land from Native Americans. However, early in the new country's political history, the

United States also developed its interventive military style and professed ideology of anti-imperialism, in the essentially defensive War of 1812 and most notably, in the Monroe Doctrine of 1823. Thereafter the United States combined its insistence on the New World's political independence and distance from Europe with a developing pattern of political interventions in the Americas, a pattern that might be summarized as willingness to overthrow but not to conquer and colonize the societies that were, derisively, dubbed *banana republics* by the U.S. media.

In the late nineteenth century, Alfred Thayer Mahan's arguments for the importance of developing naval power and global reach led to the main exceptions to this developing pattern of U.S. military deployment. The United States provoked a war with Spain that enabled it to take possession of the Philippines, Guam, Cuba, and Puerto Rico, and more enduringly, to build naval bases in Manila Bay, in Guam, at Guantánamo Bay, and in Puerto Rico. While the United States did not pursue colonization on a Dutch, French, or British scale, abjuring opportunities to conquer China or even Mexico, it did avidly continue to collect naval bases that would sustain continuing global military power projection. These included the strategically crucial Pearl Harbor and eventually the rest of Hawaii, and also the only island suitable for a coaling station along the steamship route from Hawaii to Guam, an island the United States fortified and renamed "Midway."

By the end of World War II (1939–1945), the United States had achieved global military domination, and after the war it found itself in a position to direct most of the terms of peace. The new world order largely shaped by the United States was dubbed *Pax Americana.* Collective memory of the establishment of Pax Americana is dimmed by the nearly immediate onset of the cold war, a mushrooming set of diplomatic conflicts and wars by proxy, as the Soviet Union resisted and contested the new world order planned and instituted under U.S. leadership at the new United Nations. But the logic and reality of Pax Americana is the key to U.S. neoimperialism, which has largely achieved its main criterion, "making the world safe" and keeping global peace, despite the stresses of the long cold war. Whereas between 1850 and 1900 a world population below two billion suffered over twenty million war deaths, and between 1900 and 1950 a world population under three billion suffered over sixty million war deaths, from 1950 to 2000, there were only around ten million war deaths for a world population that grew to well over five billion. Pax Americana is thus very real, and should be understood as a reaction to a history of European imperial rivalry and recurrent warfare—using ever more deadly military technologies—beginning in the eighteenth century and culminating in World War II. The key to neoimperialism, and its difference from older imperialisms, is the limitation of political will. In the

United Nations era, no conquest of states by other states, or nations by other nations, is tolerable. The new United Nations and a growing network of global economic regulatory organizations oversaw the largely peaceful breakup of the European empires, including finally the Soviet Union, into what became the only legitimate political form, the nation-state. UN membership grew from 50 members in 1945 to over 150 in the 1970s and over 175 by the early 1990s.

That this Pax Americana is a U.S. neoimperialism has become clearer again after 9/11 and more especially, in the wake of the troubled, and troubling, U.S. overthrow of Saddam Hussein and occupation of Iraq. Is the United States really, in the last analysis, another imperial power? While some "realists" suggest that the problems and behaviors of all Great Powers are essentially similar, it is important to notice consequential differences. As Frantz Fanon once observed, it was always important to European colonizers to stay different from the colonized, to maintain an imagined superiority of race and civilization, and to imagine that their true society and history was that of their European "homeland," even when they lived their whole lives in Africa or Asia. The European ideology of the "civilizing mission" created an illusion of the cultural superiority of "civilized" Europeans over allegedly backward natives. In the era of the United Nations, a far different ideology developed and was instituted. In this ideology, all nations are formally equal, free, territorial, and sovereign, and every nation-state becomes a "melting pot," rather than the essentialist "homeland" of any particular racial or ethnic group. Economists and economic modeling, not historians and cultural education, are thought to be vital to the explanation and eradication of poverty and inequality.

While in the UN era the political will and reach of nations and states have been limited for good reasons, less has been done to trim the sails of the "other Leviathans," the large corporations. On occasion, wealthy and powerful nation-states do legally restrain, and rarely even break up, corporations (from Standard Oil to Microsoft) whose power comes to threaten state sovereignty. But no similar leverage is afforded the smaller and economically weaker states, which are greatly pressured to take whatever global markets offer. Similarly, the poor states cannot stop the United States, Europe, and Japan from writing unequal and self-serving tariff rules into global trade agreements. Thus it is no surprise that in the era of Pax Americana, the rich nation-states have tended to get richer, and wealth gaps generally increase almost regardless of the internal economic policies of poor countries.

Other social and political developments in the era of Pax Americana have been more surprising, and unforeseen by the planners of this new world order. Elites in poor countries increasingly migrate to wealthier centers, creating unprecedented elite diasporas. These elite diasporas from poorer countries to centers of wealth are often actively encouraged by the governments of poor countries, and increase the "multicultural" character of centers of wealth. Many ex-colonial nation-states abandon democracy, temporarily or perduringly, with army leadership claiming to represent the nation better than ideologically driven and divisive political parties can, a pattern that perplexes planners who expect nations always to behave democratically. And the states in some nation-states collapse altogether, creating complex and violent situations that are rarely resolved through direct military intervention by "peace-keepers."

U.S. neoimperialism certainly resembles the European imperialism of prior generations in its political manipulation, economic domination, and willingness to resort to military force. But there are also major differences. Through decolonization, many former colonial subjects gained formal rights and freedoms as citizens of new states. Yet nation-states created new, specifically postcolonial predicaments. Ironically, nation-states created by decolonization limit the political reach of the world's poor to the boundaries of their own nation-states. At the same time, nongovernmental organizations (NGOs) dedicated to uplift are more responsible to their donors than to their clients. It is unlikely that the entrenched problems of neoimperialism will be solved by new and further intervention by wealthy and powerful states into the political and economic affairs of poorer states. Inequalities will continue to grow until, one way or another, the globe's poorest citizenries find means to intervene into, influence, and reorient economic and social policies in the centers of wealth.

SEE ALSO *Cold War; Colonialism; Decolonization; Empire; Imperialism; Nation-State; Neocolonialism; Neoconservatism; Neoliberalism*

BIBLIOGRAPHY

Anderson, Benedict. 1991. *Imagined Communities: Reflections on the Origin and Spread of Nationalism.* Rev. ed. London and New York: Verso.

Ashcroft, Bill, Gareth Griffiths, and Helen Tiffin, eds. 1995. *The Post-Colonial Studies Reader.* London: Routledge.

Benjamin, Walter. [1940] 2003. On the Concept of History. In *Selected Writings, Volume 4: 1938–1940*, eds. Howard Eiland and Michael W. Jennings, trans. Edmund Jephcott et al., 389–400. Cambridge, MA: Harvard University Press.

Calhoun, Craig, Frederick Cooper, and Kevin W. Moore, eds. 2006. *Lessons of Empire: Imperial Histories and American Power.* New York: New Press.

Duara, Prasenjit, ed. 2004. *Decolonization: Perspectives from Now and Then.* New York: Routledge.

Duffield, Mark. 2001. *Global Governance and the New Wars: The Merging of Development and Security*. London and New York: Zed Books.

Fanon, Frantz. 1963. *The Wretched of the Earth*. New York: Grove Press.

Ferguson, Niall. 2005. *Colossus: The Rise and Fall of the American Empire*. New York: Penguin.

Ikenberry, G. John. 2001. *After Victory: Institutions, Strategic Restraint, and the Rebuilding of Order after Major Wars*. Princeton, NJ: Princeton University Press.

Kelly, John D. 2003. U.S. Power, after 9/11 and before It: If Not an Empire, Then What? *Public Culture* 15 (2): 347–369.

Kelly, John D., and Martha Kaplan. 2001. *Represented Communities: Fiji and World Decolonization*. Chicago: University of Chicago Press.

Koonings, Kees, and Dirk Kruijt, eds. 2002. *Political Armies: The Military and Nation Building in the Age of Democracy*. London: Zed Books.

Kuznetsov, Yevgeny, ed. 2006. *Diaspora Networks and the International Migration of Skills: How Countries Can Draw on Their Talent Abroad*. New York: World Bank Publications.

Nkrumah, Kwame. 1966. *Neo-Colonialism: The Last Stage of Imperialism*. New York: International Publishers.

Nye, Joseph S. Jr. 2003. *The Paradox of American Power: Why the World's Only Superpower Can't Go It Alone*. New York: Oxford University Press.

John Kelly

NEOINSTITUTIONALISM

Neoinstitutionalism (at times also termed *state-centered theory* or *historical institutionalism*) is a nebulous set of social scientific theories that emphasize the role of institutions as important variables for explaining social phenomena. Of particular importance within economics, sociology, and political science, neoinstitutionalism rose to prominence in the 1970s and 1980s as a response to the perceived society-centric character of the social sciences. It continues as a prominent component within social science today, many of its basic points having been accepted into various popular theoretical approaches—but it has also come under attack from competing traditions within each social science discipline.

Obviously, the study of institutions is nothing new, but this is not the defining characteristic of institutionalism. The term *old institutionalism* usually refers to the formalist scholarship of the late nineteenth and early twentieth centuries that produced descriptive accounts of institutions and laws. By 1950, this institutionalism had largely been replaced by behaviorist and functionalist social science, as developed by such theorists as Talcott Parsons and David Easton. From the point of view of neoinstitutionalism, behaviorist social science and its main competitor, Marxism, were society-centric in that they failed to allow for the causal roles that institutions played in society. It was argued that institutions and the state had been reduced to a "black box": Everything they did was understood as little more than an outcome of the preferences and actions of social actors. Thus, neoinstitutionalism took shape in the attempt to overturn the perceived social reductionism of the main approaches of the day. Two interrelated characteristics differentiate this "new" institutionalism from the "old" one. First, the new institutionalism is analytic in character, not descriptive; it wants to explain things, not just describe them. Second, it does not seek to understand institutions as such but, rather, to understand the role(s) they play in the production of social phenomena (such as public policies, economic development, democracy, and so on).

Neoinstitutionalism can be divided into two general tendencies: the view of institutions as autonomous actors, and the view of institutions as constraining or enabling structures. Within the first tendency, the less common of the two, key examples include works by Theda Skocpol, Charles Tilly, Fred Block, and Margaret Levi. In this conception of institutions as actors, often originating in selective readings of Max Weber, it is assumed that individuals who occupy positions within the state bureaucracy come to share a "bureaucratic rationality"—that is, they come to think and act in accordance with and in support of the institutional interests of the bureaucracy. In this way, this branch of neoinstitutionalism understands institutions, and the state as a whole, as being "autonomous" from society. This tendency treats state institutions as self-interested agents who, at times in opposition to and at times in alliance with various social actors, seek to maximize revenues, power, legitimacy, and so on. Understanding the complex interactions between these institutional actors and other (social) actors thus becomes the key, for those within this tradition, to understanding such phenomena as revolutions, the rise of the welfare state, taxation policy, and war-making.

The second, and more common, tendency within neoinstitutionalism understands institutions to be structures that limit, condition, and/or direct social agency. Key figures include Douglas North, James March and Johan Olson, and Walter Powell and Paul DiMaggio. There are a great many variations on this approach, but most focus on the task of trying to understand the problem of structure and agency within particular fields of inquiry. In large part, neoinstitutionalism has meant that approaches such as neoclassical economics, rational choice theory, systems theory, or pluralism have been augmented by considerations of the impact of institutions upon actors. Some versions of this tendency have a very broad definition of *institutions*, as being rules of conduct and routines within cultural as well as political and economic fields. In this very broad context, the term *institutions* basically refers to social structures, and the key question typically concerns how these sets of rules or practices structure the thinking and preferences of actors, producing what is often referred to as "bound rationality." Neoinstitutionalism within economics usually holds this broad understanding of institutions and the key question becomes how this ensemble of formal and informal arrangements and rules structures social behavior by virtue of the "transaction costs" they involve. Thus, economists such as Ronald Coase, Oliver Williamson, and Douglas North have attempted to augment neoclassical economics by showing how, given the reality of transaction costs, institutions structure and direct social behavior by making it more or less costly to engage in certain types of social actions. In more narrow versions, characteristic of neoinstutionalism within sociology and political science, the term *institutions* may refer to the mode of organization of a political regime (corporatist, coalitional, single-party, etc.), or serve simply to designate self-identified bureaucratic organizations (ministries, state agencies, corporations, labor unions, and so on). Typical of this vein of neoinstitutionalism are examinations of the ways in which the internal organization of these institutions affects the capacity of various actors and interests to realize their goals through or within them. Also typical is a focus on understanding how inter-institutional relations and structures may help shape such phenomena as political conflicts, public policies, and markets.

Neoinstitutionalism has been critiqued by some on the grounds that there is little, if anything, "new" about it: Institutions, critics claim, were always taken seriously within social science. It could be argued, however, that being "new" is not the goal of neoinstitutionalism. More pointedly, neoinstitutionalism has often not lived up to its name: By studying social structures or types of political regimes, for example, it has shed little light on the specificity and dynamics of actual institutions. The tendencies of neoinstitutionalism discussed here have also failed to supersede the structure/agent dualism of the theories it critiqued. Regardless of the relative attention given to agents and structures, neoinstitutionalism has remained bound within the dualistic thinking that typifies behaviorism, rational choice theory, and systems theory. By comparison, the radical materialism of so-called "structuralists," such as Louis Althusser and Pierre Bourdieu (with whom neoinstitutionalism is sometimes conflated), understands "agency" and "structure" as being synchronic with each other. Whereas structuralists have developed new concepts for understanding how agents are produced in modern societies (the concepts of *habitus* and *interpellation*, for example), neoinstitutionalism of all stripes has

stayed within the older model in which "agents" are assumed to be external to "structures."

SEE ALSO *Institutionalism; State, The; Structuralism*

BIBLIOGRAPHY

Evans, Peter B., Dietrich Rueschemeyer, and Theda Skocpol, eds. 1985. *Bringing the State Back In.* Cambridge, U.K.: Cambridge University Press.

March, James G., and Johan P. Olsen. 1989. *Rediscovering Institutions: The Organizational Basis of Politics.* New York: Free Press.

Powell, Walter W., and Paul J. DiMaggio, eds. 1991. *The New Institutionalism in Organizational Analysis.* Chicago: University of Chicago Press.

Weaver, R. Kent, and Bert A. Rockman, eds. 1993. *Do Institutions Matter?: Government Capabilities in the United States and Abroad* Washington, DC: Brookings Institution Press.

Peter Bratsis

NEOLIBERALISM

The term *neoliberalism* is used to describe a political and economic doctrine as well as a set of economic policies that have become hegemonic in the last quarter of the twentieth century. Originally coined by its proponents, the term today is usually employed by neoliberalism's critics to refer to a set of policy prescriptions that includes an emphasis on free markets, deregulation, conservative monetary policies, the lowering of tariffs, and the privatization of state assets and services.

HISTORY AND INTELLECTUAL TRADITION

The term *neoliberalism* was first used in the 1930s and 1940s in a context in which the crisis of laissez-faire economics as well as the rise of socialism and fascism had marginalized earlier liberal projects. At a 1938 Paris meeting of concerned liberal intellectuals including figures such as Friedrich August von Hayek, Ludwig von Mises, and Wilhelm Röpke, it was argued that the rise of statism and planned economies needed to be counterposed by a new liberal project that would reassert the values of individual and economic freedom perceived to be under siege. Following on from this meeting and inspired by Hayek's influential anticollectivist treatise *The Road to Serfdom* (1944), in 1947 an international liberal think tank, the Mont Pelerin Society, was founded to further the production and dissemination of neoliberal thought. However, the neoliberal program remained marginal and overshadowed by the dominance of Keynesian economics for decades, and it was not until the 1970s, in a context of global economic crisis, that neoliberal thought gained a wider currency.

Neoliberalism is defined by a diversity of positions, including most prominently the Austrian school of economics associated with the economists Hayek and von Mises, the Chicago school strongly influenced by Milton Friedman's 1962 doctrine of monetarism, and the German Ordoliberals, who were central in the construction of Germany's postwar social market economy. Despite the variety of traditions, most neoliberals share key basic assumptions such as a methodological individualism, a skepticism of centralized state planning, and a belief in the greater efficiency of the market. Neoliberal thought draws on the classical liberal tradition associated with the Scottish Enlightenment and in particular on Adam Smith's 1776 critique of mercantilism (*An Inquiry into the Nature and Causes of the Wealth of Nations*) to provide a critique of twentieth-century Keynesian interventionist economic paradigms. Key to neoliberal theories is a skepticism towards the state's ability to know, and hence to intervene in and direct, economic life. One of the most influential neoliberal thinkers, Friedrich August von Hayek, grounds his critique of state intervention in the limits and fallibility of human reason, and hence of knowledge of society as a whole. For Hayek, this necessitates a noninterventionist state and a reliance instead on a "spontaneous order" based on disaggregated and practical forms of knowledge (Hayek 1952, 1973). The market in Hayek's framework becomes both the test and the corrective for the evolutionary development of order in society. However, unlike the classical liberal tradition, which regarded the market as a natural entity guided by an "invisible hand," neoliberal thinkers suggest that the role of the state should be the establishment of conditions favorable to the development of a free-market economy and the avoidance of monopolies.

NEOLIBERALISM AS A POLITICAL PROJECT

Neoliberal thought found its practical application in the early 1970s when an economic crisis in the form of "stagflation" increasingly cast doubt on the basic premises of the Keynesian paradigm, leading to a rethinking of received ideas regarding the relationship between the state and the economy. Starting with the neoliberal experiments in Chile in the mid-1970s by the "Chicago Boys," a group of economists educated at the University of Chicago, and the elections of U.K. Prime Minister Margaret Thatcher and U.S. President Ronald Reagan in the late 1970s and early 1980s, neoliberal thought gained hegemony and often direct influence in policy circles.

Policies associated with the welfare state and Fordist emphasis on domestic mass production and consumption were increasingly replaced by monetarist approaches, the restructuring of state services, and severe measures against trade unions. In the postcolonial world, state-led development paradigms were increasingly succeeded by "structural adjustment" policies often introduced through loan conditionalities imposed by the World Bank and the International Monetary Fund (IMF). Policies such as fiscal austerity, trade liberalization, the privatization of state functions, and deregulation became staple ingredients of policy advice from international donor agencies and the increasingly influential supranational trade and financial institutions such as the World Trade Organization (WTO), the World Bank, and the IMF. With the end of the cold war, this convergence of neoliberal policy agendas of Washington-based financial institutions became known as the "Washington Consensus." Since the late 1990s, the hegemony of the Washington Consensus has been challenged by severe financial crises, the rise of social movements, and the elections of a number of governments with explicitly antineoliberal stances in Latin America.

CRITICS OF NEOLIBERALISM

Scholarly as well as nonscholarly critics argue that neoliberal policies produce increasing inequality and lead to a reduction in democratic accountability. In one of the earliest and most influential critiques, Karl Polanyi argued that economic liberalism is a utopian project that seeks to disembed and superimpose the economy in relation to society, which is henceforth seen as merely an "adjunct to the market" (Polanyi 1944). Most contemporary critiques of neoliberalism similarly take as their target the social consequences of neoliberal policies. Pierre Bourdieu argued that neoliberalism destroys the social solidarities associated with the welfare state and thus leads to permanent state of existential insecurity (Bourdieu 1998). One of the most influential critiques from a Marxist perspective has been provided by David Harvey, for whom neoliberalism is a project of the reorganization of capitalist accumulation in a context of economic crisis (Harvey 2005). Neoliberal policies of privatization, Harvey suggests, turn ever increasing spheres of life into new loci of capital accumulation that are ultimately in the service of the restoration of the power of economic elites. Foucauldian analyses of neoliberalism have pointed to the ways in which neoliberal projects are not simply defined by the removal of state intervention, but rather inaugurate new indirect forms of power that seek to extend the enterprise form to all spheres of life and encourage the production of self-governing individuals (Foucault 2004; Barry et al. 1996).

Neoliberalism also has been subject to critique and protest outside the realm of the academy. Movements against "neoliberal globalization," organized in groups such as the World Social Forum, gained in strength since the 1990s. These critics argue that the globalization of neoliberalism through organs such as the WTO is undemocratic and increases global inequality through the institution and promotion of unfair trading regimes.

SEE ALSO *Conservatism; Empire; Globalization, Social and Economic Aspects of; Liberalism; Liberalization, Trade; Neoconservatism; Privatization; Washington Consensus*

BIBLIOGRAPHY

Barry, Andrew, Thomas Osborne, and Nicholas Rose. 1996. *Foucault and Political Reason: Liberalism, Neo-Liberalism, and Rationalities of Government.* Chicago: University of Chicago Press.

Bourdieu, Pierre. 1998. *Acts of Resistance: Against the Tyranny of the Market.* New York: New Press.

Foucault, Michel. 2004. *Naissance de la biopolitique* [The Birth of Biopolitics]. Paris: Éditions Gallimard.

Friedman, Milton. 1962. *Capitalism and Freedom.* Chicago: University of Chicago Press.

Harvey, David. 2005. *A Brief History of Neoliberalism.* New York: Oxford University Press.

Hayek, Friedrich August von. [1944] 1962. *The Road To Serfdom.* London: Routledge.

Hayek, Friedrich August von. 1952. *The Sensory Order: An Enquiry into the Foundations of Theoretical Psychology.* Chicago: University of Chicago Press.

Hayek, Friedrich August von. 1973. *Law, Legislation, and Liberty,* vol. 1.: *Rules and Order.* Chicago: University of Chicago Press.

Polanyi, Karl. 1944. *The Great Transformation: The Political and Economic Origins of Our Time.* New York: Rinehart.

Smith, Adam. [1776] 2000. *An Inquiry into the Nature and Causes of the Wealth of Nations.* New York: Modern Library.

Antina von Schnitzler

NEONATAL BEHAVIORAL ASSESSMENT SCALE

SEE *Brazelton, T. Berry.*

NEO-WALRASIAN SYNTHESIS

SEE *Patinkin, Don.*

NERVOUSNESS

SEE *Anxiety.*

NESTED HYPOTHESES

SEE *Hypothesis, Nested.*

NET WORTH

SEE *Wealth.*

NETWORK ANALYSIS

Network analysis is a cluster of methodological techniques for the mathematical description and investigation of networks. It has applications across both the natural and the social sciences. Electronic networks, river networks, etymological networks, epidemiological networks, and networks of economic transactions have all been subjects for network analysis. In the social sciences, the concern is with the investigation of social networks. A *social network* is any articulated pattern of connections in the social relations of individuals, groups, and other collectivities. Social networks include friendship and kinship networks, interorganizational networks, communication networks, scientific citation networks, and policymaker networks. Social network analysis, then, deals with relational data in all areas of social life. It handles the contacts, ties, and connections, group attachments, and meetings that relate one person or group to another and that cannot be reduced to the properties of the individual agents themselves. Such relational data are central to the building of models of the structures through which action is organized. Social network analysis is not limited to small-scale and interpersonal structures, and there have been many applications to such phenomena as global trading relations in world systems.

Social network analysis developed independently in the social anthropology of small societies and the social psychology of small groups. Anthropologists such as Alfred Radcliffe-Brown (1881–1955) pioneered a view of social structure as a "web" of social relations and an idea of actions "interweaving" and "interlocking" through such a network of connections. Anthropologists in this tradition began to investigate the "density" of these social networks and the "centrality" of individuals within them. Small group researchers in the Gestalt tradition developed ways of investigating the pattern of relations within the "life space" of social groups, the most influential example of this being Jacob Moreno's (1892–1974) sociometric studies of schoolroom friendship choices. The study of "group dynamics" developed rapidly from the 1950s with more formal applications of the network idea.

Contemporary network analysis grew markedly from the early 1970s, when a group of students and researchers working with Harrison White began to explore the use of more formal mathematical models for the analysis of small group and anthropological data and began to extend these investigations to wider sociological phenomena. A landmark study from this burgeoning work was Mark Granovetter's *Getting a Job* (1974). Granovetter showed that people's chances of getting information about job opportunities depended not on the formal methods of job search that they used but on their location in informal social networks. Counterintuitively, he also showed that having a small number of "weak" ties was far more important than having many "strong" ties: information came from "acquaintances" rather than close "friends" and relatives. This group of researchers used algebraic models from set theory and ideas from the mathematical theory of graphs, along with methods of multidimensional scaling. Together, this cluster of methods established a framework of network analysis that spread rapidly across sociology and into the other social sciences.

The basic idea in social network analysis is that a social network can be modeled as a set of "points" connected by "lines," the points representing the individuals and groups, and the lines representing their social relations. The simplest applications involve drawing a graph of points and lines to represent a social network and then visually examining the pattern of lines for its structural properties. When dealing with more than a small number of points, however, more abstract methods are necessary, and the mathematical methods allow the points and lines to be recorded in a matrix ready for mathematical processing. This has allowed the investigation of such structural properties as the density of relations, the centrality of agents, the formation of cliques and components, and the assessment of social distance. A measure of density, for example, assesses the proportion of all possible relations that actually exist in a network and is an important indicator of solidarity and cohesion. *Cliques* are subnetworks into which networks may be divided and that may comprise groups capable of independent action. Centrality concerns the strategic positions that actors may hold in the overall pattern of connections and the consequent flow of influence, support, or power.

Important applications of network analysis have been undertaken in many areas of the social sciences. Claude Fischer (1982) and Barry Wellman (1979) investigated community networks in cities with high levels of geographical mobility, and they explored the increasing reliance that people have placed on electronic methods and virtual channels of communication for maintaining interpersonal cohesion. The work of Robert Putnam was influential in advocating the idea that people's networks of social relations could be regarded as forms of social capital. This view has been elaborated in the competing approaches of Nan Lin (2001) and Ron Burt (2005). Lin stresses individual investments in social relations and the rational actions that are involved in the accumulation of social capital. Burt has looked at processes of brokerage and social closure—rooted in measures of centrality and prominence—for the creation of social capital.

Jim Bearden and various coworkers have explored structures of interlocking directorships in business, examining the nature and significance of bank centrality within financial networks (Mintz and Schwartz 1985). David Knoke has pioneered methods for studying networks of political connection and influence, leading to numerous studies of policy networks and the role of power in the policy process (Knoke et al. 1996). Peter Bearman (1993) is one of a number of researchers who has demonstrated the uses of network analysis for historical data on stratification and power relations. Many important studies have been undertaken on organizational networks in business, and these have been extended into work on knowledge management by Rob Cross (Cross and Parker 2004) and David Snowden (Kurtz and Snowden 2005). Important methodological work includes that of Linton Freeman on approaches to network visualization, using methods of pictorial display for the analysis of large social networks. These have been used in his own study of the development of social network analysis (Freeman 2004).

Applications of social network analysis have tended to be both descriptive and static, leading many to ask whether network analysts are doing anything more than producing pretty pictures and arbitrary numbers. This has been reinforced by the incursions of many physicists into the area of network analysis. These physicists have argued—often in ignorance of what work has actually been undertaken by social network analysts—that their methods have far more to offer in the analysis of social relations (Watts 2003). What is clear, however, is that these discussions have begun to shift social network analysis toward a greater concern for explanation, rather than simply description, and toward the investigation of dynamic processes in social networks.

The need to combine network analysis with agent-level models has been emphasized by Mustafa Emirbayer and his colleagues (Emirbayer 1997; Emirbayer and Goodwin 1994), who stress the interdependence of cultural, structural, and agency analyses. Network analysis must be combined with an awareness of the culturally formed subjective motivations and commitments of actors, whose intentional actions produce, reproduce, and transform network structures. This model of the structuration of social networks stresses the iterative nature of rule-governed actions. This is echoed in the growth of agent-based computational methods of network analysis that propose ways of linking microlevel decision making with macrolevel structural change (Monge and Contractor 2003).

SEE ALSO *Networks*

BIBLIOGRAPHY

Bearman, Peter. 1993. *Relations into Rhetorics: Local Elite Social Structure in Norfolk, England, 1540–1640.* New Brunswick, NJ: Rutgers University Press.

Burt, Ronald S. 2005. *Brokerage and Closure: An Introduction to Social Capital.* New York: Oxford University Press.

Carrington, Peter J., John Scott, and Stanley Wasserman, eds. 2005. *Models and Methods in Social Network Analysis.* New York: Cambridge University Press.

Cross, Rob, and Andrew Parker. 2004. *The Hidden Power of Social Networks: Understanding How Work Really Gets Done in Organizations.* Cambridge, MA: Harvard Business School Press.

Emirbayer, Mustafa. 1997. Manifesto for a Relational Sociology. *American Journal of Sociology* 103 (2): 281–317.

Emirbayer, Mustafa, and Jeff Goodwin. 1994. Network Analysis, Culture, and the Problem of Agency. *American Journal of Sociology* 99 (6): 1411–1454.

Fischer, Claude S. 1982. *To Dwell Among Friends: Personal Networks in Town and City.* Chicago: Chicago University Press.

Freeman, Linton S. 2004. *The Development of Social Network Analysis: A Study in the Sociology of Science.* Vancouver, BC: Empirical Press.

Granovetter, Mark. 1974. *Getting a Job: A Study of Contacts and Careers.* Cambridge, MA: Harvard University Press. 2nd ed. 1995. Chicago: University of Chicago Press.

Knoke, David, Franz U. Pappi, Jeffrey Broadbent, and Youtaka Tsujinaka. 1996. *Comparing Policy Networks: Labor Politics in the U.S., Germany, and Japan.* New York: Cambridge University Press.

Kurtz, Cynthia F., and David J. Snowden. 2005. The New Dynamics of Strategy: Sense-making in a Complex and Complicated World. *IBM Systems Journal* 42 (3): 462–483.

Lin, Nan. 2001. *Social Capital: A Theory of Social Structure and Action.* Cambridge, U.K.: Cambridge University Press.

Mintz, Beth, and Michael Schwartz. 1985. *The Power Structure of American Business.* Chicago: University of Chicago Press.

Monge, Peter R., and Noshir Contractor. 2003. *Theories of Communication Networks.* New York: Oxford University Press.

Scott, John. 2000. *Social Network Analysis: A Handbook.* 2nd ed. London: Sage.

Scott, John. 2002. *Social Networks: Critical Concepts in Sociology.* 4 vols. London: Routledge.

Wasserman, Stanley, and Katherine Faust. 1994. *Social Network Analysis: Methods and Applications.* New York: Cambridge University Press.

Watts, Duncan J. 2003. *Six Degrees: The Science of a Connected Age.* New York: Norton.

Wellman, Barry. 1979. The Community Question: The Intimate Networks of East Yorkers. *American Journal of Sociology* 84: 1201–1231.

Wellman, Barry, and Stephen D. Berkowitz, eds. 1988. *Social Structures: A Network Approach.* Cambridge, U.K.: Cambridge University Press.

John Scott

NETWORKS

Social networks are social relationships between two or more people (known as nodes) who have developed some kind of tie with each other (Wasserman and Faust 1994). "The social network perspective focuses on relationships among social entities; examples include communications among members of a group, economic transactions between corporations, and trade or treaties among nations" (Wasserman and Faust 1994, p. i). People use social networks to acquire new information, exchange information, find jobs, learn about new opportunities, and exchange new ideas, among other purposes. Individuals can acquire social ties in a number of social settings such as jobs, social organizations, religious organizations, political organizations, sports groups, a group of friends, and so on.

Wasserman and Faust (1994, p. 4) argue that the social network perspective should take into account the following:

- Actors and their actions are viewed as interdependent rather than independent, autonomous units.

- Relational ties (linkages) between actors are channels for transfer or "flow" of resources (either material or nonmaterial).

- Network models focusing on individuals view the network structural environment as providing opportunities for or constraints on individual action.

- Network models conceptualize structure (social, economic, political, and so forth) as lasting patterns of relations among actors.

In general, social networks are seen as providing individuals or larger groups or social entities with positive outcomes as a result of the information and social support the individuals who belong to a specific social network receive. Those who belong to a social network enjoy the advantages of social capital. The concept of social capital (Loury 1977; Bourdieu 1986; Coleman 1988) has been used to account for the advantages that network members accrue as a result of their inclusion.

According to the organizational literature, the position of the actors in a network or the network structure in which those ties are embedded would in most cases dictate the extent to which belonging to a social network can provide individuals with new information and opportunities that can help them perform better in society or facilitate their upward socioeconomic mobility. For example, central actors can influence how information gets distributed to other members in the network, referred as network *centrality* (Wasserman and Faust 1994). Also, a key actor could control the information that flows between two independent groups, a situation known in the organizational literature as *structural holes* (Burt 2001). Also, network homogeneity or *structural equivalence* (if ties are similar), or network heterogeneity (if ties are different), can influence the kinds of advantages or disadvantages network members might experience as a result of their membership in the network (Wasserman and Faust 1994).

Besides the structure and/or the position in the network, tie strength could also dictate the network's effectiveness. Mark Granovetter, first in his work *The Strength of Weak Ties* and later on in his book *Getting a Job*, revolutionized the organizational literature by introducing the concept of the "strength of weak ties" (Granovetter 1973, 1995). He argues that belonging to an open network and having access to weak ties (or acquaintances) can provide individuals with new valuable information that can help them get better jobs. Even though one might not have a strong relationship with those individuals, they are able to share new knowledge and important information that otherwise would not be available in a closed network with mostly strong ties. Those who belong to closed networks with mostly strong ties are considered to be at a disadvantage given the limited amount of information shared by the members of such networks. Studies on racial segregation (Massey and Denton 1993) have suggested that members of closed networks or cliques have less chance to learn about new important information and that the information that flows in those networks tends to be redundant and inefficient.

According to Granovetter (1982), strong ties and closed networks could be advantageous only for those who face risk and high levels of uncertainty. However, studies of entrepreneurial networks among Asian immigrants in the United States have shown that for certain immigrant groups, having access to strong ties in a closed network of highly educated or high status individuals who share high levels of socioeconomic status tend to receive the social support necessary to be successful as new entrepreneurs (Light, Sabagh, Bozorgmehr, and Der-Martirosian 1994).

Also, the distinction between kin and nonkin ties is fundamental to the understanding of how social networks operate (Adams 1967; Fischer 1982). While individuals can pick their neighbors, friends, or coworkers, they cannot pick the members of their kin (Wierzbicki 2004). In addition, kin ties are everlasting, while any other kind of ties can be dropped at any time (Wierzbicki 2004). Kin ties can be extremely important because they can provide assistance in times of crises, while any other kind of tie might not.

Neighbors can also be important ties in social networks depending on the relationship between neighbors. According to Fischer (1982), neighbors tend to be similar in race and socioeconomic status, and the individual has the freedom to develop or avoid strong ties with neighbors. Proximity is the most important factor in ties between neighbors. Such proximity can become important because it allows for social interactions that could be more difficult to achieve with other kinds of ties.

Today, technological advances such as the development of personal computers, Internet access, e-mail, and cell phones has provided advantages and disadvantages to the development of social ties. While individuals can communicate more often through e-mail and share more information, physical contact has become less frequent. People who are far from each other, even on the other side of the planet, can be in touch every day through the Internet, while those who work together next to each other can also communicate through the computer, limiting their physical and social contact.

Organizational and management literature also uses social networks as the basis for the distribution of information, which could lead to the spread of ideas and innovations and the development of new enterprises (Coleman, Katz, and Menzel 1957; Burt 1987).

Several topics have been studied using the social network perspective approach, including occupational mobility (Breiger 1981, 1990), networks of friends in urban cities (Fischer 1982), the world political and economic system (Snyder and Kick 1979), markets (Berkowitz 1988; White 1981), six degrees of separation (Watts 2003), social networks and international migration (Wierzbicki 2004), and the networks of elite Americans and politicians (Domhoff 1998), among many other. Most people around the world are now aware of the power of social networks and how knowing someone or meeting someone could change one's future. Advances in technology are helping this task, greatly facilitating communication among actors from any part of the world.

SEE ALSO *Bureaucracy; Crony Capitalism; Network Analysis; Networks, Communication; Organization Theory; Organizations; Social Capital*

BIBLIOGRAPHY

Adams, Bert N. 1967. Interaction Theory and the Social Network. *Sociometry* 30: 64–78.

Berkowitz, S. D. 1988. Markets and Market-Areas: Some Preliminary Formulations. In *Social Structures: A Network Approach*, eds. B. Wellman and S. D. Berkowitz, 261–303. Cambridge, U.K.: Cambridge University Press.

Bourdieu, P. 1986. The Forms of Capital. In *Handbook of Theory and Research for the Sociology of Education*, ed. J. G. Richardson, 241–258. New York: Greenwood Press.

Breiger, R. L. 1981. The Social Class Structure of Occupational Mobility. *American Journal of Sociology* 87 (3): 578–611.

Breiger, R. L., ed. 1990. *Social Mobility and Social Structure.* Cambridge, U.K.: Cambridge University Press.

Burt, Ronald S. 1987. Social Contagion and Innovation: Cohesion versus Structural Equivalence. *American Journal of Sociology* 92 (6): 1287–1335.

Burt, Ronald S. 2001. Structural Holes versus Network Closure as Social Capital. In *Social Capital: Theory and Research*, eds. Nan Lin, Karen S. Cook, and Ronald S. Burt, 31–56. New York: Aldine de Gruyter.

Coleman, James S., E. Katz, and H. Menzel. 1957. The Diffusion of an Innovation among Physicians. *Sociometry* 20: 253–270.

Coleman, J. S. 1988. Social Capital in the Creation of Human Capital. *American Journal of Sociology* 94: S95–S120.

Domhoff, G. William. 1998. *Who Rules America? Power and Politics in the Year 2000*, 3rd ed. Mountain View, CA: Mayfield.

Fischer, Claude S. 1982. *To Dwell among Friends: Personal Networks in Town and City.* Chicago: University of Chicago Press.

Granovetter, Mark. 1973. The Strength of Weak Ties. *American Journal of Sociology* 78 (6): 1360–1380.

Granovetter, Mark. 1982. The Strength of Weak Ties: A Network Theory Revisited. In *Social Structure and Network Analysis*, eds. Peter V. Marsden and Nan Lin, 105–130. London: Sage.

Granovetter, Mark. 1995. *Getting a Job: A Study of Contacts and Careers.* Chicago: University of Chicago Press.

Light, Ivan, Georges Sabagh, Mehdi Bozorgmehr, and Claudia Der-Martirosian. 1994. Beyond the Ethnic Enclave Economy. *Social Problems* 41: 65–79.

Loury, G. C. 1977. A Dynamic Theory of Racial Income Differences. In *Women, Minorities and Employment Discrimination*, eds. P. A. Wallace and A. M. LaMond, 153–186. Lexington, MA: Heath.

Massey, Douglas S., and Nancy A. Denton. 1993. *American Apartheid: Segregation and the Making of the Underclass.* Cambridge, MA: Harvard University Press.

Snyder, D., and E. Kick. 1979. Structural Position in the World System and Economic Growth 1955–1970: A Multiple-Network Analysis of Transnational Interactions. *American Journal of Sociology* 84 (5): 1096–1126.

Wasserman, Stanley, and Katherine Faust. 1994. *Social Network Analysis: Methods and Applications.* Cambridge, U.K., and New York: Cambridge University Press.

Watts, Duncan J. 2003. *Six Degrees: The Science of a Connected Age.* New York: Norton.

White, H. C. 1981. Where Do Markets Come From? *American Journal of Sociology* 87: 517–547.

Wierzbicki, Susan. 2004. *Beyond the Immigrant Enclave: Network Change and Assimilation.* New York: LFB Scholarly Publishing.

Nadia Y. Flores

NETWORKS, COMMUNICATION

A communication network is a set of individuals (or *nodes*) connected by communicative interaction. For example, an organizational communication network could consist of those seeking advice from others within the organization, and those giving the advice. Communication networks are social networks and are analyzed using the many theories, techniques, and procedures developed in the field of social network analysis. Though the earliest studies of social networks date from the 1930s, the modern study of communication networks originated in the 1950s with studies of how workgroups function (see Freeman 2002). For example, Alex Bavelas conducted studies in which small workgroups were given a task to complete, and then communication structure was altered to determine if a change in workgroup structure would affect task performance (it did) (Bavelas 1951).

Communication network study did not progress very much in the ensuing decades, because social scientists concentrated on taking random population samples that disconnected people from their social and communication networks (Rogers and Kincaid 1981). There was little research centered on how a person's relationships, as measured by their communication patterns or partners, affected their behavior. Gradually, however, a science of social networks has emerged, using two different research methodologies: *local* and *global*.

Local network research is conducted by asking people to name others they are close to or talk to about important matters (Burt 1985). The names provided (and they can be first names only or initials) comprise what is known as an *egocentric network*; the respondent is then asked for information about each of the persons named. Typically, the list is confined to five or six network part-

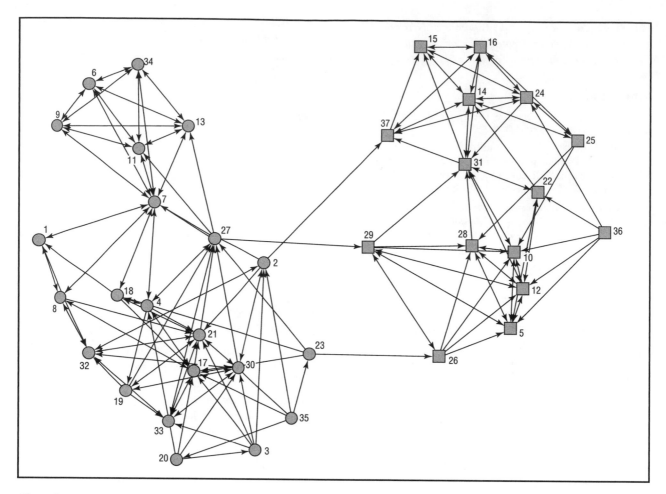

Figure 1.

ners. Researchers can then describe respondents based on the characteristics of their egocentric network. For example, respondent networks can be characterized according to the number or percent of males, people of the same religious affiliation, or people living near or far from the respondent. Importantly, one can also measure the behaviors exhibited in the network, by, for example, considering whether each network partner provides social support, expresses opinions, or engages in behaviors relevant to the respondent or study.

Global network research is conducted by defining a boundary around a set of respondents and asking everyone to name others in the network they talk to or seek advice from (the researcher can also provide a roster for the respondent to refer to). Full names or other identifying information are provided so that the researcher can draw a map (see Figure 1) of the relations within the network. This so-called *sociometric* or census approach is the most powerful network methodology. The network data are used to describe individuals and/or the entire network (Scott 2001; Wasserman and Faust 1994).

Individual network indicators include a person's *centrality*, defined as: (1) how many choices they are given by others in the network; (2) how close they are to everyone else in the network (defined as the average number of steps in the linkages to others); or (3) the degree to which they lie on paths connecting others in the network. Network analysis has developed over a dozen methods of identifying central nodes in a network. At the individual level, factors considered include, in addition to the ones mentioned above, whether a person is a member of a group, whether their ties are reciprocated, and whether they span different groups. Factors measured at the group or network level include the density of the network (the number of ties as a percent of the number of possible ties), centralization (whether the ties are concentrated around one or a few members), and clustering (whether connections between two people imply a connection to a third).

A significant finding of communication network analysis is the importance of peer influence: An individual's likelihood of engaging in a behavior increases with the percentage of their peers who engage in the behavior.

At the same time, some researchers have discovered that individuals' *network thresholds*—that is, the degree of peer influence needed to change their behavior—vary according to their personal characteristics (Valente 1995). In some cases, being integrated into a network puts one in a privileged position with regard to access to information, but in other settings it may be deleterious, for example by putting some at risk (Valente et al. 2005). Research has shown that so-called *opinion leaders* serve as important filters and conduits for information and its diffusion by influencing the adoption decisions of others. The influence of opinion leaders may depend on group norms, however, as leaders adopt innovations early if the behavior is compatible with group norms. Denser and more centralized networks may accelerate diffusion by creating more and more efficient pathways for information to flow through, but may also hinder diffusion when the density is so great that it reduces the community's access to outside information (Granovetter 1973).

Network analysis has been suggested as a methodology useful for measuring *social capital*. Social capital is defined both as the social resources available to a person via their social contacts (Lin 2001), and as a perception by the community that a person is trustworthy and civically engaged (Putnam 1995). Social network measures can provide a direct assessment of individual and communal social capital (Borgatti et al. 1998).

The tools and technology used to analyze communication networks have improved considerably in their ability to handle large datasets (such as the Internet). The field of network analysis continues to grow rapidly, aided in part by the International Network for Social Network Analysis (INSNA), which provides a Web site for access to more information.

SEE ALSO *Communication; Network Analysis; Networks; Social Capital*

BIBLIOGRAPHY

Bavelas, Alex. 1950. Communication Patterns in Task Oriented Groups. *Journal of the Acoustical Society of America* 22 (6): 725–730.

Borgatti, Stephen P., Candace Jones, and Martin G. Everett. 1998. Network Measures of Social Capital. *Connections* 21 (2): 36–44.

Burt, Ronald S. 1984. Network Items and the General Social Survey. *Social Networks* 6 (4): 293–339.

Freeman, Linton C. 2004. *The Development of Social Network Analysis: A Study in the Sociology of Science.* Vancouver, B.C.: Empirical Press.

Granovetter, M. 1973. The Strength of Weak Ties. *American Journal of Sociology* 78: 1360–1380.

Lin, Nan. 2001. *Social Capital: A Theory of Social Structure and Action.* Cambridge, U.K.: Cambridge University Press.

Putnam, Robert D. 1995. Bowling Alone: America's Declining Social Capital. *Journal of Democracy* 6 (1): 65–78.

Rogers, Everett M., and D. Lawrence Kincaid. 1981. *Communication Networks: Toward a New Paradigm for Research.* New York: Free Press.

Scott, John. 2000. *Network Analysis: A Handbook.* 2nd ed. Newbury Park, CA: Sage.

Valente, Thomas W. 1995. *Network Models of the Diffusion of Innovations.* Cresskill, NJ: Hampton Press.

Valente, Thomas W., Jennifer B. Unger, and C. Anderson Johnson. 2005. Do Popular Students Smoke? The Association between Popularity and Smoking among Middle School Students. *Journal of Adolescent Health* 37 (4): 323–329.

Wasserman, Stanley, and Katherine Faust. 1994. *Social Networks Analysis: Methods and Applications.* Cambridge, U.K.: Cambridge University Press.

Thomas W. Valente

NEUMANN, FRANZ
1900–1954

The German-born political theorist Franz Leopold Neumann was prominent in the cohort of exile scholars who brought the contested legacy of German social theory to American social and political science after 1933, especially in the study of modern democratic and dictatorial states.

Neumann was born to a Jewish family on May 23, 1900, in Kattowitz in Silesia (now Katowice, Poland). After completing his doctoral dissertation and his qualification for legal practice, he apprenticed with the leading Social Democratic labor lawyer, Hugo Sinzheimer (1875–1945), in Frankfurt. In the last years of the Weimar Republic, Neumann, in practice in Berlin, served as lead counsel for the building trade union, as well as for the Social Democratic Party. His name was reputedly high on the National Socialist (Nazi) arrest list, and he left for London in May 1933. There, he studied at the London School of Economics with Harold Laski (1893–1950) and Karl Mannheim (1893–1947), and he earned a second doctorate with a political theory dissertation on "The Governance of the Rule of Law," directed above all against the national socialist jurist Carl Schmitt (1888–1985), who had earlier intrigued him. In 1936 he came to Max Horkheimer's (1895–1973) Institute of Social Research in New York, initially as a legal advisor and eventually as a collaborator in the research program. Between 1943 and 1947, impelled by a contraction of the Institute's activities and the less-than-perfect fit between his political focus and the philosophical preoccupations of the Institute's core, he was—somewhat uncomfortably—in U.S. government service, involved above all in vainly planning a reformed social-democratic future for Germany. In 1949, after two years as a visitor, he became a professor in the Department of Public Law and Government at Columbia University in New York City. Neumann died in an automobile accident on September 2, 1954.

Neumann's publications may be divided into three periods, and key writings from all three phases have been variously retrieved by later generations of scholars in Germany, Italy, and the United States. During his years as a labor lawyer in Weimar Germany, following a methodological dissertation designed to permit a critique of German socialism's failure to move beyond its pre–World War I (1914–1918) tactical individualism in matters of criminal law, Neumann published several important articles, as well as a book, on the place of labor law in the scheme of the Weimar constitution, with labor law being taken, following Sinzheimer, as a body of socially initiated law that runs progressively against the liberal property law foundations of the civil code. The collective efforts of organized labor were an integral presupposition of this laborist approach, and the Weimar constitution was understood as a composite of democratic majoritarian parliamentary rule and a pluralistic social bargaining regime.

In the first years of exile after 1933, in his well-known *Behemoth* (1942), as well as in his posthumously published second dissertation—both of which harshly criticized in the light of events his own earlier assumptions about organized labor—Neumann offered a diagnosis of National Socialism as a political malformation arising from the legal and political order of monopoly capitalism, which neither liberalism nor laborism can comprehend. His structural analysis led him to deny the view, not alien to some of his Institute associates, that the regime should be understood as a brutally overdeveloped state with an all-encompassing bureaucracy. The Fascist slogans of "corporatism" and "totalitarian state" were mere ideological cover for a condition of incoherent conflict, according to Neumann. Nazi Germany was not to be likened to Thomas Hobbes's *Leviathan* (1651) but to his *Behemoth* (1682), the account of civil war and "confusion."

Notwithstanding the Marxist sociological tools he applied to its structure, Neumann's critique focused on the absence of a rational state in Nazi Germany and the dynamic destructive consequences of the unresolvable power struggles that constituted the system of rule. Expansionary and exploitative war without limit was the only way for such a regime, and such overreach cannot achieve a settled victory. The frame of Neumann's argument recalls the reading of G. W. F. Hegel (1770–1831) advanced at nearly the same time by his friend Herbert

Marcuse (1898–1979) in *Reason and Revolution* (1941), but Neumann lacked Marcuse's philosophical interests and he placed the weight of his work on the conjunction of his political theses with his detailed and authoritative analyses of current social, political, and economic information from German sources. It was the latter aspect that won him the greatest recognition from the dozen or more academics that reviewed *Behemoth*, but the more conjectural frame fascinated younger political writers, such as C. Wright Mills (1916–1962), who welcomed the work as an inspiration for a fresh, unhackneyed start for leftist diagnosis of trends whose dangers were not limited to Germany. Mills's influential *Power Elite* (1956) applies the analytical features that he most appreciated in Neumann's study to the American conditions of the 1950s. Neumann's mix of high humanistic ideals and tough-minded acceptance of stubborn facts recurrently intrigue a constituency on the independent Left, notably in Germany.

Neumann's writings after his years of wartime government service were constructive in aspiration, notwithstanding his occasional evocations of the critical theory formulas of the Institute of Social Research; but the work remained inconclusive. On balance, it represented an attempt to develop a theory of liberal democracy that would be responsive to the social and cultural concerns of the radical thinkers he took as his models, but that would, at the same time, support a secure constitutional order. The distinguishing feature of his work throughout is the conviction, first, that law is a mode of power and, second, that not all power in legal form is simply reducible to domination by force or fear. In its aspect as a pattern of guaranteed rights, the rule of law has a minimum ethical function beyond its ideological and economic roles; in its character as rule by democratic enactment, it has the possibility of transforming society. Neumann's central puzzle was how a political force, subject to the logic of power and confronted with the totalitarian threat immanent in all advanced societies, could serve the objectives implicit in the idea of a free and rational humanity.

SEE ALSO *Corporatism; Frankfurt School; Hegemony; Imperialism; Mills, C. Wright; Nazism; Power Elite; Totalitarianism; World War II*

BIBLIOGRAPHY

PRIMARY WORKS

Neumann, Franz L. 1929. Gegen ein Gesetz zur Nachprüfung der Verfassungsmäßigkeit von Reichsgesetzen. *Die Gesellschaft: Internationale Revue für Sozialismus und Politik* 6 (6–1): 517–536.

Neumann, Franz L. 1930. Die soziale Bedeutung der Grundrechte in der Weimarer Verfassung. *Die Arbeit* 7 (9): 569–582. Reprinted in Franz L. Neumann. 1978. *Wirtschaft,*

Staat, Demokratie: Aufsätze, 1930–1954. Ed. Alfons Söllner. Frankfurt, Germany: Edition Suhrkamp. Translated as Tribe, Keith, ed. 1987. The Social Significance of the Basic Laws in the Weimar Constitution. In *Social Democracy and The Rule of Law.* Trans. Leena Tanner and Keith Tribe. London: Allen and Unwin.

Neumann, Franz L. 1932. *Koalitionsfreiheit und Reichsverfassung.* Berlin: Heymann.

Neumann, Franz L. 1932. Reichsverfassung und Wohlfahrtsstaat. *Das Freie Wort* 4 (26): 6–11.

Neumann, Franz L. (as Leopold Franz). 1935. Zur marxistischen Staatstheorie. *Zeitschrift für Sozialismus* 2 (26/7): 865–872. Reprinted in Franz L. Neumann. 1978. *Wirtschaft, Staat, Demokratie: Aufsätze 1930–1954.* Ed. Alfons Söllner. Frankfurt, Germany: Edition Suhrkamp.

Neumann, Franz L. [1936] 1986. *[The Governance of] The Rule of Law.* Leamington Spa, U.K.: Berg.

Neumann, Franz L. 1944. *Behemoth: The Structure and Practice of National Socialism, 1933–1944.* 2nd ed. New York: Oxford University Press.

Neumann, Franz L. 1957. *The Democratic and the Authoritarian State: Essays in Political and Legal Theory.* Ed. Herbert Marcuse. Glencoe, IL: Free Press.

SECONDARY WORKS

Buchstein, Hubertus. 2003. A Heroic Reconciliation of Freedom and Power: On the Tension between Democratic and Social Theory in the Late Work of Franz L. Neumann. *Constellations* 10 (2): 228–246.

Intelmann, Peter. 1996. *Franz L. Neumann: Chancen und Dilemmas des politischen Reformismus.* Baden-Baden, Germany: Nomos.

Iser, Mattias, and David Strecker, eds. 2003. Franz L. Neumann: Power, Constitution, Critique. *Constellations* 10 (2): 211–263.

Kettler, David. 2001. Works Community and Workers' Organizations: A Central Problem in Weimar Labour Law. In *Domestic Regimes, the Rule of Law, and Democratic Social Change*, 23–43. Glienicke/Berlin and Cambridge, MA: Galda+Wilch.

Mills, C. Wright. 1942. The Nazi Behemoth: Book Review of *Behemoth* by Franz Neumann. *Partisan Review* (September/October). Reprinted in C. Wright Mills. 1967. *Power, Politics, and People: The Collected Essays of C. Wright Mills.* Ed. Irving Louis Horowitz, 170–178. London and New York: Oxford University Press.

Perels, Joachim, ed. 1984. *Recht, Demokratie, und Kapitalismus: Aktualität und Probleme der Theorie Franz L. Neumanns.* Baden-Baden, Germany: Nomos.

Scheuerman, William E. 1994. *Between the Norm and the Exception. The Frankfurt School and the Rule of Law.* Cambridge, MA: MIT Press.

Söllner, Alfons. 1996. *Deutsche Politikwissenschaftler in der Emigration.* Opladen, Germany: Westdeutscher Verlag, 1996.

David Kettler

NEUROECONOMICS

Neuroeconomics is a new and emerging approach in the social sciences that integrates theories, methodologies, and ideas from neuroscience, economics, and psychology to study how individuals make economic decisions. Typically, research in this field involves observing neurological activity in experimental tasks and situations, through brain imaging in humans (which monitors electrical activity or blood flow in clusters of neurons) and single neuron measurements in animals (which monitors individual neurons firing via tiny electrodes inserted into an animal's brain). By linking observed behaviors with the neurons and brain regions that activate during such actions, neuroeconomic researchers seek to discover not only the functionality of various brain regions, but also the underlying processes that occur in decision-making as different neural systems interact. While the full benefits of this new interdisciplinary approach are still unclear, neuroeconomics has generated excitement due to its potential to advance the existing behavioral theories of its contributing disciplines. Particularly, as neuroscience and psychology are closely related fields, neuroeconomics strongly supplements behavioral economics, a subfield that seeks to integrate psychology into the rational-choice framework of neoclassical economics. Indeed, by providing a window into what was previously regarded as the "black box" of the brain, neuroeconomics can improve the accuracy of our existing decision-making models and generate new insights into the basis of economic behavior.

One illustration of the potential insights derived from neuroeconomics can be found in the neuroscientific version of the classic two-player "ultimatum game" from game theory. In the traditional game, the first player is asked to decide how much of a sum of money he wishes to keep for himself and how much he wishes to offer to a second player. The second player can either accept this offer, in which both players receive the amount allocated to him by the offer, or reject it, in which neither party receives any money. While economic theory suggests that the second partner will rationally accept any nonzero offer, in behavioral economic experiments the second player typically rejects low offers (e.g., two dollars, when the other player receives eight dollars). When the experiment is conducted using functional magnetic resonance imaging (fMRI), brain scans of participants who face unfair offers indicate heightened neural activity in two competing brain regions: the bilateral anterior insula, a region associated with the emotions of anger, distress, and disgust, and the dorsolateral prefrontal cortex (dlPFC), a region associated with reasoning and deliberation. Interestingly, when insular activation exceeded dlPFC activation, participants typically rejected low offers, whereas when dlPFC activation exceeded insular activation, participants typically accepted these same offers. This finding expands our knowledge of decision-making in the traditional game theory experiment by revealing the presence of multiple, competing processes in the brain (in this case, representing affect versus cognition) that directly determine the subject's final choice.

Neuroeconomics currently faces some criticism from skeptics in its parent disciplines who are uncertain about the utility that can be gained from combining such dissimilar approaches to decision-making and behavioral analyses. Some neuroscientists question the usefulness of research involving fMRI—the most common neuroscientific technology employed in the field—because such techniques only capture images of the brain every few seconds (while neural activity occurs in milliseconds) and cannot detect activity that is less than 3 millimeters long (while neural activity can occur at 0.1 millimeters). Even among supporters of this new field, there are general inconsistencies in the perceived goals and purpose of neuroeconomics. Within this field, some neuroscientists apply the most basic elements of rational choice theory to explain neural activity—emphasizing findings such as the existence of neurons in monkeys that calculate physiological or expected utility—while some economists use neuroscience to expand upon rational choice theory and incorporate non-orthodox perspectives of economic behavior (e.g., from psychology and sociology). Overall, neuroeconomics is a new interdisciplinary field with many questions still left to answer. With likely advances in neuroscience technologies in the future, we may soon know much more about how useful the neuroeconomic approach is to decision-making research, and how individuals truly arrive at the economic decisions that they make.

SEE ALSO *Decision-making; Economics; Economics, Behavioral; Game Theory; Neuroscience; Psychology; Rationality*

BIBLIOGRAPHY

Camerer, Colin, George Loewenstein, and Drazen Prelec. 2005. Neuroeconomics: How Neuroscience Can Inform Economics. *Journal of Economic Literature* 43: 9–64.

Cassidy, John. 2006. Mind Games: What Neuroeconomics Tells Us about Money and the Brain. *The New Yorker* (18 September): 30–37.

Glimcher, Paul W., Michael Dorris, and Hannah M. Bayer. 2005. Physiological Utility Theory and the Neuroeconomics of Choice. *Games and Economic Behavior* 52: 213–256.

Sanfey, Alan G., George Loewenstein, Samuel M. McClure, and Jonathan D. Cohen. 2006. Neuroeconomics: Cross-currents in Research on Decision Making. *TRENDS in Cognitive Science* 10 (3): 108–116.

Jeffrey K. Lee

NEUROMANCER
SEE *Matrix, The.*

NEUROSCIENCE

The field of neuroscience reflects the interdisciplinary effort to understand the structure, function, physiology, biology, biochemistry, and pathology of the nervous system. From a social science perspective, however, neuroscience primarily refers to the study of the brain. Of interest is how the brain gives rise to learning, cognition, and behavior. The research of neuroscientists crosses many levels of analysis, ranging from molecular studies of genes to the study of social and ethical behavior. Within psychology, for example, behavioral neuroscientists use animal models to gain a better understanding of how genetic and brain processes influence behavior. Since the late 1980s, there has been a dramatic rise in the field of cognitive neuroscience, which combines cognitive psychology, neurology, and neuroscience to examine how brain activity gives rise to cognitive abilities (for example, memory, emotion, attention, language, consciousness).

Most recently, social neuroscience is an emerging field that uses the methods of neuroscience to understand how the brain processes social information. It involves scholars from widely diverse areas (for instance, social psychology, neuroscience, philosophy, anthropology, economics, sociology) working together and across levels of analysis to understand fundamental questions about human social nature. Social neuroscience merges evolutionary theory, experimental social cognition, and neuroscience to elucidate the neural mechanisms that support social behavior. From this perspective, just as there are dedicated brain mechanisms for breathing, walking, and talking, the brain has evolved specialized mechanisms for processing information about the social world, including the ability to know one's self, to know how one responds to another, and to regulate actions in order to coexist with other members of society. The problems that are studied by social neuroscience have been of central interest to social scientists for decades, but the methods and theories that are used reflect recent discoveries in neuroscience. Although in its infancy, there has been rapid progress in identifying the neural basis of many social behaviors (for reviews, see Adolphs 2003; Heatherton et al. 2004).

METHODS OF NEUROSCIENCE

The principles of how cells operate in the brain to influence behavior have been studied with great progress for more than a century, but it is only since the late 1980s that researchers have been able to study the working brain as it performs its vital mental functions. Brain activity is associated with changes in the flow of blood as it carries oxygen and nutrients to active brain regions. Brain imaging methods track this flow of blood to understand which areas of the brain are most active for a given task. Positron emission tomography (PET), the first imaging method developed, involves a computerized reconstruction of the brain's metabolic activity by using a relatively harmless radioactive substance that is injected into the blood stream. A PET scanner detects this radiation and therefore can be used to map out brain activity in real time, which is a direct measure of blood flow. The use of radioactive substances, however, places an inherent limitation on the number of trials that can be conducted in a PET study, a potential limitation that is not present in functional magnetic resonance imaging (fMRI). Like PET, fMRI measures brain activity, but it is noninvasive (that is, nothing is injected into the blood stream). The fMRI process employs a strong magnetic field to assess changes in the oxygen level of blood at particular sites after they have become active, which is an indirect measure of blood flow.

Another set of techniques for assessing brain activity involves measuring electrical activity in the brain using an electroencephalogram (EEG). As a measure of specific mental states, an EEG is limited because the recordings reflect all brain activity and therefore are too noisy to isolate specific responses to particular stimuli. A more powerful method involves averaging together many trials and measuring the brain activity evoked for the brief periods of time following the start of the trial, resulting in measurements known as event-related potentials (ERPs). ERPs have proven to be especially useful for assessing the time course of cognitive processes, such as which aspects of a stimulus are processed first. A related method, magnetoencephalography (MEG), measures magnetic fields produced by the electrical activity of the brain. Both EEG and MEG provide excellent temporal resolution (that is, timing), yet limited spatial resolution (that is, the precise location of the activation). Brain imaging methods, such as fMRI and PET, provide much better spatial resolution than EEG or MEG, but at the cost of temporal resolution (that is, blood flow changes occur over several seconds following brain activity).

APPLICATIONS OF NEUROSCIENCE TO THE SOCIAL SCIENCES

The use of brain imaging techniques has allowed scientists to discover a great deal regarding the neural correlates of mental activity. For instance, cognitive neuroscientists have used these methods to better understand which brain regions are involved in memory, attention, visual perception, language, and many other psychological processes. More recently, neuroscience methods have been used to study topics of interest across the social sciences, such as political attitudes and decision-making, moral judgments,

cooperation and competition, behavioral economics, addiction, and social cognition. For example, social psychologists have long been interested in understanding whether stereotypes reflect automatic (unconscious) or controlled (conscious) processes. Thus, social neuroscientists have begun to examine how various brain regions respond when people are making judgments of other people from various racial groups or people who possess various forms of stigma (such as status, class, disfigurement). A common finding is greater activity in the amygdala (a brain region associated with fear-based emotional responding) in response to observing faces of different races for people high in racial bias than for people low in racial bias (Eberhardt 2005).

Research within social neuroscience has often focused on the trade-off between primitive emotional responses and higher-level cognitive control. The latter reflects unique human capacities for self-reflection, understanding the minds of others, and engaging in self-control; each of these capacities ultimately depends on the intact functioning of the frontal lobes. It is likely that the methods of neuroscience will expand throughout the social sciences to address questions at a new level of analysis. As such, these methods can augment the traditional methods used to understand social behavior.

SEE ALSO *Altruism; Depression, Psychological; Dopamine; Drugs of Abuse; Generosity/Selfishness; Hallucinogens; Happiness; Memory; Neuroeconomics; Semantic Memory; Sex and Mating*

BIBLIOGRAPHY

Adolphs, Ralph. 2003. Cognitive Neuroscience of Human Social Behaviour. *Nature Reviews Neuroscience* 4 (3): 165–178.

Eberhardt, Jennifer L. 2005. Imaging Race. *American Psychologist* 60 (2): 181–190.

Heatherton, Todd F., C. Neil Macrae, and William M. Kelley. 2004. A Social Brain Sciences Approach to Studying the Self. *Current Directions in Psychological Science* 13 (5): 190–193.

Todd F. Heatherton
Anne C. Krendl

NEUROSCIENCE, SOCIAL

Social neuroscience is an interdisciplinary field that considers the mutual implications of neuroscience and social science for understanding of social and affective aspects of behavior. Specifically, social neuroscience determines the biological mechanisms underlying social processes and behavior, considered by many to be one of the major problem areas for the neurosciences in the twenty-first century, and uses biological concepts and methods to develop and refine theories of social processes and behavior in the social and behavioral sciences.

Contemporary work has demonstrated that neuroscientific theory and methods can constrain and inspire hypotheses, foster experimental tests of otherwise indistinguishable theoretical explanations, and increase the comprehensiveness and relevance of behavioral theories. Several principles from social neuroscience suggest that understanding social behavior requires the joint consideration of social, cognitive, and biological levels of analysis in an integrated fashion. The principle of *multiple determinism*, for instance, specifies that a target event specified at one level of organization, but especially at molar or abstract (e.g., social) levels of organization, can have multiple antecedents within or across levels of organization. For instance, one might consume a considerable quantity of pizza in an effort to either remedy a low blood-sugar condition (biological determinant) or win a food-eating contest (social determinant).

The principle of *nonadditive determinism* specifies that properties of the whole are not always readily predictable from the properties of the parts. In an illustrative study, the behavior of nonhuman primates was examined following the administration of either an amphetamine or a placebo. No clear pattern emerged until each primate's position in the social hierarchy was considered. When this social factor was taken into account, the amphetamine was found to increase dominant behavior in primates high in the social hierarchy and to increase submissive behavior in primates low in the social hierarchy. A strictly physiological (or social) analysis, regardless of the sophistication of the measurement technology, may not have unraveled the orderly relationship that existed.

Finally, the principle of *reciprocal determinism* specifies that there can be mutual influences between microscopic (e.g., biological) and macroscopic (e.g., social) factors in determining behavior. For example, not only has the level of testosterone in nonhuman male primates been shown to promote sexual behavior, but also the availability of receptive females influences the level of testosterone. That is, the effects of social and biological processes can be reciprocal.

One important implication of these principles is that comprehensive accounts of human behavior cannot be achieved if the biological, cognitive, or social level of organization is considered unnecessary or irrelevant.

In sum, throughout most of the twentieth century social and biological explanations were cast as incompatible. Advances in recent years have led to the development of a new view synthesized from the social and biological sciences. The new field of social neuroscience emphasizes the complementary nature of the different levels of organization spanning the social and biological domains (e.g., molecular, cellular, system, person, relational, collective, societal) and demonstrates how multilevel analyses can foster understanding of the mechanisms underlying the human mind and behavior.

SEE ALSO *Determinism, Nonadditive*

BIBLIOGRAPHY

Cacioppo, John T. 2002. Social Neuroscience: Understanding the Pieces Fosters Understanding the Whole and Vice Versa. *American Psychologist* 57: 819–830.

John T. Cacioppo
Gary G. Berntson

NEUROTICISM

Neuroticism (N) is one of the broad dimensions or traits of human personality. Individuals with high levels of N are emotionally sensitive and more likely to experience psychological distress and negative emotions, such as sadness, worry, or fear. They find it difficult to cope with stress and to control their emotions. In contrast, individuals who score low on N are characterized by low levels of emotional arousal. They are described as emotionally stable. Even when faced with stressful situations, they remain calm and relaxed and report low levels of negative emotions.

The concept of N emerged from the lexical tradition of personality research that used statistical techniques to identify the basic underlying dimensions of personality descriptions found in everyday language. Although most researchers agree that N is one of the core personality dimensions, there are some differences in its conceptualization across theoretical frameworks.

The five-factor model of personality considers N (together with Extraversion, Openness to Experience, Agreeableness, and Conscientiousness) as one of the "Big Five" dimensions of normal personality. According to Robert McCrae and Paul Costa (2003), N is composed of six facets: Anxiety, Angry Hostility, Depression, Self-Consciousness, Impulsiveness, and Vulnerability. Hans Eysenck and Sybil B. G. Eysenck (1976) identified N, together with Extraversion and Psychoticism, as one of three major dimensions of personality.

N is typically measured by asking individuals to indicate their agreement with a list of self-descriptive statements. Observer ratings obtained from peers, relatives, or medical professionals may be used as well. Two commonly used questionnaires are the Eysenck Personality Questionnaire—Revised (EPQ-R; Eysenck, Eysenck, and

Barrett 1985) and the Revised NEO Personality Inventory (NEO PI-R; Costa and McCrae 1992). The EPQ-R consists of 100 items and provides separate scales for N, Psychoticism, and Extraversion. The NEO PI-R consists of 240 items that measure each of the 5 personality domains. Scores for the six facets that define each domain are provided as well.

N is a genetically influenced (Bouchard and Loehlin 2001; Pilia et al. 2006), stable characteristic that manifests itself consistently across age groups, gender, and cultural contexts. An adult's level of N remains fairly constant across time, but there are gradual declines in N across the adult life span (Roberts, Walton, and Viechtbauer 2006). N and its facets can be sharply increased by adverse life conditions and medical disorders, though it is quite responsive to various treatment strategies as well.

Although N acquired its name through its close association with the traditional diagnosis of neurosis, N is a dimension of normal personality. Even extremely high scores on the N scale do not necessarily indicate the presence of psychopathology, and even people with low levels of N may have psychiatric disorders. That being said, high scores on N are nevertheless related to a range of problems in living. Especially in combination with low extraversion, high N is associated with lower life satisfaction and greater risk for clinical depression and other psychiatric disorders. People high in N are also prone to use maladaptive strategies (e.g., self-blame) when coping with stressors. In combination with low conscientiousness, N is also a risk factor for smoking and abuse of alcohol and drugs.

SEE ALSO *Anxiety; Depression, Psychological; Personality; Psychopathology; Self-Consciousness, Private vs. Public*

BIBLIOGRAPHY

Bouchard, Thomas J., Jr., and John C. Loehlin. 2001. Genes, Evolution, and Personality. *Behavior Genetics* 31 (3): 243–273.

Costa, Paul T., Jr., and Robert R. McCrae. 1992. *Revised NEO Personality Inventory (NEO PI-R) and the NEO Five-Factor Inventory (NEO-FFI) Professional Manual.* Odessa, FL: Psychological Assessment Resources.

Eysenck, Hans J., and Sybil B. G. Eysenck. 1976. *Psychoticism as a Dimension of Personality.* London: Hodder and Stoughton.

Eysenck, Hans J., Sybil B. G. Eysenck, and Paul Barrett. 1985. A Revised Version of the Psychoticism Scale. *Personality and Individual Differences* 6 (1): 21–29.

McCrae, Robert R., and Paul T. Costa Jr. 2003. *Personality in Adulthood: A Five-Factor Theory Perspective.* 2nd ed. New York: Guilford.

Pilia, Giuseppe, Weimin M. Chen, Angelo Scuteri, et al. 2006. Heritability of Cardiovascular and Personality Traits in 6,148 Sardinians. *PLoS Genetics* 2 (8): 1207–1223.

Roberts, Brent W., Kate Walton, and Wolfgang Viechtbauer. 2006. Patterns of Mean-Level Change in Personality Traits across the Life Course: A Meta-Analysis of Longitudinal Studies. *Psychological Bulletin* 132 (1): 1–25.

Corinna E. Löckenhoff
Paul T. Costa Jr.

NEUTRAL POLICIES, RACE

SEE *Race-Blind Policies.*

NEUTRAL RATE OF INTEREST

SEE *Interest, Neutral Rate of.*

NEUTRAL SOCIAL SCIENCE

SEE *Social Science, Value Free.*

NEUTRAL STATES

As long as states (or statelike entities) and warfare between them have existed, there have been states that did not participate in a current war and thus displayed *neutral* behavior (derived from the Latin *ne-uter,* "neither of the two"). The modern tradition of neutrality dates back to the development of the state system in the sixteenth and seventeenth centuries. The interaction of state practice, scholarly thought, and international treaties crystallized into an institution of international law.

One can distinguish at least three or even four types of "neutral" behavior of states. The first is *occasional* neutrality, a state's neutrality in a particular war between other states. Its legal rules were codified in 1907 at the second Hague Peace Conference. *Permanent* neutrality under customary international law commits a state to neutrality in all present *and* future wars and obliges it to avoid such peacetime ties and policies as would make its neutrality in war impossible. *Conventional* neutrality without an international legal basis is followed by states that tend to call their foreign policies neutral. They follow a more or less neutral course in practice, but fail to commit themselves to permanent neutrality under international law. Whereas these three types of neutrality have been practiced mostly by European states, a distant fourth variant, *nonalignment,* evolved above all in countries that during the cold war wanted to avoid entanglements in the conflict between the United States and the Soviet Union. These countries formed the *nonaligned movement*.

The Hague Conventions require the *occasional* neutral state to prevent the use of its territory, including its airspace and waters, by belligerent states; the neutral must not allow the passage of troops, munitions, or supplies through its territory. The neutral state has to refrain from any support for belligerents and may not deliver war materials or extend loans for military purposes. In contrast, the neutral is not bound to prevent private persons and companies from exporting war materials to belligerent states. If the neutral regulates trade with military goods, these provisions must treat the belligerents equally and be implemented without discrimination.

These rules originated in the liberal era when it was seen as feasible to keep apart public space (the state) and private sphere (the economy). But during the twentieth century, this distinction became more and more blurred. In addition, many armed conflicts like internal wars, guerilla wars, and massive terrorist attacks are not the type of interstate wars that are the subject matter of the international law of neutrality. Enforcement measures by the United Nations Security Council (UN Charter, chap. VII) are regarded as "police operations" and also not relevant to neutrality.

The rules for the behavior of *permanently* neutral states have never been codified. In 1815 Switzerland's status of permanent neutrality was recognized by the powers of the Congress of Vienna. As comparable buffers between France and Germany, Belgium and Luxembourg agreed to legally based permanent neutrality in the first half of the nineteenth century, but abandoned it in the aftermath of World War I (1914–1918).

The customary rules of permanent neutrality include three basic duties in peacetime: (1) not to begin a war; (2) to defend the status of permanent neutrality; and (3) to do everything to avoid being drawn into a war and to abstain from any action that could lead to involvement in a war. The range of this last set of duties, the "antecedent effects" of permanent neutrality, have been controversial. In the 1950s the Swiss authorities interpreted these duties to encompass a prohibition against concluding any treaty that would oblige it to wage war (like a military alliance). Switzerland would also not be allowed to conclude any customs or economic union with any other country because it would thereby relinquish its political independence and thus could not credibly forestall participation in a future war. As a quid pro quo for ending the four-power occupation installed after World War II (1939–1945), Austria in 1955 assumed the status of permanent neutrality according to the Swiss model.

About the same time, after the Soviet Union relinquished its naval base at Porkkala near Helsinki, Finland started to practice neutrality in its foreign relations. Sweden had followed this type of neutrality policy since the first half of the nineteenth century. Ireland had adhered to a limited "military" neutrality since World War II. These *conventional* neutrals rejected all legal obligations during peacetime, but followed a foreign policy similar to that of the permanently neutral states.

The European neutrals did not join the European Economic Community (EEC), founded in 1957, although Austria and Sweden, for example, had close economic ties with its members. During the years of détente between East and West, these neutral countries played a role in moderating international conflicts through their "active neutrality." Ireland joined the EEC in 1973. In the late 1980s and early 1990s, economic difficulties forced the other neutrals to rethink their position vis-à-vis the European Union (EU). The end of the cold war and a less-strict interpretation of permanent neutrality helped Austria, Sweden, and Finland finally join the EU in 1995. Together with Ireland, they refused a military assistance clause, as foreseen in the Constitutional Treaty of the EU. But otherwise, the foreign policy behavior of the neutral states is similar to that of the other members of the EU. They fully participate in the Common Foreign and Security Policy of the EU. In situations where military force is used without a UN Security Council mandate, their positions can become awkward, as the 1999 Kosovo crisis showed. Austria regarded the NATO bombing of Serbia as "necessary and warranted" in the EU context, but at the same time refused the overflight of NATO war planes on their way from the U.S. bases in southern Germany to the Balkans. The status of permanent or conventional neutrality has lost most of its functions at the beginning of the twenty-first century. But since neutrality is still favored by their populations (as numerous public opinion polls show), the governments of the neutral states are reluctant to change this status.

SEE ALSO *European Union; Nation-State; North Atlantic Treaty Organization; State, The; United Nations; War; War and Peace*

BIBLIOGRAPHY

Doherty, Róisín. 2002. *Ireland, Neutrality, and European Security Integration.* Aldershot, U.K.: Ashgate.

Gehler, Michael, and Rolf Steininger, eds. 2000. *Die Neutralen und die europäische Integration, 1945–1995: The Neutrals and the European Integration, 1945–1995.* Vienna: Böhlau.

Malmborg, Mikael af. 2001. *Neutrality and State-Building in Sweden.* New York and Basingstoke, U.K.: Palgrave.

Ojanen, Hanna, ed. 2003. *Neutrality and Non-alignment in Europe Today*. FIIA Report 6/2003. Helsinki: Finnish Institute of International Affairs.

Verdross, Alfred. 1978. *The Permanent Neutrality of Austria*. Trans. Charles Kessler. Vienna: Verlag für Geschichte und Politik.

Paul Luif

NEUTRALITY, POLITICAL

Political neutrality is a position a nation-state adopts regarding a particular conflict. Politically neutral countries maintain a neutral stance toward warring parties for the duration of a conflict, although certain countries, such as Sweden and Switzerland, and Belgium until 1914, extend neutrality to all conflicts so that such stances become permanent over time. Political neutrality has its basis in international law and common principles of international society, but it is termed political in the sense that it is influenced by domestic political factors, and as a chosen policy serves a country's national interests.

Politically neutral parties are not indifferent to conflict (they may still provide humanitarian assistance or other forms of nonmilitary aid to needing parties). For instance, while many countries did not provide military assistance in any form to the recent American-led Iraq War, several neutral countries have provided (and continue to provide) large amounts of bilateral humanitarian assistance. Furthermore, politically neutral countries are not necessarily pacifist in principle, as they still maintain armies for protection and they will fight for reasons of self-defense, as Belgium did in World War I when Germany invaded in 1914.

INTELLECTUAL TRADITION, INTERNATIONAL LAW, AND PRINCIPLES SERVING "NEUTRALITY"

In order for neutrality to be viable, it must be granted and respected by other states. This assumes that nation-state behavior is rule-governed. As an intellectual approach to international politics, the Grotian tradition (named after Hugo Grotius, a seventeenth-century jurist) assumes that rules and principles operate within international politics. Also termed the international society tradition, and developed by scholars such as Hedley Bull, Martin Wight, Adam Watson, R. J. Vincent, Robert H. Jackson, and Nicholas Wheeler, this perspective still assumes that states operate within anarchy—or the lack of a central, over-arching political authority that can adjudicate grievances. Additionally, the Grotian tradition does not assume that these rules will inevitably abolish interstate conflicts. Yet it asserts that in certain contexts (both spatial and temporal), nation-states hold in common certain values and interests that are binding upon members of the international society. Political neutrality is one such recognized common interest.

While many international principles have informed how neutrality has been understood in international politics, three are noteworthy. First, states that are neutral toward the internal conflict of another nation-state (civil wars) do so out of respect for the sovereignty of that country. Sovereign states have exclusive political authority throughout the geographic regions they occupy. A second and related principle is pluralism, or that there are multiple conceptions and ways of life (rather than one universal) that any state may wish to pursue. Third, there is the principle of *pacta sunt servanda*, which translates, "pacts must be respected." This principle assumes states keeping their promises. Agreements among states can only be binding if there is the assumption that, once entered, states will maintain those agreements through time.

The most explicit example of international recognition for neutrality, the Second Hague Convention (1907), grew out of what Grotian scholar Bull termed a European international society in his *Anarchical Society* (1977, pp. 31–36). Throughout the eighteenth, nineteenth, and early twentieth centuries European countries developed a body of international settlements and laws that were expressed in certain institutions (such as the Concert of Europe). At the Second Hague Convention, neutral countries such as Belgium, Sweden, and Switzerland were granted formal recognition in Articles V (The Rights and Duties of Neutral Powers and Persons in Case of War on Land) and XIII (Naval War). These articles declared, most importantly, that the land of neutral countries was "inviolable." The Second Hague Convention is still recognized law and the most important statement recognizing the rights of neutral countries.

REASONS FOR, AND FORMS OF, POLITICAL NEUTRALITY

While international recognition is important for a nation-state's political neutrality to be viable, there are many domestic influences that pressure states into neutrality (either permanently or temporarily). Three key sets of reasons for political neutrality include:

Instrumentalist Neutrality is the most cost-effective position a country can take regarding a conflict. A nation-state remains uninvolved in a dispute because the dispute is unpopular with and costly for nationally important economic and political interest groups. In instrumentalist situations, one or more warring parties may try to induce countries out of neutral positions by providing economic incentives that would therefore make political neutrality no longer cost-effective. In other words, when such material incentives successfully induce neutral countries into conflicts, an instrumentalist set of influences was probably most responsible for the original politically neutral position.

Isolationist Neutrality is based upon both a cultural and economic component that influences a country's conception of its national interest. Isolationists assert that their country should have only limited interaction with other countries. This stance has been especially popular with certain domestic interest groups that benefit from protectionist economic policies, but it also permeates the fabric of a country's larger political culture. Isolationism prevailed in the United States, for example, during the interwar period (1919–1941). This particular form of isolationism was based in the concept of American exceptionalism, or the belief that the United States held a unique place in the world and that, therefore, America could remain neutral toward, and removed from, the balance of power politics underpinning European conflicts.

Normative Neutrality is chosen as a policy because there is no position for a country to take that would not threaten its own national vision. Normative political neutrality was the British policy toward the United States during the American Civil War (1861–1865). While the British had recognized the Confederacy as a legitimate "belligerent" party, and many Brits identified with the aristocratic landholders of the American South, the Emancipation Proclamation redefined (in British society) the American Civil War as a war over slavery. Even though neutrality proved materially very costly to Britain's strategic and economic interests, the British could not side with the Confederacy as such an action would have engendered British anxiety over slavery.

In certain cases, like Switzerland, Sweden, and Belgium until 1914, neutrality is inherited as a political attribute that serves to define its social identity as a state. Belgium, from independence in 1830 until World War I, declared itself a "perpetually neutral" country. In this case political neutrality informs all decisions a state makes, during times of peace and war, and determines even the legal basis for whether and how to resist invading armies.

While neutrality seems to carry no guarantees, it should be noted that the territories of most neutral countries have been respected through time. Even in cases where neutrality has been compromised, the offending party often incurs widespread international condemna-

tion for such a violation, as Germany did following the invasion of then-neutral Belgium in 1914.

SEE ALSO *Neutral States; Neutrality of Money*

BIBLIOGRAPHY

Bull, Hedley. [1977] 2002. *The Anarchical Society: A Study of Order in World Politics.* New York: Columbia University Press.

Global Humanitarian Assistance: Update 2004–05. http://www.globalhumanitarianassistance.org/GHAupdFinal2inccov.pdf.

Brent J. Steele

NEUTRALITY OF MONEY

The (classical) quantity theory of money represents a central organizing principle for macroeconomic analysis. It goes back hundreds of years, to the writings of David Hume (Hume 1970) and Irving Fisher (Fisher 1922).

The theory posits that one-time permanent shifts in nominal variables have no effect on real variables in the long run. The simplest quantity-theoretic proposition, known as the *long-run monetary neutrality proposition*, specifies that a permanent, stochastic, (that is, purely random) shock to the money supply has a one for one effect on prices and a zero effect on real output in the long run. Another quantity-theoretic proposition is that of long-run monetary superneutrality, specifying that a permanent change in the rate of growth of nominal money (that is, money measured in current dollar magnitudes) has no long-run effect on the level of real output. In sum, changes in the money supply affect the price level (inflation) but have no effect on relative prices, the volume of employment, output, or real income (purchasing power).

Over the years, the long-run monetary neutrality propositions have been investigated in a large number of studies (McCandless and Weber 1995). However, as Lucas (1996, p. 661) puts it in his Nobel lecture, "so much thought has been devoted to this question [of proving long-run neutrality] and so much evidence is available that one might reasonably assume that it had been solved long ago. But this is not the case." In fact, Fisher and Seater (1993) and King and Watson (1997), using state-of-the-art advances in the field of applied econometrics, have shown that meaningful long-run neutrality tests can only be constructed if both nominal (measured in current dollar magnitudes) and real (measured in units of commodities) variables satisfy certain nonstationarity conditions (regarding, for example, variance, trends, and seasonal patterns) and that much of the older literature violates these requirements.

In the spirit of Fisher and Seater (1993) and King and Watson (1997), Serletis and Koustas (1998) provide international evidence for the long-run neutrality and superneutrality propositions. Using the eclectic approach of King and Watson (1997) and the Backus and Kehoe (1992) data, consisting of over one hundred years of annual observations on real output and money for ten countries—Australia, Canada, Denmark, Germany, Italy, Japan, Norway, Sweden, the United Kingdom, and the United States—they show that the data are generally supportive of monetary neutrality.

In a similar study testing the long-run neutrality of money and using the King and Watson (1997) methodology, Serletis and Koustas (2001) pay particular attention to the gains that can be achieved by rigorous use of microeconomic- and aggregation-theoretic foundations in the construction of money measures. To address disputes about the relative merits of different monetary aggregation procedures, they make comparisons among simplesum, Divisia (named after the French economist Francois Divisia), and currency-equivalent money measures for the United States, obtained from the monetary services indices (MSI) database, maintained by the Federal Reserve Bank of St. Louis as a part of the bank's Federal Reserve Economic Database. The results show that the hypothesis of long-run monetary neutrality finds support in the United States data, irrespective of how money is measured.

Finally, another long-run neutrality proposition is the Fisher relation. According to the Fisher equation, $R = r + \pi$, where R is the nominal (dollar) interest rate, r the real interest rate (the rate that determines the growth over time in the real value of assets), and π the inflation rate, the Fisher relation states that the nominal interest rate moves one-for-one with inflation in the long-run, meaning that a permanent change in the rate of inflation has no long-run effect on the level of the real interest rate. The Fisher relation holds in models in which the real interest rate is determined by a relation like the modified golden rule (according to which the marginal product of capital in steady state equals the sum of the rate of time preference and the population growth rate) and therefore does not depend on monetary variables (Sidrauski 1967). It is violated, however, in models in which the Tobin (1965) effect applies; in such models, an increase in the inflation rate results in a decrease of the real interest rate and therefore in a less than one-to-one increase of the nominal interest rate (this is known as the Tobin effect).

Koustas and Serletis (1999) have investigated the Fisherian link between inflation and nominal interest rates using postwar quarterly data for eleven countries—Belgium, Canada, Denmark, France, Germany, Greece, Ireland, Japan, the Netherlands, the United Kingdom, and the United States—and the King and Watson (1997) methodology. Their results are consistent with most of the existing literature on the Fisher effect, which mostly shows that fully anticipated inflation has less than a unit effect on the nominal interest rate, and thus reduces the real interest rate even in the longest of runs. In view of the inability to reject long-run monetary neutrality by examining the effects of money shocks on real output, we are thus left with a puzzle that needs to be addressed by future theoretical and empirical work.

SEE ALSO *Economics, Keynesian; Economics, New Classical; Interest Rates; Monetarism; Monetary Theory; Money; Money, Demand for; Policy, Monetary; Quantity Theory of Money*

BIBLIOGRAPHY

Backus, David K., and Patrick J. Kehoe. 1992. International Evidence on the Historical Properties of Business Cycles. *American Economic Review* 82 (4): 864–888.

Fisher, Irving. 1922 *The Purchasing Power of Money: Its Determination and Relation to Credit, Interest, and Crises.* 2nd ed. New York: Macmillan. Reprint, New York: Augustus Kelley, 1971.

Fisher, Mark E., and John J. Seater. 1993. Long-Run Neutrality and Superneutrality in an ARIMA Framework. *American Economic Review* 83 (3): 402–415.

Hume, David. 1955. *Writings on Economics*. Ed. Eugene Rotwein. Madison: University of Wisconsin Press.

King, Robert G., and Mark W. Watson. 1997. Testing Long-Run Neutrality. Federal Reserve Bank of Richmond, *Economic Quarterly* 83 (3): 69–101.

Koustas, Zisimos, and Apostolos Serletis. 1999. On the Fisher Effect. *Journal of Monetary Economics* 44 (1): 105–130.

Lucas, Robert E., Jr. 1996. Nobel Lecture: Monetary Neutrality. *Journal of Political Economy* 104 (4): 661–682.

McCandless, George T., Jr., and Warren E. Weber. 1995. Some Monetary Facts. Federal Reserve Bank of Minneapolis, *Quarterly Review* 19 (3): 2-11.

Serletis, Apostolos, and Zisimos Koustas. 1998. International Evidence on the Neutrality of Money. *Journal of Money, Credit, and Banking* 30 (1): 1–25.

Serletis, Apostolos, and Zisimos Koustas. 2001. Monetary Aggregation and the Neutrality of Money. *Economic Inquiry* 39 (1): 124–138.

Sidrauski, Miguel. 1967. Rational Choice and Patterns of Growth in a Monetary Economy. *American Economic Review* 57 (2): 534–544.

Tobin, James. 1965. Money and Economic Growth. *Econometrica* 33 (4): 671–684.

Apostolos Serletis

NEW CLASS, THE

The New Class is a term made popular by Milovan Djilas's book *The New Class* (1957), which describes the privileged ruling group of top government bureaucrats and party functionaries that typically arises in all Stalinist "party-states." The idea of a new technocratic and non-proletarian ruling class in Communist societies has been used to criticize the centralized social-welfare state of Soviet-type socialism. But it is also linked to the notion that a new influential class of skilled intellectuals, technocrats, and managers has emerged in modern capitalist societies to reshape the traditional class conflict between capital and labor, as well as to the proposition that the rise of such a technocratic-managerial class signals the emergence of a new, post-capitalist social order.

In the first half of the twentieth century, neo-Marxist theories of a new social stratum of managers, engineers, and other technocrats—sometimes called the "intellectual proletariat"—became popular among left-wing intellectuals, especially in Western Europe. In his famous novel *Nineteen Eighty-Four*, George Orwell predicted that this new social stratum "would control this world.… The new aristocracy was made up for the most part of bureaucrats, scientists, technicians, trade-union organizers, publicity experts, sociologists, teachers, journalists, and professional politicians" (1984, p. 169). Anarchists, anarcho-syndicalists, Left Communists, Trotskyists, and other leftist critics of Soviet-style socialism associated this technocratic meaning of the term with the "new class" of top government and party bureaucrats, industrial managers, professional propagandists, and so forth, that had emerged to dominate the Soviet Union under Stalin's system of state capitalism.

A very similar notion of a new ruling class was advanced by Milovan Djilas (1911–1995), a dissident politician in post–World War II (1939–1945) Yugoslavia. Djilas was purged from the Communist hierarchy in 1954 for advocating democratic and egalitarian ideals, which he believed permeated the original theories of Marxism, socialism, and communism, but ran counter to the dominant Stalinist dogma and practice of his day. Djilas observed that the leading government and party officials in all Stalinist regimes assumed the role of a new ruling class—a heretical idea that was at variance with the ideological claims of the governing Communists, who argued that the Communist revolution had resulted in the extinction of the dominant capitalist class and its replacement by the "dictatorship of the proletariat." He claimed that the new class exercised collective political control over the means of production as a new form of "monopoly ownership," which allowed capitalist-style relations of inequality, domination, and exploitation to persist even in the absence of a hegemonic capitalist class and its private ownership of economic production. Djilas's "new class" thus overlaps with the so-called "*nomenklatura* class," a term used in other critical descriptions of the governing bureaucracy in the Soviet Union (see Voslensky 1984).

A somewhat similar claim has been made about the "three-way polarization" of advanced capitalist societies between the capitalist class of private corporate owners, the working class, and an influential "new class" of college-trained technocrats, which Barbara and John Ehrenreich called the "Professional-Managerial Class" (PMC). This wage-earning technocratic class is generally hostile to the capitalist socioeconomic order over the issue of private ownership and control of the means of production, as well as over the unequal and unfair distribution of the fruits of material production. This anticapitalist hostility has turned the PMC into "an enduring reservoir of radicalism"—from Progressivism and the Socialist Party to the New Left (Ehrenreich and Ehrenreich 1979, p. 42). But there are also tensions with the blue-collar workforce due in part to the interest of the highly educated "new class" in extending its cultural and technological hegemony over the working classes. Their mutual antagonism has been "over the issues of knowledge, skills, culture" (Ehrenreich and Ehrenreich 1979, p. 45)—that is, over the PMC's elitism and patronizing attitude vis-à-vis working-class people. Without the pivotal assistance of the PMC, however, the ruling capitalists cannot effectively dominate the working classes, nor can the latter resist being controlled and exploited by the capitalist class.

In *The Future of Intellectuals and the Rise of the New Class* (1979), neo-Marxist sociologist Alvin Gouldner similarly challenged the central political and theoretical premise of Marxism—namely, the historical class conflict between the bourgeoisie and the proletariat—by claiming that a "New Class" has emerged under modern capitalism, comprising intellectuals, managers, and the technical intelligentsia. The New Class is not a ruling class yet and is also internally riven by important tensions between the technical intelligentsia and the humanistic intellectuals. But as an embryonic new "universal class," these bearers of specialized knowledge are the best hope for social progress in contemporary capitalist societies given the historical failure of the traditional working class (or the "industrial proletariat") to bring about a social revolution and progressive change. A basic strategy of the New Class is to cultivate an alliance with the mass working class in order to undermine and supplant the ruling capitalists and their hegemonic position in the old social order.

In like manner, Robert Reich (who served as secretary of labor under President Bill Clinton) has suggested the idea of a new class consisting of what he calls "symbolic analysts"—engineers, attorneys, scientists, university professors, business executives, journalists, consultants, and other "knowledge workers," who engage in processing information and manipulating symbols for a living. These well-educated individuals occupy a privileged position in society because they can sell their valued professional services in the global economy. According to Reich,

> Symbolic analysts solve, identify, and broker problems by manipulating symbols. They simplify reality into abstract images that can be rearranged, juggled, experimented with, communicated to other specialists, and then, eventually, transformed back into reality. The manipulations are done with analytic tools, sharpened by experience. These tools may be mathematical algorithms, legal arguments, financial gimmicks, scientific principles, psychological insights about how to persuade or to amuse, systems of induction or deduction, or any other set of techniques for doing conceptual puzzles. (1991, p. 178)

Given the worldwide drift toward "laissez-faire cosmopolitism," Reich believes that only "symbolic analysts"—because of their more advantageous position in the globalized economy—can be confident of being the "winners" of twenty-first-century capitalism.

SEE ALSO *Anarchism; Bahro, Rudolf; Bourgeoisie, Petty; Bureaucracy; Bureaucrat; Capitalism, State; Class; Communism; Credentialism; Democracy; Egalitarianism; Elite Theory; Left Wing; Managerial Class; Marxism; Meritocracy; Middle Class; Oligarchy; Power Elite; Professionalization; Socialism; Stalin, Joseph; Stalinism; Syndicalism; Totalitarianism; Trotsky, Leon; Union of Soviet Socialist Republics*

BIBLIOGRAPHY

Djilas, Milovan. 1957. *The New Class: An Analysis of the Communist System.* New York: Praeger.

Ehrenreich, Barbara, and John Ehrenreich. 1979. The Professional-Managerial Class. In *Between Labour and Capital*, ed. Pat Walker, 5–45. Brighton, U.K.: Harvester Press.

Gouldner, Alvin W. 1979. *The Future of Intellectuals and the Rise of the New Class: A Frame of Reference, Theses, Conjectures, Arguments, and an Historical Perspective on the Role of Intellectuals and Intelligentsia in the International Class Contest of the Modern Era.* New York: Seabury Press.

Orwell, George. 1949. *Nineteen Eighty-Four.* New York: Penguin, 1984.

Reich, Robert B. 1991. *The Work of Nations: Preparing Ourselves for 21st-Century Capitalism.* New York: Knopf.

Voslensky, Michael. 1984. *Nomenklatura: The Soviet Ruling Class.* Trans. Eric Mosbacher. Garden City, NY: Doubleday.

Rossen Vassilev

NEW DEAL, THE

The term *New Deal* refers collectively to the sweeping economic reforms and government programs pushed by President Franklin D. Roosevelt and enacted by Congress to combat the Great Depression and relieve its impacts on wide swaths of American society. The New Deal comprised two major waves of reforms: the First New Deal (1933–1934) and the Second New Deal (1935–1936). The First New Deal was more experimental and focused on relief efforts; the Second New Deal was more focused on class conflict. Together, they permanently changed the relationship between government and business and promoted government as an agent of the common good, a role not widely accepted before 1933. The New Deal also fundamentally reorganized the contours of American politics, erasing Republican dominance and creating a majority coalition for the Democratic Party that would last a generation.

1929–1933: THE STOCK MARKET CRASH, THE DEPRESSION, AND THE HUMAN TOLL

The 1928 election produced victory for Herbert Hoover and his Republican Party—the party's third presidential election win in a row. Hoover's first year in office, 1929, saw continued economic prosperity for the business and manufacturing sectors of the economy—but distress for the agricultural economy. The October 1929 stock market collapse brought the prosperous era of the 1920s to a crashing end and raised doubts about Republican claims of being "the party of prosperity." As eminent New Deal historian William E. Leuchtenburg notes:

> In the three years of Herbert Hoover's presidency, the bottom had dropped out of the stock market and industrial production had been cut more than half.... [S]teel plants were operating at a sickening 12 percent of capacity, with "an almost complete lack" of signs of a turn for the better. In three years, industrial construction had slumped from $949 million to an unbelievable $74 million.... By 1932, the unemployed numbered upward of 13 million. Many lived in the primitive conditions of a preindustrial society stricken by famine. In the coal fields of West Virginia and Kentucky, evicted families shivered in tents in midwinter; children went barefoot. In Los Angeles, people whose gas and electricity had been turned off were reduced to cooking over wood fires in back lots. (Leuchtenburg 1963, p. 1)

Leuchtenburg's account further documents the massive human toll of the Depression: famished children; at least one million men wandering the country in an often fruitless search for work; "Hoovervilles," or large settlements of makeshift shacks of boxes and scrap metal, housing hundreds or more in many American cities; children kept out of school because they had nothing to wear. Conditions in rural America were also desperate owing to falling crop prices and a breakdown of transportation networks for farm products. Farm foreclosures and evictions of farm families were widespread. As Leuchtenburg notes (1963, pp. 23–24):

> As farm income dipped sharply while taxes and mortgage obligations remained constant, thousands of farmers lost their land for failure to pay taxes or meet payments.... [O]n a single day in April 1932, one-fourth of the entire area of the state of Mississippi went under the hammer of auctioneers.

By early 1933, unemployment reached 25 percent, with fifteen million out of work. Five thousand banks had folded, wiping out nine million savings accounts. The venerable U.S. Steel Corporation saw its full-time workforce collapse from 229,000 in 1929 to 0 in 1933.

Presidential elections are often, in part, a referendum on the national economy. The 1932 election was very much so, creating conditions ripe for a Democratic victory—a rarity during the Republican-dominated era since 1896. In November 1932, Herbert Hoover was defeated decisively, and Democrats gained a Senate majority as well, after already having won a House majority in the 1930 congressional elections. Franklin D. Roosevelt would begin his first term working with sizable Democratic majorities in both houses of Congress.

1933–1934: THE FIRST NEW DEAL

Roosevelt entered office March 4, 1933, at a time of almost wartime crisis. The collapse of banks and the rush of depositors had prompted bank holidays nationwide. The first priority was a banking bill to reopen the banks. During Roosevelt's first 100 days in office, Congress passed fifteen major pieces of legislation, including what some critics derided as an "alphabet soup" of new government agencies and programs. The First New Deal was pragmatic: It met demands from and benefited many sectors of society, such as bank depositors, bankers, farmers, opponents of Prohibition, the unemployed, organized labor, and business interests. The most important legislation was the business-supported National Industrial Recovery Act (NIRA, 1933), which authorized companies to form cartels and created provisions for the president to regulate businesses to promote fair competition, raise prices and wages, and create jobs for the unemployed. NIRA also included the first federal minimum wage and maximum workweek, which remain today. Though struck down by the Supreme Court in 1935, NIRA's provisions

for collective bargaining were reinstated in the Wagner Act (1935).

The First New Deal also offered something for farmers: the Agricultural Adjustment Act (AAA, 1933). This program provided federal subsidies to farmers to leave some of their land idle. The effect was to reduce crop surpluses and raise crop prices, ultimately providing greater economic stability for farmers. Since the agricultural season was already under way in May 1933, the program began with the controversial large-scale destruction of crops and slaughter of livestock, overseen by the Agricultural Adjustment Administration. Some southern farmers were asked to plow under one-fourth of their cotton crop, again to raise prices. Federal farm programs in the mid-2000s still embodied the AAA's underlying principle of preventing crop overproduction that can cause severe price drops.

Given the rash of bank failures in early 1933, protecting bank deposits from being wiped out was a major priority. The First New Deal, then, included creation of the Federal Deposit Insurance Corporation (FDIC), a federal agency that guarantees checking and savings deposits in the event a bank folds. The FDIC remained in place into the twenty-first century, insuring deposits up to $100,000.

To provide large-scale relief to the unemployed, the First New Deal also included the Public Works Administration (PWA), an agency that contracted with private firms for, and funded, construction of large public projects such as airports, bridges, hospitals, schools, streets, and highways. The PWA encouraged contractors to hire the unemployed. Another work relief program was the Civilian Conservation Corps (CCC), which put young men to work planting trees, building trails and logging roads, erecting fences, raising telephone and power lines, and completing projects to prevent soil erosion. Similarly, a government corporation, the Tennessee Valley Authority (TVA), was established to provide flood control, economic development, and hydroelectric power to many of the southern states—a largely agricultural and impoverished region at the time. Congress also repealed Prohibition in 1933.

1935–1936: THE SECOND NEW DEAL

The 1934 congressional elections strengthened Democratic control of Congress, providing Roosevelt with additional political capital to pursue further reforms. The Second New Deal, more openly prolabor and antibusiness than the First New Deal had been, fostered more class conflict. The Second New Deal included three major legislative acts: the Social Security Act, the National Labor Relations Act (Wagner Act), and the Works

Progress Administration. The first two of these remain today.

The Social Security Act (1935) created a social insurance program, funded through a payroll tax paid by workers and employers alike. The program provides benefit payments for retirement, disability, death (i.e., for widows and survivors), and unemployment. Social Security established the framework for the social welfare state in the United States and provided philosophical support for the Great Society programs in the 1960s.

The National Labor Relations Act (Wagner Act, 1935) was passed following a wave of tumultuous strikes in major cities, as well as years of labor unrest in southern textile mills, including a massive general strike in 1934. The act established workers' right to collectively bargain with employers—that is, to establish and join labor unions. The Wagner Act granted workers the right to strike, declared certain employer actions as prohibited "unfair labor practices," and established procedures for lodging complaints and determining whether or not workers wish to join a union. Later, Congress amended the Wagner Act to extend the prohibition against unfair labor practices to unions.

The Works Progress Administration (WPA, 1935) was a federal program to provide jobs and income for the unemployed. Although most jobs provided construction work, the WPA included programs for writers, artists, and musicians and provided some work for women as well. A component program, the National Youth Administration, provided job training and employment for teenagers. The WPA was disbanded in 1943 during World War II, an era of nearly full employment. The Rural Electrification Administration (REA) provided electricity to remote and rural areas, especially in the more agriculture-dominated South and Plains states.

Overall, the New Deal overturned, for most Americans, prevailing notions of limited government and laissez-faire economic policies by creating government programs and agencies on an unprecedented scale. New Deal defenders argued that new rules, and a vast expansion in the size and scope of the federal government, were necessary to address an economic crisis and attendant human misery that were equally unprecedented.

DEBATES SURROUNDING THE NEW DEAL

The New Deal did have its critics, particularly because it represented a massive change in prevailing ideas of limited government, minimal regulation of business, and emphasis on state, local, and private charity for the needy. Before and during the 1920s, the "old economic order" of most wealthy Americans, financiers, industrialists, and railroad and banking interests, among others, allied with the probusiness Republican Party and argued against major government relief efforts to combat poverty and unemployment. Government relief was thought to reward laziness and discourage individual initiative. Before 1933, the prevailing philosophy of Social Darwinism held that wealth indicated virtue (hard work, initiative, and energy), and poverty indicated moral failings (lack of thrift, laziness, or both)—both individual characteristics, not remediable by government action. The "old order" also resisted government regulation, including the Wagner Act, fearing that government was openly siding against businesses and with workers in labor disputes. Before 1933, federal government policy also often reflected Social Darwinist thinking: Business regulation was limited, government was small in size, agencies were few in number, and preferred policies emphasized free markets and a hands-off, laissez-faire government that should not hinder market competition. (However, earlier Progressive-era reforms included a ban on child labor, food and drug safety laws, and prohibited direct corporate contributions to federal election campaigns.)

Ideological opposition to the New Deal, then, derived from prevailing notions of the proper relationship between government and business. New Deal advocates responded by noting the massive human costs of the depression, coupled with a conviction that the old rules could no longer work. One analysis, by A. A. Berle Jr., notes the rise of large economic organizations (corporations) that could, absent government restraint, use their economies of scale to squeeze out competition. According to Berle:

> The old economic forces do still work and they do produce a[n economic] balance after a while. But they take so long to do it and they crush so many men in the process that the strain on the social system becomes intolerable. Leaving economic forces to work themselves out as they stand will produce an economic balance, but in the course of it you may have half the entire country begging in the streets or starving to death.

> The New Deal [is] a recognition of the fact that human beings cannot indefinitely be sacrificed by millions to the operation of economic forces … [producing a] shocking toll on life and health and happiness. (Berle 1933, pp. 4–9, 19)

Berle summarizes the New Deal as an effort to "counterbalance the effects of organization gone wrong, to make sure the burdens of readjustment are equitably distributed, and that no group of individuals will be ground to powder in order to satisfy the needs of an economic balance." Historical accounts, too, often characterize the New Deal as an effort to restore balance to the economic system. Leuchtenburg (1963) characterizes New Deal theorists as seekers of balance: "the best society was one in which no important element held preponderant power" (p. 35) But New Dealers were especially worried about the "disproportionate power wielded by business in comparison to that possessed by agriculture" (p. 35). In addition, as the labor unrest of the 1920s and 1930s showed, the imbalance between the political and economic power of business versus that of organized labor was also a concern. This informed the Wagner Act (1935) and its provisions guaranteeing rights for workers seeking to organize or join a union.

While not the focus of much philosophical debate, one additional innovation of the New Deal era is noteworthy: the major infusion of scientific and academic experts into government. Roosevelt relied heavily on a "brain trust" of professors, including Raymond Moley, Rexford Tugwell, Harold Ickes, and other experts in formulating and justifying New Deal policies and in serving in senior cabinet positions. The emphasis on scientists and experts in government was a novelty at the time but rested on then-emerging doctrines of "neutral competence" in public administration.

THE NEW DEAL'S LEGACY AND IMPACTS

It is not clear whether New Deal policies "lifted" the nation out of the Great Depression, but the political impacts are clearer. It both reorganized the relationship between federal and state governments and triggered a political realignment that made the Democratic Party the majority party in American politics for a generation.

Economic Impacts of the New Deal Economically, the country hit "rock bottom" in March 1933, when the banking crisis had brought the financial system to the brink of collapse, even shutting down Wall Street and the Chicago Board of Trade by Roosevelt's Inauguration Day. Economic indicators tended to recover from mid-1933 to 1937, but then a second recession hit, worsening conditions again. Full economic recovery would wait until the United States entered World War II in 1941. In other respects, the New Deal did fundamentally transform the economic system. The New Deal swept away the "old economic order" of business domination over government policy and minimal government intervention in economics and business. The New Deal's critics feared the United States was moving toward a socially engineered economy, with some comparisons to communist planned economies appearing. New Deal supporters, however, argued that the new rules meant that government would not dominate the economic system but only become a partner with business, agriculture, and labor in fostering economic growth and prosperity. What

is certain is that the New Deal era institutionalized expectations of more active government intervention in the economy than was previously considered tolerable. Although some individual New Deal programs (NIRA, CCC, WPA) no longer exist, some others do (Social Security, FDIC, the National Labor Relations Act, the minimum wage). The notion that government properly is a partner in promoting economic health and growth is now widely accepted, and a return to strictly laissez-faire economic policy is effectively outside the boundaries of political acceptability. Likewise, the notion that government should shrug off assistance or protection to most of society's most vulnerable members was discredited during the New Deal era, resulting in Social Security.

Minimal Impacts: The New Deal and American Blacks
However, New Deal advocates did not always extend the philosophy of aiding the disadvantaged to one especially vulnerable group: black Americans. The New Deal had very little to offer blacks, considering the widespread racism, forced segregation, and discrimination and denial of voting rights they faced around the country, but especially in the South, where most blacks lived. For example, the New Deal encouraged the formation of labor unions, but most unions refused to admit blacks. New Deal programs benefited farmers and the jobless, but their benefits focused on the white jobless; racial discrimination in employment sometimes meant blacks would benefit little from jobs programs. Furthermore, Roosevelt refused to support both federal antilynching legislation and racially egalitarian voting laws. Thus, the New Deal left the festering problems of civil rights and rampant racial discrimination, especially in the South, virtually untouched. As nearly all white southerners were a key, and thoroughly racist, component of the Democratic majority coalition, any effort to push the Democratic Party toward favoring civil rights for blacks would certainly prompt a furious backlash. Later events, such as the Dixiecrat walkout at the 1948 Democratic Party's national convention and the white southern backlash to President Lyndon Johnson's support for civil rights laws in 1964–1965, showed how readily fears of white southern backlash would become reality. Given the New Deal's near total failure to address the desperate circumstances facing southern blacks (then comprising a large majority of blacks nationwide), the transformation of blacks into a solidly Democratic voting bloc during the 1930s seems puzzling.

Historian Nancy Weiss (1983) focuses on the economic benefits the New Deal provided to lower-income Americans, regardless of race. Her analysis indicates that despite Roosevelt's poor record on racial issues and the glaring racial inequalities built into the administration of many New Deal programs, blacks still perceived the Roosevelt administration as more friendly to their interests than any since that of Ulysses S. Grant (1869–1877). Another historian, Patricia Sullivan (1996), studied the rise and fall of a liberal movement in the South, the nation's most racially repressive region. She concluded that while a southern liberal movement, centered in the Popular Front, flowered in the 1930s and 1940s, it eventually collapsed by 1950 under the combination of racist and anti-Communist ideologies. The southern Popular Front movement, which attracted both black and white support, coincided with the growing visibility of a notably racially progressive wing of the Democratic Party, as historian David L. Chappell notes in reviewing Sullivan's work (1999). In the Roosevelt administration, the liberals were represented by Interior Secretary Harold Ickes, National Youth Administration director Aubrey Williams, and First Lady Eleanor Roosevelt, among others. While the liberals' impact on national racial policies was limited, they did provide hope and a sense of having "friends in high places" to millions of black Americans.

In short, explanations of why blacks moved into the Democratic Party vary. Weiss's account focuses on the New Deal's economic benefits for the poor, white and black, while Sullivan's account focuses on a bond of emotional solidarity between many blacks and the Democratic Party. The 1936 election made clear that black partisan loyalties had shifted from majority Republican to majority Democratic. During the civil rights era (1960–1968), the national Democratic Party's strong embrace of federal civil rights laws further cemented this alliance. Since 1964, blacks have been the most overwhelmingly Democratic voting bloc in American politics.

Political Impacts of the New Deal Politically, the New Deal had two major impacts: a reorientation of the proper relationship between the national and state governments and a political realignment that established the Democratic Party as the new majority party in national politics.

The New Deal changed the relationship between the national and state governments. Before 1933, the system of "dual federalism" prevailed; the national government was responsible for defense, currency, and post offices, for example. The state governments were responsible for education, social welfare, law enforcement, voting, and elections, among other things. Under dual federalism, the federal government provided little financial assistance to the states. And the policy spheres of the federal and state governments were generally separate and distinct.

The New Deal's programs meant the federal government would assume a much greater role in social welfare and economic regulation than it had previously. The PWA and other works programs marked a dramatic increase in federal aid to the states. Future programs would be based

on this new philosophy: that the federal government should financially assist states and communities. Thus, the size and scope of the federal government grew dramatically, and the federal government would provide assistance to the poor and unemployed.

In partisan politics, the effects of the New Deal were profound. In many Americans' minds, the Great Depression had destroyed the Republican Party's credibility as being the "party of prosperity." While President Herbert Hoover had taken some steps to combat the economic crisis, other actions fostered impressions that Hoover little understood the human costs of the Depression or was actively callous to human suffering. In 1932, Hoover deployed soldiers to evict an encampment on the outskirts of Washington, D.C., of "bonus marchers"—World War I veterans seeking payment of long-delayed war pensions. The images and news reports of troops rousting nonviolent squatters from the Anacostia Flats, forcing them out of their shacks at gunpoint, and burning the settlements to the ground incensed many Americans. This action was probably a major contributor to Hoover's defeat that fall. Roosevelt had offered few specifics during the 1932 campaign but displayed pragmatism and a willingness to experiment once in office. The New Deal was not initially conceived as an ideological program; it was an effort to "try out" potential solutions to the crisis.

That said, Roosevelt also projected a very appealing public persona. Although he had been stricken with polio in 1921, his disability was usually not visible to the public because television did not yet exist. Roosevelt excelled in communicating with Americans by radio. In the first of his "fireside chats," or radio addresses, Roosevelt set out to calm public fears: "The only thing we have to fear is fear itself." During his first 100 days in office, Roosevelt persuaded Congress to approve fifteen major pieces of legislation—a feat unprecedented at the time and never duplicated since.

Therefore, Roosevelt hardly needed to convince Americans that he was taking concerted action in a time of economic crisis. Roosevelt excelled at soothing Americans' fears and convincing them he understood their concerns and trials.

While Roosevelt's persona endeared him to many, his New Deal programs fundamentally realigned American politics, largely along social-class lines and in the Democratic Party's favor. In 1934, Democrats gained more congressional seats; it is unusual in a midterm election for the president's party to gain strength in Congress. In 1936, Roosevelt won a landslide reelection over Republican Alf Landon, winning 61 percent of the popular vote and carrying every state except New Hampshire and Maine. Although Democratic strength in Congress would drop sharply after the 1938 midterm election, Roosevelt won four consecutive terms as president (in the elections of 1932, 1936, 1940, and 1944). In April 1945, Roosevelt died, and his vice president, Harry S. Truman, became president. The strength of Roosevelt's political coalition was apparent even in 1948, when Truman, defying virtually all predictions, defeated Republican Thomas Dewey, extending Democratic control of the presidency to five consecutive terms (twenty years). Not until 1952 would a Republican again win the White House. Democrats also controlled Congress continuously from 1932 to 1946, with huge Democratic majorities after the 1934 and 1936 elections. Republicans, the dominant party from 1896 to 1932, were now the clear minority party in American politics and would remain so until 1968.

Roosevelt's "New Deal coalition" consisted of three major groups of voters: white southerners, urban ethnics and immigrants, and working-class Americans. White southerners had long-standing loyalties to the Democratic Party and hostility toward the Republican Party, both dating from the Civil War and Reconstruction eras. Urban ethnics and immigrants, many of them Catholic, swung decisively toward the Democratic Party between 1928 and 1936, partly because of anti-Catholic sentiments apparent in some elements of the Republican Party, partly because "white ethnic" groups such as Polish, Irish, German, and Italian Americans tended to reside in cities where largely Democratic political machines held sway, exchanging favorable votes for city jobs or other favors, and partly because their communities gained valuable public works projects from the PWA and other programs. Also, many white ethnics were also members of labor unions or worked in blue-collar jobs, making Social Security, jobs programs, and federal labor protections attractive policies. Finally, working-class Americans were strongly attracted by Roosevelt's public criticisms of financiers and corporate executives and by his policies that supported organized labor, minimum wages, maximum hours, and jobs programs for the unemployed. A major political effect of the New Deal, then, was to position Democrats as a party friendly to working-class Americans and committed to fairness for many (but rarely for blacks): jobs for the unemployed, decent wages and working conditions, the right to organize collectively, and benefits for vulnerable Americans such as the elderly and disabled. Blacks also supported Democratic candidates when and where they could vote—but most blacks lived in the South, where they faced brutal repression and near total voting discrimination in much of the region.

Meanwhile, Democrats portrayed Republicans as a party of and for the richest Americans, bent on canceling or cutting New Deal programs and reverting to laissez-faire economic policies. During the 1936 election, voting was very strongly structured along social class lines:

Republicans won majorities of the vote among the wealthiest Americans, but Democrats won lopsidedly among those with lower incomes—and in 1936, there were many more lower-income than higher-income Americans. Political scientists James Sundquist (1983) and Walter Dean Burnham (1970) both identify the 1932–1936 period as a "critical" or realigning period in American politics, in which a previous Republican majority was replaced by a Democratic majority.

Overall, the New Deal fundamentally changed the relationship between government and business in the United States, from minimal regulation to selective regulation; expanded the federal role in assisting people buffeted by economic forces beyond their control, and wrought a new era of Democratic Party dominance in national politics. The New Deal era brought great challenges and great changes to the political and economic systems, along with many new government programs to face those challenges.

SEE ALSO *Banking; Business Cycles, Real; Democratic Party, U.S.; Economic Crises; Economics, Keynesian; Federalism; Great Depression; Inequality, Racial; Politics; Politics, Black; Politics, Southern; Racism; Republican Party; Roosevelt, Franklin D.; Social Welfare Functions; Supreme Court, U.S.; Welfare State*

BIBLIOGRAPHY

Berle, A. A., Jr. 1933. The Social Economics of the New Deal. *New York Times Magazine*, October 29, pp. 4–9, 19.

Burnham, Walter Dean. 1970. *Critical Elections and the Mainsprings of American Politics.* New York: Norton.

Chappell, David L. 1999. Review of *Days of Hope: Race and Democracy in the New Deal Era*, by Patricia Sullivan. *African American Review* 33 (1): 149–151.

Leuchtenburg, William E. 1963. *Franklin D. Roosevelt and the New Deal, 1932–1940.* New York: Harper and Row.

Sullivan, Patricia. 1996. *Days of Hope: Race and Democracy in the New Deal Era.* Chapel Hill: University of North Carolina Press.

Sundquist, James L. 1983. *Dynamics of the Party System: Alignment and Realignment of Political Parties in the United States.* Rev ed. Washington, DC: Brookings Institution.

Weir, Margaret. 2005. States, Race, and the Decline of New Deal Liberalism. *Studies in American Political Development* 19: 157–172.

Weiss, Nancy J. 1983. *Farewell to the Party of Lincoln: Black Politics in the Age of FDR.* Princeton, NJ: Princeton University Press.

Fred Slocum

NEW IMMIGRANT SURVEY

The *New Immigrant Survey* (NIS) is a new plan for nationally representative, longitudinal studies of immigrants to the United States and their children that promises to provide new kinds of data that will help answer many of the important questions about migration and its impacts and also shed light on fundamental aspects of human development. The basic design calls for taking representative samples of cohorts of new legal immigrants and following them over time, with new cohorts selected every four or five years or whenever developments in U.S. immigration policy or conditions worldwide warrant. The sampling frame for each cohort is based on the electronic administrative records compiled for new immigrants by the U.S. government, formerly through the U.S. Immigration and Naturalization Service (INS) and now through its successor agencies, the U.S. Citizenship and Immigration Services (USCIS) and the Office of Immigration Statistics (OIS). It consists of all adult immigrants admitted to legal permanent residence during a specified period and two types of child immigrants who would not, or might not, be found in the households of adult immigrants. The sampling frame thus includes both new-arrival immigrants—immigrants arriving in the United States with immigrant documents acquired abroad—and adjustee immigrants—immigrants who are already in the United States with a temporary nonimmigrant visa (or, in some cases, illegally) and adjust to lawful permanent residence.

Interviews are conducted with sampled adult immigrants and their spouses and with the sponsor-parents of sampled child immigrants and the spouses of the sponsor-parents; sampled children and other children (both foreign-born and U.S.-born children) in the households of both sampled adult and child immigrants are interviewed or given assessments based on an age-eligibility schedule. Two key elements of the design are that interviews for the baseline round are conducted as soon as possible after admission to legal permanent residence and that respondents are interviewed in the language of their choice (e.g., eighty-six languages were used in the baseline round of the first full cohort, NIS-2003).

Information obtained in the interviews covers a wide range of topics, including health, schooling, marriage and family, skills, languages and English-language skills, labor force participation, earnings, financial help given to and received from relatives and friends, use of government services, networks, travel, and religion. In successive rounds, the instruments will track changes over time. A large component of the NIS survey instruments is comparable to instruments used in the major U.S. longitudinal surveys, thus facilitating comparisons of immigrants and the native born. Special attention is paid to immigrant children and the children of immigrants, including assessment of their academic abilities, skills, and achievements. As well the instruments seek immigrants' ideas about the migration and incorporation process, including assessment of the helpfulness of various sources of information.

New rounds of data collection will be conducted regularly for each cohort. The design calls for reinterview every three to five years (e.g., round 2 of NIS-2003 was in the field in 2007).

The design of the New Immigrant Survey was sharpened in discussions among immigration researchers and policy makers over a period of many years. Successive panels and workshops in both the public and private sectors developed the idea of a multiple-cohort, longitudinal survey of immigrants and their children, obtaining both retrospective and prospective data and including child assessments as well as information on extended family members. Because the NIS design, based on sampling named individuals from administrative records, with its attendant challenges of locating the immigrant and providing instruments and interviewers in several languages, had never been tried before, a pilot—the NIS-P—was carried out in 1996. The pilot both confirmed the soundness of the design, highlighted the importance of contacting sampled immigrants as soon as possible after admission to permanent residence, and provided new information on immigrants never before available (Jasso, Massey, Rosenzweig, and Smith 2000a, 2000b, 2003).

Both the pilot (NIS-P) and the first full cohort (NIS-2003, rounds 1 and 2) were investigator-initiated projects submitted to the National Institutes of Health (NIH) for support and were peer reviewed. Principal investigators are Guillermina Jasso, Douglas S. Massey, Mark R. Rosenzweig, and James P. Smith. Support has been provided by NIH, via the National Institute for Child Health and Human Development (NICHD) and the National Institute on Aging (NIA), the National Science Foundation (NSF), and the INS and its successor agency USCIS. Additional support for NIS-2003 has been provided by the assistant secretary for planning and evaluation (ASPE) in the Department of Health and Human Services and by the Pew Charitable Trusts. The data are available for public use at http://nis.princeton.edu. A growing number of researchers worldwide are using the data (approximately 700 as of April 2007).

New data—and the possibility of further new data—are a catalyst for scientific imagination. Thus not only is there a reinvigorated and rigorous attack on the classical questions about immigration (e.g., selectivity and skill transferability) and incorporation (e.g., emigration, naturalization, and language acquisition) but also new themes are emerging. These include (1) a deeper exploration of the migration process, including lost documents and visa stress and their aftermath; (2) the physical and social effects of illegality; (3) the transition to English, a dynamic and democratic language; (4) shedding the habits of illegality; (5) shedding the habits of elitism; (6) a richer understanding of health changes, taking into account the separate effects of visa stress, migration stress, and the physical and social environment; and (7) the impacts of immigration on the American stratification structure.

For example, it will be possible to assess the effects of immigration on economic inequality (via the inflow both of very low-skilled and very high-skilled individuals), on racial inequality (via the inflow of highly accomplished black African immigrants, which may overturn associations of skill with race and color and ensuing stereotypes), and on gender inequality (depending on the gender gap in skills among new immigrants and within new immigrant couples). As well in the years ahead it will be possible to gain new insight into the fabled phenomenon of "falling in love with English," as new immigrants and their children discover a language free of (grammatical) gender and formal-familiar distinctions (such as *tu-vous* in French) and limitlessly flexible. Future rounds of the New Immigrant Survey will provide a window into the twenty-first-century version of processes that built the United States, making it possible to learn how immigrants and natives increase the positive impacts of migration and mitigate its negative impacts.

SEE ALSO *Colorism; Immigration; Naturalization; Phenotype; Surveys, Sample*

BIBLIOGRAPHY

Jasso, Guillermina, Douglas S. Massey, Mark R. Rosenzweig, and James P. Smith. 2000a. Assortative Mating among Married New Legal Immigrants to the United States: Evidence from the New Immigrant Survey Pilot. *International Migration Review* 34 (2): 443–459.

Jasso, Guillermina, Douglas S. Massey, Mark R. Rosenzweig, and James P. Smith. 2000b. The New Immigrant Survey Pilot (NIS-P): Overview and New Findings about U.S. Legal Immigrants at Admission. *Demography* 37 (1): 127–138.

Jasso, Guillermina, Douglas S. Massey, Mark R. Rosenzweig, and James P. Smith. 2003. Exploring the Religious Preference of Recent Immigrants to the United States: Evidence from the New Immigrant Survey Pilot. In *Religion and Immigration: Christian, Jewish, and Muslim Experiences in the United States*, eds. Yvonne Yazbeck Haddad, Jane I. Smith, and John L. Esposito, 217–253. Walnut Creek, CA: AltaMira Press.

Guillermina Jasso

NEW INTERNATIONAL ECONOMIC ORDER
SEE *International Economic Order.*

NEW JEWEL MOVEMENT
SEE *Grenadian Revolution.*

NEW SCHOOL FOR SOCIAL RESEARCH

The *New School for Social Research* was founded in New York City in 1918 by a group of prominent Columbia University scholars—Charles A. Beard (1874–1948), James Harvey Robinson (1863–1936), Wesley C. Mitchell (1874–1948), and John Dewey (1859–1952), among others—in conjunction with a wider circle of dissident intellectuals, such as *New Republic* editor Herbert Croly (1869–1930) and iconoclastic economist Thorstein Veblen (1857–1929), who were dissatisfied with the state of the social sciences and academic freedom in the United States. With donations from well-wishers in liberal circles, the New School opened for classes in the spring of 1919 in a set of rented row houses in the Chelsea district of New York.

The founders envisaged an institution of higher learning simultaneously capable of serious independent research, accessible to the intelligent lay public, and engaged in progressive social and political reform. But the founders held distinct visions of how to apply this in practice. Disagreements led to a sharp crisis in 1922 that culminated in a spate of resignations that nearly ended the school. The reins fell into the lap of Alvin S. Johnson (1874–1971), a former academic economist and editor of the *New Republic*, who set the New School's focus on the "continued education of the educated," bringing in a host of leading lecturers from the social sciences, arts, and other fields. At a time when "adult education" was narrowly thought of as the teaching of basic education or technical skills, the advanced academic fare the New School offered was a novelty for the American public. By 1929 the New School was back on sound footing and moved to new facilities on 12th Street.

Johnson maintained the necessity of revitalizing the New School's roots as an academic research center and had launched the *Encyclopedia of the Social Sciences* in 1927 with this in mind. In April 1933, the Nazi Party began its purge of the German academia. Johnson, who was familiar with many of the scholars through the *Encyclopedia*, helped form a rescue committee to place the expelled academics in U.S.

universities. But the response from American institutions was lukewarm, so Johnson decided to have the New School host the scholars itself. It seemed natural: The Weberian emphasis in the German academic tradition on the unity of the social sciences and the willingness to engage the adult public and promote policy and reform echoed the philosophy of the New School's own creation. Working closely with the Berlin economist Emil Lederer (1882–1939), Johnson created the University in Exile, soon renamed the Graduate Faculty of Political and Social Science. The first wave of scholars assembled for the Graduate Faculty's opening in the fall of 1933 included the economists Eduard Heimann (1889–1967), Gerhard Colm (1897–1968), Karl Brandt (1899–1975), and Arthur Feiler (1879–1942); the sociologists Hans Speier (1905-1990) and Albert Salomon (1891–1966); the jurist Hermann Kantorowicz (1877–1940); and Gestalt psychologist Max Wertheimer (1880–1943). As the 1930s progressed, more displaced scholars found their way to the New School, including jurists Arnold Brecht (1884–1977) and Erich Hula (1900–1987); economists Hans Staundinger (1889–1980) and Fritz Lehmann; political scientists Hans Simons (1893–1972) and Max Ascoli (1898–1978); philosophers Felix Kaufmann (1895–1949), Alfred Schütz (1899–1959), and Leo Strauss (1899–1973); and Weimar dramatist Erwin Piscator (1893–1966).

The outbreak of World War II (1939–1945) prompted the New School and the Rockefeller Foundation to launch a vigorous, coordinated rescue plan to secure the immediate entry of a hundred European scholars into the United States, their permanent academic positions to be determined later. In all, it is estimated that between 1933 and 1945 the New School actively helped over 183 displaced European scholars and artists find their way to the United States (Krohn 1993).

The refugee scholars continued the continental tradition of interdisciplinary research, and a general seminar and journal, *Social Research*, were launched in 1934. The fall of France led to the formation of the École Libre des Hautes Études (free school of advanced studies), a French-language division of the New School chartered by Charles de Gaulle (1890–1970), which housed prominent French thinkers such as Jacques Maritain (1882–1973) and Claude Lévi-Strauss. The New School also transplanted virtually the entire Kiel school of economists—Adolph Löwe (1893–1995), Jacob Marschak (1898–1977), Hans Neisser (1895–1975), and Gerhard Colm. Their Weltwirtschaftsinstitut was recast under the New School as the Institute of World Affairs in 1941, and they resumed their distinct research program on structural growth, business cycles, and long-run economic policy.

This period also saw the gradual separation of the Graduate Faculty from the New School adult division. In 1943 the New School had been reorganized and undergraduate degree programs introduced. But increasing academic specialization in the 1950s meant that fewer Graduate Faculty professors were willing or able to cross the lines from research to adult education. So the New School adult division organized its own curriculum, offering lecture courses delivered by giants like Erich Fromm (1900–1980) and Karen Horney (1885–1952) in psychology, Sidney Hook (1902–1989) and Ernest Nagel (1901–1985) in philosophy, Margaret Mead (1901–1978) in anthropology, Max Lerner (1902–1992) in contemporary politics, Robert Frost (1874–1963) in literature, Seymour Lipton (1903–1986) in the plastic arts, and John Cage (1912–1992) in music. In 1962 the New School established the Institute for Retired Professionals, the first major effort by an institution of higher learning on behalf of senior students and, in 1964, the J. M. Kaplan Center for New York City Affairs, the first to focus on a single metropolitan area.

As the 1960s arrived, the Graduate Faculty struggled to transform itself into a regular American graduate school without losing the distinctiveness of its continental legacy. In psychology, Wertheimer's Gestalt program was upheld by the appointments of Solomon Asch (1907–1996), Rudolf Arnheim, and Mary Henle. In economics, the torch was passed from Löwe to Robert Heilbroner (1919–2005). The New School's philosophy department catapulted to distinctive prominence with the appointments of Aron Gurwitsch (1901–1973) and Hans Jonas (1903–1993) and, in 1967, Hannah Arendt (1906–1975), thereby cementing the school's continued emphasis on continental philosophy and theory.

In 1970 the New School acquired the Parsons School of Design (originally founded by painter William Merritt Chase [1849–1916] in 1896) and, in 1975, created a fourth academic division, the Milano School of Management and Urban Policy. In 1978 the New School established a full-time undergraduate liberal arts division, renamed Eugene Lang College in 1985. It established two music divisions, the School for Jazz and Contemporary Music (founded in 1986) and the Mannes College of Music (founded in 1916, acquired in 1989). In 1994 the Actor's Studio joined the New School to form a new master's program in theater, which laid the groundwork for the establishment of the New School for Drama in 2005.

The rapid expansion of the New School into areas beyond "social research" prompted a search for a new name consistent with its multiple divisions. The first rebranding attempt in 1995 yielded the unfortunate New School University. This was dropped in 2005 in favor of merely The New School, with the divisions renamed accordingly. Since 2005 the term New School for Social Research has been limited to the former Graduate Faculty.

BIBLIOGRAPHY

Coser, Lewis A. 1984. *Refugee Scholars in America: Their Impact and Their Experiences*. New Haven, CT: Yale University Press.

Fermi, Laura. 1971. *Illustrious Immigrants: The Intellectual Migration from Europe, 1930–41*. 2nd ed. Chicago: University of Chicago Press.

Johnson, Alvin S. 1952. *Pioneer's Progress: An Autobiography*. New York: Viking.

Krohn, Claus-Dieter. 1993. *Intellectuals in Exile: Refugee Scholars and the New School for Social Research*. Trans. Rita and Robert Kimber. Amherst: University of Massachusetts Press.

Rutkoff, Peter M., and William B. Scott. 1986. *New School: A History of the New School for Social Research*. New York: Free Press.

Gonçalo Fonseca

NEW SCHOOL UNIVERSITY

SEE *New School for Social Research.*

NEZ PERCE

SEE *Chief Joseph.*

NIAGARA MOVEMENT

SEE *Civil Rights Movement, U.S.*

NICENE CREED

SEE *Church, The.*

NICOTINE

SEE *Smoking.*

NIETZSCHE, FRIEDRICH
1844–1900

Friedrich Nietzsche was born into a family of Lutheran pastors but later repudiated the Christian faith. He entered Bonn University in 1864 as a theology and philology student. His interests turned more to the latter, concentrating on classical and biblical texts. He read David Strauss's skep-tical *Life of Jesus* (1835–1836), discovered Arthur Schopenhaur's atheistic philosophy, and became friends with Richard Wagner, leading to a stormy relationship.

Nietzsche became a professor in classical philology in Basel, Switzerland, in 1869. His university career lasted ten years. He resigned in 1879 for health reasons. His final decade of sanity produced his major works, including his attacks on Christianity, Wagner, traditional morality, and most aspects of the European philosophical tradition and its greatest icons, such as Socrates, Plato, and Immanuel Kant (strangely, he said little about Aristotle).

While he despised Christianity, Nietzsche admired Jesus himself, or at least the historical Jesus who, Nietzsche thought, the church had distorted. As a classical philologist he developed theories about the origin of tragedy (from music) and of ethics in ancient Greece. The latter led him to contrast Apollonian and Dionysian lifestyles, aristocratic and slave moralities, and life-affirming, ascending values versus life-denying, descending values. He shares with Max Weber the credit (or blame perhaps) for switching ethical discourse from virtues to values. Nietzsche went mad in 1889 and died in 1900.

NIHILISM, CHRISTIANITY, AND THE ÜBERMENSCH

Nietzsche's philosophy is mostly based on three components: his ontology, his theory of ethics, and his views on intellectual history. His ontology includes his best known saying, "God is dead"; truth is subjective; the will to power; and eternal recurrence. His ethics involve a preference for aristocratic values over slave morality, the Übermensch, and the claim that we create our values. Contrary to traditional religious and philosophical ideas, we do not discover them or receive them from God or nature, reason, conscience, intuition, or a moral sense. The last point leads to the problem of nihilism. *Nihilism* (from *nihil*, Latin for nothing) can be defined as consisting of three main components, atheism, moral skepticism, and the claim that life has no meaning.

From this one might conclude that therefore "anything goes." While Nietzsche clearly endorsed all three of the above, he is best classified as an aesthetic, amoral atheist. He did not accept the apparent corollary of nihilism that Fyodor Dostoyevsky (among others) claimed followed from its premises. Instead, it is our task to create or invent our own values and also to create the meaning of life for ourselves, a view repeated in the twentieth century by philosophers as diverse as Karl Popper and Jean-Paul Sartre.

Nietzsche's first book proposed an instinctual, amoral, Dionysian creative energy that has been submerged and repressed by an Apollonian force of logic and sobriety (an anticipation perhaps of subsequent work on the left brain versus the right brain). He rejected several ideas he saw as intrinsic to European philosophy, such as self-consciousness, free will, and either/or thinking. However, some may claim that his own thinking often exhibits either/or thinking: life-affirming or life-denying, ascending or descending, Apollonian or Dionysian, slave versus master morality.

Nietzsche certainly went counter to the main trends of both nineteenth-century and twentieth-century political thought, making it rather curious why so many left-wing thinkers were so enthused about him. He challenged the moral idea that exploitation, domination, injury to the weak, destruction, and appropriation are universally evil behaviors.

Nietzsche argued in *The Anti-Christ* (1895) that noble values in Roman society were corrupted by the rise of Christianity, and he discussed many of its main figures, concluding that Christianity is a religion for the weak and unhealthy whose effect has been to undermine the healthy qualities of more noble peoples. This is in striking contrast to Karl Marx's opposite argument (made by many leftist thinkers) that the real problem is that the church has taken the side of the powers that be, sanctifying their exploitation of the weak and vulnerable members of society.

Nietzsche's Übermensch idea can be misunderstood if it is taken in a collectivist rather than a radical individualist sense. It has been translated as both "superman" and "overman." The former is highly misleading and the latter unclear. The best term might seem to be "superior man." But this also is misleading. It is neither racist nor nationalist nor class nor genetically based. Nietzsche had ambiguous attitudes toward Charles Darwin and definitely was not a social Darwinist. It is arguable that everyone, or at least anyone, could be an Übermensch, a person who mastered her or his passions and became a creator rather than a creature. It is used basically as a this-worldly alternative to traditional piety.

Übermensch is related to both the weakest points in Nietzsche's philosophy, lack of systematic, logical argument, and the strongest point, his brilliant critique of egalitarianism, especially anarchism, socialism, and democracy. But again this must not be confused with later Nazi or other racial, anti-Semitic, nationalist, genetic based theories of group superiority. While it is unfair to see him as a precursor of National Socialism, he can be seen as a precursor of postmodernism and theories of social construction with their subjectivist theories of truth. In addition nothing in his theories seems to rule out racist, fascist, or even Communist ideologies (unlike Kant, utility, that is, all the theories he despises).

SCHOLARLY RESPONSES

Many Nietzsche scholars respond to criticism about the unsystematic and even contradictory nature of his ideas by claiming he was not propounding a system but proposing ideas and hypotheses. This would explain his method of aphorisms, bald assertions, and diatribes without argument and also why his twentieth-century appeal was to such a wide variety of literary and philosophical figures of differing views, from far right to far left. Many would say the same about Plato, who is also contentiously associated with twentieth-century totalitarian ideologies.

However, it can then still be asked, "If it is true that we invent our values then we invented the perverse one such as slave morality, human equality, Platonism. Thus, one can ask of preferences for affirming life versus denying life, why is the former preferable?" What is the basis for this other than Nietzsche's own opinions? Why cannot revenge, resentment, and hatred be noble under some circumstances if people create their own values? This is a problem not unique to Nietzsche because it rests on the fact-value distinction Weber and Nietzsche helped formulate.

There is also a question of the coherence of his critique of Christianity. In his ultimate critique of Christianity, *On the Genealogy of Morals* (1887), he argues that Christian morals have emerged from revenge, resentment, hatred, impotence, and cowardice. He may well be correct about this and claims that Paul or the church or someone else distorted the original message of Jesus, but perspectivism and subjectivism regarding truth rule out any argument that this is correct. Finally, it is arguable that his compatriot, Gottlob Frege, father of modern mathematical logic, had an effective critique of subjectivist theories of truth.

SEE ALSO *Atheism; Christianity; Epistemology; Ethics; Knowledge; Morality; Philosophy; Plato; Popper, Karl; Subjectivity: Overview; Weber, Max*

BIBLIOGRAPHY

Allison, David B. 2001. *Reading the New Nietzsche.* Lanham, MD: Rowman and Littlefield.

Babich, Babette E. 1994. *Nietzsche's Philosophy of Science.* Albany: State University of New York Press.

Danto, Arthur C. 1965. *Nietzsche as Philosopher: An Original Study.* New York: Macmillan.

Kaufmann, Walter Arnold. 1950. *Nietzsche: Philosopher, Psychologist, Antichrist.* Princeton, NJ: Princeton University Press.

Mandel, Siegfried. 1998. *Nietzsche and the Jews.* Amherst, NY: Prometheus Books.

Nietzsche, Friedrich. 1968. *The Portable Nietzsche.* Ed. Walter Arnold Kaufmann. New York: Viking. Contains major works such as *The Antichrist, Nietzsche contra Wagner, Thus Spoke Zarathustra,* and *Twilight of the Idols.*

Calvin Hayes

NIHILISM

SEE *Nietzsche, Friedrich.*

1984

SEE *New Class, The; Personality, Cult of.*

NINTENDO

SEE *Video games.*

NIRVĀNA

In the fifth century BCE a thirty-year old Indian prince called Siddartha (c. 566–486 BCE) abandoned royal status, family life, and all the comforts of civilization. For six years he wandered through the forests of what is today northern India, living as a celibate ascetic and seeking a solution to the problem of human suffering, which he framed within the endless round of being born, growing old, and dying, only to be reborn once again. This cycle is known in Sanskrit as *samsāra* (transmigration). Prince Siddartha wanted to know if there was a way out—*nirvāna* ("extinction")—of *samsāra* (for an extensive discussion of *nirvāna* and its synonyms, see Collins 1998, pp. 191–233). He sought a solution by studying with various ascetic teachers, none of whom could fully satisfy his questions, and by meditating and practicing severe asceticism, such as eating only one sesame seed, one grain of rice, and one juniper berry a day. His determination attracted five male disciples who looked after him.

The world of the forest recluse was predominantly male. A significant part of what Prince Siddartha had rejected in leaving city life was contact with women. Gender has been a contested issue since the earliest days of Buddhism, with many denying that women can achieve *nirvāna*, asserting they must first reincarnate as men. Ironically, as Siddartha sat meditating and wasting away, a woman, his dead mother, Queen Māyā, appeared and reminded him of the prediction at the time of his birth that he would achieve *nirvāna*, which was in jeopardy because of his continued austerities. He reassured her that he would attain his goal, and she returned to heaven. It is at this point that Prince Siddartha began to change his regimen, began to turn back toward the world and, indeed, began his reconciliation with women.

Realizing that his body was too weak to achieve *nirvāna*, he decided to eat solid food. His five male disciples, believing he had abandoned asceticism, deserted him.

But some young village women came and offered him a dish of rice and milk, which he accepted. Several other women, human and divine, also helped to restore his strength so that he could take his seat under the Bo tree where he would achieve *nirvāna* (Young 2004, pp. 1–19).

He then proceeded through a series of ever-deepening states of meditation throughout the night. It has long been debated exactly what he experienced on that night (Collins 1998, pp. xiii–xiv; Spiro 1982, pp. 56–59; Welbon 1968, passim), but its outcome, his achievement of *nirvāna*, is a defining principle of Buddhism that changed the religious face of much of Asia. After this experience he was given the title of *Buddha*, the "awakened" or "enlightened one."

Two points need to be made: First, when the Buddha achieved *nirvāna* he became an enlightened being, and second, when he died he achieved *parinirvāna*, meaning he would never be reborn. This understanding postulates that *samsāra* and *nirvāna* are two different kinds of existence, one ruled by desire and the other a realm where desire is extinguished. This is the general view of Theravāda Buddhism. A later tradition, Mahāyanā Buddhism, postulates instead that these are radically different states of mind. Whatever the metaphysical nature of *nirvāna*, its social reality was and remains structured by a celibate, male hierarchy that seeks *nirvāna* while being supported by a lay community for whom they perform various religious and educational tasks.

Theravāda Buddhism has received the most anthropological attention, beginning with Melford Spiro in 1970 dividing it into Nibbanic (nirvanic) and Kammatic (karmatic) Buddhism. Nibbanic Buddhism is practiced by some monks—in Max Weber's terms the "religious virtuosi"—who renounce the world in order to seek *nirvāna*, and Kammatic Buddhism is practiced by most monks and members of the laity who follow Buddhist precepts and practices in order to improve their karma and be reborn in a better situation for pursuing *nirvāna*. A third category, apotropaic Buddhism, offers protective practices against adversity and promotes well-being (Spiro [1970] 1982, pp. 9–12). All three types are of necessity interrelated. Richard Gombrich in 1971 published similar findings for Buddhist Ceylon (present-day Sri Lanka) (pp. 16–17 and 214–224). Both Spiro and Gombrich were interested in how pivotal religious ideas, such as *nirvāna*, are maintained and yet also reinterpreted by those unable to live up to them. Spiro contrasted what the canonical text contained with actual practices. Gombrich contrasted what people said they did with what they actually did.

The main point, though, is that most Buddhists are pursuing *nirvāna* in their various ways, and a significant number of them are living celibate lives either permanently or as temporary monks. Steven Collins has drawn out the economic advantages of an agrarian society that delays or limits marriage and thus the population, thereby creating surplus food production (Collins 1998, pp. 92–93). In his analysis the ideology of *nirvāna* created an *imaginaire* that produced a hope for salvation that shaped social and economic realities. In other words, Collins repositioned *nirvāna* as central to all forms of Buddhist practice (Collins 1998, pp. 116–117).

The achievement of *nirvāna* is believed to be accompanied by omniscience and magical powers, and it raises an individual's esteem as well as that of his religious followers and his religious community. Powerful and famous people come to visit an enlightened monk, seeking his advice and blessing as well as to establish themselves publicly as devout Buddhists, especially around election time. Stanley Tambiah's study of the cult of amulets among Thai Buddhists reveals that the most esteemed amulets were those blessed by enlightened forest saints, monks who had withdrawn from village life to pursue *nirvāna* (Tambiah 1984, pp. 3, 135–136). Similarly, in Mahāyanā Buddhism those monks believed to be enlightened attract more followers and receive far greater contributions than other monks. Consequently, many of those believed to have achieved *nirvāna* wield wealth and influence.

BIBLIOGRAPHY

Collins, Steven. 1998. *Nirvana and Other Buddhist Felicities: Utopias of the Pali Imaginaire.* Cambridge, U.K.: Cambridge University Press.

Gombrich, Richard F. 1971. *Precept and Practice: Traditional Buddhism in the Rural Highlands of Ceylon.* Oxford: Oxford University Press.

Spiro, Melford E. [1970] 1982. *Buddhism and Society: A Great Tradition and Its Burmese Vicissitudes.* 2nd ed. Berkeley: University of California Press.

Tambiah, Stanley Jeyaraja. 1984. *The Buddhist Saints of the Forest and the Cult of Amulets.* Cambridge, U.K.: Cambridge University Press.

Welbon, Guy R. 1968. *The Buddhist Nirvana and Its Western Interpreters.* Chicago: University of Chicago Press.

Young, Serinity. 2004. *Courtesans and Tantric Consorts: Sexualities in Buddhist Narrative, Iconography, and Ritual.* New York: Routledge.

Serinity Young

NIXON, RICHARD M.
1913–1994

Richard Milhous Nixon, U.S. representative and senator, vice president, and thirty-seventh president of the United States, was an influential, but flawed political figure in American politics. Born in poverty in Yorba Linda, California, Nixon was a diligent student who graduated from Whittier College, then Duke Law School. He was ambitious and felt, at an early age, a strong desire to prove himself, a personality trait that some scholars think contributed to his downfall.

Nixon's political career began in 1947 when he defeated five-term incumbent Democrat Jerry Voorhis to become U.S. representative. After winning reelection, Nixon achieved national prominence as chair of the Un-American Activities Committee by relentlessly questioning Alger Hiss for purportedly being a communist spy while working for the U.S. State Department. In winning election to the U.S. Senate in 1950, Nixon successfully branded his opponent Helen Gahagan Douglas a communist (calling her the "Pink Lady") and cemented his national reputation as a staunch anticommunist. His reputation as an anticommunist crusader early in his career undoubtedly helped Nixon achieve political and international prominence. It secured him a place on the Republican Party presidential ticket in 1952 and gave him the credibility to support China's admission to the United Nations in October 1971 and open relations with China when he visited it—the first president to do so—in early 1972.

As the sitting vice president of popular president Dwight D. Eisenhower from 1953 to 1961, Nixon was the early favorite to become the thirty-fifth president of the United States in a campaign against the Democratic but little known junior senator from Massachusetts, John F. Kennedy. Nixon was clearly the more experienced, especially in foreign affairs. But presidential politics was becoming less about experience at the beginning of the television age, and more about perception and style. Although Nixon won the first televised presidential debate among radio listeners, he did not look as "presidential" as his opponent, who won the debate among television viewers. Nixon narrowly lost the 1960 presidential election to Kennedy by less than 120,000 popular votes.

Eight years later, Nixon was elected president in another close contest against sitting Democratic vice president Hubert Humphrey, on a campaign of ending the war in Vietnam and courting moderate Republicans on civil rights and law and order. Nixon achieved numerous domestic policy successes with the Clean Air Act of 1970 and omnibus crime legislation. But his major successes related to his expertise and his life-long interest in foreign policy.

Despite being raised as a Quaker, Nixon rejected the Quaker principle of pacifism and was decidedly hawkish in his foreign policy positions. He criticized the Truman administration for being too passive in its handling of the Korean War, disagreed publicly with Truman's decision to fire General Douglas MacArthur, and, as president, expanded the war in Vietnam by sending Marines into Laos and bombing Cambodia.

In a blow to the presidency's unilateral foreign policy authority, Congress overrode Nixon's veto of the War Powers Act, which attempted to limit presidential war power in the face of mounting public and congressional opposition to the war in Vietnam by insuring that "the collective judgment of both the Congress and the President will apply to the introduction of United States Armed Forces into hostilities." Nixon and subsequent presidents argued that the War Powers Act is an unconstitutional violation of separation of powers, in part because it requires presidents to consult with Congress before U.S. armed forces engage in military hostilities and remove forces from conflict if Congress has not declared war or issued a resolution authorizing the use of force within sixty days.

Nixon was the consummate politician, a fighter for office and for his own political survival. This aggressive style assisted Nixon, at times, but did not endear him to his political opponents. He fought for his political career early—to remain Eisenhower's running mate in 1952—when he responded to charges that he had a campaign slush fund to defray personal expenses in the so-called "Checker's Speech." He admitted to having the fund, but only to pay political, not personal, expenses save one: a cocker spaniel he accepted as a gift for his daughter, Tricia. Eisenhower praised Nixon afterward and kept him on the ticket. This shrewd political maneuvering could not save him when he failed to win the presidency in 1960, to become governor of California in 1962, or to overcome the largest scandal of his political career: Watergate.

Rejected by the White House as a "third-rate burglary attempt," the arrest of five members of the Committee to Reelect the President (CREEP) at the Democratic Party Headquarters at the Watergate Hotel in Washington, D.C., "Watergate" evolved into a president-led cover up, which resulted in the first and only resignation of a sitting president in U.S. history. The extent of Nixon's involvement became evident after revelation in House judiciary committee hearings of a secret taping system in the White House. Nixon claimed executive privilege and refused to submit the tapes to Congress. But the U.S. Supreme Court, in *US v. Nixon* (1974), rejected this claim, precipitating Nixon's resignation less than three weeks later.

On August 9, 1974, Nixon was succeeded by Gerald Ford, who had replaced Nixon's elected vice president, Spiro Agnew, who had resigned in October 1973 and pleaded no contest to tax evasion in a plea-bargained deal for charges of accepting bribes while governor of Maryland and vice president of the United States. Ford was the first unelected vice president in U.S. history, in compliance with the Twenty-Fifth Amendment to the U.S. Constitution. In September 1974 he pardoned Richard Nixon for "all offenses against the United States which he … has committed or may have committed or taken part in" while president.

Although Watergate damaged the president, Nixon overcame its physical and mental tolls and became a respected leader abroad after his presidency. During and after his political career, Nixon was also a prolific writer and author. Beginning with his account of his early political career, including the Checker's Speech and Alger Hiss affair, Nixon wrote *Six Crises* (1962). Along with his presidential memoirs (1978), after his resignation he wrote several other books, including *No More Vietnams* (1985) and *1999: Victory without War* (1988), that confirm his personal interest in foreign affairs and attempts to shape and frame popular discourse on American involvement in international conflicts.

SEE ALSO *Eisenhower, Dwight D.; Kennedy, John F.; Khrushchev, Nikita; Vietnam War; Watergate*

BIBLIOGRAPHY

PRIMARY WORKS

Nixon, Richard M. 1962. *Six Crises.* Garden City, NY: Doubleday.

Nixon, Richard M. 1978. *RN: The Memoirs of Richard Nixon.* New York: Grosset and Dunlap.

Nixon, Richard M. 1985. *No More Vietnams.* New York: HarperCollins Publishers.

Nixon, Richard M. 1988. *1999: Victory without War.* New York: Simon & Schuster.

SECONDARY WORKS

Barber, James D. 1972. *The Presidential Character: Predicting Performance in the White House.* Englewood Cliffs, NJ: Prentice-Hall.

Matthew Eshbaugh-Soha

NKRUMAH, KWAME
1909–1972

It is an unquestionable fact that the political leader with the most profound impact on Africa in the twentieth century was Kwame Nkrumah, the founder and first president of the independent nation of Ghana. He was born on or about September 21, 1909, in Nkroful in the southwest part of the Gold Coast, now Ghana. The force that impelled his behavior and unleashed his energies was the ideology of pan-Africanism, which took root in him through his discipleship of Marcus Garvey (1887–1940) during his student days in the United States from 1935 to 1945. The ideology's core objective was to break the African universe away from the powerlessness and degradation that had accompanied five centuries of slavery, colonialism, and other forms of domination suffered by Africans universally at the hands of Western capitalistic imperialism. Returning to his native Gold Coast in 1947, Nkrumah soon proved himself, as the African nationalist Amílcar Cabral (1924–1973) observed, "the strategist of genius in the struggle against classical colonialism" (Davidson 1973, p. 13), bringing the British colony to independence in 1957. From then on, he made the liquidation of colonialism in Africa and the unification of the emergent states into a federal union the primary goals of the new Ghanaian state. In this schema, the freeing of Ghana from colonial rule remained always "the servant" of the second goal of Africa's total liberation and unity. He tirelessly proclaimed this credo: "I will commit all the resources and energies of Ghana towards achieving Africa's independence and unity" (Legum 1962, p. 44).

With a federal continental government, he proclaimed, Africa would be able to tackle every emergency, every enemy, and every complexity. This is not because Africans are a race of supermen, but because "we have emerged in the age of science and technology in which poverty, ignorance, and disease are no longer the masters, but the retreating foes of mankind. We have emerged in the age of socialized planning, where production and distribution are not governed by chaos, greed and self-interest, but by social needs" (Nkrumah 1973, p. 240). Above all, he continued, Africans had emerged at a time when a continental land mass such as Africa was "necessary to the economic capitalization and profitability of modern productive methods and techniques" (Nkrumah 1973, p. 240).

In a campaign based on, in the words of Colin Legum, a "passionate, informed and urgent advocacy," (Gardiner 1970, p. 53) Nkrumah assailed the gradualist, incrementalist, economistic, region-bound approach to integration, making it clear that African unity was, in the last analysis, "a political kingdom" that could only be gained by political means—that the social and economic development of Africa would come only within the political kingdom, not the other way around.

Nkrumah's single-minded challenge and overthrow of imperial power in Ghana (as the Gold Coast was renamed in 1957) greatly stimulated the forces of nationalism across Africa. The West answered back by creating the appearance of political liberation in diverse African places to hide the reality of the maintenance of old colonial relationships. This way, the West continued to rule and control Africa's economic destiny surreptitiously, using puppet regimes suitably dressed in the counterfeit trappings of sovereignty. Nkrumah characterized this new phenomenon *neocolo-*

nialism, and he went on to castigate it as the most irresponsible form of imperialism in the sense that, for those who imposed it, it meant "power without responsibility," whereas for those victimized by it, it meant "exploitation without redress" (Nkrumah 1965, p. xi).

There was no denying the reality of neocolonialism. Certainly, as Rupert Emerson noted, the territories left behind following the deliberate breakup by France of the French West Africa and French Equatorial Africa Federations seemed "hopeless experiments in endowing with life" artificial political entities that had no prospect of economic and political viability and stability (Emerson 1962, p. 286). And yet, Nkrumah was deemed "to have offended against all international proprieties" by making a battle against neocolonialism his "daily preoccupation," and by writing a book on its dangers (Bing 1968, p. 32) entitled *Neo-Colonialism: The Last Stage of Imperialism* (1965). The British prime minister, Alex Douglas-Hume, called the concept a slander, and the U.S. State Department officially summoned the Ghanaian charge d'affaires in Washington, D.C. to formally protest the publication of the book in the United States. In the end, Nkrumah's crusade for genuine decolonization and pan-African unification resulted in a foreign-instigated overthrow of his government. In the categorical statement of Jeffrey Sachs, "The CIA had its hand on the violent overthrow of President Kwame Nkrumah of Ghana in 1966" (Sachs 2005, p. 190).

Nkrumah linked pan-Africanism (as a movement for one United Africa that could countervail imperialism, and as an ideology of egalitarianism committed to the creation of opportunities for the development and uplift of all African people) with socialism: "At the core of the concept of African unity," he wrote, "lies socialism and the socialist definition of the new African society. Socialism and African unity are organically complementary" (Nkrumah 1968, p. 28). Because colonial rule precluded the accumulation of capital among the colonial subjects, a postcolonial system based on private enterprise would result in the overwhelming foreign capitalist domination of the national economy. On his postulate that capitalism "is but the gentleman's method of slavery," he insisted that pan-Africanism needed to harness the "scientific," "abiding," and "universal" principles of socialism to contain it (Nkrumah 1968, p. 29; Nkrumah 1970[b], p. 26). Among these principles are the public ownership of the means of production geared toward "the fulfillment of the people's needs," and recognition of the reality of the class struggle.

Nkrumah's heroic role in the decolonization struggle in Africa, and his enormous importance as the symbol of Ghanaian national unity in an ethnically fragmented land, produced a wave of oftentimes irrational adulation around him, reminiscent of the uncritical hero-worship that Americans once heaped on George Washington as the first president of the incipient American republic. In effect, a personality cult nourished by Nkrumah's own penchant for flamboyant style sought for him the same kind of legitimacy rooted in history, religion, and ancestral spiritual practices that was afforded his powerful rival, the Asante King. But, when all is said and done, it was Nkrumah's grand vision of a united African superstate, much like what animates and drives the European Union today, that drew the racist accusation of megalomania from the West, and not anything to do with his supposedly inflated sense of personal grandeur or fondness for adulation.

Following his ouster, Nkrumah took up residence in Conakry, Guinea, at the invitation of President Ahmed Sékou Touré (1922–1984) and spent a good deal of his time reading and writing, polishing his speaking French, and holding heated discussions on salient African issues with visiting companions-in-arms such as Cabral and Kwame Ture (Stokeley Carmichael, 1941–1998). He made several radio broadcasts to Ghana drawing attention to the neocolonial character of the February 1966 military coup, all as part of a spirited effort to rally support for his return to power. Astoundingly, during this hectic period he also managed to publish several significant books, among them *Challenge of the Congo* (1967), *Dark Days in Ghana* (1968), *Handbook of Revolutionary Warfare* (1968), *Class Struggle in Africa* (1970), and *Revolutionary Path* (1973), all of which he dedicated, characteristically, to the "African Nation That Must Be." Nkrumah died on April 27, 1972, in Bucharest, Romania, while receiving treatment for skin cancer.

Even though his dedication to the pan-African vision entailed the sacrifice of some short-term Ghana national interests, it is still the resounding verdict that the most impressive economic, social, and political achievements in Ghana to date took place during his leadership. And although he failed to achieve the goal of African political unification, what gave Nkrumah his lasting importance "is that he failed in trying to reach the right goal, and not, like many of his time and later, in trying to reach the wrong one" (Davidson 1973, p. 207). After all, this is a historical juncture "when policies aimed at … unity can alone solve Africa's problems, so that all other alternatives can be no more than temporary diversions from the pathway to those aims" (Davidson 1973, p. 37).

BIBLIOGRAPHY

PRIMARY WORKS

Nkrumah, Kwame. 1965. *Neo-Colonialism: The Last Stage of Imperialism.* London: Nelson.

Nkrumah, Kwame. 1967. *Challenge of the Congo.* New York: International Publishers.

Nkrumah, Kwame. 1968. *Dark Days in Ghana.* New York: St. Martin's Press.

Nkrumah, Kwame. 1968. *Handbook of Revolutionary Warfare.* New York: International Publishers.

Nkrumah, Kwame. 1970(a). *Class Struggle in Africa.* New York: International Publishers.

Nkrumah, Kwame. 1970(b). *Consciencism: Philosophy and the Ideology for Decolonization.* New York: Monthly Review Press.

Nkrumah, Kwame. 1973. *Revolutionary Path.* New York: International Publishers.

SECONDARY WORKS

Bing, Geoffrey. 1968. *Reap the Whirlwind: An Account of Kwame Nkrumah's Ghana from 1950 to 1966.* London: McGibbon and Kee.

Davidson, Basil. 1973. *Black Star: A View of the Life and Times of Kwame Nkrumah.* New York: Praeger Publishers.

Emerson, Rupert. 1962. Pan-Africanism. *International Organization* 16 (Spring): 275–290.

Gardiner, Robert, Margaret Joan Anstee, and C. L. Patterson, eds. 1970. *Africa and the World.* Addis Ababa: Oxford University Press.

Legum, Colin. 1962. *Pan-Africanism: A Short Political Guide.* New York: Praeger.

Sachs, Jeffrey D. 2005. *The End of Poverty: Economic Possibilities for Our Time.* New York: Penguin Press.

Smertin, Yuri. 1987. *Kwame Nkrumah.* New York: International Publishers.

Opoku Agyeman

NOBEL PEACE PRIZE

The *Nobel Peace Prize* is an annual award established by Alfred Nobel and, according to his will, given to "the person who shall have done the most or best work for fraternity among nations, for the abolition or reduction of standing armies and for the holding and promotion of peace congresses." Nobel gave the Norwegians the exclusive task of selecting each year's recipient, as opposed to the Swedes, who award each of the other Nobel Prizes. The Nobel Committee consists of five members selected by the Norwegian parliament (known as the "Storting"). Since the prize's inception, all committee members have been Norwegian nationals. Prize recipients, therefore, generally share the liberal internationalist ideals of the Norwegian Nobel Committee.

Over the years prizes have been given to a wide range of individuals and organizations that promote a variety of peace and human-rights issues. Recipients of the prize have included government officials, dissidents, nongovernmental organizations, and intergovernmental organizations. Between 1901—when the first prizes were awarded to Henry Dunant, founder of the Red Cross, and Frédéric Passy, founder and president of the French Peace Society—and 2006, there have been 112 Nobel Peace Prizes awarded to ninety-three individuals and nineteen organizations. The International Committee of the Red Cross has received the prize three times (1917, 1944, and 1963). Branches and leaders of the United Nations as well as individuals and organizations that have worked toward conventional and nuclear disarmament have been frequent recipients of the prize.

Nobel Peace Prize recipients

1901 – Henry Dunant (Switzerland), Frédéric Passy (France)
1902 – Élie Ducommun (Switzerland), Charles Albert Gobat (Switzerland)
1903 – William Randal Cremer (United Kingdom)
1904 – Institute of International Law
1905 – Bertha von Suttner (Austria)
1906 – Theodore Roosevelt (United States)
1907 – Ernesto Teodoro Moneta (Italy), Louis Renault (France)
1908 – Klas Pontus Arnoldson (Sweden), Fredrik Bajer (Denmark)
1909 – Auguste Beernaert (Belgium), Paul Henri d'Estournelles de Constant (France)
1910 – Permanent International Peace Bureau
1911 – Tobias Michael Carel Asser (the Netherlands), Alfred Hermann Fried (Austria)
1912 – Elihu Root (United States)
1913 – Henri La Fontaine (Belgium)
1914 – No prize given
1915 – No prize given
1916 – No prize given
1917 – International Committee of the Red Cross
1918 – No prize given
1919 – Thomas Woodrow Wilson (United States)
1920 – Léon Victor Auguste Bourgeois (France)
1921 – Karl Hjalmar Branting (Sweden), Christian Lous Lange (Norway)
1922 – Fridtjof Nansen (Norway)
1923 – No prize given
1924 – No prize given
1925 – Sir Austen Chamberlain (United Kingdom), Charles Gates Dawes (United States)
1926 – Aristide Briand (France), Gustave Stresemann (Germany)
1927 – Ferdinand Buisson (France), Ludwig Quidde (Germany)
1928 – No prize given
1929 – Frank Billings Kellogg (United States)
1930 – Nathan Söderblom (Sweden)
1931 – Jane Addams (United States), Nicholas Murray Butler (United States)
1932 – No prize given
1933 – Sir Norman Angell (United Kingdom)
1934 – Arthur Henderson (United Kingdom)
1935 – Carl von Ossietzky (Germany)
1936 – Carlos Saavedra Lamas (Argentina)
1937 – Robert Cecil (United Kingdom)
1938 – Nansen International Office for Refugees
1939 – No prize given
1940 – No prize given
1941 – No prize given
1942 – No prize given
1943 – No prize given
1944 – International Committee of the Red Cross
1945 – Cordell Hull (United States)
1946 – Emily Greene Balch (United States), John Raleigh Mott (United States)
1947 – Friends Service Council (United Kingdom), American Friends Service Committee (United States)
1948 – No prize given
1949 – Lord Boyd Orr (United Kingdom)
1950 – Ralph Bunche (United States)
1951 – Léon Jouhaux (France)
1952 – Albert Schweitzer (France)
1953 – George C. Marshall (United States)
1954 – Office of the United Nations High Commissioner for Refugees

1955 – No prize given
1956 – No prize given
1957 – Lester Bowles Pearson (Canada)
1958 – Georges Pire (Belgium)
1959 – Philip J. Noel-Baker (United Kingdom)
1960 – Albert John Lutuli (South Africa)
1961 – Dag Hammarskjöld (Sweden)
1962 – Linus Pauling (United States)
1963 – International Committee of the Red Cross, League of Red Cross Societies
1964 – Martin Luther King Jr. (United States)
1965 – United Nations Children's Fund
1966 – No prize given
1967 – No prize given
1968 – René Cassin (France)
1969 – International Labour Organization
1970 – Norman E. Borlaug (United States)
1971 – Willy Brandt (West Germany)
1972 – No prize given
1973 – Henry A. Kissinger (United States), Le Duc Tho (North Vietnam)
1974 – Seán MacBride (Ireland), Eisaku Sato (Japan)
1975 – Andrei Sakharov (Soviet Union)
1976 – Betty Williams (United Kingdom), Mairead Corrigan (United Kingdom)
1977 – Amnesty International
1978 – Mohamed Anwar al-Sadat (Egypt), Menachem Begin (Israel)
1979 – Mother Teresa (India)
1980 – Adolfo Pérez Esquivel (Argentina)
1981 – Office of the United Nations High Commissioner for Refugees
1982 – Alva Myrdal (Sweden), Alfonso García Robles (Mexico)
1983 – Lech Walesa (Poland)
1984 – Desmond Tutu (South Africa)
1985 – International Physicians for the Prevention of Nuclear War
1986 – Elie Wiesel (United States)
1987 – Oscar Arias Sánchez (Costa Rica)
1988 – United Nations Peacekeeping Forces
1989 – The Fourteenth Dalai Lama (Tibet)
1990 – Mikhail Gorbachev (Soviet Union)
1991 – Aung San Suu Kyi (Burma)
1992 – Rigoberta Menchú (Guatemala)
1993 – Nelson Mandela (South Africa), Frederik Willem de Klerk (South Africa)
1994 – Yassir Arafat (Palestine), Shimon Peres (Israel), Yitzhak Rabin (Israel)
1995 – Joseph Rotblat (United Kingdom), Pugwash Conferences on Science and World Affairs
1996 – Carlos Filipe Ximenes Belo (East Timor), José Ramos-Horta (East Timor)
1997 – International Campaign to Ban Landmines, Jody Williams (United States)
1998 – John Hume (United Kingdom), David Trimble (United Kingdom)
1999 – Médecins Sans Frontieres
2000 – Kim Dae-Jung (South Korea)
2001 – United Nations, Kofi Annan (Ghana)
2002 – Jimmy Carter (United States)
2003 – Shirin Ebadi (Iran)
2004 – Wangari Muta Maathai (Kenya)
2005 – International Atomic Energy Agency, Mohamed ElBaradei (Egypt)
2006 – Muhammad Yunnus Bangladesh

Controversy has surrounded some selections, as the committee has tried to balance between complying with Nobel's will and using the prize to promote Norwegian interests and values. The awarding of the 1906 Peace Prize to Theodore Roosevelt is one early example of this balance. Roosevelt was the first head of state to be so honored. While the prize was given because of his involvement in the mediation of the Japanese-Russian war, the former Rough Rider enjoyed a rather bellicose reputation. Nevertheless, Roosevelt was chosen in part because Norway, which had just received its independence from Sweden in 1905, was, as one Norwegian newspaper put it, in need of a "large, friendly neighbor." In addition, the prize signaled the willingness of the committee to at times award prizes based on specific actions rather than the overall "peacefulness" of the person in question. Prizes to such figures as Henry Kissinger and Le Duc Tho (1973), Yasir Arafat (1994), and Anwar Sadat and Menachem Begin (1978) similarly reflect this tendency.

The Nobel Committee has also used the prize to punish, rather than reward, behavior. For example, the 1935 prize was given to Carl von Ossietzky, a German journalist and dissident who wrote scathing articles against the Nazi Party for which he was sent to a German concentration camp. The prize was given to Ossietzky as much to condemn German behavior as it was to honor Ossietzky. Other cases in which the committee has used the prize to highlight atrocities being carried out by specific governments include Shirin Ebadi of Iran in 2003, Carlos Filipe Ximenes Belo and Jose Ramos-Horta of East Timor in 1996, Aung San Suu Kyi of Myanmar (Burma) in 1991, Desmond Tutu of South Africa in 1984, Lech Walesa in 1983, Martin Luther King Jr. of the United States in 1964, and Albert Lutuli of South Africa in 1960.

SEE ALSO *Arafat, Yasir; Bunche, Ralph Johnson; Carter, Jimmy; Gorbachev, Mikhail; Microfinance; Peace; Rabin, Yitzhak; Truth and Reconciliation Commissions; War; War and Peace*

BIBLIOGRAPHY

Abrams, Irwin. 2003. *The Words of Peace: The Nobel Peace Prize Laureates of the Twentieth Century*, 3rd ed. New York Newmarket Press.

Lundestad, Geir. 2001. The Nobel Peace Prize 1901–2000. In *The Nobel Prize: The First 100 Years*, eds. Agneta Wallin Levinovitz and Nils Ringertz, 163–196. London: Imperial College Press and World Scientific Publishing. http://nobelprize.org/nobel_prizes/peace/articles/lundestad-review/index.html.

David R. Andersen

NO CHILD LEFT BEHIND ACT
SEE *Accountability; Education, Unequal.*

NO FAULT DIVORCE
SEE *Divorce and Separation.*

NODE, STABLE

If all the paths of equilibrium noncyclically converge to it, the equilibrium is a *stable node*. The conditions for the equilibrium to be a stable node are a function of the system being evaluated, in particular, whether the issue of concern involves discrete versus continuous change or is a linear versus nonlinear system. If the dynamic system is discrete and linear,

$$\dot{y} = ay + b$$

The equilibrium is stable if and only if $a > 0$.

For continuous linear dynamic systems, an equilibrium is defined as a stable node if the slope of the differential equation in the neighborhood of the equilibrium is negative. For nonlinear discrete or continuous dynamic systems, the Taylor expansion about x_i^*, a nonzero equilibrium, must satisfy the following for x_i^* to be stable: $|f'(x_i^*)| < 1$. The concept of a stable node can be extended to simultaneous systems of discrete or continuous equations. The condition for a stable node is the same for discrete and continuous simultaneous systems of equation. If $|\lambda_i| < 0$, where λ_i are the eigenvalues that solve equation, then λ_i is stable. If the eigenvalues are complex, the real part must be negative for the eigenvalues to be stable.

The concept of a stable node is used to describe the dynamics of (1) an oligopoly—stability of a Cournot solution; 2) the IS-LM—stability after monetary and/or fiscal shocks; (3) the model of inflation and unemployment—stability of fiscal or employment policies; and (4) population models—stability of growth. The characterization of a node as stable is most useful in the qualitative analysis of differential equations using phase diagrams, which describes the paths of a system in and out of equilibrium.

SEE ALSO *Matrix Algebra*

BIBLIOGRAPHY

Hoy, Michael, John Livernois, Chris McKenna, and Ray Rees. 2001. *Mathematics for Economics*, 2nd ed. Cambridge, MA: MIT Press.

Shone, Ronald. 2002. *Economic Dynamics: Phase Diagrams and Their Economic Application*, 2nd ed. Cambridge, U.K., and New York: Cambridge University Press.

Rhonda V. Sharpe
Idrissa A. Boly

NOISE POLLUTION
SEE *Pollution, Noise.*

NOMENCLATURA
SEE *New Class, The.*

NOMINAL INCOME

Many societies strive to improve the well-being of their members by increasing incomes. The statement "Canadian household incomes have increased," may give an immediate impression that these households are better off. However, this may not necessarily be the case if nominal income is considered because inflation may completely erode any nominal income gains.

Nominal income is income that is not adjusted for changes in purchasing power, the amount of goods or services that one can afford with the income, owing to inflation. Adjusting nominal income for inflation is important because inflation decreases the amount of goods or services that one can afford with a given amount of nominal income. To see how inflation can erode nominal income gains, suppose that nominal income rises by 50 percent this year over last year. An individual is, in fact, better (worse) off if prices rise by less (more) than 50 percent over the same period, since the amount of goods or services that person can afford with the higher nominal income is more (less). Since nominal income is not adjusted for changes in the cost of living due to inflation, it is not a fully satisfactory measure of well-being. Fortunately, nominal incomes (e.g., wages, pensions) can be successfully adjusted to avoid loss in purchasing power due to inflation, provided that inflation is correctly anticipated.

Problems may arise when making international comparisons of nominal incomes. Suppose that the nominal income of a U.S. resident rises by $1 and that of a Ugandan resident also rises by the same amount. If the amount of goods or services that one can afford with the $1 is higher in Uganda than in the United States, then the $1 received in Uganda should be considered to be the higher income. Therefore, for international comparisons of nominal incomes (and other variables expressed in monetary terms), adjustments for purchasing power differences among countries are necessary. It is therefore not surprising that, for poverty comparison purposes, the World Bank (2005) reports the percentage of the population living on less than $1 a day after adjusting for purchasing power parity (PPP).

Even if nominal income is successfully adjusted for inflation (or PPP), some philosophical issues exist surrounding the appropriateness of nominal income as a measure of well-being. For example, according to the Capabilities Approach attributed to Amartya Sen, winner of the 1998 Nobel Prize in economics, functional capabilities (i.e., what a person can do or can be) are more important than income improvements.

The concept of nominal income is also commonly used in national income accounting to refer to nominal gross domestic product (GDP), the nominal value of all goods and services produced within a country's borders during a given time period. In evaluating nominal GDP, the output for a given year is evaluated using that year's prices. The practice of using nominal income to refer to nominal GDP is reflected in the vast literature on nominal income targeting, including the work of Henrik Jensen.

SEE ALSO *Gross Domestic Product; Gross National Income; Inflation; Money Illusion; Nominal Wages; Real Income*

BIBLIOGRAPHY

Jensen, Henrik. 2002. Targeting Nominal Income Growth or Inflation? *American Economic Review* 92 (4): 928–956.

Sen, Amartya. 1985. *Commodities and Capabilities.* Amsterdam, New York: North-Holland.

World Bank. 2005. *World Development Report 2006: Equity and Development.* New York: World Bank. http://econ.worldbank.org/.

Tomson Ogwang

NOMINAL RATE OF INTEREST
SEE *Interest Rates, Nominal.*

NOMINAL WAGES

Nominal wages, or "money wages," are pay rates unadjusted for inflation. In contrast, "real wages" are adjusted for inflation. When real wages increase, recipients can buy more with them. When nominal wages increase less than do price levels, recipients can buy less with them.

Classical economists believed that economic behavior is rational in the sense that it responds to real rather than nominal values. In labor markets, this implies that workers interpret a given decrease in real wages identically whether it was caused by a rise in inflation or by a fall in nominal wages. One of the key departures of John Maynard Keynes in his *General Theory of Employment, Interest, and Money* (1936) was that "a situation where labour stipulates (within limits) for a money-wage rather than a real wage, so far from being a mere possibility, is the normal case. Whilst workers will usually resist a reduction of money-wages, it is not their practice to withdraw their labour whenever there is a rise in the price of wage-goods" (p. 9). Nominal wages matter because nominal cuts typically occur in piecemeal fashion, which, in turn, alters any single group of workers' relative wage position. Thus, resistance to nominal wage cuts is a defense of one's relative wage position. If money wages could be lowered universally by the same percentage, Keynes's analysis suggests that there would be no more resistance on the part of labor than to the effects of a general inflation.

Early evidence of the downward nominal wage rigidity, or "sticky wages," was found in observed macroeconomic relationships. Increasing real wages during the Great Depression was attributed to falling prices combined with downward nominal wage rigidity. The post–World War II Phillips curve—the negative relationship between nominal wage changes and unemployment rates—was also explained by sticky wages, as was the non-neutrality of money supply, whereby money supply cuts caused recessions. Later studies have countered this "evidence" with alternative explanations—not based on nominal wages—that predict the same relationships.

Beginning in the 1980s, evidence of downward nominal wage rigidity has been sought in the time patterns of wages of individual workers within companies. This research has found many people with exactly zero nominal wage changes and very few whose nominal wages decrease, in contrast to no workers with exactly zero real wage changes and many whose real wages decrease. This holds true for low and moderate inflationary environments.

Different theoretical explanations of downward nominal wage rigidity assume different amounts of worker rationality. Many economists model nominal wage rigidities as rational responses to unanticipated shocks combined with imperfect information or costly wage changes. For instance, if workers can observe their own wage increases or decreases but not others' wages and not general inflation levels, they may temporarily erroneously interpret a nominal wage cut as a negative signal (of the match quality or of the company's health) rather than a

response to an economy-wide decline. It may take time for firms to be certain that their economic situations warrant wage responses, particularly when information arrives intermittently. Both time and administrative costs may be required to both gather the relevant information and implement changes in nominal pay levels, leading to infrequent, staggered wage adjustments. Any of these factors can have major macroeconomic implications. Many theories predict these implications to last only for a short run, although some models imply pervasive stickiness.

Downward wage rigidities have also been attributed to efficiency wages—that is, paying higher than market-clearing wages to increase productivity or worker quality—or to insider-outsider theories—where insider workers have bargaining power within firms. However, both of these explanations generate real rather than nominal rigidities, unless coupled with misperceptions or costly adjustments.

An intermediate view assumes "near-rationality." Humans have finite cognitive capacity and must edit out minor factors by using simple, unvarying rules of thumb. In environments of low inflation, individuals bear few costs if they assume that prices and nominal wage structures are constant. If many workers and/or firms behave in this way, however, it creates slowdowns that can persist.

Other psychologically based explanations emphasize that workers often infuse their nominal (money) wages with independent psychological meanings. Opinion surveys and experimental evidence have shown that many people's self-esteem or sense of self-worth depends on the level and changes of their nominal wages, particularly in comparison to the nominal wages of others within their firm. Many workers believe it unfair if employers violate social norms by decreasing nominal wages, even in response to a weak labor market. Finally, individuals have been shown to place more weight on avoiding losses than achieving gains. In this context, decreases in nominal wages lower morale, which can lead to reduced productivity and/or turnover. Given this, rational employers are reluctant to lower nominal wages, preferring to let real wages fall as prices rise.

SEE ALSO *Happiness; Inflation; Keynes, John Maynard; Money Illusion; Nominal Income; Relative Income Hypothesis; Wages*

BIBLIOGRAPHY

Akerlof, George A., William T. Dickens, and George L. Perry. 1996. Near-Rational Wage and Price Setting and the Long-Run Phillips Curve. *Brookings Papers on Economic Activity* 2000 (1): 1–60.

Bewley, Truman F. 1999. *Why Wages Don't Fall During a Recession.* Cambridge, MA: Harvard University Press.

Keynes, John Maynard. 1936. *The General Theory of Employment, Interest, and Money.* London: Macmillan.

Mankiw, N. Gregory, and Ricardo Reis. 2006. Pervasive Stickiness. *American Economic Review* 96 (2): 164–169.

Shulamit Kahn

NON-ALIGNMENT

Non-alignment is a philosophy for the conduct of international relations that was introduced into the diplomatic and scholarly vocabulary in 1961 with the founding of the Non-Aligned Movement (NAM). It was a product of the cold war, and its founders declared that they would not be aligned to either of the two competing political camps, led by the United States and the Soviet Union. The key intellectuals of Non-alignment philosophy have been Josip Tito, Fidel Castro, Julius Nyerere, Jawaharlal Nehru, Amilcar Cabral, and Léopold Senghor. The two central ideas of Non-alignment are the freedom to conduct an independent foreign policy and the eschewing of alliance politics. However, because the leading states of the NAM during its early years—such as Cuba and Yugoslavia—were closer to the USSR than to the United States, the movement has had the reputation of not promoting independent foreign policies. It has not been taken seriously in the academic power centers of international relations in North America and Europe. However, the NAM has been one of the most durable mechanisms of rhetorical mobilization for most of the former colonies of the world, and particularly powerful at the United Nations General Assembly, where the nonaligned bloc has been able to put on the agenda initiatives that the great powers would rather not debate, including, most prominently, proposals for a New International Economic Order and a New World Information and Communication Order.

It is useful to see Non-alignment as one of a variety of political strategies used by states to pursue their interests and survive in international politics. In contrast, the "power politics" strategy deployed by the most powerful states in the international system involves promoting alliances and placing military concerns ahead of economic and social development as objectives of foreign policy. In its early years (1961–1971), Non-alignment was seen as a form of neutrality, a philosophy of foreign policy conduct that eschewed international alliances of all types, even membership in the United Nations. However, the death knell of formal neutrality came with Switzerland's joining the United Nations in 2002. In contrast, Non-alignment has been durable, and its use of UN structures to pursue the collective foreign policy aims of its members is evidence of its attractiveness and viability as a "third way" of international relations. However, it is important to note that Non-alignment is not a revolutionary philosophy in international politics, because it adheres to the principle that the state is the primary actor in international affairs and it promotes the continued viability of the United Nations. The so-called "cultural turn" in international relations may mean that Non-alignment will be increasingly studied for its insights into identity construction in international politics.

SEE ALSO *Alliances; Castro, Fidel; Diplomacy; International Economic Order; Nation-State; Negotiation; Nehru, Jawaharlal; Neutral States; Nyerere, Julius; State, The; Tito (Josip Broz); United Nations; World War II*

BIBLIOGRAPHY

Simon, David. 2006. *Fifty Key Thinkers on Development.* London and New York: Routledge.

Singham, A. W., and Shirley Hune. 1986. *Non-alignment in an Age of Alignments.* New York: Lawrence Hill.

Mark D. Alleyne

NONBLACKS

Although racial and ethnic minority groups in the United States have been afforded many opportunities, they have also experienced a great deal of oppression over the course of U.S. history. Native Americans lost thousands of acres of land to early American settlers, and a large percentage of the Native population died in the process. In the mid- to late 1800s, individuals of Chinese descent were welcomed to the country to help build railroads, only to be excluded from citizenship and naturalization once the task was completed. Thousands of innocent Japanese-Americans were interned in the name of national security following the bombing of Pearl Harbor, resulting in the loss of billions of dollars worth of land and personal property. Blacks in America suffered the peculiar institution of slavery, the failure of reconstruction, and the insults and violence of Jim Crow. They also endured violence and bloodshed during the fight for civil rights, and they continue to address the backlash against affirmative action. Hispanics, likewise, have faced discrimination. They have been exploited for their labor and marginalized based upon their race, country of origin, and the continued use of their native tongue. Collectively, these groups are referred to as nonwhites.

Whites in America are the dominant racial group, and as such have historically had greater access to property, power and prestige than other racial groups. There have historically been large socioeconomic differences between whites and nonwhites, particularly in regard to wealth, income, educational attainment, and occupational opportunity and prestige. These differences have been most apparent between whites and blacks. Variations have also been observed between blacks and other racial and ethnic minority groups, and there has been an emergence of a "black" versus "nonblack" dichotomy. There are political as well as methodological implications for this distinction.

The designation "black" is used to describe a group of individuals that share not only similar phenotypical characteristics, such as skin color. Even more significantly, those labeled "black" are similar in that they are likely to receive unequal treatment compared to whites. The classification of "black" and "nonblack" persons is problematic, however, because the latter term often includes groups that may not be identified as black but have nonetheless had experiences comparable to that of blacks in terms of social and economic injustice. Cubans, Puerto Ricans, and Dominicans, for example, have suffered discrimination and unequal treatment in many arenas.

Moreover, the use of these terms to refer to various groups in quantitative analyses may provide support for the belief held by some about the inherent pathology of black culture, while also helping to mask the role of structural barriers in limiting upward social mobility among blacks and other minority groups. Instead of addressing the structural barriers that contribute to observed black-white disparities, efforts to eliminate the "black" category have emerged.

Some have questioned the usefulness of the black-nonblack dichotomy, given the successes of the multiracial movement in the late twentieth century. In 2000, for example, the U.S. Census Bureau allowed individuals to identify with more than one race. The use of this dichotomy is also deemed by some to have little use politically, given what can be described as the "Latin Americanization" of American racial norms. American society, in other words, can be seen as moving from a biracial classification system to a more complex multiracial or multicultural classification system. But the political successes associated with the multiracial movement do not render the black-nonblack dichotomy, or other racial classification scheme, empty. Instead, they highlight the fact that such classifications are multilevel and multidimensional—and often politically contested.

SEE ALSO *Minorities; Whites*

BIBLIOGRAPHY

Bonilla-Silva, Eduardo. 2001. *White Supremacy and Racism in the Post-Civil Rights Era.* Boulder, CO: Lynne Rienner.

Bonilla-Silva, Eduardo. 2003. From Bi-Racial to Tri-Racial: The Emergence of a New Racial Classification System in the United States. In *Skin Deep: How Race and Complexion Matter in the "Color-Blind" Era*, ed. Cedric Herring, Verna Keith, and Hayward Derrick Horton. Chicago: University of Illinois Press.

Keister, Lisa. 2000. *Wealth in America: Trends in Wealth Inequality.* Cambridge, U.K.: Cambridge University Press.

Massey, Douglas, and Nancy Denton. 1993. *American Apartheid.* Cambridge, MA: Harvard University Press.

Oliver, Melvin, and Thomas Shapiro. 1995. *Black Wealth/White Wealth: A New Perspective on Racial Inequality.* New York: Routledge.

Omi, Howard, and Michael Winant. 1994. *Racial Formation in the United States: From the 1960s to the 1990s.* New York: Routledge.

Zuberi, Tukufu. 2001. *Thicker than Blood: How Racial Statistics Lie.* Minneapolis: University of Minnesota Press.

Lori Latrice Sykes

NONCOMPETING GROUPS

The concept of noncompeting groups—labor that is sheltered from market competition—has a controversial history that parallels the evolution of labor markets during industrialization. Since the mid-nineteenth century, noncompeting groups have been variously defined in terms of occupation, social class, unionization, gender, race, and economic disadvantage. More recently, the microeconomic foundations of noncompeting groups have also been a topic of study.

NONCOMPETING GROUPS AND INDUSTRIALIZATION

Noncompeting groups were largely peripheral to labor market analysis at the time of the Industrial Revolution. Adam Smith (1723–1790), for example, emphasized the importance of "a competition among masters, who bid against one another in order to get workmen" when labor demand is growing and among workers who "bid against one another" when labor supply exceeds demand (Smith [1776] 1937, bk. 1, chap. 8, p. 71).

It was the Irish economist J. E. Cairnes (1823–1875) who coined the term *noncompeting groups* as applied to broad occupational categories—artisans and small retailers, highly skilled producers, and professionals (Cairnes 1874, p. 68). Cairnes saw entry into these groups as limited by law and custom, nontransferable skills, and the constraints of poverty (p. 62). Foreshadowing subsequent analysis of noncompeting groups by social class and race, John Stuart Mill (1806–1873) perceived these barriers as "so complete ... as to be almost equivalent to a hereditary distinction of caste" (Mill [1848] 1909, vol. 1, bk. 2, chap. 14, p. 480), but he also saw education and training as a source of intergenerational mobility between "grades" of labor provided that rules of social custom could be relaxed.

The turn of the century, however, lessened the importance of noncompeting groups (Fishback 1998), and English economist Alfred Marshall (1842–1924) saw technological change and the growth of mass production as reducing skill barriers to mobility and favoring transferable workforce attributes such as "sagacity and energy" and the ability "to accommodate oneself quickly to changes in detail of the work to be done" (Marshall [1890] 1930, bk. 4, chap. 6, secs. 2–3).

THE REEMERGENCE OF NONCOMPETING GROUPS

The growth of unions after World War II (1939–1945) focused attention on the role of labor market institutions, such as unions, in contributing to noncompetitive elements in labor markets and wage determinations (Dunlop 1958; Lewis 1986; Hirsch and Addison 1986). At the microlevel, these distinctions translated into the "balkanization" of labor markets (Kerr 1954) and a "new industrial feudalism" (Ross 1958). At the microeconomic level, entry into occupations was sometimes controlled by unions and licensure, hiring by firms was limited to entry jobs, and wage-setting was insulated from competitive forces by entry barriers and bargaining power (Reynolds 1951).

As unions and collective bargaining diminished and new social concerns emerged during the 1960s and 1970s, barriers to employment affecting "noncompeting" groups defined by gender, race, and class began to receive attention. Theories of discrimination reflecting segregated labor markets were developed (Becker 1957; Arrow 1972); persistent earnings differentials by race, gender, and class were identified (Blau and Kahn 2000; Cain 1987); and there was renewed interest in "dual economy" models of labor market segmentation (Lewis 1979; Doeringer and Piore 1971; Gordon, Edwards, and Reich 1982; Darity and Mason 1998). However, the importance of these noncompetitive elements in labor markets remains controversial (Cain 1976; Wachter 1974; Dickens and Lang 1993; Gordon, Edwards, and Reich 1982).

THE MICROFOUNDATIONS OF NONCOMPETING GROUPS

A parallel stream of analysis exploring the microeconomics of noncompeting groups has also flourished since the 1960s. Economists extended the 1950s research on employment practices within firms by developing the concept of internal labor markets in which long-term employment matches were formed that favored "internal" over "external" labor mobility (Doeringer and Piore 1971; Williamson, Wachter, and Harris 1975).

The legacy of this research on internal labor markets as noncompeting groups is a new focus on organizational efficiency as a response to various failures of competitive labor markets—firm-specific skills, poor information on the productive qualities of workers and the adverse aspects of jobs, principle-agent conflicts arising from difficulties in monitoring worker productivity, and the difficulty in writing employment contracts that could fully anticipate future contingencies. This approach was initially articulated in Oliver Williamson's *Markets and Hierarchies* (1975) and has been refined under the rubric of the "personnel economics" (Lazear 1999).

In this new incarnation, the limited entry, job hierarchies, and wage premiums found in internal labor markets were seen as improving the efficiency of imperfect external labor markets. Firm-specific skills led employers to offer *efficiency wages* (pay premiums above market rates for productive worker attributes) and promotions as incentives to reduce quits among trained workers; the threat of discharge from high-wage career jobs provided incentives for motivating productivity and reducing shirking; and implicit contracts providing high wages and secure employment markets were an efficient response to economic uncertainty (Katz and Summers 1989; Lang, Leonard, and Lilien 1987).

IMPLICATIONS FOR INEQUALITY AND ECONOMIC PERFORMANCE

Early theories emphasized the market distortions caused by noncompeting groups, as did subsequent work on labor markets segmented by unions, race, gender, class, and the employment practices of firms, as did much of the postwar research on the microfoundations of competing groups. In contrast, the new microeconomics of internal labor markets has tended to focus on the role of organizational efficiency in improving the economic performance of firms, and a large literature is emerging on the productivity gains to be made from sharing these efficiency gains with workers through higher wages, promotion opportunities, and participation in management decisions (Doeringer, Terkla, and Evan-Klock 2002, chap. 1).

The institutions of organizational efficiency, however, can also contribute to the ability of noncompeting groups within firms to increase their share of these gains in ways that may have adverse consequences. For example, firm-specific investments in training and labor market information, as well as unionization, can endow "insiders" with bargaining power that can be used to raise wages and limit job access by "outsiders" (Solow 1985). High wages can contribute to unemployment (Yellen 1984), and can also result in large pools of job applicants that make it easier to use race and class as exclusionary hiring criteria, while job ladders that provide efficient training can also become barriers to internal mobility by gender and race (Osterman 1979). In effect, noncompeting efficient internal labor markets can be both sources of productivity growth and enclaves of empowered insiders.

SEE ALSO *Discrimination; Ethnic Conflict; Ethnic Fractionalization; Ethnicity; White Supremacy*

BIBLIOGRAPHY

Arrow, Kenneth. 1972. Models of Job Discrimination. In *Racial Discrimination in Economic Life*, ed. Anthony Pascal, 187–204. Lexington, MA: Lexington Books.

Becker, Gary S. 1957. *The Economics of Discrimination*. Chicago: University of Chicago Press. 2nd ed. 1971.

Becker, Gary S. 1964. *Human Capital: A Theoretical and Empirical Analysis, with Special Reference to Education*. New York: Columbia University Press. 3rd ed. 1993. Chicago: University of Chicago Press.

Blau, Francine D., and Lawrence M. Kahn. 2000. Gender Differences in Pay. *Journal of Economic Perspectives* 14 (4): 75–100.

Cain, Glen G. 1976. The Challenge of Segmented Labor Market Theories to Orthodox Theory: A Survey. *Journal of Economic Literature* 14 (4): 1215–1257.

Cain, Glen G. 1986. The Economic Analysis of Labor Market Discrimination: A Survey. In *Handbook of Labor Economics*, eds. Orley Ashenfelter and Richard Layard, 693–781. New York: Elsevier.

Cairnes, J. E. 1874. *Some Leading Principles of Political Economy, Newly Expounded*. New York: Harper.

Darity, William A., Jr., and Patrick L. Mason. 1998. Evidence on Discrimination in Employment: Codes of Color, Codes of Gender. *Journal of Economic Perspectives* 12 (2): 63–90.

Dickens, William, and Kevin Lang. 1993. Labor Market Segmentation Theory: Reconsidering the Evidence. In *Labor Economics: Problems in Analyzing Labor Markets*, ed. William Darity Jr., 141–180. New York: Kluwer.

Doeringer, Peter B., and Michael J. Piore. 1971. *Internal Labor Markets and Manpower Analysis*. Lexington, MA: Heath.

Doeringer, Peter B., David Terkla, and Christine Evans-Klock. 2002. *Start-up Factories: High-Performance Management, Job Quality, and Regional Advantage*. New York: Oxford University Press.

Dunlop, John T. 1958. *Industrial Relations Systems*. New York: Henry Holt.

Fishback, Price V. 1998. Operations of "Unfettered" Labor Markets: Exit and Voice in American Labor Markets at the Turn of the Century. *Journal of Economic Literature* 36 (2): 722–765.

Gordon, David G., Richard Edwards, and Michael Reich. 1982. *Segmented Work, Divided Workers: The Historical Transformation of Labor in the United States*. Cambridge, U.K.: Cambridge University Press.

Hirsch, Barry T., and John T. Addison. 1986. *The Economic Analysis of Unions: New Approaches and Evidence*. Boston: Allen & Unwin.

Katz, Lawrence F., and Lawrence H. Summers. 1989. Industry Rents: Evidence and Implications. *Brookings Papers on Economic Activity* (Microeconomics issue): 209–247.

Kerr, Clark. 1954. The Balkanization of Labor Markets. In *Labor Mobility and Economic Opportunity*, 92–110. Cambridge, MA: Technology Press of MIT.

Lang, Kevin, Jonathan S. Leonard, and David M. Lilien. 1987. Labor Market Structure, Wages, and Unemployment. In *Unemployment and the Structure of Labor Markets*, eds. Kevin Lang and Jonathan S. Leonard, 1–16. New York: Blackwell.

Lazear, Edward. 1999. Personnel Economics: Past Lessons and Future Directions. *Journal of Labor Economics* 17 (2): 199–236.

Lewis, H. Gregg. 1986. *Union Relative Wage Effects: A Survey*. Chicago: University of Chicago Press.

Lewis, W. Arthur. 1979. The Dual Economy Revisited. *Manchester School* 47 (3): 211–229.

Marshall, Alfred. [1890] 1930. *Principles of Economics*. London: Macmillan.

Mill, John Stuart. [1848] 1909. *Principles of Political Economy*. London: Longmans.

Osterman, Paul. 1979. Sex Discrimination in Professional Employment: A Case Study. *Industrial and Labor Relations Review* 32 (4): 451–464.

Reynolds, Lloyd G. 1951. *The Structure of Labor Markets: Wages and Labor Mobility in Theory and Practice*. New York: Harper.

Ross, Arthur M. 1958. Do We Have a New Industrial Feudalism? *American Economic Review* 48 (5): 914–915.

Smith, Adam. [1776] 1937. *An Inquiry into the Nature and Causes of the Wealth of Nations*. New York: Modern Library.

Solow, Robert M. 1985. Insiders and Outsiders in Wage Determination. *Scandinavian Journal of Economies* 87: 411–428.

Wachter, Michael. 1974. Primary and Secondary Labor Markets: A Critique of the Dual Approach. *Brookings Papers on Economic Activity* 3: 637–680.

Williamson, Oliver E. 1975. *Markets and Hierarchies, Analysis and Antitrust Implications: A Study in the Economics of Internal Organization*. New York: Free Press.

Williamson, Oliver E., Michael Wachter, and Jeffrey Harris. 1975. Understanding the Employment Relation: The Analysis of Idiosyncratic Exchange. *Bell Journal of Economics* 6 (1): 250–278.

Yellen, Janet. 1984. Efficiency Wage Models of Unemployment. *American Economic Review* 74 (2): 200–205.

Peter B. Doeringer

NONCOOPERATIVE GAMES

Strategic games model conflict and cooperation, with the payoff to any player depending on the choice of strategy (a rule for selecting an action given each possible information set) not only by that player, but by all players. Strategic games can either be cooperative games, where some external authority exists that could enforce an agreement among the players, or noncooperative games, where no such external enforcement of agreements is available. Only self-enforcing agreements are possible in noncooperative games. Because binding agreements cannot be made, players in a noncooperative game may end up in a Pareto-inferior outcome, as in prisoner's dilemma (q.v.), because a strategy combination that would produce a better outcome for all players would leave at least one player with an incentive to deviate. Most game theory emphasizes noncooperative games, because there is no consensus about how to choose among the various solution concepts proposed for cooperative games (such as the core, kernel, nucleolus, and Shapley value). Noncooperative game theory builds primarily upon refinements of one solution concept, Nash equilibrium.

A Nash equilibrium is a strategy combination for which no player has an incentive to be the only player to switch to another strategy. John Nash, in articles from 1950 and 1951 and his 1996 volume of essays, proved that any strategic game with a finite strategy space and arbitrarily many players will have at least one equilibrium point, provided that players are allowed to choose mixed strategies (strategies that assign probabilities to the possible pure strategies, so that a player's action at a particular decision node cannot be predicted with certainty). Nash equilibrium has been interpreted as a generalization of A. Cournot's analysis of duopoly in 1838, where each of two mineral water suppliers chooses its profit-maximizing output as a best response to the other's output, taking the other firm's quantity as given, and equilibrium occurs where their reaction functions intersect and neither firm can profit by being the only one to change its quantity produced. However, Robert Leonard, in his 1994 article, suggests that this view reads too much into Cournot. The minimax mixed-strategy solution for two-person zero-sum games, whose existence was proved by John von Neumann in 1928, is a special case of Nash equilibrium for n-person, general sum games. Nash equilibrium need not be unique, and so refinements have been introduced to eliminate as unreasonable some of the Nash equilibria in a game with multiple equilibria, such as considering as reasonable only those Nash equilibria that are subgame perfect. A subgame perfect Nash equilibrium is a strategy combination that would still be a Nash equilibrium if the game was started at any decision node (even one that

would never be reached in equilibrium), so that players make only credible threats (that is, a player does not adopt a strategy implying that, if he or she were ever to be at particular off-equilibrium point, the player would do something that would decrease the player's expected payoff). For a game with multiple subgame perfect Nash equilibria, the concept of trembling hand equilibrium, where a player attaches a small probability to another player making a mistake, permits further restriction of the equilibria admitted as reasonable.

Because a Nash equilibrium is self-enforcing (no player can gain from being the only one to deviate), it is widely accepted as a plausible solution concept when there is preplay communication among players (especially if the Nash equilibrium is unique). As David G. Pearce's 1984 article argues, if players cannot talk, or cannot reach agreement on which of multiple Nash equilibria to select, other strategy combinations that are Nash equilibria may be rationalizable. A strategy is rationalizable if there exists a consistent set of beliefs about the strategies and beliefs of all the other players for which that strategy is optimal, with each player maximizing his or her expected payoff subject to his or her subjective beliefs. However, rationalizability greatly extends the range of admissible solution concepts (as the possibility of binding agreement does for cooperative games), so that players, and game theorists analyzing the games they play, may fall back on Nash equilibrium as a focal point. Nash equilibrium, together with its refinements (especially subgame perfection in multistage games), remains the workhorse of noncooperative game theory, which in turn is the most developed and most widely influential form of game theory, spreading across disciplinary boundaries.

SEE ALSO *Evolutionary Games; Game Theory; Nash Equilibrium; Nash, John; Prisoner's Dilemma (Economics); Strategy and Voting Games; Subgame Perfection*

BIBLIOGRAPHY

Dimand, Mary Ann, and Robert W. Dimand. 1996. *From the Beginnings to 1945.* Vol. 1 of *A History of Game Theory.* London and New York: Routledge.

Dimand, Mary Ann, and Robert W. Dimand, eds. 1997. *The Foundations of Game Theory.* 3 vols. Cheltenham, U.K., and Lyme, NH: Edward Elgar Publishing.

Leonard, Robert J. 1994. Reading Cournot, Reading Nash: The Creation and Stabilisation of the Nash Equilibrium. *Economic Journal* 104 (424): 492–511.

Nash, John F., Jr. 1950. Equilibrium Points in n-Person Games. *Proceedings of the National Academy of Sciences* 36 (1): 48–49.

Nash, John F., Jr. 1951. Noncooperative Games. *Annals of Mathematics* 54: 286–295.

Nash, John F., Jr. 1996. *Essays on Game Theory*. Cheltenham, U.K., and Brookfield, VT: Edward Elgar Publishing.

Pearce, David G. 1984. Rationalizable Strategic Behavior and the Problem of Perfection. *Econometrica* 52 (4): 1029–1050.

Rasmusen, Eric. 2007. *Games and Information*. 4th ed. Malden, MA: Blackwell.

Von Neumann, John, and Oskar Morgenstern. 1944. *Theory of Games and Economic Behavior*. Princeton, NJ: Princeton University Press. Expanded 60th anniversary edition with contributions by Harold W. Kuhn, Ariel Rubinstein, et al., Princeton, NJ: Princeton University Press, 2004.

Weintraub, E. Roy, ed. 1992. *Toward a History of Game Theory*. Annual Supplement to Vol. 24 of *History of Political Economy*. Durham, NC: Duke University Press.

Robert W. Dimand

NONDECISION-MAKING

Peter Bachrach and Morton Baratz (1970) first introduced the concept of *nondecision-making*, contesting the dominant explanation of the use of power in decision-making by asking how issues are suppressed and the scope of decision-making restricted. This was a challenge to Robert Dahl's conceptualization of power, which tended to focus on how decisions are made. Bachrach and Baratz suggested that to fully understand power, researchers should also consider decisions that are not made—nondecisions. Nondecision-making involves suppressing challenges to the status quo and suppressing the addition of new issues to an agenda. Issues are excluded from an agenda because they are threatening in some direct way, or because of the competition for the limited space for agenda items.

The concept of nondecision-making is best understood in relation to the concept of decision-making. Nondecision-making differs from decision-making in that direct and even tacit confrontation is avoided. Prior to the introduction of nondecision-making, power often was conceptualized as a conflict relationship—that is, a "power over" relationship. Traditional conceptualization of power, as suggested by Dahl, among others, posits that *A* gets *B* to do what *B* would not otherwise have done. Nondecision-making focuses not on such direct use of power, but on its indirect manifestations. As such, power can be exercised in the absence of a direct and overt threat. For example, assume that *A* gets *B* to engage in action *X*. As a consequence of *B*'s engagement in action *X*, it becomes unlikely that *C* will get *B* to engage in action *Y*; this is an indirect conflict relationship because *A* and *C* are not engaged in direct competition. What this suggests is that power relations can be both direct and indirect, and that they can involve the use of threats or not.

A primary function of nondecision-making is to maintain a *mobilization of bias*. Mobilization of bias represents a dominant set of beliefs, values, and institutional processes and procedures that work to privilege some groups in relation to others. This is in direct contrast to the pluralist view, which suggests that the marketplace of policy ideas is relatively open and accessible to various groups. Pluralists further argue that due to competition, the various groups possess the opportunity to influence the policy agenda, provided there has been sufficient political mobilization. Thus, groups hoping to influence policy decisions will not necessarily succeed in all of their attempts to influence policy, but neither will they be systematically denied access to influence the decisionmaking process. On the contrary, the theory of nondecision-making suggests that through a mobilization of bias, some groups are systematically denied access to the decision-making process. There are multiple forms by which the privileging of some can be achieved through nondecision-making; the threat of sanctions is one such form. Norms, rules, routines and procedures, values, and myths are often employed in the threat of sanctions. Nondecision-making can also employ the use of force. Another form of nondecision-making involves the use of the "rule of anticipated reactions": Anticipated reactions result from situations where *B*, who has relatively less power than *A*, decides not to make a demand upon *A* in an effort to avoid confrontation, or out of the fear that such behavior would result in *A*'s invoking sanctions against him or her.

The result of nondecision-making is that certain persons, perspectives, issues, or conflicts are excluded or suppressed. Consequently, the scope of the debate is limited and contained to include issues perceived as "safe." However, it is possible to challenge the mobilization of bias: To do so involves expanding the scope of participation of the decision-making process, and this requires enhancing the knowledge of participants. Community development corporations and progressive coalitions, among other groups, can all play a key role in expanding the scope of the democratic process.

SEE ALSO *Game Theory; Power; Power, Political; Schattschneider, E. E.*

BIBLIOGRAPHY

Bachrach, Peter, and Morton S. Baratz. 1970. *Power and Poverty*. New York: Oxford University Press.

Dahl, Robert A. 1961. *Who Governs?* New Haven, CT: Yale University Press.

Frey, Frederick. 1971. Comment: On Issues and Nonissues in the Study of Power. *American Political Science Review* 65 (4): 1081–1101.

Julia S. Jordan-Zachery

NON-EXPECTED UTILITY THEORY

The expected utility/subjective probability model of risk preferences and beliefs has long been the preeminent model of individual choice under conditions of uncertainty. It exhibits a tremendous flexibility in representing aspects of attitudes toward risk, has a well-developed analytical structure, and has been applied to the analysis of gambling, games of strategy, incomplete information, insurance, portfolio and investment decisions, capital markets, and many other areas. This model posits a cardinal utility function over outcomes (usually alternative wealth levels) and assumes that an individual evaluates risky prospects on the basis of the expected value of his or her utility function. In situations of objective uncertainty (e.g., roulette wheels), this expectation is based on the objective probabilities involved. In situations of subjective uncertainty (e.g., horse races) likelihood beliefs are represented by the individual's personal or subjective probabilities of the various alternative occurrences. First proposed by the Dutch mathematician Daniel Bernoulli in 1738 as a solution to the well-known Saint Petersburg paradox, the expected utility model has since been axiomatized under conditions of both objective and subjective uncertainty. Many consider these axioms and the resulting model to be the essence of rational risk preferences and beliefs.

In spite of its flexibility, the expected utility/subjective probability model has refutable implications, and beginning in the 1950s, psychologists and economists have uncovered a growing body of experimental evidence that individuals do not necessarily conform to many of the key axioms or predictions of the model. One well-known example, first demonstrated by the French economist Maurice Allais in 1953, consists of asking subjects to express their preferred option from each of two pairs of objective gambles. The majority of subjects express preferences that are inconsistent with expected utility, and they directly violate its primary empirical axiom, the so-called independence axiom. Although initially dismissed as an isolated example, the Allais paradox has been replicated by numerous researchers and found to be a special case of at least two forms of systematic violations of the independence axiom. Such departures have also been replicated using real-money gambles.

Starting in the early 1960s, researchers have also uncovered a class of systematic violations of the subjective probability hypothesis. The most well-known example, offered by Daniel Ellsberg in 1961, consists of an urn with ninety balls, thirty of which are red, with the remaining sixty being black or yellow in an unknown proportion. Subjects are asked to select from each of two pairs of bets on this urn, and they typically select in a manner inconsistent with well-defined likelihood beliefs in regard to obtaining a black versus a yellow ball. This finding was also originally dismissed, but the phenomenon has since been replicated by many researchers in a number of different examples. Choices in such experiments reveal a general preference for betting on objective rather than subjective events, a phenomenon that has been termed "ambiguity aversion."

In response to these empirical violations, researchers have developed, axiomatized, and analyzed a number of alternative models of risk preferences and beliefs, most of which replace the expected utility formula with alternative formulas that individuals are assumed to maximize. The earliest of these models, proposed by Ward Edwards in the 1950s and adopted by Daniel Kahneman and Amos Tversky in the 1970s as part of their well-known "prospect theory," was found to generate implausible predictions (namely that individuals would select some gambles with lower payoffs than other gambles). Economists have since developed and axiomatized non-expected utility models of risk preferences that avoid these difficulties, are consistent with the broad class of Allais-type violations of the independence axiom, and are capable of formal analysis and application to economic and other decisions. The most notable of these is the "rank-dependent expected utility model" of the Australian economist John Quiggin.

Researchers have also developed models of preferences over subjective prospects that are consistent with both Allais-type departures from expected utility risk preferences and Ellsberg-type departures from probabilistic beliefs. One such model, long informally discussed in the literature, axiomatized by Itzhak Gilboa and David Schmeidler, and known as "maximin expected utility," posits a utility function and a set of subjective probability distributions over events. It assumes that individuals evaluate each bet on the basis of its minimum expected utility over this class of distributions. Another important model, again axiomatized by Gilboa and Schmeidler and known as "Choquet expected utility," posits a utility function but replaces the classical (i.e., additive) probability measure of subjective expected utility with a nonadditive measure over events. It also replaces the standard expected utility formula with an alternative notion of expectation in respect to this nonadditive measure. Both models have been successfully applied to economic decision-making.

SEE ALSO *Expected Utility Theory; Probability; Probability, Subjective; Prospect Theory; Rationality; Risk; Uncertainty*

BIBLIOGRAPHY

Kahneman, Daniel, and Amos Tversky. 1979. Prospect Theory: An Analysis of Decision under Risk. *Econometrica* 47 (2): 263–291.

Machina, Mark. 1987. Choice under Uncertainty: Problems Solved and Unsolved. *Journal of Economic Perspectives* 1 (1): 121–154.

Quiggin, John. 1982. A Theory of Anticipated Utility. *Journal of Economic Behavior and Organization* 3 (4): 323–343.

Schmeidler, David. 1989. Subjective Probability and Expected Utility without Additivity. *Econometrica* 57 (3): 571–587.

Mark J. Machina

NONGOVERNMENTAL ORGANIZATIONS (NGOs)

The term *nongovernmental organization*, or *NGO*, refers to a vast range of nonprofit organizations that are not a part of any government. They vary in size from a few people operating on a shoestring budget to huge globe-spanning organizations. Highlighted below are some crucial questions and controversies that are salient in shaping the political economy of NGOs as social actors, particularly in relation to their often assumed status as expressions of civil society; their relationship to social movements; and the ways they both constrain and enable progressive social change.

The number and visibility of NGOs have expanded dramatically since the 1970s, in part because neoliberal policies have reduced the role of the state in many areas. NGOs commonly work in numerous fields, including humanitarian and other social services; research, monitoring, and information provision; and advocacy around particular issues, such as the environment, health, the empowerment of marginalized communities, human rights, and the status of women and minorities. Many NGOs contract with states and intergovernmental organizations to provide services. During the early decades of NGO growth, they were celebrated as efficient providers of services and deliverers of empowerment. As a result, they became consultants to governmental and international agencies, particularly as representatives of the "grass roots."

NGOs are sometimes called *voluntary organizations*, highlighting a presumption that social values, rather than profit or political power, are the primary motivators in the functioning of such organizations. These notions of values and voluntarism have led observers to see NGOs as expressions of civil society, similar to social movements, and to interpret their increased visibility as a strengthening of the influence of civil society in the affairs of the state and the economy.

QUESTIONS AND CONTROVERSIES

Since the mid-1990s, the popular perception that NGOs are potential agents for diffusing development and enabling empowerment has increasingly been subjected to critical scrutiny in academia and in the community spaces where NGOs operate. Critics have pointed out that it is incorrect to assume that NGOs are automatically accountable to the "target groups" in whose name they work. Indeed, some pseudo-grassroots, or "astroturf," NGOs have been set up by business or political interests to provide a misleading impression of grassroots action to advance their own agendas. Often astroturf groups try to hide their status as a vested interest.

More generally, the NGO form itself can blunt its potential for social activism for several reasons. First, NGOs commonly have an organizational hierarchy with paid staff and offices, so they must raise funds, either from donors or through contracting to provide services. This financial dependency frequently renders NGOs accountable to their funders. It also promotes a tendency toward professionalization. These factors often create tensions with movement-based models of social change that rely on mass mobilization.

Second, when NGOs rely on donors for funding, it becomes difficult for them to support alternative visions and local initiatives. For instance, David Hulme and Michael Edwards, in *NGOs, States and Donors* (1997), ask whether the interests, values, methods, and priorities of NGOs have become so tied with those of northern-government donors and "developing country-states" that they have now been "socialized" into the development industry. Have NGOs gained so much leverage, Hulme and Edwards wonder, because "they now have the social grace not to persist with awkward questions and the organizational capacity to divert the poor and disadvantaged from more radical ideas about how to overcome poverty?" (p. 3).

Third, NGO structures and project funding often lead to increased standardization and constrain the spaces for NGOs to learn in response to local concerns, leading to major gaps between advocacy and practice. As states increasingly outsource their functions to them, NGOs find themselves in a race "to do" rather than to "reflect." As David Lewis and Tina Wallace put it in *New Roles and Relevance* (2000), "Finding ways of becoming learning organizations—as well as finding ways to increase accountability at all levels—largely continue to evade NGOs, yet the successful search lies at the heart of NGOs' ability to respond in ways that are truly relevant" (p. xiv).

These processes, through which organizations working at the grassroots level lose their connection with their prime constituency and support base, have been called "NGOization." There is thus an implicit or explicit critique that NGOs and their ties with the state are significantly reshaping, or even replacing, community-based activism. For Arundhati Roy, such "NGO-ization of politics threatens to turn resistance into a well-mannered, reasonable, salaried, 9-to-5 job. With a few perks thrown in" (Roy 2004).

NGOization is by no means confined to the "Third World." For example, Sabine Lang argues in "The NGO-ization of Feminism" (2000) that the NGOization of German women's movements brought with it: (1) a structural emphasis on professionalized but decentralized small-scale organizations; (2) a turn from antihierarchical to more hierarchical structures; and (3) the partitioning of a complex feminist agenda of emancipation and equality into specific single issues with a state-oriented politics. While feminist movement-building prioritized the making of a new democratic counterculture, new feminist NGOs have aimed for issue-specific intervention and pragmatic strategies that have a strong employment focus.

On a global level, "gender mainstreaming" and "poor women's empowerment" have been important features of NGOization, with issues such as violence against women, adult literacy, HIV/AIDS, and microcredit being addressed (in isolated forms) as significant priorities. At the same time, issues that had been prominent in women's movements in the prestructural-adjustment era, such as price inflation of basic foods, women's unions, and land reforms, have been pushed aside. Thus, the structure and social location of NGOs can situate them as diffusers of the hegemonic values, ideologies, and knowledge to people at the grass roots, rather than as challengers of existing hierarchies of power that advance broader visions of social change.

NGOs WITHOUT "-IZATION"?

In a context in which NGOs have increasingly been called upon to help manage the problems produced by neoliberal policies and to pacify those who have been hardest hit by such policies, many small movements have found it impossible to exist without engaging with donor agencies or local and national NGOs in one form or another. The challenge before such organizations is to find creative ways to support their political work while also maintaining their accountability and transparency before the people they work for and work with. Despite the countless challenges, resistance to NGOization continues in many small organizations.

SEE ALSO *Accountability; Feminism; Human Rights; International Nongovernmental Organizations (INGOs); Marginalization; Microfinance; Minorities; Organizations; Poverty; Resistance; Third World; Volunteer Programs; Volunteerism; Women's Movement*

BIBLIOGRAPHY

Hulme, David, and Michael Edwards. 1997. NGOs, States and Donors: An Overview. In *NGOs, States and Donors: Too Close for Comfort?*, ed. David Hulme and Michael Edwards, 3–32. New York: St. Martin's.

Lang, Sabine. 2000. The NGO-ization of Feminism: Institutionalization and Institution Building within the German Women's Movements. In *Global Feminisms since 1945*, ed. Bonnie Smith, 290–304. New York: Routledge.

Lewis, David, and Tina Wallace. 2000. Introduction. In *New Roles and Relevance: Development NGOs and the Challenge of Change*, ed. David Lewis and Tina Wallace, ix–xvii. Bloomfield, CT: Kumarian Press.

Roy, Arundhati. 2004. Tide? Or Ivory Snow? Public Power in the Age of Empire. Speech given in San Francisco, California, on August 16, 2004. http://www.democracynow.org/static/Arundhati_Trans.shtml.

Sangtin Writers, and Richa Nagar. 2006. *Playing with Fire: Feminist Thought and Activism through Seven Lives in India*. Minneapolis: University of Minnesota Press.

David R. Faust
Richa Nagar

NONLINEAR REGRESSION

A brief discussion of linear regression is essential in understanding nonlinear regression. One of the assumptions of the classical linear regression model is linearity of the functional form. A linear regression model can be written as:

$$Y = \beta_1 X_1 + \beta_2 X_2 + \dots + \beta_k X_k + \varepsilon,$$

where Y is the dependent variable, X_1, X_2, …, X_k are the explanatory variables, and ε is the error term. A popular statistical technique to estimate the value of the parameters of this model is the classical linear regression where the optimization algorithm applies the least squares errors method to find the best fit. Given the classical assumptions, according to the Gauss-Markov theorem, the least squares coefficients are the best linear unbiased estimator (BLUE) of the population of regression coefficients.

Some regression models are intrinsically nonlinear in their parameters; therefore, application of linear regression estimates generates biased results. Nonlinear regression is an extension of the linear least squares regression for a much larger and general class of functions where the relationship between dependent and independent variable is not linear. As a result, the first-order conditions for least squares estimation of the parameters are nonlinear functions of the parameters. A general form of nonlinear regression equation is:

$$Y_i = f(\mathbf{x}_i, \theta) + \varepsilon_i,$$

where $\mathbf{x}_i$ is a $(N \times 1)$ vector of independent variables, θ is a $(K \times 1)$ parameter vector, and ε_i is an additive error term. A common example of intrinsically nonlinear functions is the Cobb-Douglas production function:

$$Q_i = \alpha L_i^{\beta_1} K_i^{\beta_2} \varepsilon_i,$$

where Q_i is the output of firm i, L_i is the labor input, K_i is the capital input, and ε_i is a multiplicative error term. Parameters of β_1 and β_2 are the elasticities of output with respect to labor and capital. Another example is the consumption function:

$$C_t = \alpha_t + \beta_1 Y_t^{\beta_2} + e_t,$$

which reflects the uncertainty with respect to the way income affects consumption expenditures. In these examples, the terms in the models cannot be rearranged to apply the linear least squares.

Pioneers such as Jennrich (1969) and Malinvaud (1970) have advanced the econometric theory for nonlinear statistical models, while development of computing technology in the last few decades has allowed application of nonlinear models to statistical analysis of complicated relationships between variables. When the nonlinear functions cannot be transformed into linear form, econometricians use two common methods, the nonlinear least squares or the maximum likelihood, to estimate the parameters of the model. These approaches essentially search for a solution to the nonlinear optimization problem by minimizing the sum of squared errors or maximizing the likelihood function. Although there are very few limitations on the functional form of nonlinear regression, the parameters of the model are conceptually estimated in the same way as the linear least squares.

However, reaching a solution to a nonlinear optimization problem is a difficult task. A number of computational methods are available. The Gauss-Newton algorithm, a special case of the more general Newton-Raphson algorithm, is a popular method that linearizes the regression model by approximating $F(\theta)$ from a Taylor series expansion around an initial θ to minimize the residual sum of squares function. In the iterative linearization process, the nonlinear least squares method typically begins with guessed starting values for the parameters and computes the corresponding sum of squared residuals to reach a global minimum. Although the Gauss-Newton algorithm is more efficient in reaching a global minimum, it is less likely than the Newton-Raphson algorithm to locate the global minimum instead of a local one. Of course, since nonlinearity of the functional form violates the classical assumptions, the Gauss-Markov theorem does not apply to the nonlinear regression.

Econometricians typically ignore the possibility that the new error term created in the process of linearization may not meet the classical linear regression model assumption. Also, the nonlinear least squares method can become computationally expensive when the number of parameters to be estimated exceeds two. Since desirable properties of classical linear regression do not necessarily remain in the nonlinear least square estimator, the maximum likelihood estimator is often preferred. In fact, the two techniques are computationally similar.

In selecting functional form, several factors must be considered, including theoretical consistency, applicability, flexibility, computational difficulty, and factual conformity (Lau, 1986). While the underlying theoretical relationship between variables is important, various statistical techniques are used to allow the data to determine the appropriate functional form. In spite of its problem with the log of zero and negative values, the most popular technique for testing nonlinearity is the Box-Cox transformation method, which tests restrictions on a more general functional form. Some nonlinear equations, however, can be transformed into classical linear form, which would facilitate the estimation of their parameters through the classical least squares procedure. For example, taking the natural log of the Cobb-Douglas production function results in the following function, which is linear in parameters:

$$\ln Q_i = \alpha + \ln \beta_1 L_i + \ln \beta_2 K_i + \ln \varepsilon_i.$$

In this case, the least squares estimates of the transformed variables would have the traditional desirable properties.

Nonlinear regression models are sometimes more consistent with the true relationship between variables and have found many applications in models such as the random parameter, continuous regime switching, and time-varying random parameter. Also, in spite of an over-identification tendency in the nonlinear models, the General Method of Moments (GMM) provides a mechanism to arrive at consistent parameter estimates without the normality assumption requirement. However, the use of nonlinear regression models has a few disadvantages. First, estimation procedures for nonlinear models are more complicated because of minimization of sum of square errors, especially when the number of parameters is large, because of minimization of sum of square errors and difficulty of finding the starting values for the iterative linearization process. Second, some measures of goodness of fit, such as the t-statistic and the F-statistic, are not directly compatible and cannot be used or require modification. Compatibility of other measures of goodness of fit such as the R^2 is debatable. Third, there is more ambiguity in the interpretation of the coefficients in nonlinear models because the derivatives of the regression are usually a function of θ rather than being constant. Overall, although the parsimony rule suggests that computationally more demanding estimators do not have better statistical properties, nonlinear maximum likelihood estimators tend to have better finite sample properties than simple alternatives.

SEE ALSO *Econometric Decomposition; Linear Regression; Linear Systems; Nonlinear Systems; Regression; Regression Analysis; Statistics*

BIBLIOGRAPHY

Amemiya, T. 1991. Nonlinear Regression Models. In *Handbook of Econometrics*, ed. Zvi Griliches and Michael Intriligator, 1: 333–389. Amsterdam: North-Holland.

Davidson, Russell, and James MacKinnon. 1993. *Estimation and Inference in Econometrics*. Oxford: Oxford University Press.

Gallant, Ronald A. 1987. *Nonlinear Statistical Models*. New York: Wiley.

Granger, Clive W. J. 1993. Strategies for Modeling Nonlinear Time Series Relationship. *Economic Record* 69: 233–238.

Greene, William H. 2003. *Econometrics Analysis*, 5th ed. Upper Saddle River, NJ: Prentice Hall.

Jennrich, Robert I. 1969. Asymptotic Properties of Nonlinear Least Squares Estimators. *Annals of Mathematical Statistics* 40 (2): 633–643.

Judge, George G., R. Carter Hill, William E. Griffiths, et al. 1985. *Introduction to the Theory and Practice of Econometrics*, 2nd ed. New York: Wiley.

Lau, Lawrence J. 1986. Functional Forms in Econometric Model Building. In *Handbook of Econometrics*, eds. Zvi Griliches and Michael Intriligator, 3: 1514–1566. Amsterdam: North-Holland.

Malinvaud, Edmond. 1970. The Consistency of Nonlinear Regressions. *Annals of Mathematical Statistics* 41: 956–969.

Quandt, Richard E. 1983. Computational Problems and Methods. In *Handbook of Econometrics*, eds. Zve Griliches and Michael Intriligator, 1: 699–764. Amsterdam: North-Holland.

Akbar Marvasti

NONLINEAR SYSTEMS

All real world systems are nonlinear: Straight lines cannot, in practice, go on forever, nor can forces and interactions in natural or social systems. Nonlinearity arises in real economic systems both from human behavior—for example, wage demands varying as a function of the rate of employment—and from the interaction of economic variables—for example, the multiplication of wage rates by the number of workers to calculate the wage bill. Any model that omits these nonlinearities, either by assuming linear behavioral functions or by assuming that a variable remains constant in order to avoid interactive nonlinearities, necessarily reduces its capacity to model the actual economy.

Idealized linear systems can be hypothesized, and the mathematical analysis of these is long established, well-known, and generally results in closed-form symbolic solutions in which the system state at any point in time is a function of the system's parameters. Moreover, in the vicinity of an equilibrium, the linear component of a system, which can be extracted from a mathematical model by a polynomial expansion, dominates the nonlinear components. Thus if a system is stable about an equilibrium, or can be constrained to remain in the vicinity of an equilibrium, its dynamics can be modeled using linear methods.

The mathematical analysis of nonlinear systems, on the other hand, is a recent development, and in general does not result in symbolic solutions. Instead, a nonlinear system must be numerically simulated, and in the subsets classed as either chaotic or structurally unstable, the time path of a system depends upon its initial conditions. Scientists in general therefore had a strong incentive to remain in the linear realm.

Since many real world systems did not meet the conditions for linear analysis, nonlinear analytic techniques were gradually developed, leading to what was initially called chaos theory and is now known as complexity theory. Nonlinear methods play a major role in most sciences today, but their uptake in economics has been noticeably more limited.

NONLINEAR ECONOMICS

Nonlinear economics began in the 1940s, when Hungarian economist Nicholas Kaldor (1908–1986) made the prescient observation that a model with linear ex-ante investment and savings functions could not explain the trade cycle. With savings and investment modeled as linear functions of employment, if the savings function were the steeper of the two, the model displayed "*more* stability than the real world appears, in fact, to possess." On the other hand, if the investment function were steeper, then the system "would always be rushing either towards a state of hyper-inflation with full employment, or towards a state of complete collapse with zero employment, with no resting-place in between" (Kaldor 1940, p. 80). Since neither result could be justified, Kaldor surmised that "we are left with the conclusion that the $I(x)$ and $S(x)$ functions cannot both be linear, at any rate over the entire range" (Kaldor 1940, p. 81).

The adoption of nonlinear methods in economics after this insight was very limited, and Kaldor later argued that this was because economics took for granted "that the economy always approaches, or is near to, a state of equilibrium" (Kaldor 1972, p. 1239). Economists therefore tended to rely upon comparative statics methods, even when the relevant linear model was unstable under reasonable parameter values—as in the case of the linear model of supply and demand, which is unstable under the realistic condition that the price elasticity of supply exceeds that of demand.

While Kaldor pointed out the need for nonlinear analysis in economics, the main pioneer of nonlinear models in economics was Richard Goodwin (1913–1996). Drawing his inspiration from the French mathematicians Henri Poincaré and Philippe Le Corbeiller (b. 1911), Goodwin developed many nonlinear models, with his signature contribution implementing Karl Marx's class-struggle cycle model as a predator-prey system—in which technically, the capitalists were the prey and workers the predators.

There is now a substantial research tradition in nonlinear dynamics within economics that overlaps with the application of chaos, complexity, and evolutionary theories, and fractal analysis to economics. There are numerous nonlinear dynamical models of macroeconomics, microeconomics, and finance market phenomena, including the aggregate business cycle, the individual market cobweb cycle, and stock market crashes. Many econometric methods to test economic time series for nonlinear data structures (e.g., the Hurst exponent, the Brock–Dechert–Scheinkman (BDS) statistic, Smooth Transition Auto-Regression) exist, though their robustness at determining whether nonlinear causal structures exist in noisy linear time series is limited.

There are journals devoted to nonlinear economic analysis—such as *Studies in Nonlinear Dynamics & Econometrics*, and *Nonlinear Dynamics, Psychology, and Life Sciences*—as well as others where nonlinear analysis features frequently—such as the *Journal of Economic Dynamics and Control*, *Macroeconomic Dynamics*, the *Review of Economic Dynamics*, and *Structural Change and Economic Dynamics*. Most contributions from the developing field of econophysics could be characterized as essentially nonlinear, including those applying nonextensive statistical mechanics to the analysis of financial market data.

Despite this flowering, nonlinear analysis in economics is hampered by two dilemmas. The first, peculiar to economics, is that the dominant pedagogic and research tendency in economics is to model economic processes as equilibrium phenomena. The second, generic problem is best captured by John von Neumann's (1903–1957) apocryphal aphorism that a general theory of nonlinear phenomena is akin to "a theory of non-elephants": While linear analysis is well defined, the variety of nonlinear phenomena is so enormous that it bedevils systematic analysis (Bak and Paczusku 1995, p. 6690).

SEE ALSO *Linear Systems*

BIBLIOGRAPHY

Asada, Toichiro, Pu Chen, Carl Chiarella, and Peter Flaschel. 2006. Keynesian Dynamics and the Wage-Price Spiral: A Baseline Disequilibrium Model. *Journal of Macroeconomics* 28 (1): 90–130.

Bak, Per, and Maya Paczuski. 1995. Complexity, Contingency, and Criticality. *Proceedings of the National Academy of Sciences of the United States of America* 92 (15): 6689–6696.

Blatt, John M. 1983. *Dynamic Economic Systems: A Post Keynesian Approach*. Armonk, NY: M. E. Sharpe.

Holt, Matthew T., and Lee A. Craig. 2006. Nonlinear Dynamics and Structural Change in the U.S. Hog-Corn Cycle: A Time-Varying STAR Approach. *American Journal of Agricultural Economics* 88 (1): 215–233.

Goodwin, Richard M. 1951. The Nonlinear Accelerator and the Persistence of Business Cycles. *Econometrica* 19 (1): 1–17.

Goodwin, Richard M. 1967. A Growth Cycle. In *Socialism, Capitalism and Economic Growth*, ed. C. H. Feinstein, 54–58. Cambridge, U.K.: Cambridge University Press.

Kaldor, Nicholas. 1934. A Classificatory Note on the Determinateness of Equilibrium. *Review of Economic Studies* 1 (2): 122–136.

Kaldor, Nicholas. 1940. A Model of the Trade Cycle. *Economic Journal* 50 (197): 78–92.

Kaldor, Nicholas. 1972. The Irrelevance of Equilibrium Economics. *Economic Journal* 82 (328): 1237–1255.

Kyrtsou, Catherine, and Apostolos Serletis. 2006. Univariate Tests for Nonlinear Structure. *Journal of Macroeconomics* 28 (1): 154–168.

Marx, Karl. *Capital I*. Marxists Internet Archives. http://www.marxists.org/archive/marx/works/1867-c1/.

Rose, Hugh. 1967. On the Non-Linear Theory of the Employment Cycle. *Review of Economic Studies* 34 (2): 153–173.

Rosser, J. Barkley. 2000. *Mathematics, Microeconomics and Finance*. Vol. I of *From Catastrophe to Chaos: A General Theory of Economic Discontinuities*. New York: Springer.

Zhou, Wei-Xing, and Didier Sornette. 2003. Evidence of a Worldwide Stock Market Log-Periodic Anti-Bubble since Mid-2000. *Physica A* 330 (3–4): 543–583.

Steve Keen

NONPARAMETRIC ESTIMATION

Nonparametric estimation is a methodology for estimating density functions or conditional moments of distributions without making any prior assumptions about functional forms. The data are allowed to speak for themselves in determining the shape of the unknown functions (Silverman 1986).

NONPARAMETRIC DENSITY ESTIMATION

In parametric estimation, if the underlying distribution is known to be normal, the data are used to calculate the mean μ and variance σ^2 of the distribution, substituting them into the formula for the normal density. Suppose

X is a continuous random variable, $f(x)$ is the probability density function, and $F(x)$ is the cumulative density function when $X = x$. With h as the width of a bin or interval, the nonparametric naive estimate of $f(x)$ is

$$\hat{f}(x) = \lim_{h \to 0} \left[\frac{\left(F\left(x + h/2\right) - F\left(x - h/2\right) \right)}{h} \right] = 1/h^*(\text{prob-}$$

ability that X belongs to the interval $[x - h/2, x + h/2]) = 1/h^*$(probability that $(X - x)/h$ belongs to the interval $[-1/2, 1/2])$.

In other words,

$$\hat{f}(x) = \frac{1}{nh} \sum_{i=1}^{n} I\left(\frac{X_i - x}{h}\right) \qquad (1)$$

where,

$$I(.) = 1 \quad \text{if} \quad -\frac{1}{2} < \left(\frac{X_i - x}{h}\right) < \frac{1}{2}$$
$$= 0 \quad \text{if} \ \text{otherwise}$$

Alternately,

$$\hat{f}(x) = \frac{1}{nh} \sum_{i=1}^{n} K\left(\frac{X_i - x}{h}\right) \qquad (2)$$

The graph of the estimated density function (Figure 1) from equation (1) is not a smooth curve. Thus the weight function I(.) is replaced by a kernel density function K(.) that satisfies the condition $\int_{-\infty}^{+\infty} K(x)\,dx = 1$. The revised nonparametric estimate of the density function is expressed in equation (2). Alternative choices on the kernel density function are provided in equations (4) through (6). The graph of a density function using kernel density weights is smooth and differentiable as illustrated by Figure 2.

NONPARAMETRIC REGRESSION

A *regression function* is an equation that explains and predicts movements in one variable (the *dependent* variable) as a function of movements in another variable or a set of other variables (the *independent* or *explanatory* variables). Having observed the independent variable X_i, the regression function provides an average or expected value of the dependent variable Y_i. For a set of n data points $\{(X_i, Y_i)\}_{i=1}^{n}$ the regression function can be modeled as

$$Y_i = E(Y_i \mid X_i) + \varepsilon_i = m(X_i) + \varepsilon_i \qquad i = 1, \dots, n \qquad (3)$$

In equation (3), m is the unknown regression equation and ε represents unknown stochastic disturbances. The aim of regression analysis is to estimate the regression function m. The *parametric* approach assumes that the regression function has some prespecified functional form (such as logarithmic, inverse, quadratic, or cubic).

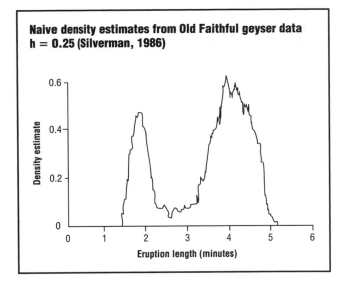

Naive density estimates from Old Faithful geyser data h = 0.25 (Silverman, 1986)

Figure 1

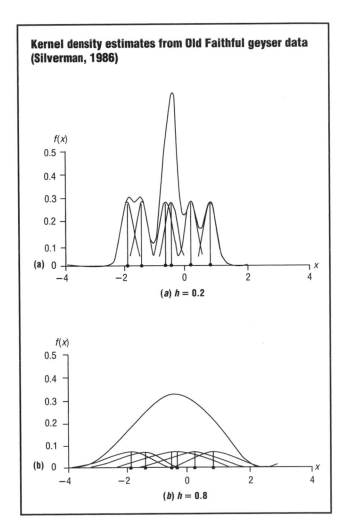

Kernel density estimates from Old Faithful geyser data (Silverman, 1986)

(a) *h* = 0.2

(b) *h* = 0.8

Figure 2

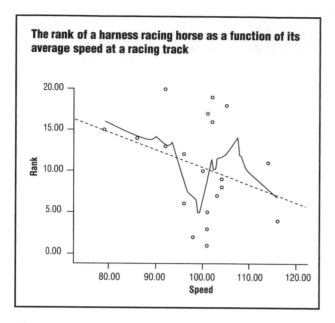

The rank of a harness racing horse as a function of its average speed at a racing track

Figure 3

Nonparametric econometrics estimates the regression function *m* without assuming any specific form.

An example of the two different approaches is illustrated by Figure 3. The straight, negatively sloped, dotted line represents a linear parametric function, while the other curve is a nonparametric estimate. Both curves model the rank of a harness racing horse (1 being high and 20 being low) as a function of its average speed at a racing track. The linear model is unable to represent a U-shaped regression relationship between the rank and speed of racing horses for certain ranges of horse speed.

The assumption that the estimate of the regression function is linear, that is, $m(X_i) = \beta_0 + \beta_1 X_i$, implies certain assumptions about the underlying data-generating process (Pagan and Ullah 1999). For example, if $\{X_i, Y_i\}_{i=1}^n$ is a bivariate normal density, then it can be shown that the mean of the conditional density of Y_i given X_i is $E(Y_i | X_i) = \alpha + \beta X_i$, where $\alpha = EY_i - \beta(EX_i)$ and $\beta = (\mathrm{Var}(X_i))^{-1}\mathrm{Cov}(X_i, Y_i)$. Thus, the linear specification for the regression function is valid only if the underlying data-generating process is normal. If the true distribution is not normal, then the true functional form of $m(X_i)$ is not linear, and least square estimates of the same, assuming a linear functional form, may be *biased* and *inconsistent*.

The question of which approach should be taken in data analysis was a key issue in a bitter feud between the statisticians Karl Pearson (1857–1936) and Ronald Aylmer Fisher (1890–1962) in the 1920s (summarized by Tapia and Thompson 1978). Fisher pointed out that the nonparametric approach gave generally poor efficiency that increased with the number of explanatory variables, thus

giving rise to the well-known *curse of dimensionality* and requiring large data samples for accuracy. Moreover, the size of the required sample increases rapidly with the number of explanatory variables. At the same time, Pearson pointed out that the price paid for pure parametric fitting is the possibility of gross misspecification resulting in high model bias. The parametric and nonparametric estimation techniques support two different and yet very interesting viewpoints. The *semiparametric estimation* technique combines the two. Here, the relationship governing Y_i is expressed as a linear function of some explanatory variables and a nonlinear function of remaining explanatory variables where the nonlinearity is unknown. The coefficients of interest are the slope coefficients of the linear part. P. M. Robinson (1988) shows that it is possible to construct estimators of the linear part that exhibit $\sqrt{n}$ consistency.

The basic principle behind the nonparametric estimation technique is to fit a window *h* around every observation of the dataset and estimate the relationship or moment of interest in each window. A kernel density function $K(.)$ is used to give high weights to data points close to the window and low weights to data points far from the window. Thus the regression relationship is estimated, piece by piece or window by window, as shown in Figure 4. One of the advantages of nonparametric estimation is that it estimates the regression coefficients at every data point. For example, if the researcher is interested in estimating the relationship between a firm's size and its export intensity, the nonparametric estimation technique will provide an estimate of the *slope coefficient* for every firm at every time period, thus giving a broader picture for analysis. Both parametric and nonparametric techniques share a common foundation. Parametric estimates are obtained by minimizing the sum of squares of residuals (SSR). Nonparametric estimates are obtained by minimizing the SSR weighted

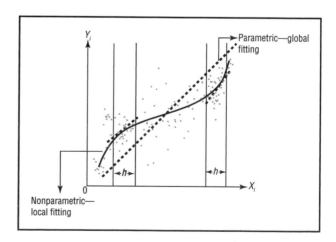

Figure 4

by the kernel density function at every data point. That is the reason why parametric estimates are a product of global fitting, while nonparametric estimates are obtained by local fitting. The conditional mean at point x is a weighted average $\sum_{i=1}^{n} w\left(X_i; x\right) Y_i$ of n data points, where $w = \sum_{i=1}^{n} K\left(X_i - x/h\right) \big/ \sum_i K\left(X_i - x/h\right)$. The weights $w(X_i; x)$ depend upon the kernel density function, the window width, X_i, and the point x at which the conditional expectation is evaluated.

CHOICE OF KERNELS AND WINDOW WIDTHS

Some examples of kernels commonly used in the literature (Silverman 1986) are:

Epanechnikov:
$$K(t) = \frac{3}{4}\left(1 - \frac{1}{5}t^2\right)\Big/ \sqrt{5} \; for \, |t| < \sqrt{5}$$
$$= 0 \qquad\qquad\qquad otherwise \qquad (4)$$

Gaussian:
$$K(t) = \frac{1}{\sqrt{2\pi}}\exp(-(1/2)t^2) \qquad (5)$$

Rectangular:
$$K(t) = 1/2 \; for \, |t| < 1 \qquad (6)$$
$$= 0 \quad otherwise$$

It is well known in the literature that the choice of kernels does not influence significantly the efficiency of estimates. The choice of window width is, however, crucial. Small values of h cause oversmoothing and high values lead to undersmoothing of the estimates. The optimum h is the one that minimizes the integrated mean squared error of $m(x) - \int_{-\infty}^{+\infty} \left(\hat{m}(x) - m(x)\right)^2 dx$.

SCOPE OF NONPARAMETRIC ESTIMATION

The scope of applications for the nonparametric estimation technique is endless (Härdle 1990). It is particularly useful in time series applications, in treatment of extreme observations known as *outliers*, and in smoothing the gap of missing data by interpolating between adjacent data points. In general, nonparametric econometrics provides a versatile method of exploiting a general relationship between two or more variables without reference to a fixed parametric model.

SEE ALSO *Functional Form; Properties of Estimators (Asymptotic and Exact); Semiparametric Estimation*

BIBLIOGRAPHY

Härdle, Wolfgang. 1990. *Applied Nonparametric Regression.* Cambridge, U.K.: Cambridge University Press.

Pagan, Adrian, and Aman Ullah. 1999. *Nonparametric Econometrics.* Cambridge, U.K.: Cambridge University Press.

Robinson, P. M. 1988. Root-N-Consistent Semiparametric Regression. *Econometrica* 56 (4): 931–954.

Silverman, B. W. 1986. *Density Estimation for Statistics and Data Analysis.* London: Chapman and Hall.

Tapia, Richard, and James Thompson. 1978. *Nonparametric Probability Density Estimation.* Baltimore, MD: Johns Hopkins University Press.

Monica Das

NONPARAMETRIC REGRESSION

A regression model may be written generally as

$$y_i = m(x_i \mid \theta) + \varepsilon_i \qquad (1)$$

where the subscript $i = 1, \ldots, n$ indexes observations, ε_i is a random error term, uncorrelated with the regressor x_i and with zero expectation, and θ represents a vector of parameters. Given $E(\varepsilon_i) = 0$, $E(y_i \mid x_i) = m(x_i \mid \theta)$; consequently, the function $m(x_i \mid \theta)$ is often called the *conditional mean function*.

In ordinary least squares regression, the parameter vector is assumed to be of length $K < \infty$ and the conditional mean function is assumed to be linear in parameters, e.g.,

$$m(x_i \mid \theta) = \theta_1 + x_{i2}\theta_2 + \ldots + x_{iK}\theta_K.$$

Moreover, in small samples the errors are typically assumed to be normally distributed in order to facilitate inference. With maximum likelihood estimation, the parameter vector is again assumed to be of finite length K, and a particular form is assumed for the conditional mean function, although linearity in parameters is not necessary. In addition, the errors are assumed to come from a particular family of distributions (e.g., normal, beta, gamma, etc.); with independent sampling, the likelihood function can then be derived as a product of marginal probability density functions, each evaluated at one of n sample observations.

Nonparametric regression involves using one of several techniques to avoid the need to assume specific functional forms for the conditional mean function as well as the distribution of the error terms in (1). By making fewer assumptions, one avoids the risk of mis-specifying either the conditional mean function or the distribution of the errors, which can lead to biased and inconsistent estimation. Moreover, with nonparametric regression techniques, the underlying, true model that is estimated can itself be viewed as nonparametric, in the sense that it can-

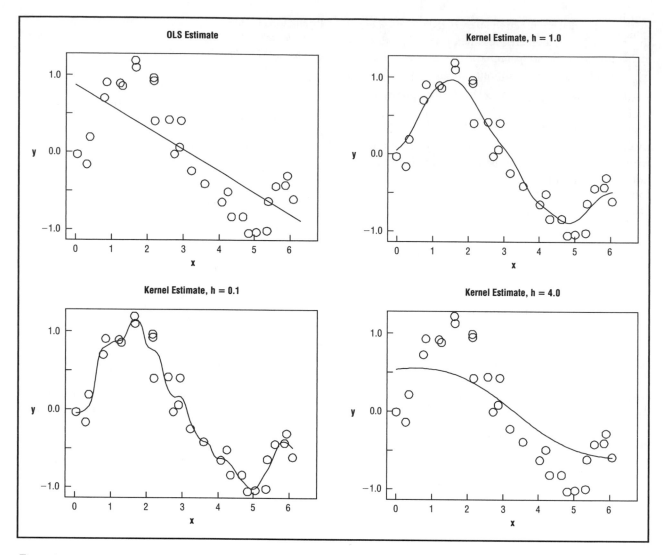

Figure 1

not be represented by a function involving a finite number of parameters. In other words, the parameter vector θ can be assumed to have an infinite number of elements. Consequently, the variety of shapes of conditional mean functions that can be estimated by nonparametric regression methods is far greater than what is possible with more conventional parametric estimation methods such as ordinary least squares or maximum likelihood. However, the increased flexibility comes with some costs; in particular, inference is often more difficult, computational burdens are greater, and rates of convergence are slower with nonparametric methods than with parametric methods.

Several nonparametric regression estimators have been developed. One of the most widely used is the Nadarya-Watson estimator (Nadarya, 1964; Watson, 1964) given by

$$\hat{m}_h(x) = \sum_{i=1}^{n} K_h(x - X_i) Y_i / \sum_{i=1}^{n} K_h(x - X_i), \qquad (2)$$

where h is a smoothing parameter or bandwidth and $K_h(\cdot) = K(\cdot/h)$ is a weighting, or kernel, function that is symmetric and integrates to 1; i.e., $K(-t) = K(t)$ and $\int K(t)\, dt = 1$. A wide variety of functions satisfy these conditions; for example, any symmetric probability density function can be used as a kernel function, as well as any even-order polynomial over some interval from $-\zeta$ to $+\zeta$ with coefficients chosen so that the polynomial integrates to 1 over this interval.

Although researchers using the Nadarya-Watson estimator (as well as other nonparametric estimators) must choose both a kernel function and a value for the smoothing parameter, the choice of kernel function is less important in determining estimation error than the choice of a value for the bandwidth. The bandwidth *h* determines the degree of smoothness of the estimator. As $h \rightarrow 0$, bias of the estimator diminishes but variance increases; as $h \rightarrow \infty$, bias increases while variance decreases. A number of data-driven techniques have been developed to optimize the choice of *h* with respect to one of several criteria; for example, cross-validation methods can be used to choose a value for *h* that minimizes either mean integrated square error or asymptotic mean integrated square error; see Pagan and Ullah (1999) for details. Alternatively, less computationally burdensome plug-in procedures proposed by Sheather and Jones (1991) can be used to choose an optimal value for the bandwidth.

Figure 1 provides an example illustrating the Nadarya-Watson estimator. With the same data displayed in each panel of Figure 1, estimated regression lines are shown for the ordinary least squares (OLS) estimate of the model

$$y_i = \theta_1 + \theta_2 x_i + \varepsilon_i \qquad (3)$$

and Nadarya-Watson kernel estimates of (1) with the standard normal density function used as the kernel function and with three different values of *h* : 0.1, 1.0, and 4.0. The data clearly follow a nonlinear pattern, which the OLS estimator of (3) cannot replicate. With $h = 1$, the kernel estimator captures the pattern of the data nicely, providing a reasonably smooth estimate of the regression curve.

When the bandwidth is reduced to 0.1, the kernel estimate becomes jagged, while increasing the bandwidth to 4.0 results in an estimated curve that is much flatter than the estimates obtained with smaller bandwidths. The two panels in the bottom row of Figure 1 illustrate the tradeoff between bias and variance associated with larger or smaller values of *h* as discussed above.

The Nadarya-Watson estimator, when evaluated at an arbitrary point *x*, is simply a weighted average of values Y_i in a neighborhood of *x* ; the size of the neighborhood and the weights given to each Y_i are determined jointly by the kernel function $K(\cdot)$ and the bandwidth *h*. Local polynomial estimators, by contrast, estimate the conditional mean function by fitting locally a *p* th-order polynomial to the data. This approach offers several advantages over the earlier Nadarya-Watson estimator, as discussed by Fan and Gijbels (1996). Setting $p = 1$ yields a local linear estimator, which has less bias but no greater variance than the Nadarya-Watson estimator. In addition, while the Nadarya-Watson estimator is inconsistent near boundaries of support for *x*, local polynomial estimators remain consistent near such boundaries. While estimation of regression derivatives is possible using modifications of the Nadarya-Watson estimator, estimation of derivatives is straightforward with local polynomial estimators. As with

the Nadarya-Watson estimator, a number of techniques have been developed to optimize the choice of bandwidth when local polynomial estimators are used, as discussed by Fan and Gijbels (1996).

SEE ALSO *Data; Econometric Decomposition; Frequency Distributions; Linear Regression; Ordinary Least Squares Regression; Regression; Regression Analysis; Statistics*

BIBLIOGRAPHY

Fan, Jianqing, and Irène Gijbels. 1996. *Local Polynomial Modelling and Its Applications.* London: Chapman and Hall.

Nadarya, E. A. 1964. On Estimating Regression. *Theory of Probability and Its Applications* 10: 186–190.

Pagan, Adrian, and Aman Ullah. 1999. *Nonparametric Econometrics.* Cambridge, U.K.: Cambridge University Press.

Sheather, S. J., and M. C. Jones. 1991. A Reliable Data-Based Bandwidth Selection Method for Kernel Density Estimation. *Journal of the Royal Statistical Society,* Series B 53 (3): 683–690.

Watson, G. S. 1964. Smooth Regression Analysis. *Sankhya,* Series A 26: 359–372.

Paul W. Wilson

NON-PROFITS

SEE *Social Economy.*

NONPROLIFERATION TREATIES

SEE *Arms Control and Arms Race.*

NONTRADED GOODS

SEE *Goods, Nontraded.*

NONVERBAL COMMUNICATION

By virtue of a series of discoveries and conceptual departures in the social sciences, our understanding of the process of human communication has been expanded to include nonverbal communication. In the words of Ashley Montagu and Floyd Matson in *The Human Connection* (1979): "It is not merely a hidden dimension or a silent language that has been uncovered by the new wave of scientific explorers; it is more like a neglected universe of discourse and intercourse. We are becoming aware that the verbal domain is only the tip of the iceberg of communicative experience—that there is more, much more, to human dialog than meets the ear" (p. xiii). This entry discusses key ideas from the vast research literature on nonverbal communication (NVC).

Nonverbal behavior (NVB) is usually divided into several categories. One category is *paralanguage*, which refers to the content-free vocalizations and pauses associated with speech. Research conducted by Starkey Duncan and Donald Fiske (1979) shows how paralinguistic behaviors serve as regulators of social interaction. Another category is *facial expressions*. Paul Ekman's research has shown how expressions indicate primary emotions (for example, see his 1992 article). A third category is *kinesics* or *body language*. The research reported by Ray Birdwhistell in *Kinesics and Context* (1970) is an example of the value of detailed recording of gestures and bodily movements. A fourth category is *visual behavior*, which includes gazing. Michael Argyle's research, reported in *Bodily Communication* (1975) and elsewhere, has elucidated the meaning of and social functions served by various patterns of eye contact between people. The study of spatial behavior or *proxemics* is another aspect of NVB research. Edward Hall's categories of interpersonal distance influenced the study of communication and culture (see *The Hidden Dimension*, 1966). Georg Simmel's writing about spatial relations throws light on how space can reflect a group's social standing as being dominant or marginal in a society (see Allen, 2000). The synergistic effects of these categories are illustrated by Albert Mehrabian's multiple-channel research summarized in his 1972 book *Nonverbal Communication*.

Each of the nonverbal channels is understood in terms of both interpretation—referred to as *decoding*—and communication, known as *encoding*. These functions are related: The interpretive function leads observers to infer the communicator's intentions; the communicative function is used to influence the observers' attribution of intentions. The knowledge generated by research provides a tool for agents of influence such as advertising executives and politicians. Certain NVBs have been shown to provide a window into emotions and intentions: For example, in her 2006 article, Christine Harris shows the NVBs and muscle activations that indicate the feeling of embarrassment (in succession—eyes down, smile control, head away, gaze shifts, face touch); and, in their 1982 book on *Nonverbal Communication*, Daniel Druckman, Richard Rozelle, and James Baxter show that deceivers displayed more frequent leg movements, less time looking at the interviewer, and more fidgeting with objects than honest and evasive role-players in their experiments. These are some of the cues that can be used to diagnose psychological states and lying (referred to as decoding); they are also the cues that can be used to disguise one's feelings or intentions (referred to as encoding).

It would seem then that the research findings provide useful information for managing impressions. However, the research also suggests that the process may be more difficult than it seems. In a 1985 chapter, Bella DePaulo and her colleagues review evidence on the impact of controlling NVBs in order to perpetrate a lie. Pointing to a phenomenon referred to as *leakage*, these findings show that when certain nonverbal channels, such as facial expressions, are orchestrated to hide an intention, other channels, subject to less conscious control, can be revealing. Words and facial expressions have been found to be easier to control than body movements and such paralinguistic behaviors as tone of voice. These researchers also show that highly motivated liars may be easier to catch than their less motivated counterparts: When the stakes for pulling off a lie are high, more-difficult-to-control nonverbal channels are more revealing than verbal clues; less motivated liars are more likely to give themselves away with words. Thus, both context and channel are important for diagnosis. Likewise, they are important for the communicator's attempts to create certain impressions.

Another issue is the extent to which the findings are universal. Culture has been shown to influence expressions: Based on a review of the research, Randall Gordon and his colleagues concluded that "the events that elicit emotions vary from culture to culture, but the particular facial muscle movements triggered when a given emotion is elicited may be relatively universal" (2006, p. 85). Cultural influences are referred to as *display rules*. These rules serve to control expressions that would be inappropriate in certain settings. Numerous studies have found differences among cultures in each of the NVB channels: Many of these studies focus on preferences for spacing or interaction distances; some show differences between cultures in gazing behavior, while others examine paralinguistic behaviors. (See, for example, Michael Argyle's 1986 article on display rules dealing with intimacy.) However, while the cross-cultural comparisons are informative, the studies provide limited insight into the situations that arouse such feelings as guilt, shame, or stress within cultures. Cultural interpretations of situations—for example, as social transgressions—are central to the idea of display rules and have implications for the way we diagnose leaked NVBs.

Professional cultures also influence expressions and their interpretation. For example, when considering the field of international politics, four questions can be asked: What is the state of the leader's health? To what extent do the statements made by national representatives reflect actual policies? How committed are representatives to the positions put forward? How secure is the representative's political status? Clues about what to look for are provided by NVC studies. A furrowed brow and raised eyelids together with change in vocal tone and heightened pitch suggest pain; deviations from baseline NVBs may indicate deception; an increase in the amount of NVBs expressed in several channels may signal strong commitment; and spatial behavior may provide clues to political status. These indicators direct attention to relationships between nonverbal channels, abrupt changes in expressions, and the intensity of nonverbal displays. They provide a structure for focusing attention on relevant details—that is, they suggest where to focus attention and what to look at. But they can also be misleading. Professional politicians are adept at masking intentions and feelings, particularly in the channels that are easier to control (facial expressions, spatial behavior). For this reason, knowledge about professional socialization and norms provides a broadened appreciation for the meaning of communication. (For more on NVC in the context of international politics, see the 2006 chapter by Gordon and his coauthors.)

SEE ALSO *Communication*

BIBLIOGRAPHY

Allen, John. 2000. On Georg Simmel: Proxemics, Distances, and Movement. In *Thinking Space*, ed. Mike Crang and Nigel Thrift, 54–70. London: Routledge.

Argyle, Michael. 1975. *Bodily Communication*. New York: International Universities Press.

Argyle, Michael. 1986. Rules for Social Relationships in Four Cultures. *Australian Journal of Psychology* 38 (3): 309–318.

Birdwhistell, Ray L. 1970. *Kinesics and Context: Essays on Body Motion Communication*. Philadelphia: University of Pennsylvania Press.

DePaulo, Bella M., J. I. Stone, and G. D. Lassiter. 1985. Deceiving and Detecting Deceit. In *The Self and Social Life*, ed. Barry R. Schlenker, 323–370. New York: McGraw-Hill.

Druckman, Daniel, Richard M. Rozelle, and James C. Baxter. 1982. *Nonverbal Communication: Survey, Theory, and Research*. Beverly Hills, CA: Sage.

Duncan, Starkey, and Donald W. Fiske. 1979. Dynamic Patterning in Conversation. *American Scientist* 67 (January-February): 90–98.

Ekman, Paul. 1992. Facial Expression of Emotions: New Findings, New Questions. *Psychological Science* 3 (1): 34–38.

Gordon, Randall, Daniel Druckman, Richard M. Rozelle, and James C. Baxter. 2006. Non-Verbal Behaviour as Communication: Approaches, Issues, and Research. In *Handbook of Communication Skills*, ed. Owen Hargie, 73–119. London: Routledge.

Hall, Edward T. 1966. *The Hidden Dimension*. New York: Doubleday.

Harris, Christine R. 2006. Embarrassment: A Form of Social Pain. *American Scientist* 94 (6): 524–533.

Mehrabian, Albert. 1972. *Nonverbal Communication*. Chicago: Aldine-Atherton.

Montagu, Ashley, and Floyd Matson. 1979. *The Human Connection*. New York: McGraw-Hill.

Daniel Druckman

NON-WALRASIAN ECONOMICS

SEE *Barro-Grossman Model; Patinkin, Don.*

NONWHITES

Social scientists often classify and study individuals and groups based upon shared characteristics. A racial group is comprised of individuals who share similar physical characteristics including skin color. The U.S. Census uses the following racial categories: American Indian or Alaska Native; Asian; Black or African American; Native Hawaiian or Other Pacific Islander; White and Some Other Race. There are also two minimum categories for ethnicity: Hispanic or Latino and Not Hispanic or Latino. Hispanics and Latinos may be of any race. The labels as well as the definition for the aforementioned racial groups have changed over time. For decades, individuals could only identify with one racial group. A historic change took place with Census 2000 that permitted individuals to identify with more than one race. This change to the enumeration questionnaire is indicative of how definitions about race can change over time and that these changes are often politically contested. Collectively, individuals identifying themselves as multiracial, Asian, black, Native American, or "other" are referred to by sociologists as "nonwhites." This typology has its strengths and weaknesses, particularly for conducting research.

Research has shown that nonwhites have relatively less access to wealth, status, and power and thus fewer life chances, relative to whites that in American society are considered the dominant racial group. It is for that reason that sociologists as well as other social scientists, in conducting research, study these populations and changes over time jointly. Yet the categorical grouping together by social scientists of all minority groups often fails to recognize the diversity within and between racial groups.

For example, while blacks, Native Americans, Asians and "others" are relatively disadvantaged when compared with their white counterparts, all nonwhites are not equally disadvantaged. On selected social and demographic indicators some Asian ethnic groups, for instance, fare better than individuals who the U.S. Census would consider white. Still other nonwhites such as blacks and Native Americans have been shown to be relatively disadvantaged when compared with their white counterparts. These findings have been observed consistently on selected social and demographic variables including on educational attainment, homeownership, housing values, income, and occupational prestige.

Various Asian ethnic groups, for example, are not equally advantaged relative to whites nor are blacks or Native Americans equally disadvantaged relative to whites. While Asians with Indian ancestry may have relatively high levels of education, Asians of Vietnamese descent may have relatively low levels of education. Similarly, blacks with recent ancestry in Africa or in the Caribbean may have higher incomes relative to native-born blacks. Consolidating individuals who do not possess physical characteristics that are similar to those of the dominant group also means that certain ethnic groups within the larger racial classifications are understudied due to their relatively small population size.

The term nonwhite can also be used to describe a group of people whose skin color is distinctive from the dominant racial group in America, despite the contention by scholars that there are no pure races. Social sciences tend to view racial categories not as purely biological rather as socially constructed. Nonwhites, therefore, share distinguishing physical characteristics that are the basis for the unequal treatment they may experience.

The term nonwhite highlights the relative disadvantages experienced by individuals with less power over their lives than the dominant group. At the same time, the term nonwhite ignores both subpopulations and within group differences on various social outcomes.

SEE ALSO *Assimilation; Minorities; Negro*

BIBLIOGRAPHY

Dodoo, F. Nii-Amoo. 1997. Assimilation Differences among Africans in America. *Social Forces* 76 (2): 527–546.

Grieco, Elizabeth, and Rachel Cassidy. 2001. *Overview of Race and Hispanic Origin: Census 2000 Brief.* Washington, DC: United States Census Bureau.

Grodsky, Eric, and Devah Pager. 2001. The Structure of Disadvantage: Individual and Occupational Determinants of the Black-White Wage Gap. *American Sociological Review* 166 (4): 542–567.

Oliver, Melvin, and Thomas Shapiro. 1995. *Black Wealth/White Wealth.* New York: Routledge.

Lori Latrice Sykes

NONZERO-SUM GAME

In game theory, *nonzero-sum games* (more precisely known as *nonconstant-sum games*) include many examples in which the sum of the payoffs to the players varies according to the strategies chosen. These cases are often more relevant to issues in social science and public policy than are *zero-sum* (and more generally *constant-sum*) games. From a mathematical point of view, however, they raise problems of solution that do not arise when the sum of payoffs is a constant.

An example arises in the case of *public goods.* Suppose that two agents acting independently can each earn payoffs of ten. However, each has the option of contributing three units from his wealth to produce two units of a "public" good that benefits both players equally. The strategies then are "contribute" or "do not contribute," and the game can be summarized in tabular *normal* form as shown in Table 1.

The Table is read as follows: Agent 1, by choosing his strategy, chooses the row, and Agent 2 chooses the column. In the chosen cell, the first payoff is to Agent 1 and the second to Agent 2. For example, at the top left, both agents contribute, leaving seven units each of private wealth, but four units of the public good are produced, adding four additional units of benefits for each of the two agents.

A game of this sort admits two broad classes of solution: *cooperative* and *noncooperative.* Cooperative solutions allow for the possibility that the agents may form a *coalition* and enter into a binding agreement to choose a joint strategy. In this case, it seems likely that they would both choose to contribute, because this choice makes both better off, while each would refuse to contribute if the other does not. Noncooperative solutions assume instead that there are no trustworthy commitments to joint action. In the case of the public goods dilemma, each agent can reason that he is better off choosing not to contribute, whatever the other may do, and moreover that the other player can reason in the same way. As a consequence, it seems that each would choose not to contribute. Therefore, "do not contribute" is the *equilibrium* of the game. The fact

		Agent 2	
		contribute	do not contribute
Agent 1	contribute	11,11	7,12
	do not contribute	12,7	10,10

Table 1. Public Goods Dilemma

that each agent has an unconditional motive to choose the equilibrium makes this game an instance of a *social dilemma*. In addition to public goods, noncooperative equilibrium concepts are applied to competition in industry, international rivalries, population dynamics in evolutionary biology, and many other issues.

In cooperative solutions of larger and more complex games, questions may arise with respect to bargaining and the division of the benefits from the common strategy and the stability of coalitions and agreements, leading to a number of alternative concepts of solution. Among noncooperative solutions, the equilibrium concept is dominant, but ambiguities can arise with respect to information and learning, and some alternative solution concepts have been explored.

A half-century of experimental work in social psychology, political science, and economics has indicated that both cooperative and noncooperative solutions influence human behavior, but also that real human beings often reason less carefully than the hypothetical agents of game theory.

SEE ALSO *Equilibrium in Economics; Game Theory; Nash Equilibrium; Nash, John; Public Goods; Von Neumann, John; Zero-sum Game*

BIBLIOGRAPHY

McCain, Roger A. 2004. *Game Theory: A Nontechnical Introduction to the Analysis of Strategy.* Mason, OH: Thomson South-Western.

Nash, John. 1951. Non-Cooperative Games. *Annals of Mathematics* 54 (2): 286–295.

von Neumann, John, and Oskar Morgenstern. 1944. *Theory of Games and Economic Behavior.* Princeton, NJ: Princeton University Press.

Roger McCain

NORM OF RECIPROCITY

SEE *Reciprocity, Norm of.*

NORMAL ACCIDENT THEORY

SEE *Accidents, Industrial.*

NORMAL PROBABILITY DENSITY FUNCTION

SEE *Probability Distributions.*

NORMAL SCIENCE

SEE *Paradigm.*

NORMALIZATION

The issue of normalization arises when the nature of an economic model is unaffected by a vector of structural parameters (coefficients) that can be arbitrarily scaled. This scaling is formally defined as *normalization*. A primary example is the simultaneous-equation framework of money supply and money demand:

$$\alpha_M M_t + \alpha_R R_t = \epsilon_t^S \quad \text{(Money Supply)} \qquad (1)$$

$$\beta_M M_t + \beta_R R_t = \beta_Y Y_t + \beta_P P_t + \epsilon_t^D \quad \text{(Money Demand)} \qquad (2)$$

In equations (1) and (2), M_t stands for money stock, R_t for the nominal interest rate, y_t for real output or real income, and P_t for the price level. All variables are expressed in log value. The money-supply and money-demand shocks, ϵ_t^S and ϵ_t^D, are random variables with zero mean and are independent of each other in probability distribution.

It has been long recognized that the parameter αs and βs in equations (1) and (2) can be normalized (scaled) in any way, with no consequence on economic interpretations of this equation. The conventional rule is to normalize the supply equation (1) as

$$R_t = \tilde{\alpha}_M M_t + \tilde{\epsilon}_t^S \qquad (3)$$

with $\tilde{\alpha}_M = -\dfrac{\alpha_M}{\alpha_R}$ and $\tilde{\varepsilon}_t^S = \dfrac{\varepsilon_t^S}{\alpha_R}$, and to normalize the demand equation (2) as

$$M_t = \tilde{\beta}_R R_t + \tilde{\beta}_Y Y_t + \tilde{\beta}_P P_t + \tilde{\epsilon}_t^D \qquad (4)$$

with $\tilde{\beta}_R = -\dfrac{\beta_R}{\alpha_M}$, $\tilde{\beta}_y = \dfrac{\beta_y}{\alpha_M}$, $\tilde{\beta}_P = \dfrac{\beta_P}{\alpha_M}$, and $\tilde{\varepsilon}_t^D = \dfrac{\varepsilon_t^D}{\beta_R}$. The coefficient $\tilde{\alpha}_M$ is often interpreted as an interest elasticity of the money supply, $\tilde{\beta}_R$ as an elasticity of demand for money, $\tilde{\beta}_y$ as a money-demand elasticity with respect to changes in output or income, and $\tilde{\beta}_P$ as an elasticity of demand for money with respect to changes in the price level. The following analysis for this example applies to any supply-demand framework in which M_t is replaced by the *quantity* of a commodity under consideration, R_t replaced by the *price* of this commodity, and y_t and P_t replaced by any variables that affect supply but not demand.

In the 1970s econometricians began to recognize that how the supply or demand equation is normalized affects the estimator of the supply or demand elasticity ($\tilde{\alpha}_M$ or $\tilde{\beta}_R$) when the two-stage least squares (2SLS) approach is employed. The quality of this estimator is sensitive to the strength of instruments used in the 2SLS estimation, which in turn depends on whether the price variable or the quantity variable is normalized to be on the left-hand side of the supply or demand equation, as in (3) or (4). There are other methods that one can use to estimate the supply and demand equations. One dominating alternative is the full-information maximum likelihood (ML) approach. This approach used to be computationally infeasible for many practical problems. As computing technology improves over time, the ML approach has become more feasible to implement. One advantage of the ML approach over the 2SLS approach is that the economic meaning of the ML estimates will *not* be affected by normalization.

Not until the 1990s, however, did it become known that normalization matters to small-sample statistical inference about the ML estimates. Likelihood-based small-sample inferences are affected because normalization governs the *likelihood shape* around the ML estimates. A poor normalization can lead to multimodal distribution, disjoint confidence intervals, and very misleading characterizations of the true statistical uncertainty.

Related to this discovery, in the Bayesian econometric literature there have been theoretical results showing that normalization can lead to ill-behaved posterior distributions when a flat or symmetric prior is used. The empirical and policy significance of these results has been largely unexplored until very recently. Daniel Waggoner and Tao Zha (2003) and James Hamilton, Waggoner, and Zha (2007) show that normalization can alter economic interpretations of dynamic responses of the variables M_t and R_t to a supply or demand shock ϵ_t^S or ϵ_t^D in the above example. They use this and other examples to demonstrate that inadequate normalization may confound statistical and economic interpretations.

There are a variety of economic applications in which normalization plays an important role in likelihood-based statistical inferences. Unfortunately, there is no mechanical way to implement the best normalization across different models. As a practical guide, therefore, it is essential to report the small-sample distributions of parameters of interest rather than the mean and standard deviation only. Bimodal and wide-spread distributions are the first clue that the chosen normalization may be inadequate. Carefully chosen normalization should follow the principle of preserving the likelihood shape around the ML esti-

mate. A successful implementation of this principle for normalization is likely to maintain coherent economic interpretations when statistical uncertainty is summarized.

SEE ALSO *Bayesian Econometrics; Demand; Econometrics; Matrix Algebra; Maximum Likelihood Regression; Regression Analysis; Simultaneous Equation Bias*

BIBLIOGRAPHY

Hamilton, James D., Daniel F. Waggoner, and Tao Zha. 2007. Normalization in Econometrics. *Econometric Reviews* 26 (2–4): 221–252.

Waggoner, Daniel F., and Tao Zha. 2003. Likelihood Preserving Normalization in Multiple Equation Models. *Journal of Econometrics* 114: 329–347.

Tao Zha

NORMATIVE SOCIAL SCIENCE

Early in the educational process, the novice social science student is typically introduced to two kinds of research: positive and normative. Positive social science is allegedly about what is—the unbiased, objective facts of the world, untainted by value judgments of an ethical, political, or aesthetic sort. By contrast, normative social science is about what ought to be. Apparently unlike positive science, normative social science admits to bias, subjectivity, the moral taint. Much confusion has arisen from the alleged positive/normative distinction, a distinction that is known in philosophy circles as the fact/value dichotomy.

Advanced students of social science, excluding some students of sociology and most students of anthropology, are not encouraged any more than are beginners to clarify the nature of the confusion. Most philosophers, but to repeat, only a few social scientists, reply that this is because the distinction between positive and normative, facts and values, what is and what ought to be, cannot be clarified; they are inextricably entangled.

The word *normative* descends from the Latin *norma*, meaning a carpenter's T-square, a rule, or a prescription. In ordinary English, a norm is what is expected, what is customary, what is habitual. In mathematics, the norm is a standard unit. In economic discourse, ever since John Neville Keynes (1852–1949) published his influential *On the Scope and Method of Political Economy* (1891), *normative* conflates the Latin *norma* and the ordinary English *norm*, yielding something like, as Keynes put it, a "regulative science … a body of systematized knowledge discussing criteria of what ought to be." Like his muse, David Hume (1711–1776), Keynes (father of the great economist John Maynard Keynes [1883–1946]) believed that "confusion between [positive and normative] has been the source of many mischievous errors" and urged "a distinct positive science of political economy" (Keynes 1891, quoted in Friedman 1953, p. 3).

NORMATIVE SOCIAL SCIENCE AND NOVELTY IN ECONOMICS

While contemporary social scientists take a liking to Keynes's prescription and the allure of the distinctly positive, historians and philosophers have settled on something like the exact opposite: they argue that the failure to acknowledge the normative element in the allegedly positive social sciences has been the source of mischievous errors.

The distinguished economist and philosopher Amartya Sen provides an example of such an error. For much of his career Sen (the 1998 Nobel laureate in economics) has been preoccupied with four areas of research: social choice, preference theory, capabilities, and the economics of poverty and famine. For example, in *Inequality Reexamined* (1992), he brings attention to a contradiction in "positive" preference theory, an error with ethical and political ramifications. Sen observes that economists and an increasingly large number of sociologists and political scientists accept "individual choice" and "revealed preference" to be foundational concepts in their positive science. Therefore, they argue, statistical measurements of income and consumption, and even the data from social surveys, are capable of extracting the parameters of "desire" or, to use the utilitarian term, of "happiness" achieved at various levels. Utility functions themselves cannot be observed. But the choice set of a rational economic actor is, by the logic of choice, relative price, and revealed preference, de facto observable, and so (indirectly) is a person's desire. But, Sen observes, impoverishment and deprivation can so reduce a person's desire and self-worth that what they say and do about their own desire is far below—and different from—what they would actually do (let alone what they "should" do) were they in fact flourishing at normal levels. According to Sen:

> The problem is particularly acute in the context of entrenched inequalities and deprivations. A thoroughly deprived person, leading a very reduced life, might not appear to be badly off in terms of the metric of desire and its fulfillment, if the hardship is accepted with non-grumbling resignation. In situations of long-standing deprivation, the victims do not go on grieving and lamenting all the time, and very often make great efforts to take pleasure in small mercies and to cut down personal desires to modest—"realistic"—proportions.... The extent of a person's deprivation may not at all show up in the metric of desire-fulfill-

ment, even though he or she may be quite unable to be adequately nourished, decently clothed, minimally educated, and properly sheltered. (Sen 1992, quoted in Putnam 2002, p. 59)

As the philosopher Hilary Putnam puts it, " 'Capabilities,' in Sen's sense, are not simply value functionings"; that is, they are not continuous utility functions derived from a preexisting and exogenously given preference ordering. They are "freedoms to enjoy valuable functionings"; that is, they are social and economic preconditions for performing a job well, keeping a clean house, casting a democratic vote, or reading a book by Adam Smith (Putnam 2002, p. 59). Social scientists disagree about what counts as a value functioning, and, importantly, on how one would go about measuring them in a capabilities approach. For example, will an annual income of $20,000 (in constant 2008 dollars) suffice, by Sen's standards, for a family of four living in the United States? Or is income level alone a lame metric of deprivation? What, if anything, should society do to help expose and heal any wounds of deprivation? The point of the example is not to answer a policy question; it is to suggest that normative judgments reside deep in the heart of the neoclassical preference-theoretic approach.

Thomas Schelling, Albert O. Hirschman, and other economists have found it easy to identify other mischievous errors in economics caused by an unexamined faith in positive analysis. For example, in "Against Parsimony: Three Easy Ways of Complicating Some Categories of Economic Discourse" (1984), Hirschman, working in a vein similar to his Princeton colleague, the philosopher Harry Frankfurt, shows that metapreferences—preferences over preferences—are a proper object of economic analysis, more realistic, more humane, but also capable of some prediction.

Metapreferences are about the kind of self one would like to be in the future, not the self one is today, at current prices and budget constraints. Metapreferences require reflection, the ability to step back and evaluate the spiritual and material constitution and direction of one's life. Bigots, for example, may find on reflection that they prefer human equality and the Golden Rule; party animals may decide on reflection that they are better off sober (or at least drinking less and at home with family and friends rather than in expensive nightclubs with strangers). If the metapreferences differ from the actual, Hirschman notes, then eventually, of course, one could expect to observe a preference change. How to observe a preference change is a matter of usual scientific debate and invention (Hirschman 1982 [2002]; Kuran 1995). But the main point here is that reflection about one's future self is itself a value judgment, even if one does not change one's preferences. So if an economist assumes in an economic model, following the positive approach of Milton Friedman (1912–2006) and Gary S. Becker, that people have, for instance, a "taste for discrimination" (Becker [1957] 1971) or excessive partying or nationalism, then at minimum economists are obliged to state that they are examining the wanton, and not the reflective, side of human life. But that move, Hirschman and Sen would probably agree, reveals a normative judgment in positive economics. It makes transparent the assertion of human wantonness.

Normative and positive continue to figure prominently in social science discourse and education. But the distinction rests on the so-called fact/value dichotomy, long collapsed.

SEE ALSO *Ethics; Methodology; Positive Social Science; Social Welfare Functions*

BIBLIOGRAPHY

Becker, Gary. [1957] 1971. *The Economics of Discrimination.* 2nd ed. Chicago: University of Chicago Press.

Cullenberg, Stephen, Jack Amariglio, and David F. Ruccio, eds. 2001. *Postmodernism, Economics, and Knowledge.* London: Routledge.

Friedman, Milton. 1953. *Essays in Positive Economics.* Chicago: University of Chicago Press.

Gordon, Scott. 1991. *The History and Philosophy of Social Science.* London: Routledge.

Hirschman, Albert O. [1982] 2002. *Shifting Involvements: Private Interest and Public Action.* Princeton, NJ: Princeton University Press.

Hirschman, Albert O. 1984. Against Parsimony: Three Easy Ways of Complicating Some Categories of Economic Discourse. *American Economic Review* 74 (2): 89–96.

Keynes, John Neville. 1891. *The Scope and Method of Political Economy.* London, New York: Macmillan.

Kuran, Timur. 1995. *Private Truths, Public Lies: The Social Consequences of Preference Falsification.* Cambridge, MA: Harvard University Press.

Megill, Allan, ed. 1994. *Rethinking Objectivity.* Durham, NC: Duke University Press.

Putnam, Hilary. 2002. *The Collapse of the Fact/Value Dichotomy, and Other Essays.* Cambridge, MA: Harvard University Press.

Sen, Amartya. 1992. *Inequality Reexamined.* New York: Sage; Cambridge, MA: Harvard University Press.

Taylor, Charles A. 1996. *Defining Science: A Rhetoric of Demarcation.* Madison: University of Wisconsin Press.

Stephen Ziliak

NORMS

Social scientists invoke the concept of norms to explain a broad range of human behaviors. No universally agreed-upon definition of *norms* exists, but many definitions share three components (Horne 2001, pp. 3–5). First, norms are rules that prescribe or proscribe a behavior or set of behaviors. Second, norms are enforced by external sanctions (rewards and punishments furnished by a source other than their target). These sanctions can be material (e.g., financial bonuses or fines) or symbolic (e.g., expressions of approval or disapproval). Third, norms are consensual, group-level phenomena. Group members recognize the existence of norms and feel entitled to enforce them. Some debate remains over whether norms, once established, are unconditional, clear, and generally followed (as in many rational choice theories), or conditional, unclear, and constantly negotiated (as in many symbolic interactionist theories) (Hechter and Opp 2001, pp. 394–396).

This definition distinguishes between norms and similar concepts, such as *values* and *attitudes*. Norms differ from values in that they are enforced by external sanctions, whereas values are enforced only by internal sanctions, such as feelings of pride or shame (Hechter and Horne 2003). Norms differ from attitudes in that norms are consensually held and legitimated by the group, whereas attitudes are a property of individuals. Norms also differ from *laws* in that a central authority (such as the state) formally creates and enforces laws, while people informally create and enforce norms. Some scholars distinguish between norms and *conventions*, the primary difference being that the direction of conventions is arbitrary (Coleman 1990). For example, it does not matter whether people drive on the left or the right side of the road, so long as everyone follows the convention of driving on the same side.

Norms shape social behavior by constraining action, and may be beneficial or harmful. Beneficial norms make society possible by protecting people from exploitation. Humans existed for thousands of years without the protections of a formal legal system (de Quervain et al. 2004), and the actual exercise of law remains limited due to resource constraints (Ellickson 1991). In the absence of law, norms regulate behavior and prevent people from routinely using force and fraud for private gain (Ellis 1971). Such norms include those that ensure that people look after their neighbors' children or livestock, punish laziness at work, respect cease-fire and arms-control agreements, reciprocate favors, help strangers, and otherwise contribute to a stable society.

Harmful norms may constrain individual achievements. Such norms include *leveling norms* that prevent advancement by members of disadvantaged ethnic groups (Portes 1998, pp. 15–18), or norms mandating that women confine their activities to domestic pursuits and forego the labor market. Norms can also sustain harmful practices that a majority of the group opposes, including informing on one's neighbors in repressive regimes and binge drinking on college campuses (Centola et al. 2005). Some norms also encourage dangerous practices such as dueling (e.g., Axelrod 1986, p. 1095).

Norms constrain the behavior of corporate actors as well as individuals. Firms sometimes adopt rules or structural changes that conform to norms in order to enhance their legitimacy, even when these practices run counter to market pressures (Meyer and Rowan 1977). Territories gain recognition as states in part by conforming to international norms defining the requirements for statehood. Failure to do so can result in loss of statehood and the attendant privileges (Meyer et al. 1997).

Given the widespread use of norms as an explanatory device, an important task for the social sciences is to explain the conditions under which norms emerge, change, and persist. Early functionalist explanations of social norms argued that norms arise because they benefit society, but this view has been discredited and generally abandoned. Because actors enforce norms through sanctioning, a number of theories seek to understand why actors sanction particular behaviors.

Structural features of situations can influence norm emergence. Conformity tends to increase as the size of the majority in favor of the norm increases (Asch 1951). Such factors as low levels of trust and a high risk of exploitation motivate the creation of norms that reduce the risk of exploitation (Yamagishi 1988). Network density may help coordinate sanctioning (Coleman 1990), and the threat of collective punishment can produce norms that mitigate that risk (Heckathorn 1988). In addition, actors with greater structural power possess greater ability to create, enforce, or undermine norms that serve their own interests at the expense of vulnerable actors (Coleman 1990).

People also follow and enforce norms in order to gain approval and signal that they are trustworthy interaction partners, thus encouraging others to profitably exchange with them (Homans [1951] 1992; Horne 2004). People increasingly enforce metanorms (by rewarding those who sanction deviants) as the direct and indirect benefits of exchanging with others increases (Horne 2004). Enforcing norms to gain approval can backfire, as when people enforce norms that the majority privately disdains because they falsely believe the norm to be popular (Centola et al. 2005).

Norms may also develop through a process of cultural evolution in which a norm, once established, provides greater average benefits to those who follow the norm than those who do not (Axelrod 1986; Bendor and Swistak 2001). Similarly, people may also learn to support norms via trial and error (Macy 1993).

Affective processes motivate norm enforcement. Emotional responses lead people to punish theft, walk away from profitable but unethical business deals, and help strangers in need, even when these actions contradict their short-term material interest (Frank 1988). Neurologically, people experience greater levels of activation in a reward center in the brain when they punish people who have behaved in an untrustworthy manner (de Quervain et al. 2004).

A number of important questions regarding norms remain. Broadly, it is important to continue to develop explanatory theories and empirical tests of norm emergence. Other pressing questions include how norms acquire content (Hechter and Opp 2001), how harmful norms emerge (e.g., Centola et al. 2005), and how norms and laws interrelate. Answers to these and related questions will deepen our knowledge of this fundamental but often opaque concept.

SEE ALSO *Culture; Lay Theories; Social System; Values*

BIBLIOGRAPHY

Asch, Solomon E. 1951. Effects of Group Pressure upon the Modification and Distortion of Judgments. In *Groups, Leadership, and Men: Research in Human Relations*, ed. Harold Guetkow, 177–190. Pittsburgh, PA: Carnegie Press.

Axelrod, Robert. 1986. An Evolutionary Approach to Norms. *American Political Science Review* 80: 1095–1111.

Bendor, Jonathan, and Piotr Swistak. 2001. The Evolution of Norms. *American Journal of Sociology* 106: 1493–1545.

Centola, Damon, Robb Willer, and Michael W. Macy. 2005. The Emperor's Dilemma: A Computational Model of Self-enforcing Norms. *American Journal of Sociology* 110: 1009–1040.

Coleman, James S. 1990. *Foundations of Social Theory.* Cambridge, MA: Belknap.

de Quervain, Dominique J.-F., et al. 2004. The Neural Basis of Altruistic Punishment. *Science* 305: 1254–1258.

Ellickson, Robert C. 1991. *Order without Law: How Neighbors Settle Disputes.* Cambridge, MA: Harvard University Press.

Ellis, Desmond P. 1971. The Hobbesian Problem of Order: A Critical Appraisal of the Normative Solution. *American Sociological Review* 36: 692–703.

Frank, Robert H. 1988. *Passions within Reason: The Strategic Role of the Emotions.* New York: Norton.

Hechter, Michael, and Christine Horne. 2003. Values and Norms. In *Theories of Social Order: A Reader*, eds. Michael Hechter and Christine Horne, 91–100. Stanford, CA: Stanford University Press.

Hechter, Michael, and Karl-Dieter Opp. 2001. What Have We Learned about the Emergence of Social Norms? In *Social Norms*, eds. Michael Hechter and Karl-Dieter Opp, 394–415. New York: Russell Sage Foundation.

Heckathorn, Douglas D. 1988. Collective Sanctions and the Creation of Prisoner's Dilemma Norms. *American Journal of Sociology* 94: 535–562.

Homans, George C. [1951] 1992. *The Human Group.* New Brunswick, NJ: Transaction.

Horne, Christine. 2001. Sociological Perspectives on the Emergence of Social Norms. In *Social Norms*, eds. Michael Hechter and Karl-Dieter Opp, 3–44. New York: Russell Sage Foundation.

Horne, Christine. 2004. Collective Benefits, Exchange Interests, and Norm Enforcement. *Social Forces* 82: 1037–1062.

Macy, Michael W. 1993. Backward Looking Social Control. *American Sociological Review* 58: 819–836.

Meyer, John W., John Boli, George M. Thomas, and Francisco O. Ramirez. 1997. World Society and the Nation-State. *American Journal of Sociology* 103: 144–181.

Meyer, John W., and Brian Rowan. 1977. Institutionalized Organizations: Formal Structure as Myth and Ceremony. *American Journal of Sociology* 83: 340–363.

Portes, Alejandro. 1998. Social Capital: Its Origins and Applications in Modern Sociology. *Annual Review of Sociology* 24: 1–24.

Yamagishi, Toshio. 1988. Seriousness of Social Dilemmas and the Provision of a Sanctioning System. *Social Psychology Quarterly* 51: 32–42.

Stephen Benard

NORTH, DOUGLASS
1920–

The American economist Douglass Cecil North shared the 1993 Nobel Memorial Prize in Economic Sciences with Robert W. Fogel, "for having renewed research in economic history by applying economic theory and quantitative methods in order to explain economic and institutional change" (Nobel Foundation 1993). North's work spans decades of inquiry into American economic history, European economic history, and economic development. His most recent research explores the intersection of economics and cognitive science.

North was born on November 5, 1920, in Cambridge, Massachusetts. He graduated from the University of California, Berkeley in 1942 and, following a stint in the merchant marine, he received his PhD from Berkeley in 1952. He started his career at the University of Washington in 1950, where he remained until 1983, when he moved to Washington University in Saint Louis. The influence of his colleagues, such as Yoram Barzel and Stephen N. S. Cheung, is apparent in North's emphasis on property rights, transaction costs, and culture.

North has also held visiting positions at Cambridge University, Rice University, and Stanford University's Center for Advanced Studies in the Behavioral Sciences. He currently holds an appointment as the Bartlett Burnap Senior Fellow at Stanford University's Hoover Institution. A former president of the Economic History Association and the Western Economic Association, North has also served as a member of the board of directors of the National Bureau of Economic Research and as editor of the *Journal of Economic History*.

North helped found two influential professional organizations: the Cliometric Society in 1983 and the International Society for New Institutional Economics (ISNIE) in the 1990s. The field of cliometrics, which applies quantitative methods and neoclassical economic theory to history, was at first controversial among traditional historians. North followed the 1991 Nobel Laureate Ronald Coase as the second president of ISNIE, which focuses scholarly attention on the role of institutions in economic development.

North shifted his focus away from insurance and toward American economic development in the mid-1950s. His research on the U.S. balance of payments, conducted under the auspices of the National Bureau of Economic Research in 1956 and 1957, formed the basis for his first two books on the history of the American economy.

North's first studies of institutions assumed that institutions—which he defines as "formal rules," "informal norms," and "enforcement characteristics" that define a society's property rights—are efficient. His research on Western ascendancy, however, showed him that narrowly applied neoclassical economic theory, which also assumes efficient institutions, is an inadequate framework for understanding economic change. He thus spent the 1970s studying the emergence of inefficient institutions. This culminated in his influential 1981 book, *Structure and Change in Economic History*.

North's major contributions in the 1980s included estimates (with his student John Wallis) that an increasing share of the gross national product was devoted to the cost of transactions and research, suggesting that changes in institutions and property rights may lead to economic growth. North refined his theory, and in 1989 he published an influential study in which he and coauthor Barry Weingast argued that certain institutional arrangements may solve what is called the "sovereign debt problem." First analyzed by Jeremy Bulow and Kenneth Rogoff, this problem suggests that any state strong enough to win a war is quite likely strong enough to renege on its promises (including loans), while any state so weak that it cannot successfully renege is also unlikely to last. North and Weingast showed how institutional change emanating from the Glorious Revolution of 1688 provided a partial solution to this problem.

In 1990 North published one of his most influential studies, *Institutions, Institutional Change, and Economic Performance*, which offered "a political-economic framework to explore long-run institutional change." This contribution began to explicitly incorporate questions of culture and ideology into a more general social-scientific framework.

North's ideas have attracted a certain amount of criticism. For example, one of his most important works, *The Rise of the Western World* (coauthored with Robert P. Thomas), was criticized for basing a theory of institutional change on a Malthusian model in which resource scarcity leads to alternative bargains for property rights. His ideas have endured, however, and they continue to shape research in economic history and development. The breadth of North's influence is perhaps most apparent through the distinctive mark it has left on widely cited research in development economics. North continues to push the frontiers of social science in his quest to understand why some people are rich and other people are poor, and it is perhaps most appropriate to close with a quote from his prologue to a 1997 collection of essays published in his honor:

> We still have a long way to go. I believe that an understanding of how people make choices, under what conditions the rationality postulate is a useful tool, and how individuals make choices under conditions of uncertainty and ambiguity are fundamental issues that we must address in order to make further progress in the social sciences. But we are making progress. (*Frontiers of the New Institutional Economics* 1997)

SEE ALSO *Cliometrics; Coase, Ronald; Development Economics; Economics, Nobel Prize in; Institutionalism; Neoinstitutionalism; Property Rights; Transaction Cost*

BIBLIOGRAPHY

PRIMARY WORKS

North, Douglass. 1961. *The Economic Growth of the United States 1790–1860*. Englewood Cliffs, NJ: Prentice Hall.

North, Douglass. 1966. *Growth and Welfare in the American Past*. Englewood Cliffs, NJ: Prentice Hall.

North, Douglass. 1971. *Institutional Change and American Economic Growth* (with Lance E. Davis). Cambridge, U.K.: Cambridge University Press.

North, Douglass. 1973. *The Rise of the Western World: A New Economic History* (with Robert Paul Thomas). Cambridge, U.K.: Cambridge University Press.

North, Douglass. 1981. *Structure and Change in Economic History*. New York: Norton.

North, Douglass. 1986. Measuring the Transaction Sector of the American Economy (with John Joseph Wallis). In *Income and Wealth: Long-Term Factors in American Economic Growth*, ed. Stanley Engerman and Robert E. Gallman. Chicago: University of Chicago Press.

North, Douglass. 1989. Constitutions and Commitment: The Evolution of Institutions Governing Public Choice in Seventeenth-Century England (with Barry Weingast). *Journal of Economic History* 49 (4): 803–832.

North, Douglass. 1990. *Institutions, Institutional Change, and Economic Performance*. Cambridge, U.K.: Cambridge University Press.

North, Douglass. 1997. Prologue. In *The Frontiers of the New Institutional Economics*, ed. John N. Drobak and John V. C. Nye, 3–12. San Diego, CA: Academic Press.

North, Douglass. 2005. *Understanding the Process of Economic Change*. Princeton, NJ: Princeton University Press.

SECONDARY WORKS

Coelho, Philip R. P. 2001. *The Rise of the Western World, A New Economic History*. Review Essay. EH.Net Project 2001 Reviews. http://eh.net/bookreviews/library/coelho.

Fogel, Robert W. 1997. Douglass C. North and Economic Theory. In *The Frontiers of the New Institutional Economics*, ed. John N. Drobak and John V. C. Nye, 13–28. San Diego, CA: Academic Press.

Nye, John V. C. 2003. North, Douglass Cecil. In *Oxford Encyclopedia of Economic History*, ed. Joel Mokyr, 107–108. New York: Oxford University Press.

Nobel Foundation. The Sveriges Riksbank Prize in Economic Sciences in Memory of Alfred Nobel, 1993. http://nobelprize.org/nobel_prizes/economics/laureates/1993/.

Art Carden

NORTH, OLIVER

SEE *Sandinistas.*

NORTH AMERICAN FREE TRADE AGREEMENT

On January 1, 1994, the North American Free Trade Agreement (NAFTA) went into effect, creating the largest free-trade area in the world. Many view NAFTA as a major policy victory for the architects of a new era of trade liberalization and economic globalization. Yet proponents of this view did not go unchallenged. NAFTA's departure from several traditional trade concerns opened political opportunities for challengers to ally across borders and overcome longstanding political divisions, making it the most contentious trade policy initiative to date (Dreiling 2001).

NAFTA AS A POLITICAL AND ECONOMIC PROCESS

At the most explicit level, NAFTA is a treaty designed to liberalize trade and investment activity in North America. The trade agreement sets timetables for significant reductions in duties and a steady elimination of tariffs between the three trading partners (Canada, the United States, and Mexico). Partly as a result of these reduced transaction costs, trade between the three countries has increased significantly. According to International Monetary Fund (IMF) data, the three NAFTA countries traded over $620 billion in goods and services in 2004, nearly doubling total trade volume in the ten years since NAFTA was implemented. Combined, the three countries produced over $12 trillion in goods and services in 2004 and, with more than 425 million people, constitute a major economic bloc in the world economy.

Literature on globalization portrays NAFTA as one of three distinct trading blocs in the world economy (Dicken 2003). The concentration of trade flows studied by sociologists, geographers, and economists reveals a growing tripolar configuration of world trade relations and policy agendas of leading states. This research suggests that NAFTA and the Maastricht Treaty on European Union (1992) were driven by global economic forces as well as strategic political responses to globalization. NAFTA, seen from this perspective, reflects a trade-policy response to the regionalization of capitalist competition at a global level. Content rule, tariff reduction schedules, and other NAFTA provisions are designed to favor North American capital. Premised on an improved capacity to export commodities produced under low-cost conditions in Mexico into the high-price consumer markets of North America, western Europe, and Japan, NAFTA is an attempt to reclaim economic power in a capitalist world system. James Petras and Morris Morley argue that "NAFTA is the centerpiece of a new economic strategy … which Washington hopes to use as a springboard for its reemergence as a more competitive player in the world market" (1995, pp. 128–129).

During the debate over NAFTA, considerable attention was addressed to the question of "jobs." Ross Perot's presidential bid and famous claim of an impending "giant sucking sound" helped frame the political debate, but also alluded to important economic trends in all three countries. Prior to the conclusion of NAFTA, a steady erosion in manufacturing employment in the United States, coupled with a rapid increase of manufacturing employment by U.S. multinational corporations operating in Mexico, aroused fears of a decline of American industrial supremacy. Economists, such as Robert Blecker and William Spriggs (1992), showed how these patterns would likely continue with NAFTA, particularly in the *maquila* sector. The maquiladoras—literally meaning "twin plants"—generally refer to export industries along the U.S.-Mexico border, though the term is also used in reference to export processing industries in El Salvador, Guatemala, and elsewhere in Central America. After NAFTA's ratification, the increase in manufacturing employment in Mexico by U.S. multinationals certainly did not create a "giant sucking sound," but the movement of industrial-sector jobs has continued.

In a policy context, NAFTA represents an economic integration plan that extended the deregulation and free-market agendas of governments in the United States, Canada, and Mexico. Administrations under presidents Ronald Reagan and George H. W. Bush in the United States, Prime Minister Brian Mulroney in Canada, and President Carlos Salinas in Mexico initiated national reform agendas where market principles supplanted other institutional goals and organization. Known as *neoliberalism*—where market forces are believed to be the most efficient and least costly mechanism for allocating all societal goods—this ideological context all but guaranteed a free-market approach to North American integration. In this way, NAFTA emerged as a neoliberal counterpart to Europe's more social democratic Maastricht Treaty.

NAFTA extends and accelerates market deregulation and trade liberalization efforts across the continent by creating supranational institutions and binding agreements between signatory governments. For example, one feature of NAFTA contained in Chapter Eleven prevents governments from discriminating against cross-border investors—all North American capital is to be treated as domestic capital, eventually. These provisions also establish an investor-state arbitration system that permits companies from one NAFTA country to seek monetary damages for actions or policies of another NAFTA government (national, state/provincial, or local). One often-cited case began in 1997 when the Ethyl Corporation, a U.S. company, challenged Canada's environmental ban of a known carcinogenic gasoline additive, methylcyclopentadienyl manganese tricarbonyl (MMT)—a chemical made by Ethyl. In July 1998 the arbitration panel ruled against Canada, forcing Canada to reverse its environmental ban on MMT and pay $13 million in damages and legal fees to Ethyl. As of 2005, five Chapter Eleven cases have settled in favor of investors, leaving critics wary of NAFTA's bias in favor of capital at the expense of national sovereignty and environmental protection. From an analytical standpoint, the neoliberal framework of NAFTA helps investor rights trump environmental or national rights.

Neoliberal defenders of NAFTA, and free markets more generally, praise this "deepening and widening" of markets in the hemisphere, calling for an extension of NAFTA to Central America and throughout the Western Hemisphere as envisioned in the Free Trade Area of the Americas. Elaborate hemispheric plans for subregional and continental integration are discussed among elite policy organizations, from the Council on Foreign Relations to the highly influential Business Roundtable (Dreiling 2001). May 2005 discussions by elite supporters of

NAFTA alluded to a new "security perimeter" around North America, known as the North American Initiative.

THE IMPACT OF NAFTA

Migration from Mexico to the United States has risen significantly under NAFTA. Growing rural unemployment in Mexico and the instability of small farming in Mexico stem in part from NAFTA's liberalization of trade in agricultural goods. With cheaper corn and grains imported from Canada and the United States into Mexico, small, often indigenous farmers are hurt economically. Worries persist that these pressures will also hurt peasant communities throughout Central America with the adoption of the Dominican Republic-Central America Free Trade Agreement in 2005. While pressure to migrate has increased, anti-immigrant politics persist in the United States, and the number of people found dead along the U.S.-Mexico border rose to a peak in 2003. Other U.S.-Mexico border problems were compounded by NAFTA. Mexico's environment and urban infrastructure remain inadequate to support the growing population and heavy concentrations of export-oriented industry. The number of labor-intensive, export-processing factories along the border in Mexico increased by about 73 percent between 1993 and 2000, putting strain on both the environment and the mostly female workforce in those factories.

The expectation that greater wealth and income growth in Mexico would increase political pressures to limit environmental pollution remains unrealized. Arguments that refer to the environmental Kuznets curve—that pollution increases with per capita gross domestic product (GDP) at lower levels of national income while pollution decreases with per capita GDP at higher levels of national income—suggest that increased trade, and hence increased wealth pollution, will decrease in Mexico (Grossman and Krueger 1993). More research is needed to address this important question about the relationship between trade, economic growth, and political pressure to improve and enforce environmental regulations in Mexico and elsewhere.

Perhaps the most significant impact of NAFTA flowed not from the agreement itself, but the conflicts that arose in NAFTA's wake. NAFTA, like its close relative and successor, the World Trade Organization (WTO), significantly departed from the direction of previous multilateral trade initiatives and inadvertently opened political opportunities for challengers to question neoliberal trade policy. Advancing new language on investment protections, institutionalizing language and protocols for protecting *trade related intellectual property rights* (TRIPs), and promoting a series of policy shocks to liberalize trade in agriculture, NAFTA drew a line that subsequent conflicts over trade policy would brave. These three concerns remain

pivotal dividing lines within the WTO and in the ongoing discussions for a Free Trade Area of the Americas. Confrontations over patents on seeds and other "intellectual property," nontariff agricultural subsidies in richer countries, and investment rules have, for example, stalled agendas at the WTO ministerial meetings in Seattle in 1999 and in Cancun, Mexico, in 2003. NAFTA anticipated and presaged these same divisions, prompting conflict both prior to and following its implementation.

The conflict over NAFTA catalyzed a mobilization of forces for and against the agreement. For over two years, the NAFTA negotiations faced challenges and changes, from a legal decision at a U.S. district court that required an environmental impact statement on NAFTA (which was subsequently appealed and overruled) to negotiations for two-side agreements on labor and the environment. Critics nearly stopped the passage of NAFTA. By the time that NAFTA went public in 1991, a broad spectrum of groups—from farmers to human rights organizations—began meeting to develop both national and international strategies to stop NAFTA in its tracks. Three years later, voices against NAFTA had developed a transnational movement, providing a supportive, if not encouraging, backdrop for the armed insurgency in Chiapas, Mexico, that initiated its mobilization with deliberate intent on January 1, 1994, NAFTA's birthday.

Beyond the contentious interests mobilized for and against NAFTA, the agreement and the historical stage it set caught the eye of scholars. NAFTA, at a social scientific level, came to represent a triumph of markets, a continentalization of economies, and a window into the political struggles over globalization. As Jeremy Brecher and Tim Costello argued (1998), this neoliberal "globalization from above"—via free trade and corporate-sponsored multilateral institutions—is being resisted not only by "older" nationalist and protectionist foes of free trade, but also by a "globalization from below." NAFTA helped set this stage.

SEE ALSO *Barriers to Trade; Liberalization, Trade; Quotas, Trade; Tariffs; World Trade Organization*

BIBLIOGRAPHY

Blecker, Robert A., and William E. Spriggs. 1992. Manufacturing Employment in North America: Where the Jobs Have Gone. Briefing paper. Washington, DC: Economic Policy Institute. http://www.epinet.org/briefingpapers/1992_bp_manufacturing.pdf.

Brecher, Jeremy, and Tim Costello. 1998. *Global Village or Global Pillage: Economic Reconstruction from the Bottom Up.* 2nd ed. Boston: South End.

Dicken, Peter. 2003. *Global Shift: Reshaping the Global Economic Map in the 21st Century.* 4th ed. New York: Guilford.

Dreiling, Michael. 2001. *Solidarity and Contention: The Politics of Security and Sustainability in the NAFTA Conflict*. New York: Garland.

Grossman, Gene M., and Alan B. Krueger. 1993. Environmental Impacts of a North American Free Trade Agreement. In *The Mexico-U.S. Free Trade Agreement*, ed. Peter M. Garber, 13–56. Cambridge, MA: MIT Press.

NAFTA Secretariat. http://www.nafta-sec-alena.org/DefaultSite/index.html.

Office of the United States Trade Representative. North American Free Trade Agreement. http://www.ustr.gov/Trade_Agreements/Regional/NAFTA/Section_Index.html.

Petras, James, and Morris Morley. 1995. *Empire or Republic: American Global Power and Domestic Decay*. New York: Routledge.

Michael Dreiling

NORTH AMERICAN FREE TRADE AREA

SEE *North American Free Trade Agreement*.

NORTH AND SOUTH, THE (GLOBAL)

The terms *the North* and *the South*, when used in a global context, are alternative designations for "developed" and "developing" countries. Together, the North and South constitute virtually the entire global population. As terms, *the North* and *the South* emerged during the 1970s, probably simultaneously, and in contrast with each other. This article thus discusses these two terms together.

While the countries that make up *the North* and the countries that comprise *the South* share broadly similar economic and historical characteristics with the other countries in their category, there is no precise definition of either term. Two generations ago, the North could have been approximately defined as Europe and its offshoots (such as Canada, the United States, Australia, and New Zealand), but Japan has also, clearly, been a developed country for many years. Several other East Asian countries, including Singapore, South Korea, and Taiwan have shifted into the North in recent decades. While there are no recent examples of countries that have moved in the opposite direction (i.e., to the South from the North), the economic position of Argentina shifted from being one of the richest countries in the world, a century ago, to its middle-ranked position today.

Precise categorization is difficult for several contemporary nations, such as Russia and Saudi Arabia. Russia

was recently admitted to the G-8 (previously the G-7), whose other members (the United States, Canada, France, Germany, Italy, the U.K., and Japan) are the richest and most economically powerful nations on earth. In contrast, Russia has a comparatively low life expectancy, which has fallen in recent decades. It also has limited political freedom and transparency in comparison to most countries in the G-8, and the North more generally.

The North and South have other names. No name is perfect, and neither *the North* nor *the South* is geographically precise. Several countries in the South are entirely in the Northern hemisphere (e.g., India, Nigeria), while Australia and New Zealand, each in the geographic South, are part of the global North, as evidenced by their long-standing membership of the Organisation for Economic Co-operation and Development (OECD). Such geographic imprecision is not unique. For example, *the West* (another synonym for developed countries) now includes Japan, as well as Australasia.

As terms, *the North* (also called *the First World*) and *the South* emerged during the 1970s in recognition of the greater economic and political power of the Third World, and in reaction to growing dissatisfaction with earlier terms, which were increasingly seen as pejorative. (This is discussed further below.) Although the South has long been home for the majority of the global population, its fraction of the global population is rising, as fertility rates have declined by a greater amount in the North. Reflecting this, the South is now sometimes called *the majority world*.

THE ORIGINS OF THE *THIRD WORLD* CONCEPT

In 1940 Colin Clark published "Conditions of Economic Progress," which showed the world to be, as one reviewer commented, "a wretchedly poor place." Two centuries earlier, almost the whole world had been "wretchedly poor," and it is unlikely that the concept of "developing countries" would then have been much appreciated. The world had largely been divided into several empires, each of which possessed a "civilized" center and peripheries that were more or less considered primitive or even "barbaric." Before the 1940s it is unlikely that the citizens of what would later be described as the North would have given much thought to the inhabitants of what was to become known as the South. When they did, most would have considered these peoples to be inferior in some way, by virtue of being non-white, less educated, or even "primitive." Many people in the Third World were subjects in European colonies, living far from the global sources of economic, political, and military power. It is even less likely that the subjugated inhabitants of these Third World lands, many of whom were illiterate, would have been aware that, even then, they formed a substantial part of the world population.

But such an awareness was growing among leaders within these poor countries, many of whom had been educated, at least partly, in Europe or America. This awareness and exposure to Western culture raised expectations and hopes, and inspired many Third World leaders to try to improve colonial living conditions and win political independence. Opposition to domination by the First World was also fed by increasing migration and travel, which had been stimulated by the two World Wars. Many troops who had participated in these wars, particularly on the allied side, were from the South. In addition, many Europeans served in Asia, and their exposure to conditions in the colonies probably helped erode the resolve of the colonial powers to keep their empires unbroken.

As the twentieth century progressed, the global decolonization movement strengthened, empowered by each country that achieved independence. An increasing number of countries in the South developed a national identity. The newly formed United Nations, born in the period of comparative hope and idealism that briefly flowered following World War II (1939–1945), also provided a forum for developing countries to share ideas and to argue their position before a wider audience.

The term *the Third World* was coined in 1952 by the French demographer, anthropologist, and economic historian Alfred Sauvy, who compared it with the *Third Estate*, a concept that emerged in the context of the French Revolution. (*First Estate* refers to the clergy and the monarch, *Second Estate* to the nobility, and *Third Estate* to the balance of the eighteenth-century French population—as much as 98 percent.) *The Third World*, as a phrase, also achieved acceptance because it usefully contrasted the poor countries to the First World (the non-Communist, high-income, "developed" countries) and the Second World (Communist countries, which though not as wealthy as those of the First World, were then characterized by greater order, higher incomes, and longer life expectancies.)

The decades that followed saw many attempts to form coalitions of Third World countries, to counter the vastly superior power of the "developed" First World countries. With hindsight, it is clear that these were only partly successful.

In 1955 Egypt, Indonesia, Burma, and the three powers of the Indian subcontinent (India, Pakistan, and Sri Lanka) organized the Asian-African Conference, held in Bandung, Indonesia. Twenty-nine countries, representing over half the world's population, sent delegates—including the charismatic Chinese premier, Zhou Enlai—to Bandung. At this meeting, Indian Prime Minister Jawaharlal Nehru explicitly rejected both sides in

the ongoing cold war between the United States and the USSR, expanding on the principles of *non-alignment*, a term he is credited with coining and first using in 1954. The meeting led to the development of the Non-Aligned Movement (NAM), which held its first formal meeting in 1961. Five charismatic Third World leaders—Nehru, Yugoslavia's Marshal Tito, Indonesia's Sukarno, Egypt's Gamal Abdel Nasser, and Ghana's Kwame Nkrumah—are credited with its establishment. China, despite its Communist ideology, has also been a member of the NAM at times.

In 1960, parallel to these developments, five other developing countries (Iran, Iraq, Kuwait, Saudi Arabia, and Venezuela) founded the Organisation of Petroleum Exporting Countries (OPEC), at the Baghdad Conference. Soon after, OPEC was enlarged to include Nigeria and several smaller and poorer African states. Indonesia, the only NAM founder with substantial oil reserves, also joined OPEC.

In 1964 another coalition of developing nations was formed, called the Group of 77. India was instrumental in the formation of this group, which was also joined by Brazil, the most populous and economically powerful South American country and never part of the Non-Aligned Movement. The Group of 77 now has over 130 members. Although the People's Republic of China has never been a formal member, it has been loosely affiliated since the 1970s.

THE EMERGENCE OF THE TERM *THE SOUTH*

The 1970s was a period of foment in the developing countries. Many improvements in living standards and life expectancy rates had been achieved in the 1950s, but by the 1970s these advances were stalling. Impatience in the Third World was growing. In 1973 OPEC substantially raised the price of oil, triggering the first global oil crisis. This had a major adverse economic effect upon the non-oil-exporting countries of the Third World, and revealed a lack of solidarity within the Third World overall. Parallel to this, the developed countries (prior to the discovery and development of the North Sea oil fields) were becoming increasingly dependent on the Third World for energy, due to the decline of U.S. oil reserves. These factors increased the economic power of part of the Third World. In 1974 the first UN-hosted population mega-conference was held in Bucharest. At this meeting the Group of 77 refused to accept responsibility for their poverty, instead blaming colonialism and ongoing Western exploitation. Famously, the Indian delegation called development "the best contraceptive." This rebellious spirit was also reflected in calls from the Third World for a New International Economic Order (NIEO).

It is unlikely to be coincidental that the terms *the South* and *the North* were first widely used around this time. These terms appear to have entered common usage as an alternative to the long-standing geographical and cultural partition of the world into West and East. The new names avoided the stigma associated with the term *the Third World*, and created the hope that a new world order—one in which the North would be fairer to the South—was underway.

REASONS FOR THE PERSISTENT DISADVANTAGE OF THE SOUTH

However, new terms alone were insufficient to bring about fundamental change. Despite the aspirations and efforts of many people, in both South and North, most of the population of the South remains terribly poor. The reasons for this are complex, but several important interlocking factors can be identified. They include the South's historical legacy of disadvantage, much of it stemming from the colonial system. Also significant are the economic and development costs associated with enduring and fighting various diseases, especially malaria, tuberculosis, and HIV/AIDS, all of which affect a substantial number of adults, who would otherwise be more productive. High levels of Southern indebtedness, poor governance, and corruption are also important causes.

Other factors warrant mention as well. One is the comparatively high fertility rate in most developing countries, especially those that are the poorest. This leads to a proportionately large number of children and young adults, many of whom are poorly educated, un- or underemployed, and vulnerable to disease and economic exploitation. Another point is that, on the whole, populations and governments in the North have shown little interest in the social and economic fate of the South. For example, while for several decades many countries in the North have pledged to increase development aid to the South, very few large countries (and none of the members of the G-7) have followed through on these promises. In fact, Northern countries have behaved collectively as though it is just and proper that the economic and social privileges of Northern populations be enhanced by Southern poverty.

Also significant is the great diversity of the countries of the South. They are united by comparative disadvantage and poverty, but divided by differences in culture, language, religion, fertility rates, and stocks of oil and other natural resources. The two most populous nations in the South—China and India—have fought two wars with each other, and have had a continuous border dispute since the early 1960s. India is a secular democracy, which aspires to be a permanent member of the UN Security Council, a status long granted to its great rival China. Totalitarian

China for its part seems as preoccupied with Russia and the United States as with the issues of the South. The South has also been divided by the policies of OPEC, a cartel whose richest countries have shown little interest in promoting the broader interest of the South.

SEE ALSO *Dependency Theory; Globalization, Anthropological Aspects of; Globalization, Social and Economic Aspects of; North-South Models*

BIBLIOGRAPHY

Arnold, Guy. 1993. *The End of the Third World.* London and New York: St Martin's Press.

Clark, Colin. 1940. *Conditions of Economic Progress.* London: Macmillan.

Coale, Ansley J., and Edgar M. Hoover. 1958. *Population Growth and Economic Development in Low-Income Countries: A Case Study of India's Prospects.* Princeton, NJ: Princeton University Press.

Editorial. 2006. A Global Famine. *Lancet* 367 (9514): 876.

Fanon, Frantz. 1963. *The Wretched of the Earth.* Trans. Constance Farrington. New York: Grove Press.

Finkle, Jason L., and Barbara B. Crane. 1975. The Politics of Bucharest: Population, Development, and the New International Order. *Population and Development Review* 1 (1): 87–114.

Hosle, Vittorio. 1992. The Third World as a Philosophical Problem. *Social Research* 59 (2): 227–262.

Kahin, George McTurnan. 1956. *The Asian-African Conference.* Ithaca, NY: Cornell University Press.

Rothbarth, Erwin. 1941. Review of *The Conditions of Economic Progress,* by Colin Clark. *Economic Journal* 51 (201): 120–124.

Sachs, Jeffrey D. 2006. How to Help the Poor: Piecemeal Progress or Strategic Plans? Review of *The White Man's Burden: Why the West's Efforts to Aid the Rest Have Done So Much Ill and So Little Good,* by William Easterly. *Lancet* 367 (9519): 1309–1310.

Sachs, Jeffrey D., and Pia Malaney. 2002. The Economic and Social Burden of Malaria. *Nature* 415 (6872): 680–685.

Sinding, Steven W. 2000. The Great Population Debates: How Relevant Are They for the 21st Century? *American Journal of Public Health* 90 (12): 1841–1845.

Colin D. Butler

NORTH ATLANTIC TREATY ORGANIZATION

The North Atlantic Treaty Organization (NATO) is one of the longest-running alliances in history. It has been one of the fixed points in international relations since 1949 and is the most influential of the regional security organizations sanctioned under the United Nations Charter (Article 51). While to most casual observers it is a military arrangement, its founders' prime purpose was political. They intended the alliance to provide an appearance of collectivity and strength that would both deter the enemy (the Soviet Union) and strengthen the determination of individual members to resist Soviet subversive infiltration. Members retain national control of armed forces but are prepared to submit them to command by foreign supreme commanders and command organizations manned by foreigners, and cooperate closely on usually sensitive issues such as security and intelligence.

The essentially intergovernmental nature of the alliance means that such military cooperation necessitates a high level of political cooperation. The central forum for this is the North Atlantic Council (NAC). The NAC is staffed by permanent ambassadorial representatives. It is chaired by the secretary-general, who acts as the spokesman for the alliance and is effectively its chief executive. The essentially intergovernmental nature of NATO is maintained by twice-yearly meetings of foreign ministers. These meetings make the large policy decisions, which the secretary-general is then required to implement, with the NAC acting as a channel of communication. Since 1952 the NAC has developed permanent and ad hoc subcommittees dealing with a range of issues. The most important is the Military Committee, whose relation to the NAC is a little anomalous in that while it reports to the NAC, it is also directed by biennial meetings of NATO defense ministers. In addition, sitting atop the whole structure are summits of heads of government when deemed necessary.

The North Atlantic Treaty (signed in Washington, D.C., on April 4, 1949) pledged that an attack on one of the twelve signatories—the United States, Canada, Iceland, Denmark, Norway, Belgium, Netherlands, Luxembourg, France, Britain, Portugal, and Italy—was an attack on all and would lead them to take whatever measures they deemed necessary, including armed action. Effectively it placed the European members under American nuclear protection. While military planners were initially skeptical of the defensive capabilities of the alliance, for the politicians the main point was to increase the Western European sense of security.

The emphasis changed during the early 1950s as a result of the Korean War. With the fear that Korea would quickly be followed by a Soviet attack in Germany, the overtly military aspect of the alliance was moved to the foreground, where it was to remain until the cold war ended. Supreme Headquarters, Allied Powers Europe (SHAPE) was established in 1951 in France. NATO has three commands, Atlantic, English Channel, and Europe, but the commander of Europe (SACEUR) is the senior. Greece and Turkey, which had been under NATO guarantees, became members in 1952. Most significantly, West Germany was admitted in 1955 and was allowed to contribute forces under the command of the West European Union.

NATO's function and structure came under scrutiny in the 1960s. Some in the United States believed that since Western Europe had recovered economically, it should shoulder a greater share of its own defense. American advocacy of "flexible response" also caused problems with the allies, who feared the expense of competing with the Soviets in conventional forces and who felt the American nuclear guarantee was being compromised. Moreover, French president Charles de Gaulle saw NATO as an instrument of Anglo-American hegemony, and in 1966 France left NATO's military structures. NATO headquarters had to relocate to Belgium.

Against the background of these developments, the Belgian foreign minister produced the Harmel Report, *The Future Tasks of the Alliance* (1967). While committing NATO to engage actively in the process of détente—reducing tensions with the Warsaw Pact—it also stated firmly that NATO was an organization serving the security needs of its members rather than a purely defensive military alliance whose existence was dependent on a specific threat.

Détente gave way to increased tension during the early 1980s, and NATO deployed intermediate-range nuclear weapons (INF) and cruise missiles in some European countries. Relations between NATO and the Warsaw Pact warmed once Mikhail Gorbachev came to power in the USSR, and in December 1987 the United States and the USSR agreed to eliminate all land-based INF missiles.

In 1982 NATO added its sixteenth member with the accession of newly democratic Spain. In 1990 the reunification of Germany moved NATO's frontiers significantly eastward. In 1991 the Soviet Union ceased to exist, and some in the West felt that NATO should follow suit, arguing it no longer had a purpose. However, NATO supporters were able to point to the Harmel Report and depict NATO as an organization to promote general security through stability and collective action. At Rome in 1991 a new Strategic Concept declared that instability was often caused by the activities of nationalist or terrorist groups. The North Atlantic Cooperation Council was set up, with sixteen NATO countries and nine others, becoming in 1997 the European Atlantic Partnership Council with forty members (forty-six by 2001). At Brussels in 1994 the Partnership for Peace was formed to promote defense cooperation.

The first test of the reality of NATO's ability to manage instability in Europe was the long crisis as Yugoslavia disintegrated. NATO proved to be hesitant and divided. It was not until 1997 that the implications of NATO's new role were properly addressed, using the forum of the Partnership for Peace. NATO began to make significant contributions to UN peacekeeping efforts, beginning with missions to the former Yugoslav republics. The partnership also made possible the NATO-Russia Founding Act signed in Paris in 1997, establishing the NATO-Russia Permanent Joint Council (PJC). This reduced Russian hostility to NATO expansion, easing the accession of Poland, Hungary, and the Czech Republic in 1999. Through the PJC, Russian troops took part in peacekeeping forces in Bosnia. Tensions remained with the Russians, especially when the crisis flared up in Kosovo in 1999 and the Russians remained cautious about NATO's role.

There was a show of solidarity by NATO members after the September 2001 terrorist attacks on the United States, but this was undermined by the unilateralism of the Bush administration. NATO did agree to operate out of area—for the first time—taking control in August 2003 of the International Security Assistance Force in Afghanistan, following American and British operations against the Taliban. Germany and France, however, disliked Bush's approach and opposed the attack on Iraq in 2003. This became a NATO issue when they vetoed American requests to strengthen Turkey in advance of the attack. Pessimists predicted NATO's immediate demise. The solidity of NATO's permanent structures, however, meant that it survived this crisis. Thus, although as an intergovernmental alliance it had become somewhat dysfunctional, ironically, its extensive multilateral structures proved a binding force, if only out of inertia and the practical difficulties of untangling integrated military structures, especially regarding intelligence. Indeed, NATO continued to expand, with seven new members joining formally in 2004—Bulgaria, Estonia, Lithuania, Latvia, Romania, Slovakia, and Slovenia.

SEE ALSO *Alliances; Coalition; Cold War; Communism; Deterrence; Genocide; Nationalism and Nationality; Taliban; Terrorism; Terrorists; Union of Soviet Socialist Republics; Weaponry, Nuclear*

BIBLIOGRAPHY

Rupp, Richard E. 2006. *NATO after 9/11: An Alliance in Continuing Decline.* New York: Palgrave Macmillan.

Schmidt, Gustav, ed. 2001. *A History of NATO: The First Fifty Years.* 3 vols. New York: Palgrave Macmillan.

Smith, Martin A. 2000. *NATO in the First Decade after the Cold War.* Boston: Kluwer Academic Publishers.

Yost, David S. 1998. *NATO Transformed: The Alliance's New Roles in International Security.* Washington, DC: United States Institute of Peace Press.

Martin H. Folly

NORTH-SOUTH MODELS

The large difference in the levels of economic development between the countries has made many view the world as being divided between the rich North and the poor South. North-South models divide the world economy along these lines and examine the interaction of the two regions through trade and other economic relationships.

The classical economists, including Adam Smith (who discussed the importance of increasing productivity due to the division of labor as economies grew) and David Ricardo (who examined the role of trade in postponing the arrival of the stationary state in rich countries by enabling cheap food imports and in having the opposite effect for poor countries), discussed North-South issues. Subsequently, Marxist writers on imperialism and dependency theorists, and development economists more generally, stressed the role of the South in providing markets and investment outlets for the North, and examined the problems of surplus transfers from the South, the deterioration of the southern terms of trade, and of uneven development.

MODELS WITH STRUCTURAL ASYMMETRIES

More mathematically explicit North-South models emerged from the early 1980s. In a 1980 article for the *American Economic Review*, Ronald Findlay examined capital accumulation in a global economy with the North growing with full employment and the South with unlimited supplies of labor at a fixed real wage. In 1983 Lance Taylor allowed for unemployment in the North as well, assuming that effective demand determines northern growth. These and other models can be thought of as special cases of a general framework, in which the northern good is a consumption-cum-investment good, and the South a consumption good. The models embody specific behavioral and institutional assumptions for the North and the South, thereby highlighting their structural differences. They have been used to examine the effects of changes in such things as technology, consumption expenditure patterns, and savings rates. Of particular interest are results which demonstrate that southern growth depends on northern growth (which is determined independently of the South), the relationship between the southern terms of trade and southern growth, and the possibility of uneven development (reflected by a rise in the relative size of the North) due, for instance, to technological change and changes in consumer preferences. Some of these mechanisms of uneven development have been endogenized to model processes of cumulative causation due to factors such as the income-inelastic demand for southern products, international demonstration effects, and endogenous technological change, as expressed in Amitava Krishna Dutt's book *Growth, Distribution, and Uneven Development* (1990). These results confirm some of the informal ideas of earlier writers on uneven development, but they depend on some of the specific assumptions made about the structures of the northern and southern economies.

The basic trade models have also been extended in several directions. For instance, international capital movements from the North to the South in search of higher profits have been shown to exacerbate uneven development, due to a fall in the price of the southern good because of increases in southern production, and to profit repatriation to the North, although under certain circumstances foreign direct investment, by making possible the production of the northern good in the South, can result in greater North-South equality.

The models stressing structural asymmetries between the North and the South do not explain why such asymmetries arise. Implicitly they assume that events in the past, such as the Atlantic slave trade or colonial domination, create and lock in these structural differences. Models which assume identical structures for the two regions have also been developed to show how small historical events can make one region (the North) end up exporting manufactured goods exhibiting increasing returns to scale, while the other region (the South) becomes more agriculturally oriented, so that there is uneven development.

NEOCLASSICAL MODELS

The models discussed so far can be seen as reactions to the dominant neoclassical Heckscher-Ohlin-Samuelson (HOS) trade models, which contain optimizing agents, are usually static in nature, and assume that markets clear so that labor and other resources are fully employed everywhere. However, the neoclassical approach has also contributed to the development of North-South models. For instance, environmental factors have been introduced into them to examine how stricter pollution control in the North can lead to a movement of "dirty" industries to the South, thereby exacerbating southern environmental problems, as seen in Brian Copeland and Scott Taylor's 1994 article for the *Quarterly Journal of Economics*. Most

of the North-South models from the neoclassical perspective, however, have followed the contributions of new growth theory, which emphasize the role of increasing returns and externalities in the growth process; this can be seen, for example, in William A. Darity and Lewis S. Davis's 2005 article for the *Cambridge Journal of Economics*.

Many new growth theory models imply economic divergence between rich and poor countries due to economies of scale along Smithian lines even without any interaction between the two. These results often carry over to models with North-South trade. For instance, trade can increase (reduce) the wage of skilled labor, the abundant factor in the North (South), thereby increasing (reducing) the incentives for education, labor productivity, and growth. This is not a necessary outcome, however; the increase in the wage of skilled labor may slow down research and development and hence technological change and growth in the North and increase it in the South.

Neoclassical models have also been used for examining North-South technology transfers. It may be supposed that if knowledge is something that all countries can share, the South will eventually catch up to the North. However, those who have studied the process of technology transfer recognize that it is not very easy to transfer technology and it requires southern countries to build up technological capability to be able to learn from, and adapt to, foreign technology. Moreover, the protection of international property rights (IPR) can serve as a barrier to technology transfers. The protection of IPR has been a major source of conflict between the North and the South, and it has been claimed that the lack of such protection will slow down innovation in the North and hence the world. A number of models, however, suggest that weaker protection of IPR will not only speed up technology transfers, but also accelerate innovation in the North as northern resources are devoted more to innovation activity than to production.

North-South models are useful for understanding the nature and consequences of the interaction between rich and poor countries, and to address key issues concerning international inequality and global growth. They can be criticized for downplaying the differences within rich and poor countries, and the possibility that poor countries may grow and join the ranks of the rich. However, two-region models have been extended to include a third, consisting of newly industrialized countries, to explore the causes of its growth and to analyze whether its growth results in the end of uneven development or the exacerbation of the gap between the rest of the South and the North.

SEE ALSO *Development; Economics; Heckscher-Ohlin-Samuelson Model; Trade; Trade, Anglo-Portuguese; Unequal Exchange*

BIBLIOGRAPHY

Copeland, Brian R., and Scott M. Taylor. 1994. North-South Trade and the Environment. *Quarterly Journal of Economics* 109 (3): 755–787.

Darity, William A., and Lewis S. Davis. 2005. Growth, Trade, and Uneven Development. *Cambridge Journal of Economics* 29: 141–170.

Dutt, Amitava Krishna. 1990. *Growth, Distribution, and Uneven Development.* Cambridge, U.K., and New York: Cambridge University Press.

Findlay, Ronald. 1980. The Terms of Trade and Equilibrium Growth in the World Economy. *American Economic Review* 70 (3): 291–299.

Grossman, Gene, and Elhanan Helpman. 1991. *Innovation and Growth in the Global Economy.* Cambridge, MA: MIT Press.

Krugman, Paul. 1990. *Rethinking International Trade.* Cambridge, MA: MIT Press.

Taylor, Lance. 1983. *Structuralist Macroeconomics.* New York: Basic Books.

Amitava Krishna Dutt

NOUVEAUX RICHES

Nouveaux Riches translates literally to "new rich," and it refers to individuals or families who have recently risen to higher economic standing but have not gained full social acceptance by members of the established upper class or elite. While the nouveaux riches do possess substantial economic wealth, they are regarded as lacking the prerequisite cultural skills and dispositions to fully become members of society's elite. To signify their membership in elite status groups, the nouveaux riches may mimic the cultural consumption of the established upper class; however, these efforts are often not entirely successful. Pierre Bourdieu in *Distinction* (1984) describes the new bourgeoisie as possessing a similarly large degree of economic capital but less cultural capital relative to the old bourgeoisie.

The Industrial Revolution played an important role in the rise of the nouveaux riches, notably through the expansion of a highly educated, urban middle class with considerable time and resources for leisure activities. These upwardly mobile, wealthy individuals then worked to legitimize their elite status by adopting the styles and tastes of the established upper class.

For much of British history, for example, "old money" has been gentrified and titled, with large estates and hereditary seats in the House of Lords. The nouveaux riches mimicked the old aristocracy to an extent by buying estates and sending their children to the same elite boarding schools. However, they also developed their own, often indulgent, sense of style that was in contrast to the more refined sensibilities of the established elite

(Crook 1999). In his critical analysis of the late-nineteenth-century American upper classes, Thorstein Veblen in *The Theory of the Leisure Class* ([1899] 1932) finds that the nouveaux riches worked to emulate European aristocratic families by engaging in "conspicuous consumption." However, they were considered by "old money" to lack taste, manners, and discretion:

> Many a gentleman of the old school has been provoked to remark regretfully upon the under-bred manners and bearing of even the better classes in the modern industrial communities; and the decay of the ceremonial code ... among the industrial classes proper has become one of the chief enormities of latter-day civilization in the eyes of all persons of delicate sensibilities. (p. 46)

More recently, in the former Soviet republics a class of nouveaux riches emerged, largely composed of former Communist Party bureaucrats who made fortunes during the transition to market capitalism and privatization (Brucan 1998, pp. 69–94).

While in previous eras the nouveaux riches were considered to demonstrate a distinctive set of artistic tastes, attitudes toward culture, political views, and the like, it appears that many of these differences have reduced over time. As Max Weber in *Economy and Society* ([1922] 1968) describes, while status groups do often draw on cultural attributes to achieve social closure and advance their own interests, ultimately "at some point economic conditions become causally important and often decisive" (p. 341). Over time, the common economic conditions and shared class interests of the new and old rich may serve to overcome social differences and create a unified elite class.

SEE ALSO *Aristocracy; Bourdieu, Pierre; Class, Leisure; Culture, Low and High; Distinctions, Social and Cultural; Elites; Gentility; Industrialization; Stratification; Upward Mobility; Veblen, Thorstein; Weber, Max*

BIBLIOGRAPHY

Bourdieu, Pierre. 1984. *Distinction: A Social Critique of the Judgement of Taste.* Cambridge, MA: Harvard University Press.

Brucan, Silviu. 1998. *Social Change in Russia and Eastern Europe: From Party Hacks to Nouveaux Riches.* Westport, CT: Praeger.

Crook, J. Mordaunt. 1999. *The Rise of the Nouveaux Riches: Style and Status in Victorian and Edwardian Architecture.* London: Trafalgar Square Publishing.

Lamont, Michèle. 1992. *Money, Morals, and Manners: The Culture of the French and the American Upper-Middle Class.* Chicago: University of Chicago Press.

Veblen, Thorstein. [1899] 1932. *The Theory of the Leisure Class.* New York: Vanguard Press, 1932.

Weber, Max. [1922] 1968. *Economy and Society: An Outline of Interpretive Sociology,* eds. Guenther Roth and Clays Wittich. 3 vols. New York: Bedminster.

Nathan D. Martin

NOZICK, ROBERT

SEE *Justice, Distributive.*

NUCLEAR PROLIFERATION

SEE *Proliferation, Nuclear.*

NUREMBURG TRIALS

SEE *War Crimes.*

NURSERY RHYMES

Although popular collections of nursery rhymes were widespread from the eighteenth century on, and academic collections have been published since the nineteenth century, their academic study really began in the twentieth century. Several approaches have been taken by scholars over the past four or five generations, and these have been largely determined by the academic climate of their day. One such early tack was the expounding, or even invention, of a rhyme's "history" trying to answer the question deriving from adult wonder about children's lore: Where does it come from? Contemporary folklorists have been more likely to try to understand the meanings of folklore in use than to plumb its history; centuries of looking closely at the phenomena of folklore have taught them that folklore—including children's rhymes—is so fluid and changeable, while by dint of its orality being so undocumented in the written record, that the search for its history can at best be quixotic.

The English term *nursery rhyme* covers a somewhat larger group of folklore than a simple reading of the term would suggest. Although many thus-categorized rhymes are indeed used in the nursery (that is, with children under, say, four years old as audience), a much larger number of them are used by adults with somewhat older children, by children themselves no matter their age, and by adults. Nonetheless, the term *nursery rhyme* has great utility and has been retained by most authors.

Twentieth-century approaches to nursery rhymes have included attempts to understand variation, to read rhymes as expressions of psychosexual maturation, to show how they introduce children to the tools of language and intellectual thought, and, most recently, to see them as agents of empowerment for children and vehicles of cultural conservation. All of these approaches have attracted many authors and have been fruitful.

Despite academic findings to the contrary, it has often been claimed that earlier generations' nursery rhymes were "originally" coded messages about political events and historical eras. Such interpretations may be seen as the "folklore of folklore" and most often can be dismissed as modern *euhemerism.* (Euhemerus was a fourth-century BCE Greek who claimed that myths of the gods were actually transformed stories about real historical people.) Euhemerist traditions about nursery rhymes have circulated, especially in the educated classes, for a hundred years, floating around like migratory legends and—also like legends—localizing from time to time.

It is understandable that such interpretations arise. It is popularly known that much folklore is "old." Interested and creative people look for ways to show how old it is. New folklore grows as easily as old folklore did, and now it finds itself an explanation of the older folklore. Folklore items have a text (their words or other formal shape), but they also often carry a more variable set of traditional beliefs and understandings as a kind of corona around the text. These secondary texts can take the form of localized legends explaining the "history" of the item.

The Humpty Dumpty rhyme is a good example of this process; in its euhemerist form, Humpty Dumpty has become a local legend in at least a half-dozen places, mainly in Great Britain. In Gloucester, Humpty Dumpty has come to represent a siege ramp built in 1643 by Charles I's forces to cross the River Severn and take the city from Cromwell. But the ramp, according to the euhemerist tradition, collapsed under the cavalry's weight:

> Humpty Dumpty sat on the wall,
> Humpty Dumpty had a great fall,
> All the king's horses and all the king's men,
> Couldn't put Humpty together again.

Similar readings have been attached to, among others, the English kings James I, King John, and Richard III, the last because of his hunchback (= Humpty).

Likewise "Pop Goes the Weasel" is interpreted as being about a piece of nineteenth-century textile equipment, or a cobbler's bench. All folklore varies by text, and the different texts of this rhyme—"carpenter's bench," "vinegar bush," "vinegar jug," and so on—produce different euhemerist readings. One reading has it in a pawnbroker's shop and provides a foundation legend for some

Salvation Army followers. Often the rhyme's own words are given as examples of now-obsolete slang that seems to "prove" the truth of the legend. All of these readings are attempts by modern people to connect to historical figures that which would otherwise appear to be "mere" children's nonsense. But modern texts are commonly used in these attempts to come up with "older" readings.

Interpretations sometimes have contemporary political undertones. In early 2000, in England, Birmingham's city council banned "Baa Baa Black Sheep" from local schools because, the council said, "the history of the rhyme … is offensive to black people due to the fact it originates from slavery." In fact, as the research by Peter and Iona Opie has shown, it is most likely not related to slavery, but simply an amusing, and largely nonsensical rhyme. Children, in any era, are amused by nonsense.

The euhemerist belief that "Ring around the Rosie" comes from one of the great plagues seems to have arisen in the 1960s, and was given greater weight by academic promulgations. The claim gained popularity in a 1961 biology textbook about rats and the plague, James Leasor's *The Plague and the Fire*. Leasor did not consult folklorists but, based on folklore from his own relatives, assumed the rhyme was known centuries before it was. More recently, Norman Cantor, a historian of the plague, did the same in his *In the Wake of the Plague* (2001). There are two main regional forms of the rhyme: "Ring a Ring of Rosie," which is mainly British, and "Ring around the Rosie," which is mainly North American. The two traditions are not entirely separate; examination of historical texts shows a great deal of overlap. Kate Greenaway's text (in her little book *Mother Goose*) was the first in print, appearing in Britain in 1881. William Wells Newell published a second version in North America several years later, in an academic collection of children's rhymes. He said it dated back to the 1790s but he does not say who his informant was, or how he knew that fact. This is Newell's "earliest" text, using the now-British form of the first line:

> Ring a ring a rosie,
> A bottle full of posie,
> All the girls in our town
> Ring for little Josie.

Newell included another more contemporary version, probably circulating in Massachusetts in the 1880s or 1890s:

> Round the ring of roses,
> Pots full of posies,
> The one who stoops the last
> Shall tell whom she loves the best.

This text represents very clearly a typical "forfeits" game with an "all fall in" section in the third line. The

lack of plague references is apparent here, as in all the pre-twentieth century texts. Only in the mid-twentieth century do the "Ashes ashes" (or "A tissue!") forms start to appear; such late texts are the "evidence" (clearly inadmissible) of being about the plague.

In the late twentieth and into the twenty-first century, the rhyme grew in symbolic value, giving a human face to plagues. HIV-AIDS groups in the United States used the rhyme to bring attention to the need for research into AIDS and support for HIV+ people. Rock musician Dave Matthews used it in his popular song "Gravedigger" to indicate how disillusioned a child is when she learns her childhood song is "about death." In an interview in *Rolling Stone* in February 2004, he said, "It's the classic of classics about dying." Not just for activists and artists, it had become a symbol of plague, of death, disease, and the corruption of flesh.

Children's folklore is a rich area for contemporary scholarly study partly because it continues to pick up traditions and generate symbols. But symbol is not history. The history of "Ring around the Rosie" is much shorter than the plague interpretation would have it. The symbols are modern, not "old," folklore—but they also show nursery rhymes to be living, contemporary culture.

SEE ALSO *Children; Death and Dying; Ethnology and Folklore*

BIBLIOGRAPHY

Bauman, Richard. 1982. Ethnography of Children's Folklore. In *Children in and out of School: Ethnography and Education*, eds. Perry Gilmore and Allan A. Glatthorn, 172–186. Washington, DC: Georgetown University Press.

Bronner, Simon J. 1990. "Left to Their Own Devices": Interpreting American Children's Folklore as an Adaptation to Aging. *Southern Folklore* 47: 101–115.

Crystal, David. 1998. *Language Play*. Chicago: University of Chicago Press.

Dundes, Alan. 1980. Projection in Folklore: A Plea for Psychoanalytic Semiotics. In his *Interpreting Folklore*, 33–61. Bloomington: Indiana University Press.

Fine, Gary Alan. 1980. Children and Their Culture: Exploring Newell's Paradox. *Western Folklore* 39 (3): 170–183.

Gomme, Alice Bertha. 1894–1898. *The Traditional Games of England, Scotland, and Ireland*. 2 vols. London: David Nutt.

Greenaway, Kate. 1881. *Mother Goose*. London: Warne.

Kirshenblatt-Gimblett, Barbara, ed. 1976. *Speech Play: Research and Resources for Studying Linguistic Creativity*. Philadelphia: University of Pennsylvania Press.

Mechling, Jay. 1986. Children's Folklore. In *Folk Groups and Folklore Genres*, ed. Elliott Oring, 91–120. Logan: Utah State University Press.

Newell, William Wells. 1883. *Games and Songs of American Children*. New York: Harper.

Opie, Iona, and Peter Opie. 1959. *The Lore and Language of Schoolchildren.* Oxford: Clarendon.

Opie, Iona, and Peter Opie, eds. 1997. *The Oxford Dictionary of Nursery Rhymes.* Rev. ed. Oxford: Oxford University Press.

Sutton-Smith, Brian. 1970. Psychology of Children: The Triviality Barrier. *Western Folklore* 29 (1): 1–8.

Sutton-Smith, Brian. 1984. The Origins of Fictions and the Fictions of Origins. In *Text, Play, and Story: The Construction and Reconstruction of Self and Society,* ed. Edward Bruner, 117–132. Washington, DC: American Ethnological Society.

Widdowson, John D. A. 1977. *"If You Don't Be Good": Verbal Social Control in Newfoundland.* ISER Study 21. St. John's: Memorial University of Newfoundland.

Zumwalt, Rosemary Lévy. 1999. The Complexity of Children's Folklore. In *Children's Folklore: A Source Book,* ed. Brian Sutton-Smith et al, 23–47. Logan: Utah State University Press.

Philip Hiscock

NUTRITION

Nutrition is a vital physiologic process necessary for the development and maintenance of the human body, its organs, and its physiological processes. In order to maintain good health, individuals require daily intake of protein, fat, and carbohydrates—nutrients that provide energy, vitamins, minerals, and water. Nutrition provides necessary nutrients that are not produced by the body. The daily requirements of these nutrients vary depending on individuals' age, sex, and physiologic state (that is, pregnancy).

In the United States dietary guidelines are updated every five years and are the basis for the Food Guide Pyramid. These guidelines are issued by the U.S. Department of Agriculture (USDA) and the U.S. Department of Health and Human Services (HHS). The Food Guide Pyramid groups foods into major categories (fruit, vegetable, dairy, grain, meat, and bean) and recommends serving sizes and the number of servings needed to achieve balanced nutrition and health. In 2005, to address the dramatic rise in obesity, the USDA modified the Food Guide Pyramid to emphasize lower energy intake and more physical activity and provide an individualized approach. The USDA promotes nutrition based on the fact that certain dietary patterns may place individuals at risk of chronic diseases, such as cardiovascular disease, diabetes, and cancer. Diets rich in saturated fat and low in fruits and vegetables are associated with heart disease, cancer, and diabetes, while diets rich in fruits and vegetables may protect individuals from these conditions.

The balance between energy intake and energy expenditure determines weight maintenance or weight gain and loss. When regular energy intake is greater than the expenditure, the body stores the surplus of energy as extra body fat or adipose tissue. Energy expenditure is a result of the basal metabolic rate, the thermic effect of food (energy spent in processing food), and the energy spent in physical activity. The contribution of physical activity to energy balance is small compared to food intake. Energy intake and dietary patterns are influenced by hormonal mechanisms and psychosocial factors. People eat in response to hunger signals that the body creates, such as changes in blood glucose levels. Hunger can also be experienced in response to sensory cues, such as the smell or sight of favorite foods.

Satiety is regulated by a complex hormonal signaling system with input from proteins secreted by the brain, the gastrointestinal tract, and the liver. In the brain the hypothalamus secretes small proteins called neuropeptides. The neuropeptides inhibit food intake after receiving input from hormones and proteins synthesized in the stomach and intestines. Ghrelin, which is synthesized predominantly by the stomach, stimulates feeding. In the fasting state ghrelin levels are high, and levels fall after eating. The intestine releases cholecystokinin (CCK) after a meal, which stimulates gut motility, the contractions of gastrointestinal muscles that enable food to move along the digestive tract and ensure absorption of nutrients and inhibits food intake by signals to the brain. Other organs and hormones are also involved in the regulation of food intake and satiety. After a meal, the pancreas secretes insulin, which in turn signals the brain to inhibit feeding. Leptin is a hormone synthesized in adipose (fat) cells, and its secretion is regulated by the obese (ob) gene. Leptin levels are low during starvation and high when nutrients are plentiful and in obesity. High levels of leptin signal the brain to reduce appetite. In obesity people are resistant to the effects of leptin. The hormone adiponectin is secreted by adipose cells, and its secretion is stimulated by food restriction. Adiponectin is also a factor that increases energy expenditure, and low levels may contribute to the development of obesity.

The body seems to tolerate positive energy balance, that is, when energy intake is higher than expenditure. The mechanisms described above strongly defend from weight loss but not from weight gain because of an evolutionary process that favored intake of nutrients when food was easily accessible and in preparation of times when food was scarce. This evolutionary perspective can explain in part the obesity epidemic that emerged during the last decades of the twentieth century when, in developed countries, there was abundance of food without periods of scarcity.

Nutrition is not only influenced by biological factors. Environment, culture, and social factors also play important roles in nutrition. The environment determines the type and quality of foods accessible to individuals and communities. A diet rich in refined sugars, carbohydrates, and fat is related to increased availability of fast foods, sugared beverages, and low-nutritional value snacks and decreased access to produce (fruits and vegetables). A positive energy balance in turn is caused by increasing calorie intake, especially when reinforced with a sedentary lifestyle. Social factors, such as low income and low socioeconomic status, are associated with less healthy dietary patterns with higher saturated fat intake and lower intake of fruits and vegetables possibly due to the facts that low-income individuals are more likely to live in communities with less access to healthy foods and that healthier food items are proportionally more expensive that unhealthy ones. Industrialized societies eat a diet rich in meat and saturated fat and lower in fiber compared to agrarian societies, who consume more fruits, vegetables, and grains. Research indicates that immigration changes dietary patterns of individuals, who over time adopt the diet of their host country.

In people with excess weight, a diet restricting calories but maintaining balanced nutrient composition can achieve healthy weight loss and reduce the risk of diabetes and cardiovascular disease, which are conditions associated with obesity. However, when the calorie restriction is severe and the diet does not allow for sufficient amounts of essential nutrients, dieting can lead to metabolic and heart problems and even death. The psychological factors that are associated with nutrition are best exemplified by obesity and eating disorders. Obese individuals frequently have low self-esteem and depression. Whether these are causes or consequences of obesity is still under debate. Some individuals may increase their food intake in response to feelings of stress, loneliness, and anxiety, which place them at risk of overweight and obesity. Eating disorders include anorexia, characterized by being severely underweight from excessive food intake restriction, and bulimia, characterized by purging. Either disorder may also have periods of binge eating. Eating disorders, especially anorexia, are associated with body image dissatisfaction, depression, and low self-esteem.

SEE ALSO *Body Image; Depression, Psychological; Disease; Food; Malnutrition; Obesity; Overeating; Self-Esteem; Stunted Growth; Undereating*

BIBLIOGRAPHY

Geissler, Catherine, and Hilary Powers. 2005. *Human Nutrition.* Edinburgh: Elsevier Churchill Livingstone.

Shils, Maurice E., James A. Olson, Moshe Shike, et al., eds. 2005. *Modern Nutrition in Health and Disease.* Baltimore, MD: Lippincott Williams and Wilkins.

Temple, Norman J., Ted Wilson, and David R. Jacobs. 2006. *Nutritional Health: Strategies for Disease Prevention.* Totowa, NJ: Humana.

U.S. Department of Agriculture. 2005. *My Pyramid: Steps to a Healthier You.* http://www.MyPyramid.gov.

U.S. Department of Health and Human Services and U.S. Department of Agriculture. 2005. *Dietary Guidelines for Americans 2005.* http://www.healthierus.gov/dietaryguidelines.

Wynnes, Katie, Sarah Stanley, Barbara McGowan, and Steve Bloom. 2005. Appetite Control. *Journal of Endocrinology* 184: 291–318.

Carmen R. Isasi

NUYORICANS

The term *Nuyorican* refers to Puerto Ricans born or raised in New York City, or more broadly in the mainland United States, as distinguished from those from the island of Puerto Rico. Indeed, the word in a range of other spellings—"neorrican," "neorrriqueno," and "newyorquino," among others—was first used by those from the island, notably in the glossary of Guillermo Cotto-Thorner's early novel about Puerto Rican life in New York, *Trópico en Manhattan* (1952) and, in more direct anticipation of the usage familiar today, in Jaime Carrero's long poem *NeoRican Jetliner* (1965). But in those early, island-based occurrences the term often carried a derogatory or at least derisive connotation. It signified cultural inauthenticity and evoked a paternalistic sympathy for the cultural loss, or even blame for the betrayal involved in the migrants' adaptation to North America. It also could imply significantly negative qualities in terms of class (usually very poor and lazy), sometimes described with the idea of "lumpen" (proletarian), and race (generally identified as black, perhaps tainted with the proximity of African Americans). Many were the young New York Puerto Ricans who experienced painful rejection and discrimination on occasions of their temporary or permanent return to their ancestral homeland, especially in the 1970s and more recent decades.

Nuyorican in its present spelling and usage emerged in the early 1970s in part as a reaction to this negative characterization. The founding of the Nuyorican Poets' Café on New York's Lower East Side in 1973 and the publication of the anthology *Nuyorican Poetry* in 1975 were the major events in this historical emergence, in both cases resulting from the collaboration between writers Miguel Algarín and Miguel Piñero. But it was rapidly adopted by many other writers, artists, and other New York–born youth of Puerto Rican extraction. It became the name of a vibrant poetic and artistic movement of those vibrant years of ethnic awakening, capturing as it did the zeitgeist of the Puerto Rican community in the 1960s and early 1970s, and featuring such poetic talents as Victor Hernández Cruz, Sandra María Estevez, and the quintessential Nuyorican poet Pedro Pietri. Algarín and Piñero both recount the indignities they endured at the hands of members of the island's cultural elite, and how they then took the negative term and threw it back at them with a sense of cultural pride, much as African Americans did in those same years with the word *black*. A dramatization of this act of resignifying occurs in the more recent film *Piñero* (2002), in a vivid scene depicting Piñero's encounter with that elite on his visit to the island in the mid-1970s. Though another Loisaida (Lower East Side) cultural institution of the times, the New Rican Village, may be considered an even more significant center of experimental expression in those same years, it was the word *Nuyorican* spelled in that idiosyncratic way that has continued as the identifying cultural nomenclature for subsequent generations of Puerto Ricans in the U.S. diaspora. In its combination of Spanish and English phonetics, its semantic mix of "newness" and geographical location, and its intertwining of the New York and the "Rican" reference, that spelling has turned out to be ideally appropriate to epitomize a fully hybrid, bicultural field of personal and group identity, corresponding to the term *Chicano* among Mexican American youth of the same period.

In more recent times some objections to the usage have emerged because of the dispersal of U.S.-based Puerto Ricans and the emergence of significant communities in other places, notably Philadelphia, Chicago, Florida, and other cities in the Northeast such as Hartford, Connecticut; Jersey City, New Jersey; and Springfield, Massachusetts. Though no new word has arisen to replace the geographically specific *Nuyorican*, some writers and others have toyed with such neologisms as *diasporican* and *AmeRícan*, the latter a signature poem by well-known writer Tato Laviera. Terms clearly modeled after Nuyorican, such as *ChicagoRican* and *PhillyRican*, have also cropped up, as has nomenclature such as *Dominican Yorks* and *MexYorks* to name newer Latino groups in New York City. In more recent times, change is also evident even in Puerto Rico, where the concept first emerged in its less sanguine usage: The diaspora cultural experience has gained greater acceptance, receiving frequent coverage in the media and cultural institutions, though often still in reluctant or paternalistic terms. Among the youth on the island, many of whom are from families of return migrants who were raised on the mainland, *Nuyorican* has come to be a term of strong admiration and even emulation. Significantly, Old San Juan now boasts the Nuyorican Café among its cultural nightspots. In the days of hip hop, reggaetón, and spoken-word poetry, the long-standing gap between island and diaspora cultural realities has finally come to narrow, and the ironic, deeper meaning of the highly charged expression *Nuyorican* to come full turn.

SEE ALSO *African Diaspora; Blackness; Boricua; Culture; Immigrants, New York City; Latinos; Nationalism and Nationality; Natives; Politics, Identity; Popular Culture; Protest; Race; Racism; Radicalism; Resistance*

BIBLIOGRAPHY

Algarín, Miguel, and Miguel Piñero, eds. 1975. *Nuyorican Poetry: An Anthology of Puerto Rican Words and Feelings*. New York: Morrow.

Flores, Juan. 1993. *Divided Borders: Essays on Puerto Rican Identity*. Houston, TX: Arte Público.

Mohr, Eugene. 1982. *The Nuyorican Experience: Literature of the Puerto Rican Minority*. Westport, CT: Greenwood.

Juan Flores

NYERERE, JULIUS
1922–1999

Julius Kambarage Nyerere, the first president of the East African country of Tanzania, was born on April 13, 1922, in a town called Butiama, located on the eastern shore of Victoria Falls. His father, Nyerere Burito, was the chief of the Zanaki tribe and had twenty-five other children. Being raised in such a large family allowed Julius to experience directly the benefits and costs of "communal living"—an idea later made central to his political philosophy. Life in such a family structure also affected the development of his educational philosophy, in which Nyerere sought to combine the epistemologies of Africa and Europe. From Europe, where he studied at Edinburgh University, Nyerere absorbed the socialism of the British Fabians. From Africa, where he combined his early communal life with a Catholic primary school education, Nyerere developed a philosophy not unlike that of the American William James in terms of an emphasis on pragmatics. These experiences constituted the foundation of his personal philosophy, perhaps best epitomized in the pamphlet "Development is for Man, by Man, and of Man" (1978): "Man does not develop himself in a vacuum, in isolation from his society and his environment. And he certainly cannot be developed by others. Man's consciousness is developed in the process of thinking, and deciding, and acting. His capacity is developed in the process of doing things."

Nyerere thus challenged the idea that a scholar should not get involved in the practical affairs of politics. As a committed activist, he had a number of critics, both European and African. The former were upset because Nyerere was a leader of the African liberation movement that sought to remove the injustices inherent in the British colonial system. The latter were upset because they feared that Nyerere was an example of yet another African whose body was in Africa but whose mind was conditioned in Europe and whose ultimate loyalties were therefore suspect.

Nyerere's political decisions were not, however, entirely predictable. He was not an ideologue, although he was an unabashed socialist and his plans for land redistribution did not endear him to Western powers. His support of the overthrow of Uganda's President Idi Amin was condemned by many African political observers as a cavein to the demands of the American/Israeli interests rather than African interests. Yet the decision was cheered by the European/Western press, which described it as a noble act of gratitude for foreign economic assistance to Tanzania. The same set of observers winced when Nyerere offered unconditional support for the armed struggle to free Southern Africa. Some observers have minimized this militaristic side of Nyerere's presidential reign and have instead focused on his pragmatic embodiment of the nonviolent spirit of India's Mahatma Gandhi.

The Gandhian influence was also reflected in Nyerere's support of the unification of the offshore island of Zanzibar with the mainland, as well as in other personal efforts of reconciliation between the East Indian immigrants and the indigenous African communities.

Nyerere did not take his African constituency for granted. He championed the incorporation of the local language, Kiswahili, into every facet of Tanzanian life. One legacy of that decision is the appearance of the Kiswahili language in the widely celebrated holiday of Kwanza among African Americans in the United States today.

Like many other post-independence leaders, Nyerere's exposure to Western education was both a blessing and a curse. Its blessings were evident in that it equipped him with the skills necessary to negotiate the treacherous waters of independence from Britain, and a curse because it sometimes tied him too closely with the oppressors of his people.

Nyerere's handling of the ever-present duality was reflected in his early support of both the Commonwealth (of former British colonies) and the OAU (Organization of African Unity). The support of both required a considerable degree of deftness because the organizations' goals were often incompatible. Such political deftness earned Nyerere the respect and admiration of many world leaders. His decision, in 1985, to relinquish the presidency and to retire to his farm for a life of reflection and international peace-making activities—a role later played by South Africa's first president, Nelson Mandela—further enhanced his international reputation.

South African leader Nelson Mandela was one of several future leaders whom Nyerere nurtured as president of Tanzania. Robert Mugabe, whose own efforts at land redistribution resembled Nyerere's, was another who was given refuge as a leader in the liberation struggle of Southern Africa.

Julius Nyerere died in London on October 14, 1999, after a short battle with leukemia. He left behind a wife and seven children and a well-deserved legacy befitting the title *Mwalimu* (teacher).

SEE ALSO *Amin, Idi; Commonwealth, The; Decolonization; Development; East Indian Diaspora; Fabianism; Gandhi, Mohandas K.; James, William; Liberation Movements; Mandela, Nelson; Organization of African Unity (OAU); Pan-African Congresses; Pan-Africanism; Socialism, African*

BIBLIOGRAPHY

Kassam, Yusuf. 1995. Julius Nyerere. In *Thinkers on Education,* ed. Zaghloul Morsy. Paris: UNESCO.

Nyerere, Julius. 1978. Development is for Man, by Man, and of Man. In *Adult Learning: A Design for Action*, eds. B. Hall and J. R. Kidd. Oxford; New York: Pergamon Press.

Carolyn Murray